VIRGINIA WOOLF A TO Z

A Comprehensive Reference
for Students, Teachers and Common Readers
to Her Life, Work and Critical Reception

Mark Hussey

OXFORD UNIVERSITY PRESS
New York Oxford

To Evelyn

Oxford University Press

Oxford New York
Athens Auckland Bangkok Bombay
Calcutta Cape Town Dar es Salaam Delhi
Florence Hong Kong Istanbul Karachi
Kuala Lumpur Madras Madrid Melbourne
Mexico City Nairobi Paris Singapore
Taipei Tokyo Toronto

and associated companies in
Berlin Ibadan

First published in 1995 by Facts On File, Inc., 11 Penn Plaza, New York, NY 10001

First issued as an Oxford University Press paperback, 1996

Oxford is a registered trademark of Oxford University Press

Library of Congress Cataloging-in-Publication Data

Hussey, Mark, 1956–
Virginia Woolf A to Z : a comprehensive reference for students,
teachers and common readers to her life, work and critical
reception / Mark Hussey.
p. cm.
Includes bibliographical references and index.
ISBN 0-19-511027-7 (Pbk)
1. Woolf, Virginia, 1882–1941—Encyclopedias. 2. Women novelists,
English—20th century—Biography—Encyclopedias. I. Title.
PR6045.072Z729 1996
823'.912—dc20 96-26824

10 9 8 7 6 5 4 3 2 1

Printed in the United States of America on acid-free paper

CONTENTS

LIST OF ILLUSTRATIONS

PREFACE

> "They only allow one seventy thousand words, you see."
> "Only seventy thousand words!" Terence exclaimed.
> "Yes, and one has to say something about everybody," Miss Allan added.
>
> (TVO 316)

This book is addressed primarily to readers who are new to the work of Virginia Woolf, although old hands may also find it useful when a name or fact has slipped their mind. It is intended to provide both a quick reference to and also a more leisurely and comprehensive overview of Woolf's writings and life, her contemporaries and times. It is not a work of scholarship, but rests—I hope securely—on the scholarship of many others. Like Mr. HILBERY in Woolf's second novel, *NIGHT AND DAY*, I have seen "the humour of these researches," but that has not prevented me "from carrying them out with the utmost scrupulosity" (ND 108).

Woolf herself was pretty scathing about the profession of English literature, and regarded the alphabetical codifying of knowledge as something of a joke. Yet, having neither her genius nor her extraordinary command of literary history, most of us must depend upon such secondary sources as we can find to help us when our memory or understanding falter. *Virginia Woolf A to Z* is no substitute for the adventure of reading Woolf's writing itself, but it should assist you on your travels through the mind of a writer whose time, as Margaret Homans wrote recently, is "always about to come" (*Virginia Woolf* 11).

PREFACE

> "They only allow one seventy thousand words, you see."
> "Only seventy thousand words!" Terence exclaimed.
> "Yes, and one has to say something about everybody," Miss Allan added.
>
> (TVO 316)

This book is addressed primarily to readers who are new to the work of Virginia Woolf, although old hands may also find it useful when a name or fact has slipped their mind. It is intended to provide both a quick reference to and also a more leisurely and comprehensive overview of Woolf's writings and life, her contemporaries and times. It is not a work of scholarship, but rests—I hope securely—on the scholarship of many others. Like Mr. HILBERY in Woolf's second novel, ***NIGHT AND DAY,*** I have seen "the humour of these researches," but that has not prevented me "from carrying them out with the utmost scrupulosity" (ND 108).

Woolf herself was pretty scathing about the profession of English literature, and regarded the alphabetical codifying of knowledge as something of a joke. Yet, having neither her genius nor her extraordinary command of literary history, most of us must depend upon such secondary sources as we can find to help us when our memory or understanding falter. *Virginia Woolf A to Z* is no substitute for the adventure of reading Woolf's writing itself, but it should assist you on your travels through the mind of a writer whose time, as Margaret Homans wrote recently, is "always about to come" (*Virginia Woolf* 11).

HOW TO USE *VIRGINIA WOOLF A TO Z*

Entries

Entries on Woolf's novels and long essays are divided into four sections: Outline, which gives a description of what happens; Genesis, which traces the evolution and development of Woolf's writing of the work; Background, which identifies relevant biographical material and influences on the work; and Critical Responses, which summarizes contemporary reviews and major critical approaches to the work. In some cases there is a section on Adaptations. An asterisk after the first mention of an author's name indicates that the reference is specific to that entry; such references are listed at the end of the entries.

Some shorter works by Woolf do not have their own entries but are referred to in other entries; if you are looking for a work and cannot find its entry, check the Index. Often, reference to essays by Woolf on literary or historical figures will be found in the entries on those figures.

Cross-References

A name, title, or term appearing in SMALL CAPITALS the first time it is mentioned in an entry signifies that it has an entry of its own.

Works Cited

Reference is made throughout the *A to Z* to those editions of Woolf's works most likely used in U.S. classrooms. Complete bibliographical details will be found in the alphabetical and topical lists of works cited. References specific to an entry are listed at the end of that entry. All works by Woolf are referred to by the abbreviations listed on p. x. Page numbers in any references correspond to the editions listed in the Works Cited.

Appendixes

If you can't remember a fictional or factual name, scanning the appropriate appendix might help. Appendix A arranges all the entries in the following categories: **Allusions in Woolf's Work and Subjects of Her Essays (including characters, myths, phrases, titles;** excluding authors); **Acquaintances (including doctors and nurses), friends, lovers; Bloomsbury Group: clubs, events, organizations, terms, topics** (excluding people); **Characters in Woolf's Fiction** (listed by novel); **Clubs, Groups, Organizations; Historical Figures and Events Mentioned in Woolf's Writing** (excludes writers); **Library Collections and Archives; Locations** (including Woolf's houses); **Performers, Photographers, Composers; Publishing: assistants, editors, newspapers, periodicals, presses, prizes, publishers; Terms; Woolf's Inventions, Flowers, Key Phrases, and Objects in Essays and Novels; Woolf's Relatives and Households, Nicknames, Pets, and Servants; Woolf's Works; Works by Writers Other Than Woolf; Writers (critics, dramatists, novelists, philosophers, poets) and Painters.** Appendix B features a number of family trees.

Index

The index identifies titles, names, and terms that are mentioned in entries but do not have entries of their own. For example, a reader wondering what Woolf thought of the French poet Charles Baudelaire would not find an entry under "B," but would learn from the index that Baudelaire is mentioned in the entry on Thomas DE QUINCEY. References to minor works by Woolf that do not warrant entries of their own can be located with the index, as can references to the work of various critics. Themes—for example, androgyny, incest—that are treated in multiple entries also can be traced with the index.

Conventions

Virginia Woolf is referred to throughout as Woolf, even when the reference is to the time before she was married to Leonard WOOLF. To avoid confusion between members of the same family, I have usually used first names: e.g., Vanessa and Clive for Vanessa

BELL and Clive BELL, or Leslie and Julia for Sir Leslie STEPHEN and Julia Prinsep STEPHEN.

When she wrote LETTERS or wrote in her DIARY, Woolf frequently omitted apostrophes and often punctuated and spelled erratically, sacrificing accuracy to speed. I have, as all her editors do, preserved these eccentricities; so, for example, "don't" usually appears as "dont" in a diary entry.

In referring to chapters or parts of works I have used Roman numerals or Arabic numerals according to the published text.

ACKNOWLEDGMENTS

My greatest debt is to the scholarly community upon whose work much of this book is founded. For their help with illustrations, I would also like to thank Linda J. Langham for her extraordinary generosity, Jean Moorcroft Wilson, Henrietta Garnett, Louise H. Tucker, Christopher Naylor, Sarah Blessington, Gillian Ellis, Wayne Furman, Sir Rupert Hart-Davis, Philip Milito, Elizabeth Neubauer and Lucinda Stewart. For other assistance my thanks to Quentin Bell, John Bicknell, Toni DeVito, Elisabeth Birnbaum, Tina Erickson, Michelle Fanelli, Antonía García-Rodriguez, Vereena Jones, Karen V. Kukil, Eleanor McNees, Vara Neverow, Nigel Nicolson, Marine Olsson, Trekkie Parsons, Maria Ptakowski and Qu Shijing. I must also thank Caroline Sutton, Jeffrey Golick and Anne Dubuisson for their indispensable support. Evelyn Leong has listened to almost every word and went well beyond duty and affection to prepare the genealogies when they had me defeated. So, to the dedicatee, *wo aini.*

ABBREVIATIONS

(see Alphabetical List of Works Cited and Topical List of Works Cited for complete bibliographical details)

AROO	Virginia Woolf, *A Room of One's Own*
BP	Virginia Woolf, *Books and Portraits*
BTA	Virginia Woolf, *Between the Acts*
CDB	Virginia Woolf, *The Captain's Death Bed and Other Essays*
CE1–4	Virginia Woolf, *Collected Essays* (4 vols.)
CH	Robin Majumdar and Allen McLaurin, eds. *Virginia Woolf: The Critical Heritage*
CM1–	*The Charleston Magazine*
CHN1–24	*Charleston Newsletter*
CR1	Virginia Woolf, *The Common Reader*
CR2	Virginia Woolf, *The Common Reader, Second Series*
CS	Virginia Woolf, *Congenial Spirits. The Selected Letters of Virginia Woolf*
CW	Virginia Woolf, *Contemporary Writers*
D1–5	Virginia Woolf, *The Diary of Virginia Woolf* (5 vols.)
DM	Virginia Woolf, *The Death of the Moth and Other Essays*
E1–3	Virginia Woolf, *The Essays of Virginia Woolf*
F	Virginia Woolf, *Flush, A Biography*
GR	Virginia Woolf, *Granite & Rainbow, Essays*
JR	Virginia Woolf, *Jacob's Room*
L1–6	Virginia Woolf, *The Letters of Virginia Woolf* (6 vols.)
LW1/2	Leonard Woolf, *An Autobiography* (2 vols.)
M	Virginia Woolf, *The Moment and Other Essays*
MD	Virginia Woolf, *Mrs. Dalloway*
MDP	Virginia Woolf, *Mrs. Dalloway's Party*
MELYM	Virginia Woolf, *Melymbrosia. An Early Version of the Voyage Out*
MOB	Virginia Woolf, *Moments of Being*
ND	Virginia Woolf, *Night and Day*
O	Virginia Woolf, *Orlando: A Biography*
OED	Oxford English Dictionary
PA	Virginia Woolf, *A Passionate Apprentice. The Early Journals. 1897–1909*
Pargiters	Virginia Woolf, *The Pargiters. The Novel-Essay Portion of "The Years"*
PH	Virginia Woolf, *Pointz Hall. The Earlier and Later Typescripts of Between the Acts*
QB1/2	Quentin Bell, *Virginia Woolf: A Biography* (2 vols.)
RF	Virginia Woolf, *Roger Fry, A Biography*
RN	Brenda R. Silver, *Virginia Woolf's Reading Notebooks*
SF	Virginia Woolf, *The Complete Shorter Fiction of Virginia Woolf*
TG	Virginia Woolf, *Three Guineas*
TLS	*Times Literary Supplement*
TTL	Virginia Woolf, *To the Lighthouse*
TVO	Virginia Woolf, *The Voyage Out*
TW	Virginia Woolf, *The Waves*
TY	Virginia Woolf, *The Years*
VWM1–	*Virginia Woolf Miscellany*
WF	*Women & Fiction*

CHRONOLOGY

1882 Woolf born January 25 at 22 HYDE PARK GATE.

1895 Julia Prinsep STEPHEN (Woolf's mother) dies.

1896 Stella DUCKWORTH agrees to marry John Waller ("Jack") HILLS.

1897 Stella and Jack marry on April 10; Stella dies July 19. Woolf attends Greek and history classes at King's College in London.

1898 Woolf takes Latin lessons with Clara PATER.

1899 Thoby STEPHEN goes up to Trinity College, Cambridge, where he meets Clive BELL, Lytton STRACHEY, Saxon SYDNEY-TURNER and Leonard WOOLF.

1904 Sir Leslie STEPHEN dies; Woolf, Vanessa BELL, George DUCKWORTH, Adrian STEPHEN and Thoby go to MANORBIER for a vacation, then to Venice and Florence. Thoby, Vanessa and Woolf, with Violet DICKINSON, stay in Paris where they are entertained by Clive Bell. In May, Woolf has a nervous breakdown and stays at Dickinson's house under the care of Nurse TRAILL.

In October, Vanessa moves the family to 46 GORDON SQUARE in BLOOMSBURY. Woolf stays with her aunt Caroline Emilia STEPHEN and assists F. W. MAITLAND by writing a chapter for his biography of her father. Woolf's first published writing, a review of William Dean Howells's *Son of Royal Langbrith,* appears in December in the *GUARDIAN.*

1905 Woolf begins teaching once a week at MORLEY COLLEGE. Thoby begins "Thursday Evenings" at Gordon Square.

1906 Woolf goes to Greece in September with her siblings and Violet Dickinson; Vanessa falls ill; Thoby returns early to England. In October, Adrian, Dickinson, Vanessa and Woolf return to England and find Thoby ill. Thoby dies November 20; Vanessa agrees on November 22 to marry Clive Bell.

1907 Clive and Vanessa marry on February 7. Woolf and her brother Adrian move to 29 FITZROY SQUARE where they continue the "Thursday Evenings." By now Woolf is at work on her first novel, *THE VOYAGE OUT* (called *MELYMBROSIA* at this point).

1909 Lytton Strachey proposes marriage to Woolf. She dines for the first time with Lady Ottoline MORRELL. Woolf receives a legacy of £2,500 on the death of Caroline Emilia Stephen in April.

In August, Woolf goes to Bayreuth with Adrian and Saxon Sydney-Turner.

1910 The DREADNOUGHT HOAX (February). In the summer, Woolf spends time at Jean THOMAS's nursing home. First POST-IMPRESSIONIST exhibition (opened November). Woolf works for women's SUFFRAGE.

1911 Woolf rents LITTLE TALLAND HOUSE. In April, she travels to Broussa in Turkey where Vanessa has had a miscarriage. Leonard Woolf returns from Ceylon (Sri Lanka). In November, Woolf and Adrian move to 38 BRUNSWICK SQUARE, sharing the house with John Maynard KEYNES, Duncan GRANT and Leonard.

1912 Woolf takes ASHEHAM HOUSE. In February she spends a few days at Jean Thomas's nursing home. In May she agrees to marry Leonard. They are married on August 10. In October, they move to 13 CLIFFORD'S INN. They spend Christmas at Asheham.

1913 The manuscript of *The Voyage Out* is delivered to Gerald Duckworth. Woolf travels with Leonard to the north of England for his research on the Co-operative Movement. Woolf increasingly unwell; she enters Thomas's home again in July. In September she attempts suicide. She stays at DALINGRIDGE PLACE, George Duckworth's house, September to November, then goes to Asheham.

1915 *The Voyage Out* published. Woolf again goes to a nursing home, having taken violently against men in general and Leonard in particular. Leonard moves to HOGARTH HOUSE, where Woolf joins him in April.

1916 Woolf discovers CHARLESTON and Vanessa Bell moves there in October with her sons Julian and Quentin BELL and with David GARNETT and Duncan Grant.

1917 The first printing press is delivered to Hogarth House; the HOGARTH PRESS is established. *TWO STORIES* published, including Leonard's "Three Jews" and Woolf's "THE MARK ON THE WALL." 1917 CLUB founded.

1918 Katherine MANSFIELD's *Prelude* published by Hogarth Press. Woolf meets T. S. ELIOT.

1919 *NIGHT AND DAY* published. The Woolfs buy MONK'S HOUSE.

1920 The MEMOIR CLUB meets for the first time.

1921 *MONDAY OR TUESDAY* published. Woolf finishes *JACOB'S ROOM.*

1922 *Jacob's Room* published. Woolf meets Vita SACKVILLE-WEST for the first time in December.

1924 The Woolfs move to 52 TAVISTOCK SQUARE. Woolf delivers "MR. BENNET AND MRS. BROWN" to the HERETICS society at Cambridge. The essay is published in October by the Hogarth Press.

1925 *THE COMMON READER* and *MRS. DALLOWAY* published. Woolf stays with Vita at LONG BARN.

1927 *TO THE LIGHTHOUSE* published. Vanessa writes from her house at CASSIS about the giant moths flying into the house, inspiring Woolf to think about what will become *THE WAVES.* In June, the Woolfs travel with Vita and Harold NICOLSON to Yorkshire to see a total eclipse of the sun.

1928 *To the Lighthouse* wins the FEMINA-VIE HEUREUSE prize. *ORLANDO, A BIOGRAPHY* is published. In October, Woolf travels twice to Cambridge to deliver the lectures on which *A ROOM OF ONE'S OWN* is based.

1929 *A Room of One's Own* published.

1930 Woolf meets Ethel SMYTH for the first time in February.

1931 Woolf meets John LEHMANN for the first time in January. *The Waves* is published.

1932 Lytton Strachey dies in January; Dora CARRINGTON kills herself. "A LETTER TO A YOUNG POET" and *THE COMMON READER, SECOND SERIES* published.

1933 *FLUSH, A BIOGRAPHY* published.

1934 *WALTER SICKERT: A CONVERSATION* published. Woolf very depressed over *THE YEARS.*

1937 *The Years* published. Woolf at work on *ROGER FRY: A BIOGRAPHY* and *THREE GUINEAS.* Julian Bell is killed in the SPANISH CIVIL WAR.

1938 *Three Guineas* published.

1939 The Woolfs visit Sigmund FREUD, who is in London having fled the Nazis in Austria. They move to 37 MECKLENBURGH SQUARE.

1940 *Roger Fry: A Biography* published. Woolf delivers a lecture, "THE LEANING TOWER," to the Workers' Educational Association in Brighton. Woolf refuses E. M. FORSTER's request to join the board of the LONDON LIBRARY.

1941 Woolf finishes *BETWEEN THE ACTS* in February. On March 28 she drowns herself in the river Ouse. *Between the Acts* published in July.

A

A to Z In *TO THE LIGHTHOUSE,* intellectual achievement is ironically figured as the alphabet and Mr. RAMSAY as being stuck at the letter Q. Mr. Ramsay knows that he does not have the genius to "lump all the letters together in one flash," but he believes he might have had the power to plod steadily on to Z were it not for the demands made upon him by his wife and children. This image is one of several examples of Woolf's mocking of rational, linear thought and of any attempt to systematize knowledge. In "Where Does Q Leave Mr. Ramsay?" Sandra M. Donaldson points out that Woolf is very likely to have known "conventional notation and illustrations for the syllogism" through conversations with her Cambridge University friends and her husband, Leonard WOOLF, as well as through her own wide reading. Donaldson notes that Sir Leslie STEPHEN, Woolf's father, "contributed to the wide-ranging debate among Victorians about logic and the significance of the syllogism" (330) that culminated in Alfred North Whitehead and Bertrand RUSSELL's publication of *Principia Mathematica* (1910–13). Whitehead and Russell used the following conventionalized notation of the syllogism to discuss its form:

All P are Q
R is P
Therefore R is Q

Mr. Ramsay, therefore, is "stuck in the major premise of the syllogism" (Donaldson 331). Donaldson also points to the way the alphabet metaphor in *To the Lighthouse* alludes to Leslie Stephen's *DICTIONARY OF NATIONAL BIOGRAPHY,* an alphabetically arranged reference work.

A. B. C. The Aerated Bread Company operated numerous tearooms throughout London where Woolf's characters can often be found having tea and writing or reading. Katharine HILBERY in *NIGHT AND DAY,* for example, takes refuge in an A. B. C. shop when she goes to meet Ralph DENHAM and misses him (ND 440), and FLORINDA in *JACOB'S ROOM* props her love letters against the milk pot in an A. B. C. (JR 78).

Abercorn Terrace The street on which Abel PARGITER and his family live in *THE YEARS.* Their house is described near the end of the novel by Delia PARGITER as "Hell!" (TY 417). There is no Abercorn Terrace in London, but there is an Abercorn Place in St. John's Wood.

Abrahamson In *THE YEARS,* he is the Jew in Sara PARGITER's lodgings who leaves hairs in the bath (TY 340).

Adaptations See entries on individual works.

Addison, Joseph (1672–1719) A close friend of Jonathan SWIFT and Richard Steele, Addison joined Steele from 1711 to 1712 in publishing the *Spectator,* a daily periodical intended "to enliven morality with wit, and to temper wit with morality." Addison was a politician, poet and essayist and appears in *ORLANDO.* Nick GREENE tells Orlando that her poem "The Oak Tree" reminds him of Addison's tragedy "Cato" (1713). Woolf's essay "Addison" was published in the *TIMES LITERARY SUPPLEMENT* in June 1919 and reprinted in the COMMON READER (CR1 132–45; CE1 85–94). Beverly Ann Schlack points out that Leslie STEPHEN, in *English Literature and Society in the Eighteenth Century* (the Ford Lectures, written as Stephen lay dying in 1903–04), wrote of Addison's "air of gentle condescension, especially when addressing ladies who cannot even translate his mottoes." In *Pope,* a biography of Alexander POPE for the English Men of Letters series, Stephen described Addison's "tone of superiority to women which is sometimes offensive. It is taken for granted that a woman is a fool."

Admiralty Arch In *A ROOM OF ONE'S OWN,* Woolf uses Admiralty Arch as an example of patriarchy's celebration of war (AROO 38). Built in 1910 and designed by Sir Aston Webb, the Admiralty Arch forms part of the National Monument to Queen Victoria, together with the Memorial in front of Buckingham Palace. Five houses on the southwest side of Trafalgar Square were demolished to make room for the edifice, which gives access to the Mall. Above the Arch were rooms used by the Admiralty.

Affable Hawk Pseudonym of Desmond MACCARTHY for his column in the *NEW STATESMAN.* One of Woolf's most notable engagements with Affable Hawk followed his column agreeing with Arnold BENNETT that women were inevitably intellectually inferior to men. Her protest was published in October 1920 under the heading "The Intellectual Status of Women," and is reprinted as appendix III in *The Diary of Virginia Woolf,* volume 2 (339–42).

Aislabie, Mrs. A guest of Kitty LASSWADE's in the "1914" chapter of *THE YEARS* who says she has heard that Tony ASHTON's lectures on Stéphane MALLARMÉ were wonderfully interesting (TY 257).

Aitken, Helen Mentioned in *JACOB'S ROOM* as a friend of Rose SHAW who is upset that "a man called Jimmy" will not marry Helen. Jimmy is killed in Flanders and "Helen visits hospitals" (JR 96–7).

Alardyce, Cyril Katharine HILBERY's cousin in *NIGHT AND DAY.* He is living with a woman who has borne him two children and to whom he is not married. Another child is on the way and these circumstances outrage Katharine's aunt, Mrs. MILVAIN.

Alardyce, Richard In *NIGHT AND DAY,* he is "the great poet" whose biography his granddaughter Katharine HILBERY and her mother, Margaret HILBERY, are supposed to be writing. His "relics" are kept in a curtained alcove off the Hilbery drawing room and visitors are taken to be shown them by Katharine. Several people remark on how similar Katharine looks to the poet's portrait that hangs in the alcove, the poet looking out beyond the horizon. Among the relics are the poet's huge slippers, an example of the way Woolf satirizes the Victorian cult of the great man. At times Katharine feels a kinship with her grandfather, imagining his life at the time the portrait was painted, when he might have been her brother (ND 319–20).

Albee, Edward See *WHO'S AFRAID OF VIRGINIA WOOLF?*

Albert The village idiot in *BETWEEN THE ACTS* who takes part in the annual pageant and whose antics make Etty SPRINGETT and Lynn JONES nervous.

Alexandra, Queen (1844–1925) In *THE WAVES,* JINNY, RHODA and SUSAN attend a school where Miss LAMBERT sits under a portrait of this Danish wife of Britain's King Edward VII. Masami Usui has discussed the way in which Woolf embeds Alexandra's biography in the soliloquies of the six "characters" in *The Waves,* reading that biography as part of the novel's critique of Empire ("A Portrait" 121–27).

Alfred A waiter in *THE YEARS* who tries to cheat Martin PARGITER (TY 233).

"All About Books" (CE2 263–67; CDB 120–26) An essay in the *NEW STATESMAN AND NATION* on February 28, 1931, reprinted in the *NEW REPUBLIC* the following month, in which Woolf considers young critics represented in *Scrutinies* (a collection of articles reprinted from F. R. and Q. D. LEAVIS's journal *Scrutiny*) and dismisses them as the "erudite and eugenic offspring" of university teachers who homogenize their thinking and lead them to lose any individuality they might have had.

Allan, Miss Character in *THE VOYAGE OUT.* In her introduction to *MELYMBROSIA,* Louise DeSalvo notes that Woolf had met a woman on a trip to Italy in 1908 who was probably the model for this character (MELYM xxxv). Miss Allan is writing a short *Primer of English Literature*—"Beowulf to Swinburne" (TVO 103). Before the end of *The Voyage Out,* Miss Allan finishes her book, though she has decided to stop at Robert BROWNING and omit A. C. SWINBURNE (TVO 316). Woolf probably also drew on her old tutor Janet CASE in creating Miss Allan, an English spinster who is rewarding herself in *The Voyage Out* with a trip to South America after "fifteen years of punctual lecturing and correcting essays upon English literature" (TVO 179). In chapter XIX, Miss Allan invites Rachel VINRACE to her room, thinking she is lonely, and shows her a bottle of crème de menthe, which she has named Oliver, and which she has taken with her every time she has traveled abroad for twenty-six years. Jane Wheare likens Miss Allan to Lucy CRADDOCK in *THE YEARS* (Wheare 63).

Ambrose, Helen Character in *THE VOYAGE OUT.* She and her husband Ridley AMBROSE travel to SANTA MARINA on the *EUPHROSYNE,* a ship owned by Willoughby VINRACE whose dead wife, Theresa, was Ridley's sister. Helen invites her niece Rachel VINRACE to stay with her and her husband at her brother's villa while her father continues his business down the Amazon. At first bored at the prospect of spending time with a naive young woman of twenty-four, Helen later decides to take responsibility for broadening Rachel's horizons and rescuing her from her father's wish to make his daughter a substitute for his wife, acting as his hostess when he runs for political office.

Jane Dunn notes that both Vanessa BELL and Woolf herself accepted that Helen was "a portrait in some salient respects of Vanessa," and Clive BELL wrote

Woolf that he supposed she "would make Vanessa believe in herself" (Dunn 88). Mitchell Leaska describes Helen as "a personality characterized by a heavily veiled and highly controlled aggressiveness" (*Novels* 14), seeing her as resenting Rachel's growing independence because it deprives her "of her most cherished substitute for real satisfaction: transitory fulfillment through others" (18).

At the beginning of *The Voyage Out,* Helen is seen to be distressed at leaving her children (although as Louise DeSalvo has pointed out, she leaves it to a nurse to tell them that their mother will be gone for several months!). On board the *Euphrosyne,* Helen reads G. E. MOORE's *Principia Ethica* and embroiders. She gradually gains Rachel's confidence, taking some of the lustre off Clarissa and Richard DALLOWAY after they have disembarked by telling her niece that she thought from the first that they were not particularly admirable people. Later, on Santa Marina, Helen develops a friendship with St. John HIRST, who is there with his friend Terence HEWET, to whom Rachel becomes engaged.

Some readers have seen Helen as the first incarnation of the goddess-like maternal figures that populate Woolf's novels, the most famous of whom is Mrs. RAMSAY in *TO THE LIGHTHOUSE.* Alice van Buren Kelley, for example, calls Helen the "goddess who oversees the action" (10) and a "ruling deity" (11). Madeline Moore, in "Some Female Versions of Pastoral," has discussed the possible influence of the scholarship of Jane Ellen HARRISON on *The Voyage Out,* especially in relation to the depiction of Helen: "In an effort to imbue Helen with the attributes of the original Great Mother, Woolf initially associates her with vegetation" (89) and shows several people attracted to her beauty (the striking nature of which is emphasized throughout the novel). In this, Moore suggests, Woolf was transferring her idealized image of her sister Vanessa to the character. As the novel progresses, Moore argues, Helen is "trapped in the maternal role typical in a traditional family" (90). Symbolically, she is "Jocasta to St. John and Terence and Demeter to Rachel" (92), embodying opposing myths. Moore suggests it is plausible "to imagine Helen as the embodiment of Theresa Vinrace's ghost come back to haunt Rachel" (94).

In earlier drafts of *The Voyage Out,* and in *MELYMBROSIA,* the intimacy between Rachel and Helen is much more explicit. A crucial scene in *The Voyage Out* occurs in chapter XXI where Rachel apparently hallucinates as Terence and Helen loom above her in the jungle and kiss. Several critics have pointed out that in earlier versions of the novel, the scene is clearer about Rachel and Helen's physical intimacy at this point; in the published version the scene remains obscure, although when Rachel comes back to consciousness it is "Helen's soft body, the strong and hospitable arms, and happiness swelling and breaking in one vast wave" that she becomes aware of, not Terence (TVO 284).

Ambrose, Ridley Character in *THE VOYAGE OUT.* His deceased sister Theresa's daughter, Rachel VINRACE, is the protagonist of the novel. Ridley and his wife, Helen AMBROSE, travel with Rachel on her father Willoughby VINRACE's ship the *EUPHROSYNE* to SANTA MARINA, where Rachel stays with the Ambroses. Ridley is editing the Odes of the Greek lyric poet Pindar (*c.* 522–442 B.C.) and frequently offers to teach classical Greek to anyone who seems even slightly interested. Like Mr. RAMSAY in *TO THE LIGHTHOUSE,* for whom he is a prototype, Ridley moans that his work goes unrecognized and depends upon female sympathy to soothe his frequent discomforts. In earlier drafts of the novel, Ridley was called Geranium.

"Am I a Snob?" (MOB 204–20) A paper read by Woolf to the MEMOIR CLUB on December 1, 1936. Having decided that Desmond MACCARTHY and Maynard KEYNES are not snobs, as they lack that desire to impress other people that Woolf acknowledges in herself, she admits to being a snob. "If you ask me would I rather meet Einstein or the Prince of Wales, I plump for the Prince without hesitation" (MOB 208).

"Anabasis" In *THE VOYAGE OUT,* the narrator remarks that the congregation at the Sunday service in chapter XVII read a passage from the Old Testament "as schoolboys translate an easy passage from the *Anabasis* when they have shut up their French grammar" (TVO 227). "Anabasis" was written by the Athenian general Xenophon and was an account of the expedition of the younger Cyrus and the retreat of the Greeks after the war with Artaxerxes in 401 B.C. T. S. ELIOT's translation of the *Anabase* of Saint-John Perse (1924) was published in 1930.

"Ancestors" See *MRS. DALLOWAY'S PARTY.*

Anderson Named in *JACOB'S ROOM,* a student at Cambridge with Jacob FLANDERS.

Andrews, Dr. Mentioned in *THE YEARS* as a great scholar and the author of *The Constitutional History of England* (TY 62). This does not impress Kitty LASSWADE (who refers to him as "Old Chuffy"), as she has felt his hand on her knee under the dinner table at her parents' house (TY 66).

Androgyny In *A ROOM OF ONE'S OWN,* the narrator, Mary BETON, wonders if the mind has two sexes as the body does, and "amateurishly" sketches an ideal fusion of male and female inspired by the sight of a man and a woman getting into a taxi together below her window. She thinks that Samuel Taylor COLERIDGE may have had such a fusion in mind when he said that "a great mind is androgynous" (AROO 98). Woolf had noted Coleridge's thought when she read *The Table Talk and Omniana of Samuel Taylor Coleridge* in 1918, preparing to review it for the *TIMES LITERARY SUPPLEMENT* ("Coleridge as Critic" E2 221–25); the line is from Coleridge's entry for September 1, 1832 (E2 224n6). In *A Room of One's Own,* Woolf extends the concept of androgyny to argue that "sex-consciousness" is fatal to the creative instinct in both men and women. She presents William SHAKESPEARE as the supremely androgynous artist, and also says that John KEATS, Laurence STERNE, William COWPER, Charles LAMB, and Coleridge were androgynous; of her contemporaries, only Marcel PROUST "was wholly androgynous, if not perhaps a little too much of a woman" (AROO 103).

Androgyny is a very ancient idea, representing unity and wholeness in many philosophical and religious systems (see Elémire Zolla, *The Androgyne: Reconciliation of Male and Female*). The concept has been discussed in critical writing on Woolf from Winifred HOLTBY's 1932 biography onwards. Herbert Marder argues that Woolf's novels were a "kind of record of this search for wholeness; each new experiment is an attempt to embody and express this elusive unity of being," a unity she at times called "the androgynous mind" (Marder 108). Marder traces the concept of androgyny through several of Woolf's novels and short fictions, and notes that Holtby said that Woolf makes her characters "manly-womanly and womanly-manly" (Holtby 182). Marder points out that Woolf uses the image of the lighthouse in several works and he finds that it is "related to the idea of androgyny." He cites Katharine HILBERY in *NIGHT AND DAY* as an early example of Woolf's concern with androgyny, and refers also to "the manliness in their girlish hearts" of the Ramsay daughters in *TO THE LIGHTHOUSE,* and to BERNARD in *THE WAVES,* who imagines how his future biographer will say that he combined masculine and feminine qualities. In *ORLANDO,* Marder writes, "the truth of androgyny that releases from the bondage of intellect plays lightly upon scene after scene, turning everything into fantasy" (113); Orlando, he points out, is androgynous from the beginning of the book (Marder 114). Marilyn R. Farwell points out that the "history of androgyny is one of eloquent but at times conflicting statements, and Woolf's place in that history is important because her work is the basis of many contemporary definitions" (433). Farwell, closely studying the term as Woolf uses it in *A Room of One's Own,* gives a brief history of attempts to define androgyny and stresses the ambivalence of Woolf's definition. "While we are left with an ambivalent and limited concept of androgyny" by *A Room of One's Own,* writes Farwell, "we are also given the tools to go beyond that" (451).

Phyllis Rose, in her biography of Woolf, notes also how significant androgyny is to Woolf's major works of the 1920s and points out that it was during this time that Woolf's love for Vita SACKVILLE-WEST was most intense. *To the Lighthouse, Orlando* and *A Room of One's Own,* says Rose, "are all in different ways concerned with sex roles, and all in different ways suggest the desirability of an end to rigid designations of what is masculine and what is feminine, an ideal which we might—very cautiously—refer to as androgyny" (Rose 176). Rose calls the androgynous mind in *A Room of One's Own* a "temporary metaphor" which employs sexual terms "to signify the transcendence of sex" (188); what Keats meant by "negative capability" and Woolf meant by "the androgynous mind" Rose suspects are much the same thing (188).

A very significant exploration of the concept of androgyny in Woolf and other writers was Carolyn Heilbrun's 1973 book *Toward a Recognition of Androgyny* in which she argued that "masculinity" had led to continual war and that the BLOOMSBURY GROUP offered an example of a group of people "in which masculinity and femininity were marvelously mixed in its members" (118). Heilbrun saw Woolf's "androgynous character" as part of the reason for public vituperation after her death (136) and praised the early work of Holtby as "vital to a discussion of Woolf's androgyny" (152).

The opposition between masculine and feminine, often serving as a paradigm for other dualisms, structured several critical works published on Woolf in the early 1970s, including Nancy Topping Bazin's *Virginia Woolf and the Androgynous Vision* and Alice van Buren Kelley's *Novels of Virginia Woolf: Fact and Vision.* Harvena Richter also writes that Woolf's mind "embraced the duality of the creative mind" (Richter 18). Roger Poole later argued against androgyny's being anything more than "a symbol that stood for resolution without in fact being any sort of resolution"; androgyny, for Poole, is only "a conceptual possibility" (Poole, *Unknown* 261).

Maria DiBattista, on the other hand, follows Heilbrun in making the argument that Woolf's "theory of anonymity naturally formulated itself as poetic fable, the myth of androgyny" (DiBattista, *Major Novels* 17). Arguing that androgyny was "essentially a comic myth" (122), DiBattista describes the concept as "a serviceable myth that released [Woolf] from the confines of the appropriate" (20). She points out that Woolf's androgynous mind was a way of freeing thought from "its subservience to the established body of biological and social 'facts of life' " (20), those same "facts" that Poole describes as the different male and female "embodiment" that renders androgyny "a kind of wish fulfillment" (Poole 262). DiBattista concurs with Heilbrun that *To the Lighthouse* presents "the daughter as the true inheritor," the creator who has "found her mother and made peace with her father": "The bereaved and obsessed self of *To the Lighthouse* becomes the dream self of *Orlando*—the androgyne" (DiBattista 110). In *The Waves,* also, DiBattista finds Woolf's "own version of a 'myth of the body' whose proper symbol is the androgyne. In the androgynous poetic body, male and female speak from 'a centre of some different order and system of life' " (DiBattista 167).

A contrary view of *The Waves* is offered by Eileen B. Sypher in "*The Waves:* A Utopia of Androgyny?" where she examines how Bernard "suggests himself as a representation of the androgynous artist Woolf speaks of in *A Room of One's Own*" (187). Marder argues that "androgyny was a kind of parable containing a solution to the dilemma of the feminist war with herself" that Woolf was riven by (Marder 108), and Sypher concurs, seeing the androgynous Bernard in *The Waves* as "a more earnest and even desperate attempt to achieve balance without reliving the conflict—an attempt, in other words, to suppress any sign of that potential feminist anger that began to emerge in *To the Lighthouse*" (Sypher 190). Sypher disagrees with DiBattista that *The Waves* presents a female myth, arguing that androgyny is "problematic politically" and "can be represented only in a highly contradictory manner in a literary text because of its utopian character" (Sypher 196). Sypher eventually finds the concept of androgyny in *The Waves* to be "associated with the suppression of female ambition" (205) and Bernard to be, in fact, Woolf's parody of not only artists "but, more deeply, the concept of androgyny itself" (208).

Sypher aligns herself with Elaine Showalter, to whom she refers as "one of the pioneers" in criticizing the concept of androgyny. Showalter directly counters Heilbrun's positive representation of androgyny, writing that when "we think about the joy, the generosity, and the absence of jealousy and domination attributed to Bloomsbury, we should also remember the victims of this emotional utopia: Mark Gertler, Dora Carrington, Virginia Woolf. They are the failures of androgyny; their suicides are one of Bloomsbury's representative art forms" (*Literature of Their Own* 264–65). In her chapter "Virginia Woolf and the Flight Into Androgyny," Showalter is usually concerned with Woolf's biography, but uses this as an argument against her feminist political writings: "Androgyny was the myth that helped her evade confrontation with her own painful femaleness and enabled her to choke and repress her anger and ambition" (264). She argues also against Bazin's interpretation of Woolf's suicide as "a beautiful act of faith, or a philosophical gesture toward androgyny," saying this view is a betrayal of "the human pain and rage that she felt" (*Literature of Their Own* 278). Agreeing with other critics that androgyny is central to Woolf's thinking not only in *A Room of One's Own* but also in her novels, Showalter criticizes the concept as a "strategic retreat" from the bitterness of female experience and from the anger that, she says, Woolf feared as "the first symptom of mental collapse" (287). The "ultimate room of one's own," for Showalter, "is the grave" (297).

Other critics, however, have interpreted Woolf's use of the concept of androgyny much more positively and have sought to understand it in the context of the complex discourses around sexuality prevalent in the 1920s. Ellen Bayuk Rosenman finds that androgyny offered Woolf "a way of rejecting biological determinism and undoing the privileging of the masculine over the feminine" ("Sexual Identity" 647), a privileging she explains was left intact by the lesbian model of the 1920s. Elizabeth Abel has drawn attention to the "tension between the discourses of androgyny and maternity" in the 1920s, finding that Woolf's discussion of androgyny in *A Room of One's Own* is implicitly weighted toward the maternal: "The very sexuality on which her language insists . . . returns to the metaphor of birth. The site of textual production is figuratively the womb. . . . Androgyny is proposed as a corrective to the masculinization of discourse" (Abel 87). Sandra Gilbert and Susan Gubar have suggested that the influence of the ideas of the writer Edward Carpenter (1844–1929) on Bloomsbury, particularly on E. M. FORSTER, accounts to some extent for Woolf's ideas of the "man-womanliness" of some artists (*Sexchanges* 364). Barbara Fassler also notes that "theories familiar to Bloomsbury hold homosexuality to be caused by a unique fusion of masculine and feminine elements. Notions about androgyny were closely intertwined with ideas about homosexuality" (Fassler 237).

Fassler points out how Woolf's use of androgyny would have intimated homosexuality to her contemporaries, drawing as it did on "current theories of the homosexual as a person who uniquely combines both masculine and feminine qualities to achieve artistic creativity and personal integration" (Fassler 251). Noting the popularity of the "trapped soul theory" as an explanation of homosexuality (and its significant exposition in Radclyffe Hall's *WELL OF LONELINESS,* the obscenity trial of which is frequently alluded to in *A Room of One's Own*), Fassler finds significant Woolf's mention of Proust in *A Room of One's Own* as the only modern writer she considers androgynous, because Proust's character Charlus in *À la recherche du temps perdu* is an example of a "trapped soul." Writing on a similar theme, Rosenman notes that androgyny carries "different implications in a historical context that defined 'lesbian' as 'masculine' " (Rosenman 649). Responding to those critics who have interpreted Woolf's use of androgyny as a retreat from feminism, Rosenman asserts that the concept was in fact a "historically specific version" of feminism (649). She also refers to the special issue of *Women's Studies* published in 1974 under the title "The Androgyny Papers," edited by Cynthia Secor, where, despite some dissenting articles—including ones by Carolyn Heilbrun and Nancy Topping Bazin—feminist opinion was seen to be turning against the concept of androgyny. Cynthia Secor herself argued that androgyny perpetuated the "old dualities" of masculine and feminine, and Daniel A. Harris described Woolf's "much-touted vision of androgyny" as "actually a compromise, a retreat from the more radically feminist fury Woolf feared to express" (Harris 175). Rosenman recommends as rebuttals to such arguments the reevaluations of Woolfian androgyny to be found in Toril Moi and Mary Jacobus.

Moi, like several recent critics writing from a perspective informed by poststructuralist theory, argues that Woolf's use of androgyny is a recognition of the "falsifying metaphysical nature" of fixed gender categories (Moi 13). "Far from fleeing such gender identities because she fears them," says Moi, "Woolf rejects them because she has seen them for what they are" (Moi 13). Makiko Minow-Pinkney makes a similar point when she says that Woolf calls into question the very sexual identities that androgyny depends upon, "opening up the fixed unity into a multiplicity, joy, play of heterogeneity, a fertile difference" (Minow-Pinkney 12). Rachel Bowlby, also, meets Showalter's criticism by pointing out that the scene in *A Room of One's Own* of the couple getting into a taxi is "set in the form of a *fantasy* of completeness and complementarity" (Bowlby 44). Of this often-cited scene, Jane Marcus has written that "every woman reader I know sees this passage as Woolf's mnemonic device to force herself out of her feminist and lesbian fantasy world, back to a realization of 'heterosexuality makes the world go round' " (*Languages* 159). Mary Jacobus argues that Woolf's remarks on androgyny should be read in the light of what *A Room of One's Own* has said about anger, seeing androgyny "not as a naive attempt to transcend the determinants of gender and culture (though it is that too), but rather as a harmonizing gesture, a simultaneous enactment of desire and repression by which the split is closed with an essentially Utopian vision of undivided consciousness" (Jacobus 39). Seeing Woolf's gesture toward androgyny as "millennial," Jacobus reads the androgynous mind in a way very similar to that in which Minow-Pinkney does, as "a mind paradoxically conceived of not as one, but as heterogeneous, open to the play of difference" (Jacobus 39).

"Angel in the House, The" In her essay "PROFESSIONS FOR WOMEN" Woolf says that before she could write she had to kill this phantom of Victorian womanhood that dictated that she must be sympathetic to men whose books she was reviewing. The phrase comes from the title of a long sequence of poems by Coventry Kersey Dighton Patmore (1823–96), a friend of Alfred, Lord TENNYSON and John RUSKIN, intended as an expression of the Victorian ideal of married love. Woolf's mother, Julia Prinsep STEPHEN, owned a copy of the fourth edition of *The Angel in the House* (1866) inscribed to "Julia Jackson with the kind regard of Coventry Patmore" (Gillespie & Steele 11).

"Angel in the house," a play by Eureka of the Ridiculous Theatrical Company based on the lives of Vanessa BELL and Duncan GRANT, was first performed in 1993 in New York. (See also POPULAR CULTURE.)

Angelo The name of the head waiter at the hotel on SANTA MARINA in *THE VOYAGE OUT*.

"Anon" The first chapter of a projected critical history of English literature that Woolf was working on just before her death in March 1941. "Reading at Random" or "Turning the Page" were titles she was considering for this work. "Anon" and a few pages of the second chapter, possibly to be called "The Reader," are all that survive, apart from her reading notes for the work. Woolf was concerned with the original "song" of the natural world from which, she speculated, literature evolved. The voice of the artist was originally the anonymous voice of a community, and she saw "common emotion" as the heart of literature. Elements of her thinking in "Reading at Random" as well as references to books she was reading for it find their way into Woolf's last work of fiction, *BETWEEN THE ACTS*, which is also concerned with England's literary history (see Mark Hussey, "Reading and Ritual" 92–93). The surviving text of "Reading at Random" has been edited and annotated by Brenda R. Silver ("Anon" 356–441).

Anrep, Boris von (1883–1969) Russian mosaicist who married Helen Maitland in 1917. In 1912, he brought the work of several contemporary Russian artists to London for the Second Post-Impressionist Exhibition organized by Roger FRY. According to Annabel Farjeon, he was "the only artist who consistently worked with mosaic in Britain during the 20th century" (15).

Anrep, Helen (1885–1965) Woolf met Helen Anrep (née Maitland), one of the circle of people around the painter Augustus JOHN, at a party given by Ottoline MORRELL in 1925. Helen was married to the Russian mosaicist Boris ANREP, with whom she had two children, Igor and Anastasia, but she left him (and the young woman he had brought from Russia to live with him as a second wife) in 1926 when she moved in with Roger FRY. Fry and Anrep remained together until Fry's death in 1934. Woolf wrote in her DIARY in November 1934 that Anrep had tentatively asked her to write Fry's biography (D4 258). In *ROGER FRY,* she describes Fry's relationship with Anrep as "what he had lacked for so many years—a centre, the intimacy between two people that grows with the years" (RF 254) and quoted from some of his letters to her.

Antaeus Son of Poseidon and Gaea in Greek mythology, he gained strength whenever he touched the earth (his mother). He was beaten by Hercules, who held him in the air. In *BETWEEN THE ACTS* Antaeus is mentioned when Lucy SWITHIN asks her brother Bart OLIVER the origin of the expression "touch wood" (28).

Antigone Herbert Marder has described the *Antigone* of Sophocles as being for Woolf "a primer of resistance to masculine tyranny" (105). Allusions to the play abound in Woolf's writing and she re-read the play many times during her life (as her reading notebooks, described by Brenda R. Silver, attest).

In *THE VOYAGE OUT,* Clarissa DALLOWAY says that she will never forget seeing a performance of Sophocles's play *Antigone* at Cambridge, a statement belied by her referring to the character CLYTEMNESTRA, who does not appear in *Antigone.* An early critic, Joan Bennett, says that the mistake is Woolf's, but this seems very unlikely. When Clarissa says she does not know Greek, William PEPPER recites part of a famous chorus from *Antigone,* identified by Avrom Fleishman as lines 332–37 of the translation by Sir Richard Jebb (the 1888 and 1904 editions of which Woolf frequently read).[1] Fleishman writes that the quotation "serves to universalize the novel's action as a voyage of human enterprise and a passage in man's mortality" (Fleishman 18). The allusion to *Antigone* was inserted in *The Voyage Out* at a late stage of the novel's development, replacing an earlier allusion to the *Agamemnon* of Aeschylus (in which Clytemnestra *does* appear). Louise DeSalvo writes that in this novel the allusion to *Antigone* makes "less sense in relationship to Rachel Vinrace than it does in relationship to Virginia Woolf" (*First Voyage* 155).

In *A ROOM OF ONE'S OWN,* Antigone is an example of women who have "burnt like beacons in all the works of all the poets from the beginning of time" (AROO 43) whom Woolf uses to stress the difference between fictional and real women. In *THREE GUINEAS,* Woolf cites Sophocles's portrayal of the tyrant Creon as a profound analysis "of the effect of power and wealth upon the soul" (TG 81). In a note she remarks that although the *Antigone* can be made to fit all kinds of modern situations, ultimately great art cannot be used as propaganda without mutilating it; "when the curtain falls we sympathize, it may be noted, even with Creon himself" (TG 170).

Silver points out that the *Antigone* "plays an important part in the description of Edward [PARGITER]'s emotional life" in *THE PARGITERS* (RN 68). In *THE YEARS,* he is first seen reading it in his rooms at Oxford but his thoughts quickly turn to his cousin Kitty. In the "1907" chapter, his cousin Sara PARGITER reads the translation of the play Edward has published (TY 135), but at the end of the novel, in "Present Day," when Edward quotes a line from the play to his sister Eleanor PARGITER, he tells his nephew North PARGITER that he cannot translate the line (which is "I cannot share in hatred, but in loving" [TY 413–14]). The plot and "buried alive" theme of *Antigone* are said by Jane Marcus to provide "the mythology and structure" of the novel (*Languages* 102).

Antiquary, The One of the Waverly novels (named for the Waverly family) of Sir Walter SCOTT, and the book that Mr. RAMSAY in *TO THE LIGHTHOUSE* reads after dinner. Louise DeSalvo has written extensively on the relation of Scott's novel to *To the Lighthouse.* She points out that according to John Gibson Lockhart's life of Scott, one of the prototypes for the character of Jonathan Oldbuck, the Antiquary, was John Ramsay of Ochertyre. *The Antiquary,* which is set in Scotland, also contains the image of a lighthouse which, as in Woolf's novel, "is associated with a need for parental protection" (DeSalvo, *Impact* 224). DeSalvo points out that the chapter Mr. Ramsay reads in section XIX of part 1 opens with a poem alluding to a "secret sin" that turns out to be Evelina Neville's mistaken belief that she has had an incestuous relationship with her half-brother; Evelina throws herself off a cliff (*Impact* 225–26).

In "1897: Virginia Woolf at Fifteen," DeSalvo traces a source of the characterization of Mr. Ramsay to Leslie Stephen's having read *The Antiquary* to his children in 1897, and finds a parallel between Cam RAMSAY's ambivalent feelings toward her father and Scott's character Isabella Wardour's ambivalence toward *her* father in the novel. DeSalvo also points out that in her 1924 essay on *The Antiquary* (E3 454–58) Woolf misreads an episode of suspected incest as actual incest. It is the episode concerning Evelina

[1] The lines in Greek are missing from the Signet Classic edition of the novel.

Neville that Mr. Ramsay feels he must re-read, and this leads DeSalvo to write that it is "horrifying to speculate that Evelina Neville in *The Antiquary* was the model Woolf would emulate many years later when she committed suicide" (97).

Antonio A "manservant" in *THE YEARS* who works for Sir Digby PARGITER.

Apostles, The A secret and exclusive undergraduate society at Cambridge University, also known as the Cambridge Conversazione Society and often referred to by its members simply as "The Society." The Apostles were the cradle of the BLOOMSBURY GROUP as Lytton STRACHEY, Saxon SYDNEY-TURNER and Leonard WOOLF were elected to the Society in 1902, a time when E. M. FORSTER, Desmond MACCARTHY, and Roger FRY were also members; John Maynard KEYNES was elected in 1903. The Apostles were founded in 1820 by George Tomlinson and were not at first a secret society (Levy 65). Membership was by election only and was for life. The Apostles had their own special language and rituals: undergraduates being considered for membership, for example, were known as "embryos," and the world beyond the Society was called "phenomenal" (as opposed to the "real" world of the Society). At the turn of the century, Cambridge, and the Apostles in particular, were under the profound influence of G. E. MOORE, whose book *Principia Ethica* (1903) was regarded by many of the intellectuals there as their "bible." The correspondence between Leonard Woolf and Lytton Strachey between 1904 and 1911 (see Spotts 65–151) is full of references to the world and language of the Apostles.

Apsley House Mentioned at the beginning of *THE YEARS,* the residence of the Duke of Wellington since 1820, originally built in 1785 for Lord Apsley. In the "1914" chapter Martin PARGITER observes that someone has written "God is Love" in pink chalk upon its gates (TY 226).

Argento, Dominick (b. 1927) American composer who in 1975 won a Pulitzer Prize for his song-cycle *From the Diary of Virginia Woolf.* The cycle is in eight parts: I: The Diary (April 1919); II: Anxiety (October 1920); III: Fancy (February 1927); IV: Hardy's Funeral (January 1928); V: Rome (May 1935); VI: War (June 1940); VII: Parents (December 1940); VIII: Last Entry (March 1941).

Aristotle In *JACOB'S ROOM,* a waiter at the hotel Jacob FLANDERS stays at in Greece.

Army and Navy Stores In *MRS. DALLOWAY,* Doris KILMAN takes Elizabeth DALLOWAY with her to the Army and Navy Stores when she needs to buy a petticoat, and in *THE YEARS,* the Stores make an appearance on the first page as evidence of the bustle of the West End of London. The Stores were founded in 1872, initially to serve officers and non-commissioned officers, and were on Victoria Street. By the 1920s they were open to the public (Abbott 205).

Arnold, Matthew (1822–88) In *THE VOYAGE OUT,* Richard DALLOWAY invokes Arnold's phrase "what a set!" in denouncing the poet Percy Bysshe SHELLEY; Ridley AMBROSE responds by calling Arnold "a detestable prig!" (TVO 44). Arnold, with whom Woolf's father, Sir Leslie STEPHEN, was acquainted, was professor of poetry at Oxford University from 1857 to 1867 and author of several volumes of poetry. Among his well-known works are "Sohrab and Rustum" and "The Scholar Gypsy" (the latter, Woolf wrote, was one of her father's "greatest favourites" [E1 129]). After 1860 he published very influential works of literary criticism as well as essays on social and political life, most notably "Culture and Anarchy" (published in the *CORNHILL MAGAZINE* 1867–68). The son of a famous headmaster of Rugby school, Arnold was also very concerned with the reform of secondary education in England.

In "*Flumina Amem Silvasque*" (1917; Andrew McNeillie translates the title as "Let me adore the rivers and the woods" [E2 164]) Woolf wrote that "if one takes a bird's-eye view of Arnold's poetry, the background seems to consist of a moonlit lawn, with a sad but not passionate nightingale singing in a cedar tree of the sorrows of mankind" (E2 162), a judgment that McNeillie points out led to correspondence in the *TIMES LITERARY SUPPLEMENT* in subsequent weeks disagreeing with her. In 1924, Woolf wrote a brief notice of *Unpublished Letters of Matthew Arnold* in the *NATION & ATHENAEUM* (E3 397). In "Indiscretions," an essay in American *Vogue* in 1924, she included Arnold among writers who "are not men when they write, nor are they women. They appeal to that large tract of the soul which is sexless" (E3 462).

Arnold-Forster, Katherine See COX, Katherine.

Arnold-Forster, William Edward (1885–1951) A second cousin of Aldous HUXLEY, he married Katherine ("Ka") COX in 1918. Will, as Ka called him, studied painting at the Slade School of Art in 1904–08 (D1 130n28). Woolf was not very impressed by him, feeling the Arnold-Forster–Cox marriage would be "merely a decorous & sympathetic alliance" (D1 172).

"Art of Fiction, The" (CE2 51–55; M 106–12) A review of E. M. FORSTER's *Aspects of the Novel* (1927), first published in the *New York Herald Tribune* on October 16, 1927, as "Is Fiction an Art?" and reprinted in a revised, slightly shorter version as "The Art of Fiction" in the Literary Supplement of the *NATION & ATHENAEUM* about a month later. Forster had quoted Woolf's "THE MARK ON THE WALL" in his Clark lectures at Cambridge, published as *Aspects of the Novel,* comparing her to Laurence STERNE and calling them both "fantasists." He included Woolf among novelists whose work depends upon what he called "the fantastic-prophetic axis" (*Aspects* 102). Woolf's review is titled in contrast to Percy Lubbock's 1921 book *The Craft of Fiction,* and she takes Forster to task in her review for not treating fiction as an art. She notes that he omits any consideration of language, the medium of fiction, and she expresses frustration with English novelists' adherence to a conception of "life" which limits the scope of their writing to the "eternal tea-table" (CE2 55). Woolf's argument is that fiction should be treated as an art just as painting, music, or sculpture would be, not just as social commentary or entertainment.

Arthur's Education Fund In *THREE GUINEAS,* Woolf uses this phrase (abbreviated to "AEF") from William Makepeace THACKERAY's novel *Pendennis* (1848–50) to illuminate one difference between the sons and daughters of educated men, that fund for the education of young men to which sisters have had for centuries to sacrifice their own education and its rewards.

"Artist and Politics, The" (CE2 230–32; M 225–28) The original version of this essay was an article entitled "Why Art Today Follows Politics" in the *DAILY WORKER* December 14, 1936 (see Jane Marcus, *Art and Anger* 105). A friend of Quentin BELL's, a young Communist named Elizabeth Watson, had asked Woolf to write the article (D5 30n4). Woolf begins with the question, why are artists interested in politics? and answers that it is because "art is the first luxury to be discarded in times of stress; the artist is the first of the workers to suffer" (M 227). When society is in chaos, she concludes, the artist is besieged by voices asking or ordering him to put his art in the service of the state or to take up another, more "useful" occupation. In her DIARY for November 10, 1936, she wrote, "But I am tired this morning: too much strain & racing yesterday. The Daily Worker article. Madrid not fallen. Chaos. Slaughter. War surrounding our island" (D5 32).

Asheham House (sometimes spelled Asham or Ascham) Woolf's first house outside London, discovered on a walk over the Sussex Downs with Leonard WOOLF in October 1911. Woolf asked her sister Vanessa BELL to share the lease, but it seems that Leonard and Virginia took over the house completely from very early on. Woolf lived at Asheham during the period of their courtship. Leonard was a guest at her housewarming party over the weekend of February 3–5, 1912, "the coldest day for 40 years." Described by Quentin BELL as "a strange and beautiful house in a lovely and romantic situation," Asheham had been built as a summer retreat between 1820 and 1825 by a Lewes solicitor who had bought neighboring Itford Farm. In 1919 Woolf's landlord decided not to renew the lease as he wished to move to the house with his elderly mother; this precipitated the search for another house that led the Woolfs to find MONK'S HOUSE. The legend that Asheham was haunted is supposed to be the germ of Woolf's short story "A HAUNTED HOUSE." In the late 1980s, the East Sussex County Council Planning Department began considering demolishing Asheham to increase the landfill site at Beddingham. In July 1992 it was reported that Asheham would be demolished "to make way for a rubbish dump," and in 1994, the East Sussex County Council having refused the Blue Circle Cement Company's offer to move and rebuild the house, Asheham was destroyed. Quentin Bell and others speculated that a persistent antipathy to the BLOOMSBURY GROUP might have influenced the Council's disregard of the house's place in England's literary history (*Sunday Telegraph* May 15, 1994: 18).

Asheham House. Photograph by Louise H. Tucker.
The Woolfs discovered Asheham House while walking on the Sussex Downs in October 1911, and this was their country home until 1919. The legend that Asheham was haunted is supposed to be the germ of Woolf's short story "A Haunted House." In 1994 the house was destroyed by the East Sussex County Council.

Ashford, Miss Mentioned attending a SUFFRAGE meeting in the "1910" chapter of *THE YEARS.*

Ashley Mentioned in *THE YEARS* as a friend of Edward PARGITER's at Oxford University (TY 52). There may be elements of Lytton STRACHEY in his characterization.

Ashton, Tony At Kitty LASSWADE's party in the "1914" chapter of *THE YEARS,* he is mentioned as lecturing on Stéphane MALLARMÉ at Mortimer House (TY 261). Mrs. AISLABIE has heard his lectures were wonderfully interesting (TY 257).

Askew, Helen Named in *JACOB'S ROOM,* observing Jacob FLANDERS and Dick GRAVES at a party. She thinks their friendship "so much more beautiful than women's friendships" (JR 111).

Aspasia See MONK'S HOUSE PAPERS.

Asquith, Emma Alice Margaret (Margot), Lady Oxford (née Tennant) (1864–1945) Wife of Herbert Henry ASQUITH, Liberal prime minister from 1908 to 1916. She was a regular guest at Ottoline MORRELL's house, GARSINGTON, where Woolf met her. Leonard WOOLF describes her in his autobiography as "a very English mixture of tomboy, enfant terrible, and great lady" (LW2 145). The Asquiths' daughter was Princess Elizabeth BIBESCO.

Asquith, Herbert Henry (1852–1928) Herbert Henry, first Earl of Oxford and Asquith, entered Parliament as a Liberal in 1886, becoming home secretary in 1892, and chancellor of the exchequer in 1905. In 1907 he became prime minister of England, remaining in power until 1916, when he retired after arguing with David LLOYD GEORGE. In *THE VOYAGE OUT,* Helen AMBROSE finds it "incredible" that people should "care whether Asquith is in or Austen Chamberlain out" (TVO 96), identifying the time the novel is taking place as 1905, when the general election was held. In *NIGHT AND DAY,* Mary DATCHET asks Ralph DENHAM whether he does not agree that "Mr. Asquith should be hanged" because he has once again blocked women's SUFFRAGE. Asquith is also mentioned in *JACOB'S ROOM*; Jacob plans to write an essay on civilization "with some pretty sharp hits at Mr. Asquith" (136).

Astell, Mary (1668–1731) Woolf mentions Astell in *THREE GUINEAS* as an example of how the desire for education exists in women as well as men (TG 25). In 1694, Mary Astell, "self-styled 'Lover of Her Sex', published the first considered plea by an Englishwoman for the establishment of an institution of higher learning for women, *A Serious Proposal to the Ladies for the Advancement of Their True and Greatest Interest*" (Kinnaird 29). Elizabeth Elstob, an Anglo-Saxon scholar whom Woolf mentions in her note on Astell in *Three Guineas* (note 21 to chapter 1), supplied George Ballard with many details of Astell's life for his biography of her, included in *Memoirs of British Ladies* (1775). Denise Riley describes Astell's *Some Reflections upon Marriage* (1700) as "an extraordinary piece of writing" whose "surface of piety and devotion is constantly ripped across by the most bitter irony" (Riley 32). Joan Kinnaird places Astell "in the ranks of those seventeenth-century reformers who promoted an enlightened ideal of marriage as rational and compassionate" (36–37), and stresses the importance of Astell's wish to found an *institution* of higher learning for women rather than just advocating private education. Woolf took notes on Astell from *Mary Astell* by Florence M. Smith (Columbia University Press, 1916) (RN 141).

Atalanta's Garland *Atalanta's Garland, Being the Book of the Edinburgh University Women's Union* included in 1926 Woolf's story "A WOMAN'S COLLEGE FROM THE OUTSIDE" (SF 139–42; BP 6–9). The Women's Union took the name for their journal from the myth of Atalanta, who was warned by an oracle never to marry. To deal with suitors, Atalanta said anyone who could beat her in a race could marry her, but those who lost would be killed. Venus gave Hippomenes three golden apples with which to distract Atalanta, and he beat her in the race. Unfortunately for Hippomenes, he forgot to thank the goddess and she had him turned into a lion.

Athenaeum Literary and artistic review founded in 1828 which published many of the leading English writers of the nineteenth century. John Middleton MURRY became its editor in 1919 and revived it from a slump, publishing work by Woolf, T. S. ELIOT, E. M. FORSTER, Roger FRY, Katherine MANSFIELD, Lytton STRACHEY and Leonard WOOLF. The *Athenaeum* was merged with the *Nation* in 1921 (see *NATION & ATHENAEUM*).

Atkins, Eileen (b. 1934) English actress who portrayed Woolf in a 1991 performance of *A ROOM OF ONE'S OWN* adapted, abridged and directed by Patrick Garland. Her two-woman show "Vita and Virginia," adapted from the correspondence between Woolf and Vita SACKVILLE-WEST, was performed first in London in 1993 with Penelope Wilton playing the part of Sackville-West, and in New York in 1994 with Vanessa Redgrave in that part.

A to Z See p. 1.

Aubrey, Uncle Character in *NIGHT AND DAY* who proudly says he does not understand Russian novelists and would rather have written the works of Charles DICKENS than spent his life as he had, ruling "a large part of the Indian Empire" (ND 348).

Auden, W. H. (Wystan Hugh) (1907–73) English poet. The left-wing poets of the 1930s have sometimes been called the "Auden generation" and Woolf came to know several of them through John LEHMANN and Stephen SPENDER. Woolf saw in Auden's poetry of the 1930s the egotism that characterized his generation's writing. She discusses their work in general terms in both "LETTER TO A YOUNG POET" and "THE LEANING TOWER." Woolf was introduced to Auden by Spender in June 1937 at an Albert Hall meeting of the National Joint Committee on Spanish Relief during the SPANISH CIVIL WAR. Later that year, an idea developed that the "young Brainies," as the Woolfs referred to this younger generation of writers, should take over the HOGARTH PRESS as a collective, but Lehmann's friends could not raise enough money and only Lehmann himself bought into the Press. Auden promised a book to the Press, but forgot that he was bound by his contract to Faber & Faber, T. S. ELIOT's firm. In 1939 Auden and Christopher ISHERWOOD left for the United States, shocking many of their former supporters in England by their decision to remain there. In 1954, reviewing *A WRITER'S DIARY* for the *New Yorker,* Auden wrote that "even in the palmiest days of social consciousness, [Woolf] was admired and loved much more than she realized" by his generation (Auden 417).

Aurora Leigh See BROWNING, Elizabeth Barrett.

Austen, Jane (1775–1817) English novelist of manners. Austen's six novels were published a number of years after they were written, and not in the order they were written: *Sense and Sensibility* (1811); *Pride and Prejudice* (1813); *Mansfield Park* (1814); *Emma* (1816); *Persuasion* (1818); and *Northanger Abbey* (1818). In *THE VOYAGE OUT,* Clarissa DALLOWAY gives Rachel VINRACE a copy of *Persuasion* inscribed with her name and address. Her pompous husband, Richard DALLOWAY, tells Rachel that "our Jane" is "incomparably the greatest female writer we possess" (TVO 62), but falls asleep soon after his wife begins to read aloud from *Persuasion.* Rachel dislikes Austen, finding her "like a tight plait" (TVO 58). In her later incarnation in *MRS. DALLOWAY,* Clarissa calls Richard Dalloway "Wickham" when she first meets him; Wickham is a character in *Pride and Prejudice* (and there is a Willoughby—the first name of Rachel Vinrace's father—in *Sense and Sensibility*). The opening of *NIGHT AND DAY* recalls the opening of Austen's *Emma.*

In *A ROOM OF ONE'S OWN,* Woolf remarks that when the middle-class woman began to write fiction at the end of the eighteenth century, a cultural change was wrought "of greater importance than the Crusades or the Wars of the Roses" (AROO 65). Woolf sees Austen as taking up the mantle of her predecessors such as Fanny BURNEY, and creates a portrait of her in *A Room* as writing secretly "in the general sitting-room," covering her manuscripts with blotting paper if anyone came in (AROO 67). Woolf likens Austen to William SHAKESPEARE as a writer who has consumed all impediments and writes "without hate, without bitterness, without fear, without protest, without preaching" (AROO 68). Jane Austen "devised a perfectly natural, shapely sentence proper for her own use" (AROO 77), having looked at what Woolf calls the "man's sentence" and laughed.

Woolf wrote several reviews of books about Austen, and an essay, "Jane Austen," in the *COMMON READER.* In 1913, she reviewed William Austen-Leigh's *Jane Austen. Her Life and Letters. A Family Record. With a Portrait* for the *TIMES LITERARY SUPPLEMENT* ("Jane Austen" E2 9–16). In October 1920, also for the TLS, she reviewed Mary Augusta Austen-Leigh's *Personal Aspects of Jane Austen* under the title "Jane Austen and the Geese" (E3 268–71); the "geese" were reviewers who "have been hissing inanities in chorus" since Austen became famous (E3 268). In "Jane Austen Practising" Woolf reviewed for the *NEW STATESMAN* *Love and Freindship [sic] and Other Early Works* of Austen's, published with a preface by G. K. CHESTERTON (E3 331–35). ("Love and Freindship" is included in Sandra M. Gilbert and Susan Gubar, *Norton* 209–32.) Austen was also one of the writers included in Woolf's "ON RE-READING NOVELS" in 1922. Woolf incorporated her 1923 review for the *NATION & ATHENAEUM* of *The Works of Jane Austen,* edited by R. W. Chapman, "Jane Austen at Sixty," into her *Common Reader* essay, "Jane Austen" (CR1 168–83; CE1 144–54).

"Jane Austen" defines the novelist's strength as knowing the boundaries of her world from an early age and not venturing beyond them. Woolf notes *Love and Freindship,* written when Austen was fifteen, as evidence that she was a writer of shapely, rhythmic sentences even then. A substantial portion of the essay concerns Austen's fragment "The Watsons," which Woolf considers important because the "second-rate works of a great writer . . . offer the best criticism of his masterpieces" (CE1 147). (Margaret DRABBLE described "The Watsons" as "a tantalizing, delightful and highly accomplished fragment, which surely must have proved the equal of her other six novels had she finished it" [Introduction to Jane Austen, *Lady Susan, The Watsons, Sanditon.* Harmondsworth: Penguin, 1974].) Woolf describes Austen as "a mistress of much deeper emotion than appears on the surface" (CE1 148), arguing that she stimulates readers to supply "what is not there." The essay closes with a speculation about how Austen might have developed her art had she lived longer and had more experience of society. Like Woolf's own character Terence HEWET in *THE VOYAGE OUT* wishes to do, Austen, Woolf suggests, would have "devised a method . . . for conveying not only what people say, but what they leave unsaid" (CE1 153).

B

Baedeker The name of a famous series of guide books founded by Karl Baedeker (1801–59) in Coblenz and transferred by his son, Fritz, to Leipzig. Several MODERNIST writers allude to the Baedeker, the most famous literary reference probably being T. S. ELIOT's poem "Burbank with a Baedeker: Bleistein with a Cigar." Mina Loy titled a book of poems *The Lunar Baedeker* (1923). In *JACOB'S ROOM,* Jacob FLANDERS gets up early in Greece to look at statues "with his Baedeker" (145).

Bagenal, Barbara (née Hiles) (1891–1985) A friend of Dora CARRINGTON's, with whom she attended the Slade School of Art in 1913–14. Woolf referred to Bagenal, Carrington and others as "the cropheads" on account of their bobbed hair. Beginning early to earn a reputation as useful, Bagenal helped out at the OMEGA WORKSHOPS; worked briefly at the HOGARTH PRESS in 1917, helping to typeset Katherine MANSFIELD's *Prelude;* and helped decorate HAM SPRAY, where Lytton STRACHEY, Carrington, and Ralph PARTRIDGE lived. Bagenal first met Vanessa BELL, whom she described as a "lifelong friend" (Noble 145), at a party at Ottoline MORRELL's house, and later met Woolf. Saxon SYDNEY-TURNER was in love with Bagenal but she married Nicholas Beauchamp Bagenal (1891–1974) in 1918, after suggesting she might share herself between the two men. Woolf described the proposed marriage à trois in a letter to her sister, writing that she could not understand the young (L2 213–14). Nicholas (who became a horticulturalist after leaving the army) and Barbara had a daughter, Judith, in 1918 and a son, Michael, in 1921. In 1944, Barbara became Clive BELL's companion, and she remained so until his death in 1964.

Bailey, Mrs. Sutton Mentioned in *NIGHT AND DAY,* a guest at tea in chapter 1 to whom Mr. HILBERY talks, leaving Katharine HILBERY and Ralph DENHAM sitting next to each other in uncomfortable silence.

Balaclava Thinking in *A ROOM OF ONE'S OWN* of how women's lives have not formed part of recorded history, Woolf describes how an old woman would remember the streets being lit for the battle of Balaclava, but would not remember what she was doing on a particular day that had no "historic" significance (AROO 89). A small seaport on the coast of the Crimea, Balaclava was the site of the "Charge of the Light Brigade" on September 26, 1854, which Alfred, Lord TENNYSON memorialized in a famous poem. Mr. RAMSAY in *TO THE LIGHTHOUSE* blurts out lines of this poem throughout the novel.

Baldwin, Stanley (1867–1947) Leader of the Conservative Party and prime minister from 1923 to 1929 and again from 1935 to 1937. Woolf refers to Baldwin in *THREE GUINEAS,* quoting from a speech he gave at Downing Street concerning the NEWNHAM COLLEGE Building Fund (TG 48–49); Baldwin also appears in the third illustration in *Three Guineas* in his ceremonial robes as chancellor of Cambridge University.

Balfour, Arthur James, First Earl (1848–1930) In *THE VOYAGE OUT,* Mrs. FLUSHING remarks that politicians would not understand that the Irish poor lose their teeth after they are twenty, and uses Arthur Balfour as her example of such an obtuse politician (TVO 199). Balfour entered Parliament in 1874 and became prime minister in 1902. In 1915 he was first lord of the Admiralty.

Ball, Mrs. Mentioned in *BETWEEN THE ACTS.* A woman who lived with another man during World War I while her husband was at the front (64).

Ballad of the Queen's Marys [or Maries] In *A ROOM OF ONE'S OWN,* Woolf tells her audience to "call me Mary Beton, Mary Seton, Mary Carmichael or by any name you please" (AROO 5), referring to three of the "Queen's Marys"—the fourth is Mary Hamilton—who were the attendants of Mary, Queen of Scots and are mentioned frequently in Scottish ballads. The ballad is number 173 in *English and Scottish Popular Ballads,* collected by Francis James Child (1825–96) and published 1883–98. There are varying accounts of the last names of the four Marys, some versions giving Mary Livingstone and Mary Fleming. Woolf would probably have been aware of the ballad in Sir Walter SCOTT's *Minstrelsy of the Scottish Border* (3 vols., 1802–03):

> Last night there were four Marys,
> Tonight there'll be but three,
> There was Mary Beaton and Mary Seton,
> And Mary Carmichael, and me.

Isobel Grundy, in " 'Words Without Meaning—Wonderful Words' ", notes that in "FRIENDSHIPS GALLERY" Woolf had "specifically linked the popularity of the name Mary with the power of the Church" (Grundy 215–16). Grundy also notes, as other critics have, that Leonard WOOLF "connected [Mary] with the romance of women's names" in his novel *THE WISE VIRGINS* (220n19). Seton and Carmichael were names that Woolf had already used, for Sally SETON in *MRS. DALLOWAY,* and Augustus CARMICHAEL in *TO THE LIGHTHOUSE.* Grundy and Harvena Richter (VWM 24:1) both argue that Judith SHAKESPEARE is a "stand-in" for the unnamed Mary Hamilton in the ballad, who was killed because she bore the king's illegitimate child.

According to Jane Marcus, who describes Woolf's use of the ballad as a "shocking feminist rhetorical strategy which excludes the male reader and directly addresses the female reader" (*Languages* 78), the ballad was actually based on the story of a Scottish lady-in-waiting to Queen Catherine of Russia who had a child by Tsar Peter and was hanged (*Languages* 197). Marcus also points out that Scott's version of the story derived from John Knox's *Monstrous Regiment of Women,* an attack on the Queen and her attendants (*Languages* 197). Further deepening the "generic power" of the name Mary, Marcus links it with Mary Llewelyn, Stephen Gordon's lover in Radclyffe Hall's novel, *THE WELL OF LONELINESS.* Mary Carmichael, the fictitious author in *A Room* of *Life's Adventure,* was the pseudonym under which Marie Stopes published her novel *Love's Creation* (1928), which opens with two women in a laboratory (Marcus, *Languages* 175).

Ballets Russes See RUSSIAN BALLET.

Balzac, Honoré de (1799–1850) French novelist best known for *La Comédie Humaine* and considered by Henry JAMES to be the greatest novelist. In *A ROOM OF ONE'S OWN,* Balzac is mentioned with Charles DICKENS and William Makepeace THACKERAY as writing "a natural prose" that exemplifies the masculine style for which women writers have no use (AROO 76). Other significant works by Balzac include *Père Goriot* and *Eugénie Grandet.* In *THE VOYAGE OUT,* Rachel VINRACE borrows *La cousine Bette* from her Uncle Ridley AMBROSE (TVO 172). Woolf wrote in her DIARY in 1937 that she was reading Balzac "with great pleasure" (D5 77).

Bankes, Mrs. Vermont An American visitor to the Hilberys in *NIGHT AND DAY.* Katharine HILBERY shows her the shrine to Richard ALARDYCE far too quickly because she is distracted, but Mrs. Bankes is enthralled all the same. Through Mrs. Bankes Woolf pokes fun at those who organize themselves into societies for author worship, to which happy failing Americans are particularly prone.

Bankes, William Character in *TO THE LIGHTHOUSE,* a guest of Mr. and Mrs. RAMSAY. He and Lily BRISCOE are staying in the village near the Ramsays' summer home because there is no room at the house, and this leads to a friendship between them (although Mrs. Ramsay is convinced they will marry). Mr. Bankes has brought a valet with him to prepare his meals. A widowed and childless botanist, Mr. Bankes was once a close friend of Mr. Ramsay's, but their friendship has stagnated. Bankes feels that Mr. Ramsay "had made a definite contribution to philosophy in one little book" when he was twenty-five (TTL 23). Lily has mixed feelings about Bankes in part 1, respecting him on the one hand, but exasperated also by the way he can "prose for hours . . . about salt in vegetables and the iniquity of English cooks" (TTL 24). At the dinner in section XVII of part 1, Mrs. Ramsay is particularly gratified when Bankes praises the BOEUF EN DAUBE (TTL 100). Bankes worships Mrs. Ramsay from afar, captivated by her beauty (TTL 29).

Banting, Mrs. ORLANDO's midwife.

Bard, Miss A schoolmistress mentioned in *THE WAVES.*

Barfoot, Captain Character in *JACOB'S ROOM* who pays attentions to Betty FLANDERS, Jacob's widowed mother, and to whom she is writing as the novel opens. He becomes a town councillor in Scarborough when Edward JENKINSON retires.

Barfoot, Ellen The wife of CAPTAIN BARFOOT in *JACOB'S ROOM* who is wheeled into the sun in her Bath chair by Mr. DICKENS while her husband goes every Wednesday to visit Betty FLANDERS. She is the daughter of one James Coppard who was mayor of Scarborough.

Barnet A gardener mentioned in *JACOB'S ROOM.*

Barouche Landau An early nineteenth-century four-wheeled carriage. In *THE WAVES,* BERNARD invents an explanation for a crane attached to a building that involves hauling a large woman out of one (TW 115).

Barrett, Miss In *JACOB'S ROOM,* she observes Fanny ELMER from inside a map store where she is waiting impatiently to be served, and thinks Fanny has a hard face.

Bartholomew, Percy The Woolfs' gardener at MONK'S HOUSE from 1928 until after World War II. He moved from Brighton with his wife, Lydia, to Rodmell where his brother William and sister Rose lived; Rose and Lydia both worked on occasion in Monk's House. In "A SKETCH OF THE PAST," Woolf records the proof of her theory that certain memories are "more real" than the present when she looks at Percy digging the asparagus bed but sees him through her childhood memory of her nursery and the road to the beach at ST. IVES. In her DIARY and LETTERS, Percy makes appearances working and chatting with Leonard WOOLF ("on and on they go—like old gaffers in gaiters") and is a source of village gossip and rumor.

Bartholomew, Widow Takes over from Mrs. GRIMSDITCH as ORLANDO's housekeeper.

Bartolus, Captain Nicholas Benedict Character in *ORLANDO,* the captain of the merchant ship upon which Orlando sails back to England after having become a woman and whose attentions make apparent to Orlando the difference of her sex from her previous incarnation.

Basket ORLANDO's butler.

Basnett, Mr. Horace Character in *NIGHT AND DAY* who has formed the Society for the Education of Democracy which Mary DATCHET joins. He is interrupted in his discussions with Mary once by Katharine HILBERY and once by Ralph DENHAM.

Bast, Mrs. In the "Time Passes" section of *TO THE LIGHTHOUSE,* Mrs. MCNAB is assisted by Mrs. Bast and her son George in getting the Ramsays' house ready for their return in part 3. It is possible Woolf took the name from E. M. FORSTER's character Leonard Bast in *Howards End.*

Batty One of Lucy SWITHIN's nicknames in *BETWEEN THE ACTS* and also the name of one of Isa OLIVER's dentists.

Bax, Mr. Character in *THE VOYAGE OUT.* In chapter XVII he conducts a Sunday service for the English guests at the hotel on SANTA MARINA.

Baxter Kitty LASSWADE's maid in *THE YEARS.*

Bayreuth See WAGNER, Richard.

Beadle See *ROOM OF ONE'S OWN, A.*

Beckwith, Mrs. Character in *TO THE LIGHTHOUSE.* In part 3, "The Lighthouse," she is a guest with Lily BRISCOE and Augustus CARMICHAEL at the Ramsays' summer home, described by Lily as "kind old Mrs. Beckwith" (TTL 148).

Beerbohm, Sir Max (1872–1956) A critic, essayist and caricaturist (see his caricature of Lytton STRACHEY) who succeeded George Bernard SHAW as drama critic for the *Saturday Review* in 1898. His successful novel *Zuleika Dobson* was published in 1911. Woolf reviewed his *Seven Men* in the *TIMES LITERARY SUPPLEMENT* in November 1919 ("The Limits of Perfection" E3 124–26) and *And Even Now* in the TLS in December 1920 ("A Flying Lesson" E3 275–77). In "The Modern Essay," she discusses Beerbohm as an essayist, describing him as "the prince of his profession" (CE2 46). Woolf first met Beerbohm at a dinner given by Ethel SANDS in December 1928 (D3 212).

Beethoven, Ludwig van (1770–1827) In *THE VOYAGE OUT,* Rachel VINRACE falls asleep thinking of "the spirit of Beethoven Op. 111" (TVO 37). In some editions of the novel (notably, the first English edition) "Op. 112" is the work Rachel is thinking about, and there has been some critical discussion of which work Woolf had in mind. In January 1920, after she had sent a revised text of the novel to New York for the first U.S. edition, Woolf wrote to Saxon SYDNEY-TURNER asking him to tell her again which was the correct opus number (L2 418), and a few days later wrote to Robert TREVELYAN that she was "altering op. 112 to 111" (L2 419). Elizabeth Heine points out that Woolf was writing in a time before typewriters were equipped with a key for the Arabic numeral 1, which may have contributed to confusion at the printer.

In 1975, Louise DeSalvo wrote that it was difficult to tell if "Op. III" was a printer's error or Woolf's revision. Comparing Opus 3 and Opus 112, DeSalvo argued that 112 was the preferred reading (VWM 3: 9–10). Opus 3 is a string trio, and Opus 112 is a cantata entitled *Meerestille* [*Calm sea*] *und glückliche Fahrt* [*and Prosperous voyage*] based upon two poems by Goethe. Opus 112, wrote DeSalvo, "reinforces, through repetition, Rachel's brooding preoccupation with death associated by water" (VWM 3:10). In the Fall 1975 issue of *VIRGINIA WOOLF MISCELLANY,* James Hafley advised consideration of Opus 111, "the celebrated last of the piano sonatas," which he described as "a demanding and famous piece that Rachel, like

Caricature of Lytton Strachey, 1925. Max Beerbohm. Courtesy of Mrs. Eva Reichmann.
Elizabeth Richardson notes Clive Bell's description in Old Friends *of Strachey's "air of flexible endlessness which was his prevailing physical characteristic" and which the caricature well illustrates.*

any young pianist, would yearn to play well" (VWM 4:4). The same point was made by S. P. Rosenbaum, who also noted the letters to Sydney-Turner and to Trevelyan that clear up the mystery (VWM 5: 3–4).

Woolf wrote in June 1928 of listening to Beethoven's late sonatas in the evenings while she was thinking about *THE WAVES*. Gerald Levin points out that Beethoven was "much discussed by writers" in the late 1920s, one of whom, J. W. N. Sullivan, Woolf knew (and disliked) and whose 1927 book *Beethoven: His Spiritual Development* may have influenced Woolf. "Sullivan's characterization of the Opus 130 fugue [the B flat quartet] as the 'reconciliation of freedom and necessity, or of assertion and submission,' suggests the major theme of the final section" of *The Waves* (Levin 166). Mitchell Leaska explores the connections between the string music RHODA hears at a concert in *The Waves*, and notes that Leonard WOOLF in his autobiography says that he told Woolf that if music were to be played at one's cremation, it should be the cavatina from Beethoven's B flat quartet, Op. 130 (LW2 436–37). This leads Leaska to interpret Rhoda's "square" as the crematorium door and "oblong" as a coffin (*Novels* 185n9).

Beginning Again, An Autobiography of the Years 1911–1918 The third volume of Leonard WOOLF's autobiography, published by the HOGARTH PRESS in 1964 and reprinted in the Oxford University Press two-volume edition, *An Autobiography* (1980). This volume begins with Leonard's return to England from Ceylon and his marriage to Woolf and covers the period to the end of World War I.

Behn, Aphra (1640–1689) Considering the work of seventeenth-century women writers, Woolf's narrator says in *A ROOM OF ONE'S OWN* that an important turning point is reached with the work of Aphra Behn, a middle-class woman who wrote for money. All women should "let flowers fall upon the tomb of Aphra Behn," she continues, "for it was she who earned them the right to speak their minds" (AROO 66). In "PROFESSIONS FOR WOMEN," Woolf included Behn with those predecessors who had cut the way for women like herself to make their livings by writing.

Aphra Behn spent some time in Surinam as a child, probably providing her with the situation and plot of her best-known work *Oroonoko, or the History of the Royal Slave* (1688), which is an important early example of the nascent genre of the novel. After the death of her husband in 1665, Behn became a spy for King Charles II, assigned to work in Antwerp. As she was not properly paid, she began to write plays, many of them comedies, and produced fifteen between 1671 and 1689. Among her plays were *The Forc'd Marriage* (1670), *The Rover* (1677), *Sir Patient Fancy* (1678), *The*

Roundheads (1681), and *The City Heiress* (1682); Behn was also recognized as a poet. Behn's "given name, date of birth, marital status, nationality, class, and religion have all been questioned" by Mary Ann O'Donnell (in Greer 240). She was buried as Astrea Behn in the cloisters of WESTMINSTER ABBEY (Greer 243).

In 1927, when Vita SACKVILLE-WEST was working on her biography *Aphra Behn* (1927), Woolf wrote asking to borrow Behn's most romantic novel (Sackville-West, *Letters* 226); Vita asked if she had read *Oroonoko.* Vita had written to Woolf earlier that her reading of Behn had turned her "into the complete ruffling rake. No more than Mrs. A. B. do I relish, or approve of, chastity" (Sackville-West, *Letters* 220). Angeline Goreau, in "Aphra Behn: A Scandal to Modesty," remarks that Behn, "in addition to inventing herself as the first woman to make a profession of writing in the English language, . . . also proved herself to be the first woman to openly discuss sexual matters in print" (Goreau 26).

Bell, Angelica See GARNETT, Angelica.

Bell, Anne Olivier (b. 1916) The daughter of Brynhild Olivier (a NEO-PAGAN) and A. E. Popham (keeper of prints and drawings at the BRITISH MUSEUM), and granddaughter of Sydney Olivier, a founding father of the Fabians (see Beatrice and Sidney WEBB) and a member of Britain's first Labour government. She trained as an art historian at the Courtauld Institute and worked as a civil servant during World War II. Later, she was on the staff of the Arts Council of Great Britain.

Vanessa BELL wrote her daughter Angelica GARNETT in 1951 that she thought Anne Olivier, whom she had invited to CHARLESTON after meeting her through Helen ANREP, "very nice and obviously very intelligent and beautiful" (Spalding 345). Anne and Quentin BELL were married in 1952 and have three children, Cressida, Virginia and Julian. Having spent ten years assisting her husband with his biography of Woolf, Anne Olivier became the editor of Woolf's DIARY for 1915–1941, published in five volumes between 1977 and 1984.

Bell, (Arthur) Clive (Heward) (1881–1964) Clive Bell, who married Woolf's sister Vanessa BELL in 1907, grew up in Wiltshire, the son of William Heward Bell and Hannah Cory, in a "newly-built old-world" home, Cleeve House (CM2 23). After education at Marlborough, he went up to Cambridge in 1899 and soon met Saxon SYDNEY-TURNER, who had rooms on the same staircase at Trinity College. Through Sydney-Turner, Clive met Leonard WOOLF, Lytton STRACHEY, and Woolf's brother Thoby STEPHEN, whom he called his "first real friend." Thoby and Clive were drawn together by a mutual fondness for hunting and riding, pursuits which their more cerebral friends regarded with some bemusement. Thoby himself said that Clive was a cross between Shelley and a country squire and this sense of his being a mixture of opposites was to become a theme in others' estimations of Clive's character. Lytton Strachey, for example, writing to a friend in 1905, found Clive a mass of contradictions:

> His character has several layers, but it is difficult to say which is the *fond.* There is the country gentleman layer, which makes him retire into the depths of Wiltshire to shoot partridges. There is the Paris decadent layer, which takes him to the quartier latin where he discusses painting and vice with American artists and French models. There is the eighteenth-century layer, which adores Thoby Stephen. There is the layer of innocence which adores Thoby's sister. There is the layer of prostitution, which shows itself in an amazing head of crimped straw-coloured hair. And there is the layer of stupidity, which runs transversely through all the other layers. [Holroyd 139]

This group of friends, together with another undergraduate, A. J. Robertson, formed the MIDNIGHT SOCIETY, which met in Clive's rooms on Saturdays to read plays aloud. The Society met at midnight because another group to which they all belonged—the X SOCIETY—met earlier in the evening. The short-lived Midnight Society was, according to Clive, the origin of the BLOOMSBURY GROUP, but there are several other contenders for that title. When Strachey and Leonard Woolf were invited to join the APOSTLES, the Midnight petered out. Quentin BELL has remarked that "Cambridge at the turn of the century was aesthetically blind," and to this very literary group of students, Clive brought a passionate appreciation of the visual arts and was an influence on their visual tastes. Ellen Hawkes Rogat, however, points out that Leonard Woolf in his autobiography wrote that at Cambridge Clive "was not yet an intellectual" (Rogat 105), and believed that Clive's interest in art developed only after he left Cambridge.

Through his friendship with Thoby, Clive visited the Stephen family during the summer of 1902 at Fritham House, Hampshire, where they were on vacation. The first letter to Clive from his future wife thanks him for a gift of partridges, "such delicious food and such a splendid topic of conversation" (Spalding 38).

In 1904, Clive went to Paris, ostensibly to continue the research into British policy at the Congress of Verona he had begun on coming down from Cambridge in 1902. There were, however, other things in Paris he found more interesting. In the company of three English-speaking artists living in Paris, Gerald Kelly, J. W. Morrice, and Roderick O'Connor,

Clive came to know many young artists and writers. Thoby, Vanessa, and Virginia Stephen, with their friend Violet DICKINSON, stopped for a week in Paris on their way back to England in May 1904, after touring Italy. There Clive entertained them, escorting them to Rodin's studio, to the Salons, and to the lively society of the Chat Blanc café. "It gave them their first glimpse, in their quest for a new way of living, of the sort of life and conversation and informal deportment which both sisters were to cultivate so successfully with their friends" (Dunn 84).

Back in England the next year, Clive was a frequent visitor to 46 GORDON SQUARE, where Thoby had begun to hold open "Thursday Evenings" as a way of keeping in touch with his Cambridge friends. "Home and found Bell, & we talked the nature of good till almost one," wrote Woolf on March 8, 1905 (PA 249). "Clive Bell to tea—a nice garrulous old man, with his odd information oozing out—rather pouring buckets full, so that we sit & are pumped into," she wrote the following month. A privately published collection of poetry, *EUPHROSYNE,* was compiled by Clive in 1905. Clive himself, Leonard Woolf, Saxon Sydney-Turner, Lytton Strachey, Walter LAMB and others contributed to it and were mocked by Woolf in an unpublished commentary she wrote on the volume in 1906 (QB1 App. C). Woolf had more fun with this rather precious collection of verse when she named the ship in which her characters sail in *THE VOYAGE OUT* *Euphrosyne.*

In 1905, Clive proposed to Vanessa and was refused. The following year, after a trip to Greece, Thoby Stephen fell ill and died in London of typhoid on November 20. Vanessa had again refused Clive's proposal in 1906, but two days after Thoby's death, she agreed to marry him. They were married at St. Pancras Registry Office February 7, 1907. It was agreed that the Bells would remain at 46 Gordon Square and that Woolf and Adrian STEPHEN would look for a new house. They moved in April to 29 FITZROY SQUARE, not far from the Gordon Square house. The move was perhaps the least profound effect on Woolf of her sister's marriage. She felt abandoned and alone, having lost, it seemed to her, a sister as well as a brother in swift succession. She wrote to Violet Dickinson in 1907, "I did not see Nessa alone, but I realise that this is all over, and I shall never see her alone any more; and Bell is a new part of her, which I must learn to accept" (L1 276).

Soon after the Bells' first child, Julian BELL, was born at Gordon Square in February 1908, they went, with Woolf, to Cornwall. There, Clive and Woolf found they could not tolerate the noise and mess of a newborn and, further, they both felt distanced by Vanessa's new maternal feelings. On long walks together, their flirtation developed into an intense relationship. Throughout his life, Clive would have many affairs and his flirtation with Woolf was, perhaps, only typical of his usual relations with women he found attractive. For Woolf, however, the affair was deeply entangled with her feelings for her sister, as she came to understand more clearly in later years.

Clive had been initiated into the delights of sex by a neighbor, Annie Raven-Hill (who was married to a *Punch* cartoonist), in 1899, just prior to his going up to Cambridge. His affair with her resumed in 1909 and continued until 1914, a fact Woolf was surprised to learn some years later, realizing Clive had been seeing Mrs. Raven-Hill at the same time he was involved with her. The most significant and lengthy of Clive's affairs was with Mary HUTCHINSON. Woolf found herself the confidante of both Clive and Mary in 1927–28 when the affair was coming to an end, an awkward situation typical of the many intrigues involving her brother-in-law by which she was both exasperated and (less frequently) delighted throughout her life.

Woolf was certainly attracted to Clive; in 1925 she wrote to Jacques RAVERAT, "Being bred a Puritan, (in the main—but I had a French great grandmother to muddle me) I warm my hands at these red-hot-coal men. I often wish I had married a foxhunter" (L3 163). Of more significance, however, was his influence on her early literary efforts. Woolf showed Clive several drafts of her first novel, *The Voyage Out* (which at the time was titled *MELYMBROSIA*). He was a sensitive, caring critic, giving her work detailed and thoughtful appraisal (see QB1 App. D), but his understanding of her writing was severely limited by his obtuseness about her feminism (Rogat 106). Long before she had finished *Melymbrosia,* Woolf had stopped showing her drafts to Clive. In 1918 she wrote that he seemed "to have little natural insight into literature" (D1 151). While he criticized as "bad art" the sharp differences between her male and female characters, Clive also wrote of Woolf's "power . . . of lifting the veil & showing inanimate things in the mystery & beauty of their reality." Later in his life, Clive often said how proud he was of having been the first to recognize Woolf's literary talents, calling her one of only two geniuses he had known (the other being Picasso).

In 1911, on his return from Ceylon, Leonard Woolf quickly sought out his Cambridge friends, dining with the Bells at Gordon Square and reacquainting himself with Virginia. Clive was apparently rather jealous when he discovered that Leonard was to marry Virginia (as Leonard had been jealous when he heard from Lytton Strachey that Clive was to marry Vanessa), and just before their marriage wrote to her, "You know, whatever happens, I shall always cheat myself in to believing that I appreciate and love you better than your husband does." Leonard himself found Clive rather trying and presented an unfavorable picture of him in the character of Arthur Woodhouse in his 1914 novel *THE WISE VIRGINS*.

In 1910 Clive and Vanessa met Roger FRY and Clive became an enthusiastic defender of the first POST-IMPRESSIONIST Exhibition that Fry organized to general establishment derision that year. In *ROGER FRY: A BIOGRAPHY*, Woolf describes a caricature that showed "Roger Fry, with his mouth very wide open and his hair flying wildly, proclaim[ing] the religion of Cézannah, with Clive Bell in attendance as St. Paul" (RF 156). This meeting with Fry also marked the beginning of the transformation of the Bells' marriage into a friendship. Vanessa's affair with Fry, together with the marriage of Leonard and Virginia, eased the triangular tensions between Woolf, Clive and Vanessa, and by 1914, the Bells' marriage was effectively over. Nevertheless, "Vanessa was correct in her assumption that he would never remarry as there was no woman whose company he preferred to her own" (Spalding 242), and they did not divorce. Vanessa's biographer Frances Spalding writes that Clive wept for "the wife he had never ceased to love" when he heard she had died (Spalding 362).

Clive's reputation as an art critic during his lifetime was founded on the many books and articles he wrote and his early championing of French contemporary painting. Roger Fry used often to complain—justifiably—that Clive had poached many of his aesthetic ideas, and Clive admitted in his memoir *Old Friends* (1956) that Fry was much cleverer than he. However, it was Clive's book *Art* (1914) that "was the first book published in England to propound a cogent, easily understandable formalist theory of art" (Spalding 115). Although Leonard Woolf said that Clive was not really a disciple of G. E. MOORE, the influence of Moore on *Art*'s aesthetic theory is unmistakable: Clive believed art promotes good as an end in itself. It was in *Art* that the phrase SIGNIFICANT FORM was first used, a notion that has since been developed by theorists in other fields (e.g., the American philosopher Suzanne K. Langer in her *Philosophy in a New Key* [1942]) and that succinctly expresses the characteristic FORMALIST aesthetic of Bloomsbury. "The one quality without which a work of art cannot exist," significant form evoked what Clive called the "aesthetic emotion." Gillian Naylor has explained that Clive and Roger Fry were both "concerned with the nature of aesthetic judgment, with the formal or formalistic elements in art and design, and with what might be described as the spiritual in art; both believed Cézanne to be the 'Christopher Columbus of a new continent of form' [*Art*] and both were preoccupied with an idea of society, or with the qualities that contribute to an Ideal State" (Naylor 249).

In addition to writing books on painting and sculpture (including *Since Cézanne* [1922] and *An Account of French Painting* [1931]), and the first book in English on Marcel PROUST (1928), Clive was also outspoken on political issues. His 1915 pamphlet *Peace At Once*, published by the National Labour Press, was seized and destroyed by order of the Lord Mayor of London; other works on politics included *On British Freedom* (1923) and *Warmongers* (1938). Although he believed that "to associate art with politics is always a mistake," Clive himself always saw a connection between his notion of a civilized society and the cultivation of a leisured class able to appreciate art. He expounded this view most fully in *Civilization* (1927), a work elaborately dedicated to Woolf. In a letter, she drily remarked that Clive's idea of civilization amounted to not much more than "a lunch party at 50 Gordon Square." Leonard Woolf wrote in the *NATION & ATHENAEUM* in June 1928 that Clive's method and assumptions in *Civilization* were wrong and would lead to wrong conclusions (D3 184n7).

Clive's love of everything French is summed up in *Civilization:* "In a universal Honours List for intellectual and artistic prowess the number of French names would be out of all proportion to the size and wealth of the country. Furthermore, it is this traditional basis that has kept French culture up to a certain level of excellence. France has never been without standards. Therefore it has been to France that the rest of Europe has always looked for some measure of fine thinking, delicate feelings, and general amenity."

Civilization was written in CASSIS, where Clive had gone to nurse his hurt feelings after his affair with Mary Hutchinson was over. Although he lived primarily at 50 Gordon Square, Clive also continued throughout his life to use CHARLESTON and Cassis for sojourns away from London. His mixture of "Don Juan of Bloomsbury," outspoken and opinionated art critic, passionate defender and proselytizer of the avant-garde, and bon vivant gave him access to many of the important figures of European MODERNISM. Clive's parties often brought together many of the iconoclastic European artists and writers of the period just following World War I. In 1919, for example, he and John Maynard KEYNES hosted a large informal supper party for the RUSSIAN BALLET at 46 Gordon Square, where the guests included Picasso, André Derain, and Lydia LOPOKOVA. The critic John Russell, writing shortly after Clive's death, said that following *Art*, "all subsequent writing on art in this country has benefited by the climate of freedom which Clive Bell initiated" (Rosenbaum, *Bloomsbury Group* 199). For Woolf, Clive was an early mentor, an early passion, and a continuing link to a world she was at once attracted to and repelled by. In a letter to Gerald BRENAN in 1923, she summed up her feelings about her brother-in-law, saying that he was "a great source of pleasure to me" and that there had never been someone "so petty, conceited, open and good at bottom of heart." Although "no one more annoys and outrages me," she wrote Brenan, she was on "perfectly friendly terms with him; and he pays my cabs, and stands me 'Cold Snacks' at the Café Royale, where the waiter brings him the cold red beef to look at before he cuts it—" (L3 79–80).

Bell, Gertrude Lowthian (1868–1926) In *A ROOM OF ONE'S OWN,* Woolf begins chapter 5 with Mary BETON looking at the shelves which hold books by living writers, among which she finds Gertrude Bell's books on Persia. Bell published *The Desert and the Sown* in 1907, reprinted in 1919 as *Syria: The Desert and the Sown,* and *Poems. English and Persian. Selections,* a collection of fourteenth-century sonnets from the Divan of Hafez. Traveling in Persia in 1926, Vita SACKVILLE-WEST had stayed with Bell in Baghdad, where she was Director of Antiquities and political adviser to King Faisal and was helping to establish a national museum (Sackville-West, *Passenger* 59). Bell died four months after Sackville-West's visit, possibly a suicide as she knew she was gravely ill. In *THREE GUINEAS,* Woolf cites Bell's girlhood as an example of the restricted life led by late Victorian women (TG 76–77).

Bell, Julian Heward (1908–37) The first child of Clive and Vanessa BELL, named for Vanessa's brother (Julian) Thoby STEPHEN, he was born on February 4, 1908, at 46 GORDON SQUARE. By all accounts Julian was an exuberant, "rampageous" (LW2 375) child, prone to hitting his nursemaids and sticking compass points into the forehead of his younger brother Quentin BELL. After an unsuccessful attempt at educating him and some other children at home, Vanessa sent Julian to a Quaker boarding school, Leighton Park, in 1922. There his developing interest in politics became apparent; in 1926 he was heckled and laughed at when he spoke on the General Strike at speech-day (Spalding 207).

In 1927, Julian went to Paris and lived with a schoolmaster, Pinault, and his family. He attended lectures at the Sorbonne, including some on China, and made friends with a Chinese student. Pinault encouraged his interest in politics; Julian did not find the artistic attractions of Paris as enthralling as his father had twenty years earlier.

At King's College, Cambridge, in 1927, studying history, Julian became friends with John LEHMANN and Anthony Blunt (later Keeper of the Queen's Pictures who became notorious in the late 1970s as a KGB spy). Julian was elected to the APOSTLES in 1929. After graduation, he worked on a thesis on Alexander POPE that he hoped would win him a fellowship, but it did not; a second dissertation on philosophical themes also failed to win him a fellowship and was turned down by Leonard WOOLF when Julian offered it to the HOGARTH PRESS.

At Cambridge, as he would throughout his brief life, Julian had several affairs, with both married and unmarried women. In 1931, he had proposed to a woman whom everyone in his family disapproved of; his mother eventually talked him out of his marriage plans. Writing his fellowship, he became involved with Lettice Ramsey, a widow with two small children (she later became well known as a photographer with the studio of Lettice and Muspratt; two of her photographs are included in Peter Stansky and William Abrahams's *Journey to the Frontier*). Julian was uncertain of a career, although his commitment to politics was strong. His first book of poetry, *Winter Movement,* was published in 1930, and in 1932 he was included in Michael Roberts's landmark anthology *New Signatures.* This book, published by the Hogarth Press, announced the new generation of poets who would become known as the "thirties" writers and included John Lehmann, W. H. AUDEN, Cecil Day LEWIS, and Stephen SPENDER. Lehmann had been introduced to the Woolfs by Julian, and through him they had access to a generation whose politics were often at odds with Bloomsbury liberalism. In 1936 Julian's second and final book, *Work for the Winter and Other Poems,* was published in the Hogarth Living Poets Series.

In November 1933 Julian took part in a Cambridge antiwar demonstration, his car decorated like a tank, Guy Burgess at his side. At this point in his life, he identified with the No More War movement, a group dedicated to absolute pacifism and non-resistance to aggression. Unlike many of his friends at the time, however, Julian never became a Communist. In the following years, his political involvements increasingly distanced him from the pacifism of his parents' generation.

In 1935, he accepted a post as Professor of English at the National University of Wuhan at Hankow, China. Despite homesickness, he felt that the three-year stay he was contracted for would help him find the direction in his life that was lacking. While in China his already close relationship with Vanessa deepened as they wrote to each other every week.

An affair with LING Shu-Hua, the wife of a Chinese colleague, prematurely ended Julian's stay. He had, in any case, been anxiously following news of the SPANISH CIVIL WAR and wrote to Vanessa that she must feel glad he was safely in China as he would otherwise certainly be fighting in Spain. In 1935 Julian had edited and written an introduction for *We Did Not Fight,* a collection of eighteen autobiographical essays by CONSCIENTIOUS OBJECTORS that also included a poem by Siegfried SASSOON, but in 1937 he returned from China determined that the antifascist cause justified violent action.

Dissuaded by his family from joining the International Brigade, Julian applied to Spanish Medical

Aid. He left for Spain on June 7 to work as an ambulance driver and was killed by shrapnel on July 18. He was buried at Fuencarral, just north of Madrid. Julian Bell's story has been told by Peter Stansky and William Abrahams in *Journey to the Frontier*.

In letters written to Julian while he was in China, Woolf often said she missed discussing Roger FRY with him, whose biography she was working on at the time. Julian had sent her an essay on Fry for possible use as one of the Hogarth Letters and to assist her with the biography, but Woolf did not think very highly of it and did not use it, which, Julian told his mother, irritated him. In a memoir of her nephew (QB2 App. C), Woolf regretted that she had not encouraged him more as a writer. She told her sister that *THREE GUINEAS* was inspired by Julian: "I'm always wanting to argue it with Julian—in fact I wrote it as an argument with him" (L6 159). In 1938, Julian's brother, Quentin, edited a volume for the Hogarth Press, *Julian Bell. Essays, Poems and Letters*.

Bell, Quentin (Claudian Stephen) (b. 1910) The second son of Clive and Vanessa BELL and best known as the biographer of his aunt, Virginia Woolf. Vanessa and Clive, convinced they would have a daughter, had chosen the name Clarissa for their new child; when Quentin was born they hurriedly named him Gratian. Later, he was registered as Claudian; during the Woolfs' marriage ceremony, Vanessa suddenly interrupted to ask the Registrar how she might change her son's name to Quentin.

Quentin Bell is mentioned in the preface to *ORLANDO* as Woolf's "old and valued collaborator in fiction," a reference perhaps to their "indecent and vulgar lives of the living" concocted for Christmas editions of the *Charleston Bulletin* (a family newspaper along the lines of the *HYDE PARK GATE NEWS*). In several letters Woolf praises Quentin's abilities as a writer, once jokingly imploring him to abandon painting for the greater advantages of literature: "Think how many things are impossible in paint; giving pain to the Keynes', making fun of one's aunts, telling libidinous stories, making mischief—" (L3 493). Woolf usually doted on her sister's children, encouraging them and extolling their virtues to many of her correspondents.

Like most young men of his generation, Quentin was caught up in the political ferment of the 1930s, writing in bitter paraphrase of William WORDSWORTH that "In those twilight days it was bloody to be alive and to be young was very hell" (LW2 372). Pulmonary illness, for which he had been sent to a Swiss sanatorium in 1933, kept Quentin out of World War II.

In 1936, Quentin went to Stoke-on-Trent to study pottery with Thomas Fennemore. Many examples of Quentin's pottery are displayed at CHARLESTON, in addition to his contributions to the painted decorations of the house. Another significant example of his work can be found in BERWICK CHURCH. Quentin Bell has had a distinguished career as writer and art historian, as well as having made his own artistic contribution to what Leonard WOOLF called "newer Bloomsbury." In addition to his two-volume biography of Woolf, Quentin Bell is also author of *On Human Finery* (1947), *Those Impossible English* (with Helmut Gernsheim), *Roger Montané, The Schools of Design* (1963), *Ruskin* (1963), *Victorian Artists* (1967), *Bloomsbury* (1968), and *A New and Noble School: The Pre-Raphaelites* (1982). In 1985, Quentin Bell published a novel, *The Brandon Papers*, a tale of sexual intrigue and suspense that tantalizes anyone who knows Woolf's work with its many playful allusions and that deals with, among other themes, a biographer's withholding facts so as not to hurt the living. The novel owes several elements of its plot to *Orlando* and also makes some play with *THREE GUINEAS*.

Quentin Bell has also held many university positions: lecturer in art education at King's College, Newcastle, 1952–62; professor of fine art, Leeds University, 1962–67; Slade Professor of Art, Oxford University, 1964–65; professor of the history and theory of fine art, University of Sussex, 1967–75. In 1952, he married Anne Olivier Popham (see Anne Olivier BELL).

In 1964, Leonard Woolf wrote to Quentin that several people had asked him to authorize a biography of Woolf (including Leon Edel, whom Leonard found "somewhat dessicated"). Leonard, always concerned about the reputation of Bloomsbury in general and his wife in particular, asked Quentin to consider writing his aunt's biography, and pointed out that he and his sister Angelica GARNETT would become executors of Woolf's literary estate upon Leonard's death. Quentin replied that the work "better not be done by a member of the family or anybody who knows as little about English literature as I do" (Spotts 535), but went on to say he thought the next ten years would be the best time for such a work to appear.

Quentin Bell's two-volume biography of his aunt was published in 1972. It has been the subject of controversy and fierce debate, seen by many critics in the United States in particular as seriously weakened by its omission of any consideration of Woolf's writing. Ellen Hawkes Rogat was an early critic, commenting on the "marked Victorian accent" of the biography (Rogat 98) and arguing that Quentin Bell seemed "obsessed by virginity and his own interpretation of its meaning" (Rogat 102). Others who have criticized the biography include Blanche Wiesen Cook, Susan M. Kenney, Jane Marcus, Cynthia Ozick and Roger Poole. Quentin Bell himself has remarked that "although the book has been fiercely attacked by those who feel that it should have been written in a different spirit and by a person of Virginia's own sex, it has hardly been criticized upon the score of accuracy" (CM2 27). For the material details of Woolf's day-to-day life, Quentin Bell's biography is an essential reference, but it should be supplemented by other biographical studies such as those by Poole, Thomas Caramagno, Louise DeSalvo, Jane Dunn, Lyndall Gordon and Phyllis Rose.

Bell, Vanessa (1879–1961) Woolf's sister, the eldest child of Leslie STEPHEN and Julia Prinsep STEPHEN, born at HYDE PARK GATE on May 30. In "Notes on Virginia's Childhood," a paper she read to the MEMOIR CLUB in 1949, Vanessa recalled how her sister was "not very old when speech became the deadliest weapon as used by her," and described the misery she felt as a child when Woolf gave her the nickname "The Saint." Different in temperament, the Stephen sisters were bound by complex emotional ties that had their roots in early childhood. In her memoir, Vanessa said she could not "remember a time when Virginia did not mean to be a writer and I a painter. It was a lucky arrangement, for it meant that we went our own ways and one source of jealousy at any rate was absent" (*Notes* np). At Hyde Park Gate, while Vanessa painted, Woolf would read aloud; Vanessa noted she could "still hear much of George Eliot and Thackeray in her voice."

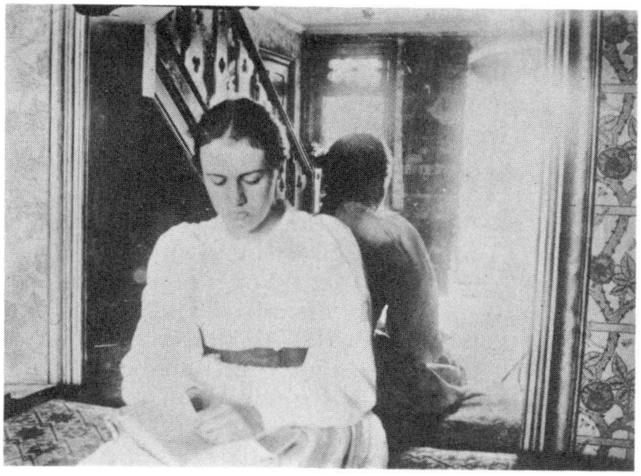

"Vanessa Reading" from Stella Duckworth Hills's album of photographs. Courtesy Henry W. and Albert A. Berg Collection, The New York Public Library, Astor, Lenox and Tilden Foundations.

Self-portrait *by Vanessa Bell, 1958 (19 x 15½"). Courtesy of The Charleston Trust.*
*Diane Gillespie remarks that this is a somewhat more detailed self-portrait than Vanessa usually painted (*Sisters' *341n43).*

Woolf characterized her sister in "REMINISCENCES" as one who always spoke unpleasant truths plainly. She illustrated what she termed "Old Nessa's honesty" with an anecdote about how, after their mother's death, the children pretended one evening not to hear their father calling them while they played in the garden; on his asking whether they had not heard him, only Vanessa admitted that they had ignored him. Woolf's representation of her sister's forthrightness is borne out in the memoirs of several other contemporaries.

As teenagers, Vanessa and Woolf divided their time between their own pursuits of painting and reading and the social demands made upon them by the Victorian mores of their family. Vanessa, to Woolf's envy, was able to escape in 1896, three afternoons a week, to Arthur Cope's School of Art in South Kensington. In July 1897, however, their half-sister Stella DUCKWORTH suddenly died, probably from peritonitis. She had been married that April to John Waller "Jack" HILLS, with Vanessa and Woolf as bridesmaids.

Woolf recalled that Vanessa was "exalted, in the most tragic way, to a strange position, full of power and responsibility" (MOB 53) as she replaced Stella in the maternal and wifely role her father had demanded after the death of their mother in 1895. Leslie Stephen's demands on Vanessa were met with her characteristic stoicism, but, like the other Stephen children, she seems to have been prone to crippling depressions. Vanessa's daughter, Angelica GARNETT, has described her mother's intermittent bouts of deep depression, sometimes lasting two years; in 1894 (the year Thoby STEPHEN threw himself out of a window), for example, Leslie Stephen reported that both Vanessa and her sister were "seriously depressed."

More alarming to certain members of the family, however, was the deep intimacy that developed between Vanessa and Jack Hills following Stella's death (at the time it was against British law to marry a deceased sibling's spouse). Partly to distract Vanessa from Jack, her half-brother George DUCKWORTH, who had taken responsibility for introducing his sister to "society," took her to Paris in 1900, where she visited the Louvre for the first time. The next year she was one of twenty students accepted into the Painting School of the Royal Academy of Art.

Leslie Stephen's death in 1904 marked an escape for Vanessa from the responsibilities of his household. With Violet DICKINSON, Thoby, and her sister, Vanessa took a trip to Italy, where she delighted in Venice and Florence. Stopping in Paris for a week on the way back to England, the Stephens were shown around by Clive BELL, a Cambridge friend of Thoby's whom Vanessa had met in 1902 at her family's summer vacation home, Fritham, when he visited Thoby.

In October 1904 Vanessa oversaw the move of the Stephen household from Hyde Park Gate to 46 GORDON SQUARE, a neighborhood of London that many of her relatives and friends of her parents considered unsuitable for people of their class. There Vanessa and her siblings were to begin a new life; she sold the old furniture to Harrods and painted the walls white; Thoby began holding open house on Thursday evenings to keep in touch with his Cambridge friends.

Vanessa's first painting to be exhibited, a portrait of Lady Robert CECIL ("Nelly"), was shown in the 18th Summer Exhibition of Works by Living Artists at the New Gallery in 1905. It was in that year, too, that Vanessa founded the FRIDAY CLUB, a disparate group of artists, mainly women, for the purpose of discussion and exhibition of the members' work.

Clive Bell, a frequent visitor to Thoby's Thursday evenings, lectured on art to the Club, and in August that year he proposed to Vanessa for the first time; she refused him. The following year he proposed again and was again refused, but then on November 20, following a trip to Greece, Thoby Stephen died in London of typhoid fever, and Vanessa agreed two days later to marry Clive.

The marriage of her sister so soon after her brother's death seemed a double loss to Woolf. It was agreed that she and her brother Adrian STEPHEN would look for a new house and that the Bells would remain in 46 Gordon Square. In 1907 Woolf and Adrian moved to 29 FITZROY SQUARE, not far from their sister.

Vanessa's career as a painter began to develop rapidly, and in 1907–08 she exhibited with the New English Art Club, the Allied Artists Association and the Friday Club. Vanessa's lifestyle, according to her biographer Frances Spalding, was also making social history as she not only was a married woman with a career but also one who entertained and established close friendships with such men as Lytton STRACHEY and others of the BLOOMSBURY GROUP.

Vanessa's first child, Julian Thoby BELL, was born in 1908 and for a while she withdrew from painting and from Clive. He was not prepared for the demands of a newborn and began a flirtation with Woolf that eventually caused a scar on the sisters' relationship that would never properly heal. When their second child, Quentin BELL, was born in 1910 Vanessa was concerned because the baby failed to put on weight. She found no support in Clive, but she had recently become reacquainted with the critic and painter Roger FRY and found him to be not only an intellectual companion but a man of great sensitivity to her worries about her child. Traveling in Turkey with Clive, Fry, and H. T. J. (Harry) NORTON in 1911, Vanessa suffered a miscarriage at Broussa and was nursed by Fry, who proved his competence in a crisis, in marked contrast to Clive. As her marriage to Clive became a marriage in name only, Vanessa began an affair with Fry that lasted until about 1913.

The year 1910 was also significant for the first POST-IMPRESSIONIST exhibition at the Grafton Galleries, which opened in November to great excitement. The show had a liberating effect on Vanessa as a painter, although she had, of course, already seen works in Paris by Cézanne, Matisse and others. When Fry organized the second Post-Impressionist exhibition in 1912, Vanessa's *Asheham* and *Nosegay* were included in the English section. Her involvement with Fry's art-world entrepreneurship continued in 1913 when she and Duncan GRANT joined him as co-directors of the OMEGA WORKSHOPS.

By 1914 Vanessa was finding herself in love with Grant, a homosexual who had lived with her brother Adrian, having begun an affair with him in 1910. When Adrian married Karin COSTELLOE, Grant began to return Vanessa's affection. However, soon after this Grant began an affair with David GARNETT. Beginning a pattern she would follow for most of the rest of her life, Vanessa became close to Garnett, realizing he was her link to Grant. During World War I, following the Military Service Act that introduced conscription, Vanessa did volunteer work for both the No Conscription Fellowship and the National Council for Civil Liberties. She, Grant and Garnett lived at Wissett Lodge in Suffolk, a property that had belonged to an aunt of Grant's, which they farmed while the men awaited the outcome of their request for exemption from military service as CONSCIENTIOUS OBJECTORS.

In 1916, on a walk in Sussex, Woolf saw a house that she thought her sister would like. In October, Vanessa moved, with Grant and Garnett and her two sons, to CHARLESTON, where she would stay for most of the rest of her life, living and working alongside Duncan Grant. It was at Charleston on Christmas Day, 1918, that Angelica, Vanessa and Duncan Grant's child, was born. Partly from fear of offending his parents, Clive Bell was said to be her father. David Garnett, who wrote prophetically to Lytton Strachey on Angelica's birth that he thought "of marrying it" when she was twenty, told his mother, Constance GARNETT, that Clive was "very glad it is a girl; so will Virginia be for she thinks very highly of her own sex. Vanessa doesn't and is probably rather disappointed" (Naylor 147). Angelica herself was not told that Duncan was her father until she was seventeen, a fact that she later ascribed to Vanessa and Duncan's insensitivity to others (MacWeeney vii).

Vanessa had been relieved when in 1912 her sister married Leonard WOOLF, writing to him, "You're the only person I know whom I can imagine as her husband" (Spotts 170). In 1915 she wrote to Fry that Woolf's first novel, *THE VOYAGE OUT,* was "extraordinarily brilliant" and said that "if it's art it seems to me art of a quite different sort from making a picture" (Spalding 137). Throughout her life Woolf would always say that her sister's opinion of her writing was the most important to her ("I always feel I'm writing more for you than for anybody," she wrote Vanessa in 1931 [L4 390]).

In 1927, Vanessa found La Bergère, her house at CASSIS, "another Charleston in France," and it was here that she received her copy of her sister's novel *TO THE LIGHTHOUSE,* writing to Woolf that "it is so shattering to find oneself face to face with these two again [i.e., her parents] that I can hardly consider anything else" (Spalding 219). She wrote to Woolf from Cassis that year about a huge moth that had been knocking one evening against the window and that they had captured for Julian's collection. Woolf later noted in her DIARY that this story was the inspiration for what would eventually become *THE WAVES.*

A most significant aspect of the collaboration and artistic interaction between Vanessa and her sister was the jacket designs she made for all of Woolf's books after *JACOB'S ROOM* in 1922 (except *ORLANDO* and "LETTER TO A YOUNG POET"). Leonard Woolf recalled in his autobiography how several book buyers laughed at Vanessa's "post-impressionist" cover for *Jacob's Room.* Vanessa also designed the wolf's-head colophon for the HOGARTH PRESS as well as covers for many other books. The uniform edition of Woolf's novels brought out by the Hogarth Press in 1929 all had the same pale blue cover designed by Vanessa.

Even more closely involved with her sister's art are the four woodcuts Vanessa made for *MONDAY OR TUESDAY,* Woolf's 1921 short-story collection. Diane Gillespie has pointed out that Vanessa's painting "The Conversation" also seems to be linked to the subject matter of Woolf's story "A SOCIETY" (Gillespie 110). Their collaboration was not always easy, however. When working on the illustrations for *KEW GARDENS,* Vanessa upset her sister by making disparaging remarks about the Hogarth Press: "But Nessa & I quarrelled as nearly as we ever do quarrel over the get up of Kew Gardens, both type & woodcuts; she firmly refused to illustrate any more stories of mine under those conditions, & went so far as to doubt the value of the Hogarth Press altogether. . . . This both stung & chilled me. Not that she was bitter or extreme; its her reason & control that give her blame its severity" (D1 279).

As well as Vanessa's designing covers for her sister's books, their collaboration was furthered by Woolf's writing introductions to exhibitions of her sister's paintings. In the foreword to *RECENT PAINTINGS BY VANESSA BELL* in 1930, Woolf described the silence of her sister's art: "Mrs. Bell says nothing. Mrs. Bell is as silent as the grave" (Rosenbaum, *Bloomsbury Group* 172). In 1934, in the catalogue to a show of Vanessa's work at the Lefevre Gallery, Woolf again stressed a silence that words are unable to describe as the characteristic quality of the art of painting. This is also the theme of her best-known writing on the visual arts, "WALTER SICKERT: A CONVERSATION," a pamphlet published in 1934 with a cover design by Vanessa.

Gillespie notes that Vanessa's illustrations for Woolf's writing (e.g., her drawings for *FLUSH* in 1933) often reflect the latter's experiments with point of view. Woolf's thinking on her sister's medium is well exemplified by her character Lily BRISCOE in *To the Lighthouse,* who struggles with what Woolf saw as Vanessa's aesthetic choices.

The sisters' nursery rivalry and intense artistic relationship continued until Woolf's death in 1941, with Woolf often comparing her financial and professional success with what she saw as her sister's domestic success. When the studio at 8 Fitzroy Street that Vanessa and Grant had taken together in 1929 was destroyed in 1940 by an incendiary bomb, Woolf wrote in her diary of this as her sister's "Trump card" in evoking her sympathy. In 1937, though, when Julian Bell was killed, Vanessa told Vita SACKVILLE-WEST that her sister was the only person who could be any comfort to her in great grief. It was a rare occasion when Woolf was able to feel Vanessa depended on her.

In 1952, Frances PARTRIDGE found that Vanessa was still "bewitching" and the "belle of the ball" (*Everything* 169). She died at Charleston in 1961 and is buried in Firle churchyard nearby.

Belloc, Hilaire (Joseph Hilary Pierre) (1870–1953) In *NIGHT AND DAY*, Mrs. COSHAM is pleased to learn that Ralph DENHAM reads Thomas DE QUINCEY, thinking that his generation only reads Belloc, G. K. CHESTERTON and George Bernard SHAW. Hilaire Belloc was a popular writer of light verse such as *The Bad Child's Book of Beasts* and *Cautionary Tales*, as well as the author of many essays and accounts of his travels. He is treated disparagingly in Woolf's 1922 "The Modern Essay" (CE2 41–50; CR1 267–81).

Bennett, Enoch Arnold (1867–1931) English novelist, author of *The Old Wives' Tale* (1908), *Clayhanger* (1910), *Hilda Lessways* (1911), *These Twain* (1916), *Riceyman Steps* (1923) and other novels and short stories. Woolf reviewed his *Books and Persons. Being comments on a past epoch* in the *TIMES LITERARY SUPPLEMENT* in July 1917 (E2 128–32) and there anticipated the argument she made famous in her essay "MR. BENNETT AND MRS. BROWN" (1923). In March 1923 Bennett had written of *JACOB'S ROOM* that its characters did not "survive vitally in the mind" ("Is the Novel Decaying?" in *Cassell's Weekly*). In her essay, Woolf grouped Bennett with H. G. WELLS and John GALSWORTHY as representative "Edwardian" writers whom the writers of her "Georgian" generation were opposed to. The techniques of the Edwardians were "tools of death," she wrote, and she focused on Bennett's *Hilda Lessways* as an example of the kind of novel she felt was outdated. Beth Rigel Daugherty has argued that "Bennett's sexism and Woolf's feminism lie at the bottom of their public wrangling" ("Whole Contention" 269).

In 1920 Woolf wrote what she termed a "counterblast" to Bennett's *Our Women* when her friend Desmond MACCARTHY wrote in the *NEW STATESMAN* that he agreed with Bennett's opinions on the intellectual inferiority of women expressed in *Our Women: Chapters on the Sex-Discord* (D2 Appendix III). Woolf met Bennett at a party given by Ethel SANDS in 1924, and again at Sands's house in 1930 (D3 334–35). Her sadness at his death surprised her and she felt that she would miss their "abuse" of each other in the press (D4 16).

Benson, Everard Named in *JACOB'S ROOM* when Jacob meets him at tea with an old family friend, Miss PERRY. Jacob thinks him a "contemptible ass" (104).

Benson, Stella (1892–1933) A writer whom Woolf met in 1932 and to whom she felt she would have

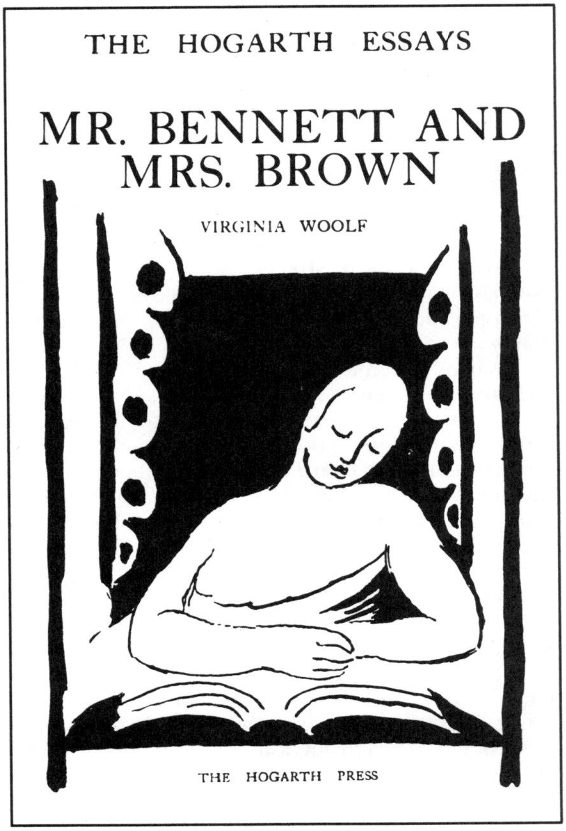

Mr. Bennett and Mrs. Brown. *Courtesy of Cecil Woolf and Jean Moorcroft Wilson.*
The first of the Hogarth Essays series, published in 1924, and one of Woolf's best-known essays. The paper wrappers were illustrated on the front by Vanessa Bell's drawing of a woman with an open book.

become closer had Benson not died the next year. Benson won the FEMINA-VIE HEUREUSE PRIZE in 1932 for her novel *Tobit Transplanted* (1931) and lived mainly in China with her husband. Her death reminded Woolf of her feelings when Katherine MANSFIELD died (D4 192–93). Benson gave Woolf a copy of *Tobit Transplanted* on August 9, 1932, writing in it, "My dear Virginia | I can't sell you my car so I give you my book. I am afraid I can't hope that either will carry you very far but it gives me an awed pleasure to think of your reading Tobit" (Holleyman I/II.3).

Bentley, Mr. Mentioned in *MRS. DALLOWAY* when he sees the skywriting airplane and thinks of it as a symbol of "man's soul" (MD 41).

Berg Collection The Henry W. and Albert A. Berg Collection of the New York Public Library has the foremost collection of Woolf's manuscripts in the world. It houses draft materials related to all Woolf's novels, as well as complete drafts of all the novels except *MRS. DALLOWAY* (the manuscript of which, chosen by Vita SACKVILLE-WEST as her bequest from Woolf, is in the library of the BRITISH MUSEUM) and *ORLANDO* (a draft of which is at KNOLE), galleys, thirty-six volumes of her DIARY, thousands of letters to and from Woolf, thirty-three volumes of her reading notebooks (see RN 345–47), first editions of her books and pamphlets, and drafts of essays and biographies, short stories, articles and reviews. In addition, the Berg has extensive materials of many other MODERNIST writers, as well as the papers of several of Woolf's relatives, and Stella DUCKWORTH's photograph album.

Much of the material at the Berg came via two Chicago rare-book dealers, Frances Hammill and Margery Barker, who approached Leonard WOOLF in the 1950s about his wife's papers. Leonard was committed to having Woolf's papers housed in an American institution because, as he wrote to his brother Philip in 1956, if the manuscripts went to an English institution they would be "stuffed away somewhere and no one would ever look at them again" (Spotts 500). The Berg made its first acquisition of Woolf materials in 1958. One of its most significant acquisitions—accomplished by the Berg's renowned curator Lola L. Szladits (1923–90)—was of Woolf's diaries, which Leonard sold with the understanding he would keep them until his death. (See John D. Gordan, "New in the Berg Collection." *Bulletin of the New York Public Library* 68, 2 [February 1964]: 77–81; and Lola L. Szladits, *Bulletin of the New York Public Library* 73, 4 [April 1969]: 237–39.)

In 1994, Research Publications International published the entire Berg Collection Woolf archive on twenty-one reels of microfilm, a project carried out under the guidance of Louise DeSalvo, S. P. Rosenbaum, James Haule, Mitchell Leaska and the present Curator of the Berg Collection, Francis O. Mattson. (See also *MELYMBROSIA, THE PARGITERS, POINTZ HALL, THREE GUINEAS* and *THE WAVES*.)

Bergson, Henri (1859–1941) French philosopher and recipient of the Nobel Prize for Literature in 1927 whose concept of "la durée" (duration) as the reality of time, demonstrated by the phenomena of memory, led several early readers and critics of Woolf to suggest that his philosophy influenced her writing. Shiv Kumar's 1953 study *Bergson and the Stream of Consciousness Novel* is an early example of the linking of Bergson's ideas with MODERNIST writing. In *Time and Western Man* (1927), Wyndham LEWIS attacked what he saw as Bergson's pernicious influence on culture.

Bernard One of the six soliloquists in *THE WAVES*. Bernard (who in drafts of the novel is called John, Johnnie, Archie and Roger) is from his childhood a storyteller, although he never seems to finish anything he writes. He speaks more than any of the others, and in the final EPISODE attempts "to sum up" the meaning of his life, an effort which involves his incorporation not only of the lives and experiences of his friends but also of the language of the INTERLUDES, as well as his description of the world "seen without a self." His friends, the five other soliloquists in the novel, frequently comment on the inadequacy of Bernard's stories or on his propensity for escaping situations by making up stories. Throughout his life, Bernard refers to the image of a woman writing in a garden at ELVEDON, sitting between two windows.

Alice Fox has pointed out that in her revisions of the novel, Woolf assigns "virtually all Shakespearian allusions to Bernard" (Fox, *Virginia Woolf* 133), and that in his summing up allusions to *Hamlet* and *King Lear* are particularly abundant (135): "Of all the minds Shakespeare reveals in the solitude of the soliloquy, it is Hamlet's that most resembles Bernard's" (Fox 137). Bernard's identification with William SHAKESPEARE is only one of several literary identifications he assumes in the course of his life. He is also, significantly, George Gordon, Lord BYRON for a time, when he is in college with NEVILLE, and in the summing up notes that he "was Hamlet, was Shelley, was the hero, whose name I now forget, of a novel by Dostoevsky" (TW 249).

Many critics have seen in Bernard an example of the androgynous mind Woolf describes in *A ROOM OF ONE'S OWN*. Madeline Moore ("Nature"), Makiko Minow-Pinkney and Harvena Richter (*Inward*), for example, all discuss Bernard as an example of the androgynous artist. In an appendix, Richter provides two diagrams showing "Bernard as the Complete Androgynous Personality" based on "Mental and Physical Aspects Drawn from a Study of Major Symbols, Images, and Leitmotifs in *The Waves*" (Richter 247). Eileen Sypher, however, finds that "one of the most disturbing things about *The Waves* is that Woolf houses a self-consciously androgynous spirit in a male body, not even attempting to alter genitalia as she does in Orlando" (Sypher 191).

For many readers, Bernard is Woolf's alter ego, and at several points in the novel he describes the vision of a fin passing far out in a waste of waters that Woolf herself noted as the original vision of *The Waves*. Bernard has been seen as "clarif[ying] the aesthetics" of *The Waves* (Bazin 143), gaining in "theoretical clarity while realizing himself in practice" (Fleishman 164), and as "a clear surrogate for Virginia Woolf herself" (Fogel 157). Irma Rantavaara, in her early study of *The Waves*, says that in the novel's final episode, "Bernard becomes Virginia

Woolf without a disguise" (19). Peter Kaye has argued that the "radical changes in Bernard's perceptions about the nature of writing . . . provide a fictionalized extension of Woolf's argument with [Arnold] Bennett about the nature of fiction writing" (VWM 27:2).

Leonard WOOLF suggested that Desmond MACCARTHY was the model for Bernard, a suggestion also made by Aileen Pippett and Mitchell Leaska. Leaska notes an early sketch for Woolf's biography of Roger FRY that saw it as divided into various stages, "all to be combined say by Desmond [MacCarthy] and me together" (Leaska, *Novels* 189). Howard Harper points out that Fry lived in Bernard Street (235n11).

Berners, Lord (Gerald Hugh Tyrwhitt-Wilson, 14th Baron Berners) (1883–1950) Mentioned in the ironic preface to *ORLANDO* as someone "whose knowledge of Elizabethan music has proved invaluable," Lord Berners was a composer, author and painter whom Woolf met in 1924.

Berwick Church St. Michaels and All Angels Church is about two miles from CHARLESTON and was decorated, beginning in 1941, by Vanessa BELL, Quentin BELL and Duncan GRANT. Frances Spalding has remarked that "Vanessa put more of herself into these paintings than into any other of her mural decorations, for she used the religious subjects as an impersonal cloak for her own feelings and experience" (*Vanessa Bell* 320).

Bessborough, Lady (1761–1821) In *A ROOM OF ONE'S OWN*, Woolf recalls Henrietta, Countess of Bessborough's deference to Lord Granville Leveson GOWER (AROO 55) and laments this example of the waste of women's talents. Lady Bessborough was the mother of Lady Caroline Lamb (1785–1828), the novelist who was passionately in love with George Gordon, Lord BYRON.

Beton, Mary The name of the subject speaking in most of *A ROOM OF ONE'S OWN*—" 'I' is only a convenient term for somebody who has no real being," says Woolf before inviting her audience to "call me Mary Beton, Mary Seton, Mary Carmichael or by any name you please" (AROO 4–5). Mary Beton is also the name of the aunt whose legacy enables the narrator to be financially independent. (See also BALLAD OF THE QUEEN'S MARYS.)

***Between the Acts* (1941)** Woolf's final novel, published in July 1941, about four months after her suicide. *Between the Acts* is set on a June day in 1939 in "a remote village in the very heart of England." The novel is structured as a series of scenes separated by space breaks. There are no chapters or section numbers and usually no transition is made between one section and the next. There are seven main characters and a host of minor ones. *Between the Acts* is concerned with public and private histories: A satirical version of the history of England is told in a pageant and is represented by both the villagers who act in it and by those who watch it, people whose families have lived in the village for centuries; the history of individuals is represented by the major characters' memories. The narrative is densely layered and is perhaps the most allusive of all Woolf's works. *Between the Acts* makes the most direct reference of all her novels to contemporary events, although these references are infrequent.

Outline

The novel opens with a brief scene on a summer evening, in which Bart OLIVER, his sister Lucy SWITHIN, and his daughter-in-law Isa OLIVER sit in a room in the Oliver family's house, Pointz Hall, discussing affairs of the village with Rupert HAINES, a local "gentleman farmer," and his wife. The rest of the novel takes place on the day of the annual village pageant, which has been written by Miss LA TROBE to be performed by the working people of the village. The audience at the pageant consists of the family at Pointz Hall, which is joined at lunch by Bart's son Giles OLIVER; Mrs. MANRESA, who lives in London and has a house in another village; a man she brings with her, William DODGE; and the rest of the local gentry.

The pageant itself is part of the novel's narrative, and tells the story of England through historical scenes that include a kind of Old English prologue, a medieval song, a tableau of Elizabeth I, a scene from a post-Shakespearean play, a tableau personifying Reason, an almost full-fledged Restoration drama called *Where there's a Will there's a Way*, a representation of the Victorian age with a prologue by an imperial policeman, and a skit depicting a picnic at which a young couple vow to marry and spend their lives converting "the heathen." The final scene of the pageant is "Present Time," when the players come on stage holding mirrors of various shapes and sizes, reflecting the audience back at itself, to its great discomfort. The pageant closes with a voice from a loudspeaker in the bushes that links the audience with the fascism menacing Europe. After the pageant, the Reverend G. W. STREATFIELD attempts to sum up its meaning and reminds the audience that it was intended to raise funds for "the illumination of our dear old church." His speech is interrupted by a flight of military aircraft.

Before and during the pageant, tensions between various characters are evident. Isa is attracted to Mr. Haines and is not happy in her marriage to Giles, whom she thinks of only as "the father of my children" (BTA 14). Giles is irritated with the people at

Pointz Hall, seeing them as "old fogies" who do nothing but sit and look at views while Europe is plunging toward war. He detests the homosexual William Dodge (although he cannot bring himself to say the word "homosexual" [60]), partly because he knows Isa is sympathetic to him. Giles is seemingly seduced by Mrs. Manresa, whom he invites to stroll to the greenhouse with him during an intermission of the pageant. A significant moment in the novel occurs when Giles comes upon a snake that is choking on a toad and stamps them both to death (BTA 99).

At the end of the novel, the family is once more alone in Pointz Hall. Finally, Isa and Giles are left alone, sitting in the dark. They seem to revert to a prehistoric setting. "Then the curtain rose. They spoke" (219) is the last line of the novel. Further details will be found in entries on the characters.

Genesis

Woolf first refers to what would become her last novel on April 12, 1938: "Last night I began making up again: Summers night: a complete whole: that's my idea" (D5 133). The short piece "THE MOMENT: SUMMER'S NIGHT" (CE2 293–97) is certainly related to her writing of *Between the Acts,* but was probably written later than this diary entry suggests. *POINTZ HALL* (in the entry on which will be found further details about the composition of *Between the Acts*) was Woolf's title for the novel from the time she began working on it in the spring of 1938 until the end of February 1941. (The name Pointz comes from a character in William Makepeace THACKERAY's *Pendennis.*) Unusually, Woolf composed most of this work on a typewriter (her usual method was to write first in longhand and then type up what she had written). Mitchell Leaska has described the evolution of the drafts of this novel (PH 3–16) and Lola L. Szladits has given a description of the manuscripts of those drafts (PH ix–xi).

In April 1938, Woolf summed up her conception of the novel in her diary, noting that she wanted to discuss "all lit. . . . in connection with real little incongruous living humour." She planned to reject "I" in favor of "We" and present a "rambling capricious but somehow unified whole" (D5 135). Since the first publication in 1953 of Woolf's DIARY, many critics have used her description of *Between the Acts* as a guide to reading the novel.

When she completed the final draft of *Between the Acts* in early 1941, Woolf decided that the work should not be published, writing to John LEHMANN that her "so-called novel" was "too slight & sketchy" (L6 482). She told Lehmann that Leonard WOOLF disagreed with her assessment of the work, and that they had decided to give Lehmann—who became Leonard's partner in the HOGARTH PRESS when Woolf sold out her share in 1938—the casting vote. Although she did not know this, Leonard had also written to Lehmann saying he was very worried about Woolf and that he thought she should not work on the novel for a while. After her death, Leonard wrote to Lehmann that he thought *Between the Acts* had more depth than her other novels and that its "strange symbolism gave it an almost terrifying profundity and beauty" (Spotts 255). Before Lehmann could reply to her, Woolf wrote him again to say that she had decided the book definitely should not be published because it was "too silly and trivial" (L6 486). She told him she planned to work on it to have it ready for publication that fall. Within days of writing this letter—perhaps even the next day—Woolf drowned herself. When the book was published, Leonard prefaced it with the following note: "The *MS.* of this book had been completed, but had not been finally revised for the printer, at the time of Virginia Woolf's death. She would not, I believe, have made any large or material alterations in it, though she would probably have made a good many small corrections or revisions before passing the final proofs." *Between the Acts* was published by the Hogarth Press on July 17, 1941, with a dust jacket designed by Vanessa BELL, and in the United States by Harcourt, Brace & Co. that October.

Background

It is helpful to know something of what Woolf called "the present state of my mind" (D5 135) as background to the novel. In the late 1930s, Woolf, like many people, was acutely aware that a way of life she had known and cherished was in imminent danger of disappearing. Although rarely referred to directly in *Between the Acts,* World War II informs the narrative's mood. Apart from seeing German planes fly low over the Sussex fields on their way to bomb London, Woolf was directly affected by the war when her house at MECKLENBURGH SQUARE was destroyed by a bomb in 1940. A few weeks after that, on a trip to London, she saw the ruins of another house she had lived in, at TAVISTOCK SQUARE.

Life in London seemed to her to be over, and she wrote in her diary of the irritations of living at MONK'S HOUSE in the small village of Rodmell where, she told her niece Judith, "We're acting village plays; written by the gardener's wife, and the chauffeur's wife; and acted by the other villagers" (L6 400). Jane Marcus has explained that pageants were very popular in England between the wars, and mentions Edith Craig (the actress Ellen TERRY's daughter) and Cicely Hamilton, both well known for putting on pageants, as possible models for Miss La Trobe (VWM 6:2).

War had impinged directly on Woolf's life earlier, in 1937 when her nephew Julian BELL was killed working as an ambulance driver during the SPANISH CIVIL WAR. Woolf's thinking on war in *THREE GUINEAS,* which she imagined partly as an argument with Julian, also influences *Between the Acts,* as Patricia Laurence* has explained ("Facts" 225–45).

Julian's death also recalled the premature death in 1906 of his namesake, Woolf's brother Julian Thoby STEPHEN. In 1939, Woolf began writing her memoir "A SKETCH OF THE PAST," focusing on memories not only of Thoby's death, but also the deaths of her mother, Julia Prinsep STEPHEN, in 1895 and her half-sister, Stella DUCKWORTH, in 1897. In the memoir she also described the incest she suffered at the hands of her half-brother Gerald DUCKWORTH, writing that her instinctive feeling that his abuse of her when she was very young was wrong "proves that Virginia Stephen was not born on the 25th January 1882, but was born many thousands of years ago" (MOB 69): the idea of a collective consciousness and that there is a "common element" in individual histories is a prevalent theme in *Between the Acts.*

"A Sketch of the Past" was only one aspect of the reliving of her past that Woolf was involved in during the mid- to late-1930s. She was also writing her biography of Roger FRY, a friend who had been important in her life for more than twenty years and who had died in 1934. The sense of a world passing was emphasized for Woolf also by the deaths in the 1930s of several others who had either been close to her throughout her life, or had been significant to her when she was young: Lytton STRACHEY had died in 1932, Janet CASE and Jack HILLS in 1937, Ottoline MORRELL and Ka COX in 1938. Penny Painter has noticed that names and places in *Between the Acts* are similar to those found in Woolf's early diary (PA) and argues that these similarities "center around Woolf's relationship with her half sister Stella Duckworth's husband John Waller 'Jack' Hills" (VWM 35:6); Mark Hussey has also compared images in "A Sketch of the Past" and *Between the Acts* (*Singing* 138–40).

Between the Acts is very much concerned with the relationship between a writer and her audience, her readers. When she died in 1941, Woolf was working on a critical history of English literature called "Reading at Random." There are very close links between *Between the Acts* and "ANON," the surviving chapter of this critical work. Several critics have discussed the relationship between the novel and Woolf's ideas about the origin of literature in the songs of "Anon." Nora Eisenberg* writes that *Between the Acts* "encourages the recapturing not only of Anon's lost song, but also of the rest of Anon's lost world" (263), and Makiko Minow-Pinkney has called Miss La Trobe a "modern anon" (195). In "Anon" Woolf described "the world beneath our consciousness: the anonymous world to which we can still return" (Silver, "Anon" 385), and this world is referred to throughout *Between the Acts.* The villagers in shirts made of sacking who pass in and out among the trees as a kind of chorus in the pageant (BTA 77–78) represent centuries of English history.

Another aspect of her last critical work that found its way into *Between the Acts* was Woolf's concern with the reader and the way in which a writer's sense of audience influences her conception. La Trobe curses her audience and despairs that she has not got across to them the message of her pageant (BTA 180). She imagines an ideal play without an audience (BTA 180). Bart remarks that being an audience is his role in the pageant (BTA 59). In June 1940, Woolf had recorded in her diary her feeling that she no longer had anyone to write for: "It struck me that one curious feeling is, that the writing 'I' has vanished. No audience. No echo. That's part of one's death" (D5 293).

Critical Responses

Early reviewers of *Between the Acts* were significantly influenced in their reading by Woolf's suicide, which many people at the time saw as a response to the war. (Probably they were misled by newspaper reports that incorrectly quoted Woolf as saying she could not "go on any longer in these terrible times" [Spotts 257] in her last letter to Leonard Woolf.) The novel was read as a protest against the war, and several critics interpreted the title as referring to the time between the two world wars. Some contemporary reviewers noted that *Between the Acts* shared themes with other novels of Woolf's and drew attention to the mysterious poetry of the book's narrative. As with contemporary reviews of her other works, *Between the Acts* was frequently described as baffling but beautiful (e.g., CH 446). One critic who did not like *Between the Acts* was F. R. LEAVIS, who wrote that "After *To the Lighthouse*" Woolf's famous preoccupation with "life itself" had culminated in a novel of "extraordinary pointlessness and vacancy." Northrop Frye, on the other hand, later wrote in *The Anatomy of Criticism* (1957) that *Between the Acts* was Woolf's "most profound" work.

In her July 1941 review of the novel for *THE NEW STATESMAN & NATION,* Elizabeth BOWEN commented that readers might "search it for some touch of finality" but she had found none (McNees 4: 173). As Woolf's last novel, *Between the Acts* has, however, attracted critical efforts to see it as the culmination of some kind of development in her fiction. Alice van Buren Kelley writes that it is "difficult not to see in it a summary statement of all that has come before" (225). Such efforts are particularly ironic in that *Between the Acts* is the least "finished" of any of Woolf's published works, existing as a version among drafts that the writer did not live to revise for publication. More recent critics have noted the novel's inherent resistance to final interpretations, Rachel Bowlby, for instance, pointing out that to see *Between the Acts* as a culmination of Woolf's art implies just that kind of teleological development that Woolf herself resolutely rejected (*Feminist* 147). Patricia Klindienst Joplin* argues that the novel "celebrates rather than mourns" the impossibility of final meaning ("Authority" 211), and Daniel Ferrer notes that it "is actually endeavoring to put in question the closure of the work of art in relation to its outside" (Ferrer 141).

Many critics have focused on the novel's mood or tone, and have paid particular attention to its ending, influenced no doubt by the fact of Woolf's suicide before the book was published. Even quite recently, opinions have varied between those who, like Gillian Beer,* find *Between the Acts* Woolf's "most mischievous and playful work" ("Introduction" 395), and those who, like Marilyn Brownstein,* describe it as "perhaps the saddest book I have ever read" (86). Mitchell Leaska goes so far as to call the draft of *Between the Acts,* "Pointz Hall," possibly "the longest suicide note in the English language" (PH 451). Susan M. Kenney's* "Two Endings" compares the ending of the novel and the ending of Woolf's life. She finds that although Woolf's "diary was full, as her mind was, of bombs and war and violence, almost none of this got into her fiction" (Kenney 273). Kenney notes that most early critics stressed the novel's pessimism (except for James Naremore, who writes of its "warm comedy"). Jean Guiguet is one of the gloomy school, finding the work "intelligible only to a reader prepared by long familiarity with Woolf's writing" (Guiguet 324). More recently, Nancy Topping Bazin and Jane Hamovit Lauter* have described the final scene of *Between the Acts* as "a dystopian vision of the future of humanity" (39) and Roger Poole* has said that "the last two pages of the novel are entirely bereft of hope" (" 'We all' " 93). Christine Froula* reads *Between the Acts* as Woolf's final rewriting of Genesis, the culmination of her "rewritings of Eden over the twenty-five-year span of her novels," and interprets the novel's ending as Woolf's creation of "a scene in which man and woman share the human condition of flesh and spirit and in which the bare fact of generation ('another life might be born') replaces imagery of fetishized maternal power." This, Froula writes, is in contrast to the Genesis myth which "creates an exclusively cultural economy that rests upon the buried mother-goddess" (Froula 217).

Kenney, like van Buren Kelley, who advises seeing beyond the gloom of the novel, gives it a more positive reading and links Woolf's suicide to the mood of the novel as showing "a kind of defiance not very different from the defiance the characters in *Between the Acts* show" (Kenney, "Two Endings" 284). In her article, Kenney suggests Woolf was resisting the "moral disapproval" implicit in Leonard's attitude to her mental instability, reacting against the element of punishment in the regimen of care he prescribed for her.

Another persistent concern of critical readings of *Between the Acts* has been with the form of the novel. Avrom Fleishman* believes that in *Between the Acts* Woolf found "a consummate means of integrating her notions of selfhood and her historical perspective" (*English Historical* 246) and describes the novel as "a phenomenological reduction of history to its elements" (246) that transcends the origins of the genre of the historical novel and "may well have achieved a limit of the genre's resources" (255). Woolf herself predicted the form of *Between the Acts* in her 1927 essay "THE NARROW BRIDGE OF ART" when she described an "unnamed variety of the novel" (CE2 228) that would be written in prose, "but in prose which has many of the characteristics of poetry" and would be "dramatic, yet not a play" (CE2 224). Mark Hussey* has noted that *Between the Acts* recalls elements of the "novel of the future" described in the essay "in so precise a way that it seems almost as if Woolf wrote the book with the essay of 1927 before her" (" 'I' Rejected" 144).

Many critics have commented on the "play within a play" aspect of the novel and the way Woolf's framing devices continually shift the reader's perspective, so that a reader of the novel often becomes identified with the audience at the pageant. Harvena Richter calls *Between the Acts* the "most graphic exposition of . . . [the] concept of the creative reader" (238), and Sallie Sears* has discussed the play within a play device. Ferrer notes that the position of the reader includes the position of the audience at the pageant, "just as *Between the Acts* includes Miss La Trobe's play" (139).

Reflecting the prevailing critical concerns of the 1960s and 1970s, several writers defended *Between the Acts* against F. R. Leavis's charge of formlessness. Naremore and Howard Harper discuss the dramatic unity of the novel, and Bazin reads the final scene between Giles and Isa as symbolizing "the hoped-for union of the masculine and feminine within the individual" (Bazin 206). In similarly dualistic readings, van Buren Kelley sees Bart Oliver as corresponding to "fact" and Lucy Swithin to "vision," while John Mepham has recently written that *Between the Acts* "portrays a simple drama" of the struggle between forces of "unity" and "Dispersity" (*Literary* 200). Postmodern critics, however, who do not hold unity as a value, have seen *Between the Acts* as Woolf's most daring formal experiment. Pamela Caughie, who has written that it is "interesting to note how our conception of the form of the novel determines our reading" (51), compares it with postmodern fiction such as Italo Calvino's *If on a winter's night a traveller*; Beth Rigel Daugherty* has called *Between the Acts* "that postmodern ancestor of [Thomas Pynchon's] *Gravity's Rainbow* and [John Barth's] *Lost in the Funhouse*" ("Face to Face" 76). Caughie also comments on the mood of the novel, finding that reading it from the perspective of postmodern art reveals its mood as "not one of despair, but one of affirmation" (Caughie 56).

It is by now a critical commonplace that Woolf—like many of her modernist contemporaries—was much less interested in plot than in form. Her novels, she said, were written to a rhythm, not to a plot, and in *Between the Acts* Woolf has her characters comment directly on this aspect of her fiction. Isa, who thinks the plot "was only there to beget emotion" (BTA 90), supposes that Miss La Trobe is saying, "Don't bother about the plot: the plot's nothing" (91). Minow-Pinkney remarks that what is true of the pageant is also true of *Between the Acts* (191). Gillian Beer* points out that *Between the Acts* is similar to most of Woolf's other novels in rejecting plot: "Plot insists on origins, sequence, consequences, discovery, exclusion, and closure" ("Beyond" 131).

Another aspect of the form of *Between the Acts* that several critics have commented on is its mixing of various genres. Avrom Fleishman notes the difficulty of summing up what happens in the novel because of its multiplicity of perspectives and also remarks on how Woolf mixes fiction and drama, satire and parody (Fleishman 202). Minow-Pinkney draws attention to what she terms the "collage" of different genres and categories in *Between the Acts,* and critics influenced by the work of Mikhail Bakhtin term the novel "carnivalesque."

In his introduction to the 1974 Folio Society edition of *Between the Acts,* Quentin BELL, as well as speculating that Woolf's despair over the novel "might well have set her upon the path to suicide," wrote that his aunt "never wrote and never could have written a political novel; but, in *Between the Acts,* she wrote a novel set, unobtrusively but definitely, within a political context." In the early 1970s, in a break with critical tradition, feminist readers began to write about the politics of Woolf's fiction and to read *Between the Acts* as a critique of fascism at home and abroad. "As Woolf revised *Pointz Hall* into *Between the Acts,*" writes Judith Johnston,* "she strengthened her political critique of British culture" ("Remediable" 256). Several writers have explored this critique in the novel: Merry Pawlowski* writes that "Woolf uncovers fascist ideology as it has shaped English history . . . paying close attention to the compliance of women in their own oppression" (189); Bonnie Kime Scott* compares Woolf's theme of fascism in *Between the Acts* with a similar aspect of Djuna Barnes's *Nightwood* (25–32); and Elizabeth Abel sees that "fascism lurks in this text, as in *Three Guineas,* in a domestic (as well as a foreign) guise," most fully realized in Giles (Abel 109). Lucio Ruotolo argues that "Woolf suggests that it is neither Luftwaffe nor Wehrmacht that constitutes the immediate threat to life and language, but rather good English folk, of all classes and professions, bound intransigently to old ideas" (*Interrupted* 206). Ruotolo also points out that the comparison in *Between the Acts* between "art's promise of wholeness" and the "absolutism of authoritarian leadership" is carried out "in terms that at times echo Freud's critique of religion" (*Interrupted* 205).

Woolf was reading Sigmund FREUD's *Group Psychology and the Analysis of the Ego* while she was writing *Between the Acts,* and both Gillian Beer (in Warner) and Merry Pawlowski have pointed out links between Freud's work and the novel. In 1939, the Hogarth Press published Freud's last great work, *Moses and Monotheism.* In "A Sketch of the Past," Woolf wrote of the ambivalence she felt toward her father, making reference to her novel *TO THE LIGHTHOUSE* as having resolved that ambivalence in a way similar to that achieved by psychoanalysis. Abel believes that the ambivalence that Woolf felt for Leslie STEPHEN she also felt toward Freud (whom Woolf had met in 1938). Woolf's response to Freud was complex, and *Between the Acts* stands in complex relation to *Moses and Monotheism*; both are "crisis texts" but each interprets the crisis differently: Freud laments the decline of patriarchy, but Woolf concedes its triumph (Abel 110). A direct link between Freud's text and Woolf's novel is the incident in the first "playlet" of La Trobe's pageant involving a baby hidden in a basket by a river (as Moses was hidden to avoid Pharaoh's decree of death to male Hebrew children [Exodus 2]). Abel discusses *Between the Acts* in terms of Woolf's rewriting of the Oedipus complex, explaining that Woolf situates love and hatred in the daughter, Isa ("Love and hate—how they tore her asunder!" [BTA 215]). "Society is 'a father' and sexual relations between men and women reproduce the father-daughter bond" (Abel 108).

Another aspect of *Between the Acts* that has received considerable attention from critics is its figuring of a prehistoric world. When Lucy Swithin wakes early on the morning of the pageant, she reads from an "Outline of History" and imagines "rhododendron forests in Piccadilly" (BTA 8).[2] The image of a prehistoric world has appeared before in Woolf's novels, in *THE VOYAGE OUT* (67) and in *MRS. DALLOWAY* (122), and Beer notes that Woolf's first and last novels "engage most directly with the idea of the primeval" (in Warner 102). Alex Zwerdling argues that the "idea of a return from civilization to barbarism is of crucial importance to an understanding of *Between the Acts*" (306). In part, *Between the Acts* is an elegy for England, for a civilization that Woolf saw tottering on the brink of disappearance. There is a peculiarly

[2] Brenda R. Silver identifies the source of what Lucy reads as G. M. TREVELYAN's *History of England* (Silver, "Anon" 401–02).

"English" sensibility about the novel, one that Woolf had occasionally described in her diary and letters. In 1928, for example, she described a country wedding, and saw the bride and groom as representing "the unconscious breathing of England" (D3 197). Poole, who traces Woolf's diary entries in the late 1930s to show "how exactly [she] is mapping current events onto the known contours of recent past history" (" 'We all' " 95), interprets the novel's title as referring to a time between a past as represented in the village pageant, and a future which will be a complete break with that history, will be in fact a return to prehistory.

For some feminist readers of Woolf, prehistory often suggests matriarchal myth. Eileen Barrett* is one of several critics who point out the influence on Woolf of Jane Ellen HARRISON's work on matriarchal mythology. Jane Marcus, in an unsigned article, "Some Sources for *Between the Acts,*" notes the influence of Harrison's work on the pageant that is mentioned in the "1911" chapter of *THE YEARS,* and points out that in the late 1930s Woolf was asked by the Rodmell Women's Institute to write a play, and was thinking of dramatizing the *Odyssey* (VWM 6:2). Evelyn Haller,* in "Isis Unveiled," says that of all Woolf's novels, "*Between the Acts* has the most palpable Egyptian ambience" (115). Mark Hussey* has also explored this dimension of the novel in "Reading and Ritual"; and in his notes to *Pointz Hall,* Leaska details many of Woolf's references to Egyptian myth and history, such as Lucy's identification (BTA 153) with CLEOPATRA (PH 231–33) and the way the legend of Isis and Osiris runs through the narrative (PH 232–33). In another article, Haller identifies Isis as "crucial among the anti-madonnas to be found in all Woolf's novels" ("Anti-Madonna" 96) and argues that the "Isis-inspired anti-madonna occurs most consistently and persuasively in *Between the Acts*"(101). Isa, Mrs. Manresa, and Lucy Swithin are all identified by Haller as anti-madonnas.

Feminist readings of *Between the Acts* have been particularly attentive to Woolf's weaving together of fact and myth. In "Liberty, Sorority, Misogyny," Marcus traces through the novel's text the way the rape that Isa reads about in the morning newspaper operates. (This rape of a girl by soldiers was reported in the *Times* of June 28, 29, and 30, 1938, as Stuart N. Clarke reports [VWM 34: 3–4].) Marcus sees *Between the Acts* as Woolf's rewriting of A. C. SWINBURNE's "Itylus," his version of the story of PROCNE AND PHILOMELA: a "story of rape and sisterly revenge set in wartime is the theme that structures *Between the Acts* with its recurrent images of the swallow and the nightingale" (*Languages* 80). Minow-Pinkney sees *Between the Acts* as "not an obviously feminist text," but one that "clearly carries a strong feminist charge" (192), and this has been borne out by feminist readings by Madeline Moore (*Short Season* 146–72), Barrett, and Diane Gillespie* ("Virginia Woolf's Miss La Trobe"). Laurence, also, points out that the "domestic rape" Isa reads about "serves as counterpoint to the political rape of lands by Hitler" ("Facts" 241).

Between the Acts draws attention to language, frequently commenting on its inadequacy. Alan Wilde* and Ruotolo both see *Between the Acts* as calling into question even the power of language to signify. Often words are blown away by the wind in the novel. For Giles, words are menacing (BTA 59) or scornful (BTA 149); to William Dodge they become "symbolical" (BTA 71). Language is also frequently represented as tangible: When the nurses who are looking after Giles and Isa's two children gossip together, their words are described as sweets rolled thin on their tongues (BTA 10); words in the pageant pepper the audience "as with a shower of hard little stones" (BTA 78). Eisenberg finds that *Between the Acts* "exposes more than ever the limitations of language as such and the virtues of different communicative forms that might better pull life together" (255). She continues by suggesting that in *Between the Acts* Woolf was trying to articulate a community that might be brought into being by "song, dance, pictures, gesture, the simplest of utterances, and the drama which includes them all" (264).

The idea of community is yet another focus of critical attention and one that has been expressed in discussions of Woolf's comedy in *Between the Acts.* Melba Cuddy-Keane,* for example, discusses the novel's radical and subversive comedy that decenters authority and creates a voice that implies a "fluid and noncoercive sense of community." Judy Little* was among the first to comment on this aspect of the novel in her essay "Festive Comedy in Woolf's *Between the Acts.*" Beer also links the comedy of the novel to its politics and its theme of a prehistoric world: "For us living in an age where we can foresee the possibility of a post-nuclear world inhabited at most by sea, grass, scorpions, and sky, the salutary comedy of *Between the Acts* realises its fullest intensity" (in Warner 122). Brenda Silver* takes the conception of manor house and playhouse as center of community that Woolf describes in "Anon" as underlying "her exploration in *Between the Acts* of the possibility of community and its survival on the eve of World War II" ("Concept of Community" 295). Silver, who sees the novel's pageant as recreating Woolf's idea of the Elizabethan playhouse, describes *Between the Acts* as affirming "the possibility of community and its ability to survive" (296).

Works Specific to This Entry

Barrett, Eileen. "Matriarchal Myth on a Patriarchal Stage: Virginia Woolf's *Between the Acts.*" *Twentieth Century Literature* 33 (1987): 18–37.

Bazin, Nancy Topping, and Jane Hamovit Lauter. "Virginia Woolf's Keen Sensitivity to War: Its Roots and Its Impact on her Novels." In Mark Hussey, ed. *Virginia Woolf and War*: 14–39.

Beer, Gillian. "Beyond Determinism: George Eliot and Virginia Woolf." In *Arguing with the Past: Essays in Narrative from Woolf to Sidney*. New York: Routledge, 1989.

———. "Introduction." *Between the Acts.* In Julia Briggs, ed. *Virginia Woolf: Introductions to the Major Works.* London: Virago, 1994: 395–424.

———"Virginia Woolf and Pre-History." In Eric Warner, ed. *Virginia Woolf: A Centenary Perspective*: 99–123.

Brownstein, Marilyn L. "Postmodern Language and the Perpetuation of Desire." *Twentieth Century Literature* 31 (1985): 73–88.

Cuddy-Keane, Melba. "The Politics of Comic Modes in Virginia Woolf's *Between the Acts*." *PMLA* 105, 2 (March 1990): 273–85.

Daugherty, Beth Rigel. "Face to Face with 'Ourselves' in Virginia Woolf's *Between the Acts*." In Vara Neverow-Turk and Mark Hussey, eds. *Virginia Woolf: Themes and Variations*: 76–82.

Eisenberg, Nora. "Virginia Woolf's Last Words on Words: *Between the Acts* and 'Anon.' " In Jane Marcus, ed. *New Feminist Essays on Virginia Woolf*: 253–66.

Fleishman, Avrom. *The English Historical Novel: Walter Scott to Virginia Woolf.* Baltimore: Johns Hopkins University Press, 1971.

Froula, Christine. "Rewriting Genesis: Gender and Culture in Twentieth-Century Texts." *Tulsa Studies in Women's Literature* 7, 2 (Fall 1988): 197–220.

Gillespie, Diane. "Virginia Woolf's Miss La Trobe: The Artist's Last Struggle Against Masculine Values." *Women and Literature* 5, 1 (Spring 1977): 38–46.

Haller, Evelyn. "The Anti-Madonna in the Work and Thought of Virginia Woolf." In Elaine K. Ginsberg and Laura Moss Gottlieb, eds. *Virginia Woolf: Centennial Essays.*

———."Isis Unveiled: Virginia Woolf's Use of Egyptian Myth." In Jane Marcus, ed. *Virginia Woolf: A Feminist Slant*: 109–31.

Hussey, Mark. " ' "I" Rejected; "We" Substituted': Self and Society in *Between the Acts*." In Bege K. Bowers and Barbara Brothers, eds. *Reading and Writing Women's Lives: A Study of the Novel of Manners.* Ann Arbor, Michigan: UMI Research Press, 1990: 141–52.

———. "Reading and Ritual in *Between the Acts*." *Anima* 15, 2 (Spring 1989): 89–99.

Johnston, Judith L. "The Remediable Flaw: Revisioning Cultural History in *Between the Acts*." In Jane Marcus, ed. *Virginia Woolf and Bloomsbury*: 253–77.

Joplin, Patricia Klindienst. "The Authority of Illusion: Feminism and Fascism in Virginia Woolf's *Between the Acts*." In Margaret Homans, ed. *Virginia Woolf*: 210–26.

Kenney, Susan M. "Two Endings: Virginia Woolf's Suicide and *Between the Acts*." *University of Toronto Quarterly* 44, 4 (Summer 1975): 265–89.

Laurence, Patricia. "The Facts and Fugue of War: From *Three Guineas* to *Between the Acts*." In Mark Hussey, ed. *Virginia Woolf and War*: 225–46.

Leavis, F. R. "After *To the Lighthouse*." *Scrutiny* 10 (1942): 295–97.

Little, Judy. "Festive Comedy in Woolf's *Between the Acts*." *Women and Literature* (Spring 1977): 26–37.

Pawlowski, Merry. "Virginia Woolf's *Between the Acts*: Fascism in the Heart of England." In Mark Hussey and Vara Neverow-Turk, eds. *Virginia Woolf Miscellanies*: 188–91.

Poole, Roger. " 'We all put up with you Virginia': Irreceivable Wisdom About War." In Mark Hussey, ed. *Virginia Woolf and War*: 79–100.

Scott, Bonnie Kime. "Woolf, Barnes and the Ends of Modernism: An *Antiphon* to *Between the Acts*." In Vara Neverow-Turk and Mark Hussey, eds. *Virginia Woolf: Themes and Variations*: 25–32.

Sears, Sallie. "Theater of War." In Jane Marcus, *Virginia Woolf: A Feminist Slant*: 212–35.

Silver, Brenda R. "Virginia Woolf and the Concept of Community: The Elizabethan Playhouse." *Women's Studies* 2, 2/3 (1977): 291–98.

Wilde, Alan. "Touching Earth: Virginia Woolf and the Prose of the World." In William E. Cain, ed., *Philosophical Approaches to Literature: New Essays on Nineteenth- and Twentieth-Century Texts.* Lewisburg: Bucknell University Press, 1984: 140–64.

Bexborough, Lady Mentioned in *MRS. DALLOWAY* as an example of English aristocracy's stoicism in the face of the tragedy of World War I. Clarissa DALLOWAY admires her because she has heard that Lady Bexborough opened a bazaar while holding in her hand the telegram that told her of her favorite son's death; Clarissa also wishes that she looked like Lady Bexborough (MD 14).

Bibesco, Princess Elizabeth (1897–1945) Only daughter of Margot and Herbert Henry ASQUITH, who married a Romanian prince, Antoine Bibesco (1879–1951), in 1919. An acquaintance of Woolf's, whom she met through Lady Robert CECIL in December 1920, Bibesco wrote fiction, plays and poetry. In 1935, she invited Woolf to support a proposed antifascist exhibition. When Woolf asked if the exhibition would take into account the "woman question," Bibesco replied that it had not occurred to her that "in matters of ultimate importance even feminists cd. wish to segregate & label the sexes" (D4 273). Woolf pasted Bibesco's letter into the second volume of clippings that she collected throughout the 1930s and used in writing *THREE GUINEAS*.

Biddy A cook mentioned in *THE WAVES*.

Bigge The cook at Dr. and Mrs. MALONE's Lodge in *THE YEARS*.

Bigham, Sir Jasper Named in *JACOB'S ROOM*.

Billycock Hat In *THE WAVES*, NEVILLE describes PERCIVAL wearing this kind of round, low-crowned felt hat (TW 60). The name may derive from hats cocked in the manner of a bully (bully cock) (OED). LOUIS in the novel also refers to people wearing billycock hats in the streets, an image of the life from which he feels alienated (TW 95; 128).

Bingham, Mrs. Mentioned in *BETWEEN THE ACTS* as suspecting that Miss LA TROBE has Russian blood (58).

Birkbeck, Miss In *JACOB'S ROOM*, a cousin of Betty FLANDERS; she bequeaths Jacob £100, which he uses to travel to Greece.

Birkenhead, Lord (1872–1930) In *A ROOM OF ONE'S OWN*, Woolf says she will not trouble to write out Lord Birkenhead's opinion of women's writing (AROO 53). S. P. Rosenbaum notes that F. E. Smith, Earl of Birkenhead, an opponent of women's SUFFRAGE, reprinted in 1928 part of a speech he had made in 1910 wherein he remarked that "the sum total of human happiness" would be unaffected had SAPPHO never sung, George ELIOT never written, Sarah Siddons never acted, and Joan of Arc never fought (WF 206).

Biron, Sir Chartres Before continuing her discussion of Mary CARMICHAEL's novel, in which "Chloe liked Olivia," in *A ROOM OF ONE'S OWN*, Woolf asks her audience to make sure that Sir Chartres Biron is not hiding behind the curtain (AROO 82). His name would have been familiar to the audience as the presiding magistrate at the trial for obscenity of Radclyffe Hall's novel *THE WELL OF LONELINESS*, a trial at which Woolf was prepared to testify on the book's behalf.

Birrell, Augustine (1850–1933) Liberal politician who knew Woolf's father, Leslie STEPHEN, and was an old friend of Ottoline MORRELL's, through whom Woolf came to know him. In 1888 he married Eleanor Locker, the widow of Alfred, Lord TENNYSON's son Lionel, and they had two sons, Anthony and Francis BIRRELL. In 1920, Woolf reviewed Birrell's edition of *Frederick Locker-Lampson: A Character Sketch* for the *ATHENAEUM* (E3 255–58), and in 1930 she reviewed *The Collected Essays and Addresses of Augustine Birrell* for the *Yale Review*. Leonard WOOLF counted Birrell among the "stars" who wrote articles for him when he was literary editor of the *NATION* (LW2 282).

Birrell, Francis Frederick Locker (1889–1935) The eldest son of Augustine BIRRELL. Known as "Frankie," he was a partner with David GARNETT in a bookstore opened after World War I (which, in 1927, the Woolfs thought briefly of buying).[3] Birrell can be considered one of the younger generation who formed a periphery to the BLOOMSBURY GROUP. Garnett took him to stay with D. H. LAWRENCE in 1915, and Lawrence, expressing his characteristic attitude to Bloomsbury, wrote, "Never bring Birrell to see me any more. There is something nasty about him like black beetles" (Bell, *Bloomsbury* 72). Birrell wrote for the *NATION & ATHENAEUM*, and in 1930, the HOGARTH PRESS published *The Art of Dying: An Anthology*, edited by Birrell and F. L. LUCAS. In 1932, Birrell's *Letter from a Black Sheep* was also published by Hogarth. Birrell is one of the friends thanked in the ironic preface to *ORLANDO*. When she learned in 1933 that Birrell had a brain tumor, Woolf wrote in her DIARY that "The sense of friends dying is a very terrible one" (D4 175). She visited Birrell frequently, finding his stoic attitude a "credit to atheism" (D4 266). His death in January 1935 added to the depression of the time during which Woolf conceived and wrote *THE YEARS*.

Bishop, Mr. A lodger at the boarding house where Annie CROSBY goes to live after the sale of the house at ABERCORN TERRACE in *THE YEARS*.

Black, William (1841–98) One of the vast mass of Victorian writers ORLANDO reads in the nineteenth-century section of *ORLANDO*, Black was war correspondent of the *Morning Star* during the Franco-Prussian war and wrote several romantic novels.

Blackfriars ORLANDO has a house at Blackfriars, and it is near there that he arranges to meet SASHA in chapter 1 on the night she leaves him. Late in the novel, the house is sold "part to the Salvation Army, part to an umbrella factory" (O 273). Blackfriars Bridge crosses the river Thames to the Victoria Embankment, connecting with the part of the City of London that bears its name. The Black Friars were a Dominican order that had a monastery in that part of London; later a theater was established in the monastery precincts by Richard Burbage. William SHAKESPEARE had a share in the theatre and his company acted there.

[3] Frances PARTRIDGE describes working there as an assistant in *Memories* (73–75).

Blanche, Jacques-Emile (1861–1942) French painter and writer whom Woolf met in 1927 through Ethel SANDS. His article *Entretien avec Virginia Woolf* ("Conversation with Virginia Woolf") was published in *Nouvelles Littéraires* in August 1927, an issue that also included his translation of Woolf's *KEW GARDENS*. In 1929 he published an article on *ORLANDO* in *Nouvelles Littéraires*.

Bletchley, Mrs. Sarah One of the people in *MRS. DALLOWAY* who tries to make out what the skywriting airplane is tracing in the sky.

Bloomsbury A neighborhood of London in which can be found the BRITISH MUSEUM, Bedford Square (where Ottoline MORRELL lived), Bernard Street (where Roger FRY lived), BRUNSWICK SQUARE, GORDON SQUARE (center of the beginnings of the BLOOMSBURY GROUP), Russell Square, TAVISTOCK SQUARE and Woburn Square.

Bloomsbury Group Definition of the Bloomsbury Group (named after a neighborhood of London in which several of its original members lived) depends on whose account is consulted, some of those who were central figures in it even denying that it ever really existed. Woolf and others used the term "Old Bloomsbury" to distinguish from later additions those thirteen people whom she and Leonard WOOLF, among others, saw as the "original" Bloomsbury Group. These thirteen, identical with the thirteen original members of the MEMOIR CLUB, were: Woolf, Leonard Woolf, Clive BELL, Vanessa BELL, E. M. FORSTER, Roger FRY, Duncan GRANT, John Maynard KEYNES, Desmond MACCARTHY, Molly MACCARTHY, Adrian STEPHEN, Lytton STRACHEY and Saxon SYDNEY-TURNER.

In *BEGINNING AGAIN*, Leonard Woolf wrote that what the outside world called "Bloomsbury" had "never existed in the form given to it by the outside world. For 'Bloomsbury' was and is currently used as a term—usually of abuse—applied to a largely imaginary group of persons with largely imaginary objects and characteristics" (LW2 9–10). In a later volume of his autobiography, *DOWNHILL ALL THE WAY*, Leonard noted that the "myth of Virginia as queen of Bloomsbury and culture, living in an ivory drawing-room or literary and aesthetic hothouse, still persists to some extent" (LW2 244). Woolf herself, in a memoir titled "OLD BLOOMSBURY," described the origins of the Bloomsbury Group in the move by the Stephen children, following Leslie STEPHEN's death, from HYDE PARK GATE to 46 Gordon Square in October 1904. There, Thoby STEPHEN, wishing to continue seeing the friends he had made at Cambridge University, began "Thursday Evenings"—a regular open invitation to his friends. Leon Edel notes that Saxon Sydney-Turner "will go down in history as the 'inaugurating guest' of Bloomsbury. On the first Thursday he was the sole visitor" (*House* 125).

Leonard described the Bloomsbury Group as "primarily and fundamentally a group of friends" the roots of whose friendship were in Cambridge University (LW2 11). In 1899, Clive Bell, Leonard Woolf, Lytton Strachey, Thoby Stephen and Saxon Sydney-Turner all entered Trinity College, Cambridge. E. M. Forster, who had entered King's College in 1897, was still there, and Keynes entered King's in 1902, the same year that Adrian Stephen went up to Trinity. In 1902, Duncan Grant attended the Westminster School of Art. Desmond MacCarthy had left Trinity College in 1897.

An early claim for the origin of the Bloomsbury Group was made in *Old Friends* by Clive Bell, who described the meetings in his rooms of the MIDNIGHT SOCIETY, a reading group consisting of himself, Strachey, Sydney-Turner, Leonard Woolf and Thoby Stephen. Certainly, the friendships formed among these men at Cambridge were central to the Bloomsbury Group. Leonard Woolf remarked that "Bloomsbury

Oil sketch of Virginia Woolf, 1927 (16 x 13"). Jacques-Emile Blanche. Courtesy Museum of Art, Rhode Island School of Design; Museum Works of Art Fund.
This sketch was made while Woolf was staying a few days in the summer of 1927 with Nan Hudson and Ethel Sands at the latter's château at Auppegard in France. Blanche had a house nearby.

grew directly out of Cambridge" (LW1 99), and noted also the influence of the APOSTLES, a secret society to which he, Strachey and Sydney-Turner were elected in 1902. In 1903, with Leonard and Strachey's influence, Keynes was elected to the Apostles. Older members of the Apostles at this time included Forster, MacCarthy and Fry (who had graduated from King's in 1888 and began writing on art in 1893). The Society (as it was usually called, short for "Cambridge Conversazione Society," another name for the Apostles) was in 1902–03 to undergo a transformation due to the influence of the philosopher G. E. MOORE, whose *Principia Ethica* was published in 1903.

Leonard Woolf described Moore as the only great man he ever met, and the writings—particularly the early writings—of the Cambridge core of Bloomsbury often acknowledge or demonstrate his influence. Gillian Naylor points out that Moore's philosophy "is frequently summed up by a quotation from *Principia Ethica*'s final chapter, on *The Ideal*: 'By far the most valuable things, which we can know or can imagine, are certain states of consciousness, which can be roughly described as the pleasures of human intercourse and the enjoyment of beautiful objects' " (Naylor 11). Paul Levy has objected that "Moore's Bloomsbury followers, when they read *Principia Ethica,* took from it only that which interested them" (Levy 7). Leonard Woolf, while acknowledging Moore's and the Apostles' profound influence on him and his peers, also argued that the work of the Bloomsbury Group members was individual, not communal, and that the basis for the group was always friendship rather than shared doctrine (LW2 11).

In what Edel terms Bloomsbury's "first phase," around 1905—the phase of "Thursday Evenings"—Vanessa Bell founded the FRIDAY CLUB, described by Quentin BELL as "the first sign that Bloomsbury was going to be interested in the visual arts" (QB1 105). The death of Thoby Stephen in 1906 caused a brief rupture in the friends' society, but it was soon repaired as the Thursday Evenings were continued. Clive and Vanessa Bell's marriage in 1907 began what Edel terms the "second phase" of Bloomsbury. In 1910 (according to Clive Bell; 1908 according to Vanessa), Roger Fry, Vanessa and Clive Bell met on a train traveling from Cambridge to London and found they shared a passionate interest in art, particularly in what was new. That year—the year in which, Woolf wrote, "human character changed" (CE1 320)—Fry organized the first POST-IMPRESSIONIST exhibition, with Desmond MacCarthy acting as secretary (a post Leonard Woolf would occupy in 1912 for the second Post-Impressionist exhibition). In 1911 (marking the start of what Edel terms the "third phase") Leonard Woolf returned from Ceylon. According to Leonard, the Bloomsbury Group came into existence between 1912 and 1914, centered around the Cambridge friends and the Stephen sisters.

Woolf's "Old Bloomsbury" is the source of a famous anecdote in which Lytton Strachey, noticing a stain on Vanessa Bell's dress, inquired whether it was "Semen?" (MOB 195). Woolf refers to the story as inaugurating a freedom about sexual matters that contrasted sharply with the Victorian mores that the Bloomsbury Group members grew up with. The young men who gathered at 46 Gordon Square were unused to "mixed company" and the presence of Vanessa Bell and Woolf had a significant effect upon them. Woolf's realization that most of the young men were homosexual led her to reflect that this enabled a certain freedom in her behavior, but also inhibited her from "showing off" (MOB 194).

Desmond and Molly (Mary) MacCarthy, although they lived in Chelsea, were considered members of Old Bloomsbury. They had married in 1906 ("the first Bloomsbury marriage," as Edel puts it [*House* 131]) and, as S. P. Rosenbaum, Bloomsbury's most comprehensive historian, points out, "Mary's uncle had married Anny Thackeray Ritchie, who was thus Aunt Anny to both her and Virginia" (*Edwardian* 217). It was Molly MacCarthy who, around 1910, coined the term "Bloomsberries" to describe the group of friends who were beginning to make their mark by that date. The first Post-Impressionist exhibition had made Fry notorious, and Clive Bell, its ardent defender, was also becoming known for his writing on art. Christopher Reed sees Fry and Bell as having "opened the way for the creation and reception of modern art in the first decades of this century" ("Through Formalism" 20). In 1913, Fry, with Vanessa Bell and Duncan Grant as co-directors, opened the OMEGA WORKSHOPS, an enterprise that lasted until 1919 but the influence of which on decorative arts persists even today.

Also in 1910, Woolf, her brother Adrian and Duncan Grant (who was living with Adrian) took part in what became known as the DREADNOUGHT HOAX. The public "did not then think of the incident as 'Bloomsbury' . . . [i]n retrospect, however, the historical connections would be made" (Edel, *House* 157). Quentin Bell writes that by 1910 "Bloomsbury had become an object of public disapproval, a centre of disaffection, of Abyssinian Emperors and of incomprehensible aesthetics" (QB1 168). The *Dreadnought* Hoax, as Rosenbaum writes, "displays the Group's emerging anti-military outlook, which is closely related to an increasing disillusionment with imperialism. . . . It is not difficult to trace the line in [Woolf's] development that runs from the *Dreadnought* Hoax to *Three Guineas*" (*Edwardian* 223). During World War I, also, Bloomsbury's pacifism was demonstrated by several of its members becoming CONSCIENTIOUS OBJECTORS; a pamphlet against the war by Clive Bell was ordered seized and burned in 1915.

Among the several clubs associated with the Bloomsbury Group, the most significant was the Memoir Club, founded by Molly MacCarthy probably as one of several attempts to induce or inspire her husband to write the great novel his friends were sure he would one day produce (he never did). The Memoir Club first met on March 4, 1920 (and in 1960 Frances PARTRIDGE wrote in her diary that "I must pull up my socks and write something for the next Memoir Club meeting" [*Everything* 357]). For some, such as Clive Bell, World War I disintegrated the Bloomsbury Group and Old Bloomsbury ended in 1918 (*Old Friends* 130); Leonard Woolf, on the other hand, describes Strachey's death in 1932 as "the beginning of the end of what we used to call Old Bloomsbury" (LW2 373). The original members usually distinguished between "Old" and "newer" or "younger" Bloomsbury. Woolf's "Old Bloomsbury" ends with the Gordon Square group being swept off by Lady Ottoline MORRELL, who brought them into contact with a very different, more glamorous society. The distinction between Old and newer Bloomsbury has often been blurred and, as several of its members have remarked, there have been people who would never have considered themselves or even wanted to be part of Bloomsbury included in it by various commentators.

Leonard Woolf described "newer Bloomsbury" as consisting of the original members plus the Bell children—Julian, Quentin and Angelica—and David GARNETT. In *Bloomsbury*, Quentin Bell describes Garnett and his friend Francis BIRRELL as "marginal" members. Bell draws a diagram of "the sort of pattern that existed in the year 1913" that includes all those so far mentioned, with the addition of Gerald Shove, James and Marjorie STRACHEY, Sydney WATERLOW, and H. T. J. NORTON (*Bloomsbury* 15). In his introduction to the first volume of Woolf's DIARY, Bell refers to "almost a second generation of Bloomsbury" consisting of Rupert BROOKE, Katherine COX, Frances Darwin (later Cornford), Jacques RAVERAT, and Brynhild, Margery and Noel Olivier (D1 xxiv), young people whom Woolf referred to collectively as the NEO-PAGANS. After World War I many of the original group of friends no longer lived in Bloomsbury, and outposts such as CHARLESTON, where Vanessa, Grant, and Garnett had moved in 1916, and the Woolfs' Sussex home, MONK'S HOUSE, became new centers of Bloomsbury activity. Vanessa wrote in 1927 to Roger Fry about "an extraordinary notice in the Westminster Gazette the other day headed 'Bloomsbury in Sussex' " (Marler 323), a headline that uncannily prefigures the very term by which Charleston has been marketed in the last couple of decades as the house and its unique decorations were restored and preserved. The connection with Gordon Square was maintained when Keynes took over number 46 from the Bells in 1916.

The Bloomsbury Group, according to Quentin Bell, "can hardly be said to have had any common ideas about art, literature or politics" (*Bloomsbury* 12). "It had no body of doctrine, no code of conduct, no masters" (Rosenbaum, *Bloomsbury Group* x), and yet the friends found each other sympathetic and were linked by their commitment to lives of "mental fight." It is also possible to trace the common elements in their thinking and intellectual backgrounds.

Rosenbaum's compendium *The Bloomsbury Group* offers the best introduction to its various points of view and contains key documents in its history, such as Keynes's memoir "My Early Beliefs" (*Bloomsbury Group* 48–65). Rosenbaum is also writing a literary history of the Bloomsbury Group, two volumes of which, *Victorian Bloomsbury* and *Edwardian Bloomsbury*, have been published. In his biography of Leslie Stephen, Noel Annan describes the Bloomsbury Group as the fourth generation of the CLAPHAM SECT, remarking that although Bloomsbury "naturally repudiated the moral code of their forefathers" (Annan 161), "one can still see the old Evangelical ferment at work, a strong suspicion of the worldly-wise, an unalterable emphasis on personal salvation and a penchant for meditation and communion among intimate friends" (Annan 162). Both Forster and Woolf had great-grandfathers in the Clapham Sect, and Rosenbaum points out that Woolf also had a relative (Caroline Emelia STEPHEN) who was in the Society of Friends. G. E. Moore's mother and members of Fry's family were Quakers. Rosenbaum traces the influence of the Clapham and Quaker traditions on Bloomsbury, citing also Keynes as an exemplar of its puritan tradition. He identifies four influences that contributed to Bloomsbury "philosophy"—puritanism, Utilitarianism, liberalism, and aestheticism—and argues that "Bloomsbury modified their puritanism with atheism, their Utilitarianism with Platonism, their liberalism with pacifism, and their aestheticism with love" ("Virginia Woolf" 24).

The idea that the Bloomsbury Group did not really exist was promulgated by its members almost from its start, yet those same people were well aware that "Bloomsbury" had entered the language as descriptive of a certain attitude to culture and society. In 1918, Woolf wrote that "the dominion that 'Bloomsbury' exercises over the sane & the insane alike seems to be sufficient to turn the brains of the most robust. Happily, I'm 'Bloomsbury' myself, & thus immune; but I'm not altogether ignorant of what they mean" (D1 106). In a letter replying to the inquiries of an American researcher, Harmon H. Goldstone, Woolf wrote of Bloomsbury in terms that her husband would continue to employ in all such replies: "I feel that Bloomsbury is a word that stands for very little. The Bloomsbury group is largely a creation of the journalists" (L5 91). Woolf was, however, sensitive to criticism of Bloomsbury, and in the 1930s those criticisms became increasingly vicious.

After World War I, Annan tells us, Bloomsbury was popular with the younger generation and by the end of the 1920s those affiliated with it had wide influence. There were also, however, powerful detractors, the most significant of which were the Cambridge literary critics grouped around F. R. and Q. D. LEAVIS and their journal *Scrutiny*. Annan describes Q. D. Leavis's vituperative review of *THREE GUINEAS*, entitled "Caterpillars of the Commonwealth Unite," as "a high example of modern invective" (Annan, "Bloomsbury" 26). In "Keynes, Lawrence and Cambridge," an article in *Scrutiny* (September 1949) later incorporated into his influential book *The Common Pursuit*, F. R. Leavis sharply criticized Keynes's memoir "My Early Beliefs" in terms that encapsulated much of the anti-Bloomsbury feeling common in England: "Articulateness and unreality cultivated together; callousness disguised from itself in articulateness; conceit casing itself safely in a confirmed sense of high sophistication; the uncertainty as to whether one is serious or not taking itself for ironic poise: who has not at some time observed the process?" (257).

As she contemplated writing Roger Fry's biography, Woolf wondered whether she should "include a note, a sarcastic note, on the Bloomsbury baiters" (D4 288–89). Among the most prominent Bloomsbury baiters she would have had in mind were the Marxist Prince Dmitri Mirsky (*The Intelligentsia of Great Britain* [1935]; see Rosenbaum, *Bloomsbury Group*: 380–87), Wyndham LEWIS, whose *Men Without Art* appeared in 1934, and Frank Swinnerton. In *The Georgian Literary Scene* (1935) Swinnerton wrote that "Bloomsbury (as the embodiment of an assumption) feels strongly its superiority to the rest of British mankind" (McNees 1: 335–36). The criticism that "Bloomsbury" had insinuated itself into the opinion-forming and taste-regulating media of Britain was widespread in the 1930s and persisted for the next few decades. Sometimes, the criticism even came from very close quarters, as when Vita SACKVILLE-WEST's son Benedict NICOLSON wrote Woolf about her generation's passive attitude toward social change. The editors of Woolf's letters inform us that she worked more carefully at her reply to Ben Nicolson than on any other letter. In a draft of her reply, Woolf said that in books such as *THE COMMON READER, A ROOM OF ONE'S OWN* and *THREE GUINEAS* she had done "her best to make them reach a far wider circle than a little private circle of exquisite and cultivated people" (L6 420) and argued that Roger Fry's lectures on art had had enormous influence on society.

The attitude that Bloomsbury was a côterie jealously guarding its power began as early as the 1920s. When Leonard Woolf was literary editor of the *NATION*, the editor, Hubert Henderson, complained about the young reviewers Leonard was commissioning, and Leonard wrote that he "naturally" thought he was right and Henderson wrong, "but not, I assure you, in the supercilious sense that is thought to be characteristic of 'Bloomsbury' " (Spotts 285). Throughout the 1950s and 1960s, Leonard continued to defend Bloomsbury against friend and foe. When Gerald BRENAN sent him draft pages of *South from Granada* in 1955, Leonard complained that he had repeated the "quite untrue" charge that Bloomsbury " 'regarded all but a chosen few people as being beyond the pale' " (Spotts 497), and in 1959 he turned down David Garnett's proposal to publish a Bloomsbury picture book because it would be "met by the usual chorus of anti-Bloomsburiansis" (Spotts 507). Leonard did not find matters helped by the publication of Garnett's memoir *Flowers of the Forest* or Clive Bell's *Old Friends*, both of which, he told Vita Sackville-West in 1957, "have done considerable harm to the reputation of Bloomsbury" (Spotts 503). The strong anti-Bloomsbury sentiment in England influenced Leonard's decisions about publishing Woolf's LETTERS and diary, and also about having her nephew write her biography. In 1964, he told Quentin Bell that the "fog which surrounds [Bloomsbury] has not yet sufficiently dissipated to give a biography a fair chance with the critics" (Spotts 535).

In 1973, the year that Bell's celebrated biography of Woolf was published, Carolyn Heilbrun wrote in *Toward a Recognition of Androgyny* (a book that did much to begin changing Woolf's stature in the United States) that "to admit admiration for the Bloomsbury Group still requires one to assume a posture either defensive or apologetic" (115). A few years earlier, Bell had published a book simply entitled *Bloomsbury*, written at a time when, according to his foreword to a 1986 edition of the book, Bloomsbury "seemed dead and stinking." Bloomsbury, he remarked, "has been criticised from a bewilderingly large number of points of view" (*Bloomsbury* 10). This negative attitude frequently centered on Woolf, who was regarded by the literary establishment in England as a neurasthenic "Lady of Letters" whose fiction was, for the most part, incomprehensible. Bernard Levin, for example—described by Nigel NICOLSON as "the most respected, humane and witty of our journalists" ("Bloomsbury" 7)—wrote proudly that he could and would not read Woolf's novels ("Cry, Woolf, but I Won't be Listening" [*The Times* May 8, 1980]).[4] Even in the 1980s, Bloomsbury was "regarded in England

[4] Presumably Mr. Levin has changed his mind, as he was a guest speaker at the annual Charleston Festival in May 1994.

as fair game for abuse" (Nicolson, "Bloomsbury" 8); in the 1990s, with the publication of new editions of Woolf's novels by Penguin and by Oxford University Press, with introductions written by several feminist scholars, Woolf's general reputation in her own country might be seen as improving. However, it is still possible to find Woolf referred to as a "cult" author (see, for example, Herbert Mitgang, *New York Times,* November 27, 1993).

In 1920, Vanessa Bell wrote angrily to her cousin Margaret (Madge) VAUGHAN, who was interested in renting Charleston but had raised questions about Vanessa's relationship with Clive and about the paternity of Angelica GARNETT. Her moral character, wrote Vanessa, was none of Madge's business and nothing to do with whether or not she would rent her house (Marler 235). The hostility aroused by the Bloomsbury Group since the 1920s has frequently been rooted in moral disapproval of what would now be called their "lifestyle." As Christopher Reed points out, the "anger Bloomsbury arouses today suggests that the group continues to stand for something that threatens established beliefs" ("Bloomsbury Bashing" 58). Reed critiques Charles Harrison's *English Art and Modernism 1900–1939* (1981), Gertrude Himmelfarb's *Marriage and Morals Among the Victorians* (1986), Hilton Kramer's "Bloomsbury Idols" (1984), and other articles by Kramer in the *New Criterion* for their homophobia. Reed also takes to task American feminist critics such as Phyllis Rose, Jane Marcus and Louise DeSalvo for what he sees as the heterosexism of some of their writing on Woolf.

Brenda R. Silver, in her research "into the construction of Woolf as a cultural icon in the popular realm" ("What's Woolf" 24), notes that "the performative role played by 'Virginia Woolf' as sign and image, the battles waged over her circulation and meaning, are still powerful makers and markers of our culture today" (Ibid. 56). "Bloomsbury" has become what many newspaper reviewers describe as an "industry," with new generations of Bells, Garnetts, Stephens and Stracheys still providing copy for Sunday magazines as they develop their own talents.[5] Books such as *Vanessa Bell's Family Album* and Alen MacWeeney's *Bloomsbury Reflections* are examples of the kind of publications Leonard Woolf felt had no market in the 1950s. Paul Levy has written that it is "not far-fetched to see the current domestic habits of middle-class Englishmen and Americans as owing a great deal to Bloomsbury's discovery of such things as French provincial and peasant cooking and culture" (Levy 15), and in 1987 Laura Ashley brought out "Bloomsbury," a home furnishings collection indebted to the work of Vanessa Bell and Duncan Grant.

Woolf is still at the center of much of this "industry," although the recent restoration of Charleston has also focused attention on Bloomsbury's rich legacy of visual and decorative art (to say nothing of its legacy of nontraditional family structures).[6] Silver comments on the striking breadth of Woolf's "name and face recognition, suggested by her appearance as a cultural marker in texts as divergent as *Los Angeles Times* editorials, George Will columns, ACTUP anticensorship marches, Michael Innis mysteries, the hard rock group Virginia Wolf, *Sesame Street,* and Hanif Kureishi's 1987 film *Sammy and Rosie Get Laid*" ("What's Woolf" 22). (See also POPULAR CULTURE.) "Bloomsbury" as a cultural signifier, a shorthand for a set of attitudes to art and culture, has been in circulation for more than eighty years now, and the problems of determining who was or was not in the Bloomsbury Group have long since given way to arguments with more serious implications for the relations between aesthetics and politics, art and society.

Bloomsbury Traveller's Almanac An annual guide (including dates and opening times) to properties, gardens, galleries, broadcasts, lectures, guided walks and coach tours in England that relate to figures in the BLOOMSBURY GROUP. It is edited and published in Brighton by Màire McQueeney.

Bloomsbury Workshop At 12 Galen Place, near the BRITISH MUSEUM, in London, a shop that specializes in books, exhibitions and artwork by BLOOMSBURY GROUP figures.

Blow, Nancy Character in *MRS. DALLOWAY* who attends Clarissa DALLOWAY's party with Lord GAYTON. Clarissa, although she likes the couple, thinks they will "solidify young" and be "rather dull" on their own (MD 270).

Bluebeard In *THE VOYAGE OUT,* the bearded Ridley AMBROSE is taunted by a group of children in London as "Bluebeard." The tale of Bluebeard appears in the folklore of many countries and concerns a man who murders several wives and hides their bodies in a locked room.

[5]The following is typical of the genre: "At this point, the reader might think, the subject of Bloomsbury must be pretty well exhausted. Its famous members have generated a seemingly endless series of biographies and memoirs; their letters and diaries have been repeatedly scrutinized and compared. Virginia Woolf, in particular, has spawned something of a cottage industry: her fiction is continually reissued in new editions, her journals and correspondence published in assorted versions." (Michiko Kakutani, *New York Times,* June 11, 1991: C17).

[6]As recently as March 1994, the *New York Times* reported in an article highlighting Vanessa Bell's granddaughter, Cressida Bell, that the Bloomsbury Group's "irrepressible style. . . is making a comeback, both in England and the United States." ("A House for Life, Love, Art and New Inspiration," March 31, 1994: C1 +4).

Boase, Captain In *JACOB'S ROOM,* he catches a "monster shark," which is displayed in the Aquarium at Scarborough; Mrs. BARFOOT had known Captain Boase quite well.

Bodham, Miss One of several people at a SUFFRAGE meeting in the "1910" chapter of *THE YEARS.*

Bodichon, Barbara Leigh Smith (1827–1891) The granddaughter of a colleague of William Wilberforce in the antislavery movement, William Smith, who was Radical member of Parliament for Norwich, and the daughter of Benjamin Smith, who was elected to his father's seat in Parliament in 1837, Barbara Smith grew up in a household frequented by American abolitionists such as Elizabeth Cady Stanton, English reformers such as Harriet MARTINEAU, and political refugees from around the world. In 1856 she visited Algeria and met there a doctor, Eugène Bodichon, whom she married.

Ray STRACHEY in *The Cause* describes the "first organisation of the Women's Movement" as being that formed by Barbara Bodichon in 1855 (the same year that in the United States Susan B. Anthony and Elizabeth Cady Stanton organized the Seneca Falls Convention). Bodichon, a cousin of Florence NIGHTINGALE and friend of Harriet Martineau, was George ELIOT's model for Romola (in her novel of that name). Her mother had died young and her enlightened father gave each of his children £300 per year when they came of age, thus putting his daughter in a unique position for a mid-nineteenth-century woman (a story Woolf recounts in *THREE GUINEAS* [TG 136*f.*]). She set about reforming English property law, publishing a popular pamphlet entitled *Brief Summary in Plain Language of the Most Important Laws Concerning Women,* which, according to Jacquie Matthews, "set out to rectify [John Stuart] Mill's omission of a critical consideration" of those laws (Matthews 96). A petition to reform property law that Bodichon began circulating in 1855 gathered 26,000 signatures in a year and was presented to both houses of Parliament. Matthews believes that "all the subsequent Married Women's Property Acts were based on Barbara's petition and *Brief Summary* and all the provisions therein were not passed until 1893" (Matthews 97).

In 1865, Bodichon joined Emily Davies, the founder of GIRTON COLLEGE, in supporting the election of John Stuart Mill. The following year, she worked on organizing a petition for Women's Suffrage that Mill would present to Parliament. The petition committee was, according to Ray Strachey, the first of all the SUFFRAGE committees to be established (Strachey, *The Cause* 105). Bodichon was the center of the "Langham Place Circle" of feminist activism. Matthews likens Bodichon to Woolf in "speaking about and to the daughters of educated men" with "a similar sense of rage at the waste" (Matthews 101), and calls her "a tough and shining thread in the mid-century women's network" (Matthews 92).

Bodkin, Archibald As *A ROOM OF ONE'S OWN* draws to a conclusion, Woolf starts to elaborate on the reasons she likes women, but stops herself with the thought that Sir Archibald Bodkin might be concealed among the table-napkins in a dresser (AROO 111). For her 1929 audience, Bodkin would have been a familiar name as he was director of public prosecutions responsible for bringing to trial for obscenity Radclyffe Hall's novel *THE WELL OF LONELINESS.*

Boeuf en Daube The triumphant dish (which translates as beef stew) served by Mrs. RAMSAY at her dinner in section XVII of part 1 of *TO THE LIGHTHOUSE,* which she says is from a French recipe of her grandmother's. It was a specialty of Roger FRY's (Spalding, *Fry* 128) and was "a Provençal specialty" that Vanessa BELL and her family enjoyed in CASSIS (Marler 318n3). A *daubière* is a "narrow-necked seasoned earthenware pot" available only in Provence (CM9 51). A recipe for *boeuf en daube* can be found in Linda Wolfe's *Literary Gourmet: Menus from Masterpieces* (New York: Harmony Books, 1989: 234–35). Miranda Carter has explained that a "*daube*" is "one of the great French peasant stews" (CM9 50) and that although there are "innumerable variations," its "one incontrovertible quality" is that it is cooked very slowly, never being allowed to boil, all its ingredients being gradually transformed into what the American food writer Richard Olney terms "pervasive unity" (CM9 50–51). Carter reviews several expert opinions (and their differences) on the process of cooking *daubes.*

Bonamy, Richard Character in *JACOB'S ROOM* who loves Jacob, whom he meets when they are students at Cambridge. At one point he seems to Elizabeth DURRANT to be one of her daughter Clara's suitors (JR 85). In the final scene of the novel, Bonamy accompanies Betty FLANDERS to Jacob's room after his death. He cries out Jacob's name and Mrs. Flanders asks him what she should do with a pair of her son's shoes.

Bond The cowman in *BETWEEN THE ACTS.*

Bonham, Mrs. Mentioned in *JACOB'S ROOM.*

Bonthorp Mentioned in *BETWEEN THE ACTS* as finding too heavy the mirror he is carrying in the last scene of the annual village pageant.

Books and Portraits A collection of critical essays by Woolf, subtitled "Some further selections from her Literary and Biographical Writings" and edited by Mary Lyon (London: Hogarth Press, 1977). In her preface, Lyon explains that these were mostly early reviews and speculates that "periodicals sent [Woolf] initially the sort of books they felt Sir Leslie Stephen's daughter would be best equipped to criticise. When she emerged as a novelist and critic in her own right, they perhaps tended more frequently to assign her works of contemporary fiction or books by women writers" (ix). Lyon wrote that Woolf "tends to see women within their own tradition, rather than the more general one, and this is an important fact in her treatment of them" (ix). The book is divided into two parts, "Of Writing and Writers" and "Mainly Portraits."

Lyon had met Leonard WOOLF in 1956 when she traveled to England to do research for her thesis at Radcliffe College on "Virginia Woolf as a Critic." Leonard later referred to her work as exemplifying the kind of scholarship done in the United States that was unknown in England, telling his brother Philip that it was for this reason he was going to deposit Woolf's papers in an American institution where they would be available to students like the impressive Mary Lyon. He also mentioned that Lyon's research had uncovered so many essays by Woolf that he was able to put together another collection of them in 1958, *GRANITE & RAINBOW* (Spotts 500). In her preface, Lyon acknowledges the help she received from B. J. Kirkpatrick's 1967 revision of her Woolf *Bibliography*.

Booth Family Mary (1848–1939, née Macaulay) and Charles Booth (1840–1916) were friends of Leslie and Julia Prinsep STEPHEN, Woolf's parents, and Kensington neighbors of the Stephen family. They are mentioned in "A SKETCH OF THE PAST." Charles Booth was an owner of the Booth Steamship Company, as well as a social scientist and reformer. George DUCKWORTH assisted him in writing *Life and Labour of the People of London* (1901–03). The Booths had three daughters, Antonia Mary ("Dodo"), Margaret (Meg), and Imogen, and a son, George Macaulay (1877–1971). Margaret (1880–1961) married William Thackeray Denis, the son of Anne Isabella Thackeray RITCHIE ("Aunt Anny") and Richmond Ritchie, in 1906. In 1905, Woolf wrote a brief notice of two of Margaret's stories in the *GUARDIAN*, calling them "the work of an immature writer" (E1 74). During their move from HYDE PARK GATE to GORDON SQUARE in 1904, following their father's death, Vanessa BELL and Woolf stayed with the Booths at 24 Great Cumberland Place.

Borges, Jorge Luis (1899–1986) Argentine poet, critic and short-story writer who translated *ORLANDO* (*Orlando, Una Biografía* [1937]) and *A ROOM OF ONE'S OWN* (*Un Cuarto Propio* [1956]) into Spanish for Sur, the publishing house founded by Victoria OCAMPO that published her magazine *Sur* (*South*).

Boswell, James (1740–95) Author of *Journal of a Tour to the Hebrides* (1785) and, most famously, the *Life of Samuel Johnson* (1791). He is seen by ORLANDO as a "little shadow with pouting lips" (O 222).

Bourget, Paul (1852–1935) In *THREE GUINEAS*, Woolf remarks as an example of the constraints on Victorian women that Gertrude BELL was not allowed to read *The Disciple*, a work by this French novelist who analyzed the moral issues of his time in psychological terms (TG 77).

Bournemouth Conference In *THREE GUINEAS*, Woolf refers to "the Bournemouth Conference of working men" (TG 8); her reference is to the 1937 Labour Party Annual Conference at Bournemouth where Hugh Dalton, M. P., asserted that Britain should be powerfully armed to face the fascist threat (RN 306).

Bourton In *MRS. DALLOWAY*, the family home of Clarissa DALLOWAY about which she thinks throughout the day of the novel's action. *Mrs. Dalloway* brings together a group of people who had been at Bourton a summer more than thirty years earlier, during which Clarissa decided not to marry Peter WALSH.

Bovary, Emma In *A ROOM OF ONE'S OWN*, Emma Bovary, the heroine of *Madame Bovary* by Gustave FLAUBERT, is adduced as an example of women who have "burnt like beacons in all the works of all the poets from the beginning of time" (AROO 43) and whom Woolf uses to stress the difference between fictional and real women.

Bow Windows Bookshop See *VOYAGE OUT, THE*.

Bowen, Elizabeth Dorothea Cole (1899–1973) Irish novelist and short-story writer whom Woolf met through Lady Ottoline MORRELL in 1931. Woolf became friends with "stammering, shy, conventional" Miss Bowen (D4 86). Following a misunderstanding in 1940 that led Woolf to think Bowen no longer wanted to see her, Woolf wrote regretfully in her DIARY that she had been fond of her and believed Bowen also liked her (D5 293). Among Bowen's novels are *The Last September* (1929), *To the North* (1932), *The House in Paris* (1935), *The Death of the Heart* (1938), *The Heat of the Day* (1949) and *A World of Love* (1955). She wrote an afterword for the 1960 Signet edition of *ORLANDO*.

Bowley, Mr. Character in *JACOB'S ROOM*. He is a friend of Rose SHAW, with whom he tries to engineer the marriage of Helen AITKEN and a man named Jimmy. "Ever so good with old ladies," Mr. Bowley also "liked young people" (JR 165–66). He is also a guest at Clarissa DALLOWAY's party in *MRS. DALLOWAY* and is seen early in that novel as one of the people looking up at the skywriting airplane.

Boxall In *JACOB'S ROOM*, the butler to LUCY, Countess of Rocksbier. When the Countess asks Boxall whose carriage is driving by (JR 100), Woolf is recalling a scene she describes in "AM I A SNOB?" of Lady Bath asking her butler Middleton to tell her who is driving by (MOB 207).

Boxall, Nellie (or Nelly) Hired on February 1, 1916, with her lifelong friend Lottie HOPE, as the Woolfs' cook and maid. The two women had previously worked for Roger FRY. Thus began a turbulent relationship that would continue until 1934 when Nellie finally left to work for the actor Charles Laughton. Woolf's frequent references in her DIARY and LETTERS to "the great servant question" invariably concern Nellie and Lottie, as through the years Nellie would quit or Woolf would fire her, only for the decision to be rescinded after many arguments. When Vanessa BELL found herself with no servants and three young children to look after, Woolf offered to lend Nellie and Lottie to her; but Leonard WOOLF disapproved, his concern for Woolf's well-being outweighing his sense of obligation to his sister-in-law. In November 1919, Woolf wrote in her diary that "No one could be nicer than Nelly," yet she continued by lamenting the frequency of their disagreement. "But," she went on, "the fault is more in the system of keeping two young women chained in a kitchen to laze & work & suck their life from two in the drawingroom than in her character or in mine" (D1 314). In 1956, Nellie participated in a BBC-radio Home Service program, *Portrait of Virginia Woolf*, in which she told interviewer Eileen Molony of how Woolf would roll her own cigarettes and of her preference for ice cream with hot chocolate sauce.

Brace, Donald (1881–1955) Woolf's American publishers from 1921 were Harcourt, Brace and Company, beginning with *MONDAY OR TUESDAY*. As Selma Meyerowitz has written in her discussion of the correspondence between Leonard WOOLF and Donald Brace in the BERG COLLECTION (VWM 17:7), the American publisher took a personal interest in Woolf's work and Leonard often discussed its publication with him. Gerald DUCKWORTH, the publisher of Woolf's first two novels, had arranged for their American publication with George H. Doran Company, but once the HOGARTH PRESS was established, all Woolf's American publications were (and are still) by Harcourt, Brace. Donald Brace visited England regularly and met the Woolfs several times.

Bradshaw, Sir William The "nerve specialist" in *MRS. DALLOWAY* to whom Septimus Warren SMITH goes for treatment when he gets no help from Dr. HOLMES. Probably a composite of several doctors with whom Woolf had experience, Bradshaw is one of her most savagely satirical portraits. He is depicted in a uniform shade of gray, from his powerful gray car to his subdued wife who has long ago lost the power to resist her husband's will. Lady Bradshaw sometimes takes "photographs, which were scarcely to be distinguished from the work of professionals" while she waits for her husband to see patients who can afford to have him come to them at home (MD 143), but her will has sunk, "waterlogged," into her husband's. When Bradshaw sees Septimus he tells Rezia that her husband must go to a "home," dismissing Septimus as "not fit to be about" (MD 149). In a famous passage, Woolf describes Bradshaw's worship of the goddesses of "Proportion" and "Conversion" allying the psychological discourse of power that Bradshaw speaks with the power of imperialism and the state.

At her party Clarissa overhears Bradshaw talking to her husband about Septimus, who has killed himself; Lady Bradshaw explains to her hostess that they are late to her party because just as they were leaving a "very sad case" of her husband's had committed suicide.

Bramham, Nick A painter in *JACOB'S ROOM* who is a friend of Jacob's. When his model, Fanny ELMER, and he fall out, he begins a flirtation with FLORINDA.

Brand One of Colonel Abel PARGITER's cronies in *THE YEARS*.

Breitkopf, Joseph Mentioned in *MRS. DALLOWAY* as an old man who was a guest of Clarissa DALLOWAY's family at BOURTON each summer when she was young. With Peter WALSH, Breitkopf interrupts Clarissa's moment of ecstasy with Sally SETON and also comes upon Clarissa and Peter during their final conversation at Bourton when Clarissa will not agree to marry Peter.

Brenan, Gerald (1894–1987) Noted writer on Spain who became a close friend of Ralph PARTRIDGE in 1914 when they were both in the army. *The Spanish Labyrinth* (1943), *The Literature of the Spanish People* (1951), and *South from Granada* (1957) are his well-known books on Spain. Woolf met Brenan at TIDMARSH in 1922 when he was staying with Partridge, Lytton STRACHEY and Dora CARRINGTON (for many years Brenan was sexually obsessed with Carrington). Brenan was the son of an army officer who wanted him to follow a military career, but in 1920 Brenan left to live in Spain and be a writer. His devotion to literature impressed Woolf and she wrote several long letters to him encouraging him as a writer. Reviewing the third volume of Woolf's LETTERS, Josephine O'Brien Schaefer described those to Brenan as "among the kindest she ever penned" (VWM 12:4); Brenan's biographer, however, writes that his letters to Woolf "almost uniquely in his vast surviving correspondence, have a strained, almost sycophantic quality" (Gathorne-Hardy 189). Leonard WOOLF and Woolf stayed with Brenan in Spain in the spring of 1923 (a trip described in Woolf's essay "To Spain," published in the *NATION & ATHENAEUM* on May 5, 1923 [E3 361–65]) and hoped he might write for the *NATION* or for the HOGARTH PRESS (which he did not). She described him to Mary HUTCHINSON as "a very sympathetic, but slightly blurred character, who owing to solitude and multitudes of books has some phantasmagoric resemblance to Shelley" (CS 162). Brenan writes about his relations with Woolf and others in the BLOOMSBURY GROUP in his autobiographies, *A Life of One's Own: Childhood and Youth* (1962, dedicated to David GARNETT) and *Personal Record 1920–1972* (1974).

Brett, Dorothy Eugenie (1883–1976) A painter who became close friends with Dora CARRINGTON and Mark GERTLER while studying at the Slade School of Art. She became part of a group that congregated at GARSINGTON, Lady Ottoline MORRELL's home, during World War I and was close to Katherine MANSFIELD, with whom she, Carrington and John Middleton Murry shared a house in Gower Street rented from John Maynard KEYNES in 1916. Woolf met Brett, as she was known, at Garsington and stayed in touch with her throughout her life. In 1924 Brett went with D. H. LAWRENCE and his wife to Taos, New Mexico, to help them establish a new community. She published *Lawrence and Brett: A Friendship* in 1933 and her portrait of the novelist is in the NATIONAL GALLERY. Her obituary in the *Times* stated that she had "figured in most of the Bloomsbury memoirs without having been part of their tangled relationships."

Brewer, Mr. Septimus Warren SMITH's employer at Sibleys and Arrowsmiths in *MRS. DALLOWAY* who advises Septimus to take up football to develop "manliness" (MD 129).

Brierly, Professor A guest at Clarissa DALLOWAY's party in *MRS. DALLOWAY* who quarrels with Jim HUTTON about Milton, on whom Professor Brierly is an expert.

Brigge, John Fenner Character in *ORLANDO* from whose diary is pieced together the story of the ceremony of Orlando's receiving the Order of the Bath and the revolution during which Orlando becomes a woman.

Briggs, Mrs. Martin PARGITER's landlady in *THE YEARS*.

Briscoe, Lily Character in *TO THE LIGHTHOUSE*, first mentioned at the end of section III of part 1 when Mrs. RAMSAY remembers that she is supposed to be staying in the same position while Lily paints her. Lily is about thirty-four in part 1 of the novel, and lives "off the Brompton Road" in London (49) where she looks after her father. Lily is staying in the village, with another of the Ramsays' guests, William BANKES, because there is no room for them at the house; however, it seems that Lily has stayed at least one other time with the Ramsays for she remembers Mrs. Ramsay coming to her room late at night and staying until dawn talking (49). Lily's feelings for people are complex, particularly her feelings for Mrs. Ramsay, with whom she longs for intimacy. She is a painter who shuns the fashions made popular by a Mr. PAUNCEFORTE, and she has to struggle not only against her hostess's feeling that "one could not take her painting very seriously" (17) but also against Charles TANSLEY's whispering in her ear that "women can't paint, women can't write."

In part 3 of the novel, Lily returns to the Ramsays' house ten years after the visit described in part 1 and once again attempts to paint a work that embodies her feelings about Mrs. Ramsay. She realizes, with a sense of triumph, that Mrs. Ramsay's judgment was often flawed and that her manipulations of men and women to marry were something she was fortunate and glad to have escaped. As Mr. RAMSAY sails with two of his children, James and Cam RAMSAY, to the lighthouse, Lily struggles with her aesthetic problems, finally resolving them as the Ramsays land at the lighthouse and the novel ends.

As Woolf certainly intended, Lily Briscoe's paintings have usually been read as analogous to the novel itself, implying in turn that Lily represents Woolf herself. Mitchell Leaska, for example, calls Lily a "silhouette" of Woolf (*Novels* 139) who thinks "in terms of painting, what her creator pondered in terms of the novel" (143). Howard Harper points out that Lily's is the only consciousness evoked in all three parts of the novel, identifying her with "the final, transcendent consciousness" (Harper 149). As Mrs. Ramsay's consciousness is the "norm" for part 1, so Lily's is the norm for part 3 of *To the Lighthouse* (Harper 156).

Thomas Caramagno links Lily's "deeply bifurcated" feelings to Woolf's own mood swings and suggests that readers' condemnation or eulogizing of Mr. and Mrs. Ramsay usually depends on evidence from Lily's internal monologues "as she struggles with mood swings that interfere with her ability to know her own feelings" about them (Caramagno 247). Like many critics, Caramagno sees *To the Lighthouse* as resolving Woolf's ambivalent feelings about her parents, but others, such as Alex Zwerdling (*Virginia Woolf*) and Jane Marcus (in *Art and Anger*) have questioned this.

Lily's painting has been likened to works of the POST-IMPRESSIONISTS, and her aesthetic problems have been seen in terms of the FORMALIST theories of Roger FRY—theories that rejected mimesis and emphasized abstract form (see Christopher Reed, "Through Formalism"). Avrom Fleishman and Elizabeth Abel both see similarities between Lily's work as described in the novel and that of Paul Cézanne, who was Fry's favorite painter. Abel, however, notes that Fry's aesthetic is represented by Woolf "as a factor in Lily's *struggle* with her painting, not as the adequate exposition of the painting" (Abel 72). Pamela Caughie, noting that the structure of the novel "is the progression of Lily's painting" (33), sees Woolf as checking two MODERNIST tendencies in Lily's art in part 3, "the withdrawal from the public world of facts into the private world of vision to achieve some form of order" and "the effort to synthesize the two to achieve some kind of harmony" (34). Caughie also suggests that it is Lily who narrates the scenes in the boat in part 3 of the novel and that through this narrative function, Woolf stresses "the reciprocal relation between life and art" (36).

Some readers, particularly male critics, have seen Lily as a "spinster lady who likes to paint" (Spilka 80), and as "plain, dried up, retiring, unambitious, fearful of and inexperienced in love" (Mepham, *Literary Life* 103). These dismissive evaluations of her are countered by other readings that focus on the erotics of her attachment to Mrs. Ramsay. Jane Lilienfeld elucidates the stages of Lily's mourning of Mrs. Ramsay in part 3, and shows that in doing so Lily "is able to give up Mrs. Ramsay's conception of the relations between men and women, a conception of which Lily had always been critical" (" 'Deceptiveness' " 368).

Abel represents Lily as breaking the "narrative decree" governing the fate of daughters, her narrative being a powerful alternative to the Oedipal fictions of James and Cam (Abel 47). Several recent readers have emphasized Lily's "triumph" over Mrs. Ramsay in part 3 as she wins her identity as a "new woman, professional, unmarried, independent" (Minow-Pinkney 111). For Makiko Minow-Pinkney, Mrs. Ramsay represents the "phallic mother" (the mother possessed of masculine power) whom Lily must kill in order to establish her autonomy (111). Lily is also seen by Jane Fisher as "capable of the inspiration that resolves problems 'in a flash,' " that inspiration that Mr. Ramsay knows eludes him (" 'Silent' " 103). She can lump all the letters from A to Z together instantly, as she does when she suddenly sees how to resolve a problem in her painting by moving the tree nearer the middle (TTL 84). (See also A TO Z.)

British Museum The British Museum, in Great Russell Street to the north of BLOOMSBURY, was built between 1823 and 1847. For almost her entire adult life Woolf lived within walking distance of the Museum and frequently used its library, sitting in the great domed Reading Room just as many of her novels' characters do. She wrote in 1926 of how she liked its "dusty bookish atmosphere" (D3 80) on a visit there during the General Strike. In *NIGHT AND DAY,* Mary DATCHET visits the Museum in her lunch hour to look at the ELGIN MARBLES. She is reminded of Ralph DENHAM when she looks at the statue of Ulysses as, in *JACOB'S ROOM,* Fanny ELMER visits the same statue to remind her of Jacob FLANDERS. Jacob visits the British Museum Reading Room in chapter 9 of *Jacob's Room,* and irritates Julia HEDGE, a feminist who is working there. Ms. Hedge laments that no women's names are inscribed in the band that runs around the interior of the dome (the names were later removed). It is in this chapter that Woolf's narrator describes the British Museum as enclosing "an enormous mind" wherein cultural history is hoarded "beyond the power of any single mind to possess it" (JR 108).

Recalling Julia Hedge, perhaps, the narrator of *A ROOM OF ONE'S OWN* plans in chapter 2 to continue her research into women and fiction at the British Museum. In the reading room, feeling like "a thought in the huge bald forehead" (AROO 26), she discovers how men have throughout the centuries written down their opinions of women. Woolf notes in *THREE GUINEAS* that women were "apparently excluded from the British Museum Reading-Room in the eighteenth century" (TG 174n6).

Brittain, Vera (1896–1970) A prolific writer and feminist. Brittain persuaded her father to send her to Oxford University, where she went in 1914. She left in 1915 to join the Voluntary Aid Detachment, a nursing auxiliary to the armed forces. During World War I her brother, her fiancé and her two best friends were killed. Brittain returned to Oxford in time for the last stages of the campaign to award degrees to women and there became friends with Winifred HOLTBY (the subject of Brittain's *Testament of Friendship* [1940]). Determined to be a journalist, she left Oxford in 1921 and published two novels in two years. She was a regular contributor to *Time and Tide,* of which Holtby became director in 1926. Brittain is probably best known for her memoirs *Testament of Youth* (1933) and *Testament of Experience* (1957). She wrote twenty-nine books, including novels, poetry, autobiography, biographies, travel books, and social studies. "Vera Brittain's ideas reflect the new direction of the feminist movement in the 1920s" (Mellown 317).

Brontë, Charlotte (1816–55) and Emily (1818–48) Author of *Jane Eyre* (1847), *Shirley* (1849), *Villette* (1853), and *The Professor* (1857), Charlotte Brontë at first published under the name "Currer Bell," veiling herself, as Woolf says in *A ROOM OF ONE'S OWN,* with a masculine pseudonym, a "relic of the sense of chastity that dictated anonymity to women" (AROO 50). Charlotte's sister Emily published her only novel, *Wuthering Heights* (1848), under the name Ellis Bell. With another sister, Anne, "Currer, Ellis, and Acton Bell" published a volume of poems in 1846. The Brontës lived at Haworth Parsonage in Yorkshire, England.

At the beginning of *A Room,* Woolf suggests that a talk on women and fiction might include "a tribute to the Brontës" (AROO 3). Woolf's most significant reference to Charlotte Brontë is her criticism of the "awkward break" in *Jane Eyre* (AROO 68–69) that leads her to conclude Brontë "will never get her genius expressed whole and entire" (AROO 69; and see *A ROOM OF ONE'S OWN*).

Woolf's second published work was an article in the *GUARDIAN,* "Haworth, November, 1904" (E1 5–9), written while she was staying with Margaret (Madge) VAUGHAN in Yorkshire. There she writes that visits to writers' houses can only be justified if they shed light on the writer's books; in the case of the Brontës, she concludes, this is so. There is almost nothing in the article, however, about the novels as it describes Woolf's own visit to Haworth Parsonage and her impressions. In 1917, Woolf reviewed for the *TIMES LITERARY SUPPLEMENT* a work called *Charlotte Brontë 1816–1916. A Centenary Memorial,* prepared by the Brontë Society, with contributions by thirteen writers. The year before, Woolf herself wrote a centenary essay, "Charlotte Bronte," for the TLS (E2 26–31) in which she likens Brontë's novels to *Hamlet,* as "living and changing creations" that allow different generations to see them in new ways continually. Brontë's power is such that a reader cannot lift her eyes from the page when reading *Jane Eyre,* Brontë's voice being "never absent for a moment" (E2 28). Woolf describes her sense that Brontë is "herself the heroine of her own novels" and celebrates her intensity, writing that each book was "a superb gesture of defiance" (E2 29). This article was later incorporated into " 'Jane Eyre' and 'Wuthering Heights' " for the *COMMON READER* (CR1 196–204; CE1 185–90). Here, Woolf compares Charlotte Brontë to Thomas HARDY in terms of their power of personality and narrowness of vision, although she says the mood of their fiction is very different: Brontë, unlike Hardy, "does not attempt to solve the problems of human life" (CE1 187). Woolf considers *Villette* Brontë's finest novel.

Writing of Emily Brontë, Woolf says she was a greater poet than her sister and that "there is no 'I' in *Wuthering Heights*" (CE1 188–89); Emily's is the impersonality of great poetry, a value Woolf praised in *A Room of One's Own.* In *THREE GUINEAS,* Woolf quotes Emily's poem "No coward soul is mine," and refers to her as "the spiritual descendant of some ancient prophetess" (TG 123–24). *Wuthering Heights* is one of the books that Rachel VINRACE, the heroine of Woolf's first novel, *THE VOYAGE OUT,* reads on board the *EUPHROSYNE.* In her ironic preface to *ORLANDO,* Woolf includes Emily Brontë among those writers to whom anyone writing is perpetually indebted.

Brooke, Rupert Chawner (1887–1915) A poet who died from blood poisoning at the age of twenty-seven while on active service in the Aegean. Woolf had known him since her childhood summer vacations in ST. IVES and had grown close to him in the 1910s. He was at King's College, Cambridge, between 1906 and 1909 and was elected to the APOSTLES in 1908. Brooke was at the center of the group known to Woolf as the NEO-PAGANS and had a stormy love affair with Katherine COX. In 1911, the year his first book, *Poems,* was published, Woolf stayed with Brooke at his home in Grantchester, where they swam naked together and Woolf supplied him with a phrase for the poem "Town and Country" (E2 280). Karen Levenback writes that the "depth of bonding between Woolf and Brooke has been overlooked in favor of anecdotal accounts of their friendship" and discusses Woolf's "Olympian" grief at his death (VWM 33: 5–6). Brooke's death was "most timely, his popular deification having begun with a *Times* account of Dean Inge's Easter sermon at St. Paul's, which included lines from one of Brooke's 'War Sonnets' " (VWM 33:5), and he became a symbol of English patriotism in the early stages of World War I. His *1914 and Other Poems* was published in 1915. In August 1918, Woolf reviewed *The Collected Poems of Rupert Brooke with a Memoir* by Edward Marsh in the *TIMES LITERARY SUPPLEMENT* (E2 277–84). She expressed in her DIARY the feelings about the memoir that she could not publish: "The book is a disgraceful sloppy sentimental rhapsody, leaving Rupert rather tarnished" (D1 171). In December 1917, reviewing John Drinkwater's *Prose Papers* in the TLS, she had hinted at these feelings in her conclusion, writing "[t]o the loss of him his friends have had to add the peculiar irony of his canonisation" (E2 203). Woolf also wrote on Brooke in a December 1919 TLS review of Walter de la Mare's *Rupert Brooke and the Intellectual Imagination* (E3 134–36).

Browne Street In *THE VOYAGE OUT,* Clarissa and Richard DALLOWAY live at 23 Browne Street, Mayfair,

London. In *THE YEARS,* Sir Digby PARGITER and his family live on Browne Street, Westminster. Browne Street seems to have been Woolf's invention.

Browne, Sir Thomas (1605–82) Author of *Religio Medici* ("Religion of a Doctor," 1643 in which Browne discusses his Christian faith and a large number of other subjects) and *Urn Burial* or *Hydriotaphia* (1658; a profound meditation on the various means of disposing of the dead), among other writings. In his solitude in chapter 2, ORLANDO takes a great interest in Browne's writings on mortality and death which complement his mood perfectly. Woolf's essay "READING" is partly about Browne. In her ironic preface to *ORLANDO* he is included among those writers to whom anyone who writes is perpetually indebted.

Browne, William (1591–1643) Browne wrote various pastorals and epitaphs. In *TO THE LIGHTHOUSE,* Mrs. RAMSAY joins her husband after dinner and begins to read Browne's "Siren's Song" (TTL 119). Maria DiBattista quotes the poem in full (*Major Novels* 82–83). Mrs. Ramsay also reads a sonnet by William SHAKESPEARE, moving easily between the works of the minor poet Browne and of Shakespeare without ranking them as her husband presumably would do.

Browning, Elizabeth Barrett (1806–61) English poet, wife of Robert BROWNING. Woolf's *FLUSH* is the story of her dog. Among her works are *Sonnets from the Portuguese* (1850), *Casa Guidi Windows* (1851) and *Aurora Leigh* (1857). Woolf reviewed *Elizabeth Barrett Browning in Her Letters* by Percy Lubbock for the *SPEAKER* in 1906 (E1 101–05), and wrote on "*Aurora Leigh*" for the *YALE REVIEW* in 1931 (CE1 209–18 and CR2 202–13).

Browning, Oscar (1837–1923) In *A ROOM OF ONE'S OWN,* Woolf quotes the opinion of Oscar Browning that "the best woman was intellectually the inferior of the worst man" (AROO 53). Jane Marcus has called Browning "the villain" of *A Room,* writing that his name evokes the "terrible reality of academic homosexual misogyny" (*Languages* 164). Marcus draws attention to the way Woolf uses only initials—"the great J— H—"—to refer to Jane Ellen HARRISON, while giving Browning—who was universally known as "O. B."—his full name. Woolf's anger at O. B., Marcus believes, "is displaced anger at the Stephen family's misogyny, at the covering up or 'pargetting' of family history, of misogyny, homosexuality, and madness" (*Languages* 185).

Browning was the Cambridge mentor of Woolf's cousin James Kenneth STEPHEN, who followed him to Cambridge from Eton after Browning was fired in 1875, joining Browning's homosexual circle. Browning later became president of the British Academy in Rome, where he wrote a *History of the Modern World, 1815–1910* (1912), *A General History of the World* (1913) and *A Short History of Italy* (1917). In "Some Cambridge Dons of the Nineties," Bertrand RUSSELL writes that there "were endless stories about O. B. He was fat, tubby and unusually ugly" (Russell 61).

Browning, Robert (1812–89) An English poet who married Elizabeth Barrett BROWNING in 1846. Woolf based *FLUSH* on the Brownings' story as she read it in their letters and in biographies of them. In *NIGHT AND DAY* Mrs. Hilbery remarks that Robert Browning "used to say that every great man has Jewish blood in him" (ND 123).

Brunswick Square In November 1911, the lease of 29 FITZROY SQUARE having expired, Woolf and her brother Adrian STEPHEN moved to 38 Brunswick Square, a large house which they shared with Duncan GRANT, John Maynard KEYNES, and, from December 4, Leonard WOOLF. This was an unusual living arrangement for 1911. It was at Brunswick Square, on September 9, 1913, that Woolf took an overdose of Veronal (a sedative) and was saved from death by Geoffrey KEYNES.

Brush, Milly Lady BRUTON's secretary in *MRS. DALLOWAY* who likes Richard DALLOWAY and resents the familiarity of Hugh WHITBREAD when they both come to lunch with Lady Bruton.

Bruton, Lady Millicent Character in *MRS. DALLOWAY* who invites Richard DALLOWAY and Hugh WHITBREAD to lunch so that they can advise her on a letter she wishes written to the Editor of the *Times* about her scheme for encouraging the emigration of young people to Canada. Lady Bruton is a classic imperialist and now her obsession is Emigration. Clarissa DALLOWAY is sure that Lady Bruton does not like her as she is known to have little patience with the wives of politicians. Certainly, Lady Bruton defers to men in a way she would never do to a woman. Although she reads no poetry, "she never spoke of England, but this isle of men, this dear, dear land, was in her blood" (MD 274). At Clarissa's party she is seen still worrying about the Empire, inviting Peter WALSH to lunch so that he can give her the latest news from India.

Brydges, Sir Samuel Egerton (1762–1837) In *A ROOM OF ONE'S OWN,* Woolf quotes Brydges's criticism of Margaret CAVENDISH, whose *Memoirs* he edited, that she used coarse language unbecoming a lady of the Court (AROO 62). Brydges was a bibliographer who published *Censura Literaria* (1805–09), *The British Bibliographer* (1810–14), and *Restituta: or, Titles, Extracts, and Characters of Old Books in English Literature Revived* (1814–16).

Buckhurst, Sir John Mentioned in *MRS. DALLOWAY* as observing Clarissa as she waits to cross Bond Street.

Buckle, Henry Thomas (1821–62) One of the vast mass of Victorian writers ORLANDO reads in the nineteenth-century section of *ORLANDO,* Buckle was a historian who had no formal education and was critical of the methods of previous historians. The first volume of his *History of Civilization in England* was published in 1857.

Budge Character in *BETWEEN THE ACTS*. He is the local publican who plays the part of an imperialist Victorian policeman in Miss LA TROBE's pageant.

Budgeon, Charles Named in *JACOB'S ROOM* as a passenger on a bus bound for Shepherd's Bush and observed by Mr. SPALDING in a moment reminiscent of Woolf's "AN UNWRITTEN NOVEL."

Bulteel, Professor Mentioned in *JACOB'S ROOM,* a professor at Leeds University at whom Jacob is appalled when he publishes a bowdlerized edition of the works of William WYCHERLEY.

Burchard, Mr. In *THE WAVES,* the businessman LOUIS likes to be asked to come to Mr. Burchard's private room to "report on our commitments to China" (TW 168).

Burgess, Mrs. Mentioned in *MRS. DALLOWAY,* apparently a friend of Peter WALSH in India, in whom he has confided about the affair he is having with DAISY.

Burke Commenting on the lack of available information about the lives of women, Woolf remarks in *A ROOM OF ONE'S OWN* that she can find all she needs to know about "Sir Hawley Butts" in "Burke or Debrett" (AROO 85). *A Genealogical and Heraldic History of the Peerage and Baronetage of the United Kingdom,* commonly known as "Burke's Peerage," was first compiled by John Burke and published in 1826. This reference to the aristocracy of the United Kingdom has been published annually since 1847. Butts appears to have been a name Woolf invented.

Burke, Edmund (1729–97) In *THE VOYAGE OUT,* Richard DALLOWAY asks Rachel if she has read Burke moments before he forces a kiss on her (TVO 75–76). Burke, who entered Parliament in 1765, wrote many works of philosophy and politics, including *A Philosophical Enquiry into the Origin of Our Ideas of the Sublime and Beautiful* (1756) and *Reflections on the Revolution in France* (1790). Later in *The Voyage Out,* Rachel asks her uncle Ridley if he has Burke's *Speech on the American Revolution* for her to borrow (TVO 171).

Burley, Mr. Mentioned in *JACOB'S ROOM,* discussing Charles James Fox at a party.

Burney, Frances ("Fanny," Madame d'Arblay) (1752–1840) Fanny Burney, the daughter of the historian of music Dr. Charles Burney, grew up in the midst of the literary society that included Samuel JOHNSON and Edmund BURKE. Her epistolary first novel, *Evelina,* was published anonymously in 1778; *Cecilia* (in which Jane AUSTEN found the title of *Pride and Prejudice*), was published in 1782; *Camilla; or Female Difficulties* in 1796; and *The Wanderer* in 1814. Burney edited her father's *Memoirs* for publication in 1832. Three years after her death, Burney's niece began issuing the *Diary and Letters of Madame D'Arblay* in seven volumes (Burney married General Alexandre d'Arblay in 1793); her *Early Diary: 1768–1778* was published in two volumes in 1899.

At the beginning of *A ROOM OF ONE'S OWN,* Woolf suggests that a talk about women and fiction might include "a few remarks about Fanny Burney" (AROO 3). In "PROFESSIONS FOR WOMEN," Burney is included as one of the women who cut the road for professional women writers such as Woolf herself.

In "Dr. Burney's Evening Party" (CR2 108–25; CE3 132–46), published in the *New York Herald Tribune* in July 1929, Woolf draws on Burney's diaries for an account of her early attitude to writing, and the opposition she received to her "scribbling" from her stepmother, among others. Woolf wrote in January 1929 to Vita SACKVILLE-WEST that she had to look up dates as she could not "simply invent the whole of Chelsea and King George the 3rd and Johnson and Mrs Thrale," although she believed "thats the way to write. . . . the truth of one's sensations is not in the fact, but in the reverberation" (L4 5). The essay sketches Dr. Burney, "the most sought-after, the most occupied of men" (CE3 134). Several pages are taken up with Fanny Burney's account of Fulke Greville (1794–1865), descendant of a friend of Sir Philip SIDNEY, for whom the evening party is arranged so that he and his wife might meet Mrs. Thrale, to whom Dr. Burney gives music lessons, and Dr. Johnson. The party is not a success.

Woolf also wrote "Fanny Burney's Half-sister" for the *TIMES LITERARY SUPPLEMENT* in August 1930 (GR 192–204; CE3 147–57). *Evelina* "owed much to the story of [Burney's half-sister] Maria Allen" (CE3 147), to whom Fanny was especially close. The article was republished in two parts in the *New York Herald Tribune* in September 1930 under the title " 'Evelina's' Step Sister."

Burns, Robert (1759–96) In *A ROOM OF ONE'S OWN,* commenting on the difficulty of genius emerging from an impoverished background, Woolf uses Burns as a proof that genius does exist among the working classes (AROO 48–49). The poet Burns was educated by his father and worked as a farm laborer until the success of his first volume of poetry enabled him to lead a literary life in Edinburgh. Woolf's point has its origin in a remark of Samuel Taylor COLERIDGE's, recorded in his *Table Talk*.

Burt, Louisa Annie CROSBY's landlady in *THE YEARS*.

Bussy, Dorothy (née Strachey) (1865–1960) Lytton STRACHEY's eldest sister, she married a French painter, Simon BUSSY, in 1903 and subsequently spent most of her time in France, where Woolf occasionally visited her. In the summers, the Bussys usually spent some time in England. Dorothy became a close friend of the painter Henri Matisse and the writer André Gide, whose works she translated. She had attended Les Ruches, a progressive school founded by Marie Souvestre, and later taught at another of Souvestre's schools, Allenswood, where one of her pupils was Eleanor Roosevelt. In 1948 her novel *Olivia,* described by Blanche Wiesen Cook as "an ardent novel that remains to date the only portrait of Marie Souvestre" and dedicated "To the beloved memory of V. W.," was published by the HOGARTH PRESS and became a best-seller (Cook, *Eleanor Roosevelt* 104). The Bussys had one daughter, Janie (1906–1960), who was also a painter.

Bussy, Simon (1870–1954) French painter who married Lytton STRACHEY's eldest sister Dorothy in 1903. Richard Shone explains that Bussy's influence can be seen in the early work of Duncan GRANT (*Bloomsbury* 41). He was one of the collaborators in the OMEGA WORKSHOPS and some of his portraits, such as those of Lytton Strachey and of Ottoline MORRELL, have become quite familiar. Oliver Garnett describes Bussy as "one of the many strands that linked Bloomsbury with the French avant-garde" (15).

Butler, Josephine (1828–1906) Born in Northumberland to a family with strong radical and nonconformist traditions, Josephine Butler began rescue work with prostitutes after moving with her husband, George Butler, to Liverpool in 1864. Through her friendship with Anne CLOUGH she joined the movement for education reform and from 1868 to 1873 was president of the North of England Council for the Higher Education of Women. Butler was persuaded in 1869 to lead the Ladies' National Association in its campaign against the regulation of prostitution through the Contagious Diseases Acts, the work for which she became best known. Jenny Uglow describes Butler as having made two significant contributions to late-nineteenth-century feminism: "She shifted the grounds of the debate about women's subordination from the liberal analysis in terms of legal and civil rights . . . to a more radical and comprehensive view of women's oppression within a total economic, political and sexual power relationship" and she "developed theories and methods of feminist attack which anticipated and influenced the campaigns of later activists" (Uglow 146–47). In *THREE GUINEAS,* Woolf quotes from Butler's *Personal Reminiscences of a Great Crusade* when she comments on the power of the press to "burke discussion of any undesirable subject" (TG 162n16).

Butler, Samuel (1835–1902) In "MR. BENNETT AND MRS. BROWN," Woolf cites Butler's biting attack on the Victorian family, *The Way of All Flesh* (published posthumously in 1903), as an early sign of that change in "human character" she said occurred about December 1910. Butler had a strict religious upbringing and was intended to become a priest, but he harbored a secret desire to be an artist. After refusing to be ordained on the grounds of religious doubt, he went to New Zealand in 1859, where he became a successful sheep farmer. In 1864 he returned to England and settled in CLIFFORD'S INN (where Woolf would also live for a time soon after her marriage). Among his numerous publications, Butler's other well-known works are the satire *Erewhon* (1872) and his *Notebooks,* published in 1912; *Erewhon Revisited* appeared in 1901. Also of interest to Woolf would have been Butler's *Authoress of the Odyssey* (1897). In *A ROOM OF ONE'S OWN,* Woolf refers to the *Notebooks* when, faced with the torrent of men's opinions of women in the BRITISH MUSEUM, she wonders why Butler says "Wise men never say what they think of women" as they apparently say little else (AROO 29).[7]

Following Jean Guiguet's opinion that Butler looms large in Woolf's background (CW 7), Allen McLaurin has explored his influence on Woolf, noting that several of her contemporaries, including E. M. FORSTER and James JOYCE, also expressed a debt to Butler. McLaurin finds that Butler "deals with certain aesthetic problems which Virginia Woolf also tried to solve, and the solutions embodied in her novels often have interesting features in common with his discussions" (McLaurin 3).

Woolf reviewed *Samuel Butler: Author of 'Erewhon', the Man and His Work,* by John F. Harris, for the *TIMES LITERARY SUPPLEMENT* in July 1916 ("A Man with a View" CW 28–32; E2 34–39). There she described Butler as a "very complex personality, and,

[7] "It has been said that all sensible men are of the same religion and that no sensible man ever says what that religion is. So all sensible men are of the same opinion about women and no sensible man ever says what that opinion is." *The Notebooks of Samuel Butler.* Edited by Henry Festing Jones. (London: Hogarth Press, 1985): 228.

like all great writers, finally inscrutable" (E2 37), defining his great gift as having a point of view of his own to which he adhered. She considered *The Way of All Flesh* and the *Notebooks* his best works, and in 1919 reviewed the novel for the TLS (CW 33–35; E3 57–60). Here, she points out that it was not until 1910 that interest in *The Way of All Flesh* really developed in the reading public (E3 58), and that Butler's novel has "fertilised" a large number of modern works "with well-known names upon their backs" (E3 59). In April 1925 she reviewed *The Life and Letters of Dr. Samuel Butler* by Samuel Butler in the *NATION & ATHENAEUM* ("The Two Samuel Butlers").

Byron, George Gordon (1788–1824) English Romantic poet and aristocrat known for such works as "Childe Harold's Pilgrimage" (1812, 1816, 1818), "The Corsair," "The Dream", and "Don Juan" (1818–20). Byron is also known for his association with the poet Percy Bysshe SHELLEY, with whose sister-in-law Claire Clairmont he had a child, Allegra. In *THE WAVES*, BERNARD identifies himself closely with Byron while he is a student, an affectation disdained by his friend NEVILLE. In the "1914" chapter of *THE YEARS*, Martin PARGITER alludes to Byron's "Beppo" when he thinks a young woman at a party "must have been in the nursery three months ago . . . eating bread and butter" (TY 251). In *BETWEEN THE ACTS*, Bart OLIVER recalls his mother giving him the works of Byron sixty years earlier and quotes the first lines of "Hebrew Melodies" and "So we'll go no more a-roving" (BTA 5). Mitchell Leaska writes that the introduction of Byron here is certainly not "for the merits of his poetry, for as [Woolf] said in a letter [to Julian BELL]: 'If Byron had lived to my age he would have been a great novelist. As it is, he is the worst poet' " [L4 140] (PH 191).

"Byron & Mr Briggs" In 1921, Woolf was thinking of writing a book to be called "Reading," of which this was to be the introductory chapter. "Reading" evolved into *THE COMMON READER*, and "Byron & Mr Briggs" was left in typescript form, heavily revised. A clean transcription by Edward A. Hungerford was published in the *YALE REVIEW* 48, 3 (1979), and Andrew McNeillie includes a version in appendix 2 of volume 3 of *The Essays of Virginia Woolf* (473–99) which reproduces many of Woolf's second and third thoughts.

C

C., Mrs. In *THE YEARS,* Rose PARGITER's nurse is gossiping with Mrs. C. and so does not notice that Rose goes out by herself. (Woolf refers to a HOGARTH PRESS assistant, Mrs. CARTWRIGHT, as "Mrs. C." in her LETTERS.)

***Cabinet of Dr. Caligari, The* (1919)** German Expressionist film directed by Robert Wiene the experience of watching which is the central subject of Woolf's 1926 article "Cinema" for *Arts,* a New York magazine ("The Cinema" CE2 268–72). Leslie Hankins has discussed the film's possible relation to *MRS. DALLOWAY* in "The Doctor and the Woolf."

Calthorp, Mr. In *JACOB'S ROOM* he has a seven-line conversation with Miss EDWARDS, in which he suggests she might know his brother, who is in the same regiment as Miss Edwards's brother, the Twentieth Hussars. Leonard WOOLF's brothers Cecil and Philip were in the Twentieth Hussars when Cecil was killed and Philip wounded by the same shell in 1917.

Cambridge Conversazione Society See APOSTLES.

Cameron, Julia Margaret (1815–1879) Woolf's great-aunt, one of the seven famous PATTLE sisters, Cameron was an important photographer. Julia Prinsep STEPHEN wrote her aunt's entry in the *DICTIONARY OF NATIONAL BIOGRAPHY,* in which she recorded Cameron's philanthropy and said she had been "well known in Calcutta for her brilliant conversation" (Gillespie & Steele 214). Cameron was born in Calcutta, the third daughter of James Pattle of the Bengal civil service. In 1838 she married Charles Hay Cameron, another civil servant in India. The Camerons came to England in 1848 and lived in Putney; in 1860 they settled at Freshwater on the Isle of Wight where they were neighbors of Alfred TENNYSON. While living at Putney, Cameron was a frequent visitor to Little Holland House, where her sister Sara PRINSEP entertained the leading intellectuals of the day.

Having been given a lens by her youngest son in 1864, Cameron began to make photographs at the age of 49. She won many prizes for her work, which was characterized by its unusual focus and the fact that she would not retouch any picture, even to dot out spots on the print. Her technique and its significance has been discussed, in comparison to that of her contemporary Lewis Carroll, by Lindsay Smith. Cameron photographed many Victorian luminaries, including Robert BROWNING, Thomas CARLYLE, Charles Darwin, Henry Wadsworth Longfellow, Ellen TERRY and Tennyson. When the Stephen children moved in 1904 to 46 GORDON SQUARE their great-aunt's portraits of their mother hung along one side of the hallway and her photographs of several eminent Victorians faced them on the other side. In 1926 the HOGARTH PRESS published *VICTORIAN PHOTOGRAPHS OF FAMOUS MEN & FAIR WOMEN,* which reproduced twenty-four of her photographs and had introductions by Woolf and Roger FRY. Woolf's rather dramatic introduction recounts her great-aunt's life story, prefiguring in tone her comedy *FRESHWATER,* which centered on the Camerons' life on the Isle of Wight. Fry praised Cameron's perception of character in her photographic portraits, calling her a "considerable" artist. "Mrs Cameron's photographs," he wrote, "bid fair to outlive most of the works of the artists who were her contemporaries" (Cameron 28).

Julia Margaret Cameron went to Ceylon in 1875 as her husband missed his life in the East. They were accompanied by their coffins ("in case coffins should be unprocurable in the East" [Cameron 19]), a fact that Woolf has great fun with in *Freshwater.* In 1878 they visited England, and in 1879 Cameron died in Ceylon.

Candish Bart OLIVER's servant in *BETWEEN THE ACTS.*

Captain's Death Bed and Other Essays, The A collection of Woolf's essays selected by Leonard WOOLF and published in the United States by Harcourt, Brace & Company in 1950 and a week later in England by the HOGARTH PRESS. Among the most significant essays included in this collection are: "MR.

BENNETT AND MRS. BROWN," "Leslie Stephen," "The Cinema," "Walter Sickert" and "MEMORIES OF A WORKING WOMEN'S GUILD." Jane Marcus has written about Leonard's decision to publish an unrevised version of "Memories of a Working Women's Guild" (*Art and Anger* 137).

Carlyle, Jane Baillie Welsh (1801–66) See CARLYLE, Thomas.

Carlyle, Thomas (1795–1881) Woolf wrote that when she was twenty she "read masses of Carlyle" (D2 210), a fact that is borne out by the frequent passing reference to him in her DIARY and in essays. Reviewing the *Essays* of William Ernest Henley for the *TIMES LITERARY SUPPLEMENT* in 1921, for example, Woolf wrote that Henley lacked "the peculiar power which men like Carlyle and Macaulay possess of so absorbing their subject that it grows again outside of them" (E3 286). Leslie STEPHEN knew Carlyle slightly, writing in his *MAUSOLEUM BOOK* that he "was always afraid of him without any cause except his fame" (Sir Leslie Stephen 8). Carlyle entered Edinburgh University at the age of fifteen and was subsequently a schoolmaster, before beginning his literary career. He married Jane Baillie Welsh (1801–66) in 1826, retiring with her to her farm at Craigenputtock. In 1834, the Carlyles moved to Cheyne Row in London, to the house Woolf describes in "Great Men's Houses," one of her *LONDON SCENE* essays. Among Carlyle's most important works are *Sartor Resartus: The Life and Opinions of Herr Teufelsdröckh* (1838), *The French Revolution* (1837), *Chartism* (1839), *Past and Present* (1843), *On Heroes, Hero-Worship, and the Heroic in History* (1841), *Oliver Cromwell's Letters and Speeches* (1845), *Latter-Day Pamphlets* (1850), *The History of Frederick the Great* (1858–65) and *Reminiscences* (1881). Leslie Stephen wrote the entry on Carlyle for the *DICTIONARY OF NATIONAL BIOGRAPHY* and is described by Noel Annan as having been intellectually shaken by reading Carlyle's work. Annan describes Carlyle as "an aberration in European thought," properly understood only in relation to Nietzsche and Richard WAGNER (Annan 172). Leslie Stephen thought that his brother James Fitzjames STEPHEN had been "a good deal corrupted by old Carlyle" (Annan 275).

In "CHARACTER IN FICTION," Woolf referred to the notoriously bad treatment by Carlyle of his wife, Jane Welsh Carlyle, as an example of a way of life that had passed and of a "horrible domestic tradition which made it seemly for a woman of genius to spend her time chasing beetles, scouring saucepans, instead of writing books" (E3 422). Woolf wrote about Jane Welsh Carlyle's letters for the *GUARDIAN* in 1905 (E1 54–58) and reviewed *The Love Letters of Thomas Carlyle and Jane Welsh Carlyle* for the *TIMES LITERARY SUPPLEMENT* in April 1909 (E1 257–62). She also wrote about Jane Carlyle and her close friend the novelist Geraldine Endsor Jewsbury (1812–80) in "Geraldine and Jane" for the TLS in February 1929 (CE4 27–39).

The story of the Carlyles' marriage had a particular resonance for Woolf as she had heard her father frequently ask her half-sister Stella DUCKWORTH, after Julia Prinsep STEPHEN's death in 1895, whether he had treated his own wife as badly as Carlyle had treated Jane Welsh. "I was not as bad as Carlyle, was I?," Woolf recalled him saying in "REMINISCENCES" (MOB 41). In the *Mausoleum Book,* Leslie Stephen wrote that if he felt that he "had a burthen upon my conscience like that which tortured poor Carlyle, I think that I should be almost tempted to commit suicide" (89). Woolf made it clear that she believed her father *should* have had such a burden on his conscience, likening him to Carlyle in his affectation of the Victorian "Great Man's" behavior.

Beverly Ann Schlack points out that Jacob FLANDERS's question in *JACOB'S ROOM* whether "History Consist[s] of the Biographies of Great Men" is answered affirmatively by Carlyle in *On Heroes, Hero-Worship and the Heroic*: "The history of the world is but the Biography of great men" (Schlack 41). She also describes the entire novel as "a pointed illustration of Carlyle's contention in *Sir Walter Scott*: 'The uttered part of a man's life, let us always repeat, bears to the unuttered, unconscious part a small unknown proportion. He himself never knows it, much less do others' " (Schlack 41). In *TO THE LIGHTHOUSE,* William BANKES tells Lily BRISCOE that he thinks Carlyle "one of the great teachers of mankind" (TTL 46).

Carmichael, Augustus Character in *TO THE LIGHTHOUSE,* a guest of Mr. and Mrs. RAMSAY. For most of the novel he basks in a chair in the garden, lost in an opium-induced haze, but at the very end he stands beside Lily BRISCOE as she has her "vision" and finishes her painting, leading her to think he has "crowned the occasion" (TTL 208). A poet, Mr. Carmichael dislikes Mrs. Ramsay and is the only person who seems immune to her charm and beauty. His favorite is Andrew RAMSAY, whose death in World War I causes Mr. Carmichael to lose all interest in life. At the dinner in section XVII of part 1, he irritates Mr. Ramsay by requesting a second plate of soup after everyone else has finished, but at the end of the dinner he and Mr. Ramsay join in reciting Charles ELTON's "Luriana, Lurilee" as the family and guests leave the dining room. During the war, a volume of his poetry is published and is unexpectedly successful (TTL 134), and in part 3 we learn that he is now famous and that things he had written forty years earlier are being published (TTL 194).

Makiko Minow-Pinkney describes Carmichael as "a blank or absence in the text" (114), but several critics have discussed his role in the mythic dimensions of the novel. Avrom Fleishman, for example, cites images associating him with "sea monster," poet, priest, and presiding deity. Jane Marcus has suggested George MEREDITH as a possible source for Carmichael. J. Hillis Miller discusses the significance of Carmichael's sharing his name with the "aspiring woman novelist" in *A ROOM OF ONE'S OWN*, Mary CARMICHAEL. Miller suggests that in "somewhat covertly granting Augustus Carmichael creative power too, along with Lily Briscoe," Woolf is expressing a desire for "an equivocal androgynous rhythm of style" ("Mr. Carmichael" 185).

John Ferguson has described Carmichael as one of Woolf's "most teasingly enigmatic characters" (45). He notes that several critics have discussed how Woolf links Mr. Carmichael with creativity, but says that no one has explained why this should be so. In *To the Lighthouse*, Ferguson argues, "Woolf turns [Thomas] De Quincey—opium eater, prose-poet, Romantic dreamer—into Mr. Carmichael" (47). While writing the novel, Woolf also wrote "IMPASSIONED PROSE," an essay on Thomas DE QUINCEY, and Ferguson finds that Carmichael is De Quincey's "fictional reflection," made "an instrumental figure in Lily's artistic triumph at least partly because De Quincey offers an inspiring prose model for Woolf's own work" (52). Ferguson identifies several correspondences with De Quincey's life in biographical details about Carmichael in the holograph draft of *To the Lighthouse* (cut from the published version).

Carmichael, Mary One of the names which the narrator of *A ROOM OF ONE'S OWN* says her audience may call her, derived from the BALLAD OF THE QUEEN'S MARYS. Woolf also uses the name for the fictitious author of *Life's Adventure*, the imaginary contemporary novel in chapter 5 of *A Room*. Mary Stopes published a novel entitled *Love's Creation* in 1928 under the name Mary Carmichael; the novel opens with two women in a laboratory. Elizabeth Abel finds that *Life's Adventure* "generates a discourse of merger and rupture that stands in place of a feminine psychoanalysis" (Abel 84).

Caroline, Cousin One of the interfering relatives in *NIGHT AND DAY* who comes to see Mrs. HILBERY about the shocking domestic circumstances of their nephew Cyril ALARDYCE.

Carrington, Dora de Houghton (1893–1932) A painter and lifelong friend of her fellow Slade School of Art students Barbara BAGENAL, Dorothy BRETT and Mark GERTLER (who was in love with her). John Rothenstein has written that she was "the most neglected serious painter of her time" (Noel Carrington 13). Little of her work has survived, however, and

Stories of the East. *Courtesy of Cecil Woolf and Jean Moorcroft Wilson.*
This collection of three stories by Leonard Woolf—"A Tale Told by Moonlight," "Pearls and Swine" and "The Two Brahmins"—was hand-printed by the Woolfs and published by the Hogarth Press in 1921. The cover illustration is a woodcut by Dora Carrington.

she rarely exhibited during her lifetime. She made four woodcuts for *TWO STORIES* (1917), the first publication of the HOGARTH PRESS, and also a woodcut for the cover of Leonard WOOLF's *STORIES OF THE EAST* (1921).

Woolf first met Carrington (as she became known at the Slade) owing to an incident in 1916 when Carrington, David GARNETT and Barbara Bagenal broke into ASHEHAM HOUSE and spent the night there. "For some reason Virginia placed the blame solely on Carrington" (Gerzina 96) and Carrington was summoned by Woolf to explain. It was at Asheham that Carrington first met Lytton STRACHEY in 1915 when she stayed there with Bagenal, Vanessa BELL, Duncan GRANT, and Mary HUTCHINSON; the house had been borrowed for a few days from the Woolfs (Gerzina 69). Having fallen in love with the homosexual Strachey, Carrington moved with him to TIDMARSH in 1917, beginning a companionship that would last until his death in 1932. In 1919 Carrington began an affair with Ralph PARTRIDGE, and they married in 1921, settling at Tidmarsh with Strachey. In 1922, Partridge's close friend Gerald BRENAN, who had heard about Carrington from Partridge, visited them and fell in love with her; their secret affair caused great stress on the Tidmarsh ménage when it was discovered.

Carrington wrote to Brenan in 1923, when Woolf and Leonard were visiting him in Spain, that he could not be "too enthusiastic, to please me, over Virginia! I always feel she is one of the few people it has actually been tremendously good fortune to have known in this life" (Carrington, *Letters* 242). Woolf was extremely fond of Carrington and, after Strachey's death in January 1932, she and Leonard were among the last people to see Carrington alive. Carrington shot herself on March 11, 1932.

Carslake, Jinny A friend of the "painter men" whom Jacob FLANDERS visits in Paris on his way to Greece in *JACOB'S ROOM*. She has had an affair with an American painter named Lefanu and frequents Indian philosophers. Later in life she collects pebbles, which she uses to exemplify her theory that multiplicity becomes unity if one looks at them long enough (JR 131).

Carter, Eliza (1717–1806) In *A ROOM OF ONE'S OWN*, Woolf says that George ELIOT should have "done homage" to the ghost of Eliza (Elizabeth) Carter, who tied a bell to her bedstead so that she would wake up early each morning to learn Greek (AROO 66). Carter was a member of the Blue Stocking circle (of which James BOSWELL gives an account in his *Life of Samuel Johnson*). She was a friend of Samuel JOHNSON and Samuel Richardson (author of *CLARISSA*), and she contributed to the periodical Johnson edited, the *Rambler*. Woolf reviewed *A Woman of Wit and Wisdom: a memoir of Elizabeth Carter, one of the 'Bas Bleu' Society, 1717–1806*, by Alice C. C. Gaussen, for the *GUARDIAN* in 1906 ("The Bluest of the Blue" E1 112–114). There she explains that the bell tied to Carter's bedstead was attached to a string that would be pulled by "a friendly sexton" at four or five each morning. In addition to Greek and Latin, Carter also taught herself Hebrew, Italian, Spanish, German, Portuguese, and Arabic (E1 113). Her 1758 translation of the works of the Stoic philosopher Epictetus was very successful.

Carter, Mr. and Mrs. Mentioned in *THE VOYAGE OUT* as an "opulent couple" staying at the hotel on SANTA MARINA (TVO 245).

Cartwright, Mrs. One of those friends who Woolf said "have helped me in ways too various to specify" mentioned in the ironic preface to *ORLANDO*, she was office manager of the HOGARTH PRESS 1925–30.

Case, Euphemia ("Emphie") One of those friends who Woolf said "have helped me in ways too various to specify" mentioned in the ironic preface to *ORLANDO*, she was Janet CASE's sister.

Case, Janet Elizabeth (1862–1937) One of those friends who Woolf said "have helped me in ways too various to specify" mentioned in the ironic preface to *ORLANDO*, Case was a contemporary of Margaret Llewelyn DAVIES at GIRTON COLLEGE. She tutored Woolf in Greek from 1902 to 1903 and became a lifelong friend. Her support of women's SUFFRAGE was an important early influence on Woolf, who wrote to Case on New Year's Day 1910 asking whether it would "be any use if I spent an afternoon or two weekly in addressing envelopes for the Adult Suffragists?" (L1 421). In her DIARY in 1903 Woolf wrote "a rough sketch" of Case (PA 181–84) in which she compared her with her previous Greek tutor, Clara PATER, and described her as "more professional . . . though perhaps not so cultivated" (PA 182). Perry Meisel discusses Case's influence as "a moral and political corrective to Virginia's burgeoning aestheticism" (22).

In 1911, Case came to spend a weekend with Woolf at LITTLE TALLAND HOUSE and there Woolf told her about George DUCKWORTH's incestuous "malefactions," which made Case feel sick (L1 472). Woolf and Case, who lived with her sister Emphie, maintained an affectionate relationship until Case's death in 1937. In "Miss Janet Case: Classical Scholar and Teacher. By an Old Pupil," Woolf's unsigned obituary in *The Times*, Woolf described Case as a "pioneer" (quoted in Marcus, *Languages* 48). In her diary she wrote of how she had loved her: "how great a visionary part she has played in my life, till the visionary became part of the fictitious, not of the real life" (D5 103). The character Lucy CRADDOCK in *THE YEARS* owes something to these feelings.

Cassis French village near Marseilles where in 1927 Vanessa BELL went to look after Duncan GRANT, who had fallen ill there with typhoid. Vanessa decided to rent and repair La Bergère, a small house owned by Colonel Peter Teed, and continued to go there every year. Angelica GARNETT has described La Bergère as CHARLESTON "reconstituted, albeit on a smaller scale" (CM 6:10). It was at La Bergère that Elise Anghilanti cooked BOEUF EN DAUBE for the family and from there that Vanessa wrote to Woolf about the huge moths that flew into the house in the evening, a letter that inspired *THE WAVES* (Marler 314–16).

Catullus, Gaius Valerius (*c.* 84–54 B.C.) Roman poet and writer of epigrams with whom NEVILLE in *THE WAVES* particularly identifies (though he does not imitate him). His poem "Ave Atque Vale" ("Hail and Farewell"), addressed to a dead brother, had particular significance for Woolf's feelings about her own dead brother Thoby STEPHEN. In *THE YEARS,* North PARGITER reads at random from Catullus's poem 5 during the party in the "Present Day" chapter.

Cavell, Edith In *THE YEARS,* Peggy PARGITER says to her aunt Eleanor PARGITER as they drive past a statue of "a woman in nurse's uniform" that it reminds her of an advertisement for sanitary napkins (TY 336–37). Eleanor's remark that the words engraved on the statue's base were the "only fine thing that was said in the war" identify it as the monument in St. Martin's Place to Edith Cavell, a British nurse executed by the Germans in 1915 in Belgium. Her last words, "Patriotism is not enough, I must have no hatred or bitterness for anyone," were inscribed on the statue's base (words, incidentally, that identify Cavell with ANTIGONE). Above, in larger letters, is inscribed "For God, King, and Country." A photograph of the statue can be found in the *Bulletin of the New York Public Library* 80, 2 (Winter 1977), a special issue on *The Years.*

Cavendish, Margaret Lucas, Duchess of Newcastle (1623–1674) In *A ROOM OF ONE'S OWN,* Woolf turns from the poetry of Anne FINCH, Lady Winchilsea, to her near-contemporary, Margaret Cavendish, Duchess of Newcastle, and finds that the work of both these women was "disfigured and deformed" by the anger they felt at the way women writers were treated (AROO 61). She notes that Charles LAMB praised Cavendish's work highly, but omits Samuel Pepys's condemnation of her as a "mad, conceited, ridiculous woman." Woolf notes that Pepys twice came out to see the Duchess (the indefatigable Andrew McNeillie points out that Woolf refers to Pepys's diary for May 1, 1667 [E1 351]).

Like Anne Finch an attendant at the royal Court, Cavendish published several books, including *Poems, and Fancies: Written by the Right Honourable, the Lady Margaret Countesse of Newcastle* (1653); *The Worlds Olio. Written by the Most Excellent Lady the Lady M. of Newcastle* (1655); *Nature's Pictures Drawn by Fancie's Pencil* (1656); *Female Orations* (1662); and *Plays Written by Lady Marchioness of Newcastle* (1667).

Woolf had first written on Cavendish in a 1911 review of *The First Duke and Duchess of Newcastle-upon-Tyne* by "the Author of a Life of Kenelm Digby" (identified by Andrew McNeillie as Thomas Longueville [E1 349]). A *COMMON READER* essay, "The Duchess of Newcastle" (CR1 98–109; CE3 51–58), revisits the earlier review and includes a footnote that lists the works Woolf presumably consulted in writing the essay: *The Life of William Cavendish, Duke of Newcastle, Etc.; Poems and Fancies; The World's Olio, Orations of Divers Sorts Accommodated to Divers Places; Female Orations; Plays*; and *Philosophical Letters.* Woolf's "etc., etc." at the end of the note suggests that she may have been even more widely read in Cavendish's work than this list suggests. It is likely that she consulted at least some of these works for her 1911 review. The same quotation from Cavendish appears in both pieces: "Women live like Bats or Owls, labour like Beasts, and die like Worms" (E1 349; CE3 54). Woolf also mentions in both pieces that Margaret Cavendish's volumes are to be found in the BRITISH MUSEUM, but only in the 1911 review does she say "one would be a 'Mountebank in learning', as [Cavendish] has it, to pretend that one has read them" (E1 348).

In "The Duchess of Newcastle," Woolf sums up Cavendish's life story, describing her shyness at Court, her marriage to the Duke, and how as a young woman she had written "sixteen paper books of no title" (CE3 52). Cavendish "similized, energetically, incongruously, eternally" (CE3 56), her questioning mind ranging over all sorts of subjects. Recently, Denise Riley has described Cavendish as an example of those seventeenth-century women authors who "achieved a scholastic flamboyance," noting that her "prolific writings . . . ran splendidly wild over the terrain of human knowledge known to her" (Riley 25–26). In the *Female Orations,* Riley discerns "the polarities of the mid-seventeenth-century arguments" about the nature of woman (Riley 28). Woolf's essay concludes by saying that "the laugh is not all on [her critics'] side" as Cavendish is assured of "immortal fame" (CE3 58).

Cecil, Lord (Edward Christian) David (1902–86) An undergraduate at Oxford University when Woolf met him at GARSINGTON in 1923. (His recollection of their first meeting was that it occurred at a party given by Ethel SANDS [Noble 123].) He was a nephew of Lady Robert ("Nelly") CECIL and in 1932 married Rachel, the daughter of Desmond and Molly MACCARTHY. He became a biographer and critic and was Goldsmith's Professor of English Literature at Oxford in 1948–49. His biography of the poet William COWPER, *The Stricken Deer* (1929), won the Hawthornden Prize in 1930.

Cecil, Lady Robert (Eleanor, "Nelly") (1868–1956) One of those friends who Woolf says "have helped me in ways too various to specify" in the ironic preface to *ORLANDO,* where she is referred to as "the

Viscountess Cecil." Born Lady Eleanor Lambton, "Nelly," as Woolf and Vanessa BELL called her, married Lord Robert Cecil (1864–1958) in 1889. "There is no doubt," Woolf wrote to her sister in 1911, "that she is the best of those elderly aristocrats" (L1 468). Nelly had come to know the Stephen sisters through Violet DICKINSON. She was an early supporter of their art, commissioning a portrait from Vanessa that was her first piece to be exhibited (at the Eighteenth Summer Exhibition of Works by Living Artists at the New Gallery in 1905 [Marler 28n]). Nelly wrote reviews and in 1905 shared two chapters of a novel (never published) with Woolf. Woolf and she also planned to write a joint review column for the *CORNHILL MAGAZINE* in 1907, but this was not realized. In 1916, Woolf appealed for Nelly's help on behalf of Duncan GRANT and David GARNETT, who were to appear before the Central Tribunal, of which Nelly's brother-in-law was chairman, to claim exemption from combat as CONSCIENTIOUS OBJECTORS.

Cenotaph In *MRS. DALLOWAY,* Peter WALSH is overtaken by a parade of boys marching down WHITEHALL on their way to lay a wreath on this memorial to the World War I dead. The Cenotaph, or Tomb of the Unknown Soldier, was designed by Sir Edward Lutyens and erected in 1920 to replace a temporary memorial that had been put up for the peace celebrations in 1919.

Ceres In *MRS. DALLOWAY,* Mr. BREWER's plaster cast of this goddess of the fruits of the earth in his garden is smashed by a bomb in the war. The Roman Ceres was identified with the Greek DEMETER.

Chailey, Emma Character in *THE VOYAGE OUT.* She is the Vinrace family servant and reveres the memory of her deceased mistress, Theresa Vinrace. When Helen and Ridley AMBROSE invite their niece Rachel VINRACE to stay with them on the island of SANTA MARINA, Mrs. Chailey also stays.

Chalmers, Mrs. A widow in *BETWEEN THE ACTS* who ignores Miss LA TROBE when she passes her in the street (211).

Chamberlain, [Joseph] Austen (1863–1937) The son of Joseph CHAMBERLAIN, Austen Chamberlain is referred to in *A ROOM OF ONE'S OWN* when Woolf glances at the headlines of the evening paper and sees that he is in Geneva (AROO 33). In *THE VOYAGE OUT* Helen AMBROSE finds it "incredible" that anyone should care whether "Asquith is in or Austen Chamberlain out" (TVO 96), placing the novel in about 1905 when there was a general election. A Unionist member of Parliament from 1892, Chamberlain was chancellor of the exchequer from 1919 to 1921 and foreign secretary from 1924 to 1929. In 1926 he received the Nobel Peace Prize, following his signing of the Treaty of Locarno, by which France and Germany agreed to settle future disputes by arbitration. He also signed the Kellogg Pact in 1928, by which members of the League of Nations, the United States and Russia renounced war.

Chamberlain, Joseph (1836–1914) Mentioned in *JACOB'S ROOM* by LUCY, Countess of Rocksbier. Chamberlain was mayor of Birmingham in 1873 and became member of Parliament for that city in 1876. In 1895 he became colonial secretary in the New Unionist government and was a major proponent of British imperialism.

"Character in Fiction" An essay by Woolf published in the *CRITERION* in July 1924, and substantially derived from a paper she read to the HERETICS at Cambridge on May 18, 1924. This in turn was derived from an essay she had published in the "Literary Review" of the *New York Evening Post,* November 17, 1923, called "MR. BENNETT AND MRS. BROWN." A draft of the paper appears as appendix III in volume 3 of *The Essays of Virginia Woolf.* The essay was reprinted under the title "Mr. Bennett and Mrs. Brown" in the "Books" section of the *New York Herald Tribune* in two installments on August 23 and 30, 1925, as number one in the Hogarth Essays series, and in *THE CAPTAIN'S DEATH BED* (CDB 94–119). As it is best known under the title "Mr. Bennett and Mrs. Brown," the essay is discussed under that entry.

Charles, Lady Mentioned in *JACOB'S ROOM.*

Charleston Home of Vanessa BELL and Duncan GRANT on Lord Gage's Firle Estate in Sussex. In May 1916, Woolf had seen Charleston Farmhouse while walking on the Sussex Downs near the village of Firle (she and Leonard WOOLF were living at ASHEHAM HOUSE at the time) and told her sister that she thought the house would be ideal for her. She was also obliged to tell her brother Adrian STEPHEN and his wife Karin about it, but hoped that Vanessa would take the house (L2 95). The decision to move was precipitated when David GARNETT and Duncan Grant were exempted from military service as CONSCIENTIOUS OBJECTORS on the condition they find work on a farm. At the time they were farming at Wissett, but the local people were not sympathetic to conscientious objectors. Having found they could work on a farm near Charleston, Grant, Garnett, and Vanessa Bell, with Julian BELL and Quentin BELL, moved to the house in October 1916.

Almost immediately, Grant and Vanessa began decorating the house, and over the next several decades

Charleston, the front door. Photograph by Linda J. Langham. Woolf discovered Charleston while walking on the Sussex Downs in 1916; Vanessa Bell moved there in October that year with her sons, Julian and Quentin, and with Duncan Grant and David Garnett. Charleston was Vanessa and Duncan's home in England until their deaths.

it became not only a dynamic artwork itself but also the country focus of the BLOOMSBURY GROUP. Grant, Garnett, Vanessa and the children lived there most of the time during World War I (Angelica GARNETT being born at Charleston on Christmas Day 1918), and after the war, Clive BELL, Vanessa and Grant spent their summers between Charleston and France. Lytton STRACHEY and John Maynard KEYNES were among the regular visitors who came to the house to talk and to write, and the house gradually became a living example of the decorative arts popularized by Vanessa, Grant, Roger FRY, and others. (Color photographs of several Charleston decorations can be found in Gillian Naylor's chapter on Charleston in *Bloomsbury*; see also Quentin Bell et al., *Charleston: Past and Present* [1987].) In 1919, Woolf wrote with characteristic exaggeration to Violet DICKINSON that her sister was presiding over "the most astonishing ménage; Belgian hares, governesses, children, gardeners, hens, ducks, and painting all the time, till every inch of the house is a different colour" (L2 355). Often Woolf would compare her own life to Vanessa's at Charleston, sometimes downcast by the fecundity of her sister's existence, at others exulting in the calm of her own life at MONK'S HOUSE. In 1939, Clive Bell moved his books, paintings, and furniture from London to Charleston and he, Vanessa, and Grant lived there until they died.

By the time Duncan Grant died in 1978, the house, which they had always rented, was in serious disrepair and contained nearly 2,000 works of art, including paintings, murals, decorated furniture, ceramics, and textiles. The decorations reflected the eclectic tastes of and influences on Vanessa and Grant. The task of restoring and preserving the house began in 1980 when the Charleston Trust was established. The Trust raised £1 million, bought the freehold in 1981, and began an organization called "Friends of Charleston" which attracted members from England and North America. The house was opened to the public in 1986, but work on the interior was not completed until 1992 when the hand-painted wallpapers in the dining room were restored. The progress of repairs and fundraising was reported in the *Charleston Newsletter*, edited by Hugh Lee and appearing in twenty-four issues between April 1982 and December 1989. The *Newsletter* also included reminiscences by members of several Bloomsbury generations, as well as reviews and articles about the life and work of Charleston denizens and Bloomsbury writers and artists. The *Newsletter* was succeeded in 1990 by the sumptuous *Charleston Magazine: Charleston, Bloomsbury and the Arts*, edited by Hugh Lee from 1990 to 1992 and now edited by Frances Spalding. Its aim is "to promote understanding and appreciation of Charleston in its literary and artistic contexts, as an entity and as a concept, and, more widely, of present-day art and design" (CM 1:3). The Winter/Spring 1991 issue (number 4) was a "Virginia Woolf Issue" and the magazine has often published articles on, reminiscences about, and previously unpublished works by Woolf.

Charleston Farmhouse and its beautiful gardens, augmented by the Charleston Shop and Gallery—which sells works inspired by the Charleston style, including pottery made by Quentin Bell—is open from April to October, 2 to 6 P.M. Visitor information is available at 011 44 323 811265.

Charleston Magazine See CHARLESTON.

Charleston Newsletter See CHARLESTON.

Chekhov, Anton Pavlovich (1860–1904) Russian dramatist and short-story writer among whose works are *The Seagull* (1896), *Uncle Vanya* (1897), *The Three Sisters* (1901) and *The Cherry Orchard* (1904). Constance GARNETT translated *The Tales of Tchehov* (1916–22) and *The Plays of Tchehov* (1923–24). Woolf reviewed Garnett's translation of *Wife and Other Stories, The Witch and Other Stories* for the *TIMES LITERARY SUPPLEMENT* on May 16, 1918 (E2 244–47), and remarked that Chekhov was not considered by English readers on the level of Fyodor DOSTOYEVSKY, but was "more on a level with ourselves" (E2 245). At the end of her review, she mentions his story "Gusev" as an example of Chekhov's "hinting at some order hitherto unguessed at" (E2 247). In "MODERN NOVELS" the following year—the essay later revised as Woolf's famous "MODERN FICTION"—she makes more detailed remarks on "Gusev" as an example of the Russian influence on MODERNIST fiction (E3 35).

Woolf reviewed Garnett's translation of Chekhov's *The Bishop and Other Stories* for the TLS in August 1919 ("The Russian Background" [E3 83–86]). She wrote that English readers were by this time "alive to the fact that inconclusive stories are legitimate" (E3 84). In 1920, Woolf reviewed an Arts Theatre production of *The Cherry Orchard* for the *NEW STATESMAN* (E3 246–49).

Chesterfield, Philip Dormer Stanhope, Lord (1694–1773) Known principally for the *Letters* he wrote to his son daily from 1737 onward intended to educate him, and which were published in 1774, but his name is probably more familiar in its association with a type of couch. ORLANDO recalls meeting Lord Chesterfield in the eighteenth-century section of *ORLANDO*, and quotes his remark to his son to the effect that women are large children with whom "a man of sense" only trifles (O 213). Woolf's review of Chesterfield's letters was included in *THE COMMON READER, SECOND SERIES* (CE3 80–85; CR2 86–92).

Chesterton, G(ilbert) K(eith) (1874–1936) In *NIGHT AND DAY*, Mrs. COSHAM is pleased to learn that Ralph DENHAM reads Thomas DE QUINCEY, thinking that his generation only reads [Hilaire] BELLOC, Chesterton and George Bernard SHAW. Chesterton, who was six years senior to Leonard WOOLF at St. Paul's school and whom Leonard knew through a debating society to which they both belonged (LW1 57–58), was a well-known journalist and essayist, novelist and poet. He is best known now for the "Father Brown" stories.

Chinnery, Mrs. Morris PARGITER's mother-in-law and the mother of Celia in *THE YEARS*.

Chipperfield Mentioned in *THE YEARS* by Edward PARGITER, who knew him when he was young and acted in a Greek play wearing a toga. He is now a "railway magnate" who buys old masters (TY 412–13) and comes to Delia PARGITER's party in the "Present Day" chapter.

Chloe and Olivia In *A ROOM OF ONE'S OWN*, Woolf uses an imaginary novel, *Life's Adventure* by Mary CARMICHAEL, as an example of contemporary women's writing. Quoting a scene in which "Chloe liked Olivia" (AROO 83), Woolf says that this marks a turning point in the representation of women in fiction. If "Mary Carmichael" can express the women's relationship, "she will light a torch in that vast chamber where nobody has yet been" (AROO 84). Adrienne Rich cites Chloe and Olivia as one example of the "lesbian continuum" she describes in her essay "Compulsory Heterosexuality and Lesbian Existence" (Rich 194). Dorothy BUSSY's 1948 novel *Olivia* probably derives its title from *A Room*'s Olivia.

Chubb, Eusebius Character in *ORLANDO* whose memoirs are quoted to illustrate the cloying onset of the Victorian Age.

"Cinema, The" See *CABINET OF DR. CALIGARI, THE.*

Clacton, Mr. Character in *NIGHT AND DAY* who writes pamphlets for the SUFFRAGE society for which Mary DATCHET works. He is wonderfully anatomized by Woolf when this champion of women's rights thinks that Mary's ideas probably come from "a group of very clever young men" (ND 266). Mary thinks his writing is "weak and pompous."

Clapham Sect The name given by Sydney Smith (founder of the *Edinburgh Review*) to a group of evangelical philanthropists who lived near each other on Clapham Common, London, toward the end of the eighteenth century. Among these men was James Stephen (1758–1832), Woolf's great-grandfather. He married Sarah Clarke in 1800, with whose brother, William Wilberforce, Stephen and others in the Clapham Sect worked for the abolition of the slave trade. In 1919 a plaque was built into the south wall of Clapham Parish Church to record the names of those men "sometime called 'The Clapham Sect' " who "laboured so abundantly for the increase of National Righteousness and the Conversion of the Heathen and rested not until the curse of slavery was swept away from all parts of the British Dominions" (James Stephen, *Memoirs* 14). Quentin BELL has called the Sect "the conscience of the British middle classes;" their influence as philanthropists was widely felt, inspiring such people as Lord Shaftesbury and Florence NIGHTINGALE.

Clapham families—Babingtons, Macaulays, Sykeses, Thorntons, and Venns—began to intermarry. When Woolf's grandfather James STEPHEN (1789–1859) married Jane Catherine Venn, he allied himself with a family that "stood at the centre of the Evangelical movement within the Church of England" (Annan 10). In "Liberty, Sorority, Misogyny," Jane Marcus discusses a "legacy of Stephen misogyny" going back to this James Stephen, whom she calls an "architect of an ideology of oppression" (*Languages* 82, 83).

A major influence on the group was Jane Venn's grandfather Henry Venn's book *Compleat Duty of Man*, which was held to be the best exposition of evangelical theology. Although each generation to some extent rebelled against the beliefs of the previous one, a sense of belonging to an elect group and a distrust of institutions persisted down to the fourth generation, the BLOOMSBURY GROUP. E. M. FORSTER was also a direct descendant of an original Clapham family, the Thorntons.

Clarissa In *A ROOM OF ONE'S OWN,* Clarissa Harlowe, the heroine of Samuel Richardson's long novel *Clarissa Harlowe* (1747–48), is offered as an example of women who have "burnt like beacons in all the works of all the poets from the beginning of time" (AROO 43), whom Woolf uses to stress the difference between fictional and real women. (See also Clarissa DALLOWAY [2]).

Clark, Eliza Character in *BETWEEN THE ACTS.* She runs the village shop and plays the part of Queen Elizabeth I in Miss LA TROBE's pageant.

Cleopatra In *A ROOM OF ONE'S OWN,* Cleopatra—from William SHAKESPEARE's *Antony and Cleopatra*—is an example of women who have "burnt like beacons in all the works of all the poets from the beginning of time" (AROO 43), whom Woolf uses to stress the difference between fictional and real women. In *BETWEEN THE ACTS,* Lucy SWITHIN is made by Miss LA TROBE's pageant to feel that Cleopatra is her "unacted part." Mitchell Leaska calls this Woolf's "boldest stroke in the entire novel" (PH 231) as not only is the historic Cleopatra a woman whose temperament seems far removed from Lucy's, but also because Cleopatra is linked with Isis, "the most famous of the Egyptian goddesses" (PH 232).

Clieveden In *MRS. DALLOWAY,* when Clarissa thinks how she has "failed" her husband she mentions having done so at Clieveden (MD 46), which was the family home of the Astors. Lady Nancy Astor was the first woman to take a seat in the British parliament.

Clifford's Inn In October 1912, two months after their marriage, the Woolfs took rooms at 13 Clifford's Inn, just off Fleet Street between Chancery and Fetter Lane in the City of London. This is probably the model for William RODNEY's apartment in *NIGHT AND DAY.* They moved in October 1914 to lodgings before moving to HOGARTH HOUSE, Richmond, in 1915.

Clive, (Robert) (1725–74) Among the family treasures in *NIGHT AND DAY* that Katharine HILBERY shows to visitors is a sword said to have belonged to Clive. "Clive of India," an employee of the East India Company in the eighteenth century, was a hero to the British. He was, in fact, a crook and a mercenary.

Cliveden See CLIEVEDEN.

Clough, Anne Jemima (1820–92) Woolf refers to Clough as an example of a nineteenth-century professional woman in *THREE GUINEAS.* Clough, a leader in the movement for higher education for women in the later nineteenth century, was born in Liverpool and spent much of her childhood in America (Ray Strachey, *The Cause* 149). She opened small schools and in 1866 began efforts to establish a lecture series for women. Between 1862 and 1866 she met Barbara Leigh Smith BODICHON and Emily Davies (founder of GIRTON COLLEGE). Clough was one of the twenty-five women who attended the first meeting of Emily Davies's Schoolmistresses' Association. In 1871, Henry Sidgwick persuaded Clough to preside over a house in which five female students were resident; this was the beginning of NEWNHAM COLLEGE, which was built in 1874 when the group under Clough's supervision had grown too large for her house.

Clutterbuck, Mr. Mentioned in *JACOB'S ROOM,* he seems a likely forerunner of Augustus CARMICHAEL in *TO THE LIGHTHOUSE,* possibly derived from the Mr. WOLSTENHOLME mentioned in "A SKETCH OF THE PAST" (MOB 73).

Clytemnestra Character in the *Agamemnon* of Aeschylus, incorrectly assigned by Clarissa DALLOWAY in *THE VOYAGE OUT* to Sophocles's *Antigone* (TVO 45). In *A ROOM OF ONE'S OWN,* Clytemnestra is offered as an example of women who have "burnt like beacons in all the works of all the poets from the beginning of time" (AROO 43), whom Woolf uses to stress the difference between fictional and real women. Clytemnestra was the wife of Agamemnon and when he sacrificed her daughter Iphigenia during the Trojan War, she killed him with the help of her lover Aegisthus.

Coates, Emily Mentioned in *MRS. DALLOWAY,* one of several people who try to make out what the skywriting airplane spells out in the sky. As she stands looking up, holding her baby, Mrs. Coates reads "Glaxo" (MD 29).

Cobbett of Cobbs Corner Character in *BETWEEN THE ACTS.* He has retired on a pension from a tea plantation (74). His observation of Mrs. MANRESA's flirtatious behavior leads him to reflect that human nature is the same in the East and West (110).

Cobbold, Captain The captain of the *EUPHROSYNE* in *THE VOYAGE OUT.*

"Cockney's Farming Experience, A" A story by Woolf which appeared in the *HYDE PARK GATE NEWS* in 1892 about a young Cockney couple's unsuccessful attempt to change their lives by running a farm. Louise DeSalvo summarizes the story and interprets it as a brilliant analysis of class issues and a reflection of Woolf's own family situation at the time, seeing also a subtext of a story of sexual assault (DeSalvo, *Impact* 139–47). The story, together with another piece of juvenilia, "EXPERIENCES OF A PATER-FAMILIAS," was published in 1972 by San Diego State University Press, edited by Suzanne Henig, as a gift for subscribers to the *VIRGINIA WOOLF QUARTERLY*. It was recently reissued by Cecil Woolf in the Bloomsbury Heritage series (1994). DeSalvo's reading of the story has been challenged by Anne Olivier BELL (VWM 38: 2), who has also said that the *Hyde Park Gate News* was invariably in Vanessa BELL's handwriting (VWM 39:1).

Cole Kitty LASSWADE's chauffeur in *THE YEARS*.

Cole, (William) Horace de Vere (1881–1936) A friend of Adrian STEPHEN's and organizer of the ZANZIBAR HOAX and the DREADNOUGHT HOAX. He is not to be confused with G. D. H. Cole, whose books on politics were published by the HOGARTH PRESS.

Colefax, Lady Sibyl (née Halsey) First referred to as "Coalbox" in Woolf's DIARY (D2 137), she was a prominent London hostess given to inviting literary stars to her home, Argyll House, in Chelsea. Woolf describes her relations with Colefax in "AM I A SNOB?" (MOB 204–20). She is one of the "friends [who] have helped me in ways too various to specify" mentioned in the ironic preface to *ORLANDO*.

Coleridge, Samuel Taylor (1772–1834) English Romantic poet and critic and the source of one of Woolf's most often-quoted lines, "a great mind is androgynous" (AROO 98). Woolf had noted Coleridge's thought that "a great mind must be androgynous" when reading *The Table Talk and Omniana of Samuel Taylor Coleridge* in 1918, preparing to review it for the *TIMES LITERARY SUPPLEMENT* ("Coleridge as Critic" E2 221–25); the line is from Coleridge's entry for September 1, 1832 (E2 224n6). Her reading notes (E2 App. II) also reveal that Coleridge was the source of another idea in *A Room,* that "no great poet has come from the lower classes except Burns" (E2 356; AROO 48–49).

Coleridge's well-known poetic works include "The Rime of the Ancient Mariner" (first published in 1798 in *Lyrical Ballads,* the volume on which Coleridge and William WORDSWORTH collaborated), "Kubla Khan," "Christabel," and "Dejection." He also wrote a great deal of criticism that has been extremely influential: a recent historian of literary criticism wrote that "one crucial axis of modern criticism is a series of rereadings in Coleridge" (Arac 3). Coleridge's criticism is most familiar to readers in *Biographia Literaria* ("Literary Remains"), published in 1817.

It was as a critic that Coleridge was most important to Woolf and other writers of her generation. In "Coleridge as Critic" she notes that his influence is so pervasive on other writers that "we possess a very visible ghost" (E2 221). His criticism is "the most spiritual in the language" (E2 222), and the fact that Coleridge never did write the great work he always had in mind seems to Woolf an advantage. It is arguable, she writes, "that the desire to be exhaustive, comprehensive, and monumental has destroyed more virtue than it has brought to birth" (E2 223). Woolf's description of Coleridge's method as a critic in her essay "HOW IT STRIKES A CONTEMPORARY" closely suggests her own critical method: she describes him as "brewing in his head the whole of poetry and letting issue now and then one of those profound general statements which are caught up by the mind when hot with the friction of reading as if they were the soul of the book itself" (E3 355).

In May 1940, Woolf wrote in her DIARY that she was reading "masses of Coleridge & Wordsworth letters of a night—curiously untwisting and burrowing into that plaited nest" (D5 289). She was rereading also *Biographia Literaria* and an essay by her father, Leslie STEPHEN, on Coleridge in *Hours in a Library* (1892). Woolf had many of her father's editions of Coleridge's works in her own library, copies that were filled with Leslie Stephen's pencilled notes (Holleyman and Treacher, *passim*). Later in the year she read a volume of Coleridge's poems, reading around, as was her usual practice, the subject of a review, in this case for the *NEW STATESMAN AND NATION* in October that year of *Coleridge the Talker* by Richard W. Armour and Raymond F. Howes. In "The Man at the Gate" (CE3 217–21; DM 104–10) she writes of Coleridge "the innumerable, the mutable, the atmospheric" (CE3 217), summing him up as "a man of exaggerated self-consciousness, endowed with an astonishing power of self-analysis" (CE3 218). The following week in the *New Statesman and Nation* she reviewed *Coleridge Fille: A Biography of Sara Coleridge* by Earl Leslie Griggs (CE3 222–26), describing Coleridge's daughter as an unfinished work of the poet's, like his poem "Christabel."

Collected Essays Published in four volumes (1 and 2 in 1966; 3 and 4 in 1967) by the HOGARTH PRESS in Britain and Harcourt, Brace & World in the United States, edited by Leonard WOOLF. The four volumes include all the essays published in the two volumes of the *COMMON READER,* and those in the four posthumous volumes of Woolf's essays that Leonard edited: *THE MOMENT, THE DEATH OF THE MOTH, THE CAPTAIN'S DEATH BED* and *GRANITE & RAINBOW*.

"Come away, come away Death" Spoken by BERNARD in *THE WAVES* (TW 282), a line from Feste the clown's song in William SHAKESPEARE's *Twelfth Night* (II.iv.50).

Common Reader, The (See also *COMMON READER, SECOND SERIES*)

As she completed *JACOB'S ROOM* toward the end of 1921, Woolf began to think about a book of essays, provisionally titled "Reading." She planned to revise some of her previously published essays and to work on some new ones for this book. She turned to these critical essays from time to time as she began to work on her next novel, *MRS. DALLOWAY*. The title of *The Common Reader*, as Woolf explains in a preface, comes from Samuel JOHNSON's "Life of Gray." The book was published with a jacket design by Vanessa BELL in 1925 by the HOGARTH PRESS, and by Harcourt, Brace & Company; the U.S. edition included an additional "Lives of the Obscure" essay, "Miss Ormerod." Woolf dedicated the book to Lytton STRACHEY, who thought *The Common Reader* "divine, a classic" (D3 32).

The book was generally well received by critics (see CH 148–57), Woolf noting in her DIARY that the *TIMES LITERARY SUPPLEMENT* had given her two columns of "sober & sensible praise" (D3 17). When she read through the book again in 1929, she felt "horrified by my own looseness" (D3 235), but *The Common Reader* does have a clear thematic concern with how to read works of the past, and how to bridge contemporary reality and the past. Among the important essays that appeared in *The Common Reader* are: "ON NOT KNOWING GREEK," "NOTES ON AN ELIZABETHAN PLAY," "Montaigne," "MODERN FICTION," "THE RUSSIAN POINT OF VIEW," "Joseph Conrad" and "HOW IT STRIKES A CONTEMPORARY."

The Common Reader. *Courtesy Linda J. Langham. Vanessa Bell designed the jacket of this Hogarth Press first edition (1925).*

Common Reader, Second Series, The Like its predecessor, *THE COMMON READER*, this was a collection of new and revised critical essays. Woolf worked on the book after finishing *THE WAVES* and while she was writing *FLUSH*, "for one thing," she wrote, "by way of proving my credentials" (D4 77). *The Common Reader, Second Series* was published in 1932 by the HOGARTH PRESS and, in the United States, by Harcourt, Brace & Company, with a cover designed by Vanessa BELL. The quotation from Samuel JOHNSON's "Life of Gray" mentioning the "common reader," which Woolf had written about in her preface to the first volume, appears as an epigraph to the second. The dust-jacket description of the first edition calls *The Common Reader, Second Series* "a book of unprofessional criticism dealing with books and characters that have chanced to come the author's way." Among the essays included in this volume are: "Robinson Crusoe" (see Daniel DEFOE), "THE NIECE OF AN EARL," " 'I Am Christina Rossetti' " and "HOW SHOULD ONE READ A BOOK?"

Complete Shorter Fiction Published in 1985 and edited by Susan Dick, this collection brings together all Woolf's short fiction from her earliest known short story "PHYLLIS AND ROSAMOND" (1906) to a brief sketch, "The Watering Place," that Dick speculates was written about a month before Woolf's death. Several works that have previously been included in collections of Woolf's essays (for example, "A WOMAN'S COLLEGE FROM THE OUTSIDE") are included in this edition, pointing up the occasional uncertainty of the boundary between Woolf's fiction and nonfiction. The edition contains many significant pieces, including: "THE MARK ON THE WALL," "KEW GARDENS," "SOLID OBJECTS," "AN UNWRITTEN NOVEL," "A SOCIETY," "THE STRING QUARTET," "MOMENTS OF BEING: 'SLATER'S PINS HAVE NO POINTS' " and "THE LEGACY."

Comus In chapter XXV of *THE VOYAGE OUT*, Rachel VINRACE first begins to feel the symptoms of the illness that leads to her death when Terence HEWET reads aloud to her from John MILTON's masque *Comus* (TVO 326–27). (*Comus* and "LYCIDAS" were works that Woolf described in "HOURS IN A LIBRARY" as giving a reader "absolute certainty of delight" [E2 60].) Hewet has said that the lines can be appreciated simply for their sound, but to Rachel they seem to be "laden with meaning" (TVO 326), a phrase that has encouraged many readers to interpret the relation of Milton's poem to Woolf's novel.

Comus, "A Masque Presented at Ludlow Castle," was first performed in September 1634. A Lady is separated from her two brothers in a forest and kidnapped by the lustful Comus, son of Bacchus and Circe, who casts a spell on her. Comus attempts to seduce the Lady but she resists, telling Comus he has "nor ear, nor soul to apprehend / The sublime notion, and high mystery / That must be uttered to unfold the sage / And serious doctrine of virginity." The brothers find the Lady, but they are unable to free her from Comus's spell because they break his glass but do not find his wand. A spirit, Thyrsis, tells them the Lady cannot be freed unless they capture Comus's wand. The Lady invokes the aid of Sabrina, goddess of the nearby river Severn, who comes attended by water-nymphs and frees her (Sabrina only helps women who are, like herself, pure). There has been a great deal of controversy in Milton scholarship on the doctrine of chastity in *Comus*.

Harvena Richter calls Sabrina Rachel's "myth-twin" (Richter, *Inward* 124) and interprets Rachel's death at the end of the novel as "Sabrina, the water-spirit, a lovely death-wish" coming for her (125). In her discussion of the evolution of *The Voyage Out* through its numerous drafts, Louise DeSalvo reads the allusion to *Comus* as pointing to Rachel's "inadmissible erotic attachment to her father," for which kissing Richard DALLOWAY has been a substitute (DeSalvo, *First Voyage* 140). Reviewing DeSalvo's book, Esther Klindienst Joplin argued that this interpretation "makes Rachel the scapegoat of a prior mythology, thereby obscuring the intention of Woolf's allusion" (VWM 16:3). Beverly Ann Schlack has also discussed the allusion to *Comus* in great detail (*Continuing* 20–27), arguing that the fact that it is a masque "should alert readers to the growing inappropriateness of realistic standards, to the heavily symbolic and allegorical direction in which Woolf's novel is moving" (21). *Comus*, according to Schlack, is "an allusive restatement of Rachel's dilemma" (21).

Christine Froula writes that Milton's words are fatal to Rachel "not because they represent a tradition in which bound, endangered 'ladies,' drowned nymphs, and the marriage plot with its tightwoven construction of female sexuality as virginity, domesticity, and maternity, figure woman's 'destiny'," but because the masque "figures female 'destiny' in terms of impossible alternatives: a forking path that leads to virginity, marriage, and maternity on one side and to rape, fallenness, and death on the other" ("Out of" 157).

Congreve, Lady A "sick old woman" whom Julia ELIOT in *JACOB'S ROOM* visits on "an errand of mercy" (JR 168).

Congreve, William (1670–1729) A master of the comedy of manners and a friend of Alexander POPE, Sir Richard Steele and Joseph ADDISON. Congreve is buried in WESTMINSTER ABBEY. In *NIGHT AND DAY*, seeing Katharine HILBERY approach as he waits to meet her in Kew Gardens, Ralph DENHAM thinks that she comes "like a ship in full sail." The line is from Congreve's *The Way of the World*, a play that Woolf often alludes to. In her 1937 essay "Congreve's Comedies" (CE1 76–84), Woolf wrote that to "read Congreve's plays is to be convinced that we may learn from them many lessons much to our advantage both as writers of books and—if the division is possible—as livers of life" (CE1 80). In the play, Millamant and Mirabell establish unconventional guidelines for their friendship in a way similar to that Ralph and Katharine work out during their conversation at Kew (Bazin 75).

Conrad, Joseph (Josef Teodor Konrad Korzeniowski) (1857–1924) Born in the Ukraine to Polish parents, Conrad became a member of the crew of a French ship in 1874, satisfying a long-felt urge to go to sea. He was naturalized as a British citizen in 1884 and in 1894 gave up his career as a sailor to write, choosing maritime settings for nearly all his stories and novels. Woolf greatly admired Conrad's writing, particularly his earlier works, and wrote several reviews of his books. Reviewing *Lord Jim* in 1917 for the *TIMES LITERARY SUPPLEMENT*, she spoke of Conrad's "rare and wonderful qualities" (E2 141). She also reviewed *Youth: A Narrative and Two Other Stories* for the TLS in 1917 (E2 158–60; the other two stories were "Heart of Darkness" and "The End of the Tether"), and *Nostromo: A Tale of the Seaboard* when it was reissued in 1918, following its first publication in 1904. When Conrad attempted a romance in 1920, *The Rescue: A Romance of the Shallow*, Woolf thought it very poor and struggled to say so in her review of the book for the TLS (D2 49). She felt Conrad's belief in romance had failed him in the middle (E3 232) and wrote in her DIARY that nothing could shake her opinion of a book, even Katherine MANSFIELD's praise of *The Rescue* that Woolf overheard at a literary lunch a few days after finishing her review. She reiterated in her diary her belief that other readers were "obedient sheep" praising Conrad's new book merely because of his reputation (D2 52). In "Prince of Prose," a 1921 review of Conrad's *Notes on the Life and Letters*, Woolf judged him not a genius but "a very sensible man" (E3 288).

Despite these opinions, however, Woolf expressed her deep admiration for Conrad in "Mr. Conrad: A Conversation," an article she wrote for the *NATION & ATHENAEUM* in 1923 reviewing *Almayer's Folly*, *Tales of Unrest*, *An Outcast of the Islands*, *The Nigger of the Narcissus*, *Typhoon*, *Lord Jim*, *Youth* and *Romance*, all of which had been published in J. M. Dent's uniform edition of Conrad that year. Her article took the form of a conversation between "Penelope Otway" and "David Lowe" (giving her the "brilliant idea" to use this form for her essays that would eventually be published as *THE COMMON READER*; the idea did not persist). Penelope Otway holds that Conrad is "not one and simple; no, he is many and complex" (E3 377), a phrase with which Woolf would have BERNARD describe himself almost exactly in *THE WAVES* (TW 76; Bernard says "complex and many"). With, perhaps, her criticism of Arnold BENNETT's lack of insight (in "MR. BENNETT AND MRS. BROWN") in mind, Woolf writes that Conrad "sees once and he sees for ever. His books are full of moments of vision. They light up a whole character in a flash" (E3 378). Penelope Otway responds to her old friend David Lowe's remark that there are no women in Conrad's books by saying that the ships are his women, and often "more feminine than his women" (E3 379).

Woolf later wrote that her "Conrad adventure," as she called this piece, had definitely helped her see more clearly how to write about character in the essays she was working on for *The Common Reader* (D2 265). Her work on those essays, and on *MRS. DALLOWAY*, was interrupted in the summer of 1924 when Conrad died and she was asked to contribute a lead article on him for the TLS. She included that article, "Joseph Conrad," in *The Common Reader* (CE1 309–13; CR1 282–91). There are several allusions to Conrad's work, particularly to "Heart of Darkness," in Woolf's fiction. Maisie JOHNSON in *Mrs. Dalloway,* for example, wants to cry out "Horror! horror!" an echo of Conrad's Mr. Kurtz (MD 39). *BETWEEN THE ACTS* closes with an image of a couple about to fight "in the heart of darkness" (BTA 219). *THE VOYAGE OUT* also probably owes elements of its tropical setting to Conrad's descriptions. In chapter 4 of *Rich and Strange,* Marianne DeKoven discusses the similar narrative structures of *Heart of Darkness* and *The Voyage Out.*

Conscientious Objectors In a memoir of her nephew Julian BELL, killed in 1937 in the SPANISH CIVIL WAR, Woolf wrote "We were all C. O.'s in the Great war" (QB2 258), expressing her conviction that to "fight intellectually" had always been the tradition of her friends. In 1935 Julian had edited and written an introduction for *We Did Not Fight,* a collection of eighteen autobiographical essays by World War I conscientious objectors that also included a poem by Siegfried SASSOON. Reflecting the BLOOMSBURY GROUP's pacifism, many of Woolf's contemporaries—including Clive BELL, Duncan GRANT, David GARNETT and Lytton STRACHEY—appeared before tribunals in 1916 to argue for exemption from combat duty, and her brother Adrian STEPHEN was secretary of the No Conscription Fellowship. Leonard WOOLF was given a medical exemption from military service because of his perpetually trembling hands. Strachey was given a medical exemption for numerous ailments by military doctors whom he had been required to see by his tribunal. The story of Strachey's answer to the tribunal's question as to what he would do if a German soldier were attempting to rape his sister ("I should try and come between them") became infamous (Holroyd 628–29). A common ground for exemption was that a person was doing work vital to the war effort, and several of Woolf's friends and acquaintances worked as farmers during the war. For many, such as Bertrand RUSSELL, Ottoline and Philip MORRELL's home, GARSINGTON, was a refuge where they could not only work on Philip's farm and thus satisfy the military tribunals' requirement, but also spend their time with fellow intellectuals. Vanessa BELL's move to CHARLESTON in 1916 was precipitated by the need for Duncan Grant and David Garnett to find a farm willing to employ them. Vanessa had urged Woolf to write to Lady Robert ("Nelly") CECIL on Grant and Garnett's behalf when they had to appear in 1916 before the Central Tribunal, of which Nelly's brother-in-law was chairman; Woolf did so (see L2 97–100).

Constable, Mrs. The children's nurse in the first EPISODE of *THE WAVES.* Throughout BERNARD's life, the memory of Mrs. Constable bathing him is significant.

Constantinople In *MRS. DALLOWAY,* Clarissa DALLOWAY feels that she has twice "failed" her husband, once at CLIEVEDEN and a second time at Constantinople. ORLANDO is sent by King Charles II to be ambassador in Constantinople. This Turkish city is described by David Roessel as "a multivalent symbol encompassing three of the most significant forces in [Woolf's] life, Sapphic love, death, and war" (Roessel 398). These three strands, Roessel argues, converge most prominently in *ORLANDO,* although he notes the frequency of references to both Turkey and Constantinople throughout Woolf's fiction. She visited Constantinople in 1906 (PA 348).

Vita SACKVILLE-WEST's first book of poetry was *Constantinople: Eight Poems* and Roessel points out that the surrounding area was significant in her writings up to 1927 (Roessel 399). Sackville-West's thinly disguised account of her affair with Violet TREFUSIS, the novel *Challenge,* is set in Asia Minor, a fact that leads Roessel to suggest that Orlando's sex-change takes place in Turkey because it recalls the setting of Sackville-West's novel. Roessel further argues that Constantinople is linked in *Mrs. Dalloway* and *TO THE LIGHTHOUSE* with erotic feelings between women.

Roessel connects Orlando's Turkish sex-change also with the story of Lady Hester Stanhope, about whom Woolf wrote in an essay published in the *TIMES LITERARY SUPPLEMENT* in 1910 ("'Lady Hester Stanhope'" E1 325–30): "Orlando's life with the Gipsies in Turkey . . . mirrors the career of Lady Hester" (Roessel 404). Roessel also points out that Constantinople was associated with death and disease for Woolf as it was while traveling through Greece and Turkey in 1906 that her brother Thoby STEPHEN contracted the typhoid that killed him. In 1911, Vanessa BELL suffered a miscarriage in Turkey. These facts lead Roessel to see Jacob FLANDERS's "vision of the Turkish countryside" in *JACOB'S ROOM* as a "premonition of his death" (Roessel 407).

Leonard WOOLF also wrote about the city in his 1917 book *The Future of Constantinople,* in which he explored its long history as a strategic center fought over by various states. After a crisis in 1922 when English and Turkish troops faced off against each other at Chanak, there was concern in England that this region would once again lead to a violent struggle. Roessel comments that the Chanak crisis "contributed heavily to the fall of Lloyd George's coalition government" (Roessel 409). There are references throughout Woolf's fiction to Turkey, the Balkans, and to Constantinople, indicating its prominence in English people's minds during the 1920s and later and lending significance to Woolf's use of the city in *Orlando.* Roessel argues that her setting Orlando's sex-change in Constantinople is "fitting" as it is "subversive not only sexually but politically" (Roessel 414).

Contemporary Writers A collection of Woolf's *TIMES LITERARY SUPPLEMENT* reviews (with one exception, published in the *NATION & ATHENAEUM*) of contemporary writers of fiction, edited by Jean Guiguet and published by the HOGARTH PRESS in 1965. These previously unrepublished essays include two on Samuel BUTLER ("A Man with a View" and "The Way of All Flesh"), and Woolf's reviews of E. M. FORSTER's *A Room with a View* and two of Dorothy RICHARDSON's novels, *The Tunnel* and *Revolving Lights.*

Cornhill Magazine Founded in 1860 with William Makepeace THACKERAY as its first editor and named for its place of publication. Leslie STEPHEN was editor from 1871 to 1882. The *Cornhill* was a monthly publication of fiction and general literature for which Woolf wrote several reviews in 1908.

Coryphaeus Mentioned in *THE VOYAGE OUT* by William PEPPER as a Roman authority on road building, he appears to have been invented by Woolf.

Cosham, Mrs. (Aunt Millicent) Character in *NIGHT AND DAY* who is delighted, upon meeting Ralph DENHAM, to discover that the younger generation reads Thomas DE QUINCEY and is even more thrilled to learn that Ralph writes in his spare time. She is a wonderful parody of a Victorian lady whose memories are populated more by characters from poetry and drama than figures from her own life.

Costelloe, Karin See STEPHEN, Karin.

Cowan, Erasmus One of three professors at Cambridge in *JACOB'S ROOM* who are satirically sketched, the "chubby" Cowan is a scholar of Virgil (JR 41–42).

Cowbind A plant. In *THE WAVES,* RHODA reads a poem and refers to "green cowbind and the moonlight coloured may" (TW 56; 206). She is reading Percy Bysshe SHELLEY's "The Question" (line 18).

Cowper, William (1731–1800) Woolf wrote in her DIARY on first thinking of *TO THE LIGHTHOUSE* that the "centre is father's character, sitting in a boat, reciting We perished, each alone" (D3.18). The line is from William Cowper's poem "The Castaway," and Mr. RAMSAY recites it in parts 1 and 3 of *To the Lighthouse.* Cowper, the son of a rector, suffered throughout his life from manic depression. His mother died when he was six, and he was bullied at his first school in Bedfordshire. Having led a quiet life until 1763, he was nominated by a cousin to be a clerk at the House of Lords, and as the examination approached he became increasingly terrified and tried several times to commit suicide. Subsequently, he believed himself to have been damned and declined into a religious mania. He published several successful volumes of poetry and after his death several editions of his letters were published.

Michael Lund sees "The Castaway" as "the central poetic leitmotif" of *To the Lighthouse* (75) and wonders whether "the nearly ubiquitous presence of Cowperian images of isolation and inundation do not color the narrative far more darkly" than readers have generally supposed (76). Lund also points out that Woolf was reading another of Cowper's poems, "The Task," in 1927 when she was correcting the proofs of *To the Lighthouse.* In 1929 she published "Cowper and Lady Austen" (CR2 140–47; CE3 181–87) in the *NATION & ATHENAEUM,* an article in which, Lund says, she is very sympathetic to Cowper's feelings of damnation.

Lund sees similarities between the portrayal of Mr. Ramsay and Cowper's life, the facts of which contribute to the "deep sadness" of *To the Lighthouse.* Quentin BELL points out that Cowper was one of the writers Woolf read late at night during the summer of 1897, the year which is most likely the source of part 1 of *To the Lighthouse.* Woolf mentions Cowper's *Letters* in *JACOB'S ROOM,* when Jacob FLANDERS "compares his own weak epistolary efforts with Cowper's accomplishments" (Lund 78) and in *THE VOYAGE OUT* when "the spirit of poor William Cowper" mingles with Rachel VINRACE's dreams (TVO 37).

Cox, Katherine Laird ("Ka") (1887–1938) A friend of Karin and Rachel Costelloe, Rupert BROOKE, and Gwen Darwin who graduated from NEWNHAM COLLEGE in 1910 and whom Woolf met in 1911. They became friends, Woolf addressing her as "Bruin" or "the Bear." Katherine confided in Woolf about her emotional tangles with Rupert Brooke and, for a time, Jacques RAVERAT (who was in love with her, but not she with him, and who married Gwen Darwin). It was to Ka Cox that Woolf made the infamous remark while on her honeymoon that "I find the climax greatly exaggerated" (L2 6). In 1913, Leonard WOOLF sent for Ka to come to the Plough Inn in Somerset where he and Woolf were on vacation (and where they had spent part of their honeymoon the year before) as Woolf was becoming increasingly unstable. They returned to London where, on September 9, Ka found Woolf unconscious on her bed, having taken an overdose of Veronal. For the next few months, Ka shared the duty of caring for Woolf with Vanessa BELL and Janet CASE ("Ka is very nice," Woolf wrote Leonard, "but as slow headed as an old cow" [L2 43]). In 1918 Ka married William (Will) ARNOLD-FORSTER, and they had a son, Mark, in 1920. Her relationship with Woolf faded in the 1920s, though they continued to see each other occasionally. On hearing of her death Woolf wrote in her DIARY that she wished she could feel more at the news and that she believed Ka's life had ended with Rupert Brooke's death: "After that she was acting a part very carefully" (D5 143).

Craddock, Lucy In *THE YEARS,* she tutors Kitty LASSWADE in history. There are elements in her characterization of both Clara PATER and Janet CASE. Perry Meisel has pointed out that the version of the scene between Lucy and Kitty in *The Years* is considerably shorter than that in *THE PARGITERS* (Meisel 27). He also refers to an earlier depiction of Clara Pater in the story "MOMENTS OF BEING: 'SLATER'S PINS HAVE NO POINTS' " and finds that the sexual feeling of the story is repressed in the novel.

"Craftsmanship" (CE2: 245–51; DM 198–207) A talk by Woolf broadcast on April 29, 1937, for the BBC radio series "Words Fail Me," and first published in the BBC magazine *The Listener* on May 5, 1937. She considers words, the medium of the writer's craft, remarking that "our unconsciousness is their privacy; our darkness is their light" (CE2 251). A recording of part of this talk is the only record of Woolf's voice, although Quentin BELL has said it does not give a very accurate idea of how she sounded. It may be found at the National Sound Archive of the British Library (M7060. BBC Archive No. 1328).

Craig, Dr. Maurice (1866–1935) "Nerve specialist" whom Leonard WOOLF consulted in 1912 about Woolf's having children. Roger FRY had recommended Craig to Vanessa BELL in 1911 after she suffered bouts of mental instability following a miscarriage in Turkey. Vanessa and Leonard both went to consult Craig about Woolf in 1915. Craig, who had advised against her having children, wrote in 1916 to Leonard that it was important for Woolf to "take as much milk as possible" (Spotts 220). Craig was also one of two doctors who wrote on Leonard's behalf when he sought exemption from military service in 1916, on account of his inherited nervous tremor and his wife's condition. Stephen Trombley, in his chapter "Enforced Conformity," discusses Craig's career and writings. He was successor to Sir George SAVAGE as "physician for psychological medicine" at Guy's Hospital (Trombley 183) and "held many key positions in the world of psychological medicine" (Trombley 183). Craig was also a member of the War Office Committee of Enquiry into "shell shock," accounts of the report of which influenced Woolf's conception of Septimus Warren SMITH in *MRS. DALLOWAY.* Roger Poole points out that in November 1922, Craig gave the Bradshaw Lecture to the Royal College of Physicians and speculates that as this was during the time Woolf was working on *Mrs. Dalloway* she may have derived the name of Sir William BRADSHAW, the nerve specialist who discusses shell shock with Richard DALLOWAY, from this occasion. Woolf noted in her DIARY in 1920 that her friend H. T. J. NORTON had consulted Craig and, ostensibly on his advice, "has given up mathematics . . . feels humiliated, & daren't face his friends" (D2 76).

Crane, Dr. (also called "Old Crane") The headmaster of the boys' school in *THE WAVES.*

Crane, Mrs. The wife of the headmaster of the boys' school in *THE WAVES,* whom BERNARD imagines in bed reading a French memoir and sighing "Is this all?" (TW 50).

Craster Referred to in *THE YEARS* as having won a pig at a village fête.

Craster, Kitty Mentioned in *JACOB'S ROOM* as marrying Mr. Stuart ORMOND on the strength of a remark he makes comparing real to artificial flowers (JR 83).

Crawley, Mr. A clerk in *JACOB'S ROOM* who works at Whitehall with Timothy DURRANT.

Creevey, Thomas (1768–1838) During the dinner in section XVII of part 1 of *TO THE LIGHTHOUSE,* Mrs. RAMSAY reflects on how she relies on the "admirable fabric of the masculine intelligence" to sustain her as she half-listens to the dinner conversation range across numerous subjects, one of which is "Creevey's Memoirs" (TTL 106). A Whig member of Parliament, Creevey published *The Creevey Papers* in 1903.

Cressida In *A ROOM OF ONE'S OWN,* Cressida, the story of whose love affair with Troilus has been told by Giovanni Boccaccio, Geoffrey Chaucer, William SHAKESPEARE and others, is offered as an example of women who have "burnt like beacons in all the works of all the poets from the beginning of time" (AROO 43), whom Woolf uses to stress the difference between fictional and real women.

Cressida, daughter of the priest, Calchas, who foresaw the fall of Troy, is loved by Troilus. She is sent to the Greek camp, however, in a prisoner exchange, and Diomede woos her. Troilus and Diomede do battle, but it is Achilles who eventually kills Troilus.

Criterion Quarterly founded and edited by T. S. ELIOT in the first issue of which (1922) his poem "The Waste Land" appeared. Woolf contributed a story, "In the Orchard" (SF 143–45), in 1923, "CHARACTER IN FICTION" in 1924, and "ON BEING ILL" in 1926. The *Criterion* also published as the *New Criterion* and the *Monthly Criterion* before reverting to its original name and closing in 1939.

Crome, John (1768–1821) English landscape painter mentioned in *BETWEEN THE ACTS* when Mrs. MANRESA asks why he was called "Old Crome" (BTA 55). (He was called "Old" to distinguish him from his son who was also a landscape painter.)

Crosby, Annie The Pargiter family's servant in *THE YEARS* who remains with the family for her entire working life, leaving only when the house is sold and the children disperse ("for Crosby it was the end of everything" [TY 216]). Even then she continues to do laundry for Martin PARGITER, her favorite. Crosby is still alive in the "Present Day" chapter (TY 389). The brief "1918" chapter of *The Years* is entirely devoted to Crosby. Louise Poresky has said that in this chapter Woolf "presents Crosby as a symbol of the loneliness that tortures human beings" (Poresky, *Elusive* 234). Jane Wheare suggests she may be based upon Sophie FARRELL (*Virginia Woolf*).

Many critics have commented on the direct link made between *The Years* and *THREE GUINEAS,* where Woolf writes that discussion with men about admitting women to the professions often leads to a rise in "the emotional temperature," which women avert by dragging into the conversation "some old family servant, called Crosby, perhaps, whose dog Rover has died" (TG 129). She notes that "while we are talking about Crosby, we are asking questions . . . about you" (i.e., about men) (TG 129). Mitchell Leaska has argued that the year 1913 (in which chapter of *The Years* Crosby leaves the house at ABERCORN TERRACE with the moribund Rover) "was a very important year in Virginia Woolf's life," and yet "by dragging in an old family servant called Crosby" Woolf has evaded some "strong emotion" (*Novels* 197). In September 1913, Woolf attempted suicide.

Crosby, Mr. Seen fleetingly at a party in *JACOB'S ROOM* in conversation with Mr. Burley (JR 87).

Cruttendon, Edward One of the "painter men" Jacob FLANDERS visits in Paris on his way to Greece in *JACOB'S ROOM.*

Cunard, Lady Maud "Emerald" (née Burke) (1872–1948) Society hostess fleetingly mentioned in "AM I A SNOB?" (MOB 213–14) and mother of the writer Nancy CUNARD. She was also a patron of the OMEGA WORKSHOPS.

Cunard, Nancy Clara (1896–1965) A "poet, essayist, editor, journalist, war correspondent, memoirist, translator, avant-garde publisher, African art collector and political activist" (Friedman, "Nancy Cunard" 63) whose poem *Parallax* was published by the HOGARTH PRESS in 1925. She was the daughter of Lady Maud and Sir Bache Cunard and knew many of the leading MODERNIST writers in London and Paris.

Curnow A boy in *JACOB'S ROOM* who works for Elizabeth DURRANT and is Mrs. PASCOE's nephew.

Curry, Miss In *THE WAVES,* she is apparently a governess in the first EPISODE, where she leads the six children in singing hymns and praying.

Curry, Sanders The name of the judge for whom Morris PARGITER clerks in *THE YEARS.*

Cutting, Miss A schoolmistress mentioned in *THE WAVES.*

Cymbeline A play by William SHAKESPEARE, lines from which recur in *MRS. DALLOWAY* after Clarissa DALLOWAY reads them in a book lying open in HATCHARDS' window. The lines—"Fear no more the heat o' the sun / Nor the furious winter's rages"—are from the dirge spoken by Guiderius and Arviragus over what they think is the body of Fidele, although it is in fact Imogen and she is not dead. Both Clarissa and Septimus Warren SMITH recall the lines throughout the day of the novel's action. Elizabeth Abel points out that Lucrezia SMITH's name recalls a poem of Shakespeare's, *The Rape of Lucrece,* which shares several plot elements with *Cymbeline*; she cites the villain of the latter, Jachimo, comparing himself to the rapist in the former and notes that he also refers to Imogen's reading the story of the rape of Philomela (see PROCNE AND PHILOMELA) (Abel 144n10).

D

Daily Herald A left-wing newspaper, associated with Trades Unions and the Labour Party, founded in 1912 that appeared as the *Weekly Herald* during World War I. Siegfried SASSOON became its first literary editor in 1920, and Andrew McNeillie suggests that E. M. FORSTER, who deputized for Sassoon, may have commissioned Woolf's first piece for the *Daily Herald* (E3 521), a 1920 review of a book on Mary Russell MITFORD ("The Good Daughter" E3 213–15). Woolf also reviewed in the *Herald* a book on George ELIOT in 1921, and in "MR. BENNETT AND MRS. BROWN" she illustrates the way society has changed in her lifetime by comparing the Victorian cook with the Georgian, the latter being someone likely to come upstairs to borrow the *Daily Herald* (CE1 320).

Daily Worker British Communist Party newspaper in which Woolf's "Why Art Today Follows Politics" appeared in 1936 (reprinted as "THE ARTIST AND POLITICS" [CE2 230–32]).

Daisy Name of Peter WALSH's lover in *MRS. DALLOWAY.* She is the wife of a Major in the Indian Army, and Peter has come to London to see his solicitors about her divorce.

Daladier, Edouard (1884–1970) French minister of defense in 1938, and minister of war from 1939. In *BETWEEN THE ACTS,* Bart OLIVER reads in his newspaper that M. Daladier has been successful in pegging down the franc (BTA 13; 216).

Dalingridge Place Home of George DUCKWORTH, where Woolf stayed for two months convalescing after her breakdown in 1913.

Dalloway, Clarissa (1) Character in *THE VOYAGE OUT* who also appears in the novel named for her, *MRS. DALLOWAY,* as well as in several sketches (MDP). In *The Voyage Out,* she and her husband, Richard DALLOWAY, join the *EUPHROSYNE* in Portugal as the ship is on the way to South America. Clarissa impresses Rachel VINRACE with her glamour and worldliness. She is fond of quoting lines of poetry, such as Percy Bysshe SHELLEY's "Adonais," and of appearing to be well read. Rachel finds that she wants to tell Clarissa things that she has never told anyone before (TVO 60). Christine Froula describes Clarissa as inviting Rachel "into conventional womanhood" and sees both Clarissa and her husband as defenders of the marriage plot that Rachel attempts to resist (Froula, "Out of" 145–46).

Dalloway, Clarissa (2) The title character of Woolf's fourth novel, *MRS. DALLOWAY.* She also appears in several sketches Woolf wrote that have been collected in *MRS. DALLOWAY'S PARTY,* edited as "a short story sequence" by Stella McNichol, some of which are used in the novel. In 1922 Kitty MAXSE, a figure from Woolf's Victorian adolescence, died in a fall at her home that Woolf surmised could have been a suicide. The character of Clarissa seems to draw on Woolf's memories of Kitty, a person for whom Woolf wrote in 1925 that she had a certain distaste, adding "one must dislike people in art without its mattering" (D3 32).

Clarissa is seen at the beginning of the novel preparing to go out to buy flowers for the party she is giving that evening. She has recently been ill, suffering from heart disease, which has meant her sleeping alone. From the first few lines of the novel and all the way through it, Clarissa is haunted by memories of her adolescence at BOURTON, her family home. Significant among these memories is her rejection of the marriage proposal of Peter WALSH, and the "most exquisite moment" of her life when Sally SETON kissed her. From others we learn that Clarissa's sister, Sylvia Parry, was killed in sight of Clarissa by a tree felled by their father. As a result of this, Clarissa has evolved an "atheist's religion of doing good for the sake of goodness" (MD 118). She is a complex character who seems to have chosen the safety of marriage to the rather ponderous Richard as opposed to the unpredictability of a life with Peter Walsh or the scandal of a relationship with a woman. Although Peter describes her as having been a Radical in her youth, he thinks now that Clarissa's opinions have been subsumed in Richard's.

Critics have expressed ambivalence about the character, Nancy Topping Bazin finding that her portrayal "detracts from the importance of what happens to her" (Bazin 123). Many have described Clarissa as a mythical figure with powers of unifying (Love, *Worlds* 146), someone who can regenerate a world undone by war. Throughout the novel Clarissa is linked in a variety of ways with Septimus Warren SMITH, a character she never meets but whose death has a profound effect on her when she hears about it. After his death, Suzette Henke writes, Clarissa is "ready to offer her guests the illumination that will transfigure the gathering into a beatified communion of saints" (139). Less sympathetic views are exemplified by that of John G. Hessler, who finds that Clarissa is unaware of how she is implicated in the world of class and money that defines her; he sees Clarissa's worldview as condoned by the lack of irony in the narrative.

Clarissa herself is ambivalent about her role as "Mrs. Richard Dalloway" and reflects often during the day of the novel on her own identity, as Howard Harper (112) and Mark Hussey (*Singing* 24–29), among others, have discussed. This has led at least one critic, Lucio Ruotolo, to call her an "existential hero" and others, including Susan Squier and Avrom Fleishman, to see her as transcending the limitations of her class position.

Robert Kiely has discussed the relation between Woolf's choice of her heroine's name and that other famous CLARISSA, Clarissa Harlowe, whose name is the title of Samuel Richardson's long novel (1747–48). Noting that Woolf was "certainly aware of the conventions governing the titles of novels of English domestic life," Kiely says that by calling her novel *Mrs. Dalloway* Woolf is drawing attention to the difference between her plot and the traditional plot that had marriage as its resolution: "Like Joyce and Lawrence, she has little interest in presenting marriage as a final solution to life or as a convenient stopping point for narrative fiction" (Kiely, *Beyond* 119). An interesting suggestion on the significance of Clarissa's name has been made by Jane Marcus, who points out that Clarissan nuns were an order of women who were married but took a vow of celibacy and were nuns in secret, thus not threatening the family by living as a community of women (*Languages* 118). In the novel, Clarissa goes up to her attic room "like a nun withdrawing" (MD 45).

At her party, Clarissa's eyes fill with tears when Mrs. HILBERY tells her that she looks like her mother (MD 267), but Clarissa cannot dwell on this thought while her guests are arriving. When she overhears Sir William BRADSHAW talking about Septimus's death, however, she withdraws into a little room "like the prayer closet of traditional devotion" (Fleishman 93) to contemplate alone what this death means. Feeling that somehow Septimus has died for her, Clarissa experiences a mystical sense of connection with him.

Dalloway, Elizabeth Clarissa and Richard DALLOWAY's daughter in *MRS. DALLOWAY*. Elizabeth is first seen going out to the ARMY AND NAVY Stores with Doris KILMAN, her tutor who loves her but by whom Elizabeth is somewhat repelled. As Rachel Bowlby has pointed out, Elizabeth represents a generation of women whose options were very different from those of her mother's. Riding on her own on a bus up the Strand, Elizabeth thinks that she might become a farmer, or a doctor, or even go into Parliament (MD 207).

Elizabeth, who is described as looking different from the rest of her family, "an Oriental mystery" (MD 186), feels awkward at the tension between her mother and Miss Kilman and longs to escape from the latter's intensity of feeling for her. Alone in London, Elizabeth responds quite differently from Clarissa to urban space, feeling a sense of possibility. The reader's sense of Elizabeth's own possibility is somewhat undercut by the last sight of her, standing by her father at her mother's party with her hair done up fashionably and wearing a pink dress.

Dalloway, Richard (1) Character in *THE VOYAGE OUT* who also appears in *MRS. DALLOWAY*. He and Clarissa, his wife, join the *EUPHROSYNE* in Portugal as the ship is on the way to South America. Richard is a Conservative politician temporarily out of office who is on a "fact-finding" tour of various countries. Against women's SUFFRAGE, contemptuous of art, and imperialist, Richard represents a type that Woolf's fiction often critiques. In conversation with Rachel VINRACE, he describes the state as a complicated machine in which citizens are parts and tells her that he never discusses politics with his wife because women do not have "the political instinct" (TVO 67). Following a storm at sea, Richard one day finds Rachel alone on deck and they go to her room to talk, where he suddenly kisses her, provoking in Rachel an extremity of emotion and, that night, a terrifying nightmare. Several critics have commented on the likely connection between Richard Dalloway and Woolf's half-brother George DUCKWORTH as "erotic pursuer" (Rose). When Richard discusses the danger to ships of "duckweed" (TVO 42), many readers have understood this to be an allusion to the incest suffered by Woolf. Roger Poole, for example, writes that Rachel's nightmare of being in a tunnel that leads to a vault where a deformed man gibbers on the floor establishes leitmotifs for George Duckworth (*Unknown* 36) and is linked to a passage in *THE YEARS* where Rose PARGITER sees a man exposing himself (TY 28–29) (which, Poole notes, Quentin BELL locates in an actual event [*Unknown* 37]).

Dalloway, Richard (2) A character in *MRS. DALLOWAY,* husband of Clarissa DALLOWAY. Richard is a Conservative member of Parliament described by Peter WALSH as possessed of the "public-spirited, British Empire, tariff-reform, governing-class spirit" (MD 116) yet also as someone who would be happier farming in Norfolk. Woolf wrote to Philip MORRELL that she had intended readers to like Richard (L3 195), which is perhaps why she makes him find Hugh WHITBREAD—whom she intended readers not to like—an "intolerable ass" (MD 173). After lunch with Lady BRUTON, Richard buys a bunch of roses for Clarissa and intends to tell her that he loves her, but when he gets home he finds he cannot say those words (yet she understands what his roses mean). Richard is solicitous of Clarissa, making her rest for an hour after lunch because a doctor had once advised it. At her party at the end of the novel, Sir William BRADSHAW tells Richard about Septimus's suicide as it has some bearing on a parliamentary bill concerning the deferred effects of shell shock (MD 279).

Damien, Father (Joseph Damien de Veuster) (1840–89) A Belgian priest who spent his life after 1873 ministering to the needs of 700 lepers at a colony on the island of Molokai, Hawaii. Robert Louis Stevenson wrote an entry on him for *Chamber's Biographical Dictionary* in 1890. In 1909 Woolf met a Mrs. Campbell in Florence who had set the life of Father Damien to verse (PA 401; QB1 143). Woolf used this character for Mrs. DUGGAN in *JACOB'S ROOM,* and in *THE VOYAGE OUT,* Terence HEWET tells Rachel VINRACE that he has an aunt Rachel who has put the life of Father Damien into verse (TVO 141).

Dante Alighieri (1265–1321) Principally known for his masterpiece *The Divine Comedy,* and author also of the *Vita Nuova,* which contains his poems expressing love for Beatrice. Septimus Warren SMITH in *MRS. DALLOWAY* reads Dante's *Inferno* until his wife Rezia gently shuts the book. Commenting on the meaning of Septimus's name, Beverly Ann Schlack writes that "behind Dante's use of the number *seven* loomed the collected rhetorical power of the seven deadly sins and the seven sacraments" (*Continuing* 70); she also provides much detail on the *Inferno's* relevance to Septimus. In *THE WAVES,* the *Inferno* is alluded to as JINNY descends into a Tube (subway) station.

In *THE YEARS,* Eleanor PARGITER, staying with her brother Morris PARGITER, picks up a book and reads two lines from it before she goes to sleep (TY 212). The lines are from Canto 15 of Dante's *Purgatorio.* Brenda Silver points out that several entries in Woolf's reading notebooks about Dante link her reading of him to her work on *The Years* (RN 244). On December 2, 1934, Woolf wrote that she could not read Dante after revising *THE PARGITERS,* and Mitchell Leaska notes her omission of Dante from an October 1934 list of books she was reading.

Darwin, Charles (1809–82) See *VOYAGE OUT, THE.*

Darwin, Gwen See RAVERAT, Gwen.

Datchet, Mary Character in *NIGHT AND DAY* who is a friend of Ralph DENHAM. She is first seen at her apartment where she is hosting a meeting of a group of young people who come to hear William RODNEY give a paper. Mary volunteers at the "S.G.S.", a SUFFRAGE organization, but she is doubtful of the effectiveness of this kind of work and very critical of Sally SEAL and Mr. CLACTON, with whom she works. Before the novel ends she has left to join with Mr. BASNETT in the Society for the Education of Democracy. It is likely that Woolf drew on Margaret Llewelyn DAVIES in her characterization of Mary, though there are also traces of Davies's companion and assistant Lilian Harris in the portrayal. Mary tells Katharine HILBERY, to whom she is very attracted, that she has managed to achieve an independent life in London chiefly by being "disagreeable" to her family. She has a sister, Elizabeth, who is still living at home caring for their father, the Reverend Wyndham Datchet, and two brothers, Edward and Christopher. Her father is rector of the parish of Disham and talks of nothing but trains. Mary is in love with Ralph but when she realizes he is infatuated with Katharine she resolves to dedicate her life to her work.

Davidson, Angus Henry Gordon (1898–1980) One of those friends who Woolf wrote in the ironic preface to *ORLANDO* "have helped me in ways too various to specify." He was an assistant at the HOGARTH PRESS from 1924 to 1927, succeeding George RYLANDS, and had a fairly stormy relationship with Leonard WOOLF. His biography of Edward Lear was published in 1938 and he became well known as a translator of Italian.

Davies, Margaret Caroline Llewelyn (1861–1944) General Secretary of the WOMEN'S COOPERATIVE GUILD from 1889 to 1921, in which capacity she was assisted by her lifelong companion Lilian Harris (1866–1949). Davies was the daughter of the Reverend John Llewelyn Davies, a Christian Socialist who had tutored Leslie STEPHEN before his entry into Cambridge University. Leonard WOOLF knew two of Davies's brothers, Crompton and Theodore, at Cambridge, where they were both elected to the APOSTLES. Davies herself was a contemporary of Janet CASE at GIRTON COLLEGE, graduating in 1883; her aunt Emily Davies was one of the founders of Girton. Adrian STEPHEN's daughter Ann married Davies's nephew, Richard. Leonard Woolf describes Davies in his autobiography as "one of the most eminent women I have known" (LW2 71). It was at her invitation that he and Woolf traveled to Newcastle in 1913 to attend the Women's Cooperative Guild annual conference, an event Woolf recalled in "MEMORIES OF A WORKING WOMEN'S GUILD," her introduction in the form of a letter to Davies for *Life As We Have Known It* (1931). Other works by Davies include *The Women's Cooperative Guild* (1904), *Maternity: Letters from Working Women* (1915), and an introduction to C. Webb's *The Woman with a Basket: The History of the Women's Cooperative Guild* (1927). Jane Marcus has suggested Davies as a source for both Mary DATCHET in *NIGHT AND DAY* and Eleanor PARGITER in *THE YEARS* (*Languages* 73) and comments that the "lifelong friendship between Woolf and Davies was built on family connections, feminism, socialism, and pacifism" (*Languages* 72).

Day Lewis, Cecil (1904–72) One of the "Oxford Poets" of the 1930s centered around W. H. AUDEN. The HOGARTH PRESS published several collections of his poems, beginning with *Transitional Poem* in 1929.

Day to Day Pamphlets See HOGARTH PRESS.

Death of the Moth and Other Essays, The This is the first posthumously published collection of Woolf's essays, published by the HOGARTH PRESS in Britain and Harcourt, Brace & Company in the United States in 1942. In an "Editorial Note," Leonard WOOLF explains that he has chosen essays that had been previously published and some that had not. He illustrates the fact that Woolf invariably revised even a brief review many times by relating a story about the author of a book Woolf had reviewed who requested a copy of the original typescript after her death. On looking for it, Leonard says he found "no fewer than eight or nine complete revisions of it" (DM viii). Leonard also says here that he usually corrected the punctuation and "obvious verbal mistakes" of her manuscripts before they were published. Among the essays included in this collection are: "STREET HAUNTING," "The Novels of E. M. Forster," "Middlebrow," "CRAFTSMANSHIP," "A LETTER TO A YOUNG POET," "PROFESSIONS FOR WOMEN" and "THOUGHTS ON PEACE IN AN AIR RAID."

Debrett Commenting on the lack of available information about the lives of women, Woolf remarks in *A ROOM OF ONE'S OWN* that she can find all she needs to know about "Sir Hawley Butts" in "Burke or Debrett" (AROO 85). Debrett's *Illustrated Baronage and Knightage* and *Illustrated Peerage* of Great Britain and Ireland have been published annually since 1865.

Deffand, Madame Du, Marie de Vichy-Chamrond (1697–1780) Mentioned in *ORLANDO* (O 199), she was a French literary hostess and close friend of Horace Walpole, author of *The Castle of Otranto*.

Defoe, Daniel (1660–1731) Author of *Robinson Crusoe* (1719), *Moll Flanders* (1722), *A Journal of the Plague Year* (1722) and *Roxana* (1724), among other works. On the 200th anniversary of the publication of *Robinson Crusoe*, Woolf wrote "The Novels of Daniel Defoe" for the *TIMES LITERARY SUPPLEMENT* (April 24, 1919), later revised and included in the *COMMON READER* as "Defoe" (CE1 62–68). Woolf's essay "Robinson Crusoe" was published in the *NATION & ATHENAEUM* in 1926 and was considerably revised for inclusion in the *COMMON READER: SECOND SERIES*. In this essay Woolf makes the argument that great writers impose their own perspective on their readers, a point that E. M. FORSTER found to be "a dreary Bloomsbury conclusion" (*Aspects* 164). Defoe is included in the ironic preface to *ORLANDO* as one of the writers to whom any subsequent writer is perpetually indebted.

Delaprée, Louis A French journalist in Madrid during the SPANISH CIVIL WAR whose pamphlet *The Martyrdom of Madrid* Woolf drew upon in writing *THREE GUINEAS*. Patricia Laurence has commented that Delaprée's "war front reports and the articles and pictures in the London *Times* on the bombardment and massacre in Madrid [in 1936] . . . profoundly affect Woolf's view of the Spanish civil war and her later involvement in the insurgents' and refugees' cause" ("Facts" 234).

Demeter and Persephone Demeter (the Roman Ceres) was the daughter of Saturn and Rhea. Her daughter Persephone (Roman Proserpine) became the wife of Hades, god of the underworld, who carried her off against her will. Zeus intervened and Hades had to agree to allow Persephone to spend half the year with her mother (summer) and half with him (winter). Woolf's *TO THE LIGHTHOUSE* has been discussed in terms of this mother-daughter myth by several feminist critics.

Dempster, Carrie A character in *MRS. DALLOWAY* who is eating her lunch in Regent's Park when Septimus and Lucrezia Warren SMITH sit there before his appointment with Sir William BRADSHAW (MD 39–40). Looking at Maisie JOHNSON, a young woman who has just arrived in London from Edinburgh, Mrs. Dempster reflects on her hard life and wishes she could whisper a word of advice to Maisie and get sympathy from her.

Denham, Joan Character in *NIGHT AND DAY*, the elder sister of Ralph DENHAM. She is in some ways a prototype of Eleanor PARGITER in *THE YEARS*, seeming to be the one member of the family to whom everyone turns for support and advice. She is the only member of his family that Ralph feels he can talk to, and his sister is very fond of him, finding him more interesting than anyone else she knows. Joan is one of several women in the novel whose lives have been sacrificed for their families. The characterization possibly draws on Bella WOOLF, Leonard WOOLF's sister.

Denham, Ralph Character in *NIGHT AND DAY.* Woolf probably drew on her husband, Leonard WOOLF, in the characterization of Ralph, and he also shares several characteristics with Harry Davis, the protagonist of Leonard's novel *THE WISE VIRGINS.* Ralph, a lawyer, meets Katharine HILBERY when he is invited to tea by her father, for whose *Critical Review* Ralph writes. Although he is angered by what he perceives as Katharine's upper-class innocence of life, he decides to make a conquest of her. As the novel unfolds, Ralph develops a fantasy of Katharine that frequently comes into conflict with the actual person when he meets her. This fantasy life is at odds with Ralph's image of himself as someone who has contemptuously dismissed "dreams" from his life.

Ralph hurts his friend Mary DATCHET, who is in love with him, not realizing how his infatuation with Katharine is obvious to her. Mary has undertaken Ralph's political education, turning him from Tory to Radical by taking him to public meetings (ND 129).

Unpopular at work because he is so rigid, Ralph is also tormented by family life and spends most of his time at home in his room alone with a sign reading "OUT" on the door. He brings Katharine home to meet his "six or seven" brothers and sisters (Joan DENHAM, James, Johnnie, Charles, Hester, Herbert, and Molly) and his mother. Ralph's father—like Leonard's—died prematurely, leaving the family worried about money and unable to send Ralph's brother Charles to university. His being Jewish is suggested by his family's address in Highgate, Mt. Ararat Road. Woolf probably drew on several young men of her acquaintance in developing Ralph's character. At one point, for example, he talks with a friend, Harry SANDYS, in terms highly suggestive of the philosophy of G. E. MOORE that influenced Leonard and his contemporaries at Cambridge (e.g., "I hear that Bennett has given up his theory of truth" [ND 65]).

De Quincey, Thomas (1785–1859) Among De Quincey's major works are *Confessions of an English Opium Eater* (1822, revised 1856), *Suspiria de Profundis* (1846), "The English Mail Coach" (1849), and a famous essay "On the Knocking on the Gate in *Macbeth*" (1823). De Quincey was one of Woolf's favorite writers and influenced such writers as Edgar Allan Poe and Charles Baudelaire. Woolf's essay "IMPASSIONED PROSE" exemplifies her regard for him. In *NIGHT AND DAY,* Mrs. COSHAM is delighted to learn that Ralph DENHAM still reads De Quincey. John Ferguson has suggested that the figure of Augustus CARMICHAEL in *TO THE LIGHTHOUSE* is based on De Quincey.

Diaghilev, Sergei Pavlovich See RUSSIAN BALLET.

Dial New York literary and cultural periodical (1880–1929) that began in Chicago. Woolf contributed "Mrs. Dalloway in Bond Street" (see *MRS. DALLOWAY'S PARTY*) in 1923 (SF 146–53), and "Miss Ormerod" in 1924.

Diana of the Crossways See MEREDITH, George.

Diary *The Diary of Virginia Woolf,* published in five volumes by the HOGARTH PRESS in Britain and in the United States by Harcourt Brace Jovanovich, 1977–84, comprises thirty notebooks in which Woolf kept a diary between 1915 and 1941. The notebooks are in the BERG COLLECTION, at the New York Public Library, where they were deposited in 1970, having been acquired from Frances Hamill and Margery Barker, who had bought them from Leonard WOOLF in 1956. The diary was edited with notes by Anne Olivier BELL, who was assisted on volumes 2 to 5 by Andrew McNeillie; endpaper maps of various parts of London and Sussex were drawn by Woolf's great-nephew Julian Bell for the British edition. The diary was published as follows: Volume 1, 1915–19 (1977); Volume 2, 1920–24 (1978); Volume 3, 1925–30 (1980); Volume 4, 1931–35 (1982); and Volume 5, 1936–41 (1984). Bell published corrections to some of her notes in VWM 10:7.

Reviewing the first volume in 1977, Margaret Comstock pointed out that Woolf had kept a diary for several years prior to 1915 and hoped that this might be published by the New York Public Library. Woolf's diary for the years 1897–1909 was published in 1990 with the title *A PASSIONATE APPRENTICE,* edited by Mitchell A. Leaska. A selection from Woolf's diary was published in 1990 under the title *A Moment's Liberty: The Shorter Diary,* abridged and edited by Anne Olivier Bell. Barbara Lounsberry has recently discussed a diary that Woolf kept at ASHEHAM HOUSE in 1917 and 1918 that is not included in Bell's edition; Lounsberry writes that Bell plans to publish portions of this diary in the *Charleston Magazine.* (See also Dominick ARGENTO; *A PASSIONATE APPRENTICE*; WARBOYS; *A WRITER'S DIARY.*)

Diary of a Nobody Staying with her brother Morris PARGITER in the "1911" section of *THE YEARS,* Eleanor PARGITER finds this satire by George Grossmith in her bedroom, but does not read it. Mitchell Leaska has suggested that Woolf may have had in mind Jules

Romain's *The Death of a Nobody,* translated in 1911 by Desmond MACCARTHY and Sydney WATERLOW (*Novels* 207n20).

Dickens, Charles (1812–70) Of this celebrated English novelist, Woolf's father Leslie STEPHEN wrote in the *DICTIONARY OF NATIONAL BIOGRAPHY* that "if literary fame could be safely measured by popularity with the half-educated, Dickens must claim the highest position among English novelists" (Annan 331). In two reviews concerning Dickens, Woolf made the point that his works were often read aloud to young children so that it was difficult for them to remember exactly when a particular work of his had been read for the first time. In "Dickens by a Disciple," a 1919 review for the *TIMES LITERARY SUPPLEMENT* of W. Walter Crotch's *The Secret of Dickens,* Woolf speculated that "no one has suffered more than Dickens from the enthusiasm of his admirers, by which he has been made to appear not so much a great writer as an intolerable institution" (E3 25). The "precise moment for reading Dickens seldom comes our way," she wrote in "David Copperfield," a 1926 review in the *NATION & ATHENAEUM* of *The Uncommercial Traveller; Reprinted Pieces and Christmas Stories* (CE1 191–95; M 76). She considered *David Copperfield* Dicken's "most perfect" novel, but she wrote that he failed with upper- and middle-class characters and with "mature emotions" (CE1 192). Despite these failures, however, she also wrote that we "remodel our psychological geography" when we read Dickens (CE1 193), such is his creative power. Woolf certainly considered Dickens one of the most important English novelists, remarking in *A ROOM OF ONE'S OWN* that, like William Makepeace THACKERAY and Honoré de BALZAC, Dickens wrote "a natural prose," an example of that masculine style she said was unsuitable for a woman writer's use.

Woolf herself re-read Dickens throughout her life; in the late 1930s, for example, she was re-reading several of his novels. In "ON RE-READING NOVELS," her response to Percy Lubbock's book *The Craft of Fiction,* Dickens is one of the writers she recommends people read to see how novelists have handled narrative. In "PHASES OF FICTION," including Dickens among "The Character-Mongers and Comedians," she analyzes his "prodigious" powers of creating character, using *Bleak House* as her example. She wrote in 1934 to George RYLANDS that Dickens was one of the novelists who create character through dialogue (L5 334). Throughout her life, Woolf identified Dickens with London and with a kind of Cockney vitality that she enjoyed from a distance, such as, for example, when overhearing people talk on a bus (D3 165). In 1941, in a letter to Ethel SMYTH, Woolf wrote that to her London represented "Chaucer, Shakespeare, Dickens. Its my only patriotism" (L6 460).

Dickens, Mr. The "bath-chair man" in *JACOB'S ROOM* who attends Captain BARFOOT's wife while he visits Betty FLANDERS.

Dickinson, Goldsworthy Lowes (1862–1932) Writer and proponent of international government who coined the term "League of Nations." Known as "Goldie," he was a contemporary at Cambridge University of Roger FRY, with whom he was in love; although he returned Dickinson's affection, Fry's heterosexuality led to their relationship changing to lifelong friendship. Dickinson was a member of the APOSTLES and became in 1887 a fellow of King's College, where Leonard WOOLF and Lytton STRACHEY met him when they went up to Trinity College in 1889. Among his books are *From King to King* (1891), *Revolution and Reaction in Modern France* (1892), *The Development of Parliament in the Nineteenth Century* (1895), *The Greek Way of Life* (1896), *The Meaning of Good* (1901) and *Letters from John Chinaman* (1901), a best-seller published in the United States in 1903 as *Letters from a Chinese Official, being an Eastern view of Western Civilization.* In the Woolfs' library were Dickinson's *Appearances* (1914), *The Choice Before Us* (1917), *Causes of International War* (1920) and *International Anarchy 1904–1914* (1926) (Holleyman). E. M. FORSTER wrote a biography of his friend, *Goldsworthy Lowes Dickinson* (1934), that Woolf found "quite futile" (D4 247) as it concealed his homosexuality. Leonard Woolf wrote that he was criticized by some of Dickinson's friends for including Woolf's disparaging remarks about Dickinson in *A WRITER'S DIARY,* made while she was writing her biography of Fry (see D4 361). Leonard defended his decision by explaining that Woolf was very fond of Dickinson but could be irritated by his "thin vapour of gentle high-mindedness" (LW2 137). In 1931, Woolf proudly quoted to Ethel SMYTH Dickinson's opinion that *THE WAVES* was a "great poem" that deals with "what is perpetual and universal" (L4 395). On hearing of his death, Woolf noted the "dismal details of the end of that fine charming spirit" (D4 120), and in a 1940 letter to Benedict NICOLSON defending the BLOOMSBURY GROUP against Nicolson's criticisms, Woolf said that Dickinson was among those who had done "an immense deal" (L6 414) to try to check Nazism in his own way.

Dickinson, Violet (1865–1948) A friend of Stella DUCKWORTH's who became an intimate friend of Woolf's around 1902, one of her earliest intense relationships with a woman. In 1903 Woolf wrote that she had "never kept a single letter all my life—but this romantic friendship ought to be preserved" (L1 75); a short time later she wrote to Dickinson that it was "astonishing what depths—hot volcano depths—your finger has stirred in Sparroy—hitherto entirely quiescent" (L1 85). Woolf referred to herself as Kangaroo, Sparroy, Sp., Wallaby, or Wall in letters to Dickinson, usually addressing her as My Violet, Aunt, My Beloved Woman, or My Woman. Throughout 1903, Woolf kept Dickinson informed of her father's slow decline, and, following her breakdown after Leslie STEPHEN's death in 1904, Woolf stayed at Burnham Wood, Dickinson's house in Welwyn, where she made her first attempt at suicide by throwing herself from a window.

In 1904 Dickinson proposed that Woolf should write for Margaret Lyttelton's Woman's Supplement of the *GUARDIAN*, which led to Woolf's first publications. Woolf seems to have become exasperated by Dickinson's comments on her work, as in 1905 we find her writing in her DIARY that she gets "nothing but criticism from Violet now—oh d———it" and determining to show her work only to editors, "whose criticism is important" (PA 232). In 1906 Woolf, Dickinson, and Vanessa BELL traveled together to Greece, where they met up with Adrian and Thoby STEPHEN. While Woolf and her brothers went on to stay with the Noel family, Dickinson remained in Athens to care for Vanessa, who had fallen ill. On their return to London, they found that Thoby, who had gone home earlier, was very ill with what was diagnosed too late as typhoid. Dickinson also had typhoid and when Thoby died in November 1906, Woolf continued to write to Dickinson with reports of his improvement to avoid burdening her friend. When Dickinson discovered Thoby's death, mentioned in a review of F. W. MAITLAND's biography of Leslie Stephen, Woolf wrote that she hoped Dickinson would understand that she had had to keep the news from her, fearing it would worsen her own illness (L1 266). In 1907, Woolf presented Dickinson with "FRIENDSHIPS GALLERY," a mock biography of her that also refers extensively to Dickinson's close friend Lady Robert CECIL, with whom she had gone on a world tour in 1905.

Their intimacy began to fade when the focus of Woolf's life shifted to her BLOOMSBURY GROUP friends. As Woolf recalled in "OLD BLOOMSBURY," Dickinson disapproved of her move to BRUNSWICK SQUARE in 1911, invoking her mother's ghost to deplore Woolf's lifestyle (MOB 201). They kept in touch throughout Woolf's life, Woolf writing in 1919 that "we have had our intimacy; something or other has fused; & never hardens again" (D1 273), but they did not correspond frequently (Betty Kushen points out that only two letters passed between them from 1929 to 1936 [42]). Dickinson is one of those friends who "have helped me in ways too various to specify" mentioned in the ironic preface to *ORLANDO*. In December 1936, Dickinson sent Woolf typescripts of about 350 letters she had received from Woolf nearly thirty years previously, bound in two volumes.

Dictionary of National Biography In *NIGHT AND DAY* Katharine HILBERY tells Ralph to think of her at home "looking up dates in the 'Dictionary of National Biography' " as she helps her mother write the biography of her grandfather, Richard ALARDYCE. Leslie STEPHEN, Woolf's father, was the first editor of the *Dictionary*, beginning in 1882. This "monument to the Victorian age" (Annan 87) eventually comprised sixty-three volumes and included 29,120 lives. Leslie Stephen edited the first twenty-six volumes himself and wrote 378 of the biographies. Woolf later remarked that her brother Adrian STEPHEN had been crushed in the womb by the weight of this vast work of her father's (D2 277). In *ORLANDO*, the biographer remarks that "whatever the *Dictionary of National Biography* may say," the true length of a person's life is always a matter of dispute (O 305–06). Note 36 to chapter 2 of *THREE GUINEAS* regrets that "no lives of maids . . . are to be found in the *Dictionary of National Biography*." *The Contributors' Index to the Dictionary of National Biography, 1885–1901* by Gillian Fenwick is published by St. Paul's Bibliographies and Omnigraphics, and lists both contributors and the articles they wrote.

Dixon, Richard Watson (1833–1900) One of the vast mass of Victorian writers ORLANDO reads in the nineteenth-century section of *ORLANDO*, Dixon published an elaborate *History of the Church of England from the Abolition of Roman Jurisdiction* (1877–1900) and several volumes of poems. He was a friend of Robert Bridges and Gerard Manley Hopkins.

Dodd, Francis (1874–1949) An artist who made several sketches of Woolf for a portrait between October 1907 and July 1908. He later used the sketches for etchings, one of which is in the NATIONAL GALLERY.

Dodge, William Character in *BETWEEN THE ACTS*. He is brought by Mrs. MANRESA, who introduces him as an artist, to Bart OLIVER's house on the day of the annual village pageant. He corrects her, saying he is "a clerk in an office" (BTA 38), leading Isa OLIVER to understand intuitively why he seems so tortured. Isa's husband, Giles OLIVER, despises William because he is a homosexual (60); William is attracted to Giles. During an intermission of the pageant, William is taken by Lucy SWITHIN to look round Pointz Hall, her family home, and feels drawn to tell her about his difficulties (in a way that strongly recalls Charles TANSLEY's feelings about Mrs. RAMSAY in *TO THE LIGHTHOUSE*). William also feels empathy with Isa and the two talk "as if they had known each other all their lives" (114). Isa and William feel that they are (like RHODA and LOUIS in *THE WAVES*) "conspirators."

Donne, John (1572–1631) English metaphysical poet and dean of St. Paul's from 1621 to 1631. Woolf's "Donne After Three Centuries" was written for *THE COMMON READER: SECOND SERIES*. In 1922 she reflected that Donne was one of those who had a touch of "some queer individuality" that she respected in writers and identified as a quality in herself (D2 168).

Dostoyevsky, Fyodor Mikhailovich (1821–81) Russian novelist whose major works are *Crime and Punishment* (1866), *The Idiot* (1868), *The Devils* (1871) and *The Brothers Karamazov* (1880). His work became well known in England through the translations between 1912 and 1920 by Constance GARNETT. In *NIGHT AND DAY,* Katharine HILBERY walks along the Strand repeating to herself a line from *The Idiot,* "It's life that matters" (ND 135). Later in that novel, Cassandra OTWAY mocks William RODNEY for not having read *The Idiot* (ND 347–48). Dostoyevsky is one of the literary identifications made by BERNARD in *THE WAVES*.

Woolf was profoundly influenced by Dostoyevsky, whom she considered one of "the greatest writers of our time" (E2 70). In "More Dostoyevsky," a review for the *TIMES LITERARY SUPPLEMENT* in February 1917 of Constance Garnett's translation of *The Eternal Husband and Other Stories* (E2 83–86), Woolf described Dostoyevsky's ability to render the flow of consciousness, writing that he was alone in being able to reconstruct "these most swift and complicated states of mind" (E2 85). Prefiguring an important theme of some of her best-known essays, such as "MODERN FICTION," and "MR. BENNETT AND MRS. BROWN," Woolf wrote that Dostoyevsky's was "the exact opposite of the method adopted, perforce, by most of our novelists" (E2 85). William Handley has remarked on the curious fact that Woolf shared her enthusiasm for Dostoyevsky with Arnold BENNETT (VWM 31: 3).

In "A Minor Dostoevsky," a TLS review on October 1917 of *The Gambler and Other Stories* (E2 165–67), Woolf wrote of the value of reading the "second-rate works of a great writer" because they provide "the very best criticism of his masterpieces" (E2 165). Dostoyevsky's range was so vast, she wrote, that "some new conception of the novelist's art remains with us in the end" (E2 167). Other reviews of works by or about Dostoyevsky are "Dostoevsky in Cranford" (E3 113–15), an October 1919 TLS review of *An Honest Thief and Other Stories,* and "Dostoevsky the Father" (E3 327–31), a January 1922 TLS review of *Fyodor Dostoevsky: A Study,* by the writer's daughter Aimée Dostoyevsky.

Downhill All the Way, An Autobiography of the Years 1919–1939 The fourth volume of Leonard WOOLF's autobiography, published by the HOGARTH PRESS in 1967 and reprinted in Britain and the United States in the Oxford University Press two-volume edition, *An Autobiography* (1980). This volume begins with the Woolfs moving to MONK'S HOUSE and covers the period up to the death of Leonard's mother and the outbreak of World War II.

Doyle, Minta Character in *TO THE LIGHTHOUSE,* a guest of Mr. and Mrs. RAMSAY. Mrs. Ramsay wonders how Minta's parents, whom she has nicknamed the Owl and the Poker (TTL 56), could have produced "this tomboy Minta," who is now twenty-four (TTL 60). There seems to have been some friction between Minta's mother and Mrs. Ramsay that reminds Mrs. Ramsay of someone else who had accused her of "robbing her of her daughter's affections" (57). In part 1, Minta is at the beach with Paul RAYLEY, and Andrew and Nancy RAMSAY; Minta is very upset when she loses a brooch that had belonged to her grandmother. When they are not back in time for dinner, Mrs. Ramsay is certain that Paul and Minta are engaged, a fact she verifies when they enter the dining room. Minta's glow makes Mrs. Ramsay momentarily jealous (TTL 99). Mr. Ramsay finds Minta attractive and, seated next to him at the dinner in section XVII of part 1, Minta flirts with him.

Jane Lilienfeld has noted the highly sexual "imagery of garish red and gold in which Minta is always celebrated" ("Where the Spear Plants" 164). Margaret Homans, commenting on Minta's leaving the last volume of George ELIOT's *Middlemarch* in a train, interprets this as signifying Woolf's celebration of "the abandonment of the mother as purveyor of the conventional female fate" (*Bearing* 278). She also remarks that Minta's lying about her intelligence to please Mr. Ramsay shows that she has learned the lesson of the ANGEL IN THE HOUSE (279).

In part 3 of *To the Lighthouse,* we learn from Lily BRISCOE's memories that the marriage of Paul and Minta has not been happy. They have two sons, but Paul is now involved with another woman, which has led them into a companionate marriage. Vara Neverow-Turk, commenting on this arrangement, writes that it is "not surprising that in *To the Lighthouse* the hints that Minta Doyle has lesbian inclinations are subtle and scattered about through the book rather than grouped together in an obvious fashion" (VWM 39:9).

Drabble, Margaret (b. 1939) English novelist and critic. She has discussed Woolf's influence on her in "Virginia Woolf: A Personal Debt" (Homans, *Collection* 46–51).

Dreadnought Hoax On February 10, 1910, Woolf, her brother Adrian STEPHEN, Anthony Buxton, Horace COLE, Duncan GRANT and Guy Ridley took a train to Weymouth. Woolf was wearing "a turban, a fine

Principals in the Dreadnought Hoax. Courtesy of The Bettmann Archive.
From left to right: Virginia Woolf, Guy Ridley, Adrian Stephen, Anthony Buxton, Duncan Grant, Horace de Vere Cole.

gold chain hanging to her waist, and an embroidered caftan." Her face was black and she had "a very handsome moustache and beard" (QB1 157). The friends were out to perpetrate a hoax on the British Navy: posing as the Emperor of Abyssinia and his retinue, and speaking a mixture of Swahili and whatever Latin the men could remember from school, the six managed to get a guided tour of the navy's most secret warship, the *HMS Dreadnought*. To add to Woolf's delight, one of the officers greeting the royal party with formal honors on the deck of the warship was her own cousin William FISHER, a flag commander. When the story found its way into the newspapers, the navy, understandably, was embarrassed. The first lord of the Admiralty was questioned in Parliament about the incident. For Woolf, perhaps, it provided an insight into the military's love affair with appearance and impressive costumes. J. J. Wilson has described the hoax as a "forerunner of Yippie agitprop" ("Why" 183n12) and S. P. Rosenbaum has remarked that the hoax displayed the BLOOMSBURY GROUP's emerging anti-military outlook, "which is closely related to an increasing disillusionment with imperialism." Rosenbaum traces a clear line in Woolf's development from the hoax to *THREE GUINEAS* (*Edwardian* 223).

To satisfy the navy's honor, Duncan Grant was abducted from his parents' home one morning by several officers and taken to Hampstead Heath, where he was administered a few ceremonial taps with a cane. Woolf alludes to the incident in her short story "A SOCIETY," where "Rose" tells of having "dressed herself as an Aethiopian prince and gone aboard one of His Majesty's ships." Her brother Adrian's account of the escapade was published in 1936 by the HOGARTH PRESS (Rosenbaum, *Bloomsbury Group* 32–43).

Dryden, John (1631–1700) This English poet and dramatist, appointed Poet Laureate in 1668, makes an anachronistic appearance in *ORLANDO* in the company of Alexander POPE and Joseph ADDISON. Dryden appears only as a name in *Orlando*, but Beverly Ann

Schlack notes that his influence on Woolf goes back to her sixteenth year when she wrote "a long picturesque essay, . . . called *Religio Laici*" (*Continuing* 173n63). Dryden's poem "Religio Laici, or a Laymans Faith" was published in 1682. Vita SACKVILLE-WEST recalls in *Knole and the Sackvilles* (145) that Dryden was saved from debt by Charles Sackville, who paid his pension even after he was ousted as Laureate.

"Duchess and the Jeweller, The" (SF 242–47) A short story by Woolf first published in *Harper's Bazaar* in April 1938 and reprinted in *A HAUNTED HOUSE*. It concerns Oliver Bacon, a Jew who is "the richest jeweller in England" (SF 243).

Duchess of Malfi In *A ROOM OF ONE'S OWN*, the Duchess of Malfi, eponymous heroine of the tragedy by John WEBSTER (1580?–1625?), is offered as an example of women who have "burnt like beacons in all the works of all the poets from the beginning of time" (AROO 43), whom Woolf uses to stress the difference between fictional and real women. The Duchess, a widow, secretly marries Antonio against the wishes of her brothers. The brothers eventually separate them and the Duchess and two of her children are strangled.

Duckworth, George Herbert (1868–1934) Woolf's elder half-brother, the first son of Herbert DUCKWORTH and Julia Prinsep STEPHEN. George was educated at Eton and Trinity College, Cambridge, and, after several unsuccessful attempts at entering the Foreign Service, became private secretary to Charles BOOTH in 1892, and then to Austen CHAMBERLAIN in 1902. "No more perfect fossil of the Victorian age could exist," Woolf wrote of her half-brother in "A SKETCH OF THE PAST" (MOB 151). In September 1904, he married Lady Margaret Leonora Evelyn Selina Herbert (1870–1958), second daughter of the fourth Earl of Carnarvon (father of the discoverer of Tutankhamen's tomb), with whom he had three sons. They lived at Dalingridge Place, where Woolf stayed for two months convalescing after her breakdown in 1913.

After the death of their mother, George assumed responsibility for the social education of Vanessa BELL and Woolf, escorting them to dinner parties and dances. When Vanessa proved recalcitrant, George turned his attentions to Woolf, but neither of the Stephen sisters acquiesced in his reverence for "Society."

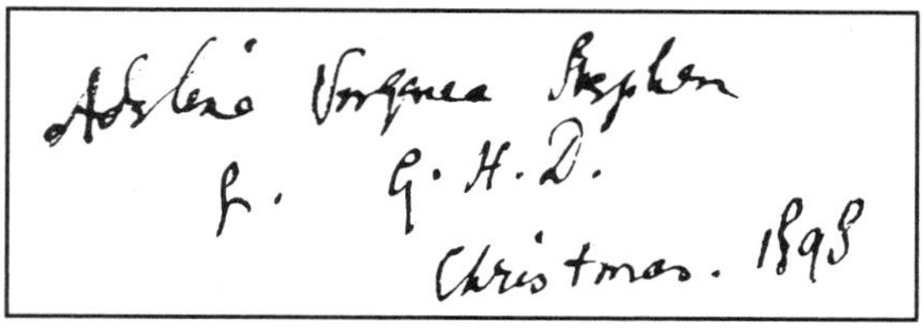

Inscription to "Adeline Virginia Stephen from G. H. D. [George Herbert Duckworth] Christmas. 1898" in Selected Poems *by Matthew Arnold. Courtesy of Cecil Woolf and Jean Moorcroft Wilson.*

Woolf wrote three portraits of her half-brother, in "REMINISCENCES," "A Sketch of the Past," and "22 HYDE PARK GATE" (all of which are in MOB, whose editor, Jeanne Schulkind, suggests George may have provided a model for Hugh WHITBREAD in *MRS. DALLOWAY*). In "Reminiscences" and "A Sketch of the Past," Woolf portrayed George as stupid, shallow, and obsessed with social proprieties. Her portrait of him in "22 Hyde Park Gate," a paper she read to the MEMOIR CLUB in about 1920–21, is more bitter and contains many images of George as a disgusting animal. This paper ends with an account of George creeping into her darkened bedroom and flinging himself on her bed, smothering her in kisses. The story is repeated in a slightly different version (which Louise DeSalvo speculates might in fact be an account of another occasion altogether) in "OLD BLOOMSBURY."

The incest that Woolf suffered has been variously euphemized by several of her biographers and other critics: for example, Quentin BELL speaks of "a nasty erotic skirmish;" Joanne Trautmann Banks speaks of Woolf being "sexually caressed" (CS 65n3); Mitchell Leaska writes of "sexual interference." Leaska and Phyllis Rose have even suggested Woolf fabricated or embellished her account of the incest she suffered. Woolf herself named George as the perpetrator of her incest in the closing paragraph of "22 Hyde Park Gate" and also told Janet CASE and Ethel SMYTH about her "incestuous brother" in detail. In "Old Bloomsbury," Woolf wrote that George had explained his behavior to Dr. George SAVAGE as his attempt to comfort Woolf for "the fatal illness of my father—who was dying three or four storeys lower down of cancer" (MOB 182).

Woolf recorded mixed emotions when she learned that George had died at Freshwater in 1934, writing in her diary and to her sister that as she had had little contact with their half-brother for so many years her feelings toward him had softened, yet also that despite his being a significant part of her childhood, his death meant very little to her.

Duckworth, Gerald de l'Etang (1870–1937) Woolf's second half-brother, the youngest child of Herbert DUCKWORTH and Julia Prinsep STEPHEN, born after his father's death. Gerald was educated at Eton and Clare College, Cambridge, and in 1898 established a publishing firm with A. R. Walker. According to Woolf's memoir "A SKETCH OF THE PAST," Gerald was rather more supportive of her resistance to entering polite Society than was his brother George DUCKWORTH, who was obsessed with decorum. When the Stephen children planned their move to 46 GORDON

SQUARE in 1904, Gerald was content to move to a "bachelor flat," while George wanted to move with his half-siblings (a fate from which they were saved by his marriage that year). Gerald married Cecil Alice Scott-Chad in 1921, when he was fifty.

In March 1913, Leonard WOOLF took the manuscript of Woolf's first novel, *THE VOYAGE OUT,* to Duckworth & Co., where it was read by Edward GARNETT, who gave the manuscript an "extremely appreciative report" (LW2). The book was not published, however, until 1915, owing to Woolf's breakdown in 1913–14. By 1913, Duckworth & Co. was well established and had published Henry JAMES, Joseph CONRAD, John GALSWORTHY, Edward Thomas, and Ford Madox Ford (Willis 47). Duckworth also published several novels by Dorothy RICHARDSON. In 1919, he published Woolf's second novel, *NIGHT AND DAY,* but according to Woolf, as she wrote to Janet CASE, Gerald did not "know a book from a beehive." The Woolfs bought the rights to her first two novels from Duckworth (Gerald was "a little cross," wrote Woolf in her DIARY) and reissued them from the HOGARTH PRESS in 1929 and 1930.

Woolf suffered extreme anxiety in 1913 when the manuscript of *The Voyage Out* was delivered to her half-brother. In 1918 she met with him to discuss her next book, and she wrote in her diary that "his likeness to a pampered overfed dog has much increased. . . . He has no opinions but merely a seaweeds drift in the prevailing current. His commercial view of every possible subject depressed me, especially when I thought of my novel destined to be pawed & snored over by him" (D1 March 1918). Her opinion of both her half-brothers was similar in that she believed them to be obtuse and shallow; in her autobiographical writings she refers to each of them in terms of animals. In 1936 she wrote of going to tea with Gerald as "like visiting an alligator in a tank, an obese and obsolete alligator."

In "A Sketch of the Past" Woolf, writing of "some of my first memories," recalled how Gerald had molested her when she was "very small," lifting her onto a slab outside the dining room and "exploring" her "private parts" (MOB 69); she connected this incident with her sense of shame of her own body and her fear of mirrors. She repeated the story in a letter to Ethel Smyth in 1941.

Duckworth, Herbert (1833–70) First husband of Woolf's mother, Julia Prinsep STEPHEN, and father of George, Stella and Gerald DUCKWORTH. Herbert was a friend of Herbert FISHER, who married Julia's sister Mary Louisa. Julia met him in 1862 with her mother on a trip to Venice to see her sister. Herbert was a barrister of no great distinction, educated at Eton and Trinity College, Cambridge. He and Julia married in 1867. In autobiographical writings, Woolf recalls that "Herbert Duckworth's barrister's wig" would turn up in her nursery closet, a dusty relic of the past. She also remarks in "A SKETCH OF THE PAST" that the great happiness her mother had known with her first husband disappeared forever upon his death.

In 1870, while staying at Upton Castle with Henry Halford Vaughan (who had married Julia's other sister, Adeline Maria; see VAUGHAN, Margaret), Herbert stretched to pick a fig, burst an abscess, and died shortly afterward. Stella later told Woolf that their mother would lie upon Herbert's grave in her grief (MOB 90). Leslie STEPHEN's description of Herbert (whom he knew slightly at Cambridge) in his *MAUSOLEUM BOOK* makes him sound a little like one of Chaucer's Canterbury pilgrims: "A man of honour, of fair accomplishments and interest in books, he was fitted to take his place in any society, without being the least of a dandy or a fop: simple, straightforward and manly" (Stephen, *Mausoleum* 35).

Duckworth, Julia See STEPHEN, Julia Prinsep.

Duckworth, Stella (1869–97) The second child of Julia Prinsep STEPHEN and Herbert DUCKWORTH, Woolf's half-sister was an important figure in her

"Virginia" ["Virginia Woolf née Stephen" written in ink along the bottom of the photograph] from Stella Duckworth Hills's album of photographs. Courtesy Henry W. and Albert A. Berg Collection, the New York Public Library, Astor, Lenox and Tilden Foundations.

childhood. In "A SKETCH OF THE PAST," Woolf says that Stella escaped "all taint of Duckworth philistinism" (MOB 97). Her father having died the year after her birth, Stella grew up in the shadow of her mother's profound grief. Even Leslie STEPHEN noticed that Julia treated her daughter much more harshly than either of her sons; the reason, Julia told him, was that Stella seemed more part of herself than either George or Gerald DUCKWORTH. As soon as Stella was of age, Julia chaperoned her to balls, but despite the attentions of several young men she remained singularly attached to her mother. Woolf wrote that "They were sun and moon to each other; my mother the positive and definite; Stella the reflecting and satellite" (MOB 96). From 1890 to 1892 Stella suffered the attentions of her cousin James Kenneth STEPHEN, who was infatuated with her and whom Julia and Leslie allowed into their house despite his evident mania. Louise DeSalvo suggests that J. K. Stephen may have raped Stella (*Impact* 52–54).

Even before her mother's death in 1895, Stella often assumed responsibility for the Stephen household while Julia was away "doing good." When Julia died, Stella had little time for her own grief as Leslie Stephen assumed she would immediately take her mother's place. In "REMINISCENCES" Woolf wrote that "I do not think that Stella lost consciousness for a single moment during all those months of his immediate need" (MOB 41). As primary caretaker for the Stephen children after 1895, Stella often appeared as drained and pale, as Julia had always seemed to Woolf: "She grew whiter and whiter in her unbroken black dress" (MOB 94). Woolf's 1897 diary (PA) records Stella's frequent visits to Laura STEPHEN, as well as the daily round of shopping for clothes and ordering meals. Woolf records Stella's plans to build cottages for the poor (PA 8n24), a philanthropic act that Woolf incorporates in her characterization of Eleanor PARGITER in *THE YEARS* (and see "chapter fifty-six" of *THE PARGITERS*). Stella gave Vanessa BELL her first music lesson and taught her the art of letter-writing. She also took responsibility for Woolf in her breakdown following Julia's death.

Much to Leslie Stephen's displeasure, Stella accepted the marriage proposal of John Waller "Jack" HILLS in 1896. He had been encouraged by Julia in his attentions to Stella, but she had refused an earlier proposal of his in 1894. Woolf was distressed early in 1897 at being made to accompany the engaged couple to Bognor Regis, and she was alarmed not long afterward at the "terrible idea" that she and Vanessa should be Stella's bridesmaids. The wedding—for which a 60-pound cake was ordered—took place on April 10, 1897, and Woolf wrote "Goodness knows how we got through it all—Certainly it was half a dream, or a nightmare" (PA 68). On the same date, her father wrote "Today Stella was married in Kensington Church to J. W. Hills. I will not put down even here the thoughts which have agitated me. Of the marriage itself there is of course nothing to say except that it is in all respects thoroughly satisfactory" (*Mausoleum* 102).

Leslie Stephen's selfish attitude toward Stella caused her marriage to be delayed, and it was only after a confrontation with him that it was agreed the couple would not live at 22 HYDE PARK GATE; a house for them was found at number 27. Soon after their marriage, Stella fell ill and in July 1897 she died. The cause of her death is unclear, but most accounts give it as peritonitis and note that Stella was pregnant at the time. The night before she died, she was operated on and the doctors pronounced the operation a success. In her diary for July 19, 1897, Woolf wrote "At 3 this morning, Georgie and Nessa came to me, & told me Stella was dead—" (PA 115). Stella was buried next to her mother in Highgate Cemetery.

In "A Sketch of the Past," Woolf wrote that her half-sister's engagement to Jack Hills provided her "first vision of love between man and woman. . . . It gave me a conception of love; a standard of love; a sense that nothing in the whole world is so lyrical, so musical, as a young man and a young woman in their first love for each other" (MOB 105). Stella is recalled in the character Prue RAMSAY in *TO THE LIGHTHOUSE.*

Dudding, Miss and Tom Dudding Mentioned in *JACOB'S ROOM,* on the hunt with Jacob FLANDERS in Essex (JR 101).

Dudley, Uncle In *NIGHT AND DAY* Katharine HILBERY forgets a basket of oysters on a bench in the STRAND, which means that Uncle Dudley, who is coming to dinner that evening, will get no oysters.

Duffus, Mr. A contractor in *THE YEARS* who has built houses (badly) for the poor under Eleanor PARGITER's direction.

Duggan, Mrs. A woman in *JACOB'S ROOM* whose story Sandra Wentworth WILLIAMS tells rather dramatically. She is putting the life of Father DAMIEN into verse, as was a Mrs. Campbell whom Woolf met in Florence in 1909 (QB1 143).

Duggins, Alfred A poacher mentioned in *NIGHT AND DAY.*

Duke of St. Simon In *THE WAVES,* LOUIS imagines himself as this French army officer and famous memoirist who served under King Louis XIII.

Dupper, Mr. One of ORLANDO's servants. A Mr. Dupper is listed in a catalog of the household of Richard Sackville, the seventeenth-century earl of Dorset, in *Knole and the Sackvilles* by Vita SACKVILLE-WEST.

Durbins The home near Guildford designed by Roger FRY for himself and his family in 1909.

Durrant, Clara Character in *JACOB'S ROOM* who comes to love Jacob, but does not ever tell him. The sister of his best friend from Cambridge, Timothy DURRANT, Clara is thought of by Jacob as "a virgin chained to a rock" and seems destined to spend her life pouring tea for polite young men and old gentlemen friends of her mother's. Mr. SALVIN thinks Clara lacks her mother's spirit (JR 86). At the end of chapter 7 it seems possible Jacob and Clara might connect, but as they go together to the kitchen during Mrs. Durrant's party, Clara is intercepted by a group of guests and has to entertain an American, Mr. PILCHER, they have brought with them. "And so Clara left him" (JR 89). Clara and her mother are also mentioned in *MRS. DALLOWAY* as guests at Clarissa DALLOWAY's party.

Durrant, Elizabeth The mother of Jacob's friend Timothy DURRANT and his sister Clara in *JACOB'S ROOM*. Mrs. Durrant is a sad and rather distant figure, loved by young people who flock to the parties she gives. When Jacob comes to stay with the Durrants for the first time, Mrs. Durrant speaks to him "as if she had known him all her life" (JR 62).

Durrant, Timothy In *JACOB'S ROOM*, Jacob's best friend while they are at Cambridge. Jacob and Timothy sail together from Falmouth to stay with Timothy's family, which consists of his sister Clara DURRANT and mother Elizabeth DURRANT, in their house that is always full of guests (rather similar to the Ramsays in *TO THE LIGHTHOUSE*). At the end of the novel, Timothy is seen working as a clerk at WHITEHALL.

E

Ebury, Mrs. Mentioned in *BETWEEN THE ACTS* as having forbidden her daughter Fanny to act in the village pageant because she has nettle-rash. The narrator remarks that there was "another name in the village for nettle-rash" (64).

Edwardians, The Vita SACKVILLE-WEST's best-selling novel was published by the HOGARTH PRESS in 1930. The story begins in 1905 and is set in "Chevron," a thinly disguised KNOLE. In her author's note, Vita wrote "No character in this book is wholly fictitious." Following the fortunes of Sebastian and his sister Viola, the narrative ends in 1910. Woolf noted its huge sales in her diary and commented that "it is not a very good book" (D3 306). Suzanne Raitt (102–07) discusses this novel in which "lesbian intensity has been displaced into an account of a male homoerotic relationship" (Raitt, *Vita & Virginia* 103).

Edwards, Miss A character in *JACOB'S ROOM* who has a brief conversation with Mr. CALTHORP. There is also a Cissy Edwards in that novel whom Sandra Wentworth WILLIAMS startles by asking if she is happy; it is not impossible they are supposed to be the same person. But Milly Edwards is a waitress who chases after Fanny ELMER when she leaves her "umberella" [sic] in a tea shop (JR 119).

Egoist, The Magazine owned and edited by Harriet Shaw WEAVER of which T. S. ELIOT was assistant editor. It is also the title of a novel by George MEREDITH in which the character Vernon Whitford is based on Leslie STEPHEN.

Eleanor, Aunt Character in *NIGHT AND DAY* who appears briefly at tea with Uncle AUBREY to announce that insanity is not a "fit subject" for fiction (ND 348), though she concedes it is a different matter in the case of poetry when Mr. Hilbery mentions "the well-known case of *Hamlet*."

Eleanor The name of one of the two aunts who have raised Rachel VINRACE (in *THE VOYAGE OUT*) in Richmond since her mother died.

Elephant and Castle In *A ROOM OF ONE'S OWN,* Judith SHAKESPEARE's body is buried at the crossroads by the Elephant and Castle after her suicide. The name derives from a famous tavern in south London that stood at one of the busiest intersections in the city, where six roads met. The tavern was destroyed by bombing during World War II. In the nineteenth century there was also an Elephant and Castle Theater in the vicinity.

Elgin Marbles The sculptures and statues that comprised the Elgin Marbles were stolen from Greece by the Earl of Elgin at the end of the eighteenth century, sold to the British government and placed in the BRITISH MUSEUM in 1816. In *NIGHT AND DAY* Mary DATCHET spends her lunch hour in the British Museum looking at the Elgin Marbles with an emotion that is not purely aesthetic (a dig on Woolf's part at her brother-in-law Clive BELL's book *Art,* which expounds the doctrine of the "aesthetic emotion"). Mary is reminded of Ralph DENHAM, whom she loves, by the statue of Ulysses, as, in *JACOB'S ROOM,* Fanny ELMER visits the same statue to remind her of Jacob FLANDERS.

Eliot, George (Marian [or Mary Anne, or Mary Ann] Evans) (1819–80) Eliot's first published work was a translation of David Friedrich Strauss's *Das Leben Jesu, The Life of Jesus* (1846). One of the leading intellectuals of her time, she was assistant editor of the *Westminster Review* from 1851 to 1853, and she began contributing "Scenes of Clerical Life" to *Blackwood's Magazine* in 1857. Her novels are *Adam Bede* (1859), *The Mill on the Floss* (1860), *Silas Marner* (1861), *Romola* (published in the *CORNHILL MAGAZINE* 1862–63), *Felix Holt* (1866), *Middlemarch* (1871–72) and *Daniel Deronda* (1874–76). Woolf's father, Leslie STEPHEN, who knew her, wrote the entry on Eliot for the *DICTIONARY OF NATIONAL BIOGRAPHY,* and also the volume on her in the "English Men of Letters" series.

Alison Booth has called Eliot "arguably [Woolf's] most substantial literary inheritance" (Booth 3), describing both writers as "palace spies, consorting with patriarchal traditions to expose their flaws" (Booth ix). Although their origins were different, Eliot and Woolf can be read, says Booth, "as heroines struggling against much the same odds with much the same success" (62). Booth points out that both women "overcame the pieties of their upbringing, whether Evangelical or humanist (and Leslie Stephen's humanism owes much to Eliot), to consort with the freethinkers of their day; both triumphed over their educational disadvantages as girls to master classical and contemporary learning and literature." She also notes that both Woolf and Eliot were "dutiful daughters" whose intellectual work had often to give way to the demands made upon them by their families, "until they escaped to homes of their own." And, finally, "both lost their somewhat remote mothers while they were in their teens" (Booth 62).

At the beginning of *A ROOM OF ONE'S OWN,* Woolf suggests that a talk on women and fiction might include "a respectful allusion" to George Eliot (AROO 3). She later compares the constraints a woman writer like Eliot lived under to the freedom of Leo TOLSTOY. Like "Currer Bell" (Charlotte BRONTË) and George SAND, Eliot, wrote Woolf, "veiled" herself with a male pseudonym, "a relic of the sense of chastity" (AROO 50). Woolf also points out in *A Room* Eliot's debt to Eliza CARTER (1717–1806), a friend of the novelist Samuel Richardson and of Samuel JOHNSON.

Woolf wrote "George Eliot (1819–1880)" for the "Great Names" series in the *DAILY HERALD* in March 1921 (E3 293–95), and she reviewed R. Brimley Johnson's selection of *The Letters of George Eliot* for the *NATION & ATHENAEUM* in 1926. For much of 1919, Woolf was re-reading Eliot's novels in preparation for the centenary article she wrote for the *TIMES LITERARY SUPPLEMENT* in November that year. This article was revised for inclusion in the *COMMON READER* (CR1 205–18; CE1 196–204). Gillian Beer describes Woolf as "an honourable and obvious exception" to the majority of critics who ignored the feminist issues of *Middlemarch* until the 1970s (*George Eliot* 148). Woolf describes *Middlemarch* as "one of the few English novels written for grown-up people" (CE1 201).

The first half of Woolf's essay concerns Eliot's life, the circumstances of which Woolf believed had a significant influence on Eliot's fiction, from the religious atmosphere of her early childhood to the ostracism resulting from her living with George Henry Lewes, a married man. Woolf writes that Eliot has had many critics, invariably men who resented the lack of charm in her fiction (CE1 197). Later in the essay, Woolf criticizes Eliot's heroines, saying that no matter what disguises she may use, we always hear Eliot's own voice speaking through them: "Their story is the incomplete story of George Eliot herself" (CE1 204).

Lyndall Gordon has written that in *THE VOYAGE OUT,* Woolf "launched herself on a problem passed on by George Eliot" (*Writer's Life* 92), and several critics have drawn attention to Eliot's legacy to Woolf of intellectual rigor and concern with patriarchy. Beer notes that the writers' most autobiographical novels, *The Mill on the Floss* and *TO THE LIGHTHOUSE,* are "also those which most emphasize the polarization of sex roles" (Beer, "Beyond Determinism" 128). Beer argues that neither Eliot nor Woolf "escaped entirely the assumptions of determinism," but each tested the patriarchal implications of that idea in their fiction, going on to explore "territories beyond it" ("Beyond Determinism" 135).

Booth links Woolf and Eliot in their common concern for women's educational reform, noting that Eliot was a friend of Barbara [Leigh Smith] BODICHON and Emily Davies (the founder of GIRTON COLLEGE), both of whom Woolf refers to in *A Room* (Booth 45). In exploring intertextualities between Woolf and Eliot's fiction, Booth argues that Bart OLIVER and Lucy SWITHIN in *BETWEEN THE ACTS* "replicate the relationship between Tom and Maggie [Tulliver] in *Mill on the Floss*. . . . They are Victorians in this novel; their childhood memories echo those of the Tullivers" (Booth 145–46). Booth also sees correspondences between Eliot's *Romola* and Woolf's *ORLANDO,* as both "register public history as private experience" (Booth 170). Booth reads *THE YEARS* as a sequel to Eliot's *Felix Holt,* and sees Woolf's last novel, *Between the Acts,* as similar to Eliot's last work, *Daniel Deronda,* in that both "raise the ominous question of what comes next for a civilization rotting from within" (Booth 236). Miss LA TROBE, Booth suggests, is "in some sense Woolf's reincarnation of Eliot" (Booth 284). Makiko Minow-Pinkney has suggested that Mr. RAMSAY in *To the Lighthouse* is a condensation of Casaubon and Lydgate from Eliot's *Middlemarch* (Minow-Pinkney 89).

Eliot, Julia A friend of Elizabeth DURRANT's in *JACOB'S ROOM* who perhaps recalls Woolf's great-aunt Julia Margaret CAMERON, as she has Jacob sit for a photograph at the end of chapter 4. She reappears throughout the novel, liking to observe rather than participate at the Durrants' parties. She is last seen on her way to visit an old woman, Lady CONGREVE, who had known her mother.

Eliot, T. S. (Thomas Stearns) (1888–1965) Poet and critic born in St. Louis who settled in England in 1915, the year he married Vivienne Haigh-Wood. In 1918, having been impressed by *Prufrock and Other Observations* (1917), Leonard WOOLF wrote inviting him to send some poems to the HOGARTH PRESS. At the time Eliot was working at Lloyd's Bank and was also assistant editor of *The Egoist.* Leonard's letter led to a meeting and in 1919 the Hogarth Press published *Poems.* This marked the beginning of a friendship that gradually deepened throughout the 1920s and '30s. The Hogarth Press also published *The Waste Land* (1923) and *Homage to John Dryden: Three Essays on Poetry of the Seventeenth Century* (1924), fourth in the Hogarth Essays series. The latter contained Eliot's influential essay on "The Metaphysical Poets" in which he discussed what he called the "dissociation of sensibility."

Woolf's first impressions were of a "polished, cultivated, elaborate young American" (D1 218). Eliot was extremely formal and reserved, and Woolf found him and his views a little intimidating at first. He was a champion of Ezra Pound, Wyndham LEWIS and James JOYCE and held "dominant and subversive" opinions about these young writers (D2 67). In "CHARACTER IN FICTION," Woolf included Eliot with E. M. FORSTER, D. H. LAWRENCE, Lytton STRACHEY, and Joyce among "the Georgians" (E3 421). The Woolfs were drawn to Eliot and began inviting him to spend weekends at MONK'S HOUSE in the early 1920s. Almost as soon as their friendship had begun, it came close to being derailed by Clive BELL and Mary HUTCHINSON's indiscreet repetition of some remarks of Eliot's about the BLOOMSBURY GROUP (D1 262), but it was soon back on track.

Eliot's admiration of Joyce cast a shadow over Woolf's work on *JACOB'S ROOM* in late 1920, leading her to reflect that "what I'm doing is probably being better done by Mr Joyce" (D2 69). Years later, Woolf had not forgotten this, writing in 1935 that Eliot could now cast no such pall over *THE YEARS* (D4 344). Through Harriet Shaw WEAVER, editor of *The Egoist,* Eliot arranged for the Woolfs to see the manuscript of *Ulysses* in the hope that the Hogarth Press could publish it; it proved to be too difficult a task for the young press.

In March 1921 Woolf wondered in her DIARY, "But what about Eliot? Will he become Tom?" (D2 100). She felt that he did not admire her writing and was "astounded" in August 1922 when he praised *MONDAY OR TUESDAY,* singling out "THE STRING QUARTET" and "A Haunted House" (D2 125). In November 1921, she remarked wryly that she was disappointed no longer to be afraid of "Tom," as he had now become.

In June 1922, Eliot read "The Waste Land" to the Woolfs and others (D2 178). Convinced of his importance as a writer, Woolf became involved in a scheme with Lady Ottoline MORRELL (to whom Eliot had been introduced by Bertrand RUSSELL) to create an endowment that would enable him to leave the bank and write full-time. This scheme was hindered by Eliot's own prevarication and finally came to an end in 1928 when the money had to be returned to the subscribers. Although Woolf admired Eliot greatly and liked him, their relationship was not always easy. In 1925, for example, Eliot annoyed the Woolfs when he failed to tell them that Faber & Gwyer was bringing out his *Collected Poems*—including "The Waste Land," which Hogarth had allowed to go out of print. Just before she saw an advertisement for the new volume, Woolf had asked him about doing a new edition of the poem. Eliot asked her to write something for his magazine *The New Criterion* (see *CRITERION*) and, despite what she considered a lukewarm response, he published "ON BEING ILL" in January 1926.

Woolf described Eliot's wife Vivienne Haigh-Wood as a "bag of ferrets" around his neck, and in 1933 Eliot in fact left her. Woolf had sympathized with him, writing in 1929 that he was "a true poet, I think; what they will call in a hundred years a man of genius" (D3 223). After Eliot left Vivienne, he seemed to Woolf to be more easygoing and their intimacy deepened. He was "a dear old fellow: one of 'us,' " she wrote in 1935; "I felt I liked him as I liked Lytton [Strachey] & Roger [FRY]—with intimacy in spite of God" (D4 324). In 1927 Eliot, with Leonard as one of his sponsors, had become a British citizen; he also joined the Anglican Church, something which mystified the Woolfs. Woolf felt that Eliot was like her in some ways (D5 112), and several critics have pointed out the influence each writer had on the other. Eliot described Woolf's death as "a change to the world which is also a damage to oneself" (Noble 120) and said that with it "a whole pattern of culture is broken" (Noble 122).

Many have seen Eliot as a model for LOUIS in*THE WAVES* and have also pointed out the echo from *The Waste Land* in JINNY's "JUG, JUG, JUG" in that novel. Eliot's influence can also be detected in *The Years,* where the atmosphere of "Gerontion" is felt in descriptions of the Jewish tenant in Sara PARGITER's lodging. Molly Hoff has discussed the influence of *MRS. DALLOWAY* on Eliot's play *The Cocktail Party* (VWM 39: 4–5). In "Our Silent Life," Lyndall Gordon examines parallels between Woolf and Eliot's "ideas about the hidden essence and structure of lives which might serve, in turn, as guidelines for biographic studies of themselves" (77–78).

Elizabeth and Essex: A Tragic History See STRACHEY, Lytton.

Elkin, Major One of Colonel Abel PARGITER's cronies in *THE YEARS.*

Ellen A maid in *TO THE LIGHTHOUSE,* whom Augustus CARMICHAEL asks for another plate of soup (to Mr. RAMSAY's annoyance). Also the name of the "discreet black maid" of Mrs. CHINNERY in *THE YEARS* (TY 209, 210) and of Mrs. MALONE's maid in the same novel.

Elliot, Hilda Character in *THE VOYAGE OUT*. She is married to Hughling ELLIOT, who thinks her "a ninny" (TVO 164). It is through her husband's knowing Ridley and Helen AMBROSE that the two worlds of the hotel and the villa on SANTA MARINA are first brought into contact in the novel. Mrs. Elliot believes that having children is "the crown, as one may call it, of a woman's life" (TVO 115–16), and wishes she had children of her own.

Elliot, Hughling Character in *THE VOYAGE OUT*. He is an Oxford University professor whom Helen and Ridley AMBROSE know, thus effecting a connection between the guests at the hotel on SANTA MARINA and those staying in the Ambroses' villa. Mr. Elliot is satirized in the novel, described by the narrator as affected and anxious to ingratiate himself with young people. Near the end of the novel, Mr. Elliot is taken ill but recovers, unlike Rachel VINRACE, who is also ill but dies.

Elmer, Fanny A character in *JACOB'S ROOM* who falls in love with Jacob FLANDERS and tries to win his favor by reading Henry FIELDING, but her love is unrequited. While Jacob is on his Grand Tour in France, Italy and Greece, Fanny resorts to going to the BRITISH MUSEUM, where she sneaks up to the head of Ulysses (one of the ELGIN MARBLES), which reminds her of Jacob, only looking at it at the last moment.

Elmhurst, Mrs. Mentioned in *BETWEEN THE ACTS* as coming from a village ten miles from POINTZ HALL. She is nervous about the behavior of ALBERT, the village idiot.

Elton, Charles (1839–1900) In *TO THE LIGHTHOUSE,* Mr. RAMSAY and Augustus CARMICHAEL recite lines from Charles Elton's "Come out and climb the garden path / Luriana, Lurilee" as the dinner in section XVII of part 1 ends. The poem was first published in *Another World Than This . . .*, an anthology compiled by Vita SACKVILLE-WEST and Harold NICOLSON (London: Michael Joseph, 1945). In 1950, Leonard WOOLF answered an inquiry about the poem made by R. G. Howarth, informing him that Elton was a relation of Lytton STRACHEY's and that Strachey had given him a copy of the poem (Spotts 488).

Elvedon In *THE WAVES,* Elvedon is either a real or imaginary place that BERNARD takes SUSAN to see when she is upset and jealous because JINNY has kissed LOUIS. Looking over the wall, Bernard describes the sight of a woman who is seated at a table between two windows writing, while gardeners with long brooms sweep the lawn (TW 16). Seen by a black-bearded gardener, Bernard and Susan flee into the woods in fright. This image recurs to Bernard throughout his life. Susan also recalls Elvedon later in her life (TW 192, 214).

Irma Rantavaara identifies Elvedon as the children's private boarding school, but this is a unique interpretation (Rantavaara 10). For many critics, Elvedon represents what Makiko Minow-Pinkney calls "a utopia of feminine writing" (179); she understands Bernard's occasional generalization of the woman to "women writing" as suggesting that Elvedon symbolizes "female creativity" (Minow-Pinkney 179). Richard Pearce identifies Elvedon with what the linguist and psychoanalyst Julia Kristeva terms the "chora," "from the Greek word for enclosed space or womb, which houses the wild and threatening semiotic rhythm that runs beneath controlled symbolic expression" (Pearce 163). Pearce argues that the walls of Elvedon not only keep Bernard out but also confine the writing woman: "Bernard's story may express his fear of the lady writing, but it is also designed . . . to 'sentence' her, imprison her between the windows of her mansion to keep her in place" (Pearce 163).

Joseph Allen Boone, who perceives "two words hidden in the name . . . 'elf-eden,' " (631), discusses Elvedon as linked to Woolf's "own attempt to articulate a meaning beyond words" in *The Waves* (629). He points out that in an earlier draft, Susan and Bernard's adventure is presented as actual, but that in the published version, "the literalness of the event is much less clear" (630). Elvedon, according to Boone, " 'suggests' the shape of Bernard's life and Woolf's vision of existence" (630).

Elvira Name of a character in *THE PARGITERS,* a prototype for Sara PARGITER in *THE YEARS*.

Eminent Victorians In 1914, Lytton STRACHEY sent Woolf the manuscript of an essay on Cardinal Manning. She and other friends of his encouraged him to write more in a similar vein, and the result was *Eminent Victorians,* published in 1918, leading to a certain degree of fame for the author. In addition to "Cardinal Manning," the book contained essays on Florence NIGHTINGALE, Thomas Arnold (the famous headmaster of Rugby School), and "The End of General Gordon." In her essay "MR. BENNETT AND MRS. BROWN," Woolf includes Strachey among her list of Georgian writers, together with James JOYCE and T. S. ELIOT, who are going against the grain in creating new conceptions of character and whose work is evidence of the "effort and strain" of iconoclastic MODERNIST writing (CE1 335). In his preface, Strachey explained his new approach to character by saying that the modern biographer "will attack his subject in unexpected places; he will fall upon the flank or the rear; he will shoot a sudden, revealing searchlight into obscure recesses, hitherto undivined" (*Eminent Victorians* 9). Just as Woolf had skewered Arnold BENNETT in her essay, so Strachey indicts the biographers of Woolf's father's generation: "Those two fat volumes, with which it is our custom to commemorate the dead—who does not know them, with their ill-digested masses of material, their slipshod style, their tone of tedious panegyric, their lamentable lack of selection, of detachment, of design?" (ibid. 10).

Emma See AUSTEN, Jane.

Episodes The nine sections of *THE WAVES* that consist of the soliloquies of BERNARD, JINNY, LOUIS, NEVILLE, RHODA and SUSAN are usually referred to as episodes, distinguished from the italicized descriptions of nature that are referred to as INTERLUDES.

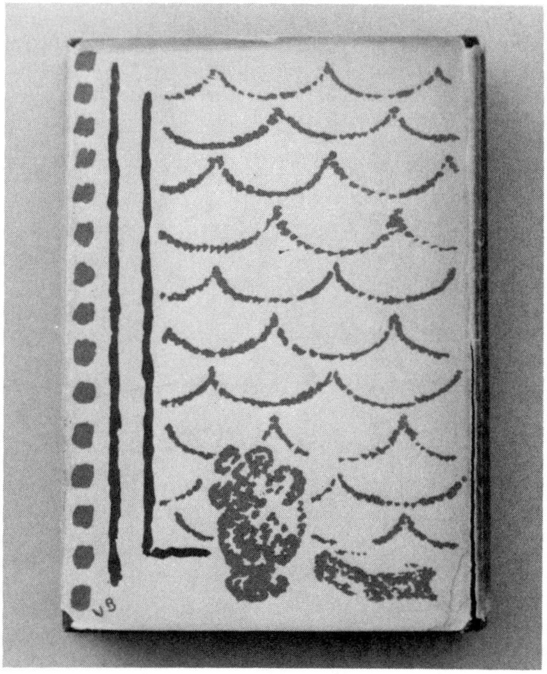

The Waves. *Courtesy Linda J. Langham.*
Vanessa Bell's dust jacket design for the first Hogarth Press edition (1931) gave an impressionistic rendering of waves on the front and back. Shown here is the back of the jacket, which suggests waves seen through a window; a vase of flowers and a book are in the foreground.

Ermyntrude, Lady In *BETWEEN THE ACTS* her bones are rumored to lie at the bottom of the pond at POINTZ HALL. In 1913 Lytton STRACHEY wrote a pornographic work called "Ermyntrude and Esmeralda" (published 1969).

Ernest A "boot boy" mentioned in *THE WAVES* when SUSAN sees him kissing Florrie, the "scullery maid."

Erridge A childhood friend of Martin PARGITER in *THE YEARS* with whom he later shares a room where they "smoke cheap cigars and tell smutty stories" (TY 222). While at lunch with his cousin Sara PARGITER in the "1914" chapter, Martin sees Erridge, who is now a stockbroker (TY 231).

Erskine, Mr. Mentioned at Elizabeth DURRANT's party in *JACOB'S ROOM.*

"Essay in Criticism, An" (CE2 252–58; GR 85–92) Woolf's review of *Men Without Women* by Ernest Hemingway, published in the *New York Herald Tribune* October 9, 1927; reprinted in *GRANITE & RAINBOW.* Woolf begins her essay with a discussion of *The Sun Also Rises,* finding that "if Mr. Hemingway is 'advanced', it is not in the way that is to us most interesting" (CE2 253). She makes clear that she is a MODERNIST critic and as such finds that Hemingway forms character in a conventional way. Commenting on the "sex consciousness" of the 1920s, Woolf finds that Hemingway's work is spoiled for women readers by a "display of self-conscious virility" similar to that she finds in James JOYCE and D. H. LAWRENCE (CE2 256). Woolf disingenuously says that she is using this essay to "reveal some of the prejudices, the instincts and the fallacies out of which what it pleases us to call criticism is made" (CE2 258). Barney Baley has pointed out Hemingway's irritation at Woolf's review, expressed in a letter to Maxwell Perkins (VWM 29:4; see also VWM 24: 2–3).

Etchells, Frederick and Jessie Painters and members of the FRIDAY CLUB. Frederick exhibited at the second POST-IMPRESSIONIST Exhibition in 1912. He and his sister were painted by Vanessa BELL that year ("Frederick and Jessie Etchells in the Studio") and both were involved in the OMEGA WORKSHOPS. Frederick attended the Woolfs' wedding in 1912.

"Etho passo tanno hai" The first line of the song sung by the caretaker's children near the end of *THE YEARS.* No one has yet been able to identify anything intelligible in the song.

Euphrosyne The name of the ship in *THE VOYAGE OUT* owned by Willoughby VINRACE on which Woolf's characters travel to SANTA MARINA. This was an in-joke on Woolf's part as *Euphrosyne* was the name of a volume of poetry privately printed in 1905 containing work by Clive BELL, Lytton STRACHEY, Walter LAMB, Saxon SYDNEY-TURNER, Thoby STEPHEN, Leonard WOOLF and others. Woolf wrote a scathing review (unpublished) of the volume in which she commented on the "advantage" of the custom "which allows the daughter to educate herself at home, while the son is educated by others abroad" (QB1 205. Appendix C in volume 1 of Quentin Bell's *Virginia Woolf: A Biography* prints Woolf's review). Euphrosyne is also the name of a "nodding mass of lace and ceremony" (O 40) mentioned as a possible wife for ORLANDO. Euphrosyne (Joy) was one of the three Graces, Greek goddesses who presided over social events.

Euphues Described by Miss ALLAN in *THE VOYAGE OUT* as "the germ of the English novel" (TVO 253), John Lyly's prose romance *Euphues: The Anatomy of Wit* was published in 1578 (part 1) and 1580 (part 2). Its peculiar and extravagant style is the origin of the term "euphuistic." The relevance of *Euphues* to *The Voyage Out* is discussed by Louise DeSalvo (*First Voyage* 21).

Euston A railway station in London mentioned in *THE WAVES* (TW 112).

Evans In *MRS. DALLOWAY,* the name of Septimus Warren SMITH's officer and friend, killed in battle, by whose ghost Septimus is haunted.

"Evening Party, The" (SF 90–95) An unfinished short story that Susan Dick dates to the period when Woolf was writing the pieces collected in *MONDAY OR TUESDAY*.

Everest, Louie (née West) (1912–77) The cook and housekeeper at MONK'S HOUSE from 1934 on, she worked for Leonard WOOLF until his death. Louie and her first husband lived in one of two cottages the Woolfs owned. She seems to have been a welcome respite from the tribulations of Nellie BOXALL and Lottie HOPE; in his autobiography Leonard wrote that she was "the only person whom I have ever known to be uniformly cheerful and with reason for her cheerfulness" (LW2 441). In 1936 she earned a Diploma in Advanced Cooking. Woolf records in a letter that Louie addressed a meeting of the Rodmell Labour Party in 1939. A photograph of her appears in LW2. In 1962 she married Konrad Mayer.

"Experiences of a Pater-familias, The" The sequel to "A COCKNEY'S FARMING EXPERIENCE," a story Woolf wrote for the *HYDE PARK GATE NEWS*. Both pieces were published in 1972 by San Diego State University Press, edited by Suzanne Henig, as a gift for subscribers to the *VIRGINIA WOOLF QUARTERLY*. Louise DeSalvo has described this story as "very subversive" and "different from anything else that Virginia wrote as a child" (*Impact* 139). It concerns the same Cockney couple as the earlier story, three years later when they have a child.

Eyres, Mr. Mentioned in *THE WAVES* as someone with whom the businessman LOUIS has an appointment (TW 168).

F

Fabian Society See WEBB, Beatrice and Sidney.

"Fade far away and quite forget . . ." In *BETWEEN THE ACTS,* Isa OLIVER recites these lines from John KEATS's "Ode to a Nightingale" to William DODGE.

Farrell, Sophie (also Sophia or Sophy) (c. 1861–1942) The Stephen family cook from the 1880s. In "A SKETCH OF THE PAST," Woolf recalls lowering a basket down from the night nursery in ST. IVES to "Sophie's kitchen," which was directly below, in the hope of getting food from the adults' dinner; if Sophie was in a good mood the basket would be laden with food, but if she were not the string would be cut! Leonard WOOLF includes a letter from Sophie to Woolf in LW2 as, he says, an illustration that her life "had become entirely absorbed in the life of the Stephen family." In the forty years she worked for the family, Sophie Farrell went from 22 HYDE PARK GATE to 29 FITZROY SQUARE, after Vanessa BELL's marriage to Clive BELL, and to 50 GORDON SQUARE, where she worked for Adrian STEPHEN and later again for Vanessa (also sometimes looking after her three children). She also worked for a time for Herbert DUCKWORTH's sister Sarah (Aunt Minna), and for George DUCKWORTH's sister-in-law, Lady Victoria Herbert. Finally, she worked for George Duckworth and his wife who, according to Quentin BELL, "still played the game in the old way." There is much of her character in the family servant CROSBY in Woolf's *THE YEARS.* In 1931, Woolf wrote a sketch drawing on Sophie's character called "The Cook," two typescript drafts of which are in the MONK'S HOUSE PAPERS (D4 48n4)

Fawcett, Millicent Garrett (1847–1929) Born to a reform-minded East Anglian family, Millicent Garrett Fawcett was described as "the Mother of Women's Suffrage." She made her first speech at the second meeting of the London Women's SUFFRAGE Committee and led the National Union of Women's Suffrage Societies (N.U.W.S.S.) from 1890 to 1919. Among her most successful writings was *Political Economy for Beginners* (1870), which quickly went through ten editions. Ann Oakley has remarked that it was Fawcett's nationalism that made her "a primary instigator of the move . . . entirely to suspend the suffrage campaign" during World War I that the N.U.W.S.S. reluctantly adopted (196). Her sister Elizabeth Garrett Anderson was the first woman to qualify as a doctor (in 1865).

"Fear no more . . ." See *CYMBELINE.*

Femina-Vie Heureuse The Prix Femina, one of France's oldest and most famous literary prizes, was founded in 1904 by the review *Femina.* The journals *Vie Heureuse* and *Vie Pratique* have also participated in sponsoring it, so it has been called Prix Femina-Vie Heureuse or Prix Femina-Vie Pratique. For twenty years, between 1920 and 1939, the prize was also awarded annually for "the best English work suitable for translation into French" (Jane Clapp, *International Dictionary of Literary Awards* [New York: Scarecrow Press, 1963]: 376). Woolf's *TO THE LIGHTHOUSE* won the 1928 prize, beating novels by Stella BENSON and Storm Jameson.

Fenwick Mentioned in *THE WAVES* when NEVILLE catches sight of him playing croquet at school (TW 51).

Fernham The "OXBRIDGE" college loosely based on NEWNHAM COLLEGE which is the setting for part of *A ROOM OF ONE'S OWN.*

Fielding, Henry (1707–54) English novelist mentioned in *THE VOYAGE OUT* when Clarissa DALLOWAY is described as having photographed Fielding's grave in Lisbon and records in her diary that she "let loose a small bird which some ruffian had trapped" because she "hates to think of anything in a cage where English people lie buried" (TVO 39–40). In 1905, Woolf herself "let loose a caged bird that was singing by Fieldings tomb—a pious act!" (PA 262). Among Fielding's works are *Joseph Andrews* (1742) and *Tom Jones* (1749).

Filmer, Mrs. The name of Septimus and Rezia Warren SMITH's landlady in *MRS. DALLOWAY*. Mrs. Filmer recommends Dr. HOLMES for Septimus when he behaves oddly. Just before he dies, Septimus and Rezia laugh about Mrs. Peters, Mrs. Filmer's married daughter, for whom Rezia makes a hat. When Septimus is dead, Mrs. Filmer flaps her apron in front of Rezia to prevent her seeing his body.

Finch, Anne, Countess of Winchilsea (1661–1720) At the beginning of chapter 4 of *A ROOM OF ONE'S OWN*, Woolf takes down from her bookshelf the poems of Lady Winchilsea expecting to find "that her mind was disturbed by alien emotions like fear and hatred and that her poems showed traces of that disturbance" (AROO 58). Anne Finch and her husband had positions at the court of the Duke of York (later King James II). After King James was exiled and replaced by William of Orange, Anne and Heneage Finch lived in what Sandra M. Gilbert and Susan Gubar describe as "a kind of political exile of their own" (*Norton* 99) until Heneage Finch inherited a distant cousin's estate, Eastwell, and title of Earl of Winchilsea; he and Anne went to live at Eastwell. There, she wrote many pastoral poems and brooded on the lot of women writers. Although she was friendly with Alexander POPE, he caricatured her as "Phoebe Clinket" in a play he coauthored with John GAY and John Arbuthnot, *Three Hours after Marriage*, and wrote a satirical "Impromptu" responding to her criticism of his "Rape of the Lock." Woolf stresses Finch's bitterness in *A Room*, noting that even though her poetry was praised, her "gift is all grown about with weeds and bound with briars" (AROO 61). Finch's *Miscellany Poems on Several Occasions, Written by a Lady* was published in 1713. Woolf bases her remarks on Finch in *A Room* on the introduction to a 1928 edition of *Poems by Anne, Countess of Winchilsea* edited by John Middleton MURRY. ORLANDO is reported to have once broken Lady Winchilsea's fan while making a rhyme (O 83).

Firle See CHARLESTON.

"Fisherman and his Wife, The" In *TO THE LIGHTHOUSE*, Mrs. RAMSAY reads this fairytale by the Brothers Grimm to her son James RAMSAY to distract him from his disappointment at being told by his father that he will not be able to go to the lighthouse the following day. Many commentators on the novel have pointed out that the tale has significant thematic resonances with Woolf's novel, although several also see the roles of husband and wife in the novel and the tale reversed. The tale concerns a magic flounder which grants wishes to a fisherman and his wife. As the wife's wishes become more and more grandiose, the sea becomes rougher and rougher, the sky darker and darker. Eventually the wife wishes to be god. In the holograph draft of *To the Lighthouse*, Mrs. Ramsay reads first "The Three Dwarves," then "The Three Bears." It is only in the published version of the novel that James is told the story of "The Fisherman and His Wife," which Jane Marcus interprets as an example of how Mrs. Ramsay helps her son work through his Oedipal conflict (*Languages* 154).

Fishers, The Woolf's first cousins. Julia Prinsep STEPHEN's sister Mary Louisa (Aunt Mary, 1841–1916) married Herbert William Fisher (1825–1903), tutor to the Prince of Wales. They had seven sons and four daughters, most of whom make frequent appearances in Woolf's early diary (PA). The Fishers lived at Brighton, where Vanessa BELL and Woolf were forced to visit them, to their displeasure. Aunt Mary was knocked down and killed by a car in 1916 ("a positive stroke of genius," Woolf wrote wickedly to her sister [L2: 114]).

Adeline Fisher married the composer Ralph Vaughan Williams in 1897. Also notable among the Fisher cousins was William Wordsworth Fisher ("Willy," 1875–1937), who received the party of the "Emperor of Abyssinia" during the DREADNOUGHT HOAX in 1910 when he was flag-commander of the Royal Navy's Home Fleet; it was William Fisher who, accompanied by three naval officers, kidnapped Duncan GRANT in revenge for the embarrassment caused the navy.

Herbert Albert Laurens Fisher (1865–1940) is the Fisher most often mentioned in Woolf's DIARY. A historian, fellow and later warden of New College, Oxford, H. A. L. Fisher served in the Cabinet of David LLOYD GEORGE during World War I, and as President of the Board of Education. In 1902 he had read Leslie STEPHEN's Ford Lectures at Oxford when Woolf's father was too weak to do so himself owing to the bowel cancer that would cause his death in 1904. Learning of the imminent end of the war from her cousin in October 1918, Woolf wrote in her diary: "I tried to think it extraordinary but I found it difficult—extraordinary, I mean, to be in touch with one who was in the very centre of the very centre, sitting in a little room at Downing Street" (D1 204). In 1933, writing to her nephew Quentin BELL, Woolf called Herbert "all that is refined and stately." Leonard WOOLF ran as the Seven Universities' Democratic Association candidate against the Liberal Herbert in the parliamentary election of 1920, Herbert being, according to Leonard, "the kind of man whom in those days I thought it to be almost a public duty to oppose in public life" (LW2 210). H. A. L. Fisher married Lettice, the great-niece of F. H. and A. C. Bradley.

Among other Fisher cousins were Florence, who married Leslie Stephen's authorized biographer,

F. W. MAITLAND; Emmeline (Emmie, 1868–1941); Hervey (c. 1873–1921); Edmund ("Jo," 1871–1918); Cordelia ("Boo," 1879–1970); Charles (1877–1916); Edwin ("Tom," 1883–1947); and Arthur ("Jack," 1868–1902). It seems highly likely that Woolf drew upon her memories of Aunt Mary and her children for her portraits of meddlesome aunts and cousins in *NIGHT AND DAY.*

Fitzgerald, Edward (1809–83) In *A ROOM OF ONE'S OWN,* Woolf thinks that it was Fitzgerald who suggested that women authored many ballads and folk songs, "crooning them to her children" (AROO 49). A friend of Thomas CARLYLE, William Makepeace THACKERAY, and Alfred, Lord TENNYSON, Fitzgerald is chiefly known for his translation of *The Rubáiyát of Omar Khayyám* (1859).

Fitzroy Square Following Vanessa BELL's marriage to Clive BELL in 1907, Woolf and her brother Adrian STEPHEN moved to 29 Fitzroy Square, where they lived until 1911, a short walk from GORDON SQUARE. Duncan GRANT had rooms at 22 Fitzroy Square, where he was joined in 1909 by John Maynard KEYNES. In 1913, Roger FRY began the OMEGA WORKSHOPS at 33 Fitzroy Square, and in 1929 Vanessa BELL rented a studio at 8 Fitzroy Street, around the corner from the Square.

Flanders, Archer Character in *JACOB'S ROOM,* Jacob's elder brother, who calls him, "Ja-cob! Ja-cob!" at the beginning of the novel. He is referred to later as being at Gibraltar, and then at Singapore, both presumably in some military capacity.

Flanders, Betty Jacob's mother in *JACOB'S ROOM.* Betty is a widow who has obscured her husband Seabrook's rather dissolute nature by having "Merchant of this city" carved on his tombstone in Scarborough; she thinks it for the best as an example to her three sons, Archer, Jacob and John. Nancy Topping Bazin sees Betty as representing all mothers whose sons were killed in World War I (Bazin 94), thus linking her with "the figure of the mother whose sons have been killed in the battles of the world" of Peter WALSH's dream in *MRS. DALLOWAY* (MD 87).

We first see Betty on the beach in Cornwall, where she has taken her sons for a vacation. She is writing one of her many-paged, tear-stained letters to Captain BARFOOT in her home town, Scarborough. Throughout the novel, she writes to Jacob as he moves through his life; in her letters she does not say what she really feels, restraining her impulse to call her son to her. Jacob, in turn, writes letters on his travels that do not tell her what she wishes to hear. As the book ends, Betty hears the dull sound of guns and thinks of her dead brother, of her dead husband, and of her sons "fighting for their country," and of the chickens Captain Barfoot advised her to buy. At the end of the novel, Betty goes with Richard BONAMY to clear out Jacob's rooms and is last seen helplessly holding up a pair of her dead son's shoes.

"8 Fitzroy Street," (26 x 19"). Vanessa Bell. Courtesy of Towner Art Gallery and Local History Museum.
Vanessa took the studio next to Duncan Grant's at 8 Fitzroy Street in 1929, hoping "to enjoy uninterrupted hours of work" after twenty-one years spent looking after her three children (Spalding, Vanessa Bell *233).*

Flanders, Jacob The title character of *JACOB'S ROOM,* he is traced through the novel from the age of about three or four until his late twenties. Jacob owes a great deal to Woolf's brother Thoby STEPHEN, though Woolf also draws on the whole circle of young male friends she met through Thoby. Jacob leads the typical life of a privileged young man, being privately tutored in Latin, educated at Rugby School and at Cambridge University, and then taking a tour through France, Italy and Greece. Jacob does not settle on a particular career, dabbling in law and thinking of articles he might write on politics. He has several affairs and falls in love with an older married woman, Sandra Wentworth WILLIAMS. He is loved by

Richard BONAMY but makes no solid connections with anyone in the novel, nor is he ever seen more than fleetingly. Jacob dies at the front during World War I. The tremendous losses in French Flanders during World War I are recalled in Jacob's last name, emphasizing, particularly for contemporary readers, the character's evocation of the generation of young men who died in that war.

Flanders, Seabrook Deceased father of Jacob FLANDERS in *JACOB'S ROOM*.

Flaubert, Gustave (1821–80) Author of *Madame Bovary* (1857), *L'Education sentimentale* (1869), *Salammbô* (1862), and the unfinished *Bouvard et Pecuchet* (1881). In *A ROOM OF ONE'S OWN*, Flaubert is offered as an example of the self-conscious nineteenth-century "man of genius" (AROO 51–52). Woolf analyzes Flaubert's short story "Un Coeur Simple" in "ON RE-READING NOVELS" as an argument against the critical theory of Percy Lubbock. In "HOW IT STRIKES A CONTEMPORARY," she refers to Flaubert's "fanaticism" (E3 355). In 1936, Woolf confided to her DIARY that only Flaubert could have been "so tortured by writing as I am" (D5 25).

Fletcher, Mr. Mentioned in *MRS. DALLOWAY*, he is in Westminster Abbey when Doris KILMAN goes there to pray. He feels sorry for her.

Florinda Character in *JACOB'S ROOM* whom Jacob meets at a bonfire party. She drinks too much and talks "more about virginity than women mostly do" (77). She has a "confidante," Mother STUART, with whom she lives. Jacob's affair with Florinda is entirely sexual as Florinda—the narrator remarks with typical Woolfian irony—"was ignorant as an owl" (JR 79). Florinda sees several men, and when Jacob sees her walking arm in arm with one of them he ends their affair. Florinda is last seen at a bar with Nick BRAMHAM; she is pregnant.

Florrie A "scullery maid" in *THE WAVES* seen by SUSAN kissing Ernest, the "boot boy."

Floyd, Reverend Andrew Character in *JACOB'S ROOM* who teaches Jacob Latin and writes a letter to Betty FLANDERS proposing marriage. Later, when Betty reads that Mr. Floyd has been made principal of Maresfield House, she recalls how she turned down his proposal. As she thinks about him, she strokes the cat that used to belong to Mr. Floyd and thinks how she had had it gelded and how one day it will have to be killed, and "how she did not like red hair in men" (JR 22–23). Mr. Floyd sees Jacob years later in the street in London, but the opportunity to talk with him slips away. There is perhaps a faint echo of Woolf's grandfather, James STEPHEN, in that Mr. Floyd also writes ecclesiastical biography.

***Flush, A Biography* (1933)** Woolf began writing *Flush* in the summer of 1931, after completing *THE WAVES*. She continued to work on it as she began writing *THE PARGITERS*, and she wrote in her DIARY at the end of 1932 that she was using *Flush* to "cool" her mind after the effort of writing *The Pargiters* (D4 132). She was, she wrote, dissatisfied with *Flush*, thinking it "too slight & too serious" (D4 134).

Flush tells the story of Elizabeth Barrett BROWNING's cocker spaniel and the Brownings from the dog's point of view, a story Woolf gleaned from the several volumes of Barrett Browning's letters and other sources that she listed in a table of "Authorities" following the text (F 171). Barrett Browning's dog was sent to her while she was in Torquay in 1841 recovering from the effects of her brother's death; she wrote three poetic tributes to Flush.

Flush was published in 1933 by the HOGARTH PRESS with "four Original Drawings by Vanessa Bell" and six other illustrations (which, unfortunately, are not

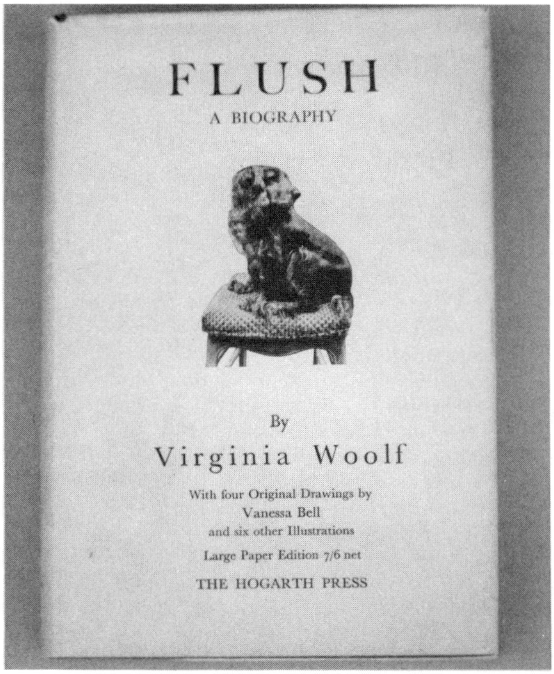

Flush, a Biography. *Courtesy of Linda J. Langham.*
Pinka, the cocker spaniel given to Woolf by Vita Sackville-West in 1926, is the cover model for this Hogarth Press first edition (1935) of Woolf's fanciful biography of Elizabeth Barrett Browning's dog.

reproduced in the paperback edition in which most people know the work). Vanessa BELL's line drawings illustrate the following scenes: "Miss Mitford takes Flush for a Walk;" "The Back Bedroom" (where Elizabeth Barrett Browning languishes, seen through the doorway); "At Casa Guidi" (Barrett Browning, again on a chaise, looks out of those windows she celebrated in her poem "Casa Guidi Windows"); and " 'So She Knitted and He Dozed,' " depicting Flush lying at his mistress's feet. The six other illustrations include National Portrait Gallery works depicting Barrett Browning, Mary Russell MITFORD, and Robert BROWNING, an unsigned nineteenth-century engraving depicting "Flush's Birthplace," and a photograph of the Woolfs' dog PINKA as the book's frontispiece.

Chapter 1, "Three Mile Cross," explains Flush's ancestry, indeed the ancestry of all cocker spaniels, and describes his birth in about 1842 at Three Mile Cross, the home of the Mitford family. Miss Mitford makes a gift of Flush to her friend, Elizabeth Barrett. From the moment Flush arrives in London at Miss Barrett's home on Wimpole Street, Woolf draws attention to the sensual world of the dog, emphasizing his acute sense of smell and the way that is his primary mode of perception.

Flush gets used to city life in chapter 2, "The Back Bedroom," but feels constrained by having to wear a leash and only run in the park. He discovers that he is "a dog of birth and breeding" (F 40) and grows to fear and detest Mr. Barrett, his mistress's father. In chapter 3, "The Hooded Man," Flush notices a growing excitement in Miss Barrett as she begins to receive letters that she reads over and over. When Robert Browning finally comes, Flush feels abandoned and resents "that man" (F 67) who hardly notices Flush even when he bites him (F 71). At the end of this chapter, Flush is stolen by a gang from Whitechapel.

"Whitechapel," chapter 4, describes Flush's imprisonment by "a hairy ruffian" (F 92) who takes him to a dank hideaway in the London slums. In defiance of Robert Browning's argument that to pay a ransom for Flush will only perpetuate dog-stealing, Barrett Browning takes her servant Wilson and goes in search of the gang's leader, Taylor. Eventually, Flush is reunited with his mistress, who is preparing to elope with Browning to Italy. And in the next chapter, "Italy," Flush discovers a new freedom: "He ran, he raced" (F 125). But then Mrs. Browning has a baby, a "horrid thing" (F 134) as far as Flush is concerned. He returns with his mistress on a visit to London, which Flush finds depressing; he longs to return to Italy.

At "The End," chapter 6, Flush is growing old. In Italy spiritualism is all the rage and Mrs. Browning spends most of her time consulting mediums, to Flush's distaste. One day he falls asleep and has a vivid dream of his life from birth at Three Mile Cross to the time he was stolen. Waking, he runs in a panic through the streets and returns to his mistress's room. As he comes in, she is reminded of the sonnet she wrote to him, "Flush or Faunus" (*Poems* 1850). He lies at her feet and dies.

Following the "Authorities," Woolf also appends ten "Notes" on her text, echoing perhaps her mock-scholarly apparatus in *ORLANDO,* to which *Flush* is a close relation in terms of its tone and genre. In the notes, Woolf buttresses her fantastic biography of a dog with facts from the biographical materials she read in preparation for writing it. The notes are frequently witty and ironic, as when she writes, "Readers of *Aurora Leigh*—but since such persons are non-existent it must be explained that Mrs. Browning wrote a poem of this name" (F 175). Woolf writes a virtual "Life of the Obscure" for Barrett Browning's servant Lily Wilson (F 176–82), looking forward, perhaps, to her comment in *THREE GUINEAS* that there are no lives of maids in the *DICTIONARY OF NATIONAL BIOGRAPHY* (TG chap. 2 n36). She wrote to David GARNETT—who had written a favorable review of *Flush* in the *NEW STATESMAN*—that she was "rather proud" of her facts (L5 231). She also told Garnett that she had written a version of the ending that was in the manner of Lytton STRACHEY's *Queen Victoria,* but "cut it out, when he was not there to see the joke" (L5 232; Strachey had died in 1932).

Flush was selected by the Book Society in England for October 1933, and by the American Book-of-the-Month Club for September as an alternate selection, both of which led to its being a best-selling book for the Hogarth Press (it sold 14,390 copies in the first six months [Willis 266]). Woolf, who had written most of it under the extreme pressure of her need to write *The Pargiters,* imagined they would "net £2000 from that six months dogged & dreary grind" (D4 176). *Flush*'s popularity soon proved a liability with some reviewers, as Woolf noted when *The Granta* mourned "the passing of a potentially great writer who perished for lack of an intelligent audience," lamenting the "deadly facility" of *Flush* combined with its popularity (D4 186).

Commenting on its status as a best-seller, Pamela Caughie speculates that its popularity is the reason *Flush* has not received very much critical attention. (An early article on *Flush* is Lola L. Szladits, "The Life, Character, and Opinions of Flush the Spaniel." *Bulletin of the New York Public Library* 74 [April 1970]: 211–18.) For Caughie, *Flush* interrogates the boundary between "high" and "low" art and she reads it as "an allegory of canon formation" (Caughie 146). Having explored the significance of *Flush* being a Book-of-the-Month Club selection, Caughie reads the work as exemplifying the instability of literary criteria; the arguments about whether *Flush* is a joke or is to be read seriously bring to the fore "the novel's very function as the excess of a canonical economy" (163).

Several critical readings of *Flush* treat it biographically in one way or another. Stephen Trombley's reading of *Flush* as autobiographical (287–95) argues that it is concerned with Woolf's resentment of Clive BELL's interruption of her relationship with her sister. Trombley comments that in Woolf's writing, "Dogs always appear against a background of unsatisfactory domestic relations" (266). Recently, Ruth Vanita has argued that *Flush* concerns Woolf's love affair with Vita SACKVILLE-WEST, and has explored the complex network of animal imagery Woolf uses in her fiction and letters (248–57). Vanita argues that the "simultaneous status of Flush as victim and offender makes him a suitable trope for the situation of the homosexual in Victorian England" (255).

Louise DeSalvo has argued that "Woolf's splendid trope is that young women are treated like dogs" (286), and she emphasizes the likeness between Barrett Browning and Flush in the text. Another critic who has read *Flush* as a critique of patriarchy is Susan Squier, who explains that "Flush occupies a marginal position in human society, and in his marginality he resembles his invalid mistress, elegantly imprisoned in her bedroom in Wimpole Street, the center—as Woolf's description makes clear—of patriarchal society" (Squier, *Virginia Woolf* 125). Squier also points out that Whitechapel was the scene of "Jack the Ripper's" murders in 1888. Woolf researched and worked on the Whitechapel chapter carefully, rewriting it several times (Lehmann, *Virginia Woolf* 95); her cousin James Kenneth STEPHEN has been mentioned as a suspect in the Ripper case.

Woolf wrote to Ottoline MORRELL in 1933 that she was so tired after writing *The Waves,* "that I lay in the garden and read the Browning letters" (L5 161). Whatever the genesis of *Flush,* it seems intricately bound up with the concerns of other works Woolf was writing concurrently with it, such as her essays in *THE LONDON SCENE* (drafts of which are in the same notebook in which she began *Flush*); also, as Squier points out, *Flush* "anticipates the serious family chronicle, *The Years*" (*Virginia Woolf* 137).

Flushing, Alice Character in *THE VOYAGE OUT.* She is based partly on Janet Ross, George MEREDITH's mistress, whom Woolf met in Florence in 1909 (PA 397–98), and also on Ottoline MORRELL, whom Woolf met for the first time that year also. She and her husband arrive late in the novel, connected to the English colony on SANTA MARINA by her acquaintance with Mrs. Raymond PARRY, whom both Helen AMBROSE and Mrs. THORNBURY know in London. Mrs. Flushing paints vivid paintings, admires Augustus JOHN, and is dedicated to the idea that art must be continually renewed. She tells dramatic stories of her harsh childhood and offends Ridley AMBROSE when she smokes a cigarette at tea. It is Mrs. Flushing's idea to take the journey up the river to see a native village during which Rachel VINRACE and Terence HEWET become engaged. When Rachel dies, Mrs. Flushing rages against death, alone in her room (TVO 359).

Flushing, Wilfred Character in *THE VOYAGE OUT.* His interest in the native art of SANTA MARINA, which he describes to Rachel VINRACE (TVO 237), is to some extent derived from Roger FRY's interest in Turkish art. Mr. Flushing and his wife buy artifacts cheaply and sell them in London for a great profit. Helen AMBROSE has heard of the Flushings and is interested to meet Alice FLUSHING as she is supposed to have made Mr. Flushing "do all the things he most disliked" (TVO 198).

Folios of New Writing John LEHMANN describes *Folios of New Writing* as the "lean war substitute" for the magazine he edited from 1936 to 1939, *New Writing* (*Thrown* 88). *New Writing* had grown out of the two successful anthologies of poetry, essays and fiction by young writers of the 1930s edited for the HOGARTH PRESS by Michael Roberts, *New Signatures* (1932) and *New Country* (1933). Woolf's "THE LEANING TOWER" was published in the second number of *Folios of New Writing* (Autumn 1940), and shortly after her death appeared "Replies" by several writers in the Spring 1941 issue.

Formalist (Formalism) A term from art criticism that derives principally from the writings of Roger FRY and refers to an analysis that focuses on the *form* of a painting rather than anything it might represent. The term also has a complex history in literary criticism.[8] Among members of the BLOOMSBURY GROUP, arguments about form in both literature and painting were common, "literary" being a derogatory term when applied to a painting. In "An Essay in Aesthetics" (1909), which Christopher Reed in his useful discussion of Bloomsbury formalism describes as "the definitive early statement of formalism" ("Through Formalism" 13), Fry wrote that "unity of some kind is necessary for our restful contemplation of the work of art as a whole" (31) and that such unity is "due to a balancing of the attractions of the eye about the central line of the picture" (31). Fry identified several "emotional elements of design" that produce the "order and variety" necessary to a work of art: the rhythm of the line, mass, space, light and shade, and color (33–34). It was these formal qualities and not any "likeness to Nature" that were, according to Fry

[8] A good account of formalism in literary criticism can be found in David H. Richter, ed. *The Critical Tradition: Classic Texts and Contemporary Trends.* NY: St. Martin's Press, 1989: 721–35.

and to Clive BELL (whose book *Art* basically summarized Fry's theories), the appropriate focus of the art critic and the viewer who wished to understand the work of art. Many Woolf critics, recognizing the importance to her of Fry's theories and the prevalence of discussions about aesthetics among her and her contemporaries, have also stressed the formal elements of design, rhythm, harmony and balance in her fiction. (See also Roger FRY.)

Forster, E. M. (Edward Morgan) (1879–1970) English novelist and one of the original members of the BLOOMSBURY GROUP. Forster's novels are *Where Angels Fear to Tread* (1905), *The Longest Journey* (1907), *A Room with a View (1908), Howards End* (1910), *A Passage to India* (1924) and *Maurice* (1970). He also wrote short stories, biographies, and criticism; his lectures on *Aspects of the Novel* (1927) influenced several generations of teachers and critics. Forster was also the first of the Bloomsbury Group to be published by the HOGARTH PRESS, in 1920 with *The Story of the Siren.* As J. H. Willis points out, he was also "the only Bloomsbury member to sustain a publishing connection with the Woolfs," publishing seven works with Hogarth. Eliza Fay's *Original Letters from India (1779–1815)* was edited with an introduction by Forster (1925); his other Hogarth publications were *Pharos and Pharillon* (1923), an account of Alexandria, where Forster served with the Red Cross in 1915–1919; *Letter to Madan Blanchard* (1931), the first of the Hogarth Letters; *Anonymity, An Enquiry* (1925), number 12 of the Hogarth Essays; *Goldsworthy Lowes Dickinson* (1934); and *What I Believe* (1939), a Hogarth Press pamphlet reprinting Forster's "Two Cheers for Democracy," first published in the New York *Nation* in July 1938 and then in the *London Mercury* in an expanded version in September 1938. The Hogarth Press also published Rose MACAULAY's study *The Writings of E. M. Forster* in 1938.

Forster was an APOSTLE and had entered King's College, Cambridge, in 1897, where Lytton STRACHEY and Leonard WOOLF met him in 1899. They nicknamed him "the taupe" (mole) because he seemed to live underground and suddenly appear from time to time. Noel Annan has described Forster as "the quintessential spirit of King's" (CHN 14:8). Forster's friendship with Leonard began to deepen only after Leonard's return from Ceylon in 1911. Woolf noted Forster's reliance on her husband (" 'Where d'you get your boots? Are Waterman pens the best?' " [D2 33]), and in "Forster and Bloomsbury," his contribution to *Aspects of E. M. Forster* (edited by Oliver Stallybrass, 1969), David GARNETT discussed his closeness to Leonard. When Forster returned from India in 1922 with *A Passage to India* unfinished, he sought advice from Leonard, who encouraged him to give up reviewing and concentrate on his novel. Forster announced the work's completion in a letter to the Woolfs of January 1924, a letter that led Woolf to reflect on how similar she and Forster were in their feelings about finishing a novel.

"I always feel him shrinking sensitively from me, as a woman, a clever woman, an up to date woman," Woolf wrote in 1919 (D1 263). She liked Forster very much, but found him "whimsical & vagulous" (D1 291).[9] Woolf and Forster, although extremely different as artists, are sometimes considered as "Bloomsbury" novelists who shared a particular aesthetic (see Dowling, for example). Although there are some who have not considered Forster a member of Bloomsbury, he was one of the thirteen members of the MEMOIR CLUB whom Leonard Woolf considered identical with "Old Bloomsbury." In "Bloomsbury, An Early Note," written in 1929 but not published until 1956, Forster described the Bloomsbury Group as "the only genuine *movement* in English civilisation" (Rosenbaum, *Bloomsbury Group* 25). Like Woolf, Forster had ancestors at the heart of the CLAPHAM SECT, and he wrote about them in *Marianne Thornton 1797–1887: A Domestic Biography* (1956). Sandra Gilbert and Susan Gubar have speculated that Edward Carpenter's theories about androgynous artists, influential on many turn-of-the-century Cambridge intellectuals, may have filtered to Woolf via Forster (*Sexchanges* 364).

Forster (as can be seen from the Critical Responses section of the entry on each of Woolf's novels) was one of Woolf's first and most important critics. Roger Poole has argued that his opinion was *the* most important to Woolf: "He was not only her mentor, he was her precursor, and to some extent her struggle to get free had to be with *him*" ("Passage to the Lighthouse" 17). Woolf wrote that Forster's liking *NIGHT AND DAY* less than *THE VOYAGE OUT* "rubbed out all the pleasure" of other, more positive responses from her friends (D1 308). In "The Novels of Virginia Woolf," an article in *The New Criterion* in 1926 (reprinted as "The Early Novels of Virginia Woolf" in *Abinger Harvest* [1936]), Forster described *Night and Day* as "a deliberate exercise in classicism" (*Abinger* 108). This article, Woolf wrote, "has cheered me very much" (D3 52).

As each of Woolf's novels appeared, she waited anxiously for Forster's comments, often relieved to get "Morgan's morganatic, evasive, elusive letter," as she described what he wrote to her about *TO THE LIGHTHOUSE* (that it was "awfully sad, very beautiful both in (non-radiant) colour and shape" [Forster, *Letters* 2: 77]). He considered *THE WAVES* "a classic" (D4 52) but was disappointed by *THE YEARS.* When *ROGER FRY* was published Woolf wrote in her DIARY

[9] In a reminiscence about Forster's visits to her father Roger FRY's house, Pamela Diamand wrote that "everyone enjoyed his whimsical conversation" (CHN 10:25).

that she would "be relieved *if* Morgan approves" (D5 305). "No review by Morgan, no review at all," she wrote a couple of days later (D5 308), and she was "slightly damped" by his review when it did appear (D5 310). In 1925, Woolf wrote about *MRS. DALLOWAY* to Gerald BRENAN and said, "I always feel that nobody, except perhaps Morgan Forster, lays hold of the thing I have done" (L3 189). In 1930, she told Ethel SMYTH that Forster's books "once influenced mine" and that she thought them "very good, . . . though impeded, shrivelled and immature" (L4 218).

A year after Woolf's death, Forster surveyed her achievement in the Rede Lecture, later published in *Two Cheers for Democracy* (an abridged version is included in Noble). There he termed *Night and Day* "a false start" and *JACOB'S ROOM* "an uneven little book" (Noble 189). *The Waves* was "an extraordinary achievement" and probably "her greatest book," although *To the Lighthouse* was his favorite (Noble 190). *The Years* he deemed a failure similar to *Night and Day*, arguing that in it Woolf had deserted the poetry that was her strength. Woolf's "problem" according to Forster was that "she is a poet, who wants to write something as near to a novel as possible" (Noble 193). Moving to consideration of what he described as "a very peculiar side of her," her feminism, Forster said it had produced both "one of the most brilliant of her books—the charming and persuasive" *A ROOM OF ONE'S OWN*, as well as "the worst of her books—the cantankerous" *THREE GUINEAS*. In a curious metaphor, Forster said there were "spots" of feminism "all over" Woolf's work (Noble 195).

Forster, a longtime champion of civil liberties, frequently sought the Woolfs' support for various political causes during the 1930s. In 1928, he and Leonard had organized a protest against the suppression of Radclyffe Hall's *THE WELL OF LONELINESS*. A joint letter from Forster and Woolf about the obscenity trial, under the title "The New Censorship," was published in the *NATION & ATHENAEUM* (September 8, 1928: 726). However, as for most of her male contemporaries (and quite a few of her female ones), Woolf's radical feminism was mystifying to Forster. In 1935, Woolf met Forster on the steps of the LONDON LIBRARY where he had just come from a committee meeting. She thought for a moment that he was going to invite her to join the Board, but he told her the committee had agreed that "ladies are impossible" (D4 297–98). Her anger inspired her to thoughts of writing "On Being Despised," but she had to suppress them in order to concentrate on finishing *The Years*: "On Being Despised" eventually found its voice as *Three Guineas*. In November 1940, Woolf got great satisfaction from turning down Forster's invitation to join the Library Board (D5 337).

Woolf first wrote about Forster before she knew him, having reviewed *A Room with a View* for the *TIMES LITERARY SUPPLEMENT* in 1908 (E1 221–22). She found the novel amusing and appreciated its modern outlook, but, anticipating her later estimate of Forster's own personality, she wrote that the novel disappointed due "to some belittlement, which seems to cramp the souls" of its characters (E1 222). In "The Novels of E. M. Forster" (1927) (CE1: 342–51; DM 162–75), Woolf pointed out his close observation of material reality and attention to detail but noted that his materialism was underpinned by his constant quest for "the soul," for "a burning core." "The neat surface is always being thrown into disarray by an outburst of lyric poetry" (CE1 344). She included him among the "Georgians" in "CHARACTER IN FICTION" (E3 421) but also wrote that he and D. H. LAWRENCE had "spoilt their early work" by trying to use the "Edwardian" tools of Arnold BENNETT, H. G. WELLS and John GALSWORTHY (E3 433). Woolf's review of Forster's *Aspects of the Novel,* "Is Fiction an Art?" appeared in October 1927 and was later reprinted as "THE ART OF FICTION" (CE2 51–55; M 106–12).

After Woolf's death, Forster wrote that she had "pushed the light of the English language a little further" (Noble 198). He wrote to Leonard in 1953 when *A WRITER'S DIARY* was published that it made him "feel so close to her. I did not feel that in our meetings, as she knew" (*Letters* 2: 255). Forster also felt that Woolf did not like his novels, but whatever the truth of that, certainly his critical thought about fiction was of enormous importance to her.

Fortescue, Mr. Character in *NIGHT AND DAY*, "the eminent novelist" (ND 10) who is based on Woolf's recollections of Henry JAMES and is served tea by Katharine HILBERY at the beginning of the novel.

Foxcroft, Mrs. Mentioned in *MRS. DALLOWAY* when Clarissa DALLOWAY thinks how she met her the night before the day on which the novel is set, at an embassy party. The war is not over for Mrs. Foxcroft because "that nice boy was killed and now the old Manor House must go to a cousin" (MD 5).

Franklin, Sir John (1786–1847) Mentioned in *NIGHT AND DAY* as one of the eminent connections of the Hilbery family (ND 36), an Arctic explorer who wrote popular "Narratives" of his voyages (published in 1823 and 1828). His last trip was with the *Erebus* and *Terror* in 1845, from which he never returned. Sir Leopold McClintock later proved that Franklin had discovered the "North West Passage."

Fraser A character in *JACOB'S ROOM* who sits next to Miss MARCHMONT on the day Jacob is reading Marlowe in the BRITISH MUSEUM Reading Room. Fraser is an atheist who has dedicated his life to destroying by the sheer force of logic the books of Dean Parker. Fraser's wife secretly baptizes their children in the wash basin.

Frazer, Sir James George (1854–1941) In the BRITISH MUSEUM scene in chapter 2 of *A ROOM OF ONE'S OWN*, one of the references Woolf consults is Frazer's *The Golden Bough*, from which she learns that some "savages" consider women half-divine "and worship them on that account" (AROO 30). Frazer was a fellow of Trinity College; his publications included *Totemism* (1887), an edition of the *Letters of William Cowper* (1912), and a large number of works on anthropology and folklore. *The Golden Bough*, a study of the rituals surrounding worship of Diana, was published in twelve volumes between 1890 and 1915; in 1936, Frazer published a supplement to the work entitled *Aftermath*.

Freshwater Woolf wrote two versions of this farcical three-act satire based on the life of her great-aunt Julia Margaret CAMERON, the first in 1923, and a revision in 1935 for a performance at Vanessa BELL's studio at 8 Fitzroy Street on January 18 attended by about eighty guests in honor of Angelica GARNETT's seventeenth birthday. On that occasion the cast included Vanessa Bell as Mrs. Cameron, Leonard WOOLF as Mr. Cameron, Julian BELL as Alfred TENNYSON, Angelica Garnett as Ellen TERRY, Duncan GRANT as G. F. WATTS, Ann Stephen (Woolf's niece) as John Craig, and Eve Younger (a friend of Angelica's) as Mary Magdalen (the maid) and Queen Victoria. Woolf had mentioned writing a play about her great-aunt as early as 1919 when she wrote in her DIARY of "the superb possibilities of Freshwater, for a comedy" (D1 237).

The action of the play concerns a group of friends who have gathered at the Camerons' house, Freshwater, on the Isle of Wight as they prepare to make a voyage to India. The voyage is considerably delayed as the Camerons await the arrival of two coffins that are to accompany them. G. F. Watts is painting his young wife Ellen Terry as Modesty at the feet of Mammon; as he does this, Tennyson strides in reading passages from *Maud*. In the second act, Ellen Terry runs off to meet a young man, the naval officer John Craig, with whom she plans to elope to live in BLOOMSBURY. The play closes with the Camerons about to leave for India, their coffins having finally arrived, and Terry announcing she is leaving with Craig. Tennyson and Watts are deserted by all but their art, when suddenly Queen Victoria arrives to bestow honors upon them.

Both versions of *Freshwater* were published in 1976, edited by Lucio P. Ruotolo. The American premiere, directed by David Richman, was held on March 3, 1974, at the Stanford Museum of Art in Palo Alto, California, to coincide with an exhibition of Julia Margaret Cameron's photographs. In 1983, a performance of the play was staged at New York University Theater with a cast that included several French literary luminaries: Eugene Ionesco as Tennyson, Alain Robbe-Grillet as Mr. Cameron, Joyce Mansour as Mrs. Cameron, Florence Delay as Ellen Terry, Jean-Paul Aron as Victoria, Tom Bishop as John Craig, Rodica Ionesco as Mary Magdalen. A mysterious butler was added to the play on this occasion to provide a part for the novelist Natalie Sarraute.

Freud, Sigmund (1856–1939) The Woolfs' primary association with Freud was through the HOGARTH PRESS's publication of the International Psycho-Analytical Library, begun in 1924. Woolf's brother Adrian STEPHEN and his wife Karin had begun training as psychoanalysts in 1919. In 1920, James STRA-

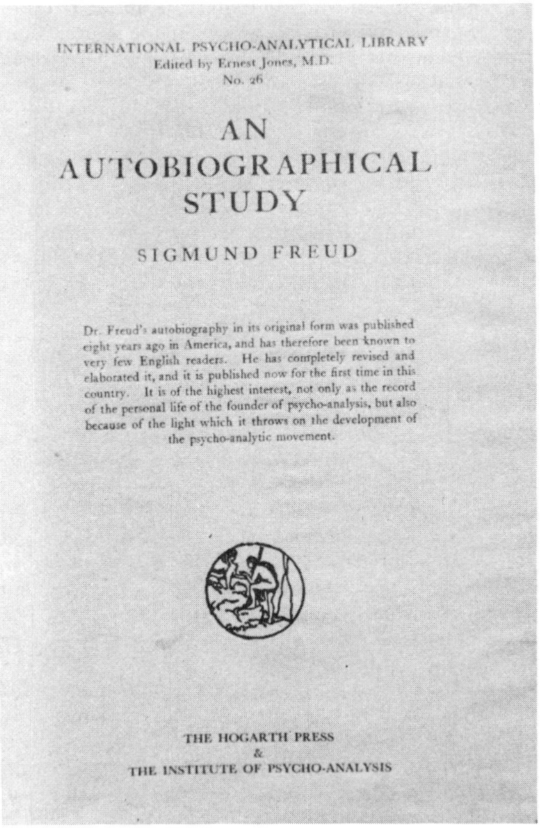
INTERNATIONAL PSYCHO-ANALYTICAL LIBRARY
Edited by Ernest Jones, M.D.
No. 26

AN AUTOBIOGRAPHICAL STUDY

SIGMUND FREUD

Dr. Freud's autobiography in its original form was published eight years ago in America, and has therefore been known to very few English readers. He has completely revised and elaborated it, and it is published now for the first time in this country. It is of the highest interest, not only as the record of the personal life of the founder of psycho-analysis, but also because of the light which it throws on the development of the psycho-analytic movement.

THE HOGARTH PRESS
&
THE INSTITUTE OF PSYCHO-ANALYSIS

Sigmund Freud, An Autobiographical Study *(1935).*
The Hogarth Press assumed publication of the papers of the International Psycho-analytical Institute in 1924 and became Freud's official English publisher.

CHEY went to Vienna to be analyzed by Freud. James and his wife Alix STRACHEY were the conduit by which Leonard Woolf came to be Freud's English publisher. Between 1953 and 1966 the Hogarth Press published James Strachey's translation of the *Standard Edition of the Complete Works of Freud* in twenty-four volumes.

In his autobiography, Leonard congratulated himself on having recognized early how important Freud's work was. He recalls the excitement of being in London in 1911 at a time when the work of Freud, Einstein and the physicist Ernest Rutherford was promising "to revolutionize our knowledge of our own minds and of the universe" (LW2 21). In June 1914, having read Freud's *Interpretation of Dreams* as preparation, Leonard reviewed *The Psychopathology of Everyday Life* in *The New Weekly*.

Woolf herself was invariably disparaging and mocking in her LETTERS and DIARY whenever she wrote about psychoanalysis or psychoanalysts. In 1925, James Strachey wrote to his wife about a dinner "with the Wolves" at which Woolf "made a more than usually ferocious onslaught upon psychoanalysis and psychoanalysts" (Meisel and Kendrick 264). As several critics have pointed out, however, Woolf was certainly aware of the debates about psychoanalysis that were intense in London in the 1920s. Elizabeth Abel has discussed in detail Woolf's sources of information about psychoanalysis, pointing out, for example, that Melanie Klein's 1925 lectures were delivered at Adrian and Karin Stephen's home at 50 GORDON SQUARE (Abel 13). Woolf demonstrated her awareness in a 1920 *TIMES LITERARY SUPPLEMENT* review of J. D. Beresford's novel *An Imperfect Mother,* entitled "Freudian Fiction" (E3 195–98), writing that Beresford "has acted the part of stepfather to some of the very numerous progeny of Dr Freud" (E3 196).

When Freud fled Austria and moved to London in 1938, Leonard arranged to visit him, and on January 28, 1939, he and Woolf went for tea with Freud and his children. Woolf wrote the next day that Freud had given her a narcissus (D5 202) and described him as an "old fire now flickering," a description echoed many years later by Leonard, who recalled Freud that day as "a half-extinct volcano" (LW2 311). In December 1939, Woolf began noting in her diary that she was "gulping up Freud" (D5 250) and from then through 1940 there are several references to his work that show her serious consideration of it. In her memoir "A SKETCH OF THE PAST" she described writing *TO THE LIGHTHOUSE* as doing for herself what psychoanalysts do for their patients, resolving the ambivalence she had felt toward her parents (MOB 81).

Freund, Gisèle (b. 1913) German photographer who met Woolf through Victoria OCAMPO in 1939 and photographed her on June 24. Woolf was very annoyed with Ocampo for, as she saw it, putting her in a position where she could not refuse Freund (D5 220). Freund has written about her own very different recollections of the sitting in *Gisèle Freund: Photographer* (96–101), where her color portrait of Woolf is also reproduced. Ocampo wrote about the incident in a 1978 article in *Review* (McNees 1:441–42). In 1965 Freund took several photographs of Leonard WOOLF.

Friday Club Organized in summer 1905 by Vanessa BELL for the discussion and exhibition of fine art. Its membership was not limited to painters and included Clive BELL (from whom Vanessa sought advice about setting it up in 1905 and who lectured to it in its early months), Henry LAMB, Pernel STRACHEY, Saxon SYDNEY-TURNER, friends of Vanessa's from the Royal Academy Schools of Art such as Margery SNOWDEN and Sylvia MILMAN, her brothers Thoby[10] and Adrian STEPHEN, and friends Katherine COX and Marjorie STRACHEY. In 1905 Woolf wrote to Violet DICKINSON that her sister would need all her diplomacy to manage the Committee as one half "shriek Whistler and French impressionists, and the other are stalwart British" (L1 201). The Friday Club is described by Quentin BELL as the first sign that Bloomsbury was to be interested in the visual arts (QB1 105). The Club also held exhibitions, and from 1910 until its dissolution in 1914, the shows received considerable attention from the press, as Frances Spalding has noted (*Vanessa Bell* 56).

"Friendships Gallery" A mock biography of her friend Violet DICKINSON, written by Woolf in 1907.[11] The typescript was edited for publication by Ellen Hawkes for a special issue of *Twentieth Century Literature* (25, 3/4 [Fall/Winter 1979]: 270–302). Also figuring prominently in "Friendships Gallery" is Lady Robert ("Nelly") CECIL, a close friend of Dickinson's. Woolf presented a copy of this humorous work to Dickinson typed in violet ink and bound in violet leather in August 1907; the copy is now in the BERG COLLECTION.

Fripp, Mr. and Mrs. Howard American guests of Dr. and Mrs. MALONE in *THE YEARS*.

Fry, Margery ("Ha") (1874–1958) The youngest of Roger FRY's six sisters. She was an important penal reformer and became Principal of Somerville College, Oxford, in 1921. Having worked in France with

[10] Woolf wrote to Madge VAUGHAN in 1906 that Thoby was to read a paper to the Friday Club on "the Decadence of Modern Art" (L1 225).

[11] Mitchell Leaska believes it to have been written "sometime in August–September of 1902" (PA 163).

the Quakers during World War I, Margery moved in with her brother in 1919 to Dalmeny Avenue. On Roger's death in 1934, Margery became his literary executor, and there was initially some confusion about whether she or Woolf would write Roger's biography. She came to discuss the biography with Woolf in November 1934 and told Woolf that she would have to guard the feelings of her sisters (D4 262). In the event, she assisted Woolf by giving her papers and arranging for her to interview people. Frances Spalding remarks that Margery never got on with the BLOOMSBURY GROUP and that this antagonism hampered Woolf's writing of *ROGER FRY*. Although in Woolf's biography "little mention is made of her important presence during the Dalmeny Avenue years" (Spalding *Roger Fry* 225), Roger himself acknowledged his sister's importance to him by dedicating *Vision and Design* to her.

Fry, Roger Eliot (1866–1934) Art critic and painter who through his lectures and writing revolutionized how people in England thought about art. Fry was the eldest member of the BLOOMSBURY GROUP and one of its original members, belonging also to the

"Roger Fry" from Twelve Original Woodcuts *by Roger Fry. Courtesy of Cecil Woolf and Jean Moorcroft Wilson.*
Fry's book of woodcuts sold out within two days of its publication by the Hogarth Press in 1921; Leonard and Virginia Woolf printed and bound the book themselves.

MEMOIR CLUB. In 1913 he founded the OMEGA WORKSHOPS. In "OLD BLOOMSBURY," Woolf described how he had been introduced by Clive BELL and "had more knowledge and experience than all of us put together" (MOB 197). Fry was from a strong Quaker family of eight children (he had six sisters, none of whom married, and a brother). At Cambridge University he became an APOSTLE and graduated from King's College with a first-class degree in Natural Science in 1888. Upon leaving Cambridge, however, he turned his attention to art and was soon established as an authority on Old Masters. His first book, *Giovanni Bellini,* was published in 1899 and he was a regular contributor to the influential *Burlington Magazine.* He married Helen Coombe, a painter, in 1896, and they had two children, Julian (1901–84), and Pamela (1902–85), who married Micu Diamand. In 1898 Helen Coombe began showing signs of the mental instability that led to her institutionalization in 1910.

Woolf came to know Fry through her sister, Vanessa BELL. Vanessa had seen Fry at Cambridge on a visit there in 1902, and had met him at a dinner given by Desmond MACCARTHY in 1904. She did not see him again until a chance meeting in 1910 brought her, Fry, and Clive BELL together on a train journey from Cambridge to London. Finding they had a great deal in common, Clive agreed to help Fry organize the first POST-IMPRESSIONIST exhibition, held at the Grafton Galleries from November 8, 1910, to January 15, 1911. Fry had just returned from several years working as a curator at the Metropolitan Museum of Art in New York City, where he had clashed with the wealthy J. Pierpont MORGAN. In 1906, after seeing two works by Paul Cézanne in a London exhibition, Fry had been converted to the cause of modern art (Bowness 10). When he met the Bells he was at a crisis in both his intellectual and personal life (QB1 167).

In April 1911, Fry, Vanessa and Clive, and H. T. J. NORTON set off for CONSTANTINOPLE. (Just before leaving, Fry had a brief affair with Lady Ottoline MORRELL [Spalding, *Roger Fry* 143].) At Broussa, Vanessa had a miscarriage and Woolf soon traveled to Turkey to be with her sister. She found Fry coping with everything, and looking after Vanessa devotedly. This incident marked the beginning of Fry and Vanessa's love affair and the gradual transformation of Vanessa's marriage to Clive (who was already involved with Mary HUTCHINSON) into a friendship. Woolf, who frequently disparaged painting when compared to literature, was resentful of Fry's intimacy with Vanessa and also grew tired of their vocal enthusiasm for visual art.

In 1912, Fry organized a second Post-Impressionist exhibition, with Leonard WOOLF, recently returned from Ceylon, as its secretary. Woolf wrote to Violet DICKINSON that "artists are an abominable race. The furious excitement of these people all the winter over their pieces of canvas coloured green and blue, is odious" (L2 15). Woolf's LETTERS, however, and Fry's (edited in two volumes by Denys Sutton), record their deepening intimacy over the years. After Fry's death, Woolf described him to her sister as "the plume in Bloomsbury's cap" and "the only civilised man I have ever met" (L5 566). In a speech opening the Roger Fry Memorial Art Exhibit at the Bristol Museum and Art Gallery in June 1934 ("Roger Fry" CE4 88–92), Woolf described how he had transformed the way people looked at art. She told an anecdote about his skill in distinguishing between fakes and authentic paintings (CE4 89) that Leonard repeated in his autobiography, except that in Woolf's version the painting in question was a Degas and in Leonard's a Poussin (LW2 67).

Several critics have discussed Woolf's work in terms of Fry's aesthetics (J. K. Johnstone, David Dowling, Allen McLaurin, and John Hawley Roberts, for example), but it is important to recognize that Fry's theories were dynamic and he continued to revise them until the end of his life. He and Clive Bell were immediately identified, following the first Post-Impressionist exhibition, with a FORMALIST aesthetic that Bell gave expression to in his 1914 book *Art*, where he emphasized the importance of SIGNIFICANT FORM. S. P. Rosenbaum has traced the complexities of the influences on Fry's aesthetics, seeing in his heritage both William Morris and John Ruskin ("Virginia Woolf" 23). In 1913, Fry wrote to Goldsworthy Lowes DICKINSON that he was "continuing my aesthetic theories and I have been attacking poetry to understand painting" (Naylor 67).

Fry's "An Essay in Aesthetics" of 1909 (in *Vision and Design*) is described by Christopher Reed as "the definitive early statement of formalism" ("Through Formalism" 13); Reed also terms Bell's *Art* "a summary of formalist principles" (13). He argues, however, that when Fry met Charles MAURON in 1919, his ideas about formalist aesthetics began to change. He became interested in the aesthetics of poetry and embarked on what would become a lifelong project of translating the works of Stéphane MALLARMÉ. (In 1927, the HOGARTH PRESS published Fry's translation of Mauron's *The Nature of Beauty in Art and Literature*.) In discussing Woolf's response to Fry, Reed argues that her first two novels, *THE VOYAGE OUT* and *NIGHT AND DAY*, are characterized by the "conspicuous rejection of formalism" (14). He believes that Woolf "took from formalism—from Fry in particular—what she admired, and moved on" (Reed, "Through Formalism" 34).

Fry reviewed Clive Bell's *Art* quite negatively in the *NATION*, feeling that Bell had been too exclusively formalist in his arguments. Jonathan Quick writes that Fry's "desire not only to include but to emphasize the familiar human element in his notion of expressive form became a principal point where Virginia Woolf saw that she stood on common ground with him" (Quick 564). As Reed remarks, "however the phrasing varies, it is clear that Woolf was very much in the thick of Bloomsbury's aesthetic theorizing in the years after World War I" (34).

Fry was an early champion of Woolf's writing, praising the short stories and sketches she wrote between 1917 and 1921. Although Leonard Woolf told the American critic Nancy Bazin in 1964 that Woolf was, "certainly in conversation, very much opposed to many of the theories of Roger Fry with regard to literature" (Spotts 528), her close engagement with post-impressionism and formalism can be seen vividly in the stories published in *MONDAY OR TUESDAY*. Panthea Reid Broughton has argued that these pieces "specifically take on the aesthetic of Roger Fry, explore its possibilities in language, and finally illustrate its limitations" ("Blasphemy" 37). Broughton believes that Fry was an enthusiastic supporter of Woolf's writing because he saw in her stories "a verbal equivalent of Post-Impressionism" (53).

"Blue & Green" (SF 136) attempts to "use words like paint to create visual objects" (Broughton 54), recalling the vivid blues and greens remarked on in 1910 by many who saw Cézanne's work for the first time. Quick regards this piece as Woolf's "brief homage and peace offering to the landscape paintings in the Cézanne manner which she had disparaged when she first saw them" (Quick 562). Broughton also reads "SOLID OBJECTS" as an ironic comment on Fry's essay "The Artist's Vision," and she sees in it Woolf's "mature assessment of and distancing from formalism" (56).

Near the end of her life, Woolf revisited the aesthetic debates of the 1910s when she agreed to write the biography *ROGER FRY*. As Fry's modern biographer, Frances Spalding, writes, Woolf's was an "insider's view" (Spalding ix) but she was hindered by several circumstances, not the least inhibiting of which was Fry's affair with her sister, Vanessa Bell. In 1918, Woolf wrote that Fry was "the centre of a whirlwind to me" (D1 134) and although the intensity of their early relationship deepened into easy intimacy, Fry's restless theorizing and inquisitiveness remained a constant source of delight to Woolf until his death, which, she wrote, made her feel that living was impoverished (D4 242).

Furse, Katharine (1875–1952) The youngest daughter of the poet, critic and historian John Addington Symonds (a close friend of Leslie STEPHEN) and sister of Margaret (Madge) VAUGHAN. Rowena Fowler points out that the Stephen and Symonds families "were connected by the various ties of kinship and social and professional acquaintance that helped define one section of the Victorian upper-middle-class" (202). Katharine married Charles Furse (1868–1904), a prominent painter who was an early influence on Vanessa BELL. After a long lapse in their acquaintance, Woolf and Katharine Furse began to correspond in the 1930s after a chance meeting in the street. Rowena Fowler has edited a previously unpublished correspondence between them concerning Furse's memoir *Hearts and Pomegranates* and Woolf's biography *ROGER FRY* (Fry had known J. A. Symonds). Louise DeSalvo, in an afterword, comments that Woolf and Furse were both "concerned at almost precisely the same time with lifting the curtain of secrecy surrounding sexuality and the mistreatment of children" (Fowler 229). Furse had struggled for several years to be allowed to read her father's manuscript autobiography at the LONDON LIBRARY, in which he discussed his homosexuality.

G

Gage, Tom A name on a tombstone in *JACOB'S ROOM,* seen by Betty FLANDERS as she walks one night with her neighbor, Mrs. JARVIS. Lytton STRACHEY and Dora CARRINGTON wrote a letter to Woolf purporting to be from "Tom Gage" and claiming he had lost his job as a lavatory attendant at Oxford Circus because she had used his name (L2 597). The tombstone next to Gage's in the novel bears the name of Bertha RUCK who, although Woolf did not know it, was a best-selling novelist who was very much alive.

Galsworthy, John (1867–1933) In Woolf's essay "MODERN FICTION," Galsworthy is one of the trio of "Edwardian" novelists (the other two are Arnold BENNETT and H. G. WELLS) whom she describes as "materialists" in contrast to the "spiritual" writers of her "Georgian" generation. The three novelists also appear in the same light in "MR. BENNETT AND MRS. BROWN." Galsworthy is best known for a series of novels published throughout his career gathered under the collective title *The Forsyte Saga,* in which the central figure is the Victorian patriarch Soames Forsyte. In *A ROOM OF ONE'S OWN,* Woolf's narrator remarks that Galsworthy is an example of a writer without "a spark of the woman in him" (AROO 102).

Galton, Francis Galton's "Hereditary Genius" is referred to in *NIGHT AND DAY* (ND 36). A cousin of Charles Darwin, Galton coined the word "eugenics" in his *Inquiries into Human Faculty and Its Development* (1883). Suzanne Raitt points out that Vita SACKVILLE-WEST's early novels are "grounded in eugenic theory and the work of Francis Galton in particular" (Raitt 90).

Gammer Gurton's Needle A sixteenth-century English verse comedy mentioned in *BETWEEN THE ACTS* as having been performed one year as the village pageant at POINTZ HALL.

Garfit A neighbor of Betty FLANDERS, in *JACOB'S ROOM,* whose acre of land Betty covets and about which Captain BARFOOT makes inquiries for her.

Garibaldi, Giuseppe (1807–82) This Italian soldier and revolutionary hero is mentioned several times in *THE VOYAGE OUT,* particularly by Evelyn MURGATROYD, who wishes there were still men like him and wishes she could have been married to him (TVO 130). Garibaldi's companion Anita Ribeiro da Silva died during their retreat across central Italy when fighting the French forces who intervened for Pope Pius IX against the Roman republic. Evelyn wonders whether Garibaldi was ever on SANTA MARINA, a possibility as he fought against Brazil in the rebellion of Rio Grande do Sul (1836–42).

Garnett, Angelica (b. 1918) Vanessa BELL's third child, born on Christmas Day; she was first called Susannah, then registered as Helen Vanessa; then her mother added Angelica when she was three months old. Almost immediately after her birth, she became seriously ill, causing extreme worry to Vanessa. Although her father was Duncan GRANT, all but a very few people were led to believe Clive BELL was Angelica's father, including Angelica herself. Later she wrote, "It seems very odd that they didn't think it was sufficiently important to tell me who my father was until I was seventeen" (MacWeeney v). This situation in effect meant Angelica grew up with no father figure as Duncan Grant, although a great friend to his child, had no interest in being a parent, and Clive Bell visited only infrequently, living in London most of the time. In an analysis of a 1924 Vanessa Bell painting of Clive and her three children, Spalding notes that Angelica is cut off from the group, "an unconscious admission of difference" (189; the painting is reproduced in Lehmann, *Virginia Woolf* 72).

Of the new baby, David GARNETT wrote prophetically to Lytton STRACHEY, "I think of marrying it; when she is twenty I shall be 46—will it be scandalous?" (To his mother, Garnett wrote, "Clive is very glad it is a girl; so will Virginia be for she thinks very highly of her own sex. Vanessa doesn't and is probably rather disappointed" [Naylor 147].) Angelica was greatly indulged as a child, continually told how beautiful she was, and encouraged to dress up

Angelica Playing the Violin, *1934 (71.5 x 65.5 cm). Duncan Grant. Courtesy Southampton City Art Gallery.*
Music was of "the greatest importance" to Angelica; she learned violin from a German woman whose method of teaching "did more to prevent than to encourage my efforts" (Angelica Garnett 88).

well into her teens; she was, for example, photographed as the young Russian princess SASHA for Woolf's *ORLANDO*. Given very little guidance as a child and teenager—not even learning the fundamentals of sex until her late teens—Angelica suffered from severe depressions later in her life. "Obviously," she wrote, "the person who was mainly responsible for my problems was Vanessa" (MacWeeney v). She was persistently treated as a child and reflected later in her life that she had no center. Of her half-brother Julian BELL's departure for China in 1935, she wrote that it "was rather like desertion at a moment when I particularly needed his understanding" (Angelica Garnett 121). She was not told in 1937 that he was going to Spain (where he would die in the SPANISH CIVIL WAR that July), and she never properly said good-bye to him.

Vanessa Bell did not believe in formal education, and she sent her daughter to Langford Grove in Essex, a school run by Elizabeth Curtis, who was far more interested in culture than the rudiments of knowledge. Angelica returned there to teach art for a term in 1941. Occasionally, Leonard WOOLF and Woolf would take Angelica out for tea from school, and Woolf went to hear Angelica give a speech there on Mrs. PANKHURST in 1934.

Woolf doted on her niece, naming her "Pixerina" in the fantasies she spun for her (in which Woolf herself was "Witcherina"). While Angelica was in her teens, Woolf gave her a £15 per quarter dress allowance. Whenever Woolf visited CHARLESTON, she would demand from Angelica "her rights"—"a kiss in the nape of the neck or on the eyelid, or a whole flutter of kisses from the inner wrist to the elbow" (Angelica Garnett 107). When Woolf went to NEWNHAM COLLEGE to give one of the lectures upon which *A ROOM OF ONE'S OWN* would be based, Vanessa and Angelica accompanied her, lunching the next day with John Maynard KEYNES and Lytton STRACHEY in George RYLANDS's rooms (the lunch reappears as an indication of the opulence of men's colleges in *A Room of One's Own*). Angelica remembered tea with Leonard and Virginia as a "rare but regular event," and noted that the only person who never indulged her was Leonard.

In 1935, Angelica played Ellen TERRY in the production of Woolf's *FRESHWATER* done at Vanessa's studio in Fitzroy Street. As well as her acting abilities, however, her talents as an artist were also encouraged. When the art director of Messrs. E. Brain and Co., a pottery in Stoke-on-Trent where Quentin BELL studied in 1936, commissioned various artists to make designs for commercial china, Duncan and Vanessa were joined by the fourteen-year-old Angelica in producing decorations for mass-produced plates. Woolf noted in her diary in 1934 that the *Star*, writing about this project, called her niece "a talented youngster" (D4 299). Angelica later reflected, however, that her artistic endeavors were more to please her parents than from any desire of her own.

After a stay in Paris in 1936, Angelica came back to London to enroll in the London Theatre Studio, run by Michel Saint-Denis. At the end-of-term student production in 1938, she danced in six mimed scenes based on Goya's *Desastros della Guerra* and acted in Benavente's *La Malguerida*, performances that were noted briefly in *The Times*. It was in this year that her affair with David Garnett—known to everybody as "Bunny"—began.

Bunny at the time was married to Rachel (Ray), the sister of Frances PARTRIDGE, with whom he had two children, William and Richard. Ray had cancer and rarely left their home, Hilton Hall, in Huntingdonshire. As Bunny had been her father's lover and was also enamored of her mother, Angelica's relation with him was, to say the least, complicated. On Bunny's side, his pursuit and seduction of Angelica seems to have been largely a way of obtaining indirectly what he could not have from Vanessa and also remaining entangled with Duncan Grant. Angelica herself has commented on the "incestuousness" of her marriage (MacWeeney viii) and wrote, "My dream of the perfect father—unrealised—possessed me, and has done so for the rest of my life. My marriage was but a continuation of it, and almost engulfed me" (Angelica Garnett 135).

Both Duncan Grant and Vanessa Bell were extremely angry when they realized what was happening, but they told very few people, not even Woolf. When she learned of the affair in 1940, Woolf wrote in her DIARY, "Pray God she may tire of that rusty surly slow old dog with his amorous ways & his primitive mind" (D5 282), but she softened in August that year when Angelica came to stay with her, writing "I see so much more of her side when I talk to her—her so reasonable & lovely side—if it weren't too, a delusion" (D5 310).

Having lost her virginity ("appropriately enough, in H. G. Wells's spare bedroom"), Angelica lived with Bunny for about three years before their marriage in 1942 (Ray Garnett died in 1940). Vanessa and Duncan were not invited to the wedding, which was witnessed by Frances and Ralph PARTRIDGE. They lived at Hilton Hall, and the marriage quickly proved unhappy. Angelica's first daughter, Amaryllis Virginia, was born in 1943; Henrietta Catherine Vanessa was born in 1945, and in 1946 came twins, Nerissa and Frances (Fanny). Henrietta Garnett's first novel, *Family Skeletons* (New York: Knopf, 1987), centers on an orphan, Catherine, who is the daughter of her mother Nellie's incestuous union with her brother, Pake. Late in the novel, a drunken Pake attempts to rape his daughter/niece. The plot also involves triangular relationships and mysterious deaths by drowning.

Angelica Bell separated from David Garnett in the late 1960s. In 1978, following Duncan Grant's death, she moved back to Charleston and fell into a severe depression. Her important memoir *Deceived with Kindness* was written at the encouragement of her friend Frank Hallman (who published Vanessa Bell's *Notes on Virginia's Childhood*) and her daughter Fanny. In it, she records her reevaluation of her mother in the light of their family history: "Vanessa shrank into a mere individual in a chain of women who, whether willingly or not, had learnt certain traits, certain attitudes from one another through the years" (Angelica Garnett 12). In 1927, Woolf had described her niece, after a children's party at Charleston, as "such an epitome of all womanliness; & such an unopened bud of sense & sensibility" (D3 167), but continued that she did not "like the physicalness of having children of one's own" and did not feel the desire to have them. Angelica Garnett saw her childhood "as a precarious paradise, slung like a cradle over a cloud, but none the less full of delight" (Angelica Garnett 176). In the late 1970s, she traveled in America, speaking about her Bloomsbury past, and she now lives in France, where she sculpts.

Garnett, Constance (1862–1946) Her translations of many Russian writers achieved great popularity in the first two decades of the twentieth century and had a profound influence on MODERNIST writers such as Woolf. Garnett studied classics at NEWNHAM COLLEGE, Cambridge University, and began to learn Russian in the early 1890s. She was married to Edward GARNETT, a publisher's reader who advised Gerald DUCKWORTH to accept Woolf's first novel, *THE VOYAGE OUT*. Their son was David GARNETT.

Garnett, David (1892–1981) The only child of Edward and Constance GARNETT, and grandson of Richard Garnett, Keeper of Books at the BRITISH MUSEUM, David Garnett was known almost universally as "Bunny." Although trained at the Royal College of Science as a botanist, he later turned to a highly successful literary career. Among his twenty-one works of fiction, *Lady into Fox* (1922) is notable for having won both the Hawthornden and Tait-Black prizes for 1923. The unexpected success of this novel led Bunny to withdraw in 1924 from the bookshop he had established in 1920 with Francis BIRRELL to devote more time to his writing. From 1923 to 1935 he was a partner in the Nonesuch Press, and from 1932 to 1935 he was literary editor of the *NEW STATESMAN AND NATION*. He wrote several memoirs and was awarded a CBE (Commander of the British Empire) in 1952.

Bunny was a friend of Adrian STEPHEN, who introduced him to Woolf in 1910. Their acquaintance was renewed in 1916 when Bunny, Barbara Hiles (see BAGENAL) and Dora CARRINGTON broke into ASHEHAM HOUSE while on their way to visit Duncan GRANT and Vanessa BELL at CHARLESTON. Finding they had no lodging for the night, and knowing Leonard and Virginia to be in London, the three "cropheads" (as Woolf called them) spent the night.

At Christmas in 1914, Bunny first met Duncan Grant while they were staying with Lytton STRACHEY. Listening to Strachey reading his sexual satire "Ermyntrude & Esmeralda" confirmed Bunny as a libertine and, he later wrote, enabled him to live a promiscuous life. Sexually adventurous, Bunny had flirted with John Maynard KEYNES, Lytton Strachey, and Francis Birrell, but he had his first physical homosexual relationship with Duncan Grant, beginning early in 1915. As a CONSCIENTIOUS OBJECTOR, Bunny had served for a time with a Quaker Relief Unit in France, but in 1916 he moved to Charleston where he and Duncan worked on a nearby farm while living with Vanessa Bell. Vanessa rejected Bunny's advances but remained close to him. Vanessa, Duncan, and Bunny formed one of several triangular relationships found among their contemporaries. Vanessa, in love with the homosexual Duncan, persuaded him to father a child with her. The child,

Angelica GARNETT, was brought up to the age of seventeen believing her father was Clive BELL. Soon after her birth, Bunny vowed he would one day marry her, which he did in 1942 much to the distress of her parents and against the advice of such friends as Virginia and Leonard Woolf and Maynard Keynes. Angelica and Bunny (who was twenty-six years older than she was) had four daughters before their marriage dissolved in the 1970s. Bunny's first wife, whom he married in 1921, was Rachel (Ray) Marshall, the elder sister of Frances PARTRIDGE.

Garnett, Edward (1868–1937) Father of David GARNETT and husband of Constance GARNETT, he was a prominent publisher's reader who in 1913 recommended that Gerald DUCKWORTH publish Woolf's first novel, *THE VOYAGE OUT.*

Garsington Home near Oxford of Lady Ottoline MORRELL which became during World War I a haven for CONSCIENTIOUS OBJECTORS and pacifists such as Clive BELL, Aldous HUXLEY, Bertrand RUSSELL and Lytton STRACHEY. After the war, Garsington continued to be the center of a wide circle of intellectuals, artists, writers and politicians (see Miranda Seymour, *Ottoline Morrell,* and Lady Ottoline Morrell, *Lady Ottoline's Album*).

Gaskell, Elizabeth Cleghorn (1810–65) At the beginning of *A ROOM OF ONE'S OWN,* Woolf suggests that a talk on women and fiction might include "a reference to Mrs. Gaskell" (AROO 3), the writer best known for her *Life of Charlotte Brontë* (1857). Gaskell grew up in Knutsford, England, on which she based the "Cranford" of her famous series of essays written between 1851 and 1853 for *Household Words,* a periodical edited by Charles DICKENS. Among Gaskell's other works are *Mary Barton* (1848), *Ruth* (1853), *North and South* (1855), *Round the Sofa* (1859), and, for the *CORNHILL MAGAZINE, Wives and Daughters* (1864–66). After her marriage in 1832, Gaskell moved to Manchester. She became "one of the nineteenth century's foremost recorders of life in England's provinces during the height of the Industrial Revolution" (Gilbert and Gubar, *Norton* 309).

Woolf reviewed *Mrs. Gaskell: Haunts, Homes and Stories,* by Mrs. Ellis H. Chadwick, for the *TIMES LITERARY SUPPLEMENT* in September 1910 ("Mrs. Gaskell" E1 340–44).

Gay, John (1685–1732) In *A ROOM OF ONE'S OWN,* Woolf notes that the poet Anne FINCH apparently offended the playwright Gay when she criticized his satirical poem *Trivia: or, the Art of Walking the Streets of London* (1716; AROO 61). Gay was a friend of Richard Steele, Joseph ADDISON and Alexander POPE (the latter's epitaph for him is inscribed on Gay's tomb in WESTMINSTER ABBEY). He was helped by Jonathan SWIFT in getting the post of secretary to Lord Clarendon, ambassador to the Court of Hanover, in 1714. Gay's most famous work is *The Beggar's Opera* (1728).

Gayton, Lord Character in *MRS. DALLOWAY* who attends Clarissa DALLOWAY's party with Miss Nancy Blow. Clarissa, although she likes the couple, thinks they will "solidify young" and be "rather dull" on their own (MD 270).

George, Henry (1839–97) Among the favorite writers of Mr. GRICE in *THE VOYAGE OUT* is this American writer on political economy and sociology.

Gerhardie, William Alexander (1895–1977) In *THREE GUINEAS,* Woolf quotes from Gerhardie's *Memoirs of a Polyglot* (Duckworth 1931) as an example of how easy it is to find men's opinions of women that concur with the fascist point of view (TG 178–79). Gerhardie was born in Russia to English parents and was military attaché to the British Embassy in Petrograd. He wrote novels, criticism and a historical biography of the Romanoff dynasty.

Gertler, Mark (1891–1939) Painter who was in love with Dora CARRINGTON, whom he had met at the Slade School of Art, and who was part of the circle around Lady Ottoline MORRELL at GARSINGTON during World War I. He was generally unpopular with the BLOOMSBURY GROUP, who found him too intense and egotistical. He was an occasional guest of the Woolfs at ASHEHAM in 1918, and his painting was admired by Vanessa BELL, Roger FRY and Duncan GRANT. Plagued by ill health, poverty and marital difficulties, he gassed himself in 1939.

Gibbon, Edward (1737–94) Author of the *History of the Decline and Fall of the Roman Empire,* the first volume of which appeared in 1776; two more volumes appeared in 1781, and the last three in 1788. In *THE VOYAGE OUT,* St. John HIRST recommends *Decline and Fall* to Rachel VINRACE, lending her his copy of the first volume. Gibbon is often used by Woolf as a paradigm of the masculine style that men are trained both to read and write by the university education from which their sisters were excluded. St. John Hirst, for example, tells Rachel that Gibbon is "the test" of whether women are able to converse with men (TVO 154). In *A ROOM OF ONE'S OWN,* Gibbon and Samuel JOHNSON are cited as the forebears of the "man's sentence" which women cannot use (AROO 76).

Woolf wrote two essays on Gibbon, "The Historian and 'The Gibbon' " for the *TIMES LITERARY SUPPLEMENT* in 1937 (CE1 115–23), and "Reflections at

Sheffield Place" for the *NEW STATESMAN AND NATION,* also in 1937 (CE1 124–30).

Gibbons, General Mentioned in *JACOB'S ROOM* at Elizabeth DURRANT's house, where the guests discuss World War I.

Gibbs, Hugh First mentioned in *THE YEARS* as a friend of Edward PARGITER's at Oxford University (TY 52). There may be elements of Clive BELL in his characterization. Presumably he is the same Gibbs who later marries Edward's sister Milly PARGITER.

Giddings, Miss Mentioned in *TO THE LIGHTHOUSE* as having almost jumped out of her skin when Mr. Ramsay bellows "Best and brightest come away!" (TTL 70).

Girton College In October 1928, Woolf spoke to the ODTAA Society at Girton College, Cambridge University, delivering one of the two papers upon which *A ROOM OF ONE'S OWN* is based. In *A Room* Woolf refers to the founding of Girton by Emily Davies when the narrator, Mary BETON, spends an evening with Mary SETON, who tells her the story of how the college came to be (AROO 20).

Emily Davies (1830–1921) was the daughter of a clergyman. With Barbara Leigh Smith BODICHON, Elizabeth Garrett, Jessie Boucheret and Rosamond Hill, Davies formed the first Women's SUFFRAGE Committee in 1858 (Ray Strachey, *The Cause* 104). In her history of the women's movement, Ray STRACHEY describes Davies as "the chief arbiter of tactics and the chief organiser of campaigns" relating to women's higher education (131). Martha Vicinus has explained that higher education for women "began modestly. Queen's College was founded in 1848. . . . In the following year Bedford College was founded by Elizabeth Reid, a determined and unswerving feminist" (Vicinus 123). It was only in 1869 that residential colleges for women were achieved with the founding of Hitchin, which later became Girton, College (Vicinus 123). In 1862, Emily Davies was secretary to a committee formed to gain admission for women to university examinations. In *A Room of One's Own,* Woolf quotes from *The Cause* that "Emily Davies took great care to secure some well-dressed and good-looking young women to fill up the front row" at a meeting of the Social Science Association called in 1863 to discuss allowing women to take university examinations (Strachey, *The Cause* 134; AROO 20n2).

Vicinus points out that the founders of the first women's colleges believed strongly that women should have their own rooms: "Davies, for example, refused to spend any money on landscaping yet insisted upon a bedroom and sitting room for each woman when Girton's first building was built" (Vicinus 141). Davies was quite single-minded about establishing Girton, even dropping her support of women's suffrage lest she jeopardize its future (Vicinus 134). Having failed to get London University to admit women to examinations, she began to plan a separate women's college, presenting her plans to Bodichon in January 1867. Woolf (in *A Room of One's Own*) and Strachey (in *The Cause*) both use as a source in retelling this story Lady Barbara Stephen's *Emily Davies and Girton College,* which Woolf reviewed for the *NATION & ATHENAEUM* in 1927 ("Two Women" CE4 61–66). In 1869, Davies settled on a site in Hitchin, half way between London and Cambridge, for her college. The lecturers traveled from Cambridge, and in 1870 five students were ready to take the University Previous Examination (known as "Little Go"); all five passed in Latin and Greek. That year, land was bought at Girton, two miles from Cambridge, and the students moved in in 1873, despite the buildings not being completely ready.

NEWNHAM COLLEGE, the other women's college at Cambridge, and Girton went separate ways as Davies differed from other reformers in believing that women should be taught and prepared for examinations in exactly the same way as men. In 1920, Strachey records, women students were admitted to full membership at Oxford University but not at Cambridge. "The course of affairs at that perverse university was long and intricate," she writes (*The Cause* 382).

Gladstone, William Ewart (1809–98) British politician who became Prime Minister in 1868, 1880, 1886, and 1892. In the "1880" chapter of *THE YEARS,* Kitty LASSWADE begins to discuss Gladstone with her mother, but the conversation is cut short because Mrs. MALONE has lost her scissors (TY 79).

Goat (also Goatus, Il Giotto) Family nickname for Woolf.

Godrevy Lighthouse The lighthouse that Woolf could see from Talland House in ST. IVES, where she spent summers as a child, and which inspires the setting of *TO THE LIGHTHOUSE.* Joseph Kessel writes that from 1859 to 1934 "the tower was fitted with the original First Order in size lens which revolved beams with regular luminosity and occurrence every ten seconds for one second duration across the line of sight of the viewer, producing a white flash" and notes that atmospheric conditions would have produced the effect of the light as a "yellow eye" recalled by James RAMSAY in Woolf's novel (VWM 18: 1–2).

Gordon Square The most densely populated by BLOOMSBURY GROUP members of the squares and streets in the area of London known as BLOOMSBURY. After Leslie STEPHEN's death in 1904, Vanessa BELL found 46 Gordon Square for herself, Woolf and their two brothers, Adrian and Thoby STEPHEN, and they moved there in October. At the time this was not considered a "proper" neighborhood for young women of the Stephens' class to live in, but over the years many Bloomsbury friends as well as people on the periphery of that network moved there. It was at 46 Gordon Square that Thoby Stephen began the "Thursday Evenings" usually described as the beginnings of the Bloomsbury Group. John Maynard KEYNES took over 46 Gordon Square in 1916 from Clive BELL and Vanessa, who had stayed there after their marriage in 1907 (Woolf and Adrian moving to FITZROY SQUARE); from 1925 he lived there with his wife, Lydia LOPOKOVA, Vanessa taking rooms at number 50. James STRACHEY and Alix STRACHEY lived at 41 Gordon Square, and from 1926 to 1933 Ralph PARTRIDGE and Frances PARTRIDGE rented rooms there. In 1919, Lady Jane Maria STRACHEY moved to 51 Gordon Square with her daughters Marjorie STRACHEY and Philippa STRACHEY; Lady Jane stayed there until her death, with various of her children living with her at different times. After their marriage in 1914, Adrian Stephen and Karin STEPHEN lived at 50 Gordon Square, where Clive Bell also rented an apartment. From 1925 to 1929 Vanessa and Duncan GRANT lived at 37 Gordon Square when they were not at CHARLESTON or CASSIS, Vanessa renting two floors to George RYLANDS and Angus DAVIDSON. Arthur WALEY and Beryl de Zoete lived at 50 Gordon Square from about 1939 until 1962.

Gorham, Mrs. Mentioned in *MRS. DALLOWAY,* praying in WESTMINSTER ABBEY when Doris KILMAN goes in to pray.

Gorky, Maxim (1868–1936) Russian novelist and short-story writer. The HOGARTH PRESS published his *Reminiscences of Tolstoi* in 1920, translated by S. S. KOTELIANSKY, and in 1921 *The Note-Books of Anton Tchekhov Together with Reminiscences of Tchekhov by Maxim Gorky,* translated by Koteliansky and Leonard WOOLF.

Gosse, Sir Edmund (1849–1928) Critic and biographer best known for his memoir *Father and Son: A Study of Two Temperaments* published anonymously in 1907. Woolf reviewed his *Some Diversions of a Man of Letters* for the *TIMES LITERARY SUPPLEMENT* in October 1919 and a new edition of his *Life of William Congreve* for the *NATION & ATHENAEUM* in 1924.

Goth, The Nickname for Thoby STEPHEN among his Cambridge friends. In letters to Leonard WOOLF, Lytton STRACHEY refers to 46 GORDON SQUARE as the "Gothic Mansion" (Spotts 75n).

Gower, Granville Leveson, Lord (1773–1846) In *A ROOM OF ONE'S OWN,* Woolf laments Lady BESSBOROUGH's deference to Lord Granville Leveson Gower, a statesman with whom she corresponded extensively.

Grace A maid in *BETWEEN THE ACTS* who finds Lucy SWITHIN "Batty" because she seems so vague (8).

Grafton Galleries See POST-IMPRESSIONIST.

Grandage, Mrs., and Tom Grandage Appear briefly in *JACOB'S ROOM* as the narrator passes over Surbiton, a London suburb, where they are preparing for the day.

Granite & Rainbow, Essays The last of four posthumous collections of Woolf's essays edited by Leonard WOOLF, published in 1958 by the HOGARTH PRESS in Britain and by Harcourt, Brace and Company in the United States. In his "Editorial Note," Leonard explains that these essays were found among Woolf's papers by B. J. Kirkpatrick and Mary Lyon (see *BOOKS AND PORTRAITS*). This volume contains several important essays, including: "THE NARROW BRIDGE OF ART," "IMPASSIONED PROSE," "WOMEN AND FICTION" and "PHASES OF FICTION."

Grant, Duncan James Corrowr (1885–1978) Painter, partner of Vanessa BELL from 1916 until her death in 1961, and father of Angelica GARNETT. Grant's Anglo-Indian army father, Major Bartle Grant, was the brother of Lady Jane Maria STRACHEY, Lytton STRACHEY's mother, and it was through this connection that Grant first came into contact with several members of the BLOOMSBURY GROUP. He grew up in India and Burma, but he attended school in England, staying with the Strachey family. Through Lady Strachey's intercession, Grant was allowed by his father to attend Westminster Art School. Vanessa was first introduced to Grant in 1905 at a meeting of the FRIDAY CLUB, and when she and Clive BELL were in Paris soon after their marriage in 1907, they saw him frequently. At the time, Grant was studying with Jacques-Emile BLANCHE. Woolf and Adrian STEPHEN also visited the Bells in Paris then, and all five would often dine together.

Simon Watney has suggested that Grant's work "would be far better known and appreciated had he been less closely associated with Bloomsbury, to whose changing critical fortunes his own reputation has been closely linked" (Watney 10). In the 1920s, however, Grant was widely recognized as one of the leading painters of the time. A co-director with Vanessa Bell and Roger FRY of the OMEGA WORK-

Drawing for a portrait of Vanessa Bell, c. *1920–21. Red and black chalk on paper. Duncan Grant. © Fitzwilliam Museum, University of Cambridge.*

SHOPS, Grant was a significant influence on Vanessa's art. He "worked in an extremely wide range of different fields, including fabric design, ceramics, book illustration, theatre work, ballet, interior decoration, and print-making, besides oil-painting and his work in other media, principally gouache, pastel and watercolour, in all of which he excelled" (Watney 11).

S. P. Rosenbaum remarks that "one of the various definitions of Bloomsbury is that of a group of women and men who were all in love with Duncan Grant" (*Edwardian* 219). His good looks and delightful personality attracted nearly all who knew him (a notable exception being the intensely homophobic D. H. LAWRENCE, who warned David GARNETT to detach himself from Grant; the character Duncan Forbes in Lawrence's *Lady Chatterley's Lover* is based on Grant). In her DIARY in August 1918, Woolf wrote, "Duncan spent the night before with us. He stumbled along until, by means which he only knows the secret of, he had us all laughing until the tears came" (D1 187).

Lytton Strachey was deeply infatuated with his cousin in 1905–06, and Grant also had affairs with John Maynard KEYNES and Adrian Stephen. When Adrian and Woolf moved to 29 FITZROY SQUARE after the Bells' marriage, Grant, who had a studio nearby, was a frequent visitor. He participated in the DREADNOUGHT HOAX in 1910, with Adrian and Woolf, and was abducted a few days later by angry and embarrassed naval officers and taken to Hampstead Heath, where they intended to beat him. Grant's mildness and lack of resistance, however, disarmed the military men and they let him go with only two ceremonial taps with a cane (QB2 Appendix E). In 1911, Grant, Adrian, Keynes, and Woolf shared a house at 38 BRUNSWICK SQUARE, where they were soon joined by Leonard WOOLF, who had just returned from Ceylon.

In May 1913, Grant accompanied Fry and the Bells to Italy. Vanessa's affair with Fry was dwindling, and she was becoming increasingly attracted to Grant, although at the time he was in love with her brother Adrian. By 1914, however, Adrian was involved with Karin COSTELLOE and his marriage (as well as the marriage of George Mallory, another of Grant's lovers) precipitated Grant's beginning to return Vanessa's feelings (Spalding, *Vanessa Bell* 133). At Christmas 1914 Grant met David Garnett while staying with Lytton Strachey, and by 1915 he and "Bunny," as Garnett was known, were involved in an affair (although Garnett also continued to have relationships with women). In 1916, Grant, Garnett and Vanessa Bell moved together to CHARLESTON, where the men did farm work as CONSCIENTIOUS OBJECTORS. Grant and Vanessa's decision to have a child was mutual (Marler 554), and on Christmas Day 1918 Angelica Bell (later Angelica Garnett) was born. Grant, though kindly, was not particularly interested in fatherhood, a responsibility he was enabled in avoiding by the fact that all but a very few people were told that Clive was Angelica's father. This included Angelica herself, who was not told the truth until she was seventeen; her memoir *Deceived with Kindness* gives a more complicated portrait of Grant than many other biographies.

As a *de facto* relative of Woolf's, Grant makes frequent appearances in her DIARY and LETTERS. He was a member of the MEMOIR CLUB and played the part of G. F. WATTS in Woolf's play *FRESHWATER*. Grant and Vanessa decorated the Woolfs' house at 52 TAVISTOCK SQUARE, and Woolf was an early collector of both their works. She described his relationship with her sister as "a left-handed marriage," one that seemed to her to work because it was based on "Bohemianism." Woolf had a tendency to disparage painting and would occasionally mock her sister's and Grant's silent absorption in their art. Nevertheless, she also wrote that she preferred nothing to sitting in their studio discussing painting. Woolf's last work, unfinished at her death, was a projected history of English literature ("ANON") which she described as an effort to explain literature to painters, Grant being her model reader.

Grant, Ethel (1863–1948) Duncan GRANT's mother. She stitched and embroidered Grant's designs for chair covers, firescreens and decorative panels. "From the 1920s to her death in 1948 she was constantly at work, not only on her son's designs but on those by Vanessa Bell and Roger Fry" (Shone 39). She was admired by many of Grant's friends, and Woolf "is thought to have had her in mind when she wrote the opening pages of *Jacob's Room* and describes Mrs. Flanders" (Shone 39).

Gratety and Hooper In *NIGHT AND DAY,* the name of the firm of solicitors where Ralph DENHAM works as a clerk. When Katharine HILBERY goes to meet Ralph the name has changed to "Hoper [sic] and Grately" (ND 438). In *MRS. DALLOWAY,* Peter WALSH has come to London to see his lawyer at "Hooper and Grately," whose offices, like Ralph's, are at Lincoln's Inn.

Gravé, Madame Lucien A Frenchwoman in *JACOB'S ROOM* who irritates Jacob at the Parthenon by pointing her camera at his head. Woolf had a dressmaker named Madame Gravé.

Graves, Dick A friend of Jacob FLANDERS in *JACOB'S ROOM.* Their friendship makes Helen ASKEW think that men's friendships are always "so much more beautiful than women's" (JR 111).

Gray, Thomas (1716–71) Although only thirteen of his poems were published in his lifetime, Gray became the most celebrated lyric poet of his day, best known perhaps for his "Elegy Written in a Country Church-Yard" (1751). Woolf alludes to a line from that poem ("Some mute inglorious *Milton* here may rest") in *A ROOM OF ONE'S OWN* when she writes that whenever we read of a woman being possessed, or ducked as a witch, or of a wise woman who sold herbs, "then I think we are on the track of a lost novelist, a suppressed poet, of some mute and inglorious Jane Austen" (AROO 49). In *THREE GUINEAS,* Woolf quotes from Gray's "Ode for Music," in which he praises the female benefactors of men's colleges at Cambridge University (TG 27–28). In 1935 Woolf was reading Gray's three-volume *Correspondence,* edited by Paget Toynbee and Leonard Whibley (Oxford: Clarendon Press, 1935), and John Mitford's "Life of Thomas Gray" in his edition of *The Works of Thomas Gray* (1836), and she was considering writing an essay on the poet (but did not). From Samuel JOHNSON's "Life of Gray," Woolf took the phrase "the common reader" as the title of two collections of her essays, *THE COMMON READER* and *THE COMMON READER: SECOND SERIES.*

Greenwich After PERCIVAL's death in *THE WAVES,* RHODA goes to a concert and then plans to go to Greenwich, where she will throw flowers into the water as a memorial. Greenwich is a borough of London on the River Thames; the Greenwich Hospital and Royal Naval College are situated there. The Royal Observatory that used to be in Greenwich Park was the source of Greenwich Mean Time. In *ORLANDO,* the Royal Court is set up on the frozen Thames at Greenwich during the Great Frost.

Greg, Mr. In *A ROOM OF ONE'S OWN,* the opinion of a "Mr. Greg" is adduced as part of the "enormous body of masculine opinion to the effect that nothing could be expected of women intellectually" (AROO 54). Probably the reference is to W. R. Greg, who published *The Creed of Christendom* in 1850–51. In "Why Are Women Redundant?" (1862), Greg lamented the "enormous and increasing number of single women in the nation" and argued that the "essentials of woman's being" were to be "supported by and to minister to men" (Vicinus 3–4). Greg's solution to the "woman question" was to ship unmarried women to Canada, Australia and the United States, where they would have better prospects of marrying.

Greene, Nick A famous writer whom ORLANDO invites to his house to discuss poetry in chapter 2 of *ORLANDO.* Greene denounces his Elizabethan contemporaries and their lack of "Glawr" ("la gloire" in French, meaning "glory") and tells Orlando that poetry is dead. A possible model for Greene is Robert Greene (1558–92), author of the earliest literary reference to William SHAKESPEARE. Greene referred to Shakespeare as "an upstart Crow" in his bitter autobiographical work *Greene's Groatsworth of Wit* (1592). In the final chapter of *Orlando,* Greene appears again, now transformed into the greatest critic of the Victorian age and still denouncing his contemporaries. It is Greene who insists that Orlando's poem *The Oak Tree* be published. In *A ROOM OF ONE'S OWN* Nick Greene is the "actor-manager" who seduces Judith SHAKESPEARE (AROO 48).

Gresham, Mr. and Mrs. People at Elizabeth DURRANT's party in *JACOB'S ROOM.*

Grice, Mr. (1) Character in *THE VOYAGE OUT.* He is the steward of the *EUPHROSYNE,* the ship owned by Willoughby VINRACE. When Clarissa DALLOWAY remarks that the life of a sailor must be fine, Mr. Grice bitterly challenges her knowledge of a seafaring life (TVO 53) and then invites her to his cabin, where he shows her his relics from the oceans of the world and recites from William SHAKESPEARE's *Tempest.* Rachel VINRACE finds Grice a bore, while her father thinks him a "very interesting fellow" (TVO 54).

Grice, Mr. (2) A real-estate agent in *THE YEARS* (TY 215).

Grice, Mrs. Referred to in *THE YEARS* as having won "the silver-plated salver" at a village fête (TY 200).

Grimsditch, Mrs. ORLANDO's housekeeper. The name comes from a list of the household of the seventeenth-century earl of Dorset, Richard Sackville, found in *Knole and the Sackvilles* by Vita SACKVILLE-WEST.

Grizzle Leonard and Virginia WOOLF's mongrel fox terrier acquired in 1922 and put down in 1926 after becoming infected with eczema.

Groves, Mrs. Mentioned in *THE YEARS* when Eleanor PARGITER visits houses for the poor with Mr. DUFFUS.

Guardian Woolf's first published work, an anonymous review of William Dean Howells's *The Son of Royal Langbrith,* appeared in this Anglo-Catholic newspaper of December 14, 1904. Founded in 1846 and from 1903 incorporating the *Churchwoman,* the *Guardian* proposed to establish in the public mind "a clear view of the ground taken by the high Church on matters religious and political." Woolf was introduced to the paper by Violet DICKINSON, who was a friend of Margaret Lyttleton, the editor of the women's pages. Between 1904 and 1909, Woolf wrote several reviews and occasional pieces for the *Guardian,* including "Haworth, November, 1904" and an obituary of her Quaker aunt, Caroline Emelia STEPHEN. Andrew McNeillie discusses in detail Woolf's relations with the *Guardian* in his introduction to E1 (xi–xiv).

Guermantes, Madame de In *A ROOM OF ONE'S OWN,* Madame (Oriane) de Guermantes, the cousin of Charlus in Marcel PROUST's *A la recherche du temps perdu (Remembrance of Things Past),* is adduced as one of the women who have "burnt like beacons in all the works of all the poets from the beginning of time" (AROO 43), whom Woolf uses to stress the difference between fictional and real women.

Gurth The STEPHEN family dog that, in 1905, replaced SHAG (subject of Woolf's obituary "On a Faithful Friend" [E1 12]).

Gwyn (or Gwynn), Nell (Eleanor) (1650–87) The mistress of King Charles II (1625–49), mentioned in *ORLANDO.*

H

Haines, Rupert Character in *BETWEEN THE ACTS.* A "gentleman farmer" to whom Isa OLIVER is attracted and whose wife Isa ignores.

Hakluyt, Richard See *VOYAGE OUT, THE.*

Hall, Radclyffe See *WELL OF LONELINESS, THE.*

Hamilton, Mary See BALLAD OF THE QUEEN'S MARYS.

Hammond Mentioned in *BETWEEN THE ACTS* as a villager taking part in the Victorian scene of the annual pageant.

Hamnett, Nina (1890–1956) Painter who worked in the OMEGA WORKSHOPS and knew the artists of the Parisian avant-garde before World War I. Frances Spalding describes her affair with Roger FRY (*Roger Fry* 200–02).

Hampton Court In *NIGHT AND DAY,* Ralph DENHAM, Katharine HILBERY, William RODNEY and Cassandra OTWAY are on an excursion to Hampton Court while Mrs. MILVAIN is telling Mr. HILBERY the shocking tale of the four young people's affairs. Lily BRISCOE and William BANKES of *TO THE LIGHTHOUSE* go to Hampton Court together. In *THE WAVES* RHODA goes to Hampton Court after the death of PERCIVAL to "recover beauty and impose order" on her soul (TW 161), and the six figures in *The Waves* (Rhoda, BERNARD, JINNY, LOUIS, NEVILLE and SUSAN) have a reunion dinner in middle age at an inn near Hampton Court in the eighth EPISODE of the novel (TW 210–35). Woolf described this section of *The Waves* as "that very difficult passage," writing of her characters that she had to show "how their lives hang lit up against the Palace" (D3 334).

Hampton Court was the center of government for King William III, who ruled England from 1689 to 1702, and was until the reign of Queen Anne the favorite royal residence. Begun in 1514 by Cardinal Wolsey, it was surrendered to Henry VIII in 1526 and partly rebuilt. William III employed the architect Christopher WREN to add to the buildings and had the gardens laid out, including the famous Hampton Court maze. It was a place Woolf herself visited many times during her life, often imagining the historic figures who had walked there. In 1903 she wrote in her DIARY an account of "An Expedition to Hampton Court" (PA 172–75).

Ham Spray House near Hungerford, Wiltshire, bought in 1924 by Lytton STRACHEY and where he lived with Dora CARRINGTON and Ralph PARTRIDGE until his death in 1932.

Harcourt, Brace & Co. See BRACE, Donald.

Hardcastle, Miss Eleanor A character in Miss LA TROBE's Victorian scene in her village pageant in *BETWEEN THE ACTS.*

Hardy, Thomas (1840–1928) English writer whose poems and novels often depict an epic struggle between people and a reasonless cosmos. Among his best-known works are *Far From the Madding Crowd* (1874), *The Return of the Native* (1878), *The Mayor of Casterbridge* (1886), *Wessex Tales* (1888), *Tess of the D'Urbervilles* (1891) and *Jude the Obscure* (1896). Woolf's father, Leslie STEPHEN, had been a friend of Hardy's and had also published his work in the *CORNHILL MAGAZINE.* In *THE VOYAGE OUT,* Terence HEWET quotes the final stanza of Hardy's poem "He Abjures Love" (from *Time's Laughingstocks*) (TVO 110).

In 1919, Bruce RICHMOND, editor of the *TIMES LITERARY SUPPLEMENT,* asked Woolf to be ready with an article when Hardy died (D2 126). Brenda Silver notes that Woolf "started reading and talking about Hardy in 1919, although her article, 'The Novels of Thomas Hardy,' was not published until January 19, 1928" (RN 111). Woolf had written to Hardy in 1915 to thank him for a poem he had published about her father, and in July 1926 she and Leonard WOOLF visited Hardy at his home (D3 96–101). They attended his funeral in February 1928 (D3 173–74). On vacation in Italy in 1908, Woolf had asked herself, "Is Thomas Hardy among the Classics?" (PA 386) and in her TLS article (CE1 256–66; reprinted in the *COMMON READER: SECOND SERIES*) she concluded that he had been "a profound and poetic genius" (CE1 266).

"Hark, hark" In his "summing up" in the ninth EPISODE of *THE WAVES*, BERNARD recites part of a well-known English nursery rhyme that goes, "Hark, hark the dogs do bark, the beggars are coming to town." The verse is heard also in *BETWEEN THE ACTS* (117) by Bart OLIVER and his sister Lucy SWITHIN.

Harriet, Archduchess (Harriet Griselda of Finster-Aarhorn and Scand-op-Boom) Character in *ORLANDO* whom Woolf intended to represent Henry, Lord Lascelles, an early suitor of Vita SACKVILLE-WEST. At the end of chapter 2, Archduchess Harriet suddenly appears to court Orlando. The Archduchess is very tall and has a knowledge of wines, firearms and sports uncommon in a woman. As she reveals herself to be in fact the Archduke Harry when she reappears in chapter 4, this knowledge is not surprising. Harry is a tiresome suitor whom Orlando gets rid of by first cheating at "Fly Loo," and then putting a frog down his shirt. Like his real-life model, Archduke Harry marries a "very great lady" (Lascelles married Mary, the only daughter of King George V).

Harris, Lilian (1866–1949) Assistant Secretary of the WOMEN'S COOPERATIVE GUILD and lifelong companion of Margaret Llewelyn DAVIES.

Harrison, Jane Ellen (1850–1928) One of the first women to graduate from NEWNHAM COLLEGE, she was lecturer in classical archaeology there from 1898 to 1922. In *A ROOM OF ONE'S OWN* "J— H— herself" is described as "the flash of some terrible reality leaping" by the narrator (AROO 17). Woolf also included her in a list of great women in her letter responding to Desmond MACCARTHY in the *NEW STATESMAN*, "The Intellectual Status of Women" (D2 Appendix III). Harrison was at the center of the "Cambridge Group," founders of myth criticism. Leonard WOOLF described her as "one of the most civilised persons I have ever known" (LW2 204), and in 1925 the HOGARTH PRESS published her *Reminiscences of a Student's Life*. Of her many books, the Woolfs' library contained *Ancient Art and Ritual* (1918), inscribed "To Virginia Woolf from Jane Harrison / Christmas 1923" (Holleyman V/s II 3), *Aspects Aorists and the Classic Tripos* (1919), and *Epilegomena to the Study of Greek Religion* (1921). From 1922 until her death, Harrison shared her life in Paris and London with Hope MIRRLEES. Her work's influence on Woolf is discussed by Patricia Cramer, Mark Hussey ("Reading and Ritual"), Jane Marcus (*Languages*) and Annabel Robinson among others.

Harrison, Lillah Mentioned in *THE VOYAGE OUT*, she is a friend of Evelyn MURGATROYD's who "runs a home for inebriate women" in London that is now the largest of its kind (TVO 248).

Hartopp, Miss Penelope When the account of ORLANDO's receipt of the Order of the Bath given in John Fenner BRIGGE's diary ends with him falling out of the tree from which he is observing the ceremony, the story is taken up in a letter Miss Hartopp writes to a friend at Tunbridge Wells.

Hatchards' A bookshop that still remains in Piccadilly, mentioned in *MRS. DALLOWAY* when Clarissa DALLOWAY looks in its window to find a gift for Hugh WHITBREAD's wife and sees there a volume of SHAKESPEARE lying open. In it she reads the lines from *CYMBELINE* that will recur throughout the day of the novel's action.

Haunted House and Other Stories, A A posthumously published collection of Woolf's short stories, edited by Leonard WOOLF. *A Haunted House* was published in January 1944 by the HOGARTH PRESS (according to Kirkpatrick), but 1943 is the date on the title page. In his foreword, Leonard explains that Woolf had planned to publish another collection of

A Haunted House and Other Stories. *Courtesy Linda J. Langham.*
The second collection of Woolf's short fiction to be published (the first being Monday or Tuesday*). The cover, printed in bright blue, was designed by Vanessa Bell. This is the American first edition (1944).*

short stories before her death. *A Haunted House* includes six of the eight pieces published in her earlier collection of short fiction, *MONDAY OR TUESDAY* (1921); omitted are "Blue & Green" and "A SOCIETY." Of the latter, Leonard writes that Woolf had decided not to include it. Among the stories in *A Haunted House* in addition to the title story are: "AN UNWRITTEN NOVEL," "THE STRING QUARTET," "KEW GARDENS," "THE MARK ON THE WALL", "LAPPIN AND LAPINOVA," "SOLID OBJECTS," "MOMENTS OF BEING: 'SLATER'S PINS HAVE NO POINTS,' " "THE SEARCHLIGHT" and "THE LEGACY."

Havelock, General Mentioned in *NIGHT AND DAY* as one of the eminent connections of the Hilbery family, whose ancestors had "ridden with Havelock to the Relief of Lucknow" (36). During the "Indian Mutiny" of 1857–58 Havelock and Sir James Outram came to the relief of Lucknow and thus ended the war. In *MRS. DALLOWAY,* Peter WALSH passes a statue of Havelock as he walks in London after his visit to Clarissa DALLOWAY (MD 77).

Hawkins, Mr. Mentioned in *JACOB'S ROOM,* an undergraduate at Cambridge who throws up his window and bawls "Jo-seph! Jo-seph!"

Hawtrey, Sir Ralph (1879–1975) R. G. Hawtrey was a friend of Thoby STEPHEN's at Cambridge and an early visitor to Thoby's "Thursday Evenings" (see BLOOMSBURY GROUP). He and Saxon SYDNEY-TURNER visited the Stephen children when they took a vacation in Cornwall in the summer of 1905. He became an economist.

Hazlitt, William (1778–1830) English essayist who was a friend of William WORDSWORTH and Samuel Taylor COLERIDGE. Hazlitt wrote on art, drama, literature and many other topics. Woolf wrote a long review of *The Complete Works of William Hazlitt* for the *New York Herald Tribune* in September 1930; the review was reprinted in the *TIMES LITERARY SUPPLEMENT* (CR2 173–85; CE1 155–64).

Head, Dr. Henry (1861–1940) Neurologist recommended to the Woolfs in 1913 by Roger FRY, who had consulted him about his wife Helen Coombe's mental instability. Stephen Trombley describes Head as a "sympathetic empiricist" and comments on the significance of his medical research. Head edited *Brain* (1905–21), "and the results of some of his most important research were published there" (Trombley 160). He also wrote poetry and did significant work on shell shock. Leonard WOOLF took Woolf to see Head in August 1913, and on September 9, having seen Head and Dr. Maurice WRIGHT that day, Woolf attempted suicide by taking an overdose of Veronal, a sedative.

Headlam, Walter (1866–1908) A protégé of Julia Prinsep STEPHEN's with whom Woolf had a mild flirtation in 1906–07 (described in her letters to Violet DICKINSON). He was a Fellow of King's College, Cambridge University, and a lecturer in classics.

Hebrides A group of about fifty, mostly uninhabited, small islands off the coast of Scotland made famous by the tales of Sir Walter SCOTT and the setting of Woolf's *TO THE LIGHTHOUSE.*

Hedge, Julia "The feminist" in *JACOB'S ROOM* who works in the BRITISH MUSEUM Reading Room, "wetting her pen in bitterness" and lamenting the absence of women's names engraved in gold around the dome above the room. She is clearly a prototype of the narrator's visit to the British Museum in *A ROOM OF ONE'S OWN,* as she observes "how composedly, unconcernedly, and with every consideration the male readers applied themselves" to their work (JR 106). She dislikes Jacob FLANDERS on sight.

Helena, Aunt Character in *MRS. DALLOWAY* recalled by Peter WALSH as having been at Bourton the summer his proposal of marriage was rejected by her niece, Clarissa DALLOWAY. He assumes she is dead, but Aunt Helena comes to Clarissa's party at the end of the novel. She is over eighty and has a glass eye and is fond of telling people what Charles Darwin said about her little book on the orchids of Burma.

Hemingway, Ernest See "ESSAY IN CRITICISM, AN."

Henderson, Ellie A character in *MRS. DALLOWAY* whom Clarissa DALLOWAY had not wanted to invite to her party but had to when Mrs. Marsham mentioned the party to her. Clarissa is exasperated at the way Ellie—who is her cousin—slouches in a corner at the party. Ellie is a little awed by the guests, particularly the prime minister, and notes everything to tell her friend Edith. Peter WALSH remembers her as cutting up underclothes "at the large table in the window" at Bourton. Ellie's anxieties about what to wear to Clarissa's annual party are prefigured in a short story by Woolf, "The New Dress," found in *MRS. DALLOWAY'S PARTY.*

Heretics A Cambridge University society to which Woolf read "CHARACTER IN FICTION" in 1924. Andrew McNeillie describes the Heretics as "a mixed society and so rather advanced by the standards of the time" and says that it was probably founded in 1909 or 1911 (E3 500).

Hewet, Terence Character in *THE VOYAGE OUT*. He is an aspiring novelist, twenty-seven years old, who wishes to write "a novel about Silence . . . the things people don't say" (TVO 216) and has come to SANTA MARINA with his friend St. John HIRST. There he meets and falls in love with Rachel VINRACE, to whom he becomes engaged. Interested in meeting other people, especially women, Hewet arranges a picnic which brings together the principal characters in the novel. On that occasion, talking with Rachel and her aunt, Helen AMBROSE, Hewet offers a brief autobiographical sketch from which the reader learns that he is the "son of a fox-hunting squire" who died when he was ten (TVO 143–44).

Most critics have assumed that Woolf drew on the character of her brother-in-law Clive BELL in creating Hewet, though some have also suggested that John Waller "Jack" HILLS also contributed to the character. Phyllis Rose sees Hewet as Rachel's alter ego, the two characters representing two sides of Woolf herself. Jane Wheare likens Hewet to Mr. Knightley in Jane AUSTEN's *Emma* and to Ralph Touchett in Henry JAMES's *Portrait of a Lady* (*Virginia Woolf* 57), and also says that Woolf puts across the "feminine point of view" primarily through Hewet. After his engagement to Rachel, however, Hewet seems to become more conventional in his outlook. According to Mitchell Leaska, there is "hazard and danger" beneath Hewet's "extremely deceptive surface simplicity" (*Novels* 22). Most critics have seen Hewet in a favorable light, but Lucio Ruotolo sees him more negatively, criticizing his merging of the roles of guardian and lover (*Interrupted* 41).

Hibbert, Lady Mentioned in *JACOB'S ROOM* at Elizabeth DURRANT's party, where she finds her old friend Julia ELIOT and exclaims that she "had all Shakespeare by heart before [she] was in her teens" (JR 86)—an echo of Mrs. HILBERY from *NIGHT AND DAY,* perhaps.

Hicks, Sir William Joynson The home secretary in England (1924–29), known to many as "Jix," who participated in banning Radclyffe Hall's novel *THE WELL OF LONELINESS* in 1928. He is mentioned in *A ROOM OF ONE'S OWN* when Woolf ironically remarks that he would probably deny that the relationships of "great men" with women have been always Platonic (AROO 86).

Higgens, Grace (née Germany) Grace Germany came to work for Vanessa BELL in 1920 when she was sixteen, first as maid, then as nurse to Angelica GARNETT, and finally as cook. She worked for Vanessa and Duncan GRANT at CHARLESTON, in London, and in CASSIS (where she learned French with Angelica from Mademoiselle Chevalier). In 1934 she married Walter Higgens, who was subsequently employed as a full-time gardener at Charleston. The low wages Vanessa paid the Higgenses meant that they could not afford a cottage of their own and so they lived, with their son John, at Charleston. Grace Higgens worked for Duncan Grant as housekeeper for several years after Vanessa's death in 1961. A photograph of her appears in Isabelle Anscombe (number 88).

Hilbery, Katharine Character in *NIGHT AND DAY* who is the primary focus of the narrative. Woolf told several people that Katharine was based upon her sister Vanessa BELL, but there are elements in Katharine's situation that correspond to Woolf's life also. In the novel, Katharine faces the problem of engagement and marriage. It is a problem because she is not at all sure she wants to marry, but societal pressure dictates that this should be her occupation in life. She has a secret passion for mathematics and would like nothing more than to be an astronomer living in isolation away from London society and, in particular, the demands of her parents. She spends her days pouring tea and helping her mother with a biography of her grandfather, the poet Richard ALARDYCE, that she knows will never be written.

The opening of *Night and Day* recalls the opening of Jane AUSTEN's *Emma* as Katharine is seen in her habitual role, pouring tea for her parents' guests. Woolf's memoir "A SKETCH OF THE PAST" describes the "tea-table training" Woolf and her sister were heirs to as Victorian young ladies and which Katharine exemplifies. Engaged to William RODNEY, she resigns herself to thinking that marriage without love is "an inevitable step" in a world in which passion is an illusion, although she clings to a vision of romantic love symbolized by a "heroic Rider." Through her friendship with Mary DATCHET Katharine glimpses a different kind of life, one of independence and work, and she gradually disengages herself from William and develops a new kind of relationship with Ralph DENHAM.

Both William and Mrs. Hilbery compare Katharine, who says she has never read SHAKESPEARE, to ROSALIND, the main character in *As You Like It.* In Shakespeare's play, Rosalind disguises herself as a man to escape the restrictions placed on women and enable her to control her relationship with Orlando. The allusion is significant as Katharine, like Rosalind, both scorns love and is tormented by her feelings of love. Further, Katharine is strongly drawn to Mary Datchet. At the end of the novel, Katharine and Ralph share their vague visions of "reality" and prepare for love in a world of new gender relations.

Hilbery, Mr. Character in *NIGHT AND DAY,* the father of Katharine HILBERY. Trevor Hilbery is the editor of the *Critical Review* and has elements of Leslie

STEPHEN in his characterization. Like Woolf's father, he does not like to involve himself in his daughter's personal relations if that means having to make any decisions, but, also like Leslie, he reacts with jealousy and possessiveness when Katharine tells him she is engaged to Ralph DENHAM.

Hilbery, Mrs. (1) A character in *NIGHT AND DAY,* Katharine HILBERY's mother. In creating Margaret Hilbery, Woolf drew heavily on her Aunt Anny (Anne Isabella Thackeray RITCHIE), to the annoyance of the Ritchie family. Mrs. Hilbery is the daughter of an eminent Victorian poet, Richard ALARDYCE, whose memory she hopes to preserve by writing a biography. She is uniquely unsuited to the task, however, as her thoughts move swiftly from one subject to another. She is a devotee of William SHAKESPEARE, to whom she refers as "my William," and has plans for bringing Shakespeare's poetry to the working class. Mrs. Hilbery recognizes that she has something of all Shakespeare's characters in her makeup and is "quite a large bit of the fool" (ND 307). As fools in Shakespeare are often wise, so Mrs. Hilbery sees what is going on in her daughter's emotional life and manages to bring the various entanglements of the young people with whom the novel is concerned to a happy resolution. She tells her daughter to marry only for love but does not fully grasp the difficulties Katharine faces in a modern world very different from that in which she grew up. There is an element of mysticism in the characterization of Mrs. Hilbery, who at the end of the novel "went on to sing her strange, half-earthly song of dawns and sunsets, of great poets, and the unchanged spirit of noble loving which they had taught" (ND 496).

Hilbery, Mrs. (2) In *MRS. DALLOWAY,* Mrs. Hilbery attends Clarissa DALLOWAY's party and tells Clarissa that she looks like her mother did when Mrs. Hilbery first saw her standing in a garden. Mrs. Hilbery suggests that Elizabeth DALLOWAY's "Oriental" looks may have been inherited from "some Mongol" ancestor wrecked on the coast of Norfolk (where the Dalloways are from).

Hillier, Ann A young woman whom Martin PARGITER sits next to in *THE YEARS* at Kitty LASSWADE's dinner party; she talks about the RUSSIAN BALLET and makes Martin feel old.

Hills, John Waller ("Jack") (1867–1938) The son of Anna (née Grove) and Herbert Augustus Hills, Jack Hills was an important figure in Woolf's early life. A protégé of Julia Prinsep STEPHEN's, he had proposed to Stella DUCKWORTH at ST. IVES some time in the 1890s but she had not accepted. As Woolf remarks in "A SKETCH OF THE PAST," "a refusal in those days was catastrophic" (MOB 99). Jack, who did not get on with his own rather unpleasant mother, was "chivalrously devoted" (Leslie Stephen, *Mausoleum* 78) to Julia Stephen and through her good offices remained in contact with the family. He was at HYDE PARK GATE the night before Julia died in 1895, and within a year after her death, he again proposed to Stella. She did not accept, but he persisted and, breaking through the "snowy numbness" that Woolf said enfolded Stella after her mother's death, he proposed again and was accepted on August 22, 1896, while the Stephen family was staying at Hindhead in a house they had been lent. This romantic event—"the black and silver night of mysterious voices" (MOB 100)—made a deep impression on the Stephen children and was vividly recalled by Woolf in her DIARY even twenty-five years later (D2 190).

Jack Hills had been at Eton with George DUCKWORTH and then went to Balliol College, Oxford. He later trained as a solicitor and for many years served as the Stephen family's lawyer. He was married to Stella on April 10, 1897. Woolf and Vanessa BELL were their bridesmaids and received gold watches inscribed with their initials and "From Stella and Jack." While Mr. and Mrs. Hills went to Florence for their honeymoon, the Stephens went to Brighton. On returning to London they found that Stella and Jack had come back early as Stella was ill. In July, Stella died, apparently from peritonitis complicated by pregnancy.

Almost immediately, the task of comforting Jack fell to Woolf and Vanessa. While the Stephens were on vacation at Painswick, Jack visited frequently. In "A Sketch of the Past," Woolf recalled sitting in a little summer house in the garden with Jack while he spoke bitterly of how her father had delayed their engagement through his jealousy and thwarted Stella's happiness. He also made clear his sexual torment at losing his wife. Woolf wrote that she would fix her gaze on a leafless tree as Jack clutched her wrist in his grief: "And the tree outside in the August summer half light was giving me, as he groaned, a symbol of his agony; of our sterile agony; was summing it all up. Still the leafless tree is to me the emblem, the symbol, of those summer months" (MOB 141). This symbol can be found, for example, in *THE YEARS* (133).

It was, however, Vanessa who became most intimate with Jack and it soon became apparent to the family that they were falling in love, a situation that appalled George Duckworth as it was at that time illegal in England for a man to marry his deceased wife's sister. While Leslie Stephen said Vanessa must make up her own mind, various other relatives made their feelings known and the affair eventually dwindled.

To Woolf, Jack was "a type—and a desirable type; the English country gentleman type" (MOB 101). He was well read, and he explained Plato to Woolf, her sister, and cousin Marny Vaughan (see Margaret [Madge] VAUGHAN); he talked frankly to Woolf about sex; and he encouraged the Stephen children's hobby of "bug-collecting," teaching them how to sugar trees to attract the moths they would put in their collection. In 1902, according to a letter Woolf wrote to Violet DICKINSON, she and Jack were planning to write "a great play" together: "There'll be oceans of talk and emotions without end" (L1 60). In "A Sketch of the Past," Woolf also writes that her half-sister's engagement to Jack gave her her "first vision of love between man and woman . . . It was to me like a ruby; the love I detected that winter of their engagement, glowing, red, clear, intense" (MOB 105).

Jack went on to write many books on fishing and sports, including *A Summer on the Test* (1924) and *My Sporting Life* (1936); he was, according to Penny Painter, "perhaps *the* English writer on fishing" (147). A lieutenant-colonel in the Durham Light Infantry, he was wounded in 1916 in France. In 1918, Woolf had dinner with Jack and Philippa STRACHEY and wrote in her DIARY that Jack's "human sympathies" had turned him "in the direction of woman's suffrage, reform, education for the poor & so on" (D1 170). From 1906 to 1922 Jack was Conservative Unionist member of Parliament for Durham City, and he was re-elected in 1925.

Woolf saw less and less of Jack after World War I, but her affection for him never diminished. On Stella's death, Jack had made over the income from her marriage settlement to the Stephen children; when he married Mary Grace Ashton in 1931, he reclaimed this, but on his death in 1938 the legacy was restored to the Stephens. In 1938, a few months before he died, Jack gave Woolf a death's head moth as a present. After his death late in 1938, Woolf wrote "of all our youthful directors he was the most open minded, least repressive, could best have fitted in with later developments, had we not gone our ways" (D5 198).

Hirst, St. John Alaric Character in *THE VOYAGE OUT*. Hirst, twenty-four, is, in his own words, "a very distinguished young man" (TVO 144) who has received several scholarships and is a fellow of King's College, Cambridge University. He and his friend Terence HEWET are staying on SANTA MARINA, where they meet Helen AMBROSE and Rachel VINRACE. St. John is socially awkward, particularly with women his own age, but he develops a friendship with Helen, in whom he confides about the pressures his family have put on him to decide on a career. Self-conscious and generally pessimistic about the prospect of being liked, Hirst eventually becomes friends with Rachel, whom he at first offends. Hirst tells Hewet that nothing repulses him more than the female breast and sees the guests at the hotel as animals in a zoo.

Most readers accept that St. John Hirst is modeled on Lytton STRACHEY, though Roger Poole has also suggested that elements of Leonard WOOLF may be detected in the characterization of both Hirst and Hewet. Mitchell Leaska describes Hirst as "a checkerboard of militance and compliance" (*Novels* 19). Rachel Blau DuPlessis notes that Hirst is the only character "unoccupied with the toils of complicity that link the central triangle" of Rachel, Helen and Terence, and remarks that through him "a nimbus of Platonized Christianity comes to settle over the love plot, gives it a peace which passeth understanding, and creates the final ambiguity" (" 'Amor vin' " 122). The novel ends with Hirst's vision of the hotel guests passing on their way to bed as indistinct objects forming a pattern.

Hiscock The Malones' butler in *THE YEARS*.

Hitler, Adolf (1889–1945) In *THREE GUINEAS*, Woolf quotes a speech of Hitler's to the Nazi Women's League (TG 53); the speech can be found in *The Speeches of Adolf Hitler*, translated by Norman H. Baynes (London: Oxford University Press, 1942) (Zwerdling 348n22). Woolf first begins to write about Hitler in her DIARY in 1932, and she mentions him directly in her essay "THOUGHTS ON PEACE IN AN AIR RAID." In 1935, she and Leonard WOOLF drove through Europe, spending three days in Germany, where they observed signs expressing hatred of Jews. In Ulken, they unwittingly became caught up in Hermann Goering's motorcade (D4 311) and drove through streets lined with cheering schoolchildren who laughed at their pet marmoset, Mitzi, which they had brought with them from England. Woolf records listening to Hitler's speeches on the radio in the late 1930s, and the "megaphonic" voices that are described near the end of *BETWEEN THE ACTS* probably owe something to her experience of hearing Hitler's ranting.

Hogarth Essays See HOGARTH PRESS.

Hogarth House Richmond home of the Woolfs from 1915 to 1924, and for which the HOGARTH PRESS was named.

Hogarth Lectures See HOGARTH PRESS.

Hogarth Letters See HOGARTH PRESS.

Hogarth Living Poets See HOGARTH PRESS.

Hogarth Press Leonard WOOLF wrote in his autobiography that the idea of owning a printing press began as a source of therapeutic activity for Woolf that would also give them the opportunity to publish "poems or other short works which the commercial publisher would not look at" (LW2 170). On her birthday in 1915, Woolf and Leonard had agreed that they would buy a printing press (D1 28). Early in 1917, the Woolfs applied for permission to learn printing at the St. Bride Foundation Institute in Fleet Street, the headquarters of the London Society of Compositors. As they did not intend to join the printers' union, however, they were denied admission and decided to teach themselves. On March 23 they ordered a small handpress from the Excelsior Printing Company in Farringdon Street; the "very sympathetic man in a brown overall" from whom they bought the press (LW2 170) also sold them some Old Face type and a sixteen-page booklet which he assured them contained all they needed to know in order to begin printing.

Fear and Politics: A Debate at the Zoo. *Courtesy of Cecil Woolf and Jean Moorcroft Wilson.*
Published in 1925 as number 7 of the Hogarth Essays series, this allegory by Leonard Woolf uses animals at a zoo to express thoughts about current politics. The paper wrappers were printed in black with a design by Vanessa Bell on the front.

The press they had ordered was small enough to fit on a kitchen table and cost less than £20. Its arrival on April 24, 1917 was met with great excitement, hardly diminished by discovering it was "smashed in half," as Woolf wrote to her sister, Vanessa BELL (L2 150). Printing, Woolf surmised, "will devour one's entire life" (L2 150).

The smashed part replaced, the Woolfs set out to teach themselves printing, beginning their first publication in May 1917: *TWO STORIES* contained Woolf's "THE MARK ON THE WALL" and Leonard Woolf's "THREE JEWS." It was bound in Japanese grass paper, some copies in dull blue, some in an overall red and white design; they bought material for the wrappers as it was needed. Ambitiously, the book also included four woodcuts by Dora CARRINGTON, and by the end of the month 124 of the 150 copies printed had been sold, mainly to their friends who had received a notice of the publication that read:

HOGARTH HOUSE
RICHMOND

THE HOGARTH PRESS

It is proposed to issue shortly a pamphlet containing two short stories by Leonard Woolf and Virginia Woolf, (price, including postage 1/2).

If you desire a copy to be sent to you, please fill up the form below and send it with a P. O. to L. S. Woolf at the above address before June

A limited edition only will be issued.

Please send copy of Publication No. 1 to

for which I enclose P. O. for

NAME
ADDRESS

Leonard Woolf decided that their next effort should be sold less formally and devised a system of subscribers: "A" subscribers would automatically be sent all the publications, and "B" subscribers would be informed of publications and given the opportunity of buying them. The subscription system was in effect until 1923, when the expansion of the Press led to a more orthodox method of sales and distribution to booksellers.

The second publication of the Press was Katherine MANSFIELD's *Prelude* (1918), but it proved too large a job for the small handpress. Borrowing larger chases from F. T. McDermott, who operated the Prompt Press, the Woolfs set the type at HOGARTH HOUSE and then carried it to the Prompt Press, where it could

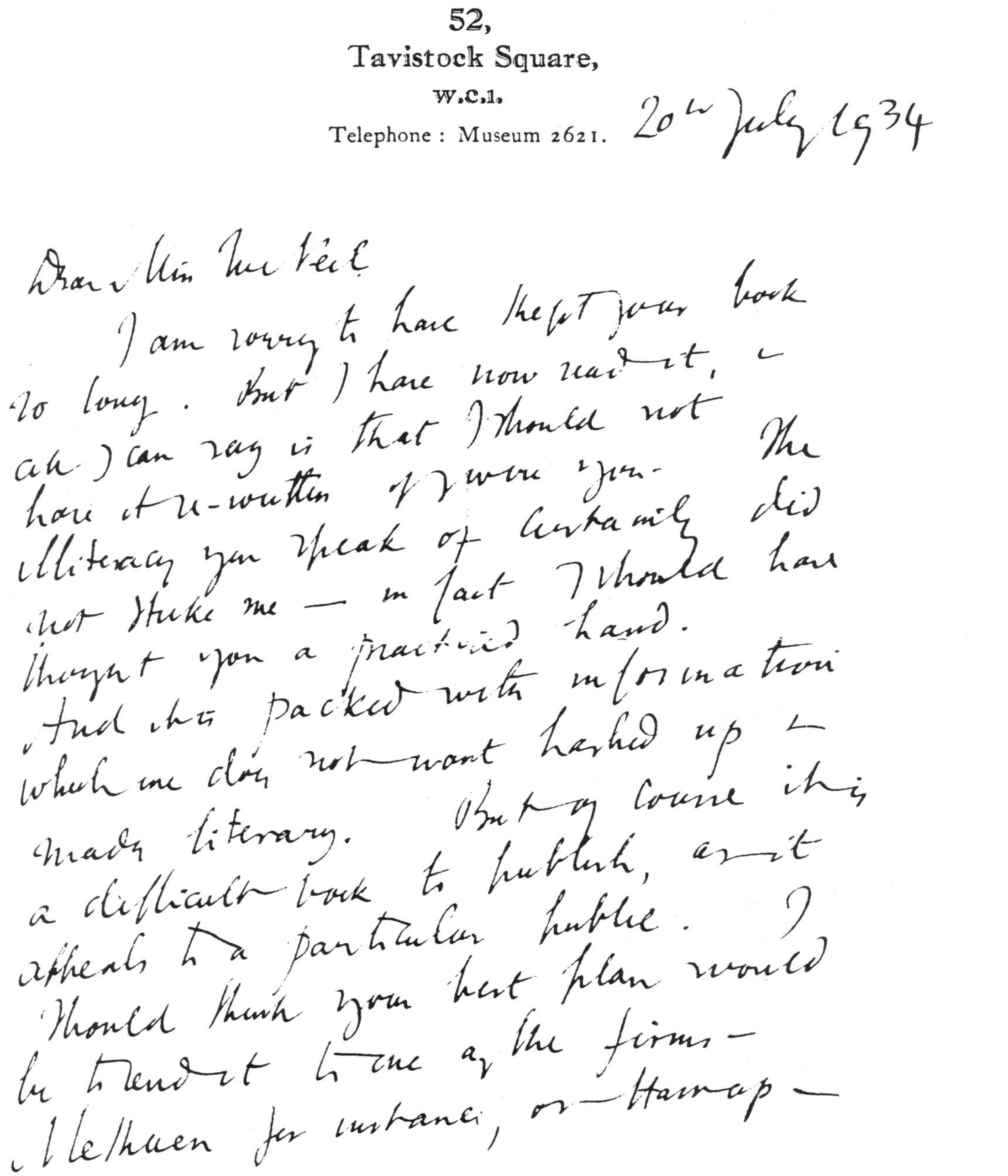

52,
Tavistock Square,
W.C.1.
Telephone : Museum 2621.

20th July 1934

Dear Miss McNeil

I am sorry to have kept your book so long. But I have now read it, & all I can say is that I should not have it re-written if I were you. The illiteracy you speak of certainly did not strike me — in fact I should have thought you a practised hand. And it is packed with information which one does not want hashed up & made literary. But of course it is a difficult book to publish, as it appeals to a particular public. I should think your best plan would be to send it to one of the firms — Methuen for instance, or Harrap —

Handwritten letter from Virginia Woolf to Miss McNeil (unidentified), July 20, 1934. Courtesy of Linda J. Langham. This letter, which has not been previously published, is a good example of how encouraging Woolf could be to young writers.
[transcription:
Dear Miss McNeil
I am sorry to have kept your book so long. But I have now read it, & all I can say is that I should not have it re-written if I were you. The illiteracy you speak of certainly did not strike me—in fact I should have thought you a practised hand. And it is packed with information which one does not want hashed up & made literary. But of course it is a difficult book to publish, as it appeals to a particular

which has a travel series. And I should lay stress upon the advantages given you by the government. Also I should certainly retain the travellers guide at the end — if anything, cut the history. I dont think you would find a general publisher to take it because of its special character.

I'm afraid this advice isn't much use; but anyhow I enjoyed reading it, & I hope soon to see it on every bookstall.

Yours
Virginia Woolf

I am having the MS sent back on Monday

public. I should think your best plan would be to send it to one of the firms—Methuen for instance, or Harrap—which has a travel series. And I should lay stress upon the advantages given you by the government. Also I should certainly retain the travellers guide at the end—if anything, cut the history. I dont think you would find a general publisher to take it because of its special character.

I'm afraid this advice isn't much use; but anyhow I enjoyed reading it, & I hope soon to see it on every bookstall.

Yours
Virginia Woolf
I am having the MS sent back on Monday]

Twelve Original Woodcuts *by Roger Fry (1921). Courtesy of Cecil Woolf and Jean Moorcroft Wilson.*
A book printed and published in 1921 by Leonard and Virginia Woolf, the first edition of which sold out in two days; here is shown the cover of the third impression (1922).

be printed four pages at a time. Three hundred copies were printed, bound at first in a plain, dark blue wrapper. Mansfield had chosen a design for the cover by a Scottish painter, J. D. Fergusson, but as Woolf disliked it, these wrappers were soon abandoned. Also in 1918, the Woolfs printed a private edition of the poems of Leonard's brother Cecil, who had been killed at the battle of Cambrai in France. His brother Philip, who had been wounded by the same shell that killed Cecil, brought the poems to the press and helped set the type for them (a task that proved therapeutic for him). This is now the rarest of the Hogarth Press publications.

In 1918, Harriet Shaw WEAVER, editor of *The Egoist* (where T. S. ELIOT was an assistant editor), brought the Woolfs a brown paper package containing part of the manuscript of James JOYCE's *Ulysses,* hoping that the Hogarth Press would publish it. Woolf commented in her DIARY on the incongruity between Miss Weaver's decorous demeanor and the "filth" of the work she was carrying under her arm (D1 140). Leonard writes that they decided they would publish it if they could find a printer, but none he approached would touch it for fear of being prosecuted for obscenity. Returning the manuscript to Harriet Weaver, Woolf did not mention this, nor give her own opinion of the work, saying only that it would be much too large a job for the Press (L2 242).

In 1919, four more works bearing the Hogarth imprint were produced. Three were hand-printed: *Poems* by T. S. Eliot; Woolf's *KEW GARDENS*; and *Paris,* a long poem by Hope MIRRLEES. The fourth, *Critic in Judgment* by John Middleton MURRY, was printed by McDermott (a job the Woolfs were not pleased with), and bound by the Woolfs. Eliot's *Poems* marked the beginning of a long friendship with the American poet and was a particularly important publication of the fledgling Press. In 1923, they published *The Waste Land,* typeset entirely by Woolf herself; Leonard described the poem as having had "greater influence upon English poetry, indeed upon English literature, than any other in the twentieth century" (LW2 176). The Hogarth Press played a very significant part in shaping the MODERNIST canon in England through its publication of new and experimental writers. Woolf herself often acted as reader for the Press, writing encouraging letters even when she was declining a manuscript (see for example the letter to Miss McNeil on pp. 114–115). Reviews of the Press's early publications were usually unfavorable, many critics sniping not only at the modernist content but also at the unusual bright paper wrappers. Leonard comments in his autobiography on the inherent conservatism of all trades and professions, including publishing and bookselling (LW2 241). Hogarth Press books were unorthodox not only in their content but also in their variety of sizes and bright wrappers.

The Hogarth Press covers were to become a distinctive feature of its books. They were of heavy paper, often of wallpaper, and very colorful. Some were made by Roger FRY, others were imported (e.g., from Czechoslovakia). The *Kew Gardens* cover was dark brown with marbled splotches of bright blue and rust. *Kew Gardens,* including woodcuts by Vanessa Bell, was so popular that a second edition of 500 had to be ordered from another printer, Richard Madley. Woolf recorded in her diary their excitement at coming back to London from ASHEHAM HOUSE to find "the hall table stacked, littered with orders" (D1 280). In 1920 she had made up her mind never to write "for publishers again" (D2 13). Beginning with *JACOB'S ROOM* (1922), all Woolf's novels, as well as her non-fiction books, were published by the Press, usually with dust jackets or covers designed by Vanessa Bell (*ORLANDO* was the only one of Woolf's novels for which Vanessa did not design the dust jacket).

Leonard Woolf later said that he and his wife found themselves in the publishing business "almost in spite of ourselves." In 1920, in addition to two hand-printed books, the Woolfs published two books that were too long for them to print themselves: Maxim GORKY's *Reminiscences of Leo Nicolayevitch Tolstoi,* and Logan Pearsall SMITH's *Stories from the Old Testament.* These were composed and printed by the Pelican Press and, as is pointed out in the foreword to the 1939 catalog of the Hogarth Press, "almost unintentionally, turned the Press into a regular publishing business." Leonard described Gorky's book as a turning point, and Woolf noted in her diary in August 1920 that the Press "is clearly too lively & lusty to be carried on in this private way any longer" (D2 55). The following year she wrote that the Press "begins to outgrow its parents" (D2 145).

Of further significance was that Gorky's book introduced what was to be a fairly regular series of original translations of notable works for which the Press would be the first English publisher. Excluding the International Psycho-Analytical Library of the works of Sigmund FREUD, of the twenty-nine translations published between 1920 and 1938 only one, *The Diary of Montaigne's Journey to Italy,* had been previously published in English.

In November 1921, Leonard bought a secondhand Minerva platen press, worked by a treadle (which can be seen today at SISSINGHURST CASTLE, where it has been since 1934 when the Woolfs gave it to Vita SACKVILLE-WEST). The increasing business of the Press had made the Woolfs realize that in addition to a larger machine, they also needed an assistant. In 1918, Barbara BAGENAL (then Barbara Hiles) had helped when the printing and binding of *Prelude* proved overwhelming. Since then, apart from a stint by Alix Sargant-Florence (see STRACHEY, Alix) that lasted the time it took for the Woolfs to walk their dog, there had been no other help. For several books, the Woolfs set up the type, printed the pages, stitched them, bound the books, made the covers, and then packed them up for mailing to subscribers. (J. Howard Woolmer's invaluable *Checklist of the Hogarth Press* includes an appendix listing the books handprinted by the Woolfs; VICTORIA UNIVERSITY LIBRARY owns a complete set of them.) Toward the end of 1920, on the recommendation of Lytton STRACHEY, they hired Ralph PARTRIDGE, who remained working part-time until March 1923. Like nearly everyone who worked for the Hogarth Press in its early years, Ralph found the exacting Leonard Woolf extremely difficult to work for. He also annoyed Woolf, who wrote to him in 1922 of her annoyance that he would have thought them "quite ready to be bamboozled with a bargain which would destroy the character of the press for the sake of money or pride or convenience" (L2 583). Ralph's departure led the Woolfs to realize they needed a full-time assistant and over the next few years a number of people came to work at the Press: Marjorie Joad worked there from 1923 to 1925; George RYLANDS for a few months in 1924; Angus DAVIDSON came at the end of 1924 and stayed until 1927. Richard KENNEDY, who at the age of sixteen came to work for the Press after Davidson, has written and illustrated an amusing account of his time there in *A Boy at the Hogarth Press.*

Despite this stream of assistants and the great success of the Press, the Woolfs decided on October 27, 1930, that they should close it down. It had become too much to cope with, given their primary work as writers. Leonard decided to try one more assistant and found John LEHMANN, who proved to be far more efficient than the previous helpers. Lehmann took an active role in seeking out new authors and brought the Woolfs into contact with the young poets of the 1930s such as Christopher ISHERWOOD and Louis MACNEICE. Lehmann worked at the Hogarth Press from early 1931 until 1932, and he returned in 1938 when he bought out Woolf's share.

At Hogarth House, the Woolfs had installed their press in the larder, printed there, bound books in the dining room, and wrapped them for mailing in the sitting room. In March 1924, the Woolfs moved to 52 TAVISTOCK SQUARE, taking a ten-year lease. At Tavistock Square the Press was separately housed in the basement, marking the end of their handprinting. Although they both continued to enjoy handprinting as a hobby, most of the work of the Press was done by commercial printers. Clark of Edinburgh and the Garden City Press at Letchworth were the most frequently used.

It was in 1924 that the Hogarth Press assumed publication of the papers of the International Psycho-Analytical Institute, thus eventually becoming the authorized publisher of Freud in English. The International Psycho-Analytical Library series was edited by Dr. Ernest Jones, later Freud's first biographer. Acting on behalf of Jones, Freud's English translator, James STRACHEY (Lytton STRACHEY's brother), had approached Leonard Woolf in early 1924 about the Hogarth Press publishing the International Psycho-Analytical Institute's books. J. H. Willis, in his recent extensive and detailed study of the Hogarth Press, points out that this was a financially risky venture at the time and also put the Press in danger of prosecution for either blasphemy or obscenity (Willis 300). Leonard Woolf's gamble, however, proved a great success.

A distinctive feature of the Hogarth Press was its publication of several series intended to bring significant ideas in literature, art, politics and criticism to a broad public. These had varying degrees of success. The first was the Hogarth Essays (First Series, 1924–26; Second Series, 1926–28). There were nineteen titles in the first series, sixteen in the second; a one-volume anthology of eleven of the essays was published in the United States by Doubleday, Doran & Company in 1928.

The Hogarth Lectures on Literature (First Series, 1927–31) included fifteen titles; the Second Series (1934) stopped after one. It was edited by George Rylands and Leonard, and began with *A Lecture on Lectures* by Sir Arthur Quiller-Couch. The series was "designed to help both students and teachers of literature, but the names of the authors of the volumes are sufficient guarantee that they are not merely handbooks for the crammers and the crammed, but will interest the ordinary reader." This description (printed on the covers of the volumes) continued by saying that the series was unlike other such series in that it treated "the whole of literature as dynamic rather than static, tracing the discovery, development and decadence of literary forms; considering fashions and imitations, revolts and revivals; expounding history rather than theory." Each volume contained six or seven lectures, except for the first, which was a general introduction to the series. Among the fifteen volumes published in the first series were *The Development of English Biography* by Harold NICOLSON (number 4); *The Structure of the Novel* by Edwin Muir (number 6); *Phases of English Poetry* by Herbert Read (number 7); *Politics and Literature* by G. D. H. Cole (number 11); and *Some Religious Elements in English Literature* by Rose MACAULAY.

The Hogarth Living Poets (First Series, 1928–32) was in twenty-four volumes (funded by Dorothy WELLESLEY); the Second Series (1933–37) in five. This differed from the other series in being collections of poems rather than essays or discussions. The Day to Day pamphlets (1930–39), in forty titles, was a series focused on contemporary social, political, and economic issues. The Hogarth Letters (1931–32) had twelve issues but was discontinued after poor sales. The letters have been published in one volume, edited and introduced by Hermione Lee, by the University of Georgia Press (1986).

After 1938, when Woolf sold her share to John Lehmann, the Press continued to grow and, in 1947, it became an allied company of Chatto & Windus. It has a significant place in the history of modernist literature, having published several then little-known writers who are now part of the modernist canon. Leonard Woolf pointed out that the "development of the Hogarth Press was bound up with the development of Virginia as a writer and with her literary or creative psychology" (LW2 232). For Woolf, the Hogarth Press meant that she could write free of any intervention by editors; in 1925 she wrote: "How my handwriting goes downhill! Another sacrifice to the Hogarth Press, yet what I owe the Hogarth Press is barely paid by the whole of my handwriting. . . . yes, I'm the only woman in England free to write what I like" (D3 42–43).

Holmes, Dr. Character in *MRS. DALLOWAY*. He is a general practitioner recommended by Mrs. FILMER who treats Septimus Warren SMITH but has no idea what Septimus's symptoms mean and tells him there is nothing the matter with him. Woolf drew on her experience of doctors in portraying Holmes, but he also exhibits characteristics of the way the medical establishment viewed shell shock in the years following World War I. Holmes causes Septimus to kill himself when he forces his way past Rezia Warren SMITH into their apartment. Holmes, who to Septimus is "human nature" come to torment him, has no idea why Septimus commits suicide.

Holmes, Oliver Wendell (1809–94) Professor of anatomy and physiology at Harvard University (1847–82) and author. Woolf reviewed Lewis W. Townsend's biography of Holmes for the *TIMES LITERARY SUPPLEMENT* in August 1909 (E1 293–301). Woolf's father, Leslie STEPHEN, had become friends with Holmes when he visited the United States in 1863.

Holtby, Winifred (1898–1935) Writer and feminist whose *Virginia Woolf* (1932) was the first major study in English of Woolf's work. Holtby acknowledges the assistance of Ethel SMYTH in her preface, and in 1932 Woolf remarked in a letter to Smyth that Holtby's book made her "roar with laughter" (L5 108). Among Holtby's novels are *The Crowded Street* (1924), *The Land of Green Ginger* (1928) and *South Riding* (1936); she also wrote *Women and a Changing Civilization* (1935). Her great friend Vera BRITTAIN wrote *Testament of Friendship* (1940) about her.

Hooper, Frances See SMITH COLLEGE.

Hope, Lottie (or Lotty) A foundling who came to work for Woolf in 1916 with her lifelong friend Nellie BOXALL. They had previously been employed by Roger FRY. Both the quick-tempered Lottie and Nellie gave and withdrew their notice many times over the years of their employment. Lottie Hope left in 1924 to work for Adrian and Karin STEPHEN and was dismissed by them (apparently for stealing) in 1930. In 1932 she became Clive BELL's cook at 50 GORDON SQUARE, and when he moved from there in 1939, Lottie went to CHARLESTON as cook.

Hopkins, Mabel Plays the part of Reason in Miss LA TROBE's village pageant in BETWEEN THE ACTS.

Horsefield, Mrs. Mentioned in JACOB'S ROOM, a friend of Miss DUDDING's at the hunt Jacob goes on in Essex; this is an example of Woolf's playful naming, similar, for example, to Mr. PAGE the reporter in *BETWEEN THE ACTS*.

"Hours in a Library" (CE2 34–40; E2 55–61; GR 24–31) Woolf borrowed the title of this 1916 essay for the *TIMES LITERARY SUPPLEMENT* from her father, Leslie STEPHEN, who used it for three collections of his critical essays (1874, 1876 and 1879). Woolf's essay is concerned with finding standards by which to evaluate contemporary writers' work: "Whatever we have learnt from reading the classics we need now in order to judge the work of our contemporaries" (E2 59). As she would also say in "Gothic Fiction," she writes here, "we owe a great deal to bad books" (E2 58).

"How It Strikes a Contemporary" (CE2 153–61; E3 353–65; CR1 292–305) An essay in the *TIMES LITERARY SUPPLEMENT* on April 5, 1923 that Woolf revised for the *COMMON READER*; the title is the same as that of a poem by Robert Browning (in *Men and Women* 1855). Reflecting on her contemporaries—one of whom, Katherine MANSFIELD, had died suddenly in January 1923—Woolf described her time as "an age of fragments. A few stanzas, a few pages, a chapter here and there, the beginning of this novel, the end of that, are equal to the best of any age or author" (CE2 156). She had rehearsed her ideas on the fragmented nature of contemporary literature in a letter to Gerald BRENAN in 1922 (L2 598), in which she described James JOYCE as "strewn with disaster." In her essay she describes *Ulysses* as "a memorable catastrophe—immense in daring, terrific in disaster" (CE2 156).

The theme of her essay is the difficulty critics have in agreeing on the value of the writing of their contemporaries, a theme similar to that she had treated in "HOURS IN A LIBRARY" several years earlier. In revising the TLS essay for the *Common Reader,* Woolf added a note illustrating what she meant, quoting from a review of Rose MACAULAY's *Told by an Idiot* that compares her to Shakespeare and Swift, and another review that describes T.S. ELIOT's *Waste Land* as "so much waste paper" (CE2 155). Having lamented the shattered literature of her contemporaries, Woolf then turns to a more optimistic note, explaining that the reason for this state of things is that she and her contemporaries are "sharply cut off from our predecessors" (CE2 157); in her revised version she omits specific reference to World War I, which she had included in the TLS version (E3 357). Much of what is best in contemporary writing, she continues, "has the appearance of being noted under pressure" (CE2 158) and if her contemporaries cannot tell stories any longer it is because they do not believe in stories. "Undoubtedly," says Woolf, surely bringing joy to the hearts of many undergraduates, "there is a dullness in great books" (CE2 158).

Woolf concludes by urging the critic to see the past in relation to the future, for the writers of her time are, she says, anonymous craftsmen "engaged upon some vast building" (CE2 161) which cannot be seen whole in the present. This idea would reappear in *A ROOM OF ONE'S OWN* where Woolf writes that masterpieces are produced by the "mass of people thinking in common" (AROO 65). A few years later, in 1929, Woolf recorded in her DIARY reading through her *Common Reader* essays and being "horrified at my own looseness," especially in "How It Strikes a Contemporary" (D3 235).

"How Should One Read a Book?" (CE2 1–11; CR2 258–70) This essay began as a talk Woolf gave at Hayes Court School for girls on January 30, 1926; she was driven there by Mary HUTCHINSON, whose daughter attended the school, as did Anastasia, the daughter of Boris and Helen ANREP. The version of "How Should One Read a Book?" reprinted in the *COMMON READER, SECOND SERIES* is a considerably revised (Kirkpatrick 165) version of that which was published in the *YALE REVIEW* in October 1926. S. P. Rosenbaum calls the essay the "critical credo" of the *Common Reader, Second Series* (*Women & Fiction* xx).

Brenda Silver has noted that "criticism and theories of criticism were clearly on [Woolf's] mind" in late 1925 (RN 97). Woolf was reading *Principles of Literary Criticism,* the influential book by I. A. Richards, and wrote in September 1925 to Janet CASE about her upcoming lecture to the schoolgirls that it was to be "on the right way of reading novels" (L3 211). This letter shows a development in Woolf's thinking since her famous essay "MR. BENNETT AND MRS. BROWN," in that she says to Case that "labelling the elderly Victorians and the young Georgians" is not a solution to the difficult critical questions surrounding the modern novel. The next month, Woolf wrote to Vita SACKVILLE-WEST that her lecture "seems to me a matter of dazzling importance and breathless excitement" (L3 220). Once the lecture was given, however, and she began to revise it for publication, Woolf wrote in her DIARY that she had to "grind out a little of that eternal How to read" for the *Yale Review* (D3 89). The version published in 1926 by which most people know "How Should One Read a Book?" is, therefore, different both from the talk from which it grew and that published in the *Yale Review.* Woolf also abridged the essay for the preface, entitled "The Love of Reading," to *Company of Books 1931–1932,* a booklist published by the Hampshire Bookshop, Northampton, Massachusetts. This and the *Yale Review* version were reprinted by SMITH COLLEGE in 1985.

Woolf's essay begins by advising readers to follow their own instincts, a theme of her criticism that she returns to in many essays. She speaks as a writer rather than a critic, asking readers to try to "become" the writers whose work they read. Perhaps the quickest way to understand the "elements of what a novelist is doing" would be to write oneself. Then, she says, readers may discover how difficult writing well is and will be better able to appreciate great writers.

Another part of reading is to judge. "But not directly." Woolf describes how once a book has been read, it is possible after a little time has passed to recall the book as a whole; "the book as a whole is different from the book received currently in separate phrases" (CE2 8). It is at this point that various books can be compared with one another, as wholes. The judgments that readers make "steal into the air" and become part of the atmosphere in which writers create. Readers and writers are, therefore, collaborators.

Hudson, Anna Hope ("Nan") (1896–1957) American painter who lived with Ethel SANDS; she is one of the friends who "have helped me in ways too various to specify" thanked in the ironic preface to *ORLANDO*. Hudson and Sands were friends of Roger FRY's and knew Vanessa BELL through him. Bell and Duncan GRANT decorated Sands's seventeenth-century French chateau in 1927, and Woolf spent four days with them that summer.

Hudson, Miss In the first EPISODE of *THE WAVES*, she gives the children their lessons.

Humanities Research Center The Harry Ransom Humanities Research Center at the University of Texas at Austin has extensive holdings of papers from members of the BLOOMSBURY GROUP, including 150 letters from Leonard WOOLF to Lytton STRACHEY, a comprehensive collection of HOGARTH PRESS books, and 130 volumes from the Woolfs' library at MONK'S HOUSE. It has also Woolf's typescripts for "KEW GARDENS" and "THOUGHTS ON PEACE IN AN AIR RAID" and 571 letters from her. Also of interest is its extensive collection of the correspondence of Dora CARRINGTON and Mary HUTCHINSON and manuscript materials for eleven of Lytton Strachey's works.

Hutchinson, Mary (née Barnes) (1889–1977) The granddaughter of Lytton STRACHEY's uncle John, she is one of the friends who "have helped me in ways too various to specify" whom Woolf thanks in the ironic preface to *ORLANDO*. Woolf's relationship with Hutchinson was stormy; she often found herself caught in the emotional tangles of Hutchinson's long (about 1915 to 1927) affair with Clive BELL. Hutchinson married St. John (Jack) Hutchinson in 1910 and had two children. She was a writer herself, although better known as a hostess; her only book, *Fugitive Pieces*, was published by the HOGARTH PRESS in 1927. She was very close to Strachey and to T. S. ELIOT and his first wife, and in 1920 was involved in a ménage à trois with Aldous HUXLEY and his wife Maria. Woolf seems to have accepted Leonard WOOLF's opinion that Hutchinson was someone she liked and disliked at different times (D2 63). In an alternative to the usual view of their relationship, Mary Mathis has discussed the archive of unpublished letters between Woolf and Hutchinson at the Harry Ransom HUMANITIES RESEARCH CENTER and finds that they "give us a fuller picture of a relationship that we might begin to consider along with Woolf's better-known relationships" with women (Mathis 340). In 1933, Woolf wrote in her DIARY that she had told Hutchinson she would put her in *THE PARGITERS* (D4 168). In *THE YEARS*, Peggy PARGITER describes Martin PARGITER as being "as sprig and spruce as a man of forty, with his canary-coloured lady in Kensington" (TY 358). Woolf frequently described Hutchinson as a "cockatoo," so this seems likely to allude to her.

Hutton, Jim Character in *MRS. DALLOWAY* who argues at Clarissa DALLOWAY's party with Professor BRIERLY about John MILTON and wears red socks.

Huxley, Aldous Leonard (1894–1963) Novelist, essayist, and poet whose best-known works are *Crome Yellow* (1921), *Antic Hay* (1923), *Point Counter Point* (1928), *Brave New World* (1932), *Eyeless in Gaza* (1936) and *Island* (1962). Woolf met him through Lady Ottoline MORRELL (whom Huxley satirized in his first novel, *Crome Yellow*) in 1917. She reviewed his *Limbo* for the *TIMES LITERARY SUPPLEMENT* in 1920 ("Cleverness and Youth" E3 176–78), and remarked that "to be aware too soon of sophisticated society makes it tempting for a young writer to use his first darts in attack and derision" (E3 176). Working on *THE YEARS* in 1935, Woolf wrote that she had "a horror of the Aldous novel: that must be avoided" (D4 281).

Huxley, Thomas Henry (1825–95) In *MRS. DALLOWAY*, Peter WALSH remembers how Clarissa DALLOWAY's favorite reading as a girl was Huxley and John TYNDALL (MD 117). Thomas Henry Huxley, a writer on many technical, philosophical and religious topics and a supporter of Charles Darwin, coined the word "agnostic" to express his own philosophical attitude. He is also among the favorite writers of Mr. GRICE in *THE VOYAGE OUT*.

Huxtable, Professor One of three professors at Cambridge satirically portrayed in *JACOB'S ROOM*; in his grumbling and groaning, particularly over money, there might be an echo of Leslie STEPHEN.

Hyde Park Gate Woolf was born and grew up at 22 Hyde Park Gate in the Kensington district of London. She describes the house in "22 HYDE PARK GATE," a contribution to the MEMOIR CLUB (MOB 164–80). After her father's death there in 1904, the Stephen children moved to GORDON SQUARE.

"Hyde Park Gate, 22" See "22 HYDE PARK GATE."

Hyde Park Gate News A newspaper written by the Stephen children in the 1880s and '90s. Its sixty-nine surviving issues are now in the Library of the BRITISH MUSEUM. According to Anne Olivier BELL, it is "almost entirely" written out in Vanessa BELL's handwriting (VWM 39:1).

Hyslop, Dr. Theophilus Bulkeley (1864–1933) Neurologist, Superintendent of the Bethlem Royal Hospital, and also a painter, composer and lecturer particularly interested in the relation between insanity and art (Trombley 212). He was one of several doctors Leonard WOOLF consulted soon after his marriage to Woolf about whether or not she should have children. In *ROGER FRY* Woolf reports that Hyslop gave a lecture about the first POST-IMPRESSIONIST exhibition in which he "gave his opinion before an audience of artists and craftsmen that the pictures were the work of madmen" (RF 156).

I

Ibsen, Henrik (1828–1906) Norwegian dramatist whose plays include *Brand* (1866), *Peer Gynt* (1867), *A Doll's House* (1879), *Ghosts* (1881), *An Enemy of the People* (1882), *The Wild Duck* (1884), *Rosmersholm* (1886), *Hedda Gabler* (1890), *The Master Builder* (1892), *Little Eyolf* (1894), *John Gabriel Borkman* (1896) and *When We Dead Awaken* (1900). In his autobiography, Leonard WOOLF describes the great importance of Ibsen to his generation, saying that in his plays the "cobwebs and veils, the pretences and hypocrisies which suppressed the truth, buttressed cruelty, injustice, and stupidity, and suffocated society in the nineteenth century, were broken through, exposed, swept away" (LW1 104).

In *THE VOYAGE OUT,* Rachel VINRACE reads Ibsen, who inspires her to act the heroine's roles in her head for days at a time (TVO 123). In the first English edition (1915) Rachel's reading is specifically identified as *A Doll's House,* drawing attention to Rachel's similarity to the confined Nora Helmer of the play, but in revising her first novel for the U.S. first edition in 1920, Woolf deleted the reference to Nora.

"Impassioned Prose" (CE1 165–72; GR 32–40) An essay in the *TIMES LITERARY SUPPLEMENT* on September 16, 1926, discussing the works of Thomas DE QUINCEY and reprinted in *GRANITE & RAINBOW.* De Quincey was a favorite author of Woolf's mother, Julia Prinsep STEPHEN, and one of Woolf's earliest published articles was on his "English Mail Coach" for the GUARDIAN in 1906 (E1 Appx. 1). Andrew McNeillie notices that Woolf's early view of De Quincey was very similar to that she expressed in her later essays on him (E1 365), and Brenda Silver has pointed out that Woolf was reading *The English Mail Coach* in 1926 (RN 89).

"Impassioned Prose," which mentions *The English Mail Coach* at the beginning, discusses De Quincey's powers of language, powers from which Woolf suggests contemporary novelists could learn. She quotes his description of his sister's death from *Suspiria de Profundis* and writes that De Quincey dreamt vividly long before he took opium. She believes his *Autobiographic Sketches* to be almost as much of a masterpiece as the more famous *Confessions of an English Opium Eater.* De Quincey was a prose writer who "made his way into precincts that are terribly difficult to approach" (CE1 172) and was able to describe states of mind in which "time is miraculously prolonged and space miraculously expanded" (CE1 171).

Indigo Girls See POPULAR CULTURE.

Inge, Dean (1860–1954) In *A ROOM OF ONE'S OWN,* one of the many men whose opinions of women Woolf finds in her researches in the BRITISH MUSEUM is Dean Inge (though she decides to "leave in peace" what he actually said [AROO 53]). The very Reverend William Ralph Inge was dean of St. Paul's Cathedral from 1911 to 1934 and published many philosophical works, the tenor of which earned him the sobriquet "The Gloomy Dean." His *Outspoken Essays* were published in two series in 1919 and 1922. In *THREE GUINEAS* Woolf refers to Inge's journalism as evidence that "bishops and deans seem to have no soul with which to preach and no mind with which to write" (TG 71).

Interior Monologue See MODERNISM.

Interludes The italicized descriptions of the natural world in *THE WAVES* are usually referred to as the interludes, as distinct from the nine sections consisting of the soliloquies of BERNARD, JINNY, LOUIS, NEVILLE, RHODA and SUSAN, which are referred to as the EPISODES.

"Introduction, The" See *MRS. DALLOWAY'S PARTY.*

"Isabella and the Pot of Basil" In *NIGHT AND DAY,* Katharine HILBERY goes into her father's study to talk to him about her second cousin Cyril ALARDYCE. While she waits for him to finish making a note she reads this work of John KEATS's (actually called "Isabella, or the Pot of Basil") published in *Lamia . . . and other Poems* (1820). The poem is based on part of the *Decameron* by Boccaccio and tells the story of Isabella's love for Lorenzo. Lorenzo is murdered by Isabella's brothers. She is led by a vision to his body buried in a forest; she places the head in a pot and puts a basil plant over it. When her brothers see what she has done, they flee.

Isherwood, Christopher (1904–86) English novelist, poet and playwright. He pleased Woolf in 1937 by telling her that she and E. M. FORSTER were the only living novelists his generation took seriously (D5 59). Isherwood was one of several young writers Woolf came to know in the 1930s through John LEHMANN, who brought their work to the HOGARTH PRESS. To Leonard WOOLF's great annoyance, Lehmann left the Press abruptly in 1932 to join Isherwood in Berlin. Woolf wrote in general terms about what came to be known as the "Auden generation" in "LETTER TO A YOUNG POET" and "THE LEANING TOWER." The Hogarth Press published Isherwood's second novel, *The Memorial* (1932), *Mr. Norris Changes Trains* (1935; published in the United States as *The Last of Mr. Norris*), *Sally Bowles* (1937), *Lions and Shadows: An Education in the Twenties* (1938) and *Goodbye to Berlin* (1939).

J

Jackson, Julia See STEPHEN, Julia Prinsep.

Jack the Ripper See STEPHEN, James Kenneth.

***Jacob's Room* (1922)** Woolf's third novel and her first to break radically with the conventional form of the genre. *Jacob's Room* is in fourteen chapters, the last being but a single page, and is a relatively short book; yet nearly 120 characters are found in it, some merely grazing the narrative as they pass Jacob in the street.

Outline

The novel begins with Jacob's mother, the widow Betty FLANDERS, sitting on a beach in Cornwall writing to her friend Captain BARFOOT, who lives in Betty's home town, Scarborough. While Jacob and his brother Archer play, an artist, Charles STEELE, paints the scene. He is exasperated when Betty gets up to fetch her sons and return to Mr. and Mrs. Pearce's lodging house, where they are staying. Jacob brings home from the beach a crab he has caught and a sheep's jawbone he found on the sand. With the help of her baby John's nurse, Rebecca, Betty puts the children to bed.

The passing of time, and, hence, Jacob's growth, is handled with extreme subtlety in this novel. Gradually, the reader becomes aware that Jacob is getting older. In chapter 2, back in Scarborough where Betty's dissolute husband Seabrook FLANDERS is buried, Jacob realizes he will be taught Latin by Reverend Andrew FLOYD. Reverend Floyd proposes to Betty by letter but she turns him down, and when he leaves to work at a parish in Sheffield he invites her three children to take anything they like from his study; Jacob chooses a one-volume edition of BYRON. Jacob hunts moths in the forest at night, coming in later than his mother would like. Captain Barfoot visits Jacob's mother, leaving his wife in the care of Mr. DICKENS, who wheels her into the sun on the promenade. After being educated at Rugby, Jacob goes up to King's College, Cambridge, in October 1906.

On the train up to Cambridge, in chapter 3, Mrs. NORMAN, with whom Jacob shares the compartment, tries, as everyone who meets him does, to fix Jacob's character, but she cannot. The nineteen-year-old Jacob is lost "as the crooked pin dropped by a child into the wishing-well twirls in the water and disappears for ever" (JR 31). He is also lost to the narrator, who comments throughout on the impossibility of summing people up. At Cambridge, Jacob attends lunch with his friend Timothy DURRANT at the home of a don, Professor PLUMER. Mrs. Plumer worries that Jacob, who arrives late, will eat all the mutton and has one of her two daughters, RHODA, hand around cigarettes. After lunch, Jacob despairs: "Had they never read Homer, Shakespeare, the Elizabethans?" (35) Back in his room, an essay entitled "Does History consist of the Biographies of Great Men?" lies on the table. His empty room is a trope in the novel of the impossibility of knowing Jacob. He is seen fleetingly in late-night arguments with university friends, discussing poetry and "Julian the Apostate." He and Timothy plan to sail from Falmouth to the Durrants' home.

At his friend's house, Jacob meets many people and an attraction between him and Clara DURRANT, Timothy's sister, seems to begin. "Poor Jacob," says Timothy's mother during a party; "They're going to make you act in their play" (62). Her words are freighted with significance in this elegy for a young man who will die in World War I.

After Cambridge, Jacob lives in London and continues to see the Durrants, going with them and their friend "the courtly Mr. Wortley" to the Opera House. In chapter 5, Richard BONAMY, whom Jacob knew at Cambridge, has become a closer friend and joins him for the kinds of discussions they had at Cambridge together. Jacob writes a stinging critique of an edition of the works of William WYCHERLEY that a Professor BULTEEL of Leeds has had the temerity to publish. Clara writes in her diary that she likes Jacob but the narrator, hovering like a hawkmoth at the mouth of a cave, remarks that Jacob is unknowable: "Such is the manner of our seeing. Such the conditions of our love" (73). In Scarborough, Captain Barfoot has become a town councillor.

Chapters 6 and 7 show Jacob's social network widening, becoming complicated. At a bonfire party on Guy Fawkes night—November 5, when England remembers the foiled plot of Guy Fawkes to blow up

King James I and the Houses of Parliament in 1605—Jacob meets FLORINDA, a woman whom he finds "horribly brainless" but sexually attractive. The female narrator—separated from Jacob by his "ten years seniority and difference of sex" (94)—comments on his relations with women and observes how he and Clara Durrant do not connect because one evening, as they are on their way to the kitchen for an ice during a party, Clara is introduced to an American, Mr. PILCHER (whom Jacob later remembers as "Mr. Pilchard"), to whom she must be polite. And so, Jacob drifts on, observed by Julia ELIOT, Rose SHAW, Mr. CLUTTERBUCK, Lady HIBBERT, Elsbeth SIDDONS, Mr. BURLEY, and a host of other people.

As chapter 8 begins it is apparent that Jacob is working as a lawyer. He is in an office at Gray's Inn and receives letters from his mother addressed to Mr. Jacob Alan Flanders, Esq. Betty's letter lies on Jacob's table while he and Florinda go into the bedroom and close the door. Despite her stupidity, Jacob cannot resist Florinda's attractions until he sees her "turning up Greek Street upon another man's arm" (JR 94). Rose Shaw, meanwhile, is upset because the match she has tried to arrange between a man named Jimmy and Helen AITKEN has not come off. "And now," comments the narrator, "Jimmy feeds crows in Flanders and Helen visits hospitals" (JR 97). The reference to Flanders in Belgium where so many died in the war makes absolutely clear the significance of Jacob's family name.

Jacob's life in London seems aimless. In chapter 9 he begins to spend time with aristocrats like LUCY, Countess of Rocksbier, and goes hunting in Essex. His servant, Mrs. PAPWORTH, listens to Jacob and Bonamy argue for hours, and in the BRITISH MUSEUM Reading Room, Jacob reads Marlowe and irritates Miss Julia HEDGE, "the feminist," who laments the absence of women's names carved in the dome above them. Jacob enjoys a visit to a brothel, where he meets Laurette. With gentle irony, the narrator notes that Jacob believes himself to be one of the "six young men" upon whom "the flesh and blood of the future depends." And so he reads the *Phaedrus* of PLATO and ignores the voices in the street below him.

A friend of Jacob's is the painter Nick BRAMHAM, whose model, a young Slade School of Art student named Fanny ELMER, falls in love with Jacob in chapter 10. To please him she begins to read Henry FIELDING, but Jacob does not notice her. He is thinking of Clara Durrant, "a virgin chained to a rock (somewhere off Lowndes Square)" (123). Florinda now flirts with Nick and Jacob is planning a trip to Greece where, Fanny sadly thinks, he will forget her. Jacob is enabled to go on this trip by a £100 legacy he receives from his mother's cousin, Miss BIRKBECK.

While his brother Archer is on his way to Gibraltar, Jacob is in Paris visiting artist friends before going on to Greece. Jacob writes home to his mother, who walks with her neighbor Mrs. JARVIS up Dods Hill in Scarborough where once she lost the garnet brooch that Jacob bought her. The next chapter, 12, finds Jacob passing through Italy and arriving in Patras, as Woolf herself had done in 1906. Jacob seems to be maturing, beginning to think about political issues such as Home Rule for Ireland (proposed by Prime Minister Herbert Henry ASQUITH in 1912) and being "puzzled" about the British Empire (JR 139). He writes home letters that Betty Flanders finds dissatisfying, and he writes to Bonamy "who couldn't love a woman and never read a foolish book" (JR 140). Bonamy, too, loves Jacob.

In Greece, Jacob meets the bored and languid Sandra Wentworth WILLIAMS, who is traveling with her defeated husband Evan. She loans Jacob her copy of a book by Anton CHEKHOV and he falls in love with her. Bonamy, in London, goes to tea with Clara Durrant to talk about Jacob, but realizing she is in love with Jacob, Bonamy says nothing about him. Fanny Elmer sighs and again the narrator comments that Jacob cannot be known. He is twenty-six. War is coming: there are soldiers in the streets of Athens; at sea, the gunners practice; and at the Durrants' they are discussing Germany. Jacob goes to the Acropolis with Sandra Wentworth Williams and gives her his copy of the poems of John DONNE.

Back in London, in chapter 13, Jacob disappoints Bonamy by not seeming pleased to see him; Bonamy senses that Jacob is in love, but with whom? His pockets are stuffed with notes he took in Greece and he receives letters from Sandra. WHITEHALL, where Timothy Durrant is a clerk, is full of the talk of war. Archer is in Singapore. The Reverend Andrew Floyd recognizes Jacob one day in London but as he hesitates, Jacob crosses the street and the opportunity to call him is lost. Mrs. Durrant, Clara and Mr. Wortley continue to go to the opera while in the Piraeus the guns on the ships are firing. Betty Flanders's sons are "fighting for their country" (JR 175).

Finally, in chapter 14, Betty and Bonamy are going through Jacob's effects, Bonamy amazed that Jacob's room has been left as if he thought he would return from the war. Echoing Archer's cry at the very beginning of the novel, Bonamy calls out "Jacob! Jacob!" but Jacob is dead.

Genesis

Woolf began to write her thoughts on her new novel in her DIARY in January 1920: "Suppose one thing should open out of another—As in An Unwritten Novel—only not for 10 pages but 200 or so . . . conceive mark on the wall, K[ew] G[ardens] & unwritten novel taking hands & dancing in unity" (D2 13). The short fictions "AN UNWRITTEN NOVEL," "THE MARK ON THE WALL" and "KEW GARDENS" were included in her collection *MONDAY OR TUESDAY,* published in April 1921. Just as Jacob Flanders is in some sense a transitional figure, so these sketches, as Woolf called them, were transitional writings carrying her from her previous novel, *NIGHT AND DAY,* to her first experiment in her new style, *Jacob's Room* (see Mark Hussey, *Singing* 70–72, 118–19, and Makiko Minow-Pinkney 25–27). After *Jacob's Room* was published, Woolf wrote "There's no doubt in my mind that I have found out how to begin (at 40) to say something in my own voice" (D2 186). Another transitional piece, this time to her next novel, *MRS. DALLOWAY,* was "Mrs. Dalloway in Bond Street," a story she had begun by April 1922. At the end of that year she noted that *Jacob's Room* had been "a necessary step" on the way to *Mrs. Dalloway* (D2 208).

Having found the form of her new fiction, in which she saw "immense possibilities," Woolf was wary of making what she saw as the mistakes made by some of her contemporaries. James JOYCE and Dorothy RICHARDSON, for example, were ruined, she thought, by "the damned egotistical self" (D2 13). Nevertheless, once she had begun to write the new work, she reflected that "what I'm doing is probably being better done by Mr Joyce" (D2 69). Joyce's *Portrait of the Artist as a Young Man* had appeared in installments in *THE EGOIST* in 1914–15, and parts of *Ulysses* had been published in the *Little Review* in 1918. *Ulysses* was published in Paris in 1922, one of the works published that year that leads Alex Zwerdling to call 1922 the "*annus mirabilis* of modern literature." In June 1922, T. S. ELIOT read his new poem *The Waste Land* to the Woolfs, who printed and published it in 1923 at the HOGARTH PRESS. The mood of Eliot's "Love Song of J. Alfred Prufrock" (1917) is also part of the atmosphere of *Jacob's Room* (particularly when Jacob meets Sandra Wentworth Williams, who hears time accumulating and asks herself, "What for? What for?" [JR 161]).

Woolf was also working on several essays concurrently with her writing *Jacob's Room,* and many of her reading notes from this period concern the essays that would eventually be published as the *COMMON READER* (RN 233–35). In literary criticism, beginning in the early 1920s, there was a particular focus on the issue of character in fiction, and Avrom Fleishman has said that *Jacob's Room* exemplifies the theories of essays Woolf wrote between 1919 and 1924, beginning with "MODERN FICTION" and up to "MR. BENNETT AND MRS. BROWN." Percy Lubbock's *Craft of Fiction* had been published in 1921, and Woolf was carefully considering "ON RE-READING NOVELS," her response to Lubbock.

Other critics have pointed out that part of the matrix from which *Jacob's Room* arose consisted of Woolf's reading of *bildungsromane*; Ralph Freedman* detects the influence of D. H. LAWRENCE's *Sons and Lovers* (1913) and sees parallels with Henry Fielding's *Tom Jones* (which, of course, Fanny Elmer reads to impress Jacob). Mark Spilka finds the method of *Jacob's Room* closer to that of Katherine MANSFIELD than that of Joyce. Edward Bishop* has recently pointed out that Woolf was reading Leonard WOOLF's *Empire and Commerce in Africa: A Study in Economic Imperialism* (1920) as she began to think about *Jacob's Room,* and soon after drafting the novel's opening scene, she read John Maynard KEYNES's *Economic Consequences of the Peace* (1919).

Jacob's Room was the first of Woolf's novels to be published by the Hogarth Press, which would subsequently publish all her work, freeing her fiction from editors and publishers' readers. In 1938, in a letter to Philip MORRELL, Woolf said that *Jacob's Room* was her favorite among her novels, "the only one I can sometimes read a page of without disgust" (L6 212). *Jacob's Room* was published in Britain by the Hogarth Press on October 22, 1922, with a dust jacket designed by Vanessa BELL, and in the United States by Harcourt, Brace & Company on February 8, 1923, also with the Vanessa Bell dust jacket.

Background

As many readers have pointed out, *Jacob's Room* is not solely an elegy for the generation of men that was slaughtered in World War I, but also an elegy for Woolf's brother, Thoby STEPHEN, who died in 1906 at the age of twenty-five. In her notebook, Woolf wrote out the last line of CATULLUS's poem "Ave Atque Vale" [Hail and Farewell] (number 101), his lament for a dead brother, and wrote "Julian Thoby Stephen 1881–1906" (as she would also think of writing on the title page of *THE WAVES*). At the beginning of the poem, Catullus writes, "I come, poor brother, with these poor offerings / To honor you at last." Nancy Topping Bazin has written that Woolf "evidently had in mind her brother Thoby" (90) in writing *Jacob's Room* and Avrom Fleishman notes the similarities between Jacob and Thoby. Fleishman estimates from the evidence of the text that Jacob was born the same year as Thoby (*Virginia Woolf* 49). Jean O. Love writes that Thoby is "divined" by "apprehending his surroundings" (*Sources* 320) and Sara Ruddick* has written on the importance of the bond between Woolf and her older brother ("Private" 185–215). In his autobiography, Leonard Woolf described a memory of his time at Cambridge with Thoby that resonates closely with *Jacob's Room*: "Late at night in the May term, I like to remember, Lytton, Saxon, Thoby Stephen, Clive Bell, and I would sometimes walk through the Cloisters of Nevilles Court in Trinity and looking out through the bars at the end on to the willows and water of the Backs, ghostly in the moonlight, listen to the soaring song of innumerable nightingales. And sometimes as we walked back through the majestic Cloisters we chanted poetry" (LW1 107).

The 1914–18 war, though, is present from the very first lines of *Jacob's Room.* "As her first readers would have known, Flanders was a synonym for death in battle" (Zwerdling 64). John McCrae's poem "In Flanders Fields" first appeared in *Punch* in 1915 and, according to Paul Fussell, became the "most popular poem of the war" (*The Great War and Modern Memory* [New York: Oxford University Press, 1977]: 248). Mrs. Flanders "represents all the mothers whose sons were killed in the war" (Bazin 94). Many readers have noticed references to the war in *Jacob's Room,* beginning with Winifred Holtby in her 1932 book on Woolf. Among others whom Zwerdling notes have remarked on this aspect of the novel are Josephine O'Brien Schaefer (*Three-fold*), Carolyn G. Heilbrun (*Toward*) and Carol Ohmann*. Daniel Ferrer remarks that we sometimes "have the impression that the entire landscape of this novel, strewn with skull and bones . . . peopled with 'death's head moths' . . . is a great corpse in the process of decomposing" (Ferrer 43).

One specific feature of the novel's web of references to the war is not so easily recognized. The Flanders's home town, Scarborough, was the object of a German bombardment in 1914, the first attack on England since 1778, as Masami Usui* has pointed out (see also Howard Harper 97). Several readers have also drawn attention to Woolf's review in 1918 of *The Collected Poems of Rupert Brooke* (E2 277–84; BP 85–89). Woolf had known Rupert BROOKE, who became an icon of British youth lost in the war, very well and was profoundly saddened by his death in 1915 (Levenback* 5).

Critical Responses

Woolf made a division in her diary between printed reviews, which she felt were unfavorable to *Jacob's Room,* and "the private people" who were enthusiastic (D2 209). Among those private people were Woolf's husband, Leonard, who called the novel "a work of genius;" "he says that the people are ghosts; he says it is very strange" (D2 209). Another was E. M. FORSTER, who wrote her that *Jacob's Room* kept his interest in the character, which he felt was "a tremendous achievement" (Forster, *Selected Letters* 2: 32). T. S. Eliot also wrote that the novel was "a remarkable success" (QB2 88), and Lytton STRACHEY—to whom the character Richard Bonamy probably owes something—"occasionally almost screamed with delight at the style." Strachey went on to say, "Jacob himself is very successful—in a most remarkable and original way. Of course I see something of Thoby in him, as I suppose was intended" (CH 93–94).

The reviewers, however, were baffled for the most part. The *TIMES LITERARY SUPPLEMENT* noticed that "it is rather like the method of *Monday or Tuesday* applied to a continuous story," but found that the method "does not create persons and characters as we secretly desire to know them" (CH 97). The *Pall Mall Gazette* expressed this view more bluntly: "no true novel can be built out of a mere accumulation of notebook entries" (CH 99). Several reviews related the novel to the influence of Impressionism or otherwise commented on its painterly style. The *Daily Telegraph* supposed that Woolf's theory of art should be called impressionist (CH 105), and the New York *Nation* called *Jacob's Room* impressionist and "a rambling, redundant affair" (CH 110). There was widespread dislike of Woolf's form, characterized by the *Yorkshire Post* review, which said the novel had "no narrative, no design, above all, no perspective" (CH 107) and that it was "a crowded little album of pictures" (CH 107).

Rebecca WEST gave a more positive expression to the link between the novel and painting when she likened *Jacob's Room* to an artist's portfolio. In the *NEW STATESMAN,* West wrote that "not only are Mrs. Woolf's contributions to her age loose leaves, but they are also connected closely with the pictorial arts" (CH 101). More recently, Zwerdling has called the style of the novel "that of the sketchbook artist rather than the academic painter" (63) and Bishop has written that *Jacob's Room* is "more profitably to be examined in terms of social drama than impressionist painting—or any purely formalist approach" (Bishop 157).

Probably the best-known contemporary criticism of *Jacob's Room* is Arnold BENNETT's, that "the characters do not vitally survive in the mind, because the author has been obsessed by details of originality and cleverness" (E3 388). This in part inspired Woolf to write "Mr. Bennett and Mrs. Brown." Zwerdling points out that this kind of criticism continued after Woolf's death, Joan Bennett (no relation!) finding that the scenes in *Jacob's Room* "build up no whole that can be held in the mind," and J. K. Johnstone complaining about the novel's lack of unity.

Concern with the form of *Jacob's Room* and the kind of characterization that form determines has dominated much of the critical writing on this novel. From Barry Morgenstern,* writing in 1972, to Edward Bishop in 1992, critics have concerned themselves with the narrator and narrative technique of *Jacob's Room.* Harper notes that the novel has "the most noticeable narrator" of all Woolf's novels, and Lucio Ruotolo remarks that *Jacob's Room* was Woolf's "first sustained assault on the omniscient narrator" (*Interrupted* 69–70). Several readers emphasize the way Woolf creates Jacob "not as a presence but as an absence" (Fleishman, *Virginia Woolf* 64). Although many readers have seen *Jacob's Room* as illustrating characteristic MODERNIST features, Zwerdling points out that "some of them are idiosyncratic" (62).

Pamela Caughie, in her discussion of *Jacob's Room,* warns against treating Woolf's characters and narrator in the same terms (Caughie 65). Reviewing the criticism on the novel, Caughie finds that there is a congruence in passages cited by various critics and in the kinds of themes they isolate, but that these critics diverge widely when it comes to attempting to account for these features of the novel. The common reading of the work's narrative uncertainty as representing Woolf's belief that we can never know another being, Caughie writes, "overlooks Woolf's emphasis on the observer's *situatedness,* both the narrator's and the character's in relation to Jacob and the reader's in relation to the narrative" (Caughie 69). Bishop, too, comments that "Woolf is not *representing* character; what she is exploring is the construction, and representation of the subject" (Bishop 148).

Some critics have seen Jacob as an "every man" and the novel itself as an immortality myth (e.g., Love, *Worlds* 133–35). Jacob has been seen by Alice van Buren Kelley as symbolic of "universal love" (81), "a universal ordering force," and a "universal type" (van Buren Kelley 82). "By combining fact and vision in himself," writes van Buren Kelley, Jacob "is of necessity an enigmatic figure" (68). Another critic who sees myth at work in Jacob's characterization is Harvena Richter, who discusses the scene of the tree falling in the forest the night Jacob goes moth-hunting in terms of the myth of Attis found in Jessie L. Weston's *From Ritual to Romance* and J. G. FRAZER'S *Golden Bough.* Richter explains the scene as a premonition of Jacob's death. She has also written on the importance of the moth as an image of the creative mind in Woolf's writing (in Freedman 13–28). Now that Woolf's early diaries are published, we can read her description of the 1899 moth-hunting expedition that is undoubtedly the source of the repeated image of the moth in *Jacob's Room* (PA 144–45); the Stephen children were led on their expedition into the forest by Thoby. Fleishman, commenting on insect imagery in the novel generally (*Virginia Woolf* 56–57), points out that the image of the captured moth is repeated in "READING," an essay Woolf projected on the day she finished *Jacob's Room.* He also mentions its appearance in "The Death of the Moth," which he quotes as a "summary statement of the theme of *Jacob's Room*" (Fleishman 67–68). The death imagery of moth, skull and empty rooms is associated also with the disintegration of time in the narrative by van Buren Kelley (74–75).

Jacob's Room is a highly self-conscious structure that has drawn attention inevitably to its form. Harper describes the novel's form thus: "Interesting patterns, almost musical in their rhythmic arrangement and in their effects, are involved in the distributions of chapters and sections of *Jacob's Room*" (88n3). He points out that the fourteen chapters consist of a varying number of sections, separated by space breaks (he also notes that several of these breaks were omitted in the U.S. edition of the book, thus reducing the number of sections in some chapters). Commenting on the scenes in particular sections, Richter describes them as experiments with perspective. On their own the scenes may be meaningless, but she finds that together they synthesize into meaningful wholes (*Inward* 109). Bazin finds that Jacob himself "functions in this larger work as the mark does in 'The Mark on the Wall' and as the snail does in 'Kew Gardens' " (Bazin 89). The form of the novel, to Bazin, represents a downplaying of the "predominantly masculine" mode of representation and an emphasis on the "predominantly feminine" non-representational aspects of reality (Bazin 91).

Although she finds the book an "aesthetic whole," Bazin's early work on Woolf is troubled by what she describes as "serious weaknesses" in the narrator's unreliability and inconsistency, which she says are "disturbing and unjustified" (Bazin 98). She thinks this inconsistency may be due to Woolf's authorial voice interrupting the text, but Woolf herself seems to offer a rebuttal to such a notion in a letter she wrote Jacques RAVERAT in 1922, responding to his comments on *Jacob's Room*: "Women may be worse, or may be better, than men, but surely the opinions of the writer of Jacobs Room on that point, or any other, are not *my* opinions. This is a very old quarrel though" (CS 151).

The effort to find unity in Woolf's fiction is a prevalent theme of much of the critical writing on it of the late 1960s and 1970s. Love calls *Jacob's Room* "an experiment in mythopoetic thought" that has "no plot or story in the empirical sense" (*Worlds* 125), but she finds in the novel "organic unity": "subject and object, person and universe, literary character and scene are totally diffuse, totally coextensive and united with each other, and the world of the novel" (*Worlds* 125). In scanning early criticism of *Jacob's Room,* Alice van Buren Kelley also found that many had seen the novel in terms of a fluctuation between subject and object (64–65). More recently, Hermione Lee has found that a "larger rhythm, made out of the constant repetition of [several] techniques, energizes the whole book" (Lee 76). An example of the technique of repetition is the way Woolf uses the same phrase at various times to describe Jacob's room: "Listless is the air in an empty room" (JR 39, 176).

The room is an important metaphor for Woolf, her "favorite symbol of personality or state of mind" according to Richter (213). Bazin quotes Dorothy Brewster's* early work on the significance of the word "room" (Bazin 92) and Schaefer (*Three-fold*) on how Woolf focuses not on Jacob but on the details of his surroundings. Love sees the room image as developed from *THE VOYAGE OUT* and *NIGHT AND DAY*, and van Buren Kelley finds that the novel itself emerges from those earlier works (though neither Love nor van Buren Kelley mentions the short fiction).

Various links with Woolf's other novels have also been suggested. Betty Flanders has been seen as a prototype of Mrs. RAMSAY in *TO THE LIGHTHOUSE* (Bazin), and Julia ELIOT as a prototype of Lily BRISCOE (van Buren Kelley). Approaching this from a different angle, Spilka suggests Woolf's mother, Julia Prinsep STEPHEN, as the maternal prototype in *Jacob's Room* and sees Woolf as extending her mother's lifeline through the war, but ostensibly removing her father from "the fictive scene" (Spilka 19).

In contrast to readings that emphasize Woolf's use of symbolism in *Jacob's Room,* Minow-Pinkney comments that although Woolf may certainly be seen in the context of Anglo-American modernism's symbolist heritage, "Woolf also has a clear-sighted awareness that the symbolist dream of organic unity is no longer easily attainable; truth and the sign have fallen asunder" (29). Minow-Pinkney refers to the postwar world as "fallen," a world in which "transcendental meaning may no longer be possible" (38).

This fallen world is the historical background to Jacob's life. Fleishman has discerned the novel's chronological structure from its references to actual events such as the Home Rule bill and a change in the constitution of the House of Lords (Fleishman 49–50). In sketching this world, several recent critics have pointed out, Woolf writes with "satiric detachment" derived from her dislike of the patriarchal privilege that Jacob's life exemplifies (and, as Zwerdling and others have remarked, that was enjoyed by her cabinet minister cousin, H. A. L. FISHER). Class identity is an important theme of *Jacob's Room* that helps shape Woolf's narrative choices (Zwerdling 75f.), a point elaborated by William R. Handley* (110–33). Nancy Topping Bazin and Jane Hamovit Lauter* ("Virginia Woolf's" 15–17) have also noted Woolf's indictment of patriarchal culture, as has Josephine O'Brien Schaefer* in her comparison of *Jacob's Room* with Willa Cather's *One of Ours,* also published in 1922 ("The Great War" 134–50). Fleishman pays attention to Jacob's class privilege that enables him to receive a good education and to travel. Jacob is heir to the "cultural brain" represented by the British Museum and to the ideal of classical Greece that he imbibes first at Rugby and then at Cambridge. His culture communicates to him a sense of the inferiority of women that persists throughout his brief life. This world was, of course, not only the world of Woolf's brothers but also that of her husband and many of her closest male friends. Her ambivalent attitude toward Cambridge is discussed by Angela Ingram* and Kathleen Dobie.* Bishop points out that although Woolf may have been reading her husband's *Empire and Commerce in Africa,* her novel "breaks up the master narrative for which Leonard Woolf searches" (Bishop 169). Zwerdling finds that "Woolf's elegy for the young men who died in the war is revisionist: there is nothing grand about Jacob; the sacrifice of his life seems perfectly pointless, not even a cautionary tale" (73).

The model that Woolf was revising in *Jacob's Room* was that exemplified by the bildungsroman, which, as many critics have said, Woolf uses in her novel. Fleishman finds *Jacob's Room* an "extension of the *Bildungsroman* form into a fitful sequence of unachieved experiences rather than a coherent process" (Fleishman 46), and Freedman reads the novel as bildungsroman combined with "comedy of manners." In describing how Woolf altered the form of the bildungsroman "to conform to the choral patterns that fashioned her 'comedy of manners,' " Freedman refers to an essay by Judy Little (later incorporated in her book, *Comedy and the Woman Writer*), wherein she notes that while early readers responded to the comedy of *Jacob's Room,* later critics have ignored it in favor of attention to the form. Little argued that the two are actually linked because *Jacob's Room* is a parody of the bildungsroman. Little noted Woolf's familiarity with the genre and explained that it was extremely popular in the nineteenth and early twentieth century. Zwerdling recognizes that, unlike the classic bildungsroman, however, *Jacob's Room* "lacks a teleology" (67); it is, he says, "a novel much more about a stage of life than about a particular person" (78).

Among several critics who have linked Woolf's narrative technique to her politics, Minow-Pinkney writes that Woolf's "critique of Edwardian realism was always in principle, if not at once in practice, a critical exposure of male ideology" (49). She points out that many of the men mentioned in *Jacob's Room* are maimed in some way (Captain Barfoot, for example, is missing fingers, and Mr. Curnow has lost an eye), seeing this as evidence that Jacob's maleness " 'kills' him in a war that is the inevitable consequence of antihumane masculine ideology" (53). As a further example of Woolf's political intent in her narrative technique, Minow-Pinkney says of names in the novel that "the connection between the name and its bearer is dubious and arbitrary . . . [putting] any belief in original truth into radical doubt" (31). Most readers have noticed the enormous number of names in *Jacob's Room,* and many have found, like Allen McLaurin, that "proper names have reference but no meaning" (McLaurin 167).

Harper calls *Jacob's Room* "a book in which people, places, and phenomena are *named,* to an extent unprecedented in *The Voyage Out* or *Night and Day,* as if these names could somehow define Jacob's 'room' " (Harper 87). Lee finds more than 160 characters in the novel, many of whom "have names which are ludicrously similar" (Lee 87), symbolic, she believes, "of the futility of public life" (Lee 87). This sense of futility is a dominant theme of critical writing on *Jacob's Room* whether the critic reads the text as symbolic or as a postmodern representation of the ideological construction of reality.

***Works Specific to This Entry:**

Bazin, Nancy Topping, and Jane Hamovit Lauter. "Virginia Woolf's Keen Sensitivity to War: Its Roots and Its Impact on Her Novels." In Mark Hussey, ed. *Virginia Woolf and War*: 14–39.

Brewster, Dorothy. *Virginia Woolf.* New York: New York University Press, 1962.

Bishop, Edward. "The Subject in *Jacob's Room.*" *Modern Fiction Studies* 38, 1 (Spring 1992): 147–75.

Dobie, Kathleen. "This Is the Room that Class Built: The Structures of Sex and Class in *Jacob's Room.*" In Jane Marcus, ed. *Virginia Woolf and Bloomsbury*: 195–207.

Freedman, Ralph. "The Form of Fact and Fiction: *Jacob's Room* as Paradigm." In Ralph Freedman, ed. *Virginia Woolf*: 123–40.

Handley, William R. "War and the Politics of Narration in *Jacob's Room.*" In Mark Hussey, ed. *Virginia Woolf and War*: 110–33.

Ingram, Angela. " 'The Sacred Edifices': Virginia Woolf and Some of the Sons of Culture." In Jane Marcus, ed. *Virginia Woolf and Bloomsbury*: 125–45.

Levenback, Karen L. "Virginia Woolf and Rupert Brooke: Poised Between Olympus and the 'Real World.' " *Virginia Woolf Miscellany* 33: 5–6.

Morgenstern, Barry. "The Self-Conscious Narrator in *Jacob's Room.*" *Modern Fiction Studies* 18 (Autumn 1972): 351–61.

Ohmann, Carol. "Culture and Anarchy in *Jacob's Room.*" *Contemporary Literature* 18 (1977): 160–72.

Richter, Harvena. "Hunting the Moth: Virginia Woolf and the Creative Imagination." In Ralph Freedman, ed. *Virginia Woolf*: 13–28.

Ruddick, Sara. "Private Brother, Public World." In Jane Marcus, ed. *New Feminist Essays*: 185–215.

Schaefer, Josephine O'Brien. "The Great War and 'This late age of world's experience' in Cather and Woolf." In Mark Hussey, ed. *Virginia Woolf and War*: 134–50.

Usui, Masami. "The German Raid on Scarborough in *Jacob's Room.*" *Virginia Woolf Miscellany* 35: 7.

James, Cousin A clergyman who reads at Rose Pargiter's funeral in *THE YEARS*. See Rose PARGITER (1).

James, Henry (1843–1916) American-born novelist who settled in Europe in 1875, lived in London for more than twenty years, and became a naturalized British citizen in 1915. In 1898 he moved to Rye, where he wrote his later novels. Among his novels are *The American* (1877), *Portrait of a Lady* (1881), *The Spoils of Poynton* (1897), *The Awkward Age* (1899), *What Maisie Knew* (1897), *The Wings of the Dove* (1902), *The Ambassadors* (1903) and *The Golden Bowl* (1904). Among the many short stories James wrote, "The Turn of the Screw" (1898) is probably the best-known. James's prefaces for a revised edition of his novels begun in 1907 are also important.

James knew Woolf's family well and she saw him often when she was young as he was a frequent guest of her parents at 22 HYDE PARK GATE. Noel Annan has remarked that Woolf's father, Leslie STEPHEN, "could claim to have nursed Henry James . . . to fame" in the pages of the *CORNHILL MAGAZINE,* which Stephen edited (Annan 67). In his autobiography, Leonard WOOLF wrote about the strong influence of James on his generation at Cambridge University; a Jamesian atmosphere, Leonard wrote, pervaded the relations of his contemporaries with one another (LW1 67). In a letter to his best friend, Lytton STRACHEY, in 1905, Leonard asked of James "Did he invent us or we him?" (Spotts 97).

Woolf first wrote about James when she reviewed *The Golden Bowl* for the *GUARDIAN* in 1905 ("Mr Henry James's Latest Novel" E1 22–24). She praised his ability to make a novel from everyday events, but commented that the work would be improved were James "content to say less and suggest more" (E1 23). Woolf complained to Violet DICKINSON that the editor of the *Guardian* had asked her to cut her review "in half" at the last moment; Andrew McNeillie transcribes Woolf's reading notes for the review in *Essays of Virginia Woolf,* vol. 1, Appendix III. In 1917, Woolf reviewed James's memoir *The Middle Years* for the *TIMES LITERARY SUPPLEMENT* ("The Old Order" E2 167–776), and in 1918, also for the TLS, she reviewed Joseph Warren Beach's *The Method of Henry James* (E2 346–49).

In 1919, Woolf reviewed for the TLS *Within the Rim and Other Essays 1914–15* (E3 22–25), a collection of essays James had written about World War I. His feelings about England when war broke out had provoked James's naturalization, and in her review Woolf draws attention to the strength of James's love of the country. Woolf's 1920 review of Percy Lubbock's edition of Henry James's *Letters* for the TLS (E3 198–207) drew an attack from A. B. Walkeley, the dramatic critic of *The Times,* who complained that the writer of the review (TLS reviews were unsigned) was too much under the influence of "the Master's" style. In 1921, Woolf wrote an essay for the TLS on "Henry James's Ghost Stories" (E3 319–26); Bruce RICHMOND, the editor of the TLS, asked her to change the word "lewd" in her review, leading Woolf to reflect on how she had to censor herself for this publication (D2 152).

Daniel Fogel sees *TO THE LIGHTHOUSE* as the most Jamesian of Woolf's novels in "its assurance, harmony, and balanced design" (Fogel 146). Both Fogel and Harvena Richter (*Inward* 224) discuss a "concealed, complex, and intricate relationship" between James RAMSAY and Henry James (Fogel 146). Richter also speculates that the central image of Mrs. RAMSAY as a fountain is subtly related to the image of Henry James's *The Sacred Fount* (*Inward* 223), pointing out that "Henry James would be associated in Virginia Woolf's mind with St. Ives in Cornwall" (223). Leon Edel, in *Henry James: The Middle Years 1882–1895* (New York: Avon, 1962), writes of James's trip to ST. IVES in 1894 (when Woolf was twelve): "For a fortnight Henry moved (as we now know) in the landscape of *To the Lighthouse* and among its people; and went striding over the moors with the future Mr. Ramsay" (380).

Fogel has also interpreted Woolf's "PHASES OF FICTION" as revealing that "an important covert subtext" of "THE NARROW BRIDGE OF ART" is that Woolf "offers an early formulation of her project for *The Waves*, giving the mind's 'soliloquy in solitude,' in sharp contradistinction to the interpersonal world of Henry James's fiction" (Fogel 118). Fogel argues that Woolf's making the figure of the novelist in *THE WAVES* a man, BERNARD, and, moreover, a figure who bears a "concealed but unmistakable identity with the very writer in opposition to whom she was trying to forge a new kind of fictional art," bespeaks "an underlying desperation in Woolf about the possibilities of her art, about the autonomy of her literary imagination, and about female literary authority" (Fogel 158). Like James, says Fogel, Bernard collects observations in notebooks as aids in writing fiction (Fogel 186n63). He identifies a specific connection in NEVILLE's repeated image of Bernard "twiddling a piece of string" whenever his stories falter, an image Fogel believes is derived from H. G. WELLS's "famous (or infamous) account of the failure of James's fiction" in *Boon* (1915) (Fogel 157). Fogel goes so far as to link RHODA's suicide to Woolf's "buried but enduring struggle with Henry James for literary identity" (159).

Jane Eyre See BRONTË, Charlotte and Emily; *A ROOM OF ONE'S OWN*.

Jarvis, Mrs. Character in *JACOB'S ROOM* who walks on the moor when she is unhappy (though she will never be unhappy enough actually to leave her husband). Betty FLANDERS likes this clergyman's wife and shows her Jacob's letters and walks with her on the moor toward the end of the novel.

Jenkinson, Edward Mentioned in *JACOB'S ROOM* as having resigned from the Town Council of Scarborough; Betty FLANDERS suggests Captain BARFOOT should stand for his place, which, apparently, he does as he does become a Councillor (JR 73).

Jenkinson, Nelly Mentioned in *JACOB'S ROOM*, a typist in a tea shop where Fanny ELMER leaves her umbrella.

Jessamy Brides, The See *ORLANDO*.

Jex-Blake, Sophia (1840–1912) As part of her history of women's struggle for rights in *THREE GUINEAS*, Woolf tells the story of Sophia Jex-Blake, who, with Elizabeth Garrett, followed the example of the American pioneer Elizabeth Blackwell in becoming a doctor (TG 64–66). Jex-Blake became lecturer in mathematics at Queen's College in 1859; at first focused on a career in education, she became committed to medicine after visiting the United States, where she met Dr. Lucy Sewell, who had opened a dispensary for women in Boston. Jex-Blake enrolled as a medical student at Edinburgh University in 1869 and in November 1870 the "Riot at Surgeons' Hall" took place (Ray Strachey, *The Cause* 179) when medical students objected to her and other female students' presence. Woolf draws on *The Life of Sophia Jex-Blake* by Margaret Todd (1918) to recount in *Three Guineas* the story of how her father refused to allow her to take paid employment (TG 131–35). Jex-Blake published *A Visit to Some American Schools and Colleges* in 1867, *Medical Women: A Thesis and a History* in 1886 and *Medical Women: Two Essays* in 1872.

Jinny One of the six soliloquists in *THE WAVES*. Jinny is immediately characterized as sensual, alert to vivid color and to the power of her own body to attract men. As a schoolgirl, Jinny says "I never cease to move and to dance" (TW 42), an image echoed later by BERNARD, who describes her as "dancing like a flame" (TW 117). (Evelyn Haller sees Jinny as closely resembling Igor Stravinsky's firebird ["Her Quill" 199–201].) One of her earliest actions in *The Waves* is to kiss LOUIS suddenly on the back of the neck, arousing painful jealousy in SUSAN, who sees her do this (TW 13). Jean Alexander writes that in Jinny Woolf "has explored the limits of eroticism and has shown its harmony with the cosmic mystery" (Alexander 153).

Woolf's father, Sir Leslie STEPHEN, called his daughter "Jinny" (or Ginny), and Howard Harper has written that Sir Leslie "would have been sexually attracted toward, and morally disapproving of, a woman like Jinny" (Harper 235n11). James Haule suggests Mary HUTCHINSON as a possible source for the characterization of Jinny ("Introduction" x), and Jean O. Love calls her "at least a descendant" of Jinny CARSLAKE in *JACOB'S ROOM* (Love, *Worlds* 212).

Joad, C. E. M. (1891–1953) A philosopher and journalist who in 1934 published two articles in the *NEW STATESMAN AND NATION* on the decline of the BLOOMSBURY GROUP as a cultural force. In *THREE GUINEAS* Woolf quotes from two of his books: *Under the Fifth Rib: A Belligerent Autobiography* (1932), in which he says men and women should not dine together (TG Ch2n4), and *The Testament of Joad* (1937), wherein he complains of the political apathy of women (TG 42–43).

John, Augustus Edwin (1879–1961) A British painter and etcher, known in the first two decades of the twentieth century for his "Bohemian" lifestyle as well as his painting; his sister was the painter Gwen John (1876–1939). In *THE VOYAGE OUT,* Mrs. Flushing refers to "a clever man called John who paints ever so much better than the old masters" (TVO 198). Woolf met him in 1909 when Lady Ottoline MORRELL invited them both to dinner.

Johnson, Maisie Character in *MRS. DALLOWAY* who is observed in Regent's Park by Carrie DEMPSTER. Nineteen-year-old Maisie has just arrived in London from Edinburgh to work at her uncle's business and asks Septimus and Rezia Warren SMITH the way to the Tube station. Septimus's "oddness" makes Maisie suddenly long to go back home; she feels like crying out, "Horror! horror!" (MD 39).

Johnson, Miss LOUIS's secretary in *THE WAVES.*

Johnson, Samuel (1709–84) A poet, essayist, biographer of poets, and, most famously, creator of the *Dictionary* (1755). Johnson's life was recorded by James BOSWELL. Johnson appears to ORLANDO as a "Roman-looking rolling shadow" (O 222). Woolf takes her notion of the "common reader" from Johnson's "Life of Gray," as she explains in her prefatory note to the *COMMON READER.* Beth Rosenberg (3) has pointed out that Woolf's prototype of the common reader, Mr. Briggs (see "BYRON & MR BRIGGS"), has a certain kind of sense defined by Johnson as "the faculty of knowing what to use, what to neglect" (E3 485).

In *A ROOM OF ONE'S OWN,* Johnson appears as but one in an unbroken line of patriarchs who have denigrated the intellectual capabilities of women, represented by his response to Boswell's telling him of hearing a woman preach at a Quaker meeting: "Sir, a woman's preaching is like a dog's walking on his hind legs. It is not done well; but you are surprised to find it done at all" (James Boswell, *The Life of Samuel Johnson, Ll.D.* New York: E. P. Dutton/Everyman's Library, 1906: 287). Woolf both gives this remark a fictional ancestor, Nick GREENE, and refers to a twentieth-century descendant, quoting from Cecil Gray's *Survey of Contemporary Music* in which he uses Johnson's line to dismiss the composer Germaine Tailleferre (AROO 54).

Jones, Brandy In *JACOB'S ROOM,* during the hunt Jacob goes into the bar with Brandy Jones "to smoke with the rustics" (JR 101).

Jones, Mrs. Lynn Character in *BETWEEN THE ACTS* who lives with Etty SPRINGETT now that both are widows. She and Etty are upset by Miss LA TROBE's satirical treatment of the Victorian family in the annual village pageant. The two women are also made nervous by the antics of ALBERT, the village idiot.

Jones, Phyllis Child in *BETWEEN THE ACTS* who personifies England at the opening of Miss LA TROBE's village pageant.

Joseph, Uncle Mentioned in *NIGHT AND DAY* when he comes to tea at Ralph DENHAM's house to offer Ralph's younger brother a job. Seeing his uncle's bowler hat and "very large umbrella" in the hall, Ralph avoids meeting him and goes up to his room.

"Journal of Mistress Joan Martyn, The" (SF 33–62) In August 1906 Woolf and her sister, Vanessa BELL, rented Blo' Norton Hall in East Harling, Norfolk, for about four weeks. While there, Woolf wrote to Violet DICKINSON that she was taking long walks and "making out brilliant stories every step of the way. One is actually being—as we geniuses say—transferred to paper at this moment" (L1 234). Woolf is most likely referring to the story which was given the title "The Journal of Mistress Joan Martyn" by Susan M. Squier and Louise A. DeSalvo, who edited it for a special Woolf issue of *TWENTIETH CENTURY LITERATURE* (237–69). About a third of the story is in the voice of Rosamond Merridew, a historian who has "exchanged a husband and a family and a house in which I may grow old for certain fragments of yellow parchment" (SF 33). Spying a house "where the owners are likely to possess exquisite manuscripts," Merridew gets invited in by Mr. and Mrs. Martyn and is shown the family papers. The rest of the story is taken up with the journal of Joan Martyn, written at the end of the fifteenth century. Joan (who was taught to write by her father Willoughby, who has the same name as Rachel VINRACE's father in *THE VOYAGE OUT*) writes an account of her daily life. In an analysis of the story, DeSalvo has written that it "explores the historical and societal causes of the tensions between the sexes" (*Impact* 269) and locates women's oppression in the land-tenure system. DeSalvo has written in "Shakespeare's *Other* Sister" that the story is "an extremely significant work in the Woolf canon because it presages many of the central concerns of Woolf's later works" (63), a view also held by Brenda Silver, who writes that the "Journal" "establishes many of [Woolf's] recurring themes" (in Scott, *Gender* 651). DeSalvo sees Joan Martyn as an early embodiment of ideas Woolf would explore in *A ROOM OF ONE'S OWN* but says that Joan is "*not* Shakespeare's sister" (referring to the figure of Judith SHAKESPEARE in *A Room*) because she *does* write and does not get ostracized or go mad or kill herself: "She is Shakespeare's *other* sister, who had another sister called Virginia Woolf" (79).

Journey Not the Arrival Matters, The. An Autobiography of the Years 1939–69 The fifth and final volume of Leonard WOOLF's autobiography, published by the HOGARTH PRESS in 1969 and reprinted in the Oxford University Press two-volume edition, *An Autobiography* (1980). This volume begins with the outbreak of World War II and Leonard's account of that descent into barbarism, and Woolf's death in 1941. He also reflects on the achievement of the Hogarth Press, and ends with an account of his return to Ceylon, where he had been a colonial administrator nearly sixty years earlier.

Joyce, James Augustine Aloysius (1882–1941) Irish novelist who spent most of his life in Paris, Trieste and Zurich. His collection of short stories, *Dubliners,* was published in 1914; *A Portrait of the Artist as a Young Man* first appeared serially in *THE EGOIST* in 1914–15; *Ulysses,* parts of which were published in the *Little Review,* was first published in Paris in 1922; and *Finnegans Wake* was published in 1939.

In her essay "MODERN NOVELS," Woolf chooses as her example of the new realities being explored and represented by the novel the work of James Joyce, naming him "spiritual" as opposed to the "materialist" trio of Arnold BENNETT, H. G. WELLS and John GALSWORTHY.

Woolf's response to Joyce was complex and inconclusive, but certain phrases of hers regarding Joyce's *Ulysses* have solidified in readers' minds over the years, their original tentativeness obscured. It is probably misguided ever to isolate a reader's responses from the cultural, literary and social contexts within which they are formed, particularly if that reader is also a writer. The "Tangled Mesh of Modernists" that appears in Bonnie Kime Scott's introduction to *The Gender of Modernism* (10) is a useful caution against such isolating of any one writer's opinion.

As she herself acknowledged, Woolf's response to *Ulysses* and to Joyce's reputation was overshadowed by its being mediated through the imposing figure of T. S. ELIOT (D2 200). The *Little Review* published parts of *Ulysses* between March and October 1918. Woolf recorded in her diary an early meeting with Eliot and her distress that his "poetic creed" set up "Ezra Pound & Wyndham Lewis as great poets, or in the current phrase 'very interesting' writers. He admires Mr Joyce immensely" (D1 219). Eliot, indeed, considered Joyce the "best living prose writer" (Eliot to Scofield Thayer, June 30, 1918, *Letters*). The notebook (RN 155–57) Woolf used in preparing her article "Modern Novels" records her thoughts on the *Little Review* extracts. She felt it was "an attempt to get thinking into literature"; despite encountering only "minor minds," it was "an effort in the right direction" (Scott, *Gender* 642). She also recorded her familiar complaint about the "egotism" of contemporary writers that impeded them from a larger view of things. Her well-known criticism of "the damned egotistical self" that "ruined" Joyce and Dorothy RICHARDSON is echoed by Katherine MANSFIELD's criticism of Richardson's *Tunnel* that no "memory" was at work: "Only we feel that until these things are judged and given each its appointed place in the whole scheme, they have no meaning in the world of art" (Scott, *Gender* 309). In "Modern Novels" Woolf wrote that Joyce "attempts to come closer to life," that he had discarded the conventions that traditionally bound novelists and that despite the work's difficulty and unpleasantness, *Ulysses* was "undeniably distinct" (E3 34). In the "Cemetery scene" we seem, she said (with characteristic irony), to be given "life itself." But, she added, in a judgment that has damned her in the eyes of many subsequent critics, *Ulysses* ultimately fails because of "the comparative poverty of the writer's mind" (E3 34).

Eliot no doubt had Woolf's essay in mind when he wrote to John Quinn in July 1919, "I am sorry to say that I have found it uphill and exasperating work trying to impose Joyce on such 'intellectual' people, or people whose opinion carries weight as I know, in London. He is far from being accepted, yet. I only know two or three people, besides my wife and myself, who are really carried away by him. There is a strong body of critical Brahminism, destructive and conservative in temper, which will not have Joyce. Novelty is no more acceptable here than anywhere else, and the forces of conservatism and obstruction are more intelligent, better educated, and more formidable" (*Letters* July 9, 1919).

Turning again to Woolf's record of her conversations with Eliot, it is easy to see that she felt threatened both by the challenge of Joyce's art and by Eliot's standing as a critic: "I kept myself from being submerged, though feeling the waters rise once or twice. I mean by this that he [Eliot] completely neglected my claims to be a writer, & had I been meek, I suppose I should have gone under—felt him & his views dominant & subversive" (D2 67). Eliot considered the work "extremely brilliant" (D2 67). An insight into the threat posed by Joyce as a rival experimental writer that undoubtedly colored

Woolf's response to his work is gained by reading what she wrote about Katherine Mansfield in 1924: "The thought of Katherine Mansfield comes to me—as usual rather reprehensibly—. . . thinking yes, if she'd lived, she'd have written on, & people would have seen that I was the more gifted—that wd. only have become more & more apparent. Indeed, so I suppose it would" (D2 317).

Thus it is not, perhaps, surprising that when in 1921 Woolf notes that "Eliot astounded me by praising Monday or Tuesday," she also can "write without cringing . . . Ulysses is prodigious" (D2 125). Joyce's book was published in Paris in February 1922 and in August of that year Woolf was reading it, "fabricating my case for & against" (D2 188). It is at this point that she makes the infamous comment that she is "puzzled, bored, irritated, & disillusioned as by a queasy undergraduate scratching his pimples." And, again, Eliot's judgment broods over her: "And Tom, great Tom, thinks this on a par with War & Peace!" (D2 188). She was in the process of reading the novel, however, and withheld her final evaluation until the next month when she finished it and declared it "a mis-fire. Genius it has I think; but of the inferior water" (D2 199). In language almost identical to that used by D. H. LAWRENCE the following year in "Surgery for the Novel—or a Bomb," she hoped that Joyce would "grow out of it; but as Joyce is 40 this scarcely seems likely." (Lawrence wrote, "It's awful. And it's childish. It really is childish, after a certain age, to be absorbedly self-conscious" [Lawrence 115].) She had not read the work carefully and, she admitted to her diary, had probably "scamped the virtue of it." Nevertheless, she still felt it was absurd to compare Joyce to Leo TOLSTOY.

The next day, Leonard Woolf showed his wife a review in the American *Nation* that led her to see how superficial her reading might have been. She wrote also of what had conditioned her reading: "Probably the final beauty of the writing is never felt by contemporaries; but they ought, I think, to be bowled over; & this I was not. Then again, I had my back up on purpose; then again I was over stimulated by Tom's praises" (D2 200). In 1935, she wrote to Stephen SPENDER that "living writers are to me like people singing in the next room—too loud, too near; and for some reason I am so exacerbated by their being flat or sharp; as if I were singing my own song, and they put me out" (L5 408).

In 1922 *Ulysses* was certainly a song heard loud and clear, with the potential of drowning out others. Eliot, however, who in August had compared the work to *War and Peace,* apparently was reconsidering his opinion. Woolf records yet another conversation with him about Joyce: "Tom said 'He is a purely literary writer. . . .' I said he was virile—a he-goat; but didn't expect Tom to agree. Tom did tho'e; & said he left out many things that were important. . . . he did not think that he gave a new insight into human nature—said nothing new like Tolstoi. Bloom told one nothing" (D2 203). In her reading notes in 1919, Woolf had concluded that "it seems possible that the big things are the big things: love, death, jealousy and so on; but must be seen again, felt again; always, perpetually" (Scott, *Gender* 645). Eliot, then, had come around to Woolf's point of view. As to her comment on Joyce's "virility," the clarity of Woolf's reading would have to wait until the 1970s for endorsement by feminist readings of Joyce (Scott, *Gender* 198–201).

Woolf continued to comment on Joyce in her essays. In "HOW IT STRIKES A CONTEMPORARY," characterizing her age, she terms *Ulysses* "a memorable catastrophe—immense in daring, terrific in disaster" (E3 356). It was important to her conception of the novel that Joyce was a "spiritual" writer as opposed to the "materialists," yet his "calculated indecency" seemed to her a trick. To Lawrence, Joyce was "too terribly would-be and done-on-purpose" (Lawrence 149), and Woolf also found an air of insincerity in his verbal pyrotechnics and, more particularly, in his "indecency." In "CHARACTER IN FICTION," she remarked "how dull indecency is, when it is not the overflowing of a superabundant energy or savagery, but the determined and public-spirited act of a man who needs fresh air!" (E3 434).

Given this history, it seems strange that when Woolf came to revise "Modern Novels" for the *COMMON READER* (giving it the more generic title "MODERN FICTION" and thus pointing attention to narrative rather than specific authors and works), she did not revise her comments on Joyce. The note that *Ulysses* was appearing serially in the *Little Review* stands as if "Modern Fiction" were a reprint and not, as it is in fact, a revision made after *Ulysses* had been published in full in 1922. Woolf's concern with Joyce as an exemplary MODERNIST is less a concern with form than with his "philosophy" or, as she usually terms it, "vision." Her snobbish disdain for the "set in a back street," as she described Joyce's intended audience, certainly contributes to her assessment of the novel, but Woolf was also measuring *Ulysses* against the Russian novelists whose journeys into the "dark places of psychology" she felt were more profound and lastingly important than anything her contemporaries had achieved, except, perhaps, for Marcel PROUST. Her comments on Proust in a letter to Roger FRY echo the passion and awe of her response a few years earlier to Fyodor DOSTOYEVSKY: having described her "amazement" at the first volume of *Remembrance of Things Past,* she went on to say, "Far otherwise is it with Ulysses; to which I bind myself like a martyr to a stake, and have thank God, now finished—My martyrdom is over" (L2 566). In 1926, she was among 167 signers of a letter protesting an American pirate edition of *Ulysses* (a letter, incidentally, that Ezra Pound would not sign). Woolf recognized and acknowledged the importance of *Ulysses* as evidence of and catalyst of the English novel's escape from restrictions of form and content; however, her own "vision of reality" was quite different from that of Joyce, as can be seen not only in her own fiction but also in her comments upon her contemporaries.

T. S. Eliot's wife, Vivienne, astutely pointed out what Woolf may have objected to in *Ulysses* in a review for the *CRITERION* of Woolf's "Character in Fiction": "Mr Bloom is real: he might almost be called, by friends of Mrs Brown, 'photographic'—a dreadful word. But what can one hang on one's walls now? What is there, unless one keeps a lodging-house, except the photographic and the abstract? And has not modern literature solved its problems by finding the symbolic in the photograph—as Mr Bloom is both a photograph and a symbol?" (CH 136). The cinema, as many have noted, had a significant influence on modernist novelists. Modernist writers such as Joyce observed and employed the montage and jump-cut techniques of filmmakers. In her notebook on *Ulysses*, Woolf wrote: "Possibly like a cinema that shows you very slowly, how a hare does jump; all pictures were a little made up before. Here is thought made phonetic—taken to bits" (Scott, *Gender* 643). Since the mid-1980s, there has been increasing attention by critics to the possibilities of seriously comparing Woolf and Joyce, although the rivalry constructed between them continues unabated in the popular press. Bonnie Kime Scott's *New Alliances in Joyce Studies*, for example, contains essays by Christine Froula and Jane Lilienfeld that explore intertextualities between works by Joyce and by Woolf.

Judd A retired shopkeeper in *THE YEARS* who attends a meeting with Eleanor PARGITER.

"Jug, jug, jug" In *THE WAVES*, JINNY "sings" like the nightingale, "jug, jug, jug," an allusion to part III of T. S. ELIOT's *Waste Land*, and also to Eliot's source in Ovid's *Metamorphoses* and the story of PROCNE AND PHILOMELA. "Jug, jug" was conventional Elizabethan slang for sexual intercourse.

K

Karenina, Anna In *A ROOM OF ONE'S OWN*, Anna Karenina, the eponymous heroine of Leo TOLSTOY's novel, is offered as an example of women who have "burnt like beacons in all the works of all the poets from the beginning of time" (AROO 43), whom Woolf uses to stress the difference between fictional and real women.

Kauffer, Edward McKnight (1890–1954) American artist who sometimes exhibited at the OMEGA WORKSHOPS but was not involved in the business (Anscombe 26). He became well known for his poster designs for the London Underground (subway). In 1928 he designed one of the wolf's-head colophons used by the HOGARTH PRESS, and he also designed a number of dust jackets for the Press.

Keats, John (1795–1821) Keats's first book of poetry was published with the assistance of Percy Bysshe SHELLEY in 1817. Among his best-known works are *Endymion, Hyperion,* "The Eve of St. Agnes," "La Belle Dame sans Merci," "ISABELLA AND THE POT OF BASIL," "Lamia" and the odes, "On a Grecian Urn," "To a Nightingale," "To Autumn," "On Melancholy," "On Indolence" and "To Psyche." His letters, of which there have been several editions, are also notable for their thoughts on poetry and Keats's analysis of his own aesthetic.

In *A ROOM OF ONE'S OWN,* Keats is first mentioned as one example of those self-conscious nineteenth-century male artists for whom writing was a struggle and who felt the world was indifferent to their work (AROO 51). Later, Woolf remarks that she would rather have the biography of a shop assistant than the seventieth study of "Keats and his use of Miltonic inversion" which "Professor Z" is at work on (AROO 90), appealing to her audience for something new in literary studies. Keats also appears in *A Room* as an example of the "androgynous" artist (AROO 103); Phyllis Rose believes that Woolf's ANDROGYNY is very similar to Keats's notion of "negative capability" (Rose 189).

Woolf was very fond of the Romantic poets and often alludes to their work in her essays. Reviewing the *Letters of Algernon Charles Swinburne* for the *TIMES LITERARY SUPPLEMENT* in 1918, she wrote that "no one would wish to sacrifice a line that Keats ever wrote; but we cling as firmly to some of his letters as to some of his poems" (E2 229). The "supreme felicities" of Keats and Shelley, she wrote in 1919, "seem to come when the engine of the brain is shut off and the mind glides serene but unconscious" ("The Intellectual Imagination" [E3 135]). Keats had a "fine and natural bearing" ("HOW IT STRIKES A CONTEMPORARY" [E3 355]), and Woolf found his attitude to criticism and sense of security about the value of his own work comforting when Wyndham LEWIS's *Men Without Art,* an attack on BLOOMSBURY GROUP writers, was published in 1934 (D4 250–51). In an article for *Vogue* in 1924, she wrote that Keats possessed "the rarest qualities that human beings can command—genius, sensibility, dignity, wisdom" (E3 461), but noted also that he treated Fanny Brawne in a typically masculine way "both as angel and cockatoo." In 1931, Woolf described her visit to Keats's house in Hampstead in "Great Men's Houses," one of her *LONDON SCENE* essays.

Clarissa DALLOWAY (1) in *THE VOYAGE OUT* quotes from Shelley's elegy for Keats, "Adonais" (TVO 58). The mood of "Adonais" can also be seen permeating *JACOB'S ROOM,* with its theme of a young man's premature death (Keats died from consumption at age 25). The same lines that Clarissa quotes in *The Voyage Out* reappear in "Mrs. Dalloway in Bond Street," one of the sketches that make up *MRS. DALLOWAY'S PARTY.* Judith P. Saunders sees the poem as a central structuring metaphor of the short story and traces how the line from the poem in Clarissa's mind, about the "contagion of the world's slow stain," becomes linked to her speculation that the girl waiting on her in the glove shop is menstruating (Saunders 45–50). Beverly Ann Schlack notes that Miss Isabel POLE in *MRS. DALLOWAY* asks of Septimus Warren SMITH, "Was he not like Keats?"

Kennedy The gardener at Mr. and Mrs. RAMSAY's summer home in *TO THE LIGHTHOUSE,* whom Mrs. Ramsay finds so handsome that she cannot fire him (TTL 65–66). After his leg is injured in a fall, Kennedy can no longer care for the garden (TTL 141).

Kennedy, Richard (1912–89) An assistant at the HOGARTH PRESS who has told the story of his time there in *A Boy at the Hogarth Press.* He started work in 1928 and left in 1930, having designed two covers as well as acted as a general assistant to Leonard WOOLF. Kennedy went on to a successful career as an illustrator.

***Kew Gardens* (SF 84–89)** Although Woolf felt that *Kew Gardens* was "slight & short" (D1 284) and wrote Vanessa BELL that it was bad, this sketch (as Woolf usually called her short fictions) was very popular when it appeared in 1919 in a limited edition of 150, hand-set and printed by Leonard and Woolf at the HOGARTH PRESS with two woodcuts by Vanessa Bell. This was the last work of Woolf's fiction that the Woolfs set by hand and printed themselves, and its publication marked the beginning of a process that would gradually turn the Hogarth Press into a commercial enterprise. *Kew Gardens* was printed in a larger second edition in 1919, and in 1927 a third (limited) edition, lavishly illustrated on each page by Vanessa Bell, was published. Leonard Woolf also included it in *A HAUNTED HOUSE* (1944).

"Kew Gardens" was also included in *MONDAY OR TUESDAY* (1921), as were "AN UNWRITTEN NOVEL" and "THE MARK ON THE WALL," all three of which Woolf identified as important in helping her make the transition to *JACOB'S ROOM* (D2 13). Set in the Royal Botanic Gardens at Kew, where Woolf had often visited since she was young, "Kew Gardens" displays many of the characteristics of her novels' style. Mark Hussey has pointed out that the story's sense of color suggests Cézanne or Monet (*Singing* 70) and is used to suggest character and mood. Some critics have noted that Anthony Alpers suggests in his biography of Katherine MANSFIELD (1980) that she was influential in helping Woolf break out of the mold of her first two novels. Mansfield wrote of "Kew Gardens" that the story belonged to another age and had a sense of leisure uncharacteristic of the frenetic pace of modern living; the flower bed which is at the heart of the piece, she said, fills "a whole world" (quoted in Baldwin 107–08). The reviewer for the *TIMES LITERARY SUPPLEMENT* was delighted with both Woolf's prose and Vanessa Bell's woodcuts (CH 66–67); and E. M. FORSTER wrote in the *Daily News* that "Kew Gardens" was "vision unalloyed" (CH 69) and quite un-English.

The sketch is structured by hovering for a moment over four couples: Eleanor and Simon, who have come to Kew with their two children, Caroline and Hubert, and are thinking of significant past moments they have experienced in the Gardens; an old man who tells his friend William that the dead from World War I are "rolling between the hills like thunder" (SF 86) and who talks to the flowers about Uruguay; two lower-middle-class women who chatter to one another (Woolf was, apparently, embarrassed at her portrayal of these women as she did not want her associates from the WOMEN'S COOPERATIVE GUILD to read this scene [D1 284]); and, finally, a young couple in love (one of whom has the name of Vanessa Bell's servant Trissie). Also, the narrative sees insects and a snail intensely for a moment. All this, as the final paragraph reveals, takes place in the heart of London against the roar of buses' engines.

Avrom Fleishman has pointed out that "Kew Gardens" exhibits a kind of organization frequently found in Woolf's short fiction in which "a series of items is set out, the final item emerging as the key one" ("Forms" 56). He identifies "voices" as this final item and notes a linear progression in the story (as he calls it). Edward L. Bishop, in "Pursuing 'It'," has suggested that "Kew Gardens" is the artistic application of the aesthetic manifesto Woolf had published a few months earlier, "MODERN NOVELS" (better known now in its revised form as "MODERN FICTION"). Jeanette McVicker suggests that if read from "an ideological position," "Kew Gardens" "provides a capsulized version of Woolf's critique of Empire" (41).

Two moments in the story stand out as foreshadowing later works: The old man tells his friend that in the ancient world heaven was called Thessaly and he describes an invention with which to communicate with spirits (SF 86); in *MRS. DALLOWAY,* Septimus Warren SMITH mutters in Regent's Park about the dead walking in Thessaly (MD 105) and feels flowers growing through his flesh (103). Eleanor tells her husband that her epiphany in the Gardens came when she was suddenly kissed on the back of the neck by an old woman with a wart on her nose, "the mother of all my kisses all my life" (SF 85). In *THE WAVES,* LOUIS is suddenly kissed by JINNY in the garden (TW 13), an event that reverberates in the children's lives.

Keymer, Mrs. Mentioned in *JACOB'S ROOM* asking who Jacob is at a party.

Keynes, Sir Geoffrey Langdon (1887–1982) Surgeon, Blake scholar, bibliographer and brother of John Maynard KEYNES. In 1913 he was lodging on the top floor of 38 BRUNSWICK SQUARE when Woolf took an overdose of Veronal. With Leonard WOOLF, Keynes took her to St. Bartholomew's Hospital where he pumped her stomach and saved her life.

Keynes, John Maynard (1883–1946) Economist and prolific writer on economics. Woolf came to know him well in 1909 when he shared rooms with Duncan GRANT at 21 FITZROY SQUARE. In 1911, he shared a house at 38 BRUNSWICK SQUARE with Woolf, Grant, Adrian STEPHEN and, a little later, Leonard WOOLF. Keynes entered King's College, Cambridge University, in 1902 and was elected to the APOSTLES in 1903 with the support of Lytton STRACHEY and Leonard Woolf. Frederic Spotts has written that Leonard initially disliked Keynes and that Leonard's "comments in his autobiography about Keynes are a masterpiece of praising with faint damn" (Spotts 578). Spotts suggests that Leonard was swayed by Strachey and Woolf, but Woolf does not seem to have been any more antipathetic to Keynes than others. Strachey may have resented him for winning the affections of Duncan Grant, with whom Strachey had himself been infatuated. Many of his friends in the BLOOMSBURY GROUP were critical of Keynes's worldliness and unabashed capitalism, criticism that is recalled in David GARNETT's memoir *The Flowers of the Forest.*

Keynes's memoir "My Early Beliefs," read to the MEMOIR CLUB in 1938, has often been taken as a definitive statement of the Bloomsbury Group's origins (Rosenbaum, *Bloomsbury Group* 48). Woolf called it "a very packed profound & impressive paper" (D5 168). It begins with the recollection of Keynes meeting D. H. LAWRENCE in Bertrand RUSSELL's rooms at Cambridge, a meeting that Lawrence described with horror in a letter to Garnett telling him to detach himself from the Bloomsbury "beetles." In the memoir, published in *Two Memoirs* (1949), Keynes describes the influence on his Cambridge generation of G. E. MOORE, describing their beliefs as a religion that was "exciting, exhilarating, the beginning of a renaissance, the opening of a new heaven on a new earth" (Rosenbaum, *Bloomsbury Group* 52). Leonard Woolf, having praised Keynes's abilities, writes in his autobiography that "most people who knew him intimately . . . would agree that there were in him some streaks of intellectual willfulness and arrogance which often led him into surprisingly wrong and perverse judgments" (LW1 92). Leonard goes on to say that Keynes's "recollections and interpretations are quite wrong about Moore's influence" (LW1 92) and give a "distorted picture of Moore's beliefs and doctrine" (LW1 93).

Despite the often abrasive relations with his Bloomsbury friends, Keynes was a lifelong part of the circle, although his government work and duties as a lecturer in economics at Cambridge often took him away. One of the early rumors in London about Bloomsbury was that Vanessa BELL and Keynes had "copulated" on a sofa during a party at GORDON SQUARE. Keynes took over 46 Gordon Square from the Bells in 1916, and it remained his London home; after his marriage, he also had a country residence at Tilton, near CHARLESTON.

Keynes joined the British Treasury in 1914 and was its chief representative at the Paris Peace Conference at the end of World War I in 1919. In May he resigned in protest at the conditions being imposed on Germany and that summer at Charleston wrote *The Economic Consequences of the Peace* (1919), a book that made him world-famous. He wrote a book or pamphlet almost every year, and published three with the HOGARTH PRESS: *The Economic Consequences of Mr. Churchill* (1925); *A Short View of Russia* (1925; number 13 in the Hogarth Essays); and *The End of Laissez-Faire* (1926). He gave financial advice freely to his friends, and was also a significant collector of modern art.

In 1925, Keynes married Lydia LOPOKOVA, a dancer with the RUSSIAN BALLET and Woolf's model for Lucrezia Warren SMITH in *MRS. DALLOWAY*. Many in Bloomsbury disapproved of the marriage, thinking Lopokova was not intelligent enough for Keynes, but Woolf came to be fond of her. Although she shared her friends' feeling that Keynes was sometimes "sensual, brutal, unimaginative" (D2 69), Woolf also admired his "remarkable mind" (D3 181). She found him "adroit & supple & full of that queer imaginative ardour about history, humanity" and enjoyed the range of his interests (D4 237). She was pleased that Keynes thought *THE YEARS* her best book (D5 77), but was nervous about his response to *THREE GUINEAS,* knowing that she was, in a way, writing about his territory. As it happened, "Maynard never said a word," a sign, she knew, of his severe disapproval of her arguments (D5 163). In 1940, Woolf speculated that of all her friends, Keynes would "interest posterity most" (D5 255).

Kilman, Doris Character in *MRS. DALLOWAY* who is a tutor and guide to Elizabeth DALLOWAY. She evokes strong feelings of distaste in Clarissa DALLOWAY and, although sympathetic to her plight, Elizabeth also finds her too intense and pitiable. Kilman feels great bitterness toward Clarissa, a bitterness which she tries to atone for by praying harder. Kilman was dismissed from her job as a teacher during the war because she would not say that all Germans were bad (MD 187). Richard DALLOWAY has taken pity on her and given her a job. Kilman is also a Quaker who has been working for the Society of Friends for more than two years (MD 187). Masami Usui points out that although most churches in England supported World War I, the Quakers, with their long radical tradition of pacifism, did not ("Female Victims" 159). Poole (*Unknown* 114) and Trombley (253) suggest that Kilman might have been modeled in part on Jean THOMAS.

Kingsley, Charles (1819–75) Professor of modern history at Cambridge University 1860–1869 and a writer concerned with social reform. Among his best-known novels are *Alton Locke* (1850), *Westward Ho!* (1857), *The Water Babies* (1863) and *Hereward the Wake* (1865). Kingsley also wrote poems and works about science, and published several volumes of his sermons. When in 1938 the *Atlantic Monthly* published a two-part summary of Woolf's ***THREE GUINEAS,*** it appeared under the title "Women Must Weep—Or Unite to End War," an allusion to a line from Kingsley's poem "The Three Fishers," "Men must work and women must weep." In her long note on chastity in *Three Guineas* (ch2n38), Woolf quotes Kingsley's comment that young middle-class women should be shielded from the realities of poverty (TG 168).

In ***THE VOYAGE OUT,*** while Rachel lies dying, her uncle Ridley AMBROSE recites lines identified by Beverly Ann Schlack as from Kingsley's "A New Forest Ballad" (TVO 350). In discussing the poem, Louise DeSalvo interprets these lines as indicating that Ridley "perceives the link between Rachel's illness and an unwitting fatal battle between Rachel's future husband and her father" (*First* 152).

Kingsley, Mary Henriette (1862–1900) In ***THREE GUINEAS,*** Woolf quotes from Stephen Gwynn's *The Life of Mary Kingsley* (Macmillan 1932) Kingsley's saying that "being allowed to learn German was *all* the paid-for education I ever had" (TG 4). Kingsley wrote widely on West Africa, publishing *Travels in West Africa* (1897), *The Story of West Africa* (1899) and *West African Studies* (1901) among other works.

Kingsway In ***NIGHT AND DAY,*** when Katharine HILBERY fails to meet Ralph DENHAM at his office in Lincoln's Inn Fields, she turns into Kingsway and stands there with the roar of traffic and swirl of people all around her (ND 439). Kingsway, in the City of London, runs into the STRAND via Aldwych and, at the northern end, into Russell Square in BLOOMSBURY via Southampton Row.

Kipling, Rudyard (1865–1936) Born in Bombay, India, Kipling had an early career as a journalist. He is best known for his stories about India, the jungle, the sea, the army and the navy, nearly all of which extol the virtues and glories of the British Empire. Among his works are *The City of Dreadful Night* (1890), *The Light That Failed* (1890), *Barrack-room Ballads* (1892), *The Jungle Book* (1894), *Captains Courageous* (1897), *Stalky & Co.* (1899), and *Kim* and *Just So Stories* (1902). Kipling was awarded a Nobel Prize for Literature in 1907. It was as the paradigmatic voice of Victorian masculinity that Woolf saw Kipling, remarking in ***A ROOM OF ONE'S OWN*** that he (like John GALSWORTHY) had not "a spark of the woman in him" and that reading his works was like being "caught eavesdropping at some purely masculine orgy" (AROO 102). Her father, Leslie STEPHEN, knew many of Kipling's ballads by heart (E1 129).

Reviewing *The Supernatural in Modern Fiction* by Dorothy Scarborough for the ***TIMES LITERARY SUPPLEMENT*** in 1918, Woolf wrote that Kipling's stories "are powerful enough to repel one by their horror, but they are too violent to appeal to our sense of wonder" (E2 220). In 1920 she reviewed Kipling's *Letters of Travel, 1892–1913* for the ***ATHENAEUM,*** finding it "quite unreadable" (E3 238). His "pictures of place," she wrote, "are painted to display the splendours of Empire and to induce young men to lay down their lives on her behalf" (E3 240).

Knole Ancestral home of Vita SACKVILLE-WEST that the law of entail prevented her from inheriting because of her sex. Sackville-West told the history of the house, one of the most famous private houses in England, in *Knole and the Sackvilles* (1922). The first known reference to Knole is in the Lambeth Palace records of 1281. Knole was bought by the Archbishop of Canterbury in 1456 and became his palace (*Knole*

Orlando, A Biography. *Courtesy Linda J. Langham. Unusual in that its jacket was not drawn by Vanessa Bell, although she may have chosen this painting, an illustration "reproduced by kind permission of the Worthing Art Gallery." This is the Hogarth Press first edition (1928).*

21). In 1566 it was granted by Elizabeth I to Thomas Sackville, Lord Buckhurst, 1st Earl of Dorset, K. G. (1536–1608).

Woolf's *ORLANDO* has often been described as giving Sackville-West Knole in a way she could never have had it in life. The house passed to her uncle on her father's death in 1928, and in 1962 to his son Edward SACKVILLE-WEST. Vita had been sad when in 1947 Knole was taken over by the National Trust (under an arrangement that allowed it to remain the Sackvilles' home [Glendinning 326]). In appendix 2 to *Knole and the Sackvilles* she quotes from an article she wrote for the *Spectator* lamenting the passing of Knole out of private hands: "Let us suggest that some of the grace of another age may seep into the consciousness of the millions wandering freely among these ancient courts, and that the new young Richards, Johns, Annes, and Elizabeths (who are also part of continuous history) may find enrichment in the gift of something so old, so courteous, and so lovely" (217–18).

Koteliansky, Samuel Solomonovitch (1892–1955) A Ukrainian Jew who came to England on a scholarship around 1910 and stayed the rest of his life. He met the Woolfs through John Middleton MURRY and Katherine MANSFIELD and was also a friend of D. H. LAWRENCE and Mark GERTLER. Through "Kot," as everyone called him, the HOGARTH PRESS came to publish several translations from the Russian, beginning in 1920 with Maxim GORKY's *Reminiscences of Leo Nicolayevitch Tolstoi.* J. H. Willis comments that with this book, the Hogarth Press "finally turned the corner from private press to small publishing house" (50). Both Leonard WOOLF and Woolf collaborated on translations with Koteliansky, polishing his rough drafts. They also both studied Russian with him. Woolf thought he resembled a character from Russian literature because he was prepared to talk at once about his "soul" (D1 108). Among other Hogarth titles on which Koteliansky and the Woolfs collaborated are: *The Note-Books of Anton Tchekhov Together with Reminiscences of Tchekhov by Maxim Gorky* (1921), *The Autobiography of Countess Sophie Tolstoi* (1922), Ivan Bunin's *The Gentleman from San Francisco* (1922) and *Stavogrin's Confession,* which also contained unpublished chapters of *The Possessed* by Fyodor DOSTOYEVSKY (1922).

L

Labour Party See WOOLF, Leonard.

Ladies of Llangollen Woolf mentioned the Ladies as she began to conceptualize what would eventually be *ORLANDO* (D3 131). Lady Eleanor Butler and Sarah Ponsonby met in 1768 and eloped ten years later, settling in Wales, where they became famous and were sought out during the next fifty years by such people as William WORDSWORTH, Lady Caroline Lamb, Edmund BURKE and the Duke of Gloucester. Danell Jones has explained Woolf's probable sources of information on this famous eighteenth-century lesbian couple ("The Chase of the Wild Goose"). Their story is told in Elizabeth Mavor's *Ladies of Llangollen* (New York: Penguin, 1971), and there is an entry on the Ladies in the *DICTIONARY OF NATIONAL BIOGRAPHY*. In 1936, the HOGARTH PRESS published Mary Gordon's fictionalized biography of the women, *The Chase of the Wild Goose*. Makiko Minow-Pinkney has written that the wild goose that appears above Marmaduke Bonthrop SHELMERDINE's head at the end of *Orlando* represents "all that Orlando tries to body forth in her poetry" (145).

"Lady in the Looking-Glass, The: A Reflection" (SF 215–19) A short sketch by Woolf published in *Harper's Magazine* in December 1929, in *Harper's Bazaar* in January 1930 (as "In the Looking Glass") and in *A HAUNTED HOUSE*. Susan Dick notes that Woolf incorporates a scene Woolf recalled from her visit to Ethel SANDS in France in 1927, of Sands not looking at her letters (D3 157). The narrator is a guest at Isabella Tyson's house and is lying in the drawing-room looking at the scene reflected in a mirror. At the end of the piece, the narrator sees Isabella reflected in the mirror and has a vision of her as "perfectly empty" with no thoughts and no friends (SF 219).

Lamb, Charles (1775–1834) English writer whose essays Woolf admired. He was a friend of Samuel Taylor COLERIDGE and wrote poetry, drama, criticism and tales. With his sister Mary (whom Lamb cared for after she killed their mother in a fit of insanity in 1796), Lamb wrote "Tales from Shakespeare" (1807). In *A ROOM OF ONE'S OWN*, Mary BETON recalls Lamb's essay on John MILTON's "LYCIDAS" (AROO 6–7) and later notes that he praised the work of Margaret CAVENDISH. (AROO 61).

Lamb, Henry (1883–1960) Painter, and younger brother of Walter LAMB. On the periphery of Bloomsbury, he was influenced by Augustus JOHN, was part of the circle around Lady Ottoline MORRELL, and also was a member of the FRIDAY CLUB. He had an affair with Helen ANREP during World War I. Vanessa BELL liked him, as at the beginning of her career he was "one of the very few people who will talk intelligently about painting to me" (Marler 75). For a time, Lytton STRACHEY was in love with him; Lamb's portrait of Strachey is in the NATIONAL GALLERY. In 1912 he painted an oil portrait of Leonard WOOLF. To Woolf, he was one of the denizens of what she called "the underworld" (a "barely definable" term used by both Woolfs to denote the world of journalists and literary hacks, but, adds Anne Olivier BELL, "with a suggestion of social inferiority" [D1 156]).

Lamb, Walter Rangely Maitland (1882–1968) A contemporary at Trinity College, Cambridge University, of Clive BELL, Thoby STEPHEN, Lytton STRACHEY, Saxon SYDNEY-TURNER and Leonard WOOLF, with whom he contributed to the verse collection *EUPHROSYNE*. From 1905 to 1907 and 1909 to 1913 he lectured in classics at NEWNHAM COLLEGE. A letter to Leonard from Strachey in 1905 informs him that Lamb was having an affair with his brother, James STRACHEY. In 1911 Lamb proposed to Woolf, as she describes in a letter to Vanessa BELL (L1 469–70). He became Secretary of the Royal Academy in 1913.

Lambert, Miss The girls' schoolteacher in *THE WAVES*, who RHODA feels makes everything change and "become luminous" (TW 45). Her glowing purple ring perhaps derives from Woolf's memory of her mother's ring flashing "as it moved across the page of the lesson book when she taught us" (MOB 81).

Lamley's The shop in *THE YEARS* where Rose PARGITER buys a box of toy ducks the night she is accosted in the street, and where Eleanor PARGITER later buys a necklace for her father to give his niece Maggie PARGITER.

***Land, The* (1926)** Vita SACKVILLE-WEST's most acclaimed work, a poem of about 2,500 lines divided into four sections, each named for a season of the year. *The Land,* which Vita had begun in 1923, won the Hawthornden Prize for 1926. Woolf wrote in her DIARY that she could not take seriously the talk of Vita's poem as great poetry, but thought this might be because she disliked the subject matter and the smooth manner of Vita's writing (D3 141). (See Louise A. DeSalvo, "Every Woman is an Island: Vita Sackville-West, the Image of the City, and the Pastoral Idyll." In Susan M. Squier, ed. *Women Writers and the City: Essays in Feminist Literary Criticism.* [Knoxville: University of Tennessee Press, 1984].)

Landor, Walter Savage (1775–1864) Landor makes a fleeting appearance near the end of *A ROOM OF ONE'S OWN* in Woolf's quotation from Sir Arthur Quiller-Couch, who refers to him as one of "the great poetical names of the last one hundred years or so" (AROO 107). Although he wrote poetry throughout his career, Landor was best known as a prose writer whose merits were "recognised as unsurpassable by all the best judges" according to Leslie STEPHEN (E3 112). Landor's *Imaginary Conversations* (1824, 1828, 1829) were his most popular works. Woolf reviewed *A Day-Book of Landor* chosen by John Bailey, in 1919 for the *TIMES LITERARY SUPPLEMENT* ("Landor in Little" E3 110–12), wherein she acknowledged that he was a "master, but one of those solitary potentates who rule over an almost deserted land" (E3 110).

Langley, Mr. Mentioned in *TO THE LIGHTHOUSE* as having suffered when Mr. RAMSAY took him on a sail to the lighthouse, despite his having "been round the world dozens of times" (TTL 91).

"Lappin and Lapinova" (SF 255–62) Susan Dick (SF 303) suggests that Woolf's comment to her sister Vanessa BELL that "marriage . . . reduces one to damnable servility" (L6 294) is probably related to this story that Woolf published in *Harper's Bazaar* in April 1939. Woolf herself said that it was a piece she had begun "at Asheham 20 years ago or more" (D5 188) when she was working on *NIGHT AND DAY.* Now, in the throes of writing *ROGER FRY: A BIOGRAPHY,* she was "rehashing" (D5 188) this story of a young couple, Ernest and Rosalind Thorburn.

Rosalind is not comfortable with the idea of being married, nor with being absorbed into Ernest's large family (like Leonard WOOLF, he has nine siblings). She invents a fantasy world in which she is Queen Lapinova and Ernest King Lappin. All is fine for about two years and then Ernest comes home from the office and won't play any more: "So that was the end of that marriage" (SF 262).

Selma Meyerowitz analyzes "Lappin and Lapinova" as one of four stories that "reveal the role of deception in women's lives" ("What Is . . ." 241) and links it to "THE LEGACY" as exploring the "conflict between the public and private self" seen in the context of "the social institution of marriage" (241). Leonard reprinted the story in *A HAUNTED HOUSE* (1943). In 1965 he wrote to Edward Albee that he had gone with the actor Peggy Ashcroft to see "WHO'S AFRAID OF VIRGINIA WOOLF?" and wondered if Albee had read "Lappin and Lapinova," as he thought its theme was the same as that of the imaginary child in Albee's play (Spotts 536–37).

Larpent The name of a boy at school with BERNARD, LOUIS and NEVILLE in *THE WAVES* whom Bernard sees years later in Rome (TW 190).

Larpent, Mrs. Mentioned in *THE YEARS* as a guest at a dinner the Malones give for Mr. and Mrs. Howard FRIPP to meet Dr. ANDREWS.

Lasswade, Kitty Character in *THE YEARS.* She is a cousin of the children of Abel and Rose PARGITER, and daughter of Dr. and Mrs. Malone. She grows up in Oxford, where her father is the Master of an Oxford University college, but she knows that she does not want to marry a professor and spend her life there. She knows that her cousin Edward PARGITER thinks he is in love with her. She takes history lessons with Lucy CRADDOCK. As her mother had hoped she would, Kitty marries Charles, Lord Lasswade, with whom she has three sons. In the "1914" chapter she gives a party attended by Martin PARGITER. People call her "The Grenadier" behind her back because she does things abruptly (TY 257). Her second son is "with the fleet at Malta" in 1914 (TY 257). At the end of the novel she comes to Delia PARGITER's party but now lives alone in the north of England, "with just a boy to chop wood" (TY 418).

Lathom, Mrs. Mentioned in *THE YEARS,* the wife of a professor of Divinity at Oxford University.

La Trobe, Miss Character in *BETWEEN THE ACTS.* She has written the village pageant that is performed on the day the novel takes place and which forms part of the narrative. The last of Woolf's artist figures, La Trobe is alienated from the community partly because she "wasn't presumably pure English" (BTA 57) and partly because she is a lesbian (BTA 211).

The villagers call her "Bossy" (63) and do not understand her vision. Only Lucy SWITHIN seems to understand whatever it is La Trobe is trying to convey (153). La Trobe longs to write the ideal play, "without an audience" because the incomprehension of the audience tortures her. At the end of the day on which the novel is set she goes alone to the village pub where the locals are gossiping about her, and there she hears the first words of her next work.

Laurette A prostitute visited by Jacob FLANDERS in chapter 9 of *JACOB'S ROOM.*

Lawrence, D. H. (David Herbert) (1885–1930) English novelist, short-story writer and poet whose books include *The White Peacock* (1911), *Sons and Lovers* (1913), *The Rainbow* (1915), *Women in Love* (1920), *Aaron's Rod* (1922) and *Lady Chatterley's Lover* (1928; not published in full in England until 1960). Lawrence was a friend of David GARNETT but was virulently opposed to BLOOMSBURY GROUP figures. He was part of the circle around Lady Ottoline MORRELL and caricatured her as Hermione Roddice in *Women in Love.* Woolf disliked his work, often expressing boredom with what she saw as his obsession with sex (L2 474), and wrote to Hugh WALPOLE in 1931 that she was tired of being "caged" with Aldous HUXLEY, James JOYCE and Lawrence (L4 402). In 1932 she was reading *The Letters of D. H. Lawrence* "with the usual sense of frustration" (D4 126) and wrote that she disliked Lawrence's preaching. She had reviewed his novel *The Lost Girl* for the *TIMES LITERARY SUPPLEMENT* in 1920 (E3 271–73), finding little positive to say about it. In 1931, she wrote "Notes on D. H. Lawrence" (M 93–98; CE1 352–55), concentrating on *Sons and Lovers.* She found it vivid but concluded that "Lawrence lacks the final power which makes things entire in themselves" (CE1 354) and that as a writer he lacked a tradition.

Lazenby, Mrs. Mentioned in *THE YEARS* attending a meeting with Eleanor PARGITER.

League of Nations See WOOLF, Leonard.

"Leaning Tower, The" (CE2 162–81; M 128–54) A lecture given by Woolf to the Workers' Educational Association in Brighton on April 27, 1940 and subsequently published in *FOLIOS OF NEW WRITING,* Autumn 1940. The paper begins with a caveat about the danger of making theories, and proceeds by characterizing nineteenth-century literature as unconsciously bound to the class of the writer. Nineteenth-century society was rigidly divided into classes that were taken for granted by writers, as the more class-conscious readers of the twentieth-century can see. These conditions, Woolf writes, persisted until 1914. English literature has all been written by the middle class, raised as they are by income and education—a tower of stucco and gold—above the masses.

The writers who began to publish around 1925, she continues (writers sometimes referred to now as the "Auden generation" and including W. H. AUDEN, Louis MACNEICE, Stephen SPENDER and Christopher ISHERWOOD), also survey the world from a tower of privilege; but because the world has changed so radically in their lifetimes, the tower has begun to lean to the left. This leaning of their tower makes those writers self-conscious. Woolf quotes MacNeice's autobiographical poem "Autumn Journal" as typical of this generation's attack on the bourgeoisie they come from themselves, and she criticizes them for hunting for scapegoats while still enjoying their middle-class comforts. The work of the "leaning tower writers" has suffered, she believes, from self-consciousness, but this has also been beneficial, for, with the help of Freud, these writers have freed literature from nineteenth-century superstitions.

Looking to the future, Woolf ends the paper with a vision of a classless society that will lead to "the end of the novel as we know it" (CE2 179). The English education system is elitist, ignoring the needs of the masses while educating only a few. Public libraries, she writes, are the key to democratizing literature, but with reading comes the obligation to be a critic, to make judgments. She sees the hope for the future in those who have been shut out of the tower trespassing freely on the "common ground" (CE2 181) of literature.

When Vita SACKVILLE-WEST's son Benedict NICOLSON wrote to Woolf in the summer of 1940 and criticized Roger FRY and the BLOOMSBURY GROUP, as Woolf had represented them in her biography of Fry published that July, she referred to "The Leaning Tower" in her reply to him: "It seemed to me useless to tell people who left school at 14 and were earning their livings in shops and factories that they ought to enjoy Shakespeare" (L6 421). The most pressing problem as she saw it, she wrote to Ben, was "What is the kind of education people ought to have?" (L6 420). She told him that in *THREE GUINEAS* she had done her best to "destroy the Sackvilles and Dufferins," that is, the aristocratic elite from which Ben Nicolson himself had derived all the privileges of his upbringing. (Incidentally, the editors of Woolf's LETTERS say that she worked on this letter to Ben Nicolson "more carefully than any other private letter of which we have a record," making several drafts [L6 419].) In note 13 to chapter 3 of *Three Guineas,* Woolf adumbrated the ideas expressed in "The Leaning Tower" when she wrote that "it would be interesting to know what the true-born working man or woman thinks of the playboys and playgirls of the educated class who adopt the working-class cause without sacrificing middle-class capital, or sharing working-class experience" (TG 177). Beth Daugherty has commented that the lectures Woolf gave that she later revised as essays, of which "The Leaning Tower" is the last, "all have a pedagogical sub-text that can be traced back to Morley" ("Taking a Leaf" 34), referring to MORLEY COLLEGE where Woolf taught between 1905 and 1907.

John LEHMANN had persuaded Woolf to let him publish "The Leaning Tower," and in the next issue of *Folios of New Writing* (Spring 1941) several "Replies" to it were published. Lehmann himself added "A Postscript," as by the time the replies were published Woolf was dead. In "The Falling Tower," the novelist and critic Edward Upward argued that Woolf had distorted the writers of his generation, saying "falling tower" would be a more apt description of their perspective. Giving a standard Marxist response to Woolf's essay, he wrote that her idea that writers should throw away their bourgeois privilege "might accord with bourgeois conceptions of saintliness," but to a socialist this was a useless argument. Writers, he argued, should struggle for a socialist future.

B. L. Coombes, a Welsh miner who had published his autobiography *These Poor Hands* in 1939, was more receptive to Woolf's essay, although he argued that there was no real division between the "working class" and "the Poor" as she had stated. In "Below the Tower," Coombes described the suspicion of his class for the tower dwellers, but argued that the working-class writer should help bridge the gap between the classes. The people in the tower, he wrote, should come down and teach those below the tower what they lack.

Louis MacNeice, whom Woolf had singled out in "The Leaning Tower," wrote in "The Tower That Once" that Woolf had oversimplified literary history when she said all nineteenth-century writers were unconscious of class, and that she had distorted his writing and that of his contemporaries. In his "Postscript," Lehmann emphasized Woolf's strong interest in younger writers and quoted letters he had received from her about writers who had submitted work to the HOGARTH PRESS (see, for example, the letter to Miss McNeil [pp. 114–115]). He also mentioned as evidence of her concern with the issues raised in "The Leaning Tower" and the responses to it, her "LETTER TO A YOUNG POET" and the introductory letter to *Life as We Have Known It* (reprinted as "MEMORIES OF A WORKING WOMEN'S GUILD"), remarking that Woolf was always conscious of her own privileged class position.

Leavis, F. R. (Frank Raymond) See LEAVIS, Q. D.

Leavis, Q. D. (Queenie Dorothy) (1906–81) Q. D. Leavis and her husband, F. R. (Frank Raymond) Leavis (1895–1978), were bitter critics of the BLOOMSBURY GROUP in general and of Woolf in particular. They had a profound influence on English literary criticism and the teaching of literature in the late 1930s to the 1970s through their rigid views on what was great literature and what was not, expressed in many books. Their journal *Scrutiny* (1932–53) published several dismissive reviews of Woolf's works, most significantly Q. D. Leavis's "Caterpillars of the Commonwealth Unite!" (September 1938), a review of *THREE GUINEAS.*

Lee, Sir Sidney (1859–1926) At the end of *A ROOM OF ONE'S OWN,* Woolf tells her audience that they should not look for mention of Judith SHAKESPEARE in Lee's *Life of William Shakespeare* (1898, revised in 1915). This was one of several works on William SHAKESPEARE by Lee, who was a member of the editorial staff of the *DICTIONARY OF NATIONAL BIOGRAPHY.* He became joint editor with Leslie STEPHEN in 1890, and sole editor in 1891.

Lee, Vernon (1856–1935) Pseudonym of the English writer Violet Paget. In *A ROOM OF ONE'S OWN,* Woolf's narrator begins chapter 5 by looking at the shelves holding books by living writers, among which she finds Lee's books on aesthetics. Lee, who lived in Florence, where Woolf may have met her in 1909 (D1 266n14), was a prolific writer, particularly on Italian cultural history. Anne Olivier BELL calls her *Studies of the Eighteenth Century in Italy* (1880) a pioneering work. Woolf did not care for her writing, finding it sentimental. She reviewed two of Lee's books for the *TIMES LITERARY SUPPLEMENT*: *The Sentimental Traveller. Notes on Places* in 1908 (E1 157–59), and *Laurus Nobilis: Chapters on Art and Life* in 1909 (E1 277–80).

"Legacy, The" (SF 275–81) A short story that Woolf wrote for *Harper's Bazaar* in late 1940, but that they did not take (which angered her; see L6 463, 469). In it Gilbert Clandon discovers in his wife's diary after her death that she had been having an affair with "B. M.," who killed himself when she would not decide to leave her marriage. On the day recording B. M.'s threat, presumably to end his own life, Angela Clandon has scribbled "Egypt. Egypt. Egypt." all over the page (SF 280). At the end of the story, Gilbert, who is shown never to have known his wife, realizes that she killed herself "to escape from him" (SF 281). Selma Meyerowitz has analyzed this story and three others—"LAPPIN AND LAPINOVA," "The New Dress" and "The Introduction"—as exemplifying Woolf's concern with the way women's lives are distorted by "social institutions in a patriarchal and class society" ("What Is . . ." 241). Mitchell Leaska points out that in Vita SACKVILLE-WEST's *Pepita* (1937) she describes her mother, who was blind in the last years of her life, writing over and over, having forgotten to turn the page, "so that it looked like sentences someone had wished to obliterate, like writing Egypt, Egypt, Egypt over an indiscretion" (PH 13). Leaska also notes that "B. M." were initials used by Sackville-West to refer to her mother, whom she called Bonne Mama.

Lehmann, John Frederick (1907–87) Poet, editor and publisher who became a partner in the HOGARTH PRESS in 1938. His sister was the novelist Rosamond LEHMANN. Lehmann was a close friend of Julian BELL and George RYLANDS, whom he had met at Cambridge, and was associated with many of the young writers of the 1930s Woolf called the "Brainies": e.g., W. H. AUDEN, Christopher ISHERWOOD, Cecil DAY LEWIS, Louis MACNEICE and Stephen SPENDER. Leonard WOOLF had accepted Lehmann's *A Garden Revisited and Other Poems* for the Hogarth Living Poets series in 1930. It was published in 1931, the year Lehmann came to work as manager at the Hogarth Press. To Leonard's great annoyance, he left abruptly in 1932 and went to join Isherwood in Germany. He later arranged the Hogarth Press's publication of Isherwood's second novel, *The Memorial,* and the Press went on to publish several other works by Isherwood. In 1936, Lehmann launched the magazine *New Writing,* which he brought to the Press when he became a partner in 1938. Lehmann persisted in asking Woolf to contribute to *New Writing,* which she did not want to do, and eventually got her to allow him to publish "THE LEANING TOWER" in *FOLIOS OF NEW WRITING* (a wartime substitute for *New Writing*).

Lehmann's relationship with Leonard was difficult, as indeed was the relationship with Leonard of nearly all the assistants at the Hogarth Press; he has told the story of his time there in *Thrown to the Woolfs.* Despite his difficulties with Leonard, Lehmann brought many younger writers to the Press and created new series that built on what Leonard had established. Woolf often had to mediate between her husband and his business partner, but in general she liked Lehmann and appreciated his literary opinions. She was delighted in 1932 when Lehmann told her he loved *THE WAVES* (D4 44) and she addressed her "LETTER TO A YOUNG POET" to him. Late in his life, Lehmann said that both Leonard and Woolf had been very important to him, "but Virginia was particularly so. I admired her and worshipped her. Artistically and spiritually her novels and writing meant more to me than did the work of anyone else in that generation" (MacWeeney np).

Lehmann played a significant role in bringing *BETWEEN THE ACTS* to publication. When Woolf felt the novel was not worth publishing, she and Leonard agreed to give Lehmann the "casting vote" (L6 482). He wrote to her praising it, but Woolf had already decided it was "too silly and trivial" (L6 486). She committed suicide soon after writing this to Lehmann and in his memoir, Lehmann speaks of bringing the book out as a kind of homage to her (*Thrown* 111–12).

Lehmann, Rosamond Nina (1901–90) Novelist and sister of John LEHMANN and of the actress Beatrix Lehmann. Married twice, Lehmann also had a long affair with the poet Cecil DAY LEWIS. Her first novel, *Dusty Answer* (1927), made her famous. Woolf met her through Lord David CECIL in 1931 and they continued to see each other occasionally. Woolf had read her second novel, *A Note in Music* (1930), "with some interest & admiration" (D3 314). In 1931 the HOGARTH PRESS published Lehmann's *A Letter to a Sister* (number 3 in the Hogarth Letters). Other works of Lehmann's include the novels *Invitation to the Waltz* (1932) and *The Weather in the Streets* (1936). Her complete fiction was reprinted by Virago in 1980.

Lenare Portrait studio where Woolf had several photographs taken of herself at Vita SACKVILLE-WEST's request in 1929. Sackville-West kept one of the Lenare portraits on her desk in her tower study at SISSINGHURST until she died.

Lesage, Dr. Character in *THE VOYAGE OUT.* When Dr. RODRIGUEZ proves incompetent in treating Rachel VINRACE, St. John HIRST is sent to find another doctor and tracks down Dr. Lesage, who is on vacation with his wife. Dr. Lesage takes over Rachel's care but too late to save her.

"Letter to a Young Poet, A" (CE2 182–95; DM 208–95) First published in the *YALE REVIEW* in June 1932, this "letter" was number 8 in the Hogarth Letters series published by the HOGARTH PRESS. The Letters, several of which, including this one, were published in one volume in 1933, were planned by Woolf, Leonard WOOLF and John LEHMANN, and Woolf addressed hers to Lehmann as a representative "young poet." Woolf later wrote to Lehmann that she thought the letter form was not conducive to good criticism "because it seems to invite archness and playfulness" and she told him she was not satisfied with her letter and "would like to tear [it] up, or entirely re-write" (L5 83).

She begins the "Letter" by playfully suggesting what prose writers say about poetry "when they are alone": that poetry is easy because there are so many rules to follow, whereas prose has no rules, leading prose writers to believe that they are the "creators" and "explorers" in literature (CE2 183). Young poets—those poets of the 1930s whom she would criticize in "THE LEANING TOWER"—need to realize, she wrote, that they are part of a whole society and culture: "The more you begin to take yourself seriously as a leader or as a follower, as a modern or as a conservative, then you become a self-conscious, biting, and scratching little animal whose work is not of the slightest value or importance to anybody" (CE2 184). The poet, she complained, is "much less interested in what we have in common than in what he has apart" (CE2 189).

At the beginning of the letter, Woolf introduces "Mrs. Gape," a charwoman who seems to function for her similarly to "Mrs. Brown" in "MR. BENNETT AND MRS. BROWN" as representing life itself. The young poet seems to have forgotten that he is part of a tradition that could use poetry to take in a much broader sweep, could include "Mrs. Gape," the actual and colloquial (CE2 189). Woolf also says that young poets' work lacks "beauty" and advises them not to publish too early.

The "Letter," unsurprisingly, was not very popular; Woolf wrote in her DIARY, "my poet letter passes unnoticed" (D4 119). In her introduction to *The Hogarth Letters* (Athens, Georgia: University of Georgia Press, 1986), Hermione Lee calls Woolf's contribution a "wary exploration of modern poetry, which noticeably ignores Auden" (xx) and points out that the quotations Woolf included were "not the most impressive illustrations she could have chosen from the early Thirties" (xxi), a criticism with which Woolf agreed in a letter to Lehmann (L5 83). The poet, biographer and critic Peter Quennell responded to Woolf for his generation in "A Letter to Mrs. Virginia Woolf" (*Hogarth Letters*: 327–46), but Woolf was rather annoyed at the choice of Quennell as respondent and wished Lehmann could have done it in print (L5 82).

Letters of Virginia Woolf, The A collection of 3,767 letters written by Woolf, published by the HOGARTH PRESS in Britain and by Harcourt Brace Jovanovich in the United States in six volumes, edited by Nigel NICOLSON, who was assisted by Joanne Trautmann. In their editorial note to the first volume, the editors state that Quentin BELL's biography has formed the basis of their chronology for the edition and is also the basis for their "interpretation of her character" (L1 xi). In his introductions to the various volumes, Nigel Nicolson dismisses Woolf's accounts of the incest she suffered from her half-brothers George and Gerald DUCKWORTH (L1 xvi–xvii), suggests that Woolf sometimes loved her sister Vanessa BELL "almost to the point of thought-incest" (L1 xvii), dismisses the notion that Woolf was a political writer (L2 xvi–xviii), discounts the argument and influence of *THREE GUINEAS* (L5 xiv–xviii), and praises the "careful analysis" of Susan M. Kenney's article on Woolf's suicide, "Two Endings" (L6 xvii).

The letters were published as follows (only the English editions were given titles): Volume 1, *The Flight of the Mind,* 1888–1912 (1975); Volume 2, *The Question of Things Happening,* 1912–1922 (1976); Volume 3, *A Change of Perspective,* 1923–1928 (1977); Volume 4, *A Reflection of the Other Person,* 1929–1931 (1978); Volume 5, *The Sickle Side of the Moon,* 1932–1935 [co-edited by Nicolson and Trautmann] (1979); and Volume 6, *Leave the Letters Till We're Dead,* 1936–41 (1980).

S. P. Rosenbaum (VWM 7:8) pointed out that cuts were made at the proof stage in certain letters in Volume 2 that referred to Clive BELL and Mary HUTCHINSON. Nigel Nicolson acknowledged this and explained that he had had a pang of conscience at the last minute over certain passages; as Mary Hutchinson died in April 1977, however, the omitted passages were published in the *VIRGINIA WOOLF MISCELLANY* (VWM 8:2). Volume 3 includes a letter from Vanessa Bell to Woolf on first reading *TO THE LIGHTHOUSE,* and one from Vita SACKVILLE-WEST on first reading *ORLANDO* (L3 Appendix). Volume 6 includes two appendixes: appendix A concerns the editors' dating of Woolf's three surviving suicide notes, which differs from that given in the second volume of Quentin Bell's biography and in the second volume of Leonard WOOLF's *Autobiography.* Nicolson and Trautmann suggest that her note to Vanessa Bell was written on March 23, 1941, and the two to Leonard were written March 18 and March 28 (and see Roger Poole, *Unknown* viii). Appendix B consists of about sixty additional letters, discovered after publication of the series began.

In 1953, Leonard Woolf had been annoyed by the publication of Aileen Pippett's *The Moth and the Star,* in which she had included several letters written by Woolf to Vita Sackville-West. Although Pippett thanked Leonard in her preface for his permission to quote the letters, he wrote to Vita that he had in fact not granted permission and had only seen the book when it was already in proofs (Spotts 494–5). He prevented the book from being published in England, although Vita herself was in favor of publishing Woolf's letters to her (*The Letters of Vita Sackville-West to Virginia Woolf* was published in 1985 by William Morrow & Co., edited by Louise A. DeSalvo and Mitchell A. Leaska). In 1956, Leonard Woolf and James STRACHEY published an expurgated edition of *Virginia Woolf and Lytton Strachey: Letters,* pointing out in their preface that "neither side of this correspondence is completely typical of its author" (vi). This volume, appearing at about the same time as Clive Bell's memoir *Old Friends* (1956) and David GARNETT's *The Flowers of the Forest* (1955), fell victim to the strong anti-BLOOMSBURY GROUP sentiment of England in the 1950s, discouraging Leonard from plans to publish any more of Woolf's correspondence. Joanne Trautmann has explained that she and Nigel Nicolson were invited to edit the letters by Quentin Bell in 1973 (VWM 3: 1).

A further nineteen letters were published in *MODERN FICTION STUDIES* 30, 2 (Summer 1984): 175–202. These were selected by Joanne Trautmann from about 100 letters that came to light after volume 6 of the *Letters* was published; she also noted that she had deposited a list of those letters she had not chosen for this publication in the BERG COLLECTION, the MONK'S HOUSE PAPERS at the University of Sussex Library, and the Harry Ransom HUMANITIES RESEARCH CENTER in Austin, Texas. The nineteen published in *Modern Fiction Studies* are to eleven recipients and include seven to Julian BELL. Joanne Trautmann Banks has also edited *Congenial Spirits: The Selected Letters of Virginia Woolf* (London: Hogarth Press; San Diego: Harcourt Brace Jovanovich 1989). This volume includes twelve letters found too late for inclusion in *Modern Fiction Studies,* including one to Katherine MANSFIELD, one to George Bernard SHAW, and four letters to editors written for publication: one to the *WOMAN'S LEADER,* one to the *NEW REPUBLIC* and two to the *NEW STATESMAN.* In her introduction to the volume, Trautmann Banks, author herself of *The Jessamy Brides: The Friendship of Virginia Woolf and V. Sackville-West,* writes about the "manners" of Woolf's correspondence, her love of Vita Sackville-West and Ethel SMYTH, and Woolf's sense of humor, concluding that "[g]iven her griefs, it was a courageous life" (CS xiv). Rowena Fowler has edited "Virginia Woolf and Katharine Furse: An Unpublished Correspondence" for *Tulsa Studies in Women's Literature* (1990), which includes nine letters from Woolf to Katharine FURSE and ten from Furse to Woolf.

In the summer of 1994, four recently discovered letters from Woolf to Vita Sackville-West were published in a special issue of the *Virginia Woolf Miscellany* (VWM 43: 1–3) and in the *Charleston Magazine* (CM 10: 25–31). In a note introducing the letters, Joanne Trautmann Banks explained that they had been hidden in Sackville-West's desk and were found by a Dutch student, Patty Brandhorst, who was cataloging Sackville-West's manuscripts. Trautmann Banks notes that one of the letters, written in 1938, "extends for years longer than we had thought Virginia's expressed physical interest in Vita" (VWM 43: 1).

Levine, David See POPULAR CULTURE.

Levys, The One of the families whom Eleanor PARGITER in *THE YEARS* visits out of charity.

Lewes See MONK'S HOUSE.

Lewis, Cecil Day See DAY LEWIS, Cecil.

Lewis, Percy Wyndham (1882–1957) Critic, novelist, artist and, with Ezra Pound, leader of the Vorticist Movement, a short-lived offshoot of Futurism, and one of the many European avant-garde art movements of the early twentieth century (see MODERNISM). His work was included in the second POST-IMPRESSIONIST exhibition. He was associated with the OMEGA WORKSHOPS but left after a dispute with Roger FRY over a commission from the *Daily Mail* for the 1913 "Ideal Home" exhibition that he claimed had been given to him, not the Omega. Soon after this he founded *Blast, Review of the Great English Vortex* (1914–15), in which he continued to attack the Omega and Fry. Persistently and virulently against anyone associated with the BLOOMSBURY GROUP, Lewis satirized and criticized those he saw as his antagonists. His novel *The Apes of God* (1930) is a satire on Bloomsbury, and in *Men Without Art* (1934) he scathingly criticized Woolf and others (D4 250–52). In his chapter on Woolf, Lewis referred to her as "a purely feminist phenomenon" who was "taken seriously by no one any longer today" (159). Stephen SPENDER defended Woolf in his review of the book in the *Spectator* (D4 254). In a book written in the 1930s but not published until 1973, *The Roaring Queen,* Lewis caricatured Woolf as, in Margaret DRABBLE's description, "Rhoda Hyman, the Empress of High-brow London, a lanky and sickly lady in Victorian muslins with a drooping intellect-ravaged exterior" (Margaret Drabble, *Arnold Bennett* [New York: Alfred A. Knopf, 1974]: 291).

Lidgett, Mrs. Mentioned in *JACOB'S ROOM,* she sits on "the great Duke's tomb" to rest from her job of cleaning the steps of the Prudential Society's office.

"Life and the Novelist" (CE2 131–36; GR 41–47) A review by Woolf in the *New York Herald Tribune* for November 7, 1926, of *A Deputy Was King* by G. B. Stern. Woolf uses this review for a discussion of the art of the novelist. The writer, she says, never ceases to work, because writing consists of two processes: receiving impressions and then selecting from them so that the experience can be transmitted. Because "the more one looks the more there is to see" (CE2 135), it is the task of the novelist to select one thing that will stand for many. This, she says, demands a higher literary skill than that which the critic employs. The processes of the novelist's art, done in isolation in "that mysterious room," are what hold such fascination for the critic.

Life As We Have Known It See "MEMORIES OF A WORKING WOMEN'S GUILD."

Life's Adventure See CARMICHAEL, Mary.

"Lighthouse, The" See *TO THE LIGHTHOUSE.*

Lily of the day In the *THE WAVES,* BERNARD recalls comparing PERCIVAL to a lily, and recites "the lily of the day is fairer far in May" (TW 265), slightly misquoting a line from Ben Jonson's "To the immortal memorie, and friendship of that noble paire, Sir Lucius Cary, and Sir Henry Morison."

Ling, Shu-Hua (1900–90) Chinese writer and artist with whom Julian BELL had an affair when he taught at Wuhan University in 1935; she was the wife of a Professor Chen Yuan at the university. She corresponded with Woolf in 1938–39 and sent her chapters of a memoir eventually published in 1953 by the HOGARTH PRESS, *Ancient Melodies.* Selma Meyerowitz has discussed *Ancient Melodies* in *Virginia Woolf Miscellany.* (18:2–3).

Little Holland House See PRINSEP FAMILY.

Little Talland House The name Woolf gave to a house she rented in the Sussex village of Firle in 1911 and to which she invited friends to stay, including Janet CASE, Marjorie STRACHEY and Leonard WOOLF.

Living Age Boston journal in which in 1908 Woolf first published an essay in America (a review of a biography of John Delane reprinted from the *CORNHILL MAGAZINE*). In 1909, *Living Age* reprinted another of her reviews, of *The Journal of Lady Holland,* and in 1924 it reprinted "MR. BENNETT AND MRS. BROWN."

Lloyd George, David (1863–1945) David, first Earl Lloyd George of Dwyfor, entered Parliament in 1890 and became president of the Board of Trade in 1905 and chancellor of the exchequer in 1908, when he instituted a National Insurance Bill. During World War I he worked in the War Office, and he became prime minister in 1916. In 1918 he was the principal British delegate at the Paris Peace Conference that led to the signing of the Treaty of Versailles (a conference also attended by John Maynard KEYNES). In *THE VOYAGE OUT,* Miss ALLAN receives a letter from her sister informing her, among other news, that "Lloyd George has taken the Bill up" (TVO 179). Later in the novel, Evelyn MURGATROYD tells Rachel VINRACE about the SATURDAY CLUB she belongs to, where such important matters as the Insurance Bill are discussed (TVO 248).

Loder, Millie In *BETWEEN THE ACTS* she plays the part of Flavinda in Miss LA TROBE'S "WHERE THERE'S A WILL THERE'S A WAY" in the village pageant.

London Library In 1935, Woolf met E. M. FORSTER on the steps of the London Library in St. James's Square, where he had just come from a committee meeting. She thought for a moment that he was going to invite her to join the Board, but he told her the committee had agreed that "ladies are impossible" (D4 297–98). Her anger inspired her to thoughts of writing "On Being Despised," but she had to suppress them in order to concentrate on finishing *THE YEARS*: "On Being Despised" eventually found its voice as *THREE GUINEAS.* In November 1940, Woolf got great satisfaction from turning down Forster's invitation to join the Library Board of which her father, Leslie STEPHEN, had been made President in 1892 (D5 337).

London Mercury A monthly founded in 1919 by J. C. Squire (1884–1958) which, Andrew McNeillie informs us, "quite belligerently opposed modernism and all things 'highbrow' " (E3 521). Woolf's "AN UNWRITTEN NOVEL" was published in the *Mercury* in 1920, and "Lives of the Obscure" appeared there in 1924.

London Scene, The Five articles by Woolf about London, published in a limited edition by Frank Hallman in 1975 and by the HOGARTH PRESS in 1982. The five essays were originally written for the magazine *Good Housekeeping* between 1931 and 1932 and appeared as follows: "The Docks of London," December 1931; "Oxford Street Tide," January 1932; "Great Men's Houses," March 1932; "Abbeys and Cathedrals," May 1932; and "This is the House of Commons," October 1932. A sixth essay, "Portrait of a Londoner," not included in the Hallman collection, appeared in *Good Housekeeping* in December 1932. Susan Squier has drawn attention to two "drastic deletions" from the first essay which she believes completely changed the character of "The Docks of London" (Squier, *Virginia Woolf* 53). According to Squier, the theme that runs through the six essays is that of the contrast between two Londons, the surface world of comfort and respectable convention enjoyed by the middle and upper classes, and the "underworld" of the poor and working classes (Squier 63). Squier also points out that Woolf may have drawn on her own experience of being robbed in a store (D3 339–40) for the passages about the robber in "Oxford Street Tide." Woolf's theme of the class dichotomy of the modern city is given gendered expression in "Great Men's Houses," in which she describes how Thomas CARLYLE wrote at the top of his house while his wife and the maid struggled to keep the house warm and clean. Pamela Caughie also discusses the series of articles (Caughie 52–70).

Long Barn House near KNOLE bought by Vita SACKVILLE-WEST and Harold NICOLSON in 1915, and where Woolf's affair with Sackville-West was consummated in December 1925.

Lopokova (Lopukhova), Lydia (1892–1981) A dancer with Diaghilev's RUSSIAN BALLET and wife of John Maynard KEYNES. Lopokova came to London for the 1918–19 season and was then married to Randolfo Barocchi, but she left him while in London. She returned in 1921 with the Diaghilev company and was persuaded by Keynes to move into 46 GORDON SQUARE, as he had fallen in love with her when they met at a party in 1918. Although many of Keynes's friends were disapproving of his marriage to her in 1925, Woolf was fond of Lopokova (D3 18, 181), admired her as an actress, and studied her as a "type" for the character Lucrezia Warren SMITH in *MRS. DALLOWAY*. In the preface to *ORLANDO,* Woolf acknowledges "Madame Lopokova's" assistance with correcting her Russian.

Louis One of the six soliloquists in *THE WAVES*. Louis (who in earlier drafts of the novel is called Nicholas and Nathaniel) is immediately set apart from the other children because he is not English but Australian, the son of a banker in Brisbane (TW 19). His life is defined by his need to overcome the sense of inferiority his Australian accent gives him, but although he becomes a successful businessman this sense never leaves him. For a time he and RHODA are lovers, or "conspirators," as he describes it. Even after he has amassed a fortune, Louis keeps a garret where he goes to write poetry that no one else sees. Throughout his life, Louis is haunted by the sound of a great beast stamping on the shore, an image that links him directly to the world of the INTERLUDES. Howard Harper suggests this image strengthens the connection between Louis and Leonard WOOLF (228n9), as Leonard had had experience of "great beasts" such as elephants during his time in Ceylon as a colonial administrator.

Doris L. Eder first pointed out the probable connection between Louis and T. S. ELIOT. As Lyndall Gordon notes, Woolf describes Louis with the same adjectives she uses in her DIARY to describe Eliot, such as "pale" and "marmoreal" (Gordon 230). Gordon also believes that some of the external details of Louis's life derive from that of Saxon SYDNEY-TURNER, and from Leonard Woolf (230). Madeline Moore has also discussed the connection with Eliot, pointing out that the poet's father was a businessman in St. Louis ("Nature" 231n23).

Kathy Phillips compares Louis's persistent image of himself as rooted in the ancient Egyptian past with "the Italian revival of old Rome or the Nazi appropriation of an 'Aryan' history in Germanic myth" (Phillips 162). She points out that as a shipper he would know about the appropriation of Egypt by Britain to facilitate trade with India, and says that Louis "displays a broad kinship with fascism in his love for conformity, aestheticism without compassion, praise for an 'august master,' resort to simple symbols, appropriation of a validating past, sadism and militarism" (Phillips 163). As Gillian Beer has noted, Louis's pretensions toward political life are "seamed" with allusions to British politicians who were "preoccupied with the Indian enterprise" ("Introduction" xxiii). Makiko Minow-Pinkney argues that Louis's ambition is "to produce some vast totalisation, a poem which will plait into 'one cable the many threads . . . of our long history' " (160).

"Love in the Valley" See MEREDITH, George.

Lovelace, Mary, Countess of Woolf quotes in *THREE GUINEAS* (TG 157) from "The Chaperoned Age," an article by the countess about her youth published in the *Times* March 9, 1932 (RN 267).

Lowell, James Russell (1819–91) On his first visit to the United States in 1863, Leslie STEPHEN met Lowell through a mutual friend, Tom Hughes, and the two men quickly developed a close friendship. Leslie visited Lowell again in 1868, and when Lowell was ambassador to the Court of St. James from 1880 to 1885, he was a frequent visitor to 22 HYDE PARK GATE. Lowell, a poet and critic, was the "acknowledged high priest of culture in Cambridge, Massachusetts" (Annan 55). Another bond between him and Leslie was that Lowell was a great admirer of Julia Prinsep STEPHEN. He inscribed several of his books as gifts to her (e.g., *Among My Books, Among My Books: Second Series,* and *Heartsease and Rue,* a book of poems). Each of the Stephen children had "quasi-sponsors," as their father called them, in place of godparents and Lowell was Woolf's. On her birth he wrote a verse to go with his gift to her of a possett dish; the first letter in Woolf's collected LETTERS is to her "godpapa," written when she was six.

Lubbock, Percy See "ON RE-READING NOVELS."

Lucas, Frank Laurence ("Peter") (1894–1967) Woolf quotes from Lucas's *Tragedy* in *A ROOM OF ONE'S OWN* at the point where her narrator comments on the difference between the actual situation of women in history and their fictional representations (AROO 43). *Tragedy in Relation to Aristotle's "Poetics"* (1928) was the second of the Hogarth Lectures series published by the HOGARTH PRESS. Lucas dedicated it to Clive BELL. An APOSTLE and Fellow of King's College, Cambridge, Lucas was a prolific writer. Several other works of his were published by the Hogarth Press: *The River Flows* (1926), his first novel; *Time and Memory* (1929), number 7 in the Hogarth Living Poets series; and *The Art of Dying: An Anthology* (1930), edited with Francis BIRRELL. Lucas also wrote poetry (*Ariadne* was published by Cambridge University

Press in 1932), and plays, such as *The Bear Dances* (1932). Other works of his include *Studies in French and English* (1934), and *Journal Under the Terror* (1938), in which he described the nervous breakdown of his second wife, Prudence Dalzell Wilkinson, whom he had married in 1932 after separating in 1929 from the novelist E. B. C. "Topsy" Jones (1893–1966). Woolf scorned the *Journal* as a "fashionable dodge," noting that André Gide was also writing in this genre: "Neither can settle to creative art" (D5 229). Woolf always found Lucas charming and good-natured, but she wrote in her DIARY that he had an uninteresting mind (D3 256–57). He seems to have represented for her the type of a modern university English professor. In the ironic preface to *ORLANDO* Lucas is listed among those friends who "have helped me in ways too various to mention."

Lucy (1) The name of one of the two aunts who have raised Rachel VINRACE in *THE VOYAGE OUT* in Richmond since her mother died.

Lucy (2) Clarissa DALLOWAY's maid in *MRS. DALLOWAY.*

Lucy, Countess of Rocksbier Visited by Jacob in *JACOB'S ROOM,* Lucy talks at lunch of Joseph CHAMBERLAIN and other celebrities she has known. Lucy is most likely based on the Marchioness of Bath, whom Woolf wrote about in "AM I A SNOB?" (MOB 207–08).

Lushington, Katherine See MAXSE, Katherine.

"Lycidas" A pastoral elegy by John MILTON for his Cambridge contemporary Edward King, who drowned in 1637. In *A ROOM OF ONE'S OWN,* Mary BETON is prevented from seeing the manuscript of "Lycidas" in the College library because unaccompanied women are not admitted. The manuscript is in the library of Trinity College, Cambridge.

Lysistrata In *THREE GUINEAS,* Woolf points out that the only thing educated men's daughters can withhold to prevent war is children, something Lysistrata recommended two millennia earlier (ch1n10). Lysistrata, eponymous heroine of Aristophanes' play, exhorts the Athenian women to boycott their husbands to bring an end to war (and see Brenda Silver, *Virginia Woolf's Reading Notebooks,* 301). The third of Woolf's notebooks of newspaper clippings (RN LX) which she began collecting in the mid-1930s and which she used in writing *Three Guineas* contains several articles and letters to editors of newspapers on the subject of the declining birthrate and its implications for war.

M

Macalister The boatman in *TO THE LIGHTHOUSE* in whose boat Mr. RAMSAY and Cam and James RAMSAY sail to the Lighthouse in part 3.

Macaulay, Rose (1881–1958) Novelist, poet and essayist. Woolf and she had a slight acquaintance in the 1920s that developed into a friendship in the 1930s, as Jane Emery has explained (CM4 9–14): "Virginia discovered that the rational Rose, who wrote an enchanted review of *Orlando,* was, like herself, a comic fantasist, and that both were drawn to the subject of androgyny" (Emery 13). A member of the "British intellectual aristocracy" (Scott, *Gender* 252), Macaulay, like Woolf, was the daughter of an agnostic Cambridge don. She had also been a friend of Rupert BROOKE and based the hero of her first novel, *Non-Combatants and Others* (1915), on him. Her first best-seller was *Potterism,* and she wrote many other novels, including *Dangerous Ages* (1922), *Told By an Idiot* (1923), *Keeping Up Appearances* (1928) and *And No Man's Wit* (1940). Emery suggests her *They Were Defeated,* published in 1932, may owe something to Woolf's story of Judith SHAKESPEARE in *A ROOM OF ONE'S OWN.* Three of her works were published by the HOGARTH PRESS: *Catchwords and Claptrap* (1926), *Some Religious Elements in English Literature* (1931) and *The Writings of E. M. Forster* (1938). Macaulay also wrote a controversial biography of John MILTON.

Macaulay, Thomas Babington (1800–59) A historian and member of Parliament who served on the Supreme Council of the British Empire in India and was partly responsible for installing there an education system modeled on the English. Macaulay is best known for his *History of England from the Accession of James II* in five volumes, which William RODNEY advises Cassandra OTWAY to read in *NIGHT AND DAY.* At the beginning of *THE VOYAGE OUT,* Ridley AMBROSE recites lines from "Horatio" from Macaulay's *Lays of Ancient Rome* (1842). In her ironic preface to *ORLANDO,* Woolf includes Macaulay among those writers to whom anyone writing is perpetually indebted.

MacCarthy, Sir (Charles Otto) Desmond (1877–1952) Editor, drama critic and literary journalist, one of the original members of the BLOOMSBURY GROUP. MacCarthy had left Trinity College, Cambridge University, by the time Leonard WOOLF entered in 1899, but Leonard came to know him through meetings of the APOSTLES, remarking that MacCarthy was "in many ways [G. E.] Moore's favourite apostle" (LW2 98). MacCarthy was one of the guests at the "Thursday Evenings" at 46 GORDON SQUARE begun by Thoby STEPHEN (PA 273), and Woolf attended when in 1906 he married Mary (Molly) Warre-Cornish—the "first Bloomsbury marriage," in Leon Edel's words (*House* 131). Mary MACCARTHY and Desmond had three children, Michael (1907–73); Rachel (1909–82), who married Lord David CECIL; and Dermod (b. 1911).

MacCarthy accompanied Roger FRY to Paris in 1910 to help him choose works for the first POST-IMPRESSIONIST exhibition. He had begun to publish drama criticism several years earlier and went on to have a distinguished career as a critic. He was literary editor of the *NEW STATESMAN* in 1920–27 and senior literary critic of the *Sunday Times* from 1927 until his death. *Remnants,* a collection of his articles, was published in 1918, and another, *Criticism,* in 1923. From 1928 to 1933 he edited *Life and Letters.*

His "Books in General" page for the *New Statesman* was written under the pseudonym "Affable Hawk." MacCarthy's comments on contemporary literature frequently irritated Woolf, and in 1920, when MacCarthy praised Arnold BENNETT's *Our Women* and concurred with his disparaging view of women's intellectual abilities, Woolf responded with two letters on "The Intellectual Status of Women" (D2 Appendix III), protesting her friend's views and pointing out the obstacles that had inhibited women's intellectual achievement. Although MacCarthy was extremely popular among his friends (Woolf referring to him in 1920 as "the oldest friend . . . perhaps the best" [D2 21]), Woolf often found him depressing and irritating: "the egotism of men surprises & shocks me even now," she wrote in 1928 after a particularly taxing visit from the self-involved MacCarthy. Woolf was frequently disappointed by MacCarthy's references to her writing in his articles; when, for example, he referred to *MRS. DALLOWAY* in a 1931 piece, she wrote that "a snub—even praise—from Desmond, depresses me more than the downright anger of Arnold Bennett—it saps my vitality" (D4 43). Throughout his life, MacCarthy's friends expected him to produce a great novel, but he never did. Leonard Woolf suggests that there is something of MacCarthy in the character BERNARD in *THE WAVES* (LW2 101).

MacCarthy, Mary Josefa (Molly) (née Warre-Cornish) (1882–1953) A daughter of Dr. Francis Warre-Cornish, the Vice-Provost of Eton, and Blanche Ritchie, Molly married Desmond MACCARTHY in 1906. She and Woolf were both nieces by marriage of Anne Thackeray RITCHIE (see Elizabeth Boyd, chapter 6). The founder of the MEMOIR CLUB (which evolved from the Novel Club), Molly MacCarthy coined the term "Bloomsberries" around 1910 to describe the members of the BLOOMSBURY GROUP. Both the Novel Club and the Memoir Club were intended to somehow induce Desmond to write the great novel Molly and their friends were sure he could write, but neither they nor anything else succeeded. Molly MacCarthy is best known for her memoir *A Nineteenth-Century Childhood* (1924). Her only novel, *A Pier and a Band,* was published in 1918, and she also published collections of biographical sketches: *Fighting Fitzgerald and Other Papers* (1930), *Handicaps* (1936) and *Festival* (1937).

Mackenzie Mentioned by Mr. FLUSHING in *THE VOYAGE OUT* as an explorer who died in the jungle, having been further inland than any other white man (TVO 277). On the trip up river, his abandoned hut is seen from the boat by the Flushings, Helen AMBROSE, Rachel VINRACE, Terence HEWET and St. John HIRST. The story seems likely to have derived from Joseph CONRAD's *Heart of Darkness.*

MacNeice, Louis (1907–63) An Irish poet associated with W. H. AUDEN and Stephen SPENDER in the 1930s. In "THE LEANING TOWER" Woolf quotes his autobiographical poem "Autumn Journal" (1939).

Maitland, Frederic W. (1850–1906) The authorized biographer of Leslie STEPHEN and Downing Professor of the Laws of England at Cambridge University, Maitland was married (after the intervention of Julia Prinsep STEPHEN) to Woolf's first cousin, Florence FISHER (1863–1920); they had two daughters, Ermengard (1888–1966) and Fredegond (1889–1949; see Fredegond SHOVE). Maitland was a good friend of Leslie Stephen's, one of the "Sunday Tramps" who would often join Woolf's father on a twenty-mile stroll. In the *MAUSOLEUM BOOK,* Stephen wrote that Maitland was "the only living person who could say anything to the purpose at present" about his life (4). Maitland, whom Noel Annan says "professional historians revere perhaps above all other Victorian historians" (xi), invited Woolf to help him with her father's biography by selecting letters to be included and also by writing a "Note" on his life. Woolf was very pleased at this, and she worked on the biography at her aunt Caroline Emelia STEPHEN's house while recovering from the breakdown she suffered after her father's death. Her work occasioned a sharp disagreement with Jack HILLS, who wrote as the family solicitor to warn Woolf against indiscretion. Woolf was happy in early 1905 that her sister Vanessa BELL and brother Thoby STEPHEN both approved of what she had written, but she was soon after depressed at the reaction of Kitty MAXSE, who did not like it. However, a good review from Lady Robert CECIL ("Nelly"), who thought Kitty's point of view absurd, dispelled the gloom. When Maitland read it, he wrote to Woolf that it was "beautiful." *Life and Letters of Leslie Stephen* was published in 1906.

Woolf was extremely fond of the Maitlands. Florence seemed to her "a true descendant of our beloved old French grandmothers and great grandmothers" (L1 34) and was "one of the most delightful, original, and beautiful people" Woolf knew (L1 145). After her father died, Woolf wrote to Violet DICKINSON that she was very pleased Maitland would write the biography, saying Maitland's letter of condolence was "almost the only one I have had worth keeping" (L1 136). When Maitland caught pneumonia on a voyage to Teneriffe and died in 1906—the year Woolf's brother Thoby died—she wrote to Dickinson that *Life and Letters of Leslie Stephen* was a blessing for the family, adding that Maitland "was one of the few, the very very few, who wrote me something about Thoby which seemed true and inspiring" (L1 271).

Mallarmé, Stéphane (1842–98) French Symbolist poet. Roger FRY spent much of his life working on a translation of Mallarmé's poems that was published in 1936, after Fry's death, edited by Julian BELL and Charles MAURON.

Mallett, Edwin Mentioned in *JACOB'S ROOM* as an admirer of Clara DURRANT, who runs sobbing out of the room when he proposes to her.

Malone, Dr. and Mrs. The parents of Kitty LASSWADE (née Malone) in *THE YEARS.* Dr. Malone is the Master of an Oxford University college. In describing the Malone household, Woolf probably drew on a visit to her cousins the FISHERS at Oxford that she described in letters to Ethel SMYTH and Quentin BELL (L5 254–56) in 1933.

"Man Who Loved His Kind, The" See *MRS. DALLOWAY'S PARTY.*

Mangin Mentioned in *JACOB'S ROOM* as someone Jacob is pleased to have met at a party and upon whose knee FLORINDA later sits.

Manning, Carrie Mentioned in *TO THE LIGHTHOUSE* by William BANKES. Mrs. RAMSAY is astonished that Carrie Manning and her husband Herbert could be alive when she has not seen them for twenty years (TTL 87).

Manning, George Mentioned in *TO THE LIGHTHOUSE* as a famous man who would sometimes come and talk with Mrs. RAMSAY in the evening.

Manorbier A village in Pembrokeshire, South Wales. In 1904, soon after Leslie STEPHEN's death, Woolf, Vanessa BELL, Adrian and Thoby STEPHEN and George DUCKWORTH went there for a four-week holiday. Clive BELL and Vanessa went there on honeymoon, and in August 1908 Woolf rented a cottage there for two weeks while writing *MELYMBROSIA.*

Manresa, Mrs. Character in *BETWEEN THE ACTS.* Some critics have suggested Woolf drew on her memories of Katherine MANSFIELD in creating her (see Penny Gay; Evelyn Haller, "Virginia Woolf"). It is rumored that Manresa was born in Tasmania; she is married to Ralph, a Jew, and has no children (40). Manresa arrives uninvited at Bart OLIVER's house for lunch, bringing champagne and a young man, William DODGE. She is described as a "wild child of nature" and prides herself on being down to earth and attractive. Manresa has a house in London and also has one in the country, but she is a newcomer, contrasted with the families who have lived for generations in one place. Both Bart and his son Giles OLIVER are attracted to Manresa and there is a suggestion of more than just flirtation between her and Giles when, during an intermission of the annual village pageant, he takes her alone to see the greenhouse. Haller includes Manresa among Woolf's "anti-madonnas" ("Anti-Madonna" 101–02).

Mansfield, Katharine (Beauchamp) (1888–1923) Short-story writer, second cousin of Sydney WATERLOW, and part of the circle around Lady Ottoline MORRELL through her friendship with D. H. LAWRENCE. She was born in Wellington, New Zealand and moved in 1903 to London, marrying the critic and editor John Middleton MURRY in 1918. Mansfield and Woolf first met in 1916, and Mansfield's long short story *Prelude* was the second publication of the HOGARTH PRESS (1918). Among her other works are *Bliss and Other Stories* (1920), *The Garden Party* (1922) and *The Dove's Nest* (1923). Her *Journal* (1927) and *Letters* (1928) were edited by Murry. Woolf reviewed the *Journal* for the *New York Herald Tribune* in September 1927 ("A Terribly Sensitive Mind" CE1 356–58), calling Mansfield "a born writer" (CE1 356).

Although many have focused exclusively on Woolf's first impressions in her DIARY that Mansfield stank "like a—well civet cat that had taken to street walking" (D1 58), this is to ignore that Woolf's relationship with Mansfield was complex and that she was someone whom Woolf "in my own way suppose[d] I loved" (D2 318). Woolf saw her as a rival, yet also as one of the few people, and the only woman at the time, with whom she could seriously discuss writing. The feeling was reciprocated by Mansfield, who wrote Woolf in 1917 that they had "the same job." Claire Tomalin describes their relationship as "markedly one-sided. Virginia was always the wooer, Katherine . . . elusive, difficult, unpredictable, unresponsive" (Tomalin 197). Woolf and Mansfield grew particularly close in 1918–19, but when Mansfield, who was severely ill, moved to France in August 1919, they saw each other infrequently, and Mansfield was an irregular correspondent. Woolf described her feelings for Mansfield in 1919 as a "queer balance of interest, amusement, & annoyance" (D1 243).

Woolf disliked "Bliss," commenting on its "superficial smartness," but recognized that Mansfield was a serious rival. Mansfield's 1919 review of *NIGHT AND DAY,* which, in Woolf's words, made her out to be a "decorous and elderly dullard" (D1 314), stung her and may, Louise DeSalvo has suggested, have influenced Woolf's 1919 and 1920 revisions of *THE VOYAGE OUT.* When Mansfield died, Woolf felt there was "no point in writing. Katherine won't read it" (D2 226). She reflected that "probably we had something in common which I shall never find in anyone else" (D2 227).

Ann L. McLaughlin has written that "ideas and techniques from Mansfield's work reappear in Woolf's novels as though they had taken root in her consciousness to flower again years later in a fuller, more articulate form" (152) and links *Prelude* and *THE WAVES* as elegies for dead brothers that are also linked by stylistic concerns. McLaughlin suggests other intertextualities, for example between *THE YEARS* and Mansfield's story "The Daughters of the Late Colonel" (158), and between Woolf's "The New Dress" and Mansfield's "The Fly," to which Woolf's story specifically alludes (159).

As both McLaughlin and Penny Gay have noted, Antony Alpers, in his biography of Mansfield, argues that a letter to Woolf from Mansfield describing Ottoline Morrell's garden at Garsington may have provided a technical breakthrough that Woolf realized in "KEW GARDENS." Evelyn Haller and Gay have also discussed the character Mrs. MANRESA in *BETWEEN*

THE ACTS as based to some extent on Mansfield. Haller argues that Woolf "made use of her ongoing feelings of antagonism toward Katherine Mansfield as a literary competitor by transferring them to the less unacceptable plane of class consciousness through characterizations in *Between the Acts*" (Haller "Virginia Woolf" 96), and Gay points out that when Woolf met Mansfield she was living one block west of Manresa Road (290).

Mansion House The official residence of the Lord Mayor of London.

Manx Cat Looking out of the window after the lavish lunch at a men's college of "OXBRIDGE" in *A ROOM OF ONE'S OWN*, Woolf's narrator sees a Manx cat crossing the lawn (grass she has been prohibited from walking on because she is a woman). "Manx" refers to the Isle of Man, to which the tailless Manx cat is indigenous. Patricia Joplin has argued that the figure of the cat "has its roots deep in Woolf's private store of imagery" (VWM 21:5) and sees it as an emblem of the silenced, mutilated woman who haunts *A Room*. In "The Voice of the Shuttle Is Ours," Joplin terms the Manx cat "a comic metaphor for feminist poetics" (28) that represents the "buried or stolen tales of women" (29) and links Woolf's metaphor to the myth of PROCNE AND PHILOMELA and William SHAKESPEARE's poem *The Rape of Lucrece*. In a review of Louise DeSalvo's *Virginia Woolf's First Voyage*, Joplin also noted that the metaphor appears in an early draft of *THE VOYAGE OUT* in a letter written by Helen AMBROSE (VWM 16:3).

Jane Marcus locates the source of the image in a 1920 *TIMES LITERARY SUPPLEMENT* review by Woolf of Aldous HUXLEY's *Limbo* ("Cleverness and Youth" E3 176–78), where Woolf quotes Huxley's character "Mrs. Crawister" (based on Blanche Warre-Cornish, wife of the Vice President at Eton) who talks to the "bewildered boys" of "Canteloup College" "now about eschatology, now about Manx cats" (E3 177). Disagreeing with Joplin's reading of the Manx cat as representing a castrated woman, Marcus reads the Manx cat as "a representation of women's missing tales in the men's college setting and culture at large" (Marcus, *Languages* 174). Sandra M. Gilbert has pointed out that in the "Nighttown" chapter of James JOYCE's *Ulysses*, Bella/Bello Cohen calls Leopold Bloom a Manx cat. Gilbert argues that Woolf places the Manx cat in *A Room* "as an emblem not of the deformed posterior of the old but of the reformative posture (and possibility) of the new" ("Woman's Sentence" 222).

Marable, Lady Margaret A guest at Kitty LASSWADE's 1914 dinner party in *THE YEARS* who sits next to Martin PARGITER.

Marbot, Baron In *MRS. DALLOWAY* Clarissa reads about "the retreat from Moscow" in Baron Marbot's memoirs (*Mémoires du général baron de Marbot*). Beverly Ann Schlack notes that "Marbot's descriptions of the Russian campaign, particularly of Napoleon's ignominious retreat, are harrowing" and suggests the allusion provides a metaphor for Clarissa's "retreat from sexuality" (Schlack 62–3).

Marchmont, Miss Character in *JACOB'S ROOM* who is working in the BRITISH MUSEUM Reading Room on her theory that color is sound, expounded in a pamphlet that Queen ALEXANDRA once graciously acknowledged.

Maria In *THE VOYAGE OUT,* Helen and Ridley AMBROSE have a local servant named Maria when they stay on SANTA MARINA. While Mrs. CHAILEY speaks to her in "vigorous English," Helen addresses Maria in Spanish.

"Mark on the Wall, The" (SF 77–83) One of the best-known of Woolf's short fictions, "The Mark on The Wall" exemplifies many of the characteristics of her longer works. Woolf identified this sketch, *KEW GARDENS* and "AN UNWRITTEN NOVEL" as important in the transition she made from these short prose experiments to *JACOB'S ROOM* (D2 13). "The Mark on the Wall" was published with Leonard WOOLF's "THREE JEWS" as the first publication of the HOGARTH PRESS, *TWO STORIES* (1917), illustrated with four small woodcuts by Dora CARRINGTON. A separate edition of "The Mark on the Wall" was published, slightly revised, in 1919. It was also included, further revised, in *MONDAY OR TUESDAY* and was included in *A HAUNTED HOUSE*. Susan Dick provides two paragraphs deleted from the 1917 and 1919 editions (SF 290n1).

"The Mark on the Wall" illustrates an aesthetic principle frequently found in Woolf's fiction, whereby a visual image "can take disparate elements of thought and organize them into a harmonious whole" (Richter 71). The narrator sees a mark on the wall and begins to wonder what it is, which leads to a meditation on life, time and history. At first the narrator thinks the mark might be a nail, and then that it is perhaps an object of some kind; the mark is finally revealed to be a snail when another voice interrupts the narrator's reverie with a complaint about the war and the announcement that he is going out to buy a newspaper. Early in the sketch, the narrator makes a comment about fiction that not only looks forward to Woolf's own novels, but also adumbrates the ideas she would publish in 1919 in "MODERN NOVELS" (better known as "MODERN FICTION"): "Novelists in the future will realise more and more the importance of these reflections," she writes, because the kind of reflections that compose "The

Mark on the Wall" are almost infinite. "Those are the phantoms they will pursue, leaving the description of reality more and more out of their stories" (SF 79–80).

Markham, Kit In *NIGHT AND DAY*, she is one of the pioneers of the SUFFRAGE organization for which Mary DATCHET works and is adored by Sally SEAL. Kit Markham brings her large dog, Sailor, to meetings. There is the trace of a suggestion that Miss Markham might be well connected toward the end of the novel when Mrs. MILVAIN tells Katharine that William RODNEY was observed sitting out five dances with Cassandra OTWAY at "the Markhams' dance" (ND 406).

Marsh, Edward (1872–1953) Author of a memoir of Rupert BROOKE, whose literary executor he was, and private secretary to Winston Churchill.

Marshall, Frances See PARTRIDGE, Frances.

Marsham, Mrs. Mentioned in *MRS. DALLOWAY* when she tells Ellie HENDERSON that Clarissa DALLOWAY is having a party, which results in Clarissa reluctantly having to invite Ellie.

Martin, Basil Kingsley (1897–1969) Recruited by Leonard WOOLF to review for the *NATION*, he became in 1931 editor of the *NEW STATESMAN AND NATION*, where he remained until 1960.

Martineau, Harriet (1802–76) In *NIGHT AND DAY*, Katharine HILBERY mentions Martineau in connection with the biography of her grandfather (ND 308). Born into a Unitarian family in Norwich, Harriet Martineau received the encouragement of her parents to study when she was young. She wrote her first article in 1822 and when she was thirty began to write a series of stories to explain political economy that proved extremely popular: *Illustrations of Political Economy* was published in nine volumes between 1832 and 1834. Martineau traveled widely and was, notes Gaby Weiner, "one of the first Englishwomen to travel independently to America" (Weiner 67). On her return after a two-year trip, Martineau wrote *Society in America* (1837). She was a very successful journalist, writing for the *Daily News* for fourteen years. Weiner says that one of her articles, "Female Industry" in the *Edinburgh Review*, "resulted in a fundamental public reappraisal of the role of women in Victorian society (Weiner 70) and led to the establishment at Langham Place of the Society for Promoting the Employment of Women. Although she did not identify herself closely with the women's movement, Martineau was an active campaigner throughout her life for women's education, employment and political rights. She also wrote an *Autobiographical Memoir* which commented on leading literary figures of her lifetime.

Marvell, Andrew (1621–78) English poet, assistant to John MILTON, and later a politician. In *THE YEARS*, North PARGITER recites Marvell's "The Garden" from memory to Sara PARGITER (TY 339).

Masham Mentioned in *JACOB'S ROOM* as having an aunt who makes Jacob and Timothy DURRANT laugh helplessly, as indeed had Masham himself, for he once swallowed his tie-pin; but, as Jacob observes, "He's a gentleman" (JR 51).

Matthaei, Louise Ernestine (1880–1969) Fellow and Director of Studies at NEWNHAM COLLEGE, Cambridge (1909–16), from which post she was forced to leave during World War I because her father was German. She was Leonard WOOLF's assistant editor on the *International Review* and subsequently worked for him on the *Contemporary Review*. Woolf's description of her in 1918 (D1 135–6) leads Karen Levenback to suggest Miss Matthaei as a model for Doris KILMAN in *MRS. DALLOWAY* (VWM 37: 4).

Mauretania In *THE VOYAGE OUT*, Richard DALLOWAY recalls the captain of the *Mauretania* telling him the worst hazard at sea is "sedgius aquatici"—duckweed (TVO 42). The *Mauretania*, a Cunard ship, was launched in 1906 and for many years held the "Blue Riband" for the fastest Atlantic crossing.

Mauron, Charles (1899–1966) Friend of Roger FRY and Julian BELL, with whom Fry shared a house in St.-Rémy-de-Provence. In 1924, the onset of blindness ended Mauron's career as a chemist and Fry suggested that he turn to translation work, with the help of his wife Marie. Mauron translated E. M. FORSTER's *A Passage to India* and Woolf's *ORLANDO* and *FLUSH* into French. His translation of an early version of the "Time Passes" section of *TO THE LIGHTHOUSE* appeared in the Paris magazine *Commerce* in 1926. Allen McLaurin has discussed the significance of Mauron's aesthetic theories for Woolf's fiction, theories that were expressed in *The Nature of Beauty in Art and Literature*, published by the HOGARTH PRESS in 1927 with a preface by Fry, who also translated the work. Mauron also provided commentaries on Fry's translations of the poems of Stéphane MALLARMÉ, published in 1936.

Mausoleum Book, The A long autobiographical letter by Sir Leslie STEPHEN to his second wife Julia Prinsep STEPHEN's children (George, Stella and Gerald DUCKWORTH; Vanessa [BELL], Virginia [WOOLF], Thoby and Adrian STEPHEN) following Julia's death in 1895. The large green album, marked "PRIVATE" on the cover, became known to the family as the "Mausoleum Book," under which title it was published in 1977, edited by Alan Bell. Ostensibly an account of Leslie Stephen's marriages to Harriet Marian (Minny) THACKERAY and to Julia, the *Mausoleum Book* also gives fascinating insights into the complex character of Woolf's father, his life, work, ethical and religious struggles, and his feelings and thoughts about other prominent Victorian contemporaries. Woolf was certainly influenced by the *Mausoleum Book* in writing *TO THE LIGHTHOUSE,* in which Mr. RAMSAY is based upon the character of her father. She wrote the last paragraph of the *Mausoleum Book* from her father's dictation when he was too weak to write himself.

Maxse, Katherine (Kitty) (1867–1922) The daughter of Judge Vernon Lushington (1832–1912), whose wife, Jane, had been a great friend of Julia Prinsep STEPHEN. She and her sisters, Susan Lushington and Margaret Massingberd, were frequent visitors to 22 HYDE PARK GATE at the turn of the century. In her memoir "22 HYDE PARK GATE" Woolf wrote, "The tea table however was also fertilized by a ravishing stream of female beauty—the three Miss Lushingtons, the three Miss Stillmans, and the three Miss Montgomeries—all triplets, all ravishing, but of the nine the paragon for wit, grace, charm and distinction was undoubtedly the lovely Kitty Lushington" (MOB 165).

Kitty was first a close friend of Stella DUCKWORTH and, after Stella's death, became close to Vanessa BELL. She had broken off an engagement with Lord Morpeth and was a representative of the world of aristocratic high society for Woolf and her sister. In 1920, Woolf heard from Margaret Llewelyn DAVIES that Kitty thought *NIGHT AND DAY* "very bad, the characters bloodless, the writing dull, the love insipid." While Leonard WOOLF thought that her "unfavorable opinion is a great compliment," Woolf wrote to Davies that "I used to hate her friends and her views, so it is quite right that she should find mine dull. . . . How she used to implore Nessa and me not to know people like Leonard!" (L2 412). In 1904, Kitty was one of the people who were appalled at Vanessa's decision to move with her brothers and sister to unfashionable BLOOMSBURY.

Kitty married Leopold James Maxse, editor of the *NATIONAL REVIEW,* in 1890. Woolf's "Street Music" appeared in the *National Review* in March 1905, her only contribution to the journal (E1 27). When Kitty died in 1922 after falling over a bannister in her house, Woolf wrote in her diary that she had not seen her since 1908 and could not bring herself to attend the memorial service. The elegant and worldly Kitty, whom Woolf believed to have committed suicide, provided a model for Clarissa DALLOWAY. Woolf also wrote to her sister in 1908 that "Lettice," as she was calling the character who became Clarissa Dalloway in *THE VOYAGE OUT,* "is almost Kitty verbatim" (L1 349).

May See COWBIND.

Mayer, Louie See EVEREST, Louie.

Mayhew, Colonel and Mrs. In *BETWEEN THE ACTS,* Colonel Mayhew is irritated at being kept waiting at the end of the pageant, while his wife imagines Miss LA TROBE is planning a "Grand Ensemble" around the Union Jack as a finale for the annual village pageant (BTA 179).

Mayhew, Sir Matthew Mentioned in *THE YEARS,* a "most distinguished man" whom Maggie PARGITER sits next to at a dinner party (TY 141).

McInnis, Nurse Character in *THE VOYAGE OUT.* Rachel VINRACE sees her at the Sunday service in chapter XVII of the novel, where she is referred to only as the "hospital nurse," and chooses her as a paradigm of the smug complacency of the "faithful." Later, Nurse McInnis attends Rachel when she is ill and Rachel's hallucinations transform her into a sinister woman playing cards in a dripping tunnel (TVO 330–31).

McNab, Mrs. Character in *TO THE LIGHTHOUSE* who appears in part 2, "Time Passes," looking after Mr. and Mrs. RAMSAY's house. With the help of Mrs. BAST, she gets the house ready for the family's return after World War I, salvaging it from decay and ruin just in time. Many critics have likened Mrs. McNab to the "rusty pump" in *MRS. DALLOWAY* who sings outside the Tube station (MD 122). Mary Lou Emery argues that the meaning of Mrs. McNab's "vision" of Mrs. Ramsay in section VIII of "Time Passes" is "stolen" to "facilitate Lily [BRISCOE]'s creativity" (226–27). Makiko Minow-Pinkney describes Mrs. McNab as "a chthonic being in touch with telluric powers" (101). Michael Tratner has pointed out that in "Time Passes" the women who are excluded from the rooms of the house in parts 1 and 3, the servants, enter freely and roam the house, representing a social unconscious repressed in the rest of the book (VWM 40: 3–4).

Measure For Measure A tragicomic play by William SHAKESPEARE that is alluded to in *NIGHT AND DAY.* When he first realizes that Katharine HILBERY is engaged to William RODNEY, Ralph DENHAM is listening to Mrs. COSHAM recite Claudio's lines from Act 3, scene 1 that refer to the fear of death.

Mecklenburgh Square The Woolfs moved to 37 Mecklenburgh Square in August 1939 following the demolition of houses next to theirs at TAVISTOCK SQUARE. In September 1940, while they were at MONK'S HOUSE, Mecklenburgh Square was bombed and their house badly damaged. Later that month, John LEHMANN supervised the moving of the HOGARTH PRESS from Mecklenburgh Square to Letchworth, and in December the Woolfs' furniture and books were sent to Rodmell for storage at Monk's House and in the village.

Melymbrosia Published in 1982 as "a reconstruction of the earliest nearly complete version which survives (probably in progress from 1909–1912) of the novel which was published as" *THE VOYAGE OUT* (MELYM x). "Melymbrosia" was the working title for Woolf's first novel; the word might be a combination of the Greek word for honey and *ambrosia.* Louise DeSalvo suggests that the title "might have referred not only to the ambrosial fields of [the poet Edmund] Spenser, but also to the ambrosial fields of Greece," the scene of Thoby STEPHEN's illness that resulted in his death in 1906. Isobel Grundy notes that "ambrosia" suggests "divinity and intoxication, made ominous by the prefix *mel*—black, or scholarly by memory of the Ambrosian library at Milan" ("Words" 211). Helen and Ridley AMBROSE are important characters in both *Melymbrosia* and *The Voyage Out.*

In the mid-1970s, DeSalvo and Elizabeth Heine, working independently in the BERG COLLECTION, discovered that a nearly complete draft of Woolf's first novel could be reconstructed from the typescript and holograph pages there. The text published in DeSalvo's edition was one of two "submerged texts" she had discovered; one was a 390-page typescript of what had been a 414-page draft, which was the text published; the other was a 567-page holograph and typescript version (MELYM xiii). Both DeSalvo and Heine analyzed the drafts of Woolf's first novel not only in terms of the narrative sequence and its relation to the published text of *The Voyage Out,* but also for its paper type, ink colors, typing and method of binding. They reported on their separate conclusions in a special issue of the *Bulletin of Research in the Humanities* (82, 3 [Autumn 1979]) devoted to the draft material and also including essays by Mitchell A. Leaska on the death of the novel's protagonist Rachel VINRACE, and by Beverly Ann Schlack on the way Woolf had revised literary allusions in drafts of *The Voyage Out.* Heine, in her essay in the *Bulletin,* came to different conclusions than DeSalvo about the dating of the drafts. Commenting on Woolf's long and complicated process of revision and rewriting of her first novel, Heine says of *Melymbrosia* that although it "includes pages which may have been typed as early as October 1907, and although the content of the whole must have built up gradually in the lost versions written and typed, and rewritten and retyped, between 1907 and 1912, the two dated holograph notebooks and the surviving typescripts unquestionably corroborate both the 1912 dating for the *Melymbrosia* version and the later, post-marriage dating for the massive revisions of 1912–13" ("New Light" 228).

Of the significance of the recovery of *Melymbrosia,* Jane Marcus wrote in the special issue of the *Bulletin* that it was "quite clear that this was a very political Edwardian novel. . . . Wouldn't it be odd if one could show that in response to Clive Bell and the other members of her circle, [Woolf] suppressed her propagandistic instincts in favor of revolutions in form, but that the instincts are still there, and quite radical?" ("Virginia Woolf" 270). Critics are agreed that *Melymbrosia* is a very different work from *The Voyage Out.* Heine says that Woolf "rewrote the novel almost completely after her marriage, changing the heroine, Rachel Vinrace, from an intelligent, outspoken, critical young feminist to the vague and innocently naive dreamer of the published text" ("Earlier" 294). Comparing the two texts, Heine says that "readers can easily appreciate the vast difference between the novel as Virginia Stephen finished it just before her marriage and the novel Virginia Woolf at last allowed to be published in 1915" ("Virginia Woolf's Revisions" 402).

In her introduction to *Melymbrosia,* DeSalvo describes Woolf's struggle to achieve what she called "a view of one's own" in her first novel. Woolf's letters from 1907 to 1912 to Vanessa BELL, Violet DICKINSON, Lytton STRACHEY and, in particular, Clive BELL frequently mention the novel she was working on. In February 1909, Woolf wrote a long letter to Clive Bell responding to his criticisms of pages she had sent him and telling him that his objection that her "prejudice against men" was didactic did not have "quite the same force with me" (L1 383). DeSalvo regards this letter as a turning point and suggests that Woolf sent no more extracts from her work in progress to others to comment on after this (MELYM xxiii). Woolf, according to DeSalvo, "was writing an angry novel about how the power of women had eroded since the time of the Egyptians, since pre-Olympian Greece," and was suggesting "that another tradition, that of the negative power of the force of a woman, had grown up and supplanted that more ancient tradition" (MELYM xxxiii). Many elements of *Melymbrosia,* DeSalvo writes, suggest that Woolf was writing a female version of the *Odyssey.* DeSalvo also draws attention to Woolf's early fictions as precursors of *Melymbrosia,* mentioning in particular "A COCKNEY'S FARMING EXPERIENCES" and "THE JOURNAL OF MISTRESS JOAN MARTYN" (MELYM xxiv–xxvi).

Like DeSalvo, Heine has said that the identification and dating of the extant drafts of *Melymbrosia* is important "in understanding the biographical influences affecting this protean novel, which grew and changed with its author's experience" ("Virginia Woolf's Revisions" 401). Heine has detailed her differences with DeSalvo over the dating of various parts of the draft materials and says she had persuaded DeSalvo of the validity of some of these differences that affect the conclusions of DeSalvo's book, *Virginia Woolf's First Voyage*. When she read an early version of DeSalvo's introduction to *Melymbrosia* in 1979, Heine writes, "none of us realised then how DeSalvo's preference for an earlier date had affected her transcription" ("Virginia Woolf's Revisions" 450n7). Heine has criticized DeSalvo's editorial principles, which she says provide "a clear text of the early chapters" but cause "a silent omission of most of the handwritten insertions in the later chapters, even when they are obviously contemporaneous with the typing" ("Virginia Woolf's Revisions" 426).

The genesis of Woolf's first full-length work of fiction is an extremely complex story on which the above references, brilliant as they frequently are, can shed only a dim light. The question of just when Woolf began working on what would become her first published novel depends, of course, on the assumption that there can be such an identifiable point. Aileen Pippett, writing in 1953, said Woolf began *Melymbrosia* some time after April 1907; Jean Guiguet suggests 1908; Harvena Richter puts the beginning at just after Thoby Stephen's death in November 1906; Leonard WOOLF in his *Autobiography* says she began it in 1909 and also recalls an occasion on which Woolf, opening a closet and finding "five or six drafts" of her first novel there, burnt them; Quentin BELL has 1907–08 but also thinks Woolf may have had the idea of the novel as early as 1904; the editors of Woolf's LETTERS suggest October 1907 (L1 315–16). (Further details will be found in the "Genesis" section of the entry on *THE VOYAGE OUT*.)

Whenever she may have begun what would eventually be *The Voyage Out*, *Melymbrosia* stands in fascinating relation to Woolf's first published novel; several critics have drawn attention to the analogous relation that exists between James JOYCE's *Portrait of the Artist as a Young Man* and that work's precursor, *Stephen Hero*, as an example of how important to the study of a major writer's creative process *Melymbrosia* is.

Memoir Club Begun in 1920 by Molly MACCARTHY, a revised version of the Novel Club she had begun in 1918, in the hope of inducing her husband Desmond MACCARTHY to write the novel his friends were sure he was capable of. The original members were Woolf, Leonard WOOLF, Clive BELL, Vanessa BELL, E. M. FORSTER, Roger FRY, Duncan GRANT, John Maynard KEYNES, Desmond MacCarthy, Molly MacCarthy, Adrian STEPHEN, Lytton STRACHEY and Saxon SYDNEY-TURNER. In his autobiography, Leonard Woolf says that these thirteen people were identical with "Old Bloomsbury," the core of the BLOOMSBURY GROUP (though this is questioned by S. P. Rosenbaum). The Memoir Club first met on March 4, 1920 and continued until the mid-1960s, with younger Bloomsbury generations joining. Its members were supposed to read autobiographical papers that were written without research and to be completely honest. Molly MacCarthy remained the Club's secretary until 1946, after which leadership passed to Vanessa Bell, Quentin Bell, and eventually to Frances PARTRIDGE. No records of the Club's meetings were kept, but several papers that were read to it have been published, including Woolf's "22 HYDE PARK GATE," "OLD BLOOMSBURY" and "AM I A SNOB?" (all in *MOMENTS OF BEING*). John Maynard Keynes's "My Early Beliefs" and Vanessa Bell's "Notes on Bloomsbury" are among Memoir Club papers included in S. P. Rosenbaum's anthology, *The Bloomsbury Group*. Elizabeth French Boyd comments that "a large number of these first drafts [read to the Club] found their way into the members' published memoirs and collections of essays" (109). The post-Bloomsbury phase of the Memoir Club is described in Frances Partridge's journal, *Everything to Lose*.

"Memoirs of a Novelist" (SF 63–73) A short story Woolf wrote in 1909 and submitted to the *CORNHILL MAGAZINE* (it was rejected). It concerns the life of a "Miss Willat" as written by her friend "Miss Linsett."

"Memories of a Working Women's Guild" (CE4 134–48; CDB 228–48) An essay by Woolf that was first published in the *YALE REVIEW* in 1930. A much-revised version formed Woolf's "Introductory Letter" addressed to Margaret Llewelyn DAVIES in *Life As We Have Known It by Co-Operative Working Women*, edited by Davies and published by the HOGARTH PRESS in 1931. This book consists of five autobiographical sketches of WOMEN'S COOPERATIVE GUILD members ("Memories of Seventy Years," by Mrs. Layton; "A Plate-Layer's Wife," by Mrs. Wrigley; "In a Mining Village," by Mrs. F. H. Smith; "A Felt Hat Worker," by Mrs. Scott, J. P.; and "A Public-Spirited Rebel," by Mrs. Yearn); a profile of a Guild office clerk, Harriet A. Kidd, written by Davies; and excerpts from the letters of twenty-one working women telling about their lives, books they had read, and their views of the Guild.

Woolf based her essay on notes she had made in June 1913 when she and Leonard WOOLF attended a meeting of the Women's Cooperative Guild in Newcastle. She hurriedly wrote the version that was published in the *Yale Review*, as she had promised them an article and had nothing else ready; this was the version republished by Leonard Woolf in *THE CAPTAIN'S DEATH BED,* and subsequently in Woolf's *COLLECTED ESSAYS.*

The version in *Life As We Have Known It* is substantially different, as Jane Marcus has noted. In it, the venue of the meeting is changed from Manchester to Newcastle; two women referred to, Miss Wick and Miss Erskine, are called by their real names, Miss Kidd and Miss Harris (Lilian Harris, Davies's lifelong companion, was assistant secretary to the Guild); and where Woolf had originally written that the reforms demanded by the women "would not matter to me one jot," she now wrote that they "would not touch one hair of my capitalistic head" (Marcus, *Art* 118). Woolf had also originally written that the next great novelist or poet would not come from the working class, but in her "Introductory Letter" she deleted that sentence and replaced it with a more considered evaluation of the literary merit of the women's writing. Marcus describes the "Introductory Letter" as "another contribution to the propaganda of hope" (*Art* 119).

In both versions, although the tone is different, Woolf reflects on the fact that she is an outsider at the Guild conference and cannot share the feelings of the working-class women without pretension. In "THE LEANING TOWER" she would criticize young intellectuals who struck poses of solidarity with the working class while remaining protected from its hardships by their privileged upbringing. Mary Childers discusses Woolf's "non-preface" in "Virginia Woolf on the Outside" (66–72).

Mendoza, Signora Lola Character in *THE VOYAGE OUT.* Seen only as a woman wearing makeup, dressed in white, and then as a shadowy figure in a dressing gown crossing the hotel hallway from one room to another late at night, Lola Mendoza is referred to as a prostitute and is ejected from the hotel by the manager, Signor RODRIGUEZ, when Mr. THORNBURY and Mr. ELLIOT report her nocturnal wanderings to him. St. John HIRST and Helen AMBROSE are appalled at what they see as this example of the hypocrisy of the English middle class.

Meredith, George (1828–1909) Woolf's father, Leslie STEPHEN, first met the English novelist George Meredith in Vienna in 1865 and they became lifelong friends. Meredith based the character of Vernon Whitford in his novel *The Egoist* (1879) on Leslie Stephen, describing him as "Phoebus Apollo turned fasting friar." Meredith began his literary career as a journalist, but he published a volume of poems in 1851, dedicated to his father-in-law, Thomas Love Peacock. In 1856, he published the poetic fantasy, *The Shaving of Shagpat: An Arabian Entertainment*; another in the same genre, *Farina, A Legend of Cologne,* appeared the following year. His first novel, *The Ordeal of Richard Feverel,* was published in 1859, and Meredith began to become acquainted with writers such as Algernon Charles SWINBURNE, Dante Gabriel Rossetti and others of the Pre-Raphaelite circle. Meredith's other notable works include: *Evan Harrington* (1860); a tragic poem, *Modern Love* (1862); *Rhoda Fleming* (1865); *Vittoria* (1866); *The Adventures of Harry Richmond* (1871); *Beauchamp's Career* (1876); *Diana of the Crossways* (1885); and *Ballads and Poems of Tragic Life* (1887). *Last Poems* appeared in 1909.

Woolf remembered Meredith as one of the "great figures" in the background of her childhood (MOB 158). In her contribution to Frederic MAITLAND's *Life and Letters of Leslie Stephen,* she recalled that her father knew by heart and admired Meredith's poem "Love in the Valley" (E1 128). In a 1919 *TIMES LITERARY SUPPLEMENT* review of *George Meredith: His Life and Friends in Relation to His Work* by S. M. Ellis, a grandson of Meredith's aunt, Woolf would not discuss "the ethics or the necessity" of a biography that told "more about an author than the author himself chose to tell" (E3 5), but pointed out that any "evidence" a biographer cites is open to interpretation on the part of both writer and reader. In this unsigned review, Woolf writes as an "insider" when she remarks that she "has reason to know" that Meredith's friends may have regarded him differently than Ellis's rather unfavorable book represents; among those friends, of course, were Woolf's parents. Woolf also reviewed Alice Mary, Lady Butcher's *Memories of George Meredith, O. M.* (E3 137–39).

On a trip to Italy in 1908, Woolf recorded her opinion of Meredith's *Harry Richmond,* that it "fails to satisfy," yet she recognized the "remarkable brain" of the author. She thought Meredith might have been led into false touches in his novel by his assumption that his readership would not be clever enough to notice them (PA 391–92). Many years later, Woolf remembered her pleasure at her brother Thoby STEPHEN's approval of her remark that Meredith had derived his women characters from Peacock (D2 164). In Florence, in 1909, Woolf had met Meredith's mistress, Janet Ross, the woman on whom he based several of his heroines. In *A ROOM OF ONE'S OWN,* Meredith's *Diana of the Crossways* is singled out as one of the extremely rare efforts in English fiction to represent two women as friends (AROO 82).

In "On Re-reading Meredith," a 1918 TLS review of *George Meredith: A Study of his Works and Personality* by J. H. R. Crees, Woolf noted that the widespread enthusiasm in England for Russian novelists "seemed for a time to reduce Meredith to an insular hero bred and cherished for the delight of connoisseurs in some sheltered corner of a Victorian hothouse" (E3 273). At his best, she found Meredith went to "the very heart of emotions"; he was a great writer, but perhaps not a great novelist (E3 274). Meredith, she surmises, was really a dramatist manqué.

Woolf's most considered treatment of Meredith is her 1928 centenary essay for the TLS, "The Novels of George Meredith" (CR2 226–36; CE1 224–32), for which she re-read several of his novels and a volume of his letters (RN 219–20). There she notes E. M. FORSTER's opinion in *Aspects of the Novel* that Meredith's moment has passed. Reading his first novel, *The Ordeal of Richard Feverel,* she finds the characters "at odds with their surroundings" (CE1 226). The characters of *Harry Richmond* are also unconvincing, but she acknowledges Meredith's imaginative power of fantasy and romance that makes the reader believe in the world of the novel. Meredith's characteristic is "intermittent brilliancy," she concludes (CE1 228). He is too didactic, but that introduction of qualities of philosophy to the novel was necessary for the genre's development, she believes: George ELIOT, Meredith, and Thomas HARDY were all "imperfect novelists" (CE1 231), but their imperfection was a necessary cost of the novel's advance in the nineteenth century. Recalling again the effect of the Russian novelists on the reputations of many nineteenth-century authors, Woolf concludes her essay by stressing Meredith's peculiarly English qualities of wit and eccentricity, seeing him as part of the tradition that stems from William SHAKESPEARE.

In *THE VOYAGE OUT,* there are allusions to both "Love in the Valley" and *Diana of the Crossways* (e.g., TVO 124; 296). According to Louise DeSalvo, "Love in the Valley" deals with the same issues as Woolf's first novel; the "specter of death" haunts both texts, "but what is especially significant in the context of 1897, and in the context of how Woolf would use the poem later, is that Leslie Stephen read it to the family while Stella [DUCKWORTH] was seriously ill . . . less than a month before she died, so that the work has very personal and private associations with Stella's brief marriage to Jack Hills" (DeSalvo, "1897" 93). DeSalvo has also written that *Diana of the Crossways* had personal associations for Woolf. She had a copy of the novel that was inscribed to her mother from Meredith (DeSalvo, *First* 124). The novel functions in *The Voyage Out,* says DeSalvo, as "an analogy for Rachel [VINRACE]'s erotic impulses, for her feelings about love and marriage" (*First* 124). DeSalvo sees the character Emma in the novel as an analogue for Woolf's mother, Julia Prinsep STEPHEN, and Rachel as an analogue for Diana.

Merridew, Rosamond See "JOURNAL OF MISTRESS JOAN MARTYN, THE"

Midnight Society A reading society of undergraduates at Trinity College, Cambridge University, that began meeting in Clive BELL's rooms on Saturdays at midnight in 1900. Among the members were Thoby STEPHEN, Lytton STRACHEY, Saxon SYDNEY-TURNER and Leonard WOOLF. Bell claimed the Midnight as the origin of the BLOOMSBURY GROUP.

Mildred The cook in *TO THE LIGHTHOUSE,* who also puts James RAMSAY to bed and shares a bedroom with him and Cam RAMSAY, the two youngest children of Mr. and Mrs. RAMSAY. In "Time Passes," part 2 of the novel, Mrs. MCNAB tries to remember Mildred's name, recalling only that she was fiery "like all red-haired women" (TTL 137).

Millamant In *A ROOM OF ONE'S OWN,* Millamant, the witty heroine of *The Way of the World* by William CONGREVE, is offered as an example of women who have "burnt like beacons in all the works of all the poets from the beginning of time" (AROO 43) whom Woolf uses to stress the difference between fictional and real women.

Milman Family Childhood acquaintances whom Vanessa BELL and Woolf would visit for tea or lunch. Arthur Milman, whose father Henry Hart Milman (1791–1868) was dean of St. Paul's, lived at 61 Cadogan Square and had four daughters, Enid, Ida, Maud and Sylvia. Sylvia studied painting with Vanessa.

Milton, John (1608–74) English poet, author of *Paradise Lost* (1667) and many other poems and essays. Woolf wrote that her father, Leslie STEPHEN, knew most of the major English poets' works by heart and that he knew Milton best. The "Ode on the Morning of Christ's Nativity" (1629) was his favorite ("Impressions of Sir Leslie Stephen" [E1 128]). Milton's poetic and prose works were, Woolf noted in her essay "READING," part of the English people's cultural heritage, a copy of *Paradise Lost* invariably to be found in an English home.

Woolf wrote in her DIARY in 1918 that she was surprised to learn from Janet CASE that she was "not the only person in Sussex who reads Milton" (D1 192), and went on to set down her impressions of *Paradise Lost.* She found it a poem unlike any other, sublimely aloof and impersonal, never illuminating "the passions of the human heart": "I scarcely feel that Milton lived or knew men & women" (D1 193). She repeated this judgment in an essay, "Indiscretions" (1924), when she called Milton the leader of the impersonal writers, among whom she listed Walter Savage LANDOR, SAPPHO, Thomas BROWNE and Andrew MARVELL.

In Woolf's first novel, *THE VOYAGE OUT,* Ridley AMBROSE recites lines from Milton's "Ode on the Morning of Christ's Nativity" described by the narrator as words that are "strangely discomforting" to Terence HEWET and St. John HIRST (TVO 351). More significantly, Rachel VINRACE's death is presaged by a complex allusion to Milton's masque *COMUS*, from which Hewet reads to her.

Milton, who was married three times, wrote *The Doctrine and Discipline of Divorce* in 1643, in which he argued that it was a constraint on civil liberty for a man not to be able to rid himself of a wife who was not or could not be the "helpmeet" intended by God. Writings such as this, together with Milton's portrayal of Eve in *Paradise Lost,* led Woolf to identify Milton himself with the patriarchal god she refers to in *A ROOM OF ONE'S OWN*. She called Milton "the first of the masculinists" (D1 192).

In *A Room,* Woolf's narrator recalls how Charles LAMB had written of being shocked that Milton could have changed a word of his poem "LYCIDAS" (1637). Realizing that she is yards from the OXBRIDGE library that houses the manuscript, she sets off to look at it and finds her way barred by a "kindly gentleman" who tells her unaccompanied women are not allowed in the library (AROO 8). Later, she describes how her aunt's legacy substituted open sky for "the large and imposing figure of a gentleman, which Milton recommended for my perpetual adoration" (AROO 39). At the very end of *A Room,* Woolf returns to this figure when she describes one of the conditions for Judith SHAKESPEARE's putting on "the body which she has so often laid down" to be for women to "look past Milton's bogey" (AROO 114). Sandra M. Gilbert and Susan Gubar have taken Woolf's image as their starting point in chapter 6 of *The Madwoman in the Attic,* "Milton's Bogey: Patriarchal Poetry and Women Readers."

Jane Marcus sees this figure in *A Room* as typical of Woolf's "sidelong method," working to deflate the patriarchal God into the Victorian paterfamilias (Marcus, *Art* 201). Milton's bogey is equivalent, argues Marcus, to God the Father in *Paradise Lost.* She disagrees with Gilbert and Gubar, who write that Woolf's "perfunctory reference" to Milton in *A Room* is not developed significantly (*Madwoman* 188), and argues that the reference to Jane Ellen HARRISON's unveiling reality rather than blocking it is one example of the allusion's development (Marcus, *Art* 202). Marcus also suggests that Woolf got the idea "to use the word *bogey* to mean god" from Harrison, in whose books the word is frequently used (Marcus, *Art* 203). Gilbert and Gubar do, however, see Woolf's use of Milton in her works generally as reinforcing the idea that "for her, as for most other women writers, both he and the creatures of his imagination constitute the misogynistic essence of what Gertrude STEIN called 'patriarchal poetry' " (*Madwoman* 188). They point out that Woolf's "two most ambitious and feminist re-visions of history," *ORLANDO* and *BETWEEN THE ACTS,* "appear quite deliberately to exclude Milton from their radically transformed chronicles of literary events" (*Madwoman* 192). To the female imagination, "Milton and the inhibiting Father—the Patriarch of patriarchs—are one" (*Madwoman* 192).

Milvain, Mrs. (Aunt Celia) Character in *NIGHT AND DAY* who writes to Katharine HILBERY about her second cousin Cyril ALARDYCE, who is living with a woman who is not his wife and with whom he has had two children and is about to have a third. Mrs. Milvain follows up her letter with a visit. Later in the novel, she concerns herself with the relationships among Katharine, Ralph DENHAM, Cassandra OTWAY and William RODNEY, eventually accosting Mr. Hilbery to tell him the whole shocking affair. It is possible that in depicting Mrs. Milvain Woolf was drawing on her own cousins, one of whom, Dorothea STEPHEN, occasioned a sharp letter from Woolf in 1921 when she raised moral objections to Vanessa BELL's domestic arrangements (L2 488–89).

Mira Colonel Abel PARGITER's mistress in *THE YEARS*.

Mirrlees, (Helen) Hope (1887–1978) One of the friends who "have helped me in ways too various to specify" thanked by Woolf in the ironic preface to *ORLANDO*. A poet and novelist whose long poem *Paris* was published by the HOGARTH PRESS in 1919, Mirrlees was a contemporary of Karin STEPHEN at NEWNHAM COLLEGE, where she was taught by Jane Ellen HARRISON. Mirrlees and Harrison lived together in Paris and London from 1922 until Harrison's death in 1928. Suzanne Henig discussed Mirrlees's work in the first issue of *VIRGINIA WOOLF QUARTERLY*. Among Mirrlees's other publications are the novel *Madeleine: One of Love's Jansenists; The Counterplot; Lud-in-the-Mist* (a fantasy); and *A Fly in Amber,* the first volume of her biography of Sir Robert Bruce Coton.

Mitchell, Elise In *MRS. DALLOWAY,* she is a little girl playing in Regent's Park used to effect a narrative transition between Rezia Warren SMITH and Peter WALSH when she runs into Rezia and Peter laughs at this.

Mitford, Mary Russell (1787–1855) At the beginning of *A ROOM OF ONE'S OWN,* Woolf suggests a talk about women and fiction might include "some witticisms about Miss Mitford" (AROO 3), an author known for her collection of essays, *Our Village, Sketches of Rural Life, Character, and Scenery,* begun in *The Ladies Magazine* in 1819 and published separately between 1824 and 1832. The village in question is Three Mile Cross, the birthplace of Flush, the cocker spaniel given by Mitford to Elizabeth Barrett BROWNING, whose story Woolf tells in *FLUSH, A BIOGRAPHY*. Woolf read widely about Mitford when preparing to write *Flush* (RN 159). Mitford also wrote *Belford Regis* (1835), sketches of a country towns; *Country Stories* (1837); and a novel, *Atherton* (1854). Her *Recollections of a Literary Life* was published in 1852. Later in *A Room,* Woolf remarks that she would not mind "if the homes and haunts of Mary Russell Mitford were closed to the public for a century at least" (AROO 45).

In her 1913 essay "Jane Austen," Woolf quotes Mitford's memory of Jane AUSTEN as "the prettiest, silliest, most affected, husband-hunting butterfly she ever remembers" (E2 10). Woolf reviewed Constance Hill's *Mary Russell Mitford and Her Surroundings* for the *TIMES LITERARY SUPPLEMENT* in May 1920 ("An Imperfect Lady" E3 210–13) and later incorporated her review into the essay "Miss Mitford" (CR1 232–40; CE4 101–06), one of four "Outlines." She also reviewed Hill's book for the *DAILY HERALD* in May 1920 ("A Good Daughter" E3 213–15). Woolf wrote a third, longer review of Hill for the *ATHENAEUM* ("The Wrong Way of Reading" E3 218–23), also in May 1920, part of which she used in the *COMMON READER* essay, where she says Hill's "is not a good book" (CE4 101). In 1925, Woolf reviewed R. Brimley Johnson's edition of *The Letters of Mary Russell Mitford* for the *NATION & ATHENAEUM.*

"Modern Fiction" (CE2 103–10; CR1 184–95) An essay in the *COMMON READER,* and a slightly revised version of "MODERN NOVELS," a 1919 article in the *TIMES LITERARY SUPPLEMENT.* "Modern Fiction" is probably Woolf's best-known and most often-quoted essay. It is a manifesto of literary MODERNISM in which she compares the writers of her generation to those she called the "Edwardians," represented in the essay by H. G. WELLS, Arnold BENNETT and John GALSWORTHY.

There is no progress in literature, Woolf begins by saying, only difference. If the works of the past seem complete and effortless in a way that contemporary works do not, that is only an illusion of perspective. Wells, Bennett and Galsworthy, she continues, are "materialists," "concerned not with the spirit but with the body" (CE2 104), and it is for this reason that "we"—the generation of novelists Woolf calls the "Georgians"—have a quarrel with them. Life itself, "the essential thing," escapes these plodding writers. Woolf's criticism of the way that Wells, Bennett and Galsworthy represent "life" leads to one of the most famous passages she ever wrote, beginning, "Examine for a moment an ordinary mind on an ordinary day. The mind receives a myriad impressions—trivial, fantastic, evanescent, or engraved with the sharpness of steel" (CE2 106). This randomness, however, is lost because the Edwardian writers feel they must conform to a conventional fictional structure of plot and characterization. Life itself, Woolf goes on, is not really like the way Bennett represents it: "Life is not a series of gig lamps symmetrically arranged; life is a luminous halo, a semi-transparent envelope surrounding us from beginning to end" (CE2 106). It is *this* that novelists should try to capture.

As an example of what younger novelists are doing, Woolf chooses James JOYCE, mentioning his *Portrait of the Artist as a Young Man* (1916–17) and *Ulysses,* of which she had read seven excerpts published in the *Little Review* from March to October 1918 (RN 156–57). Joyce, she says, is "spiritual; he is concerned at all costs to reveal the flickerings of that innermost flame which flashes its messages through the brain" (CE2 107), and this is a very different concern from that followed by Bennett, Wells and Galsworthy. Nevertheless, Woolf finds that *Ulysses* is a failure when she compares it to Joseph CONRAD's *Youth* (1902) or Thomas HARDY's *The Mayor of Casterbridge* (1896), because Joyce does not have those writers' largeness of mind and breadth of interest. The fault in Joyce's fiction, she says, is not in his method; it is that the world he creates is not as rich as that found in, for example, Laurence STERNE's *Tristram Shandy* (1759–67) or William Makepeace THACKERAY's *Pendennis* (1848–50).

What distinguishes modern writers from the previous generation is their interest in "the dark places of psychology," an interest that has developed under the profound influence of Russian writers such as Anton CHEKHOV. Woolf cites as an example of the kind of fiction that has influenced her generation Chekhov's short story "Gusev" (translated by Constance GARNETT in *The Witch and Other Stories,* 1918). The Russian sense of inconclusiveness has had a tremendous effect on young novelists, Woolf writes. "Modern Fiction" ends with the remark that there is no limit to the "proper stuff of fiction" (CE2 110).

Many critics writing on Woolf or on the history of the novel in general have singled out "Modern Fiction" for particular attention. Some have noted that the passage on "life itself" bears some similarity to that passage referring to the "stream of consciousness" in William James's *Principles of Psychology,* and Perry Meisel notes the influence on Woolf's essay of Walter PATER's conclusion to *The Renaissance.* Referring to "Modern Fiction" and to "MR. BENNETT AND MRS. BROWN," Suzette Henke has said that with these two important essays, "Woolf raises a clarion call to a new aesthetics of psychological realism" (in Scott, *Gender* 623).

Modern Fiction Studies American literary critical journal published at Purdue University that has devoted three special issues to Woolf, each of which includes a checklist of selected criticism on Woolf (by Maurice Beebe, 1956; Barbara Weiser, 1972; and Laura Sue Fuderer, 1992).

"Modern Novels" (E3 30–37) An article in the *TIMES LITERARY SUPPLEMENT* on April 10, 1919 that Woolf revised for the *COMMON READER* with the title "MODERN FICTION," by which it is best known.

Modernist (Modernism) There are many opposing definitions of modernism, but all at least agree that the term refers to the early twentieth century as a time of artistic and literary experimentation. Initially seen as a radical break with nineteenth-century forms and ideologies, modernism has also been interpreted as the last phase of Romanticism. Arguments about the politics of modernism have also ranged from those that see it as a subversive movement to those that have argued its links with an authoritarian politics (e.g., Frank Kermode's *The Sense of an Ending,* 1967). Marjorie Perloff provides a useful brief overview of conflicting definitions and interpretations in her article "Modernist Studies."

The roots of much of the ferment in the arts of the early twentieth century can be found in late-nineteenth-century artists' desire to transgress the boundaries between various genres. Richard WAGNER, for example, dreamed of a "total artwork" (*Gesamtkunstwerke*) that would unite several disciplines, and in the early years of the twentieth century artists such as Wassily Kandinsky attempted to articulate what they believed was a common spiritual basis of the arts. For some historians of modernism, World War I was the definitive break with the past that ushered in the modernist era, but many of the characteristics associated with modernist art were in fact in place before 1914.

The early twentieth century witnessed many experimental movements in the arts, all of which are often subsumed under the modernist label: futurist, constructivist, Dadaist, surrealist, expressionist and POST-IMPRESSIONIST art all played significant roles in the general and sweeping changes known as modernism. Up to the late 1960s, literary modernism was identified almost exclusively with white male artists, but in the past three decades of revisionist literary and cultural history, this monolithic modernism has been replaced by a much more complex and diverse description. Works such as Bonnie Kime Scott's *The Gender of Modernism,* Sandra M. Gilbert and Susan Gubar's *No Man's Land* and Gillian Hanscombe and Virginia L. Smyers's *Writing for Their Lives: The Modernist Women 1910–1940* have complicated and enlarged the definition of modernism.

The modernist novels of Hermann Broch, William Faulkner, James JOYCE, D. H. LAWRENCE, Thomas Mann, Dorothy RICHARDSON, Woolf and many others have often been described as "stream-of-consciousness" novels, reflecting their concern with the direct representation of characters' consciousnesses. Many critics from the late 1940s on traced the turning inward of the novel from its nineteenth-century concern with external reality to the representation of what Woolf termed in her modernist manifesto "MODERN FICTION" the "flickerings of that innermost flame" (CE2 107). The term "stream-of-consciousness" derives from William James's *Principles of Psychology* (1890), in which he uses the metaphor of a river to describe the movement of human consciousness. Robert Humphrey, in an early study of modernist novelists, wrote that Dorothy Richardson had "invented the fictional depiction of the flow of consciousness" (Humphrey 9), but he pointed out that there is "no stream-of-consciousness technique. Instead, there are several quite different techniques which are used to present stream of consciousness" (Humphrey 4). Humphrey's definition of stream-of-consciousness fiction as "a type of fiction in which the basic emphasis is placed on exploration of the prespeech levels of consciousness for the purpose, primarily, of revealing the psychic being of the characters" excluded Marcel PROUST, for example; other critics have included Proust's fiction among examples of the stream-of-consciousness technique.

The definition of these "different techniques" used by Woolf and her contemporaries has been as contested as the definition of modernism itself. Dorrit Cohn, in an article later incorporated into *Transparent Minds,* wrote that the "general consensus seems to be that the designation 'stream-of-consciousness novel' should refer to a sub-genre of the novel, whereas 'interior monologue' should designate one of several techniques most often used to convey the inner world of the characters *in* a stream-of-consciousness novel" (Cohn, "Narrated Monologue" 108). Cohn found "stream-of-consciousness" to be "a very general and impressionistic label, which delineates no precise criteria that help one to determine whether a given novel is, or is not, a stream-of-consciousness novel" (108).

Cohn distinguishes between "narrated monologue" (also known by the German term *erlebte Rede* or the French *style indirect libre* because most of the early studies of narrative were by German and French critics) and "interior monologue." Narrated monologue "enables the author to recount the character's thoughts without a break in the narrative thread" (Cohn 98), as, for example, in Joyce's *Portrait of the Artist as a Young Man.* Transposing narrated monologue into first person and present tense results in interior monologue (sometimes known by the French term, *monologue intérieure*), though Cohn points out that the techniques are not interchangeable in terms of their effect in a narrative sequence. In *Transparent Minds,* Cohn illustrates interior monologue by a passage from the beginning of the third part of *TO THE LIGHTHOUSE,* when Lily BRISCOE has returned to the Ramsays' house after a ten-year absence. Cohn remarks that "the effect of using the temporal and spatial indicators of direct discourse in the narrated monologue is one of the most powerful tools available to the novelist for locating the viewpoint within the psyche of his characters" (105).

Despite the modernist novelists' technical innovations and manipulations of language in all kinds of ways to represent the movements of conscious and even subconscious thought, it is possible to find examples of such techniques being used prior to the twentieth century (in Jane AUSTEN and Laurence STERNE, for example). "Just as a symbol in a poem was a symbol long before the Symbolists made it into the purposive center of their art," writes Cohn, "the silent monologue, both in the first and in the third person, was a literary device long before Virginia Woolf's generation filled entire books with 'an ordinary mind on an ordinary day' " (Cohn 110; Woolf CE2 106).

Moffat, Mrs. BERNARD's housekeeper in *THE WAVES,* who he frequently thinks will come "and sweep it all up."

Moment and Other Essays, The The second posthumously published collection of Woolf's essays, edited by Leonard WOOLF and published in Britain by the HOGARTH PRESS and in the United States by Harcourt, Brace & Company in 1947. Among the essays in this volume are "THE MOMENT: SUMMER'S NIGHT," "ON BEING ILL," "THE ART OF FICTION," "THE LEANING TOWER," "ON RE-READING NOVELS" and "THE ARTIST AND POLITICS."

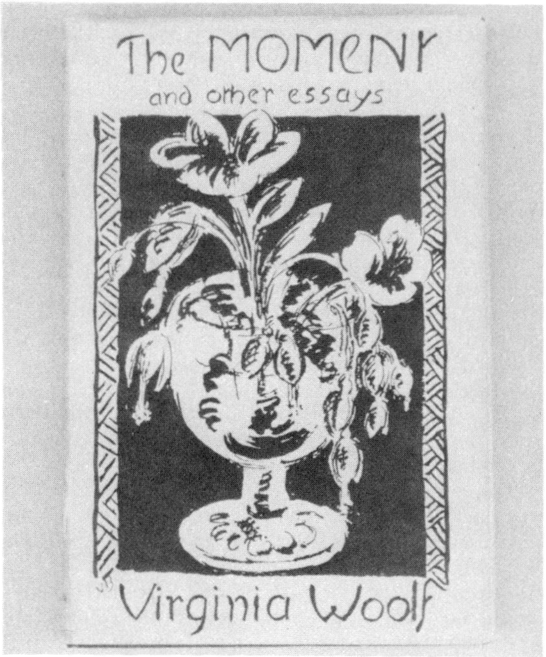

The Moment and Other Essays. *Courtesy Linda J. Langham. The pink dust jacket printed in black for this Hogarth Press first edition (1947) was designed by Vanessa Bell.*

"Moment: Summer's Night, The" (CE2 293–97; M 3–8) A sketch probably written in 1938 that is certainly related to the composition of *BETWEEN THE ACTS.* The narrative speaks of becoming aware that "we are spectators and also passive participants in a pageant" (CE2 293) as night falls on a group of people talking in a garden.

Moments of Being Title of a collection of four previously unpublished autobiographical writings by Woolf. *Moments of Being,* edited with an introduction and notes by Jeanne Schulkind from the MONK'S HOUSE PAPERS, was published in 1976 by the University of Sussex Press. It comprises "REMINISCENCES," "A SKETCH OF THE PAST," "22 HYDE PARK GATE," "OLD BLOOMSBURY" and "AM I A SNOB?" (the latter three were papers Woolf read to the MEMOIR CLUB). A second edition of *Moments of Being* was published in 1985 after a typescript acquired by the British Library added twenty-seven pages of new material to "A Sketch of the Past" as well as reworked passages of the version published in 1976. All together, this collection was an extremely important addition to available material on Woolf's life and work.

"Moments of Being: 'Slater's Pins Have No Points' " (SF 209–14) A short story by Woolf published in the New York *Forum* in January 1928 and, in a slightly revised version, in *A HAUNTED HOUSE.* As she finished writing *TO THE LIGHTHOUSE,* Woolf wrote in her DIARY that "as usual, side stories are sprouting up in great variety as I wind this up: a book of characters; the whole string being pulled out from some simple sentence, like Clara Pater's, 'Don't you find that Barker's pins have no points to them?' " (D3 106). The story is entirely sketched around a moment when a flower pinned to the dress of Fanny Wilmot, who is being taught piano by Julia Craye, drops to the floor. As she hunts for the pin, Fanny thinks about her teacher and makes clear that she is infatuated with her. As the story closes, she either has a vision of being kissed by Julia or Julia actually does kiss her. The ending of the *Forum* version is slightly different from that in the version in *A Haunted House.* Also, the rose that drops to the floor from Fanny's dress in the first paragraph becomes a carnation halfway through the story, and Fanny pins it with trembling fingers to Julia's breast at the end.

In 1927, Woolf wrote to Vita SACKVILLE-WEST that she had just rewritten "a nice little story about Sapphism, for the Americans" (L3 397). Having sent it to the Americans, she wrote again to Vita that she had been paid £60 "for my little Sapphist story of which the Editor has not seen the point, though he's been looking for it in the Adirondacks" (L3 431).

Monday or Tuesday The only collection of her short stories published in Woolf's lifetime, *Monday or Tuesday* included four woodcuts by Vanessa BELL, who also designed the cover. Although published by the HOGARTH PRESS in 1921, the book was printed by F. T. McDermott at the Prompt Press in Richmond. Woolf thought that he did a terrible job. All the stories except "A SOCIETY" and "Blue & Green" were republished in the posthumous collection *A HAUNTED HOUSE*. Among the eight stories in *Monday or Tuesday* were "AN UNWRITTEN NOVEL," "THE STRING QUARTET," *KEW GARDENS* and a revised version of "THE MARK ON THE WALL."

Monk's (or Monks) House The Woolfs' home in the Sussex village of Rodmell, near Lewes, from 1919 until their deaths. Having received notice to leave ASHEHAM HOUSE in 1919, the Woolfs bought the Round House in Lewes in June. On their way to inspect their new house, they saw a poster advertising the sale of Monk's House, which Leonard WOOLF thought would have suited them better. The next day, Woolf went to see Monk's House, "an unpretending house, long & low, a house of many doors" (D1 286). Liking what she saw, she took Leonard with her to see the house the following day. "The truth is he has the making of a fanatical lover of that garden," she wrote after they had sold the Round House and bought Monk's House at auction for £700 in July 1919 (D1 287). The name was invented by a real estate agent and the house had nothing to do with the church next to it.

The Woolfs moved to Monk's House on September 1, 1919, and spent every summer there. Gradually they added amenities to the house (which had no hot water or bath when they bought it), often financing additions with money earned by Woolf's novels. They added a bath in 1926 and two rooms in 1929, one of which was Woolf's ground-floor bedroom. Although Woolf complained about barking dogs—those perpetual enemies of writers—and the ringing church bell, Monk's House was a refuge for her from the tumult of London. It was, for example, in the solitude of a summer spent in 1926 at Monk's House, which Woolf described in her DIARY as a "retreat," that *THE WAVES* first took shape. From 1919 until 1941, her life alternated rhythmically between homes in London and Monk's House. Woolf became secretary of the Rodmell Labour Party and in 1940 was involved in helping the Rodmell Women's Institute stage a play. She and Leonard moved to Monk's House permanently after their house at MECKLENBURGH SQUARE was damaged by bombs in 1940, and it was from Monk's House that Woolf set out on March 28, 1941 and drowned herself in the River Ouse.

Leonard Woolf left Monk's House to his executor Trekkie Parsons, who donated it to Sussex University. The university eventually turned the house over to the National Trust, which now operates it. The house is open to the public during the summer.

Monk's House Papers The Virginia Woolf Manuscripts from the Monk's House Papers at the University of Sussex and additional manuscripts from the British Library, London and selected Leonard Woolf Papers were published on six reels of microfilm by Harvest Press Microform Publications in 1985. Reels 1–5 contain seventeen of Woolf's reading notebooks, together with other files of reading notes, the three scrapbooks she kept in the 1930s that she used in writing *THREE GUINEAS*, and notes for *ROGER FRY* (see RN 347–49). Also on these reels are drafts of sketches and stories, the typescripts from which the pieces in *MOMENTS OF BEING* were edited by Jeanne Schulkind, notes on Woolf's Greek and Latin studies, extensive notes and drafts for "PHASES OF FICTION," and a few pages relating to *POINTZ HALL* and *BETWEEN THE ACTS*. Also on reel 5 are several fragments by Leonard WOOLF, including papers read to the APOSTLES and to the MEMOIR CLUB, and character sketches of his friends in which he gives them Greek names (Woolf is "Aspasia"). Much of this material appears in revised form (and sometimes with names changed) in the five volumes of Leonard's autobiography. Reel 6 contains the three-volume "Mrs. Dalloway" manuscript that is in the Library of the BRITISH MUSEUM (Additional Mss. 51044–51046).

In addition to the Woolf and Leonard Woolf papers, the University of Sussex also holds the Charleston Papers, consisting of a photocopied set of letters accumulated at CHARLESTON written to or by Clive BELL, Vanesa BELL and Duncan GRANT, and letters from Roger FRY, John Maynard KEYNES, Lytton STRACHEY, Woolf, Vita SACKVILLE-WEST, E. M. FORSTER, T. S. ELIOT, Frances PARTRIDGE and others. Also at the university are the Nicolson Papers, consisting of correspondence relating to Nigel NICOLSON's editorial work on Woolf's LETTERS. Recently, the university acquired about 900 letters from Maria Jackson, Woolf's grandmother, to Julia Prinsep STEPHEN and Leslie STEPHEN.

Montaigne, Michel Eyquem de (1533–92) French author of *Essais*, which were first translated into English in 1603 by John Florio, and in 1685 by Charles Cotton. Woolf reviewed William Carew Hazlitt's five-

Monk's House gate. Photograph by Linda J. Langham.

volume edition of Montaigne's *Essays* for the *TIMES LITERARY SUPPLEMENT* in January 1924, and she slightly revised her review for inclusion in *THE COMMON READER* ("Montaigne" CE3 18–26). He was a writer whom she greatly admired, as did Leonard WOOLF. In 1931 the Woolfs visited the tower in Bergerac where Montaigne had written most of his essays.

Moore, G. E. (George Edward) (1873–1958) Philosopher who had a profound influence on Leonard WOOLF's generation of students at Cambridge, particularly through his book *Principia Ethica* (1903), and also on British philosophy in general. Moore was an APOSTLE, a fellow of Trinity College (1898–1904), university lecturer in moral sciences (1911–25) and professor of philosophy (1925–39). Together with his contemporary Bertrand RUSSELL, Moore moved the philosophical climate of Cambridge away from the Hegelian Idealism propounded by F. H. Bradley. Moore's "The Refutation of Idealism" (1903) set out to demonstrate the falsity of Idealism's notion that to be was to be perceived (*esse est percipi*). Several of the men in the BLOOMSBURY GROUP who met each other at Cambridge at the turn of the century later wrote of the transformative effect on their lives of Moore's presence and writing. Leonard Woolf described Moore as the only really great man he ever knew, and in "My Early Beliefs," John Maynard KEYNES described *Principia Ethica* as the bible of his generation's new religion (Rosenbaum, *Bloomsbury Group* 52–64).

Moore spent a weekend with the Woolfs at ASHEHAM HOUSE in June 1914, and Woolf wrote admiringly of him to her sister Vanessa BELL and brother Adrian STEPHEN. Paul Levy has written that Woolf and Moore were "in fact on more intimate terms than one would guess from the paucity of the mentions of each in the other's diaries" (Levy 276). Certainly, Woolf was aware of Moore's significance from the time she began to meet her brother Thoby STEPHEN's Cambridge friends in 1904: "Home and found [Clive] Bell, & we talked the nature of good till almost one," wrote Woolf on March 8, 1905 (PA 249), indicating that the Moorean philosophy was a staple of the "Thursday Evening" conversations at 46 GORDON SQUARE. Moore's argument that loving friendship was a "supreme good" became an important element of Bloomsbury beliefs.

In *THE VOYAGE OUT,* Richard DALLOWAY picks up the book that Helen AMBROSE is reading and reads aloud a passage from chapter 1, section 17 of *Principia Ethica,* remarking that it is "jolly to think that's going on still" (TVO 74). While writing her first novel, Woolf wrote to Clive BELL that she had been "climbing Moore like some industrious insect, who is

The church next to Monk's House. Photograph by Louise H. Tucker.
This view is from the kitchen door of Monk's House. The path would lead Woolf across the garden to her writing "Lodge" (see photo on page 230).

determined to build a nest on the top of a Cathedral spire" (L1 340).

Morgan, J. Pierpont (1837–1913) A wealthy banker and art collector whom Roger FRY periodically advised and who offered Fry the directorship of the Metropolitan Museum of Art in New York (which Fry refused, primarily as it would have meant working closely with Morgan). In *THREE GUINEAS,* Woolf asks her readers to consider the life of Pierpont Morgan as evidence that extreme wealth is as undesirable as extreme poverty (TG 69).

Morley College An evening institute for working people in South London, established in 1889, where Woolf taught a weekly class from 1905 to 1907 at the invitation of Mary SHEEPSHANKS, its vice principal. Lindsay Martin has given an account of Woolf's classes (CM 4: 21–25) and Beth Rigel Daugherty has discussed Woolf's teaching methods ("Taking" 31–40). Woolf's "Report on Teaching at Morley College" is reproduced as Appendix B in QB1.

Morrell, Lady Ottoline Violet Anne (née Cavendish-Bentinck) (1873–1938) Literary hostess whose Thursday evening parties at 44 Bedford Square, beginning in 1907, attracted many artists and writers. Ottoline was notable for her striking appearance and eccentric dress. A descendant of Margaret CAVENDISH, Duchess of Newcastle, and half-sister of the sixth Duke of Portland, Ottoline married Philip MORRELL, a Liberal member of Parliament, in 1902. In 1906, they had twins, but the boy, Hugh, died at two days; their daughter, Julian Ottoline, married first Victor Goodman and then Igor Vinogradoff. In 1914, the Morrells moved to GARSINGTON, which became a haven for many artists and writers who were CONSCIENTIOUS OBJECTORS during World War I and were able to work on the Garsington farm.

Garsington weekends (as illustrated in *Lady Ottoline's Album*) were populated by many of the leading lights of the literary, political and artistic worlds, including Augustus JOHN, Henry LAMB, Dorothy BRETT, Mark GERTLER, Katherine MANSFIELD, Lytton STRACHEY, T. S. ELIOT and W. B. YEATS, as well as younger people yet to make their mark, such as Lord David CECIL. Ottoline had a long and serious affair with Bertrand RUSSELL, as well as being involved in several other liaisons, including a brief dalliance with Roger FRY. Several of the writers in Ottoline's circle repaid her hospitality with vicious portraits of her in their novels (see Miranda Seymour, Appendix III); the most famous were D. H. LAWRENCE, who caricatured her as Hermione Roddice in *Women in Love* (1920), and Aldous HUXLEY, in whose *Crome Yellow* (1921) she appears as Priscilla Wimbush.

In "OLD BLOOMSBURY" Woolf recalled how those who gathered in 1907 at FITZROY SQUARE in a continuation of the "Thursday Evenings" begun by her brother Thoby STEPHEN were in 1908 or 1909 "swept up" by Ottoline and invited to the grander surroundings of Bedford Square (MOB 199–200). Ottoline's recent biographer, Miranda Seymour, comments that the responsibility for her subject's "spectacularly bad press lies with the Bloomsbury Group" (2) and argues that Ottoline's connection with them was actually quite limited. She also points out how selective quotation from Woolf's diaries and letters by Bloomsbury chroniclers and critics has given the false impression that Woolf despised Ottoline (2). Although Woolf shared to some extent her friends' tendency to mock Ottoline in letters to each other and to spread gossip about her, Woolf's criticisms of her were not nearly as virulent as those of, for example, Lytton Strachey, whom Ottoline believed to be one of her closest friends.

Woolf seems genuinely to have admired Ottoline, growing closer to her in the 1930s, following the Morrells' move from Garsington back to London in 1928. Woolf told Ottoline in 1932 about the incest she had suffered (Seymour 394) and during the 1930s read Ottoline's memoirs and encouraged her writing. However, she could also write of "the despicableness of people like Ott" (D2 244), as she did in 1923 when thinking about *MRS. DALLOWAY*; Molly Hoff has discussed the "collage of understated allusions [to Ottoline] scattered throughout" that novel (VWM 37: 2). In 1932 Woolf brought together Ottoline and Ethel SMYTH, two women who admired Woolf very much as Jane Marcus has explained in her account of the letters between Ottoline and Smyth that are in the Harry Ransom HUMANITIES RESEARCH CENTER (VWM 9: 4–6). Woolf wrote Ottoline's obituary for *The Times,* noting that the "great lady who suddenly appeared in the world of artists and writers before the War easily lent herself to caricature" and that the ridicule of her friends overlooked the complexity of her nature (D5 Appendix II).

Morrell, Philip Edward (1870–1943) Husband of Lady Ottoline MORRELL and a Liberal member of Parliament who spoke in Parliament against England's fighting in World War I. During the war, the Morrells' home, GARSINGTON, became a haven for CONSCIENTIOUS OBJECTORS, who were able to avoid combat duty by working on the farm there. Philip was inveterately unfaithful to Ottoline and in 1919 and 1927 urged Woolf to have an affair with him; she found him pathetic.

Morris, William (1834–96) In *MRS. DALLOWAY,* Clarissa, under Sally SETON's influence, read "Morris" (MD 49). William Morris was a poet, artist and socialist who was also well known as a designer and architect who helped effect a revolution in English domestic taste. He founded the Kelmscott Press, for which he designed type and ornamental letters.

Mortimer, (Charles) Raymond Bell (1895–1980) One of those friends "who have helped me in ways too various to specify" thanked by Woolf in the ironic preface to *ORLANDO.* He was a successful literary critic, literary editor of the *NEW STATESMAN AND NATION* (1935–47), and a close friend of Clive BELL, Harold NICOLSON (with whom he had an affair) and Francis BIRRELL.

Morty, Uncle An uncle of Jacob's in *JACOB'S ROOM* about whom family legend says he became a Mohammedan; Betty FLANDERS wonders whether the Admiralty will ever tell her what happened to her brother, who was last heard of in Rangoon.

Mozart, Wolfgang Amadeus (1756–91) The Austrian composer whose *Magic Flute* has been suggested by Jane Marcus as a structural model for *NIGHT AND DAY* (*Languages* 18–35). "The Magic Flute" is suffused with the symbols, rituals and meanings of Masonry. William RODNEY is a devotee of Mozart who moves from humming "Don Giovanni" (ND 74) to picking out the melodies from "The Magic Flute" (ND 279). Toward the end of the novel, Ralph DENHAM hears "the melody of Mozart" played by William and thinks it is expressive of the "easy and exquisite love" between William and Cassandra OTWAY (ND 424).

"Mr. Bennett and Mrs. Brown" (CE1 319–37; CDB 94–119; E3 384–89 See also "CHARACTER IN FICTION.")

A signed article by Woolf published in the "Literary Review" of the *New York Evening Post* on November 17, 1923, reprinted in the *NATION & ATHENAEUM* (of which Leonard WOOLF was Literary Editor) on December 1, 1923 and in *LIVING AGE* (Boston) on February 2, 1924. This article, one of the most influential manifestos of literary MODERNISM, formed the basis for a paper called "Character in Fiction" that Woolf read to a Cambridge society, the HERETICS, in May 1924, which was revised and published in the *CRITERION* (of which T. S. ELIOT was editor) and then was reprinted as the first of the Hogarth Essays series under the original title. Samuel Hynes has commented that the *Nation & Athenaeum* version is a "shorter and very different first draft" of the "much-anthologized" essay ("The Whole Contention"). The essay is best known in its CE1 version.

In an article entitled "Is the Novel Decaying?" in *Cassell's Weekly,* March 28, 1923, Arnold BENNETT cited *JACOB'S ROOM* as an example of the modern novel, saying that "the characters do not vitally survive in the mind, because the author has been obsessed by details of originality and cleverness" (E3 388). Woolf wrote in her DIARY that this was only the "old post-Dostoevsky argument" that "character is dissipated into shreds now" (D2 248). She had written to Janet CASE in 1922 that the "Edwardians"—among whom she included H. G. WELLS, George Bernard SHAW, Beatrice and Sidney WEBB and Arnold Bennett—had "made a pretty poor show" (L2 529) compared to the writers of her own generation, whom she termed the "Georgians." She had made an earlier criticism of Bennett in a 1917 essay, "Books and Persons," in which she singled out what she called "the far more important question of Mr Bennett's point of view" from other arguments with his opinions about the novel (E2 129). In her "Literary Review" article, she remarked that to "disagree about character is to differ in the very depths of the being" (E3 387), fixing on one of the major loci in her argument for modernist literature against that of the previous generation.

In her essay Woolf uses the figure of "Mrs. Brown" to stand for human nature, the representation of which in characters she says is the major purpose of the novel.[12] She agrees with Bennett that character is the important thing in fiction, but she disagrees with him profoundly as to how character should be expressed and what "reality" means. In the draft of the version of this essay that she read to the Heretics, Woolf explained that the generation of the 1920s was more likely to think of character than their grandparents were and to be interested in character because the world had been changed so radically by scientific theories (implying the new physics of Einstein, Bohr, Heisenberg, et al). She adds, "If you read Freud you know in ten minutes some facts—or at least some possibilities—which our parents could not possibly have guessed for themselves" (E3 504; this remark does not appear in the published version of the essay and, interestingly, belies Woolf's contention that she did not read the work of Sigmund FREUD until the late 1930s).

In "Mr. Bennett and Mrs. Brown," Woolf opposes the Edwardian generation of Bennett to her own, the Georgians. She mentions as examples of Georgian writers E. M. FORSTER, D. H. LAWRENCE, Lytton STRACHEY, James JOYCE and T. S. ELIOT. It is in this essay (which Rachel Bowlby has called "a kind of literary Clapham Junction for the crossing and potential collision of questions of representation, history and sexual difference" [2]) that Woolf makes her famous pronouncement that "in or about December, 1910, human character changed" (CE1 320). Many critics have pointed out that the first POST-IMPRESSIONIST exhibition opened that year in November; also, Edward VII died in May 1910. Woolf herself mentions as early signals of this change Samuel BUTLER's 1903 novel *The Way of All Flesh* and the plays of George Bernard Shaw. The comparison of the Victorian cook with the Georgian cook, a "creature of sunshine and fresh air" (CE1 320), is offered as a way of pinpointing the social shifts that have occurred.

At the heart of the essay is Woolf's description of a journey in a railway carriage with "Mrs. Brown" and "Mr. Smith," for whom she invents a story. Mr. Smith gets off the train at a station, and the narrator of the essay continues to imagine Mrs. Brown as a character. She points out that a writer's nationality would determine what kind of character Mrs. Brown was given, and that a writer's conception of character depends upon that writer's notion of reality. Turning to the objects of her attack, she imagines how H. G. Wells, Arnold Bennett or John GALSWORTHY would have described Mrs. Brown and says that asking one of them to teach one how to write a novel would be like going to a bootmaker for instruction in watchmaking (CE1 326). Focusing on Bennett's 1911 novel *Hilda Lessways,* Woolf remarks of his characterization of the heroine, "One line of insight would have done more than all those lines of description" (CE1 329). The tools of the Edwardians are ruin for her generation of writers, "those tools are death" (CE1 330).

The prevailing sound of the Georgian age is "breaking and falling, crashing and destruction" (CE1 334) because those writers she has mentioned—Joyce, Eliot and Strachey, for example—first have to break the old molds before making a form of their own. This is an echo of Jacob FLANDERS, that character whom Bennett found unconvincing and who deplores "Shaw and Wells and the serious sixpenny weeklies" (JR 35) and for whom "there will be no form in the world unless Jacob makes one for himself" (JR 36). In a letter to Gerald BRENAN in 1922 Woolf foreshadowed the arguments in her essay, writing that "this generation [her own] must break its neck in order that the next may have smooth going. . . . nothing is going to be achieved by us. Fragments—paragraphs—a page perhaps: but no more. Joyce seems to me strewn with disaster" (L2 598).

After a simple illustration of the way "reality" is constructed by ideology, Woolf mentions "Ulysses, Queen Victoria, Mr. Prufrock—to give Mrs. Brown some of the names she has made famous lately" (CE1 335). The essay ends with her belief that "we are trembling on the verge of one of the great ages of English literature" and an exhortation never to desert "Mrs. Brown," i. e., character in fiction (CE1 337).

***Mrs. Dalloway* (1925)** Woolf's fourth novel is set on a single day in the middle of June in 1923 and weaves together several narrative perspectives. Clarissa DALLOWAY, who is preparing for a party she will give that evening to which the prime minister is coming, remembers her rejection of Peter WALSH's marriage proposal many years earlier at her parents' house at Bourton. Peter Walsh has just returned from India to attend to the legal affairs of his lover, DAISY, who is divorcing her husband to marry Peter. As Clarissa prepares for her party, she is surprised by a visit from Peter. Parallel to these strands of the narrative is

[12] Victor Luftig has pointed out that Mrs. Brown was only lightly sketched in the *Nation & Athenaeum* version of the essay, and he argues that Woolf was playing off the article that preceded hers, "The Leaflet Touch" by A. A. Milne, which was a critique of a Unionist party pamphlet in support of protectionism that employed a dialogue between two working-class women, Mrs. Jones and Mrs. Brown (VWM 27: 1–2).

the story of Septimus Warren SMITH, a shell-shocked soldier who is taken by his wife, Rezia (Lucrezia) Warren SMITH, to see Sir William BRADSHAW, a "nerve specialist," after Rezia is dissatisfied with her husband's treatment by Dr. HOLMES. At the end of the novel, Clarissa's party brings together all the significant people from the summer at Bourton more than thirty years earlier, including Sally SETON and Hugh WHITBREAD. The two main narrative strands converge at the party when Bradshaw mentions Septimus's suicide to the politician Richard DALLOWAY, Clarissa's husband, in connection with a parliamentary bill Richard is working on concerning the deferred effects of shell shock. Other significant characters in the novel include Elizabeth DALLOWAY and her tutor Doris KILMAN; separate entries on all these characters will provide further details about the novel.

Outline

Mrs. Dalloway is structured as twelve unnumbered sections (not apparent in the U.S. edition, which has omitted some of the space breaks found in the first English edition; sections are indicated by page numbers in the following outline). The novel opens (3–19) as Clarissa Dalloway prepares to leave her house to buy flowers for her party and recalls how she felt when she was eighteen at her parents' house at Bourton. Stepping out into the London street, she hears Big Ben strike the hour, the description of its "leaden circles" setting in motion a series of identical descriptions that reverberate throughout the novel. Clarissa is delighted to be out and about in the city. She runs into Hugh Whitbread, who tells her that his wife, Evelyn, is not well. Clarissa, walking on, remembers the people who were at Bourton the summer she refused to marry Peter Walsh and reflects on her own mortality. Thinking that she would like to buy a gift for Evelyn Whitbread, she pauses by the window of HATCHARDS', a bookstore in Piccadilly, and sees among the books there a work of William SHAKESPEARE's spread open. The lines she reads from Shakespeare's *CYMBELINE* will stay in her mind throughout the day and will also come to the mind of Septimus Warren Smith much later in the novel as he lies in his sitting room watching the play of light on the wall: "Fear no more the heat o' the sun / Nor the furious winter's rages" (*Cymbeline* IV:ii:259–60). Not seeing anything suitable for Evelyn, Clarissa goes on to Bond Street, thinking of how her daughter Elizabeth cares very little for shops and shopping. Clarissa is distressed at the influence wielded by the religious Miss Kilman over Elizabeth, but she reflects that her daughter probably cares more for her dog GRIZZLE than anything else. She stops at Mulberry's, a florist, to buy flowers for her party and is deciding what to buy when everyone is startled by a loud noise from a car in the street.

Outside (19–42) a car with drawn blinds has stopped, blocking the street. Rumors begin to fly about the identity of the important person in this car and, as he waits, Septimus Warren Smith feels that everyone is looking at him. His wife, Rezia, miserable because Septimus has threatened to kill himself, gently encourages him to move on. All around is the hum and buzz of speculation about who is in the car, which Clarissa joins as she leaves the florist thinking the Queen is probably the car's occupant. Thoughts of the recent war and of the British Empire circulate from the pubs of the back streets to clubs like Brook's in St. James's Street, where men in white waistcoats look down importantly on the throngs below them.

An airplane skywriting pulls everyone's attention toward it as they try to decipher what is being advertised. In Regent's Park, Rezia tries to interest Septimus in the airplane because Dr. Holmes has told her to try and distract her husband from his self-absorption. Septimus believes "they" are signaling to him from the skies; he feels his body is intimately connected with the trees in the park. As he begins to babble about the dead and sees his dead friend EVANS behind the park railings, Rezia despairs. The narrative passes through several consciousnesses—those of Maisie JOHNSON, Carrie DEMPSTER, a "seedy-looking nondescript man" on the steps of St. Paul's cathedral—as the airplane flies above them all, linking Septimus, Clarissa and passersby together in the reader's consciousness by their shared perception of this London scene.

Clarissa returns home (42–72) to find that her husband, Richard, has gone to lunch with Lady Millicent BRUTON. Feeling abandoned, Clarissa goes up to her room, where she has been sleeping alone since being ill. "There is an emptiness about the heart of life; an attic room" (45), comments the narrator, beginning a reflection on Clarissa's coldness, her lack of "something central which permeated" (46). Yet the narrator also describes the orgasmic sensations Clarissa experiences "yielding to the charm of a woman" (46). Clarissa's thoughts turn to her old friend Sally Seton, with whom she was once in love. She remembers "the most exquisite moment of her whole life" (52) when Sally kissed her, a moment that was interrupted by Peter Walsh. Still thinking of the past, Clarissa takes down the dress she plans to wear to her party that night as it needs mending. Thanking her servant LUCY, who offers to sew it for her, Clarissa takes her dress into her drawing room and settles down on the sofa.

Clarissa falls into a reverie induced by the rhythm of her sewing and the memory of the lines from

Cymbeline she had read that morning and is suddenly interrupted by the unexpected arrival of Peter Walsh. She has not read the letter in which he told her he would be back in London. Characteristically, he plays with his pocketknife as he questions her about her husband and daughter. Running beneath their conversation all the while is their shared memory of Clarissa's rejection of Peter's proposal of marriage. He has come to London to see his lawyers, as he has fallen in love with a woman named Daisy who must divorce her husband, a major in the Indian Army, so that she may marry Peter. When Elizabeth comes in, Peter leaves with Clarissa's call to remember her party lost in the roar of the traffic as he opens the front door.

Peter walks rather aimlessly through London (72–85), thinking of Clarissa and how she would not marry him. In Trafalgar Square he catches sight of a young woman and begins to follow her, fantasizing that she is aware of him, until she enters her house. He continues walking to Regent's Park, where he falls asleep and has a strange dream (85–88) of a solitary traveler and an elderly woman who seems "to be the figure of the mother whose sons have been killed in the battles of the world" (87).

Peter wakes with a start from his dream (88–97), thinking once more about being at Bourton with Clarissa and Sally Seton, and remembering the day he realized that Clarissa would marry Richard Dalloway (92). He also remembers the bitter last conversation he had with Clarissa that led to his abruptly leaving the house.

In the park (97–125), Rezia and Septimus are waiting until it is time for their appointment with Sir William Bradshaw. Septimus continues to murmur his theories and sees the dead walking in the park. He sees a man in gray walk toward him and thinks it must be Evans, but it is Peter, who feels sorry for this young couple, imagining that they are arguing about something. Reveling in a London he finds entirely changed in the five years he has been away in India, Peter thinks about how much he liked Sally Seton because she agreed with him that Hugh Whitbread was an ass. His thoughts about Richard Dalloway are interrupted by the song of an old woman standing opposite the entrance to the Regent's Park Tube station. Peter gives her some money and gets into a cab.

Waiting to cross the road with Septimus (125–42), Rezia feels sorry for the old woman singing of her lost love. The narrator tunnels into Septimus's past, explaining that he had gone to fight in France "to save an England which consisted almost entirely of Shakespeare's plays and Miss Isabel Pole in a green dress walking in a square" (130). In the war, Septimus's best friend Evans was killed but Septimus had shown no emotion. He became engaged to Rezia at the end of the war in Italy, because "he could not feel" (131). He is appalled at the world. Rezia has taken him to see Dr. Holmes on their landlady's advice, and Septimus wants to escape from Dr. Holmes.

In his Harley Street office (142–228), Sir William Bradshaw tells Rezia that he never uses the word mad; Bradshaw "called it not having a sense of proportion" (146). He tells her he will send Septimus to a "home" where he will "rest" and Rezia feels despair, sensing that Bradshaw will crush Septimus's spirit. The narrator describes the twin goddesses of Proportion and Conversion worshipped by Bradshaw (150–54). If people cannot be taught a sense of proportion, if they cannot be converted to Sir William's way of seeing the world, then he has "to support him police and the good of society" (154).

In Oxford Street Hugh Whitbread is on his way to lunch with Lady Bruton, where he and Richard Dalloway are to help her draft a letter on emigration to the editor of the *Times*. She tells them that Peter Walsh is back in London. Having performed their function, Hugh and Richard leave together and go into a jeweler's where Hugh self-importantly asks to see the manager as he wishes to buy his wife a gift. Leaving Hugh, who irritates him somewhat, Richard buys a huge bunch of roses to take home to Clarissa. He finds her in their drawing-room fretting over Elizabeth's being "closeted" with Miss Kilman, most likely praying. Elizabeth and Miss Kilman come down shortly thereafter and prepare to go out to the ARMY AND NAVY STORES.

After shopping, Kilman and Elizabeth have tea together, Elizabeth desperate to get away and be by herself. Eventually she does, leaving a bereft Kilman, and catches a bus in Victoria Street. In his sitting room, Septimus watches light play on the walls. Rezia is making a hat and for a moment they are happy, laughing and gossiping together. Rezia decides that she will not allow Septimus to be taken away from her; she will go with him. She gets up to go and pack their things, but hears the noise of someone coming up to their rooms. Hearing Rezia attempting to stop Dr. Holmes from coming up, Septimus throws himself out of the window to his death. Just before he jumps, Septimus sees an old man coming down the stairs in the house opposite who stares at him.

As he nears his hotel (229–50), Peter hears an ambulance go by and reflects on the advances of "civilization." He finds a letter from Clarissa waiting for him at the hotel and, after his dinner, walks to her house for the party.

Peter regrets having come (250–84) and feels out of place, while Clarissa herself thinks her party will be a failure. Unexpectedly, Sally Seton, now Lady

Rosseter, arrives, thus completing the gathering of those who had been together at Bourton more than thirty years earlier. The party gradually begins to go smoothly and the prime minister drops by. Clarissa is infuriated when Lady Bradshaw explains that she and her husband were late because a young man had killed himself. She withdraws to a room by herself and thinks about the young man, gradually coming to feel that his death is somehow significant to her. Across from her house, Clarissa sees an old woman going to bed. Clarissa feels conscious of Bradshaw's oppression and momentarily identifies with the young suicide whose name, of course, she does not know. She returns to her party.

Sally and Peter are sitting together on a sofa reminiscing (284–96). The party begins to break up and Clarissa comes over to where Peter has remained sitting, filled with "extraordinary excitement" (296) as he sees her there.

Genesis

Anticipating criticisms of *JACOB'S ROOM* on the eve of its publication in 1922, Woolf wrote in her DIARY that "if they say all this is clever experiment, I shall produce Mrs Dalloway in Bond Street as the finished product" (D2 178). During 1922, Woolf was working on the essays that she would publish in 1925 as *THE COMMON READER,* reading the second volume of Marcel PROUST's *Remembrance of Things Past,* and re-reading James JOYCE's *Ulysses.* In the fall of 1922, the short story "Mrs. Dalloway in Bond Street" (see *MRS. DALLOWAY'S PARTY*) "branched into a book" and Woolf began to think of the story as the first chapter of her new novel. She had also been sketching out a story called "The Prime Minister" in which the character who eventually became Septimus Warren Smith plots to assassinate the prime minister. She thought of using both these stories as part of a novel to be called "At Home: or The Party."

As Woolf explained in a preface she wrote for the Modern Library edition of *Mrs. Dalloway* published by Random House in 1928, her first conception of the novel involved only the character of Clarissa, who was either to commit suicide or otherwise die at the end of her party (when E. M. FORSTER first read the novel he thought that Clarissa did in fact die at the end—a curiously inattentive reading!). Woolf's first reference to Septimus Warren Smith occurs in her notebook dated October 16, 1922. In the fall of that year she began thinking differently about the scope of the novel: "I adumbrate here a study of insanity & suicide: the world seen by the sane & the insane side by side" (D2 207).

Woolf continued to work on several projects as she wrote what she was calling "The Hours" (other titles she considered for the novel in its early stages were "The Life of a Lady" and "A Lady of Fashion"). At the end of 1922 she re-read the *Odyssey* and began making her own annotated translation of the plays of Aeschylus; in 1923 she was reading for the essay "ON NOT KNOWING GREEK." (Harvena Richter says that in *Mrs. Dalloway* Woolf "specifically used the idea of a Greek chorus, if we are to take seriously certain notes she made while reading Aeschylus' *Choephori*" [Richter 139; see also RN 146–47]; in the final version of the novel "only the 'elderly grey nurse' and the sleeping child remain of the chorus" [Richter 139].)

A visit to Lady Ottoline MORRELL's home, Garsington, in June 1923 gave Woolf new ideas for the novel: "A loathing overcomes me of human beings—their insincerity. their vanity—A wearisome & rather defiling talk with Ott. last night is the foundation of this complaint. . . . I am a great deal interested suddenly in my book. I want to bring in the despicableness of people like Ott: I want to give the slipperiness of the soul" (D2 243–44). Soon after this, Woolf wrote in her diary, "I want to give life & death, sanity & insanity; I want to criticise the social system, & to show it at work, at its most intense" (D2 248).

Woolf began writing her play *FRESHWATER* during the summer of 1923. She was also setting the type for T. S. ELIOT's *Waste Land,* which he had read to her and a few others the previous year and which the HOGARTH PRESS was to publish. She sent Eliot some short stories for him to consider publishing in the *CRITERION,* but he did not. By 1924, Woolf was writing to Eliot that her novel was "getting too interwoven for a chapter broken off to be intelligible" (L3 106). The short piece "Mrs. Dalloway in Bond Street" was published in the New York periodical *DIAL* in July 1923.

Charles G. Hoffman* and Jacqueline Latham* have each described the way this story was transformed into the opening section of *Mrs. Dalloway.* Several critics have also commented on how the Clarissa of "Mrs. Dalloway in Bond Street" is portrayed in a much harsher light than the character in the novel. Lucio Ruotolo remarks that Clarissa is transformed between the story and the novel from an "object of social satire to an existential heroine" (*Interrupted* 99). Although the Clarissa of the short story does quote from the dirge from *Cymbeline,* the more significant literary allusion in "Mrs. Dalloway in Bond Street" is to Percy Bysshe SHELLEY's elegy for John KEATS, "Adonais" (which was what Clarissa in her first incarnation in *THE VOYAGE OUT* recited to Rachel VINRACE). Judith P. Saunders* sees the poem as a central structuring metaphor of the short story and traces how the line from the poem in Clarissa's mind, about the "contagion of the world's slow stain," becomes linked to her speculation that the girl waiting on her in the glove shop is menstruating (Saunders 45–50).

Woolf was concerned—as with nearly all her novels after *NIGHT AND DAY*—with the form of *Mrs. Dalloway.* "Suppose one can keep the quality of a sketch in a finished & composed work?" she wondered in 1924 (D2 312). She sent the proofs of *Mrs. Dalloway* to her friend Jacques RAVERAT, a painter with whom she had corresponded about the formal difficulties she faced in her prose. Woolf had felt Raverat understood what she was trying to do when he compared the necessary linearity of writing with what could be achieved in his own medium of paint (L3 136).

Woolf had, however, come up with a solution to her difficulties with form when she discovered in late 1923 "how I dig out beautiful caves behind my characters" (D2 263). Her "tunnelling process," as she called it (D2 272), she felt satisfied exactly her needs in creating character. "The idea is that the caves shall connect, & each comes to daylight at the present moment" (D2 263). Edward A. Hungerford* has linked Woolf's "tunnelling process" to the ideas she expressed in her foreword to *RECENT PAINTINGS BY VANESSA BELL* and in an essay of 1925, "Pictures" (M 173–78). In her diary, Woolf frequently describes her composition of *Mrs. Dalloway* in terms of mining, of, for example, digging out a "seam" of "gold" with a pick.

Nearing the end of the manuscript, Woolf worried that the "reviewers will say that it is disjointed because of the mad scenes not connecting with the Dalloway scenes" (D2 323). The "mad part" had made her mind "squint so badly" (D2 248) that she found it difficult to write. Working on the scene in Regent's Park (MD 97–106), she found the only way to go forward was "by clinging as tight to fact as I can" (D2 272). It was the complex relation between Septimus and Clarissa that proved most difficult to realize in the novel. Early in the book's composition, Woolf had been dissatisfied with the character of Clarissa. Although she thought "the design is more remarkable than in any of my books," she thought that the character of Clarissa "may be too stiff, too glittering & tinselly" (D2 272). As she struggled with the creation of one of the most famous of her characters, she also wrote the first version of her essay "MR. BENNETT AND MRS. BROWN," published in 1924; later that year she further developed her ideas on character in fiction when she gave a talk with that title to the HERETICS Society at Cambridge.

Mrs. Dalloway was written relatively quickly, something Woolf congratulated herself on as "a feat" (D2 308). In March 1923, John Middleton MURRY had written an article in the *NATION & ATHENAEUM* in which he said that the English novel as it was being written by Dorothy RICHARDSON, Katherine MANSFIELD and Woolf had "reached a kind of impasse" (D2 308; CH 109). As she finished *Mrs. Dalloway* Woolf wrote, "Anyhow, I feel that I have exorcised the spell wh. Murry & others said I had laid myself under after Jacob's Room" (D2 308). *Mrs. Dalloway* confirmed Woolf's belief that she was on the right track and that she should continue to explore the possibilities of fiction in just the way she had begun to do.

Mrs. Dalloway was published in Britain by the Hogarth Press on May 14, 1925 with a dust jacket designed by Vanessa BELL, and in the United States by Harcourt, Brace & Company on the same day, with the same dust jacket.

Background

Woolf wrote to Gwen RAVERAT after her husband Jacques's death that "you can't think what a raging furnace it is still to me—madness and doctors and being forced" (L3 180). There is a clear echo here of the disquiet Clarissa feels at the end of *Mrs. Dalloway* when she imagines how "this young man who had killed himself" had been treated by Sir William Bradshaw: the "great doctor" is, she thinks, "capable of some indescribable outrage—forcing your soul, that was it" (MD 281). Woolf's long experience with and distrust of doctors informs her depiction of Holmes and Bradshaw in the novel. Stephen Trombley points out specific features in Holmes and Bradshaw of four doctors who saw Woolf as a patient, but he says the two fictional doctors are essentially composite portraits of the four—Sir George SAVAGE, Sir Henry HEAD, Sir Maurice CRAIG and Dr. T. B. HYSLOP.

When Woolf was unwell in early 1922, she went to see Dr. Harrington Sainsbury, who, as she was leaving his office, said to her, "Equanimity—practise equanimity Mrs. Woolf" (D2 189). Leonard WOOLF, who was with her, recalls the scene in his autobiography and describes their "fairly long odyssey through Harley Street and Wimpole Street which gave us a curious view of medical science and the tiptop Harley Street specialists" (LW2 222). Having had three different opinions as to what was wrong with Woolf, they "decided to forget about it and about Harley Street. [Woolf] not only recovered from three fatal and incurable diseases; the disquieting symptoms gradually disappeared" (LW2 222). Sir William Bradshaw's office is on Harley Street, where the doctors who attend to the richest patients in London still practice.

In writing the "mad scenes" of *Mrs. Dalloway* Woolf was drawing on her own experience. Roger Poole describes Septimus as an "objective correlative" for what Woolf experienced in her breakdown of 1912–13 (*Unknown* 186). As many critics have pointed out, Septimus and Woolf share several characteristics in their unbalanced state, such as hearing the birds talk in Greek. While writing the novel, Woolf reflected in her diary on the "curious vision" she had had in her room, "seeing the sunlight quivering like gold water on the wall. I've heard the voices of the dead here" (D2 283).

In the novel, Septimus lies on his sofa "watching the watery gold glow and fade" on the wall (MD 211).

Septimus is suffering from shell shock, a term introduced to the public in 1922 when the *Report of the War Office Committee of Enquiry into "Shell-shock"* was presented to the British Parliament. The report, as Sue Thomas* has noted, was quoted extensively in the *Times* in August and September 1922. Septimus first appears as a character in Woolf's notes in October 1922. Bernard Blackstone,* an early commentator on Woolf, described the major theme of *Mrs. Dalloway* as "deferred war-shock," for Septimus is only the most acute example of the suffering inflicted by war on society. Thomas details the ways in which the War Office *Report* probably contributed to Woolf's conception of the doctors in her novel and especially to the "Proportion" and "Conversion" section (MD 150–52). Shell shock was to be dealt with by discipline and moral control, as Elaine Showalter* has described in her discussion of "Male Hysteria." Showalter points out that Siegfried SASSOON, who had suffered the "treatment" given those soldiers who objected to the war, visited Woolf in 1924. Woolf had reviewed his poems in 1917. In *Mrs. Dalloway,* Showalter writes, Woolf connects "the shell-shocked veteran with the repressed woman of the man-governed world through their common enemy, the nerve specialist" (Showalter 192). Showalter's detailed description of the medical establishment's treatment of soldiers during World War I and in the years immediately following it (e.g., Showalter 176–80) makes clear how precisely Septimus Warren Smith represents those thousands of veterans. In presenting Septimus as a major character Woolf was far ahead of her time as a novelist of war.

The postwar world of *Mrs. Dalloway* was also one in which the political scene was changing radically. When Richard Dalloway visits Lady Bruton (MD 156–70) we learn that she is preparing her family papers for him as he is planning to write a history of her family when "the time came; the Labour Government she meant" (MD 168). The Labour government, putting Conservative politicians like Richard out of power, had in fact come the year before *Mrs. Dalloway* was published, when, in January 1924, Ramsay MacDonald became England's first Labour prime minister. Another aspect of Lady Bruton's discomfort is the "news from India" (MD 168), which in 1923 would have concerned the agitations there for independence from British rule. For the novel's first English readers, its social and political world would have been extremely familiar. It was a world that, as Peter Walsh notices, had changed profoundly in the five years since the end of the war.

Mrs. Dalloway is also, obviously, a London novel. Woolf's love for and intimate knowledge of the city is an important aspect of the novel's background. Her characters' routes in the course of the day can and have been plotted exactly, and the topography of the novel—Big Ben, St. Margaret's, WHITEHALL, Westminster, PICCADILLY, Trafalgar Square—plays an important role in the social criticism in which the novel is rooted. One of many sights recorded in Woolf's diary from her own walks through London makes a significant contribution to *Mrs. Dalloway*: "An old beggar woman, blind, sat against a stone wall in Kingsway holding a brown mongrel in her arms & sang aloud. There was a recklessness about her; much in the spirit of London. Defiant" (D2 47). The "rusty pump," as which this woman is described in *Mrs. Dalloway* (122), had been recalled briefly, but in terms exactly matching the description in Woolf's diary, in *Jacob's Room* (JR 67). It is the setting of the novel in a particular city on a single June day that also has led many readers to compare *Mrs. Dalloway* with Joyce's *Ulysses,* which traces its characters' movements through another capital city, Dublin, on June 16, 1904.

The hostile Wyndham LEWIS called Woolf's novel "a sort of undergraduate imitation" of *Ulysses* in his attack on Woolf in *Men Without Art* (Bloom* 20), but Lewis's is a lone voice in contrast to the majority of readers who would probably agree with Avrom Fleishman that *Mrs. Dalloway* is the "first important work of the literary period initiated by *Ulysses*" (Fleishman 69). Several early critics found other influences at work, Jean Guiguet for example finding *Mrs. Dalloway* only superficially like *Ulysses* and determining that Woolf's use of interior monologue (see MODERNISM) is "far closer to Proust than to Joyce" (Guiguet 241). Mark Spilka thinks Woolf is closer to Dorothy Richardson, while James Hafley dismisses the idea of Joyce's influence altogether. More recent critics (e.g., Maria DiBattista* Suzette Henke,* William D. Jenkins,* Richard Pearce,* Harvena Richter,* Michael Seidl*) have been concerned less with influence and more with intertextuality, tracing the various ways in which *Mrs. Dalloway* is similar to and different from *Ulysses.* Elizabeth Abel,* for example, finds that *Mrs. Dalloway* both "recalls the structure of *Ulysses* . . . and offers a female counterpart to Joyce's adaptation of an epic form" ("Narrative" 96). John Mepham follows DiBattista in singling out "The Wandering Rocks" episode of *Ulysses* as a particular influence on *Mrs. Dalloway.* In her careful comparison of the two works, "The *Ulysses* Connection," Richter notes that Stephen, the name of Joyce's major character Stephen Daedalus, was an early name for Septimus in Woolf's notes, and that Woolf occasionally slips in her notebooks in calling Sally Seton Molly, a name made famous by Joyce's Molly Bloom.

Critical Responses

In several letters written soon after *Mrs. Dalloway* was published, Woolf comments on how divergent responses to the novel were and often seems to want to explain what her intentions had been. She wrote Gerald BRENAN in 1925 that "this I certainly did mean—that Septimus and Clarissa should be entirely dependent on each other" (L3 189), and she told Philip MORRELL, who had written to her that he felt she modeled her worst characters on him, that she "meant Richard Dalloway to be liked, Hugh Whitbread to be hated" (L3 195). To explain a novel after it was published was unusual for Woolf; she eventually took the unique step of writing a special preface to explain aspects of the novel for the Modern Library edition published by Random House in 1928.

Several contemporary reviewers emphasized Peter Walsh as the other main character with Clarissa, often seeing Septimus as an impediment (as Woolf had feared reviewers would). They also occasionally complained about the "method" of the novel, finding it distracting (CH 166). A sympathetic review in the New York *Saturday Review of Literature* by Richard Hughes drew comparisons with Paul Cézanne and noted that if "in *Jacob's Room* she suggested the simultaneousness of life, here she paints not only this but its stream-like continuity" (CH 159).

Mrs. Dalloway has held the attention of critics fairly consistently, however, and, with *TO THE LIGHTHOUSE*, has probably generated more commentary than any other of Woolf's fictions. Many critics regard the novel as Woolf's first mature work (e.g., Jean O. Love, *Worlds* 145) and "her first full-length attempt to center a novel entirely within various characters' consciousnesses" (Richter, *Inward* 47). Phyllis Rose sees *Mrs. Dalloway*, which she calls "perhaps the most schizophrenic of English novels" (Rose 125), as a natural development from the concerns of "A SOCIETY," "MODERN FICTION," and *Jacob's Room*, "which all, in varying degrees of outspokenness, mock the rigidity of masculine authority" (Rose 133). From a broader perspective, Abel regards the novel as a transitional work "between the straightforward narrative of an early novel like *The Voyage Out* and the experimental structure of a late work like *The Waves*" ("Narrative" 93).

In an effort to come to some total view of *Mrs. Dalloway* several critics have stressed the way in which Woolf's narrative technique seems to bind together all the novel's disparate elements in a unified whole that has the attributes of myth. To "overstress the negative social element" for such critics is to "warp the full meaning of the work" (Alice van Buren Kelley 88). "Here, for the first time, Virginia Woolf attempts to define the different aspects of fact and vision that compose the human universe, displaying each individual element or possible combination in separate symbolic characters" (van Buren Kelley 89). The novel's dual narrative has often led critics to see Septimus and Clarissa as symbolizing different worldviews: Howard Harper, for example, describes the "essential dialectical struggle" between "opposite adaptations to the world" (Harper 127) and Blanche H. Gelfant* sees in *Mrs. Dalloway* that "love and conversion are dramatized by a double apposition of characters" (88).

For some critics this duality is resolved in some version of a "myth of preexistent unity" (Love, *Worlds* 146): "The day of the novel is not a single day; instead it is a mythic symbol of timelessness" (Love, *Worlds* 147). Fleishman believes that Woolf's 1928 preface "has somewhat misled criticism into focusing on Clarissa and Septimus as a twin center, to the detriment of the novel's compelling unity" (Fleishman 80). As Fleishman notes, a considerable literature has been built up "on the varieties of polar significance to be accorded these characters" (Fleishman 80n10). Like many other readers, nevertheless, Fleishman believes that *Mrs. Dalloway* "expresses an opposition between two views of life that Woolf alternately entertained" (Fleishman 94): that "communication is health; communication is happiness" (MD 141; or, as Woolf put it in her essay on MONTAIGNE, "Communication is health; communication is truth; communication is happiness" [CR1 93]), or that "communication" is an illusion that we construct to protect ourselves from Septimus's thought that "the world itself is without meaning" (MD 133). Herbert Marder solves the difficulty by describing Woolf's method as "to hold two mutually exclusive views in mind at once and to believe in them both."

In contrast to these efforts to resolve the novel's contradictions are more recent critical readings such as those by Rachel Bowlby, Pamela Caughie, Makiko Minow-Pinkney and Ban Wang,* who offer readings of *Mrs. Dalloway* not as revealing "some metaphysical unity but how unity is perceived and contrived" (Caughie 75). For Wang, *Mrs. Dalloway* "seems to be a depiction of various disparate, monadic consciousnesses, isolated from each other and impossible to be unified into a spiritual community" (Wang 177). For many critics *Mrs. Dalloway* is an exploration of the "inmost recesses" of consciousness, but Wang points out that the very idea of a "private consciousness" depends upon an epistemology that denies the socially constructed nature of consciousness. In discussing the scene of the stalled car in Bond Street (MD 19–28), Wang illustrates how Woolf, "far from exploring the innermost recesses of the mind . . . exposes the factitious nature of discourse and the symbolic order" (Wang 181).

The beauty of Woolf's language gives the impression to many readers that *Mrs. Dalloway* "flows in one uninterrupted stream from first word to last" (Gelfant 96). Both Gelfant and Jean Wyatt* see the novel as a metaphoric ocean whose "rhythms . . . surge through the passages describing the loss of clear distinction between the self and the world" (Wyatt 121). The images of merging that abound in *Mrs. Dalloway* culminate in Clarissa's party, which for some readers is "a grand spiritual reunion" (Love, *Worlds* 147), a synthesis of many different people. Johanna X. K. Garvey* has described the water imagery in *Mrs. Dalloway* as transforming the traditionally masculine space of the city, and she sees Clarissa, Septimus and Peter as connected by water imagery. The water imagery "subverts the 'Selfsame,' flowing into the cracks of the symbolic order and infusing it with the semiotic" (Garvey 62). Susan Squier sees Clarissa's egalitarian vision to bring people together (MD 184–85) as arising from the urban environment itself that mingles all classes in its streets (Squier 96, 99). Others, such as Alex Zwerdling, have pointed out that Clarissa's vision does not merge people from different classes (Zwerdling 127).

A significant articulation of the novel as a kind of spiritual reunion is given by J. Hillis Miller,* who sees Woolf's narrative technique in *Mrs. Dalloway* as the equivalent of a ritual raising of the dead. The reader of *Mrs. Dalloway* is "plunged within an individual mind which is being understood from inside by an ubiquitous, all-knowing mind" (Miller, *Fiction* 179). Miller identifies the song sung by the old woman outside the Tube station (MD 122–24) as Richard Strauss's "Aller Seelen," the words of which, by Hermann von Gilm, tell of the one day each year on which the dead are freed. "Like Strauss's song, *Mrs. Dalloway* has the form of an All Souls' Day in which Peter Walsh, Sally Seton, and the rest rise from the dead to come to Clarissa's party" (Miller 190). This figure of the old woman—described by Sandra Gilbert and Susan Gubar as one of "a succession of female figures [in Woolf] whose ancient voices seem to endure from a time before the neat categories of culture restrained female energy" (*War* 250)—gives a "clue to the way the day of the action is to be seen as the occasion of a resurrection of ghosts from the past" (Miller, "Virginia Woolf's" 114).

On the day of the novel, the dead have risen also for Septimus, providing just one of the many links made between him and Clarissa. In her 1928 preface Woolf was explicit that Septimus was intended to be Clarissa's double (vi). Nancy Topping Bazin finds that both characters exhibit symptoms of manic-depression, though to different degrees (Bazin 103). She also draws attention to similarities in their thinking and the way both enjoy pattern and design. Both Clarissa and Septimus, "in different ways, exhibit the failure to feel" (Richter 118) and both have been seen variously as latent or repressed homosexuals. Henke points out that "the lesbian dimension of Sally's attraction is more overt in the manuscript version" of the novel ("Communion" 136). Woolf herself had linked the two characters in her notes, "Mrs D. seeing the sane truth, Septimus the insane truth." Henke sees Clarissa's "existential vision" as the "janus-image of Septimus Smith's 'mystical madness' " ("Communion" 134). "If Clarissa is a social artist of human relations," writes Henke, "Septimus is her *Doppelgänger*—the uncontrolled, demonic side of the creative imagination" (139). Beverly Ann Schlack* has argued that Septimus shares many characteristics with Daniel Paul Schreber, Sigmund FREUD's case history of whom ("Psycho-Analytic Notes upon an Autobiographical Account of a Case of Paranoia [Dementia Paranoides]") was published in James STRACHEY's translation by the Hogarth Press in 1925.

Apart from the bird imagery that Woolf uses to describe both Clarissa and Septimus, they are further linked by allusions to Shakespeare, each thinking of the line from *Cymbeline* that Clarissa reads in a bookstore window early in the novel, and each identifying particularly with a play of Shakespeare's. Clarissa recalls *Othello* and Septimus *Anthony and Cleopatra* at various moments during the day.

The dual narrative strands of the single day of the novel's action, carrying Septimus's story on the one hand and Clarissa's on the other, have evoked a critical focus on the way Woolf effects transitions in the novel and conveys a sense that her characters belong to one world. The narrative technique of the novel seems to lend itself to diagramming, as many critics have drawn schema of either the novel's action or the movements of consciousness within it. Bazin, for example, enumerates the "connecting" devices—the car, the airplane, the bus that Elizabeth rides on and that Septimus sees dappled with sunlight, the ambulance carrying Septimus's body and the bell of which Peter Walsh hears, the child in the park, the old woman singing, Big Ben striking—and draws a diagram of the way the narrative moves between characters around these points (Bazin 114–15); diagrams are also found in Josephine O'Brien Schaefer's *Three-fold Nature of Reality,* in Roger Poole's *The Unknown Virginia Woolf,* and in David Daiches (Bloom 31, 32). Varying this theme somewhat, Richter sees links not between the objects but between the emotions those objects evoke in those who perceive them (*Inward* 53).

Another aspect of this attention to the book's structure is seen in the work of several critics who have traced out exactly the routes by which various characters traverse the city, sometimes yielding provocative insights such as the fact that Peter Walsh follows the young woman, after he has left Clarissa's house, up the aptly named Cockspur Street. Most useful is a map, "The London of Mrs. Dalloway," that Morris Beja drew and on which he has marked twenty-one points in the narrative (VWM 7:4; and see VWM 9:3 for "footnotes" to the map); Jean Moorcroft Wilson is also an enlightened source of information on the London of *Mrs. Dalloway.* The details of place contribute to the novel's social critique, as Reginald Abbott* has recently discussed in an article on the consumer culture of London represented by the novel's various shopping expeditions.

Street scenes also serve a narrative function, juxtaposing Septimus, Peter and Clarissa so that readers "must consider their interrelatedness, must connect (if only momentarily) what would otherwise remain disconnected" (Squier 120). In a novel often described as "palimpsestic" (Abel, "Narrative" 93) or "laminated," readers sometimes have difficulty in seeing just how Woolf has moved between one consciousness and another, and this has led to an emphasis in critical readings of the novel on Woolf's style and language.

Reuben Brower described the "interconnectedness of the entire novel" (52), articulating a dominant theme in various assessments of the work that have tried to see it as a whole. He wrote that Woolf's imagination was "Shakespearean" in that her "most characteristic metaphors are purely symbolic" (Brower 277). In *Mrs. Dalloway* Woolf uses repeated words and phrases so that they accrue symbolic weight as they are used in various contexts throughout the narrative. Mark Hussey (*Singing*) has described Woolf's use of "descriptive homology" as a method in which she encodes a way of reading her fiction in the fictional structure itself; Clarissa's sewing or Rezia's hat-making are metaphors of how the novel should be read, in effect, by pulling together various parts in the reader's memory. Richter comments on Woolf's use of symbols that she "gathers around those vague yet powerful symbols the secondary images which explain and expand it, giving us not only a state of mind but also the impression of a lifetime" (Richter, *Inward* 201).

Further complicating the novel's interconnecting "tunnels" of consciousness, Woolf has also encoded "her developmental plot through characters who subtly reflect Clarissa's experience," according to Abel ("Narrative" 106). Rezia, for example, like Clarissa "is plucked by marriage from an Edenic female world with which she preserves no contact" (Abel 107). Other instances of Woolf's use of the *Doppelgänger* include Doris Kilman as Clarissa's double "distanced by poverty and a superior education" (Marcus, *Art* 68). Kenneth Moon* sees the relationship between Elizabeth Dalloway and Kilman as "providing insight into the sexual nature of the earlier Clarissa-Sally one" (151).

It is, of course, primarily in the linking of Septimus and Clarissa that Woolf's use of the doubling device is most elaborately displayed. Robert Kiely* remarks that "without the intervention of Dickensian coincidence or secret blood ties, a kinship deeper than words and stronger than social classification is shown to exist between" the two characters (139). In this "war-haunted" novel (Gilbert and Gubar, *Sexchanges* 315), however, perhaps the most profound bond between Septimus and Clarissa should be understood as what Masami Usui* calls "a common sense of victimization by the war and by patriarchal values" (151).

The years 1918 to 1923 were "years in which the experiences of the Great War were absorbed into people's lives. But some of these experiences remained unassimilable, social blemishes that deface the summer scene" (O'Brien Schaefer,* "The Great War" 144). Increasingly in the last two decades, the social critique of *Mrs. Dalloway,* the intent of which Woolf had been quite clear about in her diary, has been brought into the foreground of discussion of the novel. *Mrs. Dalloway* "explores the roots of war and sexual oppression in the sexually polarized society of early modern London" (Squier 93), calling into question the division between the "public" world of men and the "private" world of women. Squier sees Peter and Clarissa as enacting this dichotomy, and Septimus as demonstrating its "tragic flaw—that such polarized sex roles and limitations on female activity and male passivity breed military aggression" (Squier 110). Zwerdling sees the characters of *Mrs. Dalloway* as ranged on a continuum, with Sir William Bradshaw at one end, the most extreme defender of the established order, and Septimus at the other. Clarissa is a "pivot" at the center of this conflict (130).

Bringing together the novel's political and mythic themes, Henke describes *Mrs. Dalloway* as a socialist and feminist critique of patriarchy, a social satire that derives "much of its force from ironic patterns of mythic reference that allow the fusion of dramatic models from Greek tragedy and from the Christian liturgy" ("Communion" 125). At the heart of both the Greek and Christian narratives, Henke points out, is the figure of the scapegoat, and it is as a scapegoat that Septimus sees himself and is seen by Clarissa: "She had once thrown a shilling into the Serpentine, never anything more. But he had flung it away. They went on living" (MD 280).

A key essay on the politics of *Mrs. Dalloway* is that by Lee R. Edwards,* who acknowledges the focus on individual isolation in the novel but sees that topic as set within a larger sociopolitical framework (99). Just as Woolf herself did, Edwards questions the conventional definition of politics: the standard definition is in terms of "precisely those qualities Virginia Woolf denounces or is at least skeptical about" (101). Edwards points out that while critics have generally agreed that *Mrs. Dalloway* is a great work, they have often overlooked the scope of the novel (Edwards 102). Summing up Woolf's achievement in *Mrs. Dalloway,* Edwards writes, "we damn ourselves if in constructing a view of the world we deny a connection between politics and feelings or values, and so create a politics lacking both beauty and joy" (111).

Adaptations

"Mrs. Dalloway," a chamber opera by Libby Larsen, libretto by Bonnie Grice, premiered July 22, 1993 by Lyric Opera Cleveland. Sopranos Mary Elizabeth Poore (Clarissa) and Fontaine Follansbee (Rezia), tenor Gary Briggle (Septimus), and baritone Richard Lewis (Peter Walsh) performed. A "reading" of David Bucknam and Lisa Peterson's oratorio "Mrs. Dalloway" was given in June 1991 at Pace University: Randy Danson (Clarissa), Claudine Cassan-Jellison (Mrs. Coates), Alan Heinberg (Septimus), Alma Cuervo (Mrs. Dempster), Theresa McCarthy (Lucrezia), John Jellison (Mr. Bowley) and Jennifer Rosin (Maisie Johnson) performed.

***Works Specific to This Entry:**

Abbott, Reginald. "What Miss Kilman's Petticoat Means: Virginia Woolf, Shopping, and Spectacle." *Modern Fiction Studies* 38, 1 (Spring 1992): 193–216.

Abel, Elizabeth. "Narrative Structure(s) and Female Development: The Case of *Mrs. Dalloway.*" In Margaret Homans, ed. *Virginia Woolf*: 93–114.

Blackstone, Bernard. *Virginia Woolf: A Commentary.* London: Hogarth Press, 1949.

Bloom, Harold, ed. *Clarissa Dalloway.* Major Literary Characters Series. New York: Chelsea House, 1990.

Brower, Reuben Arthur. "Something Central Which Permeated: Virginia Woolf and *Mrs. Dalloway.*" In *The Fields of Light: An Experiment in Critical Reading.* New York: Oxford University Press, 1951: 123–37. (Cited from Eleanor McNees 3: 276–86.)

DiBattista, Maria. "Joyce, Woolf, and the Modern Mind." In Patricia Clements and Isobel Grundy, eds. *Virginia Woolf*: 96–114.

Edwards, Lee R. "War and Roses: The Politics of *Mrs. Dalloway.*" In Arlyn Diamond and Lee R. Edwards, eds. *The Authority of Experience: Essays in Feminist Criticism.* Amherst: University of Massachusetts Press, 1977: 161–77. (Cited from Harold Bloom, ed. *Clarissa Dalloway.*)

Garvey, Johanna X. K. "Difference and Continuity: The Voices of *Mrs. Dalloway.*" *College English* 53, 1 (January 1991): 59–76.

Gelfant, Blanche H. "Love and Conversion in *Mrs. Dalloway.*" *Criticism* 8, 3 (Summer 1966): 299–45. (Cited from Harold Bloom, ed. *Clarissa Dalloway.*)

Henke, Suzette A. "Virginia Woolf Reads James Joyce." In Morris Beja, Phillip Herring, et al, eds. *James Joyce: The Centennial Symposium.* Urbana: University of Illinois Press, 1986: 39–42.

———."*Mrs. Dalloway*: The Communion of Saints." In Jane Marcus, ed. *New Feminist Essays*: 125–47.

Hoffmann, Charles G. "From Short Story to Novel: The Manuscript Revisions of Virginia Woolf's *Mrs. Dalloway.*" *Modern Fiction Studies* 14, 2 (Summer 1968): 171–86.

Hungerford, Edward A. " 'My Tunnelling Process': The Method of *Mrs. Dalloway.*" *Modern Fiction Studies* 3, 2 (Summer 1957): 164–67. (Cited from Harold Bloom, ed. *Clarissa Dalloway.*)

Jenkins, William D. "Virginia Woolf and the Belittling of *Ulysses.*" *James Joyce Quarterly* 25, 4 (1988): 513–19.

Kiely, Robert. "A Long Event of Perpetual Change." From Robert Kiely, *Beyond Egotism*: 119–30. (Cited from Harold Bloom, ed. *Clarissa Dalloway.*)

Latham, Jacqueline. "The Manuscript Revisions of Virginia Woolf's *Mrs. Dalloway*: A Postscript." *Modern Fiction Studies* 18, 2 (Summer 1972): 475–76.

Miller, J. Hillis. *Fiction and Repetition: Seven English Novels.* Cambridge, Mass.: Harvard University Press, 1982.

———."Virginia Woolf's All Souls' Day: The Omniscient Narrator in *Mrs. Dalloway.*" In M. Friedman and J. Vickery, eds. *The Shaken Realist: Essays in Honor of F. J. Hoffman.* Baton Rouge: Louisiana State University Press, 1970: 100–27.

Moon, Kenneth. "Where is Clarissa? Doris Kilman in *Mrs. Dalloway.*" *CLA Journal* 23, 3 (March 1980): 273–86. (Cited from Harold Bloom, ed. *Clarissa Dalloway.*)

Pearce, Richard. "Who Comes First, Joyce or Woolf?" In Vara Neverow-Turk and Mark Hussey, eds. *Virginia Woolf: Themes and Variations*: 59–67.

Richter, Harvena. "The *Ulysses* Connection: Clarissa Dalloway's Bloomsday." *Studies in the Novel* 21, 3 (1989): 305–19.

Saunders, Judith P. "Mortal Stain: Literary Allusion and Female Sexuality in 'Mrs. Dalloway in Bond Street.' " *Studies in Short Fiction* 15, 2 (Spring 1978): 139–44. (Cited from Harold Bloom, ed. *Clarissa Dalloway.*)

Schaefer, Josephine O'Brien. "The Great War and 'This Late Age of World's Experience' in Cather and Woolf." In Mark Hussey, ed. *Virginia Woolf and War*: 134–50.

Schlack, Beverly Ann. "A Freudian Look at Mrs. Dalloway." *Literature and Psychology* 23 (1973): 49–58.

Seidl, Michael. "The Pathology of the Everyday: Uses of Madness in *Mrs. Dalloway* and *Ulysses.*" In Vara Neverow-Turk and Mark Hussey, eds. *Virginia Woolf: Themes and Variations*: 52–59.

Showalter, Elaine. *The Female Malady: Women, Madness, and English Culture 1830–1980.* New York: Pantheon, 1985.

Thomas, Sue. "Virginia Woolf's Septimus Smith and Contemporary Perceptions of Shell Shock." *English Language Notes* 25, 2 (December 1987): 49–57.

Usui, Masami. "The Female Victims of the War in *Mrs. Dalloway.*" In Mark Hussey, ed. *Virginia Woolf and War*: 151–63.

Wang, Ban. " 'I' on the Run: Crisis of Identity in

Mrs. Dalloway." *Modern Fiction Studies* 38, 1 (Spring 1992): 177–91.

Wyatt, Jean. "Avoiding Self-Definition: In Defense of Women's Right to Merge (Julia Kristeva and *Mrs. Dalloway*)." *Women's Studies* 13 (1986): 115–26.

"Mrs. Dalloway in Bond Street." See *MRS. DALLOWAY'S PARTY.*

Mrs. Dalloway's Party Subtitled "A Short Story Sequence by Virginia Woolf," this collection of seven sketches was edited by Stella McNichol and published by the HOGARTH PRESS and Harcourt Brace Jovanovich in 1973. Versions of the seven pieces are also included in *The Complete Shorter Fiction of Virginia Woolf*: "Ancestors" (SF 175–77); "A Summing Up" (SF 202–05); "The Introduction" (SF 178–82); "The Man Who Loved His Kind" (SF 189–94); "Mrs. Dalloway in Bond Street" (SF 146–53); "The New Dress" (SF 164–71); and "Together and Apart" (SF 183–88). All the pieces bear some relation to *MRS. DALLOWAY* and various drafts of them exist in Woolf's third holograph notebook for *JACOB'S ROOM,* in papers in the BERG COLLECTION, and in the MONK'S HOUSE PAPERS. McNichol's editing of the seven pieces into a sequence was sharply criticized by John F. Hulcoop in the *VIRGINIA WOOLF MISCELLANY* (3: 3–4 and 7) in 1975. Writing as "an informed reader, stunned by the mutilated texts of Woolf's two sketches," Hulcoop particularly criticized McNichol's apparent rewriting of "Ancestors" and "The Introduction." In 1977, however, McNichol replied to Hulcoop's criticisms (VWM 9: 3) and pointed out that she had in fact been working from a text of "The Introduction" that Woolf herself had revised, but had not been permitted by Woolf's literary executors to disclose the text's whereabouts (it is in the Monk's House Papers).

"Mrs. Dalloway in Bond Street" bears the closest relation to *Mrs. Dalloway* and was intended by Woolf to be the first chapter of a novel, "to be called, perhaps, At Home: or the Party," that she began thinking about after *Jacob's Room.* The story was published in *DIAL,* a New York magazine, in July 1923. "The Man Who Loved His Kind" was published in *A HAUNTED HOUSE.* "The Introduction" appeared in the *Sunday Times* magazine in England in 1973, illustrated by Duncan GRANT. "Ancestors," listed in Woolf's 1922 manuscript notebook as the third chapter of her projected novel, exists only as a holograph draft, except for the first page, which is typed (SF 297). "Together and Apart," originally called "The Conversation," was published in *A Haunted House.* "The New Dress" is also in *A Haunted House* and was published in the New York magazine *Forum* in May 1927. "A Summing Up" was published in *A Haunted House.*

A one-woman play, "The Party," based on four of the pieces in *Mrs. Dalloway's Party,* written by Ellen McLaughlin and performed by Kathleen Chalfant, premiered in Los Angeles in 1990.

Mucklebackit Family name of characters in Sir Walter SCOTT'S *THE ANTIQUARY,* which Mr. RAMSAY reads in section XIX of part 1 of *TO THE LIGHTHOUSE.*

Murgatroyd, Evelyn Character in *THE VOYAGE OUT.* She has had many proposals of marriage but no man ever lives up to her ideal of the hero, and she leaves many bewildered men in her wake in the course of the novel. She longs to be a revolutionary, wishing she could have been married to Giuseppe GARIBALDI and planning at the end of the novel to travel on to Moscow and join the revolution against the Russian government. She explains to both Terence HEWET and to Rachel VINRACE that she is "the daughter of a mother and no father" (TVO 190), meaning that her parents—whose photographs she carries in a double frame—were not married. On SANTA MARINA, she becomes involved with Raymond OLIVER, Alfred PERROTT and a man named SINCLAIR, who threatens to shoot himself if Evelyn will not marry him. She tells Rachel that she belongs to the SATURDAY CLUB in London and is determined on her return to make the Club more political.

Isobel Grundy has discussed the significance of Evelyn's name, remarking that she has "a surname which (despite its homely significance of 'Margaret's clearing') suggests a moustachioed villain of Victorian melodrama, and a Christian name which, for readers of [Frances BURNEY'S *Evelina*], encapsulates a sentimental story of a heroine whose wronged mother is dead and whose rich and unapproachable father at the very last relents and owns his daughter's legitimacy" ("Words" 213–14).

Murry, John Middleton (1889–1957) Critic, editor and poet who met Katherine MANSFIELD in 1911 and married her in 1918. They were friends of D. H. LAWRENCE and regular guests of Lady Ottoline MORRELL'S at GARSINGTON. In 1913, Sydney WATERLOW, Mansfield's second cousin, introduced them to the Woolfs (in 1921 Leonard WOOLF wrote to Ralph PARTRIDGE that he was "on the point of quarrelling with my old friend Sydney Waterlow because I do not like Middleton Murry" [Spotts 281]). Murry's poem *The Critic in Judgment* was published by the HOGARTH PRESS in 1919. From 1919 to 1921 Murry was editor of the *ATHENAEUM,* in which he published Woolf's story "SOLID OBJECTS" in 1920. In 1923 Murry founded the *Adelphi,* where in 1926 he described both *JACOB'S ROOM* and T. S. ELIOT'S *Waste Land* as "failures" (D3 58). Woolf considered Murry a central figure in the "underworld" of literary journalism.

Among his many books are: *Dostoevsky: A Critical Study* (1916), *Countries of the Mind* (1922), *The Problem of Style* (1922), *Keats and Shakespeare* (1925), *Son of Woman, The Story of D. H. Lawrence* (1931), *The Life of Katherine Mansfield* (1933) and *William Blake* (1933).

"Mysterious Case of Miss V., The" (SF 30–32) A brief, unpublished fiction by Woolf that Susan Dick dates to 1906 as it was written on the same kind of paper and with the same kind of pen as "THE JOURNAL OF MISTRESS JOAN MARTYN" and "PHYLLIS AND ROSAMOND" (SF 289).

N

Narrated Monologue See MODERNISM.

"Narrow Bridge of Art, The" (CE2 218–229; GR 11–23) An essay by Woolf originally published in the *New York Herald Tribune* (August 14, 1927) under the title "Poetry, Fiction, and the Future." Woolf first gave the paper as a lecture on May 18, 1927 at Oxford University, where she was accompanied by Vita SACKVILLE-WEST. She wrote to Vanessa BELL that the students there were "callow" and "years behind the Cambridge young;" they asked her "innocent questions about Joyce" (L3 380).

"The Narrow Bridge of Art" is one of several essays Woolf wrote that established her as a leading advocate of the primacy of the modern novel as a genre. She begins by saying that critics usually look only to the past, leaving contemporary writing to reviewers; but no one looks to the future. Poetry fails to serve the needs of the "modern mind." People now live sealed off from life in brick boxes, connected by technological means of communication, and this has led to the "ordinary person" being "calmer, smoother, more self-contained than he used to be." Woolf's vision of the novel of the future in this essay sounds remarkably like a blueprint for her own last novel, *BETWEEN THE ACTS* (although it has also been read by some critics as a description of *THE WAVES*): "It will have something of the exaltation of poetry, but much of the ordinariness of prose. It will be dramatic, and yet not a play" (CE2 224). Prose, she continues, is now elastic enough to do all that other genres did in the past but prose writers must extend the scope of their interest to dramatize the "extraordinary number of perceptions which have not yet been expressed" (CE2 229) and move away from an excessive concern with psychology to pay attention to the impersonal aspects of the world.

Nation & Athenaeum Created in 1921 when *The Nation* absorbed the *ATHENAEUM*. It was edited by H. W. Massingham (1860–1924), who had edited *The Nation* since 1907.[13] When he began to move the periodical from a Liberal to a Labour stance, its owners, the Rowntree Trust, sold it to a consortium headed by John Maynard KEYNES. Leonard WOOLF became literary editor under Hubert Henderson in 1923, remaining in that post until 1931 when the *Nation & Athenaeum* merged with the *NEW STATESMAN* to become the *NEW STATESMAN AND NATION*. Leonard commissioned many of his friends and younger protégés to write for the *Nation & Athenaeum* and Woolf contributed many articles and reviews to it.

National Gallery After PERCIVAL's death in *THE WAVES,* Bernard consoles himself with a visit to the Italian Room of the National Gallery (TW 157), which is on Trafalgar Square in London and houses the national art collection.

National Review A right-wing political journal owned and edited by Leopold Maxse, husband of Kitty MAXSE. Woolf contributed "Street Music" to it in 1905 (E1 27–32).

Neale, Mrs. Character in *BETWEEN THE ACTS*. She runs the post office in Mrs. MANRESA's village (107).

Neo-Pagans Term used by Woolf, Vanessa BELL and other BLOOMSBURY GROUP members to describe a younger generation of friends, most of whom had been at Cambridge University, and which included Rupert BROOKE, Katherine COX, Rachel and Karin COSTELLOE, Gwen RAVERAT (née Darwin), Geoffrey KEYNES, Gerald Shove and others (see QB1 172–74).

Neville One of the six soliloquists in *THE WAVES*. An earlier name for Neville was Jasper (the name of one of the children in *TO THE LIGHTHOUSE,* Jasper RAMSAY). Various sources have been suggested for the homosexual and scholarly Neville, including John Maynard KEYNES (whose father's middle name was Neville [Haule "Introduction"]) and Lytton STRA-

[13] As "Wayfarer," Massingham wrote a column in *The Nation* on July 10, 1920 on the Plumage Bill that Woolf responded to with an article in the *Woman's Leader* (E3 241–45). The bill concerned the importation of egret feathers with which fashionable women decorated their hats, and Woolf's article attacked the torture of birds for the purposes of female adornment.

CHEY (Gordon 125). Alice van Buren Kelley places Neville in Woolf's "family of fact-driven men," among whom she includes St. John HIRST, Mr. HILBERY, Peter WALSH and Mr. RAMSAY (van Buren Kelley 154).

Described by LOUIS as the son of a gentleman, Neville is the only one of the three writers in *The Waves* who (apparently) publishes and wins some fame for his writing (Graham, "Manuscript" 315). He spends a solitary life, focused always on a single lover, having decided as a child that "there are distinctions, there are differences in this world" (TW 21), a sense of order which he appreciates. When still young, Neville knows "how to imitate Pope, Dryden, even Shakespeare" and reads CATULLUS aloud (TW 48), understanding that this sets him apart from others (TW 70–71). Even earlier, he anticipates becoming a classical scholar, exploring the writing of Virgil, Lucretius and Catullus. As a child, Neville was transfixed by the story of a dead man found in the gutter, a death he associates with the apple trees by which he found himself in the garden the night he heard about the man's death. The "immitigable" tree of death is a motif in Neville's soliloquies and is also an image that appears in Woolf's memoir "A SKETCH OF THE PAST" associated with her having overheard her parents talk about a man they knew who had committed suicide (MOB 71). A withered tree as an emblem of death is also found in *NIGHT AND DAY* and *THE YEARS*.

Newcastle, Margaret of See CAVENDISH, Margaret.

"New Dress, The" See *MRS. DALLOWAY'S PARTY*.

Newnham College In October 1928, Woolf drove to Cambridge with Leonard WOOLF, her sister Vanessa BELL and her niece Angelica GARNETT to deliver a paper to the Arts Society at Newnham College, one of the two papers on which she would base *A ROOM OF ONE'S OWN*. They stayed with Pernel STRACHEY, the principal of the College.

Newnham College developed from the work of Anne Jemima CLOUGH, who was born in Liverpool in 1820 and spent much of her childhood in America (Ray Strachey, *The Cause* 149). Having opened several small schools, Clough in 1866 began to try to establish a lecture series for women. She had met many of the pioneers of higher education for women, including the founder of GIRTON COLLEGE, Emily Davies, and was one of the twenty-five women who attended the first meeting of Davies's Schoolmistresses' Association. In 1871, Henry SIDGWICK persuaded Clough to preside over a house in which five female students were living. This group, under Clough's supervision, grew until in 1874 Newnham College was built to house the women.

New Republic Weekly which became the principal publisher of Woolf's essays and reviews in America, beginning with "To Spain" in 1923 and ending with "THOUGHTS ON PEACE IN AN AIR RAID" in 1940.

New Signatures See SPENDER, Stephen.

New Statesman Political weekly founded by Beatrice and Sidney WEBB and others in 1913. Desmond MACCARTHY became its literary editor in 1920 and contributed a column titled "Books in General" with the byline Affable Hawk (See D2 Appendix III). Woolf contributed several reviews. In 1931 it merged with the *NATION & ATHENAEUM* to become the *NEW STATESMAN AND NATION*.

New Statesman and Nation Created by the merger of the *NATION & ATHENAEUM* with the *NEW STATESMAN* in 1931 and edited until 1960 by Kingsley MARTIN. David GARNETT was Literary Editor. Woolf contributed several articles and reviews.

Nicolson, Benedict Lionel (1914–78) Eldest son of Harold NICOLSON and Vita SACKVILLE-WEST. An art historian, he was deputy surveyor of the King's pictures under Sir Kenneth Clark and became editor of the *Burlington* magazine, founded by Roger FRY and others in 1903. He offered assistance to Woolf in the early stages of her writing *ROGER FRY*, a work that he criticized when it was published. Woolf's replies to Ben's "quarrel" with the BLOOMSBURY GROUP and criticism of Fry (L6 413 and 419–21) offer a careful defense of her friends and herself.

Nicolson, Sir Harold (1886–1968) Diplomat and writer who married Vita SACKVILLE-WEST in 1913. His *Diaries and Letters* were edited in three volumes by his son Nigel NICOLSON, who also discusses his parents' relationship in *PORTRAIT OF A MARRIAGE*. Nicolson's role in *ORLANDO*, Woolf's fantastic "biography" of Vita, is that of Marmaduke Bonthrop SHELMERDINE. Like Shelmerdine, Nicolson was frequently away from home and had sailed round Cape Horn; in 1920 he flew from Paris and landed in the park at KNOLE.

His first book was *Paul Verlaine* (1920), and among his others are the novel *Sweet Waters* (1921); *Peacemaking* (1933), an account of his role in the British Delegation to the Paris Peace Conference after World War I in 1919; *Diplomacy* (1939); and several biographies, including *Tennyson* (1923), *Byron, the Last Journey* (1924) and *Swinburne* (1926). Woolf reviewed Nicolson's *Some People* in 1927 ("The New Biography" CE4 229–35; GR 149–54; and see Virginia WOOLF).

When Vita met him in 1910, Nicolson was already embarked on a career in the Foreign Service that took him to the legation in Teheran in 1925 (see *PASSENGER TO TEHERAN*) and to the British Embassy in Berlin in 1927. Vita was not interested in politics, however, and loathed being referred to as "Mrs. Harold Nicolson." Although both she and Nicolson—whom she called "Hadji"—had many homosexual affairs, they did not like being apart, and in 1929 Nicolson gave up the Foreign Service to write full-time. He returned to politics in 1935 when he was elected to Parliament as the Labour member for West Leicester, and he later became governor of the British Broadcasting Corporation.

Nicolson, Nigel (b. 1917) Younger son of Harold NICOLSON and Vita SACKVILLE-WEST and co-editor of Woolf's LETTERS. In 1962, he discovered a manuscript of his mother's telling the story of her affair with Violet TREFUSIS, which he edited and to which he added chapters discussing his parents' marriage, published as *PORTRAIT OF A MARRIAGE* in 1973. He is a co-founder of the publishing house Weidenfeld and Nicolson, was a member of Parliament for seven years, and has written books on military history and English houses.

"Niece of an Earl, The" (CE1 219–23; CR2 214–19) An essay by Woolf in *Life and Letters* (October 1928), a magazine edited by Desmond MACCARTHY. Woolf writes that English fiction would be unrecognizable without class distinctions, without the nieces of earls and the cousins of generals. Society is a "nest of glass boxes" which keep one class separate from another and determine that we can only know intimately those of our own class. This means that fiction cannot give insight into the highest or lowest classes as those classes do not write about themselves. If a working-class man is educated enough to write, he can no longer properly be called working-class. Woolf says that although the middle class may look homogeneous, it is in fact streaked with all kinds of variety. English fiction depends upon class difference for its comedy; without class, English novels would be more like Russian fiction, concerned with the immensities of the soul. The essay ends with the speculation that in a classless society of the future the novel may well be unrecognizable, demonstrating Woolf's belief in the political nature of aesthetics. She looks forward to the "art of a truly democratic age" (CE1 223) but cannot describe it.

***Night and Day* (1919)** Woolf's second (and longest) novel was published in 1919 by her half-brother Gerald DUCKWORTH's publishing house Duckworth & Company, and in 1920 in the United States by George H. Doran Company. *Night and Day* is dedicated to Woolf's sister Vanessa BELL. It is a comic novel of manners concerning five young people struggling

The Common Reader: Second Series. *Courtesy Linda J. Langham.*
Vanessa Bell designed the dust jacket for this Hogarth Press first edition (1932).

with issues of love and work, engagement and marriage, in London in the early years of the twentieth century as the Edwardian generation Woolf herself belonged to sought to escape the social and moral strictures of their parents' Victorian world. *Night and Day* is the most linear and "plotted" of Woolf's novels, developing its thirty-four chapters smoothly as the characters move toward resolution.

Outline

Chapter I: On a Sunday evening in October, Katharine HILBERY pours tea for her parents at their house in Cheyne Walk. Among Trevor and Margaret HILBERY's guests are Mr. FORTESCUE, "the eminent novelist," and Ralph DENHAM, a young lawyer who has been commissioned by Mr. Hilbery to write for the *Critical Review* which he edits. Ralph is irritated by the snobbish discussion of Manchester and Katharine senses that he does not like her or her family. At the suggestion of Mrs. Hilbery, Katharine dutifully shows Ralph the family "relics" of her grandfather, the famous poet Richard ALARDYCE. In the little chamber separated from the drawing room by a velvet curtain, Ralph and Katharine discuss families.

Chapter II: Ralph returns home to Highgate, where he lives with his large family, and goes straight to his room. His sister Joan DENHAM comes up to discuss their younger brother Charles, who has been offered a job by their Uncle Joseph. The Denhams' somewhat straitened financial circumstances, the father having died, make it impossible for Charles to go to university.

Chapter III: The Hilberys are one of a network of families similar to Woolf's own, the "intellectual aristocracy" of England. Katharine has grown up with great men of letters as constant visitors to her parents' house and a mother and aunts who speak of William SHAKESPEARE as if he were a personal friend. Katharine is a "member of a very great profession"—daughters living at home, sacrificed to the demands of their families. She is assisting her mother on a biography of Richard Alardyce that will never be written and secretly harbors a passion for mathematics. Katharine hides her calculations between the pages of a large Greek dictionary.

Chapter IV: The second set of characters is introduced. William RODNEY, an aspiring writer who is a government clerk, is to read a paper on the Elizabethan use of metaphor to a club that meets in the rooms of Mary DATCHET, a young SUFFRAGE volunteer. Ralph has arrived early to visit his friend Mary and is surprised to learn that Katharine is coming; Mary tells him she supposes Katharine will marry William. The people who come to Mary's flat are marked by their style as in rebellion against the preceding generation. Mary thinks Katharine is "a 'personality' " (ND 51) and the women are drawn to one another. Ralph continues the mission to dominate Katharine he decided on in Chapter I.

Chapter V: Leaving Mary's, Ralph follows William and Katharine and falls in step with a friend of his, Harry SANDYS. Meanwhile, William is telling Katharine he would not bother her to marry him if he could express himself as the poet he believes himself to be (ND 66). After putting Katharine into a cab, William runs into Ralph and invites him up to his rooms for a drink; there Ralph admires William's books and William shows him the poetic drama he is writing. A couple of days later, Ralph is surprised to receive from William as a gift a copy of a work of Sir Thomas BROWNE's he admired.

Chapter VI: Mary Datchet works for the "S.G.S.," a suffrage organization in Russell Square. She volunteers, while the office is staffed by Mr. CLACTON and Sally SEAL. After lunch, Mary goes to the BRITISH MUSEUM to look at the ELGIN MARBLES and is reminded of Ralph as she looks at the "Ulysses" (as Fanny ELMER is reminded of Jacob FLANDERS in *JACOB'S ROOM*); Mary thinks she might be in love with Ralph. Later that afternoon Mary is surprised in her office by a visit from Katharine. Sally Seal challenges Katharine about why she does not belong to their society if she believes women should have the vote; Mr. Clacton turns out to be a fan of the poetry of Richard Alardyce. Typical of the way characters in *Night and Day* fortuitously arrive just in time to see whom they wish to see, Ralph arrives on the scene and, to Mary's chagrin, leaves with Katharine. They get on a bus and improve their acquaintance.

Chapter VII: At dinner, Katharine tells her parents about her day. Leaving Mr. Hilbery alone to smoke his cigar and drink his port, Katharine and her mother talk about the great poet and Katharine comforts Mrs. Hilbery for her loss of the glorious past. Katharine reflects that this situation is precisely what people like Ralph and Mary do not understand about her life. She and her mother discuss marriage and the chapter closes with Katharine reading Henry FIELDING to her parents until they fall asleep in their armchairs, Katharine having made a futile attempt to interest them in hearing a modern novel. The arrival of the evening mail gives Katharine an opportunity to leave.

Chapter VIII: As well as a letter from William professing his love for her, Katharine has a letter concerning her cousin Cyril Alardyce, who is living with a woman who has borne him two children. Another child is on the way and Katharine's Aunt Celia MILVAIN is not going to stand for it. When Katharine goes to talk about this family drama with her father he will not deal with it, leaving it to Katharine to tell her mother.

Chapter IX: Working on the biography, Katharine puts off saying anything to her mother about Cyril and when Aunt Celia arrives, it is too late. As Aunt Celia is telling her sister-in-law the sordid tale, and not getting the response she desires, Cousin Caroline arrives on a similar mission.

Chapter X: Leaving the offices of GRATELY & HOOPER, where he works, Ralph sees Katharine walking along the STRAND which imparts a visionary quality to the scene for him. He goes to see Mary and they discuss suffrage and the iniquities of Mr. ASQUITH. Under the influence of his infatuation with Katharine, Ralph chastises Mary for what he tells her is a narrow life.

Chapter XI: Katharine, who did not see Ralph, is walking along the Strand repeating to herself a line from *The Idiot* by Fyodor DOSTOYEVSKY, on her way to tea with William. When she gets to William's rooms she realizes that she has left a basket of oysters on a bench in the Strand. William reads parts of his play to her and Katharine submits to the idea that she will end up marrying him, that she can hope for nothing else in life. While he is in another room she quietly says that she will marry him but, to her relief, he does not hear her. A few days later, however, we learn from a letter Mrs. Hilbery sends to Mrs. Milvain that Katharine and William have announced their engagement.

Chapter XII: Ralph comes to Cheyne Walk on the pretext of seeing Mr. Hilbery, and is, of course, pleased to find Katharine there alone. Aunt Millicent COSHAM and Aunt Celia arrive and the former is delighted to learn from Ralph that he does indeed read the works of Thomas DE QUINCEY. The aunts ramble on about the past, about relatives and poets and characters from plays, as if all were members of the family or old friends. Suddenly realizing from the conversation that Katharine and William are engaged, Ralph is thrown into turbulent emotions and leaves as soon as he can.

Chapter XIII: Every day Ralph spends his lunch hour walking in Lincoln's Inn Fields. One day he is startled by Mary, coming back from her lunch. She sees that he is depressed and preoccupied and impulsively invites him to spend Christmas with her family at Disham in Lincolnshire.

Chapter XIV: There is a committee meeting at the S.G.S. attended by Sally Seal's hero Kit MARKHAM, but Mary's mind is on Ralph. She has not been home long that evening when she is surprised by a visit from William and Katharine, who have been out "seeing old masters" at the Grafton Gallery. Katharine tells Mary of their engagement. They leave, but Katharine returns a few moments later as she forgot her purse and enigmatically tells Mary that she thinks being engaged is "very bad for the character" (176). Mary reflects that Katharine unsettles her in a way similar to Ralph.

Chapter XV: Ralph writes to Mary that he will come to Disham for Christmas, but that he wants to lodge in the village so that he can write. Mary worries about what Ralph will think of her family. Unknown to Mary, he is actually coming because he knows that the Hilberys will be staying with the OTWAY family at Stogdon House, about three miles from Disham. Mary, meanwhile, decides that Ralph will stay in her house and is relieved when he arrives and seems to get on well with her brothers.

Chapter XVI: At the Otway family seat Katharine is pacing in the garden, thinking of how to tell her cousin Henry what she really feels about marrying William. Henry OTWAY, who teaches violin to the young ladies of Bungay, at first teases Katharine when she does speak to him, but then sees that she is really upset. William is annoyed that Katharine is up in Henry's room discussing coal mines when she should be downstairs with him and the old fogies after dinner (the Coal Mines Act of 1908 that limited work in a mine to eight hours a day might be a clue to the time of the novel). Katharine insists that William stay and talk to Henry as she is going to bed, making both the men uncomfortable.

Chapter XVII: Stogdon House is faded and dilapidated. Katharine talks about marriage with Lady Otway, whose own marriage has not been happy. Mrs. Hilbery interrupts, wandering in her usual haze, and she, Katharine, William and Henry go into Lincoln in the Otway carriage.

Chapter XVIII: Meanwhile, Ralph and Mary are also on their way, on foot, to Lincoln. As Mary thinks of telling Ralph she loves him, he tells her he has decided to give up his life in London and move to a cottage in the country to write. Mary, irritated because she knows he is not being honest with her, tells him she is thinking of going to America to really learn how to do political organizing. The tension between them dissipates after a little while and they discuss their plans and go to lunch together. At lunch it suddenly dawns on Ralph that Mary is in love with him. In consternation he gets up and walks to the window and there he sees Katharine in the street. He tells Mary whom he has just seen and Mary realizes that his moodiness has all been because of his feelings for Katharine. Doing errands for the Datchets, Mary and Ralph encounter Mrs. Hilbery in a shop. Katharine is surprised and pleased to see Mary and Ralph and thinks they are probably engaged. On the way back to Stogdon House, William and Katharine get out of the carriage to walk the last couple of miles because William wants to tell Katharine how angry he is with her. She tells William she has never loved him but, after a tearful conversation, she tells him she will try to make him happy as his wife.

Chapter XIX: Ralph asks Mary to marry him, but she says she could not. They discuss their feelings more honestly but Ralph does not mention Katharine.

Chapter XX: After Christmas Mary returns to her office to find Sally Seal in a frenzy and Mr. Clacton poised with new pamphlets with which to saturate the provinces. The vote has once more slipped away, but Mary is too distracted by her thoughts of Ralph to worry about that. She leaves the office to think out her feelings and when she returns she has decided to live her life alone and plunge into her work.

Chapter XXI: Mary comes home resolved to work on her manuscript, "Some Aspects of the Democratic State," but is interrupted by a visit from Katharine, which annoys her. Katharine tells Mary she envies her her solitary life. Mary's feelings for Katharine are ambivalent and strong, irritated because Ralph loves her, yet drawn to Katharine herself. She tells Katharine that Ralph and she are not getting married but that she is in love with him. The two women sit together, Mary stroking the fur edging of Katharine's dress.

Chapter XXII: Katharine is late for dinner with William. He is thinking about Katharine's cousin Cassandra OTWAY, who appreciates music and literature as Katharine does not. He begins to write a letter to Cassandra. When Katharine arrives, William explains that they will have to postpone their marriage as he cannot get the time off from his job. Finding they have little to say to each other, William continues his letter to Cassandra. They speak detachedly about their engagement and Katharine realizes that William has fallen in love with Cassandra. William admits this is so. There is a knock at the door.

Chapter XXIII: Ralph comes in and tells them he has rented the cottage in Lincolnshire, where he will write a history of the English village from Anglo-Saxon times to the present. Once again, he leaves with Katharine, to William's dismay. Walking along the Strand, Ralph tells Katharine that while he does not "love" her, she is the "only reality in the world" to him and he is giving up his life in London because of her. He tells her of his family's financial situation and the difficulties of his younger brother Charles's future. That night Ralph stays up until dawn writing a long letter to Katharine urging her to break her engagement with William.

Chapter XXIV: Mrs. Hilbery has evolved a theory that Shakespeare's sonnets were written by Anne Hathaway and excitedly tells Katharine her latest idea, which is to buy copies of Shakespeare to distribute to working men and then open a playhouse in which she, Katharine, William and others will act the plays. In turn, Mary, William, then Ralph telephone Katharine, Ralph to arrange to meet her at Kew Gardens. Katharine writes to invite Cassandra to stay and goes out on an errand of mercy for her mother, intending to post her letter to Cassandra. All the way she thinks of her emotions and their entanglements with Ralph, Mary and William, and she returns home without having posted her letter. Visitors have arrived for tea, including William, who sees the letter lying on the table. While Katharine shows Mrs. Vermont BANKES the family relics, William is thinking about Cassandra, who has replied to his letter. Torn by his sense of propriety and his love for Cassandra, William waits for Katharine to help him out of his dilemma, which she will do.

Chapter XXV: Ralph and Katharine meet at Kew. Their conversation is desultory and Katharine loses her bag. Ralph finds it for her and they discuss the virtues of living alone and honesty in relationships with others. Gradually they work out the conditions of their friendship.

Chapter XXVI: Cassandra arrives in London. She is a little in awe of her cousin Katharine. At dinner that evening, Katharine seats her next to William so that they can flirt together. After dinner, she surprises them by deciding to visit Mary. She finds Mary with a visitor, Mr. BASNETT, with whom she is discussing the reformation of society. Going down to the street, Mary waits with Katharine for a cab and asks her if she has heard from Ralph. They discuss the meeting at Kew. Returning home, Katharine finds William just about to leave; he is clearly enthralled by Cassandra.

Chapter XXVII: Cassandra, William, Katharine and Ralph meet at the London Zoo, where, "as if the matter had been privately agreed upon," they separate into two pairs. Losing sight of each other, William and Cassandra go for tea and Ralph takes Katharine home with him to Mount Ararat Road in Highgate. There she meets his "six or seven" brothers and sisters and his mother. Katharine is rather appalled at the shabbiness and boisterousness of Ralph's home and family. When Joan comes in, however, the atmosphere changes as if she "had some mysterious and beneficent power upon her family." Hester Denham tells Katharine that she wants more than anything in the world to go to NEWNHAM COLLEGE, and soon Katharine finds herself caught up in an argument about the Salvation Army's right to disturb one's sleep by playing hymns in the street. After tea, Ralph and Katharine sit in his room and Ralph again tells her how wonderful she seems to him; Katharine demurs and leaves.

Chapter XXVIII: Ralph, who still thinks that Katharine is going to marry William, has built a kind of shrine to her in his room and for the first time admits to himself that he is in love with her. Wanting to share this news with Mary, he goes to see her and finds her with Mr. Basnett. Mary has left the S.G.S. to work full-time for Basnett's new organization. Ralph manages to make Basnett uncomfortable enough to leave after about twenty minutes and then tells Mary he is love with Katharine. Mary tells Ralph that in her opinion work is what saves us from the torments of love. Ralph leaves and wanders the streets until he comes to Cheyne Walk, where he stands outside Katharine's house fantasizing about her. William finds him there when he comes out. That afternoon William has told Cassandra how he feels about her and has been "repulsed." The two men discuss the mysterious and exasperating nature of women and Ralph tells William he loves Katharine. They agree they are both fools.

Chapter XXIX: Cassandra comes into Katharine's bedroom to tell her what William has said. Katharine tells her that she and William are no longer engaged. The next morning, "Mrs. Milvain is in the kitchen." She has come surreptitiously because "people" are talking about what is going on between William and Cassandra. Katharine is very hostile to her aunt and, when William arrives bearing flowers for Katharine, Mrs. Milvain leaves. Katharine tells William that Cassandra loves him. Cassandra then steps dramatically from behind the velvet curtain that separates the drawing room and the Alardyce chamber. She has heard everything; she agrees to marry William.

Chapter XXX: William points out to Katharine that Ralph is standing outside the house. They bring him in and tell him their marriage is off and that William is to marry Cassandra. Ralph tells Katharine that he loves her, and Katharine responds that she is in love with him: "what other word describes the state we're in?" Mrs. Hilbery comes into the dining room where Ralph and Katharine have been left alone by William and seems unsurprised to find her daughter sitting there with Ralph. Ralph senses that Mrs. Hilbery is perhaps not as vague as she seems.

Chapter XXXI: The next morning Katharine finds a note from her mother saying she has gone to Stratford-on-Avon, Shakespeare's birthplace. Cassandra is disconcerted by Katharine's demeanor when she tries to ascertain her marriage plans with Ralph. Katharine realizes, as she listens to her cousin, that Cassandra and William already have a more intimate relationship than she and William did. When William arrives to see Cassandra, Katharine leaves and goes to wait for Ralph outside his office. She misses him and stands alone in the street as the crowd of people with jobs streams around her. Not knowing what else to do, she goes to Mary's from where she telephones home and learns that Ralph has called to see her. The atmosphere between Mary and Katharine is now antagonistic as they discuss where Ralph might be. Mary makes dinner for them both and then they get into a cab, where Katharine tells Mary of her broken engagement and William's plans to marry Cassandra. Arriving at Cheyne Walk, Katharine finds Ralph waiting for her and, as Mary walks off alone, Katharine and Ralph confess their love to each other.

Chapter XXXII: On a rainy evening, with nowhere to be alone, Katharine and Ralph closet themselves in the Alardyce alcove while William and Cassandra sit in the drawing room. Eventually they all agree to go to a music-hall together, which proves so successful that they plan to go out together again. While they are out on another excursion, at HAMPTON COURT, Mrs. Milvain comes to tell her brother the shocking gossip. Mr. Hilbery is quite bewildered, and when Katharine comes home and tells him she is not going to marry William he is completely at a loss. Soon William and Cassandra come in and Mr. Hilbery hears much more about what has been going on than he ever wanted to. He bans the men from his house and says Cassandra must go home at once. To soothe his ruffled feelings he reads aloud to Katharine from the works of Sir Walter SCOTT.

Chapter XXXIII: Katharine retires to her room and absorbs herself in mathematics. Her father writes to ask his wife to come home at once, which she soon does, bearing an armful of flowers from Shakespeare's tomb. Mrs. Hilbery tells her daughter that she has known all along that Katharine was attracted to Ralph and advises her only to marry for love. Katharine tries to explain that she does not want to marry but perhaps only to live with Ralph. Mrs. Hilbery goes to Ralph's office to bring him back to Cheyne Walk, stopping on the way to pick up William. Cassandra has missed her train and lost her luggage and has come back to the house not knowing where else to go. Ralph and Katharine share their most secret expressions of life—his "dissertation" and her mathematics—and realize they share an inarticulate vision. Before long, everything is resolved as Katharine tells her father she and Ralph are engaged.

Chapter XXXIV: After dinner, Katharine and Ralph walk to Mary Datchet's house, where they stand in the street looking up at the light in her window. Ralph goes up the stairs to Mary's door but does not have the heart to knock. They walk back to the Hilberys' house recounting their past and imagining their future and on the threshold embrace before Katharine goes in.

Genesis

Woolf wrote in 1930 to Ethel SMYTH that she had composed *Night and Day* "lying in bed, allowed to write only for one half hour a day" (L4 231), a fact she repeated in 1938 in letters to Philip MORRELL and to his wife, Lady Ottoline MORRELL (L6 212, 216). Woolf's memory of writing *Night and Day* while confined to her bed (the "rest cure" Woolf experienced was exactly that described by Charlotte Perkins Gilman in her classic novella *The Yellow Wallpaper*) corroborates Elizabeth Heine's supposition that Woolf began her second novel early in 1915. References in Woolf's DIARY to "poor Effie's story" (D1 4) and to "The Third Generation" (D1 19) concern early drafts of *Night and Day* (VWM 9:10). Woolf wrote that she wanted to argue with Leonard WOOLF in the voice of her character Effie against his writing "a pamphlet about Arbitration" to "see what can be said *against* all forms of activity" (D1 22), so we may safely assume that "Effie" was an early name for Katharine Hilbery, she who amazes Sally Seal by not joining "the cause."

Most readers have found it easy to identify Katharine with Woolf's sister, Vanessa Bell, to whom Woolf wrote in 1916, "I am very interested in your life, which I think of writing another novel about" (L2 109). Woolf was explicit about the novel's source in her sister's early life: "try thinking of Katharine as Vanessa, not me," she wrote in 1919 to Janet CASE; "and suppose her concealing a passion for painting and forced to go into society by George [DUCKWORTH]" (L2 400).

Woolf said she wrote her second novel with ease and enjoyment. "In my opinion N. & D. is a much more mature & finished book than The Voyage Out," she wrote in 1919 (D1 259). Looking back to this "novel of fact" in the 1930s, Woolf saw it as a necessary exercise, using the image of a visual artist learning technique and studying anatomy by copying from plaster casts (L4 231). She likened the novel to "a minute Academy drawing" which had helped her learn "what to leave out: by putting it all in" (L6 216). To Ethel Smyth, however, she also revealed something of the reason she had turned to an apparently conventional form after *THE VOYAGE OUT:* "I was so tremblingly afraid of my own insanity that I wrote Night and Day mainly to prove to my own satisfaction that I could keep entirely off that dangerous ground" (L4 231). As well as an academic exercise, then, *Night and Day* also offered security. In "A SKETCH OF THE PAST" Woolf wrote that only in *Night and Day* and *THE YEARS* had she tried to describe "non-being"—her term for everyday life—avoiding the poetic intensities of her other works (MOB 70). *Night and Day,* an earlier title for which was "Dreams and Realities," does not eschew moments of vision altogether, though, as several critics have noted.

In writing *Night and Day* Woolf was concerned with "the whole question . . . of the things one doesn't say; what effect does that have?" (L2 400). This theme is reminiscent of her character Terence HEWET's wish in *The Voyage Out* to "write a novel about Silence; the things people don't say" (TVO 216). In describing the struggles of her characters to make new social norms, Woolf was also caught up in the problem of how to forge new narrative structures with which to represent that new world. At times there is an ambiguity in her diary entries about *Night and Day* that somewhat obscures whether she is referring to social or to narrative conventions: "as the current answers don't do, one has to grope for a new one; & the process of discarding the old, when one is by no means certain what to put in their place, is a sad one" (D1 259), This is exactly the idea behind Woolf's essay "MODERN FICTION," published in the same year as *Night and Day,* and, as Hermione Lee points out, "the relationship between the discovery of a truer life in *Night and Day* and Virginia Woolf's search for a 'truer' form of narrative realism is clear" (Lee 70). Jane Fisher* has recently written that *Night and Day* "reenacts the discarding not only of the conventions governing the behavior of unmarried women but also of the most basic narrative convention: that language has a set of comprehensible meanings that can be exchanged" (Fisher 95).

Background

Woolf overtly drew on her own experiences, family, friends, and literary heritage in composing *Night and Day.* Daniel Fogel remarks on the pervasive "Jamesian traces" of the novel, noticing as L. L. Lee did (VWM 9:1) that Mr. Fortescue, who appears only once, is based upon Henry JAMES himself. Katharine is only a "granddaughter of Jane Austen" for she is more closely related to Isabel Archer from James's *The Portrait of a Lady.* Fogel also notices that *Portrait's* Ralph Touchett is recalled by Katharine's favorite cousin, Henry Otway (Fogel 134). David GARNETT, too, has commented on the Jamesian "flavour" of *Night and Day's* opening chapters (*Great Friends* 124). In addition, although Woolf may not have liked the comparison, Katharine Hilbery shares many characteristics with Jane AUSTEN's heroines, in particular Elizabeth Bennett in *Pride and Prejudice* and Emma Woodhouse: the first few paragraphs of *Night and Day* pointedly recall Austen's *Emma.*

Several critics have explained that Mary Datchet is modeled on Margaret Llewelyn DAVIES, who headed the WOMEN'S COOPERATIVE GUILD. Sonya Rudikoff (VWM 28: 4–5) has suggested that Woolf's characterization of Cassandra Otway might have drawn on the life of Lady Dorothy Nevill, whose *Life and Letters* Woolf reviewed in 1919 (CE4 111–15). The most elaborate drawing from life was Woolf's portrait of Anne Isabella Thackeray (Anny) RITCHIE in the character of Mrs. Hilbery. Lady Ritchie read the manuscript of *Night and Day* a few months before she died, but there is no record of what she thought. The Ritchies, on the other hand, were "furious" when the book was published (L2 474). Ronald McCail* has shown that not only is *Night and Day*'s seventh chapter "a paraphrase of the most private and pathetic episode" in the life of Anny Ritchie's father, William Makepeace THACKERAY, but that Anny herself had made use of these circumstances in her novel *Old Kensington,* serialized in the *CORNHILL MAGAZINE* 1872–73 (McCail 23). McCail finds detailed parallels between *Old Kensington* and *Night and Day* (also see Carol Hanbery MacKay* 73–76).

Woolf's own life seems to have provided material for *Night and Day* also. Several critics have found Leonard Woolf to be the model for Ralph Denham and have pointed out that Katharine's visit to the Denham family at Highgate in chapter XXVII of *Night and Day* draws on Woolf's accounts of visiting Leonard's family at their home in Putney. Like Ralph, Leonard came from a large Jewish family whose father had died prematurely, leaving them in some financial difficulty. Mark Hussey* has detailed the interrelations between *Night and Day* and Leonard's 1914 novel *THE WISE VIRGINS,* pointing out that the apparently anomalous place occupied in Woolf's canon by *Night and Day* can be explained by seeing it as "a response to and a comment on her husband's *roman à clef The Wise Virgins* that takes elements from that work and recontextualizes them" (Hussey, "Refractions" 127). When *Night and Day* was published, anyone who remembered Leonard's novel, two of the principal female characters of which are named Katharine and Camilla, could see that here was the comment on it that Woolf had not made in 1915 when she first read *The Wise Virgins* in a state of extreme nervous exhaustion. Both novels explore the conventions governing heterosexual relations and the damaging effects of those conventions on their young characters.

Just as Katharine Hilbery helps her mother with the biography of her grandfather, so Woolf had helped F. W. MAITLAND with his biography of her father, Sir Leslie STEPHEN. Maitland had refused to believe that Leslie treated the women in his family badly, but Woolf's Mr. Hilbery shows traits that Woolf described her father as possessing. When Katharine tells her father she is engaged to Ralph, there are echoes in Mr. Hilbery's thoughts of Woolf's descriptions of Leslie Stephen's reaction to the news of Stella DUCKWORTH's engagement: "Had he loved her to see her swept away by this torrent, to have her taken from him by this uncontrollable force, to stand by helpless, ignored? Oh, how he loved her! How he loved her!" (ND 500). Mr. Hilbery goes "bellowing to his lair," Woolf also perhaps shooting an ironic glance in this phrase toward her husband's novel, which makes extensive use of imagery of wild beasts to describe heterosexual passions.

Circumscribing these autobiographical elements, as many readers have noticed, is Woolf's pervasive use in *Night and Day* of allusions to Shakespeare. Apart from the overt references that have both William and Mrs. Hilbery, for example, comparing Katharine to ROSALIND (a character in *As You Like It,* a play which also includes a character named ORLANDO), *Night and Day* itself is a comic celebration of love in the spirit of *Twelfth Night* or *A Midsummer Night's Dream.* Woolf uses the "primal stuff of the comic love plot" in her novel (Rachel Blau DuPlessis* 123) in which the "regenerative comedy" of Mrs. Hilbery (who likens herself to Shakespeare's wise Fool [ND 306]) solves all problems and unites true lovers at the end.

Woolf's plot, however, uses the Shakespearean happy ending awkwardly because the novel is, despite Ralph's disembodied dreams of Katharine and Katharine's longing for a "heroic Rider" to sweep her away in true passion, set firmly in the urban world of Edwardian London. Ralph and Katharine's language at the end of the novel echoes Woolf's description of the pair of young lovers in ***KEW GARDENS,*** one of those "sketches" with which she was making an effort to break away from the very narrative forms she was employing in *Night and Day.* By the time the novel was finished, Woolf "had also begun a critique of her own procedures and a program for another kind of fiction" (DuPlessis 125). Woolf seems to have written an image of herself writing *Night and Day* into "Modern Fiction," where she speaks of writers "perseveringly, conscientiously, constructing our two and thirty chapters after a design which more and more ceases to resemble the vision in our minds" (CE2 105).

Critical Responses

Leonard Woolf found the "philosophy" of *Night and Day* very melancholy, and Woolf herself later wrote of its "flatness" (D3 37). Contemporary reviewers were fairly sympathetic to the novel, seeing that in it "the Victorian age gives way to the present" (CH 76) and that "we see much more than we are shown" (CH 77). None, though, would have agreed with the elderly lady who wrote to Woolf that "she feels it, 'the forerunner of a new species of book' " (L2 400)—an opinion Woolf found "very intelligent." Clive BELL told his sister-in-law that *Night and Day* was "a work of the highest genius," but as Woolf no longer considered his opinion worth much, she waited for "the people whose judgment I respect" to give their verdict (D1 307).

One whom she greatly respected was E. M. FORSTER, who found the book "a strictly formal and classical work" (D1 310), liking it less than *The Voyage Out* (D1 307–08). The opinion that had the most profound effect was that of Katherine MANSFIELD. In her ***ATHENAEUM*** review, called "A Ship Comes Into Harbour," Mansfield wrote that it was impossible not to compare *Night and Day* with Jane Austen's work. It was, perhaps, "Miss Austen up-to-date" (CH 80) and recalled the traditional English novel, the like of which "we had never thought to look upon . . . again" (CH 82). In letters to John Middleton MURRY, Mansfield was much less reserved, and called the novel "a lie in the soul" because it was written as if World War I had not taken place; she felt also that it reeked of "intellectual snobbery." When Mansfield and Woolf saw each other soon after the review had appeared, Mansfield told Woolf that *Night and Day* was "an amazing achievement," leading Woolf to wonder "what does reviewing mean then?" (D2 44–45).

Woolf had hoped that Mansfield would not review *Night and Day* (D1 257), realizing perhaps that the author of *Prelude* would allow this stately book no quarter: "A decorous elderly dullard she describes me; Jane Austen up to date" (D1 314). Louise DeSalvo has speculated that Mansfield's review affected Woolf's revisions of *The Voyage Out* for its first U.S. edition (VWM 11: 5–6), and certainly Mansfield's opinion of the novel dominated critical responses to it for a considerable time. *Night and Day* was long seen as an oddly traditional novel by a writer about to revolutionize the form of the English novel. Nancy Topping Bazin found that it "burdens the reader with an unjustifiable number of scenes and details" (Bazin 82), and Jean Guiguet faulted the novel for "letting the reader suppose that it attempts to conform" to the type of the classical novel (Guiguet 209).

There are by now many critics who have seen *Night and Day* as only "ostensibly conventional" (Fleishman 22). Not many, probably, would go as far as Jean O. Love, who writes that the novel "in no way resembles a social comedy" in its essence, but "is a novel about knowledge, even epistemology" (*Worlds* 109), yet several readers have drawn attention to the "disturbing forces at work" behind its familiar narrative formulas (Zwerdling 220). In both *The Voyage Out* and *Night and Day* Woolf was concerned with "her own growing years and identity problems" (Richter 17). Indeed, for Roger Poole *Night and Day* is a "meta-study" of *The Voyage Out* (*Unknown* 46), and both novels draw on "the traditional concerns of love plots . . . and quest plots" (DuPlessis 115). Seeing *Night and Day* as not isolated but as an integral part of Woolf's work and vision has led to a revaluation of the novel in terms of its critique of the patriarchal family—a kind of prototype of *The Years*—and its examination of the question of women and work in the modern world.

Alex Zwerdling examines the aggressiveness, frustration and love of power inherent in the courtship ritual upon which *Night and Day*'s structure rests and sees it as a novel that, like *The Years,* details the destructiveness of the family (Zwerdling 148). For Lucio Ruotolo, the novel's "overriding purpose is to confront and resist the deadly proportion of outdated literary and social conventions" (*Interrupted* 49). The most radical analysis of *Night and Day* in these terms is to be found in Kathy Phillips' *Virginia Woolf Against Empire,* in which Ralph's socially fostered traits of domination are identified with just those qualities that drive the imperial urge. Helen Wussow* has argued that *Night and Day* shows a society that is disintegrating and, answering Katherine Mansfield's complaint, writes that the novel "reflects, or rather embodies, the very conflicts of battle" (Wussow 62). Wussow, drawing on the theoretical work of Mikhail Bakhtin, sees the ambivalence and continual misunderstandings of discourse in *Night and Day* as reflecting the conflicts of World War I.

In addition to seeing *The Voyage Out* and *Night and Day* as linked, some critics have found that *Night and Day* is integral to the whole of Woolf's work (Lee 70). The struggle to maintain a moment of vision against a chaotic world, as Ralph and Katharine do at the end of the novel, looks forward to all the rest of Woolf's fiction. According to Howard Harper, "in that final chapter, and in some other moments, the language of the book shares some of the images and symbols which constitute the larger mythic language" of Woolf's lifework (Harper 84). Ralph's little dot encircled with flames is but one example in Woolf's fiction of a symbol being imbued by a character with a particular meaning (Richter 103), and both Ralph's doodle and Katharine's vision of a "heroic Rider" reappear in *The Years. Night and Day,* then, contains most of the important themes of Woolf's fiction, themes which Herbert Marder points out "reveal her preoccupation with the problems of women" (Marder 21).

Night and Day's title alludes to dichotomies in the lives of at least three of its principal characters—Ralph, Katharine and Mary—and also to the way the novel itself poses as its problem negotiating between whatever "night" and "day" represent. Most critics have elaborated some kind of split between private and social, silent and communicable worlds to explain the significance of the title. Katharine's "inner life" is seen as separate from her "life in the world" and the novel is about this separation (Marder 53). An extended treatment of the novel's imagery of light and darkness is given by Melinda F. Cumings.* For several critics, the imagery of light and darkness that pervades the novel is a sign of Woolf's early concern with ANDROGYNY (Richter 122), the union of Ralph and Katharine at the end being seen as creating androgyny: "the function of their marriage, both as symbol and reality, is to enable them to complete each other, to help each other perfect their androgyneity" (Marder 128). Like Marder, Lee finds Ralph and Katharine's relationship "a serious early version of the light-fantastic androgynous marriage in *Orlando* and the sexless relationship between Sara and Nicholas in *The Years*" (Lee 62).

The light and darkness imagery and the narrative of Ralph and Katharine's gradual movement toward each other converge at the end of the novel. " 'The lamps are lit': the first words of the final chapter imply the reconciliation of the domains of night and day, the illumination of this new realm of knowledge" (Harper 70). As DuPlessis notes, Ralph and Katharine's final kiss is "on the limen between love and quest" (DuPlessis 124). For Avrom Fleishman the "crescendo" of *Night and Day* offers Woolf's conception of "a secular state of personal fulfillment on the model of—even borrowing the imagery of—religious transcendence" (Fleishman 42). In her provocative reading of *Night and Day* as structured "around the initiation, quest, and journey myths of [MOZART's] *The Magic Flute*" Jane Marcus brings this imagery together with what she sees as the novel's feminist theme: "For Woolf it is the patriarchs who represent the forces of darkness, while the matriarchs are as sunny as Mrs. Hilbery with her arms full of flowers from Shakespeare's tomb" (*Languages* 29).

Some readers have been confused by Woolf's satiric portrayal of the suffrage organization that Mary Datchet works for, but her purpose is illuminated by seeing *Night and Day* in the context of her later overtly political writing, in particular *THREE GUINEAS.* Marder explains that Woolf "felt doubt about the suffrage societies because she felt that they borrowed their weapons from the enemy" (Marder 92). As Audre

Lorde* would write many years later in a famous expression that Woolf might have agreed with, "The Master's Tools Will Never Dismantle the Master's House." Woolf's criticism of the suffrage movement—which Mary leaves to work for a new socialist organization—"should be seen in the light of the socialism and pacifism that always underlay her feminism" (Marcus, *Languages* 190n4). The problem that Woolf's apparently conventional novel addresses is of how to reconcile work and love in a society where, as Cicely Hamilton* put it, marriage was the only "trade" open to women.

Marcus has the "odd feeling that the only really satisfactory ending to the novel would be in Katharine Hilbery's marriage, not to Ralph but to Mary Datchet," identifying the novel's "one erotic moment" as that when Mary sits by Katharine and plays with the edge of her skirt (*Languages* 23). Shirley Nelson Garner* has also discussed how in *Night and Day* "friendship between women may subvert the romantic tale we have heard so often" (320) and argues that "the most deeply felt relationship is not between the engaged couples, but rather between Mary and Katharine" (322). Garner believes that Woolf "forces us to see that romantic fulfillment coincides with loss for Katharine" and that Woolf saw "that singleness offers possibilities for a woman that love and marriage close off" (331).

Susan Squier also identifies "a woman's struggle to do her own work" (Squier, *Virginia Woolf* 74) as the subject of *Night and Day*, finding that in it Woolf reverses the pattern of the classic city novel associated with Henry Fielding, "instead associating the city with honest work and virtue, and the country with worldly leisure and, if not vice, at least petty dishonesty" (Squier 78). Mary's story turns the traditional "spiral journey of an adventuresome young man" inside out, transforming the classic city novel and "incidentally, adapting modernist urban images to feminist themes as well" (Squier 87). In the apparently conventional *Night and Day*, what Sandra Gilbert and Susan Gubar term the "fantastic new languages" (*War* 249) of Woolf's later works such as *Orlando* and *BETWEEN THE ACTS* may not be as evident as they are in subsequent novels, but they are spoken.

Works Specific to This Entry:

Cumings, Melinda F. "*Night and Day*: Virginia Woolf's Visionary Synthesis of Reality." *Modern Fiction Studies* 18 (1972): 339–49.

DuPlessis, Rachel Blau. " 'Amor Vin—': Modifications of Romance in Woolf." In Margaret Homans, ed. *Virginia Woolf*: 115–35.

Fisher, Jane. " 'Silent as the Grave': Painting, Narrative, and the Reader in *Night and Day* and *To the Lighthouse*." In Diane Gillespie, ed. *Multiple Muses*: 90–109.

Garner, Shirley Nelson. " 'Women Together' in Virginia Woolf's *Night and Day*." In Shirley Nelson Garner, Claire Kahane, and Madelon Sprengnether, eds. *The (M)other Tongue: Essays in Feminist Psychoanalytic Interpretation*. Ithaca: Cornell University Press, 1985.

Hamilton, Cicely. *Marriage as a Trade*. London: 1909. Reprinted. Detroit: Singing Tree Press, 1971.

Hussey, Mark. "Refractions of Desire: The Early Fiction of Virginia and Leonard Woolf." *Modern Fiction Studies* 38, 1 (Spring 1992): 127–46.

Lorde, Audre. "The Master's Tools Will Never Dismantle the Master's House." In Cherríe Moraga and Gloria Anzaldúa, eds. *This Bridge Called My Back: Writings by Radical Women of Color*. New York: Kitchen Table, Women of Color Press, 1981: 98–101.

McCail, Ronald. "A Family Matter: *Night and Day* and *Old Kensington*." *Review of English Studies* 38, 149 (Fall 1987): 23–39.

MacKay, Carol Hanbery. "The Thackeray Connection: Virginia Woolf's Aunt Anny." In Jane Marcus, ed. *Virginia Woolf and Bloosmbury*: 68–95.

Murry, John Middleton, ed. *The Letters of Katherine Mansfield*. London: Constable, 1928.

Wussow, Helen. "Conflict of Language in Virginia Woolf's *Night and Day*." *Journal of Modern Literature* 16, 1 (Summer 1989): 61–73.

Nightingale, Florence (1820–1910) Famous for her reform of army hospitals during the Crimean War. Nightingale's image as the "Lady with the Lamp" remained intact until Lytton STRACHEY'S *EMINENT VICTORIANS* was published in 1918. There he contradicted the idea of Nightingale as a selfless "delicate maiden of high degree," writing that she was driven to her work by a desire to escape the enervating life of a Victorian young lady. In *A ROOM OF ONE'S OWN*, Woolf refers to Nightingale's autobiographical fragment *Cassandra* (written in 1852 but not published until it was included in *The Cause*, edited by Ray STRACHEY [1928]), calling it a loud shriek of agony (AROO 56). Alex Zwerdling describes *Cassandra* as the "most uncompromising attack on Victorian family practices as they affected women's lives" (Zwerdling 164) and notes that Nightingale anticipated Woolf's critical description of the ANGEL IN THE HOUSE (Zwerdling 219). In *THREE GUINEAS*, Woolf includes Nightingale among representative Victorian women whom, she says, were taught by "poverty, chastity, derision, and . . . freedom from unreal loyalties" (TG 78).

1917 Club Named after the February Revolution in Russia. Leonard WOOLF was involved in founding it. The Club met at 4 Gerrard Street and brought together leftist intellectuals, artists and politicians. Duncan Wilson, quoting a Labour Party colleague of Leonard's, describes the Club as "an attempt to provide the Labour Party with some equivalent to those society salons in which it was thought that much of the less formal business of the Conservative and Liberal parties was conducted" (97). Wilson notes that it "provided another place at which [Leonard] Woolf could meet his radical associates—Ramsay MacDonald in particular" (97). Jane Marcus has suggested that the Club inspired the setting for the party in the "Present Day" chapter of Woolf's *THE YEARS* and also notes that Jane Ellen HARRISON was among its members. Woolf mentions the Club frequently in the first and second volumes of *The Diary of Virginia Woolf* and in the second volume of *The Letters of Virginia Woolf* as a place where she would meet the denizens of BLOOMSBURY such as Alix, James, Lytton and Marjorie STRACHEY and several others.

Norman, Mrs. Character in *JACOB'S ROOM* who is nervous when Jacob FLANDERS gets into her railway compartment on the way to Cambridge because "it is a fact that men are dangerous" (JR 30). Mrs. Norman is reading one of the novels of W. E. Norris, of whose works Woolf wrote several reviews (E1 36–37, 66; E3 42–43, 178–80, 281–84).

Norton, H. T. J. (Henry [Harry] Tertius James) (1886–1937) Noted mathematician, APOSTLE, and Fellow of Trinity College, Cambridge. During World War I he had rooms at 46 GORDON SQUARE and had an unrequited love for Vanessa BELL. Woolf met Norton, who was part of the Cambridge circle of Lytton STRACHEY (who dedicated *EMINENT VICTORIANS* to him), Leonard WOOLF and Saxon SYDNEY-TURNER, in 1908. He accompanied Clive BELL and Vanessa to Turkey in 1911, where Vanessa had a miscarriage at Broussa and was cared for by Roger FRY. In 1918, Woolf wrote her sister that Norton was to her "the representative of old Cambridge, as we knew it, in the days of 'personal emotions' " (L2 292).

Norton, Sir Richard Makes a fleeting appearance in *THE YEARS,* where Kitty LASSWADE remembers him from her childhood as "Chingachgook" (TY 76).

Notes from Sick Rooms Apart from a letter to the *Pall Mall Gazette,* this essay was the only published writing of Julia Prinsep STEPHEN, Woolf's mother. An essay on the proper care of the sick, *Notes from Sick Rooms* was published by Smith and Elder in 1883; Constance Hunting's edition was published in 1980 by the Puckerbrush Press (Orono, Maine), and the essay is included in Diane F. Gillespie and Elizabeth Steele, eds., *Julia Duckworth Stephen* (216–40). The essay speaks of the entirely female world of the sickroom and, after Julia's self-deprecating introduction, comments that the "ordinary relations between the sick and the well are far easier and pleasanter than between the well and the well" (Gillespie and Steele 217). *Notes from Sick Rooms* casts interesting light on the characterization of Mrs. RAMSAY in *TO THE LIGHTHOUSE* as Woolf clearly drew on the memories she had of her mother visiting the sick at ST. IVES. Julia writes in her essay that nurses' treating sick people as "cases" rather than individuals is a virtue of their profession, and says that one should either be truthful or "lie freely" when dealing with a sick person. Woolf herself followed this advice in 1906 when she maintained in letters to her friend Violet DICKINSON that Thoby STEPHEN, who had died from the illness Violet herself was suffering, was in fact getting better. *Notes from Sick Rooms* covers a variety of topics: how to remove crumbs from a sick bed, how to make beds, the best kind of pillow to use, how to avoid losing handkerchiefs in the bed, the importance of urging the sick to repress the desire to wash too often, how to bathe a sick person, how to comb her hair, and so on. Visitors are instructed in the correct way to behave, and diet is explained. Finally, "if the patient should die, the nurse must remember that though her help may still be needed her place is not by the death-bed unless it is requested" (Gillespie and Steele 239).

"Notes on an Elizabethan Play" (CE1 54–61; CR1 72–83) An essay by Woolf first published in the *TIMES LITERARY SUPPLEMENT* on March 5, 1925. Brenda R. Silver finds that Woolf was reading Elizabethan writers in 1923, despite Woolf's rarely mentioning them in her DIARY and LETTERS (RN 100). Like several of her *COMMON READER* essays, "Notes on an Elizabethan Play" is concerned with how to read works of the past. She begins by pointing out that although William SHAKESPEARE's work is familiar, it is usually forgotten that he wrote in a world of many other dramatists, the "lesser Elizabethans" whose works are no longer read. Because we tend to read only the masterpieces of a "bygone age," the encounter with these lesser works can profoundly upset our cherished convictions about it. She finds the Elizabethan play boring because, she speculates, the audience demanded plot—"incessant, improbable, almost unintelligible convolutions" (CE1 56). She compares the characters of dramatists such as John Ford and John WEBSTER to Leo TOLSTOY's in *Anna Karenina* to show how flat and crude they are. Yet, Woolf continues, the lesser Elizabethans are worth reading for their sense of humanity as a whole and for the richness of their language. What their works lack is any sense of solitude, of the private self; for that, she says, readers go to John DONNE, to Michel de MONTAIGNE or to Sir Thomas BROWNE.

Notes on Virginia's Childhood See BELL, Vanessa.

"Nurse Lugton's Golden Thimble" A children's story by Woolf first published in the *TIMES LITERARY SUPPLEMENT* in June 1965 under the title "The . . ." and illustrated by Duncan GRANT. The story was found in the manuscript of *MRS. DALLOWAY*. It was separately published in 1966 by the HOGARTH PRESS with a foreword by Leonard WOOLF in which he said the story had been written for his niece Ann Stephen, daughter of Adrian and Karin STEPHEN. As Nurse Lugton dozes, the animals she has been embroidering on a curtain come alive. The story was reissued with illustrations by Julie Vivas under the title *Nurse Lugton's Curtain* by Harcourt Brace Jovanovich in 1991. An Italian translation by Enzo Siciliano, *Il Ditale D'Oro,* was published in 1976.

O

Ocampo, Victoria (1890–1979) Argentine intellectual, writer, founder and editor of the Buenos Aires-based magazine and publishing house *Sur* ("South"). Woolf and Ocampo met at an exhibit of Man RAY's photographs in London in 1934 and quickly became friends. Antonía García-Rodriguez describes Ocampo's 1954 "Virginia Woolf in Her Diary" as articulating "many of the thoughts and feelings she was unable to share with Woolf" (44). Ocampo arranged for the translation of *ORLANDO* and *A ROOM OF ONE'S OWN* by Jorge Luis BORGES, both published by Sur.

ODTAA One Damn Thing After Another was a student society at GIRTON COLLEGE, Cambridge, to which on October 26, 1928, Woolf read one of the papers on which *A ROOM OF ONE'S OWN* is based. In her DIARY, Woolf remarked that she had "blandly told them to drink wine & have a room of their own." The name derived from John Masefield's 1926 novel *Odtaa*.

"Old Bloomsbury" A paper read by Woolf to the MEMOIR CLUB in late 1921 or early 1922 and published in *MOMENTS OF BEING* (MOB 181–201). It picks up where "22 HYDE PARK GATE" (MOB 164–77) ends, with Woolf undressing in her bedroom after an evening out with her half-brother George DUCKWORTH and his coming in and flinging himself on her bed, "embracing" her while three or four floors below her father lay dying of cancer. Woolf describes the origins of the BLOOMSBURY GROUP in the move from Hyde Park Gate to 46 GORDON SQUARE in October 1904. There, Woolf's brother Thoby STEPHEN began his "Thursday Evenings," open invitations to his home, as a way of keeping in touch with his Cambridge University friends such as Lytton STRACHEY and Saxon SYDNEY-TURNER. Woolf describes how others joined the circle of friends: Leonard WOOLF, John Maynard KEYNES and Duncan GRANT. Soon she realized she was living in a society of "buggers" (MOB 194). "Old Bloomsbury" includes the famous story of Lytton Strachey looking at a stain on Vanessa's skirt and inquiring "Semen?" Woolf describes the sense of liberation she felt at the new society in Gordon Square and how it shocked their elders. The piece ends with an account of Lady Ottoline MORRELL, who swept them up into her grander society at Bedford Square.

Oliphant, Margaret Oliphant (sic) (1828–97) In *THREE GUINEAS,* Woolf cites Margaret Oliphant, a prolific novelist, as an example of a writer who prostituted her talent and "enslaved intellectual liberty in order that she might earn her living and educate her children" (TG 91–92). Oliphant described in her *Autobiography* (1899) how her voluminous writings were intended to support her own and her brother's children.

Oliver, Bartholomew Character in *BETWEEN THE ACTS.* Retired from the Indian Civil Service, Bart lives at POINTZ HALL, his family's home, where his widowed sister Lucy SWITHIN stays during the summer. His son Giles OLIVER is married to Isa OLIVER. Bart is a gruff old man who mocks his sister's Christian faith and frightens his grandson. He is usually accompanied by his Afghan hound SOHRAB, and his habit of yelling at the dog to heel whenever visitors arrive has reminded some readers that this was a habit of Leonard WOOLF's also. Some critics have seen in Woolf's portrait of Bart and Lucy an image of her own relationship with Leonard in the late 1930s. There are echoes of Mr. RAMSAY in the characterization of Bart. Jane Marcus has discussed the lines Bart quotes from A. C. SWINBURNE's "Itylus" ("O sister swallow" [BTA 115]) as Woolf's rejection of Swinburne's recasting of the myth of PROCNE AND PHILOMELA (*Languages* 76).

Oliver, Caro Baby daughter of Isa and Giles OLIVER in *BETWEEN THE ACTS.*

Oliver, George Son of Isa and Giles OLIVER in *BETWEEN THE ACTS.* He is terrified by his grandfather Bart OLIVER's mask made of newspaper and by the old man's dog, SOHRAB, leading Bart to tell his daughter-in-law that her son is a "coward" (19). In the garden at POINTZ HALL George has a vision of a flower as "complete" (BTA 11) that is almost identical to one Woolf describes in her memoir "A SKETCH OF THE PAST" (MOB 71).

Oliver, Giles Character in *BETWEEN THE ACTS*. He is a stockbroker, married to Isa OLIVER and father of George and Caro, a baby girl. On the day the novel takes place, he arrives late for lunch from London where he has been working, and is irritated to see Mrs. MANRESA's car in the driveway of his father, Bart OLIVER's, house. Giles's marriage to Isa is troubled and there are strong suggestions in the novel of his infidelity, including a moment when he goes with Mrs. Manresa, who has flirted with him, to the greenhouse. Giles is full of anger, at himself, at the "old fogies" at POINTZ HALL who sit staring at views while war is imminent in Europe, and at William DODGE, Manresa's homosexual friend. During an intermission of the annual village pageant Giles comes across a snake with a half-eaten toad stuck in its mouth and stamps both of them to death (BTA 99). The probable source of this scene can be found in Vita SACKVILLE-WEST's *Country Notes in Wartime* (a collection of pieces on gardening first published in the *NEW STATESMAN AND NATION*). "July 1940" ends with Sackville-West's description of finding a frog, "his body flattened in terror against the wall" while an adder, "a beautiful snake full of venom," waited to eat it: "I thought of Roumania and Greece, with the spiteful tongue shooting out towards them" (72).

Oliver, Isa Character in *BETWEEN THE ACTS*. She is married to Giles OLIVER, the son of Bart OLIVER, and has two children, George and Caro, a baby girl, and is thirty-nine. Isa's mother died in India (153) and Isa, we are told, is the daughter of "Sir Richard" and niece of two old ladies who are proud of their descent from the kings of Ireland (16). Isa's marriage is troubled; she is attracted to Rupert HAINES, a local farmer, and knows that her husband is unfaithful to her. Throughout the novel, Isa speaks to herself in a poetic chant, on one occasion recalling Katharine HILBERY's fantasy of a heroic Rider in *NIGHT AND DAY* (BTA 104–05) (the "withered tree" of Isa's imagery is also familiar from both *THE WAVES* and *THE YEARS*, where it is an emblem of death). She writes poetry in a book bound to look like an account book to hide it from her husband, but she considers her writing "abortive." She befriends William DODGE, who comes to the village pageant at Bart Oliver's house with Mrs. MANRESA. Isa is haunted by a longing for oblivion. At the end of the novel Isa and Giles are left alone, about to speak, in a prehistoric setting. Evelyn Haller has discussed Isa's many links with the Egyptian figure of Isis ("Anti-Madonna" 101f).

Oliver, Raymond Mentioned in *THE VOYAGE OUT* as "a tall dark boy who looks as if he had Indian blood in him" (TVO 189) whom Evelyn MURGATROYD has allowed to kiss her, thus leading him to think they are engaged.

Omega Workshops Opened on July 8, 1913, at 33 FITZROY SQUARE, the Omega Workshops were founded by Roger FRY, with Vanessa BELL and Duncan GRANT as co-directors, to produce decorative art from a background of painting rather than crafts. Fry's idea for the Omega as a way for young artists to make a living was inspired by Grant's inability to pay a train fare to DURBINS, Fry's house, where he was to meet a prospective client. The Omega brought together many young English artists who were interested in French POST-IMPRESSIONISM, including Simon BUSSY, Henri Doucet, and Frederick and Jessie ETCHELLS. Several other artists' groups probably inspired Fry to begin the Omega, including the FRIDAY CLUB, a discussion group mainly for women artists started by Vanessa Bell in 1905; the Wiener Werkstätte, a decorative arts workshop in Vienna begun in 1903; and the Atelier Martine, started in Paris in 1911 by Paul Poiret after seeing the Wiener Werkstätte. The idea of the Omega was to develop English painting by providing support for artists through the sale of decorative works. The artists were not allowed to work at the Omega for more than three and a half days a week to ensure they had time for their own painting. A huge range of products was sold, including lamps, rugs, screens, necklaces, parasols, furniture and menu cards, as well as designs for textiles, dresses, mosaics and murals. Isabelle Anscombe has told the Omega's story in her book *Omega and After*, and its influence can still be seen in home furnishings and design (see also Judith Collins, *The Omega Workshops* [1984]). After several business disagreements, most significantly involving Wyndham LEWIS, the Omega held its closing sale in July 1919.

"On Being Ill" (CE4 193–203; M 9–23) An essay by Woolf published in the *New Criterion* (see *CRITERION*) in January 1926 and under the title "Illness: An Unexplored Mine" in April 1926 in the New York *Forum*. In 1930, a revised version was published in a limited edition by the HOGARTH PRESS. Geoffrey KEYNES, who had saved Woolf's life in 1913 after she took an overdose of Veronal, says in his autobiography that Woolf gave him a holograph manuscript of the essay and also a copy of the limited edition that she had corrected in violet ink. He quotes a letter from Woolf (that does not appear in LETTERS) concerning his criticism of a sentence in the essay (Geoffrey Keynes 116–17). A letter from Leonard WOOLF to Geoffrey Keynes, however, suggests that Keynes received the manuscript in 1942, after Woolf's death (Spotts 475), and that he bequeathed it to the University Library, Cambridge.

"On Being Ill" begins by remarking that it is odd that illness, which is so common a human experience, has not become one of the "prime themes" of literature. Contrary to what literature tries to maintain, the body, says Woolf, is unavoidable. Illness alters consciousness in a way comparable to love but the English language lacks powers of expression equal to the experience of sickness. Illness contradicts the illusion that human beings are linked together, for in each person is a "virgin forest" of isolation that is only reached in illness. Sickness enables fresh perceptions, for example that Nature is entirely indifferent to humanity. Despite ages of wishing a heaven into existence, Woolf writes, the clarity of illness reveals this to be an illusion.

The last part of the essay reflects reading Woolf did in 1925 when she was considering writing a book to be called "Lives of the Obscure" (D3 37). When we are ill, we can read only poetry, for prose is too demanding; there are, though, some prose writers who can be read as poets. In the sick state we can "grasp what is beyond [the] surface meaning" of words. And so she moves from William SHAKESPEARE to Augustus J. C. Hare, for in illness, she writes, we appreciate only the finest and the worst literature. The conclusion of "On Being Ill" draws on Hare's *Story of Two Noble Lives. Being Memorials of Charlotte, Countess Canning, and Louisa, Marchioness of Waterford,* published in three volumes in 1893 (RN 98). Louisa and Charlotte were daughters of Peter Beckford (1740–1811), a famous eighteenth-century huntsman and author of celebrated books on hunting. Woolf concludes her essay with the story of Louisa, Lady Waterford, whose husband died in a fall from his horse while out hunting. The essay's final scene describes Louisa standing by a window where she crushes a heavy velvet curtain in her agony at her husband's death.

"On Not Knowing Greek" (CE1 1–13; CR1 39–59) This essay by Woolf had a long gestation. It is first referred to in August 1922 and Woolf continued to read for it for the next two and a half years (RN 101). She read the plays of Sophocles, Euripides, Aristophanes and Aeschylus, making her own "complete edition, text, translation, & notes" of the latter's "Agamemnon" (D2 215; this is now in the BERG COLLECTION). She also read dialogues of Plato and Homer's *Odyssey,* as well as biographies of the classicists Richard Bentley (1662–1742) and Sir Richard Jebb (1841–1905). The fruits of her reading are contained in the six notebooks that relate to the *COMMON READER,* where "On Not Knowing Greek" was published. Woolf had studied Greek first with Clara PATER and then with Janet CASE but remained always uncertain of her abilities. In December 1923 she wrote of her "Greek chapter" that it seemed "superficial, & not worth foisting off upon a world provided with so much knowledge already" (D2 276).

"On Not Knowing Greek" is typical of Woolf's essays in that it attempts to define the "essence" of a subject gained from the impression of a large number of texts. Woolf plunges into the essay asserting that it is "vain and foolish to talk of knowing Greek" since it is impossible to know how the Greeks spoke or how their actors acted (CE1 1). Greek literature is "impersonal" and the modern reader needs to imagine a world for it. She suggests that the Greek communities of the plays were similar in some respects to remote English villages where "life is simply sorted out into its main elements" (CE1 2), but she admits that the difference in climate is a problem in this analogy. Greek tragedy, she continues, is cruel and draws on broad emotions, the tragedians stamping well-known stories with their own peculiar accent.

To understand Sophocles requires not so much an understanding of Greek as an understanding of poetry (CE1 7). Woolf suggests that in reading Greek dramas the reader must make intuitive leaps because the exact meaning of the words can never be known. Nevertheless, she continues, it is useless to read translations because vocabulary evokes a specific cultural moment. This essay is a good example of how Woolf anticipates critical arguments that would engage readers and writers more than half a century after she wrote. It concludes by describing the "sadness" of Greek culture, a sense of mortality that is unmitigated by the kinds of consolations offered by Christianity (CE1 13).

"On Re-Reading Novels" (CE2 122–30; M 155–66) A lead article in the *TIMES LITERARY SUPPLEMENT* (TLS) July 20, 1922 (E3 336–46) that was heavily revised in subsequent appearances (it was also reprinted in the TLS in 1952 with the subtitle "Second Thoughts on the Craft of Fiction"). The essay was occasioned by J. M. Dent's publication of new editions of the novels of Jane AUSTEN; of Charlotte, Emily and Anne BRONTË; and of the works of George MEREDITH; but Woolf also used it to respond to and comment on Percy Lubbock's *The Craft of Fiction* (1921). As her reading notebooks attest, Woolf was thinking deeply about the issue of "form" in 1921 and made fourteen pages of notes on Lubbock's book (RN 145). She began to mention her "essay upon Mr. Percy Lubbock" in late 1921 (L2 494), records having disagreed "violently" with Lytton STRACHEY about Lubbock in early 1922 (D2 163), and seems to have written the essay—which she called "very laborious, yet rather gifted" (D2 179)—in June that year (RN 139).

The essay begins by wondering what is the "lasting quality" of these reissued novels (CE2 123) and says that a recent attempt at an answer to this has been made by Lubbock. He suggests that the "form" of the book is the key, but Woolf is troubled by the use of this term from the visual arts. To illustrate her difference with Lubbock she reads Gustave FLAUBERT's story "Un Coeur Simple." Her conclusion is that the "book itself" is "not form which you see, but emotion which you feel" (CE2 126); only when emotion is "feeble" can form be separated.

Woolf was grateful to Lubbock's book for advancing a language of criticism for the novel, but she disagreed with his idea that literary "devices" could be arrived at consciously. She knew from her own experience of "groping" for more than a year to find the "tunnelling process" she used in *MRS. DALLOWAY* that Lubbock was wrong about this. As in nearly all her critical essays, Woolf writes as a *writer* as well as reader; emotion, she wryly suggests, may make critics lose their heads. Where Lubbock has form, Woolf would put "art." She continues the essay by saying critics should look at how novelists have told stories, from Samuel Richardson to William Makepeace THACKERAY, Charles DICKENS, Leo TOLSTOY and, the consummate artist of the novel, Henry JAMES. Form, then, comes to mean emotions placed in "right relations" to each other. "On Re-reading Novels" ends with a hint that Marcel PROUST (whom Woolf was "trembling on the verge of reading") may take the novel in an entirely new direction, and says that readers who are critically informed have their part to play in shaping the genre, just as actors and spectators have contributed to the drama.

Orlando Eponymous hero/heroine of Woolf's 1928 novel *ORLANDO, A BIOGRAPHY* who embodies the history of the Sackville heritage of Woolf's lover Vita SACKVILLE-WEST.

***Orlando, A Biography* (1928)** Although some have hesitated to include *Orlando* among Woolf's novels, it is as much a "novel" as are any of the books after *NIGHT AND DAY;* Woolf herself was not sure what to call her long fictions, and "novel" applied to them is largely a matter of convenience. *Orlando*'s subtitle caused some difficulty for Miss Ritchie, the traveler for the HOGARTH PRESS, who had to persuade literal-minded booksellers to shelve it among the fiction.

Orlando plays with the conventions of biography in its form as well as its narrative, including as well as its six chapters, eight illustrations of its subject and various lovers, a preface, and an index. The tongue-in-cheek preface brings together many of Woolf's

Orlando. *Courtesy Linda J. Langham.*
Orlando *was first published as a Penguin paperback in England in 1942; this American edition (1946) cost 25¢.*

favorite authors as well as relatives, friends and acquaintances. She acknowledges the influence of Daniel DEFOE, Sir Thomas BROWNE, Laurence STERNE, Sir Walter SCOTT, Lord MACAULAY, Emily BRONTË and Walter PATER. Charles Percy SANGER is thanked for his knowledge of "the law of real property"; and for various other services the following are duly acknowledged in the voice of the biographer, whose persona Woolf assumes for *Orlando*: Saxon SYDNEY-TURNER, Arthur WALEY, Lydia LOPOKOVA, Roger FRY, Julian BELL, M[argery] K. Snowdon [SNOWDEN], Angus DAVIDSON, Mrs. CARTWRIGHT, Janet CASE, Lord BERNERS, Francis BIRRELL, Adrian STEPHEN, F. L. LUCAS, Mr. and Mrs. Desmond [and Molly] MACCARTHY, Clive BELL, G. H. RYLANDS, Lady [Sibyl] COLEFAX, Nellie BOXALL, John Maynard KEYNES, Violet DICKINSON, Edward SACKVILLE-WEST, Mr. and Mrs. [Mary] St. John HUTCHINSON, Duncan GRANT, Mr. and Mrs. Stephen TOMLIN, Mr. [Philip] and Lady Ottoline MORRELL, "my mother-in-law Mrs. Sidney Woolf," Osbert SITWELL, Mme. Jacques [Gwen] RAVERAT, Colonel Cory Bell (Clive's father), Valerie TAYLOR, J[ohn] T[ressider] SHEPPARD, Mr. and Mrs. T. S. ELIOT, Ethel SANDS, Nan HUDSON, Quentin BELL ("an old and valued collaborator in fiction"), Raymond MORTIMER,

Emphie CASE, Lady Gerald [Dorothy] WELLESLEY, Lytton STRACHEY, Viscountess [Lady Robert] CECIL, Hope MIRRLEES, E. M. FORSTER, Harold NICOLSON, Vanessa BELL, officials of the BRITISH MUSEUM and the Record Office, Miss Angelica Bell (Angelica GARNETT) "for a service which none but she could have rendered" (presumably the photograph of "The Russian Princess as a Child" for which Angelica posed [O 54]), and her husband, Leonard WOOLF. The preface ends with thanks to a "gentleman in America" who is in the habit of sending Woolf corrections of her novels' many errors (perhaps it was he who pointed out to Woolf that in *Night and Day* she had roses blooming in Lincolnshire in December).

Outline

Chapter 1: Orlando, a sixteen-year-old boy ("for there could be no doubt of his sex"), is slicing at the head of a Moor in the attic room of his family's vast house. Noble and attractive, Orlando can see all that his family owns from his vantage point at the root of his favorite oak tree on a hill. The biographer is somewhat distracted by Orlando's looks, which are very fine (particularly his legs). Orlando is writing "Aethelbert: A Tragedy in Five Acts," and is late to greet the Queen (Elizabeth I, who reigned from 1558 to 1603). Rushing through the servants' quarters on his way to the royal presence, Orlando catches sight of a poet sitting at TWITCHETT's table.

Two years later, Orlando is summoned to WHITEHALL to attend the Queen, who makes him a courtier and bestows on him the jeweled Order of the Garter. Loved by Elizabeth, Orlando is given lands and houses, but one day the old Queen catches sight of Orlando in her mirror kissing a girl. The biographer pauses to remark on Orlando's taste for "low company" (28), which he indulges with clandestine visits to the dockyard pubs of London's Wapping Old Stairs. Orlando tires of this, however, finding no intellectual satisfaction in lying in the arms of Sukey among the cargo of the ships from the East. Three ladies are mentioned as possible wives for Orlando: Clorinda, Favilla and EUPHROSYNE. Things look hopeful for Euphrosyne—"A nodding mass of lace and ceremony" (40)—when the Great Frost occurs, stranding the ship of the Ambassador from Moscow and the Russian Princess SASHA. We have moved quietly into the reign of James I (1603–25) as Orlando falls in love with Sasha, to the great displeasure of the English Court. Sitting opposite her, his "manhood woke; he grasped a sword in his hand" (40). His great passion is shaken, though, when he thinks he sees Sasha in the arms of a man on board her ship. Melancholy, he lingers by a performance of William SHAKESPEARE's *Othello* on the frozen River Thames, feeling a kinship with Othello in his murderous jealousy. Sasha and Orlando plan to run away together but the ice melts and Sasha sails back to Russia.

Chapter 2: In disgrace and exile from the mid-seventeenth century Court, Orlando returns to his house and falls into a trance-like slumber for seven days. Waking as if nothing extraordinary had happened, he begins to delight in morbid thoughts, spending hours in the family crypt and discovering the writing of Thomas Browne. Mourning Sasha, he reads voraciously and writes and rewrites his many plays. Before the age of twenty-five, Orlando has written forty-seven plays. He chooses two to work on, "Xenophila a Tragedy" and "The Oak Tree" (77).

A disquisition on memory by Orlando's biographer leads in to Orlando's memory of the poet at Twitchett's table (79). Comparing the exploits of his ancestors (which consist entirely of slaughtering people who are not English) with poetry, Orlando decides that only poetry is immortal and discovers that the battle to write it well is far greater than any fought by his ancestors. Through a friend, Orlando sends a letter of admiration to a famous writer, Nick GREENE, inviting him to visit. Nick Greene tells him the art of poetry is dead, which Orlando finds surprising as they are contemporaries of Shakespeare, Christopher MARLOWE, Ben Jonson, Thomas Browne and John DONNE. Greene dismisses them all (except Jonson, who is his friend) and says that the great age of literature was the Greek, when men aspired to "Glawr" (which eventually Orlando understands to be "La Gloire," French for "Glory" [89]). Greene's tales of the poets reveal Orlando's heroes to be all flawed and ordinary characters. Greene goes back to London to write a satire about Orlando, from whom he receives a quarterly pension.

At the age of thirty, Orlando is alone; he has "done with men." He burns all his writing save "The Oak Tree," refurbishes his house and entertains the local nobility. At the height of his parties, Orlando steals away to write and rewrite his poem, a palimpsest that is always with him. His style has changed because "the age of prose was congealing those warm fountains" of his earlier images (113). The landscape has changed too, as if literature and Nature reflect each other. "The Oak Tree" is now a poem.

One day a shadow falls across Orlando's page—the Archduchess HARRIET of Roumania, who tells Orlando he is the image of her long-dead sister. Suddenly overcome with lust for Harriet, Orlando asks King Charles II (1625–49) to send him as Ambassador to CONSTANTINOPLE (118).

Chapter 3: Once again the biographer apologizes for lack of information about Orlando's career and says he must "speculate, surmise, and even . . . make use of the imagination" (119). Orlando is kept busy by his duties as Ambassador but carries with him still a "much-scored manuscript" (124). King Charles confers a Dukedom and the Order of the Bath on Orlando and the ceremony takes place in a scene of great excitement and disorder, recorded only in the fragmented account of John Fenner BRIGGE and a letter to a friend from Miss Penelope HARTOPP. That night Orlando again falls into a deep sleep that lasts seven days. On his table his aides discover among his papers a deed of marriage between Orlando and Rosina Pepita (see PEPITA), a gypsy dancer (132). On the seventh day of Orlando's trance, the Turks revolt against the Sultan, only sparing Orlando's life because they assume he is already dead.

The biographer pauses, wishing that here the story could end, but "Truth, Candour, and Honesty" demand that the story continue. Three figures enter the scene: our Lady of Purity, our Lady of Chastity, and our Lady of Modesty all speak over the prone Orlando until trumpets sound, sending them away to prepare for the arrival of "THE TRUTH!"—"he was a woman" (137). While Orlando has her bath, the biographer notes that though Orlando has become a woman, "in every other respect Orlando remained precisely as he had been" (138). Leaving aside the "odious subjects" of sex and sexuality, the biographer goes on with Orlando's story (139).

Orlando puts on the androgynous costume of the Turks and goes to live with the gypsies of Broussa. All goes well until the older members of the clan begin to suspect her of worshiping Nature. When she begins to work on her poem again, their suspicions deepen. RUSTUM EL SADI scorns her few hundred years' heritage (his being so much older) and Orlando longs to go back to England. As the gypsies are planning to kill her, Orlando's decision to return home on a merchant ship comes none too soon.

Chapter 4: On the ship *Enamoured Lady,* Orlando begins to learn what it means to be a woman, her sensibility heightened by wearing feminine clothes for the first time. Femininity does not come naturally, and Orlando vacillates between the two sexes as she weighs the advantages and disadvantages of each. Her love for Sasha now deepens because at last "she knew Sasha as she was" (161).

Returning to England, once again the memory of the poet in the servants' quarters comes back to Orlando, prompted by the sight of St. Paul's, the dome of which reminds her of the poet's bald head. She has arrived in eighteenth-century London, as we learn when Captain BARTOLUS points out to her Joseph ADDISON, John DRYDEN and Alexander POPE (the anachronism of Dryden, who died when Pope was two years old, being in this company is excused in a footnote). Orlando has also returned to find herself party to several lawsuits that claim that she is dead and cannot therefore hold title to any property, that she is a woman "which amounts to much the same thing," and that she was married to Rosina Pepita, who has borne her three sons who are now claiming all Orlando's property (118). The court allows her to wait for its decision at her country house.

She returns to find her household, including Mr. DUPPER and Mrs. GRIMSDITCH, waiting for her. Reacquainting herself with her house, Orlando makes a fresh start on "The Oak Tree." As before, the shadow of Archduchess Harriet falls across the page, but she now turns out to be Archduke Harry. He explains to Orlando how he had fallen in love with Orlando's portrait and disguised himself as a woman to seduce him. Having heard that Orlando is now a woman, Archduke Harry has returned to propose marriage. After putting up with his attentions as long as she can bear, Orlando finally rids herself of Harry by offending his honor when she cheats at "Fly Loo," a game she has invented. He is about to forgive her when she drops a toad down his shirt and laughs him out of her house.

While Orlando travels up to London in search of "life and a lover," the biographer draws attention to the ways in which she is taking on the attributes of femininity, which include hiding her manuscripts whenever someone sees her writing, and looking at herself long and intently in mirrors. The biographer then discourses on the relation of clothing to sexuality. Without delay, Orlando is launched into the highest London society of the reign of Queen Anne (1702–14). Soon tiring of this, she longs to meet the writers she had caught a glimpse of from the deck of the *Enamoured Lady.* At Lady R.'s she meets Pope and invites him home with her (she still has her house in BLACKFRIARS). Orlando now spends her time in the company of Addison, Pope and Jonathan SWIFT, extracts from whose works the biographer quotes. The misogyny of the geniuses eventually wears Orlando down and she begins to amuse herself instead by dressing as a man to allow her to go out alone at night.

Orlando picks up a prostitute in Leicester Square and goes back to her room in Gerrard Street. Discovering that Orlando is a woman, Nell is delighted and brings her friends Prue, Kitty and Rose to meet Orlando. Together the women form a society of which men are ignorant. Orlando meets Samuel JOHNSON and James BOSWELL and now "enjoyed the love of both sexes equally" (221). The nineteenth century approaches suddenly as a dark cloud over the whole of London and, as the chapter ends, "The Eighteenth Century was over; the Nineteenth Century had begun" (226).

Chapter 5: The climate—in all senses of the word—has changed and dampness invades and swells everything, from people's sentences to the British Empire. Women have fifteen or twenty children. Orlando has been working on "The Oak Tree" for nearly three hundred years and decides it is time to end it. But as she writes, her pen blots the page and she finds herself writing "the most insipid verse she had ever read in her life" (238). Orlando becomes acutely conscious that she is not married, noticing wedding rings everywhere. She starts wearing one herself, but the ruse does not seem to work. Wandering her estate, she trips and falls, breaking her ankle. To the rescue comes Marmaduke Bonthrop SHELMERDINE, Esquire. "A few minutes later, they became engaged" (250). Recognizing each other's androgynous natures, they are perfectly matched.

The lawsuits are settled. Orlando's Turkish marriage is annulled and Lord PALMERSTON (the Victorian prime minister in 1855 and again in 1859–65) declares her a woman. On the day the wind rises from the Southwest—which means that Shel must set sail for Cape Horn—he and Orlando are married by Mr. Dupper.

Chapter 6: The spirit of the age apparently approves Orlando's marriage, for when she tries again to write, there are now no ink blots and she manages to conceal the "contraband" of her mind in verses that satisfy the spirit (265). The biographer is at a loss because Orlando does not behave as a woman should, does not "love" a man. What is life, asks the biographer? "Alas, we don't know" (271).

Suddenly seized with the desire for people to read her poem, Orlando goes up to London where she encounters "her very old friend, Nick Greene" (276), now "the most influential critic of the Victorian age" (277). Nick is still bemoaning the past glory of literature and dismissing his contemporaries. Now he longs for the age of Shakespeare, Marlowe and Jonson, or of Dryden, Pope and Addison, giants compared to the paltry offerings of the Victorian age, Alfred TENNYSON, Robert BROWNING and Thomas CARLYLE. He reads "The Oak Tree" and declares it must be published immediately.

Orlando sends Shel a telegram at Cape Horn, writing in their cryptic private language. She astounds a bookseller by asking him to send her everything of importance and sets herself the task of discovering what literature has become. Reading through the avalanche of books, she concludes that the rule of the Victorian age is never to say what one thinks and always to try to sound like someone else.

Now the biographer begins a digression to try and find a way of saying delicately what must be said: that Orlando gives birth to a boy. The twentieth century has also arrived and Edward VII is on the throne (1901–1910), cars are in the streets and electric lights illuminate people's houses. Orlando arrives at the present moment: 1928. She jumps into her car and goes to London to shop at Marshall & Snelgrove, where she is overcome by memories of Sasha and ponders her own middle age. On the way home, Orlando's many selves jostle in her mind and the memory of the poet seen four hundred years before still haunts her: "Was it Sh—p—re?" (313). Again she wanders through her house, which has become a museum open to the public. She goes up to her favorite oak tree intending to bury at its roots her book, *The Oak Tree,* for which she has won a prize of two hundred guineas. Nick Greene has compared it to the work of John MILTON. She leaves the book unburied and thinks of Shel, calling out his name. Suddenly an airplane appears and Shel jumps down to earth as a wild goose flies above his head. The clock strikes midnight, "Thursday, the eleventh of October, Nineteen Hundred and Twenty-eight" (329).

Genesis

Orlando is part of the enormous surge of creativity that carried Woolf from the completion of ***TO THE LIGHTHOUSE*** (published May 1927) to ***THE WAVES*** (1931). *Orlando* shares its roots with ***A ROOM OF ONE'S OWN*** (1929) and *The Waves,* although its primary motivator was Woolf's intense relationship with Vita SACKVILLE-WEST. Vita's affair with Mary Campbell, wife of the poet Roy Campbell, seems to have precipitated Woolf's jealousy (Raitt 34) and led her to "woo Vita as others could not" (CS 200) by writing Vita's life for her and, as Vita and her husband Harold NICOLSON immediately recognized, by "giving" Vita KNOLE. The laws of entail meant that Vita could not inherit the ancestral house she loved because she was a woman and when her father died in 1928, Knole passed to his brother. Vita's son Nigel NICOLSON has called *Orlando* "the longest and most charming love letter in literature" (Nicolson, *Portrait* 202) and explains that Woolf "had provided Vita with a unique consolation for having been born a girl, for her exclusion from her inheritance, for her father's death earlier that year" (Nicolson, *Portrait* 208).

Woolf first began to mention what would quickly take shape as *Orlando* in March 1927. She was suddenly struck with the idea of a "fantasy to be called 'The Jessamy Brides' " (D3 131) that would draw on, among other things, the story of the LADIES OF LLANGOLLEN and would have "satire and wildness" as its main note (D3 131). As the year went on, her conception of this fantasy changed as she began to think about writing brief biographies of all her friends: "Vita should be Orlando, a young nobleman" (D3 157). Earlier that year, in January, Woolf had been taken to Knole by Vita, and although Woolf did not care much for the house, she appreciated how much Vita loved it. In her DIARY Woolf wrote, "one or two things remain: Vita stalking in her Turkish dress, attended by small boys" (D3 125). At Knole, "All the centuries seemed lit up, the past expressive, articulate" (D3 125). In transforming Knole into Orlando's house Woolf changed few details, drawing heavily on Vita's book *Knole and the Sackvilles** (1922).

As 1927 waned, the long critical essay "PHASES OF FICTION" weighed more and more heavily on Woolf. She made a schedule, intending to ration her writing of fiction, but eventually *Orlando* pushed the critical writing aside by the sheer exuberance of its conception and Woolf abandoned her schedule. In an October 1927 letter to Vita, Woolf described how she could not write a word of "Phases of Fiction" and eventually gave up, "dipped my pen in the ink, and wrote the words, as if automatically, on a clean sheet: Orlando: A Biography" (L3 428). *Orlando* was written at high speed while *The Waves* simmered in her mind; looking back in 1933 at her description of "The Jessamy Brides," Woolf wrote in the margin of her diary, "Orlando leading to the Waves" (D3 131).

As the idea took hold that *Orlando* was to be "based on Vita, Violet Trefusis, Lord Lascelles, Knole, &c." (D3 162) and that it would be a biography "beginning in the year 1500 & continuing to the present day . . . with a change about from one sex to another" (D3 161), Woolf wrote to her subject, "But listen; suppose Orlando turns out to be Vita; and its all about you and the lusts of your flesh and the lure of your mind" (L3 428). Writing that it had occurred to her she "could revolutionise biography in a night" (L3 429), Woolf began to question Vita closely for details about her life and her family: "What used you and Lord Lascelles to talk about?" (L3 433). As Suzanne Raitt has remarked, Woolf felt that Vita summarized English history long before *Orlando* (Raitt 160).

Woolf usually kept a close eye on her creative process, recording in her diary her aims for a particular piece of writing and warning herself of pitfalls to avoid. As she began to abandon herself to the delight of making up *Orlando* she wrote that its balance of truth and fantasy had to be carefully maintained (D3 162) and that unity of tone was very important (D3 168). From quite early on Woolf saw *Orlando* as part comic, part serious. When she finished the manuscript and showed it to Leonard Woolf (who thought it "in some ways better than The Lighthouse"), she reflected that she had probably begun it "as a joke, & went on with it seriously" (D3 185), hence the book lacked unity. She tried in *Orlando* to "give things their caricature value" (D3 203) and in writing the biography of a woman writer traced through four centuries she was, from another angle, creating a narrative very similar to that she would express in *A Room of One's Own.* A few days before *Orlando* was published, Woolf wrote that she had learned from it how to write "a direct sentence" and how to provide narrative and continuity, but that she had not "got down to my depths & made shapes square up" as she had in *To the Lighthouse* (D3 203).

Orlando is dedicated to "V. Sackville-West" and appeared first in the United States on October 2, 1928, in a limited edition of 861 copies published by Crosby Gaige, of which 800 were signed by Woolf. A very few (either eleven or fifteen [Kirkpatrick 35]) were printed on green paper. The Hogarth Press edition appeared on October 11, 1928, the day on which *Orlando* ends. A copy bound in niger, lettered in gold, and inscribed "Vita from Virginia / Thursday, October the Eleventh,/ Ninetеenhundred & twenty eight" is still in Vita Sackville-West's study at SISSINGHURST. When the book was published as part of the "Uniform Edition" of Woolf's works by the Hogarth Press, *Orlando's* title page incorrectly described it as a "New Edition;" it also omitted the illustrations, as have subsequent English editions until the Definitive Edition of Woolf's novels published in 1990 by the Hogarth Press restored them. In the United States, *Orlando* was published by Harcourt, Brace & Company on October 18, 1928. A transcription by Stuart Nelson Clarke of the Knole holograph draft of *Orlando* was published in 1993.

Background

"Tomorrow I begin the chapter which describes Violet and you meeting on the ice," Woolf wrote to Vita Sackville-West in late 1927 (L3 430). The story

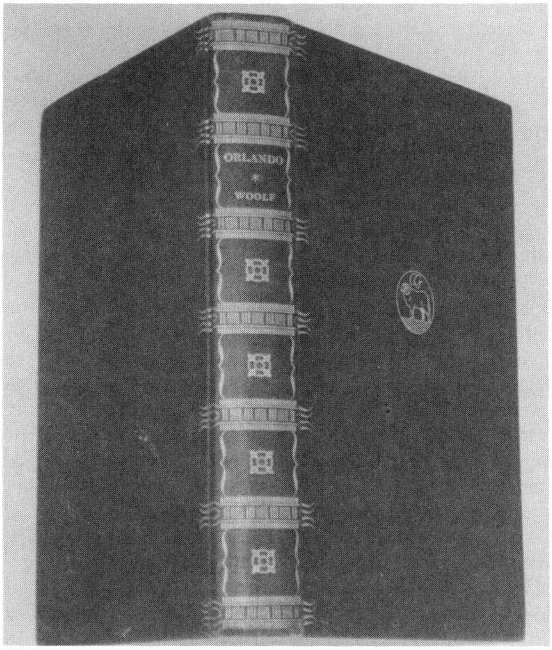

Orlando. *Courtesy Linda J. Langham.*
This limited edition, published in New York by Crosby Gaige on October 2, 1928, is the true first edition of Orlando. *Woolf signed 800 of the 861 copies printed; a very small number (11 or 15) were printed on green paper.*

of Vita's affair with Violet TREFUSIS is told in Vita's son Nigel Nicolson's book *Portrait of a Marriage,* reading which we can see how Woolf "transforms the merely personal into the mythic, the historical into the eternal" (Harper 165). Vita herself had written about the affair in her novel *Challenge* (1924), published only in the United States because both women's families found the characters so easily identifiable and had it suppressed in England. Woolf plundered Vita's life and works for *Orlando,* creating her character as a composite of the Sackville family who is writing a work, "The Oak Tree," similar to Vita's long poem "THE LAND" (for which she won the Hawthornden Prize in 1927, satirized in *Orlando* as the "Burdett Coutts' Memorial Prize" [O 312]). "The Land" is quoted early in chapter 6 of *Orlando* (265), the lines taken from the "Spring" section of Vita's poem (47–48). Rachel Blau DuPlessis* points out that the next few lines of the poem allude to lesbianism, describing the "Egyptian girl" holding to her breast "A gipsy Judith, witch of a ragged tent" (DuPlessis 133n36). Woolf also uses the story of Vita's grandmother Pepita, about whom Vita published a book with the Hogarth Press in 1937.

Frank Baldanza* has detailed the connections to be made between *Orlando* and *Knole and the Sackvilles.* Charles G. Hoffmann* also discusses how Woolf "sought to recreate the 'facts' of history as revealed in the history and temperament of the Sackvilles, who not only played a part in English history and literature but who also in their various personages and in the history of Knole House mirrored the spirit of the age in which they lived" (436). Hoffmann compares dates in the Knole manuscript with events in the Sackville family's history. David Bonnell Green* has explained the history of Knole's succession through various generations of Sackvilles and believes that "Orlando's ceasing to be a man is equivalent to the ending of the male line in the Sackville family, and his becoming a woman is equivalent to the beginning of the female representation of the family in the Sackville-Wests" (Green 268). James Naremore believes that Vita's history of her family and its house was more than just a sourcebook for Woolf, suggesting even themes and plot as well as historical detail (Naremore, *World* 206).

Knole itself—where John Donne used to preach in the family chapel, the Chapel of the Archbishops, when he was rector of Sevenoaks (Madeline Moore,* "Orlando" 343)—is a repository of English cultural and social history. The early Orlando resembles Vita's ancestor Thomas Sackville (1536–1608), treasurer to Queen Elizabeth I, who was "presented with Knole because, as legend has it, the Queen 'wished to have him nearer to her court and councils' " (Naremore 203; the quotation is from *Knole and the Sackvilles* 46). Thomas Sackville collaborated with Thomas Norton on *Gorboduc* or *Ferrex and Porrex* (1561), one of the earliest English tragedies, modeled on Seneca. Woolf asked Vita to lend it to her in November 1927 (L3 441). The description of Orlando's play "Aethelbert: A Tragedy" makes it sound rather like *Gorboduc* or, perhaps, another work of Thomas Sackville's, his "Induction" to *A Mirror for Magistrates* (1563).

Even Mr. Dupper and Mrs. Grimsditch, Orlando's servants, can be found in *Knole and the Sackvilles,* listed in a catalog of the household of Richard Sackville, the seventeenth-century earl of Dorset (Naremore 203), where they both appear among those seated "*At* the Parlour Table" for meals in the Great Hall (*Knole and the Sackvilles* 86). Naremore also points out that in the list of items Orlando buys to refurbish his house in chapter 2 (O 109), Woolf is clearly making fun of Vita's "charming pedantry" in *Knole and the Sackvilles* (Naremore 207), which includes lengthy inventories.

The Sackville family appears in some of the illustrations in *Orlando,* beginning with its frontispiece, "Orlando as a Boy," which is a portrait of the Honorable Edward Sackville, son of the fourth earl, by Cornelius Nuie (also reproduced in *Knole and the Sackvilles*). "The Archduchess Harriet" is a Tudor portrait of Mary, the fourth countess. (Archduke Harry is not represented visually in *Orlando*; he was based on Henry, Lord Lascelles [1882–1974], who had courted Vita in 1913 and who married the Princess Royal in 1922.) Woolf had made another trip with Vita to Knole in October 1927 to choose portraits for *Orlando* and took great trouble in selecting those she eventually used. The painting of "Marmaduke Bonthrop Shelmerdine, Esquire" was bought in London by Vita and was painted in about 1820 by an unknown artist of an unidentified young man. "Mar," incidentally, was Harold Nicolson's pet name for Vita. Like Shelmerdine, Harold was frequently away and had sailed round Cape Horn; in 1920 he flew from Paris and landed in the park at Knole.

Woolf also used a portrait photograph of Vita by LENARE made at the time she won the Hawthornden Prize. Vanessa BELL took "at least ten pictures of her daughter [Angelica Garnett] assuming different poses in different headdresses and robes" (Diane F. Gillespie,* " 'Her Kodak' " 136) for the picture of "The Russian Princess as a Child." "Orlando about the year 1840" was a joint production of Vanessa Bell and Duncan GRANT. "Orlando at the present time" was a snapshot taken by Leonard Woolf of Vita at her house, LONG BARN. The photographs have recently been interpreted by Talia Schaffer* as a "counterdiscourse to the novel's text" (Schaffer 26).

Woolf had visited Knole with Vita in 1924 "to lunch alone with his lordship," Vita's father. The Knole she saw then was the house as she described it at the end of *Orlando,* with rooms roped off, the chairs that Shakespeare might have sat in and the pictures looking "preserved" as if "life [had] left them" (D2 306). In the Venetian Ambassador's Bedroom, as Louise DeSalvo (VWM 13: 3–4) and Howard Harper have pointed out, Woolf would have seen tapestries depicting scenes from Ariosto's *Orlando Furioso* (1532), the poem which continues the story of Orlando's love for Angelica begun by Boiardo in the *Orlando Innamorato* (1487). In *Knole and the Sackvilles* Vita writes that the bed in this room "appears to be designed for three: it is of enormous breadth and there are three pillows in a row" (31). Harper writes that "what seems to Vita to be most touching about this room is the feeling of its emptiness, which she attributes to the huge 'matrimonial bed'. At the heart of this space, then, as at the heart of *Orlando Furioso* (and Woolf's *Orlando*), is a sexual mystery. And this mystery is at the heart of the house itself" (Harper 195). The French legends of Roland, best known in the "Chanson de Roland," tell of this paladin of the emperor Charlemagne who died at Roncevaux. "Orlando" is the Italian evolution of this figure (especially appropriate, says Harper, for Vita, who loved Italy passionately [Harper 165]).

Another source for Woolf's choice of Orlando's name might be Sir John Harington, one of Lytton Strachey's *Portraits in Miniature* (Strachey's article on Harington first appeared in the *NEW STATESMAN AND NATION*). He was "a great favourite with the ladies, who welcomed Queen Elizabeth for a day in that vast Somersetshire manor to which periodically, when out of the royal favour, he would retire to seek consolation with his dog and to translate Ariosto's *Orlando Furioso*" (Guiguet 278). In her edition of the Knole manuscript of *Orlando,* showing how it differs significantly from the published version, Madeline Moore notes the work's literary background and shows how Orlando's character draws on Ariosto's depiction of Orlando as warrior and as furiously in love and also on Shakespeare's Orlando in *As You Like It,* who is deprived of his birthright by the envy of his eldest brother, Oliver (Moore, "Orlando" 340). The indeterminacy of Woolf's Orlando is also seen as emblematized in his/her name by Françoise Defromont, who notes the "or/and (and/or) and/or" contained within it (quoted in Bowlby, *Feminist* 50).

Orlando is enormously allusive, and even self-mocking. Alex Zwerdling finds "such serious Woolfian themes as androgyny, the passage of time, and artistic dedication" to be "rather archly guyed" (Zwerdling 56). A particularly rich example occurs in chapter 2 when the biographer begins to describe the passing of time and then halts, saying all this could be more easily conveyed "by the simple statement that 'Time passed' (here the exact amount could be indicated in brackets)" (O 97–98). When she was struggling with the "Time Passes" section of *To the Lighthouse,* Woolf had written to Vita that she, as a poet, could probably achieve more easily what Woolf was attempting in prose.

Critics have found several other sources in the background of *Orlando*: Susan Squier,* for example, explains how Woolf has drawn on *Moll Flanders* while subverting the influence of Defoe's narrative (171). Squier argues that *Orlando* "may be read as a serious work of criticism as well as a love-tribute" (168) and reads it as a challenge to the "patrilineal tradition of English literature which [Leslie STEPHEN] traced in his important volume, *English Literature and Society in the Eighteenth Century*" (168). More recently Leslie Hankins* has discussed the influence on *Orlando* of René Clair's film *Entr'acte* (1924) ("'Across'" 154), and Evelyn Haller* has noted the three-hundred-year-old woman at the opening of Stravinsky's *Rite of Spring* and also found evidence of the influence on *Orlando* of his *Firebird* ("Her Quill" 199, 208). DuPlessis notes that "the Hemingway novel of adventure, the Lawrence novel of sexuality are evoked and dismissed" in *Orlando* (DuPlessis 132).

Orlando, indeed, seems to invite reference-hunting. Edward Sackville-West complained to Woolf that people might mistake him for "Mr. S. W.," but Woolf assured him that it was "(if anybody) Sydney Waterlow" that she meant (L3 559). "Lady A" bears some resemblance to Lady Colefax (Moore, "Orlando" 345). But the true subject of *Orlando,* pictured in three photographs and to whom the book is unabashedly dedicated, was Woolf's lover Vita Sackville-West. Published three months after Radclyffe Hall's *WELL OF LONELINESS* was banned, *Orlando* skirted the dangers of "sapphism" with brilliance. Raitt says that the writing of *Orlando* was "bound up with [Woolf's] desire" for Vita from the beginning (17); "far from being a way to create distance in the relationship," says Sherron Knopp,* "*Orlando* was a way to heighten intimacy—not a substitute for physical lovemaking but an extension of it" (Knopp 27).

In their correspondence while Vita was in Persia in 1926, Woolf and she drew on what Karen Lawrence* terms "a discourse of Orientalism associated with an eroticism of masquerade" (Lawrence 259) that is clearly an influence in chapter 3 of *Orlando.* Vita informs the characterization of Orlando in myriad ways, with her passion for women and for writing, her deep bond with England, her aristocratic lineage and her sense of adventure. No wonder, then, that she wrote to Woolf, "you have invented a new form of Narcissism,—I confess—I am in love with Orlando" (L3 574). When she first read the book Vita was "completely dazzled, bewitched, enchanted, under a spell" (L3 573). She wrote to Harold Nicolson that *Orlando* seemed to her unique and to have everything—"romance, wit, seriousness, beauty, imagination, style, with Sir Thomas Browne and Swift for parents" (Moore, "Orlando" 348). Vita did not tell

Woolf that she found the last part of *Orlando* disappointing, and thought that Shelmerdine as a husband was a mistake (Moore, *Short Season* 107).

One who had an extremely negative reaction to *Orlando* was Vita's mother. Lady Sackville made efforts to stop the book being reviewed and pasted a newspaper photograph of its author into her copy alongside which she wrote: "The awful face of a mad woman whose successful mad desire is to separate people who care for each other. I loathe this woman for having changed my Vita and taken her away from me" (Glendinning 206). It is very doubtful that Woolf effected any change in Vita of the kind Lady Sackville deplored, but she did influence Vita's writing, as Raitt has pointed out; motifs from *To the Lighthouse* and *Orlando* found their way into Vita's 1931 novel *All Passion Spent* (Raitt 107).

Many years after Woolf's death, Leonard Woolf still found it necessary to explain the ironic tone of *Orlando,* describing the preface as "a skit on the unpardonable snobbery of so many learned and unlearned writers who write prefaces spattered with well known people to whom they ladle out their thanks" (Spotts 543).

Critical Responses

"The book in Bloomsbury is a joke, in Mayfair a necessity, and in America a classic" said the *Daily Chronicle* in November 1928 (Glendinning 205). *Orlando* seemed to most reviewers a light entertainment. Woolf's old antagonist Arnold BENNETT called it "a high-brow lark" (CH 232) and Conrad Aiken wrote that Woolf had "expanded a *jeu d'esprit* to the length of a novel" (CH 235). Most dismissive was J. C. Squier, who called the novel "a very pleasant trifle" that would "entertain the drawing-rooms for an hour" (CH 229). A much more positive and insightful review was Rebecca WEST's "High Fountain of Genius" in the *New York Herald Tribune* (October 21, 1928), which called *Orlando* "a poetic masterpiece of the first rank" (Scott, *Gender* 592). Referring to the description at the beginning of *Orlando* of his vantage point at the roots of the oak tree from where he can see London and the mountains of Wales, West noted that Woolf combined "the frankest contempt for realism, with the profoundest reality" (Scott, *Gender* 594). The book should be read "as conscientiously and as often as one would play over a newly discovered Beethoven sonata" (Scott, *Gender* 596).

Woolf's own description of *Orlando* as having begun as a "joke" for a long time diverted critical attention from it, even when a particular critic's interests might have indicated that the work would be central to his or her study. Herbert Marder and Nancy Topping Bazin, for example, hardly mention *Orlando,* and Mitchell Leaska leaves it out entirely. Alice van Buren Kelley omits *Orlando* because it is "so formally unlike" Woolf's other fiction and because Woolf herself said it was "too long for a joke, and too frivolous for a serious book" (255n11). Lucio Ruotolo takes seriously "Woolf's designation of *Orlando* as 'A Biography' " and so does not discuss it (*Interrupted* 2n).

John Graham* sees in *Orlando* a "complex process of assessment and speculation" carried on "behind the mask of the comic fantasist" in which Woolf continues by other means, so to speak, the arguments she was expounding in her essays written between 1926 and 1929 (Graham 348). Seeing *Orlando* as primarily a parody, Graham believes Woolf used the book to play with her own themes and methods (Graham 353). Avrom Fleishman also discusses the book as "a parodic *Künstlerroman*" (Fleishman 148), but Naremore finds that it is a parody only in a very limited sense.

There are several critics who take exactly the opposite point of view from those who dismiss *Orlando* as a joke or leave it out of general considerations of Woolf's novels. These critics usually allude to the Freudian analysis of jokes as "the truth of the unconscious" (Makiko Minow-Pinkney 117) in arguing that *Orlando* should be taken seriously. Harper, who considers *Orlando* "an astonishing imaginative achievement" (202), finds the book "very serious indeed—and very revealing" (Harper 163). Maria DiBattista also takes seriously Woolf's play in *Orlando.* Raitt argues that Woolf's choice of a "joke" form for the biography of a woman with whom she was so intimately and ambivalently involved was deliberate as Woolf wished to hurt as well as to express love for Vita (Raitt 30). Knopp concurs with this reading, pointing out that what we joke about is often what "we care about too much to risk seriousness" (Knopp 25). Even Zwerdling, who finds that *Orlando* embodies "the shallower aspects of Bloomsbury," sees many parallels between it and Woolf's "darker fiction" (Zwerdling 28, 56).

Some have seen this "darkness" of *Orlando* as the weight of Woolf's literary heritage, the "largely masculine tradition" against which Orlando struggles. For Daniel Fogel, the dark subtext derives from the "difficulty of resisting [her literary heritage] and of forging for oneself a differential literary identity" (Fogel 154). The anxiety of *Orlando* is for Fogel Woolf's desire to efface Henry James. Kari Elise Lokke* also notes that *Orlando* "revisits the history and development of English literature from the Renaissance to 1928 in the spirit of feminist parody in order to free it—and by extension its author—from the burden of this largely masculine tradition" (Lokke 239). For Minow-Pinkney it is Woolf's feminism that leads to the "earnestness" of the latter part of *Orlando,* as she sees the book's "serious" tone slowly developing after Orlando becomes a woman. Woolf "becomes a victim of the 'self-consciousness' she had so often deplored in others" (Minow-Pinkney 143).

Clearly there are connections to be made between these readings of *Orlando* and the subject of *A Room of One's Own.* Lokke writes that *Orlando* "brilliantly embodies the seemingly contradictory political and aesthetic theories of *A Room of One's Own* in a vision of the comic sublime" (Lokke 236). Marder sees the two works as "companion volumes" (Marder 26) and Sandra Gilbert* notes that *Orlando* is "of course a text complementary to *A Room of One's Own*" ("Woman's Sentence" 219). Others have found links between *Orlando* and Woolf's other works of fiction, particularly *The Waves,* which both Mark Hussey (*Singing*) and Raitt see as part of the same creative impulse that produced *Orlando.* Hussey writes that *Orlando*'s tone allows Woolf to explore questions of identity more directly than in other works and links *Orlando* philosophically with *MRS. DALLOWAY* and *The Waves* in this regard. Several readers have also remarked on similarities between *Orlando* and *BETWEEN THE ACTS.* Both works, for example, in Pamela Caughie's words, "dramatize self and literature as acquiring significance within a history, within a plural past," (Caughie 84) and both celebrate or criticize (depending on the critic's point of view) English culture and poetry. Harvena Richter says *Orlando* and *Between the Acts* share an "inner tone" which is the tone of the "time of a particular moment, a vocal 'spirit of the age' " (Richter 143). To Richter, Orlando is a "questing hero in the realm of time" (154).

Returning to the issue of seriousness, J. J. Wilson* takes a critical view of many readings of *Orlando,* arguing that it is an anti-novel in the tradition of Laurence STERNE and Denis Diderot that forces readers to "rethink all our so-called givens, be they taboos, institutions, or other forms of limitations, such as gender, time, space, even death" ("Why" 179). It is, of course, the limitations of gender that have seemed to most readers *Orlando*'s significant theme. Woolf seems to many readers to be suggesting ANDROGYNY as a way of evading these limitations, as she seems to suggest also in *A Room of One's Own.*

Marder, although he does not develop the point, says that androgyny pervades *Orlando* right from the start, going so far as to say that it is "a kind of hymn to androgyny" (111). Sandra Gilbert and Susan Gubar describe Orlando as "really" androgynous "(as Tiresias, for example, is not) in the sense that she has available to her a sort of wardrobe of male and female selves" (*Sexchanges* 345). If *Orlando* is Woolf's "most successful depiction of how the dreams of the psyche are filtered into the political world" (Moore, *Short Season* 26), Woolf achieves this by aligning codes of gender with linguistic codes that "shape his/her very emotions" (Moore, *Short Season* 103). *Orlando*'s narrator, whom Bowlby describes as ending up "as something like a woman posing as a man posing as a woman to investigate the identity of a man who becomes a woman and poses as a man" (Bowlby 60), is used by Woolf to demonstrate how "lives, histories, and fictions" (Caughie 77) are constructed. The "central ambiguity" of this narrative is gender, which, says Raitt, "displaces all sorts of other certainties" (Raitt 23). For some time, androgyny was seen by several Woolf critics as a positive resolution of opposites into unity, but recently critics such as Minow-Pinkney have argued otherwise. "Androgyny in *Orlando* is not a resolution of oppositions, but the throwing of both sexes into a metonymic confusion of genders" (Minow-Pinkney 122). Carroll Smith-Rosenberg* calls Orlando a "trickster par excellence" (291) and writes that in "[t]ying gender to dress rather than dress to gender, Woolf inverts [Richard von] Krafft-Ebing's dark vision of the 'Mannish Lesbian.' Her joyous androgyne counterposes Krafft-Ebing's decadent hermaphrodite" (289). Pamela Caughie* has described Orlando's androgyny as embodying an "oscillation between positions" that is "not only a sexual ambiguity but a textual one as well" ("Double Discourse" 486). Caughie argues against feminist critics who have appropriated the androgyny in the novel as "a symbol of the more unified self" (486).

A significant effect of the critical enthusiasm for androgyny in readings of *Orlando* has been the effacement of its "lesbian subject matter" (Knopp 29). Moore sees this displacement of "the obvious lesbian base which inspired the fantasy" as occurring because of Orlando's androgyny and sees it as Woolf's covering-up of her own lesbianism. There are, Moore writes, actually two biographers telling Orlando's story: "one is the naive biographer and one is Woolf herself" (Moore, *Short Season* 102). Woolf's fantasy for Vita would render her "androgynous, immortal and the possessor of Knole. But Woolf's fantasy for herself would not result in androgyny; it would result in lesbianism" (Moore 102). The text, then, "exculpates" what was in 1928 the shocking issue of lesbianism through the fantasy of Orlando's sex-change (Minow-Pinkney 134), but lesbianism is present in the text as the "contraband" (O 265) in Orlando's mind "that marriage liberates and that itself frees writing" (DuPlessis 133). What has been missing until very recently from critical readings of *Orlando* is a discussion of those "nineteenth-century 'sexologists,' whose theories about gender and sexual identity supply common denominators for both the literary characters of Orlando and Stephen Gordon [in *The Well of Loneliness*] and the real-life self-images of Vita Sackville-West and Radclyffe Hall" (Knopp 29). *Orlando* encodes "counterstatements" to those theories of the homosexual personality prevalent in the 1920s (DuPlessis 134).

Orlando also "unpicks both the language and the narrative codes of the forms of history-writing" (Bowlby 133) and of the codes of biography upon which traditional history-writing depended. In *JACOB'S ROOM* Jacob FLANDERS ponders the question, "Does History consist of the Biographies of Great Men?" (JR 39), and *Orlando* provides the delightfully mocking answer. Some critics have seen the biographer of *Orlando* as a caricature of the omniscient consciousness Woolf would explore in *The Waves* (Graham, " 'Caricature' " 363–65), or as evolving into "a universal mythic mind" in which the drama of Orlando's life can take place (Harper 164). Wilson finds such readings miss the irony of the book in the same way, for example, that David Daiches does when he takes *Orlando*'s "Preface" seriously. Woolf was thinking about *Orlando* as she read Harold Nicolson's *Some People,* in which he crosses the boundaries between "fact" and "fantasy." Woolf reviewed the book in 1927 ("The New Biography" CE4 229–35; GR 149–54). The questions of the relations between "fact and fancy" and of how to transgress the genre/gender boundaries of prose, poetry, drama, fiction and biography were questions by which Woolf was absorbed long before and long after she wrote *Orlando.*

Adaptations

A 1981 film *Freak Orlando* is referred to in VWM 38:9. Better known is Sally Potter's 1992 film interpretation starring Tilda Swinton as Orlando and Quentin Crisp as Queen Elizabeth I. "Orlando" was written and directed by Potter, an interview with whom by Madeline Moore appears in an appendix to the Shakespeare Head Press edition of *Orlando.* The American choreographer and director Robert Wilson has staged a monologue adapted from *Orlando* by Darryl Pinckney, an American writer, in both German (1989) and French (1993) versions. The Red Shift Theatre Company premiered Robin Brooks's adaptation of *Orlando* at the Edinburgh Fringe Festival in 1992.

**** Works Specific to This Entry:***

Baldanza, Frank. "*Orlando* and the Sackvilles." *PMLA* 70 (March 1955): 274–79.

Caughie, Pamela L. "Virginia Woolf's Double Discourse." In Marleen S. Barr and Richard Feldstein, eds. *Discontented Discourses: Feminism/Textual Intervention/Psychoanalysis.* Urbana and Chicago: University of Illinois Press, 1989: 41–53. (Cited from McNees 2: 483–93.)

DuPlessis, Rachel Blau. " 'Amor Vin—': Modifications of Romance in Woolf." In Margaret Homans, ed. *Virginia Woolf*: 115–35.

Gilbert, Sandra M. "Woman's Sentence, Man's Sentencing: Linguistic Fantasies in Woolf and Joyce." In Jane Marcus, ed. *Virginia Woolf and Bloomsbury*: 208–24.

Gillespie, Diane F. " 'Her Kodak Pointed at his Head': Virginia Woolf and Photography." In Diane F. Gillespie, ed. *The Multiple Muses*: 113–47.

Graham, John. "The 'Caricature Value' of Parody and Fantasy in *Orlando.*" *University of Toronto Quarterly* 30, 4 (July 1961): 345–65.

Green, David Bonnell. "*Orlando* and the Sackvilles: Addendum." *PMLA* 71, 1 (1956): 268–69.

Haller, Evelyn. "Her Quill Drawn from the Firebird: Virginia Woolf and the Russian Dancers." In Diane F. Gillespie, ed. *The Multiple Muses*: 180–226.

Hankins, Leslie Kathleen. " 'Across the Screen of my Brain': Virginia Woolf's 'The Cinema' and Film Forums of the Twenties." In Diane F. Gillespie, ed. *The Multiple Muses*: 148–79.

Hoffmann, Charles G. "Fact and Fantasy in *Orlando*: Virginia Woolf's Manuscript Revisions." *Texas Studies in Literature and Language* 10 (1968): 435–44.

Knopp, Sherron E. " 'If I Saw You Would You Kiss Me?': Sapphism and the Subversiveness of Virginia Woolf's *Orlando.*" *PMLA* 103, 1 (January 1988): 24–34.

Lawrence, Karen R. "Orlando's Voyage Out." In *Modern Fiction Studies* 38, 1 (Spring 1992): 253–77.

Lokke, Kari Elise. "*Orlando* and Incandescence: Virginia Woolf's Comic Sublime." *Modern Fiction Studies* 38, 1 (Spring 1992): 235–52.

Moore, Madeline. "Virginia Woolf's *Orlando*: An Edition of the Manuscript." *Twentieth Century Literature* 25, 3/4 (Fall/Winter 1979): 303–55.

Sackville-West, V. *The Land and The Garden.* London: Michael Joseph, 1989.

———. *Knole and the Sackvilles.* London: Ernest Benn, 1958.

Schaffer, Talia. "Posing *Orlando.*" In Ann Kibbey, Kayann Short, and Abouali Farmanfarmaian, eds. *Sexual Artifice.* Genders 19. New York: New York University Press, 1994: 26–63.

Smith-Rosenberg, Carroll. *Disorderly Conduct: Visions of Gender in Victorian America.* New York: Alfred A. Knopf, 1985.

Squier, Susan M. "Tradition and Revision in Woolf's *Orlando*: Defoe and 'The Jessamy Brides'." *Women's Studies* 12 (1986): 167–78.

Wilson, J. J. "Why is *Orlando* Difficult?" In Jane Marcus, ed. *New Feminist Essays*: 170–84.

Ormond, Stuart Mentioned in *JACOB'S ROOM* as having made a remark comparing paper flowers to real flowers, on the strength of which Kitty CRASTER marries him.

Osborne, Dorothy (1627–95) In *A ROOM OF ONE'S OWN,* Woolf quotes Dorothy Osborne's opinion of

Margaret CAVENDISH as "a little distracted" and "rediculous" (sic) because she has written and published books, an occupation Osborne deemed unfit for a woman (AROO 62). There follows a lengthy quotation from one of Osborne's letters to her husband, the statesman Sir William Temple (1628–99), Woolf remarking ironically that letters did not count as literature. *A Room* makes clear, however, that Osborne's gift as a letter writer was a literary gift that would perhaps have resulted in other forms of writing had women not been discouraged as artists.

Dorothy Osborne married Sir William Temple in 1655. He was author of numerous political works, his secretary was the young Jonathan SWIFT, and he brought about the marriage of William of Orange and Mary. In 1668 he effected the Triple Alliance between England, Holland and Sweden. Her letters to him were published in 1888 and, in an enlarged edition, in 1928. Woolf reviewed *The Letters of Dorothy Osborne to William Temple,* edited by G. C. Moore Smith, for the *NEW REPUBLIC* in 1928; her review was reprinted the following day in the *TIMES LITERARY SUPPLEMENT.* This review was partially incorporated in her essay in the *COMMON READER: SECOND SERIES,* "Dorothy Osborne's *Letters*" (CR2 59–66; CE3 59–65). There, Woolf repeats Osborne's opinion of Margaret Cavendish, and makes explicit what is implied in *A Room*: that had she "been born in 1827, Dorothy Osborne would have written novels" (CE3 60).

Otter, Mrs. Mentioned in *BETWEEN THE ACTS.* She lives in the "End House" and plays the parts of an aged crone and of Lady Harpy Harraden in two different scenes of Miss LA TROBE's pageant.

Otway, Cassandra The twenty-two-year-old cousin of Katharine HILBERY in *NIGHT AND DAY* with whom William RODNEY falls in love. Sonya Rudikoff has suggested that Cassandra's characterization draws upon the life of Lady Dorothy Nevill, which Woolf had written about (CE4 111–15). To the despair of her mother, Cassandra is given to breeding silkworms in her bedroom. When Katharine invites her to London, Cassandra eagerly accepts not only because she greatly admires her older cousin but because she longs to escape the confines of her family home at Stogdon House. Although she is at first appalled that William Rodney, Katharine's fiancé, professes his love for her, once she learns that Katharine and William have secretly broken their engagement she happily accompanies William and soon agrees to marry him.

Apart from its obvious source in the story of Troy, in which Cassandra is daughter of Priam and Hecuba, the name was also used by Florence NIGHTINGALE in her autobiographical fragment *Cassandra* (1859). Cassandra is the narrator's name in Woolf's short story "A SOCIETY."

Otway Family In *NIGHT AND DAY,* the Otways are cousins of the Hilberys. Cassandra OTWAY is invited to London by Katharine HILBERY so that William RODNEY might woo her. The Otways—Sir Francis and Lady Charlotte Otway and their children Eleanor, Humphrey, Marmaduke, Silvia, Henry, Gilbert, Mostyn and Cassandra—live in faded glory at Stogdon House in Lincolnshire, where Katharine and her parents go to spend Christmas in chapter XVI of the novel. There may be elements of Lytton STRACHEY's family in their characterization. Henry, who teaches the young ladies of Bungay to play the violin, is the only one of her cousins in whom Katharine confides, sharing with him her unhappiness at the prospect of marrying William. Katharine also begins a conversation with Lady Otway, who implies that her own marriage has been unhappy and that for women marriage always involves sacrifice, but the conversation is cut short by the appearance of Mrs. Hilbery, in front of whom Lady Otway does not wish to continue. Her husband, Sir Francis, has retired from government service in India after a disappointing career that has left him bitter. He has turned away from his wife and is consuming the prime of his eldest daughter Eleanor's life (ND 207).

Ouse Sussex river in which Woolf drowned herself on March 28, 1941. Her body was found by children several weeks later at Piddinghoe.

Outsiders Society See *THREE GUINEAS.*

Oxbridge The university Woolf's narrator visits in *A ROOM OF ONE'S OWN.* This combination of Oxford and Cambridge, used as either noun or adjective, is a common English shorthand for the two elite universities and their products. (See Sandra Gilbert, "The Battle of the Books.")

P

Page, Mr. Local newspaper reporter in *BETWEEN THE ACTS* who is taking notes on the annual village pageant and recording the names of the gentry in attendance.

Paintings by Vanessa Bell See *RECENT PAINTINGS BY VANESSA BELL.*

Paley, Emma Character in *THE VOYAGE OUT*. Mitchell Leaska suggests Woolf modeled her on an elderly spinster she encountered traveling in Italy in 1908 (PA 389n10). One of the guests at the hotel on SANTA MARINA, the crippled Mrs. Paley is attended by her niece Susan WARRINGTON, of whose desire to be with Arthur VENNING she is completely unaware. After their engagement, however, Mrs. Paley "behaved with instinctive respect" toward her niece (TVO 180). The narrator describes Mrs. Paley as "a selfish, independent old woman, possessed of a considerable income" (TVO 180), but almost immediately softens this image of her by describing her memory of a brother who drowned before her eyes and of her best friend who died in giving birth to her first child some fifty years earlier (TVO 181).

Palmerston, Lord Henry John Temple (1784–1865) Prime minister of England from 1855 until his death (with a slight interruption in 1858 when he resigned and was then re-elected). Chapter 5 of Lytton STRACHEY's *Queen Victoria* concerns Palmerston. Palmerston's signature is on the document that pronounces "indisputably" that ORLANDO is a woman (O 255).

Pankhurst, Mrs. Emmeline See SUFFRAGE.

Papworth, Mrs. In *JACOB'S ROOM*, she is Richard BONAMY's servant. A mother of nine, she feels motherly toward Jacob FLANDERS and Bonamy.

Pargiter, Colonel Abel Character in *THE YEARS*, known to his mistress, Mira, as "Bogy." He has lost two fingers in the Indian Mutiny of 1857 and is first seen at his club in London. While his wife lies dying at home, Abel visits Mira. He is in love with his sister-in-law, Eugénie, and there is a suggestion in the novel that they have had an affair when her daughter Maggie asks his son Martin whether they might be brother and sister. After Rose Pargiter's death, Abel relies on his daughter Eleanor in much the same way that Woolf's father Sir Leslie STEPHEN relied first on Stella DUCKWORTH and, after her death, on Vanessa BELL. Mitchell Leaska, in comparing Abel's prototype in *THE PARGITERS* to the character in *The Years*, concludes that the latter "appears a more particular man whom Virginia Woolf knew well and was especially close to and fascinated by" (*Novels* 197). Several critics liken Abel to Captain BARFOOT in *JACOB'S ROOM*.

Pargiter, Charles Mentioned in *THE YEARS*, a son of Morris and Celia PARGITER who is killed in World War I (TY 336–37).

Pargiter, Delia One of Abel PARGITER's seven children in *THE YEARS*. At the beginning of the novel, Delia is anxiously waiting for her mother to die, frustrated at her constricted life as a young Victorian woman. She fantasizes about joining Charles Stewart PARNELL in winning freedom for Ireland. At her mother's funeral, she is torn by ambivalent feelings for her and thinks her brothers and sisters, and especially her father, are acting their emotions. She is not seen again until the "Present Day" chapter when she throws a large party that brings all her relatives together. She has married Patrick, an Anglo-Irish conservative who has not lived up to her fantasies, and has three children. Through a complex reading of webs of allusion, Mitchell Leaska has argued that Delia "represents all that Eleanor would not or could not be" (*Novels* 218).

Pargiter, Sir Digby The brother of Abel PARGITER in *THE YEARS*, married to Eugénie. They have two daughters, Sara and Maggie.

Pargiter, Edward One of Abel PARGITER's seven children in *THE YEARS*, nicknamed "Nigs." When the novel begins, Edward is at Oxford University, where he is studying classics and imagines himself to be in

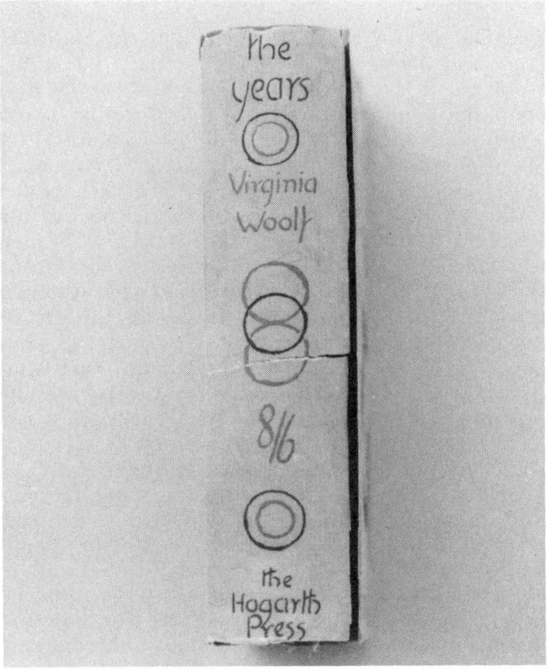

The Years. *Courtesy Linda J. Langham.*
Vanessa Bell designed the front, back and spine of the dust jacket for The Years. *Here shown is the spine of the Hogarth Press first edition (1937); "8/6" is the price—eight shillings and sixpence.*

love with his cousin Kitty LASSWADE. He toys with a friend named ASHLEY who is clearly in love with him, leaving him with another friend, GIBBS, whom Ashley detests and is jealous of. Both Jane Marcus (VWM 5:5) and James Naremore ("Nature" 253) have described Edward as a repressed homosexual. He publishes a translation of Sophocles's *ANTIGONE*, but at the party in the final chapter he tells his nephew that he cannot translate a line from the play.

Pargiter, Eleanor The eldest daughter of Abel and Rose PARGITER in *THE YEARS*. Eleanor is as close as the novel comes to a central character. When young, she sacrifices her life to caring for her family and performing charitable work, but she is adventurous and outgoing throughout the novel. She never marries, but she once thinks she would have liked to marry a man like RENNY, her cousin Maggie's husband. She travels widely, to Greece, Spain and India, and is perpetually inquisitive about life. In the habit of talking to herself in public, Eleanor can appear "a well-known type; with a bag; philanthropic; well nourished; a spinster; a virgin" (TY 102), but Woolf explores her depths. Margaret DRABBLE has written that Woolf's creation of Eleanor was "what I call heroism. To imagine an old age fulfilled and beautiful, doubting if one may ever reach it" (Drabble 51). Jane Marcus has described Eleanor as the "incarnation of an ancient Mother/Maid" (VWM 6: 1) and as a "purifying Mother Goddess" (*Languages* 44). She links Eleanor to Leonard WOOLF's description of Margaret Llewelyn DAVIES.

Pargiter, Lady Eugénie Married to Sir Digby PARGITER, Abel PARGITER's brother, in *THE YEARS*, and the mother of Sara and Maggie. Her brother-in-law is apparently in love with her, and Woolf hints that they may have had an affair when Maggie PARGITER jokingly asks her cousin Martin PARGITER if he thinks they could be brother and sister. In the "1907" chapter, Eugénie dances in Sara's bedroom to the delight of her children.

Pargiter, Maggie (Magdalena) The elder daughter of Sir Digby and Lady Eugénie PARGITER in *THE YEARS*. She marries René, whom everyone calls RENNY, and they have two children. In the "1917" chapter, she and Renny have a dinner party for Sara, Nicholas POMJALOVSKY and Eleanor PARGITER during which there is an air raid.

Pargiter, Martin One of Abel PARGITER's seven children in *THE YEARS*. He is the youngest son (born in 1868) and joins the army, becoming a captain. He later becomes a businessman.

Pargiter, Milly One of Abel PARGITER's seven children in *THE YEARS*. She and her sister Delia are seen early in the novel as bored and restless, vying with each other for eligible men who might marry them and thus rescue them from their father's house. Milly marries Hugh GIBBS and settles in Devonshire. At the end of the novel, grown fat, she and her husband cast a pall over North PARGITER's conversation with his aunt Eleanor.

Pargiter, Morris One of Abel PARGITER's seven children in *THE YEARS*. He becomes a lawyer and marries Celia Chinnery, with whom he has three children, Charles, North and Peggy.

Pargiter, North A son of Morris and Celia PARGITER in *THE YEARS*. North goes to fight in World War I in 1917, mocked by his cousin Sara as a Lieutenant in the "Royal Regiment of Rat-Catchers." After the war he farms in Africa, returning in "Present Day" (presumably around 1935) and finding London very different than when he had left. Alice Fox has noted that North moves away from war and imperialism in the course of the novel and that "as if in approbation of his views, Woolf allows North his share of Shakespearian allusions" (152). Jane Marcus, also recognizing that Woolf seems to intend North as a hopeful sign for the future, describes him as "the incarnation of the Year Spirit" (*Languages* 64).

Pargiter, Peggy The daughter of Morris and Celia PARGITER in *THE YEARS*. In "Present Day" we learn that Peggy has become a doctor, a sign of changed opportunities for women.

Pargiter, Rose (1) Abel PARGITER's wife in *THE YEARS*, mother of seven children. Her dying dominates the first chapter of the book.

Pargiter, Rose (2) The youngest daughter of Abel and Rose PARGITER in *THE YEARS*. As a child, she slips out one evening to go to a toystore and is accosted by an exhibitionist, an experience that she never forgets and that evokes nightmares. Later in the novel, she tells a story of locking herself in a bathroom and cutting her wrist with a knife after an argument with her brother Martin. Rose becomes a suffragette and is imprisoned for throwing a brick (presumably through a window), but during World War I she supports the government and is decorated for her services. Some critics have suggested she is based on Ethel SMYTH. Lucio Ruotolo remarks that Rose "remains throughout *The Years* a soldier in defense of her own class interests" (175). Grace Radin, in her study of the evolution of *The Years*, has noted that Woolf deleted from drafts the discussion of Rose's sexual nature: "While Rose's lesbianism was strongly suggested in the holograph, the published novel presents her as simply a strong, rather mannish woman who has 'felt many passions, and done many things' " (Radin 56).

Pargiter, Sara (Sally) The younger daughter of Sir Digby and Lady Eugénie PARGITER in *THE YEARS*. Set apart by a deformed shoulder, the result of being dropped as a child, Sara is a visionary character who speaks in a kind of poetic chant throughout the novel (similar to Isa OLIVER's thoughts in *BETWEEN THE ACTS*). Her laughing "Oh, to whom?" (TY 341) connects her to RHODA in *THE WAVES* (who also utters this line from Percy Bysshe SHELLEY's "The Question"). In the "Present Day" chapter, her cousin North reflects that she "has never attracted the love of men. Or had she?" (TY 317). The character Elvira in *THE PARGITERS* is an earlier version of Sara, the evolution of whom is discussed by Grace Radin in her study of *The Years*.

Pargiters, The One of the ten titles Woolf considered for her penultimate novel, *THE YEARS*, and the title of a projected book, the draft of which has been edited by Mitchell A. Leaska as *The Pargiters: The Novel-Essay Portion of The Years*. *The Pargiters* is an essential part of the complex genesis of both *The Years* and *THREE GUINEAS*. On January 20, 1931, Woolf wrote that she had conceived an "entire new book" that would be a sequel to *A ROOM OF ONE'S OWN* and would concern the sexual life of women (D4 6). She thought of calling it "Professions for Women," under which title she was to give a talk the next day to the London branch of the National Society for Women's Service, at the invitation of the branch secretary Philippa (Pippa) STRACHEY. "PROFESSIONS FOR WOMEN" was published in a drastically shortened version in *THE DEATH OF THE MOTH*, but the text of the twenty-five-page manuscript (held in the BERG COLLECTION) on which Woolf's talk was based is included in *The Pargiters* (xxvii–xliv). Leaska usefully provides in a note a report by Vera BRITTAIN in *THE NATION* on both Woolf's speech and on the one that preceded it given by Ethel SMYTH (*Pargiters* xxxv).

In November 1932 Woolf wrote that she had entirely "remodelled" her earlier conception and now planned to write "an Essay-Novel, called the Pargiters" which was to take in "everything, sex, education, life &c." (D4 129). *The Pargiters* was to be a formal experiment in which sections of "fact" that discussed the profession of writing by women would alternate with "extracts" from a supposedly published novel written by a woman. Leaska describes the remaining drafts as "among the most heavily corrected manuscripts in the entire Woolf archive" (*Pargiters* xx). Beginning in late 1932, Woolf wrote six "Essays" and five "extracts" by the end of that year. By February 1933 she had abandoned the novel-essay idea and focused solely on the novel from then on. The more than 60,000 words she had written formed the basis for the "1880" chapter of *The Years*. Grace Radin has explained that in her revisions of what became *The Years*, Woolf "deleted or obscured much of its political and social content. Eventually many of these ideas found their way into *Three Guineas*" (Radin, " 'Two Enormous Chunks' " 221).

Leaska explains in his introduction to *The Pargiters* the likely origin of the name in the word "parget," which means "to plaster with cement or mortar" and also "to whitewash." Following the suggestion of Jane Marcus (*Languages* 57), Leaska notes that Woolf was intrigued with the story of Joseph WRIGHT, in whose *English Dialect Dictionary* (six volumes, 1903) she would have found the word "parget." Woolf had read Elizabeth Mary Wright's two-volume biography of her husband, *The Life of Joseph Wright* (Oxford University Press, 1932), and had been impressed by his attitude toward women (D4 115–16). The Pargiters of *The Years* are "a family who because of the sexual premises of the age and their accompanying economic circumstances were themselves pargeters, and taught their children to be" (*The Pargiters* xix). Elsewhere, Leaska has extended his discussion of Woolf's "pargetting" to make a number of highly suggestive connections between Woolf's manuscript revisions—deletions, additions, and name changes—and events from her own biography ("Virginia Woolf, the Pargeter" 177–210). Also invaluable for "identifying the sources of [Woolf's] facts and allusions" in both *The Pargiters* and her speech on professions for women is the first of the three bound volumes of newspaper clippings and quotations that Woolf drew on in writing *Three Guineas* (RN 256f.) *The Pargiters* is a particularly important volume in any investigation of Woolf's creative processes, and it is also interesting as the "Essay" portions comment on and analyze directly the fictional "extracts" that would eventually be incorporated into *The Years*.

Leaska has described the form of *The Pargiters* as unique, but Pamela Caughie has recently argued that the form is actually that which Woolf often employs in her essays, and writes that "what most critics identify as repressions that necessitated Woolf's indirect, discontinuous, and duplicitous narrative strategies in *The Years* could well be *the thematic structures generated by the kinds of discursive strategies with which Woolf was experimenting*" (Caughie 98).

Parker, Mrs. Character in *BETWEEN THE ACTS* who lives in the village of Lathom and has come to see the annual village pageant at POINTZ HALL, Bart OLIVER's home. Mrs. MANRESA thinks Mrs. Parker is too refined to joke with (102), finding women of her own class usually boring.

Parliament Square In *A ROOM OF ONE'S OWN* Woolf remarks that, unlike women, men always feel an irresistible desire to cut their names on whatever they see (AROO 50). One example she calls to mind is Parliament Square with (at that time) its statues of Lord PALMERSTON, the Earl of Derby, Sir Robert Peel, George Canning, Lord Beaconsfield, Abraham Lincoln and Field Marshall Smuts.

Parnell, Charles Stewart (1846–91) The champion of Home Rule for Ireland whose career was ended when his affair with a married woman, Kitty O'Shea, became public and he was denounced by many in Ireland. In *THE YEARS*, he is the hero of Delia PARGITER.

Parrish, Miriam A character in *THE YEARS* involved in charity work with Eleanor PARGITER. She first appears in "1891" and is at the party in the "Present Day" chapter that concludes the novel.

Parry, Justin Mentioned in *MRS. DALLOWAY*, Clarissa DALLOWAY's father. His carelessness in cutting down a tree caused the death of Clarissa's sister Sylvia. Elizabeth Abel has suggested that the death of Sylvia Parry "echoes and revises" D. H. LAWRENCE's novella *The Fox* (Abel 33).

Parry, Lionel Mentioned in *JACOB'S ROOM* bowing to Clara DURRANT as he passes her in the street.

Parry, Mrs. Raymond Mentioned in *THE VOYAGE OUT*. A woman in London who holds "wonderful parties," she is an acquaintance that several characters in the novel discover they have in common.

Parsons, Mrs. Mentioned in *JACOB'S ROOM* as a snatch of her conversation is reported by the narrator in the tea shop where Fanny ELMER leaves her umbrella.

Partridge, Frances Catherine (b. 1900) (née Marshall) Married to Ralph PARTRIDGE, with whom in 1926 she began to live during the week at 41 GORDON SQUARE, the home of James and Alix STRACHEY (he returned to his wife, Dora CARRINGTON, at the weekends). Her first job was in the bookstore run by Francis BIRRELL and David GARNETT, where she met Ralph when he was working for the HOGARTH PRESS in 1923. Her sister Ray Marshall was Garnett's first wife, and her sister Judy was married to Lytton STRACHEY's nephew. Following the deaths of Lytton Strachey and Carrington, Ralph and Frances married in 1933. Their son, Lytton Burgo (1935–63) married Henrietta Garnett (b. 1945), daughter of David and Angelica GARNETT, in 1962. Partridge has published several volumes of memoirs and diaries.

Partridge, (Reginald) Ralph Sherring (1894–1960) Lived in a triangular relationship with his wife Dora CARRINGTON and Lytton STRACHEY, with whom Carrington was in love. Partridge met Carrington through her brother Noel in 1918, and through her met Strachey, who became extremely fond of him despite Ralph's resolute heterosexuality. Lytton dubbed Partridge "Ralph" and he was always known by that name thereafter. Partridge and Carrington married in 1921. Partridge was the first paid assistant to the HOGARTH PRESS, a position he held on to tenaciously from 1920 to 1923 through a usually stormy relationship with both Woolfs. He was a close friend of Gerald BRENAN, with whom he had served in World War I. His discovery of Brenan and Carrington's affair in 1922 severely strained his marriage, and in 1923 he began an affair with Frances Marshall. Because Strachey threatened to abandon Carrington if Partridge left her, he and Frances stayed together in London during the week in what Woolf termed a "left-handed household," and he returned to his wife at HAM SPRAY at the weekends. Following Strachey's death and Carrington's suicide in 1932, Partridge and Frances married in 1933.

Pascoe, Mrs. Mentioned in *JACOB'S ROOM.* Her nephew CURNOW works for Elizabeth DURRANT.

Passenger to Teheran A book by Vita SACKVILLE-WEST giving an account of her travels in Persia when she visited her husband, Harold NICOLSON, who was posted to the British Legation in Teheran in late 1925. Originally published by the HOGARTH PRESS in 1926, the book was reissued by Moyer Bell, Ltd. in 1990 with a new introduction by Nigel NICOLSON and photographs selected by him from Vita's album of the journey. Woolf wrote of the book that Vita's prose was "too fluent" (D3 129). Probably, however, *Passenger to Teheran* and Vita's letters to Woolf from Persia in 1926 provided some of the atmosphere for the CONSTANTINOPLE chapter (3) of *ORLANDO.*

Passionate Apprentice, A. The Early Journals 1897–1909 Woolf's early journals, omitted from the DIARY, are contained in seven holograph notebooks (six in the BERG COLLECTION and one in the Library of the BRITISH MUSEUM) and span the years 1897 to 1909. They were edited by Mitchell A. Leaska, who gave this volume its title, and published in 1990 by the HOGARTH PRESS and Harcourt Brace Jovanovich. Louise A. DeSalvo discusses the seven notebooks and considers the question of why they were omitted from the *Diary* in "As 'Miss Jan Says': Virginia Woolf's Early Journals." "Miss Jan" was a persona Woolf used in the diary that she began when she was fourteen that, DeSalvo suggests, allowed her to "explore thoughts and ideas of a theological nature" that would have been "tantamount to heresy" in her agnostic father's house ("Miss Jan" 97).

The diaries in *A Passionate Apprentice* record daily life at 22 HYDE PARK GATE with sketches of family members, friends and neighbors. In the period covered by the volume Woolf experienced the death of Stella DUCKWORTH, Leslie STEPHEN and Thoby STEPHEN. She began to write professionally in 1904 and used her diaries to keep records of her reading and books she was reviewing. She also used her diary to practice essay writing, describing places she visited and people she saw. These places include ST. IVES, Giggleswick in Yorkshire, Blo' Norton Hall in Norfolk, the New Forest, Sussex, Somerset and Wales. There are accounts of her teaching at MORLEY COLLEGE, and of her trip to Greece in 1906 where Thoby Stephen contracted the typhoid from which he would die in November that year. Her trips to Italy in 1908 and 1909 in the company of Clive BELL, whom she sketches, are described. By this time Woolf had begun work on *MELYMBROSIA,* eventually published in 1915 as *THE VOYAGE OUT,* her first novel.

Pastons The Pastons were a well-to-do Norfolk family about whom Woolf wrote in the first essay in *THE COMMON READER,* "The Pastons and Chaucer" (CR1 1–38; CE3 1–17). In late 1921 and through 1922, Woolf read *The Paston Letters. A. D. 1422–1509,* edited by Dr. James Gairdner (Chatto & Windus, 1904; Woolf also read an older edition of the letters published 1872–74 by Edward Arber), and *The Pastons and Their England. Studies in an Age of Transition* by H. S. Bennett (Cambridge University Press, 1922). The letters span three generations of the family in the era of kings Henry VI, Edward IV and Richard III and are an important record of the times. In *THREE GUINEAS,* Woolf remarks that educated English families since the Pastons have been paying money into a fund to educate their sons, to the neglect of their daughters (TG 4).

Pater, Clara (1841–1910) Sister of Walter PATER and first Classics Tutor at Somerville College, Oxford University, which she was involved in founding. She tutored Woolf in Latin and Greek beginning in 1899 and is probably the model for Julia Craye in "MOMENTS OF BEING: 'SLATER'S PINS HAVE NO POINTS.'" Perry Meisel, who sees Lucy CRADDOCK in *THE YEARS* as Woolf's second "portrait" of Pater, discusses Woolf's relations with Clara and her sister Hester Pater (17–29).

Pater, Walter Horatio (1839–94) Influential Victorian critic and associate of the Pre-Raphaelites among whose works are *Studies in the History of the Renaissance* (1873), *Marius the Epicurean* (1885), *Imaginary Portraits* (1887), *Appreciations* (1889) and *Plato and Platonism* (1893). Perry Meisel has argued that Pater's aesthetics were an unacknowledged important influence on Woolf's critical writings in particular, and also on her fiction. Pater appears in the preface to *ORLANDO* as one of the "dead and illustrious" writers in whose perpetual debt Woolf says anyone who reads or writes must be.

Patmore, Coventry See ANGEL IN THE HOUSE.

Patrick, Uncle The husband of Delia PARGITER in *THE YEARS.*

Pattle Family Woolf's great-grandparents, James Pattle (1775–1845), of the Bengal Civil Service, and Adeline (1793–1845), daughter of Antoine Chevalier de L'Etang and Thérèse Blin de Grincourt, had seven daughters of whom six were renowned for their beauty; the seventh, Julia Margaret CAMERON (1815–79), was renowned for her photographs. The family myth about James Pattle—known as "the biggest liar in India"—was that his corpse had been packed in a cask of rum to be shipped from India to England

and the cask exploded, frightening his wife out of her wits. Adeline Pattle, at any rate, sailed from India to England in 1840 with her daughters. In addition to Julia Margaret, the other six were: Adeline (1812–36); Sara (1816–87), who married Thoby PRINSEP and lived at Little Holland House; Maria Jackson (1818–92), Woolf's grandmother; Louisa (1821–73); Virginia (1827–1910); and Sophia (1829–1911). Another daughter, Eliza, died as a child (1814–18). Sara and Thoby Prinsep's daughter Alice married Charles Gurney and had two daughters, Laura and Rachel. Laura's son Ernest married Una Taylor, who later lived with Radclyffe Hall, author of *THE WELL OF LONELINESS.*

Paunceforte, Mr. Mentioned in *TO THE LIGHTHOUSE,* an artist who has made fashionable paintings in which everything is seen "pale, elegant, semitransparent" (TTL 19), a fashion resisted by Lily BRISCOE.

Pelham, Augustus Mentioned in *NIGHT AND DAY,* he is a "diarist" who is apparently a frequent guest of Mr. and Mrs. HILBERY.

Pendennis See THACKERAY, William Makepeace.

Pensions Bill In the second chapter of *THREE GUINEAS* Woolf refers to "a conspiracy of silence" by the press over the Contributory Pensions Bill and compares it to the similar silence in the nineteenth century about the Contagious Diseases Act, a silence to which Josephine BUTLER drew attention. In 1937, a letter from Philippa STRACHEY was published in the *Spectator* complaining that the press had not covered the parliamentary debate about the Contributory Pensions Bill, which discriminated against women wage-earners (TG 60; 162n16). The Bill passed by eight votes.

Pepita (Josefa Duran) (1830–71) Vita SACKVILLE-WEST's grandmother who, family legend had it, was the illegitimate daughter of a gypsy and a Spanish duke. Nigel NICOLSON (*Portrait* 47–48) says that although the facts were not as exciting as Vita would have liked, there *was* gypsy blood in Pepita's lineage. Woolf makes use of Pepita's story in *ORLANDO* when she has Orlando involved in a lawsuit relating to her alleged marriage to "Rosina Pepita" (O 168). Woolf drew on the facts of the celebrated lawsuit brought by Vita's uncle Henry that her mother successfully defended herself against in 1910. Henry Sackville-West claimed to be the legitimate heir to KNOLE, but Lady Sackville proved that she and her two sisters and two brothers were all illegitimate children of Lionel Sackville-West and Pepita, and Henry's case collapsed. Vita wrote the story of "The Star of Andalusia" and Pepita's long affair with her grandfather in her book *Pepita,* published in 1937 by the HOGARTH PRESS.

Pepper, William Character in *THE VOYAGE OUT.* A friend of Willoughby VINRACE, he is traveling on the *EUPHROSYNE* to South America. Meeting Ridley AMBROSE when the ship sets sail from London, Pepper quickly falls into conversation about the people they knew at Cambridge University in the late nineteenth century. Pepper, an eccentric and scholarly man, has never married because he has never met a woman who commands his respect, his ideal being a woman who could "read Greek, if not Persian" (TVO 25). His early life was spent in India, and he is irascible and awkward. On SANTA MARINA, he stays with the Ambroses for a week but then moves to the hotel as he believes the vegetables there will be properly washed. Woolf probably modeled Pepper at least partly on an Italian count she met in Florence in 1909 (PA 397).

Percival The silent "hero" figure in *THE WAVES* whom BERNARD, LOUIS and NEVILLE meet at school. Neville first describes Percival as "remote from us all in a pagan universe" (TW 36) and is "hopelessly in love" with him. The six "characters" of *The Waves* gather in a London restaurant to say good-bye to Percival when he leaves for India, and they are later devastated by his death there ("He fell. His horse tripped" [TW 151]). Percival and SUSAN are apparently lovers for a time, and Neville always loves Percival from a distance.

For many readers, Percival is another attempt by Woolf at writing some kind of elegy for her dead brother Thoby STEPHEN. Lyndall Gordon, for example, writes that "Thoby had been a reserved young man, and Virginia pursued his unknown ghost through two novels, trying to deduce Jacob from his room, Percival from his friends" (Gordon 125). Gordon suggests the name may have associations with Spencer Perceval, a Tory member of Parliament who was assassinated and died in the arms of Woolf's great-grandfather (Gordon 241). Many have also commented on the absence of any inner life in this figure and describe Percival as an "absent center" of *The Waves.* Sara Ruddick refers to Percival as a "silent presence and vacuum-like absence which draws to itself the other characters' fantasies of their brother/leader/opposite" ("Private" 203).

The most obvious signification of Percival's name, however, is as what Harvena Richter identifies as "the last of the Grail kings" (Richter 125). There are numerous sources for the legend of Percival, the earliest versions of which are the French *Perceval, ou le conte du graal* ("Percival, or the story of the Grail") by Chrétien de Troyes (c. 1180), and the early thirteenth-century German *Parzival* by Wolfram von Eschenbach. There is also a fifteenth-century English version, *Sir Percyvelle of Galles,* and a version by Thomas Malory in his *Morte D'Arthur* (c. 1469). Other sources include Alfred, Lord TENNYSON's *Idylls of the King* (1859–85) and Richard WAGNER's opera *Parsifal* (1882). Percival is one of the knights of legend in quest of the "Holy Grail," the chalice supposed to have been used by Jesus Christ at the Last Supper and in which his blood was collected by Joseph of Arimathea after the crucifixion. Richter notes that Percival is "also the Phrygian counterpart of Adonis" (125), the mythology surrounding whom would have been familiar to Woolf and her contemporaries in both Jessie L. Weston's *From Ritual to the Romance* (which so heavily influenced T. S. ELIOT's *The Waste Land*) and Sir James G. FRAZER's *Golden Bough.*

Percival has come to be seen by many recent critics as "the violent last of the British imperialists" (Marcus, "Britannia" 144). In the novel, according to Judy Little, he represents "a mythos, a narrative or 'sequence' that gives shape to a culture and to individuals within the culture . . . a mock grail-hero . . . [he] mocks the very notion of story, of legend, of the presumptive hero who is required to phrase a meaning for one's life" (Little 77). Although Percival exists in the novel only through the perceptions of his six friends, as Lucio Ruotolo points out, his "disappearance from the text constitutes a social crisis" (*Interrupted* 152). Judith Lee uses Woolf's essay "ON BEING ILL" (written while she was at work on *The Waves*) as a "particularly helpful gloss on Percival's role" (184). She points out that Percival is an individual who "lives in complete unconscious conformity with his culture." He is, in Makiko Minow-Pinkney's words, "a typical representative of patriarchy and imperialism" (177).

Perrott, Alfred Character in *THE VOYAGE OUT.* One of the guests at the hotel on SANTA MARINA, he is traveling with a friend, Arthur VENNING. They are both lawyers, and Perrott has come to Santa Marina on business. Described in Susan WARRINGTON's diary as not "quite" (not quite a gentleman), Perrott struggles to support an invalid sister and is the son of a grocer from Leeds. He becomes emotionally entangled with Evelyn MURGATROYD, whom he meets on the picnic arranged by Terence HEWET, and spends much of the novel trying to get Evelyn to agree to marry him.

Perry, Miss (1) Mentioned in *JACOB'S ROOM* as one of Betty FLANDERS's oldest friends. She is free to see Jacob any afternoon but Thursday.

Perry, Miss (2) A schoolmistress in *THE WAVES* whom SUSAN says loves JINNY (TW 41).

Peyton, Mr. Character in *NIGHT AND DAY,* a guest at a Hilbery tea who, as the editor of an "esteemed review," qualifies as a "minister of literature" (ND 348).

"Phases of Fiction" (CE2 56–102; GR 93–145) An essay published in three installments in the *Bookman* (New York) in April, May and June 1929 and reprinted in *GRANITE & RAINBOW.* The work was originally intended as a book and was announced in 1927 by the HOGARTH PRESS as forthcoming, but Woolf found it a difficult and tedious piece. She wrote in early 1927 to Vita SACKVILLE-WEST that she was absorbed in a "book about reading novels" (L3 325), and over the next three years her interest in "Phases" would wax and wane. In October 1927, Woolf wrote to Vita that she had been unable to write a word of "that bloody book" and, giving it up, had written the words "Orlando: A Biography" on a fresh sheet of paper. However, she did persevere with the critical work, trying as she had since at least 1925 to set down some comprehensive theory of fiction. Once "Phases" was finished she called it "a book I hate; & was, as I think, wrongly pressed to undertake" (D3 227).

Woolf proposed to read as a "common reader" because, like novelists, common readers like "to create" and are not concerned with those matters that occupy professors, critics and historians. Eschewing what E. M. FORSTER called in *Aspects of the Novel* the "demon of chronology" (*Aspects* 31), Woolf divides her essay into several sections in which novelists are grouped under different headings. "The Truth-Tellers" are first—Tobias Smollet, Daniel DEFOE and Guy de Maupassant. These writers, she says, hold in stable relation the three key elements of fiction, which are God, Man and Nature, and thus readers hold their world "in proper perspective." Next she discusses Sir Walter SCOTT, Robert Louis Stevenson and Anne Radcliffe under the heading of "Romantics" and finds them lacking. The section begins with a discussion of Scott's *Bride of Lammermoor* and moves to Stevenson's *Master of Ballantrae,* both of which she says are flawed. Radcliffe's *Mysteries of Udolpho* at least provides the reader a distinct emotion, and at the end of this section Woolf relents somewhat in conceding that the "Romantics" do realize "for us an emotion which is deep and genuine" (CE2 71). In "The Character-Mongers and Comedians" we find an illuminating discussion of how Charles DICKENS uses characters in *Bleak House* and a comparison with Jane AUSTEN's modes of characterization and use of comedy in *Pride and Prejudice.* The section closes with a discussion of George ELIOT's narrative strategies in *Silas Marner.*

Next come "The Psychologists," beginning with Henry JAMES's *What Maisie Knew.* James's being American leads Woolf to consider the relation of a novelist's culture to his art and she turns to a discussion of Marcel PROUST, finding that he is "so porous, so pliable, so perfectly receptive that we realize him only as an envelope, thin but elastic which stretches wider and wider and serves not to enforce a view but to enclose a world" (CE2 83); Proust is a persistent presence in the second half of "Phases of Fiction." Turning from Proust to Fyodor DOSTOYEVSKY, Woolf tempers her early enthusiasm for the Russian novelist, remarking that "to brush aside civilization and plunge into the depths of the soul is not really to enrich" (CE2 87).

Woolf's pose as a common reader in this essay leads her to the device of turning to a new group of writers as a refreshing contrast from those she has just discussed: after the psychologists come "The Satirists and Fantastics," beginning with Thomas Peacock's *Crotchet Castle.* Again, she stresses that the difference between novelists is due to a difference in their conceptions of reality. Laurence STERNE, she writes, was fascinated by his own mind. In "The Poets" she compares Sterne's *Tristram Shandy* to Leo TOLSTOY's *War and Peace* and to Emily BRONTË's *Wuthering Heights.* George MEREDITH's *The Ordeal of Richard Feverel* and Thomas HARDY's *Far From the Madding Crowd* provide examples of "poetic" novels whose characterization is dominated by impersonality. In *Wuthering Heights* and in Melville's *Moby Dick* Woolf finds examples of poetic works where every element of the novel is in keeping with every other element, the whole world of the novel being saturated by the writer's poetic imagination. And this leads her back to Proust, where she pauses.

There is, she says, no way to theorize the "future of fiction" for the possibilities are so wide. "Novel" in the twentieth century has no stable referent, but all novels have in common the "human element." Commenting on the "enormous growth of the psychological novel" in her own time, Woolf remarks that the novel is always tied to the contemporary conception of reality, which is why so many novels seem out of date. The novelist must simultaneously stand back from life and bring the reader closely in touch with it. Only the "most complete novelist" can achieve the necessary balance between these two opposing forces that threaten to destroy the novel as a work of art. The novelist "of merit" exerts control over readers, shaping their responses and altering their "manners." If the novelist cannot achieve this control, the novel is significant only for its own brief moment.

Phèdre In *A ROOM OF ONE'S OWN,* Phèdre, eponymous heroine of Jean RACINE's tragedy, is offered as an example of women who have "burnt like beacons in all the works of all the poets from the beginning of time" (AROO 43) whom Woolf uses to stress the difference between fictional and real women. The wife of Theseus, Phèdre (Phaedra) fell in love with his son Hippolytus and had him killed when he rejected her advances.

Philomela See PROCNE AND PHILOMELA.

"Phyllis and Rosamond" (SF 17–29) Woolf's earliest short fiction, written in 1906, concerns two sisters living at home who seem "indigenous to the drawing room" (SF 18).

Piccadilly At the beginning of *THE VOYAGE OUT,* Helen AMBROSE, struck by the innumerable poor people of London, suddenly sees herself "pacing a circle all the days of her life round Piccadilly Circus" (TVO 12), an image that perhaps has something to do with prostitution as later in the novel Helen explains to her niece Rachel VINRACE that "those women" in Piccadilly are prostitutes (TVO 81). Rachel hears about prostitution in Piccadilly also from Evelyn MURGATROYD, who has an idea to put a stop to it (TVO 249). Piccadilly is one of the great thoroughfares of London, site of many famous department stores, restaurants and other buildings. At Piccadilly Circus is a statue of Eros put up about 1890.

Pickford, Mr. Mentioned in *THE YEARS* as at a meeting with Eleanor PARGITER.

Pilcher, Mr. An American in *JACOB'S ROOM* whose arrival at Elizabeth DURRANT's party causes Clara DURRANT and Jacob to part company while she is polite to the new guest; Jacob later remembers him as "Mr. Pilchard."

Pillicock In *THE WAVES,* BERNARD in his "summing up" refers to murmuring "Pillicock sat on Pillicock's hill," a line from *King Lear* (III:iv:76).

Pinka (or Pinker) A black cocker spaniel given by Vita SACKVILLE-WEST to Woolf in 1926; the model for *FLUSH* (a photograph of Pinka is the frontispiece to that book). Pinka died in 1935.

Pinsent, Mr. Mentioned in *BETWEEN THE ACTS.* Giles OLIVER feels he and Pinsent have a similar relationship to the land (108).

Pippy Mentioned in *THE YEARS,* the Pargiter children's nurse.

Plath, Sylvia See SMITH COLLEGE.

Plomer, William (1903–73) English novelist and poet, born in South Africa, many of whose books were published by the HOGARTH PRESS between 1926 and 1932.

Plough Inn Somerset inn where the Woolfs stayed after their marriage in August 1912. In August 1913 they returned to the Plough, where Woolf became increasingly unwell and averse to food. Katherine COX came at Leonard WOOLF's request to look after Woolf on September 2, and all three returned to London on the 8th; on the 9th Woolf attempted suicide.

"The Plumage Bill" See *WOMAN'S LEADER AND THE COMMON CAUSE.*

Plumer, Mr. and Mrs. One of the Cambridge dons in *JACOB'S ROOM,* Mr. Plumer invites Jacob and three other students to his house for Sunday lunch, which experience Jacob finds excruciating. Mrs. Plumer worries that Jacob will finish all the mutton.

Pointz Hall The setting of *BETWEEN THE ACTS* and family home of Bart OLIVER and his sister Lucy SWITHIN.

Pointz Hall Woolf's working title for *BETWEEN THE ACTS,* her last novel, which she began in spring 1938, changing the title only at the end of February 1941. Mitchell A. Leaska has edited *Pointz Hall: The Earlier and Later Typescripts of Between the Acts* (PH). In his introduction to this transcription of the first and second drafts of *Between the Acts,* Leaska says that by the time Woolf "set down the first words of her last novel, [she] had approached what might be described as a creative sensibility merging with collective consciousness" (PH 14). In a provocative Afterword, Leaska suggests that *Pointz Hall* might be "the longest suicide note in the English language" (PH 451), a farewell to Vita SACKVILLE-WEST. He makes links between Woolf's final work of fiction and events and writing of thirty years earlier.

The Earlier Typescript (ETS) was begun in April 1938; Woolf stopped work on it in October 1940 and began the revision known as the Later Typescript (LTS), which she worked on from October to late November 1940. The Final Typescript, not included in Leaska's volume, is almost identical to the published novel *Between the Acts.* The typescripts transcribed by Leaska are held by the BERG COLLECTION; a "Personal Note" by Lola L. Szladits recounts some of the history of the Berg's acquisition of the manuscripts (PH ix–xi). Leaska notes that ETS and *Between the Acts* are "fundamentally different novels" (PH 29) and calls LTS a "bridge of compromise" between ETS and the published novel. The different typescripts illuminate the profound difficulties Woolf had with a satisfactory ending for her novel (see also Susan M. Kenney, "Two Endings").

Pointz Hall provides a complete transcription of the ETS and LTS, including all drafts of each page. Leaska's extensive notes and references are indispensable in tracing allusions and symbols in *Between the Acts.* Seven appendixes provide all the holograph notes and drafts of *Pointz Hall,* Holograph and Typescript revisions, and poems Woolf wrote for possible use in her novel. Leaska notes that each version—ETS, LTS, and *Between the Acts*—comprises thirty-seven scenes. In ETS there are headings for the sections (e.g., *The Lamp, The Garden*); in LTS these headings are replaced by Arabic numerals up to number 12. In the published version of the novel, scenes are indicated by space breaks but the publishers have not preserved all Woolf's demarcations.

Pole, Isabel In *MRS. DALLOWAY,* Septimus goes to fight in World War I for an England that consists "entirely of Shakespeare's plays and Miss Isabel Pole in a green dress walking in a square" (MD 130). Miss Pole seems to have introduced Septimus to Shakespeare, upon whom she lectures in Waterloo Road (MD 128). MORLEY COLLEGE, where Woolf taught working-class men and women for two years, was in Waterloo Road.

Polegate, Mr. Mentioned in *JACOB'S ROOM* when Captain BARFOOT seeks his advice about what Jacob should do on leaving Rugby School.

Pollett, Anthony Mentioned in *JACOB'S ROOM* as dancing with Helen ASKEW, who looks over his shoulder all the time at Jacob FLANDERS and his friend Dick GRAVES.

Pomjalovsky, Nicholas Character in *THE YEARS* who is an intimate of Sara PARGITER's. He is first seen at the dinner in "1917" during which there is an air raid. Later in the novel everyone calls him "Brown," presumably because they find his last name too challenging to pronounce (TY 309). Eleanor PARGITER likes him a great deal, despite an initial tremor when Sara tells her he is homosexual. Jean Alexander sees Eleanor and Nicholas as "mother" and "father" of an implied "spiritual family" which "includes but transcends the natural family, and includes but transcends a particular civilization" (Alexander 193). Herbert Marder also calls the tie that binds Sara and Nicholas " 'marriage,' although there can be no room in it for family life" (Marder 60). Lucio Ruotolo takes a more negative view of Nicholas, saying he is "uncomfortable with situations he cannot oversee" and resists ambiguity (186). Ruotolo also suggests that his ideas derive from those Woolf discusses in her essay "THE RUSSIAN POINT OF VIEW." Avrom Fleishman has suggested there may be traits of S. S. KOTELIANSKY in Nicholas. Near the end of the party in "Present Day" Nicholas wishes to drink a toast to the human race, but he is continually interrupted.

Ponting, Mr. Mentioned in *NIGHT AND DAY* as a "dreadful young man" who tells Mrs. HILBERY it is everyone's duty to live only in the present (ND 14).

Pope, Alexander (1688–1744) When ORLANDO meets this celebrated English satiric poet in the company of Joseph ADDISON and Jonathan SWIFT, she finds him a disappointment in comparison to his works. Still, he is a genius of his age, and she invites him home with her to BLACKFRIARS. His work is represented in *ORLANDO* by a few couplets from "The Rape of the Lock" (O 209). In *A ROOM OF ONE'S OWN,* Woolf refers to Pope's satirising Anne FINCH, Lady Winchilsea, as "a blue-stocking with an itch for scribbling" (AROO 61). Sandra Gilbert and Susan Gubar point out in the *Norton Anthology* that Pope coauthored a play called *Three Hours After Marriage* with John GAY and John Arbuthnot in which Finch was caricatured as "Phoebe Clinket" (98). Leslie STEPHEN wrote a biography of Pope for the English Men of Letters Series.

Popular Culture Brenda R. Silver has analyzed the use of Woolf's name and image in the marketing of various products and her circulation in popular culture as an icon ("What's Woolf Got to Do With It?"). Woolf has been used "to market products ranging from throw pillows, to fashion clothing, to the city of New Orleans, to a glossy, coffee table collection of portraits from the National Gallery in London, to the *New York Review of Books*" (Silver, "What's Woolf" 22). Silver's article discusses the way many of the mass media uses of Woolf's name obscure or ignore the feminist content of her writing. She points out, for example, that while the *New York Review of Books* uses David Levine's caricature of Woolf in its advertising, the *Review* has consistently ignored the critical studies "that made her a major cultural figure" ("What's Woolf" 23).

A special issue of *VIRGINIA WOOLF MISCELLANY* on popular culture, edited by Denise Marshall (Fall 1993, number 41), includes a discussion of Woolf's influence on contemporary musicians by Catherine Hoyser, who discusses Shakespear's Sister, The Smiths (whose song "Shakespeare's Sister" [1985] gave the former group their inspiration), and Two Nice Girls, whose 1991 recording is called "Chloe Liked Olivia" (see *A ROOM OF ONE'S OWN*). Kathryn N. Benzel also discusses the Indigo Girls' *Rites of Passage* recording (1992), which includes the song "Virginia Woolf" (VWM 41: 5). Another recent example of Woolf's presence in contemporary musicians' imaginations is the Story's "Angel in the House" (1993), the lyrics to the title song of which bear an epigraph from Woolf's "PROFESSIONS FOR WOMEN." Woolf's image also continues to appear in such unlikely places as billboard ads for Bass Ale and the fashion pages of the *New York Times* ("Virginia Woolf, Meet Anne Klein" [April 8, 1994]: B8, for example). A variation on the use of Woolf's image can be found in *Vogue* (July 1994: 176) where Claudia Schiffer, apparently exhausted by having read the first few pages of *MRS. DALLOWAY,* lies with the novel face down on a bed, modeling a pink sweater.

Porter, Major Mentioned as at a meeting with Eleanor PARGITER in *THE YEARS.*

"Portraits" (SF 236–40) Title given by Susan Dick to a group of unpublished brief sketches by Woolf that Dick believes were probably part of a collaborative work Woolf and Vanessa BELL were discussing in 1937.

Portrait of a Marriage Primarily an account of Vita SACKVILLE-WEST's affair with Violet TREFUSIS, but also including a great deal of background on Vita's family and childhood. The book alternates between chapters reproducing a manuscript written by Vita, discovered by her son Nigel NICOLSON after her death in 1962, that tells the story of her and Violet's passionate relationship, and chapters by Nigel Nicolson that provide more detailed biographical contexts for Vita's story and that discuss his parents' marriage. *Portrait of a Marriage* provides useful context for *ORLANDO.*

Post-Impressionist Name coined by Roger FRY to satisfy a journalist's request for a blanket term for the French painters he, Clive BELL and Desmond MACCARTHY had brought together for an exhibition in 1910 (Fry, *Vision and Design* 290). Alan Bowness has commented that "post-impressionism" is "a useful description of that phase in French painting from, say, 1885 to 1905" (10) and notes that it "is born out of the reaction against (or crisis within) Impressionism that occurred in the 1880s" (Bowness 10).

The first Post-Impressionist exhibition was actually called "Manet and the Post-Impressionists." It was held at the Grafton Galleries in London from November 8, 1910 to January 15, 1911, and it caused a great uproar. Jonathan Quick has described how the works of Cézanne, Denis, Derain, Gauguin, Manet, Picasso, Rouault, Seurat, Signac, van Gogh, Vlaminck and others were hung by Fry (Quick 549) in such a way that visitors were progressively more startled as they went farther into the gallery. Vanessa BELL wrote that "here was a sudden pointing to a possible path, a sudden liberation and encouragement to feel for oneself which was absolutely overwhelming" ("Memories of Roger Fry" quoted in Naylor 64). In 1945,

MacCarthy, who had written the (unsigned) preface to the show's catalog, recalled in "The Artquake of 1910" (*The Listener* February 1, 1945) how he, Clive Bell and Fry had chosen the works by visiting studios and dealers in Paris.

Many readers have taken Woolf's semi-serious remark in "MR. BENNETT AND MRS. BROWN" that "in or about December 1910, human character changed" (CE1 320) as referring to the Post-Impressionist exhibition (but see also Edwin J. Kenney, "The Moment, 1910"). In 1912, Fry organized a second Post-Impressionist exhibition, with Leonard WOOLF acting as secretary.

Potter, Mrs. A charity case of Eleanor PARGITER's in *THE YEARS* who is visited weekly by Miriam PARRISH.

Potter, Sally See *ORLANDO* (Adaptations).

Pratt, Moll A street flower-seller mentioned in *JACOB'S ROOM* and *MRS. DALLOWAY*.

Prentice The Pargiter family's doctor in *THE YEARS*.

Pride and Prejudice See AUSTEN, Jane.

Priestley Kitty LASSWADE's servant in *THE YEARS*.

Principia Ethica See MOORE, George Edward.

Prinsep Family Woolf's great-aunt Sara married H. Thoby Prinsep and in 1850 they moved to Little Holland House, where Sara's Sunday afternoon "at homes" soon became notable for their unusually casual and eclectic group of visitors. Among those visitors were politicians such as Gladstone and Disraeli; the poets TENNYSON, Rossetti and Robert BROWNING; writers such as Thomas CARLYLE, John RUSKIN and William THACKERAY; and painters Edward Burne-Jones, Millais and G. F. WATTS. Watts, whom Sara and her sisters nicknamed "Signor," actually lived at Little Holland House for more than twenty years. When the seventeen-year-old Ellen TERRY came to pose for him, Sara manipulated them into marrying, though Watts was thirty years older than Terry; the marriage lasted a year (see *FRESHWATER*). Woolf's mother, Julia Prinsep STEPHEN, lived with the Prinseps between the ages of two and nine, her own father remaining in India where he was a doctor in Calcutta. She adored Thoby Prinsep and kept his walking stick by her bedhead at 22 HYDE PARK GATE until she died.

Sara and Thoby Prinsep had four children, of whom one, Valentine (1838–1904), taught painting to Vanessa BELL when she attended the Royal Academy school in 1901.

Procne and Philomela The myth of Procne and Philomela was important to Woolf and she draws on it particularly explicitly in *BETWEEN THE ACTS*, where she inscribes an ironic revision of the retelling of the myth by Algernon Charles SWINBURNE in his poem "Itylus" (see Jane Marcus, *Languages* 75–95). The myth is best known in the version in book 6 of Ovid's *Metamorphoses* (see Patricia Klindienst Joplin, "The Voice of the Shuttle"). Tereus, king of Thrace, was given Pandion's daughter Procne to marry, with whom he had a son, Itys. Lusting after Procne's sister Philomela, Tereus locks Procne away, telling Pandion she is dead, and rapes Philomela. He cuts out her tongue to prevent her from telling anyone of his action. Philomela weaves the tale of her rape into a tapestry for her sister. Procne kills Itys and serves him to Tereus in a pie. Realizing he has eaten his son's flesh, Tereus chases the sisters and is about to kill them when all three are changed into birds by the gods: Procne becomes a swallow, Philomela a nightingale, and Tereus a hoopoe (or, in some versions, a hawk).

Marcus also sees the myth operating in the background of *A ROOM OF ONE'S OWN*, which she describes as "*still practice*, a reading of the signs, the dumb show of silence of all the women between Sappho and Jane Austen who wrote in sand with a stick between their teeth" (Marcus, *Art* 216). As a feminist critic, Woolf's narrative voice is "the swallow who sings for all the silenced nightingales. . . . In *A Room of One's Own* we hear the swallow ('Mary Hamilton') singing of the nightingale (Judith Shakespeare)" (Marcus, *Languages* 139, 145).

"Professions for Women" (CE2 284–89; DM 235–42) In 1931, Woolf was invited to address the London branch of the National Society for Women's Service by its secretary, Philippa (Pippa) STRACHEY. Her speech, "Professions for Women," exists in four versions: a seventeen-page holograph (*Pargiters* 163–67); a twenty-five-page revised typescript (*Pargiters* xxvii–xliv) (these two are both in the BERG COLLECTION); the first "essay" of *THE PARGITERS* (5–10); and the published essay "Professions for Women" in *THE DEATH OF THE MOTH*, which is much revised and considerably shorter than any of the drafts. Jane Marcus (*Art* 137–44) has compared the *Death of the Moth* version with the longer Berg version. The day before she gave the speech, Woolf recorded in her DIARY that the idea had suddenly come to her in the bath of writing a sequel to *A ROOM OF ONE'S OWN* to be called, perhaps, "Professions for Women" (D4 6). By way of *The Pargiters*, this idea eventually became *THE YEARS*, and it was also realized to some extent in *THREE GUINEAS*.

At the beginning of "Professions for Women" (in DM) Woolf reflects on those who cut the road for her own profession, writing: Fanny BURNEY, Aphra BEHN, Harriet MARTINEAU, Jane AUSTEN and George ELIOT. Writing, she says, was an obvious choice for women as it required no expensive materials or instructors and could be practiced without disturbing the household. With her first earnings from journalism, she says, she bought herself a Persian cat. An obstacle for the professional woman writer of her generation, however, was the "ANGEL IN THE HOUSE," a term she derives from Coventry Patmore's poem of that name and that sums up men's conception of Victorian womanhood. The Angel dictated to her that in reviewing the work of men she must "Be sympathetic; be tender; flatter; deceive; use all the arts and wiles of your sex" (DM 237). To write freely, she had to kill the Angel in the House, which took considerable time and energy and could only be achieved by repeatedly flinging the inkpot at her whenever she tried to interfere with what Woolf wrote.

From reviewing, Woolf moved to writing novels. She evokes the metaphor of a fisher on the bank of a deep pool who lets her line down into it, the imagination dropped into the pool of the unconscious. Again an obstacle presents itself to the woman writer: she may not tell the truth about her body. This is a problem Woolf says has still not been solved. The women she is addressing have won rooms of their own and are earning their own livings, but their rooms are still bare. The great questions for these women are how their rooms will be furnished and decorated, and with whom those rooms will be shared.

The much longer typescript published in *The Pargiters* is an altogether different document, full of a fine anger that is completely excised from the *Death of the Moth* version. Rather than the writers mentioned at the beginning of the *Death of the Moth* version as having cut the road for women like Woolf, she hails Ethel SMYTH as a pioneer, "*one of the ice breakers, the gun runners, the window smashers*" (*Pargiters* xxvii). Dame Ethel had spoken before Woolf at the meeting of the Society, and Woolf wrote to her a few days later that her speech had been "divine and entirely expressive—Leonard says about the best of its kind he ever heard" (L4 280). The Angel is described succinctly here as "*the woman that men wished women to be*" (xxix).

Woolf refers to a recent review by John Maynard KEYNES of a history of Clare College, Cambridge, on which £6,000 had been spent and laments this waste of money that could have helped the needy women's colleges (this is referred to also in note 18 to chapter 1 of *Three Guineas*). In elaborating her remarks on how women are constrained in what they can say about their own bodies and sexuality, Woolf sums up the situation thus: "The future of fiction depends very much upon what extent men can be educated to stand free speech in women" (xl). Women, she concludes, are not by nature "wives, mothers, housemaids, parlourmaids and cooks," but may be anything they wish to be. The professional women of the Society for National Service have rooms of their own and are independent through earning their own livings; it is for them to write the next chapter in the story of women's lives.

Proust, Marcel (1871–1922) French novelist, author of *A la recherche du temps perdu,* published in eight parts beginning in 1913 with *Du côté de chez Swann* and ending in 1927 with *Le temps retrouvé.* C. K. Scott-Moncrieff's translation was published between 1922 and 1931. Clive BELL wrote the first book in English on Proust (1928), and Roger FRY was an early English enthusiast. Woolf wrote in 1918 that Fry had been quoting Proust, but she could not remember the name of the novel (D1 140). In 1919 she asked Fry to bring the two volumes of *A la recherche* so far published back from France (L2 396). Early in 1922 she wrote E. M. FORSTER that "everyone" was reading Proust but she was still "shivering on the brink" (L2 499). By May she had plunged in and wrote ecstatically to Fry of how Proust stimulated her to write. She was in awe of the French writer, comparing James JOYCE's *Ulysses* to Proust's novel and finding *Ulysses* lacking (L2 566). She wondered in February 1923 whether she would be influenced by Proust, whose "command of every resource is so extravagant" (D2 234), and in 1925 she acknowledged that Proust not only would influence her but would also make her dissatisfied with her own writing (D3 7). Woolf contributed in 1923 to an "Hommage d'un groupe d'écrivains anglais" published in the *Nouvelle revue française* shortly after Proust's death. She discussed Proust in her 1929 "PHASES OF FICTION" and in 1934, having put off finishing his novel, as she told Ethel SMYTH, she again took up reading Proust while at work on *THE YEARS.*

Psychoanalysis See FREUD, Sigmund; STRACHEY, Alix.

Pullman See WASHINGTON STATE UNIVERSITY.

Purvis, Scrope Mentioned in *MRS. DALLOWAY,* a neighbor of Clarissa DALLOWAY's who gives the reader the first external perspective on her (MD 4).

Pym, Miss Mentioned in *MRS. DALLOWAY* when she waits on Clarissa DALLOWAY in Mulberry's florist.

Q

Quack, Quack! A book by Leonard WOOLF concerning the politics of the 1930s, published by the HOGARTH PRESS and by Harcourt, Brace & Co. in 1935 and in a "Cheap Edition" by the Hogarth Press in 1936. The cover of the first edition (designed by Edward McKnight KAUFFER) juxtaposed characteristic photographs of Adolf HITLER and Benito Mussolini with a photograph of the Hawaiian war god Kukailimoku. Leonard's book attacks the savage irrationality of fascism and celebrates those who have fought against totalitarianism, and includes an appendix on anti-Semitism. Interesting in the light of Woolf's *THREE GUINEAS* (1938) is that Leonard compares the "quackery" of attitudes toward German and Italian dictators with similar attitudes held by the British toward their monarchy. Josephine O'Brien Schaefer has compared Leonard's *Quack, Quack!* and Woolf's *Three Guineas* and concluded they should be "read together" (VWM 7: 2–3).

Queen Alexandra See ALEXANDRA, Queen.

Queen Victoria See STRACHEY, Lytton.

Queen's Hall Concert hall in Langham Place, London, where Woolf attended many performances. Built in 1893, the Hall accommodated nearly 3,000 people and was intimately associated with Sir Henry Wood's series of Promenade Concerts (now continued at the Albert Hall). Queen's Hall was destroyed by bombing in May 1941.

R

Racine, Jean (1639–99) French dramatic poet who was part of the literary culture flourishing around Louis XIV. He wrote three plays based on subjects from Euripides, *Andromaque* (1667), *Iphigénie* (1674) and *Phèdre* (1677); three based on historical subjects, *Britannicus* (1669), *Bérénice* (1670) and *Mithridate* (1673); and two whose subjects derived from the Bible, *Esther* (1689), and *Athalie* (1691). In *A ROOM OF ONE'S OWN*, Racine is mentioned as a writer in whose works women appear as confidantes, as they do in Greek tragedy (AROO 82). Woolf occasionally makes a passing reference to Racine in her essays, invariably linking him with William SHAKESPEARE as the great poet of another tradition.

Ramsay, Andrew One of the children of Mr. and Mrs. RAMSAY in *TO THE LIGHTHOUSE*, Andrew is killed in World War I (TTL 133). In part 1 of the novel, Lily BRISCOE remembers Andrew telling her, when she asks what Mr. Ramsay's books are about, that his father's philosophy concerns "subject and object and the nature of reality." When she does not understand what he means, Andrew tells her to "think of a kitchen table . . . when you're not there" (TTL 23), which leads Lily to see in her mind's eye a kitchen table in a tree. Andrew is the favorite of Augustus CARMICHAEL, a poet who loses "all interest in life" (TTL 194) when Andrew is killed. Another guest of the Ramsays', William BANKES, refers to Andrew as "the Just" and thinks that he will "have brains" when he is older (TTL 22). In section XIV of part 1, Andrew is seen accompanying Paul RAYLEY and Minta DOYLE to the beach, where the latter two become engaged. Mr. Ramsay, who thinks that "his gift for mathematics was extraordinary" (TTL 58), worries that Andrew will not work hard enough to attain a scholarship, while his mother says she "would be just as proud of him if he didn't" (TTL 67).

Ramsay, Cam The youngest daughter of Mr. and Mrs. RAMSAY in *TO THE LIGHTHOUSE*, named after Mrs. Ramsay's aunt Camilla (and Woolf's namesake in Leonard WOOLF's 1914 novel *THE WISE VIRGINS*). Elizabeth Abel points out that as the youngest daughter, Cam occupies the same position in her family as Woolf did in hers. Camilla is also the name of a legendary huntress mentioned by Virgil in *The Aeneid,* and the name of a river "identified with the university [Cambridge] attended by generations of Stephen males" (Abel 58). Cam is first seen in the novel picking flowers and refusing to give one to William BANKES when her nurse tells her to. Mr. Bankes privately names her "Cam the Wicked" (22).

Abel comments on Woolf's shadowy characterization of Cam but argues that "her plight brilliantly exposes the sources of the daughter's silencing" (Abel 58). Most critics who have commented on the novel as a psychoanalytic text tend to overlook its "psychoanalytic heterogeneity" (Abel 46), subsuming Cam's narrative in that of James RAMSAY. In part 3 of the novel, Cam figures more prominently as she sails with her father and brother James on the long-awaited trip to the lighthouse. In section IV of part 3, for example, the ambivalence of Cam's feelings for Mr. Ramsay is carefully delineated through what Abel calls Woolf's dramatization of "the narrative dilemma of the daughter who thinks back though her father" (46). Her story in this part of the novel is read by Abel as the "paradigmatic nineteenth-century" story of the woman writer related by Sandra Gilbert and Susan Gubar in *The Madwoman in the Attic,* and as very different from her brother's. While James remembers his mother and a garden, Cam recalls her father's study and the men there reading newspapers. "Although the father-mother-son triad that prevailed in 'The Window' [part 1] gives way in 'The Lighthouse' [part 3] to a father-daughter-son triad, the median feminine position is unchanged" (Abel 66).

Ramsay, James The youngest of Mr. and Mrs. RAMSAY's eight children in *TO THE LIGHTHOUSE*, perhaps named after Mrs. Ramsay's Uncle James (TTL 80). The novel opens with Mrs. Ramsay's words to the six-year-old James telling him he will have to be "up with the lark" if he is to go to the lighthouse the following day. Throughout part 1 of the novel, James, whom William BANKES privately calls "the Ruthless"

(22), is gripped by the fierce emotions his parents arouse in him, emotions he is shown negotiating in part 3 as he and his sister Cam RAMSAY sail to the lighthouse with their father. Leonard WOOLF suggests that James is partly modeled on Woolf's youngest brother, Adrian STEPHEN (Spotts 531). As Adrian was to his mother, Julia Prinsep STEPHEN, James is thought of by Mrs. Ramsay as more sensitive than her other children (TTL 42). Later, she also thinks of him as the most gifted (58) and wishes that he and Cam could remain children. Daniel Fogel (146) and Harvena Richter (224) have both discussed a possible connection between James and Henry JAMES, who visited Woolf's family in ST. IVES in 1894.

It is James who sees his father as a plunging "beak of brass" and his mother as a "rosy-flowered fruit tree," descriptions that have led many readers to see the Ramsays as embodying essentialist notions of masculinity and femininity. James is also seen by many readers as inhabiting a classical Oedipal triangle, fiercely contesting his father for his mother's love. This reading is supported by Lily BRISCOE's rendering of the scene of Mrs. Ramsay reading to James as a purple triangle in part 1 of the novel. As many have pointed out, James's Oedipal journey is completed in part 3 when he submits to his father's will and ceases to think about his mother (see, for example, Abel 46).

In her detailed reading of part 3, "The Lighthouse," Elizabeth Abel sees the Oedipal drama as condensed in a single scene in section VIII. Here, James recalls and revises the opening scene of the novel: "Set in the dead center of the bay, the scene on the boat is haunted by the mother whose memory must be repressed if James is to seal his identification with his father, break the stasis in the middle of the bay, and move toward the lighthouse and the future rather than remaining attached to the past" (Abel 50).

Ramsay, Jasper One of the eight children of Mr. and Mrs. RAMSAY in *TO THE LIGHTHOUSE*, Jasper is noted chiefly for shooting at starlings in the trees in part 1 of the novel. Like his mother, Jasper is prone to exaggeration (TTL 79). With his sister Rose RAMSAY he helps Mrs. Ramsay choose jewelry to wear to the dinner in section XVII of part 1, offering his mother an opal necklace (TTL 80). In part 3, Cam RAMSAY sullenly tells her father that Jasper is looking after their puppy (TTL 168).

Ramsay, Mr. Character in *TO THE LIGHTHOUSE* and probably, with his wife, Mrs. RAMSAY, the best known of Woolf's creations. He has usually been seen as a portrait of Woolf's father, Sir Leslie STEPHEN. Section VI of part 1 of *To the Lighthouse* is entirely devoted to Mr. Ramsay, and he is a prominent figure in both parts 1 and 3 of the novel. In section VI, part 1, Mr. Ramsay imagines intellectual progress as an alphabet in which he is stuck at Q, and he aggrandizes his philosophical struggles by imagining himself as the leader of a doomed company, or an arctic explorer (see A TO Z). A philosopher who feels that his marriage and large family have kept him from achieving the intellectual eminence promised by his early work, Mr. Ramsay was seen by many early critics and readers as embodying "masculine" values and ways of seeing that are opposed to Mrs. Ramsay's "feminine" outlook. In part 1, he strides around the garden mumbling or shouting out snatches of Alfred, Lord TENNYSON's "Charge of the Light Brigade," stopping repeatedly by the window of the drawing room where his wife sits with their son James RAMSAY. Famously, he incurs James's wrath by saying that the weather will certainly prevent their planned trip to the lighthouse. He demands sympathy from women by his mere presence, as Mrs. Ramsay knows in part 1, and as Lily BRISCOE feels in part 3. In the third part of the novel, Mr. Ramsay's voyage to the lighthouse with his children James and Cam RAMSAY is juxtaposed with Lily's completion of her painting. Jane Fisher has argued recently that Mr. Ramsay's effort to get from Q to R contributes equally with Lily's painting "to the degree of closure the novel achieves" (102), pointing out that the "reiterated alphabetic sequence that frustrates Mr. Ramsay in his philosophic meditation is essential for a novel's success" (Fisher 107).

In 1971, Ruth Temple was surprised to find that Glenn Pederson could believe that Mr. Ramsay is "the real hero—or victim" of the novel. Pederson's 1958 article in *PMLA* was one of the first to criticize Mrs. Ramsay, although Morris Beja has questioned Pederson's "dubious reasoning," which goes too far in seeking to make Mrs. Ramsay "a moral monster and the villain of the piece" (Beja 26). However, as critical opinion began to take a more skeptical view of Mrs. Ramsay, the interpretations of her husband also changed. Mitchell Leaska depicted "the real Mr. Ramsay" as "crowded by people and shrouded in loneliness; tyrannical with certitude and tyrannized by uncertainty. At once frightening and frightened, he is the solitary figure of a man drawn in all his naked and nervous beauty" (Leaska, *Novels* 132).

Reviewing critical writing on *To the Lighthouse*, John W. Bicknell writes that "Mrs. Ramsay has become a Madonna with feet of clay and Mr. Ramsay a tormented, ornery, but ultimately lovable and noble creature" (Bicknell 52). In his autobiography, Leonard noted that "Mr Ramsay was a pretty good fictional portrait of Leslie Stephen" (LW1 117). Certainly Mr. Ramsay owes a great deal to Leslie Stephen and to his daughter's ambivalent feelings about him, but Bicknell has cautioned that "it is impossible to use Mr. Ramsay as a guide to the complex character and work of Leslie Stephen" (54). Alex Zwerdling also sees disparities between Leslie Stephen and Mr. Ramsay as the latter exemplifies a belief in Victorian sex roles that the former did not hold. Thomas Caramagno has commented recently that Woolf's treatment of her father as Mr. Ramsay is "balanced by a recognition that he was as much victim as victimizer" (244), arguing that Woolf's care in making all perspectives in the novel provisional undercuts the negative views of, for example, James and Lily when Mr. Ramsay is presented from his own point of view. Louise DeSalvo also sees Mr. Ramsay as to some extent a victim of British society, "the oppressor, the mutilator" (*Impact* 174) that causes his own oppressive behavior.

Such views are in sharp contrast to those of critics who see Mr. Ramsay as the embodiment of masculine tyranny. Herbert Marder even goes so far as to say that he "is at least partially responsible for his wife's untimely death" (Marder 46). Maria DiBattista describes Mr. Ramsay as essentially a "resistance to the engulfment that the maternal will commends" (DiBattista 85). Like Roger Poole (*Unknown* 271–73), DiBattista reads Mrs. Ramsay's reverie in section XI of part 1 (TTL 62–65) as an idealization of drowning, and she sees Mr. Ramsay as pressing "the claims of the individual over the undifferentiated flow" of the feminine principle embodied in Mrs. Ramsay. In DiBattista's Freudian reading, Mr. Ramsay's is "a necessary tyranny," the law of the father which "socializes the libido" (DiBattista 88).

Several critics have been guided in their estimation of Mr. Ramsay by what they see as the narrative's own criticism of the character. Hermione Lee, for example, finds it "evident that Virginia Woolf did mean Mr. Ramsay to be ludicrous" (120), while Judy Little describes a narrative in which "lyrical sledgehammers of humor apply restrained taps everywhere" (Little, *Comedy* 60–61). For Howard Harper, the narrative is generally "more comfortable" with women than with men, and even when it renders the content and rhythms of Mr. Ramsay's thought, "it maintains a critical distance, criticizing explicitly what it is also showing implicitly" (Harper 144). In a more complicated view, Jane Lilienfeld finds that both Ramsays are "simultaneously presented as good and bad" (" 'Deceptiveness' " 370). She argues that Mr. Ramsay has no inner voice and that the narrative parodies his thought, transforming it by never allowing his thoughts to be rendered in his own voice (370). Commenting on Mr. Ramsay's frequent declaiming of Tennyson's "Charge of the Light Brigade," Jeanette McVicker writes that the poem and Mr. Ramsay's self-image as a tragic hero together "achieve a devastating critique of the relay between patriarchy, philosophy, imperialism, and state art in the perpetuation of power by the proponents of Empire" (42).

Isobel Grundy comments on the name Ramsay that it is "something like a norm" to which other names in *To the Lighthouse* aspire. "Its stressed vowel is repeated in Bankes and Tansley, in the peripheral Langley and Carrie Manning, in McNab, Bast, MacAlister, in the dog Badger, in four of the eight children's names: Andrew, Jasper . . . Nancy and Cam. As Tansley approaches Ramsay on one side, Rayley approaches it on another. Lily Briscoe, on the contrary, sounds nothing like it at all, and neither does Augustus Carmichael" (Grundy, " 'Words' " 213).

Ramsay, Mrs. Character in *TO THE LIGHTHOUSE* and probably, with her husband Mr. RAMSAY, the best known of Woolf's creations. She has usually been seen as a portrait of Woolf's mother, Julia Prinsep STEPHEN. Mrs. Ramsay's words to her son James RAMSAY open the novel as she tells him he will have to be up early the next morning to sail to the lighthouse. A fifty-year-old mother of eight, Mrs. Ramsay is the focus of part 1 of *To the Lighthouse,* "The Window," as she worries about her houseful of guests and children, tends to the demands of her husband, plots the marriages of certain guests, and fantasizes about the successful lives her children will lead. She is idolized by some (by William BANKES, for example), disliked by others (Augustus CARMICHAEL), and, according to the narrator, feels that she has "the whole of the other sex under her protection" (TTL 6).

In part 1 of the novel, Mrs. Ramsay sits with her son in the drawing room as Lily BRISCOE, out in the garden, paints her. She is knitting a stocking for the lighthouse keeper's son and also keeping an eye on James as he cuts out pictures from a catalog. She is shown to be continually aware of what others in the house and outside are doing, in particular her husband, who walks up and down outside the window, stopping occasionally to demand (without words) her attention and sympathy, much to his son's annoyance. To further soothe and distract her son from his disappointment when he is told by Mr. Ramsay that he will not be able to go to the lighthouse, Mrs. Ramsay reads James the Grimms' fairytale "THE FISHERMAN AND HIS WIFE." She is seen alone only once, in section XI (TTL 62–65), when she sinks into a reverie in which she imagines herself as a "wedge-shaped core of darkness" (TTL 62). Mark Hussey reads this reverie as "an act of faith" (*Singing* 32), the wedge shape "endorsed" by the purple triangle of Lily Briscoe's painting (Hussey 77). He also connects Mrs. Ramsay with Lily through the remarkable similarity between "the *states* in which Mrs. Ramsay becomes a wedge of darkness and in which Lily paints" (76). At the dinner party in section XVII,

Mrs. Ramsay presides over the scene in a way that has led many critics to identify her as both queenly and goddess-like. Jean Wyatt, among others, interprets the dinner party as a ritual, "one in a series of communal feasts" (Wyatt 160). Elizabeth Dodd, however, has recently argued that in this scene Mrs. Ramsay is a "portrait of the lady anorect," as she is never shown eating (155). Mrs. Ramsay is last seen sitting after dinner with her husband, both of them reading. In part 2, section III, Mrs. Ramsay's death is abruptly recorded in brackets (TTL 128).

Mrs. Ramsay is drawn in part at least from the figure of Woolf's mother, Julia Prinsep Stephen. In "A SKETCH OF THE PAST," Woolf wrote that she had been obsessed with her mother until she was in her forties and described how the obsession left her after she wrote *To the Lighthouse,* supposing that she had done for herself what psychoanalysts do for their patients (MOB 81). Her description in the memoir of the morning of her mother's death shows how closely the novel drew on her own experiences: "My father staggered from the bedroom as we came. I stretched out my arms to stop him, but he brushed past me" (MOB 91; see TTL 128). Vanessa BELL wrote to her sister when she had read *To the Lighthouse* in 1927 that it seemed to her Woolf had "given a portrait of mother which is more like her than anything I could ever have conceived of as possible" (L3 572).

Nevertheless, as Woolf herself took pains to point out, Mrs. Ramsay is not Julia Stephen. Alex Zwerdling has argued that Julia was "quite different from Mrs. Ramsay in important ways" (188). Woolf wrote to Vita SACKVILLE-WEST in 1927 that as her mother had died when she was 13, "probably it is a child's view of her" that Mrs. Ramsay represents (L3 374).

Herbert Marder typifies many readers in describing Mrs. Ramsay as an "ideal mother, who functions at the level of myth" (Marder 46), both a living woman and a "perfect symbolic figure" (Marder 128). A change in the generally positive view of Mrs. Ramsay occurred with the publication of Mitchell Leaska's *Virginia Woolf's Lighthouse* (1970) and Carolyn Heilbrun's *Toward a Recognition of Androgyny* (1973). In a later work, based on his earlier analysis, Leaska described Mrs. Ramsay as "an extremely isolated person" and commented on her "deceptive self-denigrating apparatus with which she first dramatically gains sympathy and then coerces people to do what she wishes" (Leaska, *Novels* 124). Leaska also calls her a "strange and aloof combination of woman, wife, mother—and Madonna" (131); Evelyn Haller sees Mrs. Ramsay as perhaps Woolf's "most compelling anti-madonna" (" 'Anti-Madonna' " 100).

Heilbrun noted that Mrs. Ramsay had "seduced" readers into worshiping her (*Toward* 156) as "the mother goddess, the earth mother in all her beauty" (158), and had been seen as the healthy counterpart to her husband's sterile worldview. However, "if his division of truth into so artificial an order as the alphabet is life-denying, no less so is her moody and dreamy mistiness which, unable to distinguish objects on the sea, comparing itself to a wedge of darkness, demands the protection of men while undermining what truths they find" (Heilbrun, *Toward* 157). This view of Mrs. Ramsay has come to be the prevalent one among commentators on *To the Lighthouse.* Daniel Ferrer notes a "sliding over" of attacks in the narrative from Mr. to Mrs. Ramsay (Ferrer 48), and writes that the "evil side of maternal protection appears fairly clearly" in the novel (Ferrer 46). Louise DeSalvo has written recently that Mrs. Ramsay is "completely oblivious to the sadness which permeates the lives of her children" (*Impact* 76). This reevaluation of the character has also influenced the interpretations of other key scenes in the novel. Most critics read the dinner scene of section XVII in part 1 as a moment embodying wholeness but Lucio Ruotolo, for example, comments that "while such events shimmer with a certain Victorian authenticity, they remain for Woolf essentially reactionary celebrations of a paradigmatic wholeness that denies every premise of modernism" (*Interrupted* 123).

An important stage in the evolution of critical views of Mrs. Ramsay is represented by Jane Lilienfeld's article " 'The Deceptiveness of Beauty,' " which argues that Woolf gave vent in *To the Lighthouse* "to the great anger and hurt that her relations with her mother had caused her" (346). Lilienfeld examines the mother-daughter relationship of Mrs. Ramsay and Lily, drawing on the work of Erich Neumann and Carl Jung to present an image of Mrs. Ramsay as the archetypal Great Mother and Terrible Mother (358). Margaret Homans, too, sees *To the Lighthouse* as embodying Woolf's ambivalence about Victorian ideologies of motherhood (*Bearing* 279).

Thomas Caramagno finds that "idealization lies at the heart of an old critical debate on the simple question of how to judge Mrs. Ramsay as a mother" (Caramagno 245) and argues that both Ramsays "have become the victims of our cultural biases about gender and parenting" (246). In Mrs. Ramsay, Caramagno sees not a portrait of Woolf's mother but a *revision* achieved by an equal (252). Although many readers have seen elements of what Woolf described as the ANGEL IN THE HOUSE in Mrs. Ramsay, Makiko Minow-Pinkney remarks that such a characterization can only ever be true up to a point: "There always remains a margin of excess female desire, jostling against the limits society imposes on it" (Minow-Pinkney 100). Minow-Pinkney finds a subversive element in Mrs. Ramsay similar to that Woolf portrays in the character of Doris KILMAN in *MRS. DALLOWAY.* As Su Reid remarks, in surveying the critical reception of

To the Lighthouse, readings of the novel in terms of classical mythology (most notably the DEMETER AND PERSEPHONE myth) have opened a debate about Mrs. Ramsay that leads into recent feminist reconsiderations of the novel (Reid 34).

Ramsay, Nancy One of the eight children of Mr. and Mrs. RAMSAY in *TO THE LIGHTHOUSE.* In section XIV of part 1, Nancy is seen at the beach where she has gone, reluctantly, with Minta DOYLE, Paul RAYLEY and her brother Andrew RAMSAY. When she learns that Nancy went with the others, Mrs. Ramsay is relieved as she has an irrational belief that no disaster will now befall the group (she had been worrying about them as night approached). Mark Hussey has analyzed the scene in which Nancy broods over a rock pool (TTL 75–76) in terms of a fragment of Blaise Pascal's entitled "Disproportion of Man" (*Pensées* 88). He finds that Pascal's description of the "movement between center and circumference" is figured in Nancy's thoughts and can be seen as a paradigm for "the tension between faith and despair" that is present throughout Woolf's writing (*Singing* 102). Hussey argues that the child at the rock pool "figures the fundamental concerns of Woolf's art," a "Pascalian dread in the face of an unresolvable problem" that is continually challenged in Woolf's fiction (104).

Ramsay, Prue The eldest daughter of Mr. and Mrs. RAMSAY in *TO THE LIGHTHOUSE.* Prue is thought of by William BANKES as "Prue the Fair," her beauty emphasized in the first part of the novel. Prue is destined for the typical life of a middle-class Victorian daughter, and her mother thinks she will be happier than other people's daughters. In part 2, "Time Passes," Prue's marriage and then death soon after "in some illness connected with childbirth" (TTL 132) are abruptly recorded in brackets, the circumstances inevitably recalling the fate of Woolf's half-sister Stella DUCKWORTH.

Ramsay, Roger One of the eight children of Mr. and Mrs. RAMSAY in *TO THE LIGHTHOUSE* and the least mentioned.

Ramsay, Rose One of Mr. and Mrs. RAMSAY's eight children in *TO THE LIGHTHOUSE.* Mrs. Ramsay, letting Rose choose the jewels she will wear to the dinner in section XVII of part 1, thinks that her daughter will suffer when she grows up from the strength of her childhood feelings for her mother. Rose arranges the bowl of fruit as a centerpiece at the dinner, leading her mother to "think of a trophy fetched from the bottom of the sea, of Neptune's banquet" (TTL 97), an element that adds to the sense of myth and ritual many readers have found in the novel.

Raverat, Gwendolen (Gwen) (née Darwin) (1885–1957) Painter and writer, granddaughter of Charles Darwin, and one of the circle around Rupert BROOKE which Woolf and others referred to as the NEO-PAGANS. She was a member of the FRIDAY CLUB and married Jacques RAVERAT in 1911. After his death (in 1925), Woolf helped Gwen find work on *Time and Tide* as a critic and illustrator. "Madame Jacques Raverat" is one of the friends "who have helped me in ways too various to specify" thanked by Woolf in the ironic preface to *ORLANDO.* Gwen Raverat's *Period Piece* was published in 1952.

Raverat, Jacques (1885–1925) French painter who was a Cambridge contemporary of Rupert BROOKE and the NEO-PAGANS and who married Gwen Darwin in 1911. In the years leading to his premature death from multiple sclerosis, Woolf wrote often to him, frequently discussing the differences between the arts of painting and writing. She sent him her books and in 1925 she sent him the proofs of *MRS. DALLOWAY* before it was published, a highly unusual act for her. Woolf idealized the Raverats' love and helped Gwen find work after Jacques' death. Joanne Trautmann Banks, introducing a selection of Woolf's LETTERS, writes that Woolf, "Seeing herself mirrored in the process of Jacques Raverat's long dying, . . . discovered her mysticism" (CS xi).

Ray, Man (1890–1976) American surrealist artist and photographer who took three photographs of Woolf in November 1934. They are reproduced in Spater and Parsons, *A Marriage of True Minds* (85–87). One was used as the cover of *Time* magazine in 1937 when *THE YEARS* was a best-seller in the United States.

Rayley, Paul Character in *TO THE LIGHTHOUSE* who is a guest of Mr. and Mrs. RAMSAY. While at the beach with Andrew and Cam RAMSAY in part 1, Paul proposes to Minta DOYLE, feeling that somehow Mrs. Ramsay is responsible for this. Jane Lilienfeld has commented that marrying Minta "is an acceptable way for Paul to show his love for Mrs. Ramsay" (" 'Deceptiveness' " 360). In part 3 of *To the Lighthouse,* Lily BRISCOE thinks about the failure of the Rayleys' marriage with a sense of triumph over Mrs. Ramsay.

Read, Herbert (1893–1968) Poet, literary and art critic and editor of the *Burlington Magazine,* 1933–39. He reviewed regularly for Leonard WOOLF in the *NATION.* The HOGARTH PRESS published several volumes of Read's poetry and criticism. In 1940 he reviewed Woolf's *ROGER FRY,* which Woolf found polite to her but "spiteful" about Roger FRY.

Virginia Woolf *by Dorothy Brewster (1962). Courtesy Linda J. Langham.*
The cover shows one of the three 1934 Man Ray photographs of Woolf.

"Reading" (CE2 12–33; CDB 151–79; E3 141–61) This essay was first published in ***THE CAPTAIN'S DEATH BED*** but appears from internal evidence to have been written in 1919 (E3 154). One of the early titles Woolf considered for the ***COMMON READER*** was *Reading* or *Reading and Writing* and it is possible that "Reading" is an early attempt at some kind of summary statement about literature of the kind she at first envisioned the *Common Reader* would be. This profound meditation on reading, time, the body, change and death includes many suggestive connections to other works of Woolf's, including "ANON" and ***BETWEEN THE ACTS***. "Reading" is a good example of Woolf's characteristic blurring of the boundaries between different genres, as it merges critical, autobiographical and fictional styles. The essay is unified by the figure of a reader who is in the library of a house that bears some resemblance to Pointz Hall in *Between the Acts*. She picks up various books and lets her mind wander through the worlds they present. Outside, a gardener walks up and down mowing the lawn (as we find also in ***THE WAVES*** and in Woolf's memoir "A SKETCH OF THE PAST") and she says that she holds the book against an escallonia hedge, as Woolf probably did at ST. IVES. Her reading consciousness blurs the boundary between the world of the book and the world she is in: "a half-shut eye can people a field much as it was before the Norman conquest," she writes (E3 142), again recalling both "A Sketch of the Past" and *Between the Acts*.

Looking up from a long meditation on Elizabethan memoirs and accounts of voyages of exploration (on many of which Woolf had already written reviews), the narrator remarks that dusk has fallen. It is time for a moth-hunting expedition, and the description that follows recalls precisely that found in Woolf's 1899 diary (PA 144–45). The description, with its recollection of a tree falling at night with the sound of "a volley of shots," is also used in chapter 2 of ***JACOB'S ROOM***.

The narrator reflects on the vein of poetry deeply sunk in English culture and manifested in every home. In small country cottages can be found the works of Sir Thomas BROWNE. Browne "brings in the whole question, which is afterwards to become of such importance, of knowing one's author" (E3 156).

Bookplate of Adeline Virginia Stephen (Virginia Woolf). Courtesy of Cecil Woolf and Jean Moorcroft Wilson.
The Latin motto translates as "In such woods the hunting is never exhausted."

This part of "Reading" in particular is closely recalled in "The Reader," the projected second chapter of the literary history Woolf was working on at the time of her death (see "ANON"). She meditates on the relation between a writer and his culture, and says she finds much of Cervantes's *Don Quixote* dull. The essay closes with a meditation on how reading has changed since the seventeenth century, on how difficult it is to think ourselves into the context of Thomas Browne, and on the mysterious "beauty" of prose.

"Reading at Random" See "ANON."

Reading Notebooks In *Virginia Woolf's Reading Notebooks* (RN), Brenda Silver describes the contents of, dates, and identifies the sources of sixty-seven volumes of Woolf's holograph notebooks ranging from her 1905 translations of Greek classics to her 1940–41 notes for "ANON." The notebooks are held in the BERG COLLECTION, the University of Sussex Library, and the Yale University Library. "Even the briefest glance at the reading notes is enough to show their crucial role in Woolf's growth as critic, biographer, historian, and feminist, and the seriousness she brought to her tasks" (RN xi). Most of the entries in the notebooks concern books Woolf was reviewing or using in one of her critical or biographical essays. There are also eleven notebooks containing notes for *THREE GUINEAS,* eight containing notes for *ROGER FRY: A BIOGRAPHY,* and many that contain her thoughts on what eventually became the *COMMON READER* and the *COMMON READER: SECOND SERIES.*

Rebecca In *JACOB'S ROOM,* she is the nurse of Betty FLANDERS's youngest son, John.

Recent Paintings by Vanessa Bell Woolf wrote forewords to two catalogues accompanying exhibitions of her sister Vanessa BELL's works: *Recent Paintings by Vanessa Bell* at the Cooling Galleries in February and March 1930, sponsored by the London Artists' Association, and *Recent Paintings by Vanessa Bell* at the Lefevre Gallery from February 4 to March 8, 1934. The former is republished in S. P. Rosenbaum's *The Bloomsbury Group* (170–73) and discussed in Diane Filby Gillespie, *The Sisters' Arts* (72–73); the latter is also discussed in Gillespie, who informs us a draft is in the BERG COLLECTION (Gillespie 329n28).

Recollections of Virginia Woolf A collection of anecdotal personal reminiscences of Woolf by friends, family members and contemporaries edited by Joan Russell Noble and first published in 1972. The volume includes memorial articles printed in *Horizon* shortly after Woolf's death, and some additional pieces. In her introduction to the first edition, Noble remarks that "little has been said in print" about Woolf's life; Quentin BELL's biography of his aunt was also published in 1972 and an enormous amount has since been said in print about Woolf's life. The contributors to *Recollections of Virginia Woolf* are as follows: Barbara BAGENAL, Clive BELL, Elizabeth BOWEN, David CECIL, Angus DAVIDSON, T. S. ELIOT, E. M. FORSTER, Madge Garland (Fashion Editor of *VOGUE* in the 1920s–'40s), Angelica GARNETT, David GARNETT, Duncan GRANT, Christopher ISHERWOOD, John LEHMANN, Rosamond LEHMANN, Frances Marshall (PARTRIDGE), Rose MACAULAY, Louie MAYER, Raymond MORTIMER, Nigel NICOLSON, William PLOMER, George RYLANDS, Vita SACKVILLE-WEST, Stephen SPENDER, Ann Stephen (daughter of Adrian STEPHEN), Alix STRACHEY, Janet Vaughan and Rebecca WEST.

A revised edition published by Penguin in 1975 replaced Noble's introduction with one by Michael Holroyd and added transcripts of conversations between Leonard WOOLF and Malcolm Muggeridge at MONK'S HOUSE that were broadcast by BBC Television in 1967 in Julian Jebb's film, "A Night's Darkness, A Day's Sail" (the title is a phrase from *TO THE LIGHTHOUSE*). Berenice Carroll has commented that the collection is "especially frustrating and even depressing" in its complete lack of any recognition of "the conscious and pervasive political character of Woolf's works" (Carroll 128n2).

"Reminiscences" (MOB 28–59) A "life" of Vanessa BELL begun by Woolf in 1907 and published in *MOMENTS OF BEING.* Woolf addressed the piece to Vanessa and Clive BELL's first child, Julian BELL, but she began writing it before he was born and probably had Clive Bell in mind as her reader. Jeanne Schulkind (MOB) points out that Woolf was in a sense continuing a family tradition of memoir writing as her grandfather James STEPHEN and her father Leslie STEPHEN had each written autobiographical works addressed to their children. S. P. Rosenbaum has commented that the text Woolf typed and corrected does not have any title: "To classify this writing as reminiscences obscures the work's generic originality and misconstrues its emphasis and tone" (*Edwardian* 383).

"Reminiscences" begins with Woolf's memories of Vanessa as a child and quickly moves on to a somewhat stilted portrait of their mother, Julia Prinsep STEPHEN. The first chapter ends with Julia's death and chapter 2 concerns the "Oriental gloom" of mourning her, and the way Stella DUCKWORTH was made by Leslie Stephen to take her place. Chapter 3 tells the story of John Waller "Jack" HILLS's courtship of Stella and ends with her death. Chapter 4, the least focused, continues the story and touches on Jack's grief after Stella's death, ending abruptly with

Woolf and Vanessa's visit to Jack's family home in Corby.

Renan, Ernest (1823–92) French historian whose *Origines du christianisme* Woolf consulted when writing *THREE GUINEAS*. Eleanor PARGITER is reading Renan on Christianity in the "1908" chapter of *THE YEARS* (TY 149).

Renny (René) Character in *THE YEARS*, married to Maggie PARGITER. He is described as a "man of science" and in World War I, despite his ostensible pacifism, helps to make shells. Eleanor PARGITER thinks he is the kind of man she would have liked to marry.

Reynolds, Sir Joshua (1723–92) The first president of the Royal Academy of Art and author of a celebrated series of *Discourses* on painting. He was also known as a portrait painter and several characters in Woolf's novels are optimistic that they own a work of Sir Joshua's: Mrs. HILBERY, for example, in *NIGHT AND DAY*, thinks she has an early work of his (ND 455).

Rhoda (1) Mentioned in *JACOB'S ROOM*, one of two daughters of Mr. and Mrs. PLUMER, she hands round cigarettes to the undergraduates who have come to lunch.

Rhoda (2) One of the six soliloquists in *THE WAVES*. As a child, she is described by LOUIS as having "no body as the others have" (TW 22) and she spends most of her life avoiding others, finding life itself a terrifying prospect. According to Louis, with whom she has a brief affair, Rhoda has no father. At school Rhoda falls in love with other girls and with her teacher, Miss LAMBERT. Throughout *The Waves*, Rhoda's leitmotif is "the nymph of the fountain always wet" (TW 117). In at least two specific instances, Rhoda describes experiences that Woolf herself describes in autobiographical writings: on one occasion, she falters before a puddle, unable to step across it, and after the news of PERCIVAL's death, Rhoda hears "the rush of the great grindstone within an inch of my head" (TW 158–59), as Woolf described herself imagining after Thoby STEPHEN's death (MOB 137). Roger Poole sees the character as derived from Woolf's own "embodiment," the "looking-glass shame" she describes in "A SKETCH OF THE PAST" (MOB 68). In BERNARD's summing up at the end of *The Waves*, we learn that Rhoda killed herself.

Harvena Richter has pointed out that the description of Rhoda as the "nymph of the fountain" allies her with the mythical Arethusa, a nymph who escaped from the river god Alpheus when Artemis turned her into a fountain (Richter 125). Annette Oxindine interprets this allusion as evidence of Rhoda's longing to escape heterosexual pursuit (Oxindine 174). She argues that Woolf's fear of being labeled lesbian after writing *A ROOM OF ONE'S OWN* affected the characterization of Rhoda, "whose sexual desires are overtly lesbian in the first draft but ambiguous in the published novel" (Oxindine 172). "Even without Woolf's expurgated references to Rhoda's lesbianism, there is much to recommend Rhoda as a 'witch,' " according to Oxindine. "Fatherless, husbandless, manless, and childless, and 'wild'—Rhoda is a 'conspirator' (TW 227) who seemingly comes from 'nowhere' to meet her friends" at HAMPTON COURT (Oxindine 179). Evelyn Haller has suggested that Rhoda's characterization may derive from *Le Spectre de la Rose*, a ballet based on a poem by Théophile Gautier and danced to Carl Maria von Weber's "Invitation to the Waltz." Rhoda is Greek for rose (Haller, "Her Quill" 213).

Several critics comment on what Howard Harper, following R. D. Laing, calls Rhoda's "ontological insecurity" (Harper 240). Madeline Moore describes Rhoda as "epistemologically and socially" the "orphan of the novel" (Moore, "Nature" 232), and Makiko Minow-Pinkney has noted that her "abhorrence of the social is largely shared by the novel itself" (Minow-Pinkney 163). Mark Hussey, who sees Rhoda as "at the furthest extreme of unembodiment of all Woolf's characters" (*Singing* 16), comments on her increasing dissociation from her body as the novel progresses, a reading disputed by Patricia Laurence, who links Rhoda to Rachel VINRACE in *THE VOYAGE OUT* and argues that in Rhoda Woolf is "simply presenting another aspect of the self . . . the dreaming self in a bodily quiescent state" (*Reading* 147). The association with Rachel Vinrace was earlier made by Moore (*Short Season* 133).

Diane Gillespie has drawn attention to the link between Vanessa BELL's faceless portraits and Rhoda's feeling that she "has no face" (*Sisters'* 176). Rhoda is also particularly associated with the Romantic poet Percy Bysshe SHELLEY, drawing her question "Oh, to whom?" (TW 206) directly from his poem "The Question." Jane Marcus contends that in *The Waves* Woolf uses Shelley's poems, "specifically 'The Indian Girl's Song,' to create a discourse for an alienated Western woman like Rhoda to have a 'heroic death,' like Indian widows in sati" ("Britannia" 137). Commenting on the association between Rhoda and Shelley, Gillian Beer has said that her language as a child and adolescent "is everywhere erotically charged" (Beer, "Introduction" xxxii).

Richardson, Dorothy Miller (1873–1957) English novelist whose *Pilgrimage* comprises thirteen novels, published between 1915 and 1938, and is the first significant example of the stream-of-consciousness technique in English, everything in the novels being mediated through the consciousness of Miriam Henderson (see MODERNISM). The first ten novels of *Pilgrimage* were published by Gerald DUCKWORTH, beginning with *Pointed Roofs* (1915). Woolf reviewed the fourth novel in the sequence, *The Tunnel,* for the *TIMES LITERARY SUPPLEMENT* in 1919 (E3 10–12), admiring the work but finding the reality represented in it ultimately superficial. In December 1919, Woolf turned down the opportunity to review *Interim,* Richardson's fifth novel, for the TLS because she thought her opinion would be influenced by professional jealousy (D1 315). Katherine MANSFIELD had recently written disparagingly of Woolf's *NIGHT AND DAY,* and this probably influenced Woolf's decision not to write about Richardson. She also refused a review of Richardson's *Deadlock* (1921) for the *NATION.* In 1920 she wrote that both Richardson and James JOYCE were ruined by the "damned egotistical self" (D2 12). In 1919, however, she reviewed *Revolving Lights,* Richardson's seventh novel, for the *NATION & ATHENAEUM* ("Romance and the Heart" E3 365–68), and she wrote that Richardson had "invented, or if she has not invented, developed and applied to her own uses, a sentence which we might call the psychological sentence of the feminine gender" (E3 367).

Richmond, Bruce Lyttelton See *TIMES LITERARY SUPPLEMENT.*

Ritchie, Lady Anne Isabella Thackeray ("Aunt Anny") (1837–1919) Leslie STEPHEN's sister-in-law by his first marriage to Harriet Marian STEPHEN (Minny) was the elder daughter of William Makepeace THACKERAY. She was a close friend of Julia Prinsep STEPHEN and Julia Margaret CAMERON, and of Lady Jane Maria STRACHEY, Lytton STRACHEY's mother. After their marriage, Leslie and Minny lived with Anny at the sisters' house in Onslow Gardens, London. Leslie found this a trial as Anny was given to exaggeration and was, to his mind, careless with her money. In a letter written in 1875, Leslie admonished her not to squander her gifts as a writer simply to make money: "Good literature has an immense influence. George Eliot has influenced people more than if she had given away millions, and you can do the same if you like" (Annan, *Leslie Stephen* 74). Despite their fractious relationship, Anny and Leslie were fond of each other, Leslie writing in his *MAUSOLEUM BOOK* that she was "the most sympathetic person I ever knew" (12). When Minny died in 1875 Anny looked after him for eighteen months. Anny also was the only person who seems ever to have shown Laura STEPHEN any love after her own mother died. Carol Hanbery MacKay has pointed out that Anny's dedication to her novel *Old Kensington* refers to Laura, "who measures the present with her soft little fingers as she beats time upon her mother's hand to her own vague music" (MacKay 77). In 1877 Anny married her second cousin, Richmond Ritchie, who was seventeen years younger and about to go to Cambridge. Their engagement caused a big family row in which Leslie was blamed by the Ritchies for encouraging what they held to be an improper relationship. The Ritchies had two children, Hester (1878–1963) and William (1880–1964). Anny became Lady Ritchie when her husband was knighted for his work in the India Office in 1907.

Anny Ritchie wrote many novels and essays. Her first novel, *The Story of Elizabeth,* was published in 1863. Others include *The Village on the Cliff* (1867); *Old Kensington* (1873), in which the character Dolly Vanborough is based on her sister Minny; and *Miss Angel* (1875), a novel based on the life of the painter Angelica Kauffmann. It was this last work that was published in Australia with the last chapter misplaced in the middle of the book owing to a confusion with the proofs; to Leslie Stephen the fact that no one noticed was convincing evidence of the haphazard way Anny approached her work. Her essays were collected in *The Blackstick Papers* (1908), which Woolf reviewed in the *TIMES LITERARY SUPPLEMENT* (E1 228), and *From the Porch* (1913). She had met many of the famous writers of the nineteenth century, including Charles DICKENS, Thomas CARLYLE, Charlotte BRONTË and George ELIOT, and she wrote about them in *Records of Tennyson, Ruskin, and Robert and Elizabeth Browning* (1892) and *Chapters from Some Unwritten Memoirs* (1894). She also contributed the entry on Elizabeth Barrett BROWNING to the *DICTIONARY OF NATIONAL BIOGRAPHY.*

When her aunt died in 1919 at her cottage, The Porch, at Freshwater on the Isle of Wight, Woolf wrote in her DIARY that she was "the last, almost, of that old 19th Century Hyde Park Gate world" and that she had "admired her sincerely" (D1 247). In an obituary for the *Times Literary Supplement* Woolf wrote that "while none of her novels can be called a masterpiece, each one is indisputably the work of a writer of genius" (E3 13). Anny possessed "the gift of an entirely personal vision of life, of which her books are the more or less complete embodiment" (E3 14). That year Woolf had published her second novel, *NIGHT AND DAY,* and acknowledged in letters to friends that the character of Mrs. HILBERY owed much to Anny. The Ritchies, according to Ronald McCail, were upset by the portrayal. She wrote about her aunt again in "The Enchanted Organ" (E3 399–403), a review for the *NATION & ATHENAEUM* of *Letters of Anne Thackeray Ritchie,* edited by Hester Ritchie (1924). There she described Anny "always escaping from the Victorian gloom and dancing to the strains of her own enchanted organ" (E3 399). Jane Marcus borrows Woolf's title for her own essay on (among other things) *Night and Day's* indebtedness to Anne Ritchie: "Enchanted Organ, Magic Bells: *Night and Day* as a Comic Opera" (*Languages* 18–35). Carol Hanbery McKay has written an important essay on the literary influence of Anny on Woolf (also noting that "in Aunt Anny, Virginia found someone who could join in friendly combat with her father" [76]). Winifred Gérin's biography *Anne Thackeray Ritchie* was published in 1981.

Robins, Elizabeth (1862–1952) American actress, feminist and writer who lived with Octavia WILBERFORCE. She brought Henrik IBSEN's plays to the London stage and acted his leading female roles. Woolf saw Robins act in the late nineteenth-century (PA 40), and Robins knew Woolf's parents. In 1905, Woolf reviewed Robins's novel *A Dark Lantern* in the *GUARDIAN* (E1 42–43). Robins wrote under the name C. E. Raimond and in 1905 had also written a play, *Votes for Women.* She became President of the Women Writers Suffrage League in 1908 and was a close adviser to Mrs. PANKHURST. Elaine Showalter describes her play as "the most influential piece of literary propaganda to come out of the suffrage movement" and notes that she adapted it as a novel, *The Convert* (1907) (*Literature* 184). In 1920, Woolf reviewed Robins's *The Mills of the Gods and Other Stories* (E3 228–29).

Woolf met Robins in 1928 at the ceremony for the FEMINA-VIE HEUREUSE prize she won for *TO THE LIGHTHOUSE* and they began an acquaintance that lasted until Woolf's death. In 1928 the HOGARTH PRESS published Robins's *Ibsen and the Actress,* and Woolf read the manuscripts of two of her autobiographical works, *Both Sides of the Curtain* (1940) and *Raymond and I* (1956). Robins's most successful novel, *The Magnetic North,* was published in 1940. Jane Marcus has compared the feminist anger of Robins's 1924 *Ancilla's Share: An Indictment of Sex Antagonism* and Woolf's *A ROOM OF ONE'S OWN* and *THREE GUINEAS* and speculated on their relationship (*Art* 122–54). A scene in *Ancilla's Share* where her enthusiasm for discovery is dashed by the contempt of the Keeper at the BRITISH MUSEUM is one example cited by Marcus of its posible influence on *A Room.*

Robinson, Grace Mentioned in *ORLANDO,* a black servant who is given the name "by way of making a Christian woman of her" (O 70); although her name might be supposed to allude to Daniel DEFOE's *Robinson Crusoe,* a Grace Robinson was listed among the servants of the household at KNOLE, and Woolf would have known this from reading Vita SACKVILLE-WEST's 1922 history of her family's house, *Knole and the Sackvilles.*

Robson, Jo Mentioned in *THE YEARS* when Kitty LASSWADE visits his sister, Nelly, and their family for tea. He is mending a hen coop when she arrives, and years later the sound of his hammering comes back to Kitty when she is at a performance of Richard WAGNER's *Siegfried,* but she does not immediately remember the young man whom she had found so attractive.

Robson, Nelly Mentioned in *THE YEARS,* a friend of Kitty LASSWADE's and the favorite pupil of Lucy CRADDOCK. In the "Present Day" chapter, Edward PARGITER tells Kitty that Nelly, who had planned to be a doctor, has died (TY 423).

Robson, Sam Character in *THE YEARS* based on Joseph WRIGHT, compiler of the *English Dialect Dictionary.*

Rodmell See MONK'S HOUSE.

Rodney, William Character in *NIGHT AND DAY* who is engaged at first to Katharine HILBERY. William is about thirty-three and works at WHITEHALL in a government office. He aspires to being a poetic dramatist but has more skill in the manipulation of meter than imagination. An effete and self-conscious man, he is reminiscent of Woolf's half-brothers, George

Virginia Woolf's "Lodge" at Monk's House. Photograph by Linda J. Langham.
In 1921, Woolf wrote to her sister that her "great excitement is that we're making a beautiful garden room out of a toolhouse with a large windows [sic] and a view of the downs" (L2 475). It was, wrote Woolf to Ethel Smyth in 1931, "the green haven where I live, solitary, praise be to the Lord, in my sitting room, looking over the marsh" (L4 302). Woolf did most of her writing during the summers in the Lodge, as she came to call it and often refers to it in letters. The Lodge, which was next to the churchyard wall, was renovated in 1934. Woolf's suicide note to Leonard Woolf, dated March 28, 1941 by the editors of her Letters, *was left in the Lodge on her writing block (L6 486).*

and Gerald DUCKWORTH, in his adherence to social propriety, but he also has a dash of Lytton STRACHEY in him both in his love of the eighteenth century and in his unsuitability as a husband for Katharine. He is first seen in the novel delivering a paper on the Elizabethan use of metaphor at Mary DATCHET's apartment, a performance which he fumbles but which seems well received. Realizing that Katharine does not love him (because she tells him so), William smoothly falls in love with her cousin Cassandra OTWAY, to whom he is engaged by the time the novel ends.

Rodriguez, Dr. Character in *THE VOYAGE OUT* who attends Rachel VINRACE when she falls ill. Mrs. Hughling ELLIOT, whose husband Dr. Rodriguez also attends, says he is not "the same as a proper [i.e., English] doctor" (TVO 317). Dr. Rodriguez keeps reassuring Terence HEWET and Helen AMBROSE that Rachel will get well, but Helen eventually persuades Terence to call for another doctor.

Rodriguez, Signor The manager of the hotel on SANTA MARINA in *THE VOYAGE OUT.*

***Roger Fry: A Biography* (1940)** Soon after Woolf's old friend the art critic Roger FRY died in September 1934, Helen ANREP (who had lived with Fry since 1926) asked Woolf to write his biography. Margery FRY, Roger's sister, had at first thought of writing a biography herself, but she quickly supported Woolf's doing it and began sending her many documents. Woolf's first thought was that several people who had known Fry should contribute their impressions and recollections of him to a book which she and perhaps Desmond MACCARTHY would put together (D4 258). Margery Fry, however, clearly wanted Woolf to write a full-length biography herself. *Roger Fry* was published by the HOGARTH PRESS and by Harcourt, Brace & Co. in 1940 with a formal portrait of Fry at his easel by Vanessa BELL on the cover and fifteen illustrations. The first edition included a foreword by Margery Fry and an appendix on Fry's painting that was unsigned but written by Vanessa Bell and Duncan GRANT; both the foreword and the appendix have been omitted in subsequent editions.

From the start, Woolf was extremely ambivalent about the project of writing the biography not only of someone who had been a close friend but who had also been her sister's lover. "I doubt that it is possible to write a friend's life," she wrote to David CECIL; "There's so much one can't say, and so much one mustn't say" (L6 426). Another consideration was that "the Frys view of Roger is completely different from ours" (L5 416), "ours" being her sister's and that of other members of the BLOOMSBURY GROUP. From early 1935 through 1938 Woolf read hundreds of letters from Fry to members of his family (his parents and six sisters) and to his friends, lovers and associates. She wrote to her nephew Julian BELL that the work was going slowly, done "in the crannies of other writing" (L6 9). The "other writing" at first was *THE YEARS,* which she was laboriously revising for publication in 1937, and then *THREE GUINEAS,* published in 1938. As she moved toward the end of the biography, she was working on *POINTZ HALL,* which would become her posthumously published last novel, *BETWEEN THE ACTS.* Whenever the "drudgery of making a coherent life of Roger" became "intolerable" (MOB 85), she turned to her memoir "A SKETCH OF THE PAST."

In several letters during this period, Woolf thinks out loud about her difficulties in writing *Roger Fry.* "How does one euphemise twenty different mistresses?" she asked Ethel SMYTH (L6 104). She asked Margaret Llewelyn DAVIES how she could publish the truth about a friend whose family was still alive (L6 169), and to Vita SACKVILLE-WEST she lamented about dealing with facts, "so many and so many and so many" (L6 226). Her affection and respect for Fry, however, spurred her on and she wrote to several people—including R. C. TREVELYAN, Sir William Rothenstein and Mark GERTLER—asking for their reminiscences about Fry and often seeking to interview them. The predominant tone of her remarks in letters and in her DIARY as she constructed the biography is one of tedium. She felt crushed by the weight of details (L6 426), and in her diary almost every entry about the biography refers to it as a "grind" (D5 191; 207; 235; 248).

When Leonard WOOLF read the first half of the book he gave Woolf "a very severe lecture. . . . It was like being pecked by a very hard strong beak" (D5 271). Leonard felt that it was dull, weighed down by quotation and of no interest to people who had not known Fry. Woolf herself had written to Ethel Smyth early in 1940 that "its not a book, only a piece of cabinet making," albeit one from which she had learned "a carpenter's trick or two" (L6 381). Leonard's criticism rankled, despite Vanessa Bell's praise for the manuscript and Margery Fry's "unbounded admiration" (D5 272). Woolf was still thinking about "that beak-pecking walk" months later, after the book was published (D5 293), and it left her open to the suggestion that the book was a failure.

Panthea Reid Broughton* has discussed Woolf's account of Leonard's criticism, pointing out that although Leonard revised the word "anal" in the Diary entry to "anal[ysis]" in *A WRITER'S DIARY* ("Its merely anal[ysis]"), Woolf probably did in fact mean "anal." Broughton notes a remark of Fry's in a 1919 letter to Vanessa Bell that Woolf read when preparing to write the biography that she believes "finally compelled Woolf to search the pages of Freud's books until she found why and how it was that Fry could describe her as 'anal'" (Broughton 156). Fry had written, "Virginia's anal & you're erotic" to Vanessa (Broughton 156).

Vanessa Bell told her sister she had "brought him back to me" (L6 385) and when Desmond MacCarthy's praising review appeared in the *Sunday Times* Woolf was very pleased. Herbert Read in the *Spectator* praised her conversion of the "débris of memories, anecdotes, letters and records into the organic shape of a work of art" (CH 420), fixing on the very issue that had most concerned Woolf in writing the book. Read went on, however, to say that *Roger Fry* was limited by Woolf's being part of the same côterie to which Fry had belonged. Fry's second biographer, Frances Spalding, has also pointed out limitations that affected Woolf, leading her, for example, to reticence about his affair with Vanessa Bell, but Woolf herself was aware of this. In her preface, Spalding writes that Woolf's *Roger Fry* at first discouraged her idea to rewrite Fry's life: "For though it is not generally considered to be among her best works, few are likely to disagree with her own opinion on it, which she confided to her diary after the biography was complete: 'I can't help thinking that I've caught a good deal of that iridescent man in my oh so laborious net' [D5 266]" (Spalding, *Roger Fry* ix).

Critics have, however, found the biography disappointing, particularly in the light of Woolf's own expressed views on biography. Elizabeth Cooley* argues that Woolf "failed to emancipate biography from the shackles of tradition. For various reasons, she was unable to deny her literary heritage and push biographical writing beyond its traditional boundaries" (72). Robert Kiely* criticizes Woolf for changing her viewpoint "repeatedly" in *Roger Fry*. She could assemble facts, he writes, "but not her own attitude toward them. Her solution, whether intended or not, was to keep herself . . . out of the book. In doing so, except for a few unguarded moments, she eliminated Fry as well" ("*Jacob's Room*" 156). A more favorable view is taken by Bathia Churgin* when she points out that Woolf wrote to R. C. Trevelyan's wife on September 4, 1940 of how she had consciously used a musical structure in writing the biography. Woolf wrote that she had stated themes in the first chapter, brought in "developments and variations" and then tried "to make them all heard together and end by bringing back the first theme in the last chapter" (VWM 40:1).

Works Specific to This Entry:

Broughton, Panthea Reid. "'Virginia Is Anal': Speculations on Virginia Woolf's Writing *Roger Fry* and Reading Sigmund Freud." *Journal of Modern Literature* 14, 1 (Summer 1987): 151–57.

Churgin, Bathia. "From the Readers." VWM 40 (Spring 1993): 1.

Cooley, Elizabeth. "Revolutionizing Biography: *Orlando, Roger Fry,* and the Tradition." *South Atlantic Review* 55, 2 (May 1990): 71–83.

Kiely, Robert. "*Jacob's Room* and *Roger Fry*: Two Studies in Still Life." In Robert Kiely, ed. *Modernism Reconsidered.* Harvard English Studies 11. Cambridge: Harvard University Press, 1983: 147–66.

Rogers, Mrs. Mentioned in *BETWEEN THE ACTS* as a villager taking part in the Victorian scene of the annual pageant.

Romney, George (1734–1802) Thinking about self-confidence in *A ROOM OF ONE'S OWN,* Woolf speculates that a source of a feeling of superiority might be "the portrait of a grandfather by Romney" (AROO 35). Romney's sojourn in Rome in 1773–75 led him to aspire to the Grand Style in his portraiture, as can be seen in his many portraits of Lady Hamilton. Alfred, Lord TENNYSON wrote "Romney's Remorse" about the painter.

A Room of One's Own. *Courtesy Linda J. Langham. Vanessa Bell's cover design incorporated a clock whose hands formed a "V" (shown here, Harcourt, Brace & Co. reimpression [1929]).*

***Room of One's Own, A* (1929)** Like Mary WOLLSTONECRAFT's *A Vindication of the Rights of Woman* (1792) before it, and Simone de Beauvoir's *The Second Sex* (1949) after it, Woolf's famous essay has had an incalculable and pervasive influence on culture. Its title alone has become a shorthand reference to a specific kind of independence. On the dust jacket of the first English edition, published by the HOGARTH PRESS in 1929, a description most likely written by Woolf herself reads: "This essay, which is largely fictitious, is based upon the visit of an outsider to a university and expresses the thoughts suggested by a comparison between the different standards of luxury at a man's college and at a woman's. This leads to a sketch of women's circumstances in the past, and the effect of those circumstances upon their writing. The conditions that are favourable to imaginative work are discussed, including the right relation of the sexes. Finally an attempt is made to outline the present state of affairs and to forecast what effect comparative freedom and independence will have upon women's artistic work in the future."

A Room of One's Own is structured as an account of the visit by Mary BETON to "OXBRIDGE," where she has been invited to give a lecture on women and fiction. The six chapters of the essay follow Mary Beton's walks through Oxbridge grounds and London streets, and her mental explorations of the history of women and fiction.

Outline

Chapter 1: Beginning *in medias res,* Woolf addresses her audience by responding to an unheard question: what has "a room of one's own" got to do with "women and fiction," the subject she was invited to speak about? Her reply is another question: what do those words "women" and "fiction" mean and how might they be related? Realizing that she will never conclusively answer such complex questions, she offers an opinion: "a woman must have money and a room of her own if she is to write fiction" (4). She will continue in the voice of a subject who has "no real being," called perhaps Mary Beton, Mary SETON, or Mary CARMICHAEL.

Mary Beton, then, comes to Oxbridge and sits by a riverbank pondering the question of women and fiction. Wandering along, deep in thought, she is startled by a "Beadle" who shoos her off the grass, which is reserved for Fellows and Scholars of the College. (A Beadle was one who executed the orders of a higher authority; at Oxford University there are four ceremonial Beadles who walk in processions, and at Cambridge University there are two; the *Oxford English Dictionary* tells us that "Beadledom" is "an embodiment of the characteristics of beadles as a class—stupid officiousness and 'red-tapeism.' ")

Mary Beton thinks of Charles LAMB, whose essays are superior even to those of Max BEERBOHM, and remembers that he wrote about the manuscript of John MILTON's "LYCIDAS," which is in the library not far from where she is walking. Also there is the manuscript of William Makepeace THACKERAY's *Esmond* (identifying the library as that of Trinity College, Cambridge, to which the manuscript in question was donated, through Woolf's aunt, Anne Isabella Thackeray RITCHIE, by Leslie STEPHEN). On getting to the door, however, her way is barred by a kindly gentleman who explains that ladies are only admitted when accompanied by a Fellow or furnished with a letter of introduction. Cursing the library, she pauses to observe the strange collection of University types going into the chapel, types, she reflects, that would not long survive outside the University's confines.[14] This College is built on a stream of gold and silver, provided over the centuries for buildings, fellowships, lectureships, libraries, laboratories and observatories, all of which cushion its denizens from the world outside.

The time of her lunch appointment arrives and Mary Beton describes the lavish fare and fine wine she enjoys. Looking out of the window after lunch, she sees a MANX CAT crossing the lawn and begins to ponder a change in the atmosphere between the sexes since World War I. To illustrate the prewar mood, she quotes from Alfred, Lord TENNYSON's *Maud* (Part I, XXII: 10) and from Christina ROSSETTI's "A Birthday" (AROO 13). After lunch, which has lasted until late in the afternoon, there is time to spare before dinner at "Fernham" (the college that Woolf loosely based on NEWNHAM COLLEGE, Cambridge) and the narrator walks along thinking of the social effects of the war.

Walking into the Fernham grounds, she catches sight of "J—H— herself"—Jane Ellen HARRISON, the great classics scholar. The dinner at Fernham is plain and there is no wine, but afterward the narrator shares a drink with her friend Mary Seton, who tells her the story of the struggle to found the women's college. A note bolsters the "fictional" account, quoting from Lady Barbara Stephen's *Life of Emily Davies* (the founder of GIRTON COLLEGE) and from Ray STRACHEY's *The Cause*. Why, the narrator asks, have not women left money with which to endow women's colleges?[15] It is because their time has been entirely taken up with bearing children, and even if women

[14]"Old Professor —," who instantly breaks into a gallop if one whistles (AROO 9), is probably derived from Woolf's memory of "a singular old cousin [Albert Venn Dicey], who trots if you whistle, and gallops if you sing" (L1 507).

[15]In an essay for the Somerville College, Oxford, student magazine *Lysistrata* in 1934, Woolf returned to the issue of the poverty of women's colleges and anticipated the "poor college" she would advocate in *THREE GUINEAS* ("Why?" CE2 278–83).

did earn money it is only in the last forty-eight years (i.e., since the Married Woman's Property Act of 1880) that they have been allowed to keep it.

And so, at the end of the day, Mary Beton reflects on the effects on the mind of poverty and of wealth, and wonders if perhaps, although it is unpleasant to be locked out of the university's life of privilege, it might not be worse to be locked in.

Chapter 2: The scene moves to London, where the narrator plans to continue her research into women and fiction at the BRITISH MUSEUM. In the great domed reading room, feeling like "a thought in the huge bald forehead" (26), she discovers that men seem to discuss in print little else than women; she is "the most discussed animal in the universe" (AROO 26). The number of books relevant to her question of why women are poor is overwhelming, and when her selection pours down onto her desk she is unsure how to proceed. A student sitting next to her, trained in research at Oxbridge, seems to know just what he is doing, but her notebook is soon filled with many more questions than she began with. She lists many headings in her notebook under "Women and Poverty."

As she begins to despair of finding a neat answer to her questions, the narrator realizes that she has been unconsciously doodling a face. It is the angry face of Professor VON X, who is writing his "monumental work," *The Mental, Moral, and Physical Inferiority of the Female Sex* (31). Her sketch has been drawn in anger, an anger she thinks she has been provoked to by the anger of men who write about women's inferiority. Later, as she eats lunch near the British Museum, she scans the headlines of the evening paper and notes their testimony to the fact that "England is under the rule of a patriarchy" (33). If men—embodied in her figure of "the professor"—are so powerful, why are they so angry? Perhaps anger is a concomitant of power. Women have served men for centuries as mirrors reflecting them at twice their natural size (35), and this is why men like Napoleon and Benito Mussolini insist on women's inferiority.

Mary Beton pays for her lunch with money she has been left by her namesake aunt, a legacy she considers much more important than women's enfranchisement (the Parliamentary Reform Act of 1918 had given votes to women of 30; the Equal Franchise Act of 1928 gave the vote to all women over 21). Her economic independence means that she need not flatter men and also reduces her feelings of bitterness. She begins to think that patriarchy also damages men, leading them to possessiveness. Her aunt's legacy has unveiled the sky to her, allowing her to ignore "the large and imposing figure of a gentleman, which Milton recommended for [her] perpetual adoration" (39). The chapter ends with Mary Beton thinking ahead 100 years to when women will no longer be the "protected sex" and gender difference will have disappeared.

Chapter 3: She turns to "facts," to history, in seeking an answer to the question of why women are poorer than men. What, for example, were the conditions of life for Elizabethan women? Reading G. M. TREVELYAN's recently published *History of England* (1926), she finds there stories of women's oppression in the fifteenth and the seventeenth centuries. Yet in fiction women "do not seem wanting in personality or character" (43). Woman "pervades poetry from cover to cover; she is all but absent from history" (43). Women's history, the narrator suggests, might be a worthwhile pursuit for "some brilliant student at Newnham or Girton" (45), because virtually nothing is known of women's lives before the eighteenth century.

She suddenly remembers a bishop who declared that a woman could never possess the genius of William SHAKESPEARE, and begins to imagine what would have been the likely biography of Shakespeare's sister had she too been as gifted as her brother. Judith SHAKESPEARE's story is a sad one that ends with her suicide, as she is pregnant by Nick GREENE (48). But genius is not a solitary gift in any case, the narrator thinks. There have probably been many geniuses who never managed to express themselves, women who were accused of witchcraft or who were tormented into madness. "Anon," she guesses, "was often a woman." The "religious importance" of chastity in a woman's life would have prevented her from following the path of the imaginary Judith Shakespeare. Even as late as the nineteenth century that sense of chastity dictated anonymity to women writers, something that distinguishes women from men, who wish everything to bear their mark.

The world, in any case, is indifferent to genius and does not ask anyone to write poetry. In the case of women, this indifference is hostility. To illustrate her point, Mary Beton returns to her earlier list of men's opinions of women, made in the British Museum, quoting that of Oscar BROWNING, whose sentiments about women carry the weight of nineteenth-century patriarchy. But these opinions of women's inferiority are centuries old and persist still, as she illustrates by quoting from a 1928 *Survey of Contemporary Music* by Cecil Gray that repeats Samuel JOHNSON's remark about the surprise he feels at women preaching (54). Again the narrator suggests a research topic for an enterprising student: the "history of men's opposition to women's emancipation" (55). This opposition has crippled women's creativity, for the mind of the artist must be "incandescent," without obstacle, as Shakespeare's mind was.

Chapter 4: As an example of the impediments to be found in the consciousness of a poet, Mary Beton takes down from her bookshelf the poems of Lady

Winchilsea (Anne FINCH), which she finds embittered. The work of her contemporary Margaret (CAVENDISH), Duchess of Newcastle, the narrator also finds "disfigured and deformed" by rage (61). Dorothy OSBORNE's letters reveal her gift as a writer, but letters do not count as "literature" and Dorothy Osborne finds the idea of a woman writing a book ridiculous. However, a landmark is reached with the work of Aphra BEHN, which signifies the ability of a woman to earn her living by writing. Mary Beton remarks that the fact that middle-class women began to write at the end of the eighteenth century is more important historically than the Crusades or the Wars of the Roses (65). Jane AUSTEN, Charlotte and Emily BRONTË and George ELIOT were able to write because others had gone before them to prepare the way: "masterpieces are not single and solitary births" (65) but grow out of the consciousness of the mass. The narrator traces a line of descent from these pioneering women to the students she is addressing.

The four women who dominate nineteenth-century literature—Austen, the Brontës, and Eliot—all wrote novels and none had children, a fact the narrator finds "possibly relevant" (66). Turning from Austen, whose mind she compares to Shakespeare's, to Charlotte Brontë, the narrator finds in *Jane Eyre* the deformity of rage and comes to ponder the effect of sex upon a novelist. In Brontë's case, she finds that anger at women's oppression has distracted the writer from her creation when she has Jane Eyre give an impassioned soliloquy about the condition of women. Only Austen and Emily Brontë "wrote as women," that is, with no thought of the opposition from men, for it took a great deal of strength in the nineteenth century to say "lock up your libraries if you like; but there is no gate, no lock, no bolt that you can set upon the freedom of my mind" (76).

Mary Beton thinks that the great difficulty for women writers of the nineteenth century was that they had no tradition behind them, "For we think back though our mothers if we are women" (76). The man's sentence was unsuited to women's purposes, and so were the forms men built with those sentences. Casting her mind forward, as chapter 4 ends, the narrator notes that "interruptions there will always be" and so the novel of the future will need to be shaped and adapted differently to suit women's lives and women's bodies.

Chapter 5: Mary Beton's wandering thoughts have led her "to the shelves which hold books by the living," and they hold many books by women "on all sorts of subjects which a generation ago no woman could have touched" (79). As an example, she takes down *Life's Adventure* by Mary Carmichael and finds that this inheritor of the tradition of women's writing is "tampering with the expected sequence" (81). Even more startling—and here the narrator asks her audience to check that Sir Chartres BIRON is not hiding behind the curtain, an allusion to the well-known obscenity trial of *THE WELL OF LONELINESS*—is that this novel describes a friendship between two women, CHLOE AND OLIVIA (82), which marks another turning point in the story of women and fiction. Much remains to be discovered about women's lives and "Mary Carmichael," Woolf's figure of the contemporary woman writer, is still fettered by class and reticent about sexuality (88). The "obscure lives" of ordinary women are not yet being expressed. The narrator goes on to advise Mary Carmichael on what she should do. Returning to *Life's Adventure,* she discovers that Mary Carmichael writes unconscious of sex and no longer thwarts her vision by using her energies to oppose men (93). Given a hundred years in which to improve, Mary Beton concludes, putting the book back on the shelf, Carmichael will become a poet.

Chapter 6: The next morning, in the hustle and bustle of London, no one gives a thought to the future of fiction. Mary Beton observes a young man and a young woman getting into a taxi beneath her window, a sight that begins a new train of thought about "the unity of the mind" (97). She wonders if the mind has two sexes as the body has, and expresses "a profound, if irrational, instinct" in favor of the theory that the greatest happiness comes from the union of the two sexes. "Amateurishly" she sketches an ideal fusion of animus and anima, a notion of ANDROGYNY that she thinks Samuel Taylor COLERIDGE might have intended when he said that "a great mind is androgynous" (98). Shakespeare's "incandescent" mind is the type of the androgynous mind. Thinking of her own time—the narrative has arrived in this last chapter at October 1928—the narrator remarks that she lives in an acutely "sex-conscious" age. She takes a book by "Mr. A" (possibly D. H. LAWRENCE) from her shelf and finds it saturated with ego, the pages shadowed by the "straight dark bar" of the letter "I" (99), a reaction to the increasing equality of the other sex. Looking at the work of "Mr. B," a critic, confirms the narrator's supposition that the women's movement has evoked self-consciousness and sex-consciousness in men. Men like John GALSWORTHY and Rudyard KIPLING write books that hold no interest for women at all. In Italy, Mary Beton notes, men are hoping that fascism will soon find its poet. She wishes for a time "when the writer used both sides of his mind," and was androgynous.

Returning to her initial task of speaking on Women and Fiction, Mary Beton says she would first say that "it is fatal for any one who writes to think of their sex" (104), and that creation occurs when the man and the woman collaborate in the mind. With this, "Mary Beton ceases to speak," having explained what led her to conclude that women need £500 a year and a room of their own with a lock on the door if they are to write fiction or poetry. Woolf points out, by quoting Sir Arthur Quiller-Couch, that for men, too, economic security and education have been relevant to success in writing. She exhorts the young women of her audience to write "all kinds of books" (109). Guarding against the possibility of being overheard by Sir Archibald BODKIN, she summarizes all she has told the students about what men think of women and returns to the fiction of Judith Shakespeare. Judith Shakespeare, Woolf says, lives in the young women she is addressing, young women who may now vote and earn their own livings (the Sex Disqualification [Removal] Act of 1919 opened to women nearly all public offices and professions); she lives also in the women who are not privileged to attend universities but wait on others or care for children. Women may now "look past Milton's bogey" and "put on the body" of Judith Shakespeare, an inheritance for which they have worked and must continue to work.

Genesis

A Room of One's Own is one flowering of Woolf's immense creative fertility following publication of *TO THE LIGHTHOUSE* in 1927, and shares its roots with both *ORLANDO,* published the year before, 1928, and *THE WAVES* (1931). The first stirrings of what would be *The Waves* can be discerned in May 1927 when Woolf was fascinated by a letter from her sister describing giant moths at her house in CASSIS, France ("The Moths" was an early title for *The Waves*). Insisting itself on Woolf's imagination at that time, however, was *Orlando,* to which she turned with relief in October 1927, feeling that she would never be able to complete the tedious "PHASES OF FICTION" that she had undertaken for the HOGARTH PRESS.

Described by many critics as the founding text of modern feminist literary theory, *A Room of One's Own* has also had a wide influence beyond the field of literature. It is impossible to separate the essay's origins from Woolf's lifelong intense concern with the damaging effects of patriarchy. Jane Marcus writes that it recalls Woolf's own "bitter battles for psychic and physical space in that all-male territory which restricted middle-class women to the private house" (*Art* 77), and Sara Ruddick has said that in *A Room* Woolf "articulated the exclusions and demeanings, implicit and explicit, which women suffered in [her brother] Thoby's world" ("Private" 191). The image of a room itself also has a profound resonance in Woolf's writing, as Harvena Richter has illustrated: "The house/room image for a state of mind or personality is indicated in the titles of *Jacob's Room* and *A Room of One's Own*; in the essay on Henry James [DM 129–55]; in the hotel rooms, which represent their occupants and which Rachel [VINRACE] visits in chapter XIX of *The Voyage Out*; in *Night and Day* (pp. 355 and 521); and in *The Waves* ('There are many rooms—many Bernards')" (Richter 213n32). Although some readers, such as Lenora Penna Smith,* have questioned Woolf's use of the room to represent liberty—because inner space has traditionally been associated with women in their domestic, restricted lives—the "room of one's own" is overwhelmingly seen as a metaphor of independence. Marcus also identifies the room as the most famous of "many vaginal creative spaces . . . which [Woolf] asserted as a response to phallocentric culture" (*Languages* 75).

A Room shares themes and style with several other works of Woolf's. Many readers have linked it with *Orlando,* J. J. Wilson, for example, calling the works "these two *soeurs jumelles* [twin sisters]" ("Why" 183), and Herbert Marder finding that *Orlando* and *A Room* "represent a summing up of Virginia Woolf's feminist ideas as of the late twenties" (Marder 24). Maria DiBattista reads *Orlando* as "a fanciful vindication of the rights of literary women," and says that it "remained for *A Room of One's Own* to convert fantasy into dogmatic prescription" (DiBattista 147). Makiko Minow-Pinkney sees Woolf's short story "A SOCIETY" as "a prototype of *A Room of One's Own* and *Three Guineas*" (Minow-Pinkney 4) and, like several others, draws parallels between *A Room* and T. S. ELIOT's well-known essay "Tradition and the Individual Talent." Many readers, of course, have linked *A Room* with *THREE GUINEAS,* which Woolf herself conceived as a "sequel" to *A Room.*

One specific example of Woolf's earlier expression of ideas she made famous in *A Room* occurs in two letters she wrote in October 1920 to the editor of the *NEW STATESMAN* in response to a column by AFFABLE HAWK (her friend Desmond MACCARTHY) in which he concurred with Arnold BENNETT's contention in *Our Women* that women would always be intellectually inferior to men. "It seems to me," Woolf wrote in her second letter, following MacCarthy's rebuttal of her argument, "that the conditions which make it possible for a Shakespeare to exist are that he shall have had predecessors in his art, shall make one of a group where art is freely discussed and practised, and shall himself have the utmost of freedom and action and experience" (CS 125). Woolf points out that such conditions have not existed for women and concludes that "the degradation of being a slave is only equalled by the degradation of being a master" (CS 127; the letters are also reprinted in D2 Appendix III). Alice Fox* has argued that "most importantly, in the *New Statesman* letters Woolf hit upon the importance of predecessors in the development of male writers, and the immense difficulties potential women writers must face precisely because these predecessors are largely absent" (Fox, "Literary Allusion" 146).

The more immediate circumstances of *A Room*'s composition can be traced in Woolf's DIARY. At Thomas HARDY's funeral in January 1928, Woolf thought about, among other things, "a lecture to the Newnhamites about women's writing" (D3 173). She had agreed that she would speak to the Newnham Arts Society in May, but she had to postpone her visit until October. In February she recorded "woolgathering away about Women & Fiction" (D3 175). On October 20, 1928, little over a week after the publication of *Orlando,* Woolf drove to Cambridge with Leonard WOOLF, Vanessa BELL and Angelica GARNETT to deliver her paper at Newnham. They stayed with Pernel STRACHEY, the principal of Newnham College. The President of the Arts Society, Elsie Elizabeth Phare, reported on Woolf's talk in the Michaelmas Term number of *Thersites,* a Newnham College magazine (WF xv–xvi). The next day, Woolf and her party had lunch in the rooms of George RYLANDS with Lytton STRACHEY and John Maynard KEYNES.

The following week, Woolf again went to Cambridge, this time accompanied by Vita SACKVILLE-WEST, to speak to the ODTAA society at Girton College. She visited her nephew Julian BELL in the afternoon, later comparing the comfort of his rooms with the poorer conditions in which the women students lived. Back from speaking at Girton, Woolf described her audience as "Starved but valiant young women. . . . Intelligent, eager, poor; & destined to become schoolmistresses in shoals" (D3 200), an estimation belied by some who were in her audience that day like Kathleen Raine, M. C. Bradbrook, and Queenie Roth (better known now as Q. D. LEAVIS), all of whom went on to distinguished writing careers. The talks Woolf gave at Cambridge have not survived.

In March 1929, the New York *Forum* published an essay of Woolf's called "WOMEN AND FICTION." According to S. P. Rosenbaum, this essay "is probably as close as we can now come to what Virginia Woolf said at Cambridge" (WF xxi), but he also notes that this essay does not have many of the features found in *A Room* and also in contemporary accounts of Woolf's visits to the women's colleges. Rosenbaum has transcribed the manuscript version of *A Room of One's Own* that he discovered in the library of Fitzwilliam College, Cambridge (see *WOMEN & FICTION*). This draft Woolf titled "Women & Fiction" and wrote in about a month after a six-week "creative illness" (WF xxii) in early 1929. While continuing to struggle with "Phases of Fiction," Woolf revised the draft, publishing it as *A Room of One's Own* in October 1929. "I shall be attacked for a feminist & hinted at for a Sapphist," she wrote in her diary on the eve of its publication (D3 262).

A Room of One's Own was published in England by the Hogarth Press on October 24, 1929 in a pale pink dust jacket printed in blue, designed by Vanessa Bell and incorporating a clock whose hands show ten to two, forming a "V." Harcourt, Brace & Co. published the book in the United States on the same day. A signed, limited edition of 492 copies was published simultaneously in England by Hogarth and in the United States by the Fountain Press. More than 22,000 copies were sold in the first six months, and a Penguin paperback edition was published in 1945.

Background

Because *A Room* is so richly allusive and refers so widely to literary characters and writers, the various elements of its background will be found in the separate entries to which the reader is directed above, and in entries on the writers and literary characters Woolf mentions in the text. (See also BALLAD OF THE QUEEN'S MARYS; ROBINS, Elizabeth.)

Critical Responses

In "Queen of the Highbrows," a review in the London *Evening Standard,* Arnold Bennett wrote that Woolf in *A Room* was "merely the victim of her extraordinary gift of fancy (not imagination)" (CH 259). The *TIMES LITERARY SUPPLEMENT* review was favorable, calling *A Room* "a delightfully peripatetic essay" (CH 255), and Vita Sackville-West, missing the point, wrote in *Listener* that "Mrs Woolf is too sensible to be a thorough-going feminist. There is no such thing as a masculinist, she seems to say, so why a feminist?" (CH 258). One of Woolf's original Girton College audience, Muriel Bradbrook,* later wrote a dismissive essay in the first issue of *Scrutiny* in which she referred to the style of *A Room* as "camouflage." (However, Bradbrook later refused Morris Beja permission to reprint her *Scrutiny* piece in his 1970 *Casebook* on *To the Lighthouse* because "she no longer agrees with it" [Beja, *Casebook* 20].)

A Room refers to the "sex-consciousness" of its contemporary context, something that clearly influenced its reception. Woolf had referred in *A Room* to Rebecca WEST, quoting the critic "z" (identified by S. P. Rosenbaum as Desmond MacCarthy) who called West an "arrant feminist" (AROO 35). West* described *A Room* as "an uncompromising piece of feminist propaganda: I think the ablest yet written" (West 211). Recognizing that Woolf was writing against the current, West called *A Room* extremely courageous because "anti-feminism is so strikingly the correct fashion of the day among the intellectuals" (West 212). Elizabeth Abel (chapter 5), and Sandra Gilbert and Susan Gubar (in *War*) have discussed in detail the "sex-conscious" cultural context in which *A Room* was written and read.

For many white U.S. feminist writers, *A Room of One's Own* has canonical status. Patricia Joplin* wrote in 1983, "It would be hard to find any major work of American feminist theory, particularly literary theory, that is not to some degree indebted to *A Room of One's Own.* There Woolf provided virtually every crucial metaphor we now use. She made available a set of questions, a way of asking them, a possible vision of what lay behind and beyond women's silence" (VWM 21:4). Echoing Joplin's theme, Marcia McClintock Folsom* has described the power of *A Room* in the classroom: "Gradually students in the course come to use it as writers do in women's studies. They discover the power of short quotations to epitomize a resonant idea ('Chloe liked Olivia,' 'we think back through our mothers if we are women,' 'interruptions there will always be,' 'anonymity runs in the blood,' 'a room of one's own,' and so on). They also use Woolf's essay to set up problems in their papers, just as feminist scholars do" (Folsom 254). Nancy Miller* also notes *A Room*'s efficacy in the classroom: "By its themes and analysis of the relations between making art and the concrete conditions of its production, *A Room of One's Own* in a course on reading and writing women's lives is exemplary" (Miller 129). Miller, however, also reports that the text is not always successful because some students find it "too foreign; too—the only word for it—elite" (Miller 129).

Many critics, following the lead of Jane Marcus, who calls the Woolf of *A Room* "the first modern socialist feminist critic" (*Art* 198), have seen *A Room* as a political work that not only has implications beyond the literary field but also demonstrates the politics *of* literature. Nancy Burr Evans* has likened Woolf in *A Room* to Karl Marx and Mahatma Gandhi (174). Selma Meyerowitz writes that Woolf "first identified the psychology of male domination that the class system creates" in *A Room* (VWM 20: 4), and Naomi Black sees *A Room* as an example of Woolf's "social feminism" (VWM 14:5). Kate Millett's* *Sexual Politics* is frequently mentioned as the most influential successor to *A Room,* for example by Abel, who says that *A Room* "anticipates (and corroborates) the argument first put forth by Kate Millett . . . and elaborated by Gilbert and Gubar [in *War of the Words*] about the impact of the suffrage movement on masculine discourse in the early twentieth century" (Abel 155n5). Jane Marcus* has remarked that the pioneering feminist critics Mary Ellmann, Kate Millett and Ellen Moers "all consciously used *A Room of One's Own* as a model for their own work" ("Daughters" 292). In a 1973 essay, the novelist Margaret DRABBLE* wrote of her discovery of *A Room,* "I read it with mounting excitement and enthusiasm. Could it be true that she herself had assembled these ideas that were my daily life? . . . A more militant, firm, concerned attack on women's subjection would be hard to find" (Drabble 46–47).

In her survey of academic feminist literary theory, Jane Gallop* frequently notes the influence of *A Room* as both precursor and structuring metaphor for feminist literary criticism published since 1970. Gallop refers to *A Room* as "the first book of feminist literary criticism" (77), "the founding text of Anglo-American feminist literary theory" (145), and "the source book of feminist literary criticism" (190). In the "path-breaking 1972 book" *Images of Women in Fiction: Feminist Perspectives,* edited by Susan Koppelman Cornillon, "Woolf represents the aesthetic summit of the last essay [by Josephine Donovan], the terminus of the book's progress" (Gallop 98). Barbara J. Williams's article on Emily Dickinson in another important anthology (Cheryl L. Brown and Karen Olson, eds. *Feminist Criticism: Essays on Theory, Poetry and Prose* [Scarecrow, 1978]), is titled "A Room of Her Own."

"We think back through our mothers if we are women": Matrilineage and *A Room*'s Daughters

One of the most significant legacies of *A Room* for feminist critics and women writers has been Woolf's phrase, "we think back through our mothers if we are women" (AROO 76). A recent collection of essays edited by Suzanne W. Jones,* *Writing the Woman Artist,* provides a telling example of the pervasiveness of this trope. Part II of the collection is entitled "Thinking Back Through Our Mothers," and the editor writes that the essays in this section "examine how women writers and the artist figures they create have perceived their relationship with their literary foremothers and biological mothers" (Jones 6). Some of the essays, she continues, "argue that thinking 'back through our mothers' can be dangerous because their lives and their work can offer their female inheritors what Margaret Homans [in *Bearing the Word*] calls 'a debilitating training' in conventional roles and techniques" (Jones 6). Glancing through the essays gathered in the volume reveals that critics in several different areas of interest rely on Woolf's trope. Margaret Diane Stetz, in "Anita Brookner: Woman Writer as Reluctant Feminist," says that Brookner "stands in the long line of twentieth-century novelists and critics who echo and interpret literally Virginia Woolf's pronouncement in *A Room of One's Own* that 'we think back through our mothers if we are women'" (Jones 102); Alison Booth, in "Incomplete Stories: Womanhood and Ambition in *Daniel Deronda* and *Between the Acts,*" argues that "If Virginia Woolf had set out to nourish her daughters in feminist literary criticism, she could hardly have offered a richer source than *A Room of One's Own,* now piously invoked by feminists of every school" (Jones 113); Mara R. Witzling, in "*Through the Flower*: Judy Chicago's Conflict," writes that it is "interesting that Chicago does not credit her biological mother with playing a role in her retrieval of her female roots. In 1928 Virginia Woolf wrote . . ." (Jones

210n20); Mary K. DeShazer, in " 'Sisters in Arms': The Warrior Construct in Writings by Contemporary U.S. Women of Color," introduces a poem by Nellie Wong with the phrase, "As a feminist thinking back through her mother . . ." (Jones 280).

In what might be called a founding text of modern feminist Woolf criticism, Jane Marcus writes that as a literary critic, "Virginia Woolf is the mother of us all" (Marcus, *New Feminist Essays* xiii). "Motherhood," she continues, "even literary 'motherhood,' remains a taboo subject, though Ellen Moers has demonstrated brilliantly how women writers influence each other across continents and centuries. And Adrienne Rich has shown the ways in which patriarchal culture has dispossessed us of motherhood and of our own mothers in literature and in life" (Marcus, *New Feminist Essays* xiv). This volume of essays is to represent "a room of our own in the British Museum, one great woman's mind throbbing under its dome" (xvi). The political implications of Woolf's trope are explored in the volume's first essay, Marcus's "Thinking Back Through Our Mothers" (1–30).

Abel describes *A Room* as Woolf's "most complete and complex interpretation of matrilineage. . . . Texts are mothered, not authored, in *A Room of One's Own,* although Woolf opposes textual maternity to biological maternity" (Abel 85, 87). *A Room* is, according to Abel, "A text that theorizes the practice of many of her contemporaries . . . a central document in the shift . . . from phallic to maternal metaphors of literary creativity in the early twentieth century" (Abel 156n7). Other critics have sought to revise, expand, or fault Woolf's trope of matrilineage. Gilbert and Gubar find Woolf's treatment of her foremothers' writings in *A Room* "at times more than implicitly dismissive" (*War* 204). Pamela Caughie, commenting on those readings that have been troubled by Woolf's lack of conclusiveness in her essay, writes that we should not see Woolf's goal "either as creating a countertradition of female works or as adding women's works to the established tradition" (Caughie 44). "Rather, the point of the essay is to introduce into the concept of tradition the concept of change, of instability" (Caughie 45). Rachel Bowlby has suggested that women also "think back, perhaps, through the very fact of having 'no tradition behind them,' think back through the *absence* of mothers" (Bowlby, *Feminist* 27). In an influential essay, "Feminist Criticism in the Wilderness," Elaine Showalter* wrote that "a woman writing unavoidably thinks back through her fathers as well; only male writers can forget or mute half their parentage" (Showalter, "Feminist" 33).

Alice Walker* has used Woolf's essay in her own meditation on matrilineage, "In Search of Our Mothers' Gardens," where she asks "What did it mean for a black woman to be an artist in our grandmothers' time?" (Walker 233). If the woman artist needs a room of her own and enough money to be independent, "What then are we to make of Phillis Wheatley, a slave, who owned not even herself?" (235). Commenting on Walker's 1974 essay, Gallop writes that where Woolf's *Room* bemoans women's past exclusion from culture, Walker's *Gardens* celebrates women's past creations not recognized by our cultural institutions. Woolf's model for future cultural production is William Shakespeare; in the inaugural text of black womanist literary theory the model is Walker's mother, a superb and impassioned gardener" (Gallop 145). In a 1985 anthology edited by Marjorie Pryse and Hortense J. Spillers, *Conjuring: Black Women, Fiction, and Literary Tradition,* Spillers refers to *A Room*'s powerful imagery. Gallop comments that "In 1974 Walker finds in her mother's garden a powerful alternative to institutionally recognized culture. A decade later, Spillers points out that black women writers are no longer locked out of the library" (Gallop 167).

Teresa de Lauretis,* introducing a collection of essays that includes one by Jessica Benjamin entitled "A Desire of One's Own: Psychoanalytic Feminism and Intersubjective Space," comments on the "semantic shift in the term *motherhood*" and refers to another essay of Walker's, "One Child of One's Own," that she says "resonates within" *A Room* "and expands it beyond the confines of an alternative—either children or writing—that most women not only are forced to make but deeply believe we are forced to make" (de Lauretis 5).

"There was no common sentence ready for her use:" Technique and Feminist Disagreements

The "notoriously puzzling concept of a woman's sentence" (Gilbert and Gubar, *War* 229) is another of *A Room*'s most celebrated and argued over ideas. Gilbert and Gubar, finding "no serious research into empirical linguistics [that] has definitively disclosed what might be the special traits of 'a woman's sentence,' " (*War* 229) argue that Woolf is using a "*fantasy* about a utopian linguistic structure" to define her desire to revise "not women's language but women's relation to language" (*War* 230). They note that Woolf "was working in a mode of linguistic fantasy that has been increasingly important since the turn of the century" (*War* 231). Recently several critics have pointed out that *A Room* itself breaks "every conceivable norm or sentence and sequence, in questioning from a multiplicity of angles the possible and impossible answers to the problems found to be lurking behind her topic" (Bowlby 48). Bowlby likens Woolf's strategy in *A Room* to that employed by the French linguist, psychoanalyst and philosopher Luce Irigaray,* in *Speculum de l'autre femme*: "She also practises a technique of 'marginal' writing, inserting her commentary literally between the lines of men's philosophical texts" (Bowlby 40). In another essay, Bowlby* has called the Woolf of *A Room* a "flâneuse" because the text "is structured throughout by an imaginary ramble" (Bowlby, "Walking" 35). Bowlby sees this topographic metaphor as "advocating a kind of female street-walking or street-writing which is clearly going to deviate from any expected routes" (36; for more on Woolf as *flâneuse* see Marcus, *New Feminist Essays* 4). Minow-Pinkney compares Woolf's strategies and notion of a "female sentence" to the "feminine writing" (*l'écriture féminine*) theorized by Hélène Cixous.*

The structure and technique of *A Room* has troubled some readers, most notably Elaine Showalter. In her chapter "Virginia Woolf and the Flight into Androgyny" (*Literature of Their Own*), Showalter complains that *A Room* is "teasing, sly, elusive" and that Woolf refuses to be "entirely serious, denying any earnest or subversive intention" (*Literature* 283); Showalter here echoes Muriel Bradbrook's *Scrutiny* criticism. Showalter's argument is mainly concerned with *A Room*'s presentation of androgyny, but she also finds that the essay's most striking feature "is its strenuous charm, its playfulness, its conversational surface" (*Literature* 282).

Showalter's critique is taken by Toril Moi* in her widely read book *Sexual/Textual Politics* as representative of "the rejection of this great feminist writer by so many of her Anglo-American feminist daughters" (Moi 1). Moi proposes to "examine some negative feminist responses to Woolf, exemplified particularly in Elaine Showalter's long, closely argued chapter on Woolf" (Moi 1). Taking Showalter as representative leads Moi to the dubious conclusion that "feminist critics cannot produce a positive political and literary assessment of Woolf's writing" (Moi 9), a conclusion belied by the thousands of words of criticism on Woolf that do just that. Commenting on Moi, Marcus suggests that Showalter's "negative view of Woolf may have been a gesture toward the Leavisite legacy of the '70s, although others feel that her attack on Woolf was meant to distinguish her work from that of feminist Woolf scholars, or, alternately, to reject the notion of 'androgyny' and its identification with Woolf which surfaced in feminist criticism at the time" (Marcus, "Daughters" 295).

Caughie finds that "what Elaine Showalter, Patricia Spacks, Diane Gillespie [in Marcus, *Feminist Slant*], and other feminist critics see as *interfering* with Woolf's argument actually *makes* her argument" (Caughie 43). *A Room*'s techniques have been seen as a deconstruction of the lecture form (Marcus, *Languages* 145), a transformation of that form "into an intimate conversation among female equals" (Marcus, *Art* 216), and, in its second chapter, as a parody of scholarship "wherein she exposes the male unitary project as a sham which depends upon the construction of a particular sort of female Other" (Denise Marshall* 270). Richter finds that *A Room* reiterates Woolf's idea that a novel is not "form which you see but emotion which you feel." Minow-Pinkney points out that Showalter's "stress on 'confrontation,' 'sexual identity,' 'experience,' posits a unified subject which is the sole agent of its own development set over against the environment" (Minow-Pinkney 12).

Peggy Kamuf* finds that Woolf herself is caught in the contradiction of arguing against a unitary subject while basing her argument upon its existence. She argues that the "fault line" running beneath Woolf's sketch of "Professor von X" "is the notion of sexual differentiation as a historical production which, if it has produced a privileged masculine subject, cannot also be understood as originating in the subject it only produces" (Kamuf 152). Kamuf, in Marcus's phrase, rejects Woolf's "role as foremother of feminist criticism in *A Room of One's Own*" (Marcus, *Art* 228) when she writes that it is precisely "because Virginia Woolf is an exemplary woman writer [that] it is important not to conclude with a too-singular version of her authority, to preclude, in other words, the authority of otherness" (Kamuf 173). Bette London* writes that Kamuf's warning against taking *A Room* as a model for feminist critical practice "has not been heeded in much of the feminist criticism that continues to draw its authority from Woolf" ("Guerrilla").

"An awkward break": Anger

Perhaps the most controversial passage in *A Room* is that where Woolf finds fault with Charlotte Brontë for letting her own anger "deform" her portrayal of Jane Eyre. Several critics have commented that Woolf's reading of Brontë was affected by her own fear of or distaste for anger in herself. Certainly many early readers of *A Room* commented on its serenity and charm. In 1933, Woolf wrote to Ethel SMYTH that in writing the essay she had forced herself "to keep my own figure fictitious; legendary. If I had said, Look here am I uneducated, because my brothers used all the family funds which is the fact—Well theyd have said; she has an axe to grind; and no one would have taken me seriously" (L5 195). Alex Zwerdling believes Woolf's "heightened awareness of a possibly hostile audience" strongly affects the tone of *A Room*: "In place of anger we have irony; in place of sarcasm, charm" (Zwerdling 255). An earlier critic, Jean Guiguet, on the contrary, found "the most striking feature is the violence of her polemic. True, the quarrel is fought on general grounds, but we feel how much it was a personal one for her" (Guiguet 169). Guiguet, typical of several early male commentators on Woolf, finds that *A Room* displays "little of the serenity and impersonality its author recommends" (170) and advises separating Woolf's "social feminism" from her "literary feminism" rather than following "the devious and tangled path of the author's impassioned pleading" (Guiguet 170). John LEHMANN found that *A Room* "made abundantly clear" Woolf "had never got over a feeling of resentment that she as a female had to learn in rather a restricted way at home, while her brother Thoby as a male was enjoying all the advantages of an expensive education at Cambridge" (Lehmann, *Virginia Woolf* 9). Woolf's brother-in-law Clive BELL "was one of the few who didn't like [*A Room*]; he thought that Virginia should stick to works of the imagination" (QB2 150).

Adrienne Rich* spoke in 1971 of her astonishment "at the sense of effort, of pains taken, of dogged tentativeness, in the tone" of *A Room.* It was the tone "of a woman almost in touch with her anger, who is determined not to appear angry, who is *willing* herself to be calm, detached, and even charming in a roomful of men where things have been said which are attacks on her very integrity" (Rich, "When We" 37). Rich pointed out that although *A Room* ostensibly addresses an audience of women, Woolf was conscious of her BLOOMSBURY GROUP contemporaries, including several homosexual anti-feminist men such as Lytton Strachey, E. M. FORSTER and John Maynard Keynes. Rich suggests also that Woolf may have felt the ghost of her father, Leslie STEPHEN, looming in the background as she wrote.

Cora Kaplan,* agreeing to a certain extent with Showalter's analysis of Woolf's "flight into androgyny," wonders what could have prompted the "excess" of Woolf's critique of Brontë in *A Room.* Kaplan points out that Woolf omitted some sentences from the rooftop speech in chapter 12 of *Jane Eyre* that she quotes (AROO 68–69), sentences in which Brontë "insists that even the confined and restless state could produce 'many and glowing' visions" (Kaplan 362). Kaplan explains Woolf's distaste for Brontë's anger as derived from Woolf's own anxiety over bringing together issues of subjectivity, class, sexuality and culture. "Like Wollstonecraft before her," Kaplan concludes, "[Woolf] cannot quite shake off the moral and libidinal economies of the enlightenment" (Kaplan 364).

Marcus, on the other hand, argues that "Woolf's anger is directed at Haworth Parsonage, not at Brontë" (*Art* 132) and finds that far more space in *A Room* is devoted to analyzing Woolf's own anger and men's anger at women. She sees Woolf as creating "an angry Charlotte Brontë as a modern Judith Shakespeare and precursor to her own angry position" ("Daughters" 286), a strategy Woolf needs in order to use Brontë "as enraged interrupter of her own discourse," a practice Woolf names as feminist. "What I am arguing then is that Woolf marks Brontë's jerks and breaks as signifiers of a woman's writing practice thus valorizing the trope of interruption in her own text, her dashes and ellipses, the violent breaks in her own narrative" (Marcus, "Daughters" 301).

Very soon after *A Room* was published, Woolf wrote to Goldsworthy Lowes DICKINSON, "I'm so glad you thought it good-tempered—my blood is apt to boil on this one subject as yours does about natives, or war; and I didnt want it to. I wanted to encourage the young women—they seem to get fearfully depressed—and to induce discussion" (L4 106). Writing about *A Room* in an early work of 1970s feminist theory, Patricia Meyer Spacks* finds "a conflict running through the entire essay . . . a clash between the need to assert and the need to apologize" (Spacks 10). In particular, Spacks believes, "she apologizes for feminine anger, which she believes an emblem of feminine limitation" (11). Spacks writes that although Woolf is correct in locating anger in those writers she cites, such as Margaret of Newcastle, her conclusions about it are wrong: often women write best out of anger, and, says Spacks, Woolf herself "writes marvelously out of personal anger" (Spacks 12). She cites the thematic "Mary" ballad as an indirect allusion throughout *A Room* to "the miserable injustice of women's condition" (Spacks 12). Recently, Mary Jacobus has read Woolf's passage about *Jane Eyre* as a comment on women and writing in which Woolf uses Brontë to say what she cannot say herself "without loss of calmness." By editing Brontë's words into her text, Woolf "creates a point of instability which unsettles her own urbane and polished decorum. The rift exposes the fiction of authorial control and objectivity, revealing other possible fictions, other kinds of writing; exposes, for a moment, its own terms" (Jacobus 35).

"Women . . . as looking-glasses . . . reflecting the figure of man at twice its natural size": Patriarchy

In *Beyond God the Father,* Mary Daly* uses the term "Looking Glass society" to refer to patriarchy, drawing on what she says is a "basic principle" expressed by Woolf: "In the Looking Glass society females, that is Magnifying Mirrors, play a crucial role" (Daly, *Beyond* 196). Daly, who also wrote in *The Church and the Second Sex* that Woolf "knew of the need for a feminist tradition, when she wrote of her hope for the eventual arrival of Shakespeare's sister" (50–51), is but one American radical feminist who sees Woolf as a "foremother." Another feminist theologian, Catherine Keller,* also refers to Woolf's trope of woman-as-mirror to criticize patriarchal religion: "Woman's support of his ego sustains his god-likeness, which together they amplify into the Infinite, thus assuring an endless return of the same cycle" (Keller 44). Andrea Dworkin* also uses the mirror trope in her analysis of pornography: "Male sexual power is the substance of culture. . . . As Woolf wrote, [woman] is [man's] mirror; by diminishing her in his use of her he becomes twice his size. In the culture he is a giant, enlarged by his conquest of her, implied or explicit. She remains his mirror and, as Woolf postulated, '. . . mirrors are essential to all violent and heroic action' " (Dworkin 23). The use of this trope is a further example of how *A Room* is a source not only of the lexicon of a major strand of contemporary American feminism, but also has shaped many of its theories. In an article on nineteenth-century women's autobiography, for example, we find the trope elaborated by Sidonie Smith*: "Product of patriarchy's binarism, the architecture of the 'self of essences' rests upon and reinforces the specularization of 'woman' as the Other through whom 'man' constructs his stature, status, and significance" (80).

The influence of *A Room,* then, cannot be overestimated, although its influence has been almost exclusively on white feminists (with some notable exceptions). Adrienne Rich* noted in a talk that she was born in 1929, the year Woolf "was writing of the necessity for a literature that would reveal 'that vast chamber where nobody has been'—the realm of relationships between women" (Rich, "Lesbian" 199). That "Chloe liked Olivia" has also become a pervasive shorthand among feminist writers referring to the hitherto silenced voices of lesbians. Marcus has named *A Room*'s "triologic" rhetoric (*Languages* 150) "sapphistry"—"when the woman writer seduces the woman reader" (*Languages* 169; see also *WELL OF LONELINESS, THE*). Ellen Bayuk Rosenman* comments that the theme of lesbianism emerges in *Life's Adventure,* the "imagined novel" of *A Room,* and refers to the draft in the MONK'S HOUSE PAPERS wherein lesbianism is "clearly present" (Rosenman 636, and see WF 114).

In its absences, ellipses and spaces, *A Room* calls forth the missing women writers of Woolf's construction of history. In her influential book *Silences,* Tillie Olsen* draws on Woolf to ponder "the silences where the lives never came to writing" (10).

Yet, as Woolf herself implicitly predicted at the end of her essay they might, many women find *A Room* valuable now more as a historic document than a strategy for the present. Trinh T. Minh-ha,* for example, who calls Woolf "our reputed foresister" (7), writes that "One has to be excessively preoccupied with the master's concerns, indeed, to try to explain why women cannot have written 'the plays of Shakespeare' as Virginia Woolf did. Such a waste of energy is perhaps unavoidable at certain stages of the struggle; it need not, however, become an end point in itself" (Trinh 85). As the editors of a recent collection of essays on writers contemporary with Woolf say, Woolf "urged her audience to write more books and to find more 'Anons'; we hope our readers will read more books and help introduce even more writers into our collective (literary) history" (Ingram and Patai* 4). Despite the sense that what Woolf called for in *A Room* has either been accomplished or is well under way, however, "the most transient visitor to this planet . . . who picked up [the news]paper could not fail to be aware" that patriarchy is still the dominant order (AROO 33). Tania Modleski* writes that although "we surely would want to go further than Woolf and imagine a time when there will *be* no classes to which the woman writer may restrict herself, we have not come close to realizing the vision which would make the radical struggle possible." Modleski's essay, taking issue with those who criticize Woolf's feminism as limited, is an example of how *A Room* still energizes feminist thinking: "Years after Woolf wrote of her hopes, the mute women remain mostly mute. . . . Woolf's prophecy of a female 'fellowship' in which women speak freely to and of one another remains to some extent a promise—and nothing less" (Modleski 24).

Works Specific to This Entry:

Bowlby, Rachel. "Walking, Women and Writing: Virginia Woolf as *flâneuse.*" In Isobel Armstrong, ed. *New Feminist Discourses: Critical Essays on Theories and Texts.* London: Routledge, 1992.

Bradbrook, M. C. "Notes on the Style of Mrs. Woolf." *Scrutiny* 1 (May 1932): 33–38.

Cixous, Hélène. "The Laugh of the Medusa." In Elaine Marks and Isabelle de Courtivron, eds. *New French Feminisms: An Anthology.* New York: Schocken, 1981.

Daly, Mary. *Beyond God the Father: Toward a Philosophy of Women's Liberation.* Boston: Beacon, 1973.

———. *The Church and the Second Sex.* Boston: Beacon, 1985.

de Lauretis, Teresa, ed. *Feminist Studies, Critical Studies.* Bloomington: Indiana University Press, 1986.

Drabble, Margaret. "Virginia Woolf: A Personal Debt." In Margaret Homans, ed. *Virginia Woolf*: 46–51.

Dworkin, Andrea. *Pornography: Men Possessing Women.* New York: Perigee, 1981.

Evans, Nancy Burr. "The Political Consciousness of Virginia Woolf: *A Room of One's Own* and *Three Guineas.*" *The New Scholar* 4 (1974): 167–80.

Folsom, Marcia McClintock. "Gallant Red Brick and Plain China; Teaching *A Room of One's Own.*" *College English* 45, 3 (March 1983): 254–62.

Fox, Alice. "Literary Allusion as Feminist Criticism in *A Room of One's Own.*" *Philological Quarterly* (Spring 1984): 145–61.

Gallop, Jane. *Around 1981: Academic Feminist Literary Theory*. New York: Routledge, 1992.

Ingram, Angela, and Daphne Patai, eds. *Rediscovering Forgotten Radicals: British Women Writers 1889–1939*. Chapel Hill: University of North Carolina Press, 1993.

Irigaray, Luce. *Speculum of the Other Woman [Speculum de l'autre femme,* 1974]. Translated by Gillian C. Gill. Ithaca: Cornell University Press, 1985.

Jones, Suzanne W. *Writing the Woman Artist: Essays on Poetics, Politics, and Portraiture*. Philadelphia: University of Pennsylvania Press, 1991.

Joplin, Patricia. " 'I Have Bought My Freedom': The Gift of *A Room of One's Own*." VWM 21 (Fall 1983): 4–5.

Kamuf, Peggy. "Penelope at Work." In *Signature Pieces: On the Institution of Authorship*. Ithaca: Cornell University Press, 1988.

Kaplan, Cora. "Pandora's Box: Subjectivity, Class and Sexuality in Socialist-Feminist Criticism." In Terry Lovell, ed. *British Feminist Thought: A Reader*. Cambridge, England: Blackwell, 1990.

Keller, Catherine. *From a Broken Web: Separation, Sexism, and Self*. Boston: Beacon, 1986.

London, Bette. "Guerrilla in Petticoats or Sans-Culotte? Virginia Woolf and the Future of Feminist Criticism." *diacritics* (Summer/Fall 1991): 11–29.

Marcus, Jane. "Daughters of Anger/Material Girls: Con/textualizing Feminist Criticism." *Women's Studies* 15 (1988): 281–308.

Marshall, Denise. "Woolf's Monumental List-Works: Transforming Popular Culture's Semiotics of Space." In Vara Neverow-Turk and Mark Hussey, eds. *Virginia Woolf: Themes and Variations*: 268–76.

Miller, Nancy. "Teaching Autobiography." In *Getting Personal: Feminist Occasions and Other Autobiographical Acts*. New York: Routledge, 1991.

Millett, Kate. *Sexual Politics*. London: Virago, 1979 (1969).

Modleski, Tania. "Some Functions of Feminist Criticism, or The Scandal of the Mute Body." *October* 49 (Summer 1989): 3–24.

Moi, Toril. *Sexual/Textual Politics: Feminist Literary Theory*. New York: Methuen, 1985.

Olsen, Tillie. *Silences*. New York: Delta/Seymour Lawrence, 1978.

Rich, Adrienne. "When We Dead Awaken: Writing as Re-Vision." In *On Lies, Secrets and Silence*. New York: W. W. Norton & Co., 1979.

———. " 'It is the Lesbian in Us . . . .' " Ibid.

Rosenman, Ellen Bayuk. "Sexual Identity and *A Room of One's Own*: 'Secret Economies' in Virginia Woolf's Feminist Discourse." *Signs: Journal of Women in Culture and Society* 14, 3 (1989): 634–50.

Showalter, Elaine. "Feminist Criticism in the Wilderness." In Elizabeth Abel, ed. *Writing and Sexual Difference*. Chicago: University of Chicago Press, 1982.

Smith, Lenora Penna. "Rooms and the Construction of the Feminine Self." In Vara Neverow-Turk and Mark Hussey, eds. *Virginia Woolf: Themes and Variations*: 216–25.

Smith, Sidonie. "Resisting the Gaze of Embodiment: Women's Autobiography in the Nineteenth Century." In Margo Culley, ed. *American Women's Autobiography: Fea(s)ts of Memory*. Madison: University of Wisconsin Press, 1992.

Spacks, Patricia Meyer. *The Female Imagination*. New York: Alfred A. Knopf, 1975.

Trinh, T. Minh-ha. *Woman, Native, Other: Writing Postcoloniality and Feminism*. Bloomington: Indiana University Press, 1989.

Walker, Alice. "In Search of Our Mothers' Gardens." In *In Search of Our Mothers' Gardens: Womanist Prose*. San Diego: Harcourt Brace Jovanovich, 1983.

———."One Child of One's Own." Ibid.

West, Rebecca. "Autumn and Virginia Woolf." *Ending in Earnest: A Literary Log*. Freeport, N.Y.: Books for Libraries, 1967. Reprint of 1931 edition.

Rosalind In *A ROOM OF ONE'S OWN*, Rosalind, from William SHAKESPEARE's *As You Like It*, is offered as an example of women who have "burnt like beacons in all the works of all the poets from the beginning of time" (AROO 43), whom Woolf uses to stress the difference between fictional and real women. Katharine HILBERY in *NIGHT AND DAY* is compared several times to Rosalind. In Shakespeare's play, Rosalind disguises herself as a man to escape the restrictions placed on women and enable her to control her relationship with Orlando. The allusion in *Night and Day* is significant as Katharine, like Rosalind, both scorns love and is tormented by her feelings of love. Further, Katharine is strongly drawn to Mary DATCHET.

Rosebery, Archibald Philip Primrose (1847–1929) During the dinner in section XVII of part 1 of *TO THE LIGHTHOUSE*, Mrs. RAMSAY reflects on how she relies on the "admirable fabric of the masculine intelligence" to sustain her as she half-listens to the dinner conversation range across numerous subjects, one of which is "Lord Rosebery" (TTL 106). Rosebery was foreign secretary in two of William GLADSTONE's governments and wrote several political biographies.

Rosseter, Miss Mentioned in *JACOB'S ROOM* at a tea Jacob attends at his mother's old friend Miss PERRY's.

Rossetti, Christina Georgina (1830–94) The sister of the Pre-Raphaelite poet and painter Dante Gabriel Rossetti, Rossetti published *Goblin Market, and Other Poems* in 1862, *The Prince's Progress, and Other Poems* in 1866, and several other works of poetry and stories. She is mentioned in *ORLANDO* when Orlando realizes that it would be "impolitic" to wrap a ten-pound note around the sugar tongs when she comes to tea. Woolf's essay " 'I am Christina Rossetti' " was published in the *NATION & ATHENAEUM* in December 1930 and reprinted in the *COMMON READER: SECOND SERIES* (CR2 237–44; CE4 54–60). In *A ROOM OF ONE'S OWN,* Rossetti's poem "A Birthday" (Gilbert and Gubar, *Norton* 882) is quoted by the narrator as an example of how women spoke to men "before the war" (AROO 13).

Ruck, Bertha A name on a tombstone in *JACOB'S ROOM* (JR 133) that led to Woolf receiving a letter from Berta (sic) Ruck's lawyer informing her that the author of *The Lad with Wings* and *The Dancing Star* was in fact alive (QB2 91). Berta Ruck (1878–1978) was married to Oliver Onions and was a hugely best-selling novelist and short-story writer; Woolf and she had a mutual friend in Lydia LOPOKOVA and got on quite well when they eventually met.

Ruff's Tour in Northumberland Mentioned in *THE YEARS,* a book Eleanor PARGITER finds in her bedroom at her sister-in-law's house. William Ruff (1801–56) wrote a series of guidebooks.

Runcorn's Boy The son of the porter at Eleanor PARGITER's flat in *THE YEARS* whom she asks her brother Edward to help get into university.

Ruskin, John (1819–1900) The author of *Modern Painters,* published in five volumes between 1843 and 1860. A defender of the Pre-Raphaelites, Ruskin was a significant influence on Victorian taste and turned in his later years to questions of social reform in works such as *Sesame and Lilies* (1865). In *NIGHT AND DAY,* Ralph DENHAM reminds Mrs. HILBERY of her "dear Mr. Ruskin" (ND 14). Woolf reviewed Ruskin's *Praeterita* in the *NEW REPUBLIC* in December 1927 (BP 59–62). Her essay "Ruskin" was included in *THE CAPTAIN'S DEATH BED* and is also in volume 1 of her *COLLECTED ESSAYS* (pages 205–08).

Russell, Bertrand Arthur William (1872–1970) Philosopher, mathematician and pacifist who is usually linked with G. E. MOORE, whom he persuaded to turn from classics to philosophy, as one of the greatest influences on British philosophy in the first half of the twentieth century. His *Principles of Mathematics* was published in 1903, the same year as Moore's *Principia Ethica.* A Fellow of Trinity College, Cambridge, and an APOSTLE, he was familiar with many of the BLOOMSBURY GROUP both at Cambridge and later in London. Russell was a member of the 1917 CLUB and his intense affair with Lady Ottoline MORRELL also brought him into continuing contact with people associated with Bloomsbury. S. P. Rosenbaum writes that Russell's "impact on Bloomsbury extends far beyond the Cambridge years, when he and Moore made their philosophical revolution, to the Great War when Bloomsbury strongly supported Russell's crusading pacifism, and on into the 1920s and 1930s" (*Victorian* 193).

Woolf first met him in 1905 with his first wife Alys, the sister of Logan Pearsall SMITH; Alys was the aunt of Rachel (see Rachel STRACHEY) and Karin Costelloe (see Karin STEPHEN). Russell lost his lectureship at Cambridge because of his opposition to World War I and was jailed in 1918 for an article he wrote in *The Tribunal,* the newspaper of the No Conscription Fellowship (of which Adrian STEPHEN was Secretary).

Russian Ballet In the "1914" chapter of *THE YEARS,* Ann HILLIER asks Martin PARGITER if he has seen "the Russian dancers," and he agrees with her that "Nijinsky's marvellous" (TY 254–55). Vaslav Fomich Nijinsky (1889–1950) performed as the rose-spirit in *Le Spectre de la Rose* between 1911 and 1918. Having formed his own company, Nijinsky danced in London in March 1914. Prior to that he had been with the company of Sergei Pavlovich Diaghilev, whose dancers enthralled London in 1911. Leonard WOOLF wrote in his *Autobiography* that in 1911, "night after night we flocked to Covent Garden, entranced by a new art, a revelation to us benighted British, the Russian Ballet in the greatest days of Diaghilev and Nijinsky" (LW2 22). In the winter 1918–19 season, Diaghilev's company shared the stage with music-hall acts at the London Coliseum, and in 1919 they performed at the Alhambra Theater. Woolf attended performances at both venues, ballet being, as Evelyn Haller remarks, "at the center of London's intellectual and cultural life" ("Her Quill" 187). In the 1918–19 visit, Lydia LOPOKOVA, who later married John Maynard KEYNES, was a new member of the Diaghilev company.

Russian Dancers See RUSSIAN BALLET.

"Russian Point of View, The" (CR1 219–31; CE1 238–46) An essay in *THE COMMON READER* that partly incorporates "The Russian View," a 1918 review in the *TIMES LITERARY SUPPLEMENT* of *The Village Priest and Other Stories* by Elena Militsina and Mikhail Saltikov, translated by Beatrix L. Tollemache (E2 341–43). The *Common Reader* essay is an important example of the profound effect on Woolf of Russian writers, many of whom were made familiar to English readers by the translations of Constance GARNETT: Anton CHEKHOV, Fyodor DOSTOYEVSKY and Ivan TURGENEV, in particular. Woolf writes that the "soul . . . is the chief character in Russian fiction," dominating the works of Dostoyevsky as "life" dominates the work of Leo TOLSTOY, and that the "soul" is alien to English readers

(CE1 242). The "incomplete" form of a Chekhov story is adduced as evidence of the difference between English and Russian fiction. Contrasting English and Russian fiction, Woolf notes that humor, particularly humor associated with the body, is characteristic in English novels and that class-consciousness constrains the English novelist to be satirical rather than offering psychological insight (CE1 244).

Rustum el Sadi The old gypsy who brings ORLANDO out of CONSTANTINOPLE on his donkey after Orlando has become a woman. He commiserates with her for her descent from a family that goes back only four or five centuries compared to his own descent of two or three millennia, and his raucous voice scorning what she had taken pride in is still sounding in Orlando's ears as the novel draws to a close (0 326). The name probably derives from Matthew ARNOLD's poem "Sohrab and Rustum."

Rylands, George Humphrey Wolferstan ("Dadie") (b. 1902) Poet and Fellow of King's College, Cambridge, a specialist in the works of William SHAKESPEARE. Known to his friends as "Dadie," Rylands attracted the attention of John Maynard KEYNES and Lytton STRACHEY when he was elected to the APOSTLES. He helped Keynes in establishing the Cambridge Arts Theatre. Woolf first met him in 1923 at TIDMARSH, where he was Strachey's guest, and liked him very much. In July 1924, Rylands began work at the HOGARTH PRESS as an assistant, but he left that December to take up his Fellowship at King's, where he remained as a teacher until his retirement in 1967. After retirement he continued to live in his rooms at King's that had been decorated for him in 1927 by Dora CARRINGTON and Douglas Davidson. The Hogarth Press published several of Rylands's books: *Russett and Taffeta* (1925, dedicated to Woolf), *Words and Poetry* (1928) and *Poems* (1931). In October 1928, Woolf gave one of the talks on which *A ROOM OF ONE'S OWN* was based to the NEWNHAM COLLEGE Arts Society, and on the following day she and Leonard WOOLF, Vanessa BELL and Angelica GARNETT had lunch with Keynes, Strachey and Rylands in the latter's rooms, a lunch extravagantly described in *A Room.*

S

Sackville-West, Edward Charles (1901–1965) The fifth Lord Sackville and cousin of Vita SACKVILLE-WEST, he became Lord Sackville and inherited KNOLE on his father's death in 1962. His *Apology of Arthur Rimbaud: A Dialogue* was published as number 7 of the second series of Hogarth Essays in 1927, and in 1931 the HOGARTH PRESS published a limited edition of his and Vita's translation of Rainer Maria Rilke's *Duineser Elegien: Elegies from the Castle of Duino.* ("The Woolfs distributed the book under the Hogarth label as a courtesy to the Sackville-Wests" [Willis 35].) He is listed among those friends "who have helped me in ways too various to specify" in Woolf's ironic preface to *ORLANDO.*

Sackville-West, Victoria Mary ("Vita") (1892–1962) Poet, novelist, biographer, travel writer and gardener, only child of the third Baron Sackville and Victoria, Lady Sackville (1862–1936). (The name West came from Sackville-West's great-grandfather George John West, fifth Earl De La Warr, who married Lady Elizabeth Sackville in 1813 [Stevens 14]). Woolf and Sackville-West had a long and serious love affair beginning in 1923. Sackville-West wrote her first novel, "Edward Sackville, Earl of Dorset," in 1906 when she was fourteen. In 1907 she won the *Onlooker* poetry prize. In 1909, her verse drama *Chatterton* was privately published. She grew up at KNOLE, her family's great house, and in 1910 was involved in a widely publicized lawsuit brought by her uncle Henry against her mother challenging the succession to the Sackville title. In that year she also met Harold NICOLSON and in 1913 they married. The first few months of their marriage were spent in CONSTANTINOPLE, and in 1914 they moved to London, where Benedict NICOLSON was born. The Nicolsons bought LONG BARN, near Knole, in 1915, and in that year Sackville-West had a stillborn son. In 1917 her *Poems of West and East* were published and Nigel NICOLSON was born.

Sackville-West became notorious for her passionate affair with Violet TREFUSIS between 1918 and 1920. When Harold told Sackville-West in November 1917 that he had a venereal infection, the result of his homosexual affairs, she "completely rewrote the ground rules of their marriage" (DeSalvo, "Tinder" 85) and soon began her affair with Violet, whom she had known since they were children. In 1920 Denys Trefusis and Harold pursued their wives, flying after them to Paris in a private plane, and eventually Sackville-West agreed to return and live with Nicolson. "They maintained their relationship, founded upon honesty about their extramarital affairs, by letters, visits, and joint holidays" (DeSalvo, "Tinder" 85). The story of this episode is told in *PORTRAIT OF A MARRIAGE,* and Sackville-West's novel *Challenge* (1923) is a fictional account of the affair.

Woolf first met Sackville-West at a dinner party given by Clive BELL on December 14, 1922, writing the next day in her DIARY of the "lovely gifted aristocratic Sackville West" (D2 216). A few days later, Sackville-West invited Woolf to dine at her house with Clive and Desmond MACCARTHY, and Woolf asked Sackville-West to send her her new book, *Knole and the Sackvilles* (1922). On December 19, Sackville-West wrote to Harold Nicolson of Woolf, "Darling, I have quite lost my heart." Ethel SANDS told Woolf that Sackville-West, a well-known "Sapphist," had her eye on her (D2 235), but Woolf did not mind. She was attracted to Sackville-West's aristocratic ease as well as her looks; in December 1924, she wrote to Jacques RAVERAT, praising Sackville-West's legs (L3 150), a feature she would make ORLANDO's prime attraction.

Sackville-West was already a well-known author by 1923, and Woolf requested a book for the HOGARTH PRESS. Sackville-West obliged by writing the novella *Seducers in Ecuador* (1924), dedicated to Woolf. She delivered the manuscript to MONK'S HOUSE herself, and when Woolf read it she found herself marvelling at Sackville-West's "skill & sensibility; for is she not mother, wife, great lady, hostess, as well as scribbling?" (D2 313). Sackville-West's books were to prove very lucrative for the Hogarth Press, which published thirteen of her works: three works of poetry, *King's Daughter* (1929), *Collected Poems* (1933) and *Solitude* (1938); the novels *Seducers in Ecuador* (1924), *All Passion Spent* (1931), *THE EDWARDIANS* (1930), *Family History* (1932) and *The Dark Island* (1934); *PASSENGER TO TEHERAN* (1926) and *Twelve Days* (1928), two books about her travels to Persia; the biographies *Pepita*

Lady with a Red Hat, *1918 (103 x 78 cm). William Strang (1859–1921). Courtesy of Glasgow Museums: Art Gallery & Museum, Kelvingrove.*
This striking portrait of Vita Sackville-West was painted at the request of her mother (who, however, later refused to buy it [Richardson 217]). In Portrait of a Marriage, *Nigel Nicolson says that Violet Trefusis sat in Strang's studio "never taking her eyes off" Vita (152) while the portrait was being painted.*

(1937) and *Joan of Arc* (1937); and a collection of her pieces for the *NEW STATESMAN AND NATION*, *Country Notes in Wartime* (1940).

Woolf was both impressed by and rather disdainful of Sackville-West's industry, but as Suzanne Raitt has written, "Woolf's experience of Sackville-West as an author is central to her gradual discovery of the woman she loves" (*Vita* 3). Both Louise DeSalvo and Victoria Glendinning suggest that Sackville-West filled the void left for Woolf by the death in January 1923 of Katherine MANSFIELD. DeSalvo has also pointed out similarities in Woolf and Sackville-West's childhoods ("Lighting" 198–99) and that they were both sexually abused as children ("Tinder" 92). Sackville-West had also suffered, and continued to suffer, at the whims of her erratic and abusive mother: "The relationship between Lady Sackville and her daughter was a struggle for possession of authentic femininity" (Raitt, "Fakes" 103).

Woolf and Sackville-West's friendship grew into love and then passion. DeSalvo argues that Sackville-West "provided Woolf with an alternative appraisal of her character to the one she had lived with for years" ("Lighting" 199), emphasizing her vitality and gregariousness rather than her frailty and sickness. In December 1925, knowing that Sackville-West would soon be leaving with Nicolson for Persia, Woolf seduced her at Long Barn. In a note to Sackville-West on December 16, 1925, Leonard WOOLF asked her to make sure his wife went to bed not a minute later than 11 and did not tire herself out talking too much (Spotts 228). They spent "a peaceful evening" on the 17th, but on the next day, Sackville-West noted in her diary that she and Woolf had stayed up talking until 3 A.M. and that it had been "Not a peaceful evening" (Glendinning 149).

The affair was at its most intense between 1925 and 1928, but already in 1927 Sackville-West was having an affair with Mary Campbell, wife of the South African poet Roy Campbell. Mitchell Leaska has argued that this precipitated Woolf's beginning *ORLANDO* (Sackville-West, *Letters* 31–32), her fantastic "biography" of Sackville-West as the young nobleman and poet who changes into a woman halfway through a four-hundred-year life. Knowing that Sackville-West, whose physical demands Woolf could not meet, was slipping away from her, she wrote *Orlando* as both a farewell and also a way of enchanting Sackville-West in a way none of her other "2nd rate schoolgirl" lovers (as Woolf described them to Ethel SMYTH) could. "In the pages of *Orlando*," also, as DeSalvo and others note, "Vita Sackville-West owned Knole in a way that she could never own it in reality" ("Lighting" 205).

Sackville-West had grown up knowing that she could never inherit Knole because she was not male. In 1928, the year *Orlando* was published, Sackville-West's father died and Knole passed to his brother; on his death it would go to Edward SACKVILLE-WEST, Sackville-West's cousin. In 1930, Vita Sackville-West and Nicolson bought SISSINGHURST, a castle that had at least a similar antiquity to Knole. At Sissinghurst Sackville-West created the spectacular garden which is still maintained by the National Trust.

The ten years of Woolf and Sackville-West's close friendship were "the most productive period of each of their lives; neither had ever before written so much so well, and neither would ever again reach this peak of accomplishment" (DeSalvo, "Lighting" 197). Sackville-West's letters to Woolf from Persia, filled with rich descriptions, formed the raw material for her successful book *Passenger to Teheran*. In the decade 1924–34, Sackville-West also published *THE LAND* (1926), her long poem for which she won the Hawthornden Prize in 1927. Other works of this time include *Aphra Behn* (1927), *Twelve Days, King's*

Daughter, Andrew Marvell (1929), *The Edwardians, All Passion Spent, Family History,* "Sissinghurst" (1931), *Thirty Clocks Strike the Hour* (1932), *Collected Poems* and *The Dark Island* (see Stevens 8–9). As DeSalvo points out, in the same period Woolf wrote "MR. BENNETT AND MRS. BROWN," *MRS. DALLOWAY, TO THE LIGHTHOUSE, Orlando, A ROOM OF ONE'S OWN, THE WAVES, FLUSH* and *A LETTER TO A YOUNG POET.* She also published *THE COMMON READER* and *THE COMMON READER: SECOND SERIES* and began working on *THE YEARS,* "while working as usual on scores of reviews and essays" (DeSalvo, "Lighting" 197).

Sackville-West wrote to Woolf in 1927 that it was "quite true that you have had infinitely more influence on me intellectually than anyone" (Sackville-West, *Letters* 165). Jane Lilienfeld has suggested that Woolf and Sackville-West's love affair "probably provided the emotional climate that allowed *To the Lighthouse* to come into being" (DeSalvo, "Lighting" 204), and Raitt points out that Sackville-West's "indirect free style owes much to Woolf's experiments in *To the Lighthouse*" (Raitt, *Vita* 91). DeSalvo and Raitt in particular have discussed the effects the two women's relationship had on their writing: "Just as the excitement and the ambivalence of her feelings for Sackville-West flooded some of Woolf's texts, particularly *Orlando,* so the unique tone of Woolf's prose resonates through much of Sackville-West's later work" (Raitt, *Vita* 91). DeSalvo argues that Woolf "temporarily at least" influenced Sackville-West's conservative political views ("Lighting" 208) and describes *All Passion Spent* as "astonishingly feminist," written perhaps under the influence of *A Room of One's Own* ("Lighting" 210). Raitt allows only that it is "perhaps an exception" to Sackville-West's customary anti-working-class views and conventional opinions on femininity and female sexual pleasure (10), but agrees that it is her most feminist novel. She adds that it "was clearly conceived with Woolf's *To the Lighthouse* in mind" (108).

DeSalvo reads Sackville-West's *Family History* as to some extent dealing with Woolf's own story ("Lighting" 198). The novel "discusses the fate of women who suppress their lesbianism" (207) and examines the marriage of "Viola and Leonard Anquetil" ("Lighting" 211). "Another remarkable feature of *Family History* is Sackville-West's gift there to Virginia Woolf of fictional children, just as Woolf had restored Knole to Sackville-West in *Orlando*" ("Lighting" 212). Raitt, however, believes DeSalvo distorts the novel and that it is "a less daring novel than many Sackville-West wrote" (113).

In 1928, Woolf and Sackville-West spent a week in France together, but the intense period of their affair was waning. Their friendship, however, continued to be close until about 1935 when, Woolf wrote in her diary, it had ended "not with a quarrel, not with a bang, but as ripe fruit falls" (D4 287). Sackville-West was by then involved with Harold Nicolson's sister, Gwen St. Aubyn, whom Woolf detested, and to whom Sackville-West dedicated *The Dark Island* and her poem *Solitude.* Woolf found that Sackville-West had also lost her physical charms by the mid-1930s, something borne out in a 1935 letter from Vanessa BELL to her sister that says she had seen Sackville-West and she "has simply become Orlando the wrong way round—I mean turned into a man, with a thick moustache, and very masterful, and surely altogether much bigger" (Marler 385).[16]

The correspondence between Woolf and Sackville-West "is one of the great love duets of contemporary letters" (DeSalvo, "Tinder" 89), and although their passion faded and friendship eventually was maintained by infrequent letters and less frequent meetings, Woolf's relationship with Vita Sackville-West was tremendously significant. Mitchell Leaska has suggested that *POINTZ HALL,* published after Woolf's death as *BETWEEN THE ACTS,* was partly a farewell to Sackville-West, with the character Mrs. MANRESA a "lusty and loving" image of her. When Woolf committed suicide, Sackville-West was the first person to whom Leonard wrote. He told her that Woolf had left one of her manuscripts to her, and Sackville-West replied that she would like that of *The Waves.* Leonard wanted to keep this for himself, however, and Sackville-West eventually accepted the manuscript of *Mrs. Dalloway.* Her poem "In Memoriam: Virginia Woolf" was published on April 6, 1941, in the *Observer.* To Leonard, Sackville-West wrote that Woolf was the "loveliest mind and spirit I ever knew, immortal both to the world and us who loved her" (Spotts 253). In the mid-1950s, Sackville-West was eager to publish Woolf's letters to her, but Leonard, wary of attacks on the BLOOMSBURY GROUP, refused to allow it. Sackville-West increasingly spent nearly all her time at Sissinghurst, rarely seeing people, working on her garden. Her LENARE portrait of Woolf remained on her writing desk for the rest of her life.

St. Ives Woolf's childhood summers were spent at Talland House in St. Ives, a seaside town in Cornwall from where the GODREVY LIGHTHOUSE can be seen. Leslie STEPHEN had discovered the house on a walking tour in 1881 and rented it from the Great Western Railway. Woolf describes the place and its significance in "A SKETCH OF THE PAST." Woolf's memories of St. Ives contributed to many of her novels, in particular *JACOB'S ROOM, TO THE LIGHTHOUSE* and *THE WAVES.* After Julia Prinsep STEPHEN's death in

[16]Joanne Trautmann Banks has written of a recently discovered letter from Woolf to Sackville-West from 1958 that it "extends for years longer than we had thought Virginia's expressed physical interest in Vita" (VWM 43: 1). See LETTERS.

1895, Leslie could no longer bear to go there and the house was sold.

Saint Paul The longest note in *THREE GUINEAS* concerns female chastity (TG 166–69n38) and begins with an extensive discussion of the teachings of Saint Paul on the matter. As well as reading Paul's epistles, Woolf also read Ernest RENAN's *Histoire des origines du christianisme* as she worked on *Three Guineas,* a work she cites in this note. At the end of 1935 Woolf was planning to buy an Old Testament. She made notes on 1 Corinthians 11: 4–15, concerning women covering their heads to pray, and 1 Corinthians 14: 34–35, on women keeping silent in church, as well as on Titus 2: 3–5, on aged women being teachers of younger women to be chaste, sober wives (RN 294). Woolf also apparently went to a Palm Sunday service at Saint Paul's Cathedral on March 21, 1937, which she describes in her reading notebook, where can also be found the program from that service (RN 293–94).

Salvin, Mr. An old gentleman who sits with Julia ELIOT at Elizabeth DURRANT's party in *JACOB'S ROOM.*

Sand, George (pen name of Amandine-Aurore-Lucile Dupin, Baronne Dudevant) (1804–76) One of those nineteenth-century women writers whom Woolf's narrator in *A ROOM OF ONE'S OWN* mentions as having veiled her identity behind a masculine name—a "relic of the sense of chastity that dictated anonymity to women" (AROO 50). Woolf's aunt Anne Thackeray RITCHIE wrote of meeting Sand in her *Chapters From Some Unwritten Memoirs* (1894), remarking that she "looked half-bored, half-faraway." Sand's relationships with the poet Alfred de Musset and the composer Frédéric Chopin have until quite recently eclipsed her writing. Among her novels are *Indiana, Lélia* and *Jacques,* published between 1831 and 1834, which are marked by a sense of rebellion against the institution of marriage; *Spiridion, Consuelo, La Comtesse de Rudolstadt* and *Les sept Cordes de la Lyre* are all distinguished by philosophical themes; her later works, such as *La Petite Fadette* and *La Mare au diable,* are pastoral. Woolf particularly admired Sand's *Histoire de ma vie* (1854–55), and she quoted from it ("the words of a half-forgotten novelist" [TG 188]) in the final note to *THREE GUINEAS:*

> All existences are interdependent, and any human being who was to present his own in isolation without attaching it to that of his fellows would only present an enigma to be unravelled. . . . Individuality has no significance or importance whatsoever on its own. It only takes on a meaning by becoming a fragment of life in general, by combining with the individuality of each one of my fellow beings, and it is thus that it becomes part of history. (Translated by Mark Hussey)

Sanders, Mary A "rustic" encountered in *JACOB'S ROOM* by Jacob FLANDERS when he goes hunting in Essex.

Sands, Ethel (1873–1962) One of the friends who "have helped me in ways too various to specify" thanked by Woolf in her ironic preface to *ORLANDO.* A wealthy American painter, friend and pupil of Walter SICKERT, she lived with Nan HUDSON, whom she met in 1894, and they divided their time between London and Normandy, France. Vanessa BELL and Duncan GRANT, to whom Roger FRY had introduced Sands, decorated her seventeenth-century French chateau in 1927, and Woolf spent four days there that summer. It was Sands who in 1923 told Woolf she thought Vita SACKVILLE-WEST might "have an eye on" her (D2 235).

Sands, Trixie The cook at Bart OLIVER's home, Pointz Hall, in *BETWEEN THE ACTS.* Her family has lived in the village for centuries.

Sandys, Harry A character in *NIGHT AND DAY,* a friend of Ralph DENHAM's who attends the gathering to hear William RODNEY's paper in chapter 4 of the novel. Following William and Katharine HILBERY, Ralph falls into step with Sandys when they all leave Mary DATCHET's apartment and has a conversation with him that seems influenced by the philosophy of G. E. MOORE. Sandys has made all his friends at university and still speaks to them as if they were undergraduates.

Sanger, Charles Percy (1871–1930) Barrister, contemporary at Trinity College, Cambridge, of Bertrand RUSSELL, and an APOSTLE. He was a visitor to the "Thursday Evenings" begun by Woolf and Adrian STEPHEN after their brother Thoby STEPHEN's death. Woolf's 1905 DIARY records Vanessa BELL and Thoby going for dinner at the Sangers' (PA 253). In 1926, the HOGARTH PRESS published Sanger's *Structure of Wuthering Heights* as number 19 of the Hogarth Essays. In the ironic preface to *ORLANDO,* Woolf thanks Sanger, "without whose knowledge of the law of real property this book could never have been written."

Santa Marina The South American location of most of the action of *THE VOYAGE OUT.* Santa Marina is another name for Saint Euphrosyne, a fifth-century Greek saint who hid from her father in a monastery after her mother died when she was eleven (DeSalvo, *First Voyage* 60).

Sappho (*c.* 610–*c.* 580 B.C.) Greek lyric poet of the 7th century B.C., born on Lesbos. She was considered by her contemporaries to be their greatest poet, but most of her work survives only as fragments. During the Sunday service in chapter XVII of *THE VOYAGE OUT,* Mrs. FLUSHING reads Sappho's "Ode to Aphrodite" which St. John HIRST has brought to the service in a translation by Algernon Charles SWINBURNE. In "A SOCIETY," a satirical feminist story by Woolf, Castalia examines a monumental edition of the works of Sappho by "Professor Hobkin," who defends Sappho's chastity against a German scholar's allegations (Jane Marcus suggests the German Sappho scholar was probably supposed to be von Wilamowitz-Moellendorff [*Languages* 88]). In the second of Woolf's letters to AFFABLE HAWK (her friend Desmond MACCARTHY) responding to his expressed concurrence in the *NEW STATESMAN* with Arnold BENNETT's views on the intellectual inferiority of women, Woolf discusses Sappho in arguing that the reason there have not been more great women poets has much more to do with patriarchal strictures than any lack of talent ("The Intellectual Status of Women" D2 Appendix III).

Sargant-Florence, Alix See STRACHEY, Alix.

Sarton, May (b. 1912) American poet and novelist. She met Woolf in 1937 through Elizabeth BOWEN (with whom Sarton was in love at the time [L6 119]) and sent Woolf flowers and her poems. She later sent Woolf her first novel, *The Single Hound* (1938), hoping she would read it ("oh how she makes me detest my own writing," wrote Woolf [D5 139]). Sarton described meeting Woolf in *I Knew a Phoenix* (1957) and has often referred to her in the several published volumes of her journals. In *Journal of a Solitude,* she writes that meeting Woolf led her to realize that "a person may be ultrasensitive and not warm" (64), and that she felt Woolf was interested in her as "a specimen young American poet" (as Woolf probably was: see D5 96). Sarton writes about first meeting Woolf in *Encore* (228). Her poem about Woolf, "Letter from Chicago," was written after Woolf's suicide in 1941. In 1939 Sarton wrote Woolf to ask for a manuscript to sell in aid of the Refugees Society (L6 314); Woolf sent her the manuscript of *THREE GUINEAS* (now in the BERG COLLECTION).

Sasha (Princess Marousha Stanilovska Dagmar Natasha Iliana Romanovitch) Character in *ORLANDO* whom Orlando meets and falls in love with when she is stranded with the Muscovite ambassador's party in London during the Great Frost. In depicting Orlando's great passion for Sasha, Woolf drew on what Vita SACKVILLE-WEST had told her of her affair with Violet TREFUSIS (described in *PORTRAIT OF A MARRIAGE*). Sasha's infidelity and abandonment of Orlando leads him to withdraw from life to his great house, where he falls into the first of his seven-day sleeps. It is interesting in light of the play with gender in *Orlando* that Sasha is a masculine name in Russian.

Sassoon, Siegfried (1886–1967) English poet and army officer who was awarded the Military Cross for bravery and protested World War I in 1917; he was sent to Craiglockhart War Hospital in Scotland to recover from his seditious views. He visited GARSINGTON in 1916 and remained friends for many years with Lady Ottoline MORRELL, who had written him praising his poetry. Woolf reviewed Sassoon's *The Old Huntsman and Other Poems* for the *TIMES LITERARY SUPPLEMENT* in May 1917, writing that what Sassoon "has felt to be the most sordid and horrible experiences in the world he makes us feel to be so in a measure which no other poet of the war has achieved" (E2 120). Lady Ottoline forwarded to Woolf a letter from Sassoon in which he said that he appreciated the review. In 1918 she reviewed his collection *Counter-attack and Other Poems* in the TLS (E2 269–72). Woolf met Sassoon socially in the mid-1920s at various parties and invited him to write for the HOGARTH PRESS, but nothing of his was published by Hogarth.

Saturday Club In *THE VOYAGE OUT,* Evelyn MURGATROYD tells Rachel VINRACE about a club she belongs to in London which meets to discuss art, but Evelyn thinks they should begin instead to talk about social and political issues. Probably Woolf is gently satirizing the FRIDAY CLUB started by her sister Vanessa BELL in 1905.

Savage, Sir George Henry (1842–1921) Physician and neurologist who was one of the Stephen family's regular doctors. One of "the most eminent physicians of his day" (Trombley 107), Savage was editor of the *Journal of Mental Science* and author of a popular late-nineteenth-century textbook, *Insanity and Allied Neuroses: Practical and Clinical* (1884). Savage advised the confinement in an asylum of Woolf's cousin James Kenneth STEPHEN, and in 1897 he recommended that Woolf create a garden to divert her from the intellectual work that he believed was disturbing her mentally. Noel Annan has written that Savage's "diagnosis in some way resembled [Leslie] Stephen's views on women because it derived from the same premise, namely that women have weaker minds as well as weaker bodies" (Annan 117). Woolf was under Savage's care during her breakdown in 1904, following her father's death, and again in 1910 and 1912, when he recommended she spend time at Burley, Jean THOMAS's rest home in Twickenham. Thomas Caramagno has pointed out that "Savage, like Weir Mitchell, evaluated his patients' progress in terms of their submission to his conservative view of reality" (16), a circumstance that makes Savage a probable model for Sir William BRADSHAW in *MRS. DALLOWAY*. Before and after their marriage, Leonard WOOLF consulted Savage about Woolf's mental health, and in January 1913, he was one of the doctors whom Leonard consulted about the advisability of Woolf's having children (Savage thought it would do her "a world of good"). Savage was pained by Leonard's having consulted other doctors about Woolf without telling him in 1913 (Spotts 194); following her suicide attempt that year he no longer saw her as a patient.

Scott, Sir Walter (1771–1832) The favorite author of Sir Leslie STEPHEN and Mr. RAMSAY (in *TO THE LIGHTHOUSE*), Scott began his writing career with an edition of Scottish Border ballads and songs, *Minstrelsy of the Scottish Border* (1802–03). Although he also wrote poetry, Scott became well known for his novels, among which are: *Waverly* (1814), *Guy Mannering* (1815), *THE ANTIQUARY* (1816), *Rob Roy* (1817), *The Heart of Midlothian* (1818), *The Bride of Lammermoor* (1819, which inspired the opera *Lucia di Lammermoor* by Gaetano Donizetti), *Ivanhoe* (1819), *Quentin Durward* (1823) and *Castle Dangerous* (1831). All his novels were published anonymously until 1827.

Scott was intimately associated with her father for Woolf. In *NIGHT AND DAY*, when Mr. Hilbery has banished the young lovers from his house and forbidden his daughter see Ralph DENHAM, he suggests that they read Scott to calm themselves. Before she can protest, Katharine finds herself "being turned by the agency of Sir Walter Scott into a civilized human being" (ND 477). It is, though, in *To the Lighthouse* that Scott figures most significantly, where a discussion of the Waverly novels (those concerning the Waverly family) at the dinner in section XVII of part 1 makes Mrs. RAMSAY suddenly alert. Following the dinner, Mr. Ramsay reads part of *The Antiquary* to reassure himself of Scott's prowess as a novelist, which has been denounced by Charles TANSLEY. In Woolf's ironic preface to *ORLANDO* Scott is among those writers to whom anyone writing is perpetually indebted.

Scrope, Sir Adrian The Admiral in *ORLANDO* who comes to CONSTANTINOPLE to award Orlando the Order of the Bath.

Scrutiny See LEAVIS, Q. D.

Seal, Sally Character in *NIGHT AND DAY* who works for the "S.G.S.," a SUFFRAGE organization for which Mary DATCHET volunteers. Woolf's portrayal of Sally satirizes enthusiasts and those who work for causes because it gives their life a purpose which it would lack entirely with nothing to be zealous about. As her "father's daughter," Mrs. Seal has served on numerous committees ("Waifs and Strays, Rescue Work, Church Work, C. O. S." [ND 87]). Sally finds it almost impossible to speak without quickly finding herself making a speech about the rights of women or the iniquities of politicians, a habit that costs her dearly as the S. G. S. fines shoptalk at tea. Sally is nonplussed by Katharine HILBERY, a young woman who does *not* belong to the Society! Although referred to throughout the novel as Mrs. Seal, Sally appears to be unmarried as she nervously asks Mary if she is going to get married and then veers away from the question "into the shades of her own shivering virginity" (ND 263). Two gold crosses are entangled around Sally's neck, and Mary reflects that Sally and her co-worker Mr. CLACTON are somehow not "in the running" for life (ND 265).

"Searchlight, The" (SF 263–66) A short story by Woolf that she began in 1929 and revised many times up until her death in 1941; it was first published posthumously in *A HAUNTED HOUSE*. J. W. Graham has traced the various drafts of the story in "Virginia Woolf's 'The Searchlight' " (*Twentieth Century Literature* 22, 4 [December 1976]: 379–93). Graham locates the genesis of the story in an episode Woolf read in *The Autobiography of Sir Henry Taylor* (1885), where he describes looking through a telescope and seeing a couple kiss. Judith Raiskin has also commented on the "ten radically different versions" of the story that can be found in the MONK'S HOUSE PAPERS (VWM 27:5).

The story is set on the balcony of a London club that was the home of an eighteenth-century earl; searchlights are wheeling through the sky, only practicing as there is no war. Mrs. Ivimey is suddenly reminded of a story told her by her great-grandfather of how he would spend lonely nights in a ruined tower on the moors stargazing through a telescope. As she describes him, the people with her lose their sense of time and place momentarily until a voice behind them abruptly recalls them to where they are. Mrs. Ivimey mimics how her great-grandfather one night swung the telescope earthward and saw a man and woman kissing outside a cottage. She recalls that he told her how he ran from his tower to find the woman, and at this point Mrs. Ivimey appears flustered for a moment, as if she is about to say the woman was herself; "She was my great-grandmother" (SF 266), she concludes.

In 1939, Woolf wrote in her DIARY that she had written "the old Henry Taylor story thats been humming in my mind these 10 years" as a relief from her work on the biography of Roger FRY (D5 204). Sir Henry Taylor had worked in the Colonial Office under Woolf's grandfather, Sir James STEPHEN, and was a close friend of Julia Margaret CAMERON (her photograph of him appears in *VICTORIAN PHOTOGRAPHS OF FAMOUS MEN & FAIR WOMEN*, Plate 12).

Henry Taylor's granddaughter was Una Elena, who married Admiral Sir Ernest Troubridge, the great-grandson of Woolf's great-aunt Sara Prinsep. Ernest Troubridge separated from Una in 1918 when she decided to live with Radclyffe Hall, author of *THE WELL OF LONELINESS.* This connection with a famous lesbian relationship gives "The Searchlight" 's reference to gazing at stars a significance similar to that in *MRS. DALLOWAY* where Clarissa DALLOWAY's moment of ecstasy with Sally SETON is interrupted by a voice that asks if they are "Star-gazing?" (see also Hussey, "Refractions" 142). Also relevant in this context is a remark in a 1929 letter from Vita SACKVILLE-WEST to Woolf about what Vita termed "SUPPRESSED RANDINESS" as the cause of Woolf's ill-health: "So there—You remember your admissions as the searchlight went round and round?" (Sackville-West, *Letters* 318). In *THE YEARS,* searchlights wheel across the sky as Eleanor PARGITER waits for a bus with the homosexual Nicholas POMJALOVSKY.

Herbert Marder connects the searchlight beams in the story with the image of the beam of a lighthouse found throughout Woolf's writing, and links that to the "theme of mystical marriage" (Marder 146).

Seton, Dr. David Elphinstone (*c.* 1827–1917) The Stephen family doctor until 1904. In her DIARY on May 5, 1924 (D2 300) and in "A SKETCH OF THE PAST" (MOB 84) Woolf recalled in almost identical terms seeing him walk slowly up the street on the morning her mother, Julia Prinsep STEPHEN, died in 1895.

Seton, Mary One of the names by which the narrator of *A ROOM OF ONE'S OWN* tells her audience they may call her. The name is also used for the narrator's friend at "Fernham" with whom she shares a drink after her dinner at the college. See BALLAD OF THE QUEEN'S MARYS.

Seton, Sally Character in *MRS. DALLOWAY* who owes something to Woolf's memories of Madge VAUGHAN. Clarissa DALLOWAY remembers being in love with Sally when she stayed at BOURTON. Sally opens the young Clarissa's eyes to the world beyond her sheltered life of privilege. When Sally kisses her on the lips one evening as they walk on the terrace, Clarissa feels it is the "most exquisite moment of her whole life" (MD 52). This scene, in which they are interrupted by Peter WALSH's question, "Star-gazing?" recalls an earlier moment of love between two women interrupted by a comment about star-gazing in *NIGHT AND DAY* when Katherine HILBERY and Mary DATCHET sit together looking out of a window (see Hussey, "Refractions" 142). At Clarissa's party at the end of the novel, Sally unexpectedly comes in. She is now Lady Rosseter, married to an industrialist in Manchester and the mother of five sons and, thinks Clarissa, she has lost her lustre.

Shadow of the Moth, The By Ellen Hawkes and Peter Manso, subtitled "A Novel of Espionage with Virginia Woolf." The novel is set in 1917 and casts Woolf in the role of detective in solving a London murder (New York: St. Martins, 1983).

Shag An Irish terrier bought in 1892 by Gerald DUCKWORTH. In 1905, Woolf's "obituary notice of poor old Shag," who was killed by a hansom cab in December 1904, was published in the *GUARDIAN* of January 18 under the title "On a Faithful Friend" (E1 12).

Shakespeare, Judith In *A ROOM OF ONE'S OWN,* Woolf invents the figure of Shakespeare's sister, Judith, to stand for the Renaissance woman artist, muted by patriarchy (AROO 46–48). She tells the tale of Judith, William's "wonderfully gifted" sister who is denied the education her brother receives, is beaten by her father when she says the marriage he has arranged is hateful to her, and runs away to London at the age of sixteen to pursue her dream of being a playwright. Rebuffed and laughed at by the men of the theater, Judith is eventually seduced by Nick GREENE and, finding that she is pregnant, kills herself—"who shall measure the heat and violence of the poet's heart when caught and tangled in a woman's body?" (AROO 48). Judith Shakespeare is buried at a crossroads by the ELEPHANT AND CASTLE.

At the end of *A Room,* Woolf returns to the figure of Judith Shakespeare to exhort the young women of her audience to become her heirs by writing, for she believes that Judith Shakespeare is a "continuing presence": "She lives in you and in me, and in many other women who are not here tonight, for they are washing up the dishes and putting the children to bed" (AROO 113). In the future, given women's liberation, Judith Shakespeare "will put on the body which she has so often laid down" (AROO 114).

William SHAKESPEARE actually had a daughter named Judith Quinney Shakespeare (1585–1662), the twin sister of Hamnet. The most likely source for Woolf's Judith is William Black's 1883 novel *Judith Shakespeare,* in which Judith is Shakespeare's daughter. Tillie Olsen, in *Silences,* notes Olive Schreiner's "little read fictional study of prostitution," *From Man to Man,* which includes a mythical female artist named Judith Shakespeare, as an "unnoted ancestor" of Woolf's *Room.* Olsen comments that the "impairment of all women resulting from exclusion, and the denial of full circumference for her own work, are recurrent threads throughout Woolf's essays, letters, diaries—and fiction" (Olsen 244).

Jane Marcus has pointed out several other resonances between Woolf's Judith and William Black's novel, including that Black's admirers built a lighthouse in his name on Duart Point in the Sound of Mull in the Hebrides (the setting of *TO THE LIGHTHOUSE*) (Marcus, *Languages* 200n30). She also notes an 1897 performance of a play by Eleanor Marx's common-law husband, Edward Aveling, called *Judith Shakespeare* mentioned in Yvonne Kapp's biography *Eleanor Marx* (New York: Pantheon, 1977). Marcus says it is reasonable to suppose Woolf would have been aware of the play as her half-brother Gerald DUCKWORTH was treasurer of an avant-garde theater group organized by Elizabeth ROBINS and Aveling was "a member of these circles, along with Olive Schreiner, Eleanor Marx, and [George Bernard] Shaw" (*Languages* 200n30).

Another level of allusion carried by the figure of Judith Shakespeare in *A Room* is the connection with Radclyffe Hall and the obscenity trial of her novel, *THE WELL OF LONELINESS*. Marcus points out that Woolf's readers would have known that Hall was a descendant of Shakespeare's daughter, Susannah Hall, and that her supporters at the trial had tried to introduce as evidence of homosexuality in great literature Shakespeare's sonnets (*Languages* 166).

Several readers, among them Sandra M. Gilbert and Susan Gubar (*War* 93) and Harvena Richter (VWM 24:1), have seen Judith Shakespeare as linked to the unnamed Mary Hamilton, the fourth "Mary" of the BALLAD OF THE QUEEN'S MARYS that Woolf uses thematically in *A Room*. Richter sees the connection as part of Woolf's thought that the woman writer must not have children, and Gilbert and Gubar point out that Woolf outlines "the violent fate that patriarchal culture would have inflicted on [Judith] for precisely Mary Hamilton's crime of bearing an illegitimate child" (*War* 93). Richter also calls Judith Woolf's "phantasy-self" (*Inward Voyage* 23), and Gilbert and Gubar find that Woolf identifies "the repressed genius . . . with the suppressed powers of ancient witches" (*War* 93). Elsewhere, Sandra Gilbert* has suggested that Miss LA TROBE in *BETWEEN THE ACTS* is "an ironic version of the lost Shakespearean sister" (Gilbert, "Costumes" 214).

Judith Shakespeare has become a powerful trope of the silenced woman artist (one example: a 1979 poetry anthology edited by Sandra M. Gilbert and Susan Gubar is entitled *Shakespeare's Sisters*). Like several other tropes from *A Room*, "Shakespeare's sister" has influenced feminist writers in fields other than the literary. Catharine A. MacKinnon,* for example, notes being "inspired" by Woolf's vision of Shakespeare's sister (MacKinnon 301n169); Carol Gilligan* entitles the preface to a recent work, "Teaching Shakespeare's Sister: Notes from the Underground of Female Adolescence."

Tania Modleski* defines Woolf's "distinctive accomplishment" as "to have given a name, a desire, and a history to one of the mute females who lived and died in obscurity" (Modleski 19–20). Modleski also argues that by giving priority to her own fiction as history, Woolf "suggests the fictiveness, and hence arbitrariness, of the patriarchal cultural tradition" (Modleski 22). Woolf's "history" has, however, been questioned by Margaret J. M. Ezell.*

Ezell argues that recent anthologies of women's writing invariably begin with eighteenth-century writers and are shaped by the "functional question" of *why* women did not write before then. This question, Ezell says, has its source in *A Room*: "Woolf and her followers view the canon as having been historically defined through silence or absence" (Ezell 582). Anthologies of women's writing have derived their concept of the female artist from Woolf's Judith Shakespeare, a fiction that Woolf develops so that it "claims the force and authority of fact" (Ezell 583). Citing as paradigmatic the *Norton Anthology of Literature by Women* (where Gilbert and Gubar include the passage about Shakespeare's sister as their selection from *A Room* [1376–83]), Ezell finds it guided by "Woolf's myth of Renaissance silence" (Ezell 584). Further, feminist literary historians have been guided by Woolf's idealization of the *professional* writer (in her remarks on Aphra BEHN) and this has led them to overlook other, less formal genres in which women writers circulated their work.

Ezell, doing the kind of historical work Woolf calls for in *A Room*, notes that Judith Shakespeare's story is based on Woolf's reading of G. M. TREVELYAN's *History of England* (1926): "since the 1920s, social historians have changed the focus and the findings of history dramatically" (Ezell 586). As a corrective to the tradition of women's writing that she believes is based on Woolf's false assumption, Ezell refers to *Kissing the Rod: An Anthology of Seventeenth-Century Women's Verse* edited by Germaine Greer et al. (1988), saying it "frees one from the necessity of continually asserting to doubting readers the inaccuracy of Woolf's belief that women did not produce a song or a sonnet in significant numbers before Behn" (Ezell 587). Responding to Ezell, Susan Bennett Smith* has recently argued that Woolf's image of the woman writer in *A Room* actually reflects the working of the patriarchal canon rather than her own idiosyncratic view (297–98nl) and that the figure of Judith Shakespeare "rejects traditional notions of authorship; instead, it focuses on the (socialist) common life and the (modernist) impersonal" (Smith 292).

Works Specific to This Entry:

Ezell, Margaret J. M. "The Myth of Judith Shakespeare: Creating the Canon of Women's Literature." *New Literary History* 21 (Spring 1990): 579–92.

Gilbert, Sandra M. "Costumes of the Mind: Transvestism as Metaphor in Modern Literature." In Elizabeth Abel, ed. *Writing and Sexual Difference.* Chicago: University of Chicago Press, 1982.
Gilligan, Carol, Nona P. Lyons, and Trudy J. Hanmer, eds. *Making Connections: The Relational Worlds of Adolescent Girls at Emma Willard School.* Cambridge: Harvard University Press, 1990.
MacKinnon, Catherine A. "Francis Biddle's Sister: Pornography, Civil Rights, and Speech (1984)." In *Feminism Unmodified: Discourses on Life and Law.* Cambridge, Mass.: Harvard University Press, 1987.
Modleski, Tania. "Some Functions of Feminist Criticism, or The Scandal of the Mute Body." *October* 49 (Summer 1989): 3–24.
Smith, Susan Bennett. "Gender and the Canon: When Judith Shakespeare At Last Assumes Her Body." In Vara Neverow-Turk and Mark Hussey, eds. *Virginia Woolf: Themes and Variations*: 291–99.

Shakespeare, William (1564–1616) Preeminent English playwright, allusions to and quotations from whose works are found throughout Woolf's writing. Alice Fox, whose chapter on Shakespeare in *Virginia Woolf and the Literature of the English Renaissance* is the most comprehensive treatment to date of Woolf's reading of Shakespeare, has remarked that he was "a part of Woolf's atmosphere" from her earliest childhood (94). Fox describes Woolf's initial resistance to Shakespeare's work, probably intimidated by his reputation. In late 1908 she began a serious reading of five tragedies: *Romeo and Juliet, Hamlet, King Lear, Othello* and *Macbeth.* Although she never wrote specifically on Shakespeare, Woolf referred to him very frequently in essays as a standard to which she held other writers and as the embodiment of the English spirit; in her fiction allusions to his work abound (see *Background* in entries on Woolf's novels). In her 1916 article "Charlotte Brontë," for example, Woolf wrote that to record "one's impressions of *Hamlet* as one reads it year after year, would be virtually to record one's own autobiography, for as we know more of life, so Shakespeare comments upon what we know" (E2 27). Christine Froula has traced how Woolf projects "her writer's self upon Shakespeare and Shakespeare upon her writer's self during forty years of sketching his image into her letters, novels, essays, and diaries" ("Virginia Woolf" 123).

In *NIGHT AND DAY*, Mrs. HILBERY speaks of "my William" and although the character is based on Woolf's aunt Anne Thackeray RITCHIE, Woolf herself felt a reverent kind of possessiveness toward Shakespeare (Fox remarks that she "venerated the man as others might worship God" [158] and see L5 422). *Measure for Measure* is the only play from which Woolf directly quotes in *Night and Day* (ND 155), but allusions to other works are plentiful (for example, the frequent comparisons of Katharine HILBERY to ROSALIND from *As You Like It*). Woolf often used quotations from Shakespeare's plays as structural devices in her fiction, as when Clarissa DALLOWAY remembers feeling like Othello when she thinks of Sally SETON ("If it were now to die, / 'Twere now to be most happy" [MD 51]). Clarissa and Septimus Warren SMITH are linked by a web of allusion and reference to Shakespeare, Septimus going to war to die for an England that to him consists of Shakespeare's plays and of the woman who had introduced them to him, Isabel POLE. Both Septimus and Clarissa at different times recall lines from the dirge of Shakespeare's *CYMBELINE*, "Fear no more the heat o' the sun."

Probably the best known of Woolf's references to Shakespeare is that in *A ROOM OF ONE'S OWN* where she speaks of his "incandescent" mind that could write without impediment (AROO 56), and of Shakespeare as the "type of the androgynous, of the man-womanly mind" (AROO 99; see ANDROGYNY). Also in *A Room,* she compares with Shakespeare's career the probable fate of his imaginary sister, Judith SHAKESPEARE.

Beverly Schlack has pointed out that Woolf's image of the reading room at the BRITISH MUSEUM as an "enormous mind" is one she most often personifies with reference to either Plato or Shakespeare. In her study of Woolf's use of allusion, Schlack notes that the image of Shakespeare working is recurrent in Woolf's writing (Schlack 171). For example, Schlack writes that when ORLANDO sees Shakespeare " 'in the pool of the mind,' the allusive circle is complete. From the sixteen-year-old Elizabethan boy who caught a glimpse of a shabby poet writing at his desk, to a thirty-six-year-old, twentieth-century wife, mother, and poet—Shakespeare bridges all" (Schlack 99).

Woolf wrote in her DIARY in 1930 that she turned to Shakespeare directly she had finished her day's work on *THE WAVES* and was astonished by his "speed & word coining power" (D3 300). She described her sense that she could keep pace with his mind at first but then felt it outpace hers utterly: "Indeed, I could say that [Shakespeare] surpasses literature altogether, if I knew what I meant" (D3 301). James Haule draws attention to the fact that Woolf saw performances of *Hamlet* and *Othello* in June 1930 and that in her subsequent revisions to *The Waves* she "gradually eliminated nearly all direct allusion to Shakespeare from the soliloquies of the other characters (Neville and Rhoda especially) to concentrate them in Bernard's summation" (Haule, "Introduction" xxix). Froula describes *The Waves* as "the flower of Woolf's autobiographical involvement with Shakespeare in its most intense phase" ("Virginia Woolf" 140).

Fox has pointed out that Woolf also deleted allusions to Shakespeare's works as she revised *THE YEARS* and changed the function of the character ELVIRA to become Sara PARGITER. Fox suggests the misanthropic hero of *Timon of Athens* as "a perfect model" for Elvira, and comments that the "contributions of *The Tempest* and *Measure for Measure,* of *Richard II,* of *Timon of Athens, Titus Andronicus, Hamlet, King Lear,* and *Macbeth,* and even much of what Woolf took from *Othello* create a rich novel grounded in a literary tradition of social criticism" (Fox 150).

In 1935, Woolf wrote to her nephew Julian BELL that she had been to see a performance of *Romeo and Juliet* and that "acting it they spoil the poetry" (L5 449). It was primarily to Shakespeare the poet rather than Shakespeare the dramatist that Woolf responded. Her last novel, *BETWEEN THE ACTS,* is infused with the melancholy mood of Prospero's speech to Ferdinand and Miranda in *The Tempest,* which, as Fox and others have pointed out, seems to sum up Woolf's own feelings as England plunged deeper into World War II: "Our revels now are ended . . . We are such stuff as dreams are made on; and our little life / Is rounded with a sleep" (IV:i:148–58).

Sharp, Becky In *A ROOM OF ONE'S OWN,* Rebecca (Becky) Sharp, the principal character in William Makepeace THACKERAY's *Vanity Fair,* is offered as an example of women who have "burnt like beacons in all the works of all the poets from the beginning of time" (AROO 43), whom Woolf uses to stress the difference between fictional and real women.

Shaw, George Bernard (1856–1950) An Irishman who came to London in 1876 and helped start the socialist Fabian Society (with Beatrice and Sidney WEBB), for which he wrote political and economic tracts. Shaw was very well known as a journalist, public speaker, playwright and critic. Shaw and Woolf met in 1916 at the Webbs'. In 1940, responding to a query of Woolf's for her biography of Roger FRY, Shaw wrote that he always connected her with his play *Heartbreak House* (1917) as he had "conceived it in that house [ASHEHAM] somewhere in Sussex where I first met you and, of course, fell in love with you, I suppose every man did" (LW2 90). Among Shaw's best-known plays are *Arms and the Man* (1898), *Mrs. Warren's Profession* (1898), *Man and Superman* (1903), *Major Barbara* (1907), *Pygmalion* (1912, on which the enormously popular musical *My Fair Lady* was based), *Heartbreak House* (1917) and *Saint Joan* (1924). Shaw's essays "The Quintessence of Ibsenism" (1891) and "The Intelligent Woman's Guide to Socialism and Capitalism" (1928) are also significant.

In *NIGHT AND DAY,* Mrs. COSHAM is relieved to learn that Ralph DENHAM reads Thomas DE QUINCEY because she suspects his generation reads only [Hilaire] BELLOC, [G. K.] CHESTERTON and Shaw. Jacob FLANDERS in *JACOB'S ROOM* deplores "Shaw and Wells and the serious sixpenny weeklies" (JR 35).

Shaw, Rose Character in *JACOB'S ROOM* who tries to arrange a marriage between Helen Aitken and a man named Jimmy and is extremely upset when this does not happen.

Sheepshanks, Mary (*c.* 1870–1958) De facto principal of MORLEY COLLEGE who invited Woolf to teach there in 1905.

Shell Shock See *MRS. DALLOWAY;* SMITH, Septimus Warren.

Shelley, Percy Bysshe (1792–1822) English Romantic poet and husband of Mary Godwin Shelley, author of *Frankenstein.* In *THE VOYAGE OUT,* Richard DALLOWAY responds to his wife Clarissa's saying that "there's almost everything one wants in" Shelley's elegy for John KEATS, "Adonais," by repeating Matthew ARNOLD's comment, "What a set! What a set!" (TVO 44). A little later, Clarissa DALLOWAY recites snatches of "Adonais" to Rachel VINRACE and says "How divine!—and yet what nonsense!" (TVO 58). Helen AMBROSE thinks her husband Ridley is what Shelley would have become had he lived to be fifty. In *THE WAVES,* RHODA recites lines from Shelley's "The Question."

Shelmerdine, Marmaduke Bonthrop A character in *ORLANDO* who bears the same relation to Harold NICOLSON that ORLANDO does to Vita SACKVILLE-WEST. Orlando meets Shelmerdine in chapter 5 of the novel and they become engaged within a few minutes. Sometimes Orlando calls him "Shel," and sometimes "Mar," which was Harold Nicolson's pet name for Vita. Like Shelmerdine, Harold Nicolson was frequently away and had sailed around Cape Horn. Nicolson flew from Paris in 1920, landing in the park at KNOLE, an event recalled in the novel's final scene (also perhaps carrying traces of Nicolson's flight *to* Paris with Denys Trefusis to bring back Vita and Violet TREFUSIS). The painting of "Marmaduke Bonthrop Shelmerdine, Esquire" used in *Orlando* was bought in London by Vita and was painted in about 1820 by an unknown artist of an unidentified young man.

Sheppard, John Tressider (1881–1968) Classical scholar who became provost of King's College, Cambridge, and who was an APOSTLE with Lytton STRACHEY and Leonard WOOLF. During World War I he lived at 46 GORDON SQUARE with John Maynard KEYNES and others. He is one of the friends who "have helped me in ways too various to specify" that Woolf thanks in her ironic preface to *ORLANDO.*

"Shooting Party, The" (SF 248–54) A short story by Woolf first published in *Harper's Bazaar* in 1938, and reprinted in *A HAUNTED HOUSE*. In 1937, Woolf wrote in her DIARY that while reading through this story she suddenly "saw the form of a new novel" (D5 114). The story concerns the memories of "Miss Antonia" as she travels in a train from the Midlands. She thinks of her life at home with her sister, Miss Rashleigh, who died when their brother, "the Squire," struck her with his whip and the family shield fell on her from above the mantelpiece.

Shove, Fredegond (née Maitland) (1889–1949) Daughter of F. W. MAITLAND and Florence Fisher, Woolf's first cousin. She was a contemporary at NEWNHAM COLLEGE of Karin STEPHEN. *Daybreak*, a collection of Fredegond's poems, was published by the HOGARTH PRESS in 1922. In 1915 she married Gerald Shove, an economist, APOSTLE, and Fellow of King's College, Cambridge, who worked on Philip and Ottoline MORRELL's farm at GARSINGTON as a CONSCIENTIOUS OBJECTOR during World War I. Quentin BELL includes Fredegond Shove among the NEO-PAGANS (QB1 173n).

Sibley, Mr. Mentioned in *JACOB'S ROOM* as a type of the professional man. (In *MRS. DALLOWAY,* Septimus Warren SMITH works for Sibleys and Arrowsmiths.)

Sickert, Walter Richard (1860–1942) One of the leading painters of his time and founder in 1911 of the Camden Town Group, which included Duncan GRANT and Augustus JOHN. Grant took over Sickert's studio at 19 FITZROY SQUARE. He was a friend of Roger FRY and was well known to Vanessa BELL and Clive BELL. Woolf met him in 1923 and in 1934, encouraged by Vanessa, she wrote to him saying how much she had enjoyed a recent exhibition of his work. Sickert replied that he would like Woolf to write about his paintings, and the result was "A Conversation About Art" published in the *YALE REVIEW*. This was slightly revised as *Walter Sickert: A Conversation* published by the HOGARTH PRESS in 1934 and reprinted as "Walter Sickert" (CE2 233–44, CDB 187–202). In the essay, Woolf discusses Sickert in FORMALIST terms and as a literary painter. She writes of the "zone of silence in the middle of every art" and says that all "great writers are great colourists" (CE2 241).

Siddons, Elsbeth Mentioned in *JACOB'S ROOM,* a friend of Clara DURRANT's who adores Clara's mother and recruits Jacob for a play when he is staying with the Durrant family.

Sidgwick, Henry (1838–1900) In *THE VOYAGE OUT,* Helen AMBROSE reads *Principia Ethica* by G. E. MOORE, and Richard DALLOWAY, picking up her book, reads aloud a passage that refers to this Cambridge University professor of moral philosophy. Sidgwick is best known for his *Methods of Ethics* (1874).

Walter Sickert: A Conversation. *Courtesy Linda J. Langham. This essay was first published in the* Yale Review *in September 1934 as "A Conversation About Art." Vanessa Bell drew this illustration for the upper cover of the Hogarth Press separate edition of the essay (1934).*

Sidney, Sir Philip (1554–86) English poet whose most famous work is the sonnet series *Astrophel and Stella* addressed to Penelope Devereux. In *NIGHT AND DAY,* William RODNEY tells Katharine HILBERY that all women should certainly be married and then slightly misquotes Sidney's sonnet 31 as they walk along the Embankment by the river Thames (ND 67).

Sieges Allee Mentioned in *A ROOM OF ONE'S OWN* as an example of men's desire to mark their possessions, a Berlin landmark embellished with statues of Hohenzollern rulers (WF 208).

Significant Form In his 1914 book *Art,* Clive BELL asked what element was common to all works of art, and stated that "Only one answer seems possible: significant form" (24). Significant form meant "relations and combinations of lines and colours, . . .

aesthetically moving forms" (*Art* 17–18) that aroused "the aesthetic emotion." S. P. Rosenbaum has pointed out that A. C. Bradley used the phrase in "Poetry for Poetry's Sake," his inaugural lecture as Oxford Professor of Poetry (Rosenbaum, "Virginia Woolf" 23–24). (See also FORMALIST.)

Simeon The name of one of Jacob's fellow students in *JACOB'S ROOM.*

Simon, Lady Shena Dorothy (née Potter) (1883–1972) A Manchester City Councillor whom Woolf met in London in 1933 and with whom she was "on impersonal good terms" (D5 137–38). Lady Simon was a social reformer who worked with her husband, Lord Simon of Wythenshawe (1879–1960), on many issues. She and Woolf corresponded in the 1930s on feminist issues and on war.

Sims, Mrs. She lets Abel PARGITER into his mistress Mira's house in *THE YEARS.* The name occurs again in *The Years* when a Miss Sims attends a meeting with Eleanor PARGITER.

Sinclair Mentioned in *THE VOYAGE OUT.* He has told Evelyn MURGATROYD that he will shoot himself if she does not marry him, and he forces a kiss on her when she tells him to leave her alone (TVO 246–47).

Sissinghurst Castle Bought by Vita SACKVILLE-WEST and Harold NICOLSON in 1930, a house in Kent of similar antiquity to KNOLE though of more modest scale. Sackville-West's poem *Sissinghurst* ("a poem of commitment and homecoming" [Glendinning 229]) was published by the HOGARTH PRESS in 1930, dedicated "To V. W." Sackville-West had her study in a tower at Sissinghurst, and she created the spectacular garden there for which she was known almost as well as for her writing. The first printing press of the Hogarth Press is in the tower at Sissinghurst, given to Sackville-West in 1930 when the Woolfs bought a new machine. The house and gardens are now administered by the National Trust.

Sitwell, Edith Louisa (1887–1964) Poet and biographer and, with her brothers Osbert (1892–1969) and Sacheverell (1897–1988), well-known participants in the 1920s London avant-garde. Woolf first met her in 1918 shortly after reviewing her poetry collection *Clowns' Houses* in the *TIMES LITERARY SUPPLEMENT* (E2 306–11) and continued to see her socially. Sitwell's first volume of poetry was *The Mother* (1915), followed in 1916 by *Twentieth-Century Harlequinade,* a collaboration with Osbert Sitwell. From 1916 to 1921 she edited *Wheels,* an annual magazine of modern poetry. On June 12, 1923 Woolf attended the infamous performance at Aeolian Hall of Sitwell's best-known work, *Façade,* in which she recited her poetry through an instrument called a "Sengerphone" to the accompaniment of music by William Walton. In 1925, the HOGARTH PRESS published Sitwell's *Poetry and Criticism* as number 11 in the Hogarth Essays.

Skelton, Oliver Mentioned at a party in *JACOB'S ROOM* where Mrs. Withers tells him about her husband's character.

"Sketch of the Past, A" (MOB 64–159) A draft memoir by Woolf published in *MOMENTS OF BEING.* Begun at Vanessa BELL's suggestion in 1939, this is Woolf's most extended autobiographical statement. She wrote it as a relief from the burden of writing *ROGER FRY, A BIOGRAPHY*; the last entry is dated November 17, 1940. "A Sketch of the Past" is of great interest not only for the biographical information it provides and insight into various characters and situations in Woolf's novels, but also because Woolf acknowledges and discusses in her memoir the "fictional" nature of all biography and autobiography. She moves back and forth between her "platform" of the present moment and her earliest memories, commenting on how memory is an active shaper of the past and how writing necessitates changing the past for fluency and interest.

Woolf begins with her earliest memory, of lying in bed at ST. IVES listening to the waves. Early in the memoir, tracing her lifelong discomfort at images of herself in mirrors, she describes how her half-brother Gerald DUCKWORTH incestuously abused her when she was "very small." This leads to one of several digressions on the function of memory.

The memoir continues with Woolf's description of what she calls "moments of being" (similar in a way to James JOYCE's notion of "epiphanies"). She describes three such moments, two of which found their way into her fiction: a vision of a flower as part of a whole comprised of flower and earth (MOB 71) is recalled in *BETWEEN THE ACTS* by Isa OLIVER's son George (BTA 11), and a memory of standing by a tree in the garden at night after overhearing the story of a man's suicide at St. Ives is recalled in *THE WAVES* (TW 24). Woolf attempts to describe what she calls her "philosophy" (MOB 72; and see Mark Hussey, *Singing passim*) in as explicit a statement as she ever made about her aesthetics.

Although "A Sketch of the Past" covers much of the same period as "REMINISCENCES," it gives a far more complex and mature view of Julia Prinsep STEPHEN. Woolf says her mother, who died when she was thirteen, obsessed her until she wrote *TO THE LIGHTHOUSE.* At the beginning of "A Sketch of the Past" Woolf says that she is not going to pause to consider the order in which she will write these memories as she is confident that an order will emerge.

As the memoir continues, she moves between memories of London and St. Ives, her half-sister Stella DUCKWORTH and early deaths of those she loved, and the present moment, which involves completing *Roger Fry* and hearing German bombers fly overhead on their way to bomb London. At one point, Woolf reflects that of the people who would have been capable of thinking about Stella in 1939 nearly all are dead (MOB 96). She writes a portrait of Stella's husband, John Waller "Jack" HILLS; describes her father Leslie STEPHEN's tyrannical behavior after Stella's death; and paints a detailed picture of 22 HYDE PARK GATE, "a complete model of Victorian society" (MOB 147).

Commenting that "scene making is my natural way of marking the past," Woolf describes her brother Thoby STEPHEN and the close relationship she had with him. In describing Thoby, the memoir returns to St. Ives and Talland House. Life in the final years of the nineteenth century, at least until Julia's death, alternated between St. Ives and London. The memoir closes with a description of George DUCKWORTH's efforts to introduce Woolf to polite society, a milieu she compares disparagingly with the intellectual world of her father.

"Slater's Pins Have No Points" See "MOMENTS OF BEING: 'SLATER'S PINS HAVE NO POINTS' "

Smith, Alexander (1830–67) One of the vast mass of Victorian writers ORLANDO reads in the nineteenth-century section of *ORLANDO*. Smith was a lace-pattern designer in Glasgow who published various poems and essays.

Smith College The Mortimer Rare Book Room of Smith College in Northhampton, Massachusetts houses the Frances Hooper Collection of Virginia Woolf Books and Manuscripts and the Elizabeth Power Richardson Collection of Bloomsbury Iconography. The Hooper Collection emphasizes Woolf as an essayist but also includes many HOGARTH PRESS first editions, limited editions of Woolf's works, and translations. Among the collection are page proofs of *ORLANDO* and *TO THE LIGHTHOUSE,* both corrected by Woolf for the first American editions; a proof copy of *THE WAVES* that Woolf inscribed to Hugh WALPOLE; and a proof copy of *THE YEARS*. The Collection also has one of the deluxe editions of *Orlando* that was printed on green paper. Other notable items include twenty-two pages of reading notes from 1926 (not included in *Virginia Woolf's Reading Notebooks*), three pages of notes for *ROGER FRY,* a six-page manuscript "As to criticism," and a typescript of "THE SEARCHLIGHT." The Hooper collection also owns 135 letters between Woolf and Lytton STRACHEY as well as other correspondence.

The Richardson Collection is a working collection of materials used by Richardson in preparing her *Bloomsbury Iconography*. It includes Leslie STEPHEN's photograph album, seventy-five original exhibition catalogs dating back to 1939, clippings and photocopies of such items as reviews of early Woolf works, and Bloomsbury material from British *Vogue* of the 1920s. The Collection also has two preliminary pencil drawings by Vanessa BELL for *FLUSH*.

Smith also has a Sylvia Plath Collection that includes eight of Woolf's books from Plath's library, several of which are underlined and annotated, as well as Plath's notes from her undergraduate English 211 class at Smith (1950–55) in which she studied *To the Lighthouse*.

Smith, Logan Pearsall (1865–1946) Writer and philologist, brother of Alys, Bertrand RUSSELL's first wife, and uncle to Rachel STRACHEY and Karin STEPHEN. The HOGARTH PRESS published his *Stories from the Old Testament Retold by Logan Pearsall Smith* (1920) and *The Prospects of Literature* (1927).

Smith, Rezia (Lucrezia) Warren Character in *MRS. DALLOWAY*, the wife of Septimus Warren SMITH. She met Septimus at the end of World War I in Italy, where he became engaged to her in a moment of panic because he could not feel. She is described as a "little woman . . . an Italian girl" (MD 21) and suffers because her husband has been traumatized by the war. She is homesick, missing her family in Milan, and wants to have a baby, but Septimus will not. She is nearly always referred to as Rezia in the novel. Woolf modeled Rezia to some extent on Lydia LOPOKOVA, the wife of John Maynard KEYNES.

Smith, Septimus Warren Character in *MRS. DALLOWAY,* a shell-shocked soldier who has fought in the worst campaigns of World War I. "One of those half-educated, self-educated men" (MD 127), Septimus seems to have attended MORLEY COLLEGE, where he fell in love with Miss Isabel POLE, who lectured on William SHAKESPEARE. He came from his hometown of Stroud, in the west of England, to London where he worked for Sibleys and Arrowsmiths and was on the path to a successful career. When war came, "Septimus was one of the first to volunteer" (MD 130). Shattered by the war, and particularly by the death of his officer, Evans, Septimus returns to England and to his former job, where he is promoted. Shakespeare's *Antony and Cleopatra,* which he had previously found beautiful, now "had shrivelled utterly" for Septimus and he reads it as an example of Shakespeare's loathing of humanity. Consumed by an indeterminate guilt, haunted by visions of the dead and possessed by an urgent need to tell what he has experienced, Septimus is taken first to Dr.

HOLMES, and then to Sir William BRADSHAW, neither of whom have any understanding of his state of mind. Despairing of "human nature," Septimus throws himself out of the window of his lodging-house onto the iron spikes of the railing below.

Throughout the novel, Septimus is linked in a variety of ways with Clarissa DALLOWAY. These characters share feelings and ways of thinking about the world, and both of them repeat lines from Shakespeare's *CYMBELINE* at different times during the day. At the party at the end of the novel, Clarissa hears about Septimus's suicide and feels that his death was an attempt to communicate to her, that he has somehow died in her place.

Septimus first appears as a character in Woolf's notebook in October 1922 (although someone called "Septimus" is also among those at Mary DATCHET's apartment in *NIGHT AND DAY* [ND 50]). It is very likely Woolf had read reports in the *Times* of the War Office Committee of Enquiry's report on shell shock that had been presented to Parliament earlier that year, for the way Septimus is treated by his doctors is typical of the blundering practices of the British medical establishment in the years following the war, when thousands of veterans applied for treatment of what is now called post-traumatic stress disorder. Sandra M. Gilbert and Susan Gubar suggest that Woolf's character was partly informed by T. S. ELIOT and that Septimus "mentally reenacts" the fate of Phlebas from Eliot's *Waste Land* (*Sexchanges* 316). Woolf also drew on her own experiences of mental breakdown in creating Septimus. As Woolf had, he hears the birds talking in Greek; as she was, he is told by doctors that he must stop thinking about himself and rest and drink milk. Woolf had thrown herself out of a window in 1904, but suffered no injury. Several commentators have drawn parallels between Woolf's and Septimus's suicide.

Smyth, Ethel Mary (1858–1944) Pioneering composer, feminist, suffragette and writer. Woolf attended the first production of Smyth's opera *The Wreckers* in 1909 and read her two-volume memoir *Impressions That Remained* in 1919. In 1921 Woolf reviewed *Streaks of Life*, another of Smyth's numerous autobiographical works, in the *NEW STATESMAN* (E3 297–300), noting there that Smyth had "friends among the Empresses and the charwomen" (E3 298). Smyth had been an intimate friend and supporter of Emmeline Pankhurst and also her lover (L5 256) (see SUFFRAGE). She had been jailed for her militant suffragette activities, and in Holloway Prison she had conducted a women's choir with her toothbrush as they sang her "March of the Women," described by Jane Marcus as the "battle song of the suffragettes" (*Languages* 51). In "The Intellectual Status of Women," Woolf's response to her friend Desmond MACCARTHY's attack in his *New Statesman* column on women's intellectual abilities, she cited Smyth as one example of women whose talents and careers had been thwarted by patriarchal opposition (D2 341).

In 1930, Smyth wrote to Woolf praising *A ROOM OF ONE'S OWN* and asking if they could meet. Woolf replied that they could, and so began an intense friendship that dominated the last decade of Woolf's life. Joanne Trautmann Banks has written that in response to Smyth's "probing questions, Virginia wrote what amounted to an epistolary autobiography" (CS 259). Their correspondence was voluminous: "I get, generally, two letters daily," Woolf wrote in 1930; "I daresay the old fires of Sapphism are blazing for the last time" (D3 306). Woolf wrote to Smyth in 1930 that "Women alone stir my imagination," and was both deeply admiring and frequently exasperated by the older woman whom she repeatedly described in her DIARY as "battered." Smyth had long been outspoken about the difficulties she had encountered in pursuing a musical career, and she continued to write about them in several memoirs, many of which she demanded that Woolf read in manuscript and comment on. *A Final Burning of Boats* had been published in 1928, and *As Time Went On*, dedicated to Woolf, was published in 1936. *What Happened Next* appeared in 1940. The articles that made up Smyth's *Female Pipings in Eden* (1934) Woolf thought too egotistic, and she advised Smyth to leave out "I" to avoid putting off readers who would see her grievances as merely personal (L5 194–95). Smyth did not follow Woolf's advice.

When they first met for tea on February 20, 1930, Smyth and Woolf "talked ceaselessly till 7," Smyth quizzing Woolf about her ancestry. This was "the basis of an undying friendship made in 15 minutes" (D3 291) as Smyth was already in love with the woman who had written *A Room of One's Own*. Although Woolf admired Smyth's "humane battered face that makes one respect human nature" (D3 313), she was not in love with her (D3 314). Their relationship was characterized by frequent arguments, usually because Smyth felt Woolf had snubbed her or avoided her (and sometimes because Leonard WOOLF, ever protective of his wife, and usually bored by Smyth, kept her away).

On January 21, 1931, Woolf and Smyth gave speeches to the London Branch of the National Society for Women's Service, where they had been invited by Philippa STRACHEY (see "PROFESSIONS FOR WOMEN" and *THE PARGITERS*; Jane Marcus discusses Smyth's speech in *Art and Anger* [94–100]). Woolf there described Smyth as "of the race of pioneers, of pathmakers. She has gone before and felled trees and blasted rocks and built bridges and thus made a way for those who come after her" (*Pargiters* xxvii–xxviii). The next month, Woolf attended rehearsals of

Smyth's *The Prison,* an oratorio based on *The Prison: A Dialogue* (1891) by Henry Brewster, who had also written the libretto for *The Wreckers* and was "the man who dominated Ethel's life" (D3 326), as Woolf had learned. Woolf was enthralled by the sight of Smyth lost in the world of her own music, although she did not particularly like the music itself. Jane Marcus has argued that *The Prison* directly influenced *THE YEARS* (*Languages* 51), but Peter Jacobs has contested this.

Woolf received "a note of ecstasy" about *THREE GUINEAS* from Smyth, when she was halfway through reading it (D5 149). Marcus suggests that Smyth was important in helping Woolf to realize the anger that fuels *Three Guineas* (*Languages* 112) and has also proposed Rose PARGITER in *The Years* as a portrait of the suffragette Smyth. She also believes that Woolf partly drew on Smyth in creating Mrs. MANRESA in *BETWEEN THE ACTS* (*Art* 99).

Snowden, Margaret Kemplay ("Snow") (1878–1966) Painter and close friend of Vanessa BELL's with whom she studied at the Royal Academy Schools of Art. In the ironic preface to *ORLANDO* Woolf acknowledges "Miss M. K. Snowdon's [sic] indefatigable researches in the archives of Harrogate and Cheltenham." In February 1930 Woolf compared Snowden's "fiddling & drifting" (D3 290) with the vitality of Ethel SMYTH, whom she had recently met.

"Society, A" (SF 118–30) A short story by Woolf in *MONDAY OR TUESDAY,* one of two from that volume that was not reprinted in *A HAUNTED HOUSE* (the other was "Blue & Green"); Leonard WOOLF writes in the preface to *A Haunted House* that he knew his wife had decided not to reprint the story. Susan Dick, in her edition of Woolf's shorter fiction, suggests "A Society" may be "in part a fictional response to [Arnold] Bennett's views on the intellectual inferiority of women" (SF 293). Woolf read AFFABLE HAWK's column on Arnold BENNETT's book *Our Women: Chapters on the Sex-Discord* in September 1920 and wrote two letters protesting both Bennett's view that women were naturally intellectually inferior to men and her friend Desmond MACCARTHY's endorsement of that view (MacCarthy wrote his column under the pseudonym Affable Hawk). (Her letters are reprinted in Appendix III of D2.) There is evidence in "A Society" that clearly supports Dick's speculation. "A Society" also foreshadows arguments that Woolf would make more explicitly in both *A ROOM OF ONE'S OWN* and *THREE GUINEAS.* As Jane Marcus has pointed out, the story parodies the Cambridge APOSTLES, that secret group to which several of Woolf's male friends and her husband belonged, known to its members as "the Society."

The story is narrated by Cassandra. Six or seven women are sitting after tea discussing men. One, Poll, bursts into tears as she has discovered men are frauds (she has been made to read the entire contents of the LONDON LIBRARY, a condition of her father's will). The women have been brought up to believe that women's duty is to bear children while men's is to produce books and civilize the world. They decide to make themselves "into a society for asking questions" (SF 119) and vow to bear no children until they have discovered the true nature of the world men have made. Over the next five years, they meet periodically to report on their findings.

Rose reports on her hoax on the British Navy—an undisguised allusion to the famous DREADNOUGHT HOAX in which Woolf herself had taken part in 1910. Fanny goes to the Law Courts and concludes that judges are either made of wood or impersonated by large animals. Helen has been to the Royal Academy of Art and when asked for her report recites snatches of patriotic poetry by Alfred, Lord TENNYSON, Robert Louis STEVENSON, Robert BURNS, Thomas Nashe, Robert BROWNING and Charles KINGSLEY. As Diane Gillespie has pointed out, Woolf's mocking view of the Royal Academy was shared by her sister, Vanessa BELL, and by Roger FRY (Gillespie, *Sisters'* 223).

Castalia spent her time at "OXBRIDGE" disguised as a charwoman. She has examined a monumental edition of the works of SAPPHO by Professor Hobkin, who defends Sappho's chastity against a German scholar's allegations (Jane Marcus suggests the German Sappho scholar was probably supposed to be von Wilamowitz-Moellendorff [*Languages* 88]). Castalia has been particularly impressed by the gentlemen's arguments over the use of something that looks to her like a hairpin. At this, Sue suggests that Hobkin was probably a gynaecologist and not a professor at all. Castalia says she will have to return to Oxbridge and try again.

Three months later, Castalia comes back and announces to Cassandra that she is pregnant. She says it was unfortunate her mother named her Castalia, the name of the pure spring at the Delphic Oracle at which the priestess, the Pythia, cleansed herself before giving prophecy. Everyone is pleased to see Castalia, however; when she asks if she should leave the society as she is pregnant a long discussion about the meaning of female chastity ensues. Judith describes her invention which will "safeguard the nation's health, accommodate its sons, and relieve its daughters" by taking the place of prostitutes (SF 124). The conversation turns to reports of the answers received from men to questions about their lives, and Jill says men despise women "too much to mind what we say" (SF 126).

They discuss men's view that there have been no great women artists since Sappho (almost certainly an allusion to Affable Hawk's correspondence with Woolf referred to above). Turning to modern literature, Elizabeth reports on her findings as a reviewer (she disguised herself as a man to get this job): H. G. WELLS is "the most popular living writer," followed by Bennett, Compton Mackenzie, Stephen McKenna and Hugh WALPOLE. Their discussion is cut short, however, by the noise from the street below—it is 1914 and war has been declared. Why men make war was a question they have not addressed.

After the war, Castalia and Cassandra look through the Society's minutes. Castalia wonders how she can bring up her daughter to believe in nothing, and Cassandra, echoing Arnold Bennett, suggests that she could teach her "that a man's intellect is, and always will be, fundamentally superior to a woman's" (SF 128). Castalia exclaims that the only hope for the good world and good books the Society hoped for is to "devise a method by which men may bear children" (SF 129). The story ends with Castalia and Cassandra solemnly giving the Society's papers to Ann, Castalia's daughter, and telling her she will be the President of the Society of the future—"upon which she burst into tears, poor little girl" (SF 130).

In her diary, Woolf imagined what the *Times* review of *Monday or Tuesday* would be like, prophesying that the reviewer would find "A Society" "too one-sided" (D2 98). The reviewer for the *TIMES LITERARY SUPPLEMENT* actually refers to the "shrewd and wicked wit of that very feminine (almost feminist) tale" (CH 88), but Affable Hawk wrote that when, as in "A Society," Woolf "writes from contempt, her work is not her best" (CH 91). Marcus, who says that in this story Woolf "made the most radical assertion of the idea that the production of culture and the reproduction of children were incompatible" (*Languages* 76), asserts that "A Society" was never reprinted "because of the hostility of male critics" (*Languages* 78). Phyllis Rose, however, finds that Woolf "cannot seem to combine in one story the sophisticated style of 'Kew Gardens' and 'Mark on the Wall' and the content of a story like 'A Society.' " Marcus actually refers to "A Society" as an essay, and in an article entitled "Is 'A Society' a Short Story?" Edward A. Hungerford has suggested that a "fruitful approach is to regard 'A Society' as a conversation, and thus as a disguised form of essay" (VWM 21: 3–4).

Sohrab Name of Bart OLIVER's Afghan hound in *BETWEEN THE ACTS*. The name recalls "Sohrab and Rustum," a poem by Matthew ARNOLD about a Persian hero, Rustum, who unwittingly kills his son Sohrab (whom he had thought was a daughter) in combat.

"Solid Objects" (SF 96–101) A short story by Woolf published in the *ATHENAEUM* in October 1920 and reprinted in *A HAUNTED HOUSE*. Woolf described the opening of the story in a letter to her sister, Vanessa BELL, in November 1918, saying she might ask her to do an illustration for it (L2 299). Dean Baldwin, who compares "Solid Objects" to Franz Kafka's story "The Hunger Artist," has located the origin of Woolf's story in a visit to the studio of the artist Mark GERTLER, whom Woolf found to be, like the character John in her story, obsessed with form.

"Solid Objects" begins with two men, Charles and John, walking on a beach arguing about politics. They stop to eat sandwiches and John digs up a piece of glass which fascinates him. John is beginning a career in politics, but he becomes gradually more and more obsessed with collecting "solid objects"—bits of broken glass and china that he finds in the streets. He is not elected and eventually no one visits him or invites him anywhere as his only interest is in adding to the collection of objects on his mantelpiece. The story ends with Charles visiting his old friend for the last time, deciding he can no longer see him.

Robert A. Watson has read the story as an allegory (VWM 16:3–4), describing the first few paragraphs as posing and answering the question "how does one transform opaque appearances, the solid objects of the world, into a story?" Charles and John represent the active and contemplative life, says Watson, and the story presents an antithesis between them.

Sophocles See *ANTIGONE*.

Sopwith, Professor One of three Cambridge dons satirically sketched in *JACOB'S ROOM*, who talks and talks to impress the young men who fill his rooms at night; the narrator notes that a woman would, involuntarily, despise Sopwith.

Sorley The lighthouse keeper in *TO THE LIGHTHOUSE*, for whose son Mrs. RAMSAY is knitting a stocking.

Spalding, James Mentioned in *JACOB'S ROOM*, a passenger on a bus going to Shepherd's Bush in a scene that recalls "AN UNWRITTEN NOVEL."

Spanish Civil War (1936–39) In 1931 the second republic was declared in Spain after the fall of the monarchy and the new government began redistributing wealth, separating church and state, and instituting reforms that generally displeased the landed aristocracy and the church. Throughout the early 1930s Spain was in turmoil as monarchists, the church, the aristocracy, a large part of the military, and the new fascist party, the Falange, joined in resistance to the government, which was also beset by the dissatisfaction of the left. In 1936 General Francisco Franco began a revolt in Morocco that was quickly followed by rightist coalitions in Spain. By November 1936, Madrid was under siege by nationalist forces and the first of several International Brigades came to the aid of the republican cause. Intellectuals, artists and writers in Europe and the United States, many of whom were Communists, were moved by the plight of the Spanish republic and began to organize relief efforts in their own countries and also to travel to Spain either to fight (as George Orwell did) or assist as ambulance drivers, as propagandists, and in other non-combatant roles. Woolf's nephew Julian BELL was killed while working as an ambulance driver in Spain in 1937. Germany and Italy sent many thousands of troops and other assistance to Franco, and throughout 1937–39 the Nationalists consolidated their victories. In April 1937, the indiscriminate bombing of the town of Guernica by German planes became an international symbol of fascist brutality and inspired one of Picasso's best-known paintings (exhibited at the 1938 World's Fair in Glasgow, Scotland). Woolf's *THREE GUINEAS* refers throughout to photographs of "dead bodies and ruined houses" that the Spanish Government sent to stir outrage and support in the international community. Despite aid to the republicans by the Soviet Union, Madrid fell on April 1, 1939, when Franco's forces entered the city. The Spanish Civil War was hugely destructive and cost many thousands of lives, and it is often regarded as laying the foundation for World War II.

Speaker The forerunner of the *NATION,* founded in 1890. Desmond MACCARTHY was its drama critic, and Woolf contributed three reviews to it in 1906.

Spender, Stephen (b. 1909) English poet and critic. In 1930 he sent some poems to Woolf (D3 318), and he first met her in 1932. Spender was one of the contributors to the landmark *New Signatures: Poems by Several Hands,* edited by Michael Roberts and published by the HOGARTH PRESS in 1932. The volume, which John LEHMANN brought to the Press (and which Leonard WOOLF later referred to as the manifesto of the thirties generation), contained works by poets of what came to be known as the "Auden generation" and was significant also in bringing together young writers affiliated with both Oxford and Cambridge universities (who were, and are still, usually wary of each other). Among the nine contributors were W. H. AUDEN, Julian BELL, Cecil DAY LEWIS, William Empson and William PLOMER. Of the younger generation of writers Woolf met through Lehmann and through her nephew Julian Bell, only Spender became a friend.

During the SPANISH CIVIL WAR, Spender introduced Woolf to Auden at a meeting at the Albert Hall of the National Joint Committee for Spanish Relief in June 1937. Christopher ISHERWOOD, another of Spender's closest friends, also was in contact with Woolf at this time, inviting her to support a delegation of writers to Spain. In 1939, the Hogarth Press published *To Spain,* a belated effort in support of the republic including poems by Spender, Auden and others. Spender went to Spain, having joined the Communist Party, in 1937 to broadcast against the fascists. In October 1937, Woolf wrote in her DIARY that she "resented" Spender, who had come to dinner, because he was still alive and her nephew, Julian, had been killed in the war (D5 115). Valentine Cunningham has written that Spender expressed doubt about his activities in the Spanish Civil War International Brigades in "a long private letter" to Woolf in 1937, where he wrote that Woolf should warn Julian off going because Spain was a "Hell . . . of narrowness and political dogmatism" (Cunningham 461).

Spender admired Woolf's work and has referred to it in many of his critical writings, such as *The Struggle of the Modern* (1965). In 1934, reviewing Wyndham LEWIS's *Men without Art,* Spender defended her against Lewis's attack. In 1931, Spender sent Woolf a novel to consider for the Hogarth Press which she rejected, telling him to concentrate on poetry. This was eventually published in 1988 as *The Temple.* Woolf had begun reading Spender's work in 1930, and she discussed her view of his generation in "THE LEANING TOWER" and in "LETTER TO A YOUNG POET." His novel *The Backward Son* (1940) was one of the texts that led her to the conception of the "Leaning Tower" school of writers as a "school of auto-analysis" (D5 266–67).

Spicer, Mr. Mentioned in *THE YEARS* as at a meeting with Eleanor PARGITER.

Springett, Etty Character in *BETWEEN THE ACTS* who lives with Lynn JONES now that both are widows. She and Lynn are upset by Miss LA TROBE's satirical treatment of the Victorian family in the annual village pageant. The two women are also made nervous by the antics of ALBERT, the village idiot.

Springett, Mr. Mentioned in *JACOB'S ROOM,* he owns a shop opposite Jacob's rooms in London.

Staël, Madame Anne Louise Germaine de (1766–1817) During the dinner in section XVII of part 1 of *TO THE LIGHTHOUSE,* Mrs. RAMSAY reflects on how she relies on the "admirable fabric of the masculine intelligence" to sustain her as she half-listens to the dinner conversation range across numerous subjects, one of which is "Voltaire and Madame de Staël" (TTL 106). Madame de Staël was an important figure in the French Revolution, gathering together many progressive thinkers in her Paris salon. She wrote on politics and literature, including an important work on German philosophy, *De l'Allemagne* (1810–13), as well as novels and memoirs.

Steele, Charles Seen on the beach at the opening of *JACOB'S ROOM* painting the scene, "an unknown man exhibiting obscurely" (JR 8).

Stein, Gertrude (1874–1946) American experimental writer who lived after 1902 in France, where she collected the work of and befriended many avant-garde painters. In 1909 she met Alice B. Toklas, with whom she subsequently lived. In 1925 Edith SITWELL sent Woolf the manuscript of Stein's "Poetry and Criticism" and *The Making of Americans* (published in Paris in 1925) in the hope that the HOGARTH PRESS would publish them in England. Woolf wrote to Vita SACKVILLE-WEST that August that she was "weighed down by innumerable manuscripts" including "the whole of Gertrude Stein" (L3 198). She did not accept them for the Press, however, but went in June 1926 to a party given by the Sitwells to introduce Gertrude Stein in England just before she went to lecture at Oxford and Cambridge universities. Woolf found Stein "rather formidable" (D3 89). In 1926, the Hogarth Press published Stein's *Composition as Explanation* as the first of the second series of the Hogarth Essays. Rachel Blau DuPlessis has discussed whether Stein knew Woolf's *A ROOM OF ONE'S OWN* and whether her 1931 "Forensics" continues Woolf's essay ("WOOLFENSTEIN" 99); DuPlessis also discusses intertextuality between *THE WAVES* and Stein's *Tender Buttons* (1911) and argues for the possible influence of Stein on Woolf's later works.

Stephen, Adeline Virginia See WOOLF, (Adeline) Virginia.

Stephen, Adrian Leslie (1883–1948) Woolf's younger brother was a favorite of their mother Julia Prinsep STEPHEN, who called him her "joy" (Leslie Stephen, *Mausoleum Book* 85). He was a delicate child, known in the family as "The Dwarf" because he was notably shorter than the other children; at sixteen, however, he began to grow rapidly and eventually reached 6 feet 5 inches. After reading law at Trinity College, Cambridge, Adrian seemed at a loss as to which career he should follow. His childhood, adolescence and student days were overshadowed by unfavorable comparisons with his good-looking and popular brother Thoby STEPHEN. Adrian also did not get on well with Leslie STEPHEN, who wrote "he is a very attractive, simple little fellow but oddly dreamy and apt to take a great deal of interest in the things which are most impractical" (Annan, *Leslie Stephen* 118). Woolf records in her 1897 diary that "Adrian had to sit up late with father doing his sums which finally about 9:30 came right" (PA 36). Adrian also attempted to compete with the *HYDE PARK GATE NEWS*, but his efforts, the *Pelican News* and its successor *The Corkscrew Gazette,* "soon petered out" (QB1 116).

Portrait of Adrian Stephen, *1910 (13½ x 10") by Duncan Grant. © The Duncan Grant Estate 1978. Courtesy of Henrietta Garnett.*
This is one of three portraits of Adrian painted by Grant at his 21 Fitzroy Square studio in 1910.

Adrian and Woolf traveled to Spain and Portugal in 1905, and in 1906, while Woolf, Vanessa BELL and Violet DICKINSON traveled through France and Italy to Greece, Adrian and Thoby rode on horseback through Albania to join them. In 1907, Adrian, Woolf, Vanessa and Clive BELL traveled together to Paris. After Vanessa married Clive in 1907, Adrian moved with Woolf to 29 FITZROY SQUARE, where they soon resumed the tradition of "Thursday Evenings" at home that Thoby had begun on coming down from Cambridge, adding more socialites to the original circle of Cambridge friends. In 1909, Adrian and Woolf accompanied Saxon SYDNEY-TURNER to the Richard WAGNER festival at Bayreuth, about which Woolf wrote "Impressions at Bayreuth" for *The Times* of August 21, 1909 (E1 288). With his friend Horace COLE, Adrian devised the DREADNOUGHT HOAX in 1910, playing the part of the interpreter "Herr Kaufmann." His account of this famous hoax was published by the HOGARTH PRESS in 1936.

In 1911, Adrian and Woolf moved to 38 BRUNSWICK SQUARE, which they shared with John Maynard KEYNES, Duncan GRANT and, on his return from Ceylon, Leonard WOOLF. Around 1910, Adrian had begun an affair with Duncan Grant that, after Adrian's death, Vanessa looked back on "as one of his happiest" relationships (Spalding, *Vanessa Bell* 88). Together they painted a mural depicting a tennis match on the wall of Adrian's apartment in the house; Adrian also decorated four panels of a closet door with female nudes, and Duncan remarked that he had some talent for painting. In 1916, Adrian put his legal training to use in arguing for the exemption from combat service as CONSCIENTIOUS OBJECTORS of Duncan Grant and David GARNETT before the tribunal in Sussex (he was joined by Philip MORRELL and Maynard Keynes, but the applications for exemption were at this point turned down). Adrian was a committed pacifist who worked as secretary of the No Conscription Fellowship and as treasurer of the National Council for Civil Liberties during World War I. In 1936 he was involved in anti-fascist marches and meetings of the "For Intellectual Liberty" group, which met in his home. After a trip to Berlin just before World War II, to rescue a German friend, he alerted the Woolfs to the savagery of the Nazis and provided them with enough morphine for suicide should the Nazis invade England (LW2 383). During World War II he served as an R.A.M.C. doctor at an army psychiatric hospital (CM2 15).

In October 1914 Adrian married Karin Costelloe (see Karin STEPHEN), with whom he had two children, Ann (b. 1916) and Judith (1918–1972). Karin was rather disliked by Vanessa and the Woolfs. In 1918, Woolf wrote of her brother and sister-in-law in her DIARY that "They live rather apart from our world; from all worlds, I can't help feeling, though this may be wrong" (D1 152). Woolf's relations with Adrian were never very easy. Later in 1918 she wrote of Adrian's seeming inability to settle into a "normal" life: "Yes, one wants to be found doing the ordinary things when one's friends call. I too have this feeling to some extent. I suppose indeed that I share many of A.'s feelings. A feeling comes over me when I am with him that instead of being comfortably obtuse we are crepuscular to each other; & thus, among other things, fearfully shy when we are alone. With other people in the room we get on much better" (D1 187). Adrian was too shy to tell her in 1919 that he had enjoyed *THE VOYAGE OUT,* which he read for the first time that year (D1 255).

In 1919, Adrian and Karin decided to train in medicine with a view to becoming psychoanalysts, which they indeed did in 1926. Adrian began his training analysis with Dr. James Glover in 1923, continuing it in 1926, after Glover's sudden death, with Ella Freeman Sharpe (1875–1947; Sharpe quotes from *A ROOM OF ONE'S OWN* in a 1931 paper, "Variations of Technique in Different Neuroses" [Abel 19]). Woolf recorded in her diary in 1923 that her brother was "altogether broken up by psycho analysis. . . . His soul is rent in pieces with a view to reconstruction" (D2 242). Adrian and Karin separated in 1923, Adrian moving in with James STRACHEY in MECKLENBURGH SQUARE (James wrote to Alix STRACHEY that he wished "Adrian were a *little* more obsessional (or obsessive). The litter & horrors in the bathroom are decidedly trying" [Meisel and Kendrick 106]). Although the couple reunited in 1926, their marriage was not a happy one, and their children were often neglected. On hearing of their separation, Woolf reflected on the truth of a remark that a friend of her father's had made to the effect that "Undoubtedly . . . the D[ictionary of] N[ational] B[iography] crushed his life out before he was born" (D2 277).

In 1925 Melanie Klein gave her famous lectures on object-relations theory at Adrian and Karin's home, 50 GORDON SQUARE, an "event that captured the attention of the British psychoanalytic world" (Abel 13). Woolf met Klein at the twenty-fifth Anniversary Dinner of the British Psycho-Analytical Society in 1939, to which Adrian took her. Woolf had thought in 1926 that her brother had at last "emerged" (D3 141) from the lethargy that so annoyed her and her family, but they saw little of each other ("Adrian I never see," she wrote in 1930 [D3 316]).

Adrian's daughter Ann Synge wrote to Leonard Woolf in 1964, when *BEGINNING AGAIN,* volume three of his autobiography, was published, saying she had "got the impression that there had been some sort of deliberate exclusion of our family from the magic circle [of the BLOOMSBURY GROUP] and that they [her parents] were trying to pretend to themselves that it was they who didn't want to be in it" (Spotts 529–30). Leonard replied that "the trouble with Adrian (and later with Karin) was pretty complicated and dated from prehistoric childhood. Some of it is used in James in *To the Lighthouse.*" Leonard then quoted the scene from *TO THE LIGHTHOUSE* in which James RAMSAY wishes to gash a hole in his father's breast (TTL 4), and continued, "He [Adrian] had a slight grudge against life, one felt, and he remained somewhat aloof and outside our circle which gradually developed into Bloomsbury" (Spotts 531). Further evidence of Adrian's influence on *To the Lighthouse* is provided by Quentin Bell, who quotes from the *Hyde Park Gate News* of September 12, 1892 concerning an invitation to Thoby and Woolf from some children in ST. IVES to go on a trip to the GODREVY LIGHTHOUSE: "Master Adrian Stephen was much disappointed at not being allowed to go" (QB1 32).

Stephen, Caroline Emelia (1834–1909) Woolf called her aunt "Nun" as she lived a cloistered life at her house, The Porch, in Cambridge. Leslie STEPHEN described his sister unflatteringly in his *MAUSOLEUM BOOK* as "making a few pathetic little attempts to turn her really great abilities to some account" (55). Caroline, whom Leslie called Milly, had come to look after him when his first wife Harriet Marian (Minny) Thackeray died; "though affectionate she was a most depressing companion," Leslie wrote (Annan 55), and after three weeks with him, she returned to her own house, writing to F. W. MAITLAND of her brother that "the action of the spoilt child in him often had to me the effect of unkindness" (Annan 129). Her first book, *The Service of the Poor* (1871), was a study of sisterhoods that argued that the preservation of the family depended upon the self-sacrifice of women. Annan describes Caroline as "a classic victim of Victorian masculinity" (129), but in her essay "The Niece of a Nun" Jane Marcus has argued for the significant influence of Caroline's mysticism and pacifism on Woolf (*Languages* 115–35). Marcus believes that the title *A ROOM OF ONE'S OWN* as well as that work's theme of an aunt's legacy came from Caroline Emelia's life (*Languages* 104–05). Caroline left Woolf £2,500, and only £100 each to Adrian STEPHEN and Vanessa BELL. Marcus has also suggested that Woolf took the "central figure of the lighthouse in her novel exorcising her mother's ghost from an eloquent passage in Caroline Stephen's essay 'Divine Guidance' in *The Vision of Faith*" (*Languages* 129).

In 1879, Caroline Stephen published *Quaker Strongholds*, describing her 1871 conversion to the Society of Friends. As well as contributing essays to the *CORNHILL MAGAZINE* and *The Nineteenth Century*, Caroline wrote several other books: *Caroline Fox and Her Family* (1883), *The First James Stephen* (1906; an edition of her father's letters), *The Light Arising: Thoughts on the Central Radiance* (1908) and *The Vision of Faith* (1911). In volume 2 of *The Later Periods of Quakerism*, Rufus M. Jones describes how she "single-handedly revived the moribund English Society of Friends" (Marcus, *Languages* 200 n23).

When Woolf had a breakdown after her father's death in 1904, she went to stay with her Quaker aunt at her house, The Porch, to recuperate. From there she wrote to her friend Violet DICKINSON that "She is a remarkable woman I always feel when I see her" (L1 230). When Caroline died in 1909, Woolf wrote her obituary for the *GUARDIAN* (E1 267), a "complete revision," according to Marcus, of her father's portrait of his sister. Marcus suggests that Caroline Stephen was an influence on several of Woolf's fictional characters, including Sally SEALE in *NIGHT AND DAY*, Eleanor PARGITER in *THE YEARS* and Lucy SWITHIN in *BETWEEN THE ACTS*.

Stephen, Dorothea Jane (1871–1965) One of seven children of Leslie STEPHEN's brother James Fitzjames STEPHEN. She was referred to by a young Woolf as "our fat religious cousin." She was a zealous Christian, became a teacher of religion in India and wrote *Studies in Early Indian Thought*, which was unfavorably reviewed in the *TIMES LITERARY SUPPLEMENT* on February 13, 1919, much to Dorothea's annoyance. In 1921 Woolf had a rather sharp exchange of letters with her cousin, who had expressed disapproval of Vanessa BELL's domestic arrangements. She wrote Dorothea, "You, for example, accept a religion which I and my servants, who are both agnostics, think wrong and indeed pernicious" (L2 489).

Stephen, Harriet Marian ("Minny") (1840–75) Leslie STEPHEN's first wife, whom he met through his mother when he was in his early thirties. Minny and her sister Anne Isabella Thackeray (Anny) RITCHIE were daughters of the novelist William Makepeace THACKERAY. Leslie and Minny were married in 1867 and took their honeymoon in the Alps. They lived at Onslow Gardens, where the Thackeray sisters had lived previously; having Anny in the household often tried Leslie's patience, especially as the sisters were devoted to each other. In 1868, Minny accompanied Leslie on his second trip to the United States. She also had a miscarriage this year. In 1870 their daughter Laura STEPHEN was born, and in 1875, during another pregnancy, Minny fell ill and died on Leslie's forty-third birthday. The night before she died, Minnie's friend and neighbor Julia Duckworth, who would become Leslie's second wife (see Julia Prinsep STEPHEN), visited them.

Stephen, James (1758–1832) See CLAPHAM SECT.

Stephen, Sir James (1789–1859) Woolf's grandfather, he married Jane Catherine Venn in 1814, thus continuing his family's involvement with the CLAPHAM SECT. They had four children, Herbert (1822–46), James Fitzjames STEPHEN (1829–1894), Leslie STEPHEN (1832–1904), and Caroline Emelia STEPHEN (1834–1909). He was appointed Regius Professor of Modern History at Cambridge in 1849 and wrote *Essays in Ecclesiastical Biography* (1842) and *Lectures on the History of France* (1852). "Mr. Over-Secretary Stephen," as he was called, was for many years Counsel to the Colonial Office and Board of Trade. His long involvement with the Colonial Office led to the newspapers calling him "Mr. Mother-Country Stephen," for it was he who used the domestic metaphor of England as mother country, likening its colonies to "unmarried daughters." Noel Annan remarks that he "was certainly one of the founders of Victorian imperialism" (*Leslie Stephen* 13). His daughter Caroline Emelia published a biography of her father in 1906 from which we learn that his son Leslie thought him a tyrant at home. Jane Marcus describes him as "the chief ideologue of British 'benevolent' imperialism" (*Languages* 83) and as a "petty patriarchal tyrant" whom Leslie remembered "dictating to his mother and sisters with a Miltonic tread" (*Languages* 83). Sir James is referred to in Woolf's "A SKETCH OF THE PAST" as the possible source of her "streak of the puritan, of the Clapham Sect" (MOB 68), when she recalls the story of how he once smoked a cigar, found he liked it, and so threw it away and never smoked another. Woolf also remembers the bust of her grandfather in the dining room at 22 HYDE PARK GATE, "an eyeless, white man who still presides in the hall of Adrian's house in Regent's Park" (MOB 117). Sir James had nervous breakdowns in 1824, 1832 and 1847, the last so severe that his friends and doctor advised his early retirement from the Colonial Office.

Stephen, Sir James Fitzjames (1829–94) Woolf's paternal uncle was known as "the Giant Grim" for his terrible pronouncements from the Bench of the High Court (1879–91) and his railings in print against those he disagreed with. Among the latter was John Stuart Mill, whom Fitzjames attacked in his "manual for the conservative politician" (Marcus, *Languages* 90), *Liberty, Equality, Fraternity*. He also published several anonymous reviews of Charles Dickens's *Little Dorritt* because he believed his father was being satirized in the "Circumlocution Office" (*Languages* 93). Among his major publications were a *General View of the Criminal Law of England* (1863), a *History of the Criminal Law* (1883) and *The Story of Nuncomar and Sir Elijah Impey* (1885).

Fitzjames overshadowed his brother Leslie STEPHEN as they grew up and was his father's favorite. Fitzjames appears as the "villain" of Jane Marcus's text in *Virginia Woolf and the Languages of Patriarchy*: "His name recurs as the signature of the language of the patriarchy, the inventor of modern legal discourse, to whom generations of law students turned for definitions of crime and punishment, the harsh discourse of discipline, the voice of an Old Testament judge" (*Languages* 16). He married Mary Cunningham ("Aunt Stephen") and had seven children who survived: Katherine STEPHEN (1856–1924), Herbert (1856–1932), James Kenneth STEPHEN (1859–92), Harry Lushington (1860–1945), Helen (1862–1908), Rosamond (1868–1951), and Dorothea Jane STEPHEN (1871–1965). Fitzjames was driven from his position as a High Court judge after a famous murder trial in which he prejudiced the jury against the defendant, Mrs. Maybrick, by accusing her of adultery and saying that women who committed adultery were naturally murderers. He had always denied that there was anything amiss with his son James Kenneth, and when this son starved himself to death in an asylum in 1892, Fitzjames deteriorated rapidly, dying two years later. Immediately after Fitzjames's death, Leslie wrote *The Life of Sir James Fitzjames Stephen* (1895).

Stephen, James Kenneth (1859–92) Woolf's cousin, the son of Sir James Fitzjames STEPHEN, her father's brother, was an outstanding student and athlete at Eton who went on to King's College, Cambridge, following his teacher Oscar BROWNING, of whose homosexual circle he was a part. In 1891 he published *The Living Languages: A Defense of the Compulsory Study of Greek at Cambridge*, in which work he coined the phrase "intellectual aristocracy." Jane Marcus suggests the work as a source for Woolf's repeated phrase "daughters of educated men" in *THREE GUINEAS* as an ironic contrast with her cousin's repetition of the phrase "highly educated men" in his "Defense" (*Languages* 200 n38; also see Woolf's "ON NOT KNOWING GREEK"). James Kenneth was well known at Cambridge as the author of *Lapsus Calami*, a collection of poems of which several are extremely misogynist.

James Kenneth was a favorite of Julia and Leslie STEPHEN's and they continued to admit him to their home when he was infatuated with Stella DUCKWORTH and was severely mentally disturbed in the early 1890s (" 'dear Jim' was a great favorite," wrote Woolf [MOB 99]). At the end of 1886 he had suffered a blow to the head while staying with friends at Felixstowe (there are various versions of exactly what happened, but a blow from some kind of machinery is a common element in the story). In his biography of his brother, Leslie attributed James Kenneth's later behavior to this blow, but Thomas C. Caramagno, who has examined James Kenneth's medical records, explains his mental state as characteristic of the manic-depressive illness suffered by several members of the Stephen family (Caramagno 101–03). Woolf describes her cousin in "A SKETCH OF THE PAST" when he was infatuated with her half-sister Stella: "That great figure with the deep voice and the wild eyes would come to the house looking for her, with his madness on him; and would burst into the nursery and spear the bread on his swordstick" (MOB 98). James Kenneth was treated by Sir William Gull and by Sir George SAVAGE (who later treated Woolf). In 1891 James Kenneth privately printed and circulated in Cambridge a pamphlet contradicting Savage's diagnosis of his condition. In that year, his behavior had become so violent and uncontrollable he was banned from his club and in November he was committed to St. Andrews Hospital in Northampton.

James Kenneth was tutor to the Duke of Clarence, Queen Victoria's grandson, while he was at Trinity College from 1883 to 1884. Michael Harrison, in *Clarence: The Life of H.R.H. the Duke of Clarence and Avondale (1864–1892)*, suggests that James Kenneth was Jack the Ripper and that the discovery of this "so broke up Leslie that he himself collapsed in 1889" (159). James Kenneth stopped eating when he heard the Duke of Clarence had died, and died himself three weeks later at St. Andrews.

Stephen, Julia Prinsep [née Jackson, quo Duckworth] (1846–95) Woolf's mother was born in India, the third daughter of Dr. John Jackson and Maria (see PATTLE family). She came to England with her mother in 1848 and was a frequent visitor to Little Holland House, where her aunt Sarah (see PRINSEP family) lived, where she was painted and drawn by Edward Burne-Jones and G. F. WATTS and photographed by her aunt Julia Margaret CAMERON. In the early 1860s she looked after her mother, who suffered from rheumatism, and it was while on a visit to her sister Mary (see FISHER family) in Venice with her mother that she met her future husband, Herbert DUCKWORTH. Having declined marriage proposals from the painter Holman Hunt and the sculptor Thomas Woolner, Julia married Herbert Duckworth in 1867. They had three children, George, Stella and Gerald DUCKWORTH, the last being born six weeks after Herbert died after bursting an abscess as he reached to pick a fig for Julia. After her husband's death, Julia lost her faith, and she found much of interest in the essays of Leslie STEPHEN on religion and agnosticism. She began to spend most of her time at Freshwater, the Camerons' house on the Isle of Wight, where she visited the poor and sick.

The Annunciation, *1879 (98 x 44). Edward Burne-Jones. Courtesy The Board of Trustees, National Museums and Galleries on Merseyside (Lady Lever Art Gallery, Port Sunlight).*
Woolf's mother, Julia Prinsep Stephen, was the model for Mary in this painting. At the time she was thirty-three and pregnant with Vanessa Bell.

In 1875, after the death of Harriet Marian ("Minny") STEPHEN, Leslie Stephen's wife and a friend of Julia's, she helped him and his sister-in-law, Anne Isabella Thackeray RITCHIE, move to HYDE PARK GATE. She developed a close friendship with Leslie and eventually agreed to marry him in 1878. After their marriage, Leslie moved, with his daughter Laura STEPHEN, into Julia's house at 13 Hyde Park Gate South (which in 1884 became 22 Hyde Park Gate), where she lived with her three children. In five years they had four children of their own, Vanessa (BELL), Julian Thoby STEPHEN, Adeline Virginia (WOOLF) and Adrian Leslie STEPHEN. Julia undertook to teach the children herself, giving them lessons in the dining room, her opal ring flashing as she turned the pages of a book. Julia nursed her father until his death in 1887, and then her mother, who frequently stayed with them. Julia's mother died in 1892 but Julia continued to exhaust herself in looking after the sick both in London and ST. IVES. In 1895 she died after a bout of influenza.

In her lifetime, Julia Stephen published only one of the essays and none of the stories that she wrote (though John Bicknell has established that she and Leslie had plans to publish some of her stories, illustrated by Leslie). Her *NOTES FROM SICK ROOMS*, an essay detailing the proper care of the sick was published in 1883. Her writing has recently been made available by Diane F. Gillespie and Elizabeth Steele in their edition *Stories for Children, Essays for Adults*. Her philanthropic work and clear-sighted ideas about nursing are exemplified in her essays, and her daughter noted in "A SKETCH OF THE PAST" that the "Julia Prinsep Stephen Nursing Association" of St. Ives was still in existence when she wrote her memoir in 1939–40 (MOB 131). Julia also exemplified what Woolf would later call the ANGEL IN THE HOUSE, after the poem of that name by Coventry Patmore, the Victorian male's ideal of a woman who could cope with a huge household and yet remain "angelic." Julia owned a copy of the fourth edition of *The Angel in the House* (1860) inscribed to "Julia Jackson with the kind regard of Coventry Patmore" (Gillespie and Steele 11). In 1889 Julia joined Octavia Hill, Mrs. Humphry WARD and many others in signing an Appeal Against Female SUFFRAGE, published in *Nineteenth Century*.

The influence of Julia on Woolf, who was thirteen when she died, was profound. In "REMINISCENCES"

Woolf described her mother's death as "the greatest disaster that could happen" (MOB 40). Twice in her DIARY she describes her vivid memory of the morning her mother died, remembering how she saw Dr. SETON walk sadly up the road, his hands folded behind his back, and her "feeling that everything had come to an end" (MOB 84). Recalling it again in 1937, she wrote, "How that early morning picture has stayed with me!" (D5 85). Julia's death plunged the family into what Woolf describes in "Reminiscences" as a period of "Oriental gloom" (MOB 40) as well as marking the beginning of Leslie's utter dependence upon first Stella and, after her untimely death, Vanessa. The *MAUSOLEUM BOOK* Leslie Stephen wrote as a memorial to Julia for her children gives an indication of the atmosphere in which Woolf spent her early teenage years. Again and again in her autobiographical writings she describes her mother as "central" in the life of her family ("there she was in the very centre of that great Cathedral space that was childhood," she writes in "A Sketch of the Past," continuing, "I suspect the word 'central' gets closest to the general feeling I had of living so completely in her atmosphere" [MOB 83]). With eight children and a demanding husband, Julia was rarely able to spend more than a few minutes alone with any one of them. This circumstance was exacerbated by her punishing schedule of visits to the poor and sick, visits on which her daughter Stella frequently accompanied her (the opening chapters of Woolf's *THE YEARS* describe the kind of Victorian applied philanthropy Julia was famous for, exemplified by Eleanor PARGITER).

Madeline Moore in "Some Female Versions of Pastoral" has suggested that Julia was the source for Rachel VINRACE's dead mother in Woolf's first novel, *THE VOYAGE OUT* ("Some" 82–104). Julia is a central presence that permeates many of Woolf's creations, but she is most famously identified with Mrs. RAMSAY of *TO THE LIGHTHOUSE*. In "A Sketch of the Past," Woolf wrote that she had been obsessed with her mother until she was in her forties; "She was one of the invisible presences who after all play so important a part in every life" (MOB 80). She described how the obsession left her after she wrote *To the Lighthouse*, supposing that she had done for herself what psychoanalysts do for their patients: "When it was written, I ceased to be obsessed by my mother" (MOB 81). Her description in the memoir of the morning of her mother's death shows how closely the novel drew on her own experiences: "My father staggered from the bedroom as we came. I stretched out my arms to stop him, but he brushed past me" (MOB 91; see TTL 128). Vanessa wrote to her sister when she had read *To the Lighthouse* in 1927 that it seemed to her Woolf had "given a portrait of mother which is more like her than anything I could ever have conceived of as possible. It is almost painful to have her so raised from the dead. You have made one feel the extraordinary beauty of her character, which must be the most difficult thing in the world to do. It was like meeting her again with oneself grown up and on equal terms and it seems to me the most astonishing feat of creation to have been able to see her in such a way" (L3 572).

Nevertheless, as Woolf herself took pains to point out, Mrs. Ramsay is not Julia Stephen. Jane Lilienfeld's essays "Where the Spear Plants Grew: the Ramsays' Marriage in *To the Lighthouse*" and "'The Deceptiveness of Beauty': Mother Love and Mother Hate in *To the Lighthouse*," are important examples of the several critical explorations of how in this novel Woolf analyzes the family, Victorian womanhood, mother–daughter relationships and other issues, drawing upon but not limiting her conception to her own memories of her mother. Alex Zwerdling also has shown that Julia was "quite different from Mrs. Ramsay in important ways" (Zwerdling 188). Writing to Vita SACKVILLE-WEST in 1927, Woolf said, "I don't know if I'm like Mrs Ramsay: as my mother died when I was 13 probably it is a child's view of her" (L3 374). To Woolf, Julia was a complex figure, as was demonstrated by her marriages to two such very different men. She was severe, disliked affectation, and seemed to her daughter always to live against a background of sadness. The last words she spoke to Woolf, from her deathbed, were "Hold yourself straight, little Goat" (MOB 84), evidence perhaps of the decorum she valued even as she lay dying. In *A ROOM OF ONE'S OWN* Woolf wrote that "we think back through our mothers, if we are women" (76), referring to other women writers, but also, certainly, to her own mother, who was a continuing presence in her life and work.

Stephen, Karin Elizabeth Conn [née Costelloe] (1889–1953) Woolf's sister-in-law, who married Adrian STEPHEN in 1914, was the daughter of Mary Pearsall Smith (Logan Pearsall SMITH's sister) and B. F. Costelloe. Karin's mother left her father to live with Bernard Berenson, whom she married when her first husband died in 1899. Karin's older sister Rachel (Ray) married Oliver STRACHEY. Karin was an outstanding philosophy student at NEWNHAM COLLEGE, Cambridge, studying under G. E. MOORE and Bertrand RUSSELL. She held a research fellowship at Newnham in 1914–15. In the early 1920s, Karin and Adrian shared the lease of 50 GORDON SQUARE with Vanessa and Clive BELL, and it was there in 1925 that Adrian and Karin hosted Melanie Klein's famous lectures on object-relations theory.

Karin and Adrian Stephen decided in 1919 to become psychoanalysts and thus studied medicine at University College Hospital, London, from 1919 to

"Mrs. Leslie Stephen" (Julia Prinsep Stephen) from Stella Duckworth Hills's album of photographs. Courtesy Henry W. and Albert A. Berg Collection, The New York Public Library, Astor, Lenox and Tilden Foundations.

1926. Karin was a prolific writer; among her most notable works are *The Misuse of the Mind: A Study of Bergson's Attack on Intellectualism* (1922), which has an introduction by Henri BERGSON, and *Psychoanalysis and Medicine: A Study of the Wish to Fall Ill* (1933), in the preface to which Ernest Jones praises her as a communicator of psychoanalytic theory to people trained in other fields (Abel 20). This book was a record of Karin's lecture series, the first ever given on psychoanalysis at Cambridge.

The Stephens' marriage was not a happy one and their two children, Ann (b. 1916) and Judith (1918–1972), were frequently neglected. Woolf wrote to Vanessa BELL in 1918, "I wish he hadn't married her. . . . A good cob of a woman; but so hearty and so without shade or softness" (L2 261). Karin's deafness, huge appetite, and penchant for flamboyant clothing offended the sensibilities of the Woolfs; she reminded Woolf of "one of our lost dogs" (D1 118). Despite this, the Woolfs went to her parties and on occasion Woolf seems to have had some tender feelings toward her sister-in-law: "But Karin was very nice: so brisk headed; & somehow <sad> pathetic" (D5 19). Karin committed suicide in 1953.

Stephen, Katherine (1856–1924) Eldest daughter of James Fitzjames STEPHEN, she was Principal of NEWNHAM COLLEGE, Cambridge, from 1911 to 1920 (when she was succeeded by Pernel STRACHEY). Leonard WOOLF recalled her being present as chaperone when he first met Woolf and Vanessa BELL at Cambridge in 1901. They had come to visit their brother Thoby STEPHEN and were staying with their cousin Katherine (Kate), who at the time was Vice Principal of Newnham. After the death of Stella DUCKWORTH in 1897, Leslie STEPHEN made Katherine Laura STEPHEN's guardian.

Stephen, Laura Makepeace (1870–1945) The daughter of Leslie STEPHEN and Harriet Marian ("Minny") Thackeray STEPHEN. In letters between Leslie and Julia Prinsep STEPHEN after Minny's death, Laura's father describes her as "perverse," but in the *MAUSOLEUM BOOK* he says she "has remained mentally deficient" (44). Leslie and Julia frequently discussed how to deal with Laura, either by punishing her or by increasing the dosage of medicine administered to her. Louise DeSalvo notes that current biographies of Woolf refer to Laura as "psychotic" (*Impact* 25), commenting that the "view of Laura as an idiot completely absolved Leslie and Julia from blame" (*Impact* 35); Thomas C. Caramagno discusses Laura's "affective disorder" (107–11) as hereditary. Leslie Stephen tried at first to teach Laura to read, but "too often lost my temper and was over-exacting" (*Mausoleum Book* 92). Noel Annan remarks that "the daughter who suffered most at Leslie's hands is usually forgotten" (122). By the late 1880s Laura was living at 22 HYDE PARK GATE apart from the rest of the family. Woolf, in her memoir "OLD BLOOMSBURY," describes the house as having rooms "built to accommodate not one family but three. For besides the three Duckworths and the four Stephens there was also Thackeray's grand-daughter, a vacant-eyed girl whose idiocy was becoming daily more obvious, who could hardly read, who would throw the scissors into the fire" (MOB 182).

Laura was institutionalized some time during the 1890s. In her 1897 diary, Woolf records Stella "away all morning and afternoon at Laura" (PA 13) and also a visit made to see Laura by her father and Stella; this latter visit is referred to by Leslie Stephen also, who wrote "When I saw her the other day, I was pained by her looks and ways" (*Mausoleum Book* 103). According to his will, Leslie designated George

DUCKWORTH and John Waller ("Jack") HILLS as guardians for Laura, but those who paid most attention to her after his death were Anny RITCHIE and Katherine STEPHEN, Leslie's niece. The four Stephen children mortgaged 22 Hyde Park Gate in 1906, raising £489 for Laura's expenses (Love, *Sources* 167), but had virtually no contact with her subsequently. When she died at The Priory Hospital, Southgate, in 1945 the administrators did not even realize she had living relatives and it was some months before Adrian STEPHEN was contacted about her estate (Love, *Sources* 168).

Stephen, Sir Leslie (1832–1904) Woolf's father was, after Matthew ARNOLD, the most important late-Victorian man of letters. He was the son of Jane Catherine Venn and Sir James STEPHEN (1789–1859). Educated at Eton and Trinity Hall, Cambridge, Leslie was ordained a deacon in 1855 and a full-fledged parson in 1859. He returned to Trinity Hall as a junior tutor in 1856 but, finding that he could no longer conduct chapel services in good conscience as he was questioning his faith, he resigned as a tutor in 1862. Although he continued some duties as a fellow his heart was not in it and he left Cambridge permanently in 1864. In 1863 he traveled to the United States at the height of the Civil War, visiting New York, Washington and the battle front. Leslie was a staunch supporter of the North and wrote that he found Lincoln "more like a gentleman to look at than I should have given him credit for from his pictures" (Annan 53). His pamphlet *The Times and the American War* (1865) has been compared by John W. Bicknell to "*exposés* of biased reporting in Vietnam or El Salvador" (Bicknell 60).[17] It was on this trip that he met James Russell LOWELL, who would later be Woolf's "godparent" and who called Leslie the "most lovable of men."

In the 1860s, Leslie published many articles on religious subjects, finding a particularly congenial home in the *Fortnightly Review*. He married Minny (Harriet Marian STEPHEN), William Makepeace THACKERAY's younger daughter, in 1867 and they had one daughter, Laura Makepeace STEPHEN. Minny died on Leslie's birthday in 1875, the same year as Leslie's mother. In 1878 he married Julia Prinsep STEPHEN, the widow of Herbert DUCKWORTH and mother of three children. Leslie and Julia had four children together, Vanessa (BELL), Thoby STEPHEN, Adeline Virginia (WOOLF) and Adrian Leslie STEPHEN.

From 1871 to 1882 Leslie was editor of the *CORNHILL MAGAZINE*, resigning to become the first editor of the *DICTIONARY OF NATIONAL BIOGRAPHY*, a task that would eventually so weaken him that he would be forced to resign in 1890. This "monument to the Victorian age" (Annan 87) eventually comprised sixty-three volumes and included 29,120 lives. Leslie edited the first twenty-six volumes himself and wrote 378 of the biographies. An eminent Victorian, Leslie was close friends with Thomas HARDY, Henry JAMES and George MEREDITH, among many others. The latter depicted Leslie in his novel *The Egoist* as the character Vernon Whitford. Leslie received honorary degrees from Cambridge, Oxford, Edinburgh and Harvard universities and in 1892 succeeded Alfred, Lord TENNYSON as President of the LONDON LIBRARY. In 1902 he was knighted.

Leslie Stephen was also a prodigious walker and in 1881 organized the "Sunday Tramps," a group eventually numbering about sixty men who would gather for what they called a "stroll" of twenty miles or more. On one occasion, when he was a student, he walked the sixty miles from Cambridge to London in twelve hours, arriving in time for dinner. He was a member of the Alpine Club and, from 1868 to 1872, editor of the *Alpine Journal*. He was the first man to climb the Schreckhorn and published a collection of accounts of his Alpine ascents in *The Playground of Europe* (1871), including "The Sunset on Mont Blanc," which, according to Woolf, he considered "the best thing he ever wrote" (CDB 70).

Leslie Stephen was a prolific writer and an important critic, "the pioneer of the sociological study of literature" (Annan 113), "one of the first Englishmen to argue that character and demands of the reading public influenced literary expression" (Annan 317), and, as Katherine C. Hill has pointed out, one of the first to embrace and support Darwin's theories ("Virginia Woolf and Leslie Stephen"). In 1873 he published *Essays on Freethinking and Plainspeaking*, in which he defined his agnosticism, and he followed this work with "An Agnostic's Apology" published in the *Fortnightly* in 1876. Among his other important works were the following: *A History of English Thought in the Eighteenth Century* (1876); *Pope*, in the English Men of Letters series (1880); *The Science of Ethics* (1882); *An Agnostic's Apology* (1893); *Social Rights and Duties* (1896); *Studies of a Biographer* (1898–1902); *The English Utilitarians* (1900); and *English Literature and Society in the Eighteenth Century* (1904). His critical essays for several periodicals were collected in *Hours in a Library* (1874, '76, and '79), a title his daughter took for an essay of her own in 1916 (E2 55). The HOGARTH PRESS published *Some Early Impressions* in 1924. After his death in 1904, F. W. MAITLAND wrote *Life and Letters of Leslie Stephen* (1906) with the assistance of Woolf, who selected letters for the biography and wrote a "Note" of reminiscence (E1 127–30).

Perhaps Woolf's best-known comment on her father is a DIARY entry for November 28, 1928:

[17] Bicknell has edited *The Selected Letters of Leslie Stephen* (London: Macmillan, 1994) in two volumes.

> 1928
> Father's birthday. He would have been 1832 96,
> 96
> yes, today; & could have been 96, like other people one has known; but mercifully was not. His life would have entirely ended mine. What would have happened? No writing, no books;—inconceivable (D3 208).

Her sister Vanessa recalled Woolf suddenly asking her "which I liked best, my father or my mother." When Vanessa answered that she preferred her mother, Woolf "went on to explain why she, on the whole, preferred my father" (*Notes* np). In her memoir "A SKETCH OF THE PAST" Woolf explores what she calls the "ambivalence" she felt toward her father. In a lengthy portrait of him she describes "the sociable father," "father as a writer," and "the tyrant father" (MOB 109–19). Bicknell has remarked that we see Woolf "conducting a recurring struggle to bring into some kind of synthesis the impulse to destroy and the impulse to understand, the claims of anger and the claims of compassionate irony, the compulsion to expose and the need to admire and love" (52–53).

In the "dreadful summer" (MOB 40) following Julia Stephen's death in 1895, Leslie depended utterly upon his step-daughter Stella DUCKWORTH (making demands that Louise DeSalvo has characterized as incestuous [*Impact* 57]). Woolf records in "REMINISCENCES" how her father used Stella up, groaning at the "blow" of her engagement to John Waller ("Jack") HILLS (MOB 50). When Stella died in 1897, Leslie turned his attentions to Vanessa, for which Woolf accuses him in "A Sketch of the Past" of "brutality" (146). When he was dying of abdominal cancer in 1903 he dictated the last paragraph of his *MAUSOLEUM BOOK* to Woolf. In her memoir Woolf wrote that "at the age of sixty-five he was a man in prison, isolated. He had so ignored, or disguised his own feelings that he had no idea of what he was; and no idea of what other people were" (MOB 146). However, she also described her father in her memoir as a lovable man, a thinker she could admire and a man with whom she felt sometimes a particular bond, for she was his favorite.

In 1891 Leslie wrote to Julia that Woolf was "certainly very like me" (Annan 135) and several critics have commented on the similarities between Woolf and her father: both were immensely well-read, both were serious and thoughtful literary critics, and both were extremely sensitive and apt to overwork. Woolf, though, was also a rebel against her father's world: "We were not his children," she wrote in "A Sketch of the Past;" "we were his grandchildren" (MOB 147). He was "not a writer for whom I have a natural taste" (MOB 115). Katherine Hill has suggested that Leslie was instrumental in educating Woolf by preparing reading lists for her (Hill 351–62) and points out "fundamental assumptions about literary criticism" they share (354–55). Woolf wrote a centenary essay for *The Times* (November 28, 1932) entitled "Leslie Stephen, The Philosopher at Home: a Daughter's Memories" (reprinted as "Leslie Stephen" CE4 76–80; CDB 69–75), in which she referred to her father's "allowing a girl of fifteen the free run of a large and unexpurgated library" (CE4 79). Hill's thesis has, however, been challenged in letters from Louise DeSalvo and Alice Fox (*PMLA* 97: 103–05), who do not share Hill's view of Leslie's positive influence.

Leonard WOOLF, who met Leslie in 1901 when he was a student at Cambridge with Thoby Stephen, and found him "formidable," gave his own satirical portrait of his wife's father in the character of Acton Lawrence in his novel *THE WISE VIRGINS* (1914). In his autobiography, Leonard noted that "Mr Ramsay was a pretty good fictional portrait of Leslie Stephen" (LW1 117). Certainly the character of Mr. RAMSAY in Woolf's *TO THE LIGHTHOUSE* owes a great deal to Leslie Stephen and to his daughter's ambivalent feelings about him, although Bicknell has cautioned that "it is impossible to use Mr. Ramsay as a guide to the complex character and work of Leslie Stephen" (54).

Thinking about her novel in 1925, Woolf wrote, "This is going to be fairly short: to have father's character done complete in it; . . . the centre is father's character, sitting in a boat, reciting We perished, each alone, while he crushes a dying mackerel" (D3 18). Woolf's memories of her father were complex, mixed with memories of her half-brother George's incest as Leslie lay "dying three or four storeys lower down of cancer" in 1904 (MOB 182), with memories of her father's tyrannical behavior toward women, of the feelings he shared with her of being "second rate" (MOB 110), of his great guilt after her mother's death, of her happiness with him in ST. IVES and in London, of the sound of books being dropped to the floor of his study as he worked hour after hour. She also read and reread his books and the books that he read aloud to her when she was a child. Although Mr. Ramsay is not an "exact portrait" (L6 517) of her father, it is difficult to separate them.

Stephen, [Julian] Thoby Prinsep (1880–1906) Woolf's older brother, Thoby, went to Clifton and then, in 1899, up to Trinity College, Cambridge, where he joined the MIDNIGHT SOCIETY in his freshman year. At Cambridge, Thoby gained notoriety by writing and circulating a pamphlet arguing against compulsory chapel. Clive BELL called Thoby his "first real friend" and the two of them differed from other members of their set such as Lytton STRACHEY, Leonard WOOLF and Saxon SYDNEY-TURNER in enjoying

"Vanessa, Virginia, and Two of Their Brothers" (Adrian and Thoby Stephen) from Stella Duckworth Hills's album of photographs. Courtesy Henry W. and Albert A. Berg Collection, The New York Public Library, Astor, Lenox and Tilden Foundations.

hunting and sports. Neither Clive nor Thoby was elected to the APOSTLES (something that Leonard Woolf and Lytton Strachey regretted, in Thoby's case, after his death). It was through Thoby—known to his friends as "The Goth" for his "monolithic" good looks—that Leonard Woolf and Clive Bell first met Woolf and Vanessa BELL (whom Lytton Strachey named "the Visigoths") when they visited their brother at Trinity.

Thoby had been a boisterous child. In 1894 while at school at Clifton he tried to throw himself out of a window (Annan 117) and in his *MAUSOLEUM BOOK* Leslie STEPHEN records laconically that "we had our anxieties: as when Thoby, for example, allowed a playful schoolfellow to stick a knife into his femoral artery, and again took to sleepwalking in an alarming way after an attack of influenza" (84). Thoby was a large, awkward young man who was immensely popular. Leonard Woolf wrote that he "had greater personal charm than anyone I have ever known" (LW1 78). Woolf was very close to Thoby, writing to him while he was at school and, when he went on to university, corresponding with him and arguing about William SHAKESPEARE (MOB 138). She later wrote that "it was through him that I first heard about the Greeks" (MOB 125). It was also from Thoby that she first heard about those Cambridge friends of his who were to become so significant in her life as members of the BLOOMSBURY GROUP. In "A SKETCH OF THE PAST" she remembered being taken with George DUCKWORTH and Vanessa to meet Thoby's train when he came home from school for their mother's funeral in 1895; she never forgot "the arch of glass burning at the end of Paddington Station" (MOB 93).

Soon after the Stephen children moved to 46 GORDON SQUARE upon their father's death in 1904, Thoby began to hold regular "at homes" on Thursday evenings as a way of staying in touch with his Cambridge friends. At this time he was reading for the Bar. The Thursday evenings were frequented by the nucleus of the Bloomsbury Group and marked a radical break with the social customs of their parents' generation in that young men and women met and spoke freely with one another. In "OLD BLOOMSBURY" Woolf wrote of these evenings, "Never have I listened so intently to each step and half-step in an argument" (MOB 190).

In September 1906 Woolf, Vanessa and their friend Violet DICKINSON left for Greece, sailing to Patras after traveling through France and Italy. Adrian STEPHEN and Thoby joined them in Olympia after traveling on horseback through Albania. (A photograph of Woolf, Thoby and Vanessa all on donkeys, taken by their brother Adrian, is reproduced in *The Charleston Magazine* 7: 34; it is a scene that suggests Woolf drew on this trip in writing *THE VOYAGE OUT*.) Vanessa fell ill and stayed in Athens with Violet Dickinson while the others went on to Euboea to stay with family friends, the Noels. (While they were there a man was murdered in a nearby field, an event Woolf described in her diary [PA 337]; the doctor who "was little better than a peasant, put into coat and trousers," may have influenced her character Dr. RODRIGUEZ in *The Voyage Out*.) Thoby returned to London in late October while the others went on to CONSTANTINOPLE, where Vanessa was again taken ill. They returned to England on the Orient Express to find that Thoby was in bed with a fever. By then, Violet Dickinson was also ill, and so Woolf and Adrian had to tend Thoby and Vanessa at 46 Gordon Square. After a misdiagnosis of malaria, Thoby was discovered to have typhoid, but the diagnosis came too late and he died on the morning of November 20. Two days later, Vanessa agreed to marry Clive Bell, who had been a constant visitor to the house while his friend was sick. From Ceylon, Leonard Woolf wrote to Lytton Strachey, "It is appalling to think that it is only death that makes it altogether clear what he was to us" (Spotts 123). All through his illness, Woolf kept up a lighthearted tone in her letters to Violet Dickinson, who seemed to be suffering from the same malady as Thoby ("Thoby swears he beats your temperature, and we are a little scornful of the Dickinson typhoid compared to the Stephen typhoid" [L1 247]). Five days after he died she wrote to Violet, "Thoby is going on splendidly. He is very cross with his nurses, because they wont give him mutton chops and beer" (L1 250). Woolf kept up the pretense that Thoby was getting better until mid-December when Violet learned of his death from a review of F. W. MAITLAND's just-published *Life* of Leslie Stephen.

Woolf memorialized her brother in *JACOB'S ROOM* and in *THE WAVES* (in the figure of PERCIVAL). Although *Jacob's Room* also owes much to the memory of the generation slaughtered during World War I, its portrait of Jacob FLANDERS, who goes up to Cambridge in October 1906, draws upon Woolf's sense of her dead brother's character. An example of what her first experimental novel owes to Thoby can be seen by comparing its third chapter, on Jacob's life at Cambridge, with the following description from Leonard Woolf's autobiography: "Late at night in the May term, I like to remember, Lytton, Saxon, Thoby Stephen, Clive Bell, and I would sometimes walk through the Cloisters of Nevilles Court in Trinity and looking out through the bars at the end on to the willows and waters of the Backs, ghostly in the moonlight, listen to the soaring song of innumerable nightingales. And sometimes as we walked back through the majestic cloisters we chanted poetry" (LW1 107). After a night of deep discussions with his undergraduate friends, Jacob walks back to his room: "Back from the Chapel, back from the Hall, back from the Library, came the sound of his footsteps, as if the old stone echoed with magisterial authority: 'The young man—the young man—the young man—back to his rooms' " (JR 46).

In her diary for 1899, Woolf wrote a lengthy description of a moth-collecting expedition ("our Sugar campaign") led by Thoby (PA 144–45). The image of this nocturnal foray into the woods, the younger children led by their elder brother, prominent in *Jacob's Room* (23–24), is also an important symbol for Woolf as Harvena Richter has explained in "Hunting the Moth: Virginia Woolf and the Creative Imagination."

Thoby's death haunted Woolf. In "A Sketch of the Past" she remembered seeing "(after Thoby's death) two great grindstones (as I walked round Gordon Square) and myself between them" (MOB 137). In 1929, as she was beginning to think about *The Waves* (which she initially called "The Moths"), she wrote "How I suffer, & no one knows how I suffer, walking up this street, engaged with my anguish, as I was after Thoby died—alone; fighting something alone" (D3 259–60). When she finished *The Waves* in February 1931, she wrote in her DIARY that she had been "sitting these 15 minutes in a state of glory, & calm, & some tears, thinking of Thoby & if I could write Julian Thoby Stephen 1881–1906 on the first page. I suppose not" (D4 10). Worried that she had been sentimental, Woolf wrote to her sister to explain that she "had him so much in my mind,—I have a dumb rage still at his not being with us always" (L4 391). When she read *The Waves,* Vanessa reassured her sister, writing, "if you wouldn't think me foolish I should say that you have found the 'lullaby capable of singing him to rest' [*Hamlet*]" (L4 391). Woolf was, however, capable of sentimentalizing Thoby: in "A Sketch of the Past" she imagined what he might have become, "Mr Justice Stephen he would be today; with several books to his credit" (MOB 140).

Thoby's premature death was painfully revisited when his namesake, Woolf's nephew Julian BELL, was killed during the SPANISH CIVIL WAR in 1937. Woolf had written of the teenage Julian that "he tells me about boys & masters as Thoby used to" (D2 308), but when Clive Bell suggested after his death that Julian was a "character" like Thoby, Woolf found she could not agree: "For some reason I did not answer, that he was like Thoby. I have always been foolish about that. I did not like any Bell to be like Thoby, partly through snobbishness I suppose; nor do I think that Julian was like Thoby, except in the obvious way that he was young & very fine to look at. I said that Thoby had a natural style, & Julian had not" (QB2 256).

Stephen, Vanessa See BELL, Vanessa.

Sterne, Laurence (1713–68) English writer and curate. His *Tristram Shandy* appeared serially between 1760 and 1767, and *A Sentimental Journey Through France and Italy* in 1768. Woolf reviewed *The Life and Times of Laurence Sterne* by Wilbur L. Cross for the *TIMES LITERARY SUPPLEMENT* in 1909 ("Sterne" E1 280–88; CE3 86–93), using the review for some of her earliest comments on the relation between a writer's life and a writer's work. In 1922 she reviewed *Sterne's Eliza* by Arnold Wright and William Lutley Sclater, a book about Eliza Draper, whom Sterne had loved ("Eliza and Sterne" E3 346–52; CE3 100–04). This review also contains reflections on biography, Woolf commenting on how changing standards of morality influence biographers' treatment of their subject. "Sterne's Ghost," a 1925 article for the *NATION & ATHENAEUM* (CE3 94–99), is a good example of Woolf's frequent practice of writing impressionistically to draw a reader imaginatively into a piece. In 1928 she wrote "A *Sentimental Journey*" for the *New York Herald Tribune* (CE1 95–101), which was reprinted, slightly revised, as "The *Sentimental Journey*" in the *COMMON READER: SECOND SERIES* and again as the introduction to the World's Classics edition of Sterne's book in 1928. There, Woolf writes of Sterne as a "forerunner of the moderns" in his interest in "silence rather than speech" (CE1 98) and notes how he transfers the reader's interest "from the outer to the inner" (CE1 97). Sterne is mentioned in the ironic preface to *ORLANDO* as among those writers to whom anyone writing is perpetually indebted.

Stewkley, Mrs. A servant in ORLANDO's household.

Stiles, Matty The caretaker of Sir Digby and Lady Eugénie PARGITER's house after their death in *THE YEARS*.

Stillman Family The three Stillman daughters, friends of Stella DUCKWORTH's, comprised one of the triplets of female beauty that fertilized the tea table at 22 HYDE PARK GATE at the end of the nineteenth century (MOB 165). Maria Stillman (1844–1927), a Pre-Raphaelite painter, and William James Stillman (1828–1901), an American painter and special correspondent for *The Times,* lived at 12 Campden Hill Gardens. W. James Stillman, author of *Autobiography of a Journalist* (1901), was a good friend of Leslie STEPHEN (*Mausoleum Book* 18). With the Stillmans lived their three daughters: Lisa, a portrait painter, Effie, a sculptress, and their eldest daughter, Bella. Mr. Stillman's first wife, Laura Mack, had committed suicide in 1869. Bella's daughter Peggy also lived with them; she was the widow of John Henry Middleton (1846–1896), Slade Professor of Fine Art at Cambridge and Art Director of the Victoria and Albert Museum from 1892 until his suicide in 1896. Woolf would often visit the Stillmans with Stella, and would sometimes go to see Lisa and Effie in their studio, "a comfortable little room at the top of a house opposite No. 12" (PA 39).

***Stories of the East* (1921)** Three stories by Leonard WOOLF hand-set and published by the HOGARTH PRESS in 1921 with a woodcut by Dora CARRINGTON on the cover. The collection was praised in a review for the *Daily Mail* by Hamilton Fyfe (who said "Pearls and Swine" would "rank with the great stories of the world" [LW2 250]), and it was also reviewed favorably in the *TIMES LITERARY SUPPLEMENT,* leading to a rush of orders for the book. The three stories—"A Tale Told by Moonlight," "Pearls and Swine" and "The Two Brahmins"—are all set in Ceylon and concern caste and race differences and imperialism. Selma Meyerowitz has summarized the stories (Meyerowitz 44–53), noting that the treatment of romantic love "set against the reality of caste and racial differences" in "A Tale Told by Moonlight" was probably influenced by Leonard's own relationships with women while he was a colonial administrator in Ceylon.

Strachey, Alix (née Sargant-Florence) (1892–1973) Psychoanalyst and translator who married James STRACHEY in 1920. According to Anne Olivier BELL, Woolf first met her when James brought her to dinner in 1916, but in a reminiscence of Woolf, Alix recalled first meeting her at a party given by Katherine COX, with whom she had been at NEWNHAM COLLEGE (1911–1914) (Noble 111). As Woolf got to know her, she was struck by Alix's melancholic demeanor, commenting on the "sepulchral despair" that seemed only just beneath the surface of her character (D1 63). In 1917 Alix came to work as an assistant at the HOGARTH PRESS but lasted only two hours, finding the work too boring. She then became Leonard WOOLF's research assistant as he worked on *Empire and Commerce in Africa* (1918). Woolf frequently saw Alix at the 1917 CLUB.

In 1920, James and Alix Strachey became the first couple to be analyzed by Sigmund FREUD in Vienna. In 1924–25, Alix went to Berlin to be analyzed by Freud's disciple Karl Abraham, and there she became an ardent supporter of Melanie Klein (Abel 9). Perry Meisel and Walter Kendrick have edited the letters that Alix and James wrote each other during this year apart (the introduction to their *Bloomsbury/Freud* contains biographical details about Alix). The Hogarth Press published her translation of Klein's *Psycho-analysis of Children* in 1932. Alix was James Strachey's assistant and collaborator on his translation of Freud's complete works, published by the Hogarth Press.

In her reminiscence of Woolf, Alix commented on the fact that Woolf had never undergone psychoanalysis and remarked that she disagreed with James that it would have been beneficial because, in her opinion, Woolf was a manic-depressive whose condition would not have improved without the use of drugs (Noble 116–17).

Strachey, Dorothy See BUSSY, Dorothy.

Strachey, James Beaumont (1887–1967) Translator and psychoanalyst. James went up to Trinity College, Cambridge, in 1905 and was elected to the APOSTLES in 1906, his way prepared by his brilliant elder brother Lytton STRACHEY. After a period as drama critic for the *ATHENAEUM,* James approached Ernest Jones, founder of the Institute of Psycho-Analysis in London, about becoming an analyst. Woolf remarked in her DIARY in November 1919 that James "proposes to earn his living as an exponent of Freud in Harley Street. For one thing you can dispense with a degree" (D1 221). Following their marriage in 1920, James and Alix STRACHEY went to Vienna, where they became the first couple to be analyzed by Sigmund FREUD (see Meisel and Kendrick 15–29). They also began that year what would be a lifelong work of translating Freud's writings. The Stracheys' translation of Freud's "A Child is Being Beaten" was published in the *International Journal of Psycho-Analysis* in 1920. In 1924, James suggested to Leonard WOOLF that the HOGARTH PRESS take over the publications of the Institute of Psycho-Analysis, and thus the Press

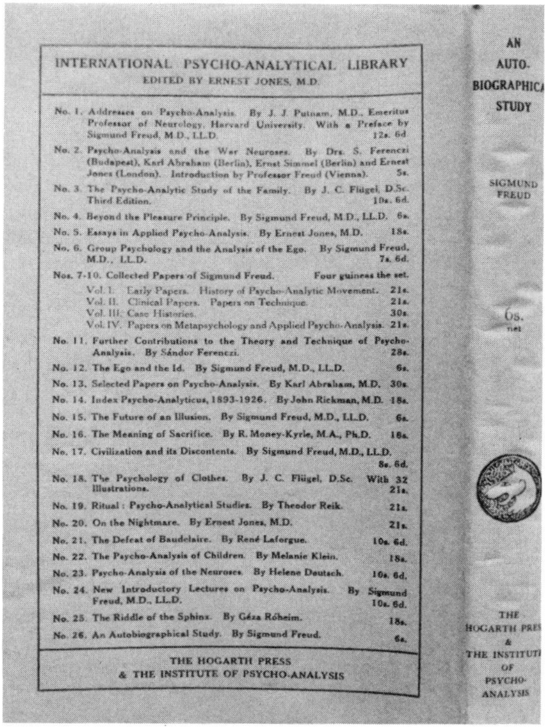

INTERNATIONAL PSYCHO-ANALYTICAL LIBRARY
EDITED BY ERNEST JONES, M.D.

No. 1. Addresses on Psycho-Analysis. By J. J. Putnam, M.D., Emeritus Professor of Neurology, Harvard University. With a Preface by Sigmund Freud, M.D., LL.D. 12s. 6d.

No. 2. Psycho-Analysis and the War Neuroses. By Drs. S. Ferenczi (Budapest), Karl Abraham (Berlin), Ernst Simmel (Berlin) and Ernest Jones (London). Introduction by Professor Freud (Vienna). 5s.

No. 3. The Psycho-Analytic Study of the Family. By J. C. Flügel, D.Sc. Third Edition. 10s. 6d.

No. 4. Beyond the Pleasure Principle. By Sigmund Freud, M.D., LL.D. 6s.

No. 5. Essays in Applied Psycho-Analysis. By Ernest Jones, M.D. 18s.

No. 6. Group Psychology and the Analysis of the Ego. By Sigmund Freud, M.D., LL.D. 7s. 6d.

Nos. 7-10. Collected Papers of Sigmund Freud. Four guineas the set.
Vol. I. Early Papers. History of Psycho-Analytic Movement. 21s.
Vol. II. Clinical Papers. Papers on Technique. 21s.
Vol. III. Case Histories. 30s.
Vol. IV. Papers on Metapsychology and Applied Psycho-Analysis. 21s.

No. 11. Further Contributions to the Theory and Technique of Psycho-Analysis. By Sándor Ferenczi. 28s.

No. 12. The Ego and the Id. By Sigmund Freud, M.D., LL.D. 6s.

No. 13. Selected Papers on Psycho-Analysis. By Karl Abraham, M.D. 30s.

No. 14. Index Psycho-Analyticus, 1893-1926. By John Rickman, M.D. 18s.

No. 15. The Future of an Illusion. By Sigmund Freud, M.D., LL.D. 6s.

No. 16. The Meaning of Sacrifice. By R. Money-Kyrle, M.A., Ph.D. 18s.

No. 17. Civilization and its Discontents. By Sigmund Freud, M.D., LL.D. 8s. 6d.

No. 18. The Psychology of Clothes. By J. C. Flügel, D.Sc. With 32 Illustrations. 21s.

No. 19. Ritual: Psycho-Analytical Studies. By Theodor Reik. 21s.

No. 20. On the Nightmare. By Ernest Jones, M.D. 21s.

No. 21. The Defeat of Baudelaire. By René Laforgue. 10s. 6d.

No. 22. The Psycho-Analysis of Children. By Melanie Klein. 18s.

No. 23. Psycho-Analysis of the Neuroses. By Helene Deutsch. 10s. 6d.

No. 24. New Introductory Lectures on Psycho-Analysis. By Sigmund Freud, M.D., LL.D. 10s. 6d.

No. 25. The Riddle of the Sphinx. By Géza Róheim. 18s.

No. 26. An Autobiographical Study. By Sigmund Freud. 6s.

THE HOGARTH PRESS
& THE INSTITUTE OF PSYCHO-ANALYSIS

AN
AUTO-
BIOGRAPHICA
STUDY
SIGMUND
FREUD
6s.
net
THE
HOGARTH PRES
&
THE INSTITUT
OF
PSYCHO-
ANALYSIS

Sigmund Freud, An Autobiographical Study.
The back of the dust jacket of the Hogarth Press first edition (1935). The Hogarth Press became Freud's official publisher in English after taking over publication of the papers of the International Psycho-Analytical Institute in 1924. The International Psycho-Analytical Library series was edited by Dr. Ernest Jones, who was Freud's first biographer.

became Freud's English publisher. In 1953, James began his translation and editing of the *Standard Edition of the Complete Psychological Works of Sigmund Freud,* completed in 1966, in which year he won the Schlegel-Tieck prize for translation. In 1956, Leonard Woolf and James, who was his brother Lytton's literary executor, edited *VIRGINIA WOOLF & LYTTON STRACHEY: LETTERS.*

Strachey, Lady Jane Maria (née Grant) (1840–1928) Mother of ten children including Lytton STRACHEY, and Duncan GRANT's aunt, she epitomized the Victorian and Anglo-Indian upper class of England (Boyd 48–75). When Sir Richard Strachey retired from active service in the (British) Indian Army in 1872, he and Lady Jane settled in London, first on Clapham Common, and later at Lancaster Gate. She began to publish in the 1880s, first *Lay Texts for the Young in English and French* (1887) and in 1893, *Nursery Lyrics.* She edited an anthology of English poetry, *Poets on Poets,* in 1894, and also wrote poetry herself. Lady Strachey was on the executive committee of the National Union of Women's Suffrage Societies, for which she wrote many pamphlets, and in 1907 she marched beside Millicent Garret FAWCETT at the head of the first major march for women's SUFFRAGE organized by her daughter Philippa STRACHEY. In 1919 she moved to 51 GORDON SQUARE with her daughters Philippa and Marjorie STRACHEY. In 1928, Woolf eulogized Lady Strachey in the *NATION & ATHENAEUM* (BP 208–11).

Strachey, (Giles) Lytton (1880–1932) Biographer and critic whose *EMINENT VICTORIANS* (1918) revolutionized the writing of biography and brought him fame. The Strachey family was part of what Leonard WOOLF described as "an intellectual aristocracy of the middle class" (LW1 119), and Strachey's nine brothers and sisters, as well as their parents, Sir Richard and Lady Jane Maria STRACHEY (Duncan GRANT's aunt), were all remarkable for their intellectual achievement. In 1899 Strachey went up to Trinity College, Cambridge, where his contemporaries in-

Lytton Strachey, *1917, writing* Eminent Victorians *at Durbins (17¾ x 15¾"). Roger Fry. Courtesy of Harry Ransom Humanities Research Center, The University of Texas at Austin. Lady Strachey, Lytton's mother, rented Durbins, Roger Fry's house, for a year in 1916, and it was probably on one of Lytton's visits there that Fry painted him (Richardson 107).*

cluded Clive BELL, Thoby STEPHEN, Saxon SYDNEY-TURNER and Leonard Woolf. He became Leonard's closest friend at this time and, with the others, was in the MIDNIGHT CLUB and contributed to a privately published collection of poems, *EUPHROSYNE.* Strachey was elected to the APOSTLES in 1902 and was influential in giving that society the homosexual character which prevailed in the first decade of the century. In a 1932 tribute to Strachey in the *NEW STATESMAN AND NATION,* Leonard Woolf described his "dominating intellectual influence upon the intellectuals of his generation" (Rosenbaum, *Bloomsbury Group* 179).

Woolf first met Strachey at Cambridge in 1901 through her brother Thoby, and in 1905 he was a regular visitor on the "Thursday Evenings" instituted by Thoby to maintain contact with his Cambridge friends. "Thoby out to dine; Sydney Turner & Strachey after dinner, & we talked till 12," Woolf wrote in March 1905 (PA 245). Leonard had left for Ceylon in 1904, where he would remain until 1911, and it was primarily through letters from Strachey that he kept abreast of what his university friends were doing. It was Strachey who told Leonard of Thoby Stephen's death and Vanessa BELL's engagement to Clive in November 1906. On the day Vanessa agreed to marry Clive, two days after Thoby's death, Woolf wrote to "Mr Strachey" inviting him to visit her and her sister whenever he wished. She wrote to Violet DICKINSON in 1907 that Walter HEADLAM and Strachey had come to tea, and that she hated "pouring out tea, and talking like a lady" (L1 284).

Strachey also kept Leonard informed about his love affairs, lamenting in 1908 when John Maynard KEYNES won the affections of Duncan Grant, with whom Strachey was infatuated. He encouraged Leonard to propose by letter to Woolf because she was the only woman clever enough to marry him. Two weeks after writing thus to Leonard in February 1909, Strachey wrote again to tell Leonard that he had proposed to Woolf himself, but, realizing this was a mistake, had got out of it "before the end of the conversation" (Spotts 147); both apparently realized their mistake immediately. By this time, however, Woolf and Strachey's friendship was firm and their brief engagement caused neither of them any further embarrassment. Woolf wrote to Molly MACCARTHY in 1912 that she would not "float into a bloodless alliance with Lytton—though he is in some ways perfect as a friend, only he's a female friend" (L1 492). Vanessa Bell had written to her sister in 1908 that she would like Strachey as a brother-in-law, but saw the only chance of this happening being his falling in love with their brother Adrian STEPHEN (Marler 67). Woolf would recall her "engagement" several times throughout her life, writing in 1924, "Oh I was right to be in love with him 12 or 15 years ago" (D2 317). In 1929 she compared Strachey and Leonard, and concluded that had she married Strachey she would "never have written anything. . . . He checks & inhibits in the most curious way" (D3 273).

In June 1912, Strachey received a postcard that said simply "Ha! Ha!" and was signed Virginia Stephen and Leonard Woolf: it was the announcement of their imminent marriage (L1 501). Leonard had immediately sought out his Cambridge friends on returning from Ceylon in 1911, and had found many of them living in BLOOMSBURY. He found also that their relations with one another were much less formal than when he had left seven years earlier, something that Clive Bell would later credit Strachey with instigating through his insistence on using first names. Strachey's social iconoclasm was also described by Woolf in her memoir "OLD BLOOMSBURY." Seeing a stain on Vanessa's dress, Strachey inquired whether it was "Semen?" (MOB 195–96) and thus inaugurated a free attitude to sexual matters that soon became associated in the public mind as characteristic of the BLOOMSBURY GROUP.

Woolf had read Strachey's letters to Leonard and commented in 1912 that the letters were "amazing!" "My God," she wrote Strachey, "what an insight I have now into that cosmogony" (L1 491). It was an insight she used in writing her first novel, *THE VOYAGE OUT,* which Phyllis Rose has described as "the book of Virginia and the clever young men—even more specifically, the book of Virginia and Lytton Strachey" (Rose 58). Woolf drew on her friend's demeanor and appearance in creating St. John HIRST in the novel, and Strachey praised it when he read it in 1915.

During World War I, Strachey was one of the CONSCIENTIOUS OBJECTORS at GARSINGTON and wrote pamphlets for the No Conscription Fellowship, of which Adrian Stephen was Secretary. Woolf found him "one of the most supple of our friends . . . the most sympathetic & understanding to talk to" (D1 89). The word "intimate" frequently occurs in her DIARY descriptions of Strachey during the war years and 1920s, but as each developed separate circles of friends, they began to see less of each other. Strachey moved in 1917 to the Mill House at TIDMARSH, Berkshire, with Dora CARRINGTON, who had fallen in love with him in 1915–16. When Ralph PARTRIDGE fell in love with Carrington and married her in 1921, he moved into the Mill House, and the three of them remained together until Strachey's death in 1932 at HAM SPRAY (where they had moved in 1924). Strachey was strongly attracted to Partridge, but, unlike most others of their circle, Partridge was exclusively heterosexual. Woolf often found herself involved as a confidante in Strachey's amours—as she did with many of her friends—but could become exasperated at the "atmosphere of buggery" in which he lived (D3 299). In 1930 she noted in her diary, "I seldom see Lytton," though she added that when they were alone together, their old intimacy was intact.

Strachey's *Landmarks in French Literature* (1912) presaged his lifelong passion for French literature and culture but had received little attention. *Eminent Victorians,* dedicated to H. T. J. NORTON, had brought Strachey fame and a reputation as an iconoclast. In her essay "CHARACTER IN FICTION," Woolf grouped Strachey with E. M. FORSTER, D. H. LAWRENCE, James JOYCE and T. S. ELIOT as "Georgians" who were in revolt against their predecessors. She noted that in *Eminent Victorians* and *Queen Victoria* "the effort and strain of writing against the grain and current of the times is visible" (E3 435). Like Leonard, though, Woolf felt that Strachey's writing did not live up to the promise of his dazzling undergraduate years: she called it "superbly brilliant journalism" (D1 236). When *Queen Victoria* (which Strachey dedicated to Woolf) was highly praised by reviewers in 1921, she noted that "altogether he's a solid celebrity, one of our leading writers" (D2 110), not necessarily regarding this as positive. Leonard "never rated his achievement as very high" (Spotts 566) and in his *New Statesman* article, written after Strachey's death in 1932, commented on Strachey's "romanticism and disregard for detailed accuracy" which, Leonard said, "account both for the enormous effect which the iconoclasm of *Eminent Victorians* had upon a generation and for the reaction against him as a biographer and historian which has been so marked in the last few years" (Rosenbaum, *Bloomsbury Group* 181).

Woolf also disliked Strachey's *Elizabeth and Essex: A Tragic History* (1928), his account of the affair between Queen Elizabeth I and the Earl of Essex, calling it a "lively superficial meretricious book" (D3 208). Alice Fox discusses Woolf's response to Strachey's *Elizabeth and Essex,* suggesting she was alienated by Strachey's "facile psychologizing" about aspects of Elizabeth's life that were similar to Woolf's own (i.e., sexual abuse), and Carolyn Heilbrun has drawn attention to the similarities between Strachey's book and Woolf's *ORLANDO* as representations of ANDROGYNY. About six months after its publication, Woolf told Strachey why she did not like *Elizabeth and Essex,* leading to an interesting discussion of the envy she felt toward other writers and her superficial pleasure when those she respected did poor work (D3 233–34). Her comments on Strachey's writing were undoubtedly colored by her rivalry with him. In 1919 she compared Stracheys with Stephens and, making extravagant claims for her own family, found the former lacking because they had not added to the world "an Omega, a Post Impressionist movement, nor even a country cottage, a Brunswick Square, or a printing press" (D1 236). Strachey, Carrington and Partridge's plans to establish the Tidmarsh Press in 1923, supposedly as a rival to the HOGARTH PRESS, were not realized (D2 232). Even in buying the Mill House, Woolf noted, Strachey had had to be "propelled from behind" by Carrington (D1 236).

Despite these critical remarks, Woolf's affection for Strachey was deep and she was devastated by his premature death from cancer in 1932. On the day he died, but before she received the news, she wrote in her diary that the death of her "old serpent" would mean "the globe of the future perpetually smashed" (D4 61). She and Leonard had sobbed on Christmas Eve 1931 when they first learned he was seriously ill. The blow of Strachey's death was compounded soon afterward when Carrington, as her friends had suspected she would, killed herself.

After Strachey's death, his brother James, his literary executor, found "masses of poems and plays" and "boxes upon boxes of letters" (L5 45) that Woolf advised him to have typed up and circulated among his friends. James demurred, saying that his brother had been very unpleasant about his friends in his letters, but, Woolf wrote her sister, "as we all do this, I dont see that it matters" (L5 45). After World War II, Strachey and Woolf came to represent what people most disliked about Bloomsbury, and were seen by the establishment as elitist intellectual backstabbers.

Michael Holroyd's biography of Strachey was "the first frank, extended biography of a member of the Bloomsbury Group" (Rosenbaum, *Bloomsbury Group* 181) and concurred with the general anti-Bloomsbury sentiment of opinion in England. The biography was published in two volumes, *The Unknown Years* (1967) and *The Years of Achievement* (1968). Leonard Woolf reviewed both volumes in the *New Statesman* and criticized the first in particular for lacking humor and taking Strachey too seriously. Leonard also drew attention to the "often devastating criticism" of James Strachey's footnotes to the biography (*New Statesman* October 6, 1967: 438). Holroyd later revised the biography for a one-volume paperback edition, *Lytton Strachey: A Biography* (1971), separating biographical chapters from those commenting on Strachey's writing, and publishing the latter as *Lytton Strachey and the Bloomsbury Group: His Work, Their Influence* (1971).

Strachey, Marjorie Colville ("Gumbo") (1882–1964) Teacher, suffragette and writer, the youngest of the Strachey daughters. She was part of the group called NEO-PAGANS by Woolf and others, and is the subject of paintings by Vanessa BELL and Duncan GRANT (notably his *Le Crime et le Châtiment* [1909]). In 1914 she fell in love with the Liberal politician Josiah Wedgwood, whose wife had left him and their seven children in 1913; he married the children's governess in 1919. Strachey's novel *The Counterfeiters* (1927), which she discussed with Woolf in 1920, is about her affair. In 1937, the HOGARTH PRESS published her

Mazzini, Garibaldi & Cavour in its World-Makers & World-Shakers series.

Strachey, (Joan) Pernel (1876–1951) Principal from 1923 to 1941 of NEWNHAM COLLEGE, Cambridge, where she had been a Tutor, Director of Studies, Vice-Principal, and also Lecturer in Modern Languages. Woolf wrote in 1918 that she imagined that Pernel's "bachelor life, with many women friends, & a great many books, & lectures to prepare on French literature" suited her perfectly (D1 189). In October 1928, Woolf stayed with her when she gave the lecture to the Newnham Arts Society on which *A ROOM OF ONE'S OWN* was partly based.

Strachey, Philippa ("Pippa") (1872–1968) Political activist who organized the first major march in London for women's SUFFRAGE on February 9, 1907, "known as the Mud March, from the state of the weather" (Boyd 73). The march (which Leonard WOOLF's sisters joined [Spotts 125]) was headed by Millicent Garrett FAWCETT; Pippa's mother, Lady Maria Jane STRACHEY, walked beside her. Pippa Strachey was Secretary of the London-National Society for Women's Service from 1914 to 1951 and founded its Library in Marsham Street, of which Woolf was an ardent supporter. In 1931, she invited Woolf and Ethel SMYTH to address the Society, and Woolf's speech became the inspiration for *THE PARGITERS,* leading to *THE YEARS,* and also to *THREE GUINEAS.* In the latter work Woolf addresses many of the issues which Pippa worked on her entire life, and on its publication Woolf wrote that Pippa's enthusiastic response, together with that of her sister-in-law Ray STRACHEY, was a "prime relief" (D5 149).

Strachey, Rachel (Ray) Conn Costelloe (1887–1940) The sister of Karin COSTELLOE (who married Woolf's brother Adrian STEPHEN) and daughter of Mary Berenson, whose second husband was Bernard Berenson. Mary had run away from Frank Costelloe, and her daughters were brought up after their father's death by Mary's mother, Hannah Whitall Smith, a Philadelphia Quaker and author of many religious books. Ray Strachey was a student at NEWNHAM COLLEGE, but her work for women's SUFFRAGE took up much of her time and she was an unsuccessful student. She married Lytton STRACHEY's brother Oliver in 1911 (as his second wife) and stood for Parliament in 1919 and 1922 but failed to win a seat. She was editor of *The Common Cause,* and from 1920 to 1923 was editor of the *WOMAN'S LEADER AND THE COMMON CAUSE* (in which she published Woolf's article on "The Plumage Bill" [D2 Appendix II]). She also founded the Women's Employment Federation. From 1916 to 1921 she was honorary Parliamentary Secretary of the National Union of Women's Suffrage Societies, and from 1916 to 1934 she chaired the Women's Service Bureau. She also advised Lady Nancy Astor when she entered Parliament, and wrote speeches for her. Ray Strachey wrote many books, including *The Cause* (1928), a history of the suffrage movement which Woolf referred to in writing both *A ROOM OF ONE'S OWN* and *THREE GUINEAS,* as well as *Millicent Garrett Fawcett* (1931). In 1936, she edited for the HOGARTH PRESS *Our Freedom and Its Results by Five Women,* contributing an article herself on changes in employment.

Strand Frequently mentioned in Woolf's novels, the Strand is one of London's major streets and runs from Charing Cross, near Trafalgar Square, to Fleet Street, close to the river Thames. In *MRS. DALLOWAY,* Elizabeth DALLOWAY takes a bus from Victoria Street up the Strand for an extra penny fare. In *THE VOYAGE OUT* Terence HEWET wishes he could be walking along the Strand "past the shops with all the new books in them" (TVO 301). In *NIGHT AND DAY* it is mentioned frequently as the five principal characters walk a great deal in London. KINGSWAY intersects with the Strand via Aldwych, often providing a route for Ralph DENHAM as he walks from his office in Lincoln's Inn Fields (ND 129).

Stream-of-Consciousness See MODERNISM.

Streatfield, Reverend G. W. Character in *BETWEEN THE ACTS.* At the end of the annual village pageant, he attempts an interpretation of what its writer, Miss LA TROBE, may have meant and reminds the audience that its purpose was to raise money for lighting in the church. His speech is interrupted by a flight of war planes (193).

"Street Haunting: A London Adventure" (CE4 155–66; DM 20–36) An essay by Woolf published in the *YALE REVIEW* in October 1927 and reprinted in a limited, signed edition of 500 copies in 1930 by the Westgate Press of San Francisco. In a letter to Helen McAfee, editor of the *Yale Review,* Woolf agrees to a change in the title of her essay—perhaps the addition of the phrase following the colon—as an improvement (L3 410).

The essay concerns "the greatest pleasure of town life in winter—rambling the streets of London" (CE4 155). The narrator, on the pretext of buying a pencil, walks in the twilight and observes various scenes: a dwarf trying on shoes, "derelicts" in the streets. She visits a second-hand bookstore, and lingers on a bridge over the river Thames, where she observes two lovers. On the way, she muses about the "true self" in language that foreshadows a similar musing in *ORLANDO,* and also prefigures *THE WAVES* in its concern with London and the city's influence on the "self." In the stationer's where she buys her pencil, the narrator senses immediately as she enters that the couple who own the shop have been quarreling, but their quarrel is silently made up as they help her choose a pencil. Finally, she returns to the familiarity and security of her own house.

Susan Squier compares "Street Haunting" with a much earlier essay of Woolf's, "Street Music," published in 1905 in the *NATIONAL REVIEW* (E1 27–32). Squier finds that the "real subject" of "Street Haunting" is "the acrobatics of a writer's consciousness as well as the spectacle of contemporary city life that the walk reveals" (Squier, *Virginia Woolf* 46). She describes an oscillation of viewpoint between "insider" and "outsider," arguing that the narrator's viewpoint is that of an outsider "only as long as it will not force her to examine her own privilege" (Squier 46). Squier finds "Street Haunting" significant "because it makes use of an urban situation to initiate a consideration of the origins of social stratification and the impact of gender, class, and material possessions upon one's sense of self" (Squier 49), but she also criticizes the essay for failing to push the analysis it begins further and sees the narrative as a "male-identified perspective" (51). Pamela Caughie, on the other hand, criticizes Squier's reading of the essay as implicating her "in a position she would have Woolf repudiate" (Caughie 132) and says that the essay is entirely described "from the writer's point of view," a perspective that is concerned only to dramatize what is seen, not to judge it morally: "The narrator is one who participates and passes on, not one who stands outside and condemns from her secure, rightful position" (Caughie 132). The multiple, indeterminate "self" of the essay is valorized, argues Caughie, not that fixed self which must, as "Street Haunting" puts it "always . . . do something or other" (CE4 164).

Stretton, Mrs. Mentioned in *JACOB'S ROOM* at Elizabeth DURRANT's party, where she talks with Mr. BURLEY.

"String Quartet, The" (SF 132–35) A short fiction published in *MONDAY OR TUESDAY* (accompanied by a woodcut by Vanessa BELL) and in *A HAUNTED HOUSE*. Woolf was "astounded" in 1925 when T. S. ELIOT singled out this piece as one he particularly admired (D2 125). Peter Jacobs remarks that this is "the only short story in which the overall presence of music is thematically important" (242) and notes that Avrom Fleishman has pointed out that Woolf "successfully tailored her prose to the alternating musical pattern of the classical Mozart quartet played by the musicians" (Jacobs 244).

Stuart, Mother Mentioned in *JACOB'S ROOM* as the "confidante" of FLORINDA, she is "dirty lodging-house wallpaper" behind the "chastity" of Florinda (JR 78).

Stubbs ORLANDO's gardener from the Elizabethan beginning to the twentieth-century end of the novel.

Sturgeon, Johnnie Mentioned in *JACOB'S ROOM* carrying a large, mysterious parcel on Oxford Street.

Suffrage In notes in her 1904–05 DIARY, Woolf "reveals that she was already thinking about women's rights in historical terms" (Zwerdling 211). Woolf notes the importance of John Stuart Mill's *Subjection of Women* (1869) and Alfred, Lord TENNYSON's "The Princess" (1847) as giving impetus to the movement for women's equality, and also jots down the names of the women's colleges at Cambridge University—GIRTON and NEWNHAM—and Oxford University—Lady Margaret Hall and Somerville (PA 279). Alex Zwerdling also remarks that Woolf's own direct involvement in the cause of women's suffrage can be precisely dated to a letter she wrote Janet CASE on January 1, 1910, asking if it would be "any use if I spent an afternoon or two weekly in addressing envelopes for the Adult Suffragists?" (L1 421).

Woolf's most explicit references in her fiction to the cause of gaining the vote for women come in *NIGHT AND DAY* and *THE YEARS*. In *Night and Day,* Mary DATCHET works for a suffrage organization called the "S.G.S." In *The Years,* Rose PARGITER (whom Jane Marcus has suggested is based on Ethel SMYTH) attends what is probably a meeting of the Women's Social and Political Union (W.S.P.U) in the "1910" chapter and in "1911" is arrested for throwing a brick. In *THREE GUINEAS,* also, Woolf refers extensively to the history of the struggle for women's equal professional opportunities, suffrage and economic independence. That history is recounted in *The Cause* by Ray STRACHEY, published in 1928, from which Woolf quotes in *A ROOM OF ONE'S OWN* (AROO 20; 56).

The Cause tells the story of the nineteenth- and early-twentieth-century pioneers of the women's movement such as Emily Davies (who founded Girton College), Florence NIGHTINGALE, Sophia JEX-BLAKE, Elizabeth Garrett and Barbara Leigh Smith BODICHON. As Sandra Gilbert and Susan Gubar have written, "women's invasion of new fields and lands was directly associated with the most ferocious battle between the sexes: the suffrage struggle. Occupying the attention of thinkers on both sides of the Atlantic between 1847 and 1920, this conflict, as amply documented by historians, was always intensely heated and often became brutally physical" (*War* 17–18). In *A Room,* Woolf's narrator remarks that the Suffrage campaign no doubt "roused in men an extraordinary desire for self-assertion" (AROO 99). The turn from nonviolence to militant activism came in July 1909 when the suffragettes of the W.S.P.U. (under the leadership of Emmeline Pankhurst [1858–1928]) began their campaign of smashing windows and, when arrested and jailed, going on hunger strikes. Zwerdling writes that what had begun as "a comprehensive movement of thought about women's nature and status—legal, educational, psychological, economic, professional, marital, and political—had been turned into a much narrower cause deliberately centered on a single issue: the vote" (Zwerdling 214). He notes that between 1911 and 1914, "the movement gradually split in two, with Christabel Pankhurst [Emmeline's daughter] taking control of the W.S.P.U. and her sister Sylvia organizing the working women of London's East End in a rival organization" (Zwerdling 234).

Ray Strachey describes the "first organisation of the Women's Movement" as being that formed by Barbara Bodichon in 1855 (the same year that in the United States Susan B. Anthony and Elizabeth Cady Stanton organized the Seneca Falls Convention). Bodichon, a cousin of Florence NIGHTINGALE and friend of Harriet MARTINEAU, was George ELIOT's model for Romola. Her mother had died young and her enlightened father gave each of his children £300 per year when they came of age, thus putting his daughter in a unique position for a mid-nineteenth-century woman. She set about reforming English property law, publishing a popular pamphlet entitled "Brief Summary in Plain Language of the Most Important Laws Concerning Women." A petition to reform property law that Bodichon began circulating in 1855 gathered 26,000 signatures in a year and was presented to both houses of Parliament. In 1865, Bodichon joined Emily Davies in supporting the election of John Stuart Mill. The following year, she worked on organizing a petition for women's suffrage that Mill would present to Parliament. The petition committee was, according to Strachey, the first of all the suffrage committees to be established (Strachey, *The Cause* 105).

The petition presented by Mill in 1866 was not signed by George Eliot or Florence Nightingale, evidence of the diversity of opinions on not only the proper role of women but also on the best way to achieve their goals. In 1889, Woolf's mother, Julia Prinsep STEPHEN, joined the wives of several other prominent men in signing "An Appeal Against Female Suffrage" published in *Nineteenth Century*; among other signatories were Mrs. Matthew Arnold; Christina ROSSETTI; Beatrice Potter (better known by her married name, Beatrice WEBB), who later changed her mind; and Mrs. Humphry WARD. The latter was the president in 1908 of the Anti-Suffrage Society of Women (Strachey, *The Cause* 319; and see Denise Riley 73f.).

In 1903, some activists who had been working among female factory-workers in Manchester decided to form a new suffrage society, the Women's Social and Political Union, under the leadership of Emmeline Pankhurst. "The Militant Suffrage Movement, which attained worldwide celebrity and became a tremendous legend, began in a simple and almost unpremeditated fashion" that year (Strachey *The Cause* 291). The period 1904–15 saw increasing militancy by the suffragettes, of whom many disapproved. In 1911, "Mrs. Pankhurst and two companions broke the windows of No. 10 Downing Street [the British Prime Minister's residence], and simultaneously hundreds of women in other parts of London smashed the plate-glass windows of shop fronts, post offices, and Government departments" (Strachey, *The Cause* 322).

The most comprehensive account of Woolf's involvement in suffrage and other women's organizations is given by Naomi Black in several articles. In "Virginia Woolf and the Women's Movement," Black explains that the organizations with which Woolf was associated were "social feminist ones" as distinct from organizations dedicated to equal rights feminism, which is premised on the essential sameness of men and women. "The majority of the British suffrage movement accepted social feminist arguments, even if sometimes accompanied by equal rights ones" (Black 183). Black identifies the group for whom Woolf did some work in 1910 as the People's Suffrage Federation, which used a MECKLENBURGH SQUARE address, close to where Woolf then lived. The P.S.F. was run in large part by Margaret Llewelyn DAVIES, and Janet Case was on its executive committee (Black 184). Woolf was also associated with the WOMEN'S COOPERATIVE GUILD and with the National Union of Women's Suffrage Societies: "Virginia Woolf's memberships thus place her squarely in the middle of the organizational network of social feminism in Britain" (Black 183).

"Summing Up, A" See *MRS. DALLOWAY'S PARTY.*

Susan One of the six soliloquists of *THE WAVES.* The adult Susan is a representation of the maternal "instinct." As a child, she is filled with jealousy when she sees JINNY kiss LOUIS, and she runs away, followed by BERNARD, who comforts her. Throughout her life, Susan is closely identified with the natural world. She marries a farmer, lives in the country, and is fiercely protective of her children. In Susan, according to Suzanne Raitt, Woolf explored "what it might mean to be so sure of who you were and what you wanted" (Raitt 162). When PERCIVAL, who loved her, dies, Susan's "passionate protectiveness" *is* her mourning, "collecting together the living in an attempt to keep away their deaths" (Raitt 165). Several critics identify traits of Woolf's sister Vanessa BELL in the characterization of Susan.

Swanwick, Helen Maria (1864–1939) The sister of Walter SICKERT, Swanwick was a student at GIRTON COLLEGE with Margaret Llewelyn DAVIES and Janet CASE. She was an enthusiastic supporter of the League of Nations, through meetings concerning which she met Leonard WOOLF (D1 157). In *THREE GUINEAS* (TG 160n5), Woolf quotes from Swanwick's memoir *I Have Been Young* (1935), but Swanwick wrote to her after publication to point out that Woolf had misquoted her: Where Woolf had said Swanwick referred to the Women's Social and Political Union, her reference was in fact to the much less militant National Union of Women's Suffrage Societies.

Sweet Alice In *TO THE LIGHTHOUSE* Cam RAMSAY is picking Sweet Alice when she refuses to give a flower to William BANKES (TTL 21). In *THE WAVES*, RHODA, playing with her bowl of water and petals which she imagines as ships, says she will "plant a lighthouse here, a head of Sweet Alice" (TW 18). Sweet Alyssum, or Sea Alyssum, is a flowering herb which grows near the sea.

Swift, Jonathan (1667–1745) A cousin of John DRYDEN, Swift is best known for his satire *Gulliver's Travels.* ORLANDO meets Swift with his friends Joseph ADDISON and Richard Steele (O 210–11) in London. Woolf also wrote about him in "Swift's 'Journal to Stella' " (CR2 67–77; CE3 71–79). Woolf's half-sister Stella DUCKWORTH and sister Vanessa BELL were named after the two significant women in Swift's life, Esther Johnson, whom he addressed as "Stella," and Esther Vanhomrigh, whom he addressed as "Vanessa." In his 1882 biography *Swift,* Leslie STEPHEN has a chapter called "Stella and Vanessa."

Swinburne, Algernon Charles (1837–1909) English Pre-Raphaelite poet and critic. In *THE VOYAGE OUT,* St. John HIRST brings Swinburne's translation of the works of SAPPHO to the Sunday service in chapter XVII. Mrs. FLUSHING, seeing the book, eagerly reads the "Ode to Aphrodite" during the service. In his poem "Itylus" Swinburne retold the story of PROCNE AND PHILOMELA, rendering it what Jane Marcus has called "a misogynist nagging whine" (*Languages* 76). In her essay "Liberty, Sorority, Misogyny" (*Languages* 75–95), Marcus argues that in *BETWEEN THE ACTS* Woolf inscribes an ironic rewriting of Swinburne's version of the myth.

Swithin, Lucy Character in *BETWEEN THE ACTS* who spends the year with her brother Bart OLIVER at POINTZ HALL, except for the winter when she goes to Hastings. Lucy is referred to by a number of nicknames in the novel: her brother calls her "Cindy" (21), and the villagers call her "Batty" (9), "Old Flimsy" (27, 59, 153) and "old mother Swithin" (34). Her own secret name is CLEOPATRA (153). She wears a crucifix and goes to church, occasioning sarcastic comments from her brother. She is a widow who has two children (53), and is the last of a number of visionary women created by Woolf in her fiction. Evelyn Haller ("Isis Unveiled") and Mark Hussey ("Reading") have discussed Lucy's identification with the Egyptian deity Isis, and Mitchell Leaska provides an extensive annotation on the significance of Lucy's telling Miss LA TROBE she has made her feel she could have played Cleopatra, which he calls Woolf's "boldest stroke in the entire novel" (PH 231–33).

Sydney-Turner, Saxon Arnoll (1880–1962) A contemporary of Clive BELL, Thoby STEPHEN, Lytton STRACHEY and Leonard WOOLF at Trinity College, Cambridge, in 1899. He was an APOSTLE, a brilliant classics scholar, and was the sole guest at the first of Thoby Stephen's "Thursday Evenings" in 1905, earning him the possible distinction of being the inaugural member of the BLOOMSBURY GROUP. He was renowned for his long silences and his encyclopedic knowledge of literature and music. In her ironic preface to *ORLANDO,* Woolf acknowledges his "wide and peculiar erudition." Sydney-Turner spent his life working at the Treasury and was in love with Barbara BAGENAL, who remained devoted to him although she married another. He was an avid opera-goer and attended hundreds of performances of Richard WAGNER's works. In 1909, he accompanied Adrian STEPHEN and Woolf to the Wagner festival at Bayreuth that Woolf described in "Impressions at Bayreuth" (E1 288–93).

T

Tagus In chapter III of *THE VOYAGE OUT,* the *EUPHROSYNE* anchors at the mouth of the river Tagus, which flows from Spain through Portugal, into the Atlantic at Lisbon.

Taine, Hippolyte (1828–93) One of the vast mass of Victorian writers ORLANDO reads in the nineteenth-century section of *ORLANDO,* Taine was a French philosopher, critic and historian whose work concerned the influences of environment and heredity on character.

Talland House See ST. IVES.

Tansley, Charles Character in *TO THE LIGHTHOUSE,* a guest of Mr. and Mrs. RAMSAY in part 1 of the novel. Tansley, who is working on his dissertation, is a protégé of Mr. Ramsay. He irritates the Ramsay children, who have dubbed him "the little atheist" (TTL 5), and tells the artist Lily BRISCOE that women can neither paint nor write (TTL 48). Mrs. Ramsay also finds Tansley a prig and a bore and is annoyed when he adds to her son James's disappointment by reiterating what her husband has said: that there will be no trip to the Lighthouse the next day. However, Mrs. Ramsay also pities Tansley and invites him with her when she runs errands in the town. This delights him and sends him into raptures over walking with a beautiful woman, leading him to wish to confess to Mrs. Ramsay the miseries of his childhood. At the dinner party in section XVII of part 1, Tansley resents having to leave his books and join the rest of the people around the table: they have all changed, but he has no other clothes to wear. He feels that women "made civilisation impossible with all their 'charm,' all their silliness" (85). Much of Tansley's hostility derives from his feeling that he has been denied the privileges the other guests have enjoyed. In part 3, Lily Briscoe recalls a day at the beach with Tansley and Mrs. Ramsay when they had got on well and she saw a much friendlier side of him (TTL 160), leading her to realize how difficult it is to sum up one's impressions of anyone. During the war, Lily remembers, she saw Tansley, who is now married, "denouncing something . . . condemning someone . . . preaching brotherly love" (197) at a public meeting.

Makiko Minow-Pinkney has suggested that Tansley draws off some of the hostility felt by readers toward Mr. Ramsay, reducing his ambivalence; "the hostility that is properly a response to Ramsay can be more readily expressed toward the meaner figure of his acolyte" (Minow-Pinkney 87). Roger Poole has detected elements of Leonard WOOLF in the characterization of Tansley (*Unknown* 65).

Tavistock Square The Woolfs bought 52 Tavistock Square in January 1924, Woolf having felt too isolated from her London friends in Richmond where she lived at HOGARTH HOUSE. The first two floors of the house were occupied by a firm of solicitors, Dollman & Pritchard, with whom the Woolfs got on so well that when in 1939 they moved to MECKLENBURGH SQUARE, the solicitors moved with them.

Taylor, Valerie (b. 1902) An actress with whom Clive BELL was involved in the 1920s and who was infatuated with Vita SACKVILLE-WEST for a time, and who also had an affair with Raymond MORTIMER. Woolf includes her among the friends who "have helped me in ways too various to specify" in the ironic preface to *ORLANDO* and briefly considered photographing her as the Russian Princess SASHA in that book.

Tchehov, Anton (or Tchekhov) See CHEKHOV, Anton.

Temple, Mrs. Mentioned in *JACOB'S ROOM* giving dubious advice on how to keep water fresh for flowers.

Tennyson, Alfred, Lord (1809–92) The poet who succeeded William WORDSWORTH as Poet Laureate in 1850 and a favorite poet of Woolf's father, Leslie STEPHEN. Among Tennyson's best-known works are *In Memoriam,* "The Charge of the Light Brigade" (from which Mr. RAMSAY declaims throughout *TO*

THE LIGHTHOUSE), *Morte D'Arthur, Maud* and *Idylls of the King.* In notes to her DIARY in 1904–05, Woolf acknowledged the importance to the SUFFRAGE movement of Tennyson's poem "The Princess" (PA 279). In *ORLANDO* Tennyson is described as the last person in the British Isles to have suffered from the "disease" of genius (O 207); he is among the contemporaries denounced by Nick GREENE in the latter's incarnation as Victorian critic. Tennyson was photographed by Woolf's great-aunt Julia Margaret CAMERON and appears as a character in Woolf's play *FRESHWATER*. In *A ROOM OF ONE'S OWN,* Woolf's narrator uses lines from *Maud* to exemplify how women spoke to men before the war (AROO 13).

Terry, Ellen Alicia (1848–1928) Celebrated English actress who appears as a character in Woolf's play *FRESHWATER*. Terry married the painter G. F. WATTS at the age of seventeen, a disastrous match that had been encouraged by Sara PRINSEP. Woolf's essay "Ellen Terry" was published in the *NEW STATESMAN AND NATION* in February 1941 (CE4 67–72). Julia Margaret CAMERON's photograph of Terry is in *VICTORIAN PHOTOGRAPHS OF FAMOUS MEN & FAIR WOMEN.*

Thackeray, Harriet Marian ("Minny") See STEPHEN, Harriet Marian.

Thackeray, Anne Isabella ("Anny") See RITCHIE, Anne Isabella Thackeray.

Thackeray, William Makepeace (1811–63) English novelist and father of Leslie STEPHEN's first wife, Minny. Thackeray was born in Calcutta and came to England at the age of six. He went to Trinity College, Cambridge, but left without taking a degree. In 1836 he married Isabella Shawe but they parted in 1840 owing to her mental breakdown; their two children, Harriet Marian (STEPHEN) and Anne Isabella (RITCHIE), went to live in Paris with their father and grandmother.

Thackeray wrote many novels, became editor of the *CORNHILL MAGAZINE* in 1860, and contributed to *Punch.* In the "Note" she wrote about her father for F. W. MAITLAND's *Life,* Woolf told of how her father would read aloud to his children and began reading Thackeray's *Vanity Fair* (1847–48) to them but stopped in the middle "because he said it was 'too terrible' " (E1 128). Among Thackeray's other notable works were *The History of Pendennis, His Fortunes and Misfortunes, his Friends and his Greatest Enemy* (1848–50); *The History of Henry Esmond* (1852); *The Newcomes, Memoirs of a Most Respectable Family* (1853–55); and *The Virginians* (1857–59).

In *A ROOM OF ONE'S OWN,* the narrator plans to go and look at the manuscript of *Esmond* to see what stylistic changes the author might have made. "The critics often say that *Esmond* is Thackeray's most perfect novel," she recalls (AROO 7). With "a flutter of black gown" her way to the "OXBRIDGE" library is barred by a "kindly gentleman" who tells her the library is not open to unaccompanied ladies. The manuscript she wishes to see was in fact donated to Trinity College, Cambridge, by Woolf's aunt Anne Ritchie (MacKay 87n2).

Thackeray makes occasional appearances in Woolf's writing, beginning with a review of "two trashy books," one of which was Lewis Melville's *The Thackeray Country,* for the *TIMES LITERARY SUPPLEMENT.* The review, "Literary Geography," was her first contribution to that periodical; in it she calls Thackeray "a cosmopolitan; with London for a base he travelled everywhere" (E1 33). In *THE VOYAGE OUT,* Terence HEWET tells Rachel VINRACE that he is a "good second-rate" writer, "about as good as Thackeray" (TVO 216). Woolf made notes on *Pendennis* as she prepared to write "MODERN NOVELS" in 1919 (RN 10) and told T. S. ELIOT in 1922 that she found *Pendennis* "more illuminating" of the psychology of character than James JOYCE's *Ulysses* (D2 203). Writing in her DIARY about how she needed to get into the right frame of mind to write by reading good literature, she said, "By the way, Thackeray is good reading, very vivacious, with 'touches' . . . of astonishing insight" (D2 193). She took from *Pendennis* the term "OXBRIDGE" and, for *THREE GUINEAS,* "Arthur's Education Fund," which she used to illuminate one difference between the sons and daughters of educated men.

Thomas, Hilda Mentioned in *JACOB'S ROOM* as she crosses Grosvenor Square "coiled in furs" (JR 100).

Thomas, Jean Proprietor of Burley, a nursing home to which Woolf was sent at the recommendation of Dr. George SAVAGE on four occasions: July–August 1910, February 1912, July–August 1913, and March–April 1915 (Trombley 255). After Woolf's first stay in 1910, she and Thomas went on a walking tour in Cornwall. In 1913, Vanessa BELL consulted Thomas about whether it would be advisable for Woolf to have children (she thought it would). After Woolf's 1913 suicide attempt, Thomas wrote to Violet DICKINSON that she thought its cause was Woolf's anxiety over her novel, *THE VOYAGE OUT,* which had been accepted for publication by Gerald DUCKWORTH. Thomas was a devout Christian, which irritated Woolf, and according to Leonard WOOLF, in Quentin BELL's account, felt "an unconscious but violent homosexual passion" for Woolf (QB2 16). Stephen Trombley suggests that Thomas is a model for Doris KILMAN in *MRS. DALLOWAY.*

Thomas, Miss A typist in *JACOB'S ROOM* who works at Whitehall and worries that if the Cabinet sits much longer she will miss her date at the movies.

Thomson, James (1700–48) Author of *The Seasons,* a long poem of the English countryside in praise of nature. ORLANDO's poem *The Oak Tree* is compared favorably with *The Seasons* (O 280) by Nick GREENE, as was its model, Vita SACKVILLE-WEST's poem *THE LAND* (which, like Thomson's, is divided into four sections named for the seasons).

Thornbury, Mrs. Character in *THE VOYAGE OUT.* She and her husband are guests at the hotel on SANTA MARINA. They have sons in the navy and army, and one at Cambridge University, as well as five daughters, and are in South America on their second honeymoon (TVO 114). She discusses maternity with Mrs. ELLIOT, who is childless, and, as Jane Wheare points out, does not subscribe to Mrs. Elliot's "conservative definition of motherhood" (Wheare 57). Mrs. Thornbury also admires Miss ALLAN for earning her own living and is optimistic about the changes in women's lives she has seen during her lifetime (TVO 319). Like her husband, she is interested in politics (TVO 158), and, at the age of seventy-five, has taken up the study of botany (TVO 324).

Thornbury, William Character in *THE VOYAGE OUT.* He and his wife are guests at the hotel on SANTA MARINA. Mr. Thornbury anxiously keeps up with political news from England by reading the *Times.*

Thorold, Edgar A character in Miss LA TROBE's Victorian scene in her village pageant in *BETWEEN THE ACTS.*

"Thoughts on Peace in an Air Raid" (CE4 173–77; DM 243–48) An essay by Woolf published in the *NEW REPUBLIC* (New York) in October 1940. Leonard WOOLF's note in *COLLECTED ESSAYS* says it was written "for an American symposium on current matters concerning women" (CE4 173). Framing her thoughts with a description of lying in bed listening to German bombers pass overhead, Woolf argues that war is an affair between men in which women are not allowed to take part (CE4 173). The only hope for an end to war is for women to engage in "mental fight," which she defines as "thinking against the current, not with it" (CE4 174). She quotes Lady Astor, who has referred to the "subconscious Hitlerism in the hearts of men" that oppresses women (174), understanding this "Hitlerism" as the desire to dominate and enslave. As an example of what she means, Woolf describes a London street where women "with crimson lips and crimson fingernails" both are enslaved and wish to enslave. Woolf makes a similar point toward the end of *BETWEEN THE ACTS* when the voice speaking through a loudspeaker asks the audience to consider "*gun slayers, bomb droppers*" who do openly what "*Mrs. E's lipstick and blood-red nails*" do slyly (BTA 187). As she argued in *THREE GUINEAS,* Woolf writes that the instinct to fight is an ancient one, fostered by centuries of education and tradition. She quotes from the autobiography of Franklin Lushington (*Portrait of a Young Man* [1940]) to illustrate how men love war and concludes that the only hope for peace is to "compensate the man for the loss of his gun" by giving him access to "the creative feelings" (CE4 175). The essay closes with an appeal to Americans, whose sleep is not disturbed by machine-gun fire, to help shape her thoughts into "something serviceable" (CE4 177).

In a letter to Lady Shena SIMON in 1940, Woolf had written, "So many of the young men, could they get prestige and admiration, would give up glory and develop what's now so stunted—I mean the life of natural happiness" (L6 380). Susan Squier sees "Thoughts on Peace" as boldly redefining "not only the social meaning of gender but also the concept of militancy" (Squier, *Virginia Woolf* 183–84), and she follows Brenda Silver ("*Three Guineas* Before and After") in seeing the influence on the essay of Woolf's reading in 1939 of Sigmund FREUD's *Group Psychology and the Analysis of the Ego.* In her reading notes on Freud's book, Woolf described how men were fighting against the masculine attributes that Adolf HITLER embodied; "Is this the first time a sex has turned against specific qualities?" (RN 116–17). John Mepham has pointed out that it is likely that around the time she was composing "Thoughts on Peace," Woolf read a collection of Freud's writings edited by John Rickman for the HOGARTH PRESS (*Civilisation, War and Death: Selections from Three Works by Sigmund Freud* [1939]) that included Freud's 1932 letter to Albert Einstein, "Why War?" Mepham suggests that it is "one very likely source for whatever is new in her thinking" in the essay, "and her new emphasis, which is a desire to emancipate men from their aggression and their desire to enslave women" (Mepham, *Literary Life* 197). Helen Cooper, Adrienne Munich and Susan Squier have explained that in her essay, Woolf "challenges the binary thinking that attributes to men responsibility for war, to women responsibility for peace. She argues that male warmaking joins female childbearing; the complex war system is grafted on to the ancient sex/gender system." In this way, they continue, Woolf is questioning "both the culturally constructed meaning of childbirth and the binary opposition between war and masculinity, peace and femininity" (Cooper, Munich and Squier 22).

***Three Guineas* (1938)** The second of Woolf's major non-fiction works, conceived as a sequel to *A ROOM OF ONE'S OWN, Three Guineas* has established Woolf as

Three Guineas. *Courtesy Linda J. Langham.*
Vanessa Bell designed the cover for both the American and English first editions. (1938); the American edition is shown here.

a significant voice in the cause of pacifism. The book is in three chapters; 124 notes elaborate its arguments and anchor them in references to Woolf's wide reading and research during the 1930s. The whole work is in the form of a letter to a barrister who has written asking how war might be prevented. In the course of her reply to the barrister's question and request for her assistance, Woolf incorporates letters and drafts of letters to other correspondents who have written for aid.

A "guinea" was originally a gold coin worth twenty shillings, first struck in 1663 but not coined after 1813; from 1717 it circulated with the value of twenty-one shillings. It was minted for the Company of Royal Adventurers to do trade with Africa, taking its name from the Guinea Coast and made with gold mined there. For over a century after the coin itself had passed out of circulation, the word guinea was used to refer to one pound sterling and one shilling. The *Oxford English Dictionary* notes that the guinea "is the ordinary unit for a professional fee and for a subscription to a society or institution; the prices obtained for works of art, racehorses, and sometimes landed property, are also stated in guineas." It is thus a term associated with luxuries.

Outline

Chapter 1: The letter from a barrister asking "How are we to prevent war?" has lain unanswered for more than three years, but its question is now more urgent than ever. Woolf remarks that it is unprecedented for a woman to be asked such a question by a man, and proceeds to sketch an image of her correspondent to help her frame her reply. He is prosperous and educated. A "gulf so deeply cut between us" is their difference of sex, which Woolf illustrates with a quotation from the biography of Mary KINGSLEY about how she had hardly any "paid-for education" (4). From William Makepeace THACKERY's novel *Pendennis,* Woolf takes the notion of "Arthur's Education Fund"—abbreviated to AEF throughout *Three Guineas*—to represent that fund for the education of young men to which sisters have had for centuries to sacrifice their own education and its rewards. AEF has enabled Woolf's correspondent to add "K. C." (King's Counsel) after his name, and to have had a life very different from that of his sisters. Such a difference in upbringing leads to a difference of view between the educated man's daughter and the educated man's son. In note 2, Woolf explains that she must use the term "educated man's daughter," clumsy though it is, because "bourgeois" is not strictly accurate for the class of women she is concerned with: middle-class women, after all, differ profoundly "in the two prime characteristics of the bourgeoisie—capital and environment" (146).

The barrister must, however, have believed her capable of understanding something of the causes of war and, indeed, her "unpaid-for education" (6) has taught her an understanding of people's natures. Women have long had to be judges of human character, a skill necessary to successful performance in the only profession available to women until 1919, that of marriage. The Sex Disqualification (Removal) Act of 1919 opened most professions to women, an event that Woolf returns to many times throughout *Three Guineas* as of momentous importance. Although an understanding of human psychology is a common attribute of both men and women, the instinct to kill, Woolf notes, has invariably been man's. In general, throughout history it has been men rather than women who have killed animals and people. Clearly men derive "some glory, some necessity, some satisfaction" from fighting.

Luckily, biographies, autobiographies and newspapers ("history in the raw" [TG 7]) provide insight into how men feel about war. Woolf quotes passages from biographies of Francis and Riversdale Grenfell and of Lord Knebworth that link manhood to war. As a contrast, she quotes the words of Wilfred Owen on the foolishness of war and its incompatibility with Christianity; she acknowledges that Owen's is a minority opinion. As "patriotism" seems to be the underlying reason men fight, she cites the definition of patriotism given by the Lord Chief Justice of England. But does patriotism mean the same to "an educated man's sister" (9)? Finding no absolute point of view on war, Woolf turns for help to the Church, but, again consulting the daily newspaper, she finds no agreement among church leaders either.

On her writing table are photographs sent by the Spanish government of dead bodies and ruined houses, victims of the fascist bombing of Madrid in the SPANISH CIVIL WAR. The point of view of all people would, Woolf thinks, be the same on seeing such photographs: "War must be stopped at whatever cost" (11). Turning again to her correspondent's letter, she considers its three requests: that she sign a letter to the newspapers; that she join his society; that she send funds to that society. These are easily done, but she feels that something more active is called for. Being a woman, she cannot fight, use economic power, or preach in church against war. Being a middle-class woman, she has no labor to withdraw that would have any serious effect. In note 10, she points out that the only thing educated men's daughters can do is refuse to produce children, as LYSISTRATA pointed out more than two millennia earlier.

Her correspondent will argue that educated women have influence over men, but she wonders if this has really been true: a glance at some memoirs reveals that aristocratic women may have had influence, but not the daughters of educated men. The struggle for women's SUFFRAGE was certainly a political cause in which women showed their influence, but that fight took so long it is doubtful that women's influence can be very effective in preventing war, which is an imminent danger. In note 11, Woolf refers to the *Letters* of D. H. LAWRENCE, Hilary Newit's *Women Must Choose* and Elizabeth Haldane's *From One Century to Another* to sketch the various kinds of influence women have been said to have. Women's work during World War I was a turning point in gaining the vote, but women are only "step-daughters" of their country because, as Woolf explains in note 12, an Englishwoman loses her nationality if she marries a foreigner.

A pernicious kind of female "influence" has been that said to be wielded by female charm. Quoting from the biography of a lawyer, Sir Ernest Wild, to illustrate her point, Woolf describes how men idealize women and how their wish to be chivalrous leads to what they call an "indirect" influence. Such influence she finds to be either beyond the reach of the "plain, poor and old" woman, or beneath the contempt of women who "would prefer to call ourselves prostitutes simply" (15). She might be content to do what her correspondent asks were it not that the right to vote was connected with the right of women to earn their own livings.

As she had in *A Room of One's Own,* Woolf emphasizes that economic independence is more valuable than the vote to women and has altered everything for the daughters of educated men, including the kind of influence she can wield. The influence of an economically independent woman is "disinterested." However, a gulf still exists between her and her correspondent, a gulf cut by the difference in their status and education. Men still own most of England and consume most of its produce. She proposes to describe her correspondent's world as an educated man's daughter sees it, "from the threshold of the private house" (a description prefigured in Woolf's short story "A SOCIETY").

In the first place, men's official clothes are extraordinary, but, as she points out in note 16, high office renders this invisible to the wearer. She describes the elaborate dress of officials and the strange ceremonies at which they wear these costumes, noting that the great variety of public attire serves to advertise the status of the wearer. Returning to the photographs of dead bodies and ruined houses, Woolf asks what connection there might be between those images and "the sartorial splendours of the educated man" (21). The connection is "not far to seek," for men's finest clothes are those they wear as soldiers. This love of display is apparent also among educated men, as a procession at a university demonstrates. One thing the daughters of educated men can easily do to support the barrister's aims is refuse all the honors that men's official clothes advertise because the distinctions between people created by such honors rouse the "feelings that lead to war" (21).

Since women have been able to earn their own livings, their help has been frequently invoked. For example, here is a letter from the honorary treasurer of a women's college asking for support. Woolf recognizes that being asked for money gives her bargaining power so she will ask that the college teach the young people to hate war. But how? Looking at the university from that "bridge" between the private house and public world, Woolf again finds it looks very different to the daughter of an educated man. Once again, men walk in procession, strangely attired.

Education is clearly of great importance, as the biographies of the ruling class and the huge sums spent on it attest. Note 18, however, refers to John Maynard KEYNES's review of a history of Clare College, Cambridge University, that reportedly cost £6,000 to produce: there is a vast disparity between the incomes of men's and women's colleges. Woolf notes that the great universities, Oxford and Cambridge, have traditionally been places where patronage and family connections too frequently have led to the monopoly of an elite on higher education. She cites the historian Edward GIBBON's criticisms of Oxford in his *Memoirs of My Life and Writing* (note 19).

The Church has been a major opponent of women's education, a fact illustrated by reference to the life of Mary ASTELL, who proposed founding a college for women but was thwarted by the Church of England. Woolf turns to the history of women's education. Thomas GRAY celebrates the aristocratic women who were benefactors of several colleges at Cambridge, but there were no such female benefactors available to the women's colleges. The struggle to found GIRTON and NEWNHAM colleges was a long and bitter one. Even in 1937, Woolf informs her correspondent, women's colleges are still not allowed to be members of Cambridge University and the number of women students admitted is severely restricted (note 26). It is, therefore, no surprise that the treasurer of a women's college has requested a donation to help rebuild the college. Recognizing that the poverty of the college allows no time for the treasurer to consider the nature of education and its effect on war, Woolf begins nevertheless to draft a letter laying out the conditions on which she will make a donation.

What is the point of rebuilding the college? Should it be built again on the traditional lines, refashioned, or burnt to the ground? Her guinea will only be sent if the education provided will help produce people who will help prevent war. Let the college be an "experimental college, an adventurous college." The new college should not perpetuate old hierarchies like those vividly illustrated by the photographs Woolf included in her text at this point (photographs that have not been reprinted in a U.S. edition since 1938). The first page of photographs in *Three Guineas* shows a soldier, a procession at Cambridge, and a group of royal heralds, all in full regalia. The new college will avoid competition by granting no honors and no degrees, giving no lectures and preaching no sermons (35).

Woolf breaks off her letter when she realizes that without degrees the women will not find jobs. To be successful, the women's college must take its place in the warmaking society where capitalists reward research that improves weaponry. The guinea will be sent, therefore, to buy rags and matches with which to "burn the college to the ground" (36). Relenting, Woolf decides finally to send her guinea with no conditions attached because women must be trained to find professional jobs. As an outsider, all Woolf feels she can do is "pour mild scorn" on the trappings of a modern university education, including the "vain and vicious system of lecturing" (37). In note 30 she explains that she is thinking principally here of lecturing on English literature, a practice made obsolete by the advent of printing.

The only hope for women's freedom is that they can escape from the private house, and education is the means by which they may escape. Until 1919, Woolf repeats, marriage was the only profession open to middle-class women and this led them to be "consciously and unconsciously in favour of war." The middle-class woman needed servants and fine clothes if she was to make a good marriage, and those luxuries depended upon the maintenance of the British Empire. The patriarchal private house sustains the division between the sexes and forces women to support the only society they know. Before she helps the barrister, Woolf concludes, she must help the women's college because to help women escape the tyranny of the private house is to contribute to the prevention of war.

Chapter 2: Perhaps even more important than education is the opportunity for influencing society against war afforded by the economic independence gained by professional women. The photographs of dead bodies and ruined houses are piling up, so it seems obvious that professional women would want to help the barrister who has written for help preventing war. But a hesitation occurs when Woolf turns to another letter from another honorary treasurer, this one requesting assistance for the daughters of educated men seeking professional employment.

Such a request draws the censure of men like C. E. M. JOAD and H. G. WELLS. Joad points out that Suffrage associations like the Women's Social and Political Union (see SUFFRAGE) received money to help in the fight for the vote and asks why there should not now be societies of women dedicated to peace. Note 2 dismisses Joad's point by referring readers to *The Story of the Disarmament Declaration,* where the list of societies "run directly or indirectly by Englishwomen in the cause of peace is too long to quote" (159). H. G. Wells, in *Experiment in Autobiography,* has also said that women are idle in the cause of peace, so, asks Woolf, how dare they demand from her a donation?

Facts once again lead to a rather different picture than that offered by Mr. Joad and Mr. Wells. The W.S.P.U. in fact operated on an "incredibly minute" budget. If £300,000,000 are spent annually on arms, what chance is there that women can have any influence? Women's earning power—despite twenty years in the professions—is still slight. Consulting *Whitaker's Almanac* (see WHITAKER), Woolf discovers that women have not advanced very far in professional hierarchies: the daughters of educated men may be in the professions but they do not make big salaries. Taking the Civil Service as an example, Woolf explains three reasons for this lack of advancement: very few women are able to gain degrees from Oxford or Cambridge, many women are burdened by the care of an elderly parent and women have a comparatively brief history of higher education. In contrast to Whitaker's representation of the low status of women civil servants, Woolf quotes the remarks of the prime minister, Stanley BALDWIN, to the effect that women are in general excellent civil servants.

In trying the case of *Baldwin* v. *Whitaker*, Woolf first points out that ability is not necessarily the reason people rise in the professions. Nepotism has an important role to play, for example. Also, the appellation "Miss" may put off those in a position to hire professionals: "What charms and consoles in the private house may distract and exacerbate in the public office" (50). The Anglican Church, for example, excludes women from the priesthood for just this reason (note 10). Three quotations from the *Daily Telegraph* exemplify the climate of opinion in England in 1936: the gist of these quotations is that women, since World War I, have excluded men from jobs that are rightfully theirs. The discrepancy between the low salaries of professional women and the high opinion of them uttered by Mr. Baldwin is due, then, to an "atmosphere" (52), that impalpable femininity that arouses men's sexism.

Woolf places her last quotation from the *Daily Telegraph* alongside another quotation, this one from a German fascist source. The English and German men share an attitude toward women, the attitude of a dictator; therefore, the Englishwoman who fights against such attitudes at home without arms is "fighting the Fascist or the Nazi as surely as those who fight him with arms" (53). Woolf asks her correspondent if they should not help the woman "crush [the dictator] in our own country" before asking her help in crushing him abroad.

If the world is divided into public and private spheres, and men are paid from taxes for the work they do in the public sphere, why are not mothers and daughters and wives paid for the work they do in the private house? The answer that a wife is entitled to half her husband's income is unsatisfactory, for clearly women do not receive that share. It now seems clearer why women in the professions need financial assistance and, certainly, that disinterested influence that might work to help prevent war will not exist until women have a disposable income similar to men's.

Is it wise, then, to encourage people to enter the professions if we wish to prevent war? Without some conditions attached to the guinea she proposes to send to the society for aiding professional women, war will continue "like a gramophone whose needle has stuck" grinding out the old tune, "Here we go round the mulberry tree . . . Give it all to me . . . Three hundred millions spent upon war" (59). The condition will be that the professions not be practiced in the same old way.

Drafting another letter to the honorary treasurer, Woolf depicts the "procession of the sons of educated men." The photographs of a judge and an archbishop in full regalia that appeared in the text at this point in the first edition of *Three Guineas* vividly illustrate her description of the procession ("One was a bishop. Another a judge. One was an admiral. Another a general" [61]). In the past twenty years, the daughters of educated men have joined the end of the procession and now must ask whether they want to remain in it and on what terms.

In the nineteenth century a great battle was fought in all the professions except that of literature. As a paradigmatic example, Woolf examines "the battle of Harley Street," that is, the struggle over admitting women to the medical profession. The life of Sophia JEX-BLAKE illustrates the story, though Woolf points out that it is a story repeated throughout the years with little variation, of men's desire to exclude women. The first condition she will attach to the second guinea, therefore, is that the receiver will do everything possible to insist that no woman entering a profession will do anything to hinder any other qualified person from entering.

The next question is where the procession of the sons of educated men is leading: are professional women to change from being "victims of the patriarchal system" to being "champions of the capitalist system" (67)? If there were rich women as there are rich men, "what could you not do?" Then, Woolf writes, there could be a women's political party, a "daily newspaper committed to a conspiracy, not of silence, but of speech" (68). If it were not for the persistence of those photographs sent by the Spanish government of dead bodies and ruined houses and the evidence of biography and history, it would be easy to agree that money is unequivocally a desirable thing. The life of a man like J. Pierpont MORGAN, however, suggests that extreme wealth may be no more desirable than extreme poverty.

Quoting from the biographies of various professional men, Woolf determines that the price of success is to become a "cripple in a cave," devoid of all sensory experience. Women entering the professions risk becoming, like men, crippled by the demands of their jobs. Women seem to be caught between the twin evils of the patriarchal private house and the possessive, greedy, pugnacious world of the professions. Looking for an example of how women might behave differently, Woolf again turns to Victorian biography, to the lives of those proto-professional women such as Anne CLOUGH, Josephine BUTLER and Octavia Hill, all of whom exhibited a selflessness that seems to Woolf desirable in her own time. Moving closer to the present, Woolf remarks on the life of Gertrude BELL, who had to be accompanied everywhere by her maid (note 36 regrets that no lives of maids are to be found in the *DICTIONARY OF NATIONAL BIOGRAPHY*). This fact prompts a long note (note 38) on female chastity and its roots in the teachings of SAINT PAUL. Woolf has already alluded twice to Paul's "pronouncement on the matter of veils," and in this note she anatomizes the misogyny of the Apostle's teachings.

Woolf returns to the statement of Mary Kingsley's that she quoted in chapter 1 and wonders what a Victorian woman's "unpaid-for education" consisted of. These women's teachers were "poverty, chastity, derision, and freedom from unreal loyalties" (78), teachers that taught women how to perform in the "unpaid-for professions" such as marriage. Woolf suggests that if these four teachers are combined with "some wealth, some knowledge, and some service to real loyalties" then women might enter the professions without risking their traditional bad effects of possessiveness, greed and pugnacity.

To understand these four teachers more clearly, Woolf tells her correspondent she must rely on intuition—"the psychometer you carry on your wrist." Failing that, "consult the findings of the public psychometer for yourself" (81), represented in art such as the *ANTIGONE* of Sophocles. Woolf assures her correspondent that the daughters of educated men will be able to avoid "the great modern sins of vanity, egotism, and megalomania" because men will continue to ridicule and censure them and hold them in contempt. In note 41 she points out that even in "a time of great political stress like the present it is remarkable how much criticism is still bestowed upon women." On such terms Woolf will send her guinea to the honorary treasurer of the society for helping the daughters of educated men enter the professions, and now she can return, having sent two guineas, to the barrister's request that began this long train of thought.

Chapter 3: The barrister has invited her to sign a manifesto pledging the protection of "culture and intellectual liberty," to join a society for the preservation of peace, and make a donation to it. Woolf understands him to be implying a connection between the protection of culture and intellectual liberty and the photographs of dead bodies and ruined houses. That the son of an educated man should ask the daughter of an educated man for help in this she likens to the Duke of Devonshire coming into his kitchen to ask the maid for help construing a difficult passage from Pindar. Woolf's response is that the daughters have already contributed more than anyone else in society to the cause of culture and intellectual liberty by going without an education of their own, sacrificing it to "Arthur's Education Fund" (86). The request for help is even more surprising in light of the fact that the daughters of educated men are not entitled to teach English literature at Oxford or Cambridge, nor do they participate in decisions concerning purchasing art for the nation: there are no women on the boards of the NATIONAL GALLERY or the Royal Academy of Art.

Culture and intellectual liberty are still, in 1938, difficult for women to obtain. Only in literature have women had any freedom and for that reason there is no official body representing the profession of literature over which influence might be wielded. Woolf begins a letter of appeal to professional women writers but is stopped by the thought of Mrs. Margaret OLIPHANT, who "prostituted her culture and enslaved her intellectual liberty" to earn her living by writing. The "disinterested" culture of the barrister's manifesto seems to be a very rare thing. The appeal must be made to professional women writers who have an independent income not to prostitute their talent for the sake of money, advertisement or publicity.

Woolf describes an educated man's daughter who is financially independent, imagining a conversation with her in which Woolf inquires why she reads so many newspapers. The answer is that there is no such thing as a "disinterested" media and their various versions of "facts" must be compared to gain an approximation of the truth. If there were enough people who would speak the truth about war and about art, if there were newspapers written by such people, then "we should not believe in war, and we should believe in art," Woolf concludes (97). Furthermore, the daughters of educated men can abstain from buying "papers that encourage intellectual slavery" and not attend "lectures that prostitute culture" (98).

A way of defending disinterested culture and intellectual liberty having been agreed on, Woolf turns to the barrister's request for money and says she will give him a guinea free of all conditions. That an educated man's daughter is able to give her brother a guinea she has earned for herself is so momentous an occurrence that a celebration is called for. Woolf proposes a ceremonial burning of the word "feminist." "Since the only right, the right to earn a living, has been won, the word no longer has a meaning" (101). The daughters of educated men who fought "the tyranny of the patriarchal state" in the nineteenth century were fighting the same enemy as the barrister is now fighting, "the tyranny of the Fascist state." Now, says Woolf, "the whole iniquity of dictatorship," wherever it is, whomever it oppresses, is clear. Her hope is that one day the words "tyrant" and "dictator" will also be destroyed "in the blaze of our common freedom" (103).

Finally, all that remains to be done is to join the barrister's society, but again Woolf hesitates. That sexual difference she has so thoroughly explored in this long letter again creates a gulf. It is from the difference, she believes, that her ability to help can come, but if she joins his society she will lose that difference. The man is a "brother" as an individual, one such as Anne Clough describes as her "best friend and adviser" (104). But the public relationship of brother to sister has been very different from the private. Joining the man's society would be to "merge our identity in yours" and perpetuate the way things have always been.

Woolf sketches "the kind of society which the daughters of educated men found and join" which will work in cooperation with the barrister's society's aims. It would be called—if it has to have a name—the "Outsiders' Society" and would have no officials and hold no meetings. The Outsiders' Society would consist of educated men's daughters working in their own class (in note 13 Woolf derides the "playboys and playgirls of the educated class who adopt the working-class cause without sacrificing middle-class capital or sharing working-class experience," a point she would repeat in her essay "THE LEANING TOWER"). The first duty of the Outsiders' Society would be not to fight with arms. Next, they would maintain "an attitude of complete indifference" to men's fighting.

If the issue of patriotism as a reason to fight should arise, the Outsider will reflect that very little, if any, of "her" country belongs to her, as she is a woman; war will make her no safer; if she marries a foreigner she loses her nationality. Any appeals to her patriotism will be dismissed by reason, for, she will say, "in fact, as a woman, I have no country. As a woman I want no country. As a woman my country is the whole world" (109). The "anonymous and secret Society of Outsiders" will thus assist the barrister by these methods of indifference, and by absenting themselves from anything to do with war.

Once again, Woolf stresses the importance of economic independence and that a wage be paid to women who work as mothers. This would transform the slavery of the patriarchal private house and benefit both men and women. The Outsiders would set themselves to learn all they could about how professions worked, and would criticize what they saw and create new ways for the professions, especially those of religion and education, to conduct themselves. The Outsiders would also dedicate themselves to freeing society from its devotion to personal distinctions, advertisement and publicity.

Woolf tells her correspondent that the Outsiders' Society already exists, citing three examples from the daily newspaper of women practicing the principles she has just outlined. Secrecy, however, is essential if only because the daughters' power is not yet great; there is also a certain fear felt by the daughters. To explain this fear, Woolf proposes to analyze the report of the Archbishops' Commission on *The Ministry of Women,* the profession of religion being, according to Whitaker, "the highest of all" the professions (121). In the *Report* it is clear that St. Paul is the reason women cannot be priests, for the archbishops agreed that Jesus held men and women to be equal in spiritual capacity. Originally there were prophets and prophetesses, but around the fourth or fifth century, religion became organized as a profession and that led to the exclusion of women from its hierarchy. To buttress their arguments, the archbishops asked the Nolloth Professor of the Philosophy of the Christian Religion at Oxford University, Professor Grensted, to "summarize the relevant psychological and physiological material" on the exclusion of women from the ministry (125). Woolf quotes at length from Grensted's appendix to the *Report,* where he analyzes the source of the antipathy to the ordination of women as being "infantile fixation" upon subconscious ideas of woman as "man manqué." The only reasons women may not be priests are psychological and emotional ones. It is such subconscious feelings, Woolf argues, that inhibit through fear the free speech of educated men's daughters.

Elaborating on Grensted's conclusions, Woolf draws parallels between the Church leaders and Adolf HITLER and Benito Mussolini, all of whom argue for women's subservient role as necessary to sustaining the social hierarchy they desire. It is men's subconscious urge to dominate that makes educated men's daughters wary of joining with them. Woolf proposes to examine "infantile fixation" in greater detail by turning once again to Victorian biography. She cites the cases of Elizabeth Barrett BROWNING's father and Charlotte BRONTË's father. A more complicated case is that of Sophia Jex-Blake's father, who did not want his daughter to be paid for a tutoring position. Mr. Jex-Blake appealed not to reason but to Sophia's "womanhood emotion," and when a man does that, says Woolf, it arouses very deep and primitive feelings. Society supports men in their "infantile fixation" for, it seems, society is also "a father" (135). An exception to the typical Victorian father was Mr. Leigh Smith, who treated his daughter Barbara Leigh Smith BODICHON and his sons equally.

Something happened in the nineteenth century to make the daughters resist the fathers, some force was apparent that changed society radically. Although the fathers yielded in private, however, in public the "infantile fixation" led to a much more formidable aggression as is attested to, Woolf argues, by the voices of dictators at home and abroad who are telling women to "go back to their homes" (141). It is the ancient voice of Creon, the dictator in Sophocles's *Antigone*—Creon who brought dead bodies and ruined houses to his land.

As she has been writing her letter to the barrister, Woolf says, another picture has come into focus in the foreground of her mind's eye, supplanting the photographs of dead bodies and ruined houses. It is the "figure of a man," "Man himself," the "Tyrant or Dictator" (142). This picture, she suggests, means that the private house and public world are connected; "that the tyrannies and servilities of the one are the tyrannies and servilities of the other;" this connection must never be forgotten if the world is to be saved from war.

The form for joining the barrister's society, then, will be returned unsigned, but the third guinea is given freely. The three guineas have been given to different causes that are the same cause: "the rights of all—all men and women—to the respect in their persons of the great principles of Justice and Equality and Liberty" (143–44).

Genesis

In June 1938, Woolf recorded in her DIARY "the end of six years floundering, striving, much agony, some ecstasy: lumping the Years and 3Gs together as one book—as indeed they are" (D5 148). At first, Woolf had attempted to write "one book," her "novel-essay" *THE PARGITERS,* which would encompass her fictional conception and the facts she had been amassing for years about the nature of patriarchy in its public and private guises. This project proved impossible to realize, and eventually the two branches of fiction and fact flowered separately.

The idea that would develop with such complexity throughout the first few years of the 1930s struck Woolf on January 20, 1931, while she was having a bath: she wrote in her diary that she had just "conceived an entire new book—a sequel to a Room of Ones own—about the sexual life of women: to be called Professions for Women perhaps" (D4 6). The idea "sprang out of" a talk Woolf was to give the next day to the London and National Society for Women's Service, an organization of which her friend Philippa (Pippa) STRACHEY was secretary. "PROFESSIONS FOR WOMEN" was published in a drastically shortened version in *DEATH OF THE MOTH,* but the text of the twenty-five-page manuscript (held in the BERG COLLECTION) on which Woolf's talk was based is included in *The Pargiters* (xxvii–xliv). Sharing the stage with Woolf that January 21 was the composer Ethel SMYTH, a new friend of Woolf's whom Jane Marcus has described as important in helping Woolf to realize the anger that fuels *Three Guineas* (*Languages* 112).

Naomi Black* has explained how *Three Guineas* includes the "specific beliefs and policy demands" of certain women's organizations, and she points out that the National Union of Women's Suffrage Societies' statement about World War I, justifying its support, alludes to Charles KINGSLEY's poem "The Three Fishers," which contains the line "Men must work and women must weep" (Black 189). Black also notes that *Three Guineas* includes "the specific policy goals of the Society for Women's Service" established by Ray STRACHEY, Philippa Strachey and others (Black 190).

Over the next several years, *Three Guineas* developed slowly in Woolf's mind, going through a number of different titles as she sought a form that would comfortably embody her arguments: "Professions for Women," "The Open Door," "Opening the Door," "A Knock [or tap] on the Door," "Men Are Like That" (rejected as "too patently feminist" [D4 77]), "On Being Despised," "P. & P.," "The Next War," "What Are We To Do?", "Answers to Correspondents," "Letter to an Englishman" and "Two Guineas." In early 1931, Woolf was writing the second draft of *THE WAVES* and had to curb her impulse to write the new work, but by early 1932 she wrote that she had "collected enough gunpowder to blow up St. Pauls" (D4 77). In the politically fraught 1930s, Woolf seemed to channel everything she saw and experienced into her two new works, warning herself in 1935 that she must not write *The Pargiters* and *Three Guineas* simultaneously "as this fiction is dangerously near propaganda" (D4 300).

As the wide-ranging references in *Three Guineas* attest, there was plenty of evidence available to Woolf in the 1930s to support her arguments about the interconnection of patriarchal and fascist tyranny. When Leonard WOOLF reviewed H. G. Wells's *The Work, Wealth and Happiness of Mankind* for the *NEW STATESMAN AND NATION* in 1932, Woolf wrote in her diary that her mind was "set running on A Knock at the Door (whats its name?) owing largely to reading 'Wells on Woman'—how she must be ancillary & decorative in the world of the future" (D4 75). By the end of 1932, Woolf wrote that she had "almost written out my first fury" (D4 132) and remarked that the new book had surprised her by releasing "such a torrent of fact as I did not know I had in me. I must have been observing & collecting these 20 years" (D4 133). Brenda R. Silver has documented twelve volumes of reading notes pertaining to *Three Guineas* (see RN). In 1933, Woolf was pleased to be able to put into practice something she advocated in *Three Guineas* when she refused the offer to deliver the Clark Lectures at Cambridge University (her father, Sir Leslie STEPHEN, had given the first Clark Lectures in 1883). She felt that to accept would compromise her ability to "tilt" at universities in her book. A few years later, she again congratulated herself when she refused offers to lecture in the United States and "to write for the larger paying magazines" (D5 96). When *Three Guineas* was finished, Woolf recorded her sense of liberation: "I shall never write to 'please' to convert; now am entirely & for ever my own mistress" (D5 105).

Three Guineas states explicitly what had been more or less implicit in Woolf's writing from very early on. A quotation from *MELYMBROSIA,* for example, illustrates how persistent in Woolf's thinking was the analysis of war she presented in *Three Guineas.* The character St. John HIRST says, "I calculate . . . that if every man in the British Isles has six male children by the year 1920 and sends them all into the navy we shall be able to keep our fleet in the Mediterranean; if less than six, the fleet disappears; if the fleet disappears, the Empire disappears; if the Empire disappears, I shall no longer be able to pursue my studies in the university of Cambridge" (quoted in Angela Ingram* 127).

In 1935, Woolf described meeting E. M. FORSTER on the steps of the LONDON LIBRARY where he had just come from a committee meeting at which it had been declared that "ladies are quite impossible" (D4 297). Woolf channeled the anger she felt at this insult into practice sentences for what she was calling at that time "On Being Despised." Later that year, reading about Mary Moore's *The Defeat of Women,* in which the author lamented women's abandonment of their "nature" after World War I and gaining the vote, Woolf felt flooded with thoughts for her "Professions book" (D4 323). In October 1935, Woolf wrote that attending the Labour Party conference in Brighton had resulted in "the breaking of the dam between me & the new book" (D4 346); in her notebook she decided that the "upshot" of the conference was that men "think war necessary" (RN 254).

The year 1935 had been particularly active for Woolf politically. She became a member of a communist-dominated committee that was organizing an anti-fascist exhibition (D4 280–81). John Mepham notes that Woolf described the group of people she met through this committee—including Anthony Blunt, Herbert READ and Henry Moore—as "respectable Bohemia" (Mepham, *Literary Life* 163). E. M. Forster invited both Woolfs to Paris for meetings of Vigilance, a group of anti-fascist intellectuals. At the end of the year, Woolf was reading St. Paul and planning to buy an Old Testament and to read the seven volumes of Ernest RENAN's *Histoire des origines du christianisme* ("History of the Origins of Christianity"). By this time, her conception of *Three Guineas* was "to pretend its all the articles editors have asked me to write during the past few years—on all sorts of subjects" (D4 361). She wrote to Ethel Smyth that she had decided to put her notes at the end of the text rather than as footnotes, "thinking people might read them, the most meaty part of the book, separately" (L6 235).

As 1936 began, Woolf was trying to suppress thoughts of "Answers to Correspondents" so that she could finish *The Years;* a year later, with the novel about to be published, she could immerse herself in "the happy tumultuous dream" of *Three Guineas* (D5 52). As the situation in Europe worsened, Woolf was increasingly sought out to lend her name to causes, to join committees, and to sign manifestoes. In the first note to the third chapter of *Three Guineas* she wrote, "It is to be hoped that some methodical person has made a collection of the various manifestoes and questionnaires issued broadcast during the years 1936–37" (172). Many of those Woolf herself collected found their way into her text, as Silver has shown in her meticulous indexing of Woolf's notebooks. Silver remarks that "when read in their entirety, the '3 bound volumes' illustrate more than the care Woolf took in preparing her books or the wealth of facts she amassed; they are an important contribution to the social history of the thirties" (RN 24; the three bound volumes of clippings are RN LVIII, LIX, and LX).

Among the many letters of the type Woolf alludes to in *Three Guineas* was one from William McNeill, pastor of the Deane Congregational Church in Bolton, Lancashire, asking her to donate one of her books to "a money-raising bazaar in aid of eight Congregational churches" (RN 279). Another came from Dame Adelaide Livingstone, Vice-Chairman of the British National Committee, requesting Woolf's signature on a manifesto of the International Peace campaign (RN 284). Monica Whately of the "Six Point Group" wrote asking Woolf to take part in a "deputation of prominent women to the German Ambassador" to help save women in German prisons (RN 307). The National Council for Equal Citizenship—a "direct descendant of the National Union of Women's Suffrage Societies" (RN 308)—and the International Association of Writers for the Defence of Culture, chaired by the poet Cecil DAY LEWIS, were among organizations soliciting Woolf's support (RN 312). After *Three Guineas* was published, May SARTON wrote Woolf to ask for a manuscript to sell in aid of the Refugees Society; Woolf sent the manuscript of *Three Guineas* (now in the BERG COLLECTION).

Leonard and Virginia Woolf signed a letter to the editor of the *Daily Express* with thirty one others on August 20, 1936, expressing "sympathy with the Spanish Government and people" and asking the English government to "take every legitimate opportunity of pursuing towards such a foreign Government the traditional British policy of sympathetic benevolence" (RN 285). As Wayne K. Chapman and Janet M. Manson* have pointed out, the Woolfs were frequent collaborators in their political thinking. Several critics have noted the congruence of interest between Leonard's *QUACK, QUACK*! (1935) and *Three Guineas.* Selma Meyerowitz, Josephine O'Brien Schaefer* and Laura Moss Gottlieb* have all discussed parallels between the two works. O'Brien Schaefer writes that, in effect, Woolf "ascribed the cause of fascism in the home to the same communal psychology to which Leonard Woolf ascribed fascism in the state" (Schaefer 2) and concludes that *Quack, Quack!* and *Three Guineas* should be read together. Gottlieb also refers to Leonard's contribution to a book he edited in 1933, *The Intelligent Man's Way to*

Prevent War. She sees a disagreement between the Woolfs about ways to end war, a view disputed by Chapman and Manson. Gottlieb speculates that Leonard may have felt threatened "by his wife's invasion of the territory he had staked out for himself" (Gottlieb 250). Referring to earlier work on the subject by Leonard, Chapman and Manson argue that *Three Guineas* "made its case to a wider audience than Leonard Woolf had attempted to reach a generation before—and did so by design" (74).

John Mepham describes 1937 as "the most political year of Virginia Woolf's life" (*Literary Life* 165). In April, Guernica in Spain was bombed and in June a meeting was held in London at the Albert Hall in support of Basque children, 4,000 of whom had been evacuated to England. The program for this meeting includes among its sponsors Woolf, Vanessa BELL and Duncan GRANT (Mepham, *Literary Life* 166). (Woolf was among the sponsors of a showing of Pablo Picasso's *Guernica* at the Burlington Gallery in 1938.) Nineteen thirty-seven was also the year in which Woolf's nephew Julian BELL was killed while serving as an ambulance driver during the Spanish Civil War. Woolf wrote to her sister in August 1937 that she had written *Three Guineas* as an argument with Julian.

As Barbara Brothers* has pointed out, however, Woolf was far from the only British woman writer who used her skills in the cause of anti-fascism. Brothers criticizes Sandra Gilbert and Susan Gubar's *Norton Anthology of Literature by Women* for "perpetuat[ing] the myth that there is a paucity of women writers concerned with politics" (Brothers 247) because they cite only *Three Guineas* and list "none of the poems, essays, or fiction that women wrote on the Spanish Civil War" (Brothers 262n14). Angela Ingram and Daphne Patai* have also made clear that Woolf, "far from being the only—or the first—writer of the time to have articulated" the connection between fascism and the patriarchal family (18), was in fact part of a widespread movement of political writing by women that has been largely obscured by literary historians until recently. Ingram and Patai cite as one example of the kind of work in whose context Woolf wrote *Three Guineas* Katharine Burdekin's *Swastika Night,* published in 1937. Judith Johnston* also points out that Winifred HOLTBY's 1935 *Women and a Changing Civilization* analyzes Hitler and Mussolini's "cult of the cradle" and "anticipated the central arguments of *Three Guineas*" (Johnston 272–73).

Another aspect of the matrix from which *Three Guineas* developed was Woolf's growing interest in the work of Sigmund FREUD. Elizabeth Abel and others mention as an influence on *Three Guineas* Freud's 1933 public letter to Albert Einstein, "Why War?," part of a League of Nations project. Abel sees the "obsession with the father" in *Three Guineas* as both reflecting and reinforcing Woolf's new interest in Freud, and argues that Woolf's "reading [in *Three Guineas*] of the Victorian family romance returns psychoanalysis to its preanalytic origins in the seduction theory, which locates desire in the father rather than in the daughter" (Abel 106).

Woolf would certainly never have claimed to be the only woman writing in the 1930s about the slow descent of Europe into another bloody war. Nevertheless, as Nancy Topping Bazin and Jane Hamovit Lauter* have argued, her "feminist opposition to war, which burst forth in *Three Guineas,* had long been a part of her thought" (27). Various critics have drawn parallels between *Three Guineas* and others of Woolf's works. Susan Squier finds that *MRS. DALLOWAY* anticipates not only *Three Guineas* but also *A Room of One's Own* and "THOUGHTS ON PEACE IN AN AIR RAID" (Squier, *Virginia Woolf* 93), and Suzette Henke* links *Mrs. Dalloway* and *Three Guineas* through their concern with war and art. Alex Zwerdling also sees similarities between the social criticism of *Mrs. Dalloway* and *Three Guineas.* Jean Guiguet describes *A Room of One's Own* and *Three Guineas* as "written as it were in the margin of *Orlando* and *The Years,*" each work providing "an ideological commentary" for the respective novels (Guiguet 167). Others have also emphasized the congruity of themes between *Three Guineas* and *BETWEEN THE ACTS,* Phyllis Rose saying that writing *Three Guineas* enabled Woolf "to write *Between the Acts,* one last novel in her own voice and style" (Rose 257). Roger Poole argues that "one of the reasons why *Three Guineas* was so unpopular was because it suggested that the whole of Europe was complicit with Hitler in acquiescing in, even wanting, armed strife. And this view lies behind *Between the Acts*" (Poole, *Unknown* 219). Catherine Smith* compares the form of *Three Guineas* to *TO THE LIGHTHOUSE:* "Part I uncovers contradictions of being female in a male world. Part II envisions the community of women and ends in the apocalypse of the daughters' dance. Part III reveals the means to a new world hidden, though scattered, in the current one" (Smith 228).

Following Woolf's own statement that *The Years* and *Three Guineas* are really "one book," many critics have sought to explain the relationship between the two works. Nancy Topping Bazin sees in each an "expansion" of the concept of ANDROGYNY to "apply not just to souls but to societies" (Bazin 167). Jane Marcus reads the political history of England in *The Years* and reads Woolf's arguments in *Three Guineas* as a commentary on that history: "In [*The Years*], as in the history of England from 1880 to 1937, the feminists, socialists, pacifists, Irish rebels, Jews, anti-fascists, are each fighting separate battles. . . . *Three Guineas* was Virginia Woolf's attempt to articulate a unified intellectual position that would connect them all" (*Languages* 55). Many readers have seen *Three Guineas* as making explicit what Woolf implied in *The Years.* Sallie Sears* writes that if "in the novel the 'dream of a world in which things would be different' is implicit in the anguish of the characters over the world as it is, in the essay the accumulated sense of the world's madness breaks finally like a great wave past the 'sanity' of the speaker, sweeping such dreams far beyond our reach" (Sears 214). Several readers also point out the way in which Woolf has used the story of Antigone as a link between the novel and the essay; Marcus, for example, writes that the "plot and the 'buried alive' theme of *Antigone* form the mythology and structure of *The Years,* and as a *novelist* Woolf makes her reader sympathize with her English Creons. It is only as a 'pamphleteer' that she chooses between good and evil" (*Art* 102).

Woolf herself described the genesis of her polemic to her friend and political colleague Margaret Llewelyn DAVIES thus: "I felt it a great impertinence to come out with my views on such a subject; but to sit silent and acquiesce in all this idiotic letter signing and vocal pacifism when there's such an obvious horror in our midst—such tyranny, such Pecksniffism—finally made my blood boil into the usual ink-spray. . . . I was writing for the very common, very reluctant, very easily bored reader" (L6 25–51).

Three Guineas was published on June 2, 1938 by the HOGARTH PRESS in England and on August 25, 1938 by Harcourt, Brace & Co. in the United States. A summary, "Women Must Weep—Or Unite to End War," was published in the May and June issues of the *Atlantic Monthly.* Vanessa Bell's cover design, printed in mauve and blue against cream paper for both the English and U.S. editions, showed three checks arranged in a fan beside an inkwell with a pen standing in it ("L. says I'm to tell you he liked your jacket very much," Woolf wrote her sister [L6 206]). The first edition included five illustrations, listed as follows: A General, Heralds and A University Procession, A Judge, and An Archbishop. Diane Gillespie has called the photographs "a powerful adjunct to feminist argumentation" ("'Her Kodak'" 113) and notes that the generic labeling of the images helps to imprint on the reader's mind "visual images of the overriding source of the problem, the patriarchy on parade" (138). In 1943 the Hogarth Press issued *Three Guineas* as part of the Uniform Edition of Woolf's works. Subsequent editions in the United States and England omitted the illustrations without comment. In 1984, Chatto & Windus/Hogarth Press published a combined edition of *A Room of One's Own* and *Three Guineas* edited by Hermione Lee, restoring the illustrations, and in 1993 Penguin (U.K.) issued another combined edition of the two works, edited by Michèle Barrett, that not only includes the photographs but also reproduces in an appendix some of the newspaper clippings from Woolf's three large notebooks from which she drew examples in *Three Guineas.*

Background

Three Guineas refers extensively to events of the 1930s, to books and newspaper articles published while Woolf was writing it, and to the history of nineteenth-century reform movements. Many of the references are explained in Woolf's own notes. Readers wishing to find out more about a particular name or event mentioned in *Three Guineas* should look for individual entries on those names or events.

Critical Responses

In her diary and in letters written just before *Three Guineas* was published, Woolf is clearly apprehensive about the reception she expects her new book will get. "I shan't, when published, have a friend left," she wrote to her sister (L6 218), and in her diary she warned herself, "I'm going to be beaten, I'm going to be laughed at, I'm going to be held up to scorn and ridicule" (D5 64). Leonard warned his wife to "expect some very angry reviews from men," and Woolf added, "from women too" (D5 146). Woolf's overriding concern was not to be dismissed; she knew her arguments in *Three Guineas* would annoy, but she wanted them to have a hearing. When Basil de Selincourt reviewed *The Years* in *The Observer* in 1937, Woolf was pleased because "this means it will be debated; & this means that 3 Gs. will strike very sharp & clear on a hot iron" (D5 68). The publication in the *Atlantic Monthly* of a summary of *Three Guineas* led Woolf to record her fear of being taunted by reviewers that while her style was charming, her arguments were empty (D5 141).

Woolf's anticipation of her book's reception was very accurate. As she had predicted, those who disliked *Three Guineas* sneered at it and at her; those who approved found it exciting and moving. She began to receive letters about the book from people in England and the United States, and she corresponded with some of their writers until her death three years later (see Brenda Silver,* "*Three Guineas* Before and After"). Woolf told Ethel Smyth that she was collecting these letters "as a valuable contribution to psychology" (L6 247; many of these letters are in the MONK'S HOUSE PAPERS at Sussex University). Silver identifies two main themes in the letters Woolf received about *Three Guineas:* praise for her use of facts and quotations, and criticisms of her arguments and suggestions as impractical. A soldier wrote in praise of *Three Guineas,* as did "a distracted middle-class woman" who wanted "to start an outsiders society among the women of Yeovil" (L6 375).

The *Sunday Referee* for May 29, 1938 printed a notice of *Three Guineas* under the headline "Woman

Starts New Sex-War/Says Men's Clothes Are 'Barbarous' " (D5 148n1). Woolf heard from Lady Shena SIMON about a meeting of the Fabian Society at which *Three Guineas* had been discussed, and wrote, "How amusing that the dress charge rankled! Of course it goes very deep; and we shan't be free to discuss it for at least a century" (L6 303). Letters from women she admired, such as Pippa Strachey, cheered Woolf immensely (D5 147n17). Lady Rhondda, the editor of *Time & Tide,* had been read extracts from an advance copy of the book and wrote in praise to Woolf. Woolf replied that she was "very glad that you call yourself an outsider—the first to take the name!" (L6 229).

Many reviewers, to say nothing of Woolf's close friends and family, were unsettled by *Three Guineas.* In June 1938, *Time & Tide* published a defense of the book which discussed the "internal conflict" of reviewers who felt they had to praise *Three Guineas* because it was by Virginia Woolf, but who were repelled by its arguments (the article is reprinted in Marcus, *Art* 261–63). Earlier that month, Theodora Bosanquet had written in *Time & Tide* that *Three Guineas,* "for all the shimmer of its surface," was "a revolutionary bomb of a book" (CH 401). The *TIMES LITERARY SUPPLEMENT* pleased Woolf by calling her "the most brilliant pamphleteer in England" (D5 148). In its review, "Women in a World of War," the TLS noted Woolf's irony and wit, but also her profound seriousness; the positive review was undercut, however, by its conclusion that war is inevitable "as long as there is flesh aware of flesh" (CH 401). The novelist Graham Greene, writing in the *Spectator,* also tried to have it both ways, calling *Three Guineas* a "clear brilliant essay" but also "a little old-fashioned . . . a little provincial, even a little shrill" (CH 407).

There were, of course, reviewers who were less circumspect. De Selincourt wrote "a terrible indictment" in the *Observer,* and the historian George Malcolm Young expostulated in the *Sunday Times* of June 19, 1938. Woolf, perhaps reflecting the sense of liberty writing *Three Guineas* had given her, wrote to Ethel Smyth that she was "glad to see I raised the hackles of that mincing old pedant" (L6 247). The reviewers might dismiss her arguments in anger, but Woolf was continually cheered by hearing from "common readers" that *Three Guineas* made sense to them. She wrote to Smyth that she had made some readers furious, but "then a Quaker or governess makes up by thanking" (L6 255).

Probably the best-known criticism of *Three Guineas* came from Q. D. LEAVIS, whose review, "Caterpillars of the Commonwealth Unite!," was published in *Scrutiny* in September 1938. Leavis's review (reprinted in full by Robin Majumdar and Allen McLaurin in CH) also gained currency from the critical climate of the 1940s and 1950s, which was dominated in England by Leavis and her husband, F. R. Leavis, and in the United States by the New Critics, both proponents of a literary critical discourse that rigidly separated art from politics. Q. D. Leavis (who had been in the audience at Girton College in 1928 when Woolf spoke to the ODTAA Society) wrote that *A Room of One's Own* "was annoying enough . . . but this book is not merely silly and ill-informed, though it is that too, it contains some dangerous assumptions, some preposterous claims, and some nasty attitudes" (CH 410). Calling *Three Guineas* "Nazi dialectic without Nazi conviction" (CH 410), Leavis had nothing positive to say about it. Woolf did not bother to read the review to the end, writing in her diary that it seemed motivated by Leavis's sense of once having been snubbed when Woolf did not reply to a letter she wrote her (D5 165). Once again, the public critique was canceled out by a letter of praise, this time from Dr. Jane Harriet Walker, who had written about *Three Guineas* for the *Journal of the Women's Medical Federation* (D5 166n2). As Francis Mulhern* has written recently, although Woolf was certainly prone to blind spots in her awareness of her own class position, "Q. D. Leavis's attack would be more sympathetic were not its terms and tone those of a far more myopic, truculently conformist femininity" (Mulhern 258). Leavis demonstrated how utterly she had missed the point of *Three Guineas* when she complained that Woolf seemed unaware that her arguments implied the necessity of a "thorough-going revolution in [men's] wage-earning pursuits, and so a regular social reorganization" (CH 416).

Although Woolf could dismiss the "poor old strumpets" of Cambridge (L6 271), she was deeply hurt by the failure of those closest to her to recognize what she had attempted in *Three Guineas.* For a while there was silence from her friends. In April 1938, she described the "horrid anticlimax of 3Gs," writing in her diary that she "didn't get so much praise from L[eonard]. as I hoped" (D5 133). "Not a word said of it by any of my family or intimates," she wrote in July (D5 156). John Maynard Keynes visited and never said a word, but his wife, Lydia LOPOKOVA, told Woolf that her friends "all put up with you" (D5 163). Woolf felt "sent to Coventry"—ostracized—by her friends, yet paradoxically drew strength from this: "I'm fundamentally, I think, an outsider. . . . Its an odd feeling though, writing against the current" (D5 189). Roger Poole* has interpreted the silence surrounding *Three Guineas* as evidence that its truths, "like the truths that Septimus Smith [in *Mrs. Dalloway*] so much wanted to communicate, . . . belonged to an order of speech that was inadmissable at the time" (Poole, " 'We all' " 96). Makiko Minow-Pinkney also sees Woolf's contemporaries' ignoring *Three Guineas* as "clearly embarrassment at a radicalism whose implications they dared not face" (Minow-Pinkney 188).

One reader of *Three Guineas* who particularly irritated Woolf was Vita SACKVILLE-WEST, who wrote to Woolf in June 1938, "at one moment you enchant one with your lovely prose and next moment exasperate one with your misleading arguments" (Sackville-West, *Letters* 412). Woolf was so angry that she wrote to say she felt she could not be an impartial reader for a manuscript of Vita's under consideration by the Hogarth Press (*Solitude,* published in 1938). Vita was alarmed at the rift between them and hurriedly wrote back that she "never for a moment questioned your *facts* or their accuracy . . . but only disagreed in some places with the deductions you drew from them" (Sackville-West, *Letters* 414). It was, of course, the very heritage of privilege and ceremony that Vita represented which Woolf was attacking in *Three Guineas.* She made this clear in the draft of a letter to Vita's son Benedict NICOLSON in August 1940, replying to his criticisms of Roger FRY and the BLOOMSBURY GROUP. In books like *Three Guineas,* Woolf wrote, she had done her best "to destroy Sackvilles and Dufferins"—aristocratic English families (L6 420).

Vita's response to *Three Guineas* was, though, typical of Woolf's intimates. Quentin Bell, in his biography of his aunt, describes Maynard Keynes as "both angry and contemptuous" about the book (QB2 204), and also describes his own reaction at the time as thinking the book wrong "to involve a discussion of women's rights with the far more agonizing and immediate question of what we were to do to meet the ever-growing menace of Fascism and war" (QB2 204–05). Bell's sentiments echo those voiced by E. M. Forster, who had said of *Three Guineas* that "there is something old-fashioned about this extreme feminism; it dates back to her suffragette youth of the 1910s. . . . By the 1930s she had much less to complain of, and seems to keep grumbling from habit" (quoted in Rose 219). In her 1938 review for *Forum and Century,* Mary M. Colum* wrote that *Three Guineas* was "the most overtly feministic book I have read since the literature of the old suffrage days" (222) and that while non-cooperation was "fine in theory," in practice "it never works out on a large enough scale to be effective" (224). Colum did, however, praise the way in which Woolf's "traditional rhythms" and "carefully chosen words" might "conceal from the casual reader the revolutionary nature of the ideas in the epistles that form the book" (225).

The line of criticism typified by Forster was revisited by Nigel NICOLSON in his introduction to the fifth volume of Woolf's LETTERS. Nicolson dismisses the arguments of *Three Guineas* as "nonsense" and "neither sober nor rational" (xvii), tracing the origin of *Three Guineas* to "the horrid masculinity of Leslie [Stephen], George and Gerald [DUCKWORTH] which had humiliated her and weakened her sexual nature" (xviii). Taken to task by Carolyn Heilbrun, Nicolson defended his introduction in a letter to *VIRGINIA WOOLF MISCELLANY* (number 16), in which he referred to his mother, Vita Sackville-West, as an "ardent feminist" and said that Woolf, "by her conduct and expressed views in 1939–41," had "recanted what she had written about war in *Three Guineas*" (VWM 16: 5).

In an important recent article, "The Authority of Anger," Brenda Silver* has traced the critical reception of *Three Guineas* to illustrate how "the reigning discourses in our century, whether political, critical, or psychological, have constructed truths that condemn anger, at least women's anger, and with it feminist critique as destructive of truth" (Silver, "Authority" 341). Silver points out that contemporary reviews of *Three Guineas* on both sides of the Atlantic "reveal a number of rhetorical strategies that deny the authority of the text by denying the authority of [its] anger" (346). Contemporary reviews in England were generally praising, but the praise was frequently of the style and tone of *Three Guineas* rather than of its arguments. Silver explains how the reception of Woolf's tone by readers depends on their construction of Woolf as "author," and this construction is crucial in the "battle for who controls the discourse of cultural criticism encoded in the history of *Three Guineas*" (347). Owing largely to the dominance of the Leavises and the New Critics in the years following World War II, *Three Guineas* remained invisible. Silver marks the revival of interest in it at the publication in 1968 of J. B. Batchelor's essay "Feminism in Virginia Woolf" and Herbert Marder's *Feminism and Art.* Batchelor* wrote that *Three Guineas* was "not an outdated echo of the suffrage movement, but draws on a spirit of resentment which was in some ways peculiar to the 'thirties" (Batchelor 169). Although these critics rescued *Three Guineas* from oblivion, Silver points out that each of them wanted Woolf to "conform to their standards and views. Ultimately, their reconstructions of Woolf and her voice subvert both the feminism and the anger through a strategy of pathologizing that denies *Three Guineas* the power to speak authoritatively in the sphere of public debate just as effectively as the strategy of praise had done in 1938" (Silver, "Authority" 356).

Marder and Batchelor both compare *Three Guineas* to *A Room of One's Own,* to the former's disadvantage. Batchelor calls *Three Guineas* "a shrill and angry work" (169) and complains of its "bitterly rancorous tone" (170). Marder, too, is unsettled by the tone of *Three Guineas,* preferring the more indirect indictments of *The Years:* "The feminist program which forms the heart of *Three Guineas* exposes Virginia Woolf's limitations as surely as the luminous narrative of *The Years* proves her mastery. Taken together, these two books encompass the best and the worst of which she was capable" (Marder 157). Calling the tone of *Three Guineas* "subtly wrong," Marder sees the polemic as a "neurotic" book compared to the "healthy" *Years* (Marder 174).

In her examination of the critical reception of *Three Guineas,* Silver suggests that male critics in particular have disliked the book. For Perry Meisel, *Three Guineas* becomes "an act of literary theft" (Silver, "Authority" 364), in which he sees Woolf as deploying the very methods she is deploring. Silver interprets Meisel's negative reading of *Three Guineas* as implicitly also a criticism of feminist literary critical practices. Many male critics have indeed found fault with Woolf's methods and tone in *Three Guineas.* Mitchell Leaska, for example, speaks of the "persuasive and lyrical *A Room of One's Own* and the harsher, more contentious *Three Guineas*" (Leaska, *Novels* 194); Leaska directly echoes E. M. Forster when he writes of finding in *Three Guineas* "Mrs. Woolf in a cantankerous mood" (Leaska 196). For Jean Guiguet, the ideas of *Three Guineas* are fused "in a surge of eloquence rather than any real logic" (Guiguet 179), and John Mepham, while acknowledging the "great and abiding value" of the book, finds that Woolf's "argument suffers from damaging over-simplification" (*Literary Life* 171). Anomalous in this gendered division of critical reception is Mark Hussey, who writes of the importance to Woolf of *Three Guineas* and *The Years,* saying that the "only truly radical politics for Woolf was sexual politics, a change in the patriarchal system of values in which the attitudes of war pervade every aspect of life" (Hussey, *Singing* 133).

Anger has often been the focus of critical writing on *Three Guineas.* Carolyn Heilbrun* acknowledges that for a long time she was "made uncomfortable by *Three Guineas,* preferring the 'nicer' *Room*" (Heilbrun 241). Alex Zwerdling points out that the drafts of *Three Guineas* are even angrier than the published version. In *Three Guineas,* he writes, Woolf "considers her male audience more carefully, more calculatedly, than in any other work" (Zwerdling 259), making rhetorical choices "to avoid offending the males in her audience so seriously that they will stop reading the book" (Zwerdling 259). Both Zwerdling and Heilbrun argue that *Three Guineas* could only have been written in Woolf's fifties. By then, says Zwerdling, "the stream of history, the stream of consciousness, and the flow of her artistic imagination had become a single current" (Zwerdling 25). Heilbrun remarks on Woolf's confidence toward the end of her life: "With great works behind her, she would no longer fear either the expression of her anger or its effects on the men who overheard her" (Heilbrun 237).

Silver identifies as "instrumental in stimulating the renewed interest" in *Three Guineas* Jane Marcus's 1974 presentation at the Modern Language Association Convention, " 'No More Horses': Virginia Woolf on Art and Propaganda" (reprinted in *Art and Anger* 101–21). *Three Guineas* now appears in debates within the peace movement and is often cited by feminist peace activists and pacifists. Silver calls it "a blueprint for a contemporary feminist analysis of culture and its institutions" ("Authority" 342); Marcus calls it a "role model" and "a major contribution to political science" (*Languages* xi), "the bible of a new generation of pacifists" (*Art and Anger* xiv); in *Sexchanges,* Sandra Gilbert and Susan Gubar refer to *Three Guineas* as "the postwar era's great text of pacifist feminism" (306). However, there are also dissenting voices, as for example Karen Rosenberg,* who writes that the image of woman as outsider is "magnetic, seductive and misleading" (453)

Sara Ruddick* calls *Three Guineas* "a feminist antimilitarist tract from the fascist thirties [that] has assumed a central place in contemporary feminist peace politics" (Ruddick 147). The book has often provided slogans as well as arguments for feminist peace activists—"As a woman I have no country," for example—but has also provoked debate within the activist community. Glynis Carr* notes that post-1960s attention to *Three Guineas* often came from peace activists and theorists of non-violence. Carr writes that Woolf's analysis has been challenged by contemporary activist feminists such as Audre Lorde and Minnie Bruce Pratt, "who believe a great deal of energy is wasted when feminists attempt to 'rank oppressions' " (Carr 14). Nevertheless, Carr concludes that *Three Guineas* "poses the essential questions for feminist theorists of war and nonviolence" (Carr 21). Nancy Burr Evans* has described similarities between the tenets of Woolf's Outsider's Society and "the basic rules for implementing the Gandhian approach" (173). In a commentary written during the Persian Gulf war of 1991, carol anne douglas* addressed Woolf directly to explain why her guinea for education must be returned: "We are not able to ensure that the educational institutions will remain free of the military-industrial establishment or that women will refrain from forming the 'unreal loyalties' you deplored to the patriarchal institutions such as the nation state, the corporations, and the military" (douglas 5).

One of Q. D. Leavis's most persistent criticisms of *Three Guineas* was that it demonstrated Woolf's blindness to the privilege her own class position afforded her. Zwerdling comments that far from being insulated by her class as Leavis charged, Woolf was in fact unusual among her peers in her awareness of class (Zwerdling 233). Marcus believes Woolf's honesty about the working class is often mistaken for snobbery by liberal critics (*Art* 116). Silver, drawing on the work of Mary Childers,* points out that those who construct *Three Guineas* "as a model for feminist politics without recognizing its exclusion of women other than those belonging to Woolf's self-defined class . . . reproduce Woolf's own class blindness and bias" (Silver, "Authority" 369–70). Childers criticizes contemporary feminists who ignore Woolf's carefully circumscribed group, the "daughters of educated men," and attempt to use *Three Guineas* to justify a totalized feminist theory (Childers 72).

Childers believes that, "in effect, Woolf chose to leave up in the air whether or not her readers would see her book as an affirmation of feminism as a political movement" (Childers 64), and argues that often Woolf's rhetorical playfulness "outdoes the content" of her text. As an example, Childers points out that the 1919 Sex Disqualification (Removal) Act frequently alluded to by Woolf in *Three Guineas* did not live up to its promise and actually resulted in little change for women in the professions. Childers sees Woolf's writing as an "impediment to the development of feminist theory in certain sectors of the academy" because Woolf insists on "aestheticized political arguments" at the same time as being impatient "with the specificity of material deprivation" (Childers 66). Childers concludes that although Woolf "wrote persuasively about being an outsider, in relation to working-class women she was often on the outside looking down" (Childers 78).

For many contemporary readers, the form of *Three Guineas* has itself been an obstacle to understanding. Zwerdling sees Woolf's rhetorical choices as dictated by her sense of the book's potential audience's hostility (257), and reads the extensive notes as Woolf's effort to "quarantine" her anger (262). Marcus, in "Thinking Back Through Our Mothers," links Woolf's 1930s notebooks with those kept by her contemporary Walter Benjamin: "The quotations she used in *A Room of One's Own, Three Guineas,* and *The Pargiters,* the scholarly footnotes in which documentation is a form of possession of the truth and exorcism of evil, are the intellectual pacifist outsider's only weapon against lies and injustice" (3). Marcus identifies *Three Guineas* as "in style and content part of the literature of the oppressed" (*Languages* 79). Several recent critics have also seen in the form of *Three Guineas* an enactment of its politics. Lynn Kramer,* for example, says that the notes "represent, in textual format, the way women's voices, especially feminist voices, have been fragmented and marginalized" (Kramer 100), and Pamela Caughie notes that Woolf's extensive use of repetition in all its aspects "exhausts the argument of the essay, resisting attempts to reduce it to a progression of logical propositions and undermining any final position, for to impose a position on others would be fascist" (Caughie 116). For Judith Johnston, the form of *Three Guineas* "embodies a polyvocal alternative to the single authoritarian voice of polemical essays and political speeches" (Johnston 255). Victoria Middleton,* who calls *Three Guineas* a "tract for our times" (415), argues that it "works not by transcending but by unsettling our ideological assumptions about culture and power" (407).

Anne Herrmann* has discussed letter-writing as "a viable rhetorical strategy for the female writer in an androcentric culture" (170). Christine Froula* also notes that the letter was "for centuries the only genre open to women" (29) in her recent analysis of *Three Guineas* as Woolf's "public reply to Paul's epistle dictating the 'veiling' or subordination of women in public life" (29). Froula argues that *Three Guineas* is a "spiritual epistle that exposes the profoundly structural role that violence and the sacred play in the masculinized public sphere" ("St. Virginia's Epistle" 28).

Catherine Smith identifies the form of *Three Guineas* as "prophecy," a "literary mode peculiar to cultural crisis" (Smith 225). One of the letters Woolf received about *Three Guineas* came from Amelia Forbes Emerson in Concord, Massachusetts, in which Emerson equated Woolf's Society of Outsiders with the Society of Friends, the Quakers. Emerson traced Woolf's "lineage and ideas to her aunt, Caroline Emelia Stephen, the Quaker theologian and mystic" (Silver, "*Three Guineas* Before and After" 266). Smith finds the "rational mysticism" of Caroline Emelia STEPHEN to have much to do with *Three Guineas,* which she calls "the spiritual autobiography of a feminist" (Smith 229). Smith argues that in *Three Guineas* Woolf "corrects" her aunt's vision because she "disagreed with Caroline Emelia's social proposals for women" (Smith 229). Linking Woolf to a tradition of English women mystics, Smith finds in *Three Guineas* a "strong tonal resemblance to seventeenth-century tracts by [Jane] Lead and her contemporaries" (Smith 233). These seventeenth-century mystics were "a neglected, diverse, early group of verbal artists in England, the link Virginia Woolf wanted to find in women's literary history between the Renaissance poets and the eighteenth-century novelists" (Smith 232). Georgia Johnston* has also read *Three Guineas* as a kind of "collective autobiography" of women's lives: "*Three Guineas* presents the lives of women as collective, instead of individual, public instead of private, referential, not to a self, but to a system" (Georgia Johnston 327).

Three Guineas, according to Elizabeth Meese, "stands in relation to contemporary cultural analysis as *A Room of One's Own* does with respect to feminist literary criticism" (Meese 100). It is, says Meese, "a meditation on the effects of difference, as well as a treatise on war or women's condition" (102). Like *A Room of One's Own, Three Guineas* has had a pervasive cultural influence, cutting a path in which have followed books such as Cynthia Enloe's *Bananas, Beaches, and Bases: Making Feminist Sense Out of International Politics* or Marilyn French's *The War Against Women.* Roger Poole has described the Woolf of *Three Guineas* as war's "greatest theoretician" (" 'We All' " 99). In *Three Guineas,* as Elizabeth Abel points out, "Woolf's political agenda . . . is less to articulate a pacifist response to the fascist threat, her stated goal, than to bring the impending war home, to resituate the battlefield in the British family and workplace" (Abel 91). The form of *Three Guineas* itself is, for Abel, "imbricated in a dialogue with psychoanalysis" (103), a dialogue that forced Woolf to abandon the maternal metaphor she had used to such effect in *A Room of One's Own:* "As the sexual and political ideologies of the 1930s underscored for Woolf both the intractability of patriarchy and the mother's position in perpetuating it, her feminism shifted from valorizing mothers to confronting the 'infantile fixation of the fathers' " (Abel 94). The "figure of a man" (whom Abel says recalls Professor VON X from *A Room of One's Own*), Woolf's generic tyrant, is sharply delineated in *Three Guineas,* but he was present in Woolf's work long before that.

Works Specific to This Entry:

Batchelor, J. B. "Feminism in Virginia Woolf." In Claire Sprague, ed. *Virginia Woolf:* 169–79.

Bazin, Nancy Topping, and Jane Hamovit Lauter. "Virginia Woolf's Keen Sensitivity to War: Its Roots and Its Impact on Her Novels." In Mark Hussey, ed. *Virginia Woolf and War:* 14–39.

Black, Naomi. "Virginia Woolf and the Women's Movement." In Jane Marcus, ed. *Virginia Woolf: A Feminist Slant:* 180–97.

Brothers, Barbara. "British Women Write the Story of the Nazis: A Conspiracy of Silence." In Angela Ingram and Daphne Patai, eds. *Rediscovering Forgotten Radicals: British Women Writers 1889–1939.* Chapel Hill: University of North Carolina Press, 1993.

Carr, Glynis. "Waging Peace: Virginia Woolf's *Three Guineas." Proteus* 3, 2 (Fall 1986): 13–21.

Chapman, Wayne K., and Janet M. Manson. "Carte and Tierce: Leonard, Virginia Woolf, and War for Peace." In Mark Hussey, ed. *Virginia Woolf and War:* 58–78.

Childers, Mary M. "Virginia Woolf on the Outside Looking Down: Reflections on the Class of Women." *Modern Fiction Studies* 38, 1 (Spring 1992): 61–80.

Colum, Mary M. "Life and Literature: Are Women Outsiders?" *Forum and Century* 100 (1938): 222–26.

douglas, carol anne. "Dear Ms. Woolf, We Are Returning Your Guinea." *off our backs* 21 (Fall 1991): 5.

Evans, Nancy Burr. "The Political Consciousness of Virginia Woolf: *A Room of One's Own* and *Three Guineas." The New Scholar* 4, 2 (1974): 167–80.

Froula, Christine. "St. Virginia's Epistle to an English Gentleman; or, Sex, Violence, and the Public Sphere in Woolf's *Three Guineas." Tulsa Studies in Women's Literature* 13, 1 (Spring 1994): 27–56.

Gottlieb, Laura Moss. "The War Between the Woolfs." In Jane Marcus, ed. *Virginia Woolf and Bloomsbury:* 242–52.

Heilbrun, Carolyn. "Woolf in Her Fifties." In Jane Marcus, ed. *Virginia Woolf: A Feminist Slant:* 236–53.

Henke, Suzette. " 'The Prime Minister': A Key to *Mrs. Dalloway."* In Elaine K. Ginsberg and Laura Moss Gottlieb, eds. *Virginia Woolf: Centennial Essays:* 127–141.

Herrmann, Anne. " 'Intimate, Irreticent and Indiscreet in the Extreme': Epistolary Essays by Virginia Woolf and Christa Wolf." *New German Critique* 38 (Spring/Summer 1986): 161–80.

Ingram, Angela. " 'The Sacred Edifices': Virginia Woolf and Some of the Sons of Culture." In Jane Marcus, ed. *Virginia Woolf and Bloomsbury:* 125–45.

Ingram, Angela, and Daphne Patai. "Introduction: 'An Intelligent Discontent with . . . Conditions.' " In Angela Ingram and Daphne Patai, eds. *Rediscovering Forgotten Radicals: British Women Writers 1889–1939.* Chapel Hill: University of North Carolina Press, 1993.

Johnston, Georgia. "Women's Voice: *Three Guineas* as Autobiography." In Vara Neverow-Turk and Mark Hussey, eds. *Virginia Woolf: Themes and Variations:* 321–28.

Johnston, Judith L. "The Remediable Flaw: Revisioning Cultural History in *Between the Acts."* In Jane Marcus, ed. *Virginia Woolf and Bloomsbury:* 253–77.

Kramer, Lynn. "One Retrospective Lupine View: A Terrified Student's View of Virginia Woolf's *Three Guineas."* In Vara Neverow-Turk and Mark Hussey, eds. *Virginia Woolf: Themes and Variations:* 97–102.

Middleton, Victoria. "*Three Guineas:* Subversion and Survival in the Professions." *Twentieth Century Literature* 8, 4 (Winter 1982): 405–17.

Mulhern, Francis. "English Reading." In Homi K. Bhabha, ed. *Nation and Narration.* New York: Routledge, 1990: 250–64.

Poole, Roger. " 'We all put up with you Virginia': Irreceivable Wisdom About War." In Mark Hussey, ed. *Virginia Woolf and War:* 79–100.

Rosenberg, Karen. "Peaceniks and Soldier Girls." *The Nation,* April 14, 1984: 453–57.

Ruddick, Sara. *Maternal Thinking: Toward a Politics of Peace.* New York: Ballantine, 1989.

Schaefer, Josephine O'Brien. "*Three Guineas* and *Quack, Quack!* Read Together." *Virginia Woolf Miscellany* 7 (Spring 1977): 2–3.

Sears, Sallie. "Notes on Sexuality: *The Years* and *Three Guineas.*" *Bulletin of the New York Public Library* 80, 2 (Winter 1977): 211–20.
Silver, Brenda R. "The Authority of Anger: *Three Guineas* as Case Study." *Signs* 6, 2 (Winter 1991): 340–70.
———. "*Three Guineas* Before and After: Further Answers to Correspondents." In Jane Marcus, ed. *Virginia Woolf: A Feminist Slant:* 254–76.
Smith, Catherine F. "*Three Guineas:* Virginia Woolf's Prophecy." In Jane Marcus, ed. *Virginia Woolf and Bloomsbury:* 225–41.

"Three Jews" The first publication of the HOGARTH PRESS was *Two Stories,* containing Woolf's "THE MARK ON THE WALL" and Leonard's "Three Jews." "Three Jews" has two narrators, the first of whom meets the second at Kew Gardens where they each acknowledge their alienation from the English scene. As with most of Leonard's fiction, the story explores racial and class tensions (see Meyerowitz 53–55).

Thursday Evenings See BLOOMSBURY GROUP.

Tidmarsh Lytton STRACHEY bought the Mill House in the village of Tidmarsh, Berkshire, in 1918. He lived there with Dora CARRINGTON, who had found the house, and, later, with her husband, Ralph PARTRIDGE, until 1924, when all three moved to HAM SPRAY.

"Time Passes" See *TO THE LIGHTHOUSE.*

Times Literary Supplement (TLS) Woolf began contributing reviews (usually unsigned) to the TLS in 1905, three years after its founding, and continued throughout her life. From 1902 to 1938 the TLS was edited by Bruce Lyttelton Richmond (1871–1964). Andrew McNeillie has written that Richmond became Woolf's "most important journalistic mentor (after her father)" (E1 xiv). In 1938, Woolf received a letter, "grateful, from Bruce Richmond, ending my 30 year connection with him & the Lit Sup." and described how pleased she had been whenever the "Major Journal" called with a commission (D5 144–45). She wrote that she had "learnt a lot of my craft" writing for Richmond (D5 145). McNeillie also points out that in the 1920s the TLS "became gradually less and less a source of reviewing work for [Woolf] and increasingly, as she wished, an outlet for full-length essays or 'leaders' " (E3 524). In her DIARY, particularly in the early years of her professional career, Woolf noted having sometimes to tailor or censor her opinions in TLS reviews (D2 30; 152).

Todd, Dorothy Editor of British *Vogue* from 1922 to 1926 who commissioned articles from Woolf and other avant-garde writers. Woolf's "Indiscretions" was published in the magazine in 1924 (E3 460–65); other contributions by her were "George Moore" (1925), a review of Arthur WALEY's translation of "The Tale of Genji" (1925), "The Life of John Mytton" (1926), and "A Professor of Life" (review of the *Letters of Walter Raleigh*) (1926).

"Together and Apart" See *MRS. DALLOWAY'S PARTY.*

Tolstoy, Count Leo Nikolayevich (1828–1910) Regarded by Woolf as one of the "masters" of the novel, Tolstoy was one of those European thinkers such as Friedrich Nietzsche and Henrik IBSEN who "sent fresh waves of thought across the Continent [while] the English slept undisturbed," she wrote in 1908 in a review of *Londoner Skizzenbuch,* by A. von Rutari, and *Londres comme je l'ai vu, texte et dessins par Charles Huard* ("The Stranger in London" E1: 203). Born into an aristocratic Russian family, Tolstoy as a young man more or less renounced his inheritance and devoted himself to writing.

Although his work was censored by the Russian Imperial government, he had a wide influence. Among his major works are *War and Peace* (1865–72), *Anna Karenina* (1875–76), *The Death of Ivan Ilyitch* (1884) and *The Kreutzer Sonata* (1890). Tolstoy's works were initially known to English-speaking readers in the twenty-two-volume series translated by Nathan Dole and published by Scribner's from 1899 to 1912 (Willis 85). Constance GARNETT's translation of *War and Peace* appeared in 1911, and her *Death of Ivan Ilyitch and Other Stories* in 1915, contributing significantly to the growing passion for Russian art in England during the 1920s.

Reviewing Tolstoy's *The Cossacks and Other Tales of the Caucasus* (1916) for the *TIMES LITERARY SUPPLEMENT* in 1917, Woolf described the "shock" of his genius on returning to his fiction after he had been slightly eclipsed for the English reader by the overwhelming popularity of Fyodor DOSTOYEVSKY and Anton CHEKHOV (E2 77). Woolf admired Tolstoy's extraordinary power of observation, and in "A Minor Dostoevsky" wrote that there was always in Tolstoy's work "a central purpose which brings the whole field into focus" (E2 166). In "CHARACTER IN FICTION," Woolf wrote that there is "hardly any subject of human experience that is left out of *War and Peace*" (E3 426). It was this aspect of Tolstoy—the breadth of his experience—that led her in *A ROOM OF ONE'S OWN* to remark that had he had to live the kind of sequestered life forced by convention upon his English contemporary George ELIOT, he could not have written *War and Peace.*

In 1920, Woolf reviewed *Reminiscences of Leo Nicolayevitch Tolstoy* by Maxim GORKY, published by the HOGARTH PRESS in a translation by Samuel Solomonovitch KOTELIANSKY and Leonard WOOLF, one of several translations from the Russian that she wrote about. In 1922, the Hogarth Press published *The Autobiography of Countess Sophie Tolstoy,* by Tolstoy's wife, also translated by Koteliansky and Leonard Woolf. Woolf herself assisted Koteliansky in the translation of two Tolstoy works published by the Hogarth Press in 1923, *Tolstoi's Love Letters with a Study of the Autobiographical Elements in Tolstoi's Work,* by Paul Biryukov, and *Talks with Tolstoi* by A. B. Goldenveizer. In 1936, the Hogarth Press published *On Socialism,* a work Tolstoy had left uncompleted at his death.

Tomlin, Stephen (1901–37) Sculptor whose 1931 bust of Woolf is in the garden at MONK'S HOUSE (one is also in the NATIONAL GALLERY; the original plaster cast is at CHARLESTON). Known as "Tommy," he became friendly with David GARNETT after visiting Garnett and Francis BIRRELL's bookstore, and through Garnett he got to know others in the BLOOMSBURY GROUP. Tomlin married Julia Strachey, Oliver Strachey's daughter by his first wife, in 1927. (Her first novel, *Cheerful Weather for the Wedding,* was published in 1932 by the HOGARTH PRESS with a jacket designed by Duncan GRANT.) In her ironic preface to *ORLANDO* Woolf includes "Mr. and Mrs. Stephen Tomlin" among those friends who "have helped me in ways too various to specify." Tomlin had a brief affair with Dora CARRINGTON in 1926.

Bust of Virginia Woolf. Stephen Tomlin. Photograph by Louise H. Tucker.
Tomlin made this bust in 1931; the original plaster cast is at Charleston, and another copy is in the National Gallery. Woolf's extreme discomfort at sitting for this work is evident from its expression.

Toms, Mrs. Mentioned in *THE YEARS,* the downstairs lodger at a house for the poor Eleanor PARGITER is involved in.

***To the Lighthouse* (1927)** Published on the thirty-second anniversary of her mother's death, Woolf's fifth novel is probably her most widely read. It concerns a large Victorian family, the Ramsays, seen before and after World War I, and is set at their summer house in the Isle of Skye in the Hebrides, a house that overflows with children and guests. The guests in part 1, "The Window," are William BANKES, Lily BRISCOE, Augustus CARMICHAEL, Minta DOYLE, Paul RAYLEY and Charles TANSLEY; in part 3, "The Lighthouse," Mr. Carmichael and Lily Briscoe return to the house together with a Mrs. BECKWITH.

In writing *To the Lighthouse* Woolf consciously used her own childhood memories of summer vacations in ST. IVES, Cornwall, at Talland House (from where she could see across the bay the GODREVY LIGHTHOUSE) and drew portraits of her parents, Leslie STEPHEN and Julia Prinsep STEPHEN, in the figures of Mr. and Mrs. RAMSAY. As in Woolf's own family, the Ramsays have eight children (though in Woolf's family, unlike the Ramsays, the children did not all share the same parents): Andrew, Cam, James, Jasper, Nancy, Prue, Roger and Rose RAMSAY.

The novel is in three titled parts—"The Window," "Time Passes" and "The Lighthouse"—each of which contains several sections of varying lengths. In part 1, there are nineteen sections; ten in part 2; and thirteen in part 3. In all HOGARTH PRESS editions of the novel up to and including 1977, the second and subsequent sections of part 1, "The Window," were misnumbered; in the U.S. editions, roman numerals are used for section numbers, and in the English editions, Arabic numerals.

Outline

"*The Window*" begins on an early evening in mid-September as Mrs. Ramsay, a fifty-year-old mother of eight, tells her six-year-old son James that, yes, he will be able to go to the lighthouse the following day if the weather is fine. "But," says her husband, a noted philosopher, it will not be fine. Mrs. Ramsay is

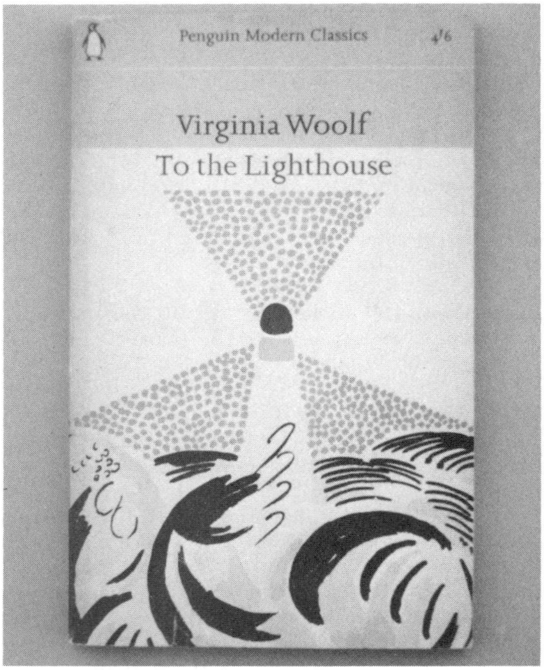

To the Lighthouse. *Courtesy of Linda J. Langham. Duncan Grant designed the cover for this Penguin Modern Classics edition, published in 1964.*

sitting in the drawing room knitting a stocking for the lighthouse keeper's son; she empathizes with the lighthouse keeper's lonely existence. Charles Tansley, a protégé of Mr. Ramsay's whom the children have dubbed "the little atheist," exacerbates James's anger when he rubs in Mr. Ramsay's pessimism about the weather. Mrs. Ramsay's daughters, Prue, Rose, and Nancy, find Tansley irritating. Although she too is annoyed by Tansley's adding to her son's disappointment, Mrs. Ramsay has earlier taken pity on Tansley, inviting him to accompany her when she runs errands in the town and pays charitable visits to the poor. Mrs. Ramsay aspires to be "an investigator, elucidating the social problem" of poverty (TTL 9). Mrs. Ramsay worries about the entire household, including "the Swiss girl" (named Marie at one point, Marthe at another) who cries because her father is dying of cancer.

(III) Trying to distract James from his disappointment, Mrs. Ramsay looks through the ARMY AND NAVY STORES catalogue for a particularly complicated picture he can cut out. In the garden, Mr. Ramsay, having "shed" Tansley, cries out a line from Alfred, Lord TENNYSON's "Charge of the Light Brigade," startling his wife. She remembers that she is supposed to be keeping her head as much as possible in the same position for Lily Briscoe, who is painting her.

Section IV begins from Lily's point of view. She is thankful that Mr. Ramsay does not come over to look at her painting; William Bankes, however, does, but she does not mind this so much. Lily and William have rooms in the village (all the rooms in the house being full) and thus have come to be allies of a sort. They go for their customary evening stroll and Lily ponders the aesthetic problems she must solve. William thinks of how his friendship with Mr. Ramsay has faded. Walking back, they encounter Cam, who refuses to give William a flower, saddening him. Discussing Mr. Ramsay's work with William, Lily thinks—as she always does since asking Andrew what his father's books were about—of a kitchen table (TTL 23); when she had not understood Andrew's explanation that Mr. Ramsay's books are about "subject and object and the nature of reality," he told her to "think of a kitchen table . . . when you're not there" (TTL 23). Suddenly, they are startled by Jasper shooting at starlings in a tree.

(V) Lily and William pass by the window as Mrs. Ramsay continues to try to console James. Seeing them, it occurs to Mrs. Ramsay that they should marry! She measures the stocking against James's leg, but he fidgets. The narrator wonders what is the source of Mrs. Ramsay's sadness and describes William Bankes's adoration of her beauty (TTL 29–30).

(VI) Mrs. Ramsay turns her attention to her husband, who stops by the window and tickles James's leg. When his wife says it may still be possible to go to the lighthouse the next day, Mr. Ramsay is enraged at her "irrationality;" "Damn you," he says (32), but then feels ashamed. Off he goes once more to walk in the garden and to wrestle with his heroic quest for "R," the letter that eludes him in the alphabetical progression from A TO Z of his philosophy. Mr. Ramsay thinks about fame, imagining himself in various heroic guises.

(VII) James hates his father for distracting Mrs. Ramsay with his demand for sympathy; he is a "beak of brass" plunging into Mrs. Ramsay's "rosy-flowered fruit tree" (38). When Mr. Ramsay resumes his pacing in the garden, Mrs. Ramsay turns to the Grimms' fairy tale of "THE FISHERMAN AND HIS WIFE," which she is reading to James. But as she reads she is troubled by the thought that people might think her husband depends upon her. Mr. Carmichael shuffles by.

(VIII) She pities Carmichael, who drops laudanum into his water at lunch, and whose wife was so mean to him. Mrs. Ramsay begins to question the motivation of her kindness to others; as she reads to James, Mr. Ramsay again walks by, now slipping into a speculation about whether the world would have been different had William SHAKESPEARE never existed, a line of thought he will follow when he talks "some nonsense to the young men at Cardiff" the following month (45). He walks to the edge of the lawn to look at the bay, observed by his wife and by Lily Briscoe.

(IX) Lily and William are still discussing Mr. Ramsay. Lily's opinion is influenced by her being in love with "staying with the Ramsays," and Mr. Bankes gazes adoringly at Mrs. Ramsay. Lily looks again at her painting and judges it "infinitely bad," hearing the voice of Charles Tansley saying "Women can't paint, women can't write . . ." (48). She recalls a nocturnal visit from Mrs. Ramsay, who wants her to be married, and thinks about the complexity of her feelings for Mrs. Ramsay, of her intense desire to become one with her. Looking at Mrs. Ramsay, Lily sees her as a dome. William Bankes is looking meanwhile at Lily's painting. They discuss it, Lily explaining that the purple triangle represents Mrs. Ramsay reading to James. Cam dashes by them.

(X) Mrs. Ramsay calls Cam to her and tells her to ask Mildred, the cook, if Andrew, Minta and Paul have come back from the beach. When she hears that they have not, Mrs. Ramsay assumes Minta and Paul are engaged. She continues reading to James, simultaneously thinking about Minta and again wondering if her motives in involving herself in other people's lives are altogether honorable. She decides they are, and again thinks of social reforms she would work toward had she the time, which, having eight children, she does not. She thinks about her children. The story finished, Mildred takes James to bed, leaving his mother alone to think of how children never forget their disappointments.

(XI) Alone, Mrs. Ramsay slips into a reverie as she continues to knit, becoming to herself a "wedge-shaped core of darkness" (62). She is startled out of her reverie by a saying—"We are in the hands of the Lord"—that pops unbidden into her mind, causing her to frown. Mr. Ramsay passes by and notes "the sternness at the heart of her beauty" (64), and feels that she is remote from him. Knowing that her husband needs to feel she needs him, Mrs. Ramsay takes her shawl and joins him in the garden.

(XII) As they stroll, they talk about their children, their house, their guests. It is just past 7 o'clock. Mr. Ramsay thinks of the better books he would have written had he not married; his wife knows he is thinking this. In the twilight Mrs. Ramsay sees William and Lily walking together, which she is certain means they will marry.

(XIII) William tells Lily about the great paintings he has seen in Europe, and they discuss the benefits for a painter of seeing masterpieces. Turning, they see the Ramsays watching Prue and Jasper throwing catches and Lily sees Mr. and Mrs. Ramsay for a moment as symbols of marriage. Mrs. Ramsay asks her daughter whether Nancy went to the beach with the others.

(XIV) A section in parentheses (presumably to suggest simultaneity with the preceding sections) moves the point of view to Nancy, who went reluctantly with Paul and Minta and her brother Andrew to the beach. Once there, Andrew and Nancy go off on their own, leaving Paul and Minta to their own devices. Nancy broods over a rock pool, turning it into a cosmos. Andrew shouts that the tide is coming in; Nancy runs up the beach and is startled to find Paul and Minta in each other's arms. Minta loses a brooch that had belonged to her grandmother, and Paul secretly resolves to slip away at dawn and buy her another in Edinburgh. Paul has asked Minta to marry him, "the worst moment of his life" (78), and feels that Mrs. Ramsay is responsible. They walk back and Paul sees the house, all lit up, people moving behind the windows, and realizes they are late for dinner.

(XVI) Prue having told her (in XV) that Nancy was with the others, Mrs. Ramsay feels irrationally that this means a disaster is less likely to have befallen them (because "holocaust on such a scale was not probable" [79]). She gets ready for dinner, sending Jasper to the kitchen to tell Mildred not to wait, inviting Rose to help her choose which jewels to wear. Outside her window, two old rooks she has named Joseph and Mary are trying to decide which tree to settle on. She comes down with Jasper and Rose and hears Paul and Minta, Andrew and Nancy coming into the house. The gong sounds to announce that dinner is ready.

(XVII) The family and guests take their seats, Mrs. Ramsay feeling suddenly weary of the effort of bringing people together. Realizing that Mrs. Ramsay pities William Bankes, Lily thinks she misjudges him. In a flash, Lily sees the solution to her aesthetic problem: she will move the tree further into the middle of her painting (84). To remind herself of this, she places the salt cellar on a flower in the pattern on the tablecloth. Tansley, who has been reading in his room, is irritated at what he feels is the superficiality of the conversation. He feels self-conscious because he has no "good" clothes to change into for dinner. William would have preferred to dine alone, his dinner prepared by his valet. Lily, resisting the urge to see what would happen were she not to soothe Tansley's feelings (as is expected of her as a woman in a social situation) is insincere, and so the conversation flows.

They discuss the state of the fishing industry, and Tansley rails against the government's iniquitous treatment of fishermen. Mr. Ramsay scowls at Augustus Carmichael's asking for a second bowl of soup, and Mrs. Ramsay feels her dinner party is running on the rocks. When the candles are lit, however, harmony ensues. Paul and Minta join them and

Minta's glow momentarily makes Mrs. Ramsay feel jealous. Their love also makes Lily flinch and remind herself that she has her painting and need not undergo the "degradation" of marriage. The cook's great triumph, BOEUF EN DAUBE, is brought in by the Swiss girl, and Mrs. Ramsay serves her guests and children. When she warms to the topic of dairy reform, Mrs. Ramsay's husband and children laugh at her, silencing her. Conversation turns to literature and as dinner ends and they leave the table, Mr. Ramsay and Mr. Carmichael recite together Charles ELTON's "Come out and climb the garden path / Luriana, Lurilee."

(XVIII) Lily observes Mrs. Ramsay going upstairs as the guests disperse. She has gone to check on James and Cam; they are still awake (it is now about 11 P.M.), quarreling about the pig's skull nailed up in the nursery. Mrs. Ramsay winds her shawl around the skull and lulls Cam to sleep by describing her shawl as a magical garden. She reassures James that the skull is still there, underneath her shawl. Coming downstairs to find Prue, Minta, Paul and Lily talking of going down to the beach to watch the waves, Mrs. Ramsay is filled with a feeling of lightheartedness and encourages them all to go. Then she goes into the room where her husband is reading.

(XIX) Mr. Ramsay is reading "one of old Sir Walter's" books—Walter SCOTT's *THE ANTIQUARY*. Mrs. Ramsay begins to knit but, hearing in her mind the lines her husband and Mr. Carmichael recited after dinner, she picks up a book of poetry and begins to read, first William BROWNE's "Siren's Song", and then Shakespeare's sonnet 98. She tells her husband that Minta and Paul are engaged. As they sit, the unspoken communication between them continues, Mrs. Ramsay realizing he wants her to tell him that she loves him, but she cannot say it. Feeling him watching her, Mrs. Ramsay turns to her husband and smiles, and thus, although she has said nothing, Mr. Ramsay knows that she loves him and, the narrator says, "she had triumphed again" (124).

"*Time Passes*" begins (I) with the return to the house of those who had gone down to the beach. The horizon between sea and sky almost disappears. Everyone goes to bed and all the lights are put out, except Mr. Carmichael's, who reads Virgil by candlelight. (II) Darkness pours down on the house and "certain airs" investigate its rooms. [At midnight Mr. Carmichael blows out his candle.] (III) The nights are destructive and wild, offering no answer to restless sleepers who go down to the beach. [Mrs. Ramsay dies.] (IV) The "airs" of (II) were "advance guards" of the forces that will begin to destroy the house. One fold of Mrs. Ramsay's shawl loosens and swings free from the skull. Mrs. MCNAB comes to air and dust the rooms. (V) While "the mystic, the visionary" seek answers on the beach, Mrs. McNab toils in the house. (VI) It is spring [Prue is married]. The summer comes [Prue dies in some "illness connected with childbirth"]. Another fold of the shawl loosens. Later in the summer comes the ominous sound of guns in the distance, "like the measured blows of hammers dulled on felt" (133). [Andrew Ramsay is killed in World War I.] The walkers on the beach see "the silent apparition of an ashen-colored ship" (133). [Mr. Carmichael brings out a volume of poems.] (VII) The days and nights run "shapelessly together." (VIII) Years have passed. Mrs. McNab has heard that the house will be sold; she remembers Mrs. Ramsay in her gray cloak and perhaps has a vision of her. There is too much work for one woman; things rot. Mrs. McNab locks the house and leaves. (IX) The fate of the house hangs in the balance, and then "one of the young ladies" writes Mrs. McNab to get the house ready for the family. With the help of Mrs. BAST and her son George, Mrs. McNab sets to work to rescue the house from the clutches of time and nature. The old women talk about the Ramsays who, they agree, will find things changed. (One late September evening, Lily Briscoe arrives at the house.) (X) Peace had come. The Ramsays come back to the house with Lily, Mr. Carmichael and Mrs. Beckwith. Lily wakes with a start, back in the house she last visited ten years before.

"*The Lighthouse*" begins early in the morning: Lily sits alone at the breakfast table trying to understand what it means to her to be staying with the Ramsays again. Mr. Ramsay, Cam and James are preparing to sail to the lighthouse. Mr. Ramsay is annoyed that the children are not ready, and strides past the window muttering lines from Tennyson. Clutching at fragments of memory, Lily decides to attempt again the painting she did not finish ten years earlier. She sets up her easel, nervous that Mr. Ramsay will approach her with his tragic demeanor, as he had the previous evening when he told her she would find them "much changed." James, now sixteen, and Cam, perhaps seventeen, clearly do not want to go to the lighthouse, but Lily sees that they are forced to acquiesce by their father's mournful appearance. As she stands before her canvas, Lily feels angry with Mrs. Ramsay, who has left "all this" behind, and with Mr. Ramsay, whose demands permeate the atmosphere.

(II) Mr. Ramsay approaches Lily, impelled by his need for female sympathy; she cannot respond as he wishes and the tension between them mounts until Lily dispels it by praising his boots. Just as she begins to feel sympathy for him, James and Cam arrive and they leave for the lighthouse, leaving Lily alone with her emotions.

(III) Lily, alone with her empty canvas, begins to paint and hears echoes of a voice saying she "couldn't create . . . couldn't paint" (159), Charles Tansley's voice she realizes. She recalls a scene from the past, on the beach with Mrs. Ramsay and Charles when he became suddenly very friendly and they got on well. Turning to her painting, Lily realizes that there is no supreme answer to life's mystery but only "little daily miracles, illuminations, matches struck suddenly in the dark" (161). She walks to the edge of the lawn and thinks she sees the boat on which Mr. Ramsay, Cam and James are preparing to set sail.

(IV) James steers the boat, Cam sits in the bow, and both feel uncomfortable because their father mutters to himself and MACALISTER and his boy will hear him. But the sail fills, Mr. Ramsay relaxes, and they are on their way. Macalister tells Mr. Ramsay about the storm at Christmas in which three ships were sunk. Mr. Ramsay "gently and mournfully" recites the final lines of William COWPER's "The Castaway," outraging Cam. But Cam murmurs to herself her father's favorite line, "We perished, each alone" (167). A silent struggle ensues between Cam and James, whose unspoken compact to resist their father's tyranny wavers when Mr. Ramsay asks Cam about their puppy. James suddenly remembers feeling angry with his mother. Cam is torn between loyalty to her brother and her love for her father. Macalister's boy catches a mackerel and Cam gazes silently at the shore, not engaging her father in conversation.

(V) Lily returns to her canvas, still thinking of Mrs. Ramsay on the beach. She brings to mind Paul and Minta, whom she has visited, who now have two sons and have had a bad marriage that has gradually resolved itself into an excellent friendship. Lily feels a little triumphant over Mrs. Ramsay, who so misjudged people and wanted her to marry William Bankes; Lily and William have been good friends. As she remembers more and more, Lily's feelings about Mrs. Ramsay grow more consciously intense and she longs to ask Mr. Carmichael, who is dozing in his chair, for his help in understanding what she is feeling. Without realizing it, Lily begins to cry, saying aloud, "Mrs. Ramsay."

(VI) [In the boat, Macalister's boy cuts bait from the fish and throws it back into the sea, still alive.]

(VII) Lily is relieved that Mr. Carmichael has not heard her; she turns again to her painting, remembering how she often pictured Mrs. Ramsay after hearing of her death. She looks again at the bay, at a boat in the middle of the expanse of water.

(VIII) The boat is becalmed. Mr. Ramsay reads and James feels his old anger at his father rising. He remembers him saying he would not be able to go to the lighthouse, and suddenly sees the lighthouse as both the "misty-looking tower" of his childhood vision and the "tower, stark and straight" that he is now sailing toward (186). As James thinks about his mother, the wind picks up and the boat moves again.

(IX) [Lily looks out across the bay; she can no longer see the boat.][18]

(X) Cam looks back at the island and remembers how she would come in from the garden to stand in the study where her father, Mr. Bankes and Mr. Carmichael would be reading *The Times.* She looks lovingly at her father, recalling how he would gently ask her if there was anything he could give her. The boat passes over the spot where a ship went down, and Cam, trailing her fingers in the water, murmurs "how we perished, each alone" (191).

(XI) Lily struggles to achieve "that razor edge of balance" (193) between the opposing forces of Mr. Ramsay and her painting. She looks at Mr. Carmichael, who is now a famous poet, and recalls how Andrew's death so profoundly affected him and how he had not liked Mrs. Ramsay. She thinks, too, of Charles Tansley, now married, whom she had heard during the war "denouncing something . . . condemning someone . . . preaching brotherly love" (197). Lily realizes that no one can be known completely; "fifty pairs of eyes" (198) would not be adequate to seeing Mrs. Ramsay whole. She thinks, too, of the Ramsays' relationship and how it would be a mistake to simplify it. Somebody comes into the drawing room, throwing a triangular-shaped shadow over the step which alters the composition of what Lily is painting, and suddenly Lily seems to see Mrs. Ramsay sitting there knitting her stocking. Lily goes again to the edge of the lawn, looking for the boat, wanting Mr. Ramsay.

(XII) James sees his father as embodying the loneliness "which was for both of them the truth about things" (203), and sees the lighthouse as "a stark tower on a bare rock." They eat their sandwiches; Macalister and Mr. Ramsay talk about their age and their children (Mr. Ramsay is 71), and when Macalister tells them they are passing over where three men drowned, Mr. Ramsay does not burst into poetry, much to the surprise of James and Cam. Mr. Ramsay praises James's steering. Nearing the lighthouse, both his children silently hope he will ask them for something, for now they long to be close to him, but he says nothing and springs from the boat onto the rock.

(XIII) Lily senses that Mr. Ramsay must have reached the lighthouse; Mr. Carmichael joins her at the edge of the lawn and confirms her feeling. Suddenly, Lily picks up her paintbrush and, drawing a line in the center, finishes her painting and thinks to herself that she has had her "vision."

Genesis

In a notebook (transcribed in Susan Dick's edition of the holograph manuscript of *To the Lighthouse* as

[18] It is likely this section should be in brackets, as in the English edition, rather than parentheses.

Appendix A) Woolf wrote that a number of sketches she had been writing, that had evolved from *MRS. DALLOWAY,* would be "a corridor . . . leading from Mrs . . . Dalloway into a new book" (*Holograph* 44–45). John Hulcoop has pointed out that while the stories published in *MRS. DALLOWAY'S PARTY* "all grow out of and look back to Woolf's work on *Mrs. Dalloway,* it is equally true that five out of the seven stories anticipate, in thematic material, recurrent images, names and other innumerable details, *To the Lighthouse,* the novel on which Virginia Woolf was already working when she wrote most of the stories" in MDP, the collection edited by Stella McNichol (VWM 3:4). One of those stories, "Ancestors," particularly prefigures *To the Lighthouse* as it concerns the memories of a "Mrs. Vallance" about her parents, John Ellis Rattray and Catherine Macdonald, and her enchanted childhood in Edinburgh (MDP 44–47). Woolf herself fixed the moment of origin of *To the Lighthouse* in "one afternoon" as she walked around TAVISTOCK SQUARE, describing that moment in her DIARY in March 1927, as she completed her revisions of the novel, and also recalling it in her memoir "A SKETCH OF THE PAST", where she wrote of making up the novel "in a great, apparently involuntary rush" (MOB 81).

In January 1925, Woolf noted in her diary a scene she had given the name "The Old Man (a character of L[eslie]. S[tephen].)" (D3 3). In May that year she succinctly set down the heart of her new novel, which, she wrote, was to be fairly short, "to have father's character done complete in it; & mothers; & St. Ives; & childhood; & all the usual things I try to put in—life, death &c. But the centre is father's character, sitting in a boat, reciting We perished, each alone, while he crushes a dying mackerel" (D3 18–19). As 1925 went on, Woolf found it difficult to concentrate on other writing projects as the new work of fiction filled her imagination. Working on a review for British *Vogue* of Lady Murasaki's *Tale of Genji* (July 1925), for example, she worried in her diary that she had thought out *To the Lighthouse* "too clearly." In June she described how she was "making up" the novel all the time and wanted the sea "to be heard all through it."

Woolf was quite clear that her experiments with form in previous novels had led her a considerable distance from the genre's conventions and she wondered whether *To the Lighthouse* could really be called a "novel." "I will invent a new name for my books to supplant 'novel,' " she wrote in June; "A new——— by Virginia Woolf. but what? Elegy?" (D3 34). The shape of the book was apparent from very early in its development, and did not change. The only existing draft shows that the three-part structure was in place at least by August 1925, although at that point Lily Briscoe had not become part of the narrative. In her notebook, Woolf drew "Two blocks joined by a corridor" (*Holograph* 48)

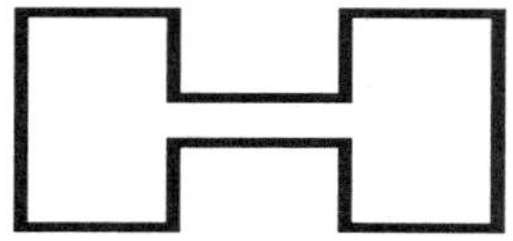

described by John Mepham as "a powerfully suggestive figure" that "holds together in one image the main themes of the book," the diagram seeming "to contain in one abstract geometry so many of the archetypal ideas, the varieties of connection and separation, that the novel was to explore" (Mepham, *Literary Life* 100). Daniel Fogel has suggested that the design "seems inspired by Henry James's geometrical figures for his novels" (Fogel 146).

Susan Dick gives a very detailed chronology of the writing of *To the Lighthouse* (Appendix D).[19] Woolf sketched the novel in her mind in late spring, but her work on it was interrupted in August 1925 when she collapsed while at CHARLESTON for her nephew Quentin BELL's birthday, and was forced by illness to remain more or less bed-ridden until December. In January 1926, she began to write and, save for what she described as "a whole nervous breakdown in miniature" in July, continued to work on the novel throughout that year, completing it in January 1927 and revising it between then and March. In October 1934, Woolf recalled that after writing *To the Lighthouse* she was "nearer suicide, seriously, than since 1913" (D4 253)—the "elegy" for her childhood and parents had brought up extremely powerful feelings.

The writing of the book, however, went "fast and fluently," Woolf feeling a new sense of ease "after that battle Jacob's Room, that agony . . . Mrs. Dalloway" (D3 59). Part 3, "The Lighthouse," presented a particular formal challenge as she tried to work out an ending that would give a sense of Lily and Mr. Ramsay simultaneously. About to leave for MONK'S HOUSE in July 1926, Woolf wrote that there she would "come to grips with the last part of that python, my book" (D3 96). Sure of her method ("It is proved, I think, that what I have to say is to be said in this manner" [D3 106]), she was nevertheless constantly worried as she wrote *To the Lighthouse* that readers would find it sentimental. "I am making some use of symbolism," she wrote in September 1926; "& I go in dread of 'sentimentality' " (D3 110). Her fear of sentimentality haunted the entire writing of the novel, yet Woolf felt confident throughout that she was on the right track. Analyzing Woolf's creative process, Dick says that she "appears to have begun

[19] Leslie Kathleen Hankins, however, notes a discrepancy between Dick's chronology and Woolf's *Diary* in the dating of the completion of part 1 and the beginning of part 2 (" 'Across' " 150–51n7).

each writing session by first reading over what she had last written" to "jog her memory" and, more importantly, to "help start a particular rhythm in her mind" (*Holograph* 14). In comparing the holograph, which is the only surviving draft, with the published novel, Dick finds that in revising Woolf eliminated many direct statements and specific details, thus enhancing the novel's poetic quality and suggestiveness (something that is certainly lost in any attempt to summarize *To the Lighthouse*). The final version is also less obviously biographical: "In the first draft she included a number of additional details directly related to the lives of her parents which are not found in the final version" (*Holograph* 21).

In "A Sketch of the Past" Woolf described writing *To the Lighthouse* as a kind of therapy. Obsessed by the memory of her mother, who had died when she was thirteen, Woolf had ceased to hear her voice after writing *To the Lighthouse.* "I suppose I did for myself what psychoanalysts do for their patients," she wrote in "A Sketch of the Past" (MOB 81), providing what many readers have taken as a vital key to understanding the novel. In the same memoir, Woolf wrote that much of the rage she felt toward her father had also been "rubbed out" by *To the Lighthouse,* yet critics have noted that Woolf's subsequent work (in particular *THE YEARS*) belies the efficacy in resolving her childhood anger Woolf claims for *To the Lighthouse.* Although Leslie and Julia Stephen were clearly to some extent the models for Mr. and Mrs. Ramsay, Woolf later became frustrated at her art's being limited to biographical interpretations, writing, for example, in 1941 to Lady Shena SIMON, that she did not like "being exposed as a novelist and told my people are my mother and father, when being in a novel, they're not" (L6 464).

On finishing the draft of *To the Lighthouse* in September 1926, Woolf felt depressed yet also that it was "easily the best of my books" (D3 117). To Vita SACKVILLE-WEST she wrote that the dinner party in section XVII of "The Window" was "the best thing I ever wrote: the one thing that I think justifies my faults as a writer" (L3 373). In September 1926, she recorded in her diary the vision of a "fin in the waste of waters" that would haunt her as she began to compose *THE WAVES* (D3 113).

The middle section of *To the Lighthouse,* "Time Passes," has a history separate from *To the Lighthouse* as a version of it was published in a French translation in 1926. Woolf found "Time Passes" a great challenge, writing in her diary in May 1926 that she could not make it out: "Here is the most difficult abstract piece of writing—I have to give an empty house, no people's characters, the passage of time, all eyeless and featureless with nothing to cling to" (D3 76). She wrote to Vita Sackville-West that she thought it "impossible as prose" (L3 374). Dick's Appendix B provides Woolf's outline for "Time Passes."

In 1983, James M. Haule* published in *Twentieth Century Literature* the typescript of "Time Passes" that Woolf had sent to Charles MAURON to be published in his French translation in the Paris-based journal *Commerce,* edited by Valéry Larbaud. Haule wrote that it was "undoubtedly an intermediary text, standing between the early Holograph and either published edition" (Haule 268). In letters provided to Haule by Mauron's daughter Alice, we learn that E. M. FORSTER had recommended that Mauron translate the work as he had done such a good job of translating Forster's novel *A Passage to India.* Haule also quotes a letter from Roger FRY to Mauron's wife, Marie, saying that "Time Passes" is not of Woolf's "best vintage": "When she tries to give her impression of inanimate objects, she exaggerates, she underlines, she poeticizes just a little bit" (Haule 268).

The translation was arranged by the publisher of *Commerce,* Princesse Bassiano. Anne Olivier BELL, in her edition of Woolf's *Diary,* suggests that Woolf made changes to "Time Passes" in response to Fry's criticisms, but Haule believes these changes to have been minimal. He writes that "it seems likely that Woolf saw periodical publication as a way to present a version of the entire section in a form that conveyed her original intention" (Haule 272). In a later essay, Haule explores the changes Woolf made in the published version of "Time Passes" and finds that there direct reference to the war "has been altered or drastically reduced," that "direct identification of the war with male destructiveness and sexual brutality has been eliminated altogether," and that the figures of the charwomen have been changed (Haule, "Evidence" 166).

To the Lighthouse was published in England by the Hogarth Press on May 5, 1927 with a cream dust jacket printed in pale blue and black designed by Vanessa BELL, depicting a lighthouse amid waves. Woolf sent a bound dummy copy to Vita Sackville-West inscribed on the flyleaf, "Vita from Virginia (In my opinion the best novel I have ever written)"—all the pages were blank. The first U.S. edition appeared on the same day as the English edition with a green dust jacket printed in black and blue, also designed by Vanessa Bell. In September 1937, The Modern Library of the World's Best Books brought out an edition with an introduction by Terence Halliday, and in 1938 a second English edition was issued by Everyman's Library with an introduction by D. M. Hoare.

Woolf used two sets of proofs for the English and

are considerable differences between the two. The 1992 Hogarth Press Definitive Collected Edition lists substantive variations. These have been discussed by J. A. Lavin.* Susan Dick (*Holograph* 34n28) agrees with Lavin that the first U.S. edition represents Woolf's final version (although she made a small number of changes also to the Everyman edition in 1938). Anne Olivier BELL, however, takes the different view that the English first edition embodies Woolf's final revisions (D3 127–28).

Background

In the summer of 1926, Woolf was choosing photographs made by her great-aunt Julia Margaret CAMERON for *VICTORIAN PHOTOGRAPHS OF FAMOUS MEN & FAIR WOMEN,* published by the Hogarth Press in October that year with introductions by both Woolf and Roger Fry. In May, Woolf had been photographed for British *Vogue* wearing a dress of her mother's (see Lyndall Gordon 215). Phyllis Rose has commented that Cameron "records in innocent approval a sexual dichotomy which Woolf questions in *To the Lighthouse*" (VWM 9:6). Rose sees both the images and text of *Victorian Photographs* as constituting "a statement of Victorian values and a critique of them, a critique which anticipates Woolf's fictional treatment of her family history, with its own Famous Man and Fair Woman, its own conflict between beauty and talent." In fact, Rose continues, "you could call *Victorian Photographs* a dry run to the lighthouse" (VWM 9:7). Another set of photographs that bear on *To the Lighthouse* are those found in Stella DUCKWORTH's album (now in the BERG COLLECTION) which date from the time part 1 of the novel is set, around 1897. Louise DeSalvo notes that *To the Lighthouse* to a great extent "explores the emotional confluence of the events of 1897," the year of Stella's death (*Impact* 222). (See photographs on pages 21, 76, 269, 272 and 376.)

To the Lighthouse. *Courtesy Linda J. Langham.*
The first American edition (1927), published by Harcourt, Brace & Co.

Despite her immersion in Victorian photographs as she worked on the novel, Woolf later wrote her sister that she had particularly refrained from reading their mother's letters or her father's biography (L3 379; it is not certain whether Woolf meant here the biography of her father by F. W. MAITLAND or Leslie Stephen's own *MAUSOLEUM BOOK,* his "biography" of Julia written for her children). Leslie Stephen's modern biographer, Noel Annan, writes that Woolf's portrait of her father in *To the Lighthouse* "was inspired by a rage which had simmered for over twenty years" (Annan 126) and, in an often-cited 1928 entry in her diary, Woolf confirms the powerful feelings evoked by her father: had he lived into old age it would have meant for her "No writing, no books" (D3 208). As she would in her 1941 memoir, Woolf here wrote that she "used to think of him & mother daily; but writing To the Lighthouse, laid them in my mind" (D3 208). In his autobiography Leonard WOOLF says that both Woolf and Vanessa were "habitually rather unfair to [Leslie] owing to a complicated variety of the Oedipus complex," a "faint streak" of which he discerns in Woolf's handling of Mr. Ramsay (LW1 117). As will be seen below (and in the entries on Mr. RAMSAY, Mrs. RAMSAY, Cam RAMSAY and James RAMSAY), critics have long debated the nature of Woolf's transformation into art of her memories of her father and mother. (See also entries on Leslie STEPHEN and Julia Prinsep STEPHEN for further biographical details relevant to *To the Lighthouse.*)

Elizabeth Abel has pointed out that Woolf's account of Cam's relationship to her father "has deeply autobiographical roots." Woolf recalled in her essay "Leslie Stephen," published in 1932 in the *TIMES LITERARY SUPPLEMENT* on the centenary of her father's birth, that she was allowed "the run of a large and quite unexpurgated library," which is "precisely Cam's experience" (Abel, *Virginia Woolf* 149n16). Other critics have sought to elucidate links between *To the Lighthouse* and Leslie Stephen's own work. Gillian Beer,* for example, sees remarkable congruities between the themes of the second volume of his *History of English Thought in the Eighteenth Century* (1876) and *To the Lighthouse* that lead her to suggest that Woolf's writing "is meditating on problems raised by her father's text" (Beer, "Hume, Stephen" 42). Hermione Lee also sees Lily Briscoe's psychology and aesthetics as adhering to principles expounded by Leslie Stephen: "Completed forms, whether made from a social and family group, an abstract painting, or the journey to the lighthouse, create the only lasting victory over death and chaos. Such forms can only be brought into being by means of the arduous search for truth which is a necessary personal responsibility" (Lee 137).

While much attention has been paid to Woolf's parents as the principal sources of *To the Lighthouse,* less has been given to her sister Vanessa's role in the background from which the novel emerged. Woolf was very anxious about her sister's response to the novel and was relieved when Vanessa wrote that she found the portrait of their mother in part 1 "more like her to me than anything I could have conceived of as possible." (L3 572). Woolf wrote her sister that there was probably a good deal of Vanessa in the character of Mrs. Ramsay, "though, in fact, I think you and mother are very different in my mind" (L3 383). Duncan GRANT thought that Woolf had combined the characteristics of Julia Stephen and Vanessa Bell in Mrs. Ramsay (Gillespie, *Sisters'* 195). Jane Dunn has recently commented that it was "precisely that sense of something solid and real in a shifting world that characterized Mrs. Ramsay, that emanated from Vanessa" (Dunn 235).

Diane Gillespie has suggested that Vanessa also informs the characterization of Lily Briscoe, saying that Lily's doubts about herself and her work could very well have been influenced by Vanessa's. Although links between Lily's aesthetics and those of Roger Fry have dominated discussions of that aspect of the novel, Gillespie believes that Lily's being a woman "is an important part of Woolf's characterization" and thus explores the links between Lily and Vanessa. She notes Lily's limited travel and education compared to that of Mr. Bankes, and remarks that "neither Lily Briscoe nor Vanessa Bell seems aware of female predecessors" (Gillespie, *Sisters'* 198). Lily's saying that faces may be left blank in paintings links her with Vanessa, who often painted such works. Gillespie notes that *To the Lighthouse* "even served as inspiration for a tile fireplace Vanessa designed in 1930 for Virginia's room at Monks House" (Gillespie, *Sisters'* 158, fig. 3.23). The design recalls Lily's final "vision" in that a lighthouse on a rocky island "provides a line down the center of Vanessa's painting and unites the two masses" (Gillespie 157). Marianna Torgovnick cites Richard Morphet,[20] "one of the few critics to comment on the formal qualities of Vanessa's paintings," who writes that she "seems to have had an obsession with verticals" and that "she would seize any opportunity that reasonably presented itself of introducing a vertical line into a painting" (Torgovnick 119).

In her letter praising the novel, Vanessa also wrote that she wondered "how Adrian will like James! Perhaps you'll finish his psycho-analysis for him. I shouldn't be surprised" (Marler 318). Quentin Bell quotes from the *HYDE PARK GATE NEWS* of September 12, 1892 concerning an invitation to Thoby STEPHEN and Woolf from some children in St. Ives to go on a trip to the Godrevy Lighthouse, the Cornish "original" of the lighthouse in the novel: "Master Adrian Stephen was much disappointed at not being allowed to go" (QB1 32). In 1964, Adrian STEPHEN's daughter Ann wrote to Leonard Woolf to ask him what had been behind her parents' exclusion from the rest of the BLOOMSBURY GROUP, and Leonard replied that Adrian had always seemed to bear a grudge since "prehistoric childhood," some of which Woolf had drawn on in her characterization of James Ramsay (Spotts 531).

Apart from Woolf's memories of her brother Adrian as a child, he is also significant in the background to the novel because he provided Woolf an intimate contact with the rapid development of psychoanalysis in England in the 1920s. Abel notes that Lily Briscoe, absent from early plans for the novel, "gains definition in conjunction with Woolf's shift of focus from the father to the mother" (Abel 151n2), a shift she notes began to occur shortly after Woolf wrote in her diary an account of a visit from Adrian, who had just attended the London lectures of Melanie Klein. "By conflating Lily's aesthetic and psychological tasks, Woolf engages issues Klein was exploring simultaneously" (Abel 69).

The discussions about Freudian and Kleinian developmental theories that were going on in the 1920s have an important bearing on *To the Lighthouse,* as Abel has demonstrated, but other concerns of Woolf's not to do with her family history also influenced the novel. Mepham cautions against confining discussion of the novel to Woolf's childhood and family life, pointing out that her love affair with Vita Sackville-West began in December 1925. He sees this as providing "the emotional context in which Virginia sketched her self-portrait as Lily Briscoe" (Mepham, *Literary Life* 103). Some critics have certainly relied too heavily on biography in reading *To the Lighthouse* (Mark Spilka, for example, finds that there is no reason in the text for Lily's grief over Mrs. Ramsay's death and concludes that the only explanation for it lies in Woolf's biography). Bette London takes issue with the tendency of critics to find author surrogates in the novel because this "glosses over the novel's relentless representation of compromised authority" (142).

[20]Richard Morphet, "The Art of Vanessa Bell." Introduction to *Vanessa Bell, Paintings and Drawings.* London: Anthony D'Offay, 1973.

As she wrote her novel, Woolf discussed it with Vita Sackville-West, writing to her in March 1926 that "style is a very simple matter; it is all rhythm." The importance of rhythm to Lily Briscoe in part 3 as she works on her painting is one of the clearest links between her aesthetics and those expounded by Roger Fry. Mark Hussey (*Singing* 165n24) points out that Fry wrote about the unconsciousness of artistic creation and emphasized rhythm in discussing Rembrandt's *Boy at Lessons* in terms that immediately call to mind Lily Briscoe: "If for a moment Rembrandt had thought about his picture he was undone; nothing but complete absorption in his vision could sustain the unconscious certainty and freedom of the gesture. Each touch, then, had to be an inspiration or the rhythm would have broken down" ("Some Questions in Aesthetics" in *Transformations: Critical and Speculative Essays on Art* [Freeport: Books for Libraries, 1968]: 40). Gillespie discusses the descriptions in Woolf's fiction of changing light and color, which show her awareness of Impressionist and POST-IMPRESSIONIST painters: in *To the Lighthouse,* "the sea again prompts Woolf to describe light and, in addition, the intermingling of water and sky which often occurs in paintings by Monet" (Gillespie, *Sisters'* 286). Many commentators on the novel agree that Fry and Clive BELL's extensive championing of the Post-Impressionists, and their writings on FORMALISM and SIGNIFICANT FORM, influenced *To the Lighthouse* considerably. Woolf was exposed to formalist aesthetics at this time through her contact with Charles Mauron, whose *Nature of Beauty in Art and Literature,* translated and with a preface by Roger Fry, was published by the Hogarth Press in 1927 as one of the Hogarth Essays.

Woolf was also exploring the aesthetic questions raised by her novel in other writings she published between 1925 and 1927 and in her reading. In "The New Biography" ([1927] CE4 229–35), she wrote that "the life which is increasingly real to us is the fictitious life." Ruth Z. Temple,* in an essay written in 1971, calls *To the Lighthouse* Woolf's "most confessional and her most Proustian novel," pointing out that Woolf was "embedded" in reading Marcel PROUST in April 1925. Of part 3 of Woolf's novel, Temple says that the "shaping of memory into art" and the "process of recovering the past" are "the two central themes of Proust's *A la recherche du temps perdu*" (Temple 100).

Hussey points out that in "IMPASSIONED PROSE", a 1926 essay on Thomas DE QUINCEY, Woolf expresses "those ideas that Lily found she could not put across to William Bankes" (*Singing* 74). Leslie Kathleen Hankins* has explored "the compelling intertextual relationship" between Woolf's 1926 essay on "Cinema" (CE2 268–72) and *To the Lighthouse,* which "indicates how film theory of the twenties informed Woolf's critical and creative projects" (" 'Across' " 150). Hankins draws attention to a letter to Vanessa on the painter's "problem of empty spaces" (L3 270–71) that Woolf wrote while she was working on "Cinema" and struggling through "the aesthetic knot of her own empty spaces in 'Time Passes' " (" 'Across' " 150n6).

In another essay, developing her investigation of how Woolf's concern with spatial arrangements and dynamics in visual art informed her fiction, Hankins examines whether the anti-sentimental aesthetics of Woolf's "peer group" stifled her experimentation. Hankins argues that Woolf was struggling to develop an aesthetics of emotion rather than form and was intrigued by experimental film of the 1920s. "Kinetic representations of sentiment could recharge an aesthetics of emotion, aiding Woolf's efforts to recapture feeling for art" (Hankins, "A Splice" 100). Woolf, she says, transferred camera techniques to fiction, particularly in "Time Passes" wherein "Woolf explored verbally the artfully disinterested perspective on home and landscape recorded by time-lapse narration" ("A Splice" 108). Hankins also believes Woolf's use of brackets in "Time Passes" anticipates "Russian film theory's influential analysis of editing as the essential element of cinema" ("A Splice" 109).

In the summer of 1926, Woolf tried in her diary to capture the sense of mystical solitude and depression she experienced while at Monk's House, referring to her time there as a "retreat." She also examined solitude in her essay "ON BEING ILL" (1926). Hussey examines her diary and biography from the inception of *To the Lighthouse* to when she began *The Waves* to illuminate the relation between the novel's exploration of identity and Woolf's own sense of self, and finds in Woolf's accounts of her solitude echoes of Mrs. Ramsay's reverie in section XI of "The Window" (see, for example, D3 111–12). At Monk's House, Woolf tried to analyze her special sense of "reality" and the soul, and to understand the mystical solitude in which much of *To the Lighthouse* was written and which would be the impulse behind *The Waves.*

Critical Responses

To the Lighthouse outsold Woolf's previous books (enabling her and Leonard to buy a car). It has also generated more critical writing than any of her other works: S. N. Clarke's *Bibliography,* for example, lists 634 entries on *To the Lighthouse,* compared with 550 for *Mrs. Dalloway,* the next most-discussed novel. Even in 1971, Temple could write that it was "probably the most written about" of Woolf's works and noted that in 1955 Norman Friedman listed six different interpretations of the last section of the novel and several diverse interpretations of its symbolism. Most recently, *To the Lighthouse* has become the only work of Woolf's for which the Modern Language

Association publishes one of its *Approaches to Teaching* . . . volumes (edited by Beth Rigel Daugherty and Mary Beth Pringle).

Roger Fry wrote to Woolf that he thought *To the Lighthouse* "the best thing you've done, actually better than Mrs Dalloway" (QB2 128) and Woolf replied that he had "kept me on the right path, so far as writing goes, more than anyone." On the question of symbolism, she wrote Fry that she "meant *nothing* by The Lighthouse. One has to have a central line down the middle of the book to hold the design together. . . . I can't manage Symbolism except in this vague, generalised way" (L3 385). It seems very likely that it is the novel's use of symbols—as well as its "universal" subject matter of family relations—that has in large part led to the amount of commentary on it, that and its "biographical" content. Gillian Beer calls it a "post-symbolist novel," and finds that symbolism is "both used and persistently brought into question" throughout ("Hume, Stephen" 48).

In January 1927 Leonard Woolf read the draft and declared the novel a masterpiece calling it "entirely new," " 'a psychological poem' " (D3 123). As always, Woolf anxiously awaited the verdicts of her closest friends, her husband, and her sister. Vanessa Bell was extremely moved, finding it "almost painful" to have their mother "so raised from the dead." Both Louise DeSalvo and Frances Spalding have suggested that Bell's painting "The Nursery" was inspired by *To the Lighthouse* (DeSalvo, *Impact* 79). Spalding writes, "One can only hint at the possible layers of meaning which *The Nursery* had for Vanessa. Inspired perhaps by *To the Lighthouse,* it presents a nostalgic evocation of motherhood" (*Vanessa Bell* 251).

E. M. Forster wrote that the book was "awfully sad, very beautiful both in (non-radiant) colour and shape, it stirs me much more to questions of whether and why than anything else you have written" (*Letters* 2: 77–78). In her diary, Woolf recorded that "with Morgan's[21] morganatic, evasive, elusive letter this morning, The Lighthouse is behind me" (D3 137). A letter that she would have been upset to read was that written by Lytton STRACHEY to Roger Senhouse in May 1927, saying that "the lack of copulation—either actual or implied" was what "worried" him about Woolf's new novel: "A marvellous and exquisite arabesque seems to be the result. I suppose there is some symbolism about the lighthouse, etc.—but I can't guess what it is. With anyone else, the suggestion would be fairly obvious, but it won't fit into the sexless pattern by any manner of means" (quoted in Holroyd 921). Stephen SPENDER, on the other hand, later wrote that "it is the most delightful book I can imagine" (L5 314n). And Vita Sackville-West professed to be "Dazzled and bewitched," asking her lover, "how did you walk along that razor edge without falling? . . . Of course it is perfectly ridiculous to call it a novel" (Sackville-West, *Letters* 196–97).

Ridiculous or not, it was as a novel that *To the Lighthouse* was awarded the FEMINA-VIE HEUREUSE prize in 1928. Presented at the South Kensington Institut Français with "£40 from the French" by Hugh WALPOLE, Woolf wrote in her diary that the prize "was an affair of dull stupid horror" (D3 183) and to Vita that it was "the most insignificant and ridiculous of prizes" (L3 479). Nevertheless, Woolf, who on principle turned down many honors in her lifetime, accepted the prize.

Contemporary reviews of *To the Lighthouse* were typical. The TLS found her characters "not completely real" (CH 194), leaving Woolf "moderately depressed" (D3 134) and the *New York Times,* comparing the novel with *Mrs. Dalloway,* found most of the characters "one-dimensional fragments that have been created with great insight but insufficient vitality" (CH 197). The reviewer did, however, find "Time Passes" the best part of the novel, as did Edwin Muir, who reviewed it in the *NATION & ATHENAEUM* (CH 209). In a review in the *Spectator* the Scottish poet Rachel A. Taylor responded to the beauty of atmosphere and language (CH 198–200), writing that "Nothing happens, everything happens" (CH 199). Conrad Aiken also wrote in *DIAL* that "Nothing happens . . . and yet all of life happens" (CH 208). Aiken found *To the Lighthouse* to have a "highly feminine style" (CH 207), by which he seems to have meant that the novel lacked conventional scenes of action. Woolf's old antagonist Arnold BENNETT, writing in the *Evening Standard,* managed to bring himself to say that "Mrs. Ramsay almost amounts to a complete person" (CH 200).

A significant moment in the history of Woolf's critical reception in general came in 1953 with the publication of Willard R. Trask's translation of Erich Auerbach's *Mimesis: The Representation of Reality in Western Literature* (first published in Switzerland in 1946). Auerbach's final chapter, "The Brown Stocking," has become a classic text in critical writing on the literature of MODERNISM. Auerbach begins by quoting the entire fifth section of "The Window" (TTL 26–30). He then asks the question, "Who is speaking?" and points out that the writer "as narrator of objective facts has completely vanished" (Auerbach 534). Auerbach distinguishes Woolf's method from the "unipersonal subjectivism" of most stream-of-consciousness writers (536) and explains that her method is not merely a question of technique but "of the author's attitude toward the reality of the world he [sic] represents" (535). He describes her method as "multipersonal . . . with synthesis as its aim."

[21] Edward Morgan Forster was called Morgan by his friends.

Setting a trend that would persist for several years, Auerbach compared Woolf to Marcel Proust and concluded that *To the Lighthouse* was "one of the few books of this type which are filled with good and genuine love but also, in its feminine way, with irony, amorphous sadness, and doubts of life" (552).

Makiko Minow-Pinkney calls Auerbach's a "seminal discussion of Woolf's narrative viewpoint" and also comments on the way Woolf can "situate herself somewhere between narrative omniscience and the characters' own consciousness, or move smoothly from one character's thought to another's within a single sentence" (Minow-Pinkney 105–06). Christopher Reed,* however, criticizes Auerbach's "frustration" at not being taken into the confidence of the author ("Through Formalism" 22) and points out that Auerbach "unselfconsciously wields a patriarchal standard to brand the domestic episodes of the novel 'minor, unimpressive, random events' " ("Through Formalism" 23). Reed also, importantly, points out how far from Bloomsbury's formalist aesthetic Auerbach is. Charles Mauron, for example, made the ability to resist being known the definitive quality of a work of art ("Through Formalism" 23).

Howard Harper speaks for many readers when he notes that *To the Lighthouse* is central in Woolf's oeuvre as fifth of nine novels and also is central "thematically." Like Nancy Topping Bazin, who finds the novel of "key importance" in understanding Woolf's "vision of reality as well as her aesthetics" (Bazin 124), Harper writes that in "both method and meaning it represents a major evolution of the symbolic language of the lifework" (Harper 135). More, perhaps, than other works of Woolf's, *To the Lighthouse* has inspired critics to interpretations that confer meaning on the work as a whole; this is partly due to the temptation offered for such readings by the symbolic lighthouse and quest-like journey to it, and partly also to the way in which Lily's painting seems to be an analogue for the novel itself.

Harvena Richter finds that "image, character, rhythm, and emotion seem fused" in *To the Lighthouse*; "the movement is more subtle, more interior, more organic" (Richter, *Inward* 219), "rhythm and symbol converge with character to convey a complexity and depth of emotion unequalled in her other novels" (224). Many critics writing in the 1950s and '60s saw the novel in terms of a struggle between masculine and feminine "principles" embodied in Mr. and Mrs. Ramsay, a reading that allowed for interpretations in terms of myth and archetype. Herbert Marder sees Mr. Ramsay's landing on the rock as "a symbol of illumination; it stands for a unity of being that can be attained only now and then by the rare individual wrestling with his soul" (Marder 153). The "masculine tower" and "feminine sea" are, for Marder and many others, opposites that are united in the "androgynous" symbol of the lighthouse. Like Marder, Bazin finds the lighthouse and Lily's tree in the center of her painting androgynous symbols (Bazin 137). Carolyn Heilbrun terms it Woolf's "best novel" of ANDROGYNY, with the "female impulse" of part 1 and the "male impulse" of part 3 united in "the androgynous vision which ends the book" (Heilbrun, *Toward* 162). Other critics who read the novel in a similar way include Jean Guiguet, Alice van Buren Kelley and Josephine O'Brien Schaefer.

Guiguet, who sees *To the Lighthouse* as the "natural sequel" to *Mrs. Dalloway,* reads the lighthouse as "the vanishing point, both material and symbolic, towards which all lines" converge (252). Less concerned than others with androgyny, Guiguet assumes the influence of the philosopher Henri BERGSON in the structure of the novel. He also detects a "kind of nostalgic yearning for a relation between women, opposed to love between man and woman" which he links, rather delicately, to Woolf's own lesbianism (257–58).

The focus of much early criticism of *To the Lighthouse,* however, was on the Ramsays rather than on Lily Briscoe. Van Buren Kelley is typical in speaking of "the marriage of two vast personalities who stand for the factual and visionary approaches to the reality of life" (114). Reviewing the work of other critics, Kelley notes that most agree the novel "treats symbolically the marriage of opposites and discusses art as an other means of combining opposing attitudes towards life" (115). Hussey writes that the relationship between the Ramsays is partly "the source of the moods and rhythm of the novel" (*Singing* 50). Many critics see the Ramsays in mythic or archetypal terms and their marriage itself as of mythical import. Maria DiBattista, for example, describes how "the cooperation of male and female wills underlies the novel's veiled myth of marriage as Eden" (DiBattista 23). Others, however, have seen in Woolf's portrayal of the Ramsays' marriage a sharp criticism of Victorian social and gender ideology.

Jane Lilienfeld* takes issue with the predominant critical views of the book up to the mid-1970s. She writes that Woolf "projects the Ramsays' relation onto the landscape" throughout the novel (" 'Where' " 148) and points out that readers have been "captivated" by Mrs. Ramsay. Despite the negative views of Mrs. Ramsay in an article by Glenn Pederson ("Vision in To the Lighthouse." *PMLA* 73 [Dec. 1958]: 585–600) and in Mitchell A. Leaska's *Virginia Woolf's Lighthouse,* Lilienfeld argues that both negative and positive views of the Ramsays "depend on a common perception: all assume the Ramsays' marriage is the eternal union of the masculine and feminine principle" (" 'Where' " 149). Most criticism of the novel, she writes, depends upon the "ideological persuasion" that the family "as structured by the patriarchy is the bulwark of morality, the state and stable human character" (149). This, she says, "obscures Woolf's point that the Ramsays' marriage is debilitating to both parties" (149).

Lilienfeld concludes that according to the novel's time scheme, the Ramsays must have been brought up in the England of the 1860s, a time of great intellectual turmoil, especially with regard to "the Woman Question." Part of the history of a struggle for a widened sphere of action for women in the late nineteenth century lies in the argument of *To the Lighthouse* (Lilienfeld, " 'Where' " 151). Lilienfeld reads the Victorian "conduct books" of writers such as Sarah Stickney Ellis as a "running commentary" on Mrs. Ramsay's behavior (151). "To many critics, the Ramsays' marriage could not conform more nearly to the ideal praised by Ruskin, Mrs. Ellis, and Leslie Stephen" (154), but Woolf, Lilienfeld argues, makes it clear that Mrs. Ramsay does not agree with this ideal. In her analysis, Lilienfeld finds that Woolf's vision of the marriage is far more subtle than most readers have noticed and that Woolf "makes it clear that it contains unresolvable ambiguities" (162).

Lilienfeld has continued to develop her analysis of the Ramsays' marriage, writing recently that an essential aspect of it "is emotional and spiritual battering" ("Like a Lion"* 155). She traces in Mr. Ramsay a classic pattern of abusive behavior as analyzed and reported by researchers working with middle- and working-class families, and concludes that "what Mr. Ramsay is furious about in his wife (and son) is that which he fears and despises in himself" ("Like a Lion" 158).

Jane Marcus has also read the marriage as reflecting the polarized gender roles of Victorian ideology, focusing in particular on section XIX of "The Window" when Mr. and Mrs. Ramsay read together after the dinner. "His reading is analytical, hers is experiential" (Marcus, *Art* 241) and in an extended analysis of what she terms an "erotics of reading," Marcus discerns how Mrs. Ramsay "dissolves differences between great and minor texts [i.e., Shakespeare and Browne], defining the reading pleasure in the sensuous experience of words, not in the knowledge of who authored them" (247). In another version of the dichotomy between Mr. and Mrs. Ramsay's ways of reading, Minow-Pinkney finds "the triumph of metaphor" to be a "*thematic* concern of the book" (85) because the "vigorous propositional discourse of the philosopher is contrasted with the symbolic language of art" (85). Drawing on Plato's denigration of fiction in *The Republic,* she writes that it "never rests quite easily under philosophy's charge that it is unconscious and seeks to gain the upper hand over its accuser on the latter's own terms" (97). The sonnet of Shakespeare's that Mrs. Ramsay reads seems to Minow-Pinkney to achieve the victory of art over philosophy.

A novel in which a major character is based upon a noted philosopher has of course encouraged readings that seek connections between it and the philosophy of Leslie Stephen or of any of the other philosophers that Woolf is supposed by some readers to have been influenced by (e.g., that of G. E. MOORE, or of Bergson). Gillian Beer believes that not only Lily Briscoe but "the entire narrative process" is engaged with the question of where to draw the line between subject and object ("Hume, Stephen" 34). Jean Wyatt* finds that *To the Lighthouse* shares its central concerns with Plato's *Symposium*: "striving for knowledge through love; the desire to create that beauty arouses; the paradox of the eternal in the midst of the transitory" (Wyatt 160). Another who sees a Platonic theme in the novel is A. C. Hoffmann,* who writes that the theme of destruction through the process of time and the subsequent threat to the individual is "rendered through a balanced tension between the Platonic concept of the world of fact and the world of value and the impressionist apprehension of the relationship between subject and object" (691). Margaret Homans interprets Lily's kitchen table image as Woolf's way of mocking "the dependence of androcentric culture on the mother's absence" (*Bearing* 1).

S. P. Rosenbaum* argues that Andrew Ramsay's description of the matter of his father's philosophy (TTL 23) is G. E. Moorean realism, not Stephenesque empiricism. Nothing survives in *To the Lighthouse* of Leslie Stephen's *Science of Ethics,* says Rosenbaum, "except maybe the faint echo of utilitarianism in Mr. Ramsay's thoughts on Shakespeare and the average man" ("Philosophical Realism" 338). Rosenbaum argues that Mr. Ramsay's A to Z of thought has been misunderstood by most readers and has led to an obscuring of the similarities between Ramsay and Moore (339). Graham Parkes* disagrees with Rosenbaum, arguing that "the philosophy embodied in Woolf's fiction is far from realism because it acknowledges the extent to which our apprehension of things and persons is mediated and conditioned by images that are precognitive and pre-rational" (Parkes 42), and he endorses Wyatt's reading of Platonic themes. Responding to Parkes, Rosenbaum points out that one of the reasons Moore had such a strong influence on members of the Bloomsbury Group "is that he reinterpreted Plato for them" (Rosenbaum, "Railing" 89); Parkes, he suggests, does not understand Moorean realism.

The conscious patterning of *To the Lighthouse,* its three-part structure, and its circularity (the journey and painting that fail in part 1 being completed in part 3, for example) have led many critics to develop readings that attempt to account for the work as a whole. James Naremore focuses on Woolf's narrative technique, describing it as "a multipersonal subjectivity, emphasizing a total emotional life composed of the feelings of different characters" (Naremore 122). As many critics have said of *The Waves,* Naremore says of *To the Lighthouse* that it is "the product of one voice which at times assumes the role of a given character and approximates his patterns of thought" (123).

In a reminiscence of Woolf, E. M. Forster remarked that *To the Lighthouse* had been referred to as "a novel in sonata form" (Noble 189), a description taken up by Jean O. Love, who speculates that "each part may have been designed deliberately to resemble the sonata form" (*Worlds* 161). The consciousness of the design has troubled some readers, however. Temple eventually decides that *Mrs. Dalloway,* not *To the Lighthouse,* is Woolf's best work because "design did not finally embody vision but was imposed on it" (Temple 100). David Dowling also finds that Woolf's aesthetic aims "overlaid and usurped the psychological or nostalgic need in the writing" (149). In contrast, Reed describes the novel as Woolf's "most eloquent investigation of the connections between formalism and feminism" ("Through Formalism" 24), and in a review of Joseph Boone's *Tradition Counter Tradition: Love and the Form of Fiction* (University of Chicago Press, 1987), Christopher Ames writes that Boone "makes a compelling connection between Woolf's formal experimentation and her challenge to traditional marriage ideology" (VWM 36:5).

A study of Woolf's narrative technique that is also noteworthy for its critical evaluation of Mrs. Ramsay is Leaska's *Virginia Woolf's Lighthouse.* Reviewing it, Quentin Bell* writes that it is not perhaps "too far-fetched to say that *To the Lighthouse* is cubist writing; it serves to give a new reality and a new complexity even to a very simple theme" ("The Biographer, The Critic" 98). In a later work, Leaska comments on the results of his statistical analysis of point of view in the novel: "Almost half the first section is transmitted through Mrs. Ramsay; more than three-quarters of the second section is given omnisciently; and more than half of the third section is filtered through Lily Briscoe. By themselves these proportions might be interesting; but they are critically worthless, unless we discern the thematic content and the emotional consistency in each section" (Leaska, *Novels* 147). Leaska discusses how Woolf implies large meanings through small events, "by the deeply-worked and difficult art of patterning" (144). "The Window," he notes, is made up of seventeen angles of perspective (148) and in his analysis he traces how subtly Woolf uses imagery in the novel, "moving into the province of poetry . . . to surmount many of the difficulties indigenous to prose expression" (148).

Of all the images, the lighthouse itself has generated the most discussion. Love points out that the lighthouse was by no means new in Woolf's fiction, seeing it as "prototypical of the author's mythopoetic imagery" and tracing its development from *THE VOYAGE OUT* through *NIGHT AND DAY, JACOB'S ROOM* and *Mrs. Dalloway* (*Worlds* 181). Avrom Fleishman assumes that the line Lily paints at the end of the novel "can only be, the Lighthouse itself" (134), and Dowling (who finds attributions of specific meanings to Lily's line "futile and irrelevant" [157]) sees the function of the lighthouse as confirming "Woolf's success in translating the spatial concerns of painters into the temporal world of print" (Dowling 159). Probably the most rigid interpretation of the lighthouse is that given by F. L. Overcarsh,* who holds that the novel "is based principally on the Bible" and that the lighthouse "has a single intended essential symbolical meaning" (he argues that the trip to the lighthouse symbolizes the ascension to heaven).

In his useful chapter on the novel, Fleishman reads the lighthouse as also referring to the Ramsays' house, seen shining in the darkness by Paul Rayley. He discusses the symbolism of house, sea and islands and the significance of waves for various characters, especially Mrs. Ramsay and Lily. When she paints, Lily enters "into the rhythm of the waves themselves, with their crests and troughs—a rhythm, it will be observed, akin to the light-dark-light of the Lighthouse and therefore suggesting pulsation, flow, and alternation in a wavelike picture of reality akin to modern physics" (Fleishman 104). Miriam Marty Clark* has also pointed out that "embedded in [*To the Lighthouse*], with its fluid notions of time and truth, is something like a wave-particle duality" (415) (and see Mark Hussey,* "*To the Lighthouse* and Physics").

Following Northrop Frye's *Anatomy of Criticism,* Fleishman develops a symbolic reading of the entire novel. "The Window," Fleishman says, creates "a consistent picture of what Frye has called 'the green world' of love (in this case, marital love) and beauty (here largely psychic rather than physical beauty) in an appropriate natural setting" (Fleishman 119). This world is threatened by storm, and the novel traces a movement of return to the green world in part 3, "The Lighthouse," through "the psychic efforts of the characters to recover prewar family happiness." Fleishman argues that these efforts are "organized by the physical activity of a journey in quest—typically, in the romance tradition, a journey by water" (Fleishman 120). He finds that Woolf has complicated the traditional romance structure, however, by drawing also on patterns of comedy, putting *To the Lighthouse* "in a tradition stretching back through Shakespeare's late romances to ancient New Comedy" (120).

Others have also discerned Woolf's use of comic patterns in the novel, among them Judy Little and Maria DiBattista. Little terms *To the Lighthouse* a "comedy of myth" in which the comedy "does from another angle what time, storms, war, and death do to the mythic values that provided an apparently sturdy and ancient order for those in the island in the first section of the novel" (Little 59). Little argues that the polarities that predominate in "The Window" are not, as many have argued, resolved in "The Lighthouse" but, rather, are "reduced to human size" in the progress of the book (58). Little also argues that "the profound liminality of landscape and attitude" in the novel precludes a conservative resolution to the comic elements (57), although she notes that DiBattista has argued otherwise.

DiBattista compares the comic treatment of the family romance in Woolf's novel to James JOYCE's *Ulysses,* seeing in both an emphasis on the disjunction between the literary characters and their "mythic ground" (78). Taking another perspective on the comedy of *To the Lighthouse,* Abel disagrees with both Fleishman and DiBattista in finding that Woolf's "insistence on repression undermines the comedy of James's reconciliation with Mr. Ramsay" in the last part of the novel (Abel 50).

Many readings of *To the Lighthouse* have stressed the archetypal significance of the principal characters and the mythic dimensions of the story. As Fleishman notes, Joseph Blotner* "brought together much of the textual evidence, along with supporting information from psychology and mythology, to establish the Demeter and Persephone myth" at the heart of the novel (Fleishman 111). Blotner argues that Mrs. Ramsay embodies the attributes of "major female figures in pagan myth" (Blotner 169), resembles Rhea, and is "almost an incarnation of Demeter" (175). Blotner also points out that Woolf and her circle were familiar with Sir James George FRAZER's *Golden Bough* (a study of the rituals surrounding worship of Diana) and with the work of Sigmund FREUD; and, of course, Woolf was very well acquainted with the work of the classicist Jane Ellen HARRISON.

Fleishman takes Blotner's analysis further, seeing the Ramsays as "the only characters to present a consistent set of mythological associations," but also noting that Mr. Carmichael has a role in the novel's play with the myth of DEMETER AND PERSPEHONE. Anne Golomb Hoffman* has also argued that Mr. Carmichael and Mrs. Ramsay are identified with Poseidon and Demeter "in ways which elaborate the system of the text and enable us to understand more fully the dilemma of its artist-protagonist" (182), seeing these mythic figures as reproducing other dualities which structure the novel. Golomb remarks that Mrs. Ramsay's identification with Demeter "underscores the ritual function of woman in marriage and maternity" (185).

Hermione Lee remarks that the novel "continually hovers on the edge of becoming a fairy tale, or, more ambitiously, a mythical or even Christian allegory, whose subject—a frequent subject of myth—is the conquest of death" (Lee 128). Naremore also describes *To the Lighthouse* as being "in the most comprehensive sense" about death (112). Helen Storm Corsa* writes that "the whole novel, in its pattern and movement evokes, recreates, and delineates the mourning process" (115). In seeking a corollary to Woolf's myth, DiBattista reads the novel as her "Winter's Tale," showing that, like Shakespeare's play, Woolf's novel is concerned with the "death of a beloved queen mother and her resurrection through art" (DiBattista 93). In Shakespeare's *Winter's Tale* and in *To the Lighthouse* the "underlying season-myth" is that of Demeter and Persephone.

The myth in terms of which the novel has most frequently been read is that of Oedipus. DiBattista remarks that if the novel is "cast in the form of an Oedipal dream, the dream work is primarily executed in the mind of the narrator" (74). As many critics have discussed, James Ramsay "inhabits a classical Oedipal triangle as philosophy and art, reality and fiction, struggle over and for him" (Minow-Pinkney 87). Annis Pratt* sees Woolf using "stock Freudian imagery whose significance she was aware of . . . in a broader way than Freud," a way Pratt says is similar to Woolf's contemporary Karen Horney. In her recent analysis of the psychoanalytic patterning of *To the Lighthouse,* Abel argues that the novel "anticipates contemporary psychoanalytic controversies" by "linking narrative, gender, and representation" and staging an "encounter" between Freud's patricentric and Melanie Klein's matricentric discourses. Rachel Bowlby also sees Woolf's explorations "of what makes the difference between the sexes [as] . . . uncannily close to Freud's in another key" (Bowlby 65). Abel, however, sets against the typical Freudian reading of the novel, which delineates the resolution of the conflict between father and son, "a darker account of the psychic, cognitive, and ethical wages of repression" (Abel 48) as she discusses the final part of the novel and closely examines not only James's experience in the boat but also Cam's. Homans returns throughout *Bearing the Word* to the scene of Mrs. Ramsay talking soothingly to Cam about the skull in her bedroom as a paradigm of what Homans terms "a daughter's language." (See also Mary Jacobus* " 'The Third Stroke.' ")

In a variation on Freudian readings focused on the son, several critics have drawn attention to the role of Lily Briscoe as a woman artist who must struggle against the ideology represented by the Ramsays, its message voiced by Charles Tansley ("Women can't paint, women can't write"). Phyllis Rose calls *To the Lighthouse* Woolf's "subtlest and most revealing exploration of autonomy, the most charged for her of all issues of identity" (Rose 154) and interprets both

Leslie and Julia Stephen as "ANGEL IN THE HOUSE" threatening Woolf's life as an artist (Rose 161). Alex Zwerdling notes that "the whole way of life embodied in the Ramsays' marriage is silently challenged by those around them" (194) even in part 1, where the Ramsay daughters dream of a different life, in Paris perhaps, not always looking after some man (TTL 6–7). However, Zwerdling finds that Woolf's criticism of Victorian ideology is complicated by the nostalgia for Victorian stability that was prevalent in the 1920s and '30s (partly due to World War I), a nostalgia also noted by Suzanne Raitt (8). The ambivalence of her feelings for her father that Woolf described in "A Sketch of the Past" has been seen by several recent critics as a structuring element of *To the Lighthouse* that further complicates the mood of the novel.

Hussey sees a shift in Woolf's concern with art to a concern with the artist as her writing career progressed, with *To the Lighthouse* marking a definite change in perspective (*Singing* 59). Many readers have described the novel as the narrative of an artist's self-definition. For DiBattista, the novel moves from "a dream of childhood through a nightmare of bereavement into the dream of freedom. That freedom, of course, is the freedom to continue in the future—writing books" (DiBattista 110). Lyndall Gordon too sees part 3 of the novel as about the making of an artist, "the task that concerned Virginia Woolf herself as she came to maturity in the mid-1920s" (Gordon 197). Zwerdling writes that all the transformations of biographical fact into fiction "have a common purpose: to suggest that work and family life are antithetical or rival commitments that simply cannot be combined" (Zwerdling 191), an idea Woolf repeats in *A ROOM OF ONE'S OWN*.

In these readings of the novel as a portrait of the artist as a woman, Lily's paintings are interpreted as exact analogues of Woolf's novel, and Lily's problems as an artist as Woolf's problems as a writer. Hussey writes that the novel "is not an exploration of whether painting and literature are commensurable, as *The Voyage Out* tentatively explored that question with regard to music and language, but Woolf uses painting to shed a light on literary creation" (*Singing* 72). Lily's "true subject," he argues, is her love for Mrs. Ramsay and "her urge to somehow bring that love into a shared world of art, out of the private world of memory" (Hussey, *Singing* 73). As Jane Fisher* has written, by concluding her novel with Lily's brushstroke, "Woolf guaranteed that virtually every critic who considered the novel would comment on the correspondence between Lily's painting and the novel's form" (Fisher 105n7). Hussey, for example, describes the moment at which Lily completes her painting as the "closing of the circle of the journey to the lighthouse," remarking that Lily's vision is thus also Woolf's (*Singing* 80), but, further, that that moment is shared by the reader; it is a moment of creation "that must be *re*created by each perceiver" (80).

Fisher sees Lily's painting as functioning as a "focal point for a series of meditations by different characters on such widely varying subjects as the claims of abstract versus representational art, vocations available to women, and Mr. Ramsay's need for sympathy" (Fisher 92), but she also argues that the focus on the painting has distracted readers from Mr. Ramsay's role in bringing the novel to a close. In this she is close to the argument of Rosenbaum, who holds that it is Mr. Ramsay's philosophy that completes Lily's vision and "brings about the reappearance of Mrs. Ramsay," combining his epistemology with Lily's "illuminations" ("Philosophical Realism" 346). Mrs. Ramsay's "most unreal return" is "dependent upon the supreme values of [G. E. Moore's] *Principia Ethica*, art and love" (Rosenbaum, "Philosophical Realism" 346).

Lily's painting has also confirmed for many readers the influence on Woolf of Roger Fry's aesthetic theories. Allen McLaurin, for example, says that Lily achieves "a successful *aesthetic* fusion of impressionism and logic in her Post-Impressionist vision" (McLaurin 184) and draws attention to Fry's description of the "physiological effect of colour as being less important than the establishment of a relation" (McLaurin 194). McLaurin argues that in Woolf's use of yellow in *To the Lighthouse*, she is "trying to come close to the 'pure' colour of a painting—colour without any literary meaning" (194). Hussey also comments on how Woolf uses colors in "relational sequences, solving Lily's problems of relation, modelling into the hollows of experience by causing words to suggest shapes beyond themselves, as Roger Fry said she had done in 'The Mark on the Wall' " (Hussey, *Singing* 79–80). Another link between Woolf and Fry's aesthetics discussed by McLaurin is the importance of framing.

Thomas G. Matro* not only examines the influence of Fry's aesthetics on *To the Lighthouse*, but also argues that the emphasis on that aspect of the novel "has obscured the presence of a major ironic theme" (212). He finds that Woolf "maintains a consistent and clear analogy between the human problem of truly knowing and experiencing another person and the aesthetic problem of creating a unified work of art" (212) and that both human and aesthetic relations in the novel are shown as similarly unsatisfactory. Matro acknowledges the early work of John Hawley Roberts,* and that of Keith M. May* and Sharon Proudfit,* among others, on the influence of Fry on Woolf, noting also that it receives lengthy discussion in J. K. Johnstone's book on the Bloomsbury Group. Extending the discussion of Lily's painting to the entire novel, Matro contends that the "design of Lily's painting is also the 'design' of her thoughts and those of the other characters, and it is, of course, the design of the novel" (222).

Abel's analysis of the paintings in *To the Lighthouse* does not concern itself primarily with aesthetics, seeing instead that painting is a medium "whose paradoxes constitute the ideal discourse for the mother-infant bond" (Abel 77). In part 1 of the novel, the painting "spatializes the psychoanalytic debate beginning to emerge in Woolf's environment" (Abel 75–76), whereas in part 3, as she paints, Lily "fashions the mother she now needs, one who, neither engulfing nor diminishing, actively joins in the creation of a shared imaginative space" (Abel 79). Lily's painting, as she says, is not "of" Mrs. Ramsay, an indeterminacy of subject and appearance that, Abel writes, is carefully preserved, "for the painting is not 'of' either woman separately but of the dual unity, mother and daughter, that has been the subject of Lily's narrative" (Abel 83). This indeterminacy has been remarked on by other critics also, Minow-Pinkney, for example, noticing that "despite the general euphoria of its last pages, the novel quietly retains certain key qualifications of Lily's vision" (Minow-Pinkney 115). As many critics have commented, the final line down the center not only joins the two sides of the painting (and the oppositions of the book), it also divides them, just as "Time Passes" separates and joins the first and third parts of the novel.

"Time Passes"

The "line down the middle" of *To the Lighthouse,* "Time Passes," is described by Richard Pearce as "a hole, an absence, that interrupts the journey, denies its power to achieve control and unity, but gives form and meaning to what the traditional journey leaves out" (Pearce 138). For Fleishman it is "a vision of cosmic destruction that bears comparison with Tolstoy's or Hardy's" (Fleishman 122). Woolf's task was to somehow hold together the experience of family life before and after World War I, something she achieves, according to Gillian Beer, by separating the two. Beer describes death as "the special knowledge of [Woolf's] entire generation through the obliterative experience of the first world war" ("Hume, Stephen" 35–36), an experience that is a powerfully felt presence in "Time Passes" although it is scarcely mentioned (something Marianne DeKoven* sees as a typical modernist strategy). "What is literally destroying the house is rain, rats and wind," writes Minow-Pinkney, "but what is figuratively destroying it is the First World War" (99). Gordon describes "Time Passes" as "a counter-history in which war is not the centre-piece but a vacant period through which time rushes, while home-makers and artists—the creators of civilization—sleep" (Gordon 161). Gordon counters those who feel that Woolf withdrew from history in writing as she did by arguing that in "Time Passes" she critiques "what histories and newspapers accustom us to define as memorable" (Gordon 161). Commenting on Woolf's use of brackets in "Time Passes" to contain the continuing "plot" of the novel, Roger Poole speculates that the device owes "something of its effectiveness to the new formalization and banalization of subjective reality that was introduced and made officially receivable by the Field Service Post Card" in World War I (" 'We all' " 84). "Democratic objectivity" has obliterated subjective experience and, Poole continues, Woolf has invented a new form of modernist mimesis to represent what Stephen Spender called the "unprecedented" nature of modern experience.

Thomas Caramagno, conversely, sees "Time Passes" as following the example of Leslie Stephen's *Mausoleum Book* in the brevity of its reference to death. In the *Mausoleum Book* Stephen only briefly mentions the deaths of Minny (Harriet Marian STEPHEN), Julia and Stella, "whereas he recounts nostalgically what has passed away generally—old times, old friends, happy occasions, opportunities gone forever, things never said that should have been said" (Caramagno 251). For DiBattista, the bracketed sections represent "the victory of the narrator in rescuing humanly decisive events from the vast stretches of indifferent time that surround them" (DiBattista 96), but she also remarks that in the face of nature's insensibility the narrative mind "approaches autism" (96).

Several critics have sought to describe the ways in which "Time Passes" is related to the other two sections of the novel. London sees "Time Passes" as making explicit "the narrative practices underwriting the novel as a whole: practices built not upon the positive representation of 'otherness' but upon the dislocation and displacement of a single system of narrative control" (151). Minow-Pinkney identifies the house itself with Mrs. Ramsay, and Marcus reads "Time Passes" as a "lament for the dead mother" (*Languages* 6). For Harper, the narrative of the middle section "moves in the realm of archetype" (146), fittingly as "in the mythic world of *To the Lighthouse* all actions are seen as archetypal" (Harper 158). In his chapter "Acquiescence," Hussey provides an extensive commentary on "Time Passes" in which he shows how the "lyric portions" (as Woolf called "Time Passes") connect with the rest of the novel, reiterating Lily's questions (*Singing* 107–08). He explains how "Time Passes" ponders the questions of the relation of nature to culture, life to art, and argues that the language of part 2 "reveals an acute struggle in Woolf's thinking: while suffused with the religious sense, it rejects the idea of any external agency, of the supernatural" but suggests "an informing spirit" (114). Hussey takes "Time Passes" as a prime example of his contention that the implicit "philosophy" of Woolf's fiction is essentially religious in character (115).

Gayatri Spivak* reads the novel as "a project to catch the essence of Mrs. Ramsay" (30), speculating that it embodies a struggle between the language of philosophy and the language of art to "catch" her. Reading "Time Passes" as a "hinge" that "narrates the production of a discourse of madness" (35), Spivak interprets Woolf's 1899 WARBOYS diary as "a desecration of the right use of reason" (35). Both Jane Marcus and Louise DeSalvo* have criticized Spivak's argument on the grounds that it relies exclusively on Quentin Bell's version of Woolf's biography and that it distorts the text of the novel (Marcus, *Art* 228). For DeSalvo, reading "Time Passes" in the context of the diary Woolf kept at Warboys in 1899 shows that the novel "does not record the psychopathology of a mad woman; rather, it details an acute sense of hopelessness which results, quite naturally, from having been unparented" ("As 'Miss Jan Says' " 104).

Recently, some critics have interpreted "Time Passes" as embodying thoughts on class struggle and social change similar to those Woolf expressed in "MR. BENNETT AND MRS. BROWN." Michael Tratner, for example, interprets Mrs. McNab and Mrs. Bast as "a repressed part of the world in which Woolf was raised" (VWM 40:3). The often-discussed unity of the dinner party in part 1 is illusory, Tratner argues, because it excludes those who cook, serve, and wash up after the dinner. These women, hidden in parts 1 and 3, emerge in part 2 into the very rooms from which they have been excluded (Tratner VWM 40:3). Mary Lou Emery* also comments that the novel, read dialogically, "sets into motion a critique of English colonialist patriarchy that simultaneously repeats colonialist assumptions about 'Englishwomen' " (Emery 218).

A reading of the novel as social critique is relatively new, and perhaps most significantly alters the more typical readings of "Time Passes" as a poetic interlude. Kathy Phillips points out that this novel in which "nothing happens," actually "casually kicks over four pillars of English society": it belittles the Empire, criticizes the institution of marriage, questions the class system, and rejects militarism. It also, she continues, "exposes intricate correspondences among colonialism, gender relations, property, and force, by describing each metaphorically in terms of the others" (Phillips 94). Gillian Beer* is led by a similar interpretation to conclude that *To the Lighthouse* is indeed an elegy, "for a kind of life no longer to be retrieved" but also a kind of life "no longer wanted back" (Beer, "The Island" 273). Lily's words—"It is finished" (TTL 208)—mean, says Beer, "also what they say. Things have come to an end. The period of empire is drawing to a close" ("The Island" 273).

Adaptations

The BBC film "To the Lighthouse" was first broadcast in 1984. Directed by Colin Gregg, produced by Alan Shallcross, and adapted by Hugh Stoddart, the film featured Rosemary Harris as Mrs. Ramsay, Michael Gough as Mr. Ramsay, Suzanne Bertish as Lily Briscoe and Kenneth Branagh as Charles Tansley.

****Works Specific to This Entry:***

Beer, Gillian. "Hume, Stephen, and Elegy in *To the Lighthouse.*" *Essays in Criticism* 34, 1 (January 1984): 33–55.

———. "The Island and the Aeroplane: The Case of Virginia Woolf." In Homi K. Bhabha, ed. *Nation and Narration.* London: Routledge, 1990: 265–90.

Bell, Quentin. "The Biographer, the Critic, and the Lighthouse." *Ariel* 2 (1971): 94–101.

Blotner, Joseph. "Mythic Patterns in *To the Lighthouse.*" *PMLA* 71 (1956): 547–62. (Cited from Morris Beja, ed. *Virginia Woolf: To The Lighthouse. A Selection of Critical Essays*: 169–88.)

Clark, Miriam Marty. "Consciousness, Stream, and Quanta, in *To the Lighthouse.*" *Studies in the Novel* 21 (Winter 1989): 413–23.

Corsa, Helen Storm. "*To the Lighthouse*: Death, Mourning, and Transfiguration." *Literature and Psychology* 21, 3 (1971): 115–31.

DeKoven, Marianne. "History as Suppressed Referent in Modernist Fiction." *ELH* 51 (Spring 1984): 137–52.

DeSalvo, Louise. "As 'Miss Jan Says': Virginia Woolf's Early Journals." In Jane Marcus, ed. *Virginia Woolf and Bloomsbury*: 96–124.

Emery, Mary Lou. " 'Robbed of Meaning': The Work at the Center of *To the Lighthouse.*" *Modern Fiction Studies* 38, 1 (Spring 1992): 217–34.

Fisher, Jane. " 'Silent as the Grave': Painting, Narrative, and the Reader in *Night and Day* and *To the Lighthouse.*" In Diane F. Gillespie, ed. *The Multiple Muses of Virginia Woolf.* Columbia: University of Missouri Press, 1993: 90–109.

Flint, Kate. "Virginia Woolf and the General Strike." *Essays in Criticism* 36 (1986): 319–34.

Hankins, Leslie Kathleen. " 'Across the Screen of My Brain': Virginia Woolf's 'The Cinema' and Film Forums of the Twenties." In Diane F. Gillespie, ed. *The Multiple Muses of Virginia Woolf*: 148–79.

———. "A Splice of Reel Life in Virginia Woolf's 'Time Passes': Censorship, Cinema, and 'the Usual Battlefield of Emotions.' " *Criticism* 35, 1 (Winter 1993): 91–114.

Haule, James M. " 'Le Temps passe' and the Original Typescript: An Early Version of the 'Time Passes' Section of *To the Lighthouse.*" *Twentieth Century Literature* 29, 3 (Fall 1983): 267–77.

———. "*To the Lighthouse* and the Great War: The Evidence of Virginia Woolf's Revisions of 'Time

Passes.' " In Mark Hussey, ed. *Virginia Woolf and War*: 164–79.
Hoffmann, A. C. "Subject and Object and the Nature of Reality: The Dialectic of *To the Lighthouse*." *Texas Studies in Literature and Language* 13, 4 (Winter 1972): 691–703.
Hoffman, Anne Golomb. "Demeter and Poseidon: Fusion and Distance in *To the Lighthouse*." *Studies in the Novel* 16 (Summer 1984): 93–110.
Hussey, Mark. "*To the Lighthouse* and Physics: The Cosmology of David Bohm and Virginia Woolf." In Helen Wussow, ed. *New Essays on Virginia Woolf*. Dallas: Contemporary Research Press, 1995.
Jacobus, Mary. " 'The Third Stroke': Reading Woolf with Freud." In Susan Sheridan, ed. *Grafts: Feminist Cultural Criticism*. London: Verso, 1988.
Lavin, J. A. "The First Editions of Virginia Woolf's *To the Lighthouse*." In Joseph Katz, ed. *Proof: The Yearbook of American Bibliographical and Textual Studies*. Vol. 2. Columbia: University of South Carolina Press, 1972: 185–211.
Lilienfeld, Jane. "Where the Spear Plants Grew: the Ramsays' Marriage in *To the Lighthouse*." In Jane Marcus, ed. *New Feminist Essays on Virginia Woolf*. Lincoln: University of Nebraska Press, 1981.
———. " 'The Deceptiveness of Beauty': Mother Love and Mother Hate in *To the Lighthouse*." *Twentieth Century Literature* 23, 3 (October 1977): 345–76.
———. " 'Like a Lion Seeking Whom He Could Devour': Domestic Violence in *To the Lighthouse*." In Mark Hussey and Vara Neverow-Turk, eds. *Virginia Woolf Miscellanies*: 154–64.
Matro, Thomas G. "Only Relations: Vision and Achievement in *To the Lighthouse*." *PMLA* 99 (1984): 212–24.
May, Keith M. "The Symbol of Painting in Virginia Woolf's *To the Lighthouse*." *Review of English Studies* 9 (1967): 91–98.
Overcarsh, F. L. "The Lighthouse, Face to Face." *Accent* 10 (Winter 1959): 107–23.
Parkes, Graham. "Imagining Reality in *To the Lighthouse*." *Philosophy & Literature* 6, 1 + 2 (Fall 1982): 33–44.
Pratt, Annis. "Sexual Imagery in *To the Lighthouse*: A New Feminist Approach." *Modern Fiction Studies* 18 (1972): 417–31.
Proudfit, Sharon. "Lily Briscoe's Painting: A Key to Personal Relations in *To the Lighthouse*." *Criticism* 13 (1971): 23–39.
Reed, Christopher. "Through Formalism: Feminism and Virginia Woolf's Relation to Bloomsbury Aesthetics." In Diane F. Gillespie, ed. *The Multiple Muses of Virginia Woolf*: 11–35.
Roberts, John Hawley. "Vision and Design in Virginia Woolf." *PMLA* 61 (1946): 835–47.
Rosenbaum, S. P. "The Philosophical Realism of Virginia Woolf." In S. P. Rosenbaum, ed. *English Literature and British Philosophy*. Chicago: University of Chicago Press, 1972.
———. "Railing Against Realism: Philosophy and *To the Lighthouse*." *Philosophy and Literature* 7, 1 (April 1983): 89–91.
Spivak, Gayatri Chakravorty. "Unmaking and Making in *To the Lighthouse*." In *In Other Worlds: Essays in Cultural Politics*. New York: Methuen, 1987: 30–45.
Temple, Ruth Z. "Never Say 'I': *To the Lighthouse* as Vision and Confession." In Clare Sprague, ed. *Virginia Woolf*: 90–100.
Wyatt, Jean. "The Celebration of Eros: Greek Concepts of Love and Beauty in *To the Lighthouse*." *Philosophy and Literature* 2 (1978): 160–75.

Toye, Mr. Mentioned in *THE YEARS*, presumably a locksmith as he has not put a new lock on Sir Digby and Lady Eugénie PARGITER's kitchen door as he had promised (TY 145).

Traill, Nurse A nurse who attended Leslie STEPHEN in his final illness and who in 1904 attended Woolf when she stayed at Violet DICKINSON's house following her breakdown after her father's death. It was under Traill's care that Woolf made her first suicide attempt.

Translations B. J. Kirkpatrick's *Bibliography of Virginia Woolf* lists translations of Woolf's works into more than twenty-five languages (Section D). Not listed there are the following translations into Chinese: *Flush* translated by Shi Po (*c.* 1948); *Night and Day* translated by Tang & Yin (Hunan 1986); *Mrs. Dalloway* translated by Sun Liang (Shanghai 1988); *Selected Essays of Virginia Woolf* translated by Qu Shi-jing (Shanghai 1986; Taiwan 1990); *To the Lighthouse* translated by Qu Shi-jing (Shanghai 1988). Sonya Rudikoff has written on "Virginia Woolf in Sweden and Finland" (VWM 27: 3). Masami Usui has surveyed translations and the reception of Woolf's work in "Discovering Woolf Studies in Japan." (See also Jorge Luis BORGES; Marguerite YOURCENAR.)

Travels with Virginia Woolf An anthology of extracts from Woolf's letters and diaries about places and traveling, edited by Jan Morris and published by the HOGARTH PRESS in 1993.

Trefusis, Violet (née Keppel) (1894–1972) Daughter of the Hon. George Keppel and Alice Keppel (King Edward VII's mistress). Trefusis was the lover of Vita SACKVILLE-WEST, whom she first met when she was ten. The story of their dramatic affair is told in *PORTRAIT OF A MARRIAGE* and in *Violet: The Letters of Violet Trefusis to Vita Sackville-West*, edited by Mitchell Leaska and John Phillips (which book Louise DeSalvo describes as "the other, far more tragic, side" to the story told in *Portrait of a Marriage*). Sackville-West's novel *Challenge* and Trefusis's *Broderie Anglaise* (1935) also concern their affair. Alexa, the central character of *Broderie Anglaise* (translated into English by Barbara Bray [1985]), is based on Woolf. Trefusis wrote six novels, three in French, three in English, and two volumes of memoirs. In *ORLANDO,* Woolf transformed Trefusis into SASHA, the fascinating and faithless Russian princess.

Trevelyan, George Macaulay (1876–1962) In *A ROOM OF ONE'S OWN,* Woolf draws on Trevelyan's *History of England* (1926) in constructing her portrait of Judith SHAKESPEARE, and also lists his chapter headings as an example of what the "history" that excludes women concerns itself with (AROO 42f.). Trevelyan's 1926 *History* was a standard work at the time Woolf wrote *A Room,* but as Margaret J. M. Ezell (see Judith SHAKESPEARE) has recently pointed out, "since the 1920s, social historians have changed the focus and the findings of history dramatically" (Ezell 586). Woolf's "ANON" begins with a quotation from Trevelyan's *History,* and Brenda Silver notes that the *History* also appears in Lucy SWITHIN's "Outline of History" at the end of *BETWEEN THE ACTS* (Silver, " 'Anon' " 401–02).

Trevelyan wrote three significant works on GARIBALDI in addition to *England under Queen Anne* (1930) and *English Social History* (1944). He was Regius Professor of Modern History at Cambridge University and master of Trinity College from 1940 to 1951. On hearing that Trevelyan, who had been an APOSTLE and fellow of the College, had been made master of Trinity, Woolf described him in her DIARY as "the complete Insider" (D5 333), repeating this description several times in the next few days as she elaborated her characterization of him as a typical product of the "University machine" she had recently analyzed in *THREE GUINEAS.* In 1905, Woolf had recorded "a dull & raucous speech" Trevelyan made at MORLEY COLLEGE (PA 218), and her opinion of him seems to have changed little over the years. She knew Trevelyan slightly as he was the younger brother of Roger FRY's friend R. C. "Bob" TREVELYAN. George Trevelyan married one of the daughters of Mrs. Humphry WARD. Leonard WOOLF, four years Trevelyan's junior at Trinity College, described him as "a rather fiercely political young man" (LW1 95n) and wrote to Lytton STRACHEY that he was one of the people at Trinity who "don't really know what literature is" (Spotts 23). Trevelyan was of the last generation influenced by thinkers such as Leslie STEPHEN, and Woolf compared him to her father in describing Trevelyan as "the glory of the 19th century. They do a great service like Roman roads. But they avoid the forests & the will o the wisps" (D5 333).

Trevelyan, Robert Calverly ("Bob") (1872–1951) A close friend of Roger FRY, with whom he shared a house in 1892, an APOSTLE, classical scholar and poet. His brother was G. M. TREVELYAN. The HOGARTH PRESS published eight volumes of his poetry and plays. *Beelzebub and other Poems* (1935) contains his poem "To V. W." (D4 233). J. H. Willis remarks that he was "the most published, if not the most distinguished, poet among the Hogarth writers" (142). Both Trevelyan and his wife, Elizabeth (Bessie), sent Woolf materials and recollections for her biography *ROGER FRY* (D5 160). When Bessie wrote Woolf in praise of the biography, Woolf thanked her for noticing the musical structure of the book and said that she always thought of her books "as music" before writing them (L6 426).

Treyer, Mrs. An "Oriental-looking woman" at Kitty LASSWADE's party in *THE YEARS.*

Trotter, Miss Mentioned in *NIGHT AND DAY,* an old woman who is an authority on the science of Heraldry and whom Ralph DENHAM visits every week at Ealing, a sign to Mary DATCHET of Ralph's lovable eccentricity (ND 129).

Tupper, Martin Farquhar (1810–89) One of the vast mass of Victorian writers ORLANDO reads in the nineteenth-century section of *ORLANDO.* Tupper's *Proverbial Philosophy* (1838–42) was immensely popular.

Turgenev, Ivan Sergeyevich (1818–83) Russian novelist, author of *Fathers and Sons* (1862), *Smoke* (1867) and *Virgin Soil* (1877), among other works. Constance GARNETT's translation of *Turgenev: The Novels and Tales* was published between 1894 and 1899. Woolf wrote "The Novels of Turgenev" in 1933 while she was in the early stages of writing what would become *THE YEARS.* The essay was published in the *TIMES LITERARY SUPPLEMENT* on December 14, 1933 (CE1 247–53; CDB 53–61). Volume I of Woolf's reading notebooks (RN 43–45) contains her notes on Turgenev.

Twentieth Century Literature American literary critical journal published at Hofstra University. The twenty-fifth-anniversary issue was a special issue on Woolf (25, 3/4 [Fall/Winter 1979]) containing several previously unpublished works: "THE JOURNAL OF MISTRESS JOAN MARTYN," "FRIENDSHIPS GALLERY," "ANON" and Madeline Moore's edition of the KNOLE manuscript of *ORLANDO.* In 1983 (29, 3 [Fall 1983]:267–311) the journal published an early version of the "Time Passes" section of *TO THE LIGHTHOUSE.*

"22 Hyde Park Gate" The title of a paper read by Woolf to the MEMOIR CLUB probably in late 1920 and published in *MOMENTS OF BEING*. She describes everyday Victorian life and focuses particularly on the "abnormally stupid" George DUCKWORTH, her half-brother. Having failed to get Vanessa BELL to enjoy the *beau monde,* George began to escort Woolf to the fashionable evenings he liked, but with no more success than he had with Vanessa. The piece ends dramatically with a description of George flinging himself on Woolf in her darkened bedroom. He was "not only father and mother, brother and sister to those poor Stephen girls; he was their lover also" (MOB 177).

Twitchett The maid of ORLANDO's mother. In Twitchett's room Orlando catches sight of a poet who might be William SHAKESPEARE sitting at the table.

Two Stories The first publication of the HOGARTH PRESS, *Two Stories* contained "THREE JEWS" by Leonard WOOLF and "THE MARK ON THE WALL" by Woolf, as well as four woodcuts by Dora CARRINGTON. "Publication No. 1" appeared at the head of the title page, and the book was bound in a variety of colors of paper-backed cloth. Entirely hand-set and printed by the Woolfs, the book was thirty-four pages long and took them about two-and-a-half months to produce. Published in July 1917, *Two Stories* had been announced earlier to the Woolfs' friends and relatives, who were the main purchasers of the book. Violet DICKINSON, for example, bought nine of the 150 copies printed.

Tyndall, John (1820–93) In *MRS. DALLOWAY,* Peter WALSH remembers how Clarissa DALLOWAY's favorite reading as a girl was "[Thomas Henry] HUXLEY and Tyndall" (MD 117). Tyndall was a popularizer of science who made a famous address on the relation between science and theology in 1874 to the British Association at Belfast.

Tyrconnel, Lady Margaret O'Brien O'Dare O'Reilly In *ORLANDO,* the proper name of EUPHROSYNE, to whom Orlando is betrothed at the time he meets SASHA.

U

Umpleby, Mary Mentioned in *THE VOYAGE OUT*, a friend of Mrs. THORNBURY of whom Terence HEWET reminds her.

Umphelby, Miss In *JACOB'S ROOM*, she is mentioned in the sketch of Erasmus COWAN as a lecturer at NEWNHAM COLLEGE. A Mr. Umphelby is mentioned in *BETWEEN THE ACTS* (199).

University of Sussex See MONK'S HOUSE PAPERS.

University of Texas See HUMANITIES RESEARCH CENTER.

"Unwritten Novel, An" (SF 106–15) A short story (or "sketch" as Woolf called it) published in the *London Mercury* in July 1920 and in the collections *MONDAY OR TUESDAY* (1921) and *A HAUNTED HOUSE* (1943). Woolf identified this sketch, most likely written at the beginning of 1920, "KEW GARDENS" and "THE MARK ON THE WALL" as important in the transition she made from these short prose experiments to *JACOB'S ROOM* (D2 13). The narrator is traveling to the south coast on a train; in her compartment are several other passengers, including a woman who catches her attention because she looks so distressed. The narrator reads in the *Times* about the signing the previous day of the Treaty of Versailles that ended World War I in 1919, and other news, but keeps looking over her newspaper at the woman. The other passengers get off at different stations, and she is left alone with the woman, who makes small talk with her and seems full of bitterness about her sister-in-law. The narrator begins to make up the woman's story, naming her Minnie Marsh and developing a setting and other characters in a stream-of-consciousness technique very similar to that in "The Mark on the Wall." When the woman is met at Eastbourne by her son, the narrator is momentarily "confounded" but then is flooded with new curiosity about these "mysterious figures" of the mother and her son (SF 115).

The situation of a narrator making up the story of a woman opposite her in a train compartment is also found in Woolf's famous essay "MR. BENNETT AND MRS. BROWN." In 1930, Woolf wrote to Ethel Smyth about the development of her fiction that "The Unwritten Novel was the great discovery . . . That—again in one second—showed me how I could embody all my deposit of experience in a shape that

Monday or Tuesday.
The only collection of her short fiction published during Woolf's lifetime, Monday or Tuesday *included four woodcuts by Vanessa Bell, who also designed the cover. Although published by the Hogarth Press (1921), the book was printed by F. T. McDermott who, Woolf thought, did a terrible job.*

fitted it" (L4 231). She had been nervous in 1920 that the story would "certainly be abused" by critics, feeling that they would disapprove of "a woman writing well, & writing in The Times" (D2 29–30); this, she wrote, slightly checked her from beginning *Jacob's Room.* Pamela Caughie has made the interesting suggestion that the title "does not refer to some phantom novel but to the process of unwriting it, taking it apart to show how it could be put together" (Caughie 93).

V

Van Dyck, Sir Anthony (1599–1641) In *A ROOM OF ONE'S OWN,* Woolf notes the satisfied feeling induced by lunch in the men's college, a feeling conveyed by the thought that "we are all going to heaven and Vandyck is of the company" (AROO 11). Her allusion is to the dying words of the painter Thomas Gainsborough to Sir Joshua REYNOLDS (WF 205n14). Van Dyck was a Flemish portrait painter who worked in Peter Paul Rubens's studio as his chief assistant. He arrived in England in 1632 as Court painter to Charles I.

Vaughan, Emma ("Toad") See VAUGHAN, Margaret (Madge).

Vaughan, Margaret (Madge) (née Symonds) (1869–1925) Julia Prinsep STEPHEN's sister Adeline Maria Jackson (1837–1881) married Henry Halford Vaughan (1811–1885); it was while they were visiting the Vaughans in 1870 that Herbert DUCKWORTH, Julia's first husband, died. Her five Vaughan cousins were friends of Woolf's in the visiting days of her Victorian childhood and young adulthood. William Wyamar Vaughan (1865–1938) was headmaster of Rugby School and married Margaret (Madge) Symonds, the daughter of John Addington Symonds, who had been a friend of Leslie STEPHEN's; her sister was Katherine FURSE. The four Vaughan daughters were Augusta (1860–1953, who married Robert Croft), Millicent (1866–1961, who married Vere Isham), Margaret ("Marny," 1862–1929); and Emma ("Toad," 1874–1960). Emma and Marny did not marry. Emma was one of the three young persons drowned in Woolf's 1899 story "Terrible Tragedy in a Duckpond" (PA 150–52; and see DeSalvo, *Impact* 255–61).

Most significant of these cousins was Madge, who had been brought up in the Swiss alps and was a writer (her *Days Spent on a Doge's Farm* was published in 1893, and *A Child of the Alps* in 1920). Woolf and Madge exchanged manuscripts and criticisms, and in "A SKETCH OF THE PAST" Woolf wrote that she would never forget her "extremity of pleasure—it was like being a violin and being played upon" when she found that her mother had sent one of her stories to Madge (MOB 95). Seventeen years younger than Madge, Woolf became passionately attached to her for a while, writing to her as "Mama Vaughan" and referring to herself as "your infant". In the 1920s Woolf's connection with the Vaughans had dwindled and Woolf found that Madge in 1921 had "become ordinary" (D2 121); as a teenager Woolf had stood in her room thrilled when Madge visited, saying to herself "at this moment she is actually under this roof" (D2 122). Woolf drew on the memory of her feelings for Madge Vaughan in creating Sally SETON in *MRS. DALLOWAY.*

Vaughan, Margaret ("Marny") See VAUGHAN, Margaret (Madge).

Venning, Arthur Character in *THE VOYAGE OUT*. He and his friend Alfred PERROTT, both lawyers, are guests at the hotel on SANTA MARINA where he meets Susan WARRINGTON and becomes engaged to her. He loathes his profession, preferring to be outdoors, and has plans, once his widowed mother dies, to take up flying seriously and become a partner in an airplane manufacturing business (TVO 119). After Arthur's engagement to Susan, Terence HEWET tells Rachel VINRACE he doubts that Arthur will ever fly.

Victoria University Library The Virginia Woolf/ Hogarth Press/Bloomsbury Collection at Victoria University Library, University of Toronto, contains more than 1,500 items, including all the books handprinted by the Woolfs at the HOGARTH PRESS and many variant issues and bindings. Among these books are the *Poems* of C. N. (Sidney) Woolf, one of the rarest Hogarth volumes; Clive BELL's *The Legend of Monte Sibilla,* with a cover designed by Duncan GRANT and Vanessa BELL and with the signatures of Grant, Vanessa Bell, Clive Bell, Leonard WOOLF and Woolf; Woolf's holograph corrections to *Paris, A Poem* by Hope MIRRLEES; and page proofs for Katherine MANSFIELD's *Prelude.* The Victoria University Collection also includes several examples of publications by the OMEGA WORKSHOPS.

Victorian Photographs of Famous Men & Fair Women A book for which Woolf selected twenty-four of her great-aunt Julia Margaret CAMERON's photographs in the summer of 1926 (while she was writing *TO THE LIGHTHOUSE*). *Victorian Photographs* was published in October that year by the HOGARTH PRESS. Woolf wrote a biographical introduction that takes some license with the facts of her great-aunt's life and anticipates the comic tone of Woolf's play *FRESHWATER*. Roger FRY also contributed an introduction to the book in which he discussed Cameron's art as a photographer, comparing her to the "greatest masters" among portrait painters (Cameron 24). In 1973, the Hogarth Press issued an expanded and revised edition of the book with twenty of the original plates and twenty-three additional works chosen by Tristram Powell, who also contributed a preface and notes on the plates. Among those portrayed are Alfred, Lord TENNYSON; Robert BROWNING; Thomas CARLYLE; Charles Darwin; Ellen TERRY; and Woolf's mother, Julia Prinsep STEPHEN.

Village in the Jungle, The Leonard WOOLF's first novel, published in 1913 by Edward Arnold. The novel draws entirely on Leonard's experience as a colonial administrator in Ceylon (now Sri Lanka) and concerns a family feud that eventually destroys the small village of Beddegama (which means literally "village in the jungle"). Leonard began writing the novel on his return to England from Ceylon in 1911. In a brief introduction to the second edition, Leonard described his years in Ceylon and his fascination with the jungle and the country's past. He dedicated the novel "To V. W." followed by a verse that reads: "I've given you all the little, that I've to give; / You've given me all, that for me is all there is; / So now I just give back to you what you have given— / If there is anything to give in this."

In his autobiography, Leonard described the novel as "the symbol of the anti-imperialism which had been growing upon me more and more in my last years in Ceylon" (LW2 29). Footnotes throughout the book explain Sinhalese words, customs, and relationships, and the plot itself demonstrates Leonard's intimate knowledge of and understanding of the people. *The Village in the Jungle* has been issued in many editions, translated into Sinhalese, Tamil and other languages, and is very popular in Sri Lanka, where it was published in 1972 by Hansa Publishers. Writing in *The Guardian* ("Woolf in the Jungle," December 1, 1979: 11), when Lester James Peries was in Sri Lanka making a film of the book, called *Beddegama*, John Cunningham gave an account of Leonard's years as a colonial administrator and pointed out that the novel, "which has elements of a Sinhalese folk tale, [has] almost no White presence; it is told entirely from the villager angle" (Lytton STRACHEY did not like Woolf's novel, because it had too many "blacks" in it [Spotts 197n2]). Cunningham also writes that it is "amazingly unlike other colonial novels" in this respect.

Vinrace, Rachel Character in *THE VOYAGE OUT* and *MELYMBROSIA*. Rachel's mother, Theresa, died when she was eleven and she has been raised by two aunts in Richmond. Her father, Willoughby VINRACE, runs a shipping line and it is on board his ship *EUPHROSYNE* that the twenty-four-year-old Rachel is first seen waiting for her aunt and uncle, Helen and Ridley AMBROSE, to arrive for a voyage to South America in Woolf's first novel, *The Voyage Out*. "Friendless, inexperienced, and sheltered, Rachel's ordinariness is the most striking thing about her" (Hussey, *Singing* 21), yet it becomes quickly apparent that Rachel has a strong desire to avoid the only profession available to women of her class and generation—marriage. The narrator remarks that Rachel's lack of formal education has left her mind "in the state of an intelligent man's in the beginning of the reign of Queen Elizabeth" (TVO 34). She is, however, an accomplished pianist.

During the voyage, Clarissa and Richard DALLOWAY join the ship for a short while. Rachel is impressed by the glamorous Mrs. Dalloway, who begins to draw her out. Richard Dalloway forces a kiss on her, leaving her extremely agitated and, that night, subject to a terrifying nightmare in which she walks down a long dripping tunnel into a vault where a little deformed man gibbers on the floor. Helen Ambrose, having decided to take over her niece's development, invites Rachel to stay with her and Ridley at their villa on SANTA MARINA. There, Rachel meets and falls in love with Terence HEWET, a young Englishman who aspires to be a novelist. They become engaged on a river journey, but soon afterward, Rachel falls ill and after several days dies. Many readers have interpreted Rachel's death as a sign of her fear of and withdrawal from sexual involvement with Terence.

The Voyage Out draws heavily on Woolf's own conflicted feelings about engagement and marriage in the decade following her father's death in 1904, and Rachel can be seen as partly an alter ego of Woolf herself. Several critics have likened Rachel to the heroines of other bildungsromane, particularly Emma Woodhouse in Jane AUSTEN's *Emma*; Dorothea Brooke, in George ELIOT's *Middlemarch*; and Isabel Archer in Henry JAMES's *Portrait of a Lady*. Phyllis Rose remarks that only Rachel "steps out so timidly to encounter the world of experience" (52). Lyndall Gordon describes Rachel as "surfacing slowly in the course of the novel" only to die "before her shape is clear" (97). Jane Wheare, who argues that Rachel's is a life of the kind that Woolf would analyze closely in *THREE GUINEAS*, compares her with Sophia Baines in

Arnold BENNETT's *The Old Wives' Tale* (Wheare 40–42). Several critics have also pointed out that the character as she was drawn in earlier versions of the novel (one of which is published as *Melymbrosia*) was much stronger, more widely read, and more feminist. In revising her first novel over several years, Woolf made Rachel a more naive and sheltered person than originally conceived.

Woolf first called her heroine Rose and then changed the name to Cynthia. In 1908 she wrote several letters to her sister Vanessa BELL and brother-in-law Clive BELL asking their help in finding another name for her heroine (see *THE VOYAGE OUT*). Louise DeSalvo points out that both Rose and Cynthia are names found throughout Elizabethan literature, "the emblem, not only of virginity, but also of true chastity" (*First Voyage* 22). Noting the association of Cynthia with the Rose in books 2 and 3 of Edmund Spenser's *Faerie Queene,* DeSalvo suggests that Rose's chastity, however, "is less admirable than one would at first suppose" (*First Voyage* 22); "the Elizabethan Rose of Spenser's *Faerie Queene,* in association with Cynthia, is the emblem of a kind of stunted sexuality" (*First Voyage* 23). Another Elizabethan analogue is pointed out by Alice Fox, who writes that the reading of William SHAKESPEARE's *Tempest* by the *Euphrosyne*'s steward, Mr. GRICE, sets up a connection between Rachel and the heroine of that play, Miranda; Fox notes that the link is ironic in light of the different fates of the two women (Fox 25). Several critics have also noted that Woolf reviewed Francis Gribble's *Rachel: Her Stage and Her Real Life,* a biography of the French actress Rachel Félix, for the *TIMES LITERARY SUPPLEMENT* in April 1911 (E1 351–54). Other possible sources of Rachel's name include the Rachel of Genesis, and the Rachel with whom Leonard WOOLF was intimate in Ceylon before his return to England in 1911 (LW1 229–34). Christine Froula has also suggested a close parallel between Rachel Vinrace and a later character, Lily Everit, who appears in "The Introduction" with Clarissa Dalloway (MDP 37–43). Some have seen Rachel as an early version of the female artist-figure so common in Woolf's fiction.

Vinrace, Theresa In *THE VOYAGE OUT,* she is the deceased mother of Rachel VINRACE and sister of Ridley AMBROSE.

Vinrace, Willoughby Character in *THE VOYAGE OUT.* He is the father of Rachel VINRACE, whose mother Theresa died when she was eleven. Alice Fox suggests his name may have been selected "in allusion to the Elizabethan voyager Sir Hugh Willoughby, who died on his voyage out" and whose story is told in the collection of tales gathered by Richard Hakluyt (Fox 31). Other possible sources for the name include Sir Clement Willoughby in Fanny BURNEY's *Evelina* and John Willoughby in Jane AUSTEN's *Sense and Sensibility.*

Willoughby Vinrace is head of a line of ten ships based in Hull trading between London and South America, apparently carrying goats. He is described by Mrs. THORNBURY as "a strong Protectionist" who made a "very able reply" to Mr. ASQUITH at the last election. Willoughby does have aspirations to Parliament, as we learn when he discusses them with Richard DALLOWAY. He also has plans for his daughter to become a hostess for him as he does the necessary entertaining to launch his political career, but Helen AMBROSE, his sister-in-law, decides to rescue Rachel from this fate.

Virginia Woolf & Lytton Strachey: Letters Leonard WOOLF and James STRACHEY edited this brief selection of the correspondence between Woolf and Lytton STRACHEY, published in England by the HOGARTH PRESS and Chatto & Windus in 1956, and in the United States by Harcourt, Brace & Company. The collection begins with a letter from Woolf inviting Strachey to 46 GORDON SQUARE two days after her brother Thoby STEPHEN's death in November 1906, and ends with a 1931 letter to Strachey that, the editors note, he most likely did not read as he was near death when it arrived. Many more letters from Woolf to Strachey are included than of his to her. In their preface, the editors comment that "neither side of this correspondence is completely typical of its author" and describe the letters as often self-conscious and stilted. Appearing at about the same time as two memoirs, Clive BELL's *Old Friends* (1956) and David GARNETT's *The Flowers of the Forest* (1955), the collection fell victim to the strong anti-BLOOMSBURY GROUP sentiment of England in the 1950s, discouraging Leonard from plans to publish any more of Woolf's correspondence. In his diary for November 10, 1956, Vita SACKVILLE-WEST's husband Harold NICOLSON wrote that he had "read the Lytton-Virginia letters and am appalled by their silliness, dirtiness and catishness."

Virginia Woolf Miscellany A newsletter founded in 1973 by Peggy Comstock, Rebecca Davidson, Ellen Hawkes, Lucio P. Ruotolo and J. J. Wilson to provide a forum for all varieties of Woolf's readers. At the time of its founding, Peggy Comstock and Ellen Hawkes were graduate students at Stanford University. Hawkes's Ph.D. dissertation, "The Lifted Veil: Virginia Woolf and Women's Consciousness," was one of the earliest efforts to address Woolf's feminist consciousness, and both the VIRGINIA WOOLF SOCIETY and the *Miscellany* (VWM) evolved concurrently with and were vital to the growth of Woolf studies in the United States. The *Miscellany* was started as an alternative to the anomalous *VIRGINIA WOOLF QUAR-*

TERLY (see J. J. Wilson, "From Solitude" 16). Published twice a year at the English Department, Sonoma State University, Rohnert Park, California, and partly supported by dues from the Virginia Woolf Society, the *Miscellany* is an indispensable and delightful resource for scholars and common readers alike. It includes notes and queries, reviews of books and performances, brief scholarly articles, personal reminiscences, correspondence (frequently about controversies in interpretations of Woolf's work and life), and has also been used by various editors to amend or update their work on, for example, Woolf's DIARY and LETTERS. The current editors are Mark Hussey, Lucio Ruotolo, Peter Stansky and J. J. Wilson, and special issues are frequently prepared by guest editors. Three detailed indexes to the *Miscellany* have been prepared by Laura Moss Gottlieb (1973–1983, Fall 1983–Spring 1988 and Fall 1988–Spring 1993).

Virginia Woolf Newsletter The first issue of this typed, mimeographed newsletter, dated March 1971, reported on the first Virginia Woolf Seminar at the Modern Language Association Convention in New York, December 29, 1970, organized by J. J. Wilson on "The Uses of Manuscripts in Virginia Woolf Studies." This seminar, which was followed by a gathering at the apartment of the poet Sharon Olds, was a turning point in Woolf studies in the United States.[22] The newsletter was produced at Columbia University by Carolyn Heilbrun with the assistance of a graduate student, Barbara Weiser (who compiled the bibliography of Woolf criticism for the second special issue on Woolf of *MODERN FICTION STUDIES* in 1972). Also included in that first number was a report from Lola L. Szladits, curator of the BERG COLLECTION, on the acquisition of twenty-seven volumes of Woolf's DIARY. J. J. Wilson reported on the successful MLA seminar, writing that "we might have known that Woolf scholars should be able to turn a moment into a work of art" and appealing to those who had a scholarly interest in Woolf to "break out of the ghetto mentality of most American scholars, who, because of the condescending contempt in which we fear others hold us, affect a superiority and self-sufficiency we do not really have or want." Forthcoming projects were announced by Nancy Topping Bazin, Morris Beja, J. W. Graham, Evelyn Haller, Suzanne Henig, Mitchell A. Leaska, Sharon L. Proudfit and Beverly Ann Schlack.

The second issue, dated November 1971, was largely occupied by John F. Hulcoop's account of his reading Woolf's diaries in the Berg Collection (this article, "Virginia Woolf's Diaries: Some Reflections After Reading Them and a Censure of Mr. Holroyd," was also published in the *Bulletin of the New York Public Library*). Hulcoop was the first person apart from Leonard WOOLF and Quentin BELL to read through Woolf's diary. He wrote that "nothing in the diaries is likely to compel radical reinterpretations of Mrs. Woolf's fiction, or her non-fiction." Hulcoop also censured Michael Holroyd for his "often wilfully spiteful caricature" of Woolf in his biography of Lytton STRACHEY. An editor's note informed readers that Hulcoop was working on a book *The Central Shadow: Life As Form and Death As Substance in the Novels of Virginia Woolf*, but this work has not appeared. Announcements of forthcoming work in late 1971 included the first volume of Quentin Bell's biography of Woolf, Jane Novak's *The Razor Edge of Balance* and Suzanne Henig's *History of the Hogarth Press* and *In Alien Corn: Virginia Woolf as a Critic* (neither of which appeared). An account of the reviews of Mitchell Leaska's *Virginia Woolf's Lighthouse: A Study in Critical Method* (to which Leonard Woolf contributed a foreword) was also in this issue.

The final issue of the *Virginia Woolf Newsletter*, dated April 1972, began with Jane Novak's discussion of Woolf and Henry JAMES, "Virginia Woolf—'A Fickle Jacobean.'" The *VIRGINIA WOOLF QUARTERLY* was announced, which publication seems to have rendered the *Newsletter* redundant. Among works in progress mentioned in this number were an essay by George Bahlke on the composition of *BETWEEN THE ACTS* and another essay on the relation between Woolf's criticism and her novels; Sydney Kaplan was writing on "feminine consciousness" in Woolf's novels, and Jean Kennard was planning a critical biography of Woolf. Ellen Hawkes Rogat's Stanford Ph.D. dissertation on George ELIOT and Woolf was announced, as was Lucio P. Ruotolo's *Six Existential Heroes: The Politics of Faith* (the first chapter of which concerns Clarissa DALLOWAY). Ruotolo was planning to teach the first graduate seminar on Woolf at Stanford in 1973.

A copy of the *Virginia Woolf Newsletter* is in the Berg Collection. (See also *VIRGINIA WOOLF MISCELLANY*; *VIRGINIA WOOLF QUARTERLY*; VIRGINIA WOOLF SOCIETY; *WOOLF STUDIES ANNUAL*.)

Virginia Woolf Quarterly *Virginia Woolf Quarterly, A Scholarly, Critical, and Literary Journal* (VWQ) was first published in Fall 1972 and was co-founded by Suzanne Henig and Mitchell A. Leaska; it ceased publication in 1977 and is generally regarded as an anomaly in Woolf studies. John LEHMANN was Honorary Co-Founding Editor, and Paul Grave was the Coordinating Editor. The *Quarterly* was published by California State University at San Diego. The editorial policy statement of the first issue explained that it was "published for the purpose of studying, documenting, appreciating, and perpetuating the memory

[22] Wilson lists those who attended the first Woolf seminar in Mark Hussey and Vara Neverow, eds. *Virginia Woolf: Emerging Perspectives:* 18.

of Virginia Woolf, one of the major writers of the twentieth century, the Bloomsbury Group, their friends, associates, acquaintances and the times in which they lived."

The contents of the *Quarterly* ranged from articles such as Leaska's "*The Voyage Out:* Character Deduction and the Function of Ambiguity" to such ephemera as Leslie STEPHEN's will and many other articles and illustrations that had at best a tenuous connection with Woolf. In 1973, the *Quarterly* experienced financial difficulties and subscribers were offered what was described as "a copy of Virginia Woolf's first novel," "A COCKNEY'S FARMING EXPERIENCE" (recently reprinted by Cecil Woolf Publishers). In 1975, California State University at San Diego withheld the *Quarterly's* subscriber list and funds and after what was termed a "hibernation period," the Aeolian Press took over publication. During this time the *VIRGINIA WOOLF MISCELLANY* (described by J. J. Wilson as an "endrun" around the "late and unlamented" *Quarterly*) had begun publication. The Quarterly ceased publication with volume 3, numbers 3 and 4 (Summer and Fall 1977). Sets of the *Quarterly* may be found in major Woolf archives such as the BERG COLLECTION.

Virginia Woolf Society The first meeting of this informal network of Woolf scholars and common readers was held in December 1976 during the Modern Language Association convention (MLA) in New York. It grew out of the interest and contacts generated by a seminar on "The Uses of Manuscripts in Virginia Woolf Studies" organized by J. J. Wilson at the 1970 MLA (see *VIRGINIA WOOLF NEWSLETTER*) and the founding of the *VIRGINIA WOOLF MISCELLANY* in 1973. Carolyn Heilbrun was the Society's first president and in her inaugural address she reminded the members of Woolf's opinion that "criticism was ideally offered late at night, over glasses of wine, in sentences which were not finished" (VWM 7:1), a tradition that the Society has carefully preserved in its various activities. In 1982, the Society formalized its relations with the *Virginia Woolf Miscellany* and instituted dues. A Society column appeared in the *Miscellany* for the first time in its Spring 1983 issue (VWM 20). The Virginia Woolf Society now sponsors two sessions on Woolf each year at the MLA convention, publishes an annual bibliography of international scholarship on Woolf and produces a membership directory. In 1994, there were about 400 members in seventeen countries. There is also a Virginia Woolf Society of Japan that holds an annual conference and publishes *Virginia Woolf Review*.

Vogue See TODD, Dorothy.

Von X, Professor The author in *A ROOM OF ONE'S OWN* of the "monumental work," *The Mental, Moral, and Physical Inferiority of the Female Sex* (AROO 31). Mary BETON, the narrator of *A Room*, doodles this professor's face in unconscious anger as she sits in the BRITISH MUSEUM contemplating the history of men's disparaging commentary on women. S. P. Rosenbaum has suggested that Woolf may have had in mind Otto Weininger's *Sex and Character* (1906), "a misogynist and anti-semitic work that influenced Ludwig Wittgenstein, Gertrude Stein, and James Joyce, among others" (WF 207). Rosenbaum also notes an article by Susan Dick in which she points out that Desmond MACCARTHY discussed *Sex and Character* in his AFFABLE HAWK column on Arnold BENNETT's *Our Women* (Susan Dick, " *'What Fools We Were!':* Virginia Woolf's *A Society*." *Twentieth Century Literature* 33 [Spring 1987]: 53). Woolf responded to MacCarthy's column in two letters that are reprinted as Appendix II in Volume 2 of the *Diary of Virginia Woolf* under the heading "The Intellectual Status of Women."

Voyage Out, The **(1915)** Woolf's first novel, dedicated "To L. W.," her husband Leonard WOOLF, is a deceptively conventional story told in twenty-seven chapters, about a young woman, Rachel VINRACE, who has been brought up by her aunts in Richmond, her mother Theresa having died when she was eleven. The story is set in about 1905. Rachel's aunt and uncle, Helen and Ridley AMBROSE, take a trip on one of Rachel's father Willoughby VINRACE's boats. Also on board are William PEPPER; the Vinraces' servant, Emma CHAILEY; and the crew, including Mr. GRICE, the ship's steward. When they stop in Lisbon, they are joined briefly by Clarissa and Richard DALLOWAY. Finding her alone one day, Mr. Dalloway kisses Rachel suddenly, provoking nightmares. Helen persuades Willoughby to allow Rachel to stay with her on SANTA MARINA, a South American island where she and Ridley have been lent a villa by her brother. Helen hopes to rescue Rachel from the fate of becoming a hostess for her father and to broaden her mind. On Santa Marina, Rachel meets and falls in love with a young Englishman, Terence HEWET, who is there with his friend St. John HIRST. The hotel on the island is full of sundry English tourists, many of whom contribute something to Rachel's sense of a world she has been sheltered from. After becoming engaged to Terence on a trip upriver to see a native village, Rachel falls ill and dies. Further details will be found in entries on individual characters.

Outline

Chapter I: Helen and Ridley Ambrose are seen walking along the Embankment by the river Thames in London. She is sad at leaving her children; young boys tease Ridley, calling him BLUEBEARD. Helen is forty, the mother of two children (a boy of six, a girl of ten), and a sensitive woman to whom London appears a brutal and sad place beneath its veneer of sophistication. Ridley, who seems to be a prototype for Mr. RAMSAY, appears as "either a Viking or a stricken Nelson" (12). They are rowed out to their ship, the *EUPHROSYNE,* where their twenty-four-year-old niece, Rachel Vinrace, is waiting for them. At dinner they are joined by another passenger, William Pepper, who engages Ridley in a conversation about the late-nineteenth-century Cambridge University they both knew. After dinner, as the ship sails down the river, Helen and Rachel walk on deck. Helen fears she will be bored on this voyage and finds herself wondering why her husband's sister, Theresa, married Willoughby.

Chapter II: At breakfast the next morning, Helen thinks again about Theresa, "perhaps the one woman Helen called friend," and about the "old wonder" of why she married such a man as Willoughby, whom she suspects of "nameless atrocities with regard to his daughter" (24). Rachel, who has in many ways come to stand in for her dead mother, is accosted by the servant, Mrs. Chailey, about the state of the guests' sheets. In Mrs. Chailey's cabin hangs a picture of Theresa Vinrace. She assists Helen in making Ridley's room comfortable, for he is irritable and needs much soothing.

They voyage on and Helen embroiders and occasionally reads a book of philosophy, G. E. MOORE's *Principia Ethica.* She wonders vaguely how Rachel spends her time. Rachel, an accomplished musician, has a room to herself, strewn with books, and where she plays the piano. The narrator comments that her "education" has left her with a mind "in the state of an intelligent man's in the beginning of the reign of Queen Elizabeth" (34). Rachel dreams, thoughts of her two aunts, Lucy and Eleanor, in Richmond, of Ludwig van BEETHOVEN, and of William COWPER "inextricably mixed in dreamy confusion" (37).

Chapter III: They reach Portugal and Willoughby goes into Lisbon on business; he returns with the news that the Dalloways are coming on board. They have been traveling in Europe while Richard Dalloway is out of political office. Their arrival unsettles everyone, Clarissa Dalloway's elegance casting everything into shadow for Rachel. At dinner conversation ranges over SUFFRAGE and the difference between politicians and artists. Afterward, Clarissa escapes to her cabin to write to a friend about the odd collection of people on board the *Euphrosyne.* Joined by her husband, they celebrate together the glories of the British Empire.

Chapter IV: Mrs. Dalloway is waylaid by the ship's steward, Mr. Grice, who takes her to his cabin and discourses on the wonders of the sea and of William SHAKESPEARE. Helen and Clarissa find common ground in discussing their children (the Dalloways have at least one daughter, but no sons), making Rachel feel excluded. She goes to her room to play a Bach fugue and is interrupted by Clarissa, who soon begins drawing her out. Seeing them thus engaged in conversation, Helen is slightly irritated, though also amused. Richard joins Rachel and his wife, and Clarissa reads aloud from Jane AUSTEN's *Persuasion.* When her husband falls asleep, Mrs. Dalloway is once again invited by Mr. Grice to further conversation. Waking, Richard begins discussing with Rachel why he never talks about politics with his wife. As Rachel begins to ask him questions about his childhood, Clarissa reappears and distracts them by pointing to two British warships of the Mediterranean fleet sailing by. At lunch Helen punctures the jingoistic conversation the ships have inspired in the Dalloways and Willoughby by saying that it is time dying on a battlefield ceased to be praised as heroic.

Chapter V: A storm breaks and Clarissa takes to her bed, where Helen ministers to her. When the storm subsides, Richard joins Helen for tea and they continue their gentle argument over the relative merits of a politician's life versus a life of the mind. Richard reads aloud a passage from Helen's book (*Principia Ethica* 1:14). Up on deck, Richard encounters Rachel and they go to her room, where, after recommending that she read Edmund BURKE on the French Revolution, he kisses her (TVO 76). Tremendously excited, Rachel goes outside to calm herself by looking at the sea. That night she dreams of walking down a long tunnel into a vault where a little deformed man with the face of an animal gibbers on the floor. All night long, Rachel feels pursued.

Chapter VI: The Dalloways disembark, Clarissa giving Rachel her copy of *Persuasion* in which she has written her address. Helen now determines to get to know her niece. Rachel tells her about Dalloway's kiss and how it had first excited and then terrified her. Helen is appalled at Rachel's ignorance of sex and reveals to her that it is because of the prostitutes that Rachel cannot walk in PICCADILLY. Helen's opinions take a little of the glamour off the Dalloways for Rachel. Helen, meanwhile, has decided she will take Rachel in hand and proposes to Willoughby that his daughter stay with her and Ridley while he continues down the Amazon on business. He agrees, thinking it will do his aspirations to Parliament good if Rachel is better able to act as a hostess for him.

Chapter VII: They arrive at Santa Marina, where Helen receives letters with news that her children are well. The narrator discourses on Empire and the failure of the seventeenth-century English colonists on this island. A British enclave has only recently been established there and it is Helen's brother who has lent them the Villa San Gervasio where they will stay. After a week, Mr. Pepper moves into the hotel on the island, preferring to have his vegetables properly washed.

Chapter VIII: The months pass, and we learn of Helen and Rachel's daily routine from a letter Helen writes to someone called Bernard. Ridley groans that his work is unrecognized; he is working on an edition of the odes of Pindar. After dinner one night, Helen and Rachel walk to the hotel, where they eavesdrop outside the windows. Helen recognizes someone she knows, Hughling ELLIOT; Terence Hewet and Susan WARRINGTON are playing cards. Old Mrs. Emma PALEY takes Susan away from the group to help her to bed, and Rachel and Helen suddenly realize that someone they cannot see who is sitting by the window has heard them outside. They run back to the villa.

Chapter IX: The guests at the hotel go to bed. Miss ALLAN reads book 5 of William WORDSWORTH's *Prelude,* Susan Warrington thinks about Arthur VENNING and writes in her diary that Alfred PERROTT is not "quite" (i.e., not quite of the right class). The narrative mind passes from room to room observing the sleepers. It is 1 A.M. St. John Hirst and Terence Hewet discuss women, and Terence proposes an expedition so that the guests can get to know one another.

The next morning, the English gather to read the *Times.* Mr. William THORNBURY is anxious to read about a Parliamentary debate; Miss Allan reads about "the discoveries in Crete" (113). Mr. Elliot goes for a walk with Terence and St. John, while Mrs. THORNBURY and Mrs. ELLIOT discuss maternity and miscarriages. At lunch, Mrs. Paley points out to Susan a woman dressed in white with a made-up face, of whom she clearly disapproves.

The day goes on. Mrs. Elliot sketches. This is the languid life of the English abroad in a hot climate, yet the ritual of tea is preserved. Susan Warrington pours for Arthur Venning and Alfred Perrott. The party is joined by Mr. Elliot, who brings with him Ridley Ambrose, whom he met on the hill. Susan decides that St. John is "a dreadful young man" (121). About to go for a walk with Arthur, Susan is called back by Mrs. Paley for help with understanding how to play a game of patience (i.e., solitaire).

Chapter X: Rachel reads the work of Henrik IBSEN in her room; on the hill, men are washing the trunks of olive trees with a white liquid. An invitation has arrived from Terence to go on a picnic to Monte Rosa. Against St. John's advice, Terence has persevered with his plan and the party assembles. Although the picnic is a success, Terence feels depressed at the thought of human beings' cruelty to one another. The sight of Helen, however, cheers him and he begins to talk to Rachel.

Chapter XI: After eating lunch, the party breaks into two groups. Arthur and Susan then go off together; he proposes to her. Rachel and Terence see them lying together, which embarrasses them. They sit down and begin to get to know each other and are joined by St. John and Helen, who have also seen Arthur and Susan. The four of them state a brief autobiography and then rejoin the rest of the party for tea. As they return, fireworks rise up from the town. That night, everyone is tired and falls asleep quickly, except for Susan, who lies awake repeating to herself that she is happy.

Chapter XII: A dance is planned to celebrate Susan and Arthur's engagement. After an awkward conversation with Rachel—whom he promises to enlighten by lending her his copy of Edward GIBBON's *Decline and Fall of the Roman Empire*—St. John finds that he can talk much more easily with Helen. They sit out a few dances together and St. John believes she is the only woman ever to have understood him. Helen asks his help in educating Rachel, and St. John tells her that "few things at the present time mattered more than the enlightenment of women" (164). When the musicians hired for the dance suddenly pack up and leave, Rachel plays, telling everyone to invent a dance to a Mozart sonata. Everyone joins in what Terence calls "the great round dance" (166) and dawn breaks.

Chapter XIII: At the villa, Ridley Ambrose is cut off from the rest of the world, alone in a room with his books. Rachel asks him for a copy of Gibbon, or something by Balzac or Burke; she gets Honoré de BALZAC's *La Cousine Bette* from her uncle and leaves him, only to find that St. John has already sent up the first volume of Gibbon as he had promised. She goes for a walk, reads a little of Gibbon, and thinks about being in love.

Chapter XIV: The next evening everyone at the hotel except Terence and St. John have mail from England. Mr. Wilfred FLUSHING arrives, a man who knows people in common with the Elliots. A large moth flies from one light to another, causing consternation among the ladies. St. John sees all the guests as animals in a zoo and tells Terence that he is repulsed by the female breast. Getting no response from his friend, St. John asks if he is in love. Terence leaves to think over his feelings and walks to the Ambroses' villa, where he overhears Rachel and Helen talking about Rachel's mother. Chanting "dreams and realities," Terence returns in a state of excitement to the hotel, where he is intercepted by Evelyn MURGATROYD, who tells him her troubles. As he goes to bed, Terence sees the woman Mrs. Paley had complained of to Susan passing from one room to another in a brightly colored dressing gown; the implication is that she is a prostitute.

Chapter XV: Ridley warns Helen to pay attention to Terence and St. John's interest in Rachel. Mrs. FLUSHING and Mrs. Thornbury pay a visit, and are followed by St. John and Terence. After tea, Terence and Rachel go for a walk, leaving St. John and Helen together to discuss St. John's future. Helen and St. John agree to call each other by their first names.

Chapter XVI: Terence and Rachel sit on the edge of a cliff and, as they have before, discuss the differences between men and women, and women's suffrage. Rachel describes a typical day in Richmond with her aunts and Terence tells her that if he were a woman he would "blow someone's brains out" (215). He tells her that he wants to write a novel "about Silence . . . the things people don't say" (216) and another in which he will show "the gradual corruption of the soul" (217). All the time, Terence is longing to take Rachel in his arms. They also agree to use first names.

Chapter XVII: It is the height of the season and more tourists arrive on Santa Marina. Gradually, the villa becomes a place of escape for some of the hotel guests. Helen has detected a change in Rachel; her relationship with Terence is developing, but Rachel is too inexperienced to understand fully what is happening. After an awkward beginning, St. John and Rachel have also become friends.

A Sunday service at the hotel draws some of the guests, though not all come to hear the words of Mr. BAX, the minister. He reads from the Old Testament, startling Susan Warrington. Rachel begins to question the unthinking faith of the congregation, concentrating on the complacent expression of a hospital nurse. At the back of the chapel, Mrs. Flushing notices that St. John is not reading a prayer book: he has A. C. SWINBURNE's translation of SAPPHO. Mr. Bax delivers a sermon on the duties of the English to their colonized subjects. After the service, Mrs. Flushing takes Rachel up to her room, where Rachel pours out her disgust at the smug churchgoers. Mrs. Flushing's room is full of her vivid paintings and of artefacts bought cheaply from the "natives" to sell to "smart women in London" at a profit. Mrs. Flushing proposes an expedition up the river to see a native village. At lunch, St. John tells Terence that he thinks Rachel is in love with him.

Chapter XVIII: Terence escapes the oppressive chatter of the lunch table and considers his feelings about Rachel and marriage, bringing to mind images of married couples, both real and imaginary. Seeing compromise as fundamental to marriage, he realizes that he loves Rachel but that conventional marriage appalls him.

Chapter XIX: Alone at the hotel after lunch, Rachel is accosted by Evelyn Murgatroyd, who takes her up to her room and excitedly tells her about her marriage proposal muddles. She tells Rachel that Terence is the only man she can trust, saying there is "something of a woman in him" (247), which causes Rachel a twinge of jealousy. Evelyn tells Rachel about the SATURDAY CLUB she belongs to in London, where they discuss art. She plans to change all that and make her club talk about things that matter: the White Slave Traffic, Woman Suffrage, and the Insurance Bill. Evelyn also has a plan to end prostitution in Piccadilly. Rachel leaves Evelyn's room and from a hallway window sees "the wrong side of hotel life," an old woman cutting off the head of a chicken. Miss Allan appears and, thinking Rachel is lonely, takes her to her room, where she shows her a lucky bottle of crème de menthe that she always travels with and has named Oliver! Extricating herself, Rachel once again wanders down a corridor, feeling miserable. At tea later, when Mrs. Flushing proposes her river expedition, Rachel enthusiastically supports the idea and is annoyed at Helen's lack of interest in the plan. Realizing that Rachel is in love, Helen agrees to go.

Chapter XX: The Flushings, St. John, Helen, Terence and Rachel set off upriver. Mrs. Flushing paints, Terence reads, St. John works on the indecent poem about God that he began during the Sunday service. When they get off the boat for a meal, Rachel and Terence walk into the jungle where, ominously and awkwardly, they declare their love for one another.

Chapter XXI: Sailing on up the river, they pass a hut where the explorer MACKENZIE died. Helen and St. John are vaguely uneasy, conscious of the new intimacy between Terence and Rachel. When they land near the village that is their destination, Terence and Rachel quickly walk ahead so they can talk. They discuss their future, but feel as if they are in a dream. Rachel seems to lose consciousness of her surroundings and suddenly sees Terence and Helen looming above her, kissing and speaking of love and marriage. When they reach the village, the stares of the women and their apparent lack of concern for the English visitors make them all feel uncomfortable. Helen has premonitions of disaster. That night, on the way back down the river, Helen talks to Rachel and Terence about marriage.

Chapter XXII: Their engagement becomes public and Rachel and Terence find they are increasingly left alone. Terence defends St. John when Rachel disparages him. They are under strain from the imposition of convention on feelings which they believe are inexplicable to other people. Terence is working on his novel and they learn more about each other, imagining their future life together in England.

Chapter XXIII: Helen has written to Willoughby with the news of his daughter's engagement. She and St. John have now firmly established a friendship. One afternoon, he comes up to the villa to gossip with Helen, telling her about a letter from his mother describing a parlor maid's suicide, and that all is not well between Arthur and Susan. He also brings the news that Signora Lola MENDOZA, the "woman of doubtful virtue," has been expelled from the hotel by the manager, Mr. Rodriguez, after being seen late at night by Mr. Thornbury. Helen and St. John are outraged at the hypocrisy of the English middle class. Terence, who seems changed since his engagement, wants Rachel to accept Mrs. Thornbury's invitation to tea at the hotel. Reluctantly, she goes, together with St. John, who feels excluded by their intimacy. He awkwardly congratulates them, saying that love seems to him "to explain everything."

Chapter XXIV: At the hotel, no one is about at first, but soon Terence and Rachel are joined by Miss Allan, who has finished writing her history of English literature, and by Mrs. Thornbury and Evelyn. Mrs. Elliot passes by on her way to speak with the head waiter about food for her husband, who has fallen ill. At tea, there seems to be no substance to St. John's rumors about Arthur and Susan. Evelyn tells Rachel she is thinking of going on to Moscow as she would like to join in a revolution against the Russian government; she describes her plans for an activists' club that she would like to gather in BLOOMSBURY. The engaged couples seem to evoke wistfulness in the old, envy in the young.

Chapter XXV: One hot afternoon, Terence reads John MILTON's "COMUS" aloud to Rachel. Her head begins to ache and she goes to bed. Quickly, she plunges into illness and Helen brings Dr. RODRIGUEZ to see her. After a few days, Helen brings Nurse MCINNIS to sit with Rachel; she is the nurse Rachel saw in the chapel. Rachel begins to hallucinate. Terence, who visits Rachel twice a day, is frustrated but has confidence in doctors, a fact that leads him to clash with Helen. After several days, Helen confronts him and says that Rachel is getting worse, not better as Rodriguez tells them. Terence confronts Rodriguez and says he will seek a second opinion, angering the doctor. He goes to Rachel's room and kisses her, but she sees only an old woman slicing off a man's head. Mrs. Flushing appears, anxious to be reassured that her expedition had nothing to do with Rachel's illness. Terence sends St. John off in search of another doctor. Eventually, he tracks down Dr. Lesage, whom he persuades to abandon his vacation and come to see Rachel. Everyone waits. Ridley can no longer work and paces up and down reciting poetry. Late one night, Dr. Lesage tells Terence to go up to Rachel's room. Alone with her, Terence feels peaceful. Rachel dies.

Chapter XXVI: The news of Rachel's death spreads through the hotel, causing grief and anger among those who knew her. Mrs. Flushing feels responsible. Evelyn is distraught. After lunch, Alfred Perrott again proposes to Evelyn, again to no avail.

Chapter XXVII: A storm. Life at the hotel continues as before, though many have left and others plan to leave soon. Mr. Pepper and Mr. Elliot play chess, Mr. Elliot prevailing for once; Mrs. Paley plays solitaire; the moth whizzes from light to light. St. John's entrance causes a brief pause before the guests go back to their customary evening occupations. As the evening draws to a close and the guests go to bed, St. John dozes, seeing them pass by, their voices and faces indistinct, a pattern of shapes.

Genesis

The story of the evolution of Woolf's first novel is complex and uncertain. Some scholars have suggested she began thinking about it soon after her father's death in 1904, others have placed its beginnings at dates ranging from 1904 to 1908. The large amount of manuscript material surviving has been studied by numerous scholars, and although there are some disagreements remaining about the dating of various drafts, there is also agreement about several issues. That Woolf rewrote the entire novel several times is clear; that her conception of it changed as her own experience changed is also clear; that her revisions were invariably deletions of autobiographical material has become clear owing largely to the work of Louise DeSalvo and Elizabeth Heine,* in particular, as well as that of critics such as Harvena Richter, Jane Novak and Mitchell Leaska, who read the BERG COLLECTION manuscripts when working on their books. Several critics, most significantly those just mentioned, have also discussed in detail the relationships between *MELYMBROSIA* and *The Voyage Out,* as well as other, unpublished versions of the novel. To further complicate matters, the English and U.S. editions of the novel are considerably different, as will be discussed below.

In "Virginia Woolf's Revisions of *The Voyage Out,*" Heine focuses on three versions of the novel: "The Earliest Version: 1907–1908;" "The 'Valentine' Version: 1908–1910" ("Valentine" was an earlier name for Ridley Ambrose; this version has not survived); and "The Later Version: 1912–1913." In *Virginia Woolf's First Voyage,* DeSalvo describes her reconstruction of "four distinct earlier versions of the novel within the manuscripts at the Berg Collection" (x) which, taken together with Woolf's other writings of the same period, "provide *the most complete account of Woolf's process of literary creation available to us*" (x). DeSalvo's appendix, "Location of the Drafts," presents a table of the Berg manuscripts. In the section of her introduction to *Melymbrosia* entitled "Recovery of the Text of *Melymbrosia,*" DeSalvo gives a detailed description of the Berg manuscripts. Also, in a special issue of *Bulletin of Research in the Humanities* (82, 3 [Autumn 1979]), DeSalvo's "Sorting, Sequencing, and Dating the Drafts of Virginia Woolf's *The Voyage Out*"* and Heine's "The Earlier *Voyage Out:* Virginia Woolf's First Novel"* provide further information on the manuscripts. These sources are essential to any thorough understanding of the tangled evolution of *The Voyage Out.* (See also entry on *MELYMBROSIA.*)

Woolf's sister Vanessa Bell had agreed to marry Clive BELL at the end of 1906, two days after the death of her brother Thoby STEPHEN; they were married in February 1907. In February 1908, their first child, Julian BELL, was born, and shortly afterward, Woolf and Clive Bell began an intense flirtation. Woolf began to show part of her work in progress to Clive and to discuss it with him. Those, like DeSalvo and Quentin BELL (QB1 125), who believe Woolf may have begun at least to imagine what would eventually be *The Voyage Out* soon after her father died in February 1904, can find confirmation in a letter of April 1908 Woolf wrote to Clive Bell. She described a dream of showing the manuscript of her novel to her father, who "snorted" and "dropped it on to a table." When she read it the following morning, she told Clive, she "thought it bad" (L1 325). Such feelings, together with the well-known comment in her diary that had her father lived there would have been "no writing, no books" for her (D3 208), suggest that her father's death allowed Woolf to begin creating a work of fiction that was very closely associated with the circumstances of her own life.

Throughout 1908, Woolf discussed the novel with her sister and brother-in-law, and also told other close friends, such as Violet DICKINSON, about her progress. In late summer that year, she wrote to Clive and to Vanessa asking for help with finding a new name for her heroine, who, having started out as Rose, was now called Cynthia; but "Cynthia dont do. All fine ladies, ingenuous young ladies, with Meredithian blood in them, are called Cynthia" (L1 343). She had written 100 pages of *Melymbrosia* and told her sister that on reading them through she had "come to the conclusion that there is something of a structure in it" (L1 343). Clive apparently suggested the name Belinda, but Woolf rejected this, saying it was "perhaps a little too dainty for my woman, and what I have come to conceive of her destiny" (L1 345). She told Clive that she looked at tombstones, hoping for inspiration, and wondered what he thought of "a Spanish name for the lady. Cintra? Andalusia? her father touched at many ports and sailors like sentimental names: he may have had other reasons, too, not to be defined" (L1 356).

As she worked on the novel, her confidence grew, as did her concern with the "conception" of the work. In late August 1908, she told Clive Bell that "the changing of names is the most trivial of occupations, and I am aware that the only thing that matters is a thing you cant control, nor I neither. . . . Whether my conception is solid is a vastly important matter to me, but at the same time, almost impersonal" (L1 361). She wrote Vanessa that she cared "less than ever before for what people say" (L1 366). Having done her hundred pages, she wondered aloud in a letter to Violet Dickinson "whether I shall ever dare to print them?" and resolved to work hard that winter to try and finish the novel (L1 367).

In October that year she sent the hundred pages to Clive. His letters, reprinted in appendix D of the first volume of Quentin Bell's *Virginia Woolf: A Biography,* "provide the most complete description available of the August 1908 draft and its revision in the following winter" (Heine, "Virginia Woolf's Revisions" 414). At this point, the Ambroses were Geranium and Lucilla and Rachel was Cynthia. Clive wrote that he saw glimpses of "the thrilling real beneath the dull apparent" (QB1 207). Heine notes that Woolf's letters indicate that "the basic story-line of the first half of the novel was in place at least by 1909" ("Virginia Woolf's Revisions" 408).

In February 1909, Woolf gave Clive a new draft, which does not survive. He wrote that the atmosphere was "more obvious" in this version and that he found the first part "too didactic." Clive objected to Woolf's portrayal of "subtle, sensitive, tactful, gracious, delicately perceptive, & perspicacious women" and "obtuse, vulgar, blind, florid, rude, tactless, emphatic, indelicate, vain, tyrannical, stupid men" (QB1 209). He also praised the picnic scene (chapter X) as her masterpiece. Woolf's reply to Clive's appraisal and criticism is regarded by DeSalvo as a turning point in Woolf's attitude toward her work.

She wrote to Clive that she had written the draft "originally in a dream like state" and that her plan was to "go over the beginning again with broad touches, keeping much of the original draft, and trying to deepen the atmosphere—Giving the feel of running water and not much else" (L1 383). She also rejected his criticism of her treatment of the sexes, suggesting that in 1909 a man was perhaps not in a very good position to judge his own sex. "I think I gather courage as I go on," she continued. "The only possible reason for writing down all this, is that it represents roughly a view of one's own. My boldness terrifies me" (L1 383). From here until the following year, we hear no more in her letters about the novel and it seems that she did not show any more drafts to anyone.

DeSalvo (*First Voyage*) says that Woolf began a new version in March 1909 and another in November 1910, referring to it as *The Voyage Out* by December that year. She began again in early 1911 and completed another version by the winter of 1912–13. A letter to Clive of April 1911 alludes to a third of the book having been rewritten (L1 461) and in May 1912 Woolf wrote to Violet Dickinson that she was working very hard and was "in sight of the end" (L1 500). In July 1912 she wrote to Violet that her novel was "at last dying. O how sad when it's done!" (L1 506). Exactly a week before her marriage to Leonard WOOLF, on August 3, 1912, she wrote to Violet that they had both finished their novels (Leonard's being *THE VILLAGE IN THE JUNGLE*). According to DeSalvo, this was a "very different version of the novel than the one Woolf had begun earlier. All overt references to Rachel's homosexual love for Helen were eradicated; all overt links between Richard Dalloway and Willoughby Vinrace were expunged . . . Helen's overt sadism was pushed underground" (*First Voyage* 102).

According to Heine, in October 1912, shortly after returning from her honeymoon, Woolf began a massive revision, adding what is now chapter XVII and replacing the earlier chapter 28 with three others: XXII, XXIII and XXIV. Leonard Woolf describes his wife "rewriting the last chapters of *The Voyage Out* for the tenth, or, it may have been, the twentieth time" (LW2 60). He recalled that she "once opened a cupboard and found in it (and burnt) a whole mountain of MSS; it was *The Voyage Out* which she had rewritten (I think) five times from beginning to end" (LW2 55). DeSalvo suggests that Woolf may have even begun a *third* version of the novel at this time, completing a final draft in February 1913: "She completed the revision, correction, and retyping of over five-hundred-eighty-nine pages of text—a complete new version of the novel—in less than two months" (*First Voyage* 104).

Leonard took Woolf's manuscript to Gerald DUCKWORTH on March 9, 1913. Earlier that year she had begun to suffer severe headaches. Duckworth's reader, Edward GARNETT, praised the book and it was accepted for publication in April. On September 9, Woolf attempted suicide by taking an overdose of Veronal. Jean THOMAS, in whose nursing home Woolf had stayed that summer, wrote a week later to Violet Dickinson that it was "the novel which has broken her up. She finished it and sent the proofs back for correction and suddenly went into a panic—couldn't sleep and thought everyone would jeer at her" (Novak 78). In January 1915, Woolf's attitude to her novel was still very negative and she was afraid of how it would be received. She wrote in her diary that she and Janet CASE had talked about the novel, "(which everyone will assure me is the most brilliant thing they've ever read; & privately condemn, as indeed it deserves to be condemned)" (D1 29). The novel stayed in proof until late 1914, and was published in England on March 26, 1915 by Duckworth & Company (the first U.S. edition was published in 1920 by George H. Doran Company; see "Publishing History" below). On March 25, Woolf again was taken to a nursing home. Quentin Bell (who draws on *The Voyage Out, MRS. DALLOWAY* and Leonard Woolf's *Beginning Again* in describing Woolf's "madness") writes that in the novel's final chapters, Woolf "had been playing with fire. She had succeeded in bringing some of the devils within her mind hugely and gruesomely from the depths, and she had gone too far for comfort" (QB2 42). Even more than twenty years later, when Woolf was struggling once again with huge revisions to a long novel, *THE YEARS,* she wrote that she had "never suffered, since The Voyage Out, such acute despair on re-reading" (D5 17) and that she had "never been so near the precipice to my own feeling since 1913" (D5 24).

Revisions

"So far as can be seen," writes Heine, "each succeeding version of *The Voyage Out* drew on its predecessors, gathering in new elements of its author's experience" ("Virginia Woolf's Revisions" 419). Heine calls it a "protean novel" (401), and others too have recognized that Woolf's own experiences changed the way she wished to present Rachel Vinrace. DeSalvo notes that in chapter XXII, Terence Hewet thinks that his novel called *Silence* will be different now that he is engaged; thus "Woolf's first novel contains the idea that a novel in progress will change as the life experiences of its author change" (*First Voyage* 1).

In a reading that looks for the psychological motivation for Woolf's revisions, DeSalvo writes that "each time Woolf completed a draft of the novel, each time she composed or revised or rewrote Rachel's delirium and death, she was staging her own punishment, delirium, and semi-suicidal death for having excited the lusts of an older man identified in the earlier version with the victim's father" (*First Voyage* 159). Nevertheless, DeSalvo goes on, "writing of Rachel's death was a way for Virginia Woolf to rejoin those taken from *her* by death" (159). Looking at the later typescript, Heine finds there more clearly than in the finished novel evidence that Woolf "is adding her own new sexual knowledge to Rachel's consciousness, or subconsciousness" ("Virginia Woolf's Revisions" 437). For DeSalvo, the published novel "is a curious amalgam of two stages of the novel's earlier phases (themselves *disguises*), feverishly, but imperfectly fused" (*First Voyage* 158). DeSalvo finds that in revising the novel, Woolf shifted a family history in which responsibility for Rachel's story lay with individuals to a social history in which that responsibility lies with a system. (Reviewing DeSalvo's book, Esther Klindienst Joplin disagreed, finding that "the manuscripts contain many signs that the later draft became a book about books, a book about education, and the ways fiction shapes life" [VWM 16: 2].)

Many of the revisions Woolf made concern literary allusions (see section on allusions in Background below). DeSalvo notes that the late addition of references to *ANTIGONE* (TVO 45) and to Charles KINGSLEY's "New Forest Ballad" (TVO 350) "indicate not only that Rachel's fate is equivalent to Sabrina's and to the Lady in [Milton's] 'Comus' . . . but also that, like Antigone and like Jane [in Kingsley], she can join those she loves only in death" (*First Voyage* 153).

Jane Novak, examining the Berg manuscripts, found that Woolf had attempted to mute emotion as she revised through "aesthetic distancing through style and point of view as well as by the deliberately restrained use of personal experience" (Novak 80). Novak describes Woolf changing her novel "more in the direction of the novel of Silence . . . which Terence wants to write, the novel that Virginia Woolf did write" (Novak 81). Novak points out that Woolf deleted references to Rachel's dead mother, Theresa, and her power over Rachel's life (Novak 81). As several other critics have noted, Woolf established a characteristic pattern of revision in writing her first novel. James Haule sees the process by which *Melymbrosia* became *The Voyage Out* as a paradigm of Woolf's "process of restricting a wealth of personal detail in favor of universal image" ("*To the Lighthouse* and the Great War" 176).

It is because this process has been so clearly recognized that critics have turned to the manuscripts in attempting to elucidate key scenes in the novel. Mitchell Leaska, for example, discussing the hallucinatory scene in the jungle when Rachel seems to see Terence and Helen above her (TVO 283–84) and the scene in which Terence reads "Comus" to Rachel (TVO 326–27), returns to the drafts and finds the published versions much more obscure: "It is through the clarity of the Holograph that we see the obscurity of the finished product insisted upon" (*Novels* 37). Another significant feature of the revisions that several critics have remarked on is that Rachel is rendered less feminist in *The Voyage Out* than in *Melymbrosia.* Haule also comments that "the powerlessness that *Melymbrosia* portrays as the fate of a single woman is extended in *The Voyage Out* to all characters" ("*To the Lighthouse* and the Great War" 175). Jessica Tvordi* points out that by the time the novel was published, most of Woolf's "obvious allusions to lesbianism—the 'Sapphist tyranny' and 'hidden Sapphist tendencies' (DeSalvo [*First Voyage*] 134) of the women in *Melymbrosia*—are barely discernible" (Tvordi 227). Following Jane Marcus's explanation of ellipsis as "a female code for lesbian love" (*Languages* 169), Tvordi reads the conversation between Evelyn Murgatroyd and Rachel in Evelyn's room as a scene of attempted seduction by Evelyn. She points out that the Evelyn of *Melymbrosia* is "significantly different" from the character in *The Voyage Out.* Woolf's revisions not only to individual characters but to the whole conception of her novel were radical, and they did not end with its publication in 1915.

Publishing History

The Voyage Out was published by Duckworth & Co., the publishing house run by Woolf's half-brother Gerald, on March 26, 1915. Two thousand copies were printed, with a gray-green dust jacket printed in navy blue. In November 1919, Woolf recorded in her diary that two American publishers were interested in publishing her first two novels in America (D1 313). One of these, Macmillan, dropped out after reading *NIGHT AND DAY,* but the other, George H. Doran Co., began negotiations. Woolf wrote that she was "considerably pleased with the American publishers, & that the old V. O. should set sail again" (D1 314).

In preparing the novel for its U.S. first edition, Woolf made revisions to a copy of the English first edition that DeSalvo believes to have been a copy sold in the mid-1970s through the Bow Windows bookshop in Lewes, Sussex. This copy has recently been located by James Haule at the Fisher Library of the University of Sydney, Australia. Haule does not believe this is the copy used by Woolf as there are annotations on only a few of its pages. It is possible that another copy used by Woolf in preparing the first U.S. edition does exist somewhere. DeSalvo has written that B. J. Kirkpatrick is mistaken in her *Bibliography* in describing a copy owned by Frederick B. Adams, Jr. as the copy-text for the U.S. first edition (Kirkpatrick 4; DeSalvo VWM 19: 3–4). There had been plans for a second English edition, but it was never published. Instead, Duckworth bought sheets from Doran and issued them in September 1920. DeSalvo believes the copy of *The Voyage Out* owned by Adams is that which Woolf revised (in holograph and typescript insertions) for the proposed second English edition; she therefore describes it as representing "Woolf's final work on how she wanted the text of her first novel set" (VWM 19: 3). (A page of the Adams copy is reproduced in Kirkpatrick, opposite page 3.) In her book on the writing of *The Voyage Out,* DeSalvo says that the copy Woolf prepared for the second English edition "is a slightly different version than the American edition. The changes are not substantially different, however, but the existence of the Adams copy establishes that Woolf intended to supplant the text of the first Duckworth edition with a new English edition that would have been very similar to the 1920 American edition" (*First Voyage* 112).

In "Virginia Woolf's Revisions for the 1920 American and English Editions of *The Voyage Out,*" DeSalvo notes that Woolf "inserted 728 words and revised mostly by deleting a total of 3,519 words" (340), 80% of the deletions being from chapter XVI. In this article she lists variations between the first American edition and changes made in the Adams copy, calling the latter "a version which has never been published" (343). At the end of her article, DeSalvo collates the American and English first editions. Heine, in an appendix on "Textual Variants" in her edition of the novel (1990), collates the first English and American editions and the variants in the Adams copy; she also notes that DeSalvo's more detailed collation of the variants in her 1977 doctoral dissertation is reproduced in the introduction to James M. Haule and Philip M. Smith Jr.'s *Concordance to The Voyage Out by Virginia Woolf* (Ann Arbor, Michigan: University Microfilms International, 1988).

For her 1990 edition of the novel, Heine chose to follow the English edition because that was what Woolf had chosen for the 1929 HOGARTH PRESS Uniform Edition of *The Voyage Out* (although she notes that the reason Woolf did this is unknown). In preparing her edition, the principle Heine follows is that "even when a change in the editions published after 1915 is known to have been made by Virginia Woolf, it is rejected unless it clarifies the sentence structure of the 1915 text" ("Virginia Woolf's Revisions" 446). Heine notes changes in the U.S. edition to the beginning of chapter X, where references to Nora in Ibsen's *Doll's House* and to "an unnamed novel about a 'woman's downfall' " are cut ("Virginia Woolf's Revisions" 437).

In February 1920, Woolf wrote in her diary that she was spending an hour a day reading *The Voyage Out,* which she had not read since July 1913. It appeared to her to be a "harlequinade," "an assortment of patches—here simple & severe—here frivolous & shallow—here like God's truth—here strong & free flowing as I could wish" (D2 17). She wrote that on the whole she liked Rachel Vinrace's mind, and remarked on her own "gift for pen & ink. . . . I can do little to amend" (D2 17). In fact, she amended, or at least altered, considerably. Chapter XVI was most heavily changed between the English and U.S. editions and the changes "drastically affected the form of the novel—tightened it—indicating that Woolf was trying to remedy structural weaknesses she and others had perceived in its first edition" (DeSalvo, *First Voyage* 113). The changes also affected the representation of Terence and Rachel's relationship as Woolf deleted specific details of their past lives. DeSalvo notes that the chapter is "the only glimpse provided of the kind of life they might have shared had Rachel lived" (*First Voyage* 113). She also notes that Woolf deleted autobiographical details in preparing the U.S. edition.

Thus, two quite different versions of *The Voyage Out* have circulated for many years. In 1978, Granada Publishing in England brought out an edition of *The Voyage Out* that DeSalvo described as "such a corrupt text that anyone who is a serious student of Virginia Woolf" should not use it. She pointed out many changes to Woolf's punctuation and spelling made by someone at Granada quite gratuitously, as well as other errors (VWM 19:3). More recently, as Woolf's English copyright expired at the end of 1991, new editions have been published of *The Voyage Out* and all Woolf's novels, as well as *A ROOM OF ONE'S OWN* and *THREE GUINEAS*. In the Penguin Twentieth Century Classics edition of *The Voyage Out* edited by Jane Wheare (1992), the English 1915 edition is used but some corrections have been made in line with the U.S. 1920 edition, and the 1920 version of chapter XVI is included in an appendix. The Shakespeare Head Press edition published by Blackwell and edited by C. Ruth Miller and Lawrence Miller (1993) compares all editions of the novel, listing all variants. Other available editions of *The Voyage Out* include the Oxford University Press/World's Classics edition, edited with an introduction by Lorna Sage (1993), and the Signet Classic edition with an introduction by Louise DeSalvo (1991).

Background

Just as most readers have accepted that *TO THE LIGHTHOUSE* has significant roots in Woolf's memories of her parents, so many have seen in *The Voyage Out* evidence of Woolf's own struggle with issues of engagement and marriage, with relations between men and women in a patriarchal society, and also the effects of several premature deaths of people she loved represented in the story of Rachel Vinrace. DeSalvo suggests that the novel may have been undertaken in an "attempt to expiate the feelings of guilt for having survived Thoby," pointing out that Rachel dies in her twenty-fourth year, Woolf's age when Thoby died (*First Voyage* 4). Harvena Richter also reads the novel as in part an effort to come to terms with Thoby's death; Thomas Caramagno, however, sees Stella DUCKWORTH "at the heart of *The Voyage Out*" (Caramagno 158).

In her introduction to the new Penguin edition of *The Voyage Out,* Jane Wheare* calls Woolf "essentially an autobiographical writer" (xiii), yet she also finds an avoidance of autobiography remarkable in a first novel. She sees the characters of the novel as taking on different characteristics of Woolf herself. Rachel Blau DuPlessis,* more typically, finds the main characters to be "displaced and realigned" members of Woolf's own family (DuPlessis 121), seeing elements of Thoby Stephen, John Waller "Jack" HILLS and Leonard Woolf in Terence; Vanessa Bell and Julia Prinsep STEPHEN in Helen; Gerald and George DUCKWORTH in Richard Dalloway; and Stella Duckworth and Woolf herself in Rachel.

To Phyllis Rose, Rachel's "pilgrimage" is a "fictionalized presentation of Virginia Woolf's own 'journey' from Hyde Park Gate to Bloomsbury" (Rose 58), and for another biographer, Lyndall Gordon, Rachel's "education follows Virginia's own" (Gordon 99). Both these biographers stress the affinities between Rachel and her creator, as well as between Helen Ambrose and Vanessa Bell: "The very names Helen and Rachel suggest a contrast of Greek and Biblical figures: Vanessa's statuesque splendor; Virginia eager, impulsive, searching" (Gordon 130). Rose sees Rachel's choice of Hewet rather than Hirst as "the same kind of willed commitment to normality that the decision to marry Leonard Woolf and the earlier flirtation with Clive Bell represented" in Woolf's life (Rose 67); presumably, by "normality" Rose means heterosexuality.

Another biographer, Stephen Trombley, goes so far as to refer to "Rachel-Virginia" in his discussion of the novel. Christine Froula* sees Rachel and Terence as two aspects of Woolf. Virginia Blain,* however, has argued against identifying Woolf with Rachel Vinrace: "Although Rachel is seen from the inside, it is not her consciousness which frames the novel, but that of Woolf's narrator, whose gender-conscious ironies operate as a constant reminder to the reader of the existence of the sex-war as a kind of grim backcloth to the romantic love story" (Blain 122). Blain believes that identifying Rachel with her author has resulted in "a denigration of the novel as the product of a prudish mind" (123).

It is, though, difficult to avoid reading *The Voyage Out* as informed by Woolf's own emotional attachments and doubts between about 1904 and 1915. As Heine has said, "no one with any knowledge of the biographical background has ever doubted that St. John Hirst is a portrayal of Lytton Strachey, or that Terence Hewet originated in Clive Bell" ("Virginia Woolf's Revisions" 416–17). Heine suggests that an early version of the Ambroses' marriage may have been based on Woolf's relationship with Walter HEADLAM. DeSalvo, on the other hand, suggests the Ambrose marriage as Woolf's image of what life might have been like with Lytton STRACHEY (*First Voyage* 35). Strachey proposed to Woolf on February 17, 1909, but within a few hours they both realized that they should not get married. Another suitor who found his way into *The Voyage Out* was Walter LAMB. In a letter to her sister on July 21, 1911, Woolf describes her "tactics in discouraging Walter Lamb's interest in marrying her in a way that suggests Evelyn M.'s response to Mr. Perrott" (Heine, "Virginia Woolf's Revisions" 425).

Jane Dunn sees the Helen-Terence-Rachel triangle of the novel as mirroring the Vanessa-Clive-Virginia triangle of 1908. Madeline Moore* also says that in *The Voyage Out* Woolf tries, "though largely unsuccessfully, to transform the psychological complexities of her relationship with Clive and Vanessa Bell into the central core of her fiction" ("Some Female" 82), and that Woolf could not gain the distance she needed. Both Frances Spalding, in her biography of Vanessa Bell, and Diane Gillespie, in *The Sisters' Arts*, discuss a letter Vanessa wrote Roger FRY in 1915 about her sister's novel in which she noted its characters' lack of distance from the author's feelings, something that she said made it difficult for her to "get outside" the novel (Marler 172–73). To Moore, the affair with Clive Bell was "the only way Woolf could re-enter the chamber of her sister's love" ("Some Female" 84).

Several journeys that Woolf made in the years immediately following her father's death are also likely to have contributed to the conception of her novel. In 1904, the Stephen children and Gerald Duckworth traveled to Italy and Paris, meeting up with Violet Dickinson in Florence. In 1905, Woolf went with her brother Adrian to Spain by sea, stopping at Oporto, Lisbon, Granada and Seville (QB1 104), a trip on which Lucio Ruotolo says she experienced "feelings of radical disengagement" to which she gave vent in her first novel (Ruotolo, *Interrupted* 19). In 1906, Woolf, Vanessa and Violet Dickinson met Thoby and Adrian in Greece and traveled together to Athens. This trip was marked by the illnesses of Vanessa and Violet and by Thoby's death on his return to London. In 1909 Woolf went to Florence with Clive and Vanessa Bell, where she encountered an English "colony" the members of which undoubtedly shaded certain characters in the novel. In August that year she traveled to the Richard WAGNER festival at Bayreuth with Adrian STEPHEN and Saxon SYDNEY-TURNER. In April 1911, Woolf went to Broussa in Turkey, where her sister, traveling with Roger Fry and H. T. J. NORTON, had fallen ill. There, she came to know Fry well, and his interest in local Turkish art is likely to have influenced the description of Mr. Flushing's dealings with the natives in *The Voyage Out*. Mrs. Flushing, on the other hand, resembles Lady Ottoline MORRELL, whom Woolf had first met in 1909.

All these journeys contributed to the setting and characterizations of *The Voyage Out*. Sometimes very specific incidents are recalled in the novel, such as when Terence and St. John, while Rachel is dying, argue about whether or not the Portsmouth road is macadamized beyond Hindhead (TVO 342). Quentin Bell recounts that Thoby and Adrian Stephen had exactly this argument in Greece in 1906 (QB1 109).

Allusions

Woolf drew on many literary sources as well. Gordon traces the germ of the idea of a sea voyage to a fantasy recorded in Woolf's 1899 "Warboys diary" (PA 138), which in turn can be traced to her reading in 1897 of Richard Hakluyt's *Collection of the Early Voyages, Travels, and Discoveries of the English Nation*

(London: R. H. Evans, 1809–12. 5 vols.) Woolf wrote about these volumes in "The Elizabethan Lumber Room" (CE1 46–53; CR1 60–71). Alice Fox has detailed how Woolf's successive drafts "reveal the author's developing awareness of how best to use Hakluyt's *Voyages* and the Elizabethan world from which it sprang and to which it contributed" (Fox 22). Fox notes that Mr. Pepper's description of the arrival of Elizabethan ships is based on Sir Francis Drake's accounts of circumnavigating the globe (Fox 23).

Fox also points out that the passage beginning "Since the time of Elizabeth very few people had seen the river" (TVO 264) was added late, "thereby drawing together the other allusions to Elizabethan voyages scattered throughout the novel, and making of *The Voyage Out* an Elizabethan voyage" (Fox 25). As Fox notes, both Winifred HOLTBY and Nancy Topping Bazin have recognized that the scene on the river where the voyagers see deer jumping (TVO 279) was found by Woolf in Sir Walter Raleigh's *Discovery of the Large, Rich, and Beautiful Empire of Guiana* (1596), one of the accounts in Hakluyt's *Voyages.* Fox points out that Woolf changes Raleigh's tame deer to wild ones (Fox 30). In 1906, Woolf reviewed Professor Walter Raleigh's *English Voyages of the Sixteenth Century* for the *SPEAKER* ("Trafficks and Discoveries" E1 120–24), the western voyages described therein providing "setting and frame" for *The Voyage Out* (Fox 36). Both Raleigh and Woolf, says Bazin, "suggest a comparison between going up the river and penetrating a female" (Bazin 52).

Another source for Woolf's setting is suggested by Gillian Beer, who finds that the novel "bears traces not only of a struggle with Victorian narrative, but of Woolf's own reading of Darwin's writing" ("Pre-History" 110), specifically *The Voyage of the Beagle,* which Beer believes "elated" Woolf: "The young Darwin, like the young Rachel, is discovering the world and in some of the same regions" ("Pre-History" 110). Elizabeth G. Lambert* has also discussed in detail Woolf's allusions to and critique of Charles Darwin's writings in *Melymbroisa* and *The Voyage Out.* Avrom Fleishman remarks on the popularity of "the novel of tropical adventure in vogue at the time" which he says modifies the "social portraiture" of Woolf's novel (Fleishman 1). One other possible source for tropical atmosphere, of course, could have been Leonard Woolf, although his influence could only have been felt after 1911 when he returned from Ceylon. Fleishman points out that in *Growing,* the second volume of his autobiography (the first chapter of which is called "The Voyage Out"), Leonard describes an intimate relationship he had in Ceylon with a young woman called Rachel (LW1 229–34).

The densely allusive character of *The Voyage Out* has encouraged readings that see the plot and setting of the novel as influenced by Woolf's own reading. For many readers, the most obvious source of *The Voyage Out*'s setting, and even elements of its plot, is Joseph CONRAD's *Heart of Darkness* (though Mark Hussey also suggests the influence of fauvist painting [*Singing* 62]). Shirley Neumann* notes the critics who have written about the novel's Conradian pattern—Dorothy Brewster, James Naremore, Avrom Fleishman, Alex Zwerdling, Hermione Lee, T. E. Apter and Rosemary Pitt* (who develops the only sustained argument about the parallels)—but she finds that "the structural similarities of the two novels weigh less than the thematic link Rosemary Pitt has labelled 'the exploration of the self' " (Neumann 62). Neumann finds Woolf's adaptation of Conrad's plot "comparatively limited" (64). Fleishman also remarks that although structurally similar to *Heart of Darkness, The Voyage Out* "is no more an exotic novel of the colonies than it is a traditional social novel" (Fleishman 2).

Daniel Fogel, while agreeing that Conrad's influence marks *The Voyage Out,* says that "the influence above all others against which Woolf was finding it very difficult to fight as she drafted and redrafted her first novel was that of Henry James" (Fogel 123), and he finds that Woolf "resists James in a variety of ways" (Fogel 128). Certainly, many readers have seen similarities between Rachel and Henry JAMES's Isabel Archer in *The Portrait of a Lady.* Jane Wheare sees "surprising affinities" between *The Voyage Out* and Alfred, Lord TENNYSON's *In Memoriam AHH* ("Introduction" xvi), remarking that "it is perhaps above all the poetry of *The Voyage Out* which distinguishes it from so much Victorian and Edwardian fiction" (xxx). (In another context, E. L. Bishop* has also remarked on how the language of Woolf's first novel "attains the concentration and suggestiveness of poetry" [343].)

Moore speculates that Jane Ellen HARRISON was an influence on *The Voyage Out,* specifically a section of her *Prolegomena to the Study of Greek Religion* (1908) entitled "Mother and Maid" ("Some Female" 88f). Moore sees Rachel as playing Persephone to Helen's DEMETER, and reads the journey up the river as tracing "the competing myths of Oedipus and of Demeter and Persephone" as they reach "a hallucinatory but definite resolution. Mother, Maiden, and lover descend into an unmediated pastoral landscape, and out of their sensual encounter emerges a revelation of their social fate" ("Some Female" 95). In another reading of classical allusion, Froula says that Richard Dalloway's kiss recalls Bruce Lincoln's discussion (in *Emerging from the Chrysalis: Studies in Ritual of Women's Initiation* [Cambridge, Massachusetts: Harvard University Press, 1981]) of "the Kore myth as a paradigm for female initiation in 'a number of male-centered, misogynistically inclined cultures, and strongly suggested in numerous Greek myths.' The Kore paradigm signals the young woman's violent abduction into male culture, where her place is in the underworld" (Froula, "Out of" 146).

The "Bloomsbury atmosphere of discussion, of Thursday 'evenings' and Cambridge friends" also found its way into *The Voyage Out* (Hussey, *Singing* 65), though Woolf mocks "Apostolic fervor" in the novel (98). The book that Helen Ambrose reads as she embroiders is *Principia Ethica,* the "bible" of Leonard Woolf's generation at Cambridge, written by G. E. Moore. Jane Marcus has described *The Voyage Out* as "a reading list of the author's influences" (*Languages* 88), as are many first novels.

Beverly Ann Schlack* writes that the "splendor of Woolf's habit of allusion is functional as well as aesthetically satisfying, and can be traced from the earliest drafts to the final, published text of any given novel" ("Novelist's Voyage" 317). In looking at Woolf's revisions of allusions as she wrote her first novel, Schlack remarks that it is "startling how little allusive material is *added* after the first fairly complete extant draft" (317). Schlack discusses how Woolf deleted many references to authors Rachel had read because they made her seem "too *informed.*" She traces the way an allusion to Thomas BROWNE's *Religio Medici* is excised, but points out that it anticipates Woolf's use of the "Comus" allusion. The "cumulative effect" of Woolf's revisions in this area, says Schlack, "is a Rachel Vinrace shorn of any wisdom or knowledge derived from reading Browne, Keats, Nietzsche, Thomas à Kempis, Whitman, and Samuel Butler, among others" ("Novelist's Voyage" 322).

Many critics agree that Woolf's allusions often link love and marriage with death. Laura Davis-Clapper* has traced the changing treatment of an allusion to *Kenilworth,* one of Walter SCOTT's Waverly novels, through *Melymbrosia* and the first English and U.S. editions, again pointing out Woolf's suppression of her novel's subtext. There are two allusions in *Melymbrosia,* one in the 1915 edition, and none in the 1920. In *Kenilworth,* Davis-Clapper says, marriage "is associated with chaos, confinement, and violence" (226). Redrafting *Melymbrosia,* "Woolf changed the book the character Susan Warrington was reading from the popular, but respectable *Kenilworth* to a fictitious, third-rate work, *Miss Appleby's Adventure*" (226).

Finally, although not strictly part of the novel's "background," it is worth mentioning a curious similarity between the words Terence speaks at Rachel's deathbed and a line in the first of two suicide notes Woolf left for Leonard in 1941: "No two people have ever been so happy as we have been" (TVO 353); "I dont think two people could have been happier than we have been" (L6 481). Howard Harper comments that "these words, from the very beginning of the lifework, are recognized as originating in the unconscious, and are associated with the dramatization of death" (Harper 53n11).

Critical Responses

Lytton Strachey, whom Blain calls Woolf's "earliest literary rival" (121), wrote to her in 1916 that *The Voyage Out* was "very, very unvictorian! The handling of the detail always seemed to me divine. My one criticism is about the conception of it as a whole—which I am doubtful about. As I read I felt that it perhaps lacked the cohesion of a dominating idea—I don't mean in the spirit—but in the action" (Woolf and Strachey 73). Replying, Woolf said his letter almost gave her the courage to reread her novel and went on to explain what she had tried to do: "to give the feeling of a vast tumult of life, as various and disorderly as possible, which should be cut short for a moment by the death, and go on again—and the whole was to have a sort of pattern, and be somehow controlled. The difficulty was to keep any sort of coherence,—also to give enough detail to make the characters interesting—which Forster says I don't do" (L2 82).

In his review on April 8, 1915, "A New Novelist," for the *Daily News and Leader,* E. M. FORSTER commented on how "Queens of the pen" (i.e., women writers) have usually been uneducated, but here was the product of an educated mind. "Here at last," he wrote, "is a book which attains unity as surely as *Wuthering Heights,* though by a different path, a book which, while written by a woman and presumably from a woman's point of view, soars straight out of local questionings into the intellectual day" (CH 52–53). The *TIMES LITERARY SUPPLEMENT* review, sounding rather like Terence Hewet, said that "never was a book more feminine, more recklessly feminine. It may be labelled clever and shrewd, mocking, suggestive, subtle, 'modern', but these terms do not convey the spirit of it—which is essentially feminine" (CH 49). The *Observer* found that it had "something startlingly like genius" (CH 50), while the *Morning Post* found it "a bewildering kind of book" (CH 51). For the *Manchester Guardian* it was "a very remarkable first novel" (CH 58), and the *Spectator* deemed it "a novel of serious artistic value" (CH 62). Woolf, as the daughter of an eminent Victorian, who had also been publishing since 1904, was sure to attract many reviews, and although many commented on the strangeness of her first novel (anticipating later critics), it was not badly received.

In February 1915 Forster sent a copy to D. H. LAWRENCE, who wrote to him that it was "Interesting but not *very* good—nothing much behind it" (Forster *Letters* 1: 220).[23] Forster described the novel to Florence Barger as "Amazingly interesting, and very funny" (*Letters* 1: 223), and to Malcolm Darling he wrote that while *The Voyage Out* was "certainly inferior" to his own novels, he did think it "fine in other ways—its feeling for adventure, its knowledge that adventure can only be undertaken alone" (*Letters* 1: 227). Woolf later wrote in her DIARY that in comparing *The Voyage Out* with *Night and Day,* Forster had called her first novel "vague and universal." In "The Early Novels of Virginia Woolf," published in *THE CRITERION* in 1926 and reprinted in *Abinger Harvest* (1936), Forster called the novel "a strange, tragic, inspired book whose scene is a South America not found on any map and reached by a boat which would not float on any sea" (*Abinger Harvest* 107).

Novak remarks that early critics (many of whose opinions are reviewed by Alice van Buren Kelley) "almost universally describe it by some variation of Clive Bell's phrase, 'a remarkable failure' " (Novak 76). While not perhaps saying directly that the novel fails, several critics writing in the 1960s and 1970s commented on the book's "strangeness." For Jean Guiguet, *The Voyage Out* is "easy enough to define, practically impossible to sum up" (Guiguet 197); "It is immediately obvious that the interest of this novel does not lie in its incidents" (198). Naremore writes that in spite of its conventional appearance, the novel "often tends to frustrate conventional expectations" (6) and finds that "an air of strangeness pervades the novel" (6). Leaska calls it "a strange, difficult, and still unpopular book" (*Novels* 12). More recently, John Mepham has written that its "satire is so accomplished that we feel ready to place Virginia Woolf somewhere in the tradition of the English comic novel, along with Jane Austen and Charles Dickens. Yet sometimes this impression is disturbed" (*Literary Life* 42).

For some readers, like Jean O. Love, *The Voyage Out* was "a poorly controlled mixture of artistic elements" (*Worlds* 86). Allen McLaurin also found that although the novel hinted at Woolf's characteristic themes and techniques, they were unconnected at this stage in her career. Caramagno, however, has recently argued that the inconsistencies of *The Voyage Out* are "part of a deliberate strategy to invite the reader to experience a *failed* reading and to deal with the frustration of pointlessness when critical acumen meets an intractable text—the first step toward understanding the manic-depressive's world" (Caramagno 157).

Setting *The Voyage Out* into its literary context, Richter points out that 1913, when Woolf finished the final draft of her novel, saw the publication of the first two volumes of Marcel PROUST's *A la recherche du temps perdu* and the "final beginnings" of James JOYCE's *Portrait of the Artist as a Young Man* (published serially in *THE EGOIST*). Gerald Duckworth also published Dorothy RICHARDSON's *Pointed Roofs* (the first volume of her novel sequence *Pilgrimage*) in 1915, the manuscript having been submitted also in 1913 (Richter 94n25). Richter describes *The Voyage Out* as a far-reaching glimpse "into internal reality and the essence of lived experience" (vii), seeing its emphasis on "the subject's experience of the object" as most clearly separating Woolf from her contemporaries (viii). Richter's examination of the Berg manuscripts leads her to conclude that Woolf's observations of subjectivity were her own, rather than the result of reading Joyce, Richardson or Proust.

Love, however, writes that the "variable subject-object relationships in *The Voyage Out* are matched by vacillation in the schematization of consciousness" (*Worlds* 89), seeing the novel as concerned with "the problem of meaninglessness" (106) and interpreting the voyage out itself and the river journey as "devices to symbolize both the lack of meaning and a search for meaning that could have occurred without them" (99). Naremore, who is unusual among critics in having written that "the passionate life, the life of the body, is central to [Woolf's] vision as a novelist" (44), writes that Woolf should be compared not with Joyce or Richardson but with Proust: "The Proustian novel shows the personality being liberated from time and space, but Mrs. Woolf goes even further until the personality itself becomes dissolved in total communion with what is 'out there' " (Naremore 36). Richter also stressed that this was a novel about identity, saying that the word "out" in the title denoted merely a physical direction: "The journey is inward" (Richter 25).

As was typical of readings of the 1960s and 1970s, several critics saw *The Voyage Out* in mythic terms. Fleishman draws on the work of Northrop Frye and Mircea Eliade in describing the novel as "a story of initiation and heroic quest" (4), but he adds that it is "not a mythological novel of the kind that was to become a major strain in modern fiction" (14). Novak also writes that in her first novel, Woolf "realized both the quest plot and the strong symbolic structure that were to persist in her work" (Novak 71). For Frederick P. W. McDowell* the world of *The Voyage Out* was one "in which chance predominates, in which the unpredictable can result in tragedy as well as in spiritual insight and ecstasy" (89), a world in which Woolf sought to show that love "can raise the inner being to its highest point" (81).

A constant theme of readings of *The Voyage Out* has been that it is a version of the bildungsroman, though Blain criticizes Naremore and Fleishman's

[23] S. P. Rosenbaum has recently written that the editors of Forster's letters are mistaken and that the novel in question was Leonard Woolf's *The Wise Virgins* (Rosenbaum, *Edwardian* 509n16). It is, though, possible Forster had an advance copy of *The Voyage Out* as he had reviewed it.

readings as limited because they do not take into account the inflection which Rachel's being a woman gives to the conventional plot of the novel of development. Woolf's subject, Blain suggests, is "the problem of a woman's disablement by fear of condemnation by the other sex" (Blain 125). *The Voyage Out* is not just another bildungsroman "detailing the metaphysical education of a heroine enacting Eliade's version of the heroic myth" (Blain 125).

As many readers commented on the "strangeness" of Woolf's first novel, so many have noted that it is "an unusual *Bildungsroman*" (Susan Dick,* "Tunnelling" 179). Ruotolo sees the novel as reversing the usual format of the bildungsroman, offering "a heroine who will not grow into the world as it is constituted" (*Interrupted* 21). In her extended discussion of the novel as a story of initiation, Froula argues that *The Voyage Out,* "depicting the initiation of a female artist-figure, captures the paradoxical relation of female initiation to female authority in the late Victorian culture of Woolf's girlhood" ("Out of" 136). She describes the paradox of Rachel's being encouraged on the one hand to imagine marriage and motherhood as her life's fulfillment, while on the other hand being endowed with a strong desire to evade that plot. Froula links the "colony" of Santa Marina with Woolf's own dream expressed in a letter to Emma Vaughan of founding "a colony where there shall be no marrying . . . no human element at all, except what comes through Art" (L1 41–42). Froula, who sees the colony on the Amazon as signaling "hostility to patriarchal marriage" (141), likens Rachel Vinrace to the character Lily Everit in Woolf's story "The Introduction" (MDP 37–43). (See *MRS. DALLOWAY'S PARTY*.)

Like all bildungsromane, writes Susan Stanford Friedman,* the narrative of *The Voyage Out* is pedagogical, but "at a metalevel," the novel "examines the place of reading in the narrative of development" (105). Friedman notes that the many scenes of reading in the novel focus on "the intertextuality of reading life and books" (108) and argues that Rachel's "reading of books shapes her reading of life" (110). It is because she is established as "a model reader who integrates and balances better than any other character the intertextual task of reading both books and life" (113) that Rachel's death is such a shock: It undermines our identification with Rachel as a reader. While many readers see her death as Woolf's "killing off" the traditional marriage plot, Friedman suggests that the novel may "have been additionally 'killing off' the kind of female reader of books and people who is most likely to be victimized" (115).

Rachel's death has long been a crux in critical readings of *The Voyage Out,* its "meaning" often posited as the meaning of the book. Some readers, like David Daiches and Hermione Lee, have found Rachel's death a shock that is totally unprepared for in the novel. Alex Zwerdling calls it "a deliberate and shocking betrayal of the conventions of the marriage plot the book seemed to accept" (Zwerdling 177). The majority of critics, however, find that there are intimations of mortality throughout the novel. Harper writes that the "final meanings of *The Voyage Out* are latent in its opening pages," for example (14). Naremore sees the central significance of death as typical of Woolf's fiction, writing that *The Voyage Out* "seems an unconscious reflection [of] the uneasy compromises [her] characters make between the will to live in the world and the temptation to dissolve all individuality and sink into a deathlike trance" (Naremore 55).

In Naremore's reading, Rachel's story personifies the theme of "elemental forces of sexuality, of life and death, that stir far down beneath the civilized and orderly exterior of British life" (55). Roger Poole reads Rachel's death as the "only close" the novel could have, representing a female abhorrence of heterosexuality and the suppression of desire (*Unknown* 45); the storm at the novel's end, then, is for Poole "meant to represent a tremendous romantic victory of the spirit over the body" (45). Trombley criticizes this reading, saying that it "reduces the existential significance" of Rachel's death (23). Remarking that her illness has no identifiable physical cause, Trombley finds that Rachel's "decline is of the nature of a lapse of *being*" (31).

That the causes of Rachel's death are left obscure has led some readers into speculating on "psychogenic" causes. Leaska argues that the causes are intentionally made ambiguous so that the death "assumes an aura of tragic pointlessness" (*Novels* 34). Froula, arguing for more complex readings of the death than those that follow psychogenic causes and see it as resulting from a fear of sexuality, finds its causes "not in Rachel's psyche but in the culture that suppresses female authority" ("Out of" 158n21). Similarly, DuPlessis interprets Rachel's death as Woolf's way of attacking the narrative conventions that would demand a resolution in marriage (" 'Amor vin—' " 119). Rachel's death "announces that [the other characters] have not investigated deeply enough what they claim to question: marriage, love, gender polarization, the formation of women" (DuPlessis 122). In an interpretation that brings together the mythic and social dimensions of the novel, Judy Little has written that for Rachel, as for other women in Woolf's fiction, "liminality, or the green world, is not a temporary, festive escape. It is a revolutionary country. It is a place from which to evaluate 'civilization,' the male civilization and its traditions which, as Woolf noted, differ considerably from those of women" (Little 34).

Jane Wheare notices that most of the characters in the novel "have experienced the death of a close friend or relative" but that they are able in time to place these deaths in perspective. "Part of Woolf's purpose in the novel," Wheare maintains, "is to assert that there is a meaning to be discovered even in a world where . . . the central characters in our lives can and will die" (*Virginia Woolf* 72). Rachel's death obliges us to "reread what has seemed to be a comic novel about love and marriage as a novel about life and death" (Wheare, *Virginia Woolf* 82). Caramagno, however, who says that the "real subject" of *The Voyage Out* is to address the question "how do we deal with a death that threatens us and a reading that defies us?" (161), argues that the novel "trivializes its own ending, undermining the significance of Rachel's death by presenting contradictory interpretations ready-made according to each character's psychological needs and strategies for dealing with threatening, pointless events" (180). Criticizing those who see Rachel's death as "caused" by sexuality, or as self-willed, Caramagno suggests the death may be simply gratuitous. Such a reading also would change the usual interpretation of Rachel's nightmare after Richard Dalloway's kiss from sexual terror to representing "the 'no exit' hell of depression" (Caramagno 167).

Many readings that have sought to explain Rachel's death as representing a psychic withdrawal from sexuality also focus on that curious scene in chapter XXI of *The Voyage Out* where Rachel seems to see Terence and Helen looming above her, kissing (TVO 283–84). Dunn calls it the "most startling and erotic passage in the book" (117); Harper describes it as the "most suddenly violent and distressing" scene (47) in which the narrative undergoes "radical disorientation" (48); several critics have detected the rhythms of orgasm in the scene (e.g., Hermione Lee 45; Neumann 63). Roger Poole, who finds the episode "very Forsterian," describes what seems to happen as that "Helen, from being an auntly figure about 50 years of age, merges into an erotic figure transmitting female desire, and thus displaces the suggestion that a satisfying relationship could ever have been achieved between Terence and Rachel, a man and a woman, in the first place" ("Passage" 27). Leaska, who seems to suggest that heterosexual intercourse is woman's "initiation," describes the scene as a "highly elliptical transcription of Rachel's *actual or imagined* initiation into womanhood" (*Novels* 30); the images "suggest erotic turbulence, a swirling mixture of sensuality and violence" (*Novels* 30).

DuPlessis points out that in an earlier version of the scene Rachel herself announced her engagement to Helen, thus it seems that "Woolf wanted us to feel that Rachel had consented" (DuPlessis 121). "But not now." In the published version, the scene ends with "the embrace of mentors over the exhausted form of the bride-to-be" (DuPlessis 121). Neumann interprets Rachel's "awakening to Helen, not her lover" as well as the orgasmic image of happiness as "swelling and breaking in one vast wave," as suggesting "not only an unwillingness to face the sexual implications of her marriage but an unresolved ambiguity about her sexual choice" (Neumann 63). In choosing marriage, Neumann suggests, Rachel may have "ventured too far." For Moore, the scene dramatizes the conflicting loyalties which "arise from Rachel's allegiance to Helen as a mother figure and to Terence as a lover" ("Some Female" 98).

Contradicting those readers who see *The Voyage Out* in terms of oppositions (which she finds overlooks the complex relativity of perspectives Woolf inscribes in her novel), Pamela Caughie criticizes readings of the jungle scene that "depend on some necessary or supposed connection between the figurative and the literal rather than looking at the place and function of this scene in the novel" (Caughie 204). Caughie argues that the disturbing and obscure quality of the scene is its point, "not some obscurity to be cleared up or dismissed" (204). Woolf herself deliberately revised the scene, as Haule notes, to evoke more effectively "dislocation, confusion, asphyxiating fear, and eroticism" (Haule, "*To the Lighthouse* and the Great War" 176).

In addition to readings that focus on individual psychology and the relations between characters, *The Voyage Out* has also been seen to inaugurate Woolf's concerns in her fiction with social critique and feminism. Herbert Marder notes that Helen expresses feminist views and that Terence "seems at times to be little more than a mouthpiece" (68) as Woolf "sketched a symbolic portrait of the patriarchy" (47). Wheare, in an extensive discussion of the feminism of the novel, argues that Woolf "dramatizes her ideas so that they become an aspect of her characterization and are integrated into the novel as a whole" (*Virginia Woolf* 37). The novel, which is probably set in about 1905 (as the election involving Herbert Henry ASQUITH and Austen CHAMBERLAIN and mention of a possible British action in Morocco suggest), is fully aware of the "sex-war" going on in England at the time as women agitated for suffrage. Various attitudes toward feminism are assigned to different characters, but Wheare finds that the characters are interesting "in their own right, and through them [Woolf] is able to reawaken the reader's interest in a cause whose arguments may well be all too familiar" (*Virginia Woolf* 38). In contrast to Hermione Lee, who finds the women at the hotel to be "callous characters" (38), Wheare writes that Woolf "emphasizes the importance not only of the heroine's life but of the lives of all her female characters" (*Virginia Woolf* 59).

Helen Wussow* notes that "Misogyny, violence, and death" are introduced as key concepts in the very first pages of the novel when the children call Ridley Ambrose "Bluebeard" (Wussow 102). Arguing that "the theme of war in Woolf's fiction has its paradigm in her first, notably prewar novel," Wussow writes that within the context of the novel, "sexual encounters between men and women in a patriarchal society frequently take on the dynamics of physical violence and international conflict" (Wussow 105). Reversing the usual view of the novel as a story about personal emotions, Kathy Phillips argues that *The Voyage Out* "subordinates personality to a range of historical and social determinants which shape individuals" (53), and also contends that rather than neglecting Conrad's setting in a European colony, "Woolf extends his examination of the effects of commerce and colonization to condemn them even more scathingly than he" (53). "Empire and its underlying values," writes Phillips, "set their stamp on all the individuals of the novel and on their relations in couples" (71).

The two views of the novel as a work of social critique and as a story of individual emotion have been succinctly articulated by DeSalvo in her introduction to the Signet Classic edition: "Over the years, Woolf vacillated between making her novel mythic and highly ambiguous, and making it a realistically drawn work of social criticism. Indeed, Woolf created the published version of the novel by quickly 'marrying' two distinct earlier versions. . . . Thus, the published text preserves both the illuminating social realism and the mythic components of her earlier, disparate versions. . . . *The Voyage Out* bristles with social commentary and impresses one with Woolf's engagement with the most significant problems of Edwardian and Georgian England" ("Introduction" xiii–xiv).

Reading *The Voyage Out* in the context of Woolf's entire oeuvre has led many critics to comment on the ways in which the novel is a precursor to Woolf's later fiction. Richter, for example, writes that "there is not a single mode of subjectivity used in her later novels which is not present in *The Voyage Out*" (93), and Marder claims that her first two novels "contain most of the important themes of her fiction" (21). Fleishman finds in the novel themes that make Woolf's fiction "distinctive and important" (2), and Naremore calls the novel "characteristic in the most profound sense" (9). Leaska notes that all Woolf's principal themes, "as well as the many technical singularities and stylistic habits" that she later developed and refined, are present in *The Voyage Out.* Several critics have pointed out that the preoccupation with pattern and rhythm in Woolf's experimental novels is also present in *The Voyage Out.* E. L. Bishop, for example, writes that in her first novel, Woolf "was already reaching toward the novel of silence" (355) and had there begun her struggle "to restore language to its metaphorical intensity" (359). Wheare writes that "the more one rereads the novel, the more one becomes aware of this complex network of repetition, binding together its diverse material and at the same time suggesting innumerable ideas beyond the central story" ("Introduction" xxxi). *The Voyage Out,* Perry Meisel remarks, "is everywhere concerned with the discovery of 'pattern' " (Meisel 183).

Hussey discerns the announcement of an important theme in Woolf's fiction in *The Voyage Out,* writing that her novels are "*about* silence, an empty space at the heart of life, but they can only point to it, imply it, shape round it. The space is ineffable and impossible to construct, for construction or words would mean filling the space; the space must come to be apprehended in the act of reading" (*Singing* 67); in strikingly similar language, Patricia Laurence writes that "because this space of being is ineffable . . . it must be apprehended by the participation of the reader" (*Reading* 119). If Woolf's fiction as a whole constitutes "the evolution of a mythic world," writes Harper, "then *The Voyage Out* is its book of Genesis, the first articulation of a language whose later forms are more familiar but also more irregular and complex" (Harper 6). Harper argues that this novel sets in place mythic patterns and a symbolic language that remain "essentially 'immovable' " throughout Woolf's work (Harper 56).

More specific features of *The Voyage Out* that reappear in later works or are developed there include what Hussey terms Woolf's investigation of "preverbal states of mind" (*Singing* 66). Her interest in music, also, Hussey comments, "is clearly from the point of view of a writer. She has already begun her search for a suitable form through which to communicate her perception of the world that . . . had at its heart an empty, silent center that eludes communication in language" (*Singing* 67). He also notes that Woolf had already begun in her first novel to use color in a characteristically "psychological" way (79). Reading *BETWEEN THE ACTS,* Hussey finds several echoes from both *The Voyage Out* and *Melymbrosia,* as if Woolf's first work of fiction announced the material she would spend her entire life working out. There are also particular images, such as that of the skeleton of the world, that appear in nearly all Woolf's novels. Trombley discusses Dr. Rodriguez as but the first appearance of the "doctor character" in Woolf's fiction, undoubtedly linked to her own experience with doctors.

A salient aspect of many readings of the novel that see it as a precursor to Woolf's later, more overtly experimental fiction is seeing it as especially related to *THE WAVES*. McDowell, for example, believes that in her "most traditional novel, Woolf's vision is closer . . . to that expressed in *The Waves* . . . than it is to any other of her novels" (McDowell 74). He sees a similar pessimism in both works and likens the vision articulated by Terence and Rachel to that of BERNARD in *The Waves* (91). In both novels, McDowell writes, Woolf "contemplated the horror of the withdrawal of the self and the attenuation of our sense of the metaphysical importance of human existence" (93). Naremore also relates the "mysterious" dialogue between Rachel and Terence in the jungle to the "unusual technique" of *The Waves* (48), and Harper notices that the travelers up the river in *The Voyage Out* are, as in *The Waves,* three men and three women (Harper 43). Louise Poresky, who reads all Woolf's novels as following "the psychological growth of one individual" (23), sees in *The Voyage Out* "the beginning of Woolf's use of a dreamlike concatenation of events that reaches its fullest expression with *The Waves*" (24).

An early title for *The Waves* was "The Moths," and as several readers have pointed out "the symbol of the moth as the struggling spirit of the visionary" is common in Woolf's writing (van Buren Kelley 28). Froula interprets the moth seen on three occasions in *The Voyage Out* as "an image of [Woolf's] own survival," the survival she could not give her character Rachel Vinrace. Froula argues that all the moths in Woolf's later writings "figure the artist-self to which Woolf gave birth through the painful labor of her first novel" ("Out of" 161). In a comment that illuminates the central importance of Woolf's first novel to understanding her art as a whole, Froula writes that the "continuing life of the moth in Woolf's writing makes legible Woolf's own great battle against that powerful antagonist, the literary and cultural tradition, to find words for the life of the female imagination, to enlarge its plots and scripts" ("Out of" 161).

Works Specific to This Entry:

Beer, Gillian. "Virginia Woolf and Pre-History." In Eric Warner, ed. *Virginia Woolf: A Centenary Perspective:* 99–123.

Bishop, E. L. "Toward the Far Side of Language: Virginia Woolf's *The Voyage Out.*" *Twentieth Century Literature* 27, 4 (Winter 1981): 343–61.

Blain, Virginia. "Narrative Voice and the Female Perspective in Virginia Woolf's Early Novels." In Patricia Clements and Isobel Grundy, eds. *Virginia Woolf: New Critical Essays.*

Davis-Clapper, Laura. "Why Did Rachel Vinrace Die? Tracing the Clues from *Melymbrosia* to *The Voyage Out.*" In Mark Hussey and Vara Neverow-Turk, eds. *Virginia Woolf Miscellanies:* 225–27.

DeSalvo, Louise. "Introduction" to Virginia Woolf, *The Voyage Out.* New York: Signet, 1991.

———. "Sorting, Sequencing, and Dating the Drafts of Virginia Woolf's *The Voyage Out.*" *Bulletin of Research in the Humanities* 82, 3 (Autumn 1979): 271–93.

———. "Virginia Woolf's Revisions for the 1920 American and English Editions of *The Voyage Out.*" *Bulletin of Research in the Humanities* 82, 3 (Autumn 1979): 338–66.

———. *Virginia Woolf's First Voyage: A Novel in the Making.* Totowa, New Jersey: Rowman & Littlefield, 1980.

Dick, Susan. "The Tunnelling Process: Some Aspects of Virginia Woolf's Use of Memory and the Past." In Patricia Clements and Isobel Grundy, eds. *Virginia Woolf: New Critical Essays:* 176–99.

DuPlessis, Rachel Blau. " 'Amor Vin—': Modifications of Romance in Woolf." In Margaret Homans, ed. *Virginia Woolf: A Collection of Critical Essays:* 115–35.

Friedman, Susan Stanford. "Virginia Woolf's Pedagogical Scenes of Reading: *The Voyage Out, The Common Reader,* and Her 'Common Readers.' " *Modern Fiction Studies* 38, 1 (Spring 1992): 101–25.

Froula, Christine. "Out of the Chrysalis: Female Initiation and Female Authority in Virginia Woolf's *The Voyage Out.*" In Margaret Homans, ed. *Virginia Woolf: A Collection of Critical Essays:* 136–61.

Heine, Elizabeth. "Virginia Woolf's Revisions of *The Voyage Out.*" In Virginia Woolf, *The Voyage Out.* London: Hogarth Press, 1990.

———. "The Earlier *Voyage Out:* Virginia Woolf's First Novel." *Bulletin of Research in the Humanities* 82, 3 (Autumn 1979): 294–316.

Lambert, Elizabeth G. " 'and Darwin says they are nearer the cow': Evolutionary Discourse in *Melymbrosia* and *The Voyage Out.*" *Twentieth Century Literature* 37, 1 (Spring 1991): 1–21.

McDowell, Frederick P. W. " 'Surely Order Did Prevail': Virginia Woolf and *The Voyage Out.*" In Ralph Freedman, ed. *Virginia Woolf:* 73–96.

Moore, Madeline. "Some Female Versions of Pastoral: *The Voyage Out* and Matriarchal Mythologies." In Jane Marcus, ed. *New Feminist Essays on Virginia Woolf:* 82–104.

Neumann, Shirley. "*Heart of Darkness,* Virginia Woolf and the Spectre of Domination." In Patricia Clements and Isobel Grundy, eds. *Virginia Woolf: New Critical Essays:* 57–76.

Pitt, Rosemary. "The Exploration of Self in Conrad's *Heart of Darkness* and Woolf's *The Voyage Out.*" *Conradiana* 10 (1978): 141–54.

Schlack, Beverly Ann. "The Novelist's Voyage from Manuscripts to Text: Revisions of Literary Allusions in *The Voyage Out.*" *Bulletin of Research in the Humanities* 82, 3 (Autumn 1979): 317–27.

Tvordi, Jessica. "*The Voyage Out:* Virginia Woolf's First Lesbian Novel." In Vara Neverow-Turk and Mark Hussey, eds. *Virginia Woolf: Themes & Variations:* 226–37.

Wheare, Jane. "Introduction" to Virginia Woolf, *The Voyage Out.* London: Penguin, 1992.

Wussow, Helen. "War and Conflict in *The Voyage Out.*" In Mark Hussey, ed. *Virginia Woolf and War:* 101–09.

W

Wagg, Miss Mentioned fleetingly in *JACOB'S ROOM,* standing on her doorstep as if expecting something to happen.

Wagner, Richard (1813–83) German composer often credited with revolutionizing modern music and the arts in general, and probably best known for the opera *Der Ring des Nibelungen* (The Ring of the Nibelungen). Among other operas Woolf refers to by Wagner are *Tristan und Isolde* and *Parsifal.* In *THE VOYAGE OUT,* Rachel VINRACE reads the score of *Tristan* (TVO 35), the sight of which prompts Clarissa DALLOWAY to tell Rachel about the first time she saw *Parsifal* at Bayreuth.

Wagner lived in the Bavarian town of Bayreuth from 1872 to 1883; an annual festival of Wagner's music takes place there in the Festspielhaus that Wagner himself planned and that was completed in 1876, when the first festival was held. Woolf attended the festival in August 1909 with her brother Adrian STEPHEN and Saxon SYDNEY-TURNER, writing an article about it for the London *Times,* "Impressions at Bayreuth" (E1 288–92).

Waley, Arthur David (1889–1966) Translator from Chinese and Japanese whose translation of *The Tale of Genji* (by Murasaki Shikibu) Woolf reviewed in *Vogue* in 1925. Waley was a friend of Roger FRY and Woolf occasionally saw him socially, but Celia Goodman has written that Waley and Woolf "had hurt each other's feelings beyond repair" (CM6: 5), presumably by their low opinion of each other's work. Waley's knowledge of Chinese is mentioned in Woolf's ironic preface to *ORLANDO.* Catherine Nelson-McDermott has discussed the possible influence of Waley's translations on Woolf's writing. From about 1939 to 1962 Waley and his lifelong companion Beryl de Zoete lived at 50 GORDON SQUARE.

Walker, Mrs. Clarissa DALLOWAY's cook in *MRS. DALLOWAY* for whom important guests make no difference, only more work.

Wallace, Mr. Mentioned in *TO THE LIGHTHOUSE* as a famous man who would come and talk with Mrs. RAMSAY in the evening.

Walpole, Hugh Seymour (1884–1941) English novelist whose book *The Green Mirror* Woolf reviewed for the *TIMES LITERARY SUPPLEMENT* in 1918 (E2 214–17), noting that he had "a true insight into the nature of domesticity" (E2 216). In 1922, Woolf wrote to Gerald BRENAN about experimental novelists of her generation that they could only hope for a glimpse of "the human soul" in their work, but that this was preferable "than to sit down with Hugh Walpole [H. G.] Wells, etc. etc. and make large oil paintings of fabulous fleshy monsters complete from top to toe" (L2 598). Woolf met Walpole in 1923 at a lunch given by Lady COLEFAX, and he made her his confidante. Although she disliked his work, she generally kept her true opinions about it from him. In 1928, he presented Woolf the FEMINA-VIE HEUREUSE prize which she had won for *TO THE LIGHTHOUSE,* making a speech which she heard as an explanation of why he did not like her novels (D3 183). Among Walpole's other novels are *The Cathedral* (1922), *Rogue Herries* (1930), *Judith Paris* (1931) and *The Fortress* (1933). Woolf appears as Jane Rose in Walpole's novel *Hans Frost* (1929).

Walsh, Peter Character in *MRS. DALLOWAY* who has recently returned from India on the day of the novel's action. Peter was in love with Clarissa DALLOWAY and had wanted to marry her more than thirty years earlier. Her refusal of him at BOURTON in favor of Richard DALLOWAY affected him deeply. Peter is known to his friends as a charming man who has never quite been the success he could have been because of his emotional temperament. He is in London again after five years in India because he has fallen in love with Daisy, the wife of a major in the Indian Army, and is seeing his lawyers about arranging her divorce. As the day of the novel goes on, it becomes apparent that Peter is not perhaps as in love with Daisy as he thinks. Peter is characterized by his continually opening and shutting the blade of a pocketknife he always carries; many Freudian critics have interpreted this as a symbol of his phallic aggression. It was Peter who interrupted the "most exquisite moment" of Clarissa's life at Bourton, when Sally SETON kissed her, by walking up to them to ask if they were star gazing.

Peter has a large share of the novel's narrative consciousness and provides the major external perspective on Clarissa, frequently comparing the Clarissa of thirty years ago with the Clarissa he finds sewing her dress when he makes a surprise visit to her on the morning of the day of her party. Peter has always been able to pierce Clarissa's social carapace, calling her, for example, "the perfect hostess," yet he is in thrall to her charms still.

Howard Harper sees Peter as existing primarily as a "reflector to illuminate Clarissa's past" (121), but Josephine O'Brien Schaefer says he is "actually one of the instruments of civilized coercion" that Woolf satirizes in *Mrs. Dalloway* ("The Great War" 145). As a colonial administrator, Peter is part of the imperial world represented in the novel by Lady BRUTON and Hugh WHITBREAD, among others. Mark Spilka speculates that Clive BELL contributed to Woolf's characterization of Peter (130n10; and, in fact, "Peter" was an early nickname of Woolf's for Clive, referring to William WORDSWORTH's Peter Bell).

"Walter Sickert" See SICKERT, Walter.

Wapping Old Stairs An area of the old London docks, still leading directly to the river, where ORLANDO clandestinely cavorts with sailors and "low" women like "Sukey." Jean Moorcroft Wilson suggests it is also from here that Helen and Ridley AMBROSE embark on their voyage to South America in *THE VOYAGE OUT* (*Virginia Woolf* 216–17).

Warboys In 1899 the Stephen family spent a summer vacation in this Huntingdonshire village. Woolf pasted the diary she kept there into a copy of Isaac Watts' *Logick|or|the right use of Reason|with a variety of rules to guard against error in the affairs of religion and human life as well as in the sciences* that she had bought because she liked its binding. The diary, incorporated into *A Passionate Apprentice,* is usually referred to as "the Warboys diary" and has been discussed by Gayatri Spivak, Louise DeSalvo ("As 'Miss Jan Says' ") and Jane Marcus (*Art* 228).

Warburton, Aunt A dowager guest at Kitty LASSWADE's "1914" party in *THE YEARS.*

Ward, Mary Augusta (Mrs. Humphry) (1851–1920) Popular English novelist, Matthew ARNOLD's niece, and active opponent of women's SUFFRAGE. Among her novels were *Miss Bretherton* (1884), *Robert Elsmere* (1888), *Marcella* (1894), *Helbeck of Bannisdale* (1898), *The Marriage of William Ashe* (1905), *The Case of Richard Meynell* (1911) and *Delia Blanchflower* (1914), an anti-suffrage novel. Woolf regarded her as the type of what she was against in both literary and political terms. Ward was a friend of Woolf's parents, Leslie and Julia Prinsep STEPHEN. In 1889, Woolf's mother joined the wives of several other prominent men in signing "An Appeal Against Female Suffrage" published in the *Nineteenth Century*. Among other signatories were Mrs. Matthew Arnold, Christina ROSSETTI, Beatrice Potter (who later changed her mind and is better known as Beatrice WEBB) and Mrs. Humphry Ward, who was the president in 1908 of the Anti-Suffrage Society of Women (Ray Strachey, *The Cause* 319).

Warrington, Susan Character in *THE VOYAGE OUT.* She is at the hotel on SANTA MARINA as a companion for her crippled aunt, Mrs. PALEY. As Jane Wheare has remarked, of all the women in the novel, Susan "most obviously epitomises Woolf's notion of 'The Angel in the House' "(Wheare, *Virginia Woolf* 63). She is thoroughly bourgeois, unimaginative, and, as St. John HIRST says, bovine. She meets and becomes engaged to Arthur VENNING, fulfilling her every dream. Louise DeSalvo suggests (MELYM xxxv) that the character is derived from a young woman Woolf encountered in Italy in 1908 (PA 390). Throughout much of the novel, Susan and Arthur's apparent simple happiness is implicitly contrasted with the complex and tortured relationship between Terence HEWET and Rachel VINRACE.

Washington State University The Leonard and Virginia Woolf Library and Bloomsbury Collection at the Washington State University Libraries contains the Woolfs' library from both MONK'S HOUSE and 24 Victoria Square (Leonard WOOLF's London residence after Woolf's death in 1941), comprising several thousand volumes (see Holleyman and Treacher). Also in the collection are photographs of the Stephen family, drawings by Leslie STEPHEN and his children, and Julia Prinsep STEPHEN's manuscripts (see Gillespie and Steele).

Waterlow, Sydney Phillip Perigal (1878–1944) A diplomat who proposed to Woolf in 1911 when his first marriage broke down (L1 485–86). A brilliant classicist, he had been a friend of Clive BELL's when both were at Trinity College, Cambridge. At Cambridge and for the rest of his life, according to Peter Levy, Waterlow was bitter about not being elected to the APOSTLES, as many in his circle of friends had been (Levy 251). He remained friends with the Woolfs, but his job as a diplomat took him out of England in the 1920s and they saw less of each other. It was Waterlow who in 1919 condensed Leonard WOOLF's *International Government* for use at the end of World War I at the Paris Peace Conference, where Leonard's ideas became incorporated into plans for establishing the League of Nations.

Watts, George Frederic (1817–1904) Victorian painter who lived for more than twenty years at Little Holland House, the home of Woolf's great-aunt Sara and great-uncle Thoby Prinsep (See PRINSEP FAMILY). Watts's disastrous and short-lived marriage to Ellen TERRY, instigated by Mrs. Prinsep, is one theme of Woolf's play *FRESHWATER*. His portrait of Julia Prinsep STEPHEN hung at Vanessa BELL's house, CHARLESTON.

Waves, The **(1931)** Woolf's seventh novel, *The Waves* is composed of nine italicized "interludes" alternating with nine "episodes." The interludes describe the passage of the sun across the sky from dawn to nightfall, and the natural world beneath it. The episodes consist of the soliloquies of BERNARD, JINNY, LOUIS, NEVILLE, RHODA and SUSAN, beginning in early childhood. The last episode is spoken by Bernard alone, an attempt "to sum up" what has gone before. The sections of *The Waves* are not numbered. Further details can be found in entries on the individual "characters."

The Waves. *Courtesy Linda J. Langham.*
The front of the dust jacket designed by Vanessa Bell for the Hogarth Press first edition (1931) suggests a female and a male figure on either side of a flower. In 1927, Woolf was toying "vaguely with some thoughts of a flower whose petals fall" as the center of the work (D3 131).

Outline

First interlude (7–8): The sun rises over the sea, as if a woman raised a lamp, lighting up the garden and house, waking the birds.

First episode (9–28): [Childhood] The six children speak of what they see and hear, using images that will recur throughout the text. Mrs. CONSTABLE, their nurse, and Biddy, a cook, prepare breakfast. Louis hides in a corner of the garden while Bernard, Jinny, Neville and Susan catch butterflies. Louis feels self-conscious because he has an Australian accent; he imagines himself connected to the roots of the world. Jinny, who has seen the leaves moving in the bushes, finds Louis and surprises him with a kiss on the back of his neck. Susan sees this and is angered by it. Seeing her run past, Bernard, who is making toy boats with Neville, follows Susan and comforts her. Together they look over the wall at ELVEDON, where a woman sits writing between tall windows while gardeners sweep the lawn with long brooms. When a black-bearded gardener sees them, Bernard and Susan run away through the woods. As Bernard's attention wanders from Susan and he begins making up phrases, Susan sees Rhoda on the path playing with petals in a bowl of water, pretending they are ships. Neville is wondering where Bernard went, taking his sharp knife.

The children have lessons with Miss HUDSON. Neville appreciates the order of tenses; Rhoda is terrified by figures. When the others are finished, she has to stay behind to complete her arithmetic. Louis says that he does not fear Rhoda as he fears the others.

All but Neville are taken for a walk by Miss CURRY. At the house, Neville tries to recapture the feeling he had the night before when he heard about a dead man found lying in the gutter. Susan sees Florrie, the kitchen maid, and Ernest, another servant, kissing in the garden. The children have tea and then say prayers and sing hymns. Mrs. Constable bathes them and they go to bed, where Rhoda dreams of being taken away by her hard-eyed aunt.

Second interlude (29): The sun rises higher. Flowers begin to open; the waves thud on the shore.

Second episode (30–72): [School] Bernard says good-bye to his mother and father and is off to school for the first time with Louis and Neville. Bernard tries not to cry as they leave London; Louis is afraid and self-conscious; Neville looks forward to studying. Old Crane, the headmaster, addresses them at their new school. Bernard says this is the first night away from their sisters (32).

Susan is sad at leaving her home and her father. The girls are also away at school, and Susan and Rhoda try not to cry as Miss LAMBERT reads to them; Jinny, however, imagines the dresses she would like to wear.

In chapel, Louis is soothed by the ritual and by the architecture, but Neville mocks the "sad religion" as he had at Easter when traveling in Rome with his father. Neville gazes admiringly at PERCIVAL, and after chapel they all follow Percival to the cricket pitch, where Bernard tells stories that tail off. Louis both resents and needs Percival.

Susan hates school and misses home and her father. She knows that Miss PERRY loves Jinny. Jinny compares herself with Rhoda and Susan. Rhoda secretly loves nameless other girls, fantasizing at night about them, and loves Miss Lambert.

Louis observes the cricket team going to play, admiring the boys yet also recognizing their brutality. Neville feels that Percival despises his weakness yet also tolerates it; he knows that he could never live with Percival. Bernard makes up a story about the domestic life of Dr. and Mrs. Crane; Neville longs to be with a lover; Louis resolves to achieve success.

Susan looks forward to the end of the term and imagines what she will do when she gets home; Jinny imagines leaving school and going to dances; Rhoda imagines herself as the Empress of Russia, imagines picking flowers to bind into a garland and wonders to whom she will offer them.

Dr. Crane presents books as prizes at the end of the term. Louis imagines that one day his name will be inscribed with the other names of poets on a wall at school; he hears a chained beast stamping on the beach. At the ceremony, Bernard is distracted by a bee and Neville thinks of how he will gradually lose touch with Percival.

On the first day of the summer vacation, Susan says she will never live in London and is moved to tears when she sees her father talking to a farmer as he waits for her at the station. Jinny takes the express train north, delighting in her body's power. Rhoda thinks of the puddle she almost could not cross. The boys have also left school, Louis thinking of all the places they will go, and how he will go into business; he still hears the beast stamping. Bernard, on his way to Edinburgh, draws a passenger into conversation, making up his story. Neville considers Bernard and how all people become characters in his story. Neville thinks of his own likely future as a professor of classics and thinks of Percival, who is on his way to Scotland.

Third interlude (73–75): The sun continues to rise; shoals of fish are seen in the sea; in the garden birds sing in chorus, taking flight at the approach of the cat or when the cook throws cinders on the ash heap. One bird pecks at a worm; rotting things fester at the grassroots, providing sustenance for the birds. The sun begins to illuminate the room. The waves drum on the shore "like turbaned warriors" with "poisoned assegais."

Third episode (76–107): [University (for Bernard and Neville)] Bernard thinks of his identity as "complex and many" and quotes his own biographer (76). He thinks what a harrowing experience it would be to call one's self and receive no answer. He considers Neville, then writes a letter to a girl with whom he is passionately in love, adopting the persona of BYRON to write to her. Bernard says that "rhythm is the main thing in writing" (TW 79). He imagines visiting his lover at her parents' house in the country, and continues to meditate on identity (76–81). Neville too thinks of writing, of being a great poet and of how identity is changed by the presence of others. Bernard tells Neville about spending time with Percival and, at tea with Bernard in his room, Neville shows Bernard his poem. After he leaves, Bernard reflects that Neville does not appreciate his complexity. From outside come sounds of revelry, of smashing china. Bernard thinks of Louis. Louis is in an "eating shop" trying to blend into the crowd, overhearing conversations, reading a book of poetry he has propped up against a bottle of sauce. He thinks of Susan, whom he respects.

Susan has been to a finishing school in Switzerland. Not yet twenty, she considers her identity and imagines the day she will meet her husband and the children she will have. She prepares food, inhabiting a fertile world, thinking of Rhoda and Jinny. Jinny finds it strange that people go to sleep at night, which is when she goes to parties, meets men, and dances. Rhoda is filled with terror at the social world and longs for her visionary world of pools and swallow. Not yet twenty-one, Rhoda feels assaulted by men and women at a party.

Fourth interlude (108–110): The sun, now risen, colors the landscape. In the garden, the birds sing "each alone" (108) and swoop to tap a snail's shell against a stone until it breaks. The room is filled with sunlight, shadows driven into the background.

Fourth episode (111–147): [The farewell dinner] Bernard, on the night train to London from the north, is engaged to be married, something that has caused profound changes in his sense of identity as he thinks of having children. He thinks of the others with whom he is to dine that night to say good-bye to Percival, who is leaving for India. Neville arrives at the restaurant early to savor Percival's entrance. Louis arrives; Susan arrives; Rhoda arrives; Jinny arrives, her beauty making them feel self-conscious and awkward. Bernard arrives. Percival arrives. He loves Susan. None of them is yet twenty-five years old. At the dinner, each recalls significant moments from childhood, and the men remember going to school ("a second severance from the body of our mother" [125]). They all recall what has happened in their lives so far. All, says Bernard, have come together, drawn by feelings they have in common, "to make one thing" (127) that will not endure. They "speak" about their feelings for the others and about themselves. Bernard pictures Percival in India; Rhoda and Louis see him there too. They all speak of their feelings for Percival. Rhoda and Louis address each other secretly, hearing savage dancing and "the drumming of naked men with assegais" (140); they imagine a festival and death woven in with the violets.

Susan says Bernard's engagement is an imposition of fixity on the group (142). Rhoda and Louis are "conspirators" (143), Louis telling Rhoda the others "talk a little language such as lovers use" (143). For a moment before leaving the restaurant, they hold the globe made of all their feelings, thoughts, experiences; then they leave. Neville is seized with agony as Percival leaves in a cab.

Fifth interlude (148–50): It is noon; the sunlight now illuminates many countries, a mosque, a village, ships on the sea, southern hills and northern fields. The birds build nests. The walls of the house gleam white; there are deep shadows within the rooms. The waves fall with the thud of a great beast stamping on the shore.

Fifth episode (151–64): [Death] Percival dies in India. Neville is bereft. Bernard is torn between joy at the birth of his son and sorrow at the death of Percival, a lost leader, dead at twenty-five (154). Bernard goes to the NATIONAL GALLERY and looks at Italian art; he decides to go and see Jinny. Rhoda hears the "rush of the great grindstone" of death by her head. She walks down Oxford Street and picks violets as an offering to Percival. She imagines the reactions of the others (except Neville) to Percival's death. Susan, she thinks, is now engaged to a farmer. Rhoda goes to a concert and has there a revelation about the dwelling place made by art. She goes to GREENWICH and flings her bunch of violets into the water.

Sixth interlude (165–66): The sun begins its decline; there is a stillness in the afternoon; the waves fall, stranding a fish in an inland pool.

Sixth episode (167–81): [Love] Louis is in his office, at the center of his world of commerce; he and Rhoda are now lovers. He thinks of the others, of Susan and her children. In the country, Susan protects and nurtures her family. Jinny seems to be talking about people at a party, filling in their stories. She describes meeting a lover at night, singing "JUG, JUG, JUG" like the nightingale (177). Neville also talks to a lover; he still hates the sadness of Christianity, still seeks order and perfection.

Seventh interlude (182–83): The sun is sinking lower, the tide is out. The birds fly; one settles on a white stake in a marsh. Petals have fallen in the garden. The red curtains and white blind are caught by the wind. Everything wavers as if the wings of a "great moth" shadow the room.

Seventh episode (184–206): [Middle age] Bernard realizes his youth is over and goes to Rome, where he reflects on his life. Far out in the water, he sees a fin turn (189). Susan also contemplates the stage of life she has reached, walking with her son—"security, possession, familiarity" (190). Yet she is sometimes sick of all this fecundity. She thinks of Percival who loved her, and of Rhoda. Jinny stands in the Tube station, extolling civilization's progress and victory over "the jungle" (194). She is still meeting new men.

Neville thinks of aging and sees drama and poetry in the everyday. In his room he reads modern poetry. Louis, successful now, still keeps his attic room where he reads "O WESTERN WIND." He has a mistress, a cockney actress; Rhoda has left him. She is in Spain, and thinks of how people terrify her, how she hates them. She remembers throwing her violets into the water at Greenwich. On a donkey, she climbs a hill from the top of which she will see Africa, and imagines the waves that will "shoulder" her under (206).

Eighth interlude (207–09): The sun is setting; the day becomes cooler; the corn is cut. Clouds darken the scene, which is reflected in a mirror. Shadows on the beach grow longer.

Eighth episode (210–35): [The reunion dinner] The friends, now middle-aged, meet at the inn at HAMPTON COURT as Bernard has arranged. Neville misses Percival. They ask each other what they have made of life. Neville tries to impress Susan with his credentials, comparing his life to hers. She responds, meeting his challenge, their clash "the necessary prelude" when old friends meet (215). Bernard speaks of his life, his stories. Louis, still self-conscious, tries to protect his vulnerable soul. Jinny, who is never alone, adapts herself to whoever she is with. Rhoda feels she has nothing to set beside the "children, authority, fame, love, society" (223) of the others, that they will let her fall into torment.

Bernard becomes conscious of silence and reflects on the cosmic insignificance of the world. The others also comment on the vast silence and then, roused by Bernard, oppose the "illimitable chaos" (226). (Louis and Rhoda still talk conspiratorially to each other.) The meal over, Bernard reflects on the comparative meaninglessness of historical events when set against eternity. As the friends walk in Hampton Court, they recover a sense of unity. They divide into pairs—Bernard with Susan, Neville with Jinny, Louis with Rhoda. Neville remarks that they are "in that passive and exhausted frame of mind when we only wish to rejoin the body of our mother from whom we have been severed" (233). Just before they leave, Bernard imagines the placid lives of the petit-bourgeoisie.

Ninth interlude (236–37): The sun has set; leaves fall; the birds are silent; darkness falls.

Ninth episode (238–97): [Summing up] Bernard, addressing a nameless and invisible dinner companion, sums up. To explain his life he must tell stories, though none of them is true. He begins at "the nursery, with windows opening on to a garden, and beyond that the sea" (239), and tells the story of his development as a separate entity. He has absorbed the experiences and memories of the others. Percival's death still weighs on Bernard. As if lifting fish from a pool, Bernard describes the characters of his friends. He also draws in the language of the interludes. It seems Bernard has had an affair with Jinny; he recalls being Byron, his marriage and children; he quotes his biographer ("long since dead"). He became "a certain kind of man" (260) and settled into complacency until Percival's death crashed into his life. Again, Bernard pictures the scene of Percival's death, recalls visiting Jinny, and how the memory of Percival began to take its place among other memories. He began then to question life just going on, seeking answers from his friends that others might seek from priests or poetry. With an effort, he despatches the "enemy" whose presence he first felt as a child. As another order to life becomes apparent to him, he goes to see Neville, but Neville is waiting for his one companion and Bernard leaves, suddenly longing for Percival. Repeating that he is not one person, Bernard says he is not sure who he is—"Jinny, Susan, Neville, Rhoda, or Louis" (276)—and does not know how to distinguish his life from theirs. At the Hampton Court dinner, Bernard thinks they "saw for a moment laid out among us the body of the complete human being whom we have failed to be" (277). After the meeting at Hampton Court, Bernard went to a barber and felt withered and forgotten. Rousing himself yet again, he opposed his vigor to Rhoda, who had killed herself (281).

One day, "the rhythm stopped" (283); no self answers Bernard's call; the world's color drains away as if there was an eclipse of the sun. Bernard sees the world without a self. Gradually color returns; Bernard wonders how to describe the "world seen without a self" because "there are no words" (287).

The dinner is over. Bernard is not sure where he is or who he is; separateness has vanished. His body has absorbed the experiences of the others. He now sees in a visionary way, describing the world of the interludes in his vision of a house at sunrise. But his vision vanishes when he catches sight of his dinner companion looking at him. The companion leaves and Bernard is alone. The waiters want to go home, so Bernard leaves. It is dawn. He feels a horse rising beneath him, a horse which he will ride against the enemy, Death.

The Waves ends with the line, "*The waves broke on the shore.*"

Genesis

Woolf wrote two complete drafts of *The Waves* (published in J. W. Graham's transcription in 1976), beginning the first in 1929; she had begun thinking about the novel at least three years before she began writing it. Graham transcribed seven bound manuscript books containing two distinct holograph drafts of the novel, as well as notebook entries and two pages from the MONK'S HOUSE PAPERS. No typed drafts of *The Waves* have survived. Graham gives a detailed account of the likely stages of composition, revision, and correction (*Holograph* 20–38; summarized page 38). Woolf also jotted down a calendar of her writing of *The Waves* in July 1931 (D4 35), which Graham refers to as "the Account" (*Holograph* 29). Woolf was particularly concerned to trace the evolution of her new work; we can thus learn a great deal about its genesis from her DIARY.

The roots of *The Waves* are found in a mystical experience of depression Woolf had during the summer of 1926 while she was at MONK'S HOUSE. In September that year she wrote in her diary of waking at 3 A.M. and feeling a wave of depression and misery rising over her, an overwhelming sense of failure (D3 110). Near the end of the month, on September 28, she analyzed the "intense depression" she felt as she wrote the last pages of *TO THE LIGHTHOUSE* (D3 111–12). On September 30, wanting to add some remarks on what she called "the mystical side of this solitude," she described a vision of "a fin passing far out" in a waste of waters (D3 113). Her depression triggered a memory of being unable once to cross a puddle in a courtyard when she was a child, transfixed by a sense of life's strangeness. This image reappears in *The Waves* as an experience of Rhoda's when identity fails her (TW 64). Bernard mentions the "fin in a waste of waters" several times in *The Waves* (189, 245, 273, 284). Describing her state of mind in late 1926, Woolf thought that this might be "the impulse behind another book" (D3 113), and three years later, in October 1929, she wrote beside the 1926 entry that perhaps that book might be "The Waves or Moths" ("The Moths" was her first title for this work). In 1933, again re-reading her diary, she noted the genesis of "Orlando leading to The Waves" in her need for a break after finishing *To the Lighthouse* (D3 131).

From the start, Woolf was preoccupied with the form of her new work. "Why not invent a new kind of play . . . prose yet poetry; a novel & a play" (D3 128) she wrote in February 1927. Her conception was very abstract: she "toyed vaguely with some thoughts of a flower whose petals fall" as the center of the work (D3 131). On May 3, 1927, Woolf's sister Vanessa BELL wrote from her house in CASSIS about the huge moths that flew in during the evening (Marler 314–16). Woolf wrote back that the story fascinated her and she could think of "nothing else but you and the moths for hour's after reading your letter" (L3 372). The moth had long been an important symbol for Woolf, often associated with death and also with the creative imagination. The brief sketch "The Death of the Moth" (DM 3–6; CE1 359–61) demonstrates the link Woolf made between moths and dying.

In June Woolf thought she would write "the story of the Moths" as a way of filling in her conception of the "play-poem." She deliberately held back from immersing herself in writing the new book, working at it a little in the evenings as she listened to BEETHOVEN's late sonatas. This book, she wrote, was to be a story of childhood, "but it must not be *my* childhood" (D3 236). By the end of 1928, "The Moths" was to be "an abstract mystical eyeless book: a playpoem" in which she would come to terms with her "mystical feelings" (D3 203). Woolf wished to convey a sense of "life itself going on" (D3 229), seen in the image of the "perpetual crumbling & renewal" of a plant. She was struggling to create an anonymous narrator but worried that this would become too "arty" (D3 229–30). Still she resisted the urge to begin writing, choosing to wait until the new book had "grown heavy" in her mind like fruit ripening on a branch. In this new work, she wanted to "escape this appalling narrative business of the realist," which she described as "false, unreal, merely conventional" (D3 209).

In March 1929, Woolf repeated that she was bored by narrative (D3 219) and, recalling her 1926 experience at Rodmell, wrote that she was going to "enter a nunnery" for the next few months. She described the new work as an "angular shape in my mind," and wrote that she was dissatisfied with its "frame" (D3 219). Always clear about her own creative intent, Woolf wrote to her nephew Quentin BELL that she was at work on "an entirely new kind of book" (L4 35). Lyndall Gordon points out that "soon after her abortive attempt to launch her first draft," Woolf read William WORDSWORTH's long autobiographical poem *The Prelude* and "resolved to follow only the internal lines of development in six lives, the unfolding of character, mind, and soul" (Gordon 204).

The idea of an anonymous narrator persisted, and in September 1929 Woolf wrote that she wanted to include "The Lonely Mind" in "The Moths" "as if it were a person" (D3 251). In the middle of that month, Woolf noted in her diary that she would have to abandon "The Moths" as a title as she had just realized that moths do not fly during the day. Increasingly, her concern was with narrative technique: "Who thinks it? And am I outside the thinker?" She wanted "some device that is not a trick" (D3 257). As the fall of 1929 went on she continued to wrestle with the form of *The Waves,* which she described as "vague yet elaborate," worrying that there might be "some radical fault" in her scheme (D3 259), some "falsity of method" (D3 264). By November 1929 she felt she was "only accumulating notes for a book" and described her writing notebook as "like a lunatic's dream" (D3 275).

As 1930 began, Woolf struggled with how to hold together the two streams of the book's movement, represented by the episodes and the interludes, and speculated that a "gigantic conversation" might be the way to conclude (D3 285), a "mosaic" that would bring together all the voices (D3 298). She was clear that this work represented the most extreme development so far of her art (D3 300) and continued to agonize over what she described as "this hideous shaping & moulding" (D3 301). *The Waves* was, she knew, "a reach after that vision I had, the unhappy summer—or three weeks—at Rodmell, after finishing The Lighthouse" (D3 302). She completed her first draft in April 1930 and began to rewrite the entire book on May 1.

By August 1930, *The Waves* was resolving itself into "a series of dramatic soliloquies," the challenge of which was to keep them running in and out of the rhythm of the waves, which Woolf wanted to have heard all through the book (D3 312). She wrote in her diary that she was writing *The Waves* "to a rhythm not to a plot" (D3 316), something she had also written a few days earlier to Ethel SMYTH, where she added that she was "casting about all the time for some rope to throw the reader" (L4 204). At the end of 1930 Woolf was still pondering how to "run all the scenes together . . . so as to make the blood run like a torrent from end to end" (D3 343).

On February 7, 1931 Woolf recorded the end of *The Waves* and described how she had "reeled across the last ten pages," often seeming only to stumble after her own voice, "or almost, after some sort of speaker (as when I was mad)" (D4 10). She wondered whether she could write "Julian Thoby Stephen 1881–1906" on the title page but told herself, "I suppose not." (D4 10). Woolf was triumphant, knowing that she had "netted that fin in the waste of waters" (D4 10).

The Waves was published in England by the HOGARTH PRESS on October 8, 1931 and in the United States by Harcourt, Brace & Company on October 22 (delayed by the late arrival of Vanessa Bell's dust jacket). Based on a computer comparison of the first English and U.S. editions and an uncorrected proof at the William Allan Neilson Library of SMITH COLLEGE, James Haule* concludes that "the first English edition is the more revised text" ("Introduction"). Vanessa Bell designed not only the front, but also the back and spine of the dust jacket. Despite the common belief that her jackets were inspired by her sister's writing, John LEHMANN has pointed out that the truth was otherwise. He quotes a letter he received from Vanessa about *The Waves:* "I've not read a word of the book—I only have had the vaguest description of it and of what she wants me to do from Virginia—but that has always been the case with the jackets I have done for her" (Lehmann, *Thrown* 27).

Background

As J. W. Graham has explained, the history of the evolution of *The Waves* "shows that it was the most carefully considered of all her experiments" (*Holograph* 14). He considers Woolf's diary entries and essays written between 1925 and when she began to write *The Waves* in 1929 as preparation. Certainly, many of Woolf's essays written in this period seem to speculate about the "entirely new" kind of fiction she wished to write. Graham cites "IMPASSIONED PROSE," her 1926 essay on Thomas DE QUINCEY, as an example of "how long and how deeply meditated, was the approach to the writing of *The Waves*" (*Holograph* 16). A key essay in the matrix from which *The Waves* evolved is "THE NARROW BRIDGE OF ART" (1927), wherein Woolf describes a work of the future in terms that many have taken as precisely anticipating *The Waves:* "It will have something of the exaltation of poetry, but much of the ordinariness of prose. It will be dramatic, and yet not a play" (CE2 224).

Graham also points out that in diary entries on September 30, 1926 and June 18, 1927 Woolf postulates "two elements in the narrative, intimately related but also in tension with each other: a fin *turning* in a waste of water and a continuous stream *intersected* by the arrival of the moths" (*Holograph* 18). This central feature of Woolf's thinking about *The Waves* was never abandoned and is seen by Graham as embodied in the structural relation between interludes and episodes in the novel, a rhythmic opposition that nearly all commentators on *The Waves* discuss. In another essay, Graham* locates the development of the difficult style of *The Waves* precisely in Woolf's need to communicate her vision of the fin. He notes that the image appears "in a ritualistic gesture towards the source of the book" after each draft was written ("Point of View" 203).

Woolf also described her vision of the kinds of books that might be written in the future in "WOMEN AND FICTION" (1929) and in "PHASES OF FICTION" (1929). All these essays, together with Woolf's examination of women's writing in *A ROOM OF ONE'S OWN,* indicate how profoundly she was considering the nature of fiction in the years immediately preceding the inception of *The Waves.* Graham describes the essays as a "constellation" of ideas and concerns that bear on *The Waves,* illustrating Woolf's dissatisfaction with contemporary prose as a medium for reflecting the complexity of modern life.

Although described by many readers as a distinctive break with even her own practice as a novelist, *The Waves* has also been seen as emerging from, or connected with, others of Woolf's works. Like *MRS. DALLOWAY* and *To the Lighthouse, The Waves* emphasizes "the dilemmas of the alienated self," although its method is strikingly different (Graham, *Holograph* 14). Perry Meisel comments that "Ironically, *To the Lighthouse* is a far more abstract account of the way the self is situated in the common life than *The Waves,*" although it is the latter that is usually regarded as Woolf's "most oblique achievement" (Meisel 200). James Hafley first pointed out that the form of *The Waves* seems to have originated in the "Time Passes" section of *To the Lighthouse.*

Several critics have noted that *The Waves* is part of an enormously rich creative phase of Woolf's life that includes *To the Lighthouse,* *ORLANDO* and *A Room.* Suzanne Raitt, for example, sees *Orlando* and *The Waves* as "phases of the same cycle" and reads the "impersonality of *The Waves* . . . [as] the obverse of the intense, if concealed, personal relevance of *Orlando*" (Raitt 151). Judy Little also finds that *The Waves* "covers much of the same psychological territory" as *Orlando*" (Little 74).

The Waves has been regarded simultaneously as anomalous in Woolf's oeuvre yet also connected by myriad filaments to nearly all her other works. Howard Harper writes that readers of *The Waves* "will recognize in 'A Sketch of the Past' . . . many of the central images and motifs of the novel" (Harper

214n5). Makiko Minow-Pinkney, writing on the drafts of the novel, sees there "thematic relationships with early stories like 'An Unwritten Novel' and 'The Mark on the Wall' that are less apparent in the final text" (Minow-Pinkney 157). Jane Wheare has even suggested that there are in *NIGHT AND DAY* "innovative sections which anticipate the poetic style of *The Waves*" (Wheare 111). Others, such as Jean Guiguet and Avrom Fleishman, have pointed out the resonances between *The Waves* and *JACOB'S ROOM,* with its pervasive moth imagery and early portrait of Woolf's dead brother Thoby STEPHEN, who most readers understand as at least partly informing Percival in *The Waves.*

THE VOYAGE OUT and *The Waves* have often been linked. Allen McLaurin sees the "rhythmical repetition and rise and fall of the mind" described at the end of chapter II of *The Voyage Out* as pointing forward to *The Waves* (McLaurin 31), and Harper argues that the "plot" of *The Waves* is "essentially a later version, more artful and sophisticated, of the story of *The Voyage Out:* the ontologically insecure must die so that the transcendent consciousness of the artist may take control" (Harper 247n14). Harper writes that the pattern for the ending of *The Waves* was first discovered in the ending of *The Voyage Out* and that Woolf's subsequent novels all follow this pattern (Harper 249).

Woolf wrote in her diary of listening in the evenings to the late quartets of Beethoven as she thought about *The Waves.* Gerald Levin* discusses Woolf's longstanding interest in Beethoven and suggests that the musical style of *The Waves* is "contrapuntal" (Levin 164). Levin also describes the musical style of *The Waves* as " 'pantonal'—in which the tonalities or six characters each become the thematic center at the moment of expression but are absorbed into a whole which the novel discloses gradually" (Levin 167). He speculates that Arnold Schoenberg's pantonal music of the 1920s might have influenced the novel's structure. Robin Gail Schulze* points out that the "provisionalizing strategies" of *The Waves* are "a hallmark of works of modernist music" (13) and likens Woolf's method to that of Schoenberg, pointing out many congruences.

Another musical influence on *The Waves* is suggested by Evelyn Haller,* who notes that the sound of the "great beast stamping" heard throughout by Louis "resembles the collective sound of the stamping feet of the dancers" in Igor Stravinsky's ballets ("Her Quill" 205). (Another possible source of this image is found in a letter Woolf wrote in January 1928 to Vita SACKVILLE-WEST describing a pump in the basement of the neighboring Imperial Hotel that spent "25 minutes pumping like the tread of a rhythmical elephant" [L4 3].) Haller argues that Woolf "appears to have composed the soundscape of *The Waves* from the physiologically imperative pulsations of Stravinsky's music" ("Her Quill" 205), and that *The Waves* was the most strongly influenced by Russian dance of Woolf's novels.

David Dowling describes *The Waves* as the "most painterly" of Woolf's novels (172), and several critics have drawn attention to the elements of Impressionism and POST-IMPRESSIONISM in the work. McLaurin writes that Woolf uses color in "quite a new way" in *The Waves,* "a use which corresponds to Cézanne's art" (77). Things in the novel are seen "in a half-light, as if through waves" similar to that found in Impressionist painting (McLaurin 79). McLaurin comments on Woolf's use of color to create "psychological volume," as she had in *To the Lighthouse,* and to establish relationships between characters. He also compares Woolf's technique in the interludes to Seurat's depiction of empty landscapes, both of which "achieve their emptiness by banishing human beings" (McLaurin 90).

Jack F. Stewart* compares Woolf's technique in the interludes of *The Waves* to that of Cézanne: in the interludes, "we see . . . not a material landscape, psychologized as in Proust, but a formal composition of color and space" ("Spatial Form" 90). Like Monet in his great series "Rouen Cathedral," Woolf emphasizes "texture and structure, prominence or recession of objects, and interrelation of colored planes" ("Spatial Form" 91). Drawing parallels between *The Waves* and the work of artists including Cézanne, Seurat, Kandinsky, Monet, and the Symbolist poet Stéphane MALLARMÉ, Stewart interprets the interludes as still-lifes, "post-impressionist studies undiluted by symbolic content" ("Spatial Form" 99). Kathleen McCluskey* compares *The Waves* to a Cubist painting "where there is an attempt to foreground everything in the picture. Background is lost and the eye has difficulty in focusing on any one thing over another" (McCluskey 131n23).

Peter Jacobs* writes that in *The Waves* Woolf "probably came closest to achieving the goal that Fry set" (230), a point also made by Irma Rantavaara* in her study of the novel. Rantavaara finds that Woolf is dealing with the same issues Roger FRY and Clive BELL addressed in their discussions of SIGNIFICANT FORM. She also notes "a striking affinity between [Woolf's] own art and that of the symbolists" (Rantavaara 76). Fry had begun translating Mallarmé's poetry during the 1920s and certainly discussed this difficult work with Woolf. Minow-Pinkney finds that Woolf frequently uses the syntax of Symbolist poetry, where "the verse is structured according to principles of sound, rhythm, imagery" (171), particularly in *The Waves.* McLaurin also describes *The Waves* as a Symbolist novel, pointing out that "in the figure of Rhoda, Virginia Woolf embodies that area of ambiguity between 'purity' and 'sterility' which is one of

Mallarmé's principal concerns" (52); like Mallarmé, McLaurin notes, Rhoda is obsessed with absence (McLaurin 83).

Woolf had to write *The Waves* to understand and overcome her own depression (Gordon 203), an experience that almost certainly informs the loss of self Bernard describes in the last episode (Raitt 156). Woolf drew on her memory of a total solar eclipse in June 1927 (D3 142–44) for the imagery of Bernard's description of the loss of self; the imagery of *The Waves* derives from many sources. Several readers have commented, for example, on the echoes from T. S. ELIOT's poetry that are found throughout the novel. McLaurin argues that *The Waves* as a whole "enlarges on certain of [Eliot's] images and ideas; and so forms a criticism of Eliot's position, and perhaps finds a place for itself in his 'tradition' " (130). Most agree that Louis is based to some extent on Eliot, but it is not only Louis who echoes the poet. Jinny's "jug, jug jug," for example, alludes to part III of *The Waste Land* ("The Fire Sermon"), which in turn alludes to Ovid's tale of PROCNE AND PHILOMELA ("jug, jug" was also conventional Elizabethan slang for sexual intercourse).

Rachel Blau DuPlessis* suggests that "in her desire to make portraits without telling stories, Woolf may be said to resist a different novel[ist] in each character: in Susan, [Thomas] Hardy; in Neville, [E. M.] Forster; in Bernard, some of herself; in Louis, [Arnold] Bennett; in Jinny, [Katherine] Mansfield" (DuPlessis, "*WOOLFENSTEIN*" 103). The focus of DuPlessis's essay is Gertrude STEIN, whose writing, she believes, may have challenged Woolf and become "part of the multiplicity of originating influences on *The Waves*" (100). Just as Woolf's early work was challenged by the critique of narrative in Dorothy RICHARDSON's *Pilgrimage,* so, DuPlessis suggests, Woolf's later work, including *The Waves* and *BETWEEN THE ACTS,* "was challenged by the formal designs, the repetitions, the grids, the critique of the center, the other otherness of the work of Gertrude Stein" (101). DuPlessis goes on to discuss the intertextuality of *The Waves* and Stein's *Tender Buttons.*

As always in Woolf's work, *The Waves* is allusively steeped in the canonical tradition of English literature. Critics have particularly noted its allusions to Romantic poetry. Frank D. McConnell* links Neville's "immitigable tree" (which seems to derive from an experience Woolf describes in "A Sketch of the Past" [MOB 71]) with the vision of single things in Wordsworth's "Intimations Ode," which inspires the poet to ask, "Whither is fled the visionary gleam? / Where is it now, the glory and the dream?" (ll. 56–57) (McConnell 126). As noted above, Woolf read Wordsworth's *Prelude* early in the process of composing *The Waves.* Kate Flint* points out that Woolf copied lines 458–66 of book 7 of the 1850 version of *The Prelude* into her diary on August 22, 1929 (Flint, "Introduction" 220); she had copied the same lines into her notebook while writing *Mrs. Dalloway,* adding the comment "Good quotation for one of my books" (RN 228). Rantavaara points out that both *The Prelude* and *The Waves* "are *Bildungsgeschichte* [histories of development] in the sense that they proceed from the simple sense-perceptions of a child to higher levels of consciousness" (Rantavaara 25).

Percy Bysshe SHELLEY's "The Question" is the source of Rhoda's question as "to whom" she should make her offering (TW 206). Gillian Beer* notes that Woolf reviewed Walter Edwin Peck's *Shelley: His Life and Work* in 1927 (" 'Not One of Us' " DM 119–28; CE4: 20–26) and describes a "submerged level of intertextuality . . . [that] bears on Woolf's feelings for her dead brother Thoby" ("Introduction" xxix).

Following the work of Catherine F. Smith in her essay "Mysticism and the Woman Clothed with the Sun," Madeline Moore has argued that Woolf may have been influenced in her conception of the interludes by the life and writing of the seventeenth-century mystic Jane Lead. Moore, who describes Woolf as creating in *The Waves* her "most abstract myth of female power as a backdrop to her drama of emerging human consciousness" (*Short Season* 27), believes Woolf's "woman in the sun" in the interludes was inspired by Lead's visions of the Virgin Sophia, "A Woman Cloathed with the Sun" (*Short Season* 30).

Moore has also written that during the time she was composing *The Waves,* Woolf's correspondence "resounds with cynicism and sadness" (*Short Season* 117). The most significant relationship of this period of Woolf's life, according to Moore, was with the composer Ethel Smyth: "Nothing, it seems, is too shocking to reflect upon, and all of it is written to Ethel Smyth" (Moore, *Short Season* 117). The mid- to late 1920s was a period in which Woolf was intensely active politically, speaking, as Beer notes, "at public and private meetings on issues of gender and class" ("Introduction" xii). *The Waves* was also conceived and written during a time that saw Woolf's love affair with Vita Sackville-West move from passionate intensity to quiet affection. Raitt has commented that, "if *The Waves* is preoccupied with death, it is also concerned with reproduction. The depression that drove Woolf to write it was partly a response to her own childlessness" (Raitt 158). Raitt sees Sackville-West as one of several important maternal presences in Woolf's life, identifying the "spectre" of Sackville-West as well as Julia Prinsep STEPHEN and Vanessa Bell behind Woolf's account of motherhood in *The Waves.*

Critical Responses

Woolf wrote to her brother-in-law Clive Bell in February 1931 that she had finished her new book but it was a failure: "Too difficult: too jerky: too inchoate altogether" (L4 294), and to Ethel Smyth she wrote that *The Waves* was "fundamentally unreadable" (L4 357). Although some readers have shared Woolf's opinion, at least on their first attempt, many more have agreed with Leonard WOOLF, who told her in July 1931 that *The Waves* was a "masterpiece . . . the best of your books" (D4 36). Later in 1931, Woolf wrote Smyth that most of "the low-brow reviewers (whose sense I respect) find The Waves perfectly simple" (L4 389). She proudly quoted to Smyth Goldsworthy Lowes DICKINSON's opinion that the book was a "great poem" that deals with "what is perpetual and universal" (L4 395). Smyth had told Woolf she found the book "profoundly disquieting, sadder than any book I ever read" (L4 395n1), and Woolf wrote that Dickinson had also found it "hopelessly sad," though that had not been her intention. Woolf was pleased and surprised at the initial response to her difficult book, a book she described in her diary as "an adventure which I go on alone" (D4 47). Harold NICOLSON called to say it was a masterpiece (D4 47), and the *Times* praised the novel's characters, although, wrote Woolf, "I meant to have none" (D4 47). As Eric Warner* has pointed out, the "six figures quickly became read as 'characters,' their progress through the world as a 'story' " (*Virginia Woolf: The Waves* 98).

Woolf was habitually concerned first with the reactions of her family and a few close friends to a new work. Vanessa Bell wrote that being moved by *The Waves* was "quite as real an experience as having a baby or anything else" (Marler 367). In reply, Woolf alluded to their brother Thoby's premature death and said she had "a dumb rage still at his not being with us always" (L4 391). She felt that it had been "a long toil to reach this beginning—if The Waves is my first work in my own style" (D4 53).

On November 12 E. M. FORSTER wrote Woolf that he had "the sort of excitement over it which comes from believing one's encountered a classic" (Forster, *Letters* 2: 110). He also wrote, however, to W. J. H. (Sebastian) Sprott that he was "*repelled* by the emotion emanating from Percival, told Leonard so, and he told Virginia. But moderate your content. With this repulsion mingles the conviction that the book will be a classic" (*Letters* 2: 111). Another contemporary who professed his admiration for *The Waves* was W. B. Yeats, whom Woolf met at Ottoline MORRELL's in 1934. He told Woolf he had been writing about her. In his introduction to *Fighting the Waves* Yeats wrote that "Certain typical books—*Ulysses,* Virginia Woolf's *The Waves,* Mr. Ezra Pound's *Draft of XXX Cantos*—suggest a philosophy like that of the *Samkara* school of ancient India" (Yeats* 210). Woolf also noted in her diary on June 1, 1937 that William Faulkner had "most intelligently (& highly)" praised *The Waves* (D5 91), but no mention by Faulkner of the novel has been traced. That year also, Vita Sackville-West told Woolf she had been re-reading *The Waves* and liked "the 2nd half best,—lovely, lovely pages" (Sackville-West, *Letters* 398).

The *TIMES LITERARY SUPPLEMENT* reviewer (identified by S. P. Rosenbaum as A. S. McDowall, author of a 1918 study of realism and a 1931 book on Hardy [Haule, "Introduction" xxxviin4]) called *The Waves* "a piece of subtle, penetrating magic" (CH 263). He saw the novel as fulfilling Woolf's description in "MODERN FICTION" of life as a "luminous halo" (CH 264), and he described it, as have many others, as a poetic novel and praised her characters. A very different opinion was offered in the *Evening News* by Frank Swinnerton, who called it "bloodless" and "not very interesting to read" in part because it was difficult to distinguish between the characters (CH 267). Gerald Bullett, reviewing *The Waves* for the *NEW STATESMAN AND NATION,* found Woolf's use of the soliloquy "little short of miraculous" (CH 270) and called Woolf "a metaphysical poet who has chosen prose-fiction for her medium" (CH 269). Several reviewers wrote that *The Waves* was the logical outcome of Woolf's developing aesthetic. In the *Weekend Review,* the novelist L. P. Hartley acknowledged the radical assault on convention that the work represented: "so much has been disrupted, standards overturned, ideas blown skywards, the great body of knowledge has been punched so full of deadly holes that there is, it seems, no authority to whom we, or they, can refer for an answer to the simplest question" (CH 272).

The sharp dichotomy between those contemporary readers who found *The Waves* "an authentic and unique masterpiece" (CH 294) and those who dismissed it as "a highly artificial trick" (CH 283) has persisted in readings of the novel, although later critics tend to be more guarded in their negative assessments. Maria DiBattista remarks that "near unanimity supports Leonard Woolf's contention that *The Waves* is Virginia Woolf's masterpiece" (146), yet it is also true, as Beer has recently noted, that many important studies of Woolf "either dismiss or avoid *The Waves,* despite general acknowledgment of it as her masterpiece" ("Introduction" xxi). For many, it is "a representative text of modernism" (Graham, *Holograph* 13), its very difficulty and strangeness placing it at the heart of MODERNISM's experimental tradition. Alice van Buren Kelley remarks that few critics "have done more than to suggest one or two themes that might prove fruitful to those who should dare more thorough exploration" (145), and Mitchell Leaska writes that to claim "anything more than a partial and imperfect understanding of *The Waves* is to run the risk of ridicule" (*Novels* 159). Leaska's description of *The Waves* is typical: "exquisitely written, supremely complex, almost incomprehensible" (160). Ian Gregor* has remarked that *The Waves* has created in its readers "a response of such marked intensity, whether of identification or rejection, that the act of critical judgment is made to seem an act of supererogation" (Gregor 52).

Several readings, nevertheless, offer interpretations of *The Waves* that respond to its sense of being about "life in general" as Woolf described it in her first draft. McConnell argues against the frequent labeling of *The Waves* as a *sui generis* masterpiece, calling it "a tough-minded and sobering examination of the chances for the shaping intellect to shape meaningfully at all" (129). Jean Alexander, one of several critics who focus on the mystical aspects of the novel, argues that Woolf "seeks a form and style to convey vision in the symbolic or anagogic sense rather than the literal sense" (147), and Pamela Transue contends that Woolf's development of a form to convey her vision constitutes a feminist act (128). Alexander writes that "the greater design—larger than persons, forces of nature, or social structures—must be considered a religious or mythic one" (175). Louise Poresky also gives a religious interpretation of the overall meaning of *The Waves* (*Elusive* 211–12). In contrast, Susan Lorsch* rejects a religious interpretation, saying that Percival "does not solve the religious difficulties and metaphysical problems posed by the disappearance of God and the designification of nature" (Lorsch 148). Suzette A. Henke* argues that *The Waves* should be understood as phenomenological rather than mystical and uses the writing of Martin Heidegger in exploring the novel.

For many readers, *The Waves* is a book "about" the creative imagination itself, or, in Harper's words, about "the drama of the intentionality of the narrative consciousness" (Harper 248). It has been described as being Terence HEWET's novel "about Silence" (TVO 216), a novel that offers "a vision of human solitude" (Zwerdling 10). Susan Gorsky* feels it is Hewet's projected novel in two senses: "both in its obvious silences . . . and in the content of the monologues themselves" (Gorsky 47). Rantavaara concludes that the novel is not about what life is like or about what human beings are like, nor about the world around us, but is "an account of a creative vision, of the artist's approach to reality" (Rantavaara 91). Jack F. Stewart closely connects the use of symbolism in *The Waves* with Woolf's understanding of the creative process ("Existence"), and novelist Carol Ascher* has commented, "How this novel is about the imagination itself! As flight, as joyful play, as a reach for order, and as relief from pain" (54); the novel's insistence on an active reader, she says, "nourishes me for my own art" (56).

Moore (*Short Season* 119) and Lucio Ruotolo have both drawn attention to the similarity between Woolf's sense of reality and Heidegger's philosophy. Ruotolo notes that Woolf began *The Waves* three weeks before Heidegger delivered his inaugural address at Freiburg on the question "What About This Nothing?" (*Interrupted* 146) and writes that "the world Woolf offers in *The Waves* exists precariously on the margins of that non-being she has tried to avoid" (*Interrupted* 148). Although frequently criticized as gratuitously esoteric, *The Waves* has, in Wheare's opinion, "not only aesthetic but also didactic importance" because it draws attention to the "arbitrariness of the contemporary world-view" (Wheare 16).

For Minow-Pinkney, it is not simply the creative imagination that is described in *The Waves,* but the *feminine* creative imagination. *The Waves* occupies what she terms "the difficult 'between' " of "two unpalatable options"—that of rejecting patriarchal notions of identity so radically that psychosis is precipitated, and that of challenging patriarchy but retaining its forms and categories of representation to do so (Minow-Pinkney 115). The "feminine writing" Woolf attempts in *The Waves* is ultimately impossible, she argues, because it must oscillate between silence and "phallocentric positionality" (186), yet *The Waves* is the "high point" of Woolf's achievement "in terms of the dialectic of symbolic and semiotic, and of the convergence of modernism and feminism" (187). Minow-Pinkney argues that "Percival, narrativity and the patriarchy must be simultaneously dislodged to allow Elvedon and women's writing to emerge" (180).

Much critical work on the novel has concerned its style and structure. Rantavaara's early study analyzed the rhetorical modes of *The Waves* in considerable detail and described Woolf's technique as "an amalgamation of impressionistic and expressionistic devices" (57). McCluskey has also analyzed the novel's structure and syntax in great detail, illuminating how Woolf associates particular devices and styles with individual characters. For Gordon, "the fixing of the book's structure is an attempt to defamiliarize lives and see them as phenomena of nature" (Gordon 203); the novel "asks what shape lifespans have in common" (Gordon 203), a task that lends itself to the kind of patterning discerned by Rantavaara and McCluskey.

Paul Ricoeur describes *The Waves* as at the limit of the "polyphonic novel;" it is "a pure novel of multiple voices . . . no longer a novel at all but a sort of oratorio offered for reading" (97). The "polyphonic" style of the novel has challenged and intrigued many readers. According to Minow-Pinkney, *The Waves* "enacts a denigration of 'general sequence' both formally and thematically" (162) as it disrupts what Bernard describes as the "military progress" of the sentence (TW 255). For many critics, the most significant feature of *The Waves* is its dialectical structure, the rhythmic opposition between the world of the interludes and that of the episodes. Stewart discusses how Woolf's need to balance consciousness with nature and to interconnect six selves "increased her tendency to see her form in spatial perspective" ("Spatial Form" 88), a form he believes was inspired "by a mystical sense of 'eternal renewal' " (89).

Moore also describes *The Waves* in terms of the dramatization of conflict between subject and object, a dialectic that moves between "a spiritual being and a social self" (Moore, "Nature"* 223). For Harper the dialectic is between the different kinds of creation represented in the interludes and in the episodes (245); Transue describes a dialectic between "vision and the compulsive but ultimately futile attempt to articulate it" (128); and Jean O. Love discusses "a dialectical repetition of movement from more to less diffusion followed by a reversion to somewhat more diffusion" (*Worlds* 195). For these and many other critics, the style of the novel is an attempt to enact a vision of the world as simultaneously individual and archetypal (Gorsky 47). As Harper remarks, the "strange, haunting formality of *The Waves* emphasizes the distance between the infinite richness of experience and the finite capacity of language to describe that experience" (Harper 204).

A specific aspect of the style of *The Waves* that has received attention is Woolf's odd choice of tenses. Graham sees this as Woolf's "most striking departure from prevailing narrative convention" ("Point of View" 194). The speakers use the pure present ("I go") which is an unnatural tense in which to represent actions "for it seems to rob them of their psychological substance, their felt duration *as actions*" ("Point of View" 195). He notes that the pure present necessitates frequent repetition of "I." For Transue, Woolf's use of the pure present in the episodes is a "feminist revision of the masculine modes of perception" (138), and Stewart points out that the present tenses in the episodes "create a flowing unity between timebound selves, while past tenses quicken the interludes with a sense of finite time" ("Spatial Form" 89). The effect of the pure present in the episodes is like that of hearing a "translator" who appears explicitly only in the use of "said" (Graham, "Point of View" 196). Graham traces the evolution of the narrative style through the drafts of *The Waves* and concludes that the root of Woolf's curious choice can be traced to her need to embody the complexity and strangeness of her 1926 experience at Rodmell. In speculating about the novel before beginning to write it, Graham notes, Woolf uses "speak" and "think" interchangeably. In another comment on the verbs of the episodes, Raitt has described them as "pseudo-performatives," a usage which "postpones accomplishment, as it postpones ending" (Raitt 157). For Woolf, she says, this usage "represented a postponement of the decision to die" (Raitt 157).

In their attempt to come to terms with the strangeness of the narrative of *The Waves,* many readers have understood the six voices as aspects of a single character, a point of view apparently endorsed by Woolf herself. Graham quotes Leonard Woolf as saying in a radio interview that Woolf had told him the six were "meant to be 'severally facets of a single complete person' " ("Point of View" 206), and Woolf wrote in 1931 to Goldie Dickinson that she "did mean in some vague way we are the same person, and not separate people. The six characters were supposed to be one" (L4 397). The idea that the monologues "often seem like one pervasive voice with six personalities" (Naremore 152) or that the six are aspects of a single being has been common in critical discussions of *The Waves* from early on. The point is made with slight variations by such differently oriented critics as Aileen Pippett, Dorothy Brewster, Guiguet, Richter, Poresky, Transue, Gorsky, Daniel Ferrer and Thomas Caramagno. McConnell, disagreeing with the notion of six characters in one, refers to Woolf's sketch "Evening Over Sussex: Reflections in a Motor-Car" (CE2 290–92; DM 7–11) as an example of her projection of six distinct "personalities" (McConnell 124).

James Naremore, commenting on the narrative technique, sees the six individuals of *The Waves* as "represented by six detached spokesmen who are continually going through a process of self-revelation . . . voices [that] seem to inhabit a kind of spirit realm from which, in a sad, rather world-weary tone, they comment on their time-bound selves below" (Naremore 173). That tone is for many readers an undifferentiated one, endorsing the idea that the six are aspects of a single personality. For Ferrer, this lack of differentiation among the characters' voices is so great "that it places us from the start outside the conventions of realism" (Ferrer 65). Harper is one of the few critics who disagrees, noting the many ways in which the voices are differentiated and also pointing out that "the differences between the sexes are usually greater than the differences between individuals within the same sex" (Harper 241). Beer argues that *The Waves* "has to do with the sexual life, with the six persons of one woman" ("Introduction" xiii).

In the first full-length English study of Woolf, Winifred HOLTBY referred to the soliloquies of the six characters as "recitatives" (Holtby 190), a term also used by David Daiches. Haule points out that the "radical shift" to soliloquy occurred as Woolf wrote the second draft ("Introduction" xxiv). The soliloquies "*are* the plot and action" of the novel (Graham, "Point of View" 194), and seem to take place "in parallel, almost chorically, somewhere on the border between speech and silence" (Raitt 150). Guiguet writes that the word "said" introducing the soliloquies "does not bear its ordinary meaning." The voice it refers to "speaks through no mouth, has no individual timbre, does not use the language of everyday. And to define that voice is to solve the whole problem of *The Waves*" (Guiguet 284). Patricia Laurence writes that the "physical voices are silent, subjectivity speaks" (*Reading* 21), and Rantavaara describes the voices as "qualities in human consciousness," rendering the characters "humors," representatives of certain types (Rantavaara 9).

The voices that speak the soliloquies also appropriate details from the interludes, as Hermione Lee notes (167). The episodes, however, are markedly different from the interludes, embodying the patterns of human development rather than those of nature. Alice Fox describes *The Waves* as Woolf's "most Elizabethan book" in its use of dramatic soliloquies (Fox 136), and Pamela Caughie finds that both *The Waves* and *Between the Acts* "bring the domain of narrative close to the domain of theater" (Caughie 51). Far from abandoning "character" in the episodes, as many have argued, Caughie believes that Woolf makes character "so highly self-conscious that the concept becomes more important, not less" (63).

The interludes and episodes are interrelated. The italicized passages "mirror the entire natural movement of the novel and infer the perceptual changes which the soliloquists articulate as they live their lives" (Moore, "Nature" 227). Van Buren Kelley also sees the interludes as mirroring the entire movement of the novel on a smaller scale (146). Fleishman believes "great care must be taken in describing these italicized passages, for to assume that they are prologues, prose poems, or any other conventional form is to prejudice our judgment of the work's unique achievement" (Fleishman 152). Guiguet, who notes that in the second draft Woolf wrote the interludes consecutively, describes them as a whole as "the overture to an opera, presenting all the essential motifs in compressed form and in their mutual relationship" (Guiguet 282). The italics, he suggests, might be read as stage directions.

Wendy B. Faris (who refers to the interludes as "preludes") and Jack F. Stewart have both drawn attention to the painterly qualities of the interludes. Faris describes them as "stationary panels in the temporal flow of words" (VWM 12:6). Stewart refers to them as still-lifes, though they are "neither technically nor spiritually mere *natures mortes*" because they are "never static" ("Spatial Form" 102). Stewart compares the nine "panels" of the interludes to Monet's "Water Lilies," creating "a dynamic field of language in which time and space are synthesized in the varicolored flow of consciousness" ("Spatial Form" 102).

The interludes, like the "Time Passes" section of *To The Lighthouse,* are an attempt to "present a phenomenal world without the intervention of human consciousness" (McConnell 126). Judith Lee* reads the interludes as mythologizing a process of invention, as well as representing "a woman-centered cosmogony" (Judith Lee 191). Despite the absence of human consciousness in the interludes, they are linked in subtle ways with the human world of the episodes. Harper, for example, points out that the first eight interludes begin with the word "*The*" and the ninth with "*Now*" which, "subliminally at least, [announces] its transcendent significance" and links it to the ninth episode which also begins with "Now" (Harper 211). Graham argues that the interludes "render not 'insensitive nature' but the hypersensitive response to it of the anonymous consciousness that narrates them" (Graham, "Manuscript" 329).

Most readers, as Madeline Moore says, think of *The Waves* as "asocial." Moore finds "an organic and inevitable relationship between Woolf's attitudes toward nature and her attitudes toward community" ("Nature" 219) and argues for the influence of G. E. MOORE on Woolf's awareness of the process of perceiving nature (224). Moore cites her namesake's 1903 essay "The Refutation of Idealism" as a possible influence on Woolf's perception of nature. Susan Lorsch, in her chapter "The Ebb and Flow of Meaning in Virginia Woolf's *The Waves:* A Structure for a Designified Landscape," writes that the responses to unmeaning nature of Matthew ARNOLD, A. C. SWINBURNE, Thomas HARDY and Joseph CONRAD are all "central" to *The Waves* (Lorsch 132). The language of the novel "resists the symbolizing or metaphorizing of nature" (132). The very structure of *The Waves,* according to Lorsch, invokes the "problem of humanity's—and the literary artist's—relation to and interaction with post-nineteenth century nature, designified and unreadable" (Lorsch 135). Moore has explained Woolf's vision of the fin, which inspired the novel, as "symbolic shorthand for the implacable otherness of nature" (*Short Season* 119). For many readers, a crux of this issue is the novel's final italicized line, but McConnell writes that to ask whether this line "is an affirmation or denial of Bernard's resolve is nugatory: it is simply and sublimely irrelevant to Bernard, as Bernard to it, and therein lies its enormous power" (McConnell 127).

The "macrostructure" of *The Waves,* its dialectical movement between interlude and episode, undoubtedly owes much to Woolf's writing "to a rhythm, not to a plot." Hermione Lee finds that the consistent and insistent rhythm of the novel "makes it difficult to read as a novel, in that its emphasis on rhythm overwhelms distinctions of character" (164), yet it is the novel's rhythmic aspect that ensures its success for many readers. McCluskey writes that it is perhaps only in the rhythm of the two movements of speech and silence that *The Waves* can be read at all (78), and McLaurin holds that the entire design of the novel "arises from the idea of repetition and rhythm" (129). Woolf relies on rhythm to "weld the book into a unity, though it was precisely rhythm that had fragmented it in the first place" (Minow-Pinkney 174). Karen Kaivola sees *The Waves* as a demonstration of "how rhythm can embody a subversive desire for liberation from confining social and political structures" (Kaivola 37), and Richter and Beer both locate the novel's rhythms in the body (Richter, *Inward* 207; Beer, "Introduction" xii).

Bernard's summing up in the ninth episode of *The Waves* draws on the language of the interludes and of the other five voices, a "strange intermixing of conversational with almost ritualistic rhythms" (Mepham, *Literary Life* 141). Graham sees the summing up as functioning analogously to the party at the end of *Mrs. Dalloway* ("Point of View" 208), but several critics have expressed dissatisfaction with this episode. Ruotolo points out that the shift to a single voice is at variance with the design of *The Waves* (*Interrupted* 163), and Minow-Pinkney says that the episode "results only in a restatement of all the previous scenes without throwing any new light on them, and thus multiplies the reader's monotony" (173). Love finds the attempt to synthesize "futile" (*Worlds* 208), and Harper describes Bernard's final soliloquy as a victory "in a very ambiguous sense" (241).

The summing up is Bernard's attempt "to reconstruct a world without Percival" (Judith Lee 195), and if it is a failure, the failure seems to rest with Bernard rather than Woolf. "Notwithstanding Bernard's sensitive rendering of modern experience," says Ruotolo, "his poetry discloses a romantic egotism that denies modern life its depth" (*Interrupted* 167). Susan Dick* argues that Woolf modified her method in the final episode because she had decided to include Bernard's experience of the loss of self. She suggests one way of reading the episode is as "an extended dramatization of the functions of memory and of the role that memory plays in the building up of the self" ("I Remembered" 38). Bernard in the final episode is similar to the narrator that Woolf created in the early stages of her composition of *The Waves* (Graham, "Point of View" 207). A more positive view of Bernard is offered by Caughie, who sees in the final episode important questions raised about Woolf's aesthetics: "*What kinds of narrative relations are possible once we have relinquished the concepts of a central self, a stable world, and an individual artist? Where are we to ground the multiform artwork if not in the artist or in the world?*" (Caughie 49).

Several critics have questioned why Woolf chose to represent the writer as male in *The Waves,* particularly if, as many believe, Bernard is Woolf's alter ego. Fogel explains the decision as due to Woolf's anxiety about the influence of Henry James and insecurity about women's writing. Annette Oxindine* argues that, particularly after publishing *A Room of One's Own,* Woolf feared being labeled lesbian. Eileen B. Sypher* wonders whether a "male narrator and then character [began] to exert a force in her conception [as Woolf evolved her drafts] because of the largeness of her own fears about revealing that 'anger and ambition' were she to give a female or even a sexually ambiguous mind as dominant a role as she had originally planned" (Sypher 192). In contrast, Richard Pearce says that in *The Waves* we hear Woolf's "most successful realization of the female authorial voice—which does not separate itself from the narrative to tell the story but em-bodies it" (Pearce 156).

In DiBattista's reading of what she calls Woolf's "comic romance in prose," Percival's name enacts in its original French denotation of piercing the veil (perce-voile) the "primary strategy" of *The Waves,* which is veiling: "Woolf's dissimulation is the dissimulation of the chaste and pure speaker who conceals herself behind a veil of anonymity in order to speak the truth" (DiBattista 151). She argues that Percival is a decoy, intended to divert attention from the novel's "real center, the 'She' not the 'He' who successfully pierces the veil" (159). The anonymous female creative mind ("Anon was often a woman" Woolf wrote in *A Room*) is the implicit source of the episodes, as the interludes explicitly depict a female creator. The woman who sits and writes in Elvedon is "as much a god" as Percival is (Little 82). "The most solemn and awesome of the 'abstract' and 'religious' emotions in *The Waves* are given, not to the Parsifal figure, but to the female figure, to the Stonehenge 'presence,' the woman writing in the threatening garden" (Little 84).

Despite the general acceptance of *The Waves* as Woolf's masterpiece, some have dissented from this point of view. Rantavaara concludes that the novel is "an interesting experiment rather than an unqualified success" (92). Phyllis Rose compares it to Gertrude Stein's more abstract pieces in its creation of "a lyric monotony into which few readers are willing to penetrate" (Rose 172). Naremore comments on the "unrelieved poetic intensity with which every experience is presented, and the static atmosphere that is created" (152); for him, the novel is a failure, "though a highly interesting one" (189). This judgment has been repeated by Fogel ("a magnificent failure" [156]) and Zwerdling ("an experiment she was not tempted to repeat" [12]). Frank Kermode* has even gone so far as to call *The Waves* "an intolerable novel, I mean I find it intolerable in that it makes me sick, in fact, to try and read it" (Kermode 150). Mark Hussey, who writes that *The Waves* "exposes a gulf between language and reality, identity and self, that is rarely acknowledged in fiction" (*Singing* 44), argues that the very difficulty of the novel has assured its reputation as a modernist classic (82). Reading the novel as a continuation of the aesthetic developed by Woolf in *To the Lighthouse* rather than as the "entirely new" work Woolf proposed, Hussey describes *The Waves* as an "aesthetic failure" (82), an "antinovel." He notes that Woolf herself worried that the novel would be "a failure from a reader's point of view" (*Singing* 86). Although many critics have argued that *The Waves* is a unified and even "universal" work of art, Hussey writes that it is not, as Fleishman describes it, "an *ars poetica* for fiction . . . but a sketchpad for an unwritten novel" (91).

These detractors have been answered by other critics who point out that to read *The Waves* as continuing from *To the Lighthouse* the quest for the "essence" of consciousness and as a search for a form "capable of expressing 'timeless unity' " (Caughie 47) is to ignore the protocols of the text itself. The frustration of some readers testifies to "the deeply ingrained forces of those conventions of plot and sequence which [*The Waves*] regards as produced by the 'totalitarianism' of the logocentric mind" (Minow-Pinkney 186). McCluskey locates any failure in the reader rather than the text, "for it seems that we simply cannot sustain the intensity required of a text so 'saturated' " (McCluskey 78).

One argument made by those who see *The Waves* as a failed experiment is that it has not led anywhere and has no imitators (Mepham, *Literary* 143). However, several critics have pointed out that the French *nouveau roman* of writers such as Alain Robbe-Grillet and Nathalie Sarraute might be seen as descended from *The Waves*. *The Waves* has also been placed by Rantavaara in a tradition that includes the work of Gustave FLAUBERT, Henri Stendahl and Marcel PROUST, and many have linked it with Joyce's *Finnegans Wake*. Fleishman sees similarities with Faulkner's *As I Lay Dying*, and McConnell, who like Richter sees *The Waves* as the precursor of Robbe-Grillet and Sarraute, mentions Jorge Luis BORGES's "Tlön, Uqbar, Orbis Tertius" as depicting a world very similar to that of *The Waves*.

The Waves is a work usually omitted from political considerations of Woolf, although some have argued that its assault on the traditional novel is a part of Woolf's general subversion of patriarchal ideology. "Oppression, Woolf implies in this text, cannot be resisted at the individual level" (Kaivola 44). DuPlessis also argues that the waves themselves "are an image of the antiauthoritarian and critical poetics that animate her later books, with their group protagonists, their political critique, their psychic boundlessness figuring in and as the necessary next step, of history" ("*WOOLFENSTEIN*" 106).

Recently the novel has received readings that place it compellingly in the context of Woolf's political consciousness. Judith Lee argues that "even this most personal and lyrical narrative is important to understanding the often problematic connection between her ethics and her aesthetics" (180). Lee notes that Woolf wrote "ON BEING ILL" while she was working on *The Waves* and that her reflections in that essay "provide a particularly helpful gloss on Percival's role" (184). In a reading informed by Elaine Scarry's *The Body in Pain*, Lee argues that Percival represents "not only the (ironically dehumanized) possibility that one can live uncritically and painlessly in the world but also all that opposes (without destroying) the impulse to create that Bernard embodies" (186–87). The imagery of battle and militarism in the interludes, Lee argues, develops the correspondence between their symbolic universe and the "cultural and psychic universe of the episodes" as well as de-idealizing and inverting the chivalric myth embodied in Percival. In her revisionist mythmaking, Woolf shows militarism and mysticism to be antithetical.

Graham also discusses the heroic myth embodied in *The Waves* in a "constellation of figures, events, relationships, statements, and images which invoke the archetypal story of the hero without ever telling it" (Graham, "Manuscript" 314). He explains the general lack of attention to this theme as due to the fact that, despite what Woolf herself believed about the novel, "the heroic theme does *not* dominate" (327). It is the vision of the fin that dominates, not the heroic theme, Graham argues ("Manuscript" 331), the mysticism that Judith Lee finds incompatible with the military imagery of the novel.

Jane Marcus* argues that the "poetic language and experimental structure of this modernist classic are vehicles for a radical politics that is both antiimperialist and anticanonical" ("Britannia" 137). *The Waves* is regarded as a "novel of the thirties that is not a thirties novel" by most critics, its reputation as a difficult text ensuring that it is read only in FORMALIST or philosophical terms. Taking as her context the legitimation of cultural studies, and the "combined methodologies of feminism, marxism, [and] revisionist Orientalism," Marcus is enabled to read *The Waves* as Woolf's critique of the process of producing culture, and as a work concerned "with race, class, colonialism, and the cultural politics of canonicity itself" (142).

In this reading the Romantic allusions noted by earlier critics are seen as exposing "the implications of race and gender in the still-living English Romantic quest for a self and definition of the (white male) self against the racial or sexual other" (Marcus, "Britannia" 137). *The Waves*, Marcus contends, is "about the ideology of white British colonialism and the Romantic literature that sustains it," such as Shelley's "Indian Girl's Song," which Woolf uses to create a discourse for a white Western woman like Rhoda to have a "heroic Death" (Marcus, "Britannia" 137). As Ruotolo remarks of the Romanticism of what Marcus describes as the "hero-poet" (represented by Percival and Bernard), "the promise of shining knights destined to lead us out of darkness invokes familiar expectations for Woolf, as it no doubt did for readers of her own culture . . . for the adult and more relevantly for the maturing artist, such myths, particularly in a secular age, supply at best an artificial coherence" (*Interrupted* 171).

Adaptations

The Waves was abridged by Louis MACNEICE for BBC Radio October 7, 1976, produced and directed by Guy Vaesen, with Dame Peggy Ashcroft as the "Choral Voice." Bruce Saylor's "*The Waves:* Three Dramatic Monologues" for voice and musical accompaniment was composed in 1985. A musical adaptation of *The Waves* by David Bucknam and Lisa Peterson premiered at New York Theatre Workshop in April 1990.

****Works Specific to This Entry:***

Ascher, Carol. "Reading to Write: *The Waves* as Muse." In Mark Hussey and Vara Neverow-Turk, eds. *Virginia Woolf Miscellanies:* 47–56.

Beer, Gillian. "Introduction" to *The Waves.* Oxford: Oxford University Press/World's Classics, 1992.

Dick, Susan. "I Remembered, I Forgotten: Bernard's Final Soliloquy in *The Waves.*" *Modern Language Studies* 13, 3 (1983): 38–52.

DuPlessis, Rachel Blau. "WOOLFENSTEIN." In Ellen G. Friedman and Miriam Fuchs, eds. *Breaking the Sequence: Women's Experimental Fiction.* Princeton: Princeton University Press, 1989: 99–114.

Flint, Kate. "Introduction" to *The Waves.* In Julia Briggs, ed. *Virginia Woolf: Introductions to the Major Works.* London: Virago, 1994.

Gorsky, Susan. " 'The Central Shadow:' Characterization in *The Waves.*" *Modern Fiction Studies* 18, 3 (Autumn 1972): 449–66 (quoted from Eleanor McNees, ed. *Virginia Woolf:* 4).

Graham, J. W. "Point of View in *The Waves:* Some Services of the Style." *University of Toronto Quarterly* 39 (April 1970): 193–211.

———. "Manuscript Revision and the Heroic Theme of *The Waves.*" *Twentieth Century Literature* 29, 3 (Fall 1983): 312–32.

Gregor, Ian. "Virginia Woolf and her Reader." In Eric Warner, ed. *Virginia Woolf:* 41–55.

Haller, Evelyn. "Her Quill Drawn from the Firebird: Virginia Woolf and the Russian Dancers." In Diane F. Gillespie, ed. *The Multiple Muses of Virginia Woolf:* 180–226.

Haule, James M. "Introduction." The Shakespeare Head Press Edition of Virginia Woolf. *The Waves.* Oxford: Basil Blackwell, 1993.

Henke, Suzette A. "Virginia Woolf's *The Waves:* A Phenomenological Reading." *Neophilologus* 73 (1989): 461–72.

Jacobs, Peter. " 'The Second Violin Tuning in the Ante-room:' Virginia Woolf and Music." In Diane F. Gillespie, ed. *The Multiple Muses of Virginia Woolf:* 227–60.

Kermode, Frank. "Panel Discussion 2." In Eric Warner, ed. *Virginia Woolf:* 146–65.

Lee, Judith. " 'This hideous shaping and moulding:' War and *The Waves.*" In Mark Hussey, ed. *Virginia Woolf and War:* 180–202.

Levin, Gerald. "The Musical Style of *The Waves.*" *Journal of Narrative Technique* 13, 3 (1983): 164–71.

Lorsch, Susan E. *Where Nature Ends: Literary Responses to the Designification of Landscape.* Rutherford, N.J.: Fairleigh Dickinson University Press, 1983.

Marcus, Jane. "Britannia Rules *The Waves.*" In Karen Lawrence, ed. *Decolonizing Tradition: The Cultural Politics of Modern Literary Canons.* Urbana: University of Illinois Press, 1991: 136–62.

McCluskey, Kathleen. *Reverberations: Sound and Structure in the Novels of Virginia Woolf.* Ann Arbor, Michigan: UMI Research Press, 1986.

McConnell, Frank D. " 'Death Among the Apple Trees:' *The Waves* and the World of Things." In Claire Sprague, ed. *Virginia Woolf:* 117–29.

Moore, Madeline. "Nature and Communion: A Study of Cyclical Reality in *The Waves.*" In Ralph Freedman, ed. *Virginia Woolf: Revaluation and Continuity:* 219–40.

Oxindine, Annette. "Sapphist Semiotics in Woolf's *The Waves:* Untelling and Retelling What Cannot be Told." In Vara Neverow-Turk and Mark Hussey, eds. *Virginia Woolf: Themes and Variations:* 171–81.

Rantavaara, Irma. *Virginia Woolf's The Waves.* Port Washington: Kennikat Press, 1960.

Schulze, Robin Gail. "Design in Motion: Words, Music, and the Search for Coherence in the Works of Virginia Woolf and Arnold Schoenberg." *Studies in the Literary Imagination* 25, 2 (Fall 1992): 5–22.

Stewart, Jack F. "Existence and Symbol in *The Waves.*" *Modern Fiction Studies* 18, 3 (Autumn 1972): 433–47.

———. "Spatial Form and Color in *The Waves.*" *Twentieth Century Literature* 28, 1 (Spring 1982): 86–107.

Sypher, Eileen B. "*The Waves:* A Utopia of Androgyny?" In Elaine Ginsberg and Laura Moss Gottlieb, eds., *Virginia Woolf:* 187–213.

Warner, Eric. *Virginia Woolf: The Waves.* Landmarks in World Literature. New York: Cambridge University Press, 1987.

Yeats, W. B. *Selected Criticism.* Edited with an introduction and notes by A. Norman Jeffares. London: Macmillan, 1964.

Weaver, Harriet Shaw (1876–1961) Champion of the work of James JOYCE and owner and editor (with Dora Marsden) of *The Egoist,* where T. S. ELIOT was her assistant editor. In 1918, at the suggestion of Roger FRY, she took the manuscript of Joyce's *Ulysses* to the Woolf's HOGARTH PRESS (D1 139–40). The Press could not cope with printing such a long manuscript, and the commercial printers they approached were too fearful of prosecution, and so the manuscript was returned to Weaver.

Webb, Beatrice (1858–1943) and Sidney (1859–1947) Founders of the *NEW STATESMAN,* the London School of Economics and the Fabian Research Bureau.[24] In 1914 Leonard WOOLF came to their attention through an article he had written for the *Manchester Guardian* on the conference of the WOMEN'S COOPERATIVE GUILD in Newcastle. The Webbs commissioned him to write a supplement to the *New Statesman* on international organizations. This work was eventually published by Allen and Unwin and the Fabian Society in 1916 as *International Government: Two reports by L. S. Woolf prepared for the Fabian Research Department, Together with a Project by a Fabian Committee for a Supernational Authority that Will Prevent War.* Woolf attended a Fabian meeting in 1915 (finding it "well worth hearing" [D1 26]) and in 1918 the Webbs came to stay at ASHEHAM HOUSE (D1 193–97). Leonard maintained a respectful friendship with the Webbs throughout their lives, enjoying their eccentricity, admiring their dedication, but finding their socialism too linked to its nineteenth-century roots.

Webster, John (1580?–1634) A Jacobean playwright, author of *The White Devil, The DUCHESS OF MALFI* and other dramas. In *NIGHT AND DAY,* Katharine HILBERY supposes that all the people at Mary DATCHET's apartment to hear William RODNEY's paper on Elizabethan use of metaphor have read Webster, but Mary tells her that is no proof of cleverness (ND 59). Later in the novel, Mrs. HILBERY is depressed by the "crudeness" of *The Duchess of Malfi* (ND 416).

***Well of Loneliness, The* (1928)** Novel about lesbian life by Radclyffe Hall (1886–1943, who lived with Una Troubridge, wife of the great-grandson of Woolf's great-aunt Sara Prinsep). An action was initiated against the book by the Home Secretary, Sir William Joynson-Hix (known as "Jix"), after an article in the *Sunday Express* by its editor, James Douglas, declared that he would "rather give a healthy boy or a healthy girl a phial of Prussic acid than this novel" (Brittain 16). Woolf and many other writers, including Vera BRITTAIN, E. M. FORSTER and Vita SACKVILLE-WEST, were prepared to defend the book at trial, but the Bow Street magistrate Sir Chartres BIRON (mentioned in *A ROOM OF ONE'S OWN*) pronounced the novel obscene in November 1928 and disallowed any testimony from defense witnesses (Desmond MACCARTHY was the only one called, and he was not allowed to give his opinion). Hall herself had required that any witnesses on her behalf testify to the book's worth as literature, which Woolf and others, whose involvement was a matter of principle, could not have done sincerely.

The Well of Loneliness tells the story of Stephen Gordon, a woman who becomes an ambulance driver in World War I and has an intense affair with Mary Llewelyn, who later marries Stephen's suitor Martin Hallam. Vera Brittain reviewed the novel in *Time and Tide,* calling it an "important, sincere and very moving study" (Brittain 48). After the trial, the novel was published in Paris by Pegasus Press and imported into England. Whenever copies were found, they were destroyed by order of Sir Archibald BODKIN, the Director of Public Prosecutions (also mentioned in *A Room*). Jane Marcus has discussed the relation between *A Room of One's Own* and the *Well* trial in "Sapphistory: The Woolf and the Well."

Wellesley, Lady Dorothy Violet (née Ashton) Poet who in 1928 financed the HOGARTH PRESS Living Poets series and helped choose works for it until withdrawing in 1933. Hogarth published several of Wellesley's collections of poetry. Wellesley first met the Woolfs through her friend Vita SACKVILLE-WEST in 1924. Wellesley is listed among the friends who have "helped me in ways too various to specify" thanked in Woolf's ironic preface to *ORLANDO.*

Wells, Herbert George (1866–1946) The author of many novels, including *The Time Machine* (1895), *The War Between the Worlds* (1898) and *The Sleeper Awakes* (1911), as well as works of history and popular accounts of science. Leonard WOOLF knew Wells from their work together on helping to establish the League of Nations, and he described in his autobiography "a friendship with him which was very pleasant and lasted until his death, though it was broken, as friendship with H. G. often was, by interludes of storm and stress" (LW2 138). Four works by Wells were published by the HOGARTH PRESS: *Democracy under Revision* (1927), *The Common Sense of World Peace*

[24]The Fabian Society, a socialist group, came into being in 1884. The name "derived from a dubious political reference to the Roman general Fabius Cunctator, whose tactics in his campaign against Hannibal were supposedly both cautious and forthright" (Norman and Jeanne MacKenzie, *The Fabians* [New York: Simon & Schuster, 1977]: 27).

(1929), *The Open Conspiracy: Blue Prints for a World Revolution* (1930) and *The Idea of a World Encyclopaedia* (1936).

Woolf also came to know Wells socially, meeting Arnold BENNETT and George Bernard SHAW at his house in 1917. She reviewed *Joan and Peter. The Story of an Education* for the *TIMES LITERARY SUPPLEMENT* in September 1918 (E2 294–98) and called Wells's characters "curiously disappointing" (E2 296). In several essays attacking those she termed the "Edwardians," Woolf included Wells in a trio whose other members were Arnold Bennett and John GALSWORTHY. These three writers were compared in "MODERN FICTION," "MR. BENNETT AND MRS. BROWN" and "CHARACTER IN FICTION" with the younger generation of writers represented by James JOYCE and Woolf herself. In "Character in Fiction," Woolf wrote that "to go to these men and ask them to teach you how to write a novel . . . is precisely like going to a bootmaker and asking him to teach you how to make a watch" (E3 427). In 1922, in a long letter to her friend Gerald BRENAN, Woolf wrote that the efforts of her generation of writers to create a new realism were doomed to failure, but even this seemed "better to me . . . than to sit down with Hugh Walpole, Wells, etc. etc. and make large oil paintings of fabulous fleshy monsters complete from top to toe" (L2 598). Her sentiments were echoed by her character Jacob FLANDERS, who deplores "Shaw and Wells and the serious sixpenny weeklies" (JR 35).

In 1932, Leonard reviewed Wells's *The Work, Wealth and Happiness of Mankind* for the *NEW STATESMAN AND NATION,* and Woolf recorded in her DIARY that reading Wells's views on women in this book had set her mind running on "A Knock at the Door," which was at that time the title of what would eventually be *THREE GUINEAS* (D4 75). In late 1934 she wrote that she was reading Wells's *Experiment in Autobiography* "with interest and distaste" (D4 262) and quotations from this work appear in *Three Guineas* (TG 43). Reflecting on a visit to Wells in 1937, Woolf described him as a "humane man in some corner; also brutal; also entirely without poetry" (D5 53).

West, Rebecca (1892–1983) Born Cicily Isabel Fairfield, West took her name from the radical feminist heroine of Henrik IBSEN's *Rosmersholm* (1886) and was an important socialist feminist writer. After a brief stint as an actor, West found a niche writing for the radical suffragist journal *Freewoman.* In the 1920s she wrote reviews for the *NEW STATESMAN.* Bonnie Kime Scott has written that the "vast corpus of West's writing defies usual categories of genre and period" (Scott, *Gender* 562). Among her works of non-fiction are a study of Henry JAMES (1916); a biography of St. Augustine (1933); *Black Lamb and Grey Falcon* (1941), about her travels in Yugoslavia and an attack on Nazism; and *The Meaning of Treason* (1949). Her works of fiction include *The Return of the Soldier* (1918), *The Judge* (1922), *Harriet Hume* (1929), *The Harsh Voice* (1935), *The Thinking Reed* (1936) and *The Fountain Overflows* (1957). West had a ten-year affair with the writer H. G. WELLS, whom she met after harshly reviewing his novel *Marriage,* and raised their son, Anthony West.

In *A ROOM OF ONE'S OWN,* Woolf's narrator describes her astonishment at a critic named "Z" calling Rebecca West an "arrant feminist" because she said men are snobs. "Z" can be identified as Woolf's friend and occasional antagonist Desmond MACCARTHY: She records an afternoon spent talking with him in 1928, remarking that West's saying men are snobs "gets an instant rise" out of him (D3 195). In "Autumn and Virginia Woolf," West described *A Room* as "an uncompromising piece of feminist propaganda: I think the ablest yet written" (West, *Ending in Earnest* 211). Recognizing that Woolf was writing against the current, West called *A Room* extremely courageous because "anti-feminism is so strikingly the correct fashion of the day among the intellectuals" (West 212). When she wrote in the *New York Herald Tribune* that *ORLANDO* was "a poetic masterpiece of the first rank" (Scott 592), Woolf wrote to thank her, saying "(what a lot more you have guessed of my meaning than anybody else)" (CS 242). Woolf met West at a party given by Dorothy TODD, the editor of *Vogue,* in 1928, and "rather liked her" (CS 235), describing her to Vanessa BELL as "very distrustful, hard as nails, and no beauty" (CS 235). They met several times, and Woolf maintained a sense that West lived in a kind of brittle society about which Woolf felt ambivalent; after a dinner with West and her husband in 1935, Woolf analyzed this sense in her DIARY: "One cd. go on having dinner every night & never know each other better" (D4 326).

When Donald BRACE, Woolf's U.S. publisher, suggested in 1932 that someone write a book on Woolf, Leonard WOOLF replied that he felt West would be the best person to do this (Spotts 239–40). Leonard later wrote to West praising her "Letter to a Grandfather," number 7 in the short-lived Hogarth Letters series, and published in 1933 by the HOGARTH PRESS. When *The Harsh Voice* appeared in 1935, Woolf wrote in its praise to West and was disappointed not to have a reply (West later explained that she had been ill). West reviewed Quentin BELL's biography of Woolf in *Vogue* in 1973.

"Western Wind, O" "O western wind when wilt thou blow" is an anonymous medieval lyric that occurs several times in Woolf's writing. It is recited by LOUIS in *THE WAVES,* and, as Alice Fox notes, is also quoted or alluded to in "HOW SHOULD ONE READ A BOOK?," in "BYRON & MR BRIGGS," and in Woolf's

DIARY (D4 204). Gillian Beer has noted that the lyric was the first poem in *The Week-end Book,* a "publishing phenomenon" in the 1920s (Beer, *The Waves* 256).

Westminster Abbey One of the great landmarks of London, Westminster Abbey appears throughout Woolf's writing. In *MRS. DALLOWAY,* Doris KILMAN goes there to pray, and in *ORLANDO* it is one of the first sights Orlando sees as she sails up the river Thames on her return from CONSTANTINOPLE. Officially called the Collegiate Church of St. Peter, Westminster Abbey is one of several important buildings on PARLIAMENT SQUARE. It was originally a Benedictine monastery and has been altered and enlarged throughout the centuries by various English monarchs. The kings and queens of England since William the Conqueror have been crowned in the Abbey, and many of them are also buried there. Of particular significance for Woolf, perhaps, is the "Poets' Corner" of the cemetery in the south transept of the Abbey, where there are memorials to many English writers, including Aphra BEHN, Geoffrey Chaucer, John MILTON, William SHAKESPEARE and Edmund Spenser.

"Where There's a Will There's a Way" The Restoration play within Miss LA TROBE's village pageant in *BETWEEN THE ACTS* (126–33; 135–38; 143–48). The dramatis personae are: Lady Harpy Harraden; Deb, her maid; Flavinda, her niece; Sir Spaniel Lilyliver; Sir Smirking Peace-be-with-you-all; Lord and Lady Fribble; and Valentine.

Whitaker Commenting on the lack of available information about the lives of women, Woolf's narrator remarks in *A ROOM OF ONE'S OWN* that she can find all she needs to know about men in various sources, one of which is "Whitaker" (AROO 86). This refers to *Whitaker's Almanac,* founded in 1868 by Joseph Whitaker (1820–1895). The *Almanac* contained general information concerning government, finances, population and commerce, with special reference to the United States and England. Also mentioned in *A Room* is the "Table of Precedency" in Whitaker (AROO 105–06), which gave the hierarchy of church and state in England from the monarch down. Woolf also referred frequently to the *Almanac* when writing *THREE GUINEAS,* gleaning statistics from it with which to support her arguments. Holleyman and Treacher list the *Almanac* for 1936 and 1938 as in the Woolfs' library.

Whitbread, Hugh A character in *MRS. DALLOWAY* whom Woolf satirizes. Clarissa DALLOWAY meets him in St. James's Park soon after she has left her house to buy flowers for her party. Hugh has a "little job at Court" and is pompous and stupid. He is the type of those "men in white waistcoats" who look down from the windows of their private club at the world they control. He tells Clarissa that his wife, Evelyn, is ill, as she seems often to be. At Clarissa's party, Peter WALSH thinks to himself that "the rascals who get hanged for battering the brains of a girl out in a train do less harm on the whole than Hugh Whitbread and his kindness" (MD 263).

Whitechapel See *FLUSH, A BIOGRAPHY.*

Whitehall Mentioned frequently in Woolf's writing, Whitehall passes from Trafalgar Square down to the Westminster Bridge in London and gives its name to the area in which the Houses of Parliament stand. Downing Street, the official address of the English prime minister, is off Whitehall, as are many government offices. In Woolf's time, particularly, Whitehall was associated with war and government. It is the site of the Admiralty, the War Office, and the Parade Ground where Woolf would have noted the statues of Field-Marshal Earl Kitchener, Viscount Wolseley and Lord Roberts. In the center of Whitehall is an equestrian statue of the Duke of Cambridge, once a commander in chief of the British Army. In *A ROOM OF ONE'S OWN,* Woolf describes a "splitting off of consciousness" that women experience walking down Whitehall (AROO 97) as they realize their alienation from power. Whitehall is the area in which Clarissa DALLOWAY lives, and it is in Whitehall that Peter WALSH in *MRS. DALLOWAY* is overtaken by a parade of boys marching to lay a wreath at the CENOTAPH, a World War I memorial erected in 1920. It was not until 1931, however, that the name Whitehall was given to the entire thoroughfare from Trafalgar Square to Parliament Street.

Whitehorn, Mrs. Mentioned in *JACOB'S ROOM,* she is Jacob's landlady and asks his advice about her son, who has been beaten by a schoolmaster.

Whitman, Walt (1819–92) American poet and author of *Leaves of Grass,* a collection that grew and changed through several editions during the poet's lifetime. During the American Civil War Whitman worked as a hospital volunteer. In *THE VOYAGE OUT,* Terence HEWET reads from the "Calamus" section of *Leaves of Grass* while on the trip upriver (TVO 267). In her 1925 article "American Fiction" (CE2 111–21) for the New York *Saturday Review of Literature,* Woolf calls Whitman the one American writer wholeheartedly admired by the English (CE2 111). In an earlier piece, a review of *An Apology for Old Maids* by Henry Dwight Sedgwick for the *TIMES LITERARY SUPPLEMENT* in February 1917, Woolf had singled out Whitman's preface to the first edition of *Leaves of Grass* (1855) as an exemplary statement of the American spirit that should silence any skepticism about the future of American art (E2 81).

Whittaker, Mr. Mentioned in *MRS. DALLOWAY,* the man who, by his preaching, has shown "the light" to Doris KILMAN.

Who's Afraid of Virginia Woolf? Play by Edward Albee (b. 1928) that concerns an all-night drinking party in which a middle-aged couple, George and Martha, torment each other verbally; they have an imaginary child that at the end of the play they "kill" by abandoning their fantasy. In 1962, Albee wrote Leonard WOOLF asking if he could use Woolf's name (Spotts 522). When Leonard saw the play in 1965, he wrote Albee that he thought it was "about the really important things in life" and asked if Albee knew Woolf's "LAPPIN AND LAPINOVA," which shared with Albee's play the theme of an imaginary child (Spotts 536–37). Lucio Ruotolo has written that the play was inspired by the conclusion of *BETWEEN THE ACTS* (VWM 27:5). In 1982, Nigel Nicolson said, "Ask the average Briton what he knows about Virginia Woolf and he will give you Albee" ("Bloomsbury" 9). Brenda R. Silver identifies the play (and the 1966 Mike Nichols film with Elizabeth Taylor and Richard Burton) as "the major event that precipitated Woolf into public awareness" ("What's Woolf" 26). In her analysis of the construction of Woolf as a cultural icon, Silver notes that the play made Woolf's name "synonymous with the power to elicit fear and wreak psychological death or destruction" (27). Silver also notes that Albee saw the phrase which he made his play's title on a blackboard in a gay bar in Greenwich Village (28).

Wickham, Mr. In *THE WAVES,* LOUIS remembers throughout his life knocking at the "grained oak door" of Mr. Wickham, a schoolmaster.

Wilberforce, Dr. Octavia Mary (1888–1963) Often referred to as Woolf's last doctor, although she saw her in a professional capacity only on March 27, 1941, the day before Woolf committed suicide. Referring to *Octavia Wilberforce: The Autobiography of a Pioneer Woman Doctor* (Pat Jalland, ed. [1989]), Thomas Caramagno reports that she "suspected in 1940 that her patient might be an alcoholic" (62). Jane Marcus refers to Wilberforce as the last of Woolf's "mother mentors" (*Languages* 113). Their families had been closely linked in the nineteenth-century CLAPHAM SECT; Wilberforce was the great-granddaughter of William Wilberforce (1759–1833), known as "The Emancipator" for his part in abolishing the slave trade. The Woolfs met Wilberforce and Elizabeth ROBINS, with whom she lived, in 1937. Wilberforce practiced medicine in Brighton and also kept cows, from which she brought milk and cream to the Woolfs at MONK'S HOUSE in 1940–41. George Spater and Ian Parsons (182–84) give an account of Wilberforce's conversations with Woolf as she related them in letters to Robins (who had returned to the United States in 1940). In the last few lines of Woolf's DIARY she wonders about "Octavia's story. Could I englobe it somehow? English youth in 1900" (D5 359).

Wilding, Charlotte Mentioned in *JACOB'S ROOM* as a friend of Clara DURRANT's, she thinks Clara's mother is sad and wins a bet that Jacob will join in a play.

Willett, Miss Character in *THE VOYAGE OUT.* She plays the harmonium during the Sunday service in chapter XVII.

William A servant of Mrs. CHINNERY's in *THE YEARS.*

William, King See HAMPTON COURT.

William, Uncle Mentioned in *MRS. DALLOWAY* as having said a lady is known by her shoes and gloves. During World War I, he apparently gives up the will to live.

Williams, Sandra Wentworth Character in *JACOB'S ROOM* whom Jacob meets when he is in Greece, where she is traveling with her husband, Evan. Jacob falls in love with the self-absorbed Mrs. Williams, who is used to having affairs. Jacob travels with the Williamses from Olympia to Corinth and on to CONSTANTINOPLE, Sandra being a great hook in his side that tugs him along. When Jacob returns to London, Sandra writes to him, remembering a significant moment they shared in the dark on the road to the Acropolis. She puts the book of DONNE's poetry Jacob gave her in her bookcase next to the dozen or so other books she has collected on her travels; and she thinks of Jacob as a small boy as she looks at her own child, Jimmy, out in her garden with his nurse.

Wilkins, Mr. Mentioned in *MRS. DALLOWAY,* a man Clarissa hires for parties to announce her guests as they arrive.

Winchilsea, Lady See FINCH, Anne.

"Window, The" See *TO THE LIGHTHOUSE.*

***Wise Virgins, The. A Story of Words, Opinions, and a Few Emotions* (1914)** Leonard WOOLF's second novel, published by Edward Arnold in 1914, was dedicated to Desmond MACCARTHY. Leonard began writing *The Wise Virgins* on his honeymoon in Spain in 1912. He notes in his autobiography that the "war killed it dead" and that he earned only £20 from the book. *The Wise Virgins* was not reissued until 1979, when the HOGARTH PRESS published a second edition with an introduction by Ian Parsons; the second edition was published in the United States by Harcourt, Brace, Jovanovich.

The Wise Virgins makes little attempt to disguise that it is based on Leonard's own circumstances and portrays his own family in a very unflattering way. Although the people and situations on which the novel is modeled could only be discerned at the time by those involved, the publication and availability now of the letters and diaries and other papers of the principals makes such identifications easy. The novel gave great offence to the WOOLF FAMILY, several members of which read drafts that Leonard sent them. Bella WOOLF, Leonard's sister, was distressed by the novel, and Leonard's mother warned her son that there might be a serious breach between them were it published (Spotts 195–96). The lasting anger at the novel in Leonard's family can be judged from a letter written by Edgar Woolf in 1953 that tells his brother he had "showed what a cad you were when you published *The Wise Virgins*—after solemnly promising not to!" (Spotts 493). Even Lytton STRACHEY, Leonard's closest friend at the time and one who might not have been thought to concern himself with Mrs. Woolf's feelings, suggested that Leonard should let the manuscript sit for six months before revising it. The publisher, Edward Arnold, also required Leonard to make a number of alterations as "concessions to the taste of the reading public" (Spotts 199). According to one of Leonard's biographers, *The Wise Virgins* was "effectively restricted" (Wilson, *Leonard Woolf* 253), but there is no clear evidence of this.

The plot of *The Wise Virgins* concerns the Jewish Davis family who have recently moved to "Richstead," a suburb of London. Their cynical and disaffected son Harry, who is clearly to be identified with Leonard himself, has met Miss Camilla Lawrence at his art class. The Lawrence family (Acton Lawrence and his daughters Camilla and Katharine) are modeled on Leslie STEPHEN and his daughters, Woolf and Vanessa BELL. Other friends of the Lawrence family are also based on people Leonard knew well, such as Clive BELL (Arthur Woodhouse in the novel) and Saxon SYDNEY-TURNER (upon whom the minor character Trevor Trevithick is probably based). To Harry Davis, Camilla Lawrence represents all that is "worth getting."

The Davises (Mr. and Mrs. Davis, Harry, and his sister Hetty) become friendly with the widowed Mrs. Garland and her four unmarried daughters. Gwen Garland catches Harry's eye, and he sets about what he terms "waking her up" by giving her the works of George MEREDITH and Henrik IBSEN to read. Gwen begins to fall in love with Harry. At the same time, Harry is pursuing Camilla but she tells him she is only interested in a friendship with him.

Harry is invited to stay with the Lawrences for a weekend in the country. He is acutely conscious of the anti-Semitism of Camilla's friends, such as Arthur Woodhouse. Harry also feels strongly drawn to Camilla's sister, the earthy Katharine, who, like Vanessa Bell, "liked men and to be with them and to talk to them better than women" (102). When Camilla later refuses Harry's marriage proposal he is very angry, feeling that he is the only man he knows who does not have a woman of his own. The Garlands and the Davises go on vacation together, accompanied by the Reverend Macausland, an odious vicar who is engaged to May Garland, one of Gwen's sisters. Macausland disapproves of Harry's influence on Gwen. While on vacation, Harry writes to Camilla asking if they can remain friends. One night, at the hotel, Gwen comes to Harry's room.

The next day, Gwen's nocturnal visit to Harry having become known, the families are distraught. Although he can now barely bring himself to look at Gwen, Harry agrees to marry her. Gwen convinces herself that he loves her. Harry receives a letter from Camilla saying they should remain friends. He goes to visit the Lawrences just before his marriage to Gwen and finds that nothing has changed: They are still sitting in their deep armchairs, talking endlessly. Harry is reminded how strongly attracted he was and still is to Katharine. On this visit, however, he rails against Acton Lawrence and the smug, monied class the Lawrences represent, seeming to blame Camilla for his fate. Camilla is upset and confused by Harry's bitterness but unable to feel any passion for him. The novel ends with a despondent Harry getting married to Gwen in a double wedding with Macausland and May Garland.

Woolf read *The Wise Virgins* on January 31, 1915 and wrote in her DIARY that it was "a remarkable book . . . a writer's book" that showed the "poetic side" of her husband. Selma Meyerowitz, in her biography of Leonard Woolf, has noted that the early novels by the Woolfs—*THE VOYAGE OUT, NIGHT AND DAY* and *The Wise Virgins*—"present their view of love, both spiritual and physical, marriage, and individual fulfillment as they portray twentieth-century English society" (Meyerowitz 17). Mark Hussey, in "Refractions of Desire," has explored the relations between *The Wise Virgins* and Woolf's second novel, *Night and Day,* arguing that *Night and Day* is a response to Leonard's novel: "What *The Wise Virgins* presents, so to speak, *Night and Day* analyzes" (Hussey, "Refractions" 129). Roger Poole treats *The Wise Virgins* extensively in *The Unknown Virginia Woolf,* arguing that in the novel Leonard analyzes the three "problems" of class, race and feeling that he himself was facing in the early years of the century (Poole 78–102).

Withers, Mrs. Mentioned in *JACOB'S ROOM* telling Oliver SKELTON about her husband's character at a party.

Wollstonecraft, Mary (1759–97) Author of *A Vindication of the Rights of Men, in a Letter to the Right Honorable Edmund Burke* (1790), *A Vindication of the Rights of Woman* (1792), and other works. Woolf's article "Mary Wollstonecraft" (CE3 193–99) was published in 1929 in the *NATION & ATHENAEUM* and is concerned mainly with the events of Wollstonecraft's life.

Wolstenholme, Joseph (1829–91) The probable model for Augustus CARMICHAEL in *TO THE LIGHTHOUSE,* Wolstenholme was a friend of Leslie STEPHEN's in his Cambridge days whom Woolf and her siblings called "The Wooly One" (MOB 73). He was "a mathematician and walker who had the gift of being able to spout thousands of lines of poetry by heart" (Annan 54) and was a professor at Cooper's Hill College. In his *MAUSOLEUM BOOK,* Leslie Stephen wrote that Wolstenholme consoled himself for a unsatisfactory life "with mathematics and opium" (79). He would stay with Leslie and Julia Prinsep STEPHEN every summer in ST. IVES, where "he could at least be without his wife" (*Mausoleum Book* 79).

"Woman's College from Outside, A" (BP 6–9; SF 139–42) A short sketch by Woolf that was first published in *ATALANTA'S GARLAND* in 1926. It describes Angela Williams, a student at NEWNHAM College. When she is kissed by Alice Avery, Angela feels emotions very similar to those Clarissa DALLOWAY feels when she is kissed by Sally SETON (MD 52–53): "She held it glowing to her breast, a thing not to be touched, thought of, or spoken about, but left to glow there" (SF 141). Susan Dick points out that the first sentence of the piece also appears in *JACOB'S ROOM* (JR 38) and that a draft of "A Woman's College" is in the first holograph notebook of *Jacob's Room* in the BERG COLLECTION (SF 294).

Woman's Leader and the Common Cause Feminist weekly edited in 1920–23 by Rachel STRACHEY, who had edited *Common Cause* before its amalgamation in 1920 with the *Woman's Leader.* Woolf contributed a signed article on "The Plumage Bill" in 1920, responding to a column in the *NATION* by H. W. Massingham. The Bill, which was to ban the importation of plumage, used by women as a fashion accessory and obtained by extremely cruel methods, had been the subject of considerable newspaper attention. Volume 3 of *The Essays of Virginia Woolf* prints the article, Massingham's response, and Woolf's further reply to him (E3 241–45).

"Women and Fiction" (CE2 141–48; GR 76–84) An essay by Woolf published in *The Forum* in March 1929 on the same subject as two talks she gave at NEWNHAM COLLEGE and GIRTON COLLEGE, Cambridge University, in October 1928, the talks she referred to as the basis for *A ROOM OF ONE'S OWN.* The title is the same as the working title for *A Room of One's Own.* According to S. P. Rosenbaum, this essay "is probably as close as we can now come to what Virginia Woolf said at Cambridge" (*Women & Fiction* xxi), but he also notes that this essay does not have many of the features found in *A Room* and also in contemporary accounts of Woolf's visits to the women's colleges.

Women & Fiction: The Manuscript Versions of A Room of One's Own S. P. Rosenbaum discovered 134 handwritten draft pages of Woolf's *A ROOM OF ONE'S OWN* in the Fitzwilliam Museum, Cambridge, where they had "lain virtually unread" since Leonard WOOLF donated them in 1942. Rosenbaum's transcription of the two different drafts, supplemented with twenty manuscript pages from the MONK'S HOUSE PAPERS, was published in 1992. He notes that the drafts, written in 1929, are informed by both the fantasy of *ORLANDO,* which Woolf had recently completed, and the mysticism of *THE WAVES,* which she had been thinking about since 1927. *Women & Fiction* shows Woolf reworking sentences and passages, trying out different words and phrases. The narrator of *A Room* begins *Women & Fiction* as a medieval peddlar, the sort of person who "gossiped with women at the cottage doors." The figure of the anonymous spirit of literature reappears in "ANON," a chapter of the projected literary history on which Woolf was working when she died in 1941.

Women and Writing A selection of Woolf's essays edited and introduced by Michèle Barrett (London: The Women's Press, 1979; New York: Harcourt, 1980).

"Women Must Weep" See KINGSLEY, Charles; *THREE GUINEAS.*

Women's Cooperative Guild An organization within the Cooperative Wholesale Societies of Great Britain—"a peculiar and enormous system of manufacture, retail trade and banking, based upon the consumers organised in retail Cooperative Societies" (LW2 71)—with which Woolf and Leonard WOOLF were closely involved from 1913. The Cooperative Movement began in 1844 and the Women's Cooperative Guild (WCG) was founded in 1883. From 1889 to 1921 Margaret Llewelyn DAVIES was the WCG's

General Secretary and it was through her that the Woolfs became involved. In her "Note on the Women's Co-operative Guild" in *Life As We Have Known It,* Davies explained that members of local Cooperative Societies owned the shops where they bought goods, and that a federation of more than 1,000 local societies with 6 million members constituted the England and Scottish Co-operative Wholesale Societies. "The local Societies are also federated into the Co-operative Union for educational, legal and propagandistic purposes, and, through the Cooperative Party, are allied politically with the Labour Party" (Davies x). In 1930, the WCG had 1,400 branches and 67,000 members, which, wrote Davies, had "given the unity and force which enable the women to become a power in the Movement and to share in its administration" (xi). She noted that there was also now an International Cooperative Guild in which twenty-seven countries participated. "Guildswomen," wrote Davies, "starting from buying bread and butter on revolutionary principles, have reached an international outlook" (Davies xiii). The WCG held an annual conference attended by 1,000 delegates and in 1913 the Woolfs went to the conference in Newcastle. In her "Introductory Letter" to *Life As We Have Known It* ("MEMORIES OF A WORKING WOMEN'S GUILD") Woolf describes her attendance at a Guild conference. Leonard Woolf wrote many pamphlets about the Cooperative Movement and published *Co-operation and the Future of Industry* in 1919 (see Luedeking and Edmonds Appendix 1). From 1917 to 1921, Woolf ran monthly meetings of the Guild in her home, HOGARTH HOUSE, for which she arranged speakers.

Women's Suffrage See SUFFRAGE.

Woolf, Bella Sidney (1877–1960) The eldest child of Sidney and Marie Woolf, Bella was emotionally Leonard WOOLF's closest sibling. A children's book writer, she encouraged Leonard to send articles to the *Jewish Chronicle.* In 1907 she visited Leonard in Ceylon and there met Robert Lock (1879–1915), whom she married in 1910. In 1921 she married Wilfrid Thomas Southorn (1879–1957), a colonial administrator who was colonial secretary of Hong Kong and later governor of Gambia.

There seems to be something of the relationship between Leonard and Bella in that between Ralph DENHAM and his sister Joan in Woolf's *NIGHT AND DAY.* In a letter to Leonard in 1901, Bella wrote, "I have hours & days when like you I feel I *must* find the key to the door, that I'm consoling myself with false hopes & buoying myself up with vain theories" (Spotts 16–17). Leonard confided most in her, and in her letters to him while he was in Ceylon she discussed marriage, writing in 1909 that "women stand to lose so much by marriage nowadays, at least women with brains, that it takes a great deal for them to go in for it" (Spotts 148).

Bella was shocked when she read a draft of Leonard's novel *THE WISE VIRGINS* in 1913, writing a nine-page critique in which she condemned it as an unfair attack on their family (Spotts 195). Like her brother Edgar, she was also hurt many years later by his *Principia Politica,* particularly by Leonard's description of his relationship with their mother (Spotts 511). In the same letter she told Leonard that she had noted "the contempt Virginia had for us" when she read *A WRITER'S DIARY,* but Leonard pointed out in his reply to her that she had completely misread the passage she referred to (D4 306). Happily for Bella she never read Woolf's 1933 letter to Stella BENSON (a novelist who was living in China) in which she said, "I should be desperate if I lived in a wilderness of Bellas—she sends home photographs of herself opening golf clubs from which I get my only idea of English life in China" (CS 321).

Woolf Family Leonard WOOLF's parents were Solomon Rees Sydney ("Sidney") Woolf (1844–92), the son of a prosperous shop-owning family in London, and Marie Bathilde de Jongh (1850–1939), born in Amsterdam, the daughter of a rich diamond merchant. Sidney was called to the bar in 1860 and became a barrister in 1864, building up one of the leading practices in bankruptcy law in the City of London. In 1890 he became a Queen's Counsel. His premature death at the age of 48 considerably reduced the family's circumstances. The Woolfs were married in 1872 (Marie was the widow of Zacharias W. A. Goldstücker) and had ten children. Sidney John died in 1878 aged three months.

Arnold Herbert Sidney (1879–1949) became head of the family upon his father's death. He started work on the stock exchange at the age of sixteen. Bella Sidney WOOLF (1877–1960) was emotionally closest to Leonard. Cecil Nathan Sidney (1887–1917) won a fellowship in history to Trinity College, Cambridge, and was considered one of the most promising scholars of his generation. He was killed by a shell in World War I at the Battle of Cambrai in France. His brother Philip Sidney (1889–1962), who had joined the same regiment, was wounded by the same shell.

Philip failed to pass the entrance exam for Trinity and also failed to get a job he wanted as an interpreter with the Foreign Office, and before the war he began to study painting. He was an estate manager from 1922 to 1952 and married Marjorie Lowndes ("Babs") in 1922. After the war Philip brought some poems of Cecil's to Leonard and Woolf for the HOGARTH PRESS to publish. Philip helped set the type for the privately printed edition of *Poems* by C. N.

Sidney Woolf (1918), a task that proved therapeutic for him. Woolf commented on the poems in her DIARY, "They're not good; they show the Woolf tendency to denunciation without the vigour of my particular Woolf" (D1 124). After his wife's suicide, Philip lived with his sister Bella, and after her death in 1960 he too killed himself. One of his three children, Cecil, assisted Leonard in researching family history for his autobiography and has continued the tradition of the Hogarth Press by establishing Cecil Woolf Publishers in London, where he and his wife, the biographer Jean Moorcroft Wilson, work at the same table on which the first Hogarth press stood (MacWeeney np).

Two of Leonard's sisters were active in the SUFFRAGE movement: Clara Henrietta Sidney (1885–1934) was a volunteer nurse during World War I and in the early 1920s worked at the New York Public Library, where she met her husband, George Walker, an American journalist; Flora Sidney (1886–1975) married an uninspiring schoolmaster, George Sturgeon, and traveled widely after his death.

Harold Benjamin Sidney (1882–1967), whom Woolf found the most lively of Leonard's siblings (D5 103), married Alice Bilson in 1913 and was extremely successful on the stock exchange; his second wife was Muriel Steedman. Lastly, Edgar Sidney (1883–1981), whom, with his wife Sylvia, Woolf found gloomy and miserable, became a partner in his brother Herbert's firm after World War I. Although Leonard did not identify the sender, Edgar wrote him what Leonard calls in his autobiography "the bitterest letter which I have ever received," complaining that in his book *Principia Politica* Leonard had gone out of his way "to disparage & hold up to ridicule our family." The letter continued by saying that as a boy Leonard had been mean and a bully; "Having always been the lickspittle of greater intellects, you suffer from the deformity of the little man" (Spotts 493). Toward the end of Leonard's life, the brothers reconciled. Edgar's second wife was Zosia Norton.

Woolf certainly found her husband's family very different from her own; they did not move in the same circles. She wrote rather wickedly to Vita SACKVILLE-WEST in 1926 of a visit to Herbert and his wife Freda that she "promptly fell in love, not with him or her, but with being a stockbroker, with never having read a book . . . with not having heard of Roger [FRY], or Clive [BELL], or Duncan [GRANT], or Lytton [STRACHEY]" (L3 243). She always found her mother-in-law childish and fretted in her DIARY often about the two-hour teas she and Leonard were obliged to attend with her. "These reunions are rather like shows of old clothes," she wrote of the gathering to celebrate Mrs. Woolf's eighty-eighth birthday. Mrs. Woolf hinted that she felt her son Leonard did not pay her as much attention as his brothers because his wife took him away from the family. Despite her frequent exasperation with "Lady" (as all her children but Leonard called their mother), Woolf wrote on her death that she had "a regret for that spirited old lady, whom it was such a bore to visit" (D5 223) and remembered that "sometimes tho' she made me feel the daughter emotion" (D5 224).

Woolf, Leonard Sidney (1880–1969) Woolf's husband was educated at St. Paul's School and Trinity College, Cambridge, to which he went on a scholarship in 1899. At Trinity Leonard made friends to whom he would always remain close in varying degrees, including Lytton STRACHEY, John Maynard KEYNES, Desmond MACCARTHY, Clive BELL, E. M. FORSTER and Saxon SYDNEY-TURNER. At Cambridge he also became friends with Thoby STEPHEN, in whose rooms he first met Vanessa BELL and Woolf in 1901. Like many of his circle, Leonard was profoundly influenced by the philosopher G. E. MOORE. Leonard was the first Jew to be elected to the APOSTLES.

Having achieved a lower class degree than he had hoped for, Leonard was uncertain what to do on graduating from Cambridge in 1904. He remarked to Lytton Strachey that it was unlikely the parents of private schoolboys in England would wish them to be taught by an atheistic Jew (Spotts 10). To his dismay, he got a job in the Colonial Civil Service, rather than the Home branch, and was posted to Ceylon (Sri Lanka) in 1904, where he remained for seven years.

Leonard was a successful colonial administrator and quickly rose in the hierarchy to run a district of his own, Hambantota province. *Growing* (1961), the second volume of his autobiography, is devoted to the years he spent in Ceylon. He gradually began to hate imperialism, and he was scathing in his letters about the white colonialists he encountered in Ceylon. He came to admire the indigenous people, however, teaching himself Sinhalese and Tamil. His first novel, *THE VILLAGE IN THE JUNGLE* (1913), is told entirely from the point of view of the Sinhalese characters, and writing it on his return on leave in 1911 helped Leonard determine that he no longer wished to perpetuate the system he had so effectively administered during his tenure in Hambantota.

Having heard from Lytton Strachey that Clive Bell had married Vanessa and that Woolf herself had had proposals of marriage, Leonard—who had told Lytton how he had fallen in love with Vanessa the first time he met her at Cambridge—returned to England in 1911 thinking of Vanessa's sister as a possible wife. He found that England had changed radically in terms of social mores during the time he had been away, and he quickly renewed his acquaintance with Cambridge friends. He met Woolf again on July 3, 1911, when she came in with Duncan GRANT and Walter LAMB after Leonard had had dinner with Vanessa and Clive Bell at 46 GORDON SQUARE. At the end of the year, Woolf invited Leonard to share a house (38 BRUNSWICK SQUARE) with her brother Adrian STEPHEN, Duncan Grant and Maynard Keynes (L1 484–85).

Leonard, who had had no correspondence with Woolf while he was in Ceylon, seems to have fallen in love with her very quickly. Their correspondence during the first half of 1912 (Spotts 167–76; L1 484–97) details Woolf's uncertainty about her feelings and Leonard's passion for her. They were both working on their first novels and shared their manuscripts with one another. During these months Woolf also had marriage proposals from Walter Lamb and Sydney WATERLOW. In May, Leonard resigned from the Colonial Service as he could no longer extend his leave without explaining why he wished to; Woolf had told him she did not wish to marry him but to go on as they had been. At the end of May, she agreed to marry him and they were married on August 10. Much to his mother's sorrow, Leonard did not invite her, nor any other members of his family, to the marriage ceremony at St. Pancras Registry Office. Leonard and Woolf spent six weeks on honeymoon in France, Spain and Italy.

In his autobiography, Leonard says that he had been made a liberal by his experiences in Ceylon, and was converted to socialism by the poverty he saw in East London, where he worked briefly with Woolf's cousin Margaret (Marny) Vaughan in 1912. At this time he also became involved in the WOMEN'S COOPERATIVE GUILD through Woolf's friend Margaret Llewelyn DAVIES, who was secretary of the Guild, and began to write for the *Co-Operative News.* In October 1912 Leonard began work as secretary to the second POST-IMPRESSIONIST exhibition at the Grafton Galleries.

At the end of 1912, Woolf began to feel unwell, complaining of severe headaches, and Leonard began keeping a daily record of her physical state. He also asked Vanessa her opinion as to whether Woolf should have children. There had been a cooling in the relationship between the sisters in 1912 owing to various broken confidences about marriage proposals and affairs and, according to Vanessa's biographer, "the breach was never wholly repaired" (Spalding 130), yet she offered her advice to Leonard, writing that she felt it would be unwise for Woolf to have children (Spotts 181–82). Before he and Woolf were married, Leonard had consulted the Stephen family doctor, Sir George SAVAGE, about her. In January 1913, he again saw Savage, who told him he thought it would be good for Woolf to have a child. Leonard also consulted several others on the same question: Dr. Maurice CRAIG (on January 16), who thought it would be too risky; Jean THOMAS, the next day, who agreed with Craig; Dr. Maurice WRIGHT, on January 22, who gave the same opinion as Savage, whom Leonard saw the next day; and, finally, Dr. T. B. HYSLOP, who advised Leonard to put off the decision for eighteen months. Leonard decided that Woolf should not have children. In April 1913, Woolf wrote to Violet DICKINSON, "We aren't going to have a baby, but we want to have one" (L2 73). Fourteen years later she wrote to Ethel SANDS that she was "always angry with myself for not having forced Leonard to take the risk in spite of doctors" (L3 329).

With the manuscript of *THE VOYAGE OUT* delivered to Gerald DUCKWORTH's publishing house, Woolf left in March 1913 with Leonard for the north of England where he was to do research on the Cooperative Movement (work that would draw him to the attention of Beatrice and Sidney WEBB and lead to his joining the Fabian Society). In June they attended the Women's Cooperative Guild Congress in Newcastle. On their return to London, Woolf was increasingly unwell and went to Jean Thomas's nursing home for two weeks at the end of July. Leonard was by now embarked on the political writing that he would continue throughout his long life and also at work on his second (and last) novel, *THE WISE VIRGINS,* which he had begun in Spain on his honeymoon. That book was published in 1914, the same year in which he published two pamphlets, *Control of Industry by Co-Operators and Trade Unionists* and *Education and the Co-Operative Movement.* Woolf had helped him with research for these pamphlets while she convalesced at ASHEHAM HOUSE, but in September 1913, in London, she took an overdose of Veronal. She was saved from death by Maynard Keynes's brother Geoffrey KEYNES, who was living at the top of 38 Brunswick Square while he was House Surgeon at St. Bartholemew's Hospital (Geoffrey Keynes 115–16). Leonard took Woolf, with two nurses, to her half-brother George DUCKWORTH's house, Dalingridge Place in Sussex, where they stayed until November when Woolf was judged well enough to return to Asheham.

Apart from the issue of her psychological condition, there is probably no aspect of Woolf's biography more argued about than her relationship with Leonard. Interpretations range from the "without Leonard there would have been no Virginia" extreme to the "Leonard was a Victorian patriarch jealous of his wife's success" school of thought at the other extreme. Cynthia Ozick suggests that Leonard was duped into being a nurse for Woolf (35); certainly he was not told the degree of her past breakdowns before their marriage by either Vanessa or Adrian STEPHEN. Jane Marcus calls Woolf's suicide notes to Leonard "the work of a great artist and a good generous woman, following the advice of her doctor to 'reassure Leonard' and absolve him of any guilt"

(*Art* 161). The *VIRGINIA WOOLF MISCELLANY,* for example, has since about 1979 published many letters and articles arguing over questions such as exactly when Leonard consulted a particular doctor. Apart from the many biographies of Woolf, works by Jane Marcus, Roger Poole, Louise DeSalvo, Susan Kenney and Ellen Rogat have all discussed Leonard's role in Woolf's life.

These arguments extend also to the issue of the Woolfs' working relationship. Josephine O'Brien Schaefer has compared Leonard's *QUACK, QUACK*! (1931) and Woolf's *THREE GUINEAS* (1938) and concluded they should be "read together" (VWM 7: 2–3). One of Leonard's biographers, Selma Meyerowitz, argues against Elaine Showalter's contention in *A Literature of Their Own* that the Woolfs' marriage was "destructive" and that Leonard saw his wife's breakdowns as examples of female hysteria, and stresses their intellectual collaboration (VWM 11: 2–3). Laura Moss Gottlieb, on the other hand, argues in "The War Between the Woolfs" that Leonard's edited volume *The Intelligent Man's Way to Prevent War* (1933) should be read as a masculine argument against *Three Guineas.* Wayne K. Chapman and Janet M. Manson have argued against Gottlieb that there is plenty of evidence for the Woolfs' close collaboration on political projects ("Carte"). Many feminist critics—for example Naomi Black, Berenice Carroll and Jane Marcus—have argued persuasively against Leonard's characterization of Woolf in his autobiography as "the least political animal that ever lived." Marcus suggests that Woolf was a more radical political thinker than Leonard and that this led to editorial bias on his part, causing him "to leave out, for example, the fact that she had written some of her essays for the *Daily Worker* and, in his selection of texts for the [*COLLECTED ESSAYS*], to remove some of her views altogether" (*Art* 117). As an example, Marcus cites Woolf's introduction to *Life as We Have Known It,* "MEMORIES OF A WORKING WOMEN'S GUILD," which Leonard printed in an unrevised, first-draft version in *Collected Essays.* Marcus also cites "PROFESSIONS FOR WOMEN," which "exists in the [BERG COLLECTION] in a version three times as long and as strong as the one Leonard Woolf printed in [*THE DEATH OF THE MOTH*] and *Collected Essays*" (Marcus, *Art* 137).

Whatever one may decide among the conflicting and contrasting interpretations of the biographical record, Leonard was Woolf's most intimate and constant companion from their marriage until her death in 1941. He was invariably the first reader of her manuscripts, and she, in turn, read and encouraged his work (of *Empire and Commerce in Africa* [1920], for example, she wrote "I'm reading it for the second time—to me it seems superb" [L2 413]). In 1915 Woolf was very supportive of Leonard's research on international organizations, done at the invitation of Beatrice Webb for a fee of £100, which eventually became his most influential book, *International Government* (1916). This book became an important part of the foundation of the League of Nations; "by relying on it, the British delegates at Versailles [at the end of World War I] ensured that the League (and later the United Nations) would foster cultural and economic co-operation rather than limit itself only to the arbitration of disputes" (Luedeking and Edmonds vii).

In 1915 the Woolfs moved to HOGARTH HOUSE, Richmond, and made plans to buy a printing press. Leonard joined the Union of Democratic Control and published *The Control of Industry by the People* and *Co-Operation and the War,* two more pamphlets for the Women's Cooperative Guild. Woolf's *The Voyage Out* was published in this year, two years after it had been accepted by Duckworth's. Leonard, whose political influence and acumen have been somewhat underrated (though this is beginning to change as scholars reread his works), was settling into what would prove to be a long career as a journalist, publisher, editor, and, after World War I, an advisor to the Labour Party (see Duncan Wilson, *Leonard Woolf, A Political Biography*). "Today I am the wife of an Editor," Woolf wrote when Leonard was appointed editor of the *International Review* in 1918 (D1 190). A few years later, when Leonard was literary editor of the *NATION,* Woolf revised her opinion of her status: "Am I not sitting waiting for L. to 'come back from the office' like other wives. It annoys me to be like other wives" (D2 241).

Rejected for military service in 1916 because of the tremor in his hands he had all his life, Leonard joined the editorial board of the journal *War and Peace,* and he published *International Government* and another pamphlet for the Women's Cooperative Guild, *Taxation.* The following year, Woolf and Leonard established the HOGARTH PRESS, inaugurating it by publishing *TWO STORIES,* Leonard's "THREE JEWS" and Woolf's "THE MARK ON THE WALL." They began setting up the type for their next publication, Katherine MANSFIELD's *Prelude,* but this was interrupted to set the *Poems* (1918) of Leonard's brother Cecil, who had been killed in France. In October, Woolf noted that, "At this moment, L. is bringing the 17 Club into existence" (D1 57). The 1917 CLUB was established as a meeting place for people with radical politics. Leonard's final publication this year was *The Future of Constantinople.*

Among Woolf's first comments in her diary upon finishing a manuscript are usually those recording Leonard's reaction. In 1919, he found the "philosophy" of *NIGHT AND DAY* "very melancholy" (D1 259), and he commented in 1922 that the characters of *JACOB'S ROOM* were all ghosts. *TO THE LIGHTHOUSE* he found "a masterpiece." "He calls it entirely new 'a psychological poem' . . . An improvement upon Dalloway: more interesting" (D2 123). Although he found *ORLANDO* "very original" (D3 185), Woolf thought he found her affair with Vita SACKVILLE-WEST "rather a bore . . . but not enough to worry him" (D3 117). Of their planned trip to France in 1928, Woolf wrote to Vita, "Leonard says he can't come. Like an angel he says, but of course go with Vita. Then somehow conveys without a word the fact of his intolerable loneliness without me—" (L3 520). Leonard wrote to her, "I hope you wont make a habit of deserting me" (Spotts 234).

Leonard, Woolf said, gave her the "maternal protection" she so often sought from women and which she received from Vanessa and, clumsily, from Vita (D3 52). In the 1930s, their marriage seems to have been especially happy: "I dont think we've ever been so happy, what with one thing & another. And so intimate, & so completely entire, I mean L. & I. If it could only last like this another 50 years—life like this is wholly satisfactory. To me anyhow" (D4 130). They argued, as do any two people living together, about the mundanities of life. Woolf did not share Leonard's devotion to the garden at MONK'S HOUSE, which they had bought in 1919 and which she loved dearly, but always with the understanding that London, with its parties, was home too. Leonard, whom no one has ever accused of not being a typical heterosexual man, did not like Woolf to wear makeup and frowned on her spending money on clothes: "Never mind," she wrote. "I adore Leonard" (D2 203).

Leonard was appointed secretary to the Labour Party Advisory Committee on International Questions in 1918, the year he published *After the War* and *A Durable Settlement after the War by Means of a League of Nations.* In 1920 he stood for Parliament as the candidate of the Seven Universities Democratic Association and became political editor of the *Nation.* As well as publishing radical political writers at the Hogarth Press, Leonard himself continued to write on imperialism. *Mandates and Empire, Economic Imperialism* and *Empire and Commerce in Africa* all appeared in 1920. When he was appointed secretary to the Labour Party Advisory Committee on Imperial Questions in 1924, he urged Sidney Webb (at the time Secretary of State for Colonial Affairs) to implement the promises made by the Labour government to fund education and roads for the indigenous peoples of Kenya.

The Hogarth Press continued to flourish, and in 1921, Leonard and Woolf hand-set his *STORIES OF THE EAST,* which proved to be a very popular title. In the years following the Woolfs' move to TAVISTOCK SQUARE in 1924, Leonard published *Fear and Politics: A Debate at the Zoo* (1925), *Hunting the Highbrow* (1927), *The Way of Peace* (1928) and *Imperialism and Civilization* (1928) and helped to establish the *Political Quarterly* in 1929.

When she showed Leonard the manuscript of *THE WAVES* in 1931, Woolf was nervous; "For one thing he will be honest" (D4 35–6). He assured her once again " 'It is a masterpiece' . . . 'And the best of your books' " (D4 36). Woolf found Leonard an impersonal and objective reader, one whom she could trust usually to tell her honestly what he thought. She commented on his manner as a critic in 1940 after showing him the first half of *ROGER FRY: A BIOGRAPHY,* when he gave her a "very severe lecture," which she found a "curious example of L. at his most rational & impersonal." Recalling the image of Mr. RAMSAY as a "beak of brass," she said Leonard's lecture "was like being pecked by a very hard strong beak" (D5 271).

In the late 1930s their political concerns seemed to come closer than ever together. Leonard published the first volume of *After the Deluge* and *Quack, Quack!* in 1931. In 1936 he helped set up the Association for Intellectual Liberty and wrote *The League and Abyssinia.* Woolf, thinking of her "Anti fascist pamphlet" in 1935, discussed her ideas with Leonard: "He was extremely reasonable & adorable, & told me I should have to take account of the economic question. His specialised knowledge is of course an immense gain, if I could use it & stand away: I mean in all writing its the person's own edge that counts" (D4 282). When he read *Three Guineas* in 1938, Leonard thought it "an extremely clear analysis" and gravely approved (D5 127), but Woolf wrote that she "didnt get so much praise from L. as I hoped" (D5 133). In his introduction to volume 5 of *The Letters of Virginia Woolf,* Nigel NICOLSON points out that Leonard does not mention *Three Guineas* in his autobiography. He had found *THE YEARS* "extraordinarily good: very strange; very interesting; very sad" (D5 30). Of Leonard's second volume of *After the Deluge,* Woolf wrote that it was "very good; full; moulded; subtle" (D5 284). In the mid-1930s Leonard wrote to his nephew Julian BELL, who was in China, discussing the European political situation in detail (Spotts 402–07, 409–11).

Woolf referred to Leonard as her "inviolable centre" (D5 183). In 1939 they moved to MECKLENBURGH SQUARE and Leonard published his play about fascism, *The Hotel,* and *Barbarians at the Gate* for the Left Book Club. They went to visit Sigmund FREUD in Hampstead. In 1914 Leonard had been one of the earliest readers of Freud in England, reviewing *The Psychopathology of Everyday Life* for the *New Weekly* and the *NEW STATESMAN,* and the Hogarth Press had published Freud's works in James STRACHEY's translation. With the outbreak of World War II, Leonard stored gasoline in the garage at Monk's House for their suicide in the case of a Nazi invasion (D5 284).

He published *The War for Peace* and *The Future of International Government* in 1940, believing more than ever in the League of Nations concept as the only way to ensure future peace. He had by this time become disgusted with the Labour Party's failures to live up to its promises and its dismal handling of foreign policy.

On March 28, 1941, Leonard found one of two suicide notes Woolf had written him in which she wrote that she owed all the happiness of her life to him (L6 481). He later found another note on her writing table in the hut in the garden in which she worked at Monk's House (the dating of these notes and the one she wrote to Vanessa is discussed in L6 Appendix A, and in Roger Poole, *Unknown,* which both question the dating given in QB2 and LW2). Woolf's body was found three weeks later in the river Ouse. Leonard attended her cremation in Brighton alone and buried her ashes at the foot of one of the two elms they had named Leonard and Virginia in the Monk's House garden.

After Woolf's death, Leonard found that he was the addressee of myriad inquiries about her and he received many visitors who were studying Woolf's life and work. He edited a collection of Woolf's essays, *The Death of the Moth and other Essays,* in 1942, and in 1944 edited *A HAUNTED HOUSE AND OTHER SHORT STORIES.* Another collection of essays selected by Leonard, *THE MOMENT AND OTHER ESSAYS,* appeared in 1947, and in 1950 he prepared a further selection, *THE CAPTAIN'S DEATH BED AND OTHER ESSAYS.* In 1953 he edited selections from Woolf's diary for publication as *A WRITER'S DIARY,* and in 1956 he edited with James Strachey a selection of letters between Woolf and Lytton Strachey. The critical climate in 1950s England was quite hostile to Bloomsbury and Leonard was discomfited by the reception of these books. He remained concerned with his wife's reputation and was irritated in 1955 when Aileen Pippett quoted letters from Woolf to Vita Sackville-West in her biography of Woolf, *The Moth and the Star,* without his permission. As the book was already in proofs when he saw it, Leonard decided to allow publication to go ahead in the United States but prevented an English edition.

Finding that no library in England was interested in Woolf's papers, Leonard arranged for most of them to go to the New York Public Library's BERG COLLECTION. He told his brother Philip that he had been most impressed by the research of an American student, Mary Lyon, on Woolf (see *BOOKS AND PORTRAITS*) and that if Woolf's papers went to Cambridge or Oxford "they would be stuffed away somewhere and no one would ever look at them again except that one would be shown from time to time to the public under a glass case" (Spotts 500). With the assistance of Lyon and B. J. Kirkpatrick, Leonard had gathered a collection of Woolf's essays published as *GRANITE & RAINBOW* in 1958. In 1964, Leonard wrote to Quentin BELL that several people had asked him to authorize a biography of Woolf. Leonard, always concerned about the reputation of Bloomsbury in general and his wife in particular, asked Quentin to consider writing her biography, and pointed out that he and his sister Angelica GARNETT would become executors of Woolf's literary estate upon Leonard's death.

After his *Principia Politica* (1953) failed to excite much interest, Leonard devoted the remainder of his life to autobiography. He visited Ceylon again in 1960 and was very well received. That year the first volume of his autobiography, *Sowing,* was published. The second volume, *Growing,* was published in 1961, and in 1963 the *Ceylon Historical Journal* published the official diaries Leonard had kept as a colonial civil servant more than fifty years before; the Hogarth Press issued them as a book also that year. He edited the four volumes of Woolf's *Collected Essays* (1966–67) and brought out an edition of her children's story *NURSE LUGTON'S GOLDEN THIMBLE,* with pictures by Duncan Grant, in 1966. The third and fourth volumes of his autobiography, *BEGINNING AGAIN* (1964) and *DOWNHILL ALL THE WAY* (1967), followed, and finally, in 1969, the year Leonard died at Monk's House (after a day showing visitors around his garden), the final installment, *THE JOURNEY NOT THE ARRIVAL MATTERS,* was published by the press he and Woolf had begun on their dining table fifty years earlier.

Woolf Studies Annual Founded in 1994 and published by Pace University Press at the beginning of each year, the *Annual* includes long articles on Woolf and related topics as well as book reviews. The first issue includes a previously unpublished letter from Woolf to St. John Hutchinson.

Woolf, (Adeline) Virginia (née Stephen) (1882–1941) Adeline Virginia Stephen was born at Sir Leslie and Julia Prinsep STEPHEN's home, 22 HYDE PARK GATE, on January 25, 1882. Woolf's father and his first wife, Harriet Marian ("Minny") THACKERAY, had had one daughter, Laura STEPHEN, before Minny's death in 1875, and when Leslie married Julia in 1878, she brought with her three children from her marriage to Herbert DUCKWORTH (who had died in 1870): George, Gerald and Stella DUCKWORTH. Leslie and Julia's first child, Vanessa [BELL], was born in 1879; their second, Thoby STEPHEN, in 1880; and their last, Adrian STEPHEN, in 1883. In her memoir "A SKETCH OF THE PAST," Woolf described the family she was born into as not rich but well-to-do, and inhabiting a "very communicative, literate, letter writing, visiting, articulate, late nineteenth-century world" (MOB 65).

The Hogarth Press

Leonard Woolf

40-42 William IV Street, London, W.C.2

Telephone: Temple Bar 5549 Cables: Hogarth, London

Home & van Thal Ltd
36 Gt Russell Street, WC1
9/7/47

Dear Sir,

I have to thank you for your letter of 4 July. I am not sure that I can at the moment find you a suitable letter, but I will have a look, and if I do I will let you know.

Yours truly

From LEONARD WOOLF
Monk's House, Rodmell, Lewes, Sussex *Tel.: Lewes* 385

11.11.53

Herbert van Thal Esq.,
Arthur Barker Ltd,
30, Museum Street,
London, W.C.1.

Dear Mr. van Thal,

Many thanks for your letter of November 2nd. I will see whether I can find you a suitable letter and let you know again.

Yours sincerely,

From LEONARD WOOLF
Monk's House, Rodmell, Lewes, Sussex *Tel.: Lewes* 385

H van Thal Esq
Arthur Barker Ltd
30 Museum Street, WC1
13 November, 1953

Dear Mr van Thal,

With mefernce to my previous letter, I now enclose a letter of Virginia Woolf which, perhaps, might do for the anthology. It was written to an old friend of hers, Violet Dickinson, who is no longer alive.

Yours sincerely

Three letters from Leonard Woolf to Herbert van Thal. Courtesy of Linda J. Langham.
After Woolf's death in 1941, Leonard for the rest of his life responded to many requests about her and her work, always concerned with preserving her reputation and overseeing the posthumous publication of many of her essays.

A Note on Biographies

The representation of Woolf's life has been a contested field since the publication in 1973 of her nephew Quentin BELL's two-volume biography, which he was asked to write by Leonard WOOLF. An earlier biography by Aileen Pippett, *The Moth and the Star,* published in the United States in 1955, had the support of Vita SACKVILLE-WEST, who gave Pippett letters from Woolf, but as Leonard was incensed when Pippett quoted from the letters without his permission, he prevented the book from being published in England. Since the early 1970s several biographies or biographical studies of Woolf have been published, in many cases becoming the subjects of fierce controversies over issues such as the nature and effects of Woolf's mental instability, the extent and effects of the sexual abuse she suffered, the extent and seriousness of her political involvements and feminist thought, and the uses and abuses of various approaches to the writing of biography. These studies include books by Alma Bond, Thomas Caramagno, Louise DeSalvo, Lyndall Gordon, Shirley Panken, Roger Poole and Phyllis Rose, as well as articles by Blanche Wiesen Cook, Susan M. Kenney, Susan M. and Edwin J. Kenney, Jane Marcus, Cynthia Ozick and Ellen Hawkes Rogat. In addition to books on Woolf herself, there have also appeared studies such as Stephen Trombley's on Woolf's doctors, and Jane Dunn's and Diane Filby Gillespie's books on the relationship between Woolf and her sister Vanessa Bell. John Mepham's *Virginia Woolf: A Literary Life* was published in 1991, and in 1994 a new full-scale biography, *Virginia Woolf* by James King, was published in England. Two more biographical works on Woolf are in preparation by the English scholars Hermione Lee and Julia Briggs.

This proliferation of biographies is accounted for by Woolf's own thinking about the nature of modern biography. In a review of Harold NICOLSON's *Some People* for the *New York Herald Tribune* in 1927 ("The New Biography" CE4 229–35) that she used as an occasion to expound thoughts on biography she had begun researching that summer (RN 84), Woolf remarked that the modern, post-Lytton STRACHEY biographer had "ceased to be the chronicler; he has become an artist" (CE4 231). Strachey had exploded the conventions of Victorian biography when he published the four essays that make up ***EMINENT VICTORIANS*** in 1918. Woolf wrote in "The New Biography" that "the life which is increasingly real to us is the fictitious life" (CE4 234) and explained that the modern biographer is "always being stimulated to use the novelist's art of arrangement, suggestion, dramatic effect to expound the private life" (CE4 234). There is a danger in bringing together the different truths of "life" and of "fiction," but the danger must be risked because, Woolf argues, modern biography is not simply about the chronology of a person's life but also in a profound sense tells the story of the biographer's values and the times in which the biography is written.

By the 1920s, as Woolf's extensive writing on biography demonstrates, the interpretation of a "fact" in a written life was understood as an ideological issue, and in recent years the arguments around this issue have intensified and grown more complicated rather than diminishing. Carolyn Heilbrun has written that in "choosing among biographers and biographies, we choose among counterfeit integrations" (*Writing* 50); the best approach to Woolf's biography would be to compare several of those "counterfeit integrations."

In the year Woolf was born her father became editor of the ***DICTIONARY OF NATIONAL BIOGRAPHY,*** a grueling job he would perform until 1891. That year, when Woolf was nine, the Stephen children began their family newspaper, the ***HYDE PARK GATE NEWS,*** which Woolf would wait for her mother to read with trembling anticipation. Julia's approval, Woolf later wrote, made her feel like a violin being played. Woolf's childhood was in many ways typical of an upper-middle-class late Victorian's, but her home was often filled with the noted artists and writers of the time, guests of her father and mother. Unlike the Strachey daughters and those of other intellectuals in the Stephens' circle, Woolf and Vanessa were not sent to school but were educated at home, initially by their mother and later, in Woolf's case, by tutors. In a 1932 essay about her father for *The Times,* Woolf recalled him allowing her as a "girl of fifteen the free

"The Family" from Stella Duckworth Hills's album of photographs. Courtesy Henry W. and Albert A. Berg Collection, The New York Public Library, Astor, Lenox and Tilden Foundations.
Back row: Gerald Duckworth, Woolf, Thoby Stephen, Vanessa Bell, George Duckworth; Seated: Adrian Stephen, Julia Prinsep Stephen, Leslie Stephen.

run of a large and unexpurgated library" (CE4 79), a form of education that was quite unusual for a young woman of the time.

Each summer, the family would go to ST. IVES in Cornwall, where the days would be spent taking long walks, reading, and playing cricket in the garden. In "A Sketch of the Past," Woolf remembered these times as idyllic, but they came to an abrupt end in 1895 when Julia Stephen died. Woolf was thirteen and had by then already been sexually abused by her half-brothers, incest that would continue into her later teenage years. Woolf's first nervous breakdown occurred following her mother's death (QB1 45). Leslie Stephen became increasingly self-pitying after Julia's death, as a reading of his *MAUSOLEUM BOOK* attests. He relied heavily on Stella Duckworth to play the maternal role in the family, delaying her marriage to John Waller ("Jack") HILLS through his possessiveness. Shortly before their marriage in 1897, Woolf was made to accompany Stella and Jack to Bognor Regis, a chaperone duty she was very upset about, as she wrote in the diary she began keeping that year (PA 27–35). By this time, Laura Stephen had been institutionalized, but Stella continued to visit her.

Stella's happiness with Jack was short-lived: she died in 1897, just three months after her marriage. This time it was Vanessa who was thrust into the maternal role by Leslie, but she refused it. She and Woolf had been growing closer, especially since their brothers had gone to school, and their relationship now began to deepen because both were committed to escaping the constraints of Victorian womanhood and pursuing their respective arts of painting and writing. Woolf began studying Greek, first at King's College in Kensington, and later with Clara PATER. Dr. George SAVAGE, however, in 1897 recommended that Woolf create a garden to divert her from the intellectual work that he believed was disturbing her mentally. In 1899, Thoby Stephen went up to Trinity College, Cambridge, where he met Clive BELL, Lytton Strachey, Saxon SYDNEY-TURNER and Leonard Woolf.

Woolf and Vanessa visited their brother at Trinity several times. Once, Vanessa caught a glimpse of Roger FRY and his wife, but did not meet him. Woolf's social circle at this point did not extend much beyond her many VAUGHAN and FISHER cousins and other family friends, but in 1902, the year she began taking Greek lessons with Janet CASE, Woolf began an intimate friendship with Violet DICKINSON, who had been a friend of Stella's, that would last for many years. That year Adrian Stephen went up to Trinity College, joining his brother, who had another year remaining.

Leslie Stephen had become ill in 1900, and late in 1902 he was operated on by Sir Frederick Treves. The following year saw his gradual decline and on February 22, 1904 he died of cancer. A week later, the Stephen children and George Duckworth went to MANORBIER in South Wales for a month, and in April they went to Italy, where Violet Dickinson joined them. That May, Violet, Vanessa and Woolf traveled from Italy to Paris, where they were entertained by Clive Bell, who was ostensibly studying there. After returning to Hyde Park Gate, Woolf had another breakdown and was put under the care of Dr. Savage. She spent three months at Violet Dickinson's house, where she was also looked after by Nurse TRAILL. It was there that Woolf attempted suicide by throwing herself out of a window, as her brother Thoby had also tried to do in 1894 when he was recovering from influenza at school.

There is no generally accepted account of what caused Woolf's breakdowns; there is, however, a great deal of disagreement about not only the causes but also what to call those times when Woolf was unable to function normally. In his biography, Quentin Bell simply uses the terms "mad" and "madness" to describe Woolf's various periods of mental instability. His approach is challenged by Roger Poole *(Unknown)*, who argues that these terms obscure the probable causes of Woolf's breakdowns in her family situation and early experiences of death and sexual abuse. Kenney and Kenney criticize Bell for failing to distinguish carefully enough "between physical and mental illnesses" (166). Several critics and biographers have argued that the incest Woolf suffered and the premature loss of her parents, half-sister and brother, together with her extreme sensitivity later in her life to the critical reception of her writing, contributed to her breakdowns. Others have just as vigorously disputed such arguments. Recently, Caramagno has contested the Freudian bias of many of Woolf's biographers and argued that Woolf's symptoms and her own descriptions of her breakdowns support a view of Woolf as a manic-depressive whose condition had a physiological basis. He further argues that her art was Woolf's attempt to explore and understand her mood swings.

Her breakdowns were usually characterized by severe headaches, often leading to blackouts, and a complex relation to food which was exacerbated by treatment that frequently involved encouraging her to eat and drink. Woolf also reported having heard birds singing in Greek and Edward VII muttering foul language in the bushes. In his autobiography, Leonard Woolf writes that none of the many doctors they consulted during Woolf's life knew the cause or nature of her "disease" (LW2 51). He says that four times Woolf "passed across the border which divides what we call insanity from sanity" (LW2 51). Leonard's usual method of dealing with Woolf's breakdowns was to keep her away from people and from work, and to ensure that she drank milk and rested as much as possible. Apart from her breakdown of

1915, when Woolf turned against men in general and Leonard in particular, he was her primary caretaker until her death.

While Woolf was convalescing in 1904, Vanessa had decided to move her siblings out of Hyde Park Gate, and in October—to the alarm of their respectable relatives and such friends as Violet Dickinson—Woolf, Adrian, Thoby and Vanessa moved to 46 GORDON SQUARE in the unfashionable BLOOMSBURY district of London. Soon after the move, Woolf went to stay with her aunt Caroline Emelia STEPHEN, where she helped F. W. MAITLAND with his biography of Leslie Stephen. In December 1904, Woolf's first publication appeared, an unsigned review in the *GUARDIAN*.

The year 1905 was the beginning of a very different kind of life for Woolf. At the invitation of Mary SHEEPSHANKS, she began to teach literature at MORLEY COLLEGE and Thoby, wishing to keep in touch with the friends he had made at Cambridge, began holding "Thursday Evenings," open invitations to his friends. Woolf began to make the acquaintance of those figures who would soon be associated with the BLOOMSBURY GROUP. In March 1905, she and Adrian sailed together to Portugal, a trip that would provide Woolf with a setting for the opening of her first novel, *THE VOYAGE OUT*. By 1906, Woolf had settled into life as a writer and, for two years, a teacher, and Vanessa was developing her career as a painter, organizing the FRIDAY CLUB as a way of providing support for artists and a place for them to show their work. Clive Bell, who joined, had proposed to Vanessa in the summer of 1905, but she had turned him down.

From around 1906, the question of whom Woolf would marry was of great concern to her friends, but not to her. She wrote to Dickinson, "I wish everyone didn't tell me to marry. Is it crude human nature breaking out?" (L1 31). Vanessa's letters to her sister between 1904 and 1908 are increasingly concerned with Woolf's sleeping and eating but also frequently discuss contraception, "George's delinquencies," and what was to become of her "poor little monkey." In 1906, Vanessa teased Woolf about getting up "a flirtation in the train" that would lead to "some lady [getting] a written promise of marriage out of you . . . & then where will we be?" (Marler 37; and see Hussey, "Refractions").

In the early fall of 1906, Woolf went to Greece with Violet Dickinson and Vanessa and met up with her brothers there. The trip was marred by Vanessa's falling ill. On their return to London, Woolf found that Thoby, who had come home earlier, was himself seriously ill. Both he and Vanessa were sick in bed at Hyde Park Gate and Violet also was ill, unable to leave her house. On November 20, Thoby died of typhoid, and, not wanting to burden Violet, Woolf continued to send her daily letters reporting on his gaining strength for the next month (until Violet discovered the truth in a review of Maitland's biography of Leslie Stephen). Two days after Thoby's death, Vanessa agreed to marry Clive Bell.

By now Woolf was writing her work of "fancy and imagination," first called *MELYMBROSIA* and published in 1915 as *The Voyage Out*. Following the Bells' marriage, Woolf and Adrian began looking for a house and moved in April 1907 to 29 FITZROY SQUARE, where they restarted the "Thursday Evenings." The birth of Julian BELL in 1908 exacerbated Woolf's sense of isolation from Vanessa, and she began a flirtation with Clive Bell, to whom she was now showing pages of her novel, that would strain her relationship with Vanessa. The friendships between Lytton Strachey, Saxon Sydney-Turner and other young Cambridge men were now firm and Woolf had moved a great distance from her Victorian young womanhood. Older Cambridge APOSTLES such as Desmond MACCARTHY and E. M. FORSTER were also important friends. She traveled to the Richard WAGNER festival at Bayreuth with Adrian and Sydney-Turner in 1909, writing about the experience in *The Times*. She was now reviewing regularly. The Thursday Evening group had also been brought into the orbit of Lady Ottoline MORRELL. Woolf received a marriage proposal from Hilton YOUNG in 1909. In February 1909 Lytton Strachey had proposed, but both he and Woolf almost immediately realized neither was serious.

Woolf's participation in the DREADNOUGHT HOAX in 1910 confirmed her aunts' worst fears about her lifestyle and her inappropriate friends, but by now Woolf was secure enough not to worry. Roger Fry became part of the growing circle, and the first POST-IMPRESSIONIST exhibition in December 1910 established that circle's iconoclastic attitudes to culture and art. In 1910 also, Woolf became involved in the SUFFRAGE movement. A sign of her independence was her renting a house in 1911, which she named LITTLE TALLAND HOUSE after the house of her childhood summers. She began to have guests for weekends, making friends with Katherine COX and other NEO-PAGANS, as Woolf called the younger generation of Cambridge University friends gathered around Rupert BROOKE.

In April 1911, Woolf went to the assistance of Vanessa, who had had a miscarriage while traveling in Turkey with Clive Bell, Roger Fry and H. T. J. NORTON. This marked the beginning of Vanessa's affair with Fry and the gradual shifting of her relationship with Clive from wife to friend. Back in London in July, Woolf dropped by her sister's house after dinner one evening and met Leonard Woolf, who had returned days earlier from Ceylon, where he had been since 1904. Soon after this, Walter LAMB proposed to Woolf. She invited Leonard to come for the weekend to Little Talland House with Marjorie STRACHEY. In November, Woolf and Adrian moved from Fitzroy Square to 38 BRUNSWICK SQUARE, where they set up a shared house that for the time was extremely unusual. John Maynard KEYNES, Duncan GRANT and, after a few weeks, Leonard Woolf joined the Stephens in their house, continuing the settlement of Bloomsbury by radical thinkers who would greatly influence English culture in the early twentieth century.

After a brief courtship, Leonard resigned from the Colonial Service in May 1912, hoping that Woolf would agree to marry him, despite her having written that she felt no physical attraction for him (L1 496). She liked and wished to continue seeing Leonard but was very dubious about marriage. Their correspondence during the first half of 1912 (Spotts 167–76; L1 484–97) details both Woolf's uncertainty about her feelings and Leonard's passion for her. On May 29, however, Woolf made her decision and they were married on August 10.

Before he and Woolf were married, Leonard had consulted the Stephen family doctor, Sir George Savage, about her and whether they should have children. In January 1913, he again saw Savage, who told him he thought it would be good for Woolf to have a child. Leonard also consulted several others on the same question: Dr. Maurice CRAIG (on January 16), who thought it would be too risky; Jean THOMAS, the next day, who agreed with Craig; Dr. Maurice WRIGHT, on January 22, who gave the same opinion as Savage, whom Leonard saw the next day; and, finally, Dr. T. B. HYSLOP, who advised Leonard to put off the decision for eighteen months. Leonard, with Vanessa's endorsement (Spotts 181–82), decided that Woolf should not have children. In April 1913, Woolf wrote to Violet Dickinson, "We aren't going to have a baby, but we want to have one" (L2 73). Fourteen years later she wrote to Ethel SANDS that she was "always angry with myself for not having forced Leonard to take the risk in spite of doctors" (L3 329). In 1923 she wrote in her DIARY, "Never pretend that children, for instance, can be replaced by other things" (D2 221), and in 1926 the thought of her childlessness, she wrote, "rakes me wretched in the early hours" (D3 107). And yet, Woolf could also write that children were nothing compared to the thrill of artistic creation.

By the end of 1912 Woolf was being troubled by severe headaches. Leonard began work studying the Cooperative Movement and writing political articles. In March 1913, the manuscript of *The Voyage Out* was delivered to Gerald Duckworth who, on the recommendation of Edward GARNETT, accepted it for publication. That summer, increasingly depressed, Woolf was taken to see Dr. Savage, who recommended a rest cure at a nursing home run by Jean Thomas. In August, she and Leonard went for a few days to the PLOUGH INN, where they had spent part of their honeymoon, but Woolf became increasingly unwell and would not eat. Leonard, who had had little idea before his marriage of the seriousness of Woolf's breakdowns, sent for Katherine Cox to come and help look after her, and they returned together to London where, on September 9, having seen Drs. Henry HEAD and Maurice Wright earlier in the day, Woolf took an overdose of Veronal, a sedative. Her life was saved on this occasion by Geoffrey KEYNES.

Just before *The Voyage Out* was published in March 1915, Woolf again had a breakdown, refusing to see Leonard. The Woolfs spent the fall at ASHEHAM HOUSE, which Woolf had taken at the end of 1911. In London, they now lived at HOGARTH HOUSE, having moved there in early 1915. In 1917, the first printing press was delivered to Hogarth House and the HOGARTH PRESS began. Woolf was writing reviews and essays for a number of periodicals and was at work on her second novel, *NIGHT AND DAY*. Her life was fully occupied by writing fiction and journalism, by publishing, and by politics—she organized monthly meetings and speakers for the WOMEN'S COOPERATIVE GUILD and went frequently to the 1917 CLUB.

In 1919 the Woolfs bought MONK'S HOUSE in the village of Rodmell, Sussex, where they would spend most summers until Woolf's death in 1941. They lived in three different houses in London, moving from Hogarth House to 52 TAVISTOCK SQUARE in 1924, and in 1939 to 37 MECKLENBURGH SQUARE. After her first two novels were published by her half-brother Gerald, Woolf published all her work at the Hogarth Press, beginning in 1921 with *MONDAY OR TUESDAY*. A short piece, "THE MARK ON THE WALL," had been published in *TWO STORIES*, the Hogarth's first publication, and that "sketch," as Woolf called it, indicated the experimental direction her fiction was taking. As the 1920s began, Woolf had begun already to articulate her innovative vision of the future of fiction in short pieces such as those published in *Monday or Tuesday* and in essays such as "MODERN FICTION," first published in the *TIMES LITERARY SUPPLEMENT* in 1919 as "MODERN NOVELS."

By 1920 Woolf was a leading literary figure and critic, and when *JACOB'S ROOM* appeared in 1922, her reputation as an important MODERNIST writer began to widen. It was in 1922 that Woolf met Vita SACKVILLE-WEST, a well-known writer who was to become a central figure in Woolf's life. Their love affair began in 1923, and in 1926 Woolf wrote that it was "a spirited, creditable affair, I think, innocent (spiritually) & all gain, I think, rather a bore for Leonard but not enough to worry him" (D3 117). The women's love and later close friendship lasted throughout a decade of extraordinary creativity by both of them. From 1923 to 1933 Woolf wrote "MR. BENNETT AND MRS. BROWN," *MRS. DALLOWAY, TO THE LIGHTHOUSE, ORLANDO, A ROOM OF ONE'S OWN, THE WAVES, FLUSH* and many other articles and reviews. Her novels seemed to open out of one another, the vision of the next work often beginning to take shape as she finished writing one. Woolf consolidated her reputation in the 1920s as one of the world's leading novelists, as well as establishing herself as a theoretician of the novel. With the publication of *A Room of One's Own* in 1929, she also assured her place in the tradition of feminist thought going back to Mary WOLLSTONECRAFT.

Woolf began work on her visionary novel *THE WAVES* in 1929, influenced both by a story her sister had told her of giant moths flying into her house at CASSIS (where Vanessa spent the time she was not at CHARLESTON), and by her own mystical experiences at Monk's House in the summer of 1926. *The Waves* was published in 1931, and already by then Woolf was becoming more closely involved with a younger generation of writers and political activists. John LEHMANN, an assistant at the Hogarth Press who later became a co-director, introduced the Woolfs to a new group of writers, including Stephen SPENDER, W. H. AUDEN and Christopher ISHERWOOD. Woolf's "LETTER TO A YOUNG POET" (1932) and "THE LEANING TOWER" (1940) are examples of her intellectual engagement with these writers. As the political situation in Europe moved inexorably throughout the 1930s to its crisis in 1939, Woolf began to collect newspaper clippings about the relations between men and women, the institutions of men and the lives of women. These would form an important source of her most overtly political book, *THREE GUINEAS* (1938). By the mid-1930s, Woolf's affair with Sackville-West had cooled to friendship, and her attentions were focused, not always pleasurably, on the composer Ethel SMYTH, whom she had come to know in 1930 after Smyth wrote her a letter praising *A Room of One's Own*.

Leonard Woolf, established as an important political journalist, editor and adviser to the Labour Party, was Woolf's constant guard against what he considered dangerous stresses and excitements. He was the first reader of all her work and monitored her health closely throughout her life. The strain, however, of writing *THE YEARS* (1937) took an enormous toll and in 1936 Woolf came perilously close to another breakdown. The following year, Woolf found herself in the role of caretaker when her nephew Julian was killed in the SPANISH CIVIL WAR and Woolf spent many weeks at his mother Vanessa's side.

There has been as much speculation and disagreement about the nature of the Woolfs' marriage as about other aspects of Woolf's biography, despite the impossibility of any accurate assessment of what is necessarily unknowable. Most accept that their relationship quickly became a loving companionship centered around writing and that the sexual element of the marriage was short-lived. Woolf's diary provides ample evidence of her happiness with her "inviolable centre," as she referred to Leonard in 1938 (D5 183). In 1919 she wrote, "I daresay we're the happiest couple in England" (D1 318), and in 1937, "after 25 years" they could not "bear to be separate. . . . our marriage is so complete" (D5 115).

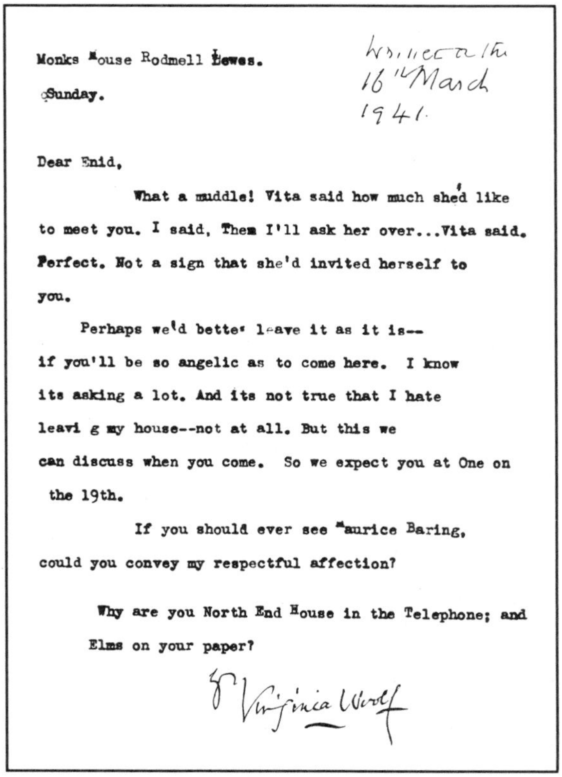
Written the 16th March 1941.

Monks House Rodmell Lewes.

Sunday.

Dear Enid,

What a muddle! Vita said how much she'd like to meet you. I said, Then I'll ask her over...Vita said, Perfect. Not a sign that she'd invited herself to you.

Perhaps we'd better leave it as it is-- if you'll be so angelic as to come here. I know its asking a lot. And its not true that I hate leavi g my house--not at all. But this we can discuss when you come. So we expect you at One on the 19th.

If you should ever see Maurice Baring, could you convey my respectful affection?

Why are you North End House in the Telephone; and Elms on your paper?

Virginia Woolf

Typed letter from Virginia Woolf to Enid Bagnold. Courtesy of Linda J. Langham.
See Volume 6 of The Letters of Virginia Woolf *(page 468), which corrects the date someone has written on the top right corner of the letter. Enid Bagnold (1889–1981) was a novelist and playwright and close friend of Desmond MacCarthy (CS 96).*

The 1930s were a time of great international turmoil, and in Woolf's life there were private sorrows also as Lytton Strachey and Roger Fry, as well as several other people she had known many years, died premature deaths. Her work on Fry's biography was grinding, and brought her little satisfaction. As World War II began, the Woolfs spent more and more time at Monk's House, moving there permanently after their house at Mecklenburgh Square was badly damaged by bombs. Woolf was at work in 1941 on the novel she called *POINTZ HALL,* but she did not live to see it published. On March 28, leaving notes for Leonard and for Vanessa saying she was certain she was "going mad again," Woolf drowned herself in the river OUSE (L6 481, 485–86). Her last novel, by then called *BETWEEN THE ACTS,* was published in July 1941.

Wordsworth, William (1770–1850) This well-known English poet is said to "sanction" the "strong thought" of the phrase "snaky flower" in ORLANDO's poem "The Oak Tree" (O 265). The lines in which the phrase occurs are actually quoted from Vita SACKVILLE-WEST's poem *The Land.* Discussing androgynous artists in *A ROOM OF ONE'S OWN,* Woolf's narrator says that Wordsworth had "too much of the male" in him (AROO 103). She earlier quotes a line from stanza 17 of Wordsworth's "Resolution and Independence" (also known as "The Leech-gatherer") in discussing how male poets have always complained of the difficulties of writing works of genius; "Mighty poets in their misery dead" (AROO 52) is identified by Alice Fox as referring to the poets Thomas Chatterton and Robert BURNS (Fox, "Literary Allusion" 151). In *THREE GUINEAS,* discussing the affection between sisters and brothers, Woolf quotes the last six lines of Wordsworth's poem "The Sparrow's Nest" (TG 104). Woolf also re-read *The Prelude,* Wordsworth's long autobiographical poem, as she began to work on *THE WAVES.*

Workers' Educational Association See "LEANING TOWER, THE"

"World's great age" In his "summing up" in the ninth EPISODE of *THE WAVES,* BERNARD refers to murmuring "The World's great age begins anew," a line from *Hellas* by Percy Bysshe SHELLEY (TW 282).

Wortley, Mr. "The courtly Mr. Wortley" is a character in *JACOB'S ROOM* who is a friend of Elizabeth DURRANT and her family. He writes plays that are acted at the Durrants' parties.

Wren, Sir Christopher (1631–1723) A few days after the Great Fire of London in 1666, the architect Wren presented a plan for rebuilding the city that was not adopted. He was, however, made surveyor in charge of the City churches and designed fifty-two of them. Probably the best-known of his buildings is St. Paul's Cathedral, which delights ORLANDO and many other characters in Woolf's novels. King William III employed Wren to add to the buildings at HAMPTON COURT.

Wright, Joseph (1855–1930) Compiler of the six-volume *English Dialect Dictionary* (1896–1905), Wright was Woolf's inspiration for a character in *THE PARGITERS,* Mr. Brook, who appears in *THE YEARS* as Sam ROBSON. The word "pargeter" is found in the *Dialect Dictionary.* Woolf read Wright's wife Elizabeth Mary's two-volume biography of this Oxford professor of Comparative Philology (1901–25) with admiration, remarking after she had finished the first volume that it was "rare . . . to meet people who say things we ourselves could have said" (D4 116).

Wright, Dr. Maurice A doctor whom Leonard WOOLF consulted in 1911 about his inherited nervous tremor, and who in 1916 wrote a letter enabling Leonard's exemption from military service. In January 1913, he was one of several doctors whom Leonard consulted about the advisability of Woolf's having children (Wright was in favor). On September 9, 1913, Leonard took Woolf to see Wright, who told her she was very ill; he then took her to see Dr. Henry HEAD, who said the same. That evening Woolf took an overdose of Veronal, a sedative.

Writer's Diary, A (See also DIARY) In 1953 the HOGARTH PRESS published *A Writer's Diary, Being Extracts from the Diary of Virginia Woolf,* edited by Leonard WOOLF. Leonard selected passages written between August 1918 and March 1941, explaining in his preface that he had chosen "practically everything which referred to her own writing" (viii), as well as extracts that showed Woolf practicing the art of writing, recording the direct impact on her of scenes and persons, and commenting on books she was reading. Leonard also wrote that he considered *THE WAVES* "far and away the greatest of her books," and he singled out *TO THE LIGHTHOUSE* and *BETWEEN THE ACTS* as her other major works. Leonard did not indicate omissions in *A Writer's Diary,* but Anne Olivier BELL's five-volume edition of Woolf's DIARY both supplies the missing passages and also corrects several misdated or misread entries in *A Writer's Diary.*

Wuthering Heights See BRONTË, Charlotte and Emily.

Wycherley, William (1631–1723) In *JACOB'S ROOM,* Jacob FLANDERS scorns Professor BULTEEL's bowdlerized edition of the works of Wycherley, a playwright, satirist and friend of Alexander POPE (who revised many of his writings). Charles LAMB believed Wycherley and William CONGREVE to be the best writers of "Artificial Comedy." Thomas Babington MACAULAY called Wycherley licentious and indecent.

X

X Society A play-reading society at Cambridge University that replaced the MIDNIGHT SOCIETY and to which belonged Clive BELL, Thoby STEPHEN, Lytton STRACHEY, Saxon SYDNEY-TURNER and Leonard WOOLF. According to Leonard's letters, the members wrote as well as read plays for the Society (Spotts 19n, 21n).

Y

Yale Review Periodical in which Woolf published several articles, beginning in 1926 with "HOW SHOULD ONE READ A BOOK?" The correspondence between Woolf and Helen McAfee, the managing editor (whom Woolf met in London in 1928), is in the Beinecke Library at Yale University. Also of particular interest is the publication in the *Yale Review* of an early version of "MEMORIES OF A WORKING WOMEN'S GUILD" (1930).

Yarmouth Mrs. FLUSHING's maid in *THE VOYAGE OUT*.

Years, The **(1931)** Woolf's eighth novel consists of eleven chapters, each titled with a year, except for the final chapter which is called "Present Day." Beginning in 1880, the novel chronicles the lives of the Pargiter family. Each chapter opens with a description of the weather, reminiscent in some ways of the INTERLUDES of *THE WAVES*.

Outline

"1880" (3–88) Colonel Abel PARGITER is at his club. His wife, Rose PARGITER, is dying at home. Abel visits his mistress, Mira, at her sordid lodging. At the

The Years family trees

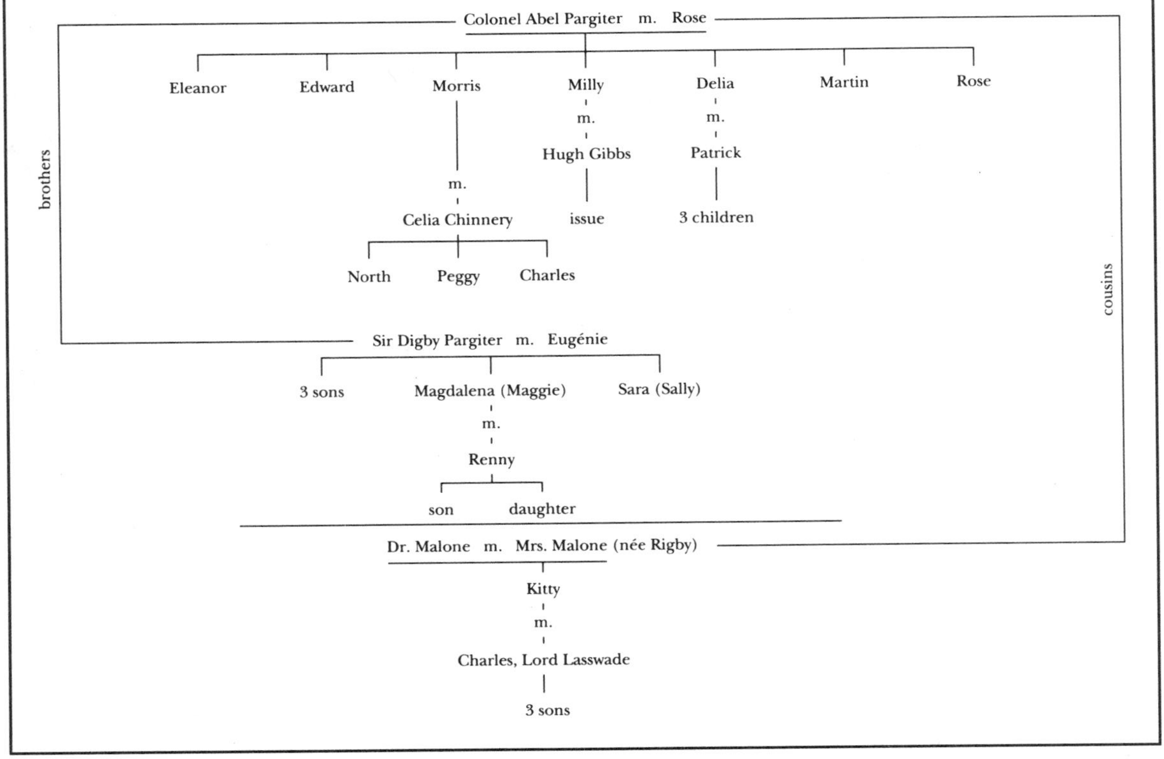

The Years. *Courtesy Linda J. Langham.*
This was one of only two jacket designs for her sister's books that Vanessa Bell signed with her full name (the other being Between the Acts*). This is the Hogarth Press first edition (1937).*

Pargiter home in ABERCORN TERRACE, Delia and Milly PARGITER wait as usual for the kettle to boil for tea. The youngest child, Rose PARGITER, and her brother Martin PARGITER are also at home. When Abel returns in a bad mood, tea is tense until the arrival of Eleanor PARGITER, who has been out doing charitable work; Eleanor has a calming influence on the family, who are anxiously awaiting their mother's death. Delia is feeling confined and secretly hopes her mother will die soon. When she sits by her mother's sickbed she fantasizes about addressing a political meeting with Charles Stewart PARNELL at her side (TY 23).

Rose asks her brother Martin to accompany her to Lamley's, a toy store, but they argue and she goes out alone. Imagining herself as her military ancestor "Pargiter of Pargiter's Horse," Rose rushes by a frightening man standing by a pillar-box (mailbox); on her return from the store, in the gloom of dusk, the man moves toward her, unbuttoning his clothes. The memory of this exhibitionist will stay with Rose throughout her life.

Morris PARGITER comes home from his job as clerk to a Judge, Sanders Curry, and the family has dinner. Eleanor is planning to write to her brother Edward PARGITER, who is studying at Oxford, and thinks that she will inherit her mother's writing table when Mrs. Pargiter dies. During dinner, Annie CROSBY comes in to say that Mrs. Pargiter has taken a turn for the worse. The relaxed feeling that Abel's good spirits had promoted evaporates and Martin leaves to fetch the family doctor. Delia observes her father carefully, thinking that, like her, he will be relieved when Rose dies. She rallies, however, to Delia's dismay.

Young Rose has a nightmare but cannot tell her sister Eleanor its cause, inhibited perhaps because she would have then to admit she had gone out alone, which she had been told not to do. Eleanor soothes her sister and goes back downstairs to write to Edward. As the family is preparing to go to bed, the nurse rings again. Their mother is dying. Delia observes the scene at her mother's deathbed dispassionately.

The scene moves to Oxford, where Edward is reading *ANTIGONE* late at night. After a glass of port, his thoughts drift to his cousin Kitty Malone (Kitty LASSWADE). Two friends of Edward who dislike each other, GIBBS and ASHLEY, come to his room. Edward knows that the cerebral and effete Ashley is jealous of the friendship that Gibbs, a hunting man, has with him, and leaves the two together knowing he will have to face a row with Ashley about it the next day.

At the Lodge, Dr. and Mrs. MALONE and their daughter Kitty are saying goodnight to American visitors, the Howard FRIPPS, after dinner with Dr. ANDREWS—"Old Chuffy," as Kitty calls him. Kitty admires the American woman's style and ease. She falls asleep thinking about Edward Pargiter and that she does not want to marry a professor and spend the rest of her life in Oxford. The next day she goes for her weekly history lesson with Lucy CRADDOCK but, as usual, has done no work. Lucy is disappointed but also is extremely fond of Kitty. From there, Kitty goes on to visit her friend Nelly ROBSON at her home, meeting her family for the first time. At tea, Kitty thinks how attractive Jo ROBSON is and warms to the entire Robson family, presided over by Jo and Nelly's father, Sam ROBSON.

Back at the Lodge, Kitty listens to the pigeons cooing and compares her life with Nelly's. Her mother knows that Kitty is dissatisfied but wonders what it is that makes her daughter restless. Mother and daughter dine alone and after dinner, a servant, Hiscock, brings in a note from Edward Pargiter saying that his mother has died. Mrs. Malone thinks about her cousin Rose, who was about her age, and about Edward, whom she likes but does not want Kitty to marry, preferring Lord Lasswade as a match for her daughter.

At Rose Pargiter's funeral, Delia thinks of "the woman she had loved and hated so" (TY 87) and believes her family is faking an emotion none of them feels.

"1891" (89–128) Kitty, now Lady Lasswade, lives in the north of England. Edward is an Oxford don, and Morris is a lawyer. Milly has married Hugh GIBBS. The narrative follows Eleanor's day. She sits at the writing table doing the family accounts, which she presents to her father. Then, she is off to a committee meeting, thinking as she goes of a visit she paid to her sister Milly in Devonshire. Her committee is concerned with good works for the poor and after the meeting she visits Rigby Cottages, houses that she has supervised for poor people. Meeting Duffus, the builder, Eleanor becomes increasingly irritated with him as she points out his shoddy work. She talks to herself on the bus home, remembering just before she gets to the house that her father had asked her to buy a birthday gift for his niece Maggie PARGITER. Eleanor buys a necklace from Lamley's. She and her father lunch alone together at home.

That afternoon, Morris is appearing in a case and Eleanor has promised to go and watch him in action. She meets his wife Celia Pargiter at the courts, but does not stay long after Morris has spoken. The newspaper headlines report the death of Parnell, and Eleanor worries about Delia. She goes to her sister's house intending to comfort her, but Delia is not home.

Abel Pargiter has also seen the news, on his way to visit his brother Sir Digby PARGITER's family, and his thoughts about Parnell—whose affair with Kitty O'Shea led to his downfall—mingle with thoughts of Mira. At Digby's house in BROWNE STREET, his wife Eugénie PARGITER and her daughters, Sara PARGITER and Maggie, are burning leaves in the back garden. Abel and Eugénie chat about the family, but when Digby arrives, Abel feels unwanted, irritated at not being able to spend time with Eugénie alone, and leaves depressed.

"1907" (129–45) Martin has returned from India. In her bedroom at Browne Street, Sara (Sally) Pargiter hears the sounds of a dance at a house down the street; outside her window is a black tree. She opens for the first time a book inscribed to her from her cousin Edward, his translation of *Antigone*. Maggie and Eugénie come home from a party and stay talking with Sara for a while. Her daughters encourage Lady Pargiter to dance for them in the bedroom, which she does, enchanting them both. Digby's voice summoning his wife to bed ends the moment.

"1908" (146–59) Eugénie and Digby both have died and the Browne Street house is sold. Martin visits his sister Eleanor, who has been reading Ernest RENAN's history of Christianity. Eleanor had liked Digby, Martin had preferred Eugénie. Rose, who has been speaking at a by-election in the north, arrives and talks about an argument she and Martin had as children that resulted in her locking herself in the bathroom and cutting her wrist with a knife. She still bears the scar.

"1910" (160–91) Rose is on her way to lunch with her cousins Sara and Maggie, something that leads her to think of the past. Sara and Maggie live in a run-down apartment together. Rose invites them to come with her to a meeting at Abercorn Terrace, hoping that Maggie will come, but only Sara does. The meeting (most likely a suffragette meeting) is in progress when they arrive. Eleanor and Martin are there, as are several others. Kitty Lasswade arrives, dressed for the opera. After the meeting breaks up, Eleanor accepts a lift from Kitty, who is going to the Covent Garden Opera House to hear Richard WAGNER's *Siegfried,* her favorite. Kitty is joined in her box by Edward and a young cousin of her husband's. The audience at the Opera House looks at the Royal Box, which is empty. The King (Edward VII) is dying. Siegfried's hammering on stage leads Kitty to remember a young man from her past, perhaps someone who kissed her when she was fifteen. She does not identify the sound as the hammering she heard the day she had tea with the Robsons when Jo was mending a chicken coop.

Back home in Hyams Place, Sara spins out the tale of her afternoon with "withered Rose, spiky Rose, tawny Rose, thorny Rose" (TY 188) for her sister Maggie. From the street comes the shout of a man who says the King has died.[25]

"1911" (192–213) Eleanor has been in Greece with Edward, who leads tours there for schoolmistresses, and on her own in Spain. She is on her annual summer visit to Morris at the home of his mother-in-law, Mrs. Chinnery. The Pargiter house at Abercorn Terrace is for sale (from which we may infer that Abel has died). As well as her niece and nephew, Peggy and North PARGITER, Eleanor is surprised to find Sir William Whatney staying with Morris and Celia, a man she remembers as "Old Dubbin" and who once praised her eyes. They discuss the situation in the Balkans. After dinner Celia asks Eleanor about her sister Rose, who has been arrested for throwing a brick (presumably as part of an action for SUFFRAGE). In bed that night, Eleanor picks up a volume of DANTE and reads lines that do "not give out their full meaning" but seem suggestive to her (TY 213).

[25] King Edward VII died suddenly on May 6, 1910.

"1913" (214–23) Eleanor says good-bye to Crosby; the Abercorn Terrace house has been sold. Crosby goes to lodgings in Richmond, taking the old dog, Rover (who promptly dies). Crosby still does Martin Pargiter's laundry, collecting it each week from his apartment in Ebury Street. Martin is insincere with Crosby when she visits, leading him to the reflection that everyone lies. After his father's death, for example, they had found letters from Mira. Martin calls family life "an abominable system" (TY 222).

"1914" (224–78) On his way to visit his stockbroker in the City of London, Martin runs into Sara at St. Paul's and invites her to lunch. Rose is in prison for throwing a brick; Sara imagines her being force-fed. After their lunch, Martin accompanies Sara to meet Maggie by the Round Pond in Hyde Park. They pause at Speakers' Corner. Maggie is waiting with her sleeping baby; drowsy from the wine she drank at lunch, Sara also falls asleep. Martin tells Maggie he is bored with his romantic life, and tells her about his father's mistress. He asks his cousin if she thinks his father was in love with Eugénie, her mother. Maggie jokingly asks if they might be brother and sister.

That evening, Martin goes to a dinner party given by Kitty Lasswade. She is upset that Eleanor declined her invitation, and is also frustrated with her guests, feeling everyone is simply going through the motions. Martin feels old and left out, failing to impress a young woman he sits next to at dinner. When everyone has left, Kitty hurries to the station to catch a night train north. The next morning, she exults in walking alone in the countryside, lying down on a hill and hearing the land "singing to itself" (TY 278).

"1917" (279–301) Eleanor dines with Maggie and her husband René, whom everyone calls RENNY, and meets there a foreigner named Nicholas [POMJALOVSKY]. Sara arrives late because North Pargiter had suddenly shown up at her door on his way to the Front. They have argued. At dinner in the basement, they discuss the war and are interrupted by sirens signaling an air raid. While Maggie soothes her children, the others take refuge in the cellar. The raid over, they drink a toast to the New World. Sara tells Eleanor that Nicholas is homosexual, causing her a frisson that immediately gives way to her sense that she likes Nicholas very much. As she says goodnight, Eleanor suddenly thinks that she would like to have married Renny twenty years ago. She goes home alone on the bus.

"1918" (302–05) Crosby hobbles along, bitterly denouncing the Belgian "Count" who leaves a dirty bathtub for her to clean. The war is over.

"Present Day" (306–435) Eleanor, who has been to India, has several visitors, including her niece and nephew, Peggy and North, and Nicholas Pomjalovsky (whom everyone calls "Brown"). North has been farming in Africa and has been back in England only ten days. He goes to dine with Sara and finds her on the phone with Nicholas when he arrives. He remembers quarreling with her the night he left for the Front in 1917. While he was in Africa, North's mother, Celia, died. Sara and he talk about the letters they wrote each other while he was away. North has returned to a society that is much changed.

Sara, now living alone in lodgings, cannot provide a very good dinner. North picks up her telephone when she ignores its ring and finds himself speaking to Eleanor, who has called to remind Sara of Delia's party that night. The narrative alternates among various characters as they move toward the office building where Delia is having her party. Eleanor is with Peggy, who is now a doctor. Peggy wants her aunt to talk about the past, feeling adrift in some way in her own life. She is startled when Eleanor, now seventy, abruptly rips a newspaper in which there is a photograph of "a fat man gesticulating," exclaiming as she does so, "Damned . . . bully!" (TY 330). Peggy and Eleanor share a cab together to Delia's. On the way, Eleanor is momentarily shocked when Peggy says a statue (of Edith CAVELL) makes her think of an advertisement for sanitary napkins, but she realizes that Peggy is bitter over the death of her brother Charles PARGITER in the war (TY 336).

North meanwhile is trying to persuade Sara to go to the party. He begins to recite for her the only poem he knows by heart, Andrew MARVELL's "The Garden." The sound of a man taking a bath interrupts them—the Jew (Abrahamson), Sara says, who will leave a line of grease around the tub.

Eleanor and Peggy arrive at Delia's and argue over who will pay the cab fare. At Sara's, she and North are startled when Maggie and Renny appear in the doorway. They have been to a play that has moved Renny to tears. He and North begin to discuss Africa, and the four of them leave together for Delia's.

At the party, Peggy talks to Delia's hard-of-hearing husband, Patrick, thinking all the time of pleasure and pain and how she hates parties. Gradually, the Pargiters all arrive: Martin, whose doctor is Peggy; Edward; Rose, now deaf. As Delia says to North and Maggie, at the party are "all your uncles and aunts; and your cousins; and your sons and daughters" (TY 364). Throughout the evening, Eleanor is prompted to think about her life and about the possibility of a "gigantic pattern" within which they all live. At times she dozes. The younger people dance. Nicholas arrives and banters with Sara, a kind of love as Eleanor recognizes. Milly and her husband Hugh throw a shadow of dullness over North and Eleanor's conversation, and North becomes irritated at the women's talk about their offspring.

Withdrawn from the crowd, Peggy takes a book at random from the bookshelf and thinks she will read there what she is thinking (which she does: that the universe is a mediocre, petty place, and that people are revolting [TY 383]). Peggy's malaise is expressed in an awkward speech she makes attacking her brother North. North too later picks up a book at random and reads "*nox est perpetua una dormienda*" ("We must sleep one endless night"), a line from CATULLUS (Poem 5, v. 6). Going down to supper, both North and Peggy feel the tension between them.

North thinks that the young men's conversation about politics is immature; he compares his experience alone in Africa with these untested young people's knowledge of life. The justice and liberty they speak of seem hollow to him. Nicholas tries to make a speech thanking Delia but is several times interrupted. As the dancing again begins on the floor above, Nicholas tells Kitty Lasswade that he would have drunk a toast to the human race, "which is now in its infancy" (TY 426), had he been able to finish his speech.

Dawn approaches and the guests at the party are suddenly surprised by the caretaker's children, who sing an unintelligible song (TY 428–29). Delia draws open the curtains; the Pargiters are framed against the window. As people begin to say good-bye, Eleanor watches a taxi pull up outside a house two doors down. A young man and young woman get out and go into the house together (TY 434). The sun has risen above the houses, and an air of calm pervades the sky.

Genesis

An account of the genesis and evolution of *The Years* is available in considerable detail; it was a book that became a huge burden to Woolf during the years of its composition and revision. On January 20, 1931—the day before she was to give a speech to the London/National Society for Women's Service, sharing the stage with Ethel SMYTH—Woolf wrote in her DIARY that she had suddenly thought of a sequel to ***A ROOM OF ONE'S OWN*** while having a bath. The book would be "about the sexual lives of women: to be called Professions for Women perhaps" (D4 6). A marginal note she made in 1934 reads "(This is *Here & Now,* I think . . .)," identifying this moment as the genesis of what would eventually be published as *The Years* ("Here & Now" was an early title for *The Years*). The speech "PROFESSIONS FOR WOMEN" exists in four versions: a seventeen-page holograph (*Pargiters* 163–67), now in the BERG COLLECTION; a twenty-five-page revised typescript (*Pargiters* xxvii–xliv), also in the Berg Collection; the first "essay" of ***THE PARGITERS*** (5–10); and the published essay "Professions for Women" (CE2 284–89; DM 235–42), which is much revised and considerably shorter than any of the drafts.

On October 11, 1932, Woolf began "The Pargiters: An Essay based upon a paper read to the London/National Society for Women's Service," and within a month she had revised "An Essay" to "A Novel-Essay," reflecting her conception of *The Pargiters,* which would intersperse "extracts" from a novel with essays analyzing the extracts. In her introduction to the recent Penguin edition of *The Years,* Jeri Johnson* distinguishes three discrete stages of development for *The Years:* (1) *The Pargiters,* which is the first volume and 84 pages of the second of the eight volumes of holograph in the Berg Collection; (2) what she calls "the Holograph"—the remaining six and one-half volumes; and (3) the novel as published (Johnson, "Introduction" 342n4). A few days after her speech, Woolf wrote to Ethel Smyth that she had had "a sudden influx of ideas" while taking a bath and wanted to develop these "perhaps in a small book, about the size of A Room" (L4 280).

Anne Olivier BELL sees the diary entry of January 20 as the genesis of both *The Years* and ***THREE GUINEAS*** and lists the following titles by which Woolf referred to *The Years* as she worked on it: *The Pargiters; Here & Now; Music; Dawn; Sons and Daughters; Daughters and Sons; Ordinary People; The Caravan; Other People's Houses; The Years* (D4 6n8). At the time Woolf recorded her "sudden influx of ideas" she was revising the second draft of ***THE WAVES***. Between February 1933 and September 1934, in addition to writing about 200,000 words of "the nameless book," she also wrote ***FLUSH***.

Throughout the composition of *The Years,* Woolf wrote frequently to Ethel Smyth about her thoughts on the book. In December 1932, she asked her for "a few facts" on suffrage and for information about Mrs. Pankhurst. By this time, Woolf had written the first draft of what would become the "1880" chapter, which consisted of six essays and five fictional "extracts" (*Pargiters* xvii). She wrote in January 1933 that she visualized the new book as "a curiously uneven time sequence—a series of great balloons, linked by straight narrow passages of narrative" (D4 142), adding that what she had learned from writing ***NIGHT AND DAY*** would help her achieve this. Soon, however, fearing that her "novel-essay" was too much like propaganda, she decided to leave out the "interchapters."

Woolf's work on *The Years* was interrupted in March 1933 when she was offered, and refused, an honorary degree by Manchester University, something that Susan Squier* has pointed out raised issues for Woolf that were identical to those she was exploring in her novel. Squier writes that "as the male Pargiters have a variety of roles in patriarchal society, so the female characters enact a whole range of responses to the question Woolf was considering—in art—when the episode of the Manchester honorary degree replicated it in life: What is the woman's right relation to the institutions of patriarchal society?" ("A Track" 199). In April, Woolf noted this confluence of art and life, writing in her diary that she hardly knew "which I am or where: Virginia or Elvira; in the Pargiters or outside" (D4 148). (Elvira was an earlier version of Sara Pargiter.)

Woolf wanted to "give the whole of the present society" in this novel, "facts, as well as the vision" (D4 151). It was somehow to combine *Night and Day* with *The Waves* (D4 152). In September 1933, Woolf woke up in the night and decided that "Here & Now" would be a better title (D4 176), and toward the end of the year she was reading her diaries from the period of World War I to "freshen" her memory of the war; "How close the tears come, again & again" (D4 193). By the next summer, she felt that she was "breaking the mould" made by *The Waves* (D4 233). In November 1934 she began to "compact" the book and wondered how to end it. "I want a Chorus.a general statement.a song for 4 voices" (D4 236).

As the spring of 1935 approached, Woolf was cutting and revising the air-raid scene in the "1917" chapter and was also beginning to think about how she might write the biography of Roger FRY. In April she met E. M. FORSTER on the steps of the LONDON LIBRARY, where he had just come from a meeting at which the board had expressed the opinion that "ladies were quite impossible" (D4 300). Woolf's anger at this spurred her to thoughts of a book to be called "On Being Despised," but she held back because *The Years* was "dangerously near propaganda" and she could not write both at once. "On Being Despised" became *Three Guineas.* The first reference to *The Years* as the title of her new novel occurs in September 1935; it was, she wrote, "psychologically, the oddest of my adventures" (D4 338). She had typed a draft of 740 pages by July 1935.

After a trip with Leonard WOOLF to the Labour Party conference in October she returned to revising what she described to Victoria OCAMPO as "a corpulent and most obstinate novel" (L5 439), completing the first revision by December 1935 (Woolf referred to this as the "last version" of *The Years*). By March 1936, convinced that the book was a failure, she took the unprecedented step of having galleys prepared before showing the new work to Leonard. "I have never suffered," she wrote in her diary, "since The Voyage Out, such acute despair on re-reading" (D5 17). That spring, Woolf was deeply depressed and ill. She wrote that she had "never been so near the precipice to my own feeling since 1913" (D5 24), describing the "almost catastrophic illness" which prevented her from doing any work from April to June 1936. Woolf spent most of the year at MONK'S HOUSE.

Having carried the galleys to Leonard as if they were "a dead cat," Woolf felt relief, sure that Leonard would agree with her that the galleys should be burned, the book abandoned. In November 1936, she wrote "Miracles will never cease—L. actually likes The Years!" (D5 28). Woolf felt that she might have exaggerated the book's badness and that this had led Leonard to exaggerate its worth (D5 30), a supposition confirmed by what Leonard Woolf wrote in his autobiography many years later: "To Virginia I praised the book more than I should have done if she had been well, but I told her exactly what I thought about its length" (LW2 301). Woolf wrote to her nephew Julian BELL that she was publishing *The Years* on Leonard's advice (L6 84) and set about further revisions.

She excised what Leonard called "two enormous chunks" (LW2 302). These have been reproduced in both the special issue on *The Years* of the *Bulletin of the New York Public Library* (80, 2 [Winter 1977]) and as an appendix in the Oxford University Press/World's Classics edition of the novel. Grace Radin* discusses the "two enormous chunks" and describes their content. "In the episodes Woolf deleted Eleanor is beginning to realize that her absorption in her family and charities has prevented her from coming to grips with the destructive forces that are overtaking her society" (Radin, " 'Two' " 227). Radin identifies the first "chunk," which depicts London in wartime, as from the "1917" chapter, but recently Karen Levenback* has demonstrated that the deleted portion is almost certainly set in 1914 ("Placing"); the second "chunk" was an entire chapter, "1921," that "chronicles the changes that have taken place in the postwar world" (Radin, " 'Two' " 235).

Woolf added the descriptive passages at the beginning of each chapter very late; they are not in the galleys.[26] She sent the proofs to the printer on December 30, 1936 and *The Years* was published by the HOGARTH PRESS on March 15, 1937 and by Harcourt, Brace & Co. in the United States on April 8. Vanessa BELL's design for the Hogarth Press dust jacket is dominated by "a large, partially opened rose" on both the front and back covers (Gillespie, *Sisters'* 251). Diane Gillespie points out that this was one of only two covers Vanessa Bell signed with her full name (the other being for *BETWEEN THE ACTS*).

The process of writing *The Years,* Woolf's second longest novel after *Night and Day,* was often linked in

[26] Marianna Torgovnick notes that "descriptions for years *after* 1910 show Impressionist and Post-Impressionist models absent in the generally realistic descriptions that introduce earlier years" (15).

her diary to the process of childbirth, as Squier* has noted ("Woolf Studies" 17), one that was long, laborious, and painful. Soon after the novel was published, Woolf wrote to Stephen SPENDER about what she had tried to achieve: to "give a picture of society as a whole" and to "give characters from every side"; she wanted to "envelop the whole in a changing temporal atmosphere" and shift the stress from present to future at the end, to "show the old fabric insensibly changing without death or violence . . . suggesting that there is no break, but a continuous development, possibly a recurrence of some pattern." "Of course," she wrote Spender, "I completely failed" (L6 116). In another letter to Spender, on April 30, Woolf again discussed her intentions, explaining that all the characters were supposed to be seen as crippled by their upbringing except for Maggie and Sara. Being a woman, she had not been able to bring into the novel the experience of battle at the Front, but being a woman was only partly the reason she did not do so: "I think action generally unreal," Woolf told Spender; "Its the thing we do in the dark that is more real" (L6 122).

Woolf continued to refer to *The Years* as a difficult and painful book to write. In June 1938, she described herself as at the end of six years' floundering, striving, and ecstasy, "lumping the Years & [*Three Guineas*] together as one book—as indeed they are" (D5 148). In 1940, at work on *POINTZ HALL* (an early title for *Between the Acts*), she still referred to "that misery The Years" (D5 340).

Background

The name Pargiter has been explained by Jane Marcus and, following her suggestion, by Mitchell Leaska as deriving from the word "parget" that can be found in the *English Dialect Dictionary* (1903) by Joseph WRIGHT. To parget means to whitewash, or plaster over cracks, and, by metaphorical extension, can be understood to mean repression or denial. Woolf introduced the figure of Joseph Wright, whose 1932 biography *The Life of Joseph Wright*, by his wife Elizabeth Mary Wright, she had read, in the sixth essay of *The Pargiters* as an "ideal model of manhood" (Leaska, *Pargiters* xii). Marcus believes that Woolf's use of the word as a surname "suggests both a moral and physical ambivalence in a novel about the patriarchal family, perhaps a combination of whitewash and filth, a true 'whited sepulchre' " (*Languages* 57). Leaska,* in "Virginia Woolf, the Pargeter," reproduces the relevant page from Wright's *Dialect Dictionary*. Woolf's description of the Robsons, whom Kitty Malone visits for tea, is based on elements from the biography of Joseph Wright.

The family chronicle of *The Years* clearly draws on Woolf's own experience of growing up in a Victorian household, the mother of which dies leaving the children with an irascible and demanding father. The young Rose Pargiter's experience of being accosted by an exhibitionist, for example, is based on a man Quentin BELL informs us hung around the Stephens' home "and was seen by both Vanessa and Virginia" when they were children (QB1 35). Leaska has interpreted this scene, and Rose's purchase of a box of ducks at Lamley's, as linked to George DUCKWORTH's sexual abuse of Woolf, his half-sister (*Novels* 200).

Woolf depended on "facts" to, as she put it in a letter to Stephen Spender, "keep one toe on the ground" (L6 116). (Many elements of the "factual" background to *The Years* will be found in individual entries on characters and persons named in the novel.) In an essay of 1933, "The Novels of Turgenev" (CE1 247–53), Woolf remarked that few novelists "combine the fact and the vision" (CE1 249), something she was consciously trying to do in this novel. Radin describes this essay as "a commentary on what she was trying to do in *The Years*" (*Virginia Woolf's The Years* xxin7). Although the emphasis in the novel is not on the events and dates that are usually emphasized by historians, the material background of European history from the late nineteenth century until about 1936 is always present. The meeting to which Rose takes Sara in the "1910" chapter, for example, is most likely a meeting of the Women's Social and Political Union, as Sharon Proudfit* has pointed out. After the meeting, Kitty Lasswade says to Eleanor Pargiter that she believes force is always wrong; in 1911, Christabel Pankhurst took control of the increasingly militant W.S.P.U., which had for some years been waging a campaign of window smashing and direct action. Ethel Smyth, who was imprisoned for her activism, was able to form a women's choir in Holloway Prison because so many suffragettes were there in 1911.

Woolf was reading R. Barry O'Brien's *Life of Charles Stewart Parnell* (2 volumes, 1898) in early 1933 (D4 143n7), and in April 1934 she and Leonard traveled to Ireland. That year also saw the publication of Leonard Woolf's study of dictators, *QUACK, QUACK*! The following year, in May, the Woolfs traveled by car through Holland, Germany, Italy and France and saw the growing evidence of fascist organization and mobilization, such as swastikas on cars in Germany. In her diary in September 1935, Woolf noted that in London there were "writings chalked up all over the walls . . . a circle with a symbol in it. Fascist propaganda, L. said" (D4 337). In *The Years*, North Pargiter, recently returned from his African farm, sees as he drives through an unfamiliar London that "somebody had chalked a circle on the wall with a jagged line in it" (TY 310). In the same month that Woolf sent the proofs of *The Years* to the printer, she published "Why Art Today Follows Politics" in the

DAILY WORKER (later reprinted as "THE ARTIST AND POLITICS").

Both Jane Marcus and Margaret Comstock* mention Olive Schreiner's *Story of an African Farm* in relation to *The Years.* Comstock describes the book as "a story of bigotry and oppression, including the particular forms of oppression suffered by women" (266), and both she and Marcus note that Woolf reviewed *The Letters of Olive Schreiner* for the *New Republic* in 1925. Comstock relates the owl seen by Eleanor and Peggy Pargiter in "1911" to the parable of the white bird of Truth in Schreiner's novel.

Other literary sources for themes and allusions in *The Years* have been noted, for example by Alice Fox, who believes that William SHAKESPEARE's *Timon of Athens* "may have provided in its misanthropic hero a perfect model" for Sara Pargiter's prototype in *The Pargiters,* Elvira (Fox 143). Fox notes that Woolf deleted allusions to Shakespeare as Elvira became the character Sara. Sophocles's *Antigone* is also significant in *The Years,* its "plot and 'buried alive' theme" forming "the mythology and structure" of the novel, according to Marcus (*Languages* 102). Several critics have also pointed out the presence of the mood of T. S. ELIOT's "Gerontion" in some characters' anti-Semitism.

Avrom Fleishman sees the sections of *The Years* as similar to the short-story form typical of MODERNISM, usually tending to an "epiphany" of some kind. He compares the scene in Sara's bedroom, when Maggie and their mother Eugénie come in from a party, with Katherine MANSFIELD's *Prelude,* and "1913" with James JOYCE's "The Dead." "Present Day," "for all its narrative turnings and mixture of modes," Fleishman compares to the "Wandering Rocks" chapter of *Ulysses* "as a grand attempt to synthesize a vision of life from the varied perspectives of a modern multitude" (Fleishman 192). Another intertextuality with Mansfield has been suggested by Ann L. McLaughlin,* who links *The Years* with Mansfield's story "The Daughters of the Late Colonel" (158).

Marcus suggests that the influence of two women who represent the conservative and radical traditions of women reformers—Mrs. Humphry WARD and Margaret Llewelyn DAVIES—"stands behind the composition of *The Years*" (*Languages* 70). The ambience of Ward's "Young Days at Oxford" suffuses the Oxford scenes of the novel and, Marcus points out, one of Mrs. Ward's novels was called *Eleanor. The Years* was written when Woolf's relationship with Ethel Smyth was in full flower, and Marcus also argues that Smyth's *The Prison* directly influenced *The Years.* For Marcus, the novel is a kind of Wagnerian opera, drawing both structure and technique, as well as ideas, from Wagner's *Ring* cycle (*Languages* 57). Peter Jacobs, on the other hand, has disputed both these claims of influence (Jacobs 236).

The Years was written at a time of acute sadness for Woolf, in years that marked the deaths of many close friends as well as of writers who had been the object of some of her most famous criticism. Lytton STRACHEY died in 1932, followed about six weeks later by the suicide of Dora CARRINGTON. In August that year, Goldsworthy Lowes DICKINSON died. George Duckworth died in 1934—not much lamented perhaps, but another reminder of passing time. Much more significant that year was the death of Roger Fry. Arnold BENNETT had died in 1931, John GALSWORTHY in 1933, and at the end of 1933, the writer Stella BENSON died. Benson had visited Woolf the previous year and her death reminded Woolf of how she had felt when Katherine Mansfield died. In 1935, another friend, Francis BIRRELL, died prematurely, and also Winifred HOLTBY, who was 37. Mitchell Leaska has pointed out that during this period, Woolf's friendship with Vita SACKVILLE-WEST faded and in 1936 Violet DICKINSON made Woolf a gift of bound typescripts of all the letters Woolf had written her many years before (Leaska, *Novels* 232).

Critical Responses

As the publication date approached, Woolf felt her usual apprehension: "I'm going to be beaten, I'm going to be laughed at, I'm going to be held up to scorn and ridicule" (D5 64). She was pleased to hear from John Maynard KEYNES that he thought *The Years* her best book (D5 77), and also from his sister-in-law Margaret that she liked some of the same characters in the novel Woolf herself did, "Sally, for instance" (L6 138). Leonard apparently kept his true feelings about the book to himself even after it was published; in 1962 he wrote to Angus Wilson that he thought *Night and Day* and *The Years* were "her worst books" (Spotts 520).

Woolf was relieved at the reviews in the *TIMES LITERARY SUPPLEMENT, The Observer* and *Time and Tide,* but she was depressed by Edwin Muir's in *The Listener.* She determined that there were "2 lines of criticism: one the Communist; the other the free mind. Had there been only one, I shd. have been damned. As it is I'm discussed (as usual) & no one has yet seen the point—*my* point" (D5 70). Madeline Moore* has explained this missing of Woolf's point as connected to many male reviewers' description of *The Years* as the product of a feminine sensibility unable or unwilling to deal with external reality. Desmond MACCARTHY wrote in *The Sunday Times* that a "Communist historian of literature would regard Mrs. Woolf's work as the hebe, the lovely doomed flower, of the bourgeois imagination when imprisoned by a civilisation which isolates it from contact with realities and communal interests" (in McNees 4: 114), a point of view that many apparently non-Communist reviewers also shared.

Basil de Selincourt wrote in the *Observer* that "no one could have written it who had not already written *The Waves*" (CH 371), and emphasized the novel's poetry. Howard Spring, in the *Evening Standard,* also stressed the poetic sensibility of the novel, finding in it "the blood and marrow of history—the thing itself, not an effigy for children" (CH 376–77). Many contemporary reviewers called the novel a poem, or at least poetic, and frequently compared it to *The Waves,* both favorably and unfavorably. The *New York Times* reviewer, for example, wrote that *The Years* went "far beyond" *The Waves,* "lovely" as that book had been (CH 391). Predictably, following the F. R. and Q. D. LEAVIS line, W. H. Mellers' review in *Scrutiny* was hostile, calling the novel "a document of purposelessness" and "fatuous" in its themes (CH 397). Woolf was, he concluded, "only a very minor sort of poet" (CH 399). Moore notes that "none of the *Scrutiny* reviews before Mellers made quite so much of the writer's sex" (252).

The Years was a popular success, probably due to the vogue for family chronicles, yet it was critically regarded as a failure after the experimentation of Woolf's previous novels. In the United States it became a best-seller, leading to a 1937 *Time* magazine cover for Woolf (which used a 1934 Man RAY photograph of the author). John Mepham notes that a United States Armed Services edition was published in 1945, but that the novel's reputation soon thereafter declined and remained low; it was "probably the least known and the least read of her novels" until the feminist revisionary readings of Woolf began to be published in the United States in the 1970s (Mepham, *Literary Life* 159).

Jean Guiguet describes *The Years* as a "novel *manqué*" and sees in it "perhaps the most significant symptom we have of the disequilibrium that made Virginia Woolf's originality and greatness—and which led to her undoing!" (Guiguet 309). Referring to Woolf's remark that she was breaking the mold made by *The Waves* in writing *The Years,* Guiguet contradicts her positive understanding of this process and sees it as the very heart of the problem of *The Years.* For many critics of the 1950s and 1960s—and, of course, beyond then—*The Years* is a "dead" novel. Quentin Bell writes that "whatever we may think of the final result . . . it was for her a pitfall, very nearly a death trap" (QB2 172). Carolyn Heilbrun* has written recently that both *The Years* and *Three Guineas* "to this day affront the sensibilities of almost all her male critics," and she sees Woolf's achievement in these works as a product of "a new and remarkable kind of courage" Woolf found in her fifties (*Writing* 124).

A common complaint about *The Years* has been that it lacks a center or central character. Phyllis Rose, while allowing that *The Years* is "a more readable novel than *The Waves,*" finds that it "ultimately suffers from a scrupulous impartiality, Woolf's refusal to define a central character or to shape a narrative, while heaping on us the kind of detail that demands such a shape" (Rose 213). Ann L. McLaughlin, reviewing Rose's book, says that this "suggests [Rose] has not considered seriously either its experiments in aesthetics or its feminist politics" (VWM 11:3). Charles G. Hoffman,* the first critic to discuss the novel's drafts, also complains that it "is diffuse at its center" (88).

Responding to this criticism, Joanna Lipking* suggests that "a center—of a sort—presents itself" in the "1914" chapter when Sara and Martin Pargiter lunch together in the City of London. Martin is seen there to be connected to the power base of the society: "The established church of financial power bears Martin to his somewhat uneasy supremacy in the universe of English civil society" (Lipking 145). Margaret Comstock sees the lack of a center as a deliberate strategy on Woolf's part, arguing that the novel might be said to have been written "on aesthetic principles that are the opposite of fascist" (Comstock 254).

For many critics, *The Years* seemed to be a disappointing return to the kind of novel Woolf had left behind with her experimental fiction of the 1920s. Hoffman explained its "failure" as "mainly the result of Virginia Woolf's attempts to free herself from the limitations of the externality of the family chronicle by using the internality of personal vision to portray the continuity of the years" (89). James Naremore* (who omits *The Years* entirely from his book on Woolf) argues that many readers misunderstand the realism of *The Years* and deem it a failure for not achieving what it does not actually set out to do ("Nature"). Rare among early writers on Woolf is James Hafley, who considers *The Years* one of Woolf's best novels (Hafley 132).

Victoria S. Middleton,* noting that the critical consensus seemed in the early 1970s to be that "whatever Woolf is saying in *The Years,* she could have said it better" (158), argues that Woolf might have "sought to write a novel that would call into question her own aesthetic" (158). Middleton suggests that *The Years* is at times self-parody (citing the end of "1914" as an example) and "is finally anti-visionary" (158). She argues that the chaos of the novel is calculated, and that the motive for this "deliberate failure" is bound up with Woolf's preoccupation with the relation between art and politics. Woolf believed "that excessive awareness of social, economic and political crises fosters excessive self-consciousness" (171), the conditions that she said would destroy art. Valentine Cunningham has suggested that the egocentricity Woolf criticizes in "THE LEANING TOWER" is just that which Peggy Pargiter encounters at the party in "Present Day."

The articles by Lipking, Comstock and Middleton were all published, with several others, in a special issue of the *Bulletin of the New York Public Library* in Winter 1977 devoted to *The Years*. In the front matter to this issue, Jane Marcus described it as "a landmark in Virginia Woolf studies" (137). More recently, Brenda Silver* has discussed the significance of Marcus's 1977 prediction that *The Years* would become a focus of study and that the special issue of the *Bulletin* would radically alter the image of Woolf: "Until this time, most critics of Woolf praised and studied her writings either in terms of psychology and 'sensibility,' or in the context of a modernism defined through formal experimentation, authorial perspective, symbolic systems, poetry, and a self-conscious attention to art itself" (Silver, "Textual Criticism" 203). This focus led to almost exclusive critical attention to *MRS. DALLOWAY, TO THE LIGHTHOUSE* and *The Waves*, Woolf's earlier novels being seen as preparation for, and later novels as a falling away from, the achievement of these works. As Heilbrun* has written, "suffice it to recognize that an understanding of [*The Years*] awaited feminist criticism, a discipline as derided and as undeservedly so, as *The Years* itself" (244).

One of the initial aims of the renewed attention to *The Years* marked by the 1977 *Bulletin* was to explore the novel's evolution. Inevitably, this led to comparisons between the published version and its earlier conception as *The Pargiters*. Grace Radin, in her analysis of the "two enormous chunks" Woolf deleted, found that in her revision, Woolf "deleted or obscured much of its political and social content" (Radin, " 'Two' " 221).

The most extensive discussion of the novel's drafts is Radin's *Virginia Woolf's The Years** in which she tells the story of "how it was written, and of how its nature changed as it was revised" (xvii). Radin notes that despite the large amount of manuscript material that exists, there were undoubtedly other typescript drafts that have not survived. As well as her detailed description of the novel's earlier drafts, Radin chooses particular trends on which to focus her discussion, "such as the deletion of sexual and ideological material and the changes in the depiction of one character, Elvira (Sara in *The Years*)" (xxiv). Remarking that *The Years*, though "quiet" in tone, is a richly meaningful novel that contains "some of Woolf's most memorable writing," Radin speculates that little attention had been paid up until the early 1970s to Woolf's social and political theories, "perhaps because they cluster around feminism, a point of view that has only recently been restored to serious consideration. For this reason *The Years* and its documents are at the heart of the current reappraisal of Woolf, since it is in these uncut documents that her social and political theories are developed most fully" (xxii–xxiii).

Susan Squier has charted Woolf's developing use of urban themes, images and settings and follows "her discussion of street love in *The Pargiters*; her revision of Cleopatra's Needle as a symbol of the feminist civilization to come, in an excised portion of '1910'; and her contrasting visions of wartime and postwar London in 'two enormous chunks' deleted from the novel's galley proofs" (Squier, *Woolf and London* 142). Squier argues that although *The Years* "contains none of the penetrating factual analysis of women's conditions in Victorian London that makes *The Pargiters* such a fascinating social document . . . it relies upon urban images to convey the same information in fiction, dramatically, indirectly, and—most importantly—uncoercively" (Squier 167–68). Squier thus also sees Woolf's aesthetics as linked to her politics in *The Years*.

A significant amount of critical attention has been given to the form of *The Years*, particularly to its uneven time sequence. Leaska believes that Woolf's irregular movement from year to year was a conscious omission of "blocks of time which were of great importance to her life and later to her work" (an assertion recently countered by Pamela Caughie, who argues that the time sequence of the novel is generated by Woolf's experimentation with discursive strategies [Caughie 98]). Naremore also remarks on the omission of the year "1919," which is frequently referred to in *Three Guineas* as "a watershed in the history of women's emancipation." Jean Alexander writes that even for those years that have an obvious historical identity (1891, 1910, 1914, 1918), "the definition Woolf has found would not be a historian's definition" (185). Critics have disagreed over whether the novel represents "an objectified vision of history as a meaningful process" (Alexander 199), or whether the novel concludes that "the search for meaning in history has failed" (Harper 265). Alex Zwerdling argues that *The Years* "can be read as a critique of the idea of progress" (304). Caughie, who writes that the past in the novel is not a model for the present but a function of it, compares *The Years* with *Night and Day*. The "unified history of objects, actions, and manners" in the earlier novel "gives way to a heterogeneous history of perspectives and relations" in *The Years*. There is "continuity without progress, coherence without unity, ending without certainty" (Caughie 102).

The ending of the novel, which has generally been read as optimistic, is for Caughie a "*structural necessity* in a narrative that conceives of history and story as a dynamic complex of relations" (106). As many have noted, the image of the arriving taxi, seen from the window by Eleanor Pargiter, is one that recalls a similar image from *A Room of One's Own* and expresses optimism about society's future. A different note is struck by Nancy Topping Bazin, who finds the novel's "tone of horror" ultimately prevails over its "naive optimism" (180). Many readers have noted that *The Years* contains Woolf's most sordid images of urban life.

Two early writers on Woolf who emphasized the novel's visionary content were Alice van Buren Kelley and Herbert Marder, and subsequent critics have also noted its combination of fact and vision. Jane Wheare finds that the novel's poetry "comes not in the individual word or image, but in the structure of the novel as a whole, with its repetitions and recollections, through which Woolf approaches the idea of *The Waves* from a new direction" (Wheare 141). Wheare gives a comprehensive catalog of the repetitions in the novel. Among others who have compared *The Years* to *The Waves* is Harvena Richter, who argues that Woolf uses the "same modes of memory" in both works, but simplifies the technique in *The Years*. There are many images in the latter work that "suggest that the most important part of our lives lies concealed in hidden memory and the unconscious" (*Inward* 176).

Richter is a critic particularly aware of Woolf's use of musical structures in her fiction, and several people have noted how in *The Years* "the techniques of realism have been subtly altered by the addition of techniques from music" (Alexander 185). Alexander argues that "vulgar music" (e.g., street music and dance music) moves against "serious music, the large sound of Wagner, for example, or the highly refined, abstract form of the quartet" (Alexander 189–90). She notes that the "musical intelligence" in the novel functions mostly through rhythm, of which repetition is a prime aspect. Fleishman writes that the repetitions of images and objects, sounds and phrases in *The Years* "create in the reader the sense of an audible music of humanity, of continuity and harmony in human life" (Fleishman 176). In a sense, writes Marcus, *The Years* "is *about* repetition as well as repetitive in style" (*Languages* 38). Perry Meisel also comments that the novel is "tied together" by the use of figures familiar in Woolf's work: the accentuation of the "common life" by the recurrent use of plurals, the "omnipresence of anonymous street singers, organ grinders, and musicians," and "the shifting status of personal pronouns" (Meisel 206).

Marcus has even suggested that *The Years* is "a kind of Greek opera, simultaneously a dirge and a dithyramb celebrating the death and rebirth of the Spirit of the year" (*Languages* 36), an idea she traces to its source in the work of Jane Ellen HARRISON. Patricia Cramer* also explores the influence of Harrison, arguing that her "discovery of the ritual origins of art provided a model for a nonpatriarchal art form that Woolf adopted as the narrative and symbolic structure for *The Years*" (Cramer 204). Another link with classical Greece may be found in the pervasive imagery of red and gold in the novel, a red and gold light that, writes Marcus, "shines into some very musty corners of British family life" (*Languages* 36). Laura Moss Gottlieb* notes that red and gold imagery is also prevalent in the poems of SAPPHO and suggests that Woolf "was interested in linking Sappho with some of the themes and characters of her novel" (Gottlieb 225).

Those themes are understood by many recent critics to concern the hidden lives of women. Howard Harper notes that the perspective at the Pargiter house in the "1880" section is always associated with one of the daughters, even when a Pargiter son is present (Harper 257). Cramer has described Woolf as working "in secret" in *The Years*, "by threading matriarchal subplots within the historical narrative" (203). In an essay indebted to the work of Berenice Carroll, Gottlieb describes *The Years* as a radical feminist vision of the world based on "woman's values," and as a work in which public events and public figures are seen only from the perspective of an "outsider" (Gottlieb 216; 221).

The "outsiders" Renny, Maggie, Sara, Nicholas and Eleanor are brought together in the air-raid scene of "1917" "to create a liminal moment when the barriers to speech and matriarchal consciousness dissolve" (Cramer 213). Hermione Lee has likened the dialogue in this scene to that found in the work of Anton CHEKHOV, and she notes that in her essay "THE RUSSIAN POINT OF VIEW," Woolf described Chekhov as exemplifying a restless generation (Lee 196–97). Michael Rosenthal sees Edward Pargiter ("Buried alive with his *Antigone*") as embodying "that quality of fearful, isolated living to which Dante's vision is opposed. Taken together, Edward and *Antigone*, Eleanor and Dante can be thought of as defining the two extremes of the novel—the suffocating facts of social and psychological isolation and the emancipating vision of wholeness and harmony—within whose confines the different Pargiters make their separate ways" (Rosenthal 180).

When Woolf first had that "sudden influx of ideas" that led to both *The Years* and *Three Guineas*, she was thinking about "the sexual lives of women" (D4 6). Sallie Sears* has written that, "whatever the reasons, the sexual interest of the novel is vested neither in marriage nor in any other form of monogamous heterosexuality" (Sears 214n6). Sexuality in *The Years* is defined always in relation to power (Sears 211). Leaska argues that the novel embodies implications of incest that are linked to Woolf's own experiences (*Novels* 200). He analyzes the experiences of the child

Rose Pargiter in this light, and also points out that when Eleanor slips in referring to Maggie as her "niece—I mean cousin" (TY 103), Woolf is "telling us that Eleanor now thinks of herself not as *Miss* but as *Mrs.* Pargiter" (*Novels* 207). David Eberly* remarks that in reading the novel "as a text of incest trauma, it is important to recognize that many of its characters exhibit the effects of sexual abuse suffered not by them but by their creator" (Eberly 149).

In her analysis of sexuality in *The Years,* Sears takes note of "the lesbian impulses in the novel" (219), citing as an example the relationship between Kitty Malone and Lucy Craddock. Women who seem "to have cut through the constraints and eluded the strictures of the private house" fascinate other women (Sears 219). The women in the novel, Sears argues, "eroticize liberty; the males, tyranny" (220). Sears points out that the politics attacked in *Three Guineas* is a sexual politics, the same that provides "the texture of a way of life" depicted in the novel (Sears 211).

Woolf's concern, most explicit in the 1930s, to show that the public and private worlds are inseparable, that sexual politics infuse public as well as private life, leads in *The Years* to what Naremore describes as "the merging of a transcendent, elegiac theme with a social radicalism [that] helps to make the novel one of Woolf's most comprehensive statements" ("Nature" 244). He argues that in the novel Woolf tried "to give a concrete demonstration" of that split in consciousness by which people deny the connection between public and private ("Nature" 246). The Pargiter sons enter the three institutions—the law, the army, and the university—that Woolf explicitly attacks in *Three Guineas* (Naremore, "Nature" 253). Cramer sees Woolf as representing "British daily life as social text" throughout the novel, the focus on rituals of family life making "conscious the political consequences of these seemingly innocuous events" (Cramer 204).

The Years is a political novel "in the feminist and pacifist senses" (Squier 141). Beverly Ann Schlack notes that "much of the scornful humor in *The Years* is directed against Establishment values like religion and science" ("Strategy" 147), values that Woolf anatomized in *Three Guineas.* In *The Years,* the concerns of the 1930s are brought together with Woolf's lifelong concern with myth, ritual, women's lives, and sexual politics. The issues were ones Woolf struggled with to the end of her life, as can be seen in her late essay "THOUGHTS ON PEACE IN AN AIR RAID."

Works Specific to This Entry

Comstock, Margaret. "The Loudspeaker and the Human Voice: Politics and the Form of *The Years.*" *Bulletin of the New York Public Library* 80, 2 (Winter 1977): 252–75.

Cramer, Patricia. "'Loving in the War Years': The War of Images in *The Years.*" In Mark Hussey, ed. *Virginia Woolf and War:* 203–24.

Eberly, David. "Incest, Erasure, and *The Years.*" In Mark Hussey and Vara Neverow, eds. *Virginia Woolf: Emerging Perspectives:* 147–56.

Gottlieb, Laura Moss. "*The Years:* A Feminist Novel." In Elaine K. Ginsberg and Laura Moss Gottlieb, eds. *Virginia Woolf: Centennial Essays.*

Heilbrun, Carolyn G. "Woolf in Her Fifties." In Jane Marcus, ed. *Virginia Woolf: A Feminist Slant:* 236–53.

———. *Writing a Woman's Life.* New York: W. W. Norton, 1988.

Hoffman, Charles G. "Virginia Woolf's Manuscript Revisions of *The Years.*" *PMLA* 84 (1969): 79–89.

Jacobs, Peter. "'The Second Violin Tuning in the Ante-room': Virginia Woolf and Music." In Diane F. Gillespie, ed. *The Multiple Muses of Virginia Woolf:* 227–60.

Johnson, Jeri. "Introduction." In Julia Briggs, ed. *Virginia Woolf: Introductions to the Major Works.* London: Virago Press, 1994.

Leaska, Mitchell. "Virginia Woolf, the Pargeter: A Reading of *The Years.*" *Bulletin of the New York Public Library* 80, 2 (Winter 1977): 172–210.

Levenback, Karen L. "Placing the First 'Enormous Chunk' Deleted from *The Years.*" *Virginia Woolf Miscellany* 42 (Spring 1994): 8–9.

Lipking, Joanna. "Looking at the Monuments: Woolf's Satiric Eye." *Bulletin of the New York Public Library* 80, 2 (Winter 1977): 141–45.

McLaughlin, Ann L. "An Uneasy Sisterhood: Virginia Woolf and Katherine Mansfield." In Jane Marcus, ed. *Virginia Woolf: A Feminist Slant:* 152–61.

Middleton, Victoria S. "*The Years:* 'A Deliberate Failure.'" *Bulletin of the New York Public Library* 80, 2 (Winter 1977): 159–71.

Moore, Madeline. "Virginia Woolf's *The Years* and Years of Adverse Male Reviewers." *Women's Studies* 4 (1977): 247–63.

Naremore, James. "Nature and History in *The Years.*" In Ralph Freedman, ed. *Virginia Woolf: Revaluation and Continuity:* 241–62.

Proudfit, Sharon. "Virginia Woolf: Reluctant Feminist in *The Years.*" *Criticism* 17 (1975): 59–73. In Eleanor McNees, ed. *Virginia Woolf: Critical Assessments,* vol. 4: 149–61.

Radin, Grace. "'Two Enormous Chunks': Episodes Excluded During the Final Revisions of *The Years.*" *Bulletin of the New York Public Library* 80, 2 (Winter 1977): 221–51.

———. *Virginia Woolf's The Years: The Evolution of a Novel.* Knoxville: University of Tennessee Press, 1981.

Schlack, Beverly Ann. "Virginia Woolf's Strategy of Scorn in *The Years* and *Three Guineas*." *Bulletin of the New York Public Library* 80, 2 (Winter 1977): 146–50.

Sears, Sallie. "Notes on Sexuality: *The Years* and *Three Guineas*." *Bulletin of the New York Public Library* 80, 2 (Winter 1977): 211–20.

Silver, Brenda R. "Textual Criticism as Feminist Practice: Or, Who's Afraid of Virginia Woolf Part II." In George Bornstein, ed. *Representing Modernist Texts: Editing as Interpretation.* Ann Arbor: University of Michigan Press, 1991: 193–222.

Squier, Susan. "A Track of Our Own: Typescript Drafts of *The Years*." In Jane Marcus, ed. *Virginia Woolf: A Feminist Slant:* 198–211.

———. "Woolf Studies Through *The Years:* Nationalism, Methodological Politics, and Critical Reproduction." In Vara Neverow-Turk and Mark Hussey, eds. *Virginia Woolf: Themes and Variations:* 16–24.

Yeats, W. B. (1865–1939) See *WAVES, THE.*

Young, Edward Hilton (1879–1960) Politician, poet, and contemporary of Clive BELL, Thoby STEPHEN, Lytton STRACHEY, Saxon SYDNEY-TURNER and Leonard WOOLF at Trinity College, Cambridge. He was a regular visitor to the "Thursday Evenings" instituted by Thoby to maintain contact with his Cambridge friends in 1905. In 1909 he proposed to Woolf, as she had expected he would.

Yourcenar, Marguerite (1903–1987) First and only woman elected to the Académie Française, and best known for her novel *The Memoirs of Hadrian* (1951). Her translation of Woolf's *THE WAVES* (*Les Vagues*) was published in 1937. Judith Johnston has argued that *The Waves* influenced Yourcenar's 1939 novel *Coup de Grâce* in its analysis of gender politics ("Necessary Bore" 125). Woolf described Yourcenar's visit to discuss her translation (D5 60–61).

Z

Zanzibar Hoax A forerunner of the DREADNOUGHT HOAX, and also organized by Adrian STEPHEN's friend Horace COLE. In 1905, the mayor of Cambridge received a telegram purporting to be from a staff member of the "Sultan of Zanzibar" saying the sultan's uncle was going to visit the city. Appendix C of *A Passionate Apprentice: The Early Journals, 1897–1909* includes newspaper reports on this successful hoax. The *Daily Mail* reported that the hoaxers were "received with civic honours" (PA 410). Woolf's brother Adrian was one of the four Cambridge undergraduates who dressed up, arrived by train from London, and fooled the mayor into giving them a tour of the city.

ALPHABETICAL LIST OF WORKS CITED, BY AUTHOR

University Press has been abbreviated U P throughout the list of works cited.

Abel, Elizabeth. "Narrative Structure(s) and Female Development: The Case of *Mrs. Dalloway*." In Margaret Homans, ed. *Virginia Woolf:* 93–114.

———. *Virginia Woolf and the Fictions of Psychoanalysis.* Chicago: U of Chicago P, 1989.

Abbott, Reginald. "What Miss Kilman's Petticoat Means: Virginia Woolf, Shopping, and Spectacle." *Modern Fiction Studies* 38, 1 (Spring 1992): 193–216.

Alexander, Jean. *The Venture of Form in the Novels of Virginia Woolf.* Port Washington, N.Y.: Kennikat Press, 1974.

Annan, Noel. "Bloomsbury and the Leavises." In Jane Marcus, ed. *Virginia Woolf and Bloomsbury:* 23–38.

———. *Leslie Stephen: The Godless Victorian.* New York: Random House, 1984.

Anscombe, Isabelle. *Omega and After: Bloomsbury and the Decorative Arts.* London: Thames & Hudson, 1981.

Apter, T. E. *Virginia Woolf: A Study of Her Novels.* New York: New York U P, 1979.

Arac, Jonathan. *Critical Genealogies: Historical Situations for Postmodern Literary Studies.* New York: Columbia U P, 1987.

Ascher, Carol. "Reading to Write: *The Waves* as Muse." In Mark Hussey and Vara Neverow-Turk, eds. *Virginia Woolf Miscellanies:* 47–56.

Auden, W. H. *Forewords and Afterwords.* Selected by Edward Mendelson. London: Faber & Faber, 1973.

Auerbach, Erich. *Mimesis: The Representation of Reality in Western Literature.* Translated by Willard R. Trask. Princeton: Princeton U P, 1968 (1953).

Baldwin, Dean. *Virginia Woolf: A Study of the Short Fiction.* Boston: Twayne, 1989.

Barrett, Eileen. "Matriarchal Myth on a Patriarchal Stage: Virginia Woolf's *Between the Acts.*" *Twentieth Century Literature* 33 (1987): 18–37.

Batchelor, J. B. "Feminism in Virginia Woolf." In Claire Sprague, ed. *Virginia Woolf:* 169–79.

Bazin, Nancy Topping. *Virginia Woolf and the Androgynous Vision.* New Brunswick, N.J.: Rutgers U P, 1973.

Bazin, Nancy Topping, and Jane Hamovit Lauter. "Virginia Woolf's Keen Sensitivity to War: Its Roots and Its Impact on Her Novels." In Mark Hussey, ed. *Virginia Woolf and War:* 14–39.

Beer, Gillian. "Beyond Determinism: George Eliot and Virginia Woolf." In Gillian Beer, *Arguing with the Past: Essays in Narrative from Woolf to Sidney.* New York: Routledge, 1989.

———. *George Eliot.* Bloomington: Indiana U P, 1986.

———. "Hume, Stephen, and Elegy in *To the Lighthouse.*" *Essays in Criticism* 34, 1 (January 1984): 33–55.

———. "Introduction" to *The Waves.* Oxford: Oxford U P/World's Classics, 1992.

———. "Introduction" to *Between the Acts.* In Julia Briggs, ed. *Virginia Woolf: Introductions to the Major Works.* London: Virago, 1994: 395–424.

———. "The Island and the Aeroplane: The Case of Virginia Woolf." In Homi K. Bhabha, ed. *Nation and Narration.* London: Routledge, 1990: 265–90.

———. "Virginia Woolf and Pre-History." In Eric Warner, ed. *Virginia Woolf: A Centenary Perspective:* 99–123.

Beja, Morris. ed. *Virginia Woolf: To The Lighthouse. A Selection of Critical Essays.* London: Macmillan, 1970.

Bell, Clive. *Art.* New York: Perigee, 1981.

———. *Old Friends.* New York: Harcourt, Brace & Co., 1956.

Bell, Quentin. "The Biographer, the Critic, and the Lighthouse." *Ariel* 2 (1971): 94–101.

———. *Bloomsbury.* London: Weidenfeld & Nicolson, 1986 (1968).

———. *The Brandon Papers.* San Diego: Harcourt Brace Jovanovich, 1985.

———. *Virginia Woolf: A Biography.* Vol. 1, *Virginia Stephen 1882–1912.* Vol. 2, *Mrs. Woolf 1912–1941.* London: Hogarth Press, 1973.

Bell, Vanessa. *Notes on Virginia's Childhood.* Edited by Richard J. Schaubeck Jr. New York: Frank Hallman, 1974.

Bennett, Joan. *Virginia Woolf: Her Art as a Novelist.* Cambridge: Cambridge U P, 1964.

Bicknell, John W. "Mr. Ramsay was Young Once." In Jane Marcus, ed. *Virginia Woolf and Bloomsbury:* 52–67.

Bishop, Edward. "Pursuing 'It' Through 'Kew Gardens.'" In Dean Baldwin, ed. *Virginia Woolf:* 109–17.

———. "The Subject in *Jacob's Room.*" *Modern Fiction Studies* 38, 1 (Spring 1992): 147–75.

Bishop, E. L. "Toward the Far Side of Language: Virginia Woolf's *The Voyage Out.*" *Twentieth Century Literature* 27, 4 (Winter 1981): 343–61.

Black, Naomi. "Virginia Woolf and the Women's Movement." In Jane Marcus, ed. *Virginia Woolf: A Feminist Slant:* 180–97.

Blackstone, Bernard. *Virginia Woolf: A Commentary.* London: Hogarth Press, 1949.

Blain, Virginia. "Narrative Voice and the Female Perspective in Virginia Woolf's Early Novels." In Patricia Clements and Isobel Grundy, eds. *Virginia Woolf: New Critical Essays.* Totowa: Barnes & Noble, 1983.

Bloom, Harold, ed. *Clarissa Dalloway.* Major Literary Characters Series. New York: Chelsea House, 1990.

Blotner, Joseph. "Mythic Patterns in *To the Lighthouse.*" *PMLA* 71 (1956): 547–62. (Cited from Morris Beja, ed. *Virginia Woolf: To the Lighthouse. A Selection of Critical Essays:* 169–88.)

Boone, Joseph Allen. "The Meaning of Elvedon in *The Waves.*" *Modern Fiction Studies* 27, 4 (Winter 1981–82): 629–37.

Booth, Alison. *Greatness Engendered: George Eliot and Virginia Woolf.* Ithaca: Cornell U P, 1992.

Bowlby, Rachel. *Virginia Woolf. Feminist Destinations.* New York: Basil Blackwell, 1988.

———. "Walking, Women and Writing: Virginia Woolf as *flâneuse.*" In Isobel Armstrong, ed. *New Feminist Discourses: Critical Essays on Theories and Texts.* London: Routledge, 1992.

Bowness, Alan. "Introduction." *Post-Impressionism: Cross-Currents in European Painting.* London: Royal Academy of Arts/Weidenfeld & Nicolson, 1979.

Boyd, Elizabeth French. *Bloomsbury Heritage: Their Mothers and Their Aunts.* New York: Taplinger, 1976.

Bradbrook, M. C. "Notes on the Style of Mrs. Woolf." *Scrutiny* 1 (May 1932): 33–38.

Brewster, Dorothy. *Virginia Woolf.* New York: New York U P, 1962.

———. *Virginia Woolf's London.* New York: New York U P, 1960.

Brittain, Vera. *Radclyffe Hall: A Case of Obscenity?* South Brunswick, N.J.: A. S. Barnes & Co, 1968.

Brothers, Barbara. "British Women Write the Story of the Nazis: A Conspiracy of Silence." In Angela Ingram and Daphne Patai, eds. *Rediscovering Forgotten Radicals: British Women Writers 1889–1939:* 244–64.

Brower, Reuben Arthur. "Something Central Which Permeated: Virginia Woolf and *Mrs. Dalloway.*" In *The Fields of Light: An Experiment in Critical Reading.* New York: Oxford U P, 1951: 123–37.

Broughton, Panthea Reid. "The Blasphemy of Art: Fry's Aesthetics and Woolf's Non-'Literary' Stories." In Diane F. Gillespie, ed. *The Multiple Muses of Virginia Woolf:* 36–57.

———. " 'Virginia Is Anal': Speculations on Virginia Woolf's Writing *Roger Fry* and Reading Sigmund Freud." *Journal of Modern Literature* 14, 1 (Summer 1987): 151–57.

Brownstein, Marilyn L. "Postmodern Language and the Perpetuation of Desire." *Twentieth Century Literature* 31 (1985): 73–88.

Butler, Samuel. *The Notebooks of Samuel Butler.* Edited by Henry Festing Jones. London: Hogarth Press, 1985.

Cameron, Julia Margaret. *Victorian Photographs of Famous Men & Fair Women.* With Introductions by Virginia Woolf and Roger Fry. Preface and Notes by Tristram Powell. London: Hogarth P, 1973.

Caramagno, Thomas. *The Flight of the Mind: Virginia Woolf's Art and Manic-Depressive Illness.* Berkeley: U of California P, 1992.

Carr, Glynis. "Waging Peace: Virginia Woolf's *Three Guineas.*" *Proteus* 3, 2 (Fall 1986): 13–21.

Carrington, [Dora]. *Letters and Extracts from her Diaries.* Edited by David Garnett. Oxford: Oxford U P, 1979.

Carrington, Noel. *Carrington: Paintings, Drawings and Decorations.* London: Thames & Hudson, 1980.

Carroll, Berenice A. " 'To Crush Him in Our Own Country': The Political Thought of Virginia Woolf" *Feminist Studies* 4 (1978): 99–131.

Carter, Miranda. "A Boeuf en Daube for *To the Lighthouse.*" *Charleston Magazine* 9 (Spring/Summer 1994): 50–53.

Caughie, Pamela L. *Virginia Woolf & Postmodernism. Literature in Quest and Question of Itself.* Urbana: U of Illinois P, 1991.

———. "Virginia Woolf's Double Discourse." In Marleen S. Barr and Richard Feldstein, eds. *Discontented Discourses: Feminism/Textual Intervention/Psychoanalysis.* Urbana and Chicago: University of Illinois Press, 1989: 41–53. (Cited from McNees 2: 483–93.)

Caws, Mary Ann. *Women of Bloomsbury: Virginia, Vanessa and Carrington.* New York: Routledge, 1990.

Chapman, Wayne K., and Janet M. Manson. "Carte and Tierce: Leonard, Virginia Woolf, and War for

Peace." In Mark Hussey, ed. *Virginia Woolf and War:* 58–78.

Childers, Mary M. "Virginia Woolf on the Outside Looking Down: Reflections on the Class of Women." *Modern Fiction Studies* 38, 1 (Spring 1992): 61–80.

Cixous, Hélène. "The Laugh of the Medusa." In Elaine Marks and Isabelle de Courtivron, eds. *New French Feminisms: An Anthology.* New York: Schocken, 1981.

Clark, Miriam Marty. "Consciousness, Stream, and Quanta, in *To the Lighthouse.*" *Studies in the Novel* 21 (Winter 1989): 413–23.

Clarke, S. N. *A Bibliography of Virginia Woolf and the Bloomsbury Group: A Computerised Database.* London: S. N. Clarke, 1993.

———. *Virginia Woolf. Orlando. The Holograph Draft.* Transcribed and edited by Stuart Nelson Clarke. London: S. N. Clarke, 1993.

Clements, Patricia, and Isobel Grundy, eds. *Virginia Woolf: New Critical Essays.* Totowa: Barnes & Noble, 1983.

Cohn, Dorrit. "Narrated Monologue: Definition of a Fictional Style." *Comparative Literature* 18 (Spring 1966): 96–112.

———. *Transparent Minds: Narrative Modes for Presenting Consciousness in Fiction.* Princeton: Princeton U P, 1978.

Colum, Mary M. "Life and Literature: Are Women Outsiders?" *Forum and Century* 100 (1938): 222–26.

Comstock, Margaret. "The Loudspeaker and the Human Voice: Politics and the Form of *the Years.*" *Bulletin of the New York Public Library* 80, 2 (Winter 1977): 252–75.

Cook, Blanche Wiesen. *Eleanor Roosevelt.* Vol. 1, 1884–1933. New York: Viking, 1992.

———. " 'Women Alone Stir My Imagination': Lesbianism and the Cultural Tradition." *Signs* 4, 4 (Summer 1979): 718–39.

Cooley, Elizabeth. "Revolutionizing Biography: *Orlando, Roger Fry,* and the Tradition." *South Atlantic Review* 55, 2 (May 1990): 71–83.

Cooper, Helen M., Adrienne Auslander Munich, and Susan Merrill Squier. "Arms and the Woman: The Con[tra]ception of the War Text." In Cooper, Munich, and Squier, eds. *Arms and the Woman: War, Gender, and Literary Representation.* Chapel Hill: U of North Carolina P, 1989.

Corsa, Helen Storm. "*To the Lighthouse:* Death, Mourning, and Transfiguration." *Literature and Psychology* 21, 3 (1971): 115–31.

Cramer, Patricia. " 'Loving in the War Years': The War of Images in *The Years.*" In Mark Hussey, ed. *Virginia Woolf and War:* 203–24.

Cuddy-Keane, Melba. "The Politics of Comic Modes in Virginia Woolf's *Between the Acts.*" *PMLA* 105, 2 (March 1990): 273–85.

Cumings, Melinda F. "*Night and Day:* Virginia Woolf's Visionary Synthesis of Reality." *Modern Fiction Studies* 18 (1972): 339–49.

Cunningham, Valentine. *British Writers of the Thirties.* New York: Oxford U P, 1988.

Daiches, David. *Virginia Woolf.* New York: New Directions, 1963.

Daly, Mary. *Beyond God the Father: Toward a Philosophy of Women's Liberation.* Boston: Beacon, 1973.

———. *The Church and the Second Sex.* Boston: Beacon, 1985.

Daugherty, Beth Rigel. "Face to Face with 'Ourselves' in Virginia Woolf's *Between the Acts.*" In Vara Neverow-Turk and Mark Hussey, eds. *Virginia Woolf: Themes and Variations:* 76–82.

———. "Taking a Leaf from Virginia Woolf's Book: Empowering the Student." In Mark Hussey and Vara Neverow-Turk, eds. *Virginia Woolf Miscellanies:* 31–40.

———. "The Whole Contention Between Mr. Bennett and Mrs. Woolf Revisited." In Elaine K. Ginsberg and Laura Moss Gottlieb, eds. *Virginia Woolf: Centennial Essays.*

Davies, Margaret Llewelyn. *Life As We Have Known It.* New York: W. W. Norton & Co., 1975.

Davis-Clapper, Laura. "Why Did Rachel Vinrace Die? Tracing the Clues from *Melymbrosia* to *The Voyage Out.*" In Mark Hussey and Vara Neverow-Turk, eds. *Virginia Woolf Miscellanies:* 225–27.

DeKoven, Marianne. "History as Suppressed Referent in Modernist Fiction." *ELH* 51 (Spring 1984): 137–52.

———. *Rich and Strange: Gender, History, Modernism.* Princeton: Princeton U P, 1991.

de Lauretis, Teresa, ed. *Feminist Studies, Critical Studies.* Bloomington: Indiana U P, 1986.

DeSalvo, Louise. "As 'Miss Jan Says': Virginia Woolf's Early Journals." In Jane Marcus, ed. *Virginia Woolf and Bloomsbury:* 96–124.

———. "Lighting the Cave: The Relationship Between Vita Sackville-West and Virginia Woolf." *Signs: Journal of Women in Culture and Society* 8, 21 (Winter 1982): 195–214.

———. "Shakespeare's *Other* Sister." In Jane Marcus, ed. *New Feminist Essays:* 61–81.

———. "Sorting, Sequencing, and Dating the Drafts of Virginia Woolf's *The Voyage Out.*" *Bulletin of Research in the Humanities* 82, 3 (Autumn 1979): 271–93.

———. " 'Tinder-and-Flint': Virginia Woolf and Vita Sackville-West." In Whitney Chadwick and Isabelle de Courtivron, eds. *Significant Others: Creativity and Intimate Partnership.* New York: Thames and Hudson, 1993.

———. "1897: Virginia Woolf at Fifteen." In Jane Marcus, ed., *Virginia Woolf: A Feminist Slant.*

———. *Virginia Woolf: The Impact of Childhood Sexual Abuse on Her Life and Work.* Boston: Beacon, 1989.

———. *Virginia Woolf's First Voyage: A Novel in the Making.* Totowa: Rowman & Littlefield, 1980.

———. "Virginia Woolf's Revisions for the 1920 American and English Editions of *The Voyage Out.*" *Bulletin of Research in the Humanities* 82, 3 (Autumn 1979): 338–66.

DiBattista, Maria. "Joyce, Woolf, and the Modern Mind." In Patricia Clements and Isobel Grundy, eds. *Virginia Woolf:* 96–114.

———. *Virginia Woolf's Major Novels: The Fables of Anon.* New Haven, Conn.: Yale U P, 1980.

Dick, Susan. "I Remembered, I Forgotten: Bernard's Final Soliloquy in *The Waves.*" *Modern Language Studies* 13, 3 (1983): 38–52.

———. "The Tunnelling Process: Some Aspects of Virginia Woolf's Use of Memory and the Past." In Patricia Clements and Isobel Grundy, eds. *Virginia Woolf:* 176–99.

———. " *'What Fools We Were!'*: Virginia Woolf's *A Society.*" *Twentieth Century Literature* 33 (Spring 1987): 53.

Dobie, Kathleen. "This is the Room that Class Built: The Structures of Sex and Class in *Jacob's Room.*" In Jane Marcus, ed. *Virginia Woolf and Bloomsbury:* 195–207.

Dodd, Elizabeth. " 'No, she said, she did not want a pear': Women's Relation to Food in *To the Lighthouse* and *Mrs. Dalloway.*" In Vara Neverow-Turk and Mark Hussey, eds. *Virginia Woolf: Themes and Variations:* 150–57.

Donaldson, Sandra M. "Where Does Q Leave Mr. Ramsay?" *Tulsa Studies in Women's Literature.* (Fall 1992): 329–36.

douglas, carol anne. "Dear Ms. Woolf, We Are Returning Your Guinea." *off our backs* 21 (Fall 1991): 5.

Dowling, David. *Bloomsbury Aesthetics and the Novels of Forster and Woolf.* New York: St. Martin's Press, 1985.

Drabble, Margaret. "Virginia Woolf: A Personal Debt." In Margaret Homans, ed. *Virginia Woolf:* 46–51.

Dunn, Jane. *A Very Close Conspiracy: Vanessa Bell and Virginia Woolf.* London: Pimlico, 1990.

DuPlessis, Rachel Blau. " 'Amor Vin—:' Modifications of Romance in Woolf." In Margaret Homans, ed. *Virginia Woolf:* 115–35.

———. "WOOLFENSTEIN." In Ellen G. Friedman and Miriam Fuchs, eds. *Breaking the Sequence: Women's Experimental Fiction.* Princeton: Princeton U P, 1989: 99–114.

Dworkin, Andrea. *Pornography: Men Possessing Women.* New York: Perigee, 1981.

Eberly, David. "Incest, Erasure, and *The Years.*" In Mark Hussey and Vara Neverow, eds. *Virginia Woolf: Emerging Perspectives:* 147–56.

Edel, Leon. *Bloomsbury. A House of Lions.* New York: J. B. Lippincott Co., 1979.

Eder, Doris L. "Louis Unmasked: T. S. Eliot in *The Waves.*" *Virginia Woolf Quarterly* 2, 1 and 2 (Winter–Spring 1975).

Edwards, Lee R. "War and Roses: The Politics of *Mrs. Dalloway.*" In Arlyn Diamond and Lee R. Edwards, eds. *The Authority of Experience: Essays in Feminist Criticism.* Amherst: U of Massachusetts P, 1977: 161–77.

Eisenberg, Nora. "Virginia Woolf's Last Words on Words: *Between the Acts* and 'Anon.' " In Jane Marcus, ed. *New Feminist Essays on Virginia Woolf:* 253–66.

Eliot, T. S. *The Letters of T. S. Eliot.* Vol. 1, 1898–1922. Edited by Valerie Eliot. San Diego: Harcourt Brace Jovanovich, 1988.

Emery, Jane. "Virginia and Rose." *Charleston Magazine* 4: 9–14.

Emery, Mary Lou. " 'Robbed of Meaning': The Work at the Center of *To the Lighthouse.*" *Modern Fiction Studies* 38, 1 (Spring 1992): 217–34.

Evans, Nancy Burr. "The Political Consciousness of Virginia Woolf: *A Room of One's Own* and *Three Guineas.*" *The New Scholar* 4 (1974): 167–80.

Ezell, Margaret J. M. "The Myth of Judith Shakespeare: Creating the Canon of Women's Literature." *New Literary History* 21 (Spring 1990): 579–92.

Farjeon, Annabel. "Mosaics and Boris Anrep." *Charleston Magazine* 7 (Summer/Autumn 1993): 15–22.

Farwell, Marilyn R. "Virginia Woolf and Androgyny." *Contemporary Literature* 16, 4 (Autumn 1975): 433–51.

Fassler, Barbara. "Theories of Homosexuality as Sources of Bloomsbury's Androgyny." *Signs* 5 (1979): 237–51.

Ferguson, John. "A Sea Change: Thomas De Quincey and Mr. Carmichael in *To the Lighthouse.*" *Journal of Modern Literature* 14, 1 (Summer 1987): 45–63.

Ferrer, Daniel. *Virginia Woolf and the Madness of Language.* Translated by Geoffrey Bennington and Rachel Bowlby. New York: Routledge, 1990.

Fisher, Jane. " 'Silent as the Grave': Painting, Narrative, and the Reader in *Night and Day* and *To the Lighthouse.*" In Diane F. Gillespie, ed. *The Multiple Muses of Virginia Woolf:* 90–109.

Fleishman, Avrom. *The English Historical Novel: Walter Scott to Virginia Woolf.* Baltimore: Johns Hopkins U P, 1971.

———. "Forms of the Woolfian Short Story." In Ralph Freedman, ed. *Virginia Woolf:* 44–70.

———. *Virginia Woolf. A Critical Reading.* Baltimore: Johns Hopkins U P, 1975.

Flint, Kate. "Introduction" to *The Waves.* In Julia Briggs, ed. *Virginia Woolf: Introductions to the Major Works.* London: Virago, 1994.

———. "Virginia Woolf and the General Strike." *Essays in Criticism* 36 (1986): 319–34.

Fogel, Daniel Mark. *Covert Relations: James Joyce, Virginia Woolf, and Henry James.* Charlottesville: U P of Virginia, 1990.

Folsom, Marcia McClintock. "Gallant Red Brick and Plain China: Teaching *A Room of One's Own.*" *College English* 45, 3 (March 1983): 254–62.

Forster, E. M. *Abinger Harvest.* San Diego: Harcourt Brace Jovanovich, 1964.

———. *Aspects of the Novel.* (1927) Harmondsworth: Penguin, 1976.

———. *Selected Letters of E. M. Forster.* Edited by Mary Lago and P. N. Furbank. Vol. 1, 1879–1920. Cambridge: Harvard U P, 1983. Vol. 2, 1921–1970. Cambridge: Harvard U P, 1985.

Fowler, Rowena. "Virginia Woolf and Katharine Furse: An Unpublished Correspondence." *Tulsa Studies in Women's Literature* 9 (Fall 1990): 201–28.

Fox, Alice. "Literary Allusion as Feminist Criticism in *A Room of One's Own.*" *Philological Quarterly* (Spring 1984): 145–61.

———. *Virginia Woolf and the Literature of the English Renaissance.* Oxford: Clarendon, 1990.

Freedman, Ralph. "The Form of Fact and Fiction: *Jacob's Room* as Paradigm." In Freedman, ed. *Virginia Woolf:* 123–40.

———, ed. *Virginia Woolf: Revaluation and Continuity.* Berkeley: U of California P, 1980.

Freund, Gisèle. *Gisèle Freund: Photographer.* New York: Harry N. Abrams, 1985.

Friedman, Susan Stanford. "Nancy Cunard (1896–1965)." In Bonnie Kime Scott, ed. *The Gender of Modernism:* 63–67.

———. "Virginia Woolf's Pedagogical Scenes of Reading: *The Voyage Out, The Common Reader,* and Her 'Common Readers.' " *Modern Fiction Studies* 38, 1 (Spring 1992): 101–25.

Froula, Christine. "The Daughter's Seduction: Sexual Violence and Literary History." *Signs* 11, 4 (1986): 621–44.

———. "Out of the Chrysalis: Female Initiation and Female Authority in Virginia Woolf's *The Voyage Out.*" In Margaret Homans, ed. *Virginia Woolf:* 136–61.

———. "Rewriting Genesis: Gender and Culture in Twentieth-Century Texts." *Tulsa Studies in Women's Literature* 7, 2 (Fall 1988): 197–220.

———. "St. Virginia's Epistle to an English Gentleman; or, Sex, Violence, and the Public Sphere in Woolf's *Three Guineas.*" *Tulsa Studies in Women's Literature* 13, 1 (Spring 1994): 27–56.

———. "Virginia Woolf as Shakespeare's Sister: Chapters in a Woman Writer's Autobiography." In Marianne Novy, ed. *Women's Revisions of Shakespeare: On Responses of Dickinson, Woolf, Rich, H. D., George Eliot, and Others.* Urbana: U of Illinois P, 1990.

Fry, Roger. "An Essay in Aesthetics." In *Vision and Design.* London: Chatto & Windus, 1920.

Gadd, David. *The Loving Friends: A Portrait of Bloomsbury.* New York: Harcourt Brace Jovanovich, 1974.

Gallop, Jane. *Around 1981: [Academic Feminist Literary Theory].* New York: Routledge, 1992.

García-Rodriguez, Antonía. "Virginia Woolf from a Latin-American Perspective." In Mark Hussey and Vara Neverow-Turk, eds. *Virginia Woolf Miscellanies:* 43–45.

Garner, Shirley Nelson. " 'Women Together' in Virginia Woolf's *Night and Day.*" In Shirley Nelson Garner, Claire Kahane, and Madelon Sprengnether, eds. *The (M)other Tongue: Essays in Feminist Psychoanalytic Interpretation.* Ithaca: Cornell U P 1985.

Garnett, Angelica. *Deceived with Kindness: A Bloomsbury Childhood.* San Diego: HBJ, 1985.

Garnett, David. *Great Friends: Portraits of Seventeen Writers.* London: Macmillan, 1979.

Garnett, Oliver. "Simon Bussy: An Anglo-French Painter." *Charleston Magazine* 6 (Winter/Spring 1992–93): 15–21.

Garvey, Johanna X. K. "Difference and Continuity: The Voices of *Mrs. Dalloway.*" *College English* 53, 1 (January 1991): 59–76.

Gathorne-Hardy, Jonathan. *Gerald Brenan: The Interior Castle. A Biography.* New York: W. W. Norton, 1992.

Gay, Penny. "Bastards from the Bush: Virginia Woolf and her Antipodean Relations." In Mark Hussey and Vara Neverow, eds. *Virginia Woolf: Emerging Perspectives:* 289–95.

Gelfant, Blanche H. "Love and Conversion in *Mrs. Dalloway.*" *Criticism* 8, 3 (Summer 1966): 299–45.

Gilbert, Sandra M. "The Battle of the Books/The Battle of the Sexes: Virginia Woolf's *Vita Nuova.*" *Michigan Quarterly Review* 23 (1984): 171–95.

———. "Costumes of the Mind: Transvestism as Metaphor in Modern Literature." In Elizabeth Abel, ed. *Writing and Sexual Difference.* Chicago: U of Chicago P, 1982.

———. "Woman's Sentence, Man's Sentencing: Linguistic Fantasies in Woolf and Joyce." In Jane Marcus, ed. *Virginia Woolf and Bloomsbury:* 208–24.

Gilbert, Sandra M., and Susan Gubar. *The Madwoman*

in the Attic: The Woman Writer and the Nineteenth-Century Literary Imagination. New Haven: Yale U P, 1979.

———. *The War of the Words.* Vol. 1 of *No Man's Land: The Place of the Woman Writer in the Twentieth Century.* New Haven: Yale U P, 1988.

———. *Sexchanges.* Vol. 2 of *No Man's Land: The Place of the Woman Writer in the Twentieth Century.* New Haven: Yale U P, 1989.

Gilbert, Sandra M., and Susan Gubar, eds. *The Norton Anthology of Literature by Women: The Tradition in English.* New York: W. W. Norton & Co., 1985.

Gillespie, Diane Filby. " 'Her Kodak Pointed at His Head:' Virginia Woolf and Photography." In Diane F. Gillespie, ed. *The Multiple Muses:* 113–47.

———. *The Sisters' Arts. The Writing and Painting of Virginia Woolf and Vanessa Bell.* Syracuse: Syracuse U P, 1988.

———. "Virginia Woolf's Miss La Trobe: The Artist's Last Struggle Against Masculine Values." *Women and Literature* 5, 1 (Spring 1977): 38–46.

Gillespie, Diane Filby, ed. *The Multiple Muses of Virginia Woolf.* Columbia: U of Missouri P, 1993.

Gillespie, Diane Filby, and Elizabeth Steele, eds. *Julia Duckworth Stephen: Stories for Children, Essays for Adults.* Syracuse: Syracuse U P, 1987.

Gilligan, Carol, Nona P. Lyons, and Trudy J. Hanmer, eds. *Making Connections: The Relational Worlds of Adolescent Girls at Emma Willard School.* Cambridge Mass.: Harvard U P, 1990.

Ginsberg, Elaine K., and Laura Moss Gottlieb, eds. *Virginia Woolf: Centennial Essays.* Troy, N.Y.: Whitston, 1983.

Glendinning, Victoria. *Vita: A Biography of Vita Sackville-West.* New York: Alfred A. Knopf, 1983.

Gordon, Lyndall. "Our Silent Life: Virginia Woolf and T. S. Eliot." In Patricia Clements and Isobel Grundy, eds. *Virginia Woolf: New Critical Essays:* 77–95.

———. *Virginia Woolf: A Writer's Life.* Oxford: Oxford U P, 1984.

Goreau, Angeline. "Aphra Behn: A Scandal to Modesty." In Dale Spender, ed. *Feminist Theorists:* 8–27.

Gorsky, Susan. " 'The Central Shadow:' Characterization in *The Waves.*" *Modern Fiction Studies* 18, 3 (Autumn 1972): 449–66.

Gottlieb, Laura Moss. "The War Between the Woolfs." In Jane Marcus, ed. *Virginia Woolf and Bloomsbury:* 242–52.

———. "*The Years:* A Feminist Novel." In Elaine K. Ginsberg and Laura Moss Gottlieb, eds. *Virginia Woolf.*

Graham, J. W. "The 'Caricature Value' of Parody and Fantasy in *Orlando.*" *University of Toronto Quarterly* 30, 4 (July 1961): 345–65.

———. "Manuscript Revision and the Heroic Theme of *The Waves.*" *Twentieth Century Literature* 29, 3 (Fall 1983): 312–32.

———. "Point of View in *The Waves:* Some Services of the Style." *University of Toronto Quarterly* 39 (April 1970): 193–211.

Green, David Bonnell. "*Orlando* and the Sackvilles: Addendum." *PMLA* 71, 1 (1956): 268–69.

Greer, Germaine, Susan Hastings, Jeslyn Medoff, and Melinda Sansone, eds. *Kissing the Rod: An Anthology of Seventeenth-Century Women's Verse.* New York: Farrar Straus Giroux, 1988.

Gregor, Ian. "Virginia Woolf and Her Reader." In Eric Warner, ed. *Virginia Woolf:* 41–55.

Grundy, Isobel. " 'Words Without Meaning—Wonderful Words:' Virginia Woolf's Choice of Names." In Patricia Clements and Isobel Grundy, eds. *Virginia Woolf: New Critical Essays.*

Guiguet, Jean. *Virginia Woolf and Her Works.* New York: Harcourt Brace Jovanovich, 1965.

Gerzina, Gretchen Holbrook. *Carrington: A Life.* New York: W. W. Norton, 1989.

Hafley, James. *The Glass Roof: Virginia Woolf as Novelist.* Berkeley: U of California P, 1954.

Haller, Evelyn. "The Anti-Madonna in the Work and Thought of Virginia Woolf." In Elaine K. Ginsberg and Laura Moss Gottlieb, eds. *Virginia Woolf: Centennial Essays.*

———. "Her Quill Drawn from the Firebird: Virginia Woolf and the Russian Dancers." In Diane F. Gillespie, ed. *The Multiple Muses of Virginia Woolf:* 180–226.

———. "Isis Unveiled: Virginia Woolf's Use of Egyptian Myth." In Jane Marcus, ed. *Virginia Woolf: A Feminist Slant:* 109–31.

———. "Virginia Woolf and Katherine Mansfield: Or, the case of the Déclassé Wild Child." In Mark Hussey and Vara Neverow-Turk, eds. *Virginia Woolf Miscellanies:* 96–104.

Hamilton, Cicely. *Marriage as a Trade.* London: 1909. Reprinted. Detroit: Singing Tree Press, 1971.

Handley, William R. "War and the Politics of Narration in *Jacob's Room.*" In Mark Hussey, ed. *Virginia Woolf and War:* 110–33.

Hankins, Leslie K. " 'Across the Screen of my Brain:' Virginia Woolf's 'The Cinema' and Film Forums of the Twenties." In Diane F. Gillespie, ed. *The Multiple Muses:* 148–79.

———. "A Splice of Reel Life in Virginia Woolf's 'Time Passes:' Censorship, Cinema, and 'the usual battlefield of emotions.' " *Criticism* 35, 1 (Winter 1993): 91–114.

———. "The Doctor and the Woolf: Reel Challenges—*The Cabinet of Dr. Caligari* and *Mrs. Dalloway.*" In Vara Neverow-Turk and Mark Hussey, eds. *Virginia Woolf: Themes and Variations:* 40–51.

Harper, Howard. *Between Language and Silence: The Novels of Virginia Woolf.* Baton Rouge: Louisiana State U P, 1982.

Harris, Daniel A. "Androgyny: The Sexist Myth in Disguise." *Women's Studies* 2 (1974): 171–84.

Harrison, Michael. *Clarence: The Life of H.R.H. the Duke of Clarence and Avondale (1864–1892).* London: W. H. Allen, 1972.

Haule, James M. "Introduction." The Shakespeare Head Press Edition of Virginia Woolf. *The Waves.* Oxford: Basil Blackwell, 1993.

———. " 'Le Temps passe' and the Original Typescript: An Early Version of the 'Time Passes' Section of *To the Lighthouse.*" *Twentieth Century Literature* 29, 3 (Fall 1983): 267–77.

———. "*To the Lighthouse* and the Great War: The Evidence of Virginia Woolf's Revisions of 'Time Passes.' " In Mark Hussey, ed. *Virginia Woolf and War:* 164–79.

Havard-Williams, Peter, and Margaret Havard-Williams. "Mystical Experience in Virginia Woolf's *The Waves.*" *Essays in Criticism* 4 (January 1954): 71–84.

Heilbrun, Carolyn G. *Toward a Recognition of Androgyny.* New York: Knopf, 1973.

———. "Woolf in Her Fifties." In Jane Marcus, ed. *Virginia Woolf: A Feminist Slant:* 236–53.

———. *Writing a Woman's Life.* New York: W. W. Norton, 1988.

Heine, Elizabeth. "The Earlier *Voyage Out:* Virginia Woolf's First Novel." *Bulletin of Research in the Humanities* 82, 3 (Autumn 1979): 294–316.

———. "New Light on *Melymbrosia.*" In Mark Hussey and Vara Neverow-Turk, eds. *Virginia Woolf Miscellanies.*

———. "Virginia Woolf's Revisions of *The Voyage Out.*" In Virginia Woolf, *The Voyage Out.* London: Hogarth Press, 1990. (The Definitive Collected Edition of the Novels of Virginia Woolf.)

Henke, Suzette A. "*Mrs. Dalloway:* The Communion of Saints." In Jane Marcus, ed. *New Feminist Essays on Virginia Woolf:* 125–47.

———. " 'The Prime Minister': A Key to *Mrs. Dalloway.*" In Elaine K. Ginsberg and Laura Moss Gottlieb, eds. *Virginia Woolf: Centennial Essays.*

———. "Virginia Woolf Reads James Joyce." In Morris Beja, Phillip Herring, et al., eds. *James Joyce: The Centennial Symposium.* Urbana: U of Illinois P, 1986: 39–42.

———. "Virginia Woolf's *The Waves:* A Phenomenological Reading." *Neophilologus* 73 (1989): 461–72.

Herrmann, Anne. " 'Intimate, Irreticent and Indiscreet in the Extreme:' Epistolary Essays by Virginia Woolf and Christa Wolf." *New German Critique* 38 (Spring/Summer 1986): 161–80.

Hessler, John G. "Moral Accountability in *Mrs. Dalloway.*" *Renascence* 30, 3 (Spring 1978): 126–36.

Hill, Katherine C. "Virginia Woolf and Leslie Stephen: History and Literary Revolution." *PMLA* 96 (1981): 351–62.

Hoffmann, A. C. "Subject and Object and the Nature of Reality: The Dialectic of *To the Lighthouse.*" *Texas Studies in Literature and Language* 13, 4 (Winter 1972): 691–703.

Hoffman, Anne Golomb. "Demeter and Poseidon: Fusion and Distance in *To the Lighthouse.*" *Studies in the Novel* 16 (Summer 1984): 93–110.

Hoffman, Charles G. "Fact and Fantasy in *Orlando:* Virginia Woolf's Manuscript Revisions." *Texas Studies in Literature and Language* 10 (1968): 435–44.

———. "From Short Story to Novel: The Manuscript Revisions of Virginia Woolf's *Mrs. Dalloway.*" *Modern Fiction Studies* 14, 2 (Summer 1968): 171–86.

———. "Virginia Woolf's Manuscript Revisions of *The Years.*" *PMLA* 84 (1969): 79–89.

Holleyman [George] and Treacher. *Catalogue of Books from the Library of Leonard and Virginia Woolf. Taken from Monk's House, Rodmell, Sussex and 24 Victoria Square, London and now in the possession of Washington State University, Pullman, U. S. A.* Brighton: Holleyman & Treacher, Ltd, 1975. [Limited edition of 250]

Holroyd, Michael. *Lytton Strachey: A Biography.* Harmondsworth: Penguin, 1971.

Holtby, Winifred. *Virginia Woolf.* London: Wishart & Co., 1932.

Homans, Margaret. *Bearing the Word: Language and Female Experience in Nineteenth-Century Women's Writing.* Chicago: U of Chicago P, 1986.

Homans, Margaret, ed. *Virginia Woolf: A Collection of Critical Essays.* Englewood Cliffs, N.J.: Prentice-Hall, 1993.

Humphrey, Robert. *Stream of Consciousness in the Modern Novel.* Berkeley: U of California P, 1962.

Hungerford, Edward A. " 'My Tunnelling Process:' The Method of *Mrs. Dalloway.*" *Modern Fiction Studies* 3, 2 (Summer 1957): 164–67.

Hussey, Mark. " ' "I" Rejected; "We" Substituted:' Self and Society in *Between the Acts.*" In Bege K. Bowers and Barbara Brothers, eds. *Reading and Writing Women's Lives: A Study of the Novel of Manners.* Ann Arbor: UMI Research Press, 1990: 141–52.

———. "Living in a War Zone: An Introduction to Virginia Woolf as a War Novelist." In Mark Hussey, ed., *Virginia Woolf and War:* 1–13.

———. "Reading and Ritual in *Between the Acts.*" *Anima* 15, 2 (Spring 1989): 89–99.

———. "Refractions of Desire: The Early Fiction of Virginia and Leonard Woolf." *Modern Fiction Studies* 38, 1 (Spring 1992): 127–46.

———. *The Singing of the Real World: The Philosophy*

of Virginia Woolf's Fiction. Columbus: Ohio State U P, 1986.

———. "*To the Lighthouse* and Physics: The Cosmology of David Bohm and Virginia Woolf." In Helen Wussow, ed. *New Essays on Virginia Woolf.* Dallas: Contemporary Research Press, 1995.

Hussey, Mark, ed. *Virginia Woolf and War: Fiction, Reality, and Myth.* Syracuse: Syracuse U P, 1991.

Hussey, Mark, and Vara Neverow-Turk, eds. *Virginia Woolf Miscellanies: Proceedings of the First Annual Conference on Virginia Woolf.* New York: Pace U P, 1992.

———. *Virginia Woolf: Emerging Perspectives. Selected Papers from the Third Annual Conference on Virginia Woolf.* New York: Pace U P, 1994.

Ingram, Angela. " 'The Sacred Edifices:' Virginia Woolf and Some of the Sons of Culture." In Jane Marcus, ed. *Virginia Woolf and Bloomsbury:* 125–45.

Ingram, Angela, and Daphne Patai, eds. *Rediscovering Forgotten Radicals: British Women Writers 1889–1939.* Chapel Hill: U of North Carolina P, 1993.

———. "Introduction: 'An Intelligent Discontent with . . . Conditions.' " In Angela Ingram and Daphne Patai, eds. *Rediscovering Forgotten Radicals: British Women Writers 1889–1939.*

Irigaray, Luce. *Speculum of the Other Woman* [*Speculum de l'autre femme,* 1974]. Translated by Gillian C. Gill. Ithaca: Cornell U P, 1985.

Jacobs, Peter. " 'The Second Violin Tuning in the Ante-room:' Virginia Woolf and Music." In Diane F. Gillespie, ed. *The Multiple Muses of Virginia Woolf:* 227–60.

Jacobus, Mary. *Reading Woman: Essays in Feminist Criticism.* New York: Columbia U P, 1986.

———. " 'The Third Stroke:' Reading Woolf with Freud." In Susan Sheridan, ed. *Grafts: Feminist Cultural Criticism.* London: Verso, 1988.

Jenkins, William D. "Virginia Woolf and the Belittling of *Ulysses.*" *James Joyce Quarterly* 25, 4 (1988): 513–19.

Johnson, Jeri. "Introduction." In Julia Briggs, ed. *Virginia Woolf: Introductions to the Major Works.* London: Virago Press, 1994.

Johnston, Georgia. "Women's Voice: *Three Guineas* as Autobiography." In Vara Neverow-Turk and Mark Hussey, eds. *Virginia Woolf: Themes and Variations:* 321–28.

Johnston, Judith L. " 'Necessary Bore' or Brilliant Novelist: What Marguerite Yourcenar Understood about Woolf's *The Waves.*" In Mark Hussey and Vara Neverow-Turk, eds. *Virginia Woolf Miscellanies:* 125–322.

———. "The Remediable Flaw: Revisioning Cultural History in *Between the Acts.*" In Jane Marcus, ed. *Virginia Woolf and Bloomsbury:* 253–277.

Johnstone, J. K. *The Bloomsbury Group: A Study of E. M. Forster, Lytton Strachey, Virginia Woolf and Their Circle.* London: Secker & Warburg, 1954.

Jones, Danell. "The Chase of the Wild Goose: The Ladies of Llangollen and *Orlando.*" In Vara Neverow-Turk and Mark Hussey, eds. *Virginia Woolf: Themes and Variations:* 181–89.

Jones, Suzanne W. *Writing the Woman Artist: Essays on Poetics, Politics, and Portraiture.* Philadelphia: U of Pennsylvania P, 1991.

Joplin, Patricia Klindienst. "The Authority of Illusion: Feminism and Fascism in Virginia Woolf's *Between the Acts.*" In Margaret Homans, ed. *Virginia Woolf:* 210–26.

———. " 'I Have Bought My Freedom:' The Gift of *A Room of One's Own.*" VWM 21 (Fall 1983): 4–5.

———. "The Voice of the Shuttle Is Ours." *Stanford Literature Review* 1 (1984): 25–53.

Jullian, Philippe, and John Phillips. *Violet Trefusis: A Biography.* London: Methuen, 1986.

Kaivola, Karen. *All Contraries Confounded: The Lyrical Fiction of Virginia Woolf, Djuna Barnes, and Marguerite Duras.* Iowa City: U of Iowa P, 1991.

Kamuf, Peggy. "Penelope at Work." In *Signature Pieces: On the Institution of Authorship.* Ithaca: Cornell U P, 1988.

Kaplan, Cora. "Pandora's Box: Subjectivity, Class and Sexuality in Socialist-Feminist Criticism." In Terry Lovell, ed. *British Feminist Thought: A Reader.* Cambridge, Mass.: Blackwell, 1990.

Keller, Catherine. *From a Broken Web: Separation, Sexism, and Self.* Boston: Beacon, 1986.

Kelley, Alice van Buren. *The Novels of Virginia Woolf: Fact and Vision.* Chicago: U of Chicago P, 1973.

Kennedy, Richard. *A Boy at the Hogarth Press.* London: Heinemann, 1972.

Kenney, Edwin J., Jr. "The Moment, 1910: Virginia Woolf, Arnold Bennett, and Turn of the Century Consciousness." *The Colby Library Quarterly* 13 (1977): 42–66.

Kenney, Susan M. "Two Endings: Virginia Woolf's Suicide and *Between the Acts.*" *University of Toronto Quarterly* 44, 4 (Summer 1975): 265–89.

Kermode, Frank. "Panel Discussion 2." In Eric Warner, ed. *Virginia Woolf.*

Keynes, Sir Geoffrey. *The Gates of Memory.* Oxford: Clarendon P, 1981.

Kiely, Robert. *Beyond Egotism: The Fiction of James Joyce, Virginia Woolf, and D. H. Lawrence.* Cambridge, Mass.: Harvard U P, 1980.

———. "*Jacob's Room* and *Roger Fry:* Two Studies in Still Life." In Robert Kiely, ed. *Modernism Reconsidered.* Harvard English Studies II. Cambridge, Mass.: Harvard U P, 1983: 147–66.

Kinnaird, Joan K. "Mary Astell: Inspired by Ideas." In Dale Spender, ed. *Feminist Theorists:* 28–39.

Kirkpatrick, B. J. *A Bibliography of Virginia Woolf.* Third edition. Oxford: Clarendon P, 1980.

Knopp, Sherron E. " 'If I Saw You Would You Kiss Me?:' Sapphism and the Subversiveness of Virginia Woolf's *Orlando.*" *PMLA* 103, 1 (January 1988): 24–34.

Kramer, Lynn. "One Retrospective Lupine View: A Terrified Student's View of Virginia Woolf's *Three Guineas.*" In Vara Neverow-Turk and Mark Hussey, eds. *Virginia Woolf: Themes and Variations:* 97–102.

Kushen, Betty. *Virginia Woolf and the Nature of Communion.* West Orange, N.J.: The Raynor Press, 1983.

Lambert, Elizabeth G. " 'and Darwin says they are nearer the cow:' Evolutionary Discourse in *Melymbrosia* and *The Voyage Out.*" *Twentieth Century Literature* 37, 1 (Spring 1991): 1–21.

Latham, Jacqueline. "The Manuscript Revisions of Virginia Woolf's *Mrs. Dalloway:* A Postscript." *Modern Fiction Studies* 18, 2 (Summer 1972): 475–76.

Laurence, Patricia Ondek. "The Facts and Fugue of War: From *Three Guineas* to *Between the Acts.*" In Mark Hussey, ed. *Virginia Woolf and War:* 225–46.

———. *The Reading of Silence: Virginia Woolf in the English Tradition.* Stanford: Stanford U P, 1991.

Lavin, J. A. "The First Editions of Virginia Woolf's *To the Lighthouse.*" In Joseph Katz, ed. *Proof: The Yearbook of American Bibliographical and Textual Studies.* Vol. 2. Columbia: U of South Carolina P, 1972: 185–211.

Lawrence, D. H. *Selected Literary Criticism.* Edited by Anthony Beal. New York: Viking, 1966.

Lawrence, Karen R. "Orlando's Voyage Out." In *Modern Fiction Studies* 38, 1 (Spring 1992): 253–77.

Leaska, Mitchell A. *The Novels of Virginia Woolf from Beginning to End.* New York: John Jay P, 1977.

———. "Virginia Woolf, the Pargeter: A Reading of *The Years.*" *Bulletin of the New York Public Library* 80, 2 (Winter 1977): 172–210.

Leavis, F. R. "After *To the Lighthouse.*" *Scrutiny* 10 (1942): 295–97.

———. *The Common Pursuit.* Harmondsworth: Pelican, 1970.

Lee, Hermione. *The Novels of Virginia Woolf.* London: Methuen, 1977.

Lee, Judith. " 'This hideous shaping and moulding:' War and *The Waves.*" In Mark Hussey, ed. *Virginia Woolf and War:* 180–202.

Lehmann, John. *Thrown to the Woolfs: Leonard and Virginia Woolf and the Hogarth Press.* New York: Holt, Rhinehart & Winston, 1978.

———. *Virginia Woolf and her World.* London: Thames & Hudson, 1975.

Levenback, Karen L. "Placing the First 'Enormous Chunk' Deleted from *The Years.*" *Virginia Woolf Miscellany* 42 (Spring 1994): 8–9.

———. "Virginia Woolf and Rupert Brooke: Poised Between Olympus and the 'Real World.' " *Virginia Woolf Miscellany* 33: 5–6.

Levin, Gerald. "The Musical Style of *The Waves.*" *Journal of Narrative Technique* 13, 3 (1983): 164–71.

Levy, Paul. *Moore: G. E. Moore and the Cambridge Apostles.* New York: Holt, Rinehart and Winston, 1979.

Lewis, Wyndham. *Men Without Art.* New York: Russell & Russell, 1964 (1934).

Lilienfeld, Jane. " 'The Deceptiveness of Beauty:' Mother Love and Mother Hate in *To the Lighthouse.*" *Twentieth Century Literature* 23 (Oct. 1977): 345–76.

———. " 'Like a Lion Seeking Whom He Could Devour': Domestic Violence in *To the Lighthouse.*" In Mark Hussey and Vara Neverow-Turk, eds. *Virginia Woolf Miscellanies:* 154–64.

———. "Where the Spear Plants Grew: The Ramsays' Marriage in *To the Lighthouse.*" In Jane Marcus, ed. *New Feminist Essays on Virginia Woolf:* 148–69.

Lipking, Joanna. "Looking at the Monuments: Woolf's Satiric Eye." *Bulletin of the New York Public Library* 80, 2 (Winter 1977): 141–45.

Little, Judy. *Comedy and the Woman Writer: Woolf, Spark, and Feminism.* Lincoln: U of Nebraska P, 1983.

———. "Festive Comedy in Woolf's *Between the Acts.*" *Women and Literature* Spring 1977: 26–37.

Lokke, Kari Elise. "*Orlando* and Incandescence: Virginia Woolf's Comic Sublime." *Modern Fiction Studies* 38, 1 (Spring 1992): 235–52.

London, Bette. *The Appropriated Voice: Narrative Authority in Conrad, Forster, and Woolf.* Ann Arbor: U of Michigan P, 1990.

———. "Guerrilla in Petticoats or Sans-Culotte? Virginia Woolf and the Future of Feminist Criticism." *diacritics* (Summer/Fall 1991): 11–29.

Lorde, Audre. "The Master's Tools Will Never Dismantle the Master's House." In Cherríe Moraga and Gloria Anzaldúa, eds. *This Bridge Called My Back: Writings by Radical Women of Color.* New York: Kitchen Table, Women of Color Press, 1981: 98–101.

Lorsch, Susan E. *Where Nature Ends: Literary Responses to the Designification of Landscape.* Rutherford: Fairleigh Dickinson U P, 1983.

Lounsberry, Barbara. "The Art of Virginia Woolf's Diaries." In Mark Hussey and Vara Neverow, eds. *Virginia Woolf: Emerging Perspectives:* 266–71.

Love, Jean O. *Virginia Woolf: Sources of Madness and Art.* Berkeley: U of California P, 1977.

———. *Worlds in Consciousness: Mythopoetic Thought in the Novels of Virginia Woolf.* Berkeley: U of California P, 1970.

Luedeking, Leila, and Michael Edmonds. *Leonard*

Woolf: A Bibliography. New Castle, Del.: Oak Knoll Books, 1992.

Luftig, Victor. "Woolf and the Leaflet Touch: A Political Context for 'Mr. Bennett and Mrs. Brown.' " *Virginia Woolf Miscellany* 27 (Fall 1986): 1–2.

Lund, Michael. " 'The Castaway' and *To the Lighthouse*." *Journal of Modern Literature* 16 (Summer 1989): 75–92.

MacKay, Carol Hanbery. "The Thackeray Connection: Virginia Woolf's Aunt Anny." In Jane Marcus, ed. *Virginia Woolf and Bloomsbury* 68–95.

MacKinnon, Catherine A. "Francis Biddle's Sister: Pornography, Civil Rights, and Speech (1984)." In *Feminism Unmodified: Discourses on Life and Law*. Cambridge, Mass.: Harvard U P, 1987.

McCail, Ronald. "A Family Matter: *Night and Day* and *Old Kensington*." *Review of English Studies* 38, 149 (Fall 1987): 23–39.

McCluskey, Kathleen. *Reverberations: Sound and Structure in the Novels of Virginia Woolf*. Ann Arbor: UMI Research Press, 1986.

McConnell, Frank D. " 'Death Among the Apple Trees:' *The Waves* and the World of Things." In Clare Sprague, ed. *Virginia Woolf:* 117–29.

McDowell, Frederick P. W. " 'Surely Order Did Prevail:' Virginia Woolf and *The Voyage Out*." In Ralph Freedman, ed. *Virginia Woolf:* 73–96.

McLaughlin, Ann L. "An Uneasy Sisterhood: Virginia Woolf and Katherine Mansfield." In Jane Marcus, ed. *Feminist Slant:* 152–61.

McLaurin, Allen. *Virginia Woolf: The Echoes Enslaved*. Cambridge, England: Cambridge U P, 1973.

McNees, Eleanor, ed. *Virginia Woolf: Critical Assessments*. 4 vols. New York: Routledge, 1994.

McVicker, Jeanette. "Vast Nests of Chinese Boxes, or Getting from Q to R: Critiquing Empire in 'Kew Gardens' and *To the Lighthouse*." In Mark Hussey and Vara Neverow-Turk, eds. *Virginia Woolf Miscellanies:* 40–42.

MacWeeney, Alen, and Sue Allison. *Bloomsbury Reflections*. New York: W. W. Norton, 1990.

Majumdar, Robin, and Allen McLaurin, eds. *Virginia Woolf: The Critical Heritage*. London: Routledge & Kegan Paul, 1975.

Mansfield, Katherine. *Journal of Katherine Mansfield*. Edited by J. Middleton Murry. New York: Ecco Press, 1983.

Marcus, Jane. *Art and Anger: Reading Like a Woman*. Columbus: Ohio State UP, 1988.

———. "Britannia Rules *The Waves*." In Karen Lawrence, ed. *Decolonizing Tradition: The Cultural Politics of Modern Literary Canons*. Urbana: U of Illinois P, 1991: 136–62.

———. "Daughters of Anger/Material Girls: Con/textualizing Feminist Criticism." *Women's Studies* 15 (1988): 281–308.

———. "Sapphistory: The Woolf and the Well." In Karla Jay and Joanne Glasgow, eds. *Lesbian Texts and Contexts: Radical Revisions*. New York: New York UP, 1990: 164–79.

———. "Thinking Back Through Our Mothers." In Jane Marcus, ed. *New Feminist Essays:* 1–30.

———. *Virginia Woolf and the Languages of Patriarchy*. Bloomington: Indiana U P, 1987.

Marcus, Jane, ed. *New Feminist Essays on Virginia Woolf*. Lincoln: U of Nebraska P, 1981.

———. *Virginia Woolf and Bloomsbury: A Centenary Celebration*. Bloomington: Indiana UP, 1987.

———. *Virginia Woolf: A Feminist Slant*. Lincoln: U of Nebraska P, 1983.

Marder, Herbert. *Feminism and Art: A Study of Virginia Woolf*. Chicago: U of Chicago P, 1968.

Marler, Regina, ed. *Selected Letters of Vanessa Bell*. New York: Pantheon, 1993.

Marshall, Denise. "Woolf's Monumental List-Works: Transforming Popular Culture's Semiotics of Space." In Vara Neverow-Turk and Mark Hussey, eds. *Virginia Woolf: Themes and Variations:* 268–76.

Mathis, Mary. " 'The Double Eye of Love:' Virginia Woolf and Mary Hutchinson." In Vara Neverow-Turk and Mark Hussey, eds. *Virginia Woolf: Themes and Variations:* 337–44.

Matro, Thomas G. "Only Relations: Vision and Achievement in *To the Lighthouse*." *PMLA* 99 (1984): 212–24.

Matthews, Jacquie. "Barbara Bodichon: Integrity in Diversity." In Dale Spender, ed. *Feminist Theorists:* 90–123.

May, Keith M. "The Symbol of Painting in Virginia Woolf's *To the Lighthouse*." *Review of English Studies* 9 (1967): 91–98.

Meese, Elizabeth A. *Crossing the Double-Cross: The Practice of Feminist Criticism*. Chapel Hill: U of North Carolina P, 1986.

Meisel, Perry. *The Absent Father: Virginia Woolf and Walter Pater*. New Haven: Yale UP, 1980.

Meisel, Perry, and Walter Kendrick, eds. *Bloomsbury/Freud: The Letters of James and Alix Strachey 1924–1925*. New York: Basic Books, 1985.

Mellown, Muriel. "Vera Brittain: Feminist in a New Age." In Dale Spender, ed. *Feminist Theorists:* 316–34.

Mepham, John. *Virginia Woolf: A Literary Life*. New York: St. Martin's P, 1991.

———. *Virginia Woolf*. Criticism in Focus Series. New York: St. Martin's, 1992.

Meyerowitz, Selma. *Leonard Woolf*. Boston: Twayne, 1982.

Middleton, Victoria S. "*The Years:* 'A Deliberate Failure.' " *Bulletin of the New York Public Library* 80, 2 (Winter 1977): 159–71.

Middleton, Victoria. "*Three Guineas:* Subversion and

Survival in the Professions." *Twentieth Century Literature* 8, 4 (Winter 1982): 405–17.
Miller, J. Hillis. *Fiction and Repetition: Seven English Novels.* Cambridge: Harvard U P, 1982.
———. "Mr. Carmichael and Lily Briscoe: The Rhythm of Creativity in *To the Lighthouse.*" In Robert Kiely, ed. *Modernism Reconsidered.* Harvard English Studies II. Cambridge: Harvard U P, 1983: 167–89.
———. "Virginia Woolf's All Souls' Day: The Omniscient Narrator in *Mrs. Dalloway.*" In M. Friedman and J. Vickery, eds. *The Shaken Realist: Essays in Honor of F. J. Hoffman.* Baton Rouge: Louisiana State U P, 1970: 100–27.
Miller, Nancy. "Teaching Autobiography." In *Getting Personal: Feminist Occasions and Other Autobiographical Acts.* New York: Routledge, 1991.
Millett, Kate. *Sexual Politics.* London: Virago, 1979 (1969).
Minow-Pinkney, Makiko. *Virginia Woolf and the Problem of the Subject: Feminine Writing in the Major Novels.* New Brunswick, N.J.: Rutgers U P, 1987.
Modleski, Tania. "Some Functions of Feminist Criticism, or The Scandal of the Mute Body." *October* 49 (Summer 1989): 3–24.
Moi, Toril. *Sexual/Textual Politics: Feminist Literary Theory.* New York: Methuen, 1985.
Moon, Kenneth. "Where is Clarissa? Doris Kilman in *Mrs. Dalloway.*" *CLA Journal* 23, 3 (March 1980): 273–86.
Moore, George Edward. *Principia Ethica.* Cambridge, England: Cambridge U P, 1903 (1980).
Moore, Madeline. "Nature and Communion: A Study of Cyclical Reality in *The Waves.*" In Ralph Freedman, ed. *Virginia Woolf: Revaluation and Continuity:* 219–40.
———. *The Short Season Between Two Silences: The Mystical and the Political in the Novels of Virginia Woolf.* Boston: George Allen & Unwin, 1984.
———. "Some Female Versions of Pastoral: *The Voyage Out* and Matriarchal Mythologies." In Jane Marcus, ed. *New Feminist Essays on Virginia Woolf:* 82–104.
———. "Virginia Woolf's *Orlando:* An Edition of the Manuscript." *Twentieth Century Literature* 25, 3/4 (Fall/Winter 1979): 303–55.
———. "Virginia Woolf's *The Years* and Years of Adverse Male Reviewers." *Women's Studies* 4 (1977): 247–63.
Morgenstern, Barry. "The Self-Conscious Narrator in *Jacob's Room.*" *Modern Fiction Studies* 18 (Autumn 1972): 351–61.
Morrell, Lady Ottoline. *Lady Ottoline's Album: Snapshots and portraits of her famous contemporaries (and of herself), photographed for the most part by Lady Ottoline Morrell.* Edited by Carolyn G. Heilbrun. New York: Alfred A. Knopf, 1976.
Mulhern, Francis. "English Reading." In Homi K. Bhabha, ed. *Nation and Narration.* New York: Routledge, 1990: 250–64.

Naremore, James. "Nature and History in *The Years.*" In Ralph Freedman, ed. *Virginia Woolf: Revaluation and Continuity:* 241–62.
———. *The World Without a Self: Virginia Woolf and the Novel.* New Haven: Yale U P, 1973.
Naylor, Gillian, ed. *Bloomsbury: The Artists, Authors and Designers by Themselves.* London: Octopus, 1990.
Nelson-McDermott, Catherine. "Virginia Woolf and Murasaki Shikibu: A Question of Perception." In Mark Hussey and Vara Neverow-Turk, eds. *Virginia Woolf Miscellanies:* 133–43.
Neumann, Shirley. "*Heart of Darkness,* Virginia Woolf and the Spectre of Domination." In Patricia Clements and Isobel Grundy, eds. *Virginia Woolf: New Critical Essays.*
Neverow-Turk, Vara, and Mark Hussey, eds. *Virginia Woolf: Themes and Variations. Selected Papers from the Second Annual Conference on Virginia Woolf.* New York: Pace U P, 1993.
Nicolson, Nigel. "Bloomsbury: The Myth and the Reality." In Jane Marcus, ed. *Virginia Woolf and Bloomsbury:* 7–22.
———. *Portrait of a Marriage.* New York: Atheneum, 1973.
Noble, Joan Russell, ed. *Recollections of Virginia Woolf by Her Contemporaries.* New York: William Morrow, 1972.
Novak, Jane. *The Razor Edge of Balance: A Study of Virginia Woolf.* Coral Gables, Fla.: U of Miami P, 1975.

Oakley, Ann. "Millicent Garrett Fawcett: Duty and Determination." In Dale Spender, ed. *Feminist Theorists:* 184–202.
Ohmann, Carol. "Culture and Anarchy in *Jacob's Room.*" *Contemporary Literature* 18 (1977): 160–72.
Olsen, Tillie. *Silences.* New York: Delta/Seymour Lawrence, 1978.
Overcarsh, F. L. "The Lighthouse, Face to Face." *Accent* 10 (Winter 1959): 107–23.
Oxindine, Annette. "Sapphist Semiotics in Woolf's *The Waves:* Untelling and Retelling What Cannot be Told." In Vara Neverow-Turk and Mark Hussey, eds. *Virginia Woolf: Themes and Variations:* 171–81.
Ozick, Cynthia. "Mrs. Virginia Woolf." *Commentary* 56 (1973): 33–44.

Painter, Penny. "The Overlooked Influence of John Waller 'Jack' Hills on Virginia Woolf." In Mark Hussey and Vara Neverow-Turk, eds., *Virginia Woolf Miscellanies:* 146–47.
Parkes, Graham. "Imagining Reality in *To the Light-*

house." *Philosophy and Literature* 6, 1 + 2 (Fall 1982): 33–44.

Partridge, Frances. *Everything to Lose. Diaries 1945–1960.* Boston: Little, Brown & Co., 1985.

———. *Memories.* London: Victor Gollancz, 1981.

Pascal, [Blaise]. *Pensées.* Translated with an introduction by A. J. Krailsheimer. Harmondsworth, England: Penguin, 1966.

Paul, Janis. *The Victorian Heritage of Virginia Woolf: The External World in Her Novels.* Norman: Pilgrim, 1987.

Pawlowski, Merry. "Virginia Woolf's *Between the Acts:* Fascism in the Heart of England." In Mark Hussey and Vara Neverow-Turk, eds. *Virginia Woolf Miscellanies:* 188–91.

Pearce, Richard. *The Politics of Narration: James Joyce, William Faulkner, and Virginia Woolf.* New Brunswick, N.J.: Rutgers U P, 1991.

———. "Who Comes First, Joyce or Woolf?" In Vara Neverow-Turk and Mark Hussey, eds. *Virginia Woolf: Themes and Variations:* 59–67.

Perloff, Marjorie. "Modernist Studies." In Stephen Greenblatt and Giles Gunn, eds. *Redrawing the Boundaries: The Transformation of English and American Literary Studies.* New York: The Modern Language Association of America, 1992: 154– 78.

Pippett, Aileen. *The Moth and the Star: A Biography of Virginia Woolf.* New York: Viking, 1957.

Pitt, Rosemary. "The Exploration of Self in Conrad's *Heart of Darkness* and Woolf's *The Voyage Out.*" *Conradiana* 10 (1978): 141–54.

Poole, Roger. "Passage to the Lighthouse." *Charleston Newsletter* 16 (September 1986):16–32.

———. *The Unknown Virginia Woolf.* 3rd ed. Atlantic Highlands: Humanities Press International, 1990.

———. " 'We all put up with you Virginia:' Irreceivable Wisdom About War." In Mark Hussey, ed. *Virginia Woolf and War:* 79–100.

Poresky, Louise A. *The Elusive Self: Psyche and Spirit in Virginia Woolf's Novels.* Newark: U of Delaware P, 1981.

———. "Eternal Renewal: Life and Death in Virginia Woolf's *The Waves.*" In Mark Hussey and Vara Neverow-Turk, eds. *Virginia Woolf Miscellanies:* 64–70.

Pratt, Annis. "Sexual Imagery in *To the Lighthouse:* A New Feminist Approach." *Modern Fiction Studies* 18 (1972): 417–31.

Proudfit, Sharon. "Lily Briscoe's Painting: A Key to Personal Relations in *To the Lighthouse.*" *Criticism* 13 (1971): 23–39.

———. "Virginia Woolf: Reluctant Feminist in *The Years.*" *Criticism* 17 (1975): 59–73. In Eleanor McNees, ed. *Virginia Woolf: Critical Assessments.* Vol. 4: 149–61.

Quick, Jonathan R. "Virginia Woolf, Roger Fry and Post-Impressionism." *Massachusetts Review* 26, 4 (Winter 1985): 547–70.

Radin, Grace. " 'Two Enormous Chunks:' Episodes Excluded During the Final Revisions of *The Years.*" *Bulletin of the New York Public Library* 80, 2 (Winter 1977): 221–51.

———. *Virginia Woolf's The Years: The Evolution of a Novel.* Knoxville: U of Tennessee P, 1981.

Raitt, Suzanne. "Fakes and Femininity: Vita Sackville-West and Her Mother." In Isobel Armstrong, ed. *New Feminist Discourses: Critical Essays on Theories and Texts.* New York: Routledge, 1992.

———. *Vita & Virginia: The Work and Friendship of V. Sackville-West and Virginia Woolf.* New York: Oxford U P, 1993.

Rantavaara, Irma. *Virginia Woolf's The Waves.* Port Washington: Kennikat Press, 1960.

Reed, Christopher. "Bloomsbury Bashing: Homophobia and the Politics of Criticism in the Eighties." *Genders* 11 (Fall 1991): 58–80.

———. "Through Formalism: Feminism and Virginia Woolf's Relation to Bloomsbury Aesthetics." In Diane F. Gillespie, ed. *The Multiple Muses of Virginia Woolf:* 11–35.

Reid, Su. *To the Lighthouse: An Introduction to the Variety of Criticism.* London: Macmillan, 1991.

Rich, Adrienne. "Compulsory Heterosexuality and Lesbian Existence." In Ann Snitow, Christine Stansell, and Sharon Thompson, eds. *Powers of Desire: The Politics of Sexuality.* New York: Monthly Review Press, 1983: 177–205.

———. " 'It is the Lesbian in Us . . .' " In *On Lies, Secrets and Silence.* New York: W. W. Norton & Co., 1979.

———. "When We Dead Awaken: Writing as Re-Vision." In *On Lies, Secrets and Silence.* New York: W. W. Norton & Co., 1979.

Richter, Harvena. "Hunting the Moth: Virginia Woolf and the Creative Imagination." In Ralph Freedman, ed. *Virginia Woolf:* 13–28.

———. "The *Ulysses* Connection: Clarissa Dalloway's Bloomsday." *Studies in the Novel* 21, 3 (1989): 305–19.

———. *Virginia Woolf: The Inward Voyage.* Princeton: Princeton U P, 1970.

Ricoeur, Paul. *Time and Narrative.* Vol. 2. Translated by Kathleen McLaughlin and David Pellauer. Chicago: U of Chicago P, 1985.

Riley, Denise. *"Am I That Name?" Feminism and the Category of "Women" in History.* Minneapolis: U of Minnesota, 1988.

Roberts, John Hawley. "Vision and Design in Virginia Woolf." *PMLA* 61 (1946): 835–47.

Roessel, David. "The Significance of Constantinople

in *Orlando*." *Papers on Language and Literature* (Fall 1992): 398–416.

Rogat, Ellen Hawkes. "The Virgin in the Bell Biography." *Twentieth Century Literature* 20, 2 (April 1974): 96–113.

Rose, Phyllis. *Woman of Letters: A Life of Virginia Woolf*. New York: Oxford UP, 1978.

Rosenbaum, S. P. *Edwardian Bloomsbury: The Early Literary History of the Bloomsbury Group*. Vol. 2. New York: St. Martin's, 1994.

———. "The Philosophical Realism of Virginia Woolf." In S. P. Rosenbaum, ed. *English Literature and British Philosophy: A Collection of Essays*. Chicago: Chicago U P, 1971: 316–56.

———. "Railing Against Realism: Philosophy and *To the Lighthouse*." *Philosophy and Literature* 7, 1 (April 1983): 89–91.

———. *Victorian Bloomsbury: The Early Literary History of the Bloomsbury Group*. New York: St. Martin's, 1987.

———. "Virginia Woolf and the Intellectual Origins of Bloomsbury." In Elaine K. Ginsberg and Laura Moss Gottlieb, eds., *Virginia Woolf: Centennial Essays*.

Rosenbaum, S. P., ed. *The Bloomsbury Group: A Collection of Memoirs, Commentary and Criticism*. Toronto: U of Toronto P, 1975.

———. Virginia Woolf. *Women & Fiction: The Manuscript Versions of A Room of One's Own*. Transcribed and edited by S. P. Rosenbaum. Oxford: Basil Blackwell, 1992.

Rosenberg, Beth. "Virginia Woolf: Conversation and the Common Reader." In Mark Hussey and Vara Neverow-Turk, eds., *Virginia Woolf Miscellanies*: 1–8.

Rosenberg, Karen. "Peaceniks and Soldier Girls." *The Nation* April 14, 1984: 453–57.

Rosenman, Ellen Bayuk. "Sexual Identity and *A Room of One's Own*: 'Secret Economies' in Virginia Woolf's Feminist Discourse." *Signs* 14, 3 (1989): 634–50.

Rosenthal, Michael. *Virginia Woolf*. New York: Columbia U P, 1979.

Ruddick, Sara. *Maternal Thinking: Toward a Politics of Peace*. New York: Ballantine, 1989.

———. "Private Brother, Public World." In Jane Marcus, ed. *New Feminist Essays*: 185–215.

Ruotolo, Lucio P. *The Interrupted Moment: A View of Virginia Woolf's Novels*. Stanford: Stanford U P, 1986.

———. *Six Existential Heroes: The Politics of Faith*. Cambridge: Harvard U P, 1973.

Russell, Bertrand. "Some Cambridge Dons of the Nineties." In *Portraits from Memory*. New York: Simon and Schuster, 1956.

Sackville-West, Vita. *Country Notes in Wartime*. 1940.

———. *Knole and the Sackvilles*. London: Ernest Benn, 1958.

———. *The Land & The Garden*. London: Michael Joseph, 1989.

———. *The Letters of Vita Sackville-West to Virginia Woolf*. Edited by Louise DeSalvo and Mitchell A. Leaska. New York: William Morrow, 1985.

———. *Passenger to Teheran*. New York: Moyer Bell, 1990.

Sarton, May. *Encore: A Journal of the Eightieth Year*. New York: W. W. Norton 1993.

———. *Journal of a Solitude*. New York: W. W. Norton, 1973.

Saunders, Judith P. "Mortal Stain: Literary Allusion and Female Sexuality in 'Mrs. Dalloway in Bond Street.' " *Studies in Short Fiction* 15, 2 (Spring 1978): 139–44.

Schaefer, Josephine O'Brien. "The Great War and 'This late age of world's experience' in Cather and Woolf." In Mark Hussey, ed. *Virginia Woolf and War*: 134–50.

———. *The Three-fold Nature of Reality in the Novels of Virginia Woolf*. The Hague: Mouton, 1965.

———. "*Three Guineas* and *Quack, Quack!* Read Together." *Virginia Woolf Miscellany* 7 (Spring 1977): 2–3.

Schaffer, Talia. "Posing *Orlando*." In Ann Kibbey, Kayann Short, and Abouali Farmanfarmaian, eds. *Sexual Artifice*. Genders 19. New York: New York U P, 1994: 26–63.

Schlack, Beverly Ann. *Continuing Presences: Virginia Woolf's Use of Literary Allusion*. University Park: Pennsylvania State U P, 1979.

———. "A Freudian Look at Mrs. Dalloway." *Literature and Psychology* 23 (1973): 49–58.

———. "The Novelist's Voyage from Manuscripts to Text: Revisions of Literary Allusions in *The Voyage Out*." *Bulletin of Research in the Humanities* 82, 3 (Autumn 1979): 317–27.

———. "Virginia Woolf's Strategy of Scorn in *The Years* and *Three Guineas*." *Bulletin of the New York Public Library* 80, 2 (Winter 1977): 146–50.

Schulze, Robin Gail. "Design in Motion: Words, Music, and the Search for Coherence in the Works of Virginia Woolf and Arnold Schoenberg." *Studies in the Literary Imagination* 25, 2 (Fall 1992): 5–22.

Scott, Bonnie Kime, ed. *The Gender of Modernism: A Critical Anthology*. Bloomington: Indiana U P, 1990.

———. "Woolf, Barnes and the Ends of Modernism: An *Antiphon* to *Between the Acts*." In Vara Neverow-Turk and Mark Hussey, eds. *Virginia Woolf: Themes and Variations*: 25–32.

———, ed. *New Alliances in Joyce Studies: 'When It's Aped to Foul a Delfian*.' Newark: U of Delaware P, 1988.

Sears, Sallie. "Notes on Sexuality: *The Years* and *Three Guineas*." *Bulletin of the New York Public Library* 80, 2 (Winter 1977): 211–20.

———. "Theater of War." In Jane Marcus, *Virginia Woolf: A Feminist Slant:* 212–35.

Seidl, Michael. "The Pathology of the Everyday: Uses of Madness in *Mrs. Dalloway* and *Ulysses.*" In Vara Neverow-Turk and Mark Hussey, eds. *Virginia Woolf: Themes and Variations:* 52–59.

Seymour, Miranda. *Ottoline Morrell: Life on the Grand Scale.* London: Hodder & Stoughton, 1992.

Shone, Richard. *Bloomsbury Portraits: Vanessa Bell, Duncan Grant, and Their Circle.* Oxford: Phaidon, 1976.

———. Review of *Bloomsbury: The Artists, Authors and Designers by Themselves.* Edited by Gillian Naylor. *Charleston Magazine* 2 (Autumn/Winter 1990): 46–48.

Showalter, Elaine. *The Female Malady: Women, Madness, and English Culture 1830–1980.* New York: Pantheon, 1985.

———. "Feminist Criticism in the Wilderness." In Elizabeth Abel, ed. *Writing and Sexual Difference.* Chicago: U of Chicago P, 1982.

———. *A Literature of Their Own: British Women Novelists from Brontë to Lessing.* Princeton: Princeton U P, 1977.

Silver, Brenda R. " 'Anon' and 'The Reader:' Virginia Woolf's Last Essays." Edited, with an introduction and commentary, by Brenda R. Silver. *Twentieth Century Literature* 25, 3/4 (Fall/Winter 1979): 356–441.

———. "The Authority of Anger: *Three Guineas* as Case Study." *Signs* 6, 2 (Winter 1991): 340–70.

———. "Textual Criticism as Feminist Practice: Or, Who's Afraid of Virginia Woolf Part II." In George Bornstein, ed. *Representing Modernist Texts: Editing as Interpretation.* Ann Arbor: U of Michigan P, 1991: 193–222.

———. "*Three Guineas* Before and After: Further Answers to Correspondents:" In Jane Marcus, ed. *Virginia Woolf: A Feminist Slant:* 254–76.

———. "Virginia Woolf and the Concept of Community: The Elizabethan Playhouse:" *Women's Studies* 2, 2/3 (1977): 291–98.

———. *Virginia Woolf's Reading Notebooks.* Princeton: Princeton U P, 1983.

———. "What's Woolf Got To Do With It? Or, The Perils of Popularity." *Modern Fiction Studies* 38, 1 (Spring 1992): 21–60.

Smith, Catherine, F. "*Three Guineas:* Virginia Woolf's Prophecy." In Jane Marcus, ed. *Virginia Woolf and Bloomsbury:* 225–41.

Smith, Lenora Penna. "Rooms and the Construction of the Feminine Self." In Vara Neverow-Turk and Mark Hussey, eds. *Virginia Woolf: Themes and Variations:* 216–25.

Smith, Lindsay. "The Politics of Focus: Feminism and Photography Theory." In Isobel Armstrong, ed. *New Feminist Discourses: Critical Essays on Theories and Texts.* London: Routledge, 1992: 238– 62.

Smith, Sidonie. "Resisting the Gaze of Embodiment: Women's Autobiography in the Nineteenth Century." In Margo Culley, ed. *American Women's Autobiography: Fea(s)ts of Memory.* Madison: U of Wisconsin P, 1992.

Smith, Susan Bennett. "Gender and the Canon: When Judith Shakespeare at Last Assumes Her Body." In Vara Neverow-Turk and Mark Hussey, eds. *Virginia Woolf: Themes and Variations:* 291–99.

Smith-Rosenberg, Carroll. *Disorderly Conduct: Visions of Gender in Victorian America.* New York: Alfred A. Knopf, 1985.

Spacks, Patricia Meyer. *The Female Imagination.* New York: Alfred A. Knopf, 1975.

Spalding, Frances. *Roger Fry: Art and Life.* Berkeley: U of California P, 1980.

———. *Vanessa Bell.* New Haven: Ticknor & Fields, 1983.

Spater, George, and Ian Parsons. *A Marriage of True Minds: An Intimate Portrait of Leonard and Virginia Woolf.* New York: Harcourt Brace Jovanovich, 1977.

Spender, Dale, ed. *Feminist Theorists: Three Centuries of Key Women Thinkers.* New York: Pantheon, 1983.

Spilka, Mark. *Virginia Woolf's Quarrel with Grieving.* Lincoln: U of Nebraska P, 1980.

Spivak, Gayatri Chakravorty. "Unmaking and Making in *To the Lighthouse.*" In *In Other Worlds: Essays in Cultural Politics.* New York: Methuen, 1987: 30–45.

Spotts, Frederic. *Letters of Leonard Woolf.* San Diego: Harcourt Brace Jovanovich, 1989.

Sprague, Claire, ed. *Virginia Woolf: A Collection of Critical Essays.* Englewood Cliffs: Prentice-Hall, 1971.

Squier, Susan Merrill. "A Track of Our Own: Typescript Drafts of *The Years.*" In Jane Marcus, ed. *Virginia Woolf: A Feminist Slant*: 198–211.

———. *Virginia Woolf and London: The Sexual Politics of the City.* Chapel Hill: U of N Carolina P, 1985.

———. "Tradition and Revision in Woolf's *Orlando*: Defoe and 'The Jessamy Brides.' " *Women's Studies* 12 (1986): 167–78.

———. "Woolf Studies Through *The Years*: Nationalism, Methodological Politics, and Critical Reproduction." In Vara Neverow-Turk and Mark Hussey, eds. *Virginia Woolf: Themes and Variations*: 16–24.

Stansky, Peter, and William Abrahams. *Journey to the Frontier: Two Roads to the Spanish Civil War.* Boston: Little, Brown & Co., 1966.

Stephen, James. *The Memoirs of James Stephen, Written by Himself for the Use of His Children.* London: Hogarth Press, 1954.

Stephen, Sir Leslie. *Sir Leslie Stephen's Mausoleum Book.* Introduction by Alan Bell. Oxford: Clarendon P, 1977.

Stevens, Michael. *V. Sackville-West: A Critical Biography.* London: Michael Joseph, 1973.

Stewart, Jack F. "Existence and Symbol in *The Waves.*" *Modern Fiction Studies* 18, 3 (Autumn 1972): 433–47.

———. "Spatial Form and Color in *The Waves.*" *Twentieth Century Literature.* 28, 1 (Spring 1982): 86–107.

Strachey, Lytton. *Eminent Victorians.* Harmondsworth: Penguin, 1975.

Strachey, Ray. *The Cause: A Short History of the Women's Movement in Great Britain.* (1928) New preface by Barbara Strachey. London: Virago, 1978.

Sypher, Eileen B. "*The Waves*: A Utopia of Androgyny?" In Elaine Ginsberg and Laura Moss Gottlieb, eds., *Virginia Woolf:* 187–213.

Temple, Ruth Z. "Never Say 'I:' *To the Lighthouse* as Vision and Confession." In Clare Sprague, ed. *Virginia Woolf: A Collection of Critical Essays*: 90–100.

Thomas, Sue. "Virginia Woolf's Septimus Smith and Contemporary Perceptions of Shell Shock." *English Language Notes* 25, 2 (December 1987): 49–57.

Tomalin, Claire. *Katherine Mansfield: A Secret Life.* New York: St. Martin's P, 1987.

Torgovnick, Marianna. *The Visual Arts, Pictorialism, and the Novel: James, Lawrence, and Woolf.* Princeton: Princeton U P, 1985.

Transue, Pamela J. *Virginia Woolf and the Politics of Style.* Albany: State U of New York P, 1986.

Trinh, T. Minh-ha. *Woman, Native, Other: Writing Postcoloniality and Feminism.* Bloomington: Indiana U P, 1989.

Trombley, Stephen. *All That Summer She Was Mad: Virginia Woolf, Female Victim of Male Medicine.* New York: Continuum, 1982.

Tvordi, Jessica. "*The Voyage Out*: Virginia Woolf's First Lesbian Novel." In Vara Neverow-Turk and Mark Hussey, eds. *Virginia Woolf: Themes and Variations*: 226–37.

Uglow, Jenny. "Josephine Butler: From Sympathy to Theory." In Dale Spender, ed. *Feminist Theorists*: 146–64.

Usui, Masami. "Discovering Woolf Studies in Japan." In Eileen Barrett and Patricia Cramer, eds. *Re: Reading, Re: Writing, Re: Teaching Virginia Woolf. Selected Papers from the Fourth Annual Conference on Virginia Woolf* (New York: Pace U P, 1995).

———. "The Female Victims of the War in *Mrs. Dalloway.*" In Mark Hussey, ed. *Virginia Woolf and War*: 151–63.

———. "The German Raid on Scarborough in *Jacob's Room.*" *Virginia Woolf Miscellany* 35: 7.

———. "A Portrait of Alexandra, Princess of Wales and Queen of England, in Virginia Woolf's *The Waves.*" In Vara Neverow-Turk and Mark Hussey, eds. *Virginia Woolf: Themes and Variations*: 121–27.

Vanita, Ruth. " 'Love Unspeakable:' The Uses of Allusion in *Flush.*" In Vara Neverow-Turk and Mark Hussey, eds., *Virginia Woolf: Themes and Variations*: 248–57.

Vicinus, Martha. *Independent Women: Work and Community for Single Women 1850–1920.* Chicago: U of Chicago P, 1985.

Walker, Alice. "In Search of Our Mothers' Gardens." In *In Search of Our Mothers' Gardens: Womanist Prose.* San Diego: Harcourt Brace Jovanovich, 1983.

———. "One Child of One's Own." Ibid.

Wang, Ban. " 'I' on the Run: Crisis of Identity in *Mrs. Dalloway.*" *Modern Fiction Studies* 38, 1 (Spring 1992): 177–91.

Warner, Eric. *Virginia Woolf: The Waves.* Landmarks in World Literature. New York: Cambridge U P, 1987.

———, ed. *Virginia Woolf: A Centenary Perspective.* New York: St. Martin's P, 1984.

Watney, Simon. "Duncan Grant." *Charleston Magazine* 1: 10–22.

Weiner, Gaby. "Harriet Martineau: A Reassessment." In Dale Spender, ed.: *Feminist Theorists*: 60–74.

West, Rebecca. *Ending in Earnest: A Literary Log.* (1931) Freeport, New York: Books for Libraries, 1967.

Wheare, Jane. *Virginia Woolf: Dramatic Novelist.* London: Macmillan, 1989.

———. "Introduction" to Virginia Woolf, *The Voyage Out.* London: Penguin, 1992.

Wilde, Alan. "Touching Earth: Virginia Woolf and the Prose of the World." In William E. Cain, ed. *Philosophical Approaches to Literature: New Essays on Nineteenth- and Twentieth-Century Texts.* Lewisburg: Bucknell U P, 1984: 140–64.

Willis, J. H. Jr. *Leonard and Virginia Woolf as Publishers. The Hogarth Press 1917–1941.* Charlottesville: U P of Virginia, 1992.

Wilson, Duncan. *Leonard Woolf: A Political Biography.* New York: St. Martin's, 1978.

Wilson, J. J. "From Solitude to Society Through Reading Virginia Woolf." In Mark Hussey and Vara Neverow, eds. *Virginia Woolf: Emerging Perspectives*: 13–18.

———. "Why is *Orlando* Difficult?" In Jane Marcus, ed. *New Feminist Essays*: 170–84.

Wilson, Jean Moorcroft. *Virginia Woolf, Life & London: A Biography of Place.* London: Cecil Woolf, 1987.

Woolf, Leonard. *An Autobiography*. Vol. 1: 1880–1911; Vol. 2: 1911–1969. New York: Oxford U P, 1980.

Woolf, Leonard, and James Strachey, eds. *Virginia Woolf and Lytton Strachey. Letters*. New York: Harcourt, Brace & Co., 1956.

Woolf, Virginia. *Between the Acts*. San Diego: Harvest/Harcourt Brace Jovanovich, 1969 (1941).

———. *Books and Portraits, Some Further Selections from her Literary and Biographical Writings*. Edited by Mary Lyon. London: Hogarth Press, 1977.

———. *The Captain's Death Bed and Other Essays*. New York: Harvest/Harcourt Brace Jovanovich, 1950.

———. *Collected Essays*. 4 vols. New York: Harcourt, Brace & World, 1967.

———. *The Common Reader*. London: Hogarth Press, 1925 (Reprinted 1975).

———. *The Common Reader, Second Series*. London: Hogarth Press, 1932 (Reprinted 1974).

———. *Congenial Spirits. The Selected Letters of Virginia Woolf*. Edited by Joanne Trautmann Banks. San Diego: Harcourt Brace Jovanovich, 1989.

———. *Contemporary Writers*. London: Hogarth Press, 1965.

———. *The Diary of Virginia Woolf*. 5 vols. Edited by Anne Olivier Bell. (Vols. 2–5 assisted by Andrew McNeillie). New York: Harcourt Brace Jovanovich, 1977–1984.

———. *The Death of the Moth and Other Essays*. New York: Harvest/Harcourt Brace Jovanovich, 1970 (1942).

———. *The Essays of Virginia Woolf*. Edited by Andrew McNeillie. 6 vols. Vol. 1: 1904–1912; Vol. 2: 1912–1918; Vol. 3: 1919–1924. San Diego: Harcourt Brace Jovanovich, 1986 (v. 1), 1987 (v. 2), 1988 (v. 3).

———. *Flush, A Biography*. New York: Harvest/Harcourt Brace Jovanovich 1961 (1933).

———. *Freshwater*. Edited by Lucio Ruotolo. New York: Harcourt Brace Jovanovich, 1976.

———. *Granite & Rainbow. Essays*. New York: Harvest/Harcourt Brace Jovanovich, 1975 (1958).

———. *Jacob's Room*. San Diego: Harvest/Harcourt Brace Jovanovich, 1950 (1922).

———. *The Letters of Virginia Woolf*. Edited by Nigel Nicolson and Joanne Trautmann. 6 vols. New York: Harcourt Brace Jovanovich, 1975–1980.

———. *Melymbrosia. An Early Version of The Voyage Out*. Edited by Louise A. DeSalvo. New York: New York Public Library, 1982.

———. *The Moment and Other Essays*. New York: Harvest/Harcourt Brace Jovanovich, 1974 (1948).

———. *Mrs. Dalloway*. San Diego: Harvest/Harcourt Brace Jovanovich, 1953 (1925).

———. *Mrs. Dalloway's Party. A Short Story Sequence*. Edited by Stella McNichol. New York: Harvest/Harcourt Brace Jovanovich, 1973.

———. *Moments of Being*. Edited by Jeanne Schulkind. Second edition. San Diego: Harvest/Harcourt Brace Jovanovich, 1985.

———. *Night and Day*. San Diego: Harvest/Harcourt Brace Jovanovich, 1948 (1920).

———. *Orlando, A Biography*. San Diego: Harvest/Harcourt Brace Jovanovich, 1956 (1928).

———. *A Passionate Apprentice. The Early Journals. 1897–1909*. Edited by Mitchell A. Leaska. San Diego: Harcourt Brace Jovanovich, 1990.

———. *The Pargiters. The Novel-Essay Portion of The Years*. Edited by Mitchell A. Leaska. San Diego: Harcourt Brace Jovanovich, 1978.

———. *Pointz Hall. The Earlier and Later Typescripts of Between the Acts*. Edited by Mitchell A. Leaska. New York: University Publications, 1983.

———. *Roger Fry, A Biography*. New York: Harvest/Harcourt Brace Jovanovich, 1976 (1940).

———. *A Room of One's Own*. Foreword by Mary Gordon. San Diego: Harvest/Harcourt Brace Jovanovich, 1989 (1929).

———. *The Complete Shorter Fiction of Virginia Woolf*. Edited by Susan Dick. San Diego: Harcourt Brace Jovanovich, 1985.

———. *Three Guineas*. New York: Harbinger/Harcourt, Brace & World, 1938.

———. *To the Lighthouse*. Foreword by Eudora Welty. San Diego: Harvest/Harcourt Brace Jovanovich, 1989 (1927).

———. *To the Lighthouse: The Original Holograph Draft*. Transcribed and edited by Susan Dick. Toronto: U of Toronto P, 1982.

———. *The Voyage Out*. San Diego: Harvest/Harcourt Brace Jovanovich, 1948 (1920).

———. *The Waves*. San Diego: Harvest/Harcourt Brace Jovanovich, 1978 (1931).

———. *The Waves. The Two Holograph Drafts*. Transcribed and edited by J. W. Graham. London: Hogarth Press, 1976.

———. *The Years*. San Diego: Harvest/Harcourt Brace Jovanovich, 1965 (1937).

———. *Women & Fiction. The Manuscript Versions of A Room of One's Own*. Edited by S. P. Rosenbaum. Cambridge, Mass.: Blackwell/Shakespeare Head Press, 1992.

Woolmer, J. Howard. *A Checklist of the Hogarth Press 1917–1938*. With a Short History of the Press by Mary E. Gaither. London: Hogarth Press, 1976.

Wussow, Helen. "Conflict of Language in Virginia Woolf's *Night and Day*." *Journal of Modern Literature* 16, 1 (Summer 1989): 61–73.

———. "War and Conflict in *The Voyage Out*." In

Mark Hussey, ed. *Virginia Woolf and War:* 101–09.

Wyatt, Jean. "Avoiding Self-definition: In Defense of Women's Right to Merge (Julia Kristeva and *Mrs Dalloway*)." *Women's Studies* 13 (1986): 115–26.

———. "The Celebration of Eros: Greek Concepts of Love and Beauty in *To the Lighthouse*." *Philosophy & Literature* 2 (1978): 160–75.

Yeats, W. B. *Selected Criticism.* Edited with an introduction and notes by A. Norman Jeffares. London: Macmillan, 1964.

Zolla, Elémire. *The Androgyne: Reconciliation of Male and Female.* New York: Crossroad, 1981.

Zwerdling, Alex. *Virginia Woolf and the Real World.* Berkeley: U of California P, 1986.

TOPICAL LIST OF WORKS CITED

Autobiographies and Biographical Studies of Woolf and Others

Annan, Noel. *Leslie Stephen. The Godless Victorian.* New York: Random House, 1984.

Bell, Quentin. *Virginia Woolf: A Biography.* Vol. 1, *Virginia Stephen 1882–1912.* Vol. 2, *Mrs. Woolf 1912–1941.* London: Hogarth Press, 1973.

Bell, Vanessa. *Notes on Virginia's Childhood.* Edited by Richard J. Schaubeck Jr. New York: Frank Hallman, 1974.

Bicknell, John W. "Mr. Ramsay Was Young Once." In Jane Marcus, ed. *Virginia Woolf and Bloomsbury:* 52–67.

Boyd, Elizabeth French. *Bloomsbury Heritage: Their Mothers and Their Aunts.* New York: Taplinger, 1976.

Cameron, Julia Margaret. *Victorian Photographs of Famous Men & Fair Women.* With introductions by Virginia Woolf and Roger Fry. Preface and notes by Tristram Powell. London: Hogarth P, 1973.

Caramagno, Thomas. *The Flight of the Mind: Virginia Woolf's Art and Manic-Depressive Illness.* Berkeley: U of California P, 1992.

Caws, Mary Ann. *Women of Bloomsbury: Virginia, Vanessa and Carrington.* New York: Routledge, 1990.

DeSalvo, Louise. "As 'Miss Jan Says': Virginia Woolf's Early Journals." In Jane Marcus, ed. *Virginia Woolf and Bloomsbury*: 96–124.

———. "1897: Virginia Woolf at Fifteen." In Jane Marcus, ed. *Virginia Woolf: A Feminist Slant.* Lincoln: U of Nebraska P, 1983.

———. "Lighting the Cave: The Relationship Between Vita Sackville-West and Virginia Woolf." *Signs: Journal of Women in Culture and Society* 8, 21 (Winter 1982): 195–214.

———. " 'Tinder-and-Flint': Virginia Woolf and Vita Sackville-West." In Whitney Chadwick and Isabelle de Courtivron, eds. *Significant Others: Creativity & Intimate Partnership.* New York: Thames and Hudson, 1993.

———. *Virginia Woolf: The Impact of Childhood Sexual Abuse on Her Life and Work.* Boston: Beacon, 1989.

Dunn, Jane. *A Very Close Conspiracy: Vanessa Bell and Virginia Woolf.* London: Pimlico, 1990.

Garnett, Angelica. *Deceived with Kindness: A Bloomsbury Childhood.* San Diego: HBJ, 1985.

Gathorne-Hardy, Jonathan. *Gerald Brenan: The Interior Castle. A Biography.* New York: W. W. Norton, 1992.

Glendinning, Victoria. *Vita: A Biography of Vita Sackville-West.* New York: Alfred A. Knopf, 1983.

Gordon, Lyndall. *Virginia Woolf: A Writer's Life.* Oxford: Oxford U P, 1984.

Hill, Katherine C. "Virginia Woolf and Leslie Stephen: History and Literary Revolution." *PMLA* 96 (1981): 351–62.

Holroyd, Michael. *Lytton Strachey: A Biography.* Harmondsworth: Penguin, 1971.

Holtby, Winifred. *Virginia Woolf.* London: Wishart & Co., 1932.

Lehmann, John. *Thrown to the Woolfs: Leonard and Virginia Woolf and the Hogarth Press.* NY: Holt, Rhinehart & Winston, 1978.

———. *Virginia Woolf and Her World.* London: Thames & Hudson, 1975.

Love, Jean O. *Virginia Woolf: Sources of Madness and Art.* Berkeley: U of California P, 1977.

MacKay, Carol Hanbery. "The Thackeray Connection: Virginia Woolf's Aunt Anny." In Jane Marcus, ed., *Virginia Woolf and Bloomsbury:* 68–95.

MacWeeney, Alen, and Sue Allison. *Bloomsbury Reflections.* New York: W. W. Norton, 1990.

Mepham, John. *Virginia Woolf: A Literary Life.* New York: St. Martin's P, 1991.

Ozick, Cynthia. "Mrs. Virginia Woolf." *Commentary* 56 (1973): 33–44.

Painter, Penny. "The Overlooked Influence of John Waller 'Jack' Hills on Virginia Woolf." Mark Hussey and Vara Neverow-Turk, eds. *Virginia Woolf Miscellanies:* 146–47.

Pippett, Aileen. *The Moth and the Star: A Biography of Virginia Woolf.* New York: Viking, 1957.

Poole, Roger. *The Unknown Virginia Woolf.* 3rd ed. Atlantic Highlands: Humanities Press International, 1990.

Raitt, Suzanne. *Vita & Virginia: The Work and Friendship of V. Sackville-West and Virginia Woolf.* New York: Oxford U P, 1993.

Rogat, Ellen Hawkes. "The Virgin in the Bell Biography." *Twentieth Century Literature* 20, 2 (April 1974): 96–113.

Rose, Phyllis. *Woman of Letters: A Life of Virginia Woolf.* New York: Oxford U P, 1978.

Sackville-West, Vita. *The Letters of Vita Sackville-West to Virginia Woolf.* Edited by Louise DeSalvo and Mitchell A. Leaska. New York: William Morrow, 1985.

Seymour, Miranda. *Ottoline Morrell: Life on the Grand Scale.* London: Hodder & Stoughton, 1992.

Spalding, Frances. *Roger Fry: Art and Life.* Berkeley: U of California P, 1980.

———. *Vanessa Bell.* New Haven: Ticknor & Fields, 1983.

Spater, George, and Ian Parsons. *A Marriage of True Minds: An Intimate Portrait of Leonard and Virginia Woolf.* New York: Harcourt Brace Jovanovich, 1977.

Stephen, James. *The Memoirs of James Stephen, Written by Himself for the Use of His Children.* London: Hogarth Press, 1954.

Stephen, Sir Leslie. *Sir Leslie Stephen's Mausoleum Book.* Introduction by Alan Bell. Oxford: Clarendon P, 1977.

Stevens, Michael. *V. Sackville-West: A Critical Biography.* London Michael Joseph, 1973.

Trombley, Stephen. *All That Summer She Was Mad: Virginia Woolf, Female Victim of Male Medicine.* New York: Continuum, 1982.

Woolf, Leonard. *An Autobiography.* Vol. 1: 1880–1911; Vol. 2: 1911–1969. New York: Oxford U P, 1980.

The Bloomsbury Group

Annan, Noel. "Bloomsbury and the Leavises." In Jane Marcus, ed. *Virginia Woolf and Bloomsbury:* 23–38.

Bell, Clive. *Old Friends.* New York: Harcourt, Brace & Co., 1956.

Bell, Quentin. *Bloomsbury.* London: Weidenfeld & Nicolson, 1986 (1968).

Edel, Leon. *Bloomsbury. A House of Lions.* New York: J. B. Lippincott Co., 1979.

Gadd, David. *The Loving Friends: A Portrait of Bloomsbury.* New York: Harcourt Brace Jovanovich, 1974.

Garnett, David. *Great Friends: Portraits of Seventeen Writers.* London: Macmillan, 1979.

Heilbrun, Carolyn G. *Toward a Recognition of Androgyny.* New York: Knopf, 1973.

Johnstone, J. K. *The Bloomsbury Group: A Study of E. M. Forster, Lytton Strachey, Virginia Woolf and Their Circle.* London: Secker & Warburg, 1954.

Naylor, Gillian, ed. *Bloomsbury: The Artists, Authors and Designers by Themselves.* London: Octopus, 1990.

Nicolson, Nigel. "Bloomsbury: the Myth and the Reality." In Jane Marcus, ed. *Virginia Woolf and Bloomsbury:* 7–22.

Noble, Joan Russell, ed. *Recollections of Virginia Woolf by Her Contemporaries.* New York: William Morrow, 1972.

Partridge, Frances. *Everything to Lose. Diaries 1945–1960.* Boston: Little, Brown & Co., 1985.

———. *Memories.* London: Victor Gollancz, 1981.

Reed, Christopher. "Bloomsbury Bashing: Homophobia and the Politics of Criticism in the Eighties." *Genders* 11 (Fall 1991): 58–80.

Rosenbaum, S. P., ed. *The Bloomsbury Group: A Collection of Memoirs, Commentary and Criticism.* Toronto: U of Toronto P, 1975.

———. *Edwardian Bloomsbury: The Early Literary History of the Bloomsbury Group.* Vol. 2. New York: St. Martin's, 1994.

———. "The Philosophical Realism of Virginia Woolf." In S. P. Rosenbaum, ed. *English Literature and British Philosophy: A Collection of Essays.* Chicago: Chicago U P, 1971: 316–56.

———. *Victorian Bloomsbury: The Early Literary History of the Bloomsbury Group.* New York: St. Martin's, 1987.

———. "Virginia Woolf and the Intellectual Origins of Bloomsbury." In Elaine K. Ginsberg and Laura Moss Gottlieb, eds., *Virginia Woolf: Centennial Essays.*

Draft Materials and Manuscripts

DeSalvo, Louise. *Virginia Woolf's First Voyage: A Novel in the Making.* Totowa: Rowman & Littlefield, 1980.

Lounsberry, Barbara. "The Art of Virginia Woolf's Diaries." In Mark Hussey and Vara Neverow, eds. *Virginia Woolf: Emerging Perspectives:* 266–71.

Radin, Grace. " 'Two Enormous Chunks:' Episodes Excluded During the Final Revisions of *The Years.*" *Bulletin of the New York Public Library* 80, 2 (Winter 1977): 221–51.

———. *Virginia Woolf's The Years: The Evolution of a Novel.* Knoxville: U of Tennessee P, 1981.

Silver, Brenda R. " 'Anon' and 'The Reader': Virginia Woolf's Last Essays." Edited, with an introduction and commentary, by Brenda R. Silver. *Twentieth Century Literature* 25, 3/4 (Fall/Winter 1979): 356–441.

———. "Textual Criticism as Feminist Practice: Or, Who's Afraid of Virginia Woolf Part II." In George Bornstein, ed. *Representing Modernist Texts: Editing as Interpretation.* Ann Arbor: U of Michigan P, 1991: 193–222.

Squier, Susan Merrill. "A Track of Our Own: Typescript Drafts of *The Years.*" In Jane Marcus, ed. *Virginia Woolf: A Feminist Slant:* 198–211.

Woolf, Virginia. *Melymbrosia. An early version of The*

Voyage Out. Edited by Louise A. DeSalvo. New York: New York Public Library, 1982.
———. *The Pargiters. The Novel-Essay Portion of The Years*. Edited by Mitchell A. Leaska. San Diego: Harcourt Brace Jovanovich, 1978.
———. *Pointz Hall. The Earlier and Later Typescripts of Between the Acts*. Edited by Mitchell A. Leaska. New York: University Publications, 1983.
———. *To the Lighthouse: The Original Holograph Draft*. Transcribed and edited by Susan Dick. Toronto: U of Toronto P, 1982.
———. *The Waves. The Two Holograph Drafts*. Transcribed and edited by J. W. Graham. London: Hogarth Press, 1976.
———. *Women & Fiction: The Manuscript Versions of A Room of One's Own*. Transcribed and edited by S. P. Rosenbaum. Oxford: Basil Blackwell, 1992.

Reference Works

Clarke, S. N. *A Bibliography of Virginia Woolf and the Bloomsbury Group: A Computerised Database*. London: S. N. Clarke, 1993.
Holleyman [George] and Treacher. *Catalogue of Books from the Library of Leonard and Virginia Woolf. Taken from Monk's House, Rodmell, Sussex and 24 Victoria Square, London and now in the possession of Washington State University, Pullman, U. S. A.* Brighton: Holleyman & Treacher, Ltd, 1975. [Limited edition of 250]
Richardson, Elizabeth P. *A Bloomsbury Iconography*. Winchester: St. Paul's Bibliographies, 1989.
Kirkpatrick, B. J. *A Bibliography of Virginia Woolf*. Third edition. Oxford: Clarendon P, 1980.
Majumdar, Robin, and Allen McLaurin, eds. *Virginia Woolf: The Critical Heritage*. London: Routledge & Kegan Paul, 1975.
McNees, Eleanor, ed. *Virginia Woolf: Critical Assessments*. 4 vols. New York: Routledge, 1994.
Schlack, Beverly Ann. *Continuing Presences: Virginia Woolf's Use of Literary Allusion*. University Park: Pennsylvania State U P, 1979.
Silver, Brenda R. *Virginia Woolf's Reading Notebooks*. Princeton: Princeton U P, 1983.
Woolmer, J. Howard. *A Checklist of the Hogarth Press 1917–1938*. With a Short History of the Press by Mary E. Gaither. London: Hogarth Press, 1976.

Studies of All or Several of Woolf's Works

a. Monographs and Essay Collections

Abel, Elizabeth. *Virginia Woolf and the Fictions of Psychoanalysis*. Chicago: U of Chicago P, 1989.
Alexander, Jean. *The Venture of Form in the Novels of Virginia Woolf*. Port Washington, N.Y.: Kennikat Press, 1974.
Apter, T. E. *Virginia Woolf: A Study of Her Novels*. New York: New York U P, 1979.
Bazin, Nancy Topping. *Virginia Woolf and the Androgynous Vision*. New Brunswick, N.J.: Rutgers U P, 1973.
Bennett, Joan. *Virginia Woolf: Her Art as a Novelist*. Cambridge, England: Cambridge U P, 1964.
Blackstone, Bernard. *Virginia Woolf: A Commentary*. London: Hogarth Press, 1949.
Bowlby, Rachel. *Virginia Woolf. Feminist Destinations*. New York: Basil Blackwell, 1988.
Brewster, Dorothy. *Virginia Woolf*. New York: New York U P, 1962.
———. *Virginia Woolf's London*. New York: New York U P, 1960.
Briggs, Julia, ed. *Virginia Woolf: Introductions to the Major Works*. London: Virago, 1994.
Caughie, Pamela L. *Virginia Woolf & Postmodernism. Literature in Quest and Question of Itself*. Urbana: U of Illinois P, 1991.
Clements, Patricia, and Isobel Grundy, eds. *Virginia Woolf: New Critical Essays*. Totowa: Barnes & Noble, 1983.
Daiches, David. *Virginia Woolf*. New York: New Directions, 1963.
DeSalvo, Louise. *Virginia Woolf: The Impact of Childhood Sexual Abuse on Her Life and Work*. Boston: Beacon, 1989.
DiBattista, Maria. *Virginia Woolf's Major Novels: The Fables of Anon*. New Haven: Yale U P, 1980.
Dowling, David. *Bloomsbury Aesthetics and the Novels of Forster and Woolf*. New York: St. Martin's Press, 1985.
Ferrer, Daniel. *Virginia Woolf and the Madness of Language*. Translated by Geoffrey Bennington and Rachel Bowlby. New York: Routledge, 1990.
Fleishman, Avrom. *Virginia Woolf. A Critical Reading*. Baltimore: Johns Hopkins U P, 1975.
Fox, Alice. *Virginia Woolf and the Literature of the English Renaissance*. Oxford: Clarendon, 1990.
Freedman, Ralph, ed. *Virginia Woolf: Revaluation and Continuity*. Berkeley: U of California P, 1980.
Gillespie, Diane F., ed. *The Multiple Muses of Virginia Woolf*. Columbia: U of Missouri P, 1993.
Ginsberg, Elaine K., and Laura Moss Gottlieb, eds. *Virginia Woolf: Centennial Essays*. Troy, New York: Whitston, 1983.
Guiguet, Jean. *Virginia Woolf and Her Works*. New York: Harcourt Brace Jovanovich, 1965.
Hafley, James. *The Glass Roof: Virginia Woolf as Novelist*. Berkeley: U of California P, 1954.
Harper, Howard. *Between Language and Silence: The Novels of Virginia Woolf*. Baton Rouge: Louisiana State U P, 1982.
Homans, Margaret, ed. *Virginia Woolf: A Collection*

of Critical Essays. Englewood Cliffs, N.J.: Prentice Hall, 1993.

Hussey, Mark. *The Singing of the Real World: The Philosophy of Virginia Woolf's Fiction.* Columbus: Ohio State U P, 1986.

Hussey, Mark, and Vara Neverow-Turk, eds. *Virginia Woolf Miscellanies: Proceedings of the First Annual Conference on Virginia Woolf.* New York: Pace U P, 1992.

———. eds. *Virginia Woolf: Emerging Perspectives. Selected Papers from the Third Annual Conference on Virginia Woolf.* New York: Pace U P, 1994.

Kelley, Alice van Buren. *The Novels of Virginia Woolf: Fact and Vision.* Chicago: U of Chicago P, 1973.

Kushen Betty. *Virginia Woolf and the Nature of Communion.* West Orange, N.J.: The Raynor Press, 1983.

Laurence, Patricia Ondek. *The Reading of Silence: Virginia Woolf in the English Tradition.* Stanford: Stanford U P, 1991.

Leaska, Mitchell A. *The Novels of Virginia Woolf from Beginning to End.* New York: John Jay P, 1977.

Lee, Hermione. *The Novels of Virginia Woolf.* London: Methuen, 1977.

Little, Judy. *Comedy and the Woman Writer: Woolf, Spark, and Feminism.* Lincoln: U of Nebraska P, 1983.

London, Bette. *The Appropriated Voice: Narrative Authority in Conrad, Forster, and Woolf.* Ann Arbor: U of Michigan P, 1990.

Love, Jean O. *Virginia Woolf: Sources of Madness and Art.* Berkeley: U of California P, 1977.

———. *Worlds in Consciousness: Mythopoetic Thought in the Novels of Virginia Woolf.* Berkeley: U of California P, 1970.

McCluskey, Kathleen. *Reverberations: Sound and Structure in the Novels of Virginia Woolf.* Ann Arbor: UMI Research Press, 1986.

McLaurin, Allen. *Virginia Woolf: The Echoes Enslaved.* Cambridge, England: Cambridge U P, 1973.

McNees, Eleanor, ed. *Virginia Woolf: Critical Assessments.* 4 vols. New York: Routledge, 1994.

Marcus, Jane. *Art and Anger: Reading Like a Woman.* Columbus: Ohio State U P, 1988.

———. *Virginia Woolf and the Languages of Patriarchy.* Bloomington: Indiana U P, 1987.

Marcus, Jane, ed. *New Feminist Essays on Virginia Woolf.* Lincoln: U of Nebraska P, 1981.

———. *Virginia Woolf and Bloomsbury: A Centenary Celebration.* Bloomington: Indiana U P, 1987.

———. ed. *Virginia Woolf: A Feminist Slant.* Lincoln: U of Nebraska P, 1983.

Marder, Herbert. *Feminism and Art: A Study of Virginia Woolf.* Chicago: U of Chicago P, 1968.

Meisel, Perry. *The Absent Father: Virginia Woolf and Walter Pater.* New Haven: Yale U P, 1980.

Mepham, John. *Virginia Woolf: A Literary Life.* New York: St. Martin's P, 1991.

———. *Virginia Woolf.* Criticism in Focus Series. New York: St. Martin's, 1992.

Minow-Pinkney, Makiko. *Virginia Woolf and the Problem of the Subject: Feminine Writing in the Major Novels.* New Brunswick, N.J.: Rutgers U P, 1987.

Moore, Madeline. *The Short Season Between Two Silences: The Mystical and the Political in the Novels of Virginia Woolf.* Boston: George Allen & Unwin, 1984.

Naremore, James. *The World Without a Self: Virginia Woolf and the Novel.* New Haven: Yale U P, 1973.

Neverow-Turk, Vara, and Mark Hussey, eds. *Virginia Woolf: Themes and Variations. Selected Papers from the Second Annual Conference on Virginia Woolf.* New York: Pace U P, 1993.

Novak, Jane. *The Razor Edge of Balance: A Study of Virginia Woolf.* Coral Gables, Fla.: U of Miami P, 1975.

Paul, Janis. *The Victorian Heritage of Virginia Woolf: The External World in Her Novels.* Norman: Pilgrim, 1987.

Pearce, Richard. *The Politics of Narration: James Joyce, William Faulkner, and Virginia Woolf.* New Brunswick, N. J.: Rutgers U P, 1991.

Poresky, Louise A. *The Elusive Self: Psyche and Spirit in Virginia Woolf's Novels.* Newark: U of Delaware P, 1981.

Raitt, Suzanne. *Vita & Virginia: The Work and Friendship of V. Sackville-West and Virginia Woolf.* New York: Oxford U P, 1993.

Richter, Harvena. *Virginia Woolf: The Inward Voyage.* Princeton: Princeton U P, 1970.

Rosenthal, Michael. *Virginia Woolf.* New York: Columbia U P, 1979.

Ruotolo, Lucio P. *The Interrupted Moment: A View of Virginia Woolf's Novels.* Stanford: Stanford U P, 1986.

Schaefer, Josephine O'Brien. *The Three-fold Nature of Reality in the Novels of Virginia Woolf.* The Hague: Mouton, 1965.

Schlack, Beverly Ann. *Continuing Presences: Virginia Woolf's Use of Literary Allusion.* University Park: Pennsylvania State U P, 1979.

Spilka, Mark. *Virginia Woolf's Quarrel with Grieving.* Lincoln: U of Nebraska P, 1980.

Sprague, Claire, ed. *Virginia Woolf: A Collection of Critical Essays.* Englewood Cliffs, N.J.: Prentice-Hall, 1971.

Squier, Susan Merrill. *Virginia Woolf and London: The Sexual Politics of the City.* Chapel Hill: U of North Carolina P, 1985.

Torgovnick, Marianna. *The Visual Arts, Pictorialism, and the Novel: James, Lawrence, and Woolf.* Princeton: Princeton U P, 1985.

Transue, Pamela J. *Virginia Woolf and the Politics of Style.* Albany: State of U of New York P, 1986.

Warner, Eric, ed. *Virginia Woolf: A Centenary Perspective*. New York: St. Martin's P, 1984.
Wheare, Jane. *Virginia Woolf: Dramatic Novelist*. London: Macmillan, 1989.
Zwerdling, Alex. *Virginia Woolf and the Real World*. Berkeley: U of California P, 1986.

b. Articles

Beer, Gillian. "The Island and the Aeroplane: The Case of Virginia Woolf." In Homi K. Bhabha, ed. *Nation and Narration*. London: Routledge, 1990: 265–90.
DuPlessis, Rachel Blau. " 'Amor Vin—:' Modifications of Romance in Woolf." In Margaret Homans, ed. *Virginia Woolf:* 115–35.
Froula, Christine. "Rewriting Genesis: Gender and Culture in Twentieth-Century Texts." *Tulsa Studies in Women's Literature* 7, 2 (Fall 1988): 197–220.
Gilbert, Sandra M. "The Battle of the Books/The Battle of the Sexes: Virginia Woolf's *Vita Nuova*." *Michigan Quarterly Review* 23 (1984): 171–95.
Gillespie, Diane Filby. " 'Her Kodak Pointed at His Head:' Virginia Woolf and Photography." In Diane F. Gillespie, ed. *The Multiple Muses:* 113–47.
Haller, Evelyn. "The Anti-Madonna in the Work and Thought of Virginia Woolf." In Elaine K. Ginsberg and Laura Moss Gottlieb, eds. *Virginia Woolf: Centennial Essays*.
———. "Her Quill Drawn from the Firebird: Virginia Woolf and the Russian Dancers." In Diane F. Gillespie, ed. *The Multiple Muses of Virginia Woolf:* 180–226.
———. "Isis Unveiled: Virginia Woolf's Use of Egyptian Myth." In Jane Marcus, ed. *Virginia Woolf: A Feminist Slant:* 109–31.
Ingram, Angela. " 'The Sacred Edifices:' Virginia Woolf and Some of the Sons of Culture." In Jane Marcus, ed. *Virginia Woolf and Bloomsbury:* 125–45.
Jacobs, Peter. " 'The Second Violin Tuning in the Ante-room:' Virginia Woolf and Music." In Diane F. Gillespie, ed. *The Multiple Muses of Virginia Woolf:* 227–60.

Studies of Specific Works by Woolf

a. Long works

BETWEEN THE ACTS

Barrett, Eileen. "Matriarchal Myth on a Patriarchal Stage: Virginia Woolf's *Between the Acts*." *Twentieth Century Literature* 33 (1987): 18–37.
Beer, Gillian. "Virginia Woolf and Pre-History." In Eric Warner, ed. *Virginia Woolf: A Centenary Perspective:* 99–123.
———. "Beyond Determinism: George Eliot and Virginia Woolf." In Gillian Beer, *Arguing with the Past: Essays in Narrative from Woolf to Sidney*. New York: Routledge, 1989.
Brownstein, Marilyn L. "Postmodern Language and the Perpetuation of Desire." *Twentieth Century Literature* 31 (1985): 73–88.
Cuddy-Keane, Melba. "The Politics of Comic Modes in Virginia Woolf's *Between the Acts*." *PMLA* 105, 2 (March 1990): 273–85.
Daugherty, Beth Rigel. "Face to Face with 'Ourselves' in Virginia Woolf's *Between the Acts*." In Vara Neverow-Turk and Mark Hussey, eds. *Virginia Woolf: Themes and Variations:* 76–82.
Eisenberg, Nora. "Virginia Woolf's Last Words on Words: *Between the Acts* and 'Anon.' " In Jane Marcus, ed. *New Feminist Essays on Virginia Woolf:* 253–66.
Froula, Christine "Rewriting Genesis: Gender and Culture in Twentieth-Century Texts." *Tulsa Studies in Women's Literature* 7, 2 (Fall 1988): 197–220.
Gillespie, Diane F. "Virginia Woolf's Miss La Trobe: The Artist's Last Struggle Against Masculine Values." *Women and Literature* 5, 1 (Spring 1977): 38–46.
Grundy, Isobel. " 'Words Without Meaning—Wonderful Words:' Virginia Woolf's Choice of Names." In Patricia Clements and Isobel Grundy, eds. *Virginia Woolf: New Critical Essays*.
Haller, Evelyn. "The Anti-Madonna in the Work and Thought of Virginia Woolf." In Elaine K. Ginsberg and Laura Moss Gottlieb, eds. *Virginia Woolf: Centennial Essays*.
———. "Isis Unveiled: Virginia Woolf's Use of Egyptian Myth." In Jane Marcus, ed. *Virginia Woolf: A Feminist Slant:* 109–31.
Hussey, Mark. " ' "I" Rejected; "We" Substituted:' Self and Society in *Between the Acts*." In Bege K. Bowers and Barbara Brothers, eds. *Reading and Writing Women's Lives: A Study of the Novel of Manners*. Ann Arbor: UMI Research Press, 1990: 141–52.
———. "Reading and Ritual in *Between the Acts*." *Anima* 15, 2 (Spring 1989): 89–99.
Johnston, Judith L. "The Remediable Flaw: Revisioning Cultural History in *Between the Acts*." In Jane Marcus, ed. *Virginia Woolf and Bloomsbury:* 253–277.
Joplin, Patricia Klindienst. "The Authority of Illusion: Feminism and Fascism in Virginia Woolf's *Between the Acts*." In Margaret Homans, ed. *Virginia Woolf:* 210–26.
Kenney, Susan M. "Two Endings: Virginia Woolf's Suicide and *Between the Acts*." *University of Toronto Quarterly* 44, 4 (Summer 1975): 265–89.
Laurence, Patricia Ondek. "The Facts and Fugue of War: From *Three Guineas* to *Between the Acts*." In Mark Hussey, ed. *Virginia Woolf and War:* 225–46.

Leavis, F. R. "After *To the Lighthouse.*" *Scrutiny* 10 (1942): 295–97.

Little, Judy. "Festive Comedy in Woolf's *Between the Acts.*" *Women and Literature* Spring 1977: 26–37.

Pawlowski, Merry. "Virginia Woolf's *Between the Acts:* Fascism in the Heart of England." In Mark Hussey and Vara Neverow-Turk, eds. *Virginia Woolf Miscellanies:* 188–91.

Scott, Bonnie Kime. "Woolf, Barnes and the Ends of Modernism: An *Antiphon* to *Between the Acts.*" In Vara Neverow-Turk and Mark Hussey, eds. *Virginia Woolf: Themes and Variations:* 25–32.

Sears, Sallie. "Theater of War." In Jane Marcus, *Virginia Woolf: A Feminist Slant:* 212–35.

Silver, Brenda R. "Virginia Woolf and the Concept of Community: The Elizabethan Playhouse." *Women's Studies* 2, 2/3 (1977): 291–98.

Wilde, Alan. "Touching Earth: Virginia Woolf and the Prose of the World." In William E. Cain, ed., *Philosophical Approaches to Literature: New Essays on Nineteenth- and Twentieth-Century Texts.* Lewisburg: Bucknell U P, 1984: 140–64.

FLUSH

DuPlessis, Rachel Blau. " 'Amor Vin—:' Modifications of Romance in Woolf." In Margaret Homans, ed. *Virginia Woolf:* 115–35.

Vanita, Ruth. " 'Love Unspeakable:' The Uses of Allusion in *Flush.*" In Vara Neverow-Turk and Mark Hussey, eds. *Virginia Woolf: Themes and Variations:* 248–57.

JACOB'S ROOM

Bishop, Edward. "The Subject in *Jacob's Room.*" *Modern Fiction Studies* 38, 1 (Spring 1992): 147–75.

Dobie, Kathleen. "This Is the Room that Class Built: The Structures of Sex and Class in *Jacob's Room.*" In Jane Marcus, ed. *Virginia Woolf and Bloomsbury:* 195–207.

Freedman, Ralph. "The Form of Fact and Fiction: *Jacob's Room* as Paradigm." In Freedman, ed. *Virginia Woolf:* 123–40.

Handley, William R. "War and the Politics of Narration in *Jacob's Room.*" In Mark Hussey, ed. *Virginia Woolf and War:* 110–133.

Ingram, Angela. " 'The Sacred Edifices:' Virginia Woolf and Some of the Sons of Culture." In Jane Marcus, ed. *Virginia Woolf and Bloomsbury:* 125–45.

Kiely, Robert. "*Jacob's Room* and *Roger Fry:* Two Studies in Still Life." In Robert Kiely, ed. *Modernism Reconsidered.* Harvard English Studies II. Cambridge, Mass.: Harvard U P, 1983: 147–66.

Levenback, Karen L. "Virginia Woolf and Rupert Brooke: Poised Between Olympus and the 'Real World.' " VWM 33: 5–6.

Morgenstern, Barry. "The Self-Conscious Narrator in *Jacob's Room.*" *Modern Fiction Studies* 18 (Autumn 1972): 351–61.

Ohmann, Carol. "Culture and Anarchy in *Jacob's Room.*" *Contemporary Literature* 18 (1977): 160–72.

Richter, Harvena. "Hunting the Moth: Virginia Woolf and the Creative Imagination." In Ralph Freedman, ed. *Virginia Woolf:* 13–28.

Ruddick, Sara. "Private Brother, Public World." In Jane Marcus, ed. *New Feminist Essays:* 185–215.

Schaefer, Josephine O'Brien. "The Great War and 'This late age of world's experience' in Cather and Woolf." In Mark Hussey, ed. *Virginia Woolf and War:* 134–50.

Usui, Masami. "The German Raid on Scarborough in *Jacob's Room.*" *Virginia Woolf Miscellany* 35: 7.

MRS. DALLOWAY

Abbott, Reginald. "What Miss Kilman's Petticoat Means: Virginia Woolf, Shopping, and Spectacle." *Modern Fiction Studies* 38, 1 (Spring 1992): 193–216.

Abel, Elizabeth. "Narrative Structure(s) and Female Development: The Case of *Mrs. Dalloway.*" In Margaret Homans, ed. *Virginia Woolf:* 93–114.

Bloom, Harold, ed. *Clarissa Dalloway.* Major Literary Characters Series. New York: Chelsea House, 1990.

Bowlby, Rachel. "Walking, Women and Writing: Virginia Woolf as *flâneuse.*" In Isobel Armstrong, ed. *New Feminist Discourses: Critical Essays on Theories and Texts.* London: Routledge, 1992.

Brower, Reuben Arthur. "Something Central Which Permeated: Virginia Woolf and *Mrs. Dalloway.*" In *The Fields of Light: An Experiment in Critical Reading.* New York: Oxford U P, 1951: 123–37.

DiBattista, Maria. "Joyce, Woolf and the Modern Mind." In Patricia Clements and Isobel Grundy, eds. *Virginia Woolf:* 96–114.

DuPlessis, Rachel Blau. " 'Amor Vin—:' Modifications of Romance in Woolf." In Margaret Homans, ed. *Virginia Woolf:* 115–35.

Edwards, Lee R. "War and Roses: The Politics of *Mrs. Dalloway.*" In Arlyn Diamond and Lee R. Edwards, eds. *The Authority of Experience: Essays in Feminist Criticism.* Amherts: U of Massachusetts P, 1977: 161–77.

Garvey, Johanna X. K. "Difference and Continuity: The Voices of *Mrs. Dalloway.*" *College English* 53, 1 (January 1991): 59–76.

Gelfant, Blanche H. "Love and Conversion in *Mrs. Dalloway.*" *Criticism* 8, 3 (Summer 1966): 299–45.

Hankins, Leslie Kathleen. "The Doctor and the Woolf: Reel Challenges—*The Cabinet of Dr. Caligari* and *Mrs. Dalloway.*" In Vara Neverow-Turk and Mark Hussey, eds. *Virginia Woolf: Themes and Variations:* 40–51.

Henke, Suzette A. "*Mrs. Dalloway:* The Communion of Saints." In Jane Marcus, ed. *New Feminist Essays on Virginia Woolf:* 125–47.

———. " 'The Prime Minister': A Key to *Mrs. Dallo-*

way." In Elaine K. Ginsberg and Laura Moss Gottlieb, eds. *Virginia Woolf: Centennial Essays*.

———. "Virginia Woolf Reads James Joyce." In Morris Beja, et al., eds. *James Joyce: The Centennial Symposium*. Urbana: U of Illinois P, 1986: 39–42.

Hessler, John G. "Moral Accountability in *Mrs. Dalloway*." *Renascence* 30, 3 (Spring 1978): 126–36.

Hoffman, Charles G. "From Short Story to Novel: The Manuscript Revisions of Virginia Woolf's *Mrs. Dalloway*." *Modern Fiction Studies* 14, 2 (Summer 1968): 171–86.

Hungerford, Edward A. " 'My Tunnelling Process:' The Method of *Mrs. Dalloway*." *Modern Fiction Studies* 3, 2 (Summer 1957): 164–67.

Jenkins, William D. "Virginia Woolf and the Belittling of *Ulysses*." *James Joyce Quarterly* 25, 4 (1988): 513–19.

Kiely, Robert. "A Long Event of Perpetual Change." From Robert Kiely, *Beyond Egotism:* 119–30.

Latham, Jacqueline. "The Manuscript Revisions of Virginia Woolf's *Mrs. Dalloway:* A Postscript." *Modern Fiction Studies* 18, 2 (Summer 1972): 475–76.

Miller, J. Hillis. "Virginia Woolf's All Souls' Day: The Omniscient Narrator in *Mrs. Dalloway*." In M. Friedman and J. Vickery, eds. *The Shaken Realist: Essays in Honor of F. J. Hoffman*. Baton Rouge: Louisiana State U P, 1970: 100–27.

———. *Fiction and Repetition: Seven English Novels*. Cambridge: Harvard U P, 1982.

Moon, Kenneth. "Where is Clarissa? Doris Kilman in *Mrs. Dalloway*." *CLA Journal* 23, 3 (March 1980): 273–86.

Pearce, Richard. "Who Comes First, Joyce or Woolf?" In Vara Neverow-Turk and Mark Hussey, eds. *Virginia Woolf: Themes and Variations:* 59–67.

Richter, Harvena. "The *Ulysses* Connection: Clarissa Dalloway's Bloomsday." *Studies in the Novel* 21, 3 (1989): 305–19.

Ruotolo, Lucio. *Six Existential Heroes: The Politics of Faith*. Cambridge: Harvard U P, 1973.

Schaefer, Josephine O'Brien. "The Great War and 'This late age of world's experience' in Cather and Woolf." In Mark Hussey, ed. *Virginia Woolf and War:* 134–50.

Schlack, Beverly Ann. "A Freudian Look at Mrs. Dalloway." *Literature & Psychology* 23 (1973): 49–58.

Seidl, Michael. "The Pathology of the Everyday: Uses of Madness in *Mrs. Dalloway* and *Ulysses*." In Vara Neverow-Turk and Mark Hussey, eds. *Virginia Woolf: Themes and Variations:* 52–59.

Thomas, Sue. "Virginia Woolf's Septimus Smith and Contemporary Perceptions of Shell Shock." *English Language Notes* 25, 2 (December 1987): 49–57.

Usui, Masami. "The Female Victims of the War in *Mrs. Dalloway*." In Mark Hussey, ed. *Virginia Woolf and War:* 151–63.

Wang, Ban. " 'I' on the Run: Crisis of Identity in *Mrs. Dalloway*." *Modern Fiction Studies* 38, 1 (Spring 1992): 177–91.

Wyatt, Jean. "Avoiding Self-definition: In Defense of Women's Right to Merge (Julia Kristeva and *Mrs. Dalloway*)." *Women's Studies* 13 (1986): 115–26.

NIGHT AND DAY

Cumings, Melinda F. "*Night and Day:* Virginia Woolf's Visionary Synthesis of Reality." *Modern Fiction Studies* 18 (1972): 339–49.

DuPlessis, Rachel Blau. " 'Amor Vin—:' Modifications of Romance in Woolf." In Margaret Homans, ed. *Virginia Woolf:* 115–35.

Fisher, Jane. " 'Silent as the Grave:' Painting, Narrative, and the Reader in *Night and Day* and *To the Lighthouse*." In Diane F. Gillespie, ed. *The Multiple Muses of Virginia Woolf:* 90–109.

Garner, Shirley Nelson. " 'Women Together' in Virginia Woolf's *Night and Day*." In Shirley Nelson Garner, Claire Kahane, and Madelon Sprengnether, eds. *The (M)other Tongue: Essays in Feminist Psychoanalytic Interpretation*. Ithaca: Cornell U P 1985.

Hussey, Mark. "Refractions of Desire: The Early Fiction of Virginia and Leonard Woolf." *Modern Fiction Studies* 38, 1 (Spring 1992): 127–46.

MacKay, Carol Hanbery. "The Thackeray Connection: Virginia Woolf's Aunt Anny." In Jane Marcus, ed. *Virginia Woolf and Bloomsbury:* 68–95.

McCail, Ronald. "A Family Matter: *Night and Day* and *Old Kensington*." *Review of English Studies* 38, 149 (Fall 1987): 23–39.

Wussow, Helen. "Conflict of Language in Virginia Woolf's *Night and Day*." *Journal of Modern Literature* 16, 1 (Summer 1989): 61–73.

ORLANDO

Baldanza, Frank. "*Orlando* and the Sackvilles" *PMLA* 70 (March 1955): 274–79.

Caughie, Pamela L. "Virginia Woolf's Double Discourse." In Marleen S. Barr and Richard Feldstein, eds. *Discontented Discourses: Feminism/Textual Intervention/Psychoanalysis*. Urbana and Chicago: University of Illinois Press, 1989: 41–53.

Clarke, Stuart Nelson. *Virginia Woolf. Orlando. The Holograph Draft*. Transcribed and edited by Stuart Nelson Clarke. London: S. N. Clarke, 1993.

Cooley, Elizabeth. "Revolutionizing Biography: *Orlando, Roger Fry*, and the Tradition." *South Atlantic Review* 55, 2 (May 1990): 71–83.

DuPlessis, Rachel Blau. " 'Amor Vin—:' Modifications of Romance in Woolf." In Margaret Homans, ed. *Virginia Woolf:* 115–35.

Gilbert, Sandra M. "Woman's Sentence, Man's Sentencing: Linguistic Fantasies in Woolf and Joyce." In Jane Marcus, ed. *Virginia Woolf and Bloomsbury:* 208–24.

Gillespie, Diane F. " 'Her Kodak Pointed at his Head:'

Virginia Woolf and Photography." In Diane F. Gillespie, ed. *The Multiple Muses:* 113–47.

Graham, J. W. "The 'Caricature Value' of Parody and Fantasy in *Orlando.*" *University of Toronto Quarterly* 30, 4 (July 1961): 345–65.

Green, David Bonnell. "*Orlando* and the Sackvilles: Addendum." *PMLA* 71, 1 (1956): 268–69.

Haller, Evelyn. "Her Quill Drawn from the Firebird: Virginia Woolf and the Russian Dancers." In Diane F. Gillespie, ed. *The Multiple Muses:* 180–226.

Hankins, Leslie Kathleen. " 'Across the Screen of my Brain:' Virginia Woolf's 'The Cinema' and Film Forums of the Twenties." In Diane F. Gillespie, ed. *The Multiple Muses:* 148–79.

Hoffman, Charles G. "Fact and Fantasy in *Orlando:* Virginia Woolf's Manuscript Revisions." *Texas Studies in Literature and Language* 10 (1968): 435–44.

Jones, Danell. "The Chase of the Wild Goose: The Ladies of Llangollen and *Orlando.*" In Vara Neverow-Turk and Mark Hussey, eds. *Virginia Woolf: Themes and Variations:* 181–89.

Knopp, Sherron E. " 'If I Saw You Would You Kiss Me?': Sapphism and the Subversiveness of Virginia Woolf's *Orlando.*" *PMLA* 103, 1 (January 1988): 24–34.

Lawrence, Karen R. "Orlando's Voyage Out." In *Modern Fiction Studies* 38, 1 (Spring 1992): 253–77.

Lokke, Kari Elise. "*Orlando* and Incandescence: Virginia Woolf's Comic Sublime." *Modern Fiction Studies* 38, 1 (Spring 1992): 235–52.

Moore, Madeline. "Virginia Woolf's *Orlando:* An Edition of the Manuscript." *Twentieth Century Literature* 25, 3/4 (Fall/Winter 1979): 303–55.

Roessel, David. "The Significance of Constantinople in *Orlando.*" *Papers on Language and Literature* (Fall 1992): 398–416.

Schaffer, Talia. "Posing *Orlando.*" In Ann Kibbey, Kayann Short, and Abouali Farmanfarmaian, eds. *Sexual Artifice.* Genders 19. New York: New York U P, 1994: 26–63.

Squier, Susan Merrill. "Tradition and Revision in Woolf's *Orlando:* Defoe and 'The Jessamy Brides.' " *Women's Studies* 12 (1986): 167–78.

Wilson, J. J. "Why is *Orlando* Difficult?" In Jane Marcus, ed. *New Feminist Essays:* 170–84.

ROGER FRY, A BIOGRAPHY

Broughton, Panthea Reid. " 'Virginia Is Anal:' Speculations on Virginia Woolf's Writing *Roger Fry* and Reading Sigmund Freud." *Journal of Modern Literature* 14, 1 (Summer 1987): 151–57.

Cooley, Elizabeth. "Revolutionizing Biography: *Orlando, Roger Fry,* and the Tradition." *South Atlantic Review* 55, 2 (May 1990): 71–83.

Kiely, Robert. "*Jacob's Room* and *Roger Fry:* Two Studies in Still Life." In Robert Kiely, ed. *Modernism Reconsidered.* Harvard English Studies II. Cambridge, Mass.: Harvard U P, 1983: 147–66.

Quick, Jonathan R. "Virginia Woolf, Roger Fry and Post-Impressionism." *Massachusetts Review* 26, 4 (Winter 1985): 547–70.

A ROOM OF ONE'S OWN

Bowlby, Rachel. "Walking, Women and Writing: Virginia Woolf as *flâneuse.*" In Isobel Armstrong, ed. *New Feminist Discourses: Critical Essays on Theories and Texts.* London: Routledge, 1992.

Bradbrook, M. C. "Notes on the Style of Mrs. Woolf." *Scrutiny* 1 (May 1932): 33–38.

DeSalvo, Louise. "Shakespeare's *Other* Sister." In Jane Marcus, ed. *New Feminist Essays:* 61–81.

Evans, Nancy Burr. "The Political Consciousness of Virginia Woolf: *A Room of One's Own* and *Three Guineas.*" *The New Scholar* 4 (1974): 167–80.

Ezell, Margaret J. M. "The Myth of Judith Shakespeare: Creating the Canon of Women's Literature." *New Literary History* 21 (Spring 1990): 579–92.

Folsom, Marcia McClintock. "Gallant Red Brick and Plain China: Teaching *A Room of One's Own.*" *College English* 45, 3 (March 1983): 254–62.

Fox, Alice. "Literary Allusion as Feminist Criticism in *A Room of One's Own.*" *Philological Quarterly* (Spring 1984): 145–61.

Joplin, Patricia Klindienst. " 'I Have Bought My Freedom:' The Gift of *A Room of One's Own.*" VWM 21 (Fall 1983): 4–5.

Kaplan, Cora. "Pandora's Box: Subjectivity, Class and Sexuality in Socialist-Feminist Criticism." In Terry Lovell, ed. *British Feminist Thought: A Reader.* Cambridge, Mass.: Blackwell, 1990.

Kamuf, Peggy. "Penelope at Work." In *Signature Pieces: On the Institution of Authorship.* Ithaca: Cornell U P, 1988.

London, Bette. "Guerrilla in Petticoats or Sans-Culotte? Virginia Woolf and the Future of Feminist Criticism." *diacritics* (Summer/Fall 1991): 11–29.

Marcus, Jane. "Daughters of Anger/Material Girls: Con/textualizing Feminist Criticism." *Women's Studies* 15 (1988): 281–308.

———. "Sapphistory: The Woolf and the Well." In Karla Jay and Joanne Glasgow, eds. *Lesbian Texts and Contexts: Radical Revisions.* New York: New York U P, 1990: 164–79.

Marshall, Denise. "Woolf's Monumental List-Works: Transforming Popular Culture's Semiotics of Space." In Vara Neverow-Turk and Mark Hussey, eds. *Virginia Woolf: Themes and Variations:* 268–76.

Miller, Nancy. "Teaching Autobiography." In *Getting Personal: Feminist Occasions and Other Autobiographical Acts.* New York: Routledge, 1991.

Modleski, Tania. "Some Functions of Feminist Criticism, or The Scandal of the Mute Body." *October* 49 (Summer 1989): 3–24.

Rosenbaum, S. P., ed. Virginia Woolf. *Women and Fiction: The Manuscript Versions of A Room of One's Own.* Transcribed and edited by S. P. Rosenbaum. Oxford: Basil Blackwell, 1992.

Rosenman, Ellen Bayuk. "Sexual Identity and *A Room of One's Own:* 'Secret Economies' in Virginia Woolf's Feminist Discourse." *Signs* 14, 3 (1989): 634–50.

Smith, Lenora Penna. "Rooms and the Construction of the Feminine Self." In Vara Neverow-Turk and Mark Hussey, eds. *Virginia Woolf: Themes and Variations:* 216–25.

Smith, Susan Bennett. "Gender and the Canon: When Judith Shakespeare At Last Assumes Her Body." In Vara Neverow-Turk and Mark Hussey, eds. *Virginia Woolf: Themes and Variations:* 291–99.

THREE GUINEAS

Batchelor, J. B. "Feminism in Virginia Woolf." In Claire Sprague, ed. *Virginia Woolf:* 169–79.

Black, Naomi. "Virginia Woolf and the Women's Movement." In Jane Marcus, ed. *Virginia Woolf: A Feminist Slant:* 180–97.

Carr, Glynis. "Waging Peace: Virginia Woolf's *Three Guineas." Proteus* 3, 2 (Fall 1986): 13–21.

Chapman, Wayne K., and Janet M. Manson. "Carte and Tierce: Leonard, Virginia Woolf, and War for Peace." In Mark Hussey, ed. *Virginia Woolf and War:* 58–78.

Childers, Mary M. "Virginia Woolf on the Outside Looking Down: Reflections on the Class of Women." *Modern Fiction Studies* 38, 1 (Spring 1992): 61–80.

Colum, Mary M. "Life and Literature: Are Women Outsiders?" *Forum and Century* 100 (1938): 222–26.

douglas, carol anne. "Dear Ms. Woolf, We Are Returning Your Guinea." *off our backs* 21 (Fall 1991): 5.

Evans, Nancy Burr. "The Political Consciousness of Virginia Woolf: *A Room of One's Own* and *Three Guineas." The New Scholar* 4 (1974): 167–80.

Froula, Christine. "St. Virginia's Epistle to an English Gentleman; or, Sex, Violence, and the Public Sphere in Woolf's *Three Guineas." Tulsa Studies in Women's Literature* 13, 1 (Spring 1994): 27–56.

Gottlieb, Laura Moss. "The War Between the Woolfs." In Jane Marcus, ed. *Virginia Woolf and Bloomsbury:* 242–52.

Heilbrun, Carolyn. "Woolf in Her Fifties." In Jane Marcus, ed. *Virginia Woolf: A Feminist Slant:* 236–53.

Herrmann, Anne. " 'Intimate, Irreticent and Indiscreet in the Extreme:' Epistolary Essays by Virginia Woolf and Christa Wolf." *New German Critique* 38 (Spring/Summer 1986): 161–80.

Ingram, Angela. " 'The Sacred Edifices:' Virginia Woolf and Some of the Sons of Culture." In Jane Marcus, ed. *Virginia Woolf and Bloomsbury:* 125–45.

Johnston, Georgia. "Women's Voice: *Three Guineas* as Autobiography." In Vara Neverow-Turk and Mark Hussey, eds. *Virginia Woolf: Themes and Variations:* 321–28.

Kramer, Lynn. "One Retrospective Lupine View: A Terrified Student's View of Virginia Woolf's *Three Guineas."* In Vara Neverow-Turk and Mark Hussey, eds. *Virginia Woolf: Themes and Variations:* 97–102.

Laurence, Patricia Ondek. "The Facts and Fugue of War: From *Three Guineas* to *Between the Acts."* In Mark Hussey, ed. *Virginia Woolf and War:* 225–46.

Middleton, Victoria. "*Three Guineas:* Subversion and Survival in the Professions." *Twentieth Century Literature* 8, 4 (Winter 1982): 405–17.

Mulhern, Francis. "English Reading." In Homi K. Bhabha, ed. *Nation and Narration.* New York: Routledge, 1990: 250–64.

Poole, Roger. " 'We all put up with you Virginia:' Irreceivable Wisdom About War." In Mark Hussey, ed. *Virginia Woolf and War:* 79–100.

Rosenberg, Karen. "Peaceniks and Soldier Girls." *The Nation* April 14, 1984: 453–57.

Schaefer, Josephine O'Brien. "*Three Guineas* and *Quack, Quack!* Read Together." *Virginia Woolf Miscellany* 7 (Spring 1977): 2–3.

Schlack, Beverly Ann. "Virginia Woolf's Strategy of Scorn in *The Years* and *Three Guineas." Bulletin of the New York Public Library* 80, 2 (Winter 1977): 146–50.

Sears, Sallie. "Notes on Sexuality: *The Years* and *Three Guineas." Bulletin of the New York Public Library* 80, 2 (Winter 1977): 211–20.

Silver, Brenda R. "The Authority of Anger: *Three Guineas* as Case Study." *Signs* 6, 2 (Winter 1991): 340–70.

———. "*Three Guineas* Before and After: Further Answers to Correspondents." In Jane Marcus, ed. *Virginia Woolf: A Feminist Slant:* 254–76.

Smith, Catherine F. "*Three Guineas:* Virginia Woolf's Prophecy." In Jane Marcus, ed. *Virginia Woolf and Bloomsbury:* 225–41.

TO THE LIGHTHOUSE

Auerbach, Erich. *Mimesis: The Representation of Reality in Western Literature.* Translated by Willard R. Trask. Princeton: Princeton U P, 1968 (1953).

Beer, Gillian. "Hume, Stephen, and Elegy in *To the Lighthouse." Essays in Criticism* 34, 1 (January 1984): 33–55.

———. "The Island and the Aeroplane: The Case of Virginia Woolf." In Homi K. Bhabha, ed. *Nation and Narration.* London: Routledge, 1990: 265–90.

Beja, Morris. ed. *Virginia Woolf: To The Lighthouse. A*

Selection of Critical Essays. London: Macmillan, 1970.
Bell, Quentin. "The Biographer, the Critic, and the Lighthouse." *Ariel* 2 (1971): 94–101.
Bicknell, John W. "Mr. Ramsay Was Young Once." In Jane Marcus, ed. *Virginia Woolf and Bloomsbury:* 52–67.
Blotner, Joseph. "Mythic Patterns in *To the Lighthouse.*" *PMLA* 71 (1956): 547–62. (Cited from Morris Beja, ed. *Virginia Woolf: To The Lighthouse. A Selection of Critical Essays:* 169–88.)
Carter, Miranda. "A Boeuf en Daube for *To the Lighthouse.*" *Charleston Magazine* 9 (Spring/Summer 1994): 50–53.
Clark, Miriam Marty. "Consciousness, Stream, and Quanta, in *To the Lighthouse.*" *Studies in the Novel* 21 (Winter 1989): 413–23.
Corsa, Helen Storm. "*To the Lighthouse:* Death, Mourning, and Transfiguration." *Literature and Psychology* 21, 3 (1971): 115–31.
DeKoven, Marianne. "History as Suppressed Referent in Modernist Fiction." *ELH* 51 (Spring 1984): 137–52.
Dodd, Elizabeth. " 'No, she said, she did not want a pear:' Women's Relation to Food in *To the Lighthouse* and *Mrs. Dalloway.*" In Vara Neverow-Turk and Mark Hussey, eds. *Virginia Woolf: Themes and Variations:* 150–57.
Donaldson, Sandra M. "Where does Q Leave Mr. Ramsay?" *Tulsa Studies in Women's Literature* (Fall 1992): 329–36.
Emery, Mary Lou. " 'Robbed of Meaning:' The Work at the Center of *To the Lighthouse.*" *Modern Fiction Studies* 38, 1 (Spring 1992): 217–34.
Ferguson, John. "A Sea Change: Thomas De Quincey and Mr. Carmichael in *To the Lighthouse.*" *Journal of Modern Literature* 14, 1 [Summer 1987]: 45–63.
Fisher, Jane. " 'Silent as the Grave:' Painting, Narrative, and the Reader in *Night and Day* and *To the Lighthouse.*" In Diane F. Gillespie, ed. *The Multiple Muses of Virginia Woolf:* 90–109.
Hankins, Leslie Kathleen. "A Splice of Reel Life in Virginia Woolf's 'Time Passes:' Censorship, Cinema, and 'the usual battlefield of emotions.' " *Criticism* 35, 1 (Winter 1993): 91–114.
Haule, James M. " 'Le Temps passe' and the Original Typescript: An early Version of the 'Time Passes' Section of *To the Lighthouse.*" *Twentieth Century Literature* 29, 3 (Fall 1983): 267–77.
———. "*To the Lighthouse* and the Great War: The Evidence of Virginia Woolf's Revisions of 'Time Passes.' " In Mark Hussey, ed. *Virginia Woolf and War:* 164–79.
Hoffmann, A. C. "Subject and Object and the Nature of Reality: The Dialectic of *To the Lighthouse.*" *Texas Studies in Literature and Language* 13, 4 (Winter 1972): 691–703.
Hoffman, Anne Golomb. "Demeter and Poseidon: Fusion and Distance in *To the Lighthouse.*" *Studies in the Novel* 16 (Summer 1984): 93–110.
Hussey, Mark. "*To the Lighthouse* and Physics: The Cosmology of David Bohm and Virginia Woolf." In Helen Wussow, ed. *New Essays on Virginia Woolf.* Dallas: Contemporary Research Press, 1995.
Jacobus, Mary. " 'The Third Stroke:' Reading Woolf with Freud." In Susan Sheridan, ed. *Grafts: Feminist Cultural Criticism.* London: Verso, 1988.
May, Keith M. "The Symbol of Painting in Virginia Woolf's *To the Lighthouse.*" *Review of English Studies* 9 (1967): 91–98.
Lavin, J. A. "The First Editions of Virginia Woolf's *To the Lighthouse.*" In Joseph Katz, ed. *Proof: The Yearbook of American Bibliographical and Textual Studies.* Vol. 2 Columbia: U of South Carolina P, 1972: 185–211.
Lilienfeld, Jane. " 'The Deceptiveness of Beauty:' Mother Love and Mother Hate in *To the Lighthouse.*" *Twentieth Century Literature* 23 (October 1977): 345–76.
———. " 'Like a Lion Seeking Whom He Could Devour': Domestic Violence in *To the Lighthouse.*" In Mark Hussey and Vara Neverow-Turk, eds. *Virginia Woolf Miscellanies:* 154–64.
———. "Where the Spear Plants Grew: the Ramsays' Marriage in *To the Lighthouse.*" In Jane Marcus, ed. *New Feminist Essays on Virginia Woolf:* 148–69.
Lund, Michael. " 'The Castaway' and *To the Lighthouse.*" *Journal of Modern Literature* 16 (Summer 1989): 75–92.
McVicker, Jeanette. "Vast Nests of Chinese Boxes, or Getting from Q to R: Critiquing Empire in 'Kew Gardens' and *To the Lighthouse.*" In Mark Hussey and Vara Neverow-Turk, eds., *Virginia Woolf Miscellanies:* 40–42.
Matro, Thomas G. "Only Relations: Vision and Achievement in *To the Lighthouse.*" *PMLA* 99 (1984): 212–24.
May, Keith M. "The Symbol of Painting in Virginia Woolf's *To the Lighthouse.*" *Review of English Studies* 9 (1967): 91–98.
Miller, J. Hillis. "Mr. Carmichael and Lily Briscoe: The Rhythm of Creativity in *To the Lighthouse.*" In Robert Kiely, ed. *Modernism Reconsidered.* Harvard English Studies II. Cambridge, Mass.: Harvard U P, 1983: 167–89.
Overcarsh, F. L. "The Lighthouse, Face to Face." *Accent* 10 (Winter 1959): 107–23.
Parkes, Graham. "Imagining Reality in *To the Lighthouse.*" *Philosophy & Literature* 6, 1 + 2 (Fall 1982): 33–44.
Poole, Roger. "Passage to the Lighthouse." *Charleston Newsletter* 16 (September 1986): 16–32.
Pratt, Annis. "Sexual Imagery in *To the Lighthouse:* A

New Feminist Approach." *Modern Fiction Studies* 18 (1972): 417–31.

Proudfit, Sharon. "Lily Briscoe's Painting: A Key to Personal Relations in *To the Lighthouse*." *Criticism* 13 (1971): 23–39.

Reid, Su. *To the Lighthouse: An Introduction to the Variety of Criticism*. London: Macmillan, 1991.

Roberts, John Hawley. "Vision and Design in Virginia Woolf." *PMLA* 61 (1946): 835–47.

Rosenbaum, S. P. "The Philosophical Realism of Virginia Woolf." In S. P. Rosenbaum, ed. *English Literature and British Philosophy*. Chicago: U of Chicago P, 1972.

———. "Railing Against Realism: Philosophy and *To the Lighthouse*." *Philosophy and Literature* 7, 1 (April 1983): 89–91.

Spivak, Gayatri Chakravorty. "Unmaking and Making in *To the Lighthouse*." In *In Other Worlds: Essays in Cultural Politics*. New York: Methuen, 1987: 30–45.

Temple, Ruth Z. "Never Say 'I': *To the Lighthouse* as Vision and Confession." In Clare Sprague, ed. *Virginia Woolf: A Collection of Critical Essays:* 90–100.

Wyatt, Jean. "The Celebration of Eros: Greek Concepts of Love and Beauty in *To the Lighthouse*." *Philosophy & Literature* 2 (1978): 160–75.

THE VOYAGE OUT

Beer, Gillian. "Virginia Woolf and Pre-History." In Eric Warner, ed. *Virginia Woolf: A Centenary Perspective:* 99–123.

Bishop, E. L. "Toward the Far Side of Language: Virginia Woolf's *The Voyage Out*." *Twentieth Century Literature* 27, 4 (Winter 1981): 343–61.

Blain, Virginia. "Narrative Voice and the Female Perspective in Virginia Woolf's Early Novels." In Patricia Clements and Isobel Grundy, eds. *Virginia Woolf: New Critical Essays*. Totowa: Barnes & Noble, 1983.

Davis-Clapper, Laura. "Why Did Rachel Vinrace Die? Tracing the Clues from *Melymbrosia* to *The Voyage Out*." In Mark Hussey and Vara Neverow-Turk, eds. *Virginia Woolf Miscellanies:* 225–27.

DeKoven, Marianne. *Rich and Strange: Gender, History, Modernism*. Princeton: Princeton U P, 1991.

DeSalvo, Louise. "Sorting, Sequencing, and Dating the Drafts of Virginia Woolf's *The Voyage Out*." *Bulletin of Research in the Humanities* 82, 3 (Autumn 1979): 271–93.

———. *Virginia Woolf's First Voyage: A Novel in the Making*. Totowa: Rowman & Littlefield, 1980.

———. "Virginia Woolf's Revisions for the 1920 American and English Editions of *The Voyage Out*." *Bulletin of Research in the Humanities* 82, 3 (Autumn 1979): 338–66.

Dick, Susan. "The Tunnelling Process: Some Aspects of Virginia Woolf's Use of Memory and the Past." In Patricia Clements and Isobel Grundy, eds. *Virginia Woolf: New Critical Essays:* 176–99.

DuPlessis, Rachel Blau. " 'Amor Vin—:' Modifications of Romance in Woolf." In Margaret Homans, ed. *Virginia Woolf:* 115–35.

Friedman, Susan Stanford. "Virginia Woolf's Pedagogical Scenes of Reading: *The Voyage Out, The Common Reader*, and Her 'Common Readers.' " *Modern Fiction Studies* 38, 1 (Spring 1992): 101–25.

Froula, Christine. "Out of the Chrysalis: Female Initiation and Female Authority in Virginia Woolf's *The Voyage Out*." In Margaret Homans, ed. *Virginia Woolf:* 136–61.

Gregor, Ian. "Virginia Woolf and Her Reader." In Eric Warner, ed. *Virginia Woolf:* 41–55.

Heine, Elizabeth. "The Earlier *Voyage Out:* Virginia Woolf's First Novel." *Bulletin of Research in the Humanities* 82, 3 (Autumn 1979): 294–316.

———. "New Light on *Melymbrosia*." In Mark Hussey and Vara Neverow-Turk, eds. *Virginia Woolf Miscellanies*.

———. "Virginia Woolf's Revisions of *The Voyage Out*." In Virginia Woolf, *The Voyage Out*. London: Hogarth Press, 1990. (The Definitive Collected Edition of the Novels of Virginia Woolf.)

Hussey, Mark. "Refractions of Desire: The Early Fiction of Virginia and Leonard Woolf." *Modern Fiction Studies* 38, 1 (Spring 1992): 127–46.

Lambert, Elizabeth G. " 'and Darwin says they are nearer the cow:' Evolutionary Discourse in *Melymbrosia* and *The Voyage Out*." *Twentieth Century Literature* 37, 1 (Spring 1991): 1–21.

McDowell, Frederick P. W. " 'Surely Order Did Prevail:' Virginia Woolf and *The Voyage Out*." In Ralph Freedman, ed. *Virginia Woolf:* 73–96.

Moore, Madeline. "Some Female Versions of Pastoral: *The Voyage Out* and Matriarchal Mythologies." In Jane Marcus, ed. *New Feminist Essays on Virginia Woolf:* 82–104.

Neumann, Shirley. "*Heart of Darkness*, Virginia Woolf and the Spectre of Domination." In Patricia Clements and Isobel Grundy, eds. *Virginia Woolf: New Critical Essays*.

Pitt, Rosemary. "The Exploration of Self in Conrad's *Heart of Darkness* and Woolf's *The Voyage Out*." *Conradiana* 10 (1978): 141–54.

Schlack, Beverly Ann. "The Novelist's Voyage from Manuscripts to Text: Revisions of Literary Allusions in *The Voyage Out*." *Bulletin of Research in the Humanities* 82, 3 (Autumn 1979): 317–27.

Tvordi, Jessica. "*The Voyage Out:* Virginia Woolf's First Lesbian Novel." In Vara Neverow-Turk and Mark Hussey, eds. *Virginia Woolf: Themes and Variations:* 226–37.

Wussow, Helen. "War and Conflict in *The Voyage Out*." In Mark Hussey, ed. *Virginia Woolf and War:* 101–09.

THE WAVES

Ascher, Carol. "Reading to Write: *The Waves* as Muse." In Mark Hussey and Vara Neverow-Turk, eds. *Virginia Woolf Miscellanies:* 47–56.

Boone, Joseph Allen. "The Meaning of Elvedon in *The Waves.*" *Modern Fiction Studies* 27, 4 (Winter 1981–82): 629–37.

Dick, Susan. "I Remembered, I Forgotten: Bernard's Final Soliloquy in *The Waves.*" *Modern Language Studies* 13, 3 (1983): 38–52.

DuPlessis, Rachel Blau. "WOOLFENSTEIN." In Ellen G. Friedman and Miriam Fuchs, eds. *Breaking the Sequence: Women's Experimental Fiction.* Princeton: Princeton U P, 1989: 99–114.

Eder, Doris L. "Louis Unmasked: T. S. Eliot in *The Waves.*" *Virginia Woolf Quarterly* 2, 1 and 2 (Winter–Spring 1975).

Gorsky, Susan. " 'The Central Shadow:' Characterization in *The Waves.*" *Modern Fiction Studies* 18, 3 (Autumn 1972): 449–66.

Graham, J. W. "Manuscript Revision and the Heroic Theme of *The Waves.*" *Twentieth Century Literature* 29, 3 (Fall 1983): 312–32.

———. "Point of View in *The Waves:* Some Services of the Style." *University of Toronto Quarterly* 39 (April 1970): 193–211.

Gregor, Ian. "Virginia Woolf and Her Reader." In Eric Warner, ed. *Virginia Woolf:* 41–55.

Haller, Evelyn. "Her Quill Drawn from the Firebird: Virginia Woolf and the Russian Dancers." In Diane F. Gillespie, ed. *The Multiple Muses of Virginia Woolf:* 180–226.

Havard-Williams, Peter, and Margaret Havard-Williams. "Mystical Experience in Virginia Woolf's *The Waves.*" *Essays in Criticism* 4 (January 1954): 71–84.

Henke, Suzette A. "Virginia Woolf's *The Waves:* A Phenomenological Reading." *Neophilologus* 73 (1989): 461–72.

Jacobs, Peter. " 'The Second Violin Tuning in the Ante-room:' Virginia Woolf and Music." In Diane F. Gillespie, ed. *The Multiple Muses of Virginia Woolf:* 227–60.

Johnston, Judith L. " 'Necessary Bore' or Brilliant Novelist: What Marguerite Yourcenar Understood about Woolf's *The Waves.*" In Mark Hussey and Vara Neverow-Turk, eds. *Virginia Woolf Miscellanies:* 125–322.

Lee, Judith. " 'This hideous shaping and moulding:' War and *The Waves.*" In Mark Hussey, ed. *Virginia Woolf and War:* 180–202.

Levin, Gerald. "The Musical Style of *The Waves.*" *Journal of Narrative Technique* 13, 3 (1983): 164–71.

Lorsch, Susan E. *Where Nature Ends: Literary Responses to the Designification of Landscape.* Rutherford: Fairleigh Dickinson U P, 1983.

McConnell, Frank D. " 'Death Among the Apple Trees:' *The Waves* and the World of Things." In Clare Sprague, ed. *Virginia Woolf:* 117–29.

Marcus, Jane. "Britannia Rules *The Waves.*" In Karen Lawrence, ed. *Decolonizing Tradition: The Cultural Politics of Modern Literary Canons.* Urbana: U of Illinois P, 1991: 136–62.

Moore, Madeline. "Nature and Communion: A Study of Cyclical Reality in *The Waves.*" In Ralph Freedman, ed. *Virginia Woolf: Revaluation and Continuity:* 219–40.

Oxindine, Annette. "Sapphist Semiotics in Woolf's *The Waves:* Untelling and Retelling What Cannot be Told." In Vara Neverow-Turk and Mark Hussey, eds. *Virginia Woolf: Themes and Variations:* 171–81.

Poresky, Louise. "Eternal Renewal: Life and Death in Virginia Woolf's *The Waves.*" In Mark Hussey and Vara Neverow-Turk, eds. *Virginia Woolf Miscellanies:* 64–70.

Rantavaara, Irma. *Virginia Woolf's The Waves.* Port Washington: Kennikat Press, 1960.

Richter, Harvena. "Hunting the Moth: Virginia Woolf and the Creative Imagination." In Ralph Freedman, ed. *Virginia Woolf:* 13–28.

Schulze, Robin Gail. "Design in Motion: Words, Music, and the Search for Coherence in the Works of Virginia Woolf and Arnold Schoenberg." *Studies in the Literary Imagination* 25, 2 (Fall 1992): 5–22.

Stewart, Jack F. "Existence and Symbol in *The Waves.*" *Modern Fiction Studies* 18, 3 (Autumn 1972): 433–47.

———. "Spatial Form and Color in *The Waves.*" *Twentieth Century Literature* 28, 1 (Spring 1982): 86–107.

Sypher, Eileen B. "*The Waves:* A Utopia of Androgyny." In Elaine Ginsberg and Laura Moss Gottlieb, eds. *Virginia Woolf.*

Usui, Masami. "A Portrait of Alexandra, Princess of Wales and Queen of England, in Virginia Woolf's *The Waves.*" In Vara Neverow-Turk and Mark Hussey, eds. *Virginia Woolf: Themes and Variations:* 121–27.

Warner, Eric. *Virginia Woolf: The Waves.* Landmarks in World Literature. New York: Cambridge U P, 1987.

THE YEARS

Comstock, Margaret. "The Loudspeaker and the Human Voice: Politics and the Form of *The Years.*" *Bulletin of the New York Public Library* 80, 2 (Winter 1977): 252–75.

Cramer, Patricia. " 'Loving in the War Years:' The War of Images in *The Years.*" In Mark Hussey, ed. *Virginia Woolf and War:* 203–24.

Eberly, David. "Incest, Erasure, and *The Years.*" In Mark Hussey and Vara Neverow, eds. *Virginia Woolf: Emerging Perspectives:* 147–56.

Gottlieb, Laura Moss. "*The Years:* A Feminist Novel."

In Elaine K. Ginsberg and Laura Moss Gottlieb, eds. *Virginia Woolf.*
Heilbrun, Carolyn G. "Woolf in Her Fifties." In Jane Marcus, ed. *Virginia Woolf: A Feminist Slant:* 236–53.
Hoffman, Charles G. "Virginia Woolf's Manuscript Revisions of *The Years.*" *PMLA* 84 (1969): 79–89.
Jacobs, Peter. " 'The Second Violin Tuning in the Ante-room:' Virginia Woolf and Music." In Diane F. Gillespie, ed. *The Multiple Muses of Virginia Woolf:* 227–60.
Leaska, Mitchell A. "Virginia Woolf, the Pargeter: A Reading of *The Years.*" *Bulletin of the New York Public Library* 80, 2 (Winter 1977): 172–210.
Levenback, Karen L. "Placing the First 'Enormous Chunk' Deleted from *The Years.*" *Virginia Woolf Miscellany* 42 (Spring 1994): 8–9.
Lipking, Joanna. "Looking at the Monuments: Woolf's Satiric Eye." *Bulletin of the New York Public Library* 80, 2 (Winter 1977): 141–45.
Middleton, Victoria S. "*The Years:* 'A Deliberate Failure.' " *Bulletin of the New York Public Library* 80, 2 (Winter 1977): 159–71.
Moore, Madeline. "Virginia Woolf's *The Years* and Years of Adverse Male Reviewers." *Women's Studies* 4 (1977): 247–63.
Naremore, James. "Nature and History in *The Years.*" In Ralph Freedman, ed. *Virginia Woolf: Revaluation and Continuity:* 241–62.
Proudfit, Sharon. "Virginia Woolf: Reluctant Feminist in *The Years.*" *Criticism* 17 (1975): 59–73.
Radin, Grace. " 'Two Enormous Chunks:' Episodes Excluded During the Final Revisions of *The Years.*" *Bulletin of the New York Public Library* 80, 2 (Winter 1977): 221–51.
———. *Virginia Woolf's The Years: The Evolution of a Novel.* Knoxville: U of Tennessee P, 1981.
Schlack, Beverly Ann. "Virginia Woolf's Strategy of Scorn in *The Years* and *Three Guineas.*" *Bulletin of the New York Public Library* 80, 2 (Winter 1977): 146–50.
Sears, Sallie. "Notes on Sexuality: *The Years* and *Three Guineas.*" *Bulletin of the New York Public Library* 80, 2 (Winter 1977): 211–20.
Silver, Brenda R. "Textual Criticism as Feminist Practice: Or, Who's Afraid of Virginia Woolf Part II." In George Bornstein, ed. *Representing Modernist Texts: Editing as Interpretation.* Ann Arbor: U of Michigan P, 1991: 193–222.
Squier, Susan Merrill. "A Track of Our Own: Typescript Drafts of *The Years.*" In Jane Marcus, ed. *Virginia Woolf: A Feminist Slant:* 198–211.
———. "Woolf Studies Through *The Years:* Nationalism, Methodological Politics, and Critical Reproduction." In Vara Neverow-Turk and Mark Hussey, eds. *Virginia Woolf: Themes and Variations:* 16–24.

b. Shorter works (fiction)

Baldwin, Dean. *Virginia Woolf: A Study of the Short Fiction.* Boston: Twayne, 1989.
Bishop, Edward. "Pursuing 'It' through 'Kew Gardens.' " In Dean Baldwin, ed. *Virginia Woolf:* 109–17.
Dick, Susan. " '*What Fools We Were!*': Virginia Woolf's *A Society.*" *Twentieth Century Literature* 33 (Spring 1987): 53.
Fleishman, Avrom. "Forms of the Woolfian Short Story." In Ralph Freedman, ed. *Virginia Woolf:* 44–70.
McVicker, Jeanette. "Vast Nests of Chinese Boxes, or Getting from Q to R: Critiquing Empire in 'Kew Gardens' and *To the Lighthouse.*" In Mark Hussey and Vara Neverow-Turk, eds. *Virginia Woolf Miscellanies:* 40–42.
Saunders, Judith P. "Mortal Stain: Literary Allusion and Female Sexuality in 'Mrs. Dalloway in Bond Street.' " *Studies in Short Fiction* 15, 2 (Spring 1978): 139–44.

c. Shorter works (essays)

Daugherty, Beth Rigel. "The Whole Contention Between Mr. Bennett and Mrs. Woolf Revisited." In Elaine K. Ginsberg and Laura Moss Gottlieb, eds. *Virginia Woolf: Centennial Essays.*
Friedman, Susan Stanford. "Virginia Woolf's Pedagogical Scenes of Reading: *The Voyage Out, The Common Reader,* and Her 'Common Readers.' " *Modern Fiction Studies* 38, 1 (Spring 1992): 101–25.
Hankins, Leslie K. " 'Across the Screen of my Brain:' Virginia Woolf's 'The Cinema' and Film Forums of the Twenties." In Diane F. Gillespie, ed. *The Multiple Muses:* 148–79.
Kenney, Edwin J. Jr. "The Moment, 1910: Virginia Woolf, Arnold Bennett, and Turn of the Century Consciousness." *The Colby Library Quarterly* 13 (1977): 42–66.
Luftig, Victor. "Woolf and the Leaflet Touch: A Political Context for 'Mr. Bennett and Mrs. Brown.' *Virginia Woolf Miscellany* 27 (Fall 1986): 1–2.
Rosenberg, Beth. "Virginia Woolf: Conversation and the Common Reader." In Mark Hussey and Vara Neverow-Turk, eds., *Virginia Woolf Miscellanies:* 1–8.

Thematic Studies

Androgyny

Farwell, Marilyn R. "Virginia Woolf and Androgyny." *Contemporary Literature* 16, 4 (Autumn 1975): 433–51.
Fassler, Barbara. "Theories of Homosexuality as Sources of Bloomsbury's Androgyny." *Signs* 5 (1979): 237–51.

Heilbrun, Carolyn G. *Toward a Recognition of Androgyny*. New York: Knopf, 1973.

Sypher, Eileen B. "*The Waves:* A Utopia of Androgyny." In Elaine Ginsberg and Laura Moss Gottlieb, eds. *Virginia Woolf:* 187–213.

***Feminism/Politics* (See also *A Room of One's Own; Three Guineas*; War)**

Batchelor, J. B. "Feminism in Virginia Woolf." In Claire Sprague, ed. *Virginia Woolf:* 169–79.

Black, Naomi. "Virginia Woolf and the Women's Movement." In Jane Marcus, ed. *Virginia Woolf: A Feminist Slant:* 180–97.

Bowlby, Rachel. "Walking, Women and Writing: Virginia Woolf as *flâneuse*." In Isobel Armstrong, ed. *New Feminist Discourses: Critical Essays on Theories and Texts*. London: Routledge, 1992.

Carroll, Berenice A. " 'To Crush Him in Our Own Country:' The Political Thought of Virginia Woolf." *Feminist Studies* 4 (1978): 99–131.

Childers, Mary M. "Virginia Woolf on the Outside Looking Down: Reflections on the Class of Women." *Modern Fiction Studies* 38, 1 (Spring 1992): 61–80.

Evans, Nancy Burr. "The Political Consciousness of Virginia Woolf: *A Room of One's Own* and *Three Guineas*." *The New Scholar* 4 (1974): 167–80.

Flint, Kate. "Virginia Woolf and the General Strike." *Essays in Criticism* 36 (1986): 319–34.

Marder, Herbert. *Feminism and Art: A Study of Virginia Woolf*. Chicago: U of Chicago P, 1968.

Reed, Christopher. "Through Formalism: Feminism and Virginia Woolf's Relation to Bloomsbury Aesthetics." In Diane F. Gillespie, ed. *The Multiple Muses of Virginia Woolf:* 11–35.

Incest

DeSalvo, Louise. *Virginia Woolf: The Impact of Childhood Sexual Abuse on Her Life and Work*. Boston: Beacon, 1989.

Eberly, David. "Incest, Erasure, and *The Years*." In Mark Hussey and Vara Neverow, eds. *Virginia Woolf: Emerging Perspectives:* 147–56.

Lesbian Studies

Cook, Blanche Wiesen. " 'Women Alone Stir My Imagination:' Lesbianism and the Cultural Tradition." *Signs* 4, 4 (Summer 1979): 718–39.

Jones, Danell. "The Chase of the Wild Goose: The Ladies of Llangollen and *Orlando*." In Vara Neverow-Turk and Mark Hussey, eds. *Virginia Woolf: Themes and Variations:* 181–89.

Knopp, Sherron E. " 'If I Saw You Would You Kiss Me?': Sapphism and the Subversiveness of Virginia Woolf's *Orlando*." *PMLA* 103, 1 (January 1988): 24–34.

Marcus, Jane. "Sapphistory: The Woolf and the Well." In Karla Jay and Joanne Glasgow, eds. *Lesbian Texts and Contexts: Radical Revisions*. New York: New York U P, 1990: 164–79.

Oxindine, Annette. "Sapphist Semiotics in Woolf's *The Waves:* Untelling and Retelling What Cannot be Told." In Vara Neverow-Turk and Mark Hussey, eds. *Virginia Woolf: Themes and Variations:* 171–81.

Raitt, Suzanne. *Vita & Virginia: The Work and Friendship of V. Sackville-West and Virginia Woolf*. New York: Oxford U P, 1993.

Tvordi, Jessica. "*The Voyage Out:* Virginia Woolf's First Lesbian Novel." In Vara Neverow-Turk and Mark Hussey, eds. *Virginia Woolf: Themes and Variations:* 226–37.

Vanita, Ruth. " 'Love Unspeakable:' The Uses of Allusion in *Flush*." In Vara Neverow-Turk and Mark Hussey, eds., *Virginia Woolf: Themes and Variations:* 248–57.

Psychoanalysis

Abel, Elizabeth. *Virginia Woolf and the Fictions of Psychoanalysis*. Chicago: U of Chicago P, 1989.

Broughton, Panthea Reid. " 'Virginia Is Anal:' Speculations on Virginia Woolf's Writing *Roger Fry* and Reading Sigmund Freud." *Journal of Modern Literature* 14, 1 (Summer 1987): 151–57.

Jacobus, Mary. " 'The Third Stroke:' Reading Woolf with Freud." In Susan Sheridan, ed. *Grafts: Feminist Cultural Criticism*. London: Verso, 1988.

Schlack, Beverly Ann. "A Freudian Look at Mrs. Dalloway." *Literature & Psychology* 23 (1973): 49–58.

Visual Art/Aesthetics

Anscombe, Isabelle. *Omega and After: Bloomsbury and the Decorative Arts*. London: Thames & Hudson, 1981.

Broughton, Panthea Reid. "The Blasphemy of Art: Fry's Aesthetics and Woolf's Non-'Literary' Stories." In Diane F. Gillespie, ed. *The Multiple Muses of Virginia Woolf:* 36–57.

Dowling, David. *Bloomsbury Aesthetics and the Novels of Forster and Woolf*. New York: St. Martin's Press, 1985.

Gillespie, Diane F. *The Sisters' Arts. The Writing and Painting of Virginia Woolf and Vanessa Bell*. Syracuse: Syracuse U P, 1988.

Laurence, Patricia Ondek. *The Reading of Silence: Virginia Woolf in the English Tradition*. Stanford: Stanford U P, 1991.

McLaurin, Allen. *Virginia Woolf: The Echoes Enslaved*. Cambridge, England: Cambridge U P, 1973.

Naylor, Gillian, ed. *Bloomsbury: The Artists, Authors and Designers by Themselves*. London: Octopus, 1990.

Quick, Jonathan R. "Virginia Woolf, Roger Fry and Post-Impressionism." *Massachusetts Review* 26, 4 (Winter 1985): 547–70.

Reed, Christopher. "Through Formalism: Feminism and Virginia Woolf's Relation to Bloomsbury Aesthetics." In Diane F. Gillespie, ed. *The Multiple Muses of Virginia Woolf:* 11–35.

Roberts, John Hawley. "Vision and Design in Virginia Woolf." *PMLA* 61 (1946): 835–47.

Shone, Richard. *Bloomsbury Portraits: Vanessa Bell, Duncan Grant, and Their Circle.* Oxford: Phaidon, 1976.

Stewart, Jack F. "Spatial Form and Color in *The Waves.*" *Twentieth Century Literature* 28, 1 (Spring 1982): 86–107.

Torgovnick, Marianna. *The Visual Arts, Pictorialism, and the Novel: James, Lawrence, and Woolf.* Princeton: Princeton U P, 1985.

War

Bazin, Nancy Topping, and Jane Hamovit Lauter. "Virginia Woolf's Keen Sensitivity to War: Its Roots and Its Impact on Her Novels." In Mark Hussey, ed. *Virginia Woolf and War:* 14–39.

Hussey, Mark. "Living in a War Zone: An Introduction to Virginia Woolf as a War Novelist." In Mark Hussey, ed. *Virginia Woolf and War:* 1–13.

Hussey, Mark, ed. *Virginia Woolf and War: Fiction, Reality, and Myth.* Syracuse: Syracuse U P, 1991.

Levenback, Karen L. "Virginia Woolf and Rupert Brooke: Poised Between Olympus and the 'Real World.' " *Virginia Woolf Miscellany* 33: 5–6.

Poole, Roger. " 'We all put up with you Virginia:' Irreceivable Wisdom About War." In Mark Hussey, ed. *Virginia Woolf and War:* 79–100.

Usui, Masami. "The Female Victims of the War in *Mrs. Dalloway.*" In Mark Hussey, ed. *Virginia Woolf and War:* 151–63.

———. "The German Raid on Scarborough in *Jacob's Room.*" *Virginia Woolf Miscellany* 35: 7.

Wussow, Helen. "War and Conflict in *The Voyage Out.*" In Mark Hussey, ed. *Virginia Woolf and War:* 101–09.

Leonard Woolf

Chapman, Wayne K., and Janet M. Manson. "Carte and Tierce: Leonard, Virginia Woolf, and War for Peace." In Mark Hussey, ed. *Virginia Woolf and War:* 58–78.

Gottlieb, Laura Moss. "The War Between the Woolfs." In Jane Marcus, ed. *Virginia Woolf and Bloomsbury:* 242–52.

Hussey, Mark. "Refractions of Desire: The Early Fiction of Virginia and Leonard Woolf." *Modern Fiction Studies* 38, 1 (Spring 1992): 127–46.

Luedeking, Leila, and Michael Edmonds. *Leonard Woolf: A Bibliography.* New Castle, Del.: Oak Knoll Books, 1992.

Meyerowitz, Selma. *Leonard Woolf.* Boston: Twayne, 1982.

Schaefer, Josephine O'Brien. "*Three Guineas* and *Quack, Quack!* Read Together." *Virginia Woolf Miscellany* 7 (Spring 1977): 2–3.

Spotts, Frederic. *Letters of Leonard Woolf.* San Diego: Harcourt Brace Jovanovich, 1989.

Willis, J. H. Jr. *Leonard and Virginia Woolf as Publishers. The Hogarth Press 1917–1941.* Charlottesville: U P of Virginia, 1992.

Wilson, Duncan. *Leonard Woolf: A Political Biography.* New York: St. Martin's, 1978.

Woolf, Leonard. *An Autobiography.* Vol. 1: 1880–1911; Vol. 2: 1911–1969. New York: Oxford U P, 1980.

Woolf and Other Writers

Beer, Gillian. "Beyond Determinism: George Eliot and Virginia Woolf." In Gillian Beer, *Arguing with the Past: Essays in Narrative from Woolf to Sidney.* New York: Routledge, 1989.

Booth, Alison. *Greatness Engendered: George Eliot and Virginia Woolf.* Ithaca: Cornell U P, 1992.

DiBattista, Maria. "Joyce, Woolf, and the Modern Mind." In Patricia Clements and Isobel Grundy, eds. *Virginia Woolf:* 96–114.

Dowling, David. *Bloomsbury Aesthetics and the Novels of Forster and Woolf.* New York: St. Martin's Press, 1985.

DuPlessis, Rachel Blau. "WOOLFENSTEIN." In Ellen G. Friedman and Miriam Fuchs, eds. *Breaking the Sequence: Women's Experimental Fiction.* Princeton: Princeton U P, 1989: 99–114.

Dowling, David. *Bloomsbury Aesthetics and the Novels of Forster and Woolf.* New York: St. Martin's Press, 1985.

Fogel, Daniel Mark. *Covert Relations: James Joyce, Virginia Woolf, and Henry James.* Charlottesville: U P of Virginia, 1990.

Fox, Allice. *Virginia Woolf and the Literature of the English Renaissance.* Oxford: Clarendon, 1990.

Froula, Christine. "Virginia Woolf as Shakespeare's Sister: Chapters in a Woman Writer's Autobiography." In Marianne Novy, ed. *Women's Revisions of Shakespeare: On Responses of Dickinson, Woolf, Rich, H. D., George Eliot, and Others.* Urbana: U of Illinois P, 1990.

García-Rodriguez, Antonía. "Virginia Woolf from a Latin-American Perspective." In Mark Hussey and Vara Neverow-Turk, eds. *Virginia Woolf Miscellanies:* 43–45.

Gay, Penny. "Bastards from the Bush: Virginia Woolf and her Antipodean Relations." In Mark Hussey and Vara Neverow, eds. *Virginia Woolf: Emerging Perspectives:* 289–95.

Gilbert, Sandra M. "Woman's Sentence, Man's Sentencing: Linguistic Fantasies in Woolf and Joyce." In Jane Marcus, ed. *Virginia Woolf and Bloomsbury:* 208–24.

Gordon, Lyndall. "Our Silent Life: Virginia Woolf and T. S. Eliot." In Patricia Clements and Isobel Grundy, eds. *Virginia Woolf: New Critical Essays:* 77–95.

Haller, Evelyn. "Virginia Woolf and Katherine Mansfield: Or, the Case of the Déclassé Wild Child." In Mark Hussey and Vara Neverow-Turk, eds. *Virginia Woolf Miscellanies:* 96–104.

Henke, Suzette A. "Virginia Woolf Reads James Joyce." In Morris Beja et al., eds. *James Joyce: The Centennial Symposium.* Urbana: U of Illinois P, 1986: 39–42.

Jenkins, William D. "Virginia Woolf and the Belittling of *Ulysses.*" *James Joyce Quarterly* 25, 4 (1988): 513–19.

Kaivola, Karen. *All Contraries Confounded: The Lyrical Fiction of Virginia Woolf, Djuna Barnes, and Marguerite Duras.* Iowa City: U of Iowa P, 1991.

Kiely, Robert. *Beyond Egotism: The Fiction of James Joyce, Virginia Woolf, and D. H. Lawrence.* Cambridge: Harvard U P, 1980.

McLaughlin, Ann L. "An Uneasy Sisterhood: Virginia Woolf and Katherine Mansfield." In Jane Marcus, ed. *Feminist Slant:* 152–61.

Meisel, Perry. *The Absent Father: Virginia Woolf and Walter Pater.* New Haven: Yale U P, 1980.

Nelson-McDermott, Catherine. "Virginia Woolf and Murasaki Shikibu: A Question of Perception." In Mark Hussey and Vara Neverow-Turk, eds. *Virginia Woolf Miscellanies:* 133–43.

Neumann, Shirley. "*Heart of Darkness,* Virginia Woolf and the Spectre of Domination." In Patricia Clements and Isobel Grundy, eds. *Virginia Woolf: New Critical Essays.*

Pearce, Richard. *The Politics of Narration: James Joyce, William Faulkner, and Virginia Woolf.* New Brunswick, N.J.: Rutgers U P, 1991.

———. "Who Comes First, Joyce or Woolf?" In Vara Neverow-Turk and Mark Hussey, eds. *Virginia Woolf: Themes and Variations:* 59–67.

Pitt, Rosemary. "The Exploration of Self in Conrad's *Heart of Darkness* and Woolf's *The Voyage Out.*" *Conradiana* 10 (1978): 141–54.

Poole, Roger. "Passage to the Lighthouse." *Charleston Newsletter* 16 (September 1986): 16–32.

Richter, Harvena. "The *Ulysses* Connection: Clarissa Dalloway's Bloomsday." *Studies in the Novel* 21, 3 (1989): 305–19.

Rosenberg, Beth. "Virginia Woolf: Conversation and the Common Reader." In Mark Hussey and Vara Neverow-Turk, eds., *Virginia Woolf Miscellanies:* 1–8.

Schaefer, Josephine O'Brien. "The Great War and 'This late age of world's experience' in Cather and Woolf." In Mark Hussey, ed. *Virginia Woolf and War:* 134–50.

Scott, Bonnie Kime, ed. *New Alliances in Joyce Studies: 'When It's Aped to Foul a Delfian.'* Newark: U of Delaware P, 1988.

Seidl, Michael. "The Pathology of the Everyday: Uses of Madness in *Mrs. Dalloway* and *Ulysses.*" In Vara Neverow-Turk and Mark Hussey, eds. *Virginia Woolf: Themes and Variations:* 52–59.

———. "Woolf, Barnes and the Ends of Modernism: An *Antiphon* to *Between the Acts.*" In Vara Neverow-Turk and Mark Hussey, eds. *Virginia Woolf: Themes and Variations:* 25–32.

Squier, Susan Merrill. "Tradition and Revision in Woolf's *Orlando:* Defoe and 'The Jessamy Brides.' " *Women's Studies* 12 (1986): 167–78.

Torgovnick, Marianna. *The Visual Arts, Pictorialism, and the Novel: James, Lawrence, and Woolf.* Princeton: Princeton U P, 1985.

APPENDIX A: TOPICAL LIST OF ENTRIES

Allusions in Woolf's Work and Subjects of Her Essays (including characters, myths, phrases, titles; excluding authors)

Anabasis
Angel in the House
Antaeus
Antigone
Antiquary, The
Aurora Leigh
Baedeker
Ballad of the Queen's Marys [or Maries]
Beton, Mary
Bluebeard
Bovary, Emma
Burke
Cabinet of Dr. Caligari
Ceres
Clarissa
Cleopatra
Clytemnestra
"Come Away, Come Away Death"
"Comus"
Cressida
Cymbeline
Debrett
Demeter and Persephone
Diana of the Crossways
Diary of a Nobody
Duchess of Malfi
Euphues
"Fade far away and quite forget . . ."
"Fear no more . . ."
"Fisherman and His Wife, The"
Gammer Gurton's Needle
Guermantes, Madame de
"Hark, Hark"
"Isabella and the Pot of Basil"
Jane Eyre
"Jug, jug, jug"
Karenina, Anna
Lily of the Day
"Love in the Valley"
Lycidas
Lysistrata
Measure for Measure
Millamant
Mucklebackit
Pendennis
Phèdre
Philomela
Pillicock
Pride and Prejudice
Procne and Philomela
Rosalind
Ruff's Tour in Northumberland
Sharp, Becky
"Western Wind, O"
"Where There's a Will There's a Way"
Whitaker
"World's Great Age"
Wuthering Heights

Acquaintances (including doctors and nurses), friends, lovers

Anrep, Boris von
Anrep, Helen
Arnold-Forster, Katherine
Arnold-Forster, William Edward
Bagenal, Barbara
Bibesco, Princess Elizabeth
Birrell, Augustine
Birrell, Francis
Blanche, Jacques-Emile
Booth Family
Brenan, Gerald
Brett, Dorothy
Bussy, Dorothy
Bussy, Simon
Carrington, Dora de Houghton
Case, Euphemia
Case, Janet Elizabeth
Cecil, Lord (Edward Christian) David
Cecil, Lady Robert ("Nelly")
Cole (William) Horace de Vere
Colefax, Lady Sibyl
Cox, Katherine Laird ("Ka")
Craig, Dr. Maurice
Cunard, Lady Maud
Cunard, Nancy
Darwin, Gwen
Davidson, Angus Henry Gordon
Davies, Margaret Caroline Llewelyn
Dickinson, Goldsworthy Lowes
Dickinson, Violet
Etchells, Frederick and Jessie
Fry, Margery ("Ha")
Fry, Roger Eliot
Furse, Katherine
Garnett, David ("Bunny")
Grant, Duncan James Corrowr
Grant, Ethel
Hamnett, Nina
Harris, Lillian
Harrison, Jane Ellen
Hawtrey, Sir Ralph
Head, Dr. Henry
Headlam, Walter
Hudson, Anna Hope ("Nan")
Hutchinson, Mary
Hyslop, Dr. Theophilus Bulkeley
Kauffer, Edward McKnight
Keynes, Sir Geoffrey
Keynes, John Maynard
Koteliansky, Samuel Solomonovitch
Lamb, Henry
Lamb, Walter Rangely Maitland
Lushington, Katherine
MacCarthy, Sir (Charles Otto) Desmond
MacCarthy, Mary Josefa (Molly)
Marsh, Edward
Maxse, Kitty
Milman Family
Morrell, Lady Ottoline Violet Anne
Morrell, Philip
Nicolson, Benedict Lionel
Nicolson, Sir Harold
Nicolson, Nigel
Partridge, Frances Catherine
Partridge, (Reginald Sherring) Ralph
Pater, Clara
Raverat, Gwendolen (Gwen)
Raverat, Jacques
Robins, Elizabeth
Rylands, George Humphrey Wolferstan ("Dadie")

Sackville-West, Edward Charles
Sackville-West, Victoria Mary ("Vita")
Sands, Ethel
Sanger, Charles Percy
Sargant-Florence, Alix
Savage, Sir George
Seton, Dr. David Elphinstone
Sheepshanks, Mary
Sheppard, John Tressider
Shove, Fredegond
Simon, Lady Shena Dorothy
Smith, Logan Pearsall
Smyth, Ethel Mary
Snowden, Margaret Kemplay
Stillman Family
Strachey, Alix
Strachey, Dorothy
Strachey, James Beaumont
Strachey, Lady Jane Maria
Strachey, (Giles) Lytton
Strachey, Marjorie Colville ("Gumbo")
Strachey, (Joan) Pernel
Strachey, Philippa ("Pippa")
Strachey, Rachel ("Ray") Conn Costelloe
Swanwick, Helen Maria
Sydney-Turner, Saxon Arnoll
Taylor, Valerie
Traill, Nurse
Trefusis, Violet
Vaughan, Margaret (Madge)
Waterlow, Sydney Phillip Perigal
Webb, Beatrice and Sidney
Wellesley, Lady Dorothy Violet
Wilberforce, Dr. Octavia
Wright, Dr. Maurice
Young, Edward Hilton

Bloomsbury Group: clubs, events, organizations, terms, topics (excluding people)

Affable Hawk
Apostles
Bloomsbury Group
Cambridge Conversazione Society
Clapham Sect
Dreadnought Hoax
Friday Club
Memoir Club
Midnight Society
1917 Club
Omega Workshops
X Society
Zanzibar Hoax

Characters in Woolf's Fiction (listed by novel)

Between the Acts

Albert
Ball, Mrs.
Batty
Bingham, Mrs.
Bond
Bonthorp
Budge
Candish
Chalmers, Mrs.
Clark, Eliza
Cobbett of Cobbs Corner
Dodge, William
Ebury, Mrs.
Elmhurst, Mrs.
Grace
Haines, Rupert
Hammond
Hardcastle, Miss Eleanor
Hopkins, Mabel
Jones, Mrs. Lynn
Jones, Phyllis
La Trobe, Miss
Loder, Millie
Manresa, Mrs.
Mayhew, Colonel and Mrs.
Neale, Mrs.
Oliver, Bartholemew
Oliver, Caro
Oliver, George
Oliver, Giles
Oliver, Isa
Otter, Mrs.
Page, Mr.
Parker, Mrs.
Pinsent
Rogers, Mrs.
Sands, Trixie
Sohrab
Springett, Etty
Streatfield, Reverend G. W.
Swithin, Lucy
Thorold, Edgar
Umphelby, Miss

Jacob's Room

Aitken, Helen
Anderson
Aristotle
Askew, Helen
Barfoot, Captain
Barfoot, Ellen
Barnet
Barrett, Miss
Benson, Everard
Bigham, Sir Jasper
Birkbeck, Miss
Boase, Captain
Bonamy, Richard
Bonham, Mrs.
Boxall
Bramham, Nick
Budgeon, Charles
Bulteel, Professor
Burley, Mr.
Calthorp, Mr.
Carslake, Jinny
Charles, Lady
Clutterbuck, Mr.
Congreve, Lady
Cowan, Erasmus
Craster, Kitty
Crawley, Mr.
Crosby, Mr.
Cruttendon, Edward
Curnow
Dickens, Mr.
Dudding, Miss and Tom Dudding
Duggan, Mrs.
Durrant, Clara
Durrant, Elizabeth
Durrant, Timothy
Edwards, Miss
Eliot, Julia
Elmer, Fanny
Erskine, Mr.
Flanders, Archer
Flanders, Betty
Flanders, Jacob
Flanders, Seabrook
Florinda
Floyd, Reverend Andrew
Fraser
Gage, Tom
Garfit
Gibbons, General
Grandage, Mrs. and Tom Grandage
Gravé, Madame Lucien
Graves, Dick
Gresham, Mr. and Mrs.
Hawkins, Mr.
Hedge, Julia
Hibbert, Lady
Horsefield, Mrs.
Huxtable, Professor
Jarvis, Mrs.
Jenkinson, Edward
Jenkinson, Nelly
Jones, Brandy
Keymer, Mrs.
Laurette
Lidgett, Mrs.
Lucy, Countess of Rocksbier
Mallett, Edwin
Mangin
Marchmont, Miss
Masham
Morty, Uncle
Norman, Mrs.
Ormond, Stuart
Papworth, Mrs.
Parry, Lionel
Parsons, Mrs.
Pascoe, Mrs.
Perry, Miss (1)
Pilcher, Mr.
Plumer, Mr. and Mrs.
Polegate, Mr.
Pollett, Anthony
Pratt, Moll
Rebecca
Rhoda (1)
Rosseter, Miss
Ruck, Bertha
Salvin, Mr.
Sanders, Mary
Shaw, Rose
Sibley, Mr.
Siddons, Elsbeth
Simeon
Skelton, Oliver
Sopwith, Professor
Spalding, James
Springett, Mr.
Steele, Charles
Stretton, Mrs.
Stuart, Mother
Sturgeon, Johnnie
Temple, Mrs.
Thomas, Miss

Thomas, Hilda
Wagg, Miss
Whitehorn, Mrs.
Wilding, Charlotte
Williams, Sandra Wentworth
Withers, Mrs.
Wortley, Mr.

Mrs. Dalloway

Bentley, Mr.
Bexborough, Lady
Bletchley, Mrs. Sarah
Blow, Nancy
Bowley, Mr.
Bradshaw, Sir William
Breitkopf, Joseph
Brewer, Mr.
Brierly, Professor
Brush, Milly
Bruton, Lady Millicent
Buckhurst, Sir John
Burgess, Mrs.
Coates, Emily
Daisy
Dalloway, Clarissa (2)
Dalloway, Elizabeth
Dalloway, Richard (2)
Dempster, Carrie
Evans
Filmer, Mrs.
Fletcher, Mr.
Foxcroft, Mrs.
Gayton, Lord
Gorham, Mrs.
Helena, Aunt
Henderson, Ellie
Hilbery, Mrs. (2)
Holmes, Dr.
Hutton, Jim
Johnson, Maisie
Kilman, Doris
Lucy (2)
Marsham, Mrs.
Mitchell, Elise
Parry, Justin
Pole, Isabel
Purvis, Scrope
Pym, Miss
Seton, Sally
Smith, Rezia (Lucrezia) Warren
Smith, Septimus Warren
Walker, Mrs.
Walsh, Peter
Whitbread, Hugh
Whittaker, Mr.
William, Uncle
Wilkins, Mr.

Night and Day

Alardyce, Cyril
Alardyce, Richard
Aubrey, Uncle
Bailey, Mrs. Sutton
Bankes, Mrs. Vermont
Basnett, Mr. Horace
Caroline, Cousin
Clacton, Mr.
Cosham, Mrs. (Aunt Millicent)
Datchet, Mary
Denham, Joan
Denham, Ralph
Dudley, Uncle
Duggins, Alfred
Eleanor, Aunt
Fortescue, Mr.
Hilbery, Katharine
Hilbery, Mr.
Hilbery, Mrs. (1)
Joseph, Uncle
Milvain, Mrs. (Aunt Celia)
Otway, Cassandra
Otway Family
Pelham, Augustus
Ponting, Mr.
Rodney, William
Sandys, Harry
Seal, Sally
Trotter, Mrs.

Orlando, A Biography

Banting, Mrs.
Bartholemew, Widow
Bartolus, Captain Nicholas Benedict
Basket
Brigge, John Fenner
Chubb, Eusebius
Dupper, Mr.
Grimsditch, Mrs.
Harriet, Archduchess
Hartopp, Miss Penelope
Orlando
Pepita
Robinson, Grace
Rustum el Sadi
Sasha
Scrope, Sir Adrian
Shelmerdine, Marmaduke Bonthrop
Stewkley, Mrs.
Stubbs
Twitchett
Tyrconnel, Lady Margaret O'Brien O'Dare O'Reilly

To the Lighthouse

Bankes, William
Bast, Mrs.
Beckwith, Mrs.
Briscoe, Lily
Carmichael, Augustus
Doyle, Minta
Ellen
Giddings, Miss
Kennedy
Langley, Mr.
Macalister
Manning, Carrie
Manning, George
McNab, Mrs.
Mildred
Paunceforte, Mr.
Ramsay, Andrew
Ramsay, Cam
Ramsay, James
Ramsay, Jasper
Ramsay, Mr.
Ramsay, Mrs.
Ramsay, Nancy
Ramsay, Prue
Ramsay, Roger
Ramsay, Rose
Rayley, Paul
Sorley
Tansley, Charles
Wallace, Mr.

Voyage Out, The

Allan, Miss
Ambrose, Helen
Ambrose, Ridley
Angelo
Bax, Mr.
Carter, Mr. and Mrs.
Chailey, Emma
Cobbold, Captain
Dalloway, Clarissa (1)
Dalloway, Richard (1)
Eleanor
Elliot, Hilda
Eliot, Hughling
Flushing, Alice
Flushing, Wilfred
Grice, Mr. (1)
Harrison, Lillah
Hewet, Terence
Hirst, St. John Alaric
Lesage, Dr.
Lucy (1)
Mackenzie
Maria
McInnis, Nurse
Mendoza, Signora Lola
Murgatroyd, Evelyn
Oliver, Raymond
Paley, Emma
Parry, Mrs. Raymond
Pepper, William
Perrott, Alfred
Rodriguez, Dr.
Rodriguez, Signor
Sinclair
Thornbury, Mrs.
Thornbury, William
Umpleby, Mary
Venning, Arthur
Vinrace, Rachel
Vinrace, Willoughby
Warrington, Susan
Willett, Miss
Yarmouth

Waves, The

Bernard
Bard, Miss
Biddy
Burchard, Mr.
Constable, Mrs.
Crane, Dr.
Crane, Mrs.
Curry, Miss
Cutting, Miss
Ernest
Eyres, Mr.
Fenwick
Florrie
Hudson, Miss
Jinny
Johnson, Miss
Lambert, Miss
Larpent
Louis
Moffat, Mrs.
Neville
Percival
Perry, Miss (2)
Rhoda (2)
Susan
Wickham, Mr.

Years, The

Abrahamson
Aislabie, Mrs.
Alfred
Andrews, Dr.
Antonio
Ashford
Ashley
Ashton, Tony
Baxter
Bigge
Bishop, Mr.
Bodham, Miss
Brand
Briggs, Mrs.
Burt, Louisa
C., Mrs.
Chinnery, Mrs.
Chipperfield
Cole
Craddock, Lucy
Craster
Crosby, Annie
Curry, Sanders
Duffus
Elkin, Major

Ellen
(Elvira)
Erridge
Fripp, Mr. and Mrs.
Howard
Gibbs, Hugh
Grice, Mr. (2)
Grice, Mrs.
Groves, Mrs.
Hillier, Ann
Hiscock
James, Cousin
Judd
Larpent, Mrs.
Lasswade, Kitty
Lathom, Mrs.
Lazenby, Mrs.
Levys
Malone, Dr. and Mrs.
Marable, Lady Margaret
Margaret
Markham, Kit
Mayhew, Sir Matthew
Mira
Norton, Sir Richard
Pargiter, Abel
Pargiter, Charles
Pargiter, Delia
Pargiter, Sir Digby
Pargiter, Edward
Pargiter, Eleanor
Pargiter, Lady Eugénie
Pargiter, Maggie
(Magdalena)
Pargiter, Martin
Pargiter, Milly
Pargiter, Morris
Pargiter, North
Pargiter, Peggy
Pargiter, Rose (1)
Pargiter, Rose (2)
Pargiter, Sara (Sally)
Parrish, Miriam
Patrick, Uncle
Pickford, Mr.
Pippy
Pomjalovsky, Nicholas
Porter, Major
Potter, Mrs.
Prentice
Priestley
Renny (René)
Robson, Jo
Robson, Nelly
Robson, Sam
Runcorn's Boy
Sims, Mrs.
Spicer, Mr.
Stiles, Matty
Toms, Mrs.
Toye, Mr.
Treyer, Mrs.
Warburton, Aunt
William

Clubs, Groups, Organizations (see also Bloomsbury Group: Clubs et al)

Bournemouth
Conference
Fabian Society
Heretics
Labour Party
League of Nations
ODTAA
Virginia Woolf Society
Women's Cooperative
Guild
Workers' Educational
Association

Historical Figures and Events Mentioned in Woolf's Writing (excludes writers)

Alexandra, Queen
Asquith, Herbert Henry
Asquith, Emma Alice
Margaret
Asquith, Mr.
Baldwin, Stanley
Balfour, Arthur James,
First Earl
Bessborough, Lady
Birkenhead, Lord
Biron, Sir Chartres
Bodichon, Barbara Leigh
Smith
Bodkin, Archibald
Browning, Oscar
Burke, Edmund
Butler, Josephine
Cavell, Edith
Chamberlain, [Joseph]
Austen
Chamberlain, Joseph
Chesterfield, Philip
Dormer Stanhope,
Lord
Clive [Robert]
Clough, Anne Jemima
Daladier, Edouard
Damien, Father
Darwin, Charles
Deffand, Madame du,
Marie de Vichy-
Chamrond
Delaprée, Louis
Duke of St. Simon
Fawcett, Millicent
Garrett
Franklin, Sir John
Garibaldi, Giuseppe
Gladstone, William
Ewart
Gower, Granville
Leveson, Lord
Gwyn, Nell
Hakluyt, Richard
Hamilton, Mary
Havelock, General
Hicks, Sir William
Joynson
Hitler, Adolf
Holmes, Oliver Wendell
Jack the Ripper
Jex-Blake, Sophia
Ladies of Llangollen
Lloyd George, David
Lovelace, Mary, Countess
of
Marbot, Baron
Morgan, J. Pierpont
Nightingale, Florence
Palmerston, Lord
Pankhurst, Emmeline
Parnell, Charles Stewart
Pastons
Pensions Bill
Saint Paul
Spanish Civil War
William, King
Wren, Sir Christopher

Library Collections and Archives

Berg Collection
Hooper, Frances
Humanities Research
Center
Monk's House Papers
Pullman
Smith College
University of Sussex
University of Texas
Victoria University
Library
Washington State
University

Locations (including Woolf's houses)

A. B. C.
Abercorn Terrace (TY)
Admiralty Arch
(AROO)
Apsley House (TY)
Army and Navy Stores
(MD, TY)
Asheham House
Balaclava (TTL)
Bayreuth (TVO)
Berwick Church
Blackfriars (O)
Bloomsbury
Bloomsbury Workshop
Bourton (MD)
Bow Windows Bookshop

British Museum (JR, AROO)
Browne Street (TY)
Brunswick Square
Cassis
Cenotaph (MD)
Charleston
Clieveden (Cliveden) (MD)
Clifford's Inn
Constantinople (MD, O)
Dalingridge Place
Durbins
Elephant and Castle (AROO)
Elvedon (TW)
Euston (TW)
Fernham (AROO)
Firle
Fitzroy Square
Garsington
Girton College (TG)
Godrevy Lighthouse
Gordon Square
Grafton Galleries
Grately & Hooper (MD, ND)
Greenwich (O, TW)
Hampton Court (TW)
Ham Spray
Hatchards' (MD)
Hebrides (TTL)
Hogarth House
Hyde Park Gate
Kew Gardens
Kingsway (ND)
Knole
Lamley's (TY)
Lewes
Little Holland House
Little Talland House
London Library
Long Barn
Manorbier
Mansion House (TG)
Mecklenburgh Square
Monk's House
Morley College
National Gallery (TW)
Newnham College (TG)
Ouse
Oxbridge (AROO)
Parliament Square (AROO, MD)
Piccadilly (TVO, ND, MD, AROO, TY)
Plough Inn
Pointz Hall (BTA)
Queen's Hall (TW)
Rodmell
St. Ives
Santa Marina
Sieges Allee (AROO)
Sissinghurst Castle
Strand (ND)
Tagus (TVO)
Talland House
Tavistock Square
Tidmarsh
Wapping Old Stairs (O)
Warboys
Westminster Abbey (MD, O)
Whitechapel (F)
Whitehall (AROO, MD)

Performers, Photographers, Composers, and Their Work

Adaptations
Albee, Edward
Argento, Dominick
Atkins, Eileen
Ballets Russes
Beethoven, Ludwig van
Berners, Lord
Diaghilev, Sergei Pavlovich
Freund, Gisèle
Indigo Girls
Lenare
Lopokova, Lydia
Mozart, Wolfgang Amadeus
Potter, Sally
Ray, Man
Russian Ballet
Russian Dancers
Wagner, Richard

Publishing: assistants, editors, newspapers, periodicals, presses, prizes, publishers

Athenaeum
Brace, Donald
Cartwright, Mrs.
Charleston Magazine
Charleston Newsletter
Cornhill Magazine
Criterion
Daily Herald
Daily Worker
Day to Day Pamphlets
Dial
Egoist, The
Femina-Vie Heureuse
Garnett, Edward
Guardian
Harcourt, Brace & Co.
Hogarth Essays
Hogarth Lectures
Hogarth Letters
Hogarth Living Poets
Hogarth Press
Hyde Park Gate News
Kennedy, Richard
Lehmann, John Frederick
Living Age
London Mercury
Martin, Basil Kingsley
Matthaei, Louise Ernestine
Modern Fiction Studies
Nation & Athenaeum
National Review
New Republic
New Signatures
New Statesman
New Statesman and Nation
Richmond, Bruce Lyttelton
Scrutiny
Speaker
Times Literary Supplement
Todd, Dorothy
Twentieth Century Literature
Virginia Woolf Miscellany
Virginia Woolf Newsletter
Virginia Woolf Quarterly
Vogue
Weaver, Harriet Shaw
Woman's Leader and the Common Cause
Woolf Studies Annual
Yale Review

Terms

Androgyny
Angel in the House
Arthur's Education Fund
Beadle
Billycock Hat
Boeuf en Daube
Conscientious Objectors
Episodes
Formalist (Formalism)
Interior Monologue
Interludes
Modernist (Modernism)
Narrated Monologue
Neo-Pagans
Suffrage
Popular Culture
Post-Impressionist
Psychoanalysis
Shell shock
Significant Form
Stream-of-Consciousness
"Thursday Evenings"
Women's Suffrage

Woolf's Inventions, Flowers, Key Phrases, and Objects in Essays and Novels

A to Z (TTL)
Arthur's Education Fund (TG)
Barouche Landau (TW)
Carmichael, Mary (AROO)
Chloe and Olivia (AROO)
Coryphaeus (TVO)
Cowbind (TW)
Elgin Marbles (JR, ND)
Ermyntrude, Lady (BTA)

Etho passo tanno hai (TY)
Jessamy Brides, The
Life's Adventure (AROO)
Manx Cat (AROO)
Mauretania (TVO)
May (TW)
Merridew, Rosamond
Outsiders Society (TG)
Saturday Club (TVO)
Seton, Mary (AROO)
Shakespeare, Judith (AROO)
Sweet Alice (TTL, TW)
Von X, Professor (AROO)

Woolf's Relatives and Households, Nicknames, Pets, and Servants

Aspasia
Bartholemew, Percy
Bell, Angelica
Bell, Anne Olivier
Bell, [Arthur] Clive [Heward]
Bell, Julian Heward
Bell, Quentin [Claudian Stephen]
Bell, Vanessa
Boxall, Nellie (or Nelly)
Cameron, Julia Margaret
Costelloe, Karin
Duckworth, George Herbert
Duckworth, Gerald de L'Etang
Duckworth, Herbert
Duckworth, Julia
Duckworth, Stella
Everest, Louie
Farrell, Sophia
Fishers, The
Garnett, Angelica
Goat
Goth, The
Grizzle
Gurth
Higgens, Grace
Hills, John Waller ("Jack")
Hope, Lottie (or Lotty)
Jackson, Julia
Mayer, Louie
Pattle Family
Pinka (or Pinker)
Prinsep Family
Ritchie, Lady Anne Isabella Thackeray
Shag
Stephen, Adrian Leslie
Stephen, Caroline Emelia
Stephen, Dorothea Jane
Stephen, Harriet Marian
Stephen, James
Stephen, Sir James
Stephen, Sir James Fitzjames
Stephen, James Kenneth
Stephen, Julia Prinsep
Stephen, Karin Elizabeth Conn
Stephen, Katherine
Stephen, Laura Makepeace
Stephen, Sir Leslie
Stephen, [Julian] Thoby Prinsep
Stephen, Vanessa
Stephen, (Adeline) Virginia
Thackeray, Harriet Marian
Thackeray, Anne Isabella ("Anny")
Vaughan, Emma ("Toad")
Vaughan, Margaret (Marny)
Woolf, Bella Sidney
Woolf Family
Woolf, Leonard Sidney
Woolf, [Adeline] Virginia

Woolf's Works

Essays, Biography, and Reviews

"Anon"
"All About Books"
"Art of Fiction, The"
"Artist and Politics, The"
Books and Portraits
"Byron & Mr Briggs"
Captain's Death Bed and Other Essays
"Character in Fiction"
"The Cinema"
Collected Essays
Common Reader, The
Common Reader, Second Series, The
Contemporary Writers
"Craftsmanship"
Death of the Moth and Other Essays, The
"Essay in Criticism, An"
"Friendships Gallery"
Granite & Rainbow, Essays
"Hours in a Library"
"How It Strikes a Contemporary"
"How Should One Read a Book?"
"Impassioned Prose"
"Leaning Tower, The"
"Letter to a Young Poet, A"
"Life and the Novelist"
Life As We Have Known It (Introductory Letter)
"London Scene, The"
"Memories of a Working Women's Guild"
"Modern Fiction"
"Modern Novels"
Moment and Other Essays, The
"Moment: Summer's Night, The"
"Mr. Bennett and Mrs. Brown"
"Narrow Bridge of Art, The"
"Niece of an Earl, The"
"Notes on an Elizabethan Play"
"On Being Ill"
"On Not Knowing Greek"
"On Re-Reading Novels"
Paintings By Vanessa Bell
"Phases of Fiction"
"Plumage Bill, The" (Letter)
"Professions For Women"
"Reading"
"Reading at Random"
Recent Paintings By Vanessa Bell (Foreword)
Roger Fry: A Biography
Room of One's Own, A
"Russian Point of View, The"
"Street Haunting"
"Thoughts on Peace in an Air Raid"
Three Guineas
Translations
Victorian Photographs of Famous Men & Fair Women (Introduction)
"Walter Sickert"
"Women and Fiction"
Women and Writing
"Women Must Weep"

Short Fiction

"Ancestors"
Atalanta's Garland
"Blue & Green"
"Cockney's Farming Experience, A"
Complete Shorter Fiction, The
"Duchess and the Jeweller, The"
"Evening Party, The"
"Experiences of a Paterfamilias, The"
Haunted House and Other Stories, A
"Introduction, The"
"Journal of Mistress Joan Martyn, The"
Kew Gardens
"Lady in the Looking-Glass, The: A Reflection"
"Lappin and Lapinova"
"Legacy, The"
"Man Who Loved His Kind, The"
Mark on the Wall, The
"Memoirs of a Novelist"
"Moments of Being: 'Slater's Pins Have No Points' "
Monday or Tuesday
Mrs. Dalloway in Bond Street"
Mrs. Dalloway's Party
"Mysterious Case of Miss V., The"
"New Dress, The"
"Nurse Lugton's Golden Thimble"
"Phyllis and Rosamond"
"Portraits"
"Searchlight, The"
"Shooting Party, The"
"Society, A"
"Solid Objects"

"String Quartet, The"
"Summing Up, A"
"Together and Apart"
Two Stories
"Unwritten Novel, An"
"Woman's College from Outside, A"

Autobiography, Diary, Letters

"Am I a Snob?"
Diary
"22 Hyde Park Gate"
Letters
Moments of Being
"Old Bloomsbury"
Passionate Apprentice, A: The Early Journals 1897–1909
"Reminiscences"
"Sketch of the Past, A"
Travels with Virginia Woolf
Virginia Woolf & Lytton Strachey: Letters
Writer's Diary, A

Long Fiction and Novels

Between the Acts
Flush, A Biography
Freshwater (play)
Jacob's Room
"Lighthouse, The"
Mrs. Dalloway
Night and Day
Orlando, A Biography
"Time Passes"
To the Lighthouse
Translations
Voyage Out, The
Waves, The
"Window, The"
Years, The

Drafts, Manuscripts, Notes, Versions

Melymbrosia
Pargiters, The
Pointz Hall
Reading Notebooks
Women & Fiction: The Manuscript Versions of "A Room of One's Own"

Works by Writers Other Than Woolf

Beginning Again: An Autobiography of the Years 1911–1918
Bloomsbury Traveller's Almanac
Dictionary of National Biography
Downhill All the Way: An Autobiography of the Years 1919–1939
Edwardians, The
Elizabeth and Essex: A Tragic History
Eminent Victorians
Emma
Folios of New Writing
Journey Not the Arrival Matters, The: An Autobiography of the Years 1939–1969
Land, The
Mausoleum Book
"Notes from Sick Rooms"
Notes on Virginia's Childhood
Passenger to Teheran
Portrait of a Marriage
Principia Ethica
Quack, Quack!
Queen Victoria
Recollections of Virginia Woolf
Shadow of the Moth, The
Stories of the East
"Three Jews"
Village in the Jungle, The
Well of Loneliness, The
Who's Afraid of Virginia Woolf?
Wise Virgins, The

Writers (critics, dramatists, novelists, philosophers, poets) and Painters

Addison, Joseph
Arnold, Matthew
Astell, Mary
Auden, W. H.
Austen, Jane
Balzac, Honoré De
Beerbohm, Sir Max
Behn, Aphra
Bell, Gertrude Lowthian
Belloc, Hilaire [Joseph Hilary Pierre]
Bennett, Arnold Enoch
Benson, Stella
Bergson, Henri
Black, William
Borges, Jorge Luis
Boswell, James
Bourget, Paul
Bowen, Elizabeth
Brittain, Vera
Brontë, Charlotte and Emily
Brooke, Rupert Chawner
Browne, Sir Thomas
Browne, William
Browning, Elizabeth Barrett
Browning, Robert
Brydges, Sir Samuel Egerton
Buckle, Henry Thomas
Burney, Frances ("Fanny", Madame d'Arblay)
Burns, Robert
Butler, Samuel
Byron, George Gordon
Carlyle, Jane Baillie Welsh
Carlyle, Thomas
Carter, Eliza
Catullus, Gaius Valerius
Cavendish, Margaret Lucas, Duchess of Newcastle
Chekhov, Anton Pavlovich
Chesterton, G. K. (Gilbert Keith)
Coleridge, Samuel Taylor
Congreve, William
Conrad, Joseph
Cowper, William
Creevey, Thomas
Crome, John
Dante (Alighieri)
Day Lewis, Cecil
Defoe, Daniel
De Quincey, Thomas
Dickens, Charles
Dixon, Richard Watson
Dodd, Francis
Donne, John
Dostoyevsky, Fyodor Mikhailovich
Drabble, Margaret
Dryden, John
Eliot, T. S.
Eliot, George
Elton, Charles
Fielding, Henry
Finch, Anne, Countess of Winchilsea
Fitzgerald, Edward
Flaubert, Gustave
Forster, E. M.
Frazer, Sir James George
Freud, Sigmund
Fry, Roger
Galsworthy, John
Galton, Francis
Garnett, Constance
Gaskell, Elizabeth Cleghorn
Gay, John
George, Henry
Gerhardie, William Alexander
Gertler, Mark
Gibbon, Edward
Gorky, Maxim
Gosse, Sir Edmund
Gray, Thomas
Greene, Nick
Greg, Mr.
Hall, Radclyffe
Hardy, Thomas
Hemingway, Ernest
Holtby, Winifred
Huxley, Aldous Leonard
Huxley, Thomas Henry
Ibsen, Henrik
Inge, Dean
Isherwood, Christopher
James, Henry
Joad, C. E. M.
John, Augustus
John, Gwen

Johnson, Samuel
Joyce, James Augustine Aloysius
Keats, John
Kingsley, Charles
Kingsley, Mary
Kipling, Rudyard
Lamb, Charles
Landor, Walter Savage
Lawrence, D. H.
Leavis, F. R.
Leavis, Q. D.
Lee, Sir Sidney
Lee, Vernon
Lehmann, Rosamond Nina
Levine, David
Lewis, Percy Wyndham
Ling, Shu-hua
Lowell, James Russell
Lubbock, Percy
Lucas, Frank Laurence ("Peter")
Macaulay, Rose
Macaulay, Thomas Babington
MacNeice, Louis
Maitland, Frederic W.
Mallarmé, Stéphane
Mansfield, Katherine
Martineau, Harriet
Marvell, Andrew
Mauron, Charles
Meredith, George
Milton, John
Mirrlees, (Helen) Hope
Mitford, Mary Russell
Montaigne, Michel Eyquem de
Moore, G. E.
Morris, William
Mortimer, (Charles) Raymond Bell
Murry, John Middleton
Newcastle, Margaret of
Ocampo, Victoria
Oliphant, Margaret Oliphant
Osborne, Dorothy
Pater, Walter Horatio
Patmore, Coventry
Plath, Sylvia
Plomer, William
Pope, Alexander
Proust, Marcel
Racine, Jean
Read, Herbert
Renan, Ernest
Reynolds, Sir Joshua
Richardson, Dorothy Miller
Romney, George
Rosebery, Archibald Philip Primrose
Rossetti, Christina Georgina
Ruskin, John
Russell, Bertrand Arthur William
Sand, George
Sappho
Sarton, May
Sassoon, Siegfried
Scott, Sir Walter
Shakespeare, William
Shaw, George Bernard
Shelley, Percy Bysshe
Sickert, Walter
Sidgwick, Henry
Sidney, Sir Philip
Sitwell, Edith Louisa
Smith, Alexander
Sophocles
Spender, Stephen
Staël, Madame Anne Louise Germaine de
Stein, Gertrude
Sterne, Laurence
Strachey, (Giles) Lytton
Swift, Jonathan
Swinburne, Algernon Charles
Taine, Hippolyte
Tchehov (Tchekhov), Anton
Tennyson, Alfred Lord
Thackeray, William Makepeace
Thomson, James
Tolstoy, Leo Nikolayevich
Tomlin, Stephen
Trevelyan, George Macaulay
Trevelyan, Robert Calverly ("Bob")
Tupper, Martin Farquhar
Turgenev, Ivan Sergeyevich
Tyndall, John
Vandyck, Sir Anthony
Waley, Arthur David
Walpole, Hugh Seymour
Ward, Mary Augusta (Mrs. Humphry)
Watts, George Frederic
Webster, John
Wells, H. G.
West, Rebecca
Whitman, Walt
Winchilsea, Lady
Wollstonecraft, Mary
Wordsworth, William
Wright, Joseph
Wycherley, William
Yeats, W. B.
Yourcenar, Marguerite

APPENDIX B: GENEALOGIES

A note on the genealogies:

(1) Woolf's mother was born Julia Prinsep Jackson. She married Herbert Duckworth and, after his death, Leslie Stephen. She is, therefore, often referred to in various sources as Julia Duckworth Stephen. I have referred to her thoughout the A to Z entries as Julia Prinsep Stephen.
(2) Names for which there are entries appear in boldface.

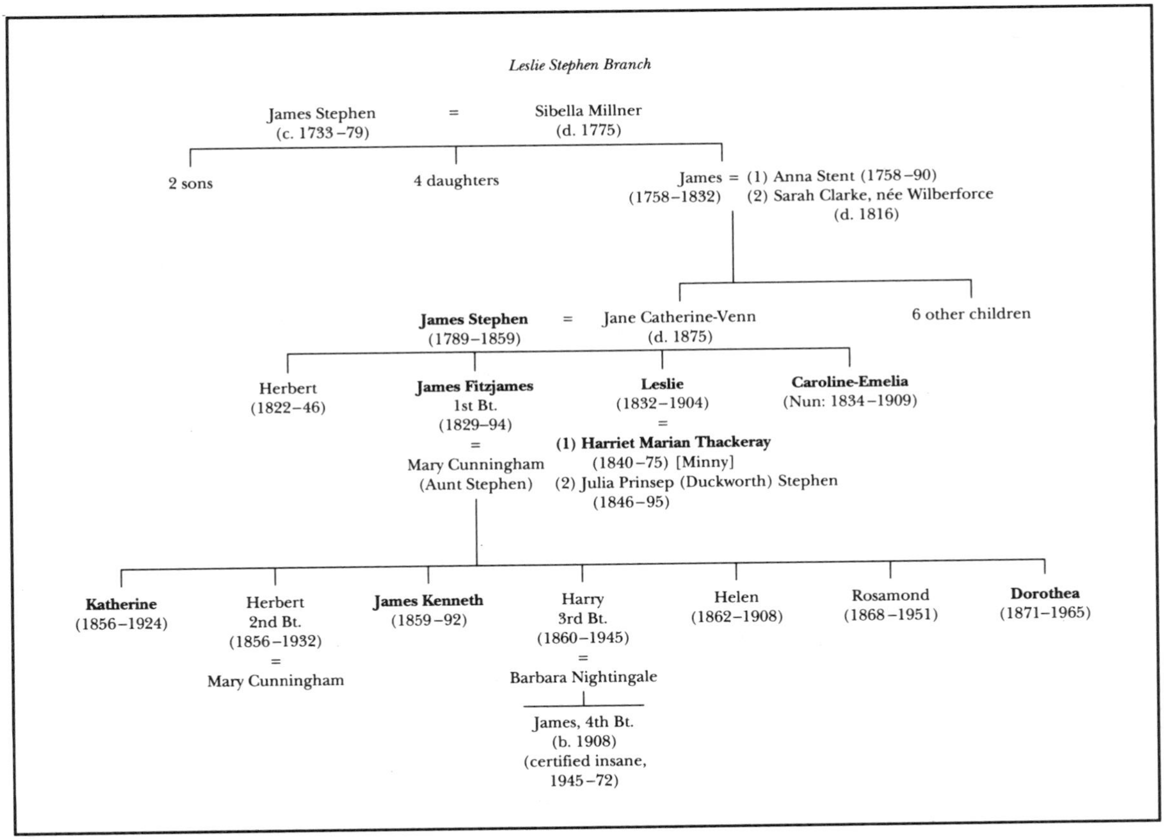

Harriet Marian Thackeray (Stephen) Branch

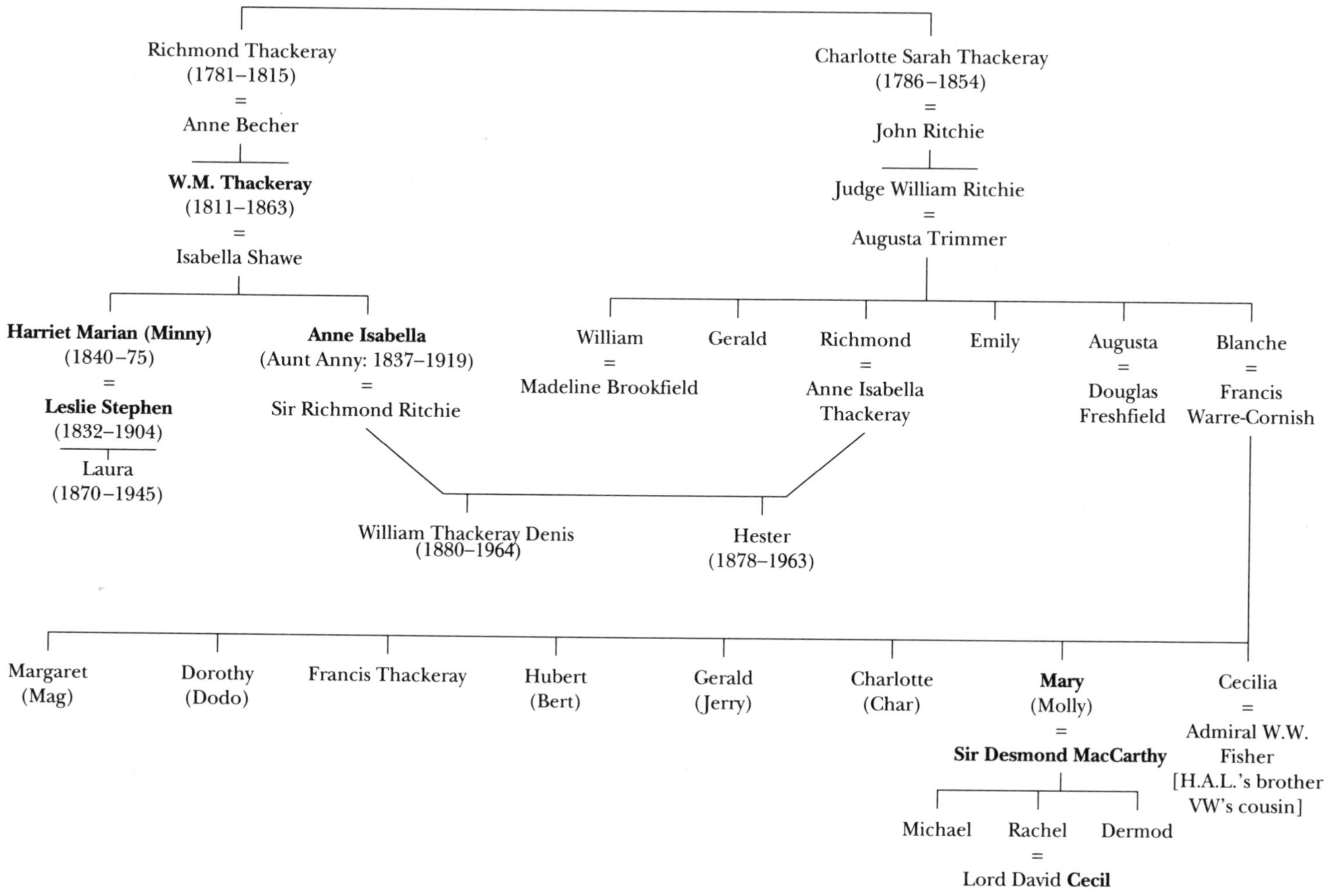

Julia Prinsep Stephen Branch

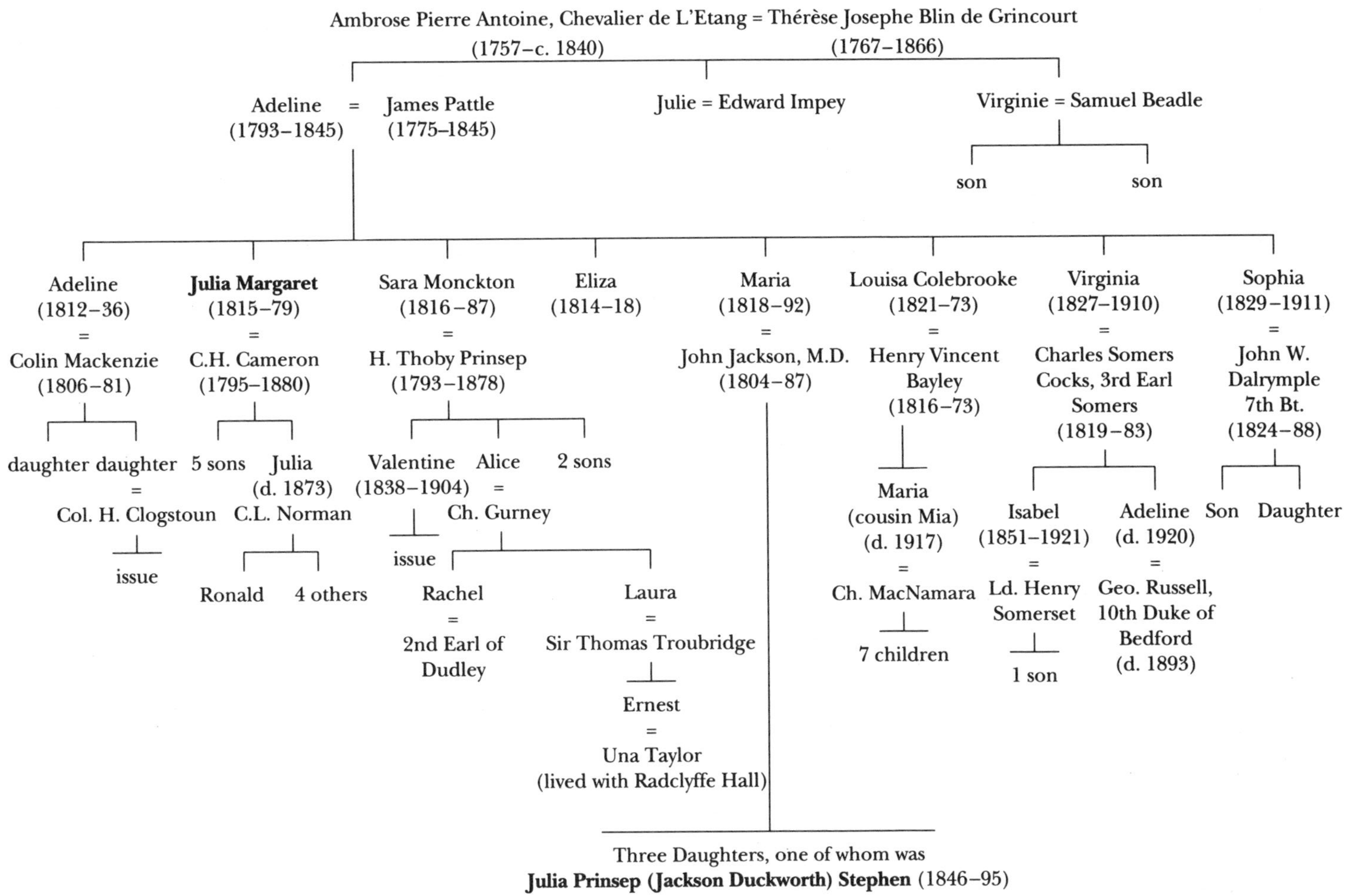

Julia Prinsep Stephen Branch (2)

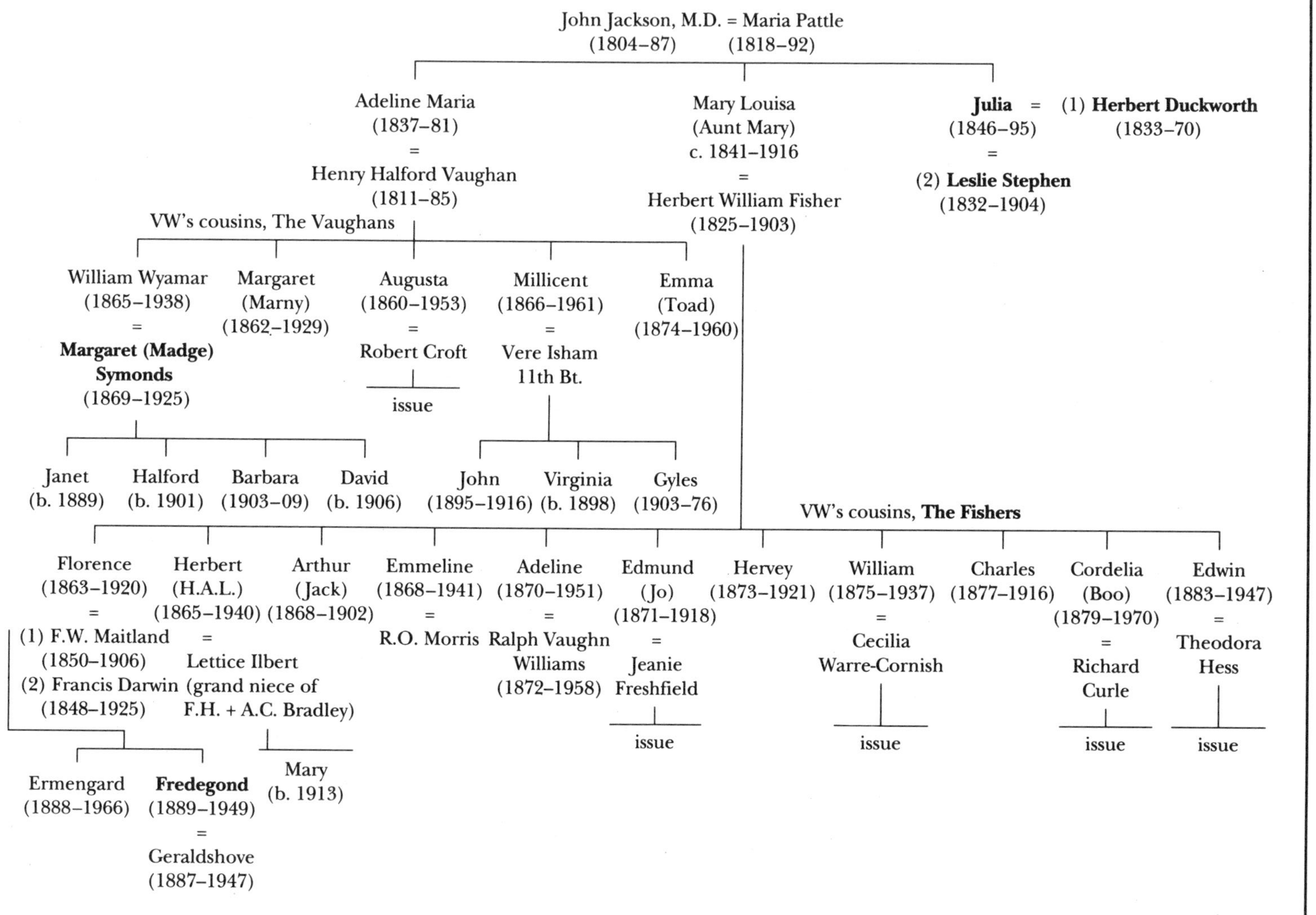
John Jackson, M.D. = Maria Pattle
(1804–87) (1818–92)
Adeline Maria
(1837–81)
=
Henry Halford Vaughan
(1811–85)
Mary Louisa
(Aunt Mary)
c. 1841–1916
=
Herbert William Fisher
(1825–1903)
Julia = (1) **Herbert Duckworth**
(1846–95) (1833–70)
=
(2) **Leslie Stephen**
(1832–1904)
VW's cousins, The Vaughans
William Wyamar
(1865–1938)
=
Margaret (Madge)
Symonds
(1869–1925)
Margaret
(Marny)
(1862–1929)
Augusta
(1860–1953)
=
Robert Croft
issue
Millicent
(1866–1961)
=
Vere Isham
11th Bt.
Emma
(Toad)
(1874–1960)
Janet
(b. 1889)
Halford
(b. 1901)
Barbara
(1903–09)
David
(b. 1906)
John
(1895–1916)
Virginia
(b. 1898)
Gyles
(1903–76)
VW's cousins, **The Fishers**
Florence
(1863–1920)
=
(1) F.W. Maitland
(1850–1906)
(2) Francis Darwin
(1848–1925)
Herbert
(H.A.L.)
(1865–1940)
=
Lettice Ilbert
(grand niece of
F.H. + A.C. Bradley)
Arthur
(Jack)
(1868–1902)
Emmeline
(1868–1941)
=
R.O. Morris
Adeline
(1870–1951)
=
Ralph Vaughn
Williams
(1872–1958)
Edmund
(Jo)
(1871–1918)
=
Jeanie
Freshfield
issue
Hervey
(1873–1921)
William
(1875–1937)
=
Cecilia
Warre-Cornish
issue
Charles
(1877–1916)
Cordelia
(Boo)
(1879–1970)
=
Richard
Curle
issue
Edwin
(1883–1947)
=
Theodora
Hess
issue
Ermengard
(1888–1966)
Fredegond
(1889–1949)
=
Geraldshove
(1887–1947)
Mary
(b. 1913)

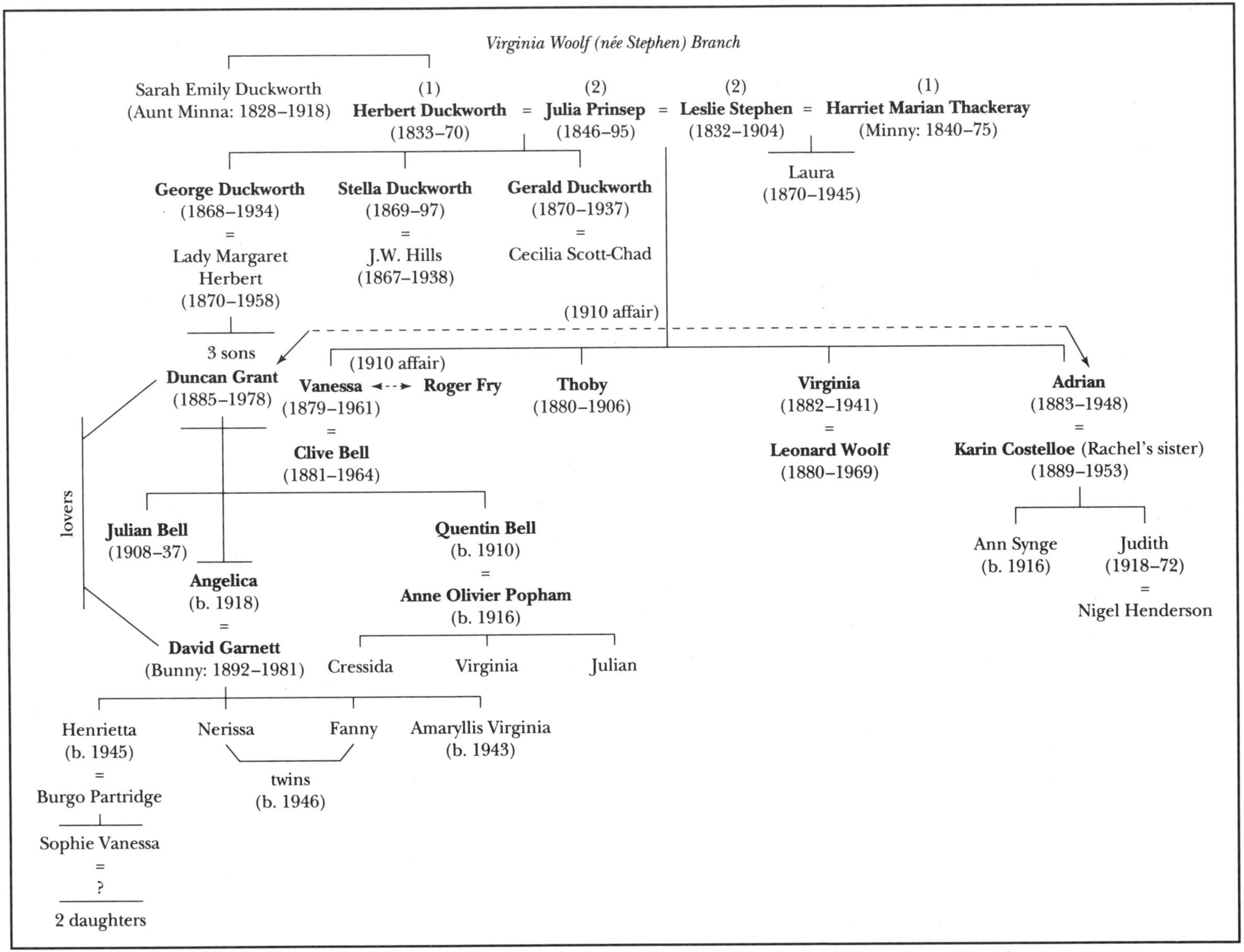

Virginia Woolf (née Stephen) Branch
Sarah Emily Duckworth (Aunt Minna: 1828–1918)
(1) Herbert Duckworth (1833–70)
=
(2) Julia Prinsep (1846–95)
=
(2) Leslie Stephen (1832–1904)
=
(1) Harriet Marian Thackeray (Minny: 1840–75)
Laura (1870–1945)
George Duckworth (1868–1934)
=
Lady Margaret Herbert (1870–1958)
3 sons
Stella Duckworth (1869–97)
=
J.W. Hills (1867–1938)
Gerald Duckworth (1870–1937)
=
Cecilia Scott-Chad
(1910 affair)
(1910 affair)
Duncan Grant (1885–1978)
Vanessa (1879–1961)
Roger Fry
=
Clive Bell (1881–1964)
Thoby (1880–1906)
Virginia (1882–1941)
=
Leonard Woolf (1880–1969)
Adrian (1883–1948)
=
Karin Costelloe (Rachel's sister) (1889–1953)
Ann Synge (b. 1916)
Judith (1918–72)
=
Nigel Henderson
lovers
Julian Bell (1908–37)
Angelica (b. 1918)
=
David Garnett (Bunny: 1892–1981)
Quentin Bell (b. 1910)
=
Anne Olivier Popham (b. 1916)
Cressida
Virginia
Julian
Henrietta (b. 1945)
=
Burgo Partridge
Sophie Vanessa
=
?
2 daughters
Nerissa
Fanny
twins (b. 1946)
Amaryllis Virginia (b. 1943)

Leonard Woolf Branch

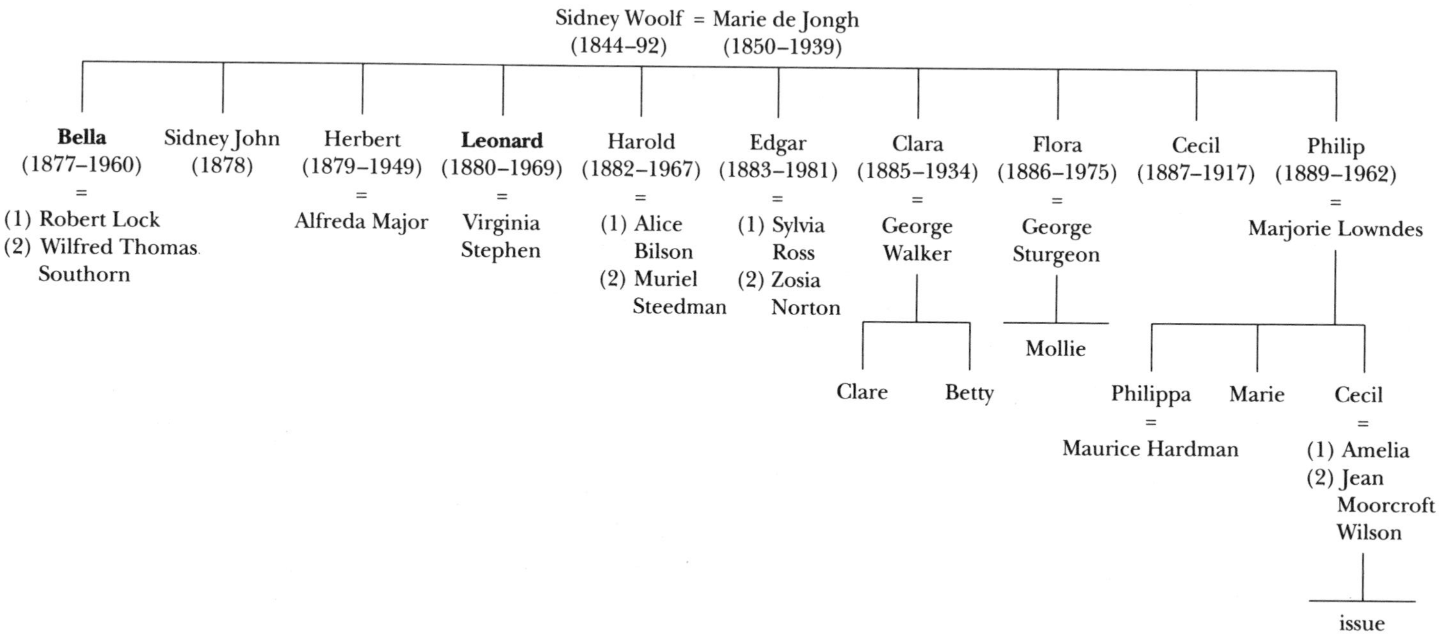
Sidney Woolf = Marie de Jongh
(1844–92) (1850–1939)
Bella (1877–1960) = (1) Robert Lock (2) Wilfred Thomas Southorn
Sidney John (1878)
Herbert (1879–1949) = Alfreda Major
Leonard (1880–1969) = Virginia Stephen
Harold (1882–1967) = (1) Alice Bilson (2) Muriel Steedman
Edgar (1883–1981) = (1) Sylvia Ross (2) Zosia Norton
Clara (1885–1934) = George Walker
Flora (1886–1975) = George Sturgeon
Cecil (1887–1917)
Philip (1889–1962) = Marjorie Lowndes
Clare
Betty
Mollie
Philippa = Maurice Hardman
Marie
Cecil = (1) Amelia (2) Jean Moorcroft Wilson
issue

Duncan Grant's and Lytton Strachey's Branches

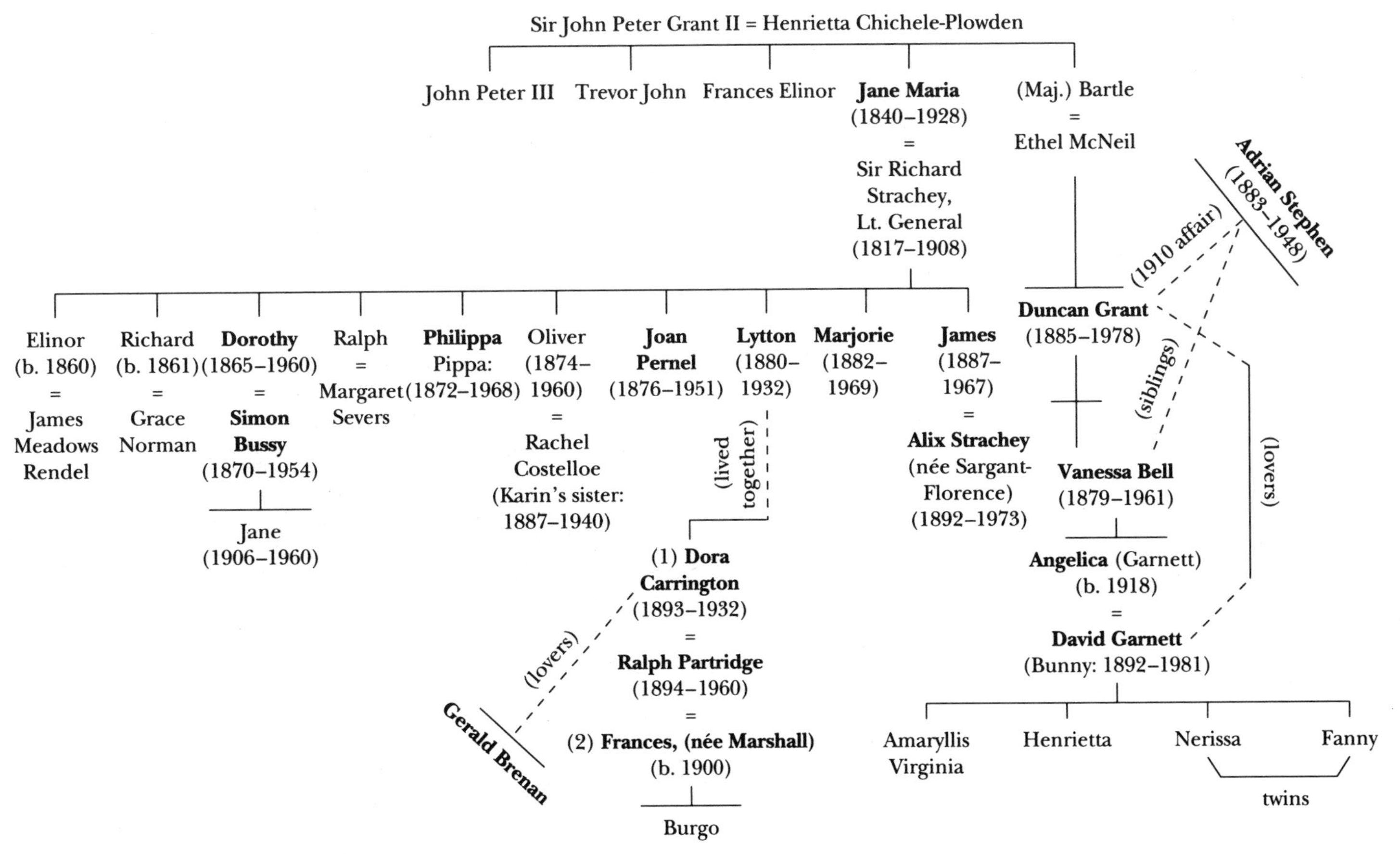

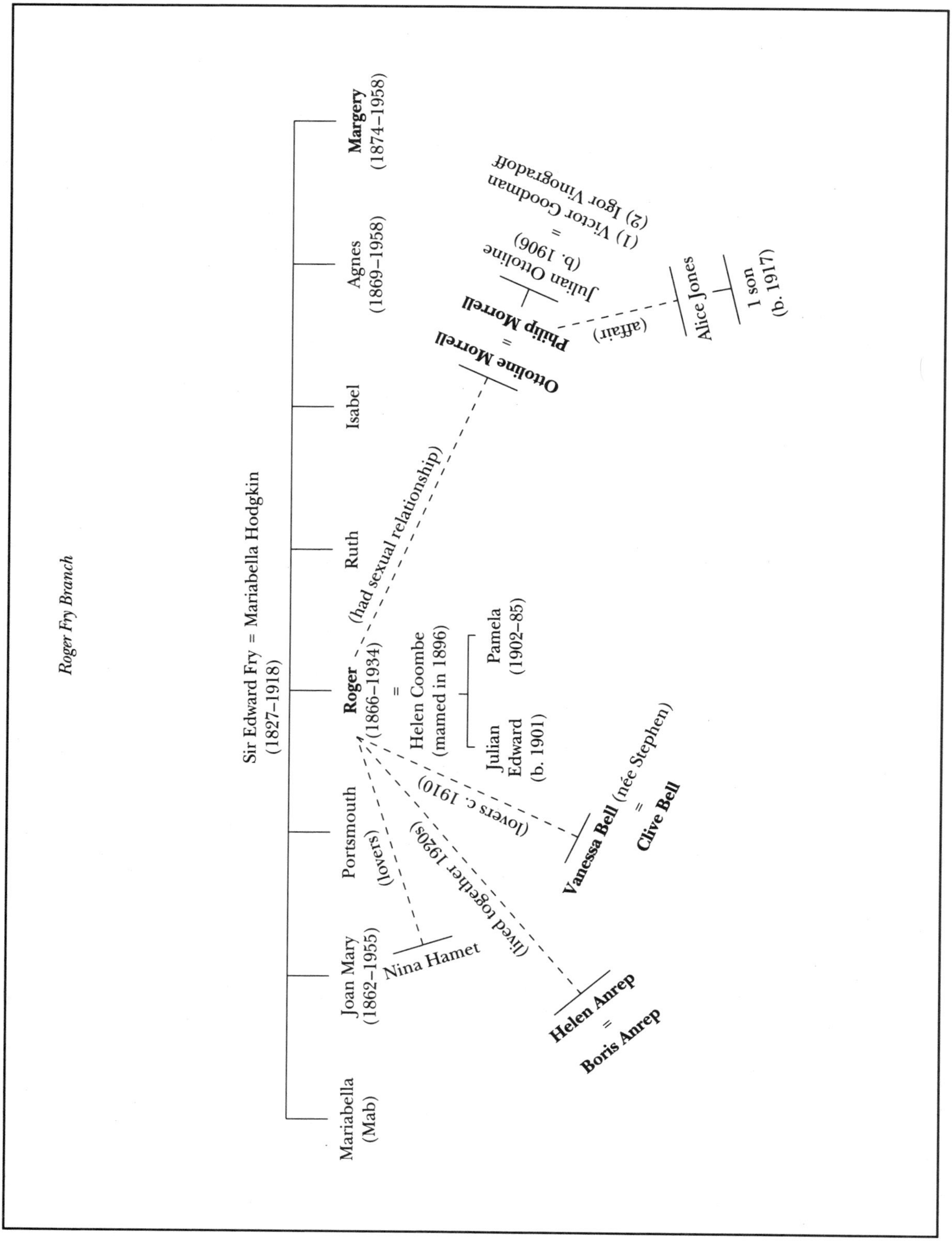

Roger Fry Branch
Sir Edward Fry = Mariabella Hodgkin
(1827–1918)
Mariabella
(Mab)
Joan Mary
(1862–1955)
Portsmouth
Roger
(1866–1934)
Ruth
Isabel
Agnes
(1869–1958)
Margery
(1874–1958)
=
Helen Coombe
(mamed in 1896)
Julian
Edward
(b. 1901)
Pamela
(1902–85)
(had sexual relationship)
Ottoline Morrell
=
Philip Morrell
Julian Ottoline
(b. 1906)
=
(1) Victor Goodman
(2) Igor Vinogradoff
(affair)
Alice Jones
1 son
(b. 1917)
(lovers c. 1910)
Vanessa Bell (née Stephen)
=
Clive Bell
(lovers)
Nina Hamet
(lived together 1920s)
Helen Anrep
=
Boris Anrep

INDEX

This index essentially serves two purposes that supplement the alphabetically arranged and cross-referenced A-to-Z entries. The index identifies titles, names, and terms that are mentioned in the A-to-Z entries but do not have entries of their own. References to minor works by Woolf that do not warrant entries of their own can be located with the index, as can references to the work of critics. Themes that are treated in multiple entries—for example, androgyny, or incest—can be traced with this index. All titles are by Virginia Woolf unless otherwise indicated. Other authors of fictional characters are identified paranthetically—for example: Wardour, Isabella (Scott). Abbreviations are explained on p. x. The letter *i* following a page number denotes illustration; the letter *n*, mention in a note. **Boldface** indicates a major entry on the term.

D

E

F

G

M

N

O

P

Q

R

S